T H I R D   E D I

Exploring Lifespan Development

Laura E. Berk
Illinois State University

PEARSON

Boston • Columbus • Indianapolis • New York • San Francisco • Upper Saddle River
Amsterdam • Cape Town • Dubai • London • Madrid • Milan • Munich • Paris • Montréal • Toronto
Delhi • Mexico City • São Paulo • Sydney • Hong Kong • Seoul • Singapore • Taipei • Tokyo

Dedication

*To Annie, Bailey, and Penny
in gratitude for wise counsel
and steadfast support*

Director, Product Development Operations: Craig Campanella
Managing Editor: Tom Pauken
Editorial Assistants: Rachel Trapp, Carla Worner
Supplements Editors: Rachel Trapp, Kim Michaud, Judy Ashkenaz
Program Manager: Linda Behrens
Senior Project Manager, Psychology: Donna Simons
Media Director: Brian Hyland
Senior Digital Product Manager: Peter Sabatini
Media Project Manager: Caitlin Smith
Director of Marketing: Brandy Dawson
Executive Marketing Manager: Wendy Albert
Senior Operations Specialist: Diane Peirano
Photo Researcher: Sarah Evertson—ImageQuest
Interior Designer: Carol Somberg
Cover Designer: Joel Gendron, PreMedia Global
Project Coordination and Editorial Services: Electronic Publishing Services Inc., NYC
Art Rendering and Electronic Page Makeup: Jouve
Copyeditor and References Editor: Margaret Pinette
Proofreader: Julie Hotchkiss
Indexer: Linda Herr Hallinger
Printer/Binder and Cover Printer: Courier Corp., Kendallville, IN
Text Font: Minion
Cover Art: "Aflame Every Autumn" by Harold Gregor

CIP data is on file with the Library of Congress.

Student Edition
ISBN 10: 0-205-95738-2
ISBN 13: 978-0-205-95738-5

Instructor's Review Edition
ISBN 10: 0-205-95880-X
ISBN 13: 978-0-205-95880-1

À la Carte Edition
ISBN 10: 0-205-95870-2
ISBN 13: 978-0-205-95870-2

About the Author

Laura E. Berk is a distinguished professor of psychology at Illinois State University, where she has taught human development to both undergraduate and graduate students for more than three decades. She received her bachelor's degree in psychology from the University of California, Berkeley, and her master's and doctoral degrees in child development and educational psychology from the University of Chicago. She has been a visiting scholar at Cornell University, UCLA, Stanford University, and the University of South Australia.

Berk has published widely on the effects of school environments on children's development, the development of private speech, and the role of make-believe play in development. Her research has been funded by the U.S. Office of Education and the National Institute of Child Health and Human Development. It has appeared in many prominent journals, including *Child Development, Developmental Psychology, Merrill-Palmer Quarterly, Journal of Abnormal Child Psychology, Development and Psychopathology,* and *Early Childhood Research Quarterly.* Her empirical studies have attracted the attention of the general public, leading to contributions to *Psychology Today* and *Scientific American.* She has also been featured on National Public Radio's *Morning Edition* and in *Parents Magazine, Wondertime,* and *Reader's Digest.*

Berk has served as a research editor of *Young Children* and as a consulting editor for *Early Childhood Research Quarterly.* Currently, she is associate editor of the *Journal of Cognitive Education and Psychology.* She is a frequent contributor to edited volumes on early childhood development, having recently authored chapters on the importance of parenting, on make-believe play, and on the kindergarten child. She has also written the article on social development for *The Child: An Encyclopedic Companion;* the article on Vygotsky for the *Encyclopedia of Cognitive Science;* and the chapter on storytelling as a teaching strategy for *Voices of Experience: Memorable Talks from the National Institute on the Teaching of Psychology* (Association for Psychological Science). She is coauthor of the forthcoming chapter on make-believe play and self-regulation in the *Sage Handbook of Play and Learning in Early Childhood.*

Berk's books include *Private Speech: From Social Interaction to Self-Regulation; Scaffolding Children's Learning: Vygotsky and Early Childhood Education; Landscapes of Development: An Anthology of Readings;* and *A Mandate for Playful Learning in Preschool: Presenting the Evidence.* In addition to *Development Through the Lifespan* and *Exploring Lifespan Development,* she is author of the best-selling texts *Child Development* and *Infants, Children, and Adolescents,* published by Pearson. Her book for parents and teachers is *Awakening Children's Minds: How Parents and Teachers Can Make a Difference.*

Berk is active in work for children's causes. In addition to service in her home community, she is a member of the national board of directors and chair of the Chicago advisory board of Jumpstart, a nonprofit organization that provides intensive literacy intervention to thousands of low-income preschoolers across the United States, using college and university students as interveners. Berk is a fellow of the American Psychological Association, Division 7: Developmental Psychology.

Features at a Glance

Contents

PART III

Infancy and Toddlerhood: The First Two Years

chapter 4

Physical Development in Infancy and Toddlerhood   91

chapter 5

Cognitive Development in Infancy and Toddlerhood   117

chapter 8
Emotional and Social Development in Early Childhood 199

chapter 9
Physical and Cognitive Development in Middle Childhood 226

PART VIII

Middle Adulthood

chapter 15

Physical and Cognitive Development in Middle Adulthood 400

chapter 16

Emotional and Social Development in Middle Adulthood 422

PART IX
Late Adulthood

chapter 17
Physical and Cognitive Development in Late Adulthood 446

chapter 18
Emotional and Social Development in Late Adulthood 478

A Personal Note to Students

My more than 30 years of teaching human development have brought me in contact with thousands of students like you—students with diverse college majors, future goals, interests, and needs. Some are affiliated with my own field, psychology, but many come from other related fields—education, sociology, anthropology, family studies, social service, nursing, and biology, to name just a few. Each semester, my students' aspirations have proved to be as varied as their fields of study. Many look toward careers in applied work—counseling, caregiving, nursing, social work, school psychology, and program administration. Some plan to teach, and a few want to do research. Most hope someday to become parents, whereas others are already parents who come with a desire to better understand and rear their children. And almost all arrive with a deep curiosity about how they themselves developed from tiny infants into the complex human beings they are today.

My goal in preparing this third edition of *Exploring Lifespan Development* is to provide a textbook that meets the instructional goals of your course as well as your personal interests and needs. To achieve these objectives, I have grounded this book in a carefully selected body of classic and current theory and research. In addition, the text highlights the lifespan perspective on development and the interacting contributions of biology and environment to the developing person. It also illustrates commonalities and differences among ethnic groups and cultures and discusses the broader social contexts in which we develop. I have provided a unique pedagogical program that will assist you in mastering information, integrating various aspects of development, critically examining controversial issues, applying what you have learned, and relating the information to your own life.

I hope that learning about human development will be as rewarding for you as I have found it over the years. I would like to know what you think about both the field of human development and this book. I welcome your comments; please feel free to send them to me at Department of Psychology, Box 4620, Illinois State University, Normal, IL 61790.

Laura E. Berk

Preface for Instructors

I wrote *Exploring Lifespan Development* with the goal of retaining all the vital features of *Development Through the Lifespan* while providing students with a clear, efficient read of the most important concepts and empirical findings in the field of lifespan development. The text has been refashioned with an exceptionally strong emphasis on applications. Classical, contemporary, and cutting-edge theories and research are made accessible to students in a manageable and relevant way. This third edition represents rapidly transforming aspects of the field, with a wealth of new content and teaching tools:

- *Diverse pathways of change are highlighted.* Investigators have reached broad consensus that variations in biological makeup and everyday tasks lead to wide individual differences in paths of change and resulting competencies. This edition pays more attention to variability in development and to recent theories—including ecological, sociocultural, and dynamic systems—that attempt to explain it. Multicultural and cross-cultural findings, including international comparisons, are enhanced throughout the text. Biology and Environment and Cultural Influences boxes also accentuate the theme of diversity in development.

- *The lifespan perspective is emphasized.* As in previous editions, the lifespan perspective—development as lifelong, multidimensional, multidirectional, plastic, and embedded in multiple contexts—continues to serve as a unifying approach to understanding human change and is woven thoroughly into the text.

- *The complex bidirectional relationship between biology and environment is given greater attention.* Accumulating evidence on development of the brain, motor skills, cognitive and language competencies, temperament and personality, emotional and social understanding, and developmental problems underscores the way biological factors emerge in, are modified by, and share power with experience. Interconnections between biology and environment are integral to the lifespan perspective and are revisited throughout the text narrative and in the Biology and Environment boxes with new and updated topics.

- *Inclusion of interdisciplinary research is expanded.* The move toward viewing thoughts, feelings, and behavior as an integrated whole, affected by a wide array of influences in biology, social context, and culture, has motivated developmental researchers to strengthen their ties with other fields of psychology and with other disciplines. Topics and findings included in this edition increasingly reflect the contributions of educational psychology, social psychology, health psychology, clinical psychology, neurobiology, pediatrics, geriatrics, sociology, anthropology, social service, and other fields.

- *The links among theory, research, and applications are strengthened.* As researchers intensify their efforts to generate findings relevant to real-life situations, I have placed even greater weight on social policy issues and sound theory- and research-based applications. Further applications are provided in the Applying What We Know tables, which give students concrete ways of building bridges between their learning and the real world.

- *The role of active student learning is made more explicit.* **TAKE A MOMENT...**, a feature built into the chapter narrative, asks students to think deeply and critically or to engage in an exercise or application as they read. Ask Yourself questions at the end of each major section have been thoroughly revised and expanded to promote four approaches to engaging actively with the subject matter—*Review, Connect, Apply,* and *Reflect.* This feature assists students in thinking about what they have learned from multiple vantage points. A new **LOOK AND LISTEN** feature asks students to observe what real children, adolescents, and adults say and do; speak with them or with professionals invested in their well-being; and inquire into community programs and practices that influence lifespan development. In addition, highlighting of key terms within the text narrative reinforces student learning in context.

Text Philosophy

The basic approach of this book has been shaped by my own professional and personal history as a teacher, researcher, and parent. It consists of seven philosophical ingredients that I regard as essential for students to emerge from a course with a thorough understanding of lifespan development. Each theme is woven into every chapter:

1. **An understanding of the diverse array of theories in the field and the strengths and shortcomings of each.** The first chapter begins by emphasizing that only knowledge of multiple theories can do justice to the richness of human development. As I take up each age period and domain of development, I present a variety of theoretical perspectives, indicate how each highlights previously overlooked aspects of development, and discuss research that evaluates it. Consideration of contrasting theories also serves as the context for an evenhanded analysis of many controversial issues.

2. **A grasp of the lifespan perspective as an integrative approach to development.** I introduce the lifespan perspective as an organizing framework in the first chapter and refer to and illustrate its assumptions throughout the text, in an effort to help students construct an overall vision of development from conception to death.

3. **Knowledge of both the sequence of human development and the processes that underlie it.** Students are provided with a discussion of the organized sequence of development

along with processes of change. An understanding of process—how complex combinations of biological and environmental events produce development—has been the focus of most recent research. Accordingly, the text reflects this emphasis. But new information about the timetable of change has also emerged. In many ways, the very young and the old have proved to be far more competent than they were believed to be in the past. In addition, many milestones of adult development, such as finishing formal education, entering a career, getting married, having children, and retiring, have become less predictable. Current evidence on the sequence and timing of development, along with its implications for process, is presented for all periods of the lifespan.

4. **An appreciation of the impact of context and culture on human development.** A wealth of research indicates that people live in rich physical and social contexts that affect all domains of development. Throughout the book, students travel to distant parts of the world as I review a growing body of cross-cultural evidence. The text narrative also discusses many findings on socioeconomically and ethnically diverse people within the United States. Furthermore, the impact of historical time period and cohort membership receives continuous attention. In this vein, gender issues—the distinctive but continually evolving experiences, roles, and life paths of males and females—are granted substantial emphasis. Besides highlighting the effects of immediate settings, such as family, neighborhood, and school, I make a concerted effort to underscore the influence of larger social structures—societal values, laws, and government policies and programs—on lifelong well-being.

5. **An understanding of the joint contributions of biology and environment to development.** The field recognizes more powerfully than ever before the joint roles of hereditary/constitutional and environmental factors—that these contributions to development combine in complex ways and cannot be separated in a simple manner. Numerous examples of how biological dispositions can be maintained as well as transformed by social contexts are presented throughout the book.

6. **A sense of the interdependency of all domains of development—physical, cognitive, emotional, and social.** Every chapter emphasizes an integrated approach to human development. I show how physical, cognitive, emotional, and social development are interwoven. Within the text narrative, and in a special series of Ask Yourself questions at the end of major sections, students are referred to other sections of the book to deepen their grasp of relationships among various aspects of change.

7. **An appreciation of the interrelatedness of theory, research, and applications.** Throughout this book, I emphasize that theories of human development and the research stimulated by them provide the foundation for sound, effective practices with children, adolescents, and adults. The link among theory, research, and applications is reinforced by an organizational format in which theory and research are presented first, followed by practical implications. In addition, a current focus in the field—harnessing knowledge of human development to shape social policies that support human needs throughout the lifespan—is reflected in every chapter. The text addresses the current condition of children, adolescents, and adults in the United States and elsewhere in the world and shows how theory and research have combined with public interest to spark successful interventions. Many important applied topics are considered, such as family planning, infant mortality, maternal employment and child care, teenage pregnancy and parenthood, domestic violence, exercise and adult health, religiosity and well-being, lifelong learning, grandparents rearing grandchildren, caring for aging adults with dementia, adjustment to retirement, optimal aging, and palliative care for the dying.

Text Organization

I have chosen a chronological organization for *Exploring Lifespan Development*. The book begins with an introductory chapter that describes the scientific history of the field, influential theories, and research strategies. It is followed by two chapters on the foundations of development. Chapter 2 combines an overview of genetic and environmental contexts into a single integrated discussion of these multifaceted influences on development. Chapter 3 is devoted to prenatal development, birth, and the newborn baby. With this foundation, students are ready to look closely at seven major age periods: infancy and toddlerhood (Chapters 4, 5, and 6), early childhood (Chapters 7 and 8), middle childhood (Chapters 9 and 10), adolescence (Chapters 11 and 12), early adulthood (Chapters 13 and 14), middle adulthood (Chapters 15 and 16), and late adulthood (Chapters 17 and 18). Topical chapters within each chronological division cover physical development, cognitive development, and emotional and social development. The book concludes with a chapter on death, dying, and bereavement (Chapter 19).

The chronological approach assists students in thoroughly understanding each age period. It also eases the task of integrating the various domains of development because each is discussed in close proximity. At the same time, a chronologically organized book requires that theories covering several age periods be presented piecemeal. This creates a challenge for students, who must link the various parts together. To assist with this task, I frequently remind students of important earlier achievements before discussing new developments, referring back to related sections with page references. Also, chapters or sections devoted to the same topic (for example, cognitive development) are similarly organized, making it easier for students to draw connections across age periods and construct an overall view of developmental change.

New Coverage in the Third Edition

Lifespan development is a fascinating and ever-changing field of study, with constantly emerging new discoveries and refinements in existing knowledge. The sixth edition represents this burgeoning contemporary literature, with over 1,500 new citations. Cutting-edge topics throughout the text underscore the book's major themes. Here is a sampling:

CHAPTER 1: Updated Biology and Environment box on resilience • Updated section on developmental cognitive neuroscience • Increased coverage of evolutionary developmental psychology, with special attention to the adaptiveness of human longevity • Updated Cultural Influences box on immigrant youths • Clarified explanation of sequential designs

CHAPTER 2: Updated Social Issues: Health box on the pros and cons of reproductive technologies • Updated section on development of adopted children • Enhanced attention to the impact of poverty on development • Expanded introduction to family influences on development, including the importance of coparenting • Updated research on neighborhood influences on children's physical and mental health • Current statistics on the condition of children, families, and the aged in the United States compared with other Western nations • Introduction to the concept of gene–environment interaction, with illustrative research findings • Expanded section on epigenesis, including new examples of environmental influences on gene expression • New Biology and Environment box highlighting a case of epigenesis—prenatal smoking modifies gene expression

CHAPTER 3: Enhanced attention to fetal brain development, sensory capacities, and behavior • Expanded and updated consideration of a wide range of teratogens • New evidence on the long-term consequences of emotional stress during pregnancy • Updated evidence on the contributions of doula support to the birth process and to newborn adjustment • New research on parenting and development of preterm and low-birth-weight infants • Expanded and updated Social Issues: Health box on health care and other policies for parents and newborn babies • New Social Issues: Health box on the Nurse–Family Partnership—reducing maternal stress and enhancing child development through social support • Updated findings on the roles of impaired brain functioning, maternal smoking, and maternal drug abuse in sudden infant death syndrome (SIDS) • New evidence on the role of sleep in infant learning • Updated research on touch sensitivity in newborns, including techniques for reducing infant stress to painful medical procedures

CHAPTER 4: Updated introduction to major methods of assessing brain functioning, including the EEG geodesic sensor net (GSN) and near-infrared spectroscopy (NIRS) • Updated discussion of advances in brain development, with special attention to the prefrontal cortex • New research on children adopted from Romanian orphanages, including neurobiological evidence bearing on the question of whether infancy is a sensitive period of development • Updated Cultural Influences box on cultural variation in infant sleeping arrangements • Updated section on breastfeeding • New dynamic systems research on development of walking and reaching • Enhanced attention to cultural influences—including infant sleep and motor development • New evidence on the perceptual narrowing effect in speech, music, and species-related face perception, and in gender- and race-related face perception

CHAPTER 5: Revised and updated section on infant and toddler imitation, revealing toddlers' ability to infer others' intentions • New section on symbolic understanding, including toddlers' developing grasp of words and pictures as symbolic tools • New Social Issues: Education box on baby learning from TV and video, including discussion of the video deficit effect • Revised section introducing information-processing concepts, including working memory, automatic processes, speed of processing, and executive function • Revised and updated section on infant and toddler categorization skills • New research on babies' joint attention and preverbal gestures, revealing their developing capacity to participate in cooperative processes necessary for effective communication • Updated findings on toddlers' earliest spoken words, including cultural variations • New findings on adult–child conversation and early vocabulary development, with special attention to SES differences

CHAPTER 6: New research on consequences of effortful control—the self-regulatory dimension of temperament—for cognitive, emotional, and social development • Special attention to the role of child genotype in parenting effects on temperament • Revised and updated section on consequences of early availability of a consistent caregiver for attachment security, emotion processing, and adjustment, highlighting studies of children adopted from Eastern European orphanages • Updated findings on employed fathers' increased involvement in caregiving • Revised and updated Social Issues: Health box on child care, attachment, and later development • New evidence on toddlers' scale errors, with implications for body self-awareness

CHAPTER 7: Increased attention to brain development in early childhood, with special attention to the prefrontal cortex and executive function • Updated statistics and research on the health status of U.S. young children, including tooth decay, immunizations, unintentional injury, and overall health status • New research on development of handedness, including cultural variations • New evidence on preschoolers' magical beliefs • Revised and updated section on preschoolers' understanding of symbol–real-world relations • New research on cultural variations in effective scaffolding • New Social Issues: Education box on children's questions as a catalyst for cognitive development • Updated discussion of gains in executive function in early childhood, including attention, inhibition, and planning • Recent findings on toddlers' early, implicit false-belief understanding and its relationship to preschoolers explicit grasp of false belief • New evidence on cognitive attainments and social experiences that contribute to mastery of false belief • Enhanced discussion of SES differences in emergent literacy and math knowledge • Updated discussion of the effects of television and computers on academic learning

CHAPTER 8: Updated consideration of emotional self-regulation in early childhood, including the influence of temperament and parenting • Enhanced Cultural Influences box on ethnic differences in the consequences of physical punishment • New section on the role of positive peer relations in school readiness • New longitudinal evidence on the relationship of early corporal punishment to later behavior problems • Enhanced attention to aggressive children's distorted view of the social world • Updated discussion of parent training programs to reduce child conduct problems, with special attention to Incredible Years • New findings on the harmful impact of parental psychological control on children's adjustment • Updated consideration of consequences of child maltreatment, including new evidence on central nervous system damage

CHAPTER 9: Revised and updated section on overweight and obesity, including current U.S. prevalence rates, international comparisons, and coverage of contributing factors and consequences • Updated statistics on physical activity and fitness among U.S. school-age children • New sections on working-memory capacity and executive function in middle childhood, with implications for academic learning • Revised and updated Biology and Environment box on children with attention-deficit hyperactivity disorder • New research on development of planning in middle childhood • Updated evidence on the school-age child's theory of mind • Discussion of secular trends in IQ, including implications for understanding ethnic variations in IQ • Attention to the impact of the U.S. No Child Left Behind Act on quality of U.S. education • New research on educational consequences of widespread SES and ethnic segregation in American schools • New Social Issues: Education box on magnet schools as a means of attaining equal access to high-quality education • Revised and updated section on U.S. academic achievement in international perspective, including comparisons with high-performing nations

CHAPTER 10: Enhanced attention to cultural variations in self-concept, with special attention to Asian versus U.S. comparisons • Updated research on parenting practices and children's achievement-related attributions, including the influence of cultural values on likelihood of developing learned helplessness • New section on children's understanding of diversity and inequality, development of racial and ethnic prejudice, and strategies for reducing prejudice • Updated evidence on implications of peer-acceptance categories for bullying and victimization • Updated Biology and Environment box on bullies and their victims • New evidence on sex differences in development of gender identity in middle childhood • Enhanced attention to the role of effective coparenting in children's adjustment to parental divorce and remarriage • New research on the implications of self-care and after-school programs for school-age children's adjustment • Revised and updated Cultural Influences box on impact of ethnic and political violence on children • Updated findings on the consequences of child sexual abuse

CHAPTER 11: New section on adolescent brain development, focusing on the imbalance between the cognitive control network and the emotional/social network, with implications for teenage reward-seeking, emotional reactivity, and risk-taking • Updated evidence on teenage pregnancy and parenthood prevention and intervention strategies • Expanded and updated research on adolescent decision making • New research on the impact of school transitions on adolescent adjustment • New Social Issues: Education box on the impact of "media multitasking" on learning

CHAPTER 12: New research on personal and social factors contributing to identity development in adolescence • Updated Social Issues: Health box on adolescent suicide • Updated evidence on adolescents' capacity to integrate moral, social-conventional, and personal concerns • Enhanced consideration of factors that promote moral identity, along with its relationship to moral behavior • New evidence on gender intensification in adolescence • Updated section on parenting and adolescent autonomy, including research on immigrant families • Expanded and updated section on Internet friendships, with special attention to teenagers' use of social networking sites • New findings on long-term outcomes of multisystemic therapy for violent juvenile offenders

CHAPTER 13: Updated Biology and Environment box on telomere length as a marker of the impact of life circumstances on biological aging • New controversial evidence on the role of free radicals in aging • New research on SES variations in adult health • Updated statistics on the continued rise in adult overweight and obesity • New findings on negative stereotyping and discrimination experienced by overweight adults • Updated discussion of treatment of adult obesity • New evidence on the Internet as a contemporary way to initiate dating relationships • Updated research on psychological stress and unfavorable health outcomes • Enhanced discussion of the psychological impact of attending college, including benefits of opportunities to interact with racially and ethnically diverse peers • New findings on the role of gender stereotypes in women's likelihood of choosing STEM careers • Updated Social Issues: Education box on men who choose nontraditional careers

CHAPTER 14: Revised and updated section on emerging adulthood, including new findings on emerging adults' religiosity, spirituality, and commitment to community service • Enhanced discussion of the controversy over whether emerging adulthood really is a distinct period of development • Special attention to parenting of emerging adults, including "helicopter parenting" • Updated consideration of increasingly flexible age-graded expectations for early adulthood life events • Updated consideration of factors that contribute to enduring romantic relationships • New findings on social networking sites as contexts for early adulthood friendship • Expanded discussion of the rise in average age of leaving the parental home • Increased attention to parent–young-adult child relationships • New findings on sharing of household tasks in dual-earner marriages, including cross-national evidence • Updated research on relationship qualities and communication skills contributing to marital satisfaction • Updated consideration of the dramatic increase in never-married single parents, including SES and ethnic variations • New findings on career development in early adulthood, with special attention to obstacles to success faced by women and ethnic minorities • Enhanced discussion of combining work and family

CHAPTER 15: Updated Biology and Environment box on anti-aging effects of dietary calorie restriction • Updated evidence on the risks of hormone therapy to reduce physical discomforts of menopause • New survey findings on sexual activity of U.S. middle-aged adults • Updated sections on risk of cancer and heart disease in midlife • New findings on midlife changes in attention and memory • New Social Issues: Education box on how lessons in the art of acting improve memory in older adults

CHAPTER 16: Enhanced consideration of the contribution of parenting to generativity in midlife • Updated Social Issues: Health box on grandparents rearing grandchildren in skipped-generation families • Updated evidence on relationships between middle-aged adults and their aging parents, including ethnic variations • New findings on midlife intergenerational assistance to both children and aging parents • Enhanced discussion of care of aging parents in poor health, with emphasis on gender disparities, ethnic variations, and emotional, physical, and financial consequences • New research on middle-aged adults' use of social networking sites • Updated discussion of the glass ceiling in career advancement faced by women and ethnic minorities • Discussion of the impact of the late-2000s recession on delayed retirement

CHAPTER 17: Updated statistics on life expectancy in late adulthood, including gender and SES variations • Updated international comparisons in healthy life expectancy • New research on brain development, including neurological changes that enable older adults to compensate for declines in central nervous system functioning • Updated findings on risk and protective factors associated with various aspects of physical aging • Updated section on assistive technologies • Expanded and updated discussion of stereotypes of aging, including stereotype threat, with implications for physical and cognitive performance • Updated consideration of SES and ethnic variations in health in late adulthood • Expanded consideration of progress in compression of morbidity • Updated survey findings on sexual activity in late adulthood • New findings on neurological changes associated with Alzheimer's disease, including efforts to understand how abnormal amyloid and tau damage neurons • New evidence on genetic and environmental risks for Alzheimer's, and on protective factors, with special emphasis on diet, education, and physical activity • Updated Social Issues: Health box on interventions for caregivers of older adults with dementia, with increased attention to respite and caregiving skills • Expanded discussion of episodic memory and prospective memory in late adulthood • Enhanced consideration of the impact of cognitive training on older adults' mental functioning, including broadening programs to target self-efficacy • New evidence on the rapid rise in use of computers and the Internet among older people

CHAPTER 18: Updated research on reminiscence in late adulthood • New findings on personality development in late adulthood, with special attention to openness to experience • Enhanced consideration of the benefits of spirituality and religiosity in late life • Consideration of sustaining an effective person–environment fit in older adults' social contexts, including caregiving and housing arrangements • New research on divorce, remarriage, and cohabitation in late adulthood, including aging baby boomers' use of online dating services • Updated findings on late-life friendships • New evidence on retirement as a dynamic process with multiple transitions and wide individual variation

CHAPTER 19: Updated research on diverse factors influencing people's adaptation to dying • Updated discussion of dying at home, in hospitals, and in nursing homes • New findings on hospice, including reducing patient suffering, improving family functioning, and increasing ability to sustain patient care at home • Updated statistics on public attitudes toward passive euthanasia, voluntary active euthanasia, and assisted suicide • New research on the role of expressions of happiness and humor in bereavement adjustment • New evidence on bereavement interventions, with special attention to support groups based on the dual-process model of coping with loss

Pedagogical Features

Maintaining a highly accessible writing style—one that is lucid and engaging without being simplistic—continues to be one of my major goals. I frequently converse with students, encouraging them to relate what they read to their own lives. In doing so, I hope to make the study of human development involving and pleasurable.

CHAPTER INTRODUCTIONS AND VIGNETTES ABOUT REAL PEOPLE. To provide a helpful preview, I include an outline and overview of chapter content in each chapter introduction. To help students construct a clear image of development and to enliven the text narrative, each chronological age division is unified by case examples woven throughout that set of chapters. For example, the middle childhood section highlights the experiences and concerns of 10-year-old Joey; 8-year-old Lizzie; their divorced parents, Rena and Drake; and their classmates. In the chapters on late adulthood, students get to know Walt and Ruth, a vibrant retired couple, along with Walt's older brother Dick, Dick's wife Goldie, and Ruth's sister Ida, a victim of Alzheimer's disease. Besides a set of main characters who bring unity to each age period, many additional vignettes offer vivid examples of development and diversity among children, adolescents, and adults.

END-OF-CHAPTER SUMMARIES. Chapter summaries are organized by learning objectives, encouraging active study. They also include bolded key terms, which help students acquire and master the vocabulary of the field.

TAKE A MOMENT... Built into the text narrative, this feature asks students to "take a moment" to think about an important point, integrate information on human development, or engage in an exercise or an application to clarify a challenging concept. *TAKE A MOMENT...* highlights and reinforces the text's strength in conversing with and actively engaging the student in learning and in inspiring critical thinking.

LOOK AND LISTEN. This **new** active-learning feature asks students to observe what real individuals say and do; speak with or observe parents, teachers, or other professionals; and inquire into community programs and practices that influence children, adolescents, and adults.

ASK YOURSELF QUESTIONS. Active engagement with the subject matter is also supported by study questions at the end of each major section. Three types of questions prompt students to think about development in diverse ways: *Review* questions help students recall and comprehend information they have just read; *Apply* questions encourage the application of knowledge to controversial issues and problems faced by children, adolescents, adults, and professionals who work with them; and *Reflect* questions help make the study of human development personally meaningful by asking students to reflect on their own development and life experiences. Each question is answered on the text's MyDevelopmentLab website.

FEATURE BOXES. Thematic boxes accentuate the philosophical themes of this book. *(See page iv for a complete listing.)*

Biology and Environment boxes highlight the growing attention to the complex, bidirectional relationship between biology and environment during development. Examples include *A Case of Epigenesis: Smoking During Pregnancy Alters Gene Expression; Children with Attention-Deficit Hyperactivity Disorder; Anti-Aging Effects of Dietary Calorie Restriction;* and *Music as Palliative Care for Dying Patients.*

Cultural Influences boxes deepen the attention to culture threaded throughout the text and accentuate both cross-cultural and multicultural variations in human development—for example, *Immigrant Youths: Adapting to a New Land; Impact of Ethnic and Political Violence on Children; Is Emerging Adulthood Really a Distinct Period of Development?;* and *The New Old Age.*

Social Issues boxes discuss the impact of social conditions on children, adolescents, and adults and emphasize the need for sensitive social policies to ensure their well-being:

New Social Issues: Education boxes focus on home, school, and community influences on learning. Examples include *Baby Learning from TV and Video: The Video Deficit Effect; Media Multitasking Disrupts Attention and Learning; Magnet Schools: Equal Access to High-Quality Education;* and *The Art of Acting Improves Memory in Older Adults.*

New Social Issues: Health boxes address values and practices relevant to physical and mental health. Examples include *The Nurse–Family Partnership: Reducing Maternal Stress and Enhancing Child Development Through Social Support; A Cross-National Perspective on Health Care and Other Policies for Parents and Newborn Babies;* and *Interventions for Caregivers of Older Adults with Dementia.*

APPLYING WHAT WE KNOW TABLES. To accentuate the link between theory and research and applications, Applying What We Know tables provide easily accessible practical advice on the importance of caring for oneself and others throughout the lifespan. The tables also speak directly to students as parents or future parents and to those pursuing child- and family-related careers or areas of study, such as teaching, health care, counseling, or social work. They include: *Do's and Don'ts of a Healthy Pregnancy, Signs of Developmentally Appropriate Infant and Toddler Child Care, Positive Parenting, Helping Children Adjust to Their Parents' Divorce, Resources That Foster Resilience in Emerging Adulthood, Relieving the Stress of Caring for an Aging Parent,* and *Fostering Adaptation to Widowhood in Late Adulthood. (See page iv for a complete listing.)*

MILESTONES TABLES. A Milestones table appears at the end of each age division of the text. These tables summarize major physical, cognitive, language, emotional, and social attainments, providing a convenient aid for reviewing the chronology of lifespan development.

ENHANCED ART AND PHOTO PROGRAM. A revised art style presents concepts and research findings with clarity and attractiveness, thereby aiding student understanding and retention. Each photo has been carefully selected to complement the text discussion and to represent the diversity of people in the United States and around the world.

IN-TEXT KEY TERMS WITH DEFINITIONS, END-OF-CHAPTER TERM LIST, AND END-OF-BOOK GLOSSARY. Mastery of terms that make up the central vocabulary of the field is promoted through in-text highlighting of key terms and concept definitions, which encourages students to review the terminology of the field in greater depth by rereading related information. Key terms also appear in an end-of-chapter page-referenced list of important terms and concepts and an end-of-book page-referenced glossary.

Acknowledgments

The dedicated contributions of many individuals helped make this book a reality and contributed to refinements and improvements in this third edition. An impressive cast of reviewers provided many helpful suggestions, constructive criticisms, and enthusiasm for the organization and content of the text. I am grateful to each one of them.

Reviewers for the Third Edition

Cheryl Anagnopoulos, Black Hills State University
Carolyn M. Barry, Loyola University
Lori Bica, University of Wisconsin, Eau Claire
Linda Curry, Texas Christian University
Manfred Diehl, Colorado State University
Mary Anne Erickson, Ithaca College
Karen Fingerman, University of Texas, Austin
Linda Halgunseth, Pennsylvania State University
Melinda Heinz, Iowa State University
Joseph Kishton, University of North Carolina, Wilmington
Dale Lund, California State University, San Bernardino
Debra McGinnis, Oakland University
Celinda Reese-Melancon, Oklahoma State University
Mathew Shake, Western Kentucky University
Kim Shifren, Towson University
Gregory Smith, Kent State University
Stephanie Stein, Central Washington University
JoNell Strough, West Virginia University
Bruce Thompson, University of Southern Maine
Laura Thompson, New Mexico State University

Reviewers for Previous Editions

Gerald Adams, University of Guelph
Jackie Adamson, South Dakota School of Mines and Technology
Paul C. Amrhein, University of New Mexico
Cheryl Anagnopoulos, Black Hills State University
Doreen Arcus, University of Massachusetts, Lowell
René L. Babcock, Central Michigan University
Sherry Beaumont, University of Northern British Columbia
W. Keith Berg, University of Florida
James A. Bird, Weber State University
Toni Bisconti, University of Akron
Joyce Bishop, Golden West College
Kimberly Blair, University of Pittsburgh
Tracie L. Blumentritt, University of Wisconsin, La Crosse
Ed Brady, Belleville Area College
Michele Y. Breault, Truman State University
Dilek Buchholz, Weber State University
Lanthan Camblin, University of Cincinnati
Judith W. Cameron, Ohio State University
Joan B. Cannon, University of Massachusetts, Lowell
Michael Caruso, University of Toledo
Susan L. Churchill, University of Nebraska—Lincoln
Gary Creasey, Illinois State University
Rhoda Cummings, University of Nevada—Reno
Rita M. Curl, Minot State University
Carol Lynn Davis, University of Maine
Lou de la Cruz, Sheridan Institute
Byron Egeland, University of Minnesota
Beth Fauth, Utah State University
Karen Fingerman, Purdue University
Maria P. Fracasso, Towson University
Elizabeth E. Garner, University of North Florida
Laurie Gottlieb, McGill University
Dan Grangaard, Austin Community College
Clifford Gray, Pueblo Community College
Marlene Groomes, Miami Dade College
Laura Gruntmeir, Redlands Community College
Laura Hanish, Arizona State University
Traci Haynes, Columbus State Community College
Vernon Haynes, Youngstown State University
Bert Hayslip, University of North Texas
Bob Heller, Athabasca University
Karl Hennig, St. Francis Xavier University
Paula Hillman, University of Wisconsin—Whitewater
Deb Hollister, Valencia Community College
Hui-Chin Hsu, University of Georgia
Lera Joyce Johnson, Centenary College of Louisiana
Janet Kalinowski, Ithaca College
Kevin Keating, Broward Community College
Wendy Kliewer, Virginia Commonwealth University
Marita Kloseck, University of Western Ontario
Karen Kopera-Frye, University of Nevada, Reno
Valerie Kuhlmeier, Queens University
Deanna Kuhn, Teachers College, Columbia University
Rebecca A. López, California State University—Long Beach
Dale Lund, California State University, San Bernardino
Pamela Manners, Troy State University
Ashley Maynard, University of Hawaii
Robert B. McLaren, California State University, Fullerton
Kate McLean, University of Toronto at Mississauga
Randy Mergler, California State University
Karla K. Miley, Black Hawk College
Carol Miller, Anne Arundel Community College
Teri Miller, Milwaukee Area Technical College
David Mitchell, Kennesaw State University
Steve Mitchell, Somerset Community College
Gary T. Montgomery, University of Texas, Pan American
Feleccia Moore-Davis, Houston Community College
Ulrich Mueller, University of Victoria
Karen Nelson, Austin College
Bob Newby, Tarleton State University
Jill Norvilitis, Buffalo State College
Patricia O'Brien, University of Illinois at Chicago
Nancy Ogden, Mount Royal College
Peter Oliver, University of Hartford
Verna C. Pangman, University of Manitoba

Robert Pasnak, George Mason University
Ellen Pastorino, Gainesville College
Julie Patrick, West Virginia University
Marion Perlmutter, University of Michigan
Warren H. Phillips, Iowa State University
Leslee K. Polina, Southeast Missouri State University
Dana Plude, University of Maryland
Dolores Pushkar, Concordia University
Leon Rappaport, Kansas State University
Pamela Roberts, California State University, Long Beach
Stephanie J. Rowley, University of North Carolina
Elmer Ruhnke, Manatee Community College
Randall Russac, University of North Florida
Marie Saracino, Stephen F. Austin State University
Edythe H. Schwartz, California State University—Sacramento
Bonnie Seegmiller, City University of New York, Hunter College
Richard Selby, Southeast Missouri State University
Aurora Sherman, Oregon State University
Carey Sherman, University of Michigan
David Shwalb, Southeastern Louisiana University
Paul S. Silverman, University of Montana
Judi Smetana, University of Rochester
Glenda Smith, North Harris College
Jacqui Smith, University of Michigan
Jeanne Spaulding, Houston Community College
Thomas Spencer, San Francisco State University
Bruce Stam, Chemeketa Community College
JoNell Strough, West Virginia University
Vince Sullivan, Pensacola Junior College
Bruce Thompson, University of Southern Maine
Laura Thompson, New Mexico State University
Mojisola Tiamiyu, University of Toledo
Ruth Tincoff, Harvard University
Joe Tinnin, Richland College
Catya von Károlyi, University of Wisconsin, Eau Claire
L. Monique Ward, University of Michigan
Rob Weisskirch, California State University, Fullerton
Nancy White, Youngstown State University
Ursula M. White, El Paso Community College
Carol L. Wilkinson, Whatcom Community College
Lois J. Willoughby, Miami-Dade Community College
Paul Wink, Wellesley College
Deborah R. Winters, New Mexico State University

I cannot begin to express what a great pleasure it has been, once again, to work with Tom Pauken, Managing Editor. His careful review of manuscript, keen organizational skills, responsive day-to-day communication, insightful suggestions, astute problem solving, interest in the subject matter, and thoughtfulness greatly enhanced the quality of the text and eased the immense challenges that arose during its preparation. Judy Ashkenaz, Development Editor, commented on each chapter, helping to ensure that every thought and concept would be clearly expressed and well-developed. She also assisted with

preparation of photo specifications, drafting of photo captions, and, as needs arose, graciously took on extra tasks, including updating of diverse aspects of the Instructor's Resource Manual. Rachel Trapp, editorial assistant, has been extraordinary. In addition to spending countless hours searching, gathering, and organizing scholarly literature, she assisted with an array of editorial and production tasks. In a pinch, she diligently took over the responsibility of preparing and editing many of the assessments in MyDevelopmentLab (MDL).

The supplements package benefited from the talents and dedication of several other individuals. Leah Shriro revised the IRM brief summaries and lecture outlines. Kimberly Michaud prepared a superb Test Bank and many of the MDL assessments. Judy Ashkenaz and Rachel Trapp assisted me in designing and writing a highly attractive PowerPoint presentation. Maria Henneberry and Phil Vandiver of Contemporary Visuals in Bloomington, IL, prepared an artistic and inspiring set of new video segments addressing diverse topics in lifespan development.

Donna Simons, Senior Production Project Manager, coordinated the complex production tasks that resulted in an exquisitely beautiful third edition. I am grateful for her keen aesthetic sense, attention to detail, flexibility, efficiency, and thoughtfulness. I thank Sarah Evertson and Tom Pauken for photo research that contributed to the exceptional photographs that illustrate the text narrative. Margaret Pinette provided outstanding copyediting and careful compilation of the references list, and Julie Hotchkiss offered meticulous proofreading.

Wendy Albert, Executive Marketing Manager, prepared the beautiful print ads and informative e-mails to the field about *Exploring Lifespan Development,* Third Edition. She has also ensured that accurate and clear information reached Pearson Education's sales force and that the needs of prospective and current adopters were met.

A final word of gratitude goes to my family, whose love, patience, and understanding have enabled me to be wife, mother, teacher, researcher, and text author at the same time. My sons, David and Peter, grew up with my texts, passing from childhood to adolescence and then to adulthood as successive editions were written. David has a special connection with the books' subject matter as an elementary school teacher. Peter is now an experienced attorney, and his vivacious and talented wife Melissa joins a new generation of university faculty dedicated to creative teaching and research. All three continue to enrich my understanding through reflections on events and progress in their own lives. Last, but certainly not least, I thank my husband, Ken, for joining me on a wonderfully fulfilling lifespan journey. Over the past two decades, he willingly made room in our lives for the immensely demanding endeavor of authoring three editions of *Exploring Lifespan Development* and six editions of its parent text, *Development Through the Lifespan.* His reflections, support, and astute counsel made all the difference during the project's final months.

Laura E. Berk

Teaching Resources

A variety of teaching tools are available to assist instructors in organizing lectures, planning demonstrations and examinations, and ensuring student comprehension.

- **MyDevelopmentLab for *Exploring Lifespan Development*.** Authored by Laura Berk, MyDevelopmentLab includes a variety of assessments that enable continuous evaluation of students' learning. Extensive video footage, multimedia simulations, "Careers in Human Development," and interactive activities—all unique to *Exploring Lifespan Development*—are also included.

- **Instructor's Resource Manual (IRM).** This thoroughly revised IRM can be used by first-time or experienced instructors to enrich classroom experiences. Each chapter includes a Chapter-at-a-Glance grid, Brief Chapter Summary, Learning Objectives, detailed Lecture Outline, Learning Activities, "Ask Yourself" questions with answers, Suggested Readings, and Media Materials list.

- **Test Bank.** The Test Bank contains over 2,000 multiple-choice and essay questions, all of which are page-referenced to the chapter content and also classified by type.

- **Pearson MyTest.** This secure online environment allows instructors to easily create exams, study guide questions, and quizzes from any computer with an Internet connection.

- **PowerPoint Presentation.** The PowerPoint presentation provides outlines and illustrations of key topics for each chapter of the text.

- ***Explorations in Lifespan Development* DVD and Guide.** This new DVD is over four hours in length and contains over 70 four- to ten-minute narrated segments, designed for classroom use, that illustrate the many theories, concepts, and milestones of human development. New additions include *Preterm Birth; Autism; First-Grade Science Education; Civic Engagement in Adolescence; Changing Parent–Adolescent Relationships; Adult Obesity;* and *Expertise, Practical Problem Solving, and Leadership in Middle Adulthood.* The DVD and Guide are available to instructors who adopt the text and to students as a supplement when packaged with the text. The DVD Guide helps students use the DVD in conjunction with the textbook, deepening their understanding and applying what they have learned to everyday life.

MyDevelopmentLab

Authored by Laura Berk, MyDevelopmentLab for *Exploring Lifespan Development* engages students through personalized learning and helps instructors with course preparation, content delivery, and assessment. It helps students better prepare for class, quizzes, and exams. It provides educators with a dynamic set of tools for tracking individual and class performance.

- A **Personalized Study Plan** analyzes students' study needs into three levels: Remember, Understand, and Apply.

- The **Gradebook** helps students track progress and get immediate feedback. Automatically graded assessments flow into the Gradebook, which can be viewed in MyDevelopmentLab or exported.

- The **eText** allows students to highlight relevant passages and add notes. Access the eText through a laptop, iPad®, or tablet—or download the free app to use on tablets.

- **Extensive video footage** includes **NEW** video segments such as *Preterm Birth; Autism; First-Grade Science Education; Civic Engagement in Adolescence; Changing Parent–Adolescent Relationships; Adult Obesity;* and *Expertise, Practical Problem Solving, and Leadership in Middle Adulthood.*

- **Multimedia simulations** include **NEW** *Reducing Gender Stereotyping, Create an Older Adult,* and *Working Memory.*

- **Careers in Human Development** explains how studying lifespan development is essential for a wide range of career paths. This tool features over 25 career overviews, which contain interviews with actual practitioners, educational requirements, typical day-to-day activities, and links to websites for additional information.

- **Biographies** of major figures in the field. Examples include Erik Erikson, Jean Piaget, Lev Vygotsky, and Lawrence Kohlberg.

- **NEW MyVirtualLife** includes two simulations. In the first, students observe the effects of their parenting decisions on a child's development. In the second, they simulate their own progress through adulthood, making personal choices and reflecting on their lives.

MyDevelopmentLab can be used by itself or linked to any learning management system. To learn more about how the new MyDevelopmentLab combines learning applications with powerful assessment, visit *www.mydevelopmentlab.com.*

About the Cover Art

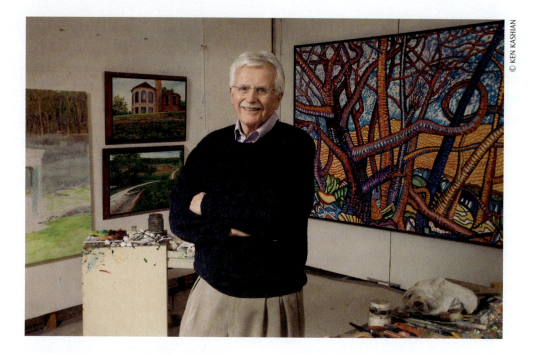

Growing up in Depression-era Detroit, Harold Gregor displayed passion for and talent in art as a child. As early as kindergarten, he drew—so much so that he recalls being placed in the corner for wasting paper. He earned his bachelor's degree from Wayne State University, master's degree from Michigan State University, and Ph.D. in painting from Ohio State University. After a decade of teaching and experimentation with diverse artistic styles in southern California, he moved to the American heartland, joining the faculty at Illinois State University in 1970.

The Illinois farm and prairie landscape quickly became a compelling source of inspiration, and Gregor gained national prominence as one of the foremost American Photorealist painters. Starting with close-up views of corn cribs, an indigenous form of architecture that fascinated him, he soon moved to panoramas and aerial views of prairie farm scenes, introducing imaginative colors that accentuated the unique and varied beauty of the Midwestern landscape.

In 2004, while climbing a cliff trail in Italy, he fell and broke his right wrist. With his right arm in a cast, he transformed an obstacle into an opportunity: He began to paint with his left hand. Once his right arm healed, he refined his left-handed paintings, eventually arriving at brilliantly colorful, abstract stylistic innovations he calls Vibrascapes, of which the dazzling, energetic image on the cover of this text is an example.

Now a distinguished professor emeritus, Harold Gregor is the epitome of "optimal aging." At age 83, he continues to paint prolifically, prepare new exhibitions, and teach. On his studio wall can be found a Chinese proverb, which reads, "What happiness to wake alive again into this same gray world of winter rain." He says the proverb reminds him that although growing older is accompanied by unforeseen challenges, he feels blessed each day to do what he enjoys most: painting and teaching.

Harold Gregor's paintings have been shown at the White House, the American Embassy in Moscow, and the Art Institute of Chicago. They have won numerous prestigious awards and can be viewed in galleries across the United States. To learn more about his life and work, visit *www.hgregor.com*; and watch the video segment, Creativity in Late Life, that accompanies this text.

Legend for Photos Accompanying Sofie's Story

Sofie's story is told in Chapters 1 and 19, from her birth to her death. The photos that appear at the beginning of Chapter 1 follow her through her lifespan and include family members of two succeeding generations.

Page 1

1. Sofie, age 18, high school graduation in 1926.
2. Sofie as a baby, with her mother in 1908.
3. Sofie, age 6, with her brother, age 8, in 1914.
4. Sofie's German passport.
5. Sofie, age 60, and daughter Laura on Laura's wedding day in 1968.
6. Sofie and Phil in 1968, less than two years before Sofie died.
7. Sofie's grandsons, David and Peter, ages 5 and 2, children of Laura and Ken.
8. Laura, Ken, and sons Peter and David, ages 10 and 13, on the occasion of David's Bar Mitzvah in 1985.
9. Peter and Melissa on their wedding day in 2007.
10. Laura, Ken, sons David and Peter, and Peter's wife Melissa, with acclaimed pianist Awadagin Pratt, at the naming of a Pratt Foundation piano scholarship in Sofie's memory.

Page 2 top

Sofie, age 61, and her first grandchild, Ellen, October 1969, less than three months before Sofie died.

Page 2 bottom

Sofie and Phil in their mid-thirties, during World War II, when they became engaged.

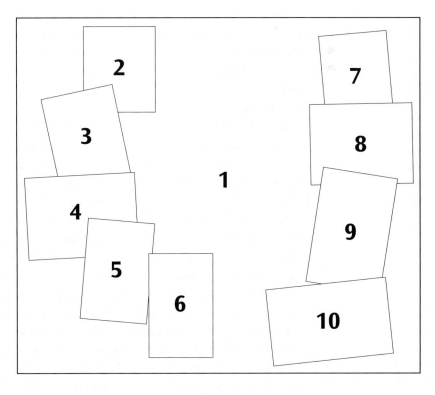

chapter
1

History, Theory, and Research Strategies

This photo essay chronicles the life course and family legacy of Sofie Lentschner. It begins in 1908 with Sofie's infancy and concludes in 2012, four decades after Sofie's death, at an event celebrating the naming of a piano scholarship in her memory. For a description of each photo, see the legend on page xxvii.

chapter outline

A Scientific, Applied, and Interdisciplinary Field

Basic Issues

Continuous or Discontinuous Development? • One Course of Development or Many? • Relative Influence of Nature and Nurture?

The Lifespan Perspective: A Balanced Point of View

Development Is Lifelong • Development Is Multidimensional and Multidirectional • Development Is Plastic • Development Is Influenced by Multiple, Interacting Forces

■ **BIOLOGY AND ENVIRONMENT** Resilience

■ **CULTURAL INFLUENCES** The Baby Boomers Reshape the Life Course

Scientific Beginnings

Darwin: Forefather of Scientific Child Study • The Normative Period • The Mental Testing Movement

Mid-Twentieth-Century Theories

The Psychoanalytic Perspective • Behaviorism and Social Learning Theory • Piaget's Cognitive-Developmental Theory

Recent Theoretical Perspectives

Information Processing • Developmental Cognitive Neuroscience • Ethology and

Evolutionary Developmental Psychology • Vygotsky's Sociocultural Theory • Ecological Systems Theory

Comparing Theories

Studying Development

Common Research Methods • General Research Designs • Designs for Studying Development

■ **CULTURAL INFLUENCES** Immigrant Youths: Adapting to a New Land

Ethics in Lifespan Research

Sofie Lentschner was born in 1908, the second child of Jewish parents who made their home in Leipzig, Germany. Her father was a successful businessman and community leader, her mother a socialite well-known for her charm, beauty, and hospitality. As a baby, Sofie displayed the determination and persistence that would be sustained throughout her life. She sat for long periods inspecting small objects with her eyes and hands. As soon as Sofie could crawl, she steadfastly pulled herself up to the keys of the piano in the parlor and marveled at the tinkling sounds.

COURTESY OF LAURA E. BERK

By the time Sofie entered elementary school, she was an introspective child, often ill at ease at the festive parties that girls of her family's social standing were expected to attend. She immersed herself in schoolwork, especially in mastering foreign languages. Twice a week, she took piano lessons from the finest teacher in Leipzig. By the time Sofie graduated from high school, she spoke English and French fluently and had become an accomplished pianist. Whereas most German girls of her time married by age 20, Sofie postponed serious courtship in favor of entering the university.

Sofie wanted marriage as well as education, but her plans were thwarted by the political turbulence of her times. When Hitler rose to power in the early 1930s, Sofie's father, fearing for the safety of his wife and children, moved the family to Belgium. Conditions for Jews in Europe quickly worsened. The Nazis plundered Sofie's family home and confiscated her father's business. By the end of the 1930s, Sofie had lost contact with all but a handful of her aunts, uncles, cousins, and childhood friends, many of whom (she later learned) were herded into cattle cars and transported to Nazi death camps. In 1939, as anti-Jewish laws and atrocities intensified, Sofie's family fled to the United States.

COURTESY OF LAURA E. BERK

As Sofie turned 30, her parents, convinced that she would never marry and would need a career for financial security, agreed to support her return to school. Sofie earned two master's degrees, one in music and the other in librarianship.

Then, on a blind date, she met Philip, a U.S. army officer. Philip's calm, gentle nature complemented Sofie's intensity and worldliness. Within six months they married. During the next four years, two daughters and a son were born.

When World War II ended, Philip left the army and opened a small men's clothing store. Sofie divided her time between caring for the children and helping Philip in the store. Now in her forties, she was a devoted mother, but few women her age were still rearing young children. As Philip struggled with the business, he spent longer hours at work, and Sofie often felt lonely. She rarely touched the piano, which brought back painful memories of youthful life plans shattered by war. Sofie's sense of isolation and lack of fulfillment frequently left her short-tempered. Late at night, she and Philip could be heard arguing.

As Sofie's children grew older, she returned to school again, this time to earn a teaching credential. Finally, at age 50, she launched a career. For the next decade, she taught German and French to high school students and English to newly arrived immigrants. Besides easing her family's financial difficulties, she felt a gratifying sense of accomplishment and creativity. These years were among the most energetic and satisfying of Sofie's life. She had an unending enthusiasm for teaching—for transmitting her facility with language and her practical understanding of how to adapt to life in a new land. She watched her children adopt many of her values and commitments and begin their marital and vocational lives at the expected time.

Sofie approached age 60 with an optimistic outlook. Released from the financial burden of paying for their children's college education, she and Philip looked forward to greater leisure. Their affection and respect for each other deepened. Once again, Sofie began to play the piano. But this period of contentment was short-lived.

One morning, Sofie felt a hard lump under her arm. Several days later, her doctor diagnosed cancer. Sofie's spirited disposition and capacity to adapt to radical life changes helped her meet the illness head on, defining it as an enemy to be fought and overcome. As a result, she lived five more years. Despite the exhaustion of chemotherapy, Sofie maintained a full schedule of teaching duties and continued to visit and run errands for her elderly mother. But as she weakened physically, she no longer had the stamina to meet her classes. Bedridden for the last few weeks, she slipped quietly into death with Philip at her side. The funeral chapel overflowed with hundreds of Sofie's students. She had granted each a memorable image of a woman of courage and caring.

One of Sofie's three children, Laura, is the author of this book. Married a year before Sofie died, Laura and her husband, Ken, often think of Sofie's message, spoken privately to them on the eve of their wedding day: "I learned from my own life and marriage that you must build a life together but also a life apart. You must grant each other the time, space, and support to forge your own identities, your own ways of expressing yourselves and giving to others. The most important ingredient of your relationship must be respect."

Laura and Ken settled in a small Midwestern city, near Illinois State University, where they have served on the faculty for many years—Laura in the Department of Psychology, Ken in the

Department of Mathematics. They have two sons, David and Peter, who carry Sofie's legacy forward. David shares his grandmother's penchant for teaching; he is a second-grade teacher. Peter, a lawyer, shares his grandmother's love of music, and his wife Melissa—much like Sofie—is both a talented linguist and a musician.

Sofie's story raises a wealth of fascinating issues about human life histories:

- What determines the features that Sofie shares with others and those that make her unique—in physical characteristics, mental capacities, interests, and behaviors?
- What led Sofie to retain the same persistent, determined disposition throughout her life but to change in other essential ways?
- How do historical and cultural conditions—for Sofie, the persecution that destroyed her childhood home, caused

the death of family members and friends, and led her family to flee to the United States—affect well-being throughout life?
- How does the timing of events—for example, Sofie's early exposure to foreign languages and her delayed entry into marriage, parenthood, and career—affect development?
- What factors—both personal and environmental—led Sofie to die sooner than expected?

These are central questions addressed by **developmental science,** a field of study devoted to understanding constancy and change throughout the lifespan (Lerner, 2006; Lerner et al., 2011). Great diversity characterizes the interests and concerns of investigators who study development. But all share a single goal: to identify those factors that influence consistencies and transformations in people from conception to death. ●

A Scientific, Applied, and Interdisciplinary Field

The questions just listed are not merely of scientific interest. Each has *applied,* or practical, importance as well. Research about development has also been stimulated by social pressures to improve people's lives. For example, the beginning of public education in the early twentieth century led to a demand for knowledge about what and how to teach children of different ages. The interest of the medical profession in improving people's health required an understanding of physical development, nutrition, and disease. The social service profession's desire to treat emotional problems and to help people adjust to major life events required information about personality and social development. And parents have continually sought expert advice about child-rearing practices and experiences that would promote their children's well-being.

Our large storehouse of information about development is *interdisciplinary.* It has grown through the combined efforts of people from many fields of study. Because of the need for solutions to everyday problems at all ages, researchers from psychology, sociology, anthropology, biology, and neuroscience have joined forces in research with professionals from education, family studies, medicine, public health, and social service, to name just a few. Together, they have created the field as it exists today—a body of knowledge that is not just scientifically important but also relevant and useful.

Basic Issues

Speculations about how people grow and change have existed for centuries. As they combined with research, they inspired the construction of *theories* of development. A **theory** is an

orderly, integrated set of statements that describes, explains, and predicts behavior. For example, a good theory of infant–caregiver attachment would (1) *describe* the behaviors of babies of 6 to 8 months of age as they seek the affection and comfort of a familiar adult, (2) *explain* how and why infants develop this strong desire to bond with a caregiver, and (3) *predict* the consequences of this emotional bond for future relationships.

Theories are vital tools for two reasons. First, they provide organizing frameworks for our observations of people, *guiding and giving meaning* to what we see. Second, theories that are verified by research provide a sound basis for practical action. Once a theory helps us *understand* development, we are in a much better position to know *how to improve* the welfare and treatment of children and adults.

As we will see, theories are influenced by the cultural values and belief systems of their times. But theories differ from mere opinion or belief: A theory's continued existence depends on *scientific verification*. Every theory must be tested using a fair set of research procedures agreed on by the scientific community, and findings must endure, or be replicated over time.

The field of developmental science contains many theories about what people are like and how they change. Humans are complex beings; they change physically, mentally, emotionally, and socially. And investigators do not always agree on the meaning of what they see. But the existence of many theories helps advance knowledge as researchers try to support, contradict, and integrate these different points of view.

This chapter introduces you to major theories of human development and research strategies used to test them. Although there are many theories, we can easily organize them by looking at the stand they take on three basic issues: (1) Is the course of development continuous or discontinuous? (2) Does one course of development characterize all people, or are there many possible courses? (3) Are genetic or environmental factors more important in influencing development?

Continuous or Discontinuous Development?

How can we best describe the differences in capacities among infants, children, adolescents, and adults? As Figure 1.1 illustrates, major theories recognize two possibilities.

One view holds that infants and preschoolers respond to the world in much the same way as adults do. The difference between the immature and mature being is simply one of *amount or complexity*. For example, when Sofie was a baby, her perception of a piano melody, memory for past events, and ability to categorize objects may have been much like our own. Perhaps her only limitation was that she could not perform these skills with as much information and precision as we can. If this is so, then changes in her thinking must be **continuous**—a process of gradually augmenting the same types of skills that were there to begin with.

According to a second view, infants and children have *unique ways of thinking, feeling, and behaving,* ones quite different from adults. If so, then development is **discontinuous**—a process in which new ways of understanding and responding to the world emerge at specific times. From this perspective, Sofie could not yet perceive, remember, and categorize experiences as a mature person can. Rather, she moved through a series of developmental steps, each of which has unique features, until she reached the highest level of functioning.

Theories that accept the discontinuous perspective regard development as taking place in **stages**—*qualitative* changes in thinking, feeling, and behaving that characterize specific periods of development. In stage theories, development is like climbing a staircase, with each step corresponding to a more mature, reorganized way of functioning. The stage concept also assumes that people undergo periods of rapid transformation as they step up from one stage to the next. In other words, change is fairly sudden rather than gradual and ongoing.

One Course of Development or Many?

Stage theorists assume that people everywhere follow the same sequence of development. Yet children and adults live in distinct **contexts**—unique combinations of personal and environmental circumstances that can result in different paths of change. For example, a shy individual who fears social encounters develops in very different contexts from those of an outgoing agemate who readily seeks out other people (Kagan, 2008a). Children and adults in non-Western village societies have experiences that differ sharply from those of people in large Western cities, which result in markedly different intellectual capacities, social skills, and feelings about the self and others (Shweder et al., 2006).

As you will see, contemporary theorists regard the contexts that shape development as many-layered and complex. On the personal side, they include heredity and biological makeup. On the environmental side, they include home, school, and neighborhood as well as circumstances more remote from everyday life: community resources, societal values, and historical time period. Finally, researchers have become increasingly conscious of cultural diversity in development.

Relative Influence of Nature and Nurture?

In addition to describing the course of human development, each theory takes a stand on a major question about its underly-

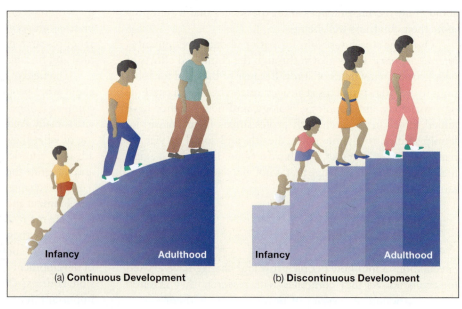

FIGURE 1.1 Is development continuous or discontinuous? (a) Some theorists believe that development is a smooth, continuous process. Individuals gradually add more of the same types of skills. (b) Other theorists think that development takes place in discontinuous stages. People change rapidly as they step up to a new level and then change very little for a while. With each new step, the person interprets and responds to the world in a reorganized, qualitatively different way. As we will see later, still other theorists believe that development is characterized by both continuous and discontinuous change.

Infancy   Adulthood
(a) Continuous Development

Infancy   Adulthood
(b) Discontinuous Development

ing causes: Are genetic or environmental factors more important? This is the age-old **nature–nurture controversy.** By *nature,* we mean the hereditary information we receive from our parents at the moment of conception. By *nurture,* we mean the complex forces of the physical and social world that influence our biological makeup and psychological experiences before and after birth.

Although all theories grant roles to both nature and nurture, they vary in emphasis. A theory's position affects how it explains individual differences. Theorists who emphasize *stability*—that individuals who are high or low in a characteristic (such as verbal ability, anxiety, or sociability) will remain so at later ages—typically stress the importance of *heredity*. If they regard environment as important, they usually point to *early experiences* as establishing a lifelong pattern of behavior. Powerful negative events in the first few years, they argue, cannot be fully overcome by later, more positive ones (Bowlby, 1980; Sroufe, Coffino, & Carlson, 2010). Other theorists, taking a more optimistic view, see development as having substantial **plasticity** throughout life—as open to change in response to influential experiences (Baltes, Lindenberger, & Staudinger, 2006; Overton, 2010).

Since the 1960s, researchers have moved from focusing only on child development to investigating development over the entire life course. This woman and her companions on a river rafting trip illustrate the health, vitality, and life satisfaction of many contemporary older adults.

The Lifespan Perspective: A Balanced Point of View

So far, we have discussed basic issues of human development in terms of extremes—solutions favoring one side or the other. But as we trace the unfolding of the field, you will see that positions have softened. Today, some theorists believe that both continuous and discontinuous changes occur. Many acknowledge that development has both universal features and features unique to each individual and his or her contexts. And a growing number regard heredity and environment as inseparably interwoven, each affecting the potential of the other to modify the child's traits and capacities (Gottlieb, 2007; Overton, 2010).

These balanced visions owe much to the expansion of research from a nearly exclusive focus on the first two decades to include adulthood. In the first half of the twentieth century, it was widely assumed that development stopped at adolescence. Adulthood was viewed as a plateau and aging as a period of decline. The changing character of the North American population awakened researchers to the idea that gains in functioning are lifelong.

Because of improvements in nutrition, sanitation, and medical knowledge, *average life expectancy* (the number of years an individual born in a particular year can expect to live) gained more in the twentieth century than in the preceding 5,000 years. In 1900, life expectancy was just under age 50; today, it is 78.5 years in the United States and even higher in most other industrialized nations. Life expectancy continues to increase; in the United States, it is predicted to reach 84 years in 2050 (U.S. Census Bureau, 2013).

Older adults are not only more numerous but also healthier and more active. Challenging the earlier stereotype of the withering person, they have contributed to a profound shift in our view of human change. Increasingly, researchers are envisioning *development as a dynamic system*—a perpetually ongoing process, extending from conception to death, that is molded by a complex network of biological, psychological, and social influences (Lerner et al., 2011). A leading dynamic systems approach is the **lifespan perspective.** Four assumptions make up this broader view: that development is (1) lifelong, (2) multidimensional and multidirectional, (3) highly plastic, and (4) affected by multiple, interacting forces (Baltes, Lindenberger, & Staudinger, 2006; Staudinger & Lindenberger, 2003).

Development Is Lifelong

According to the lifespan perspective, no single age period is supreme in its impact on the life course. Rather, events occurring during each major period, summarized in Table 1.1 on page 6, can have equally powerful effects on future change.

TABLE 1.1
Major Periods of Human Development

PERIOD	APPROXIMATE AGE RANGE	BRIEF DESCRIPTION
Prenatal	Conception to birth	The one-celled organism transforms into a human baby with remarkable capacities to adjust to life outside the womb.
Infancy and toddlerhood	Birth–2 years	Dramatic changes in the body and brain support the emergence of a wide array of motor, perceptual, and intellectual capacities and first intimate ties to others.
Early childhood	2–6 years	During the "play years," motor skills are refined, thought and language expand at an astounding pace, a sense of morality is evident, and children establish ties with peers.
Middle childhood	6–11 years	The school years are marked by improved athletic abilities; more logical thought processes; mastery of basic literacy skills; advances in self-understanding, morality, and friendship; and the beginnings of peer-group membership.
Adolescence	11–18 years	Puberty leads to an adult-sized body and sexual maturity. Thought becomes abstract and idealistic and school achievement more serious. Adolescents focus on defining personal values and goals and establishing autonomy from the family.
Early adulthood	18–40 years	Most young people leave home, complete their education, and begin full-time work. Major concerns are developing a career, forming an intimate partnership, and marrying, rearing children, or establishing other lifestyles.
Middle adulthood	40–65 years	Many people are at the height of their careers and attain leadership positions. They must also help their children begin independent lives and their parents adapt to aging. They become more aware of their own mortality.
Late adulthood	65 years–death	People adjust to retirement, to decreased physical strength and health, and often to the death of a spouse. They reflect on the meaning of their lives.

Within each period, change occurs in three broad domains: *physical, cognitive,* and *emotional/social,* which we separate for convenience of discussion (see Figure 1.2 for a description of each). Yet, as you already know from the first part of this chapter, these domains overlap and interact.

Development Is Multidimensional and Multidirectional

Think back to Sofie's life and how she continually faced new demands and opportunities. From a lifespan perspective, the challenges and adjustments of development are *multidimensional*—affected by an intricate blend of biological, psychological, and social forces.

Lifespan development is also *multidirectional.* At every period, development is a joint expression of growth and decline. When Sofie mastered languages and music as a school-age child, she gave up refining other skills. Later, when she chose to become a teacher, she let go of other career options. Although gains are especially evident early in life, and losses during the final years, people of all ages can improve current skills and develop new ones (Lang, Rohr, & Williger, 2010; Scheibe, Freund, & Baltes, 2007). Most older adults, for example, devise compensatory techniques for dealing with their increasing memory failures, such as relying more on external aids like calendars and lists.

Besides being multidirectional over time, change is multidirectional within each domain of development. Although some qualities of Sofie's cognitive functioning (such as memory) likely declined in her mature years, her knowledge of both English and French grew throughout her life. And she also developed new forms of thinking—for example, expertise in practical matters, a quality of reasoning called *wisdom.* Recall Sofie's wise advice to Laura and Ken on the eve of their wedding day. Notice how the lifespan perspective includes both continuous and discontinuous change.

Development Is Plastic

Lifespan researchers emphasize that development is plastic at all ages. Consider Sofie's social reserve in childhood and her decision to study rather than marry as a young adult. As new opportunities arose, Sofie moved easily into marriage and childbearing in her thirties. And although parenthood and financial difficulties posed challenges to Sofie's and Philip's happiness, their relationship gradually became richer and more fulfilling. In Chapter 17, we will see that intellectual performance also remains flexible with advancing age. Older people respond to special training with substantial (but not unlimited) gains in a wide variety of mental abilities (Stine-Morrow & Basak, 2011).

Evidence on plasticity reveals that aging is not an eventual "shipwreck," as has often been assumed. Instead, the metaphor

Physical Development

Changes in body size, proportions, appearance, functioning of body systems, perceptual and motor capacities, and physical health

Cognitive Development

Changes in intellectual abilities, including attention, memory, academic and everyday knowledge, problem solving, imagination, creativity, and language

Emotional and Social Development

Changes in emotional communication, self-understanding, knowledge about other people, interpersonal skills, friendships, intimate relationships, and moral reasoning and behavior

FIGURE 1.2 Major domains of development. The three domains are not really distinct. Rather, they overlap and interact.

of a "butterfly"—of metamorphosis and continued potential—provides a more accurate picture of lifespan change. Still, development gradually becomes less plastic, as both capacity and opportunity for change are reduced. And plasticity varies across individuals. Some children and adults experience more diverse life circumstances. Also, as the Biology and Environment box on page 8 indicates, some adapt more easily than others to changing conditions.

Development Is Influenced by Multiple, Interacting Forces

According to the lifespan perspective, *development is influenced by multiple forces:* biological, historical, social, and cultural. Although these wide-ranging influences can be organized into three categories, they work together, combining in unique ways to fashion each life course.

Age-Graded Influences. Events that are strongly related to age and therefore fairly predictable in when they occur and how long they last are called **age-graded influences.** For example, most individuals walk shortly after their first birthday, acquire their native language during the preschool years, reach puberty around age 12 to 14, and (for women) experience menopause in their

late forties or early fifties. These milestones are influenced by biology, but social customs—such as starting school around age 6, getting a driver's license at age 16, and entering college around age 18—can create age-graded influences as well.

For these 18-year-olds, moving into their college dorm is a major life transition, offering new freedoms and responsibilities. Entering college is an age-graded influence, occurring at about the same age for most young people.

Biology and Environment

Resilience

John and his best friend, Gary, grew up in a rundown, crime-ridden, inner-city neighborhood. By age 10, each had experienced years of family conflict followed by parental divorce. Reared from then on in mother-headed households, John and Gary rarely saw their fathers. Both dropped out of high school and were in and out of trouble with the police.

Then their paths diverged. By age 30, John had fathered two children with women he never married, had spent time in prison, was unemployed, and drank alcohol heavily. In contrast, Gary had returned to finish high school, had studied auto mechanics at a community college, and had become manager of a gas station and repair shop. Married with two children, he had saved his earnings and bought a home. He was happy, healthy, and well-adapted to life.

A wealth of evidence shows that environmental risks—poverty, negative family interactions and parental divorce, job loss, mental illness, and drug abuse—predispose children to future problems (Masten & Gewirtz, 2006; Sameroff, 2006; Wadsworth & Santiago, 2008). Why did Gary "beat the odds" and come through unscathed?

Research on **resilience**—the ability to adapt effectively in the face of threats to development—is receiving increased attention as investigators look for ways to protect young people from the damaging effects of stressful life conditions (Masten & Powell, 2003). This interest has been inspired by long-term studies on the relationship of life stressors in childhood to competence and adjustment in adolescence and adulthood (Werner, 2013). In each study, some individuals were shielded from negative outcomes, whereas others had lasting problems. Four broad factors offered protection from the damaging effects of stressful life events.

Personal Characteristics

A child's genetically influenced characteristics can reduce exposure to risk or lead to experiences that compensate for early stressful events. High intelligence and socially valued talents (in music or athletics, for example) increase the chances that a child will have rewarding experiences in school and in the

community that offset the impact of a stressful home life. Temperament is particularly powerful. Children who have easygoing, sociable dispositions and who can readily inhibit negative emotions and impulses tend to have an optimistic outlook on life and a special capacity to adapt to change— qualities that elicit positive responses from others. In contrast, emotionally reactive and irritable children often tax the patience of people around them (Vanderbilt-Adriance & Shaw, 2008; Wang & Deater-Deckard, 2013). For example, both John and Gary moved several times during their childhoods. Each time, John became anxious and angry, whereas Gary looked forward to making new friends.

A Warm Parental Relationship

A close relationship with at least one parent who provides warmth, appropriately high expectations, monitoring of the child's activities, and an organized home environment fosters resilience (Taylor, 2010). But this factor (as well as the next one) is not independent of children's personal characteristics. Children who are relaxed, socially responsive, and able to deal with change are easier to rear and more likely to enjoy positive relationships with parents and other people. At the same time, some children develop more attractive dispositions as a result of parental warmth and attention (Gulotta, 2008).

Social Support Outside the Immediate Family

The most consistent asset of resilient children is a strong bond with a competent, caring adult. For children who do not have a close bond with either parent, a grandparent, aunt, uncle, or teacher who forms a special relationship with the child can promote resilience (Masten & Reed, 2002). Gary received support in adolescence from his grandfather, who listened to Gary's concerns and helped him solve problems.

Associations with rule-abiding peers who value school achievement are also linked to resilience (Tiet, Huizinga, & Byrnes, 2010). But children who have positive relationships with adults are far more likely to establish these supportive peer ties.

This child's close relationship with his father helps shield him from the damaging effects of stressful life conditions.

Community Resources and Opportunities

Community supports—good schools, convenient and affordable health care and social services, libraries, and recreation centers— foster both parents' and children's well-being. In addition, engaging in extracurricular activities at school and in religious youth groups, scouting, and other organizations teaches important social skills, such as cooperation, leadership, and contributing to others' welfare. As participants acquire these competencies, they gain in self-reliance, self-esteem, and community commitment (Benson et al., 2006). As a student, Gary volunteered for Habitat for Humanity, joining a team building affordable housing in low-income neighborhoods. Community involvement offered Gary opportunities to form meaningful relationships, which further strengthened his resilience.

Research on resilience highlights the complex connections between heredity and environment. Armed with positive characteristics, which stem from native endowment, favorable rearing experiences, or both, children and adolescents can act to reduce stressful situations.

But when many risks pile up, they are increasingly difficult to overcome (Obradović et al., 2009). To inoculate children against the negative effects of risk, interventions must not only reduce risks but also enhance children's protective relationships at home, in school, and in the community.

History-Graded Influences.

Development is also profoundly affected by forces unique to a historical era. Examples include epidemics, wars, and periods of economic prosperity or depression; technological advances, such as the introduction of television, computers, and the Internet; and changes in cultural values, such as attitudes toward women and ethnic minorities. These **history-graded influences** explain why people born around the same time—called a *cohort*—tend to be alike in ways that set them apart from people born at other times.

Consider the *baby boomers,* a term used to describe people born between 1946 and 1964, the post–World War II period during which birth rates soared in most Western nations, with an especially sharp increase in the United States. The sheer size of the baby-boom generation made it a powerful social force from the time its members became young adults; today, the baby boomers are redefining our view of middle and late adulthood (see the Cultural Influences box on page 10).

Lessons from an inspiring music teacher is a nonnormative influence that may powerfully affect the direction of this child's life.

ELYSE LEWIN/PHOTOGRAPHERS' CHOICE/GETTY IMAGES

LOOK AND LISTEN

Identify a history-graded influence in your life, and speculate about its impact on people your age. Then ask someone a generation older than you to identify a history-graded influence in his or her life and to reflect on its impact. ●

Nonnormative Influences.

Age-graded and history-graded influences are *normative*—meaning typical, or average— because each affects large numbers of people. **Nonnormative influences** are events that are irregular: They happen to just one person or a few people and do not follow a predictable timetable. Nonnormative influences that had a major impact on the direction of Sofie's life included piano lessons in childhood with an inspiring teacher; delayed marriage, parenthood, and career entry; and a battle with cancer.

Nonnormative influences have become more powerful and age-graded influences less so in contemporary adult development. Compared with Sofie's era, much greater diversity exists today in the ages at which people finish their education, enter careers, get married, have children, and retire. Indeed, Sofie's "off-time" accomplishments would have been less unusual had she been born two generations later!

Notice that instead of a single line of development, the lifespan perspective emphasizes many potential pathways and outcomes—an image more like tree branches extending in diverse directions (see Figure 1.3). Now let's turn to scientific foundations of the field as a prelude to major theories that address various aspects of change.

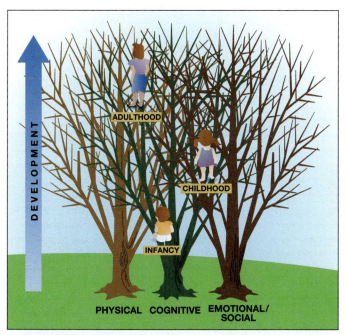

FIGURE 1.3 The lifespan view of development. Rather than envisioning a single line of stagewise or continuous change (see Figure 1.1 on page 4), lifespan theorists conceive of development as more like tree branches extending in diverse directions. Many potential pathways are possible, depending on the contexts that influence the individual's life course. Each branch in this treelike image represents a possible skill within one of the major domains of development. The crossing of the branches signifies that the domains—physical, cognitive, emotional, and social—are interrelated.

ASK YOURSELF

REVIEW Distinguish age-graded, history-graded, and nonnormative influences on lifespan development. Cite an example of each in Sofie's story.

APPLY Anna, a high school counselor, has devised a program that integrates classroom learning with vocational training to help adolescents at risk for school dropout stay in school. What is Anna's position on *stability versus plasticity* in development? Explain.

REFLECT Describe an aspect of your development that differs from a parent's or a grandparent's when he or she was your age. Using influences highlighted by the lifespan perspective, explain this difference in development.

Cultural Influences

The Baby Boomers Reshape the Life Course

Rock star Bono, born in 1960, shares his cohort's sense of social responsibility. Shown here at a health clinic in Lesotho, he is a leader in the fight against AIDS and poverty in Africa.

From 1946 to 1964, 92 percent of all American women of childbearing age gave birth, averaging almost four children each (Croker, 2007). This splurge of births, which extended for nearly two decades, yielded a unique generation often credited with changing the world. Today, the baby boomers comprise more than 80 million adults—nearly 30 percent of the U.S. population (U.S. Census Bureau, 2013). Most are middle-aged, with the oldest having recently entered late adulthood.

Several interrelated factors sparked the post–World War II baby boom. Many people who had postponed marriage and parenthood throughout the Great Depression of the 1930s started families in the 1940s, once the economy had improved. With the end of World War II, returning GIs also began to have children. And as economic prosperity accelerated in the 1950s, making larger families affordable, more people married at younger ages and had several children closely spaced (Stewart & Malley, 2004). Finally, after a war, the desire to make babies generally strengthens. Besides replacing massive loss of life, new births signify hope that "human life will continue" (Croker, 2007, p. 9).

Compared with the previous generation, many more young baby boomers were economically privileged. They were also the recipients of deep emotional investment from their parents, who—having undergone the deprivations of depression and war—often ranked children as the most enduring benefit of their adult lives. These factors may have engendered optimism, confidence, even a sense of entitlement (Elder, Nguyen, & Caspi, 1985). At the same time, their huge numbers—evident in overflowing school classrooms—may have sparked an intense struggle for individual recognition. By the time the boomers reached early adulthood, this set of traits led critics to label them a narcissistic, indulged, "me" generation.

From the mid-1960s to the early 1970s, the "leading-edge" baby boomers (born in the late 1940s and early 1950s) entered colleges and universities in record numbers, becoming better educated than any previous gen-

eration. This cohort—self-focused, socially aware, and in search of distinction—broke away from their parents' family- and marriage-centered lifestyles. Starting in the mid-sixties, marriage rates declined, age of first marriage rose, and divorce rates increased. And the baby boomers responded to the turbulence of those times—the assassination of President Kennedy in 1963, the Vietnam War, and growing racial tensions—by mobilizing around the antiwar, civil rights, and women's movements, yielding a generation of student activists.

By the time the "trailing-edge" boomers (born in the late 1950s and early 1960s) came of age, these movements had left an enduring mark. Even as they turned toward family life and career development, the boomers continued to search for personal meaning, self-expression, and social responsibility. By midlife, the generation had produced an unusually large number of socially concerned writers, teachers, filmmakers, and labor and community organizers, as well as innovative musicians and artists (Cole & Stewart, 1996; Dickstein, 1992). And a multitude of ordinary citizens worked to advance social causes.

In addition, as baby-boom women entered the labor market and struggled for career advancement and equal pay, their self-confidence grew, and they paved the way for the next generation: On average, younger women attained this same level of self-confidence at a much earlier age (Twenge, 1997, 2001). And as baby-boom activists pressed for gender and racial equality, they influenced national policy. The 1960s saw laws passed that banned discrimination in employment practices, in racial access to public accommodations, and in sale or rental of housing. By the 1970s, progress in civil rights served as the springboard for the gay and lesbian rights movement.

Today, the baby boomers are healthier, better educated, and financially better off than

any previous midlife cohort (Whitbourne & Willis, 2006). Their sense of self-empowerment and innovativeness is bringing new vitality to this period of the lifespan, including efforts to increase the personal meaningfulness of their careers and to deepen their lifelong engagement with social causes.

Nevertheless, though advantaged as a generation, the baby boomers are diverse in health status and sense of control over their lives. Those higher in education and income considerably better off. And because retirement savings were heavily hit by the economic recession of 2007 to 2009, many are working longer than they otherwise had planned.

What lies ahead as this gigantic population bulge moves into late adulthood? Most analysts focus on societal burdens, such as rising social security and health-care costs. At the same time, as the boomers could become "our only increasing natural resource" (Freedman, 1999). After retirement, they will have more time to care about others—and more relevant experience and years left to do so—than any previous generation. Policies and programs aimed at recruiting older adults into volunteer and service roles may be one of the best ways to "channel good will into good deeds," combat social ills, and enhance development during all periods of life.

Scientific Beginnings

Scientific study of human development dates back to the late nineteenth and early twentieth centuries. Early observations of human change were soon followed by improved methods and theories, contributing to the firm foundation on which the field rests today.

Darwin: Forefather of Scientific Child Study

British naturalist Charles Darwin (1809–1882) observed the infinite variation among plant and animal species. He saw that within a species, no two individuals are exactly alike. From these observations, he constructed his famous *theory of evolution.*

The theory emphasized two related principles: *natural selection* and *survival of the fittest.* Darwin explained that certain species survive in particular environments because they have characteristics that fit with, or are adapted to, their surroundings. Individuals within a species who best meet the environment's survival requirements live long enough to reproduce and pass their more beneficial characteristics to future generations. Darwin's (1859/1936) emphasis on the adaptive value of physical characteristics and behavior found its way into important developmental theories.

Darwin's theory of evolution emphasizes the adaptive value of physical characteristics and behavior. Affection and care in families promote survival and psychological well-being throughout the lifespan. Here, a son helps his father adjust to using a walker.

During his explorations, Darwin discovered that early prenatal growth is strikingly similar in many species. Other scientists concluded from Darwin's observations that the development of the human child follows the same general plan as the evolution of the human species. Although this belief eventually proved inaccurate, efforts to chart parallels between child growth and human evolution prompted researchers to make careful observations of all aspects of children's behavior. As a result, scientific child study was born.

The Normative Period

G. Stanley Hall (1844–1924), one of the most influential American psychologists of the early twentieth century, is regarded as the founder of the child study movement (Cairns & Cairns, 2006). He also wrote one of the few books of his time on aging, foreshadowing lifespan research. Inspired by Darwin's work, Hall and his well-known student Arnold Gesell (1880–1961) devised theories based on evolutionary ideas. They regarded development as a *maturational process*—a genetically determined series of events that unfold automatically, much like a flower (Gesell, 1933; Hall, 1904).

Hall and Gesell are remembered less for their one-sided theories than for their intensive efforts to describe all aspects of development. This launched the **normative approach,** in which measures of behavior are taken on large numbers of individuals, and age-related averages are computed to represent typical development. Using this procedure, Hall constructed elaborate questionnaires asking children of different ages almost everything they could tell about themselves—interests, fears, imaginary playmates, dreams, friendships, everyday knowledge, and more. Through careful observations and parent interviews, Gesell collected detailed normative information on infants' and children's motor achievements, social behaviors, and personality characteristics.

Gesell was also among the first to make knowledge about child development meaningful to parents. His books, along with Benjamin Spock's *Baby and Child Care,* became central to a rapidly expanding child-rearing literature for parents.

The Mental Testing Movement

While Hall and Gesell were developing their theories and methods in the United States, French psychologist Alfred Binet (1857–1911) was also taking a normative approach, but for a different reason. In the early 1900s, Binet and his colleague Theodore Simon were asked by Paris school officials to find a way to identify children with learning problems for placement in special classes. To address this practical educational concern, they constructed the first successful intelligence test.

In 1916, at Stanford University, Binet's test was adapted for use with English-speaking children. Since then, the English version has been known as the *Stanford-Binet Intelligence Scale.* Besides providing a score that successfully predicted school achievement, the Binet test sparked tremendous interest in individual differences in development.

Mid-Twentieth-Century Theories

In the mid-twentieth century, the study of human development expanded into a legitimate discipline. A variety of theories emerged, each of which still has followers today.

The Psychoanalytic Perspective

In the 1930s and 1940s, as more people sought help from professionals to deal with emotional difficulties, a new question had to be addressed: How and why do people become the way they are? To treat psychological problems, psychiatrists and social workers turned to an approach to personality development that emphasizes each individual's unique life history.

According to the **psychoanalytic perspective**, people move through a series of stages in which they confront conflicts between biological drives and social expectations. How these conflicts are resolved determines the person's ability to learn, to get along with others, and to cope with anxiety. Among the many contributors to the psychoanalytic perspective, two were especially influential: Sigmund Freud, founder of the psychoanalytic movement, and Erik Erikson.

Freud's Theory. Freud (1856–1939), a Viennese physician, treated emotionally troubled adults by having them talk freely about painful childhood events. Working with these recollections, he examined the unconscious motivations of his patients and constructed his **psychosexual theory**, which emphasizes that how parents manage their child's sexual and aggressive drives in the first few years is crucial for healthy personality development.

In Freud's theory, three parts of the personality—id, ego, and superego—become integrated during five stages, summarized in Table 1.2. The *id,* the largest portion of the mind, is the source of basic biological needs and desires. The *ego,* the conscious, rational part of personality, emerges in early infancy to redirect the id's impulses into acceptable behaviors.

Between 3 and 6 years of age, the *superego,* or conscience, develops as parents insist that children conform to the values of society. Now the ego faces the increasingly complex task of reconciling the demands of the id, the external world, and conscience (Freud, 1923/1974). According to Freud, relations established among the id, ego, and superego during the preschool years determine the individual's basic personality.

Freud (1938/1973) believed that during childhood, sexual impulses shift their focus from the oral to the anal to the genital regions of the body. In each stage, parents walk a fine line between permitting too much or too little gratification of their child's basic needs. If parents strike an appropriate balance, then children grow into well-adjusted adults with the capacity for mature sexual behavior and investment in family life.

Freud's theory was the first to stress the influence of the early parent–child relationship on development. But his per-

spective was eventually criticized. First, it overemphasized the influence of sexual feelings in development. Second, because it was based on the problems of sexually repressed, well-to-do adults in nineteenth-century Viennese society, it did not apply in other cultures. Finally, Freud had not studied children directly.

Erikson's Theory. Several of Freud's followers improved on his vision, the most important of whom was Erik Erikson (1902–1994). In his **psychosocial theory,** Erikson emphasized that in addition to mediating between id impulses and superego demands, the ego makes a positive contribution to development, acquiring attitudes and skills that make the individual an active, contributing member of society. A basic psychosocial conflict, which is resolved along a continuum from positive to negative, determines healthy or maladaptive outcomes at each stage. As Table 1.2 shows, Erikson's first five stages parallel Freud's stages, but Erikson added three adult stages.

Unlike Freud, Erikson pointed out that normal development must be understood in relation to each culture's life situation. For example, in the 1940s, he observed that Yurok Indians of the northwest coast of the United States deprived babies of breastfeeding for the first 10 days after birth and instead fed them a thin soup. At age 6 months, infants were abruptly weaned—an experience that, from our cultural vantage point, might seem cruel. But Erikson explained that the Yurok lived in a world in which salmon filled the river just once a year, a circumstance requiring considerable self-restraint for survival.

Contributions and Limitations of the Psychoanalytic Perspective. A special strength of the psychoanalytic perspective is its emphasis on understanding the individual's unique life history. Consistent with this view, psychoanalytic theorists accept the *clinical,* or *case study, method,* yields a detailed picture of the personality of a single person.

ANTONIA TOZER/GETTY IMAGES/AWL IMAGES RM

A child of the Kazakh people of Mongolia observes closely as her grandfather demonstrates how to train an eagle to hunt small animals, essential for the heavily meat-based Kazakh diet. As Erikson recognized, this parenting practice is best understood in relation to the competencies valued and needed in Kazakh culture.

TABLE 1.2 Freud's Psychosexual Stages and Erikson's Psychosocial Stages Compared

APPROXIMATE AGE	FREUD'S PSYCHOSEXUAL STAGE	ERIKSON'S PSYCHOSOCIAL STAGE
Birth–1 year	*Oral:* The new ego directs the baby's sucking activities toward breast or bottle. If oral needs are not met, the individual may develop such habits as thumb sucking, fingernail biting, overeating, or smoking.	*Basic trust versus mistrust:* From warm, responsive care, infants gain a sense of trust, or confidence, that the world is good. Mistrust occurs if infants are neglected or handled harshly.
1–3 years	*Anal:* Toddlers and preschoolers enjoy holding and releasing urine and feces. If parents toilet train before children are ready or make too few demands, conflicts about anal control may appear in the form of extreme orderliness or disorder.	*Autonomy versus shame and doubt:* Using new mental and motor skills, children want to decide for themselves. Parents can foster autonomy by permitting reasonable free choice and not forcing or shaming the child.
3–6 years	*Phallic:* As preschoolers take pleasure in genital stimulation, Freud's Oedipus conflict for boys and Electra conflict for girls arise: Children feel a sexual desire for the other-sex parent. To avoid punishment, they give up this desire and adopt the same-sex parent's characteristics and values. As a result, the superego is formed, and children feel guilty when they violate its standards.	*Initiative versus guilt:* Through make-believe play, children gain insight into the person they can become. Initiative—a sense of ambition and responsibility—develops when parents support their child's sense of purpose. But if parents demand too much self-control, children experience excessive guilt.
6–11 years	*Latency:* Sexual instincts die down, and the superego strengthens as the child acquires new social values from adults and same-sex peers.	*Industry versus inferiority:* At school, children learn to work and cooperate with others. Inferiority develops when negative experiences at home, at school, or with peers lead to feelings of incompetence.
Adolescence	*Genital:* With puberty, sexual impulses reappear. Successful development during earlier stages leads to marriage, mature sexuality, and child rearing.	*Identity versus role confusion:* By exploring values and vocational goals, the young person forms a personal identity. The negative outcome is confusion about future adult roles.
Early adulthood		*Intimacy versus isolation:* Young adults establish intimate relationships. Because of earlier disappointments, some individuals cannot form close bonds and remain isolated.
Middle adulthood		*Generativity versus stagnation:* Generativity means giving to the next generation through child rearing, caring for others, or productive work. The person who fails in these ways feels an absence of meaningful accomplishment.
Old age		*Integrity versus despair:* Integrity results from feeling that life was worth living as it happened. Older people who are dissatisfied with their lives fear death.

© OLIVE PIERCE/BLACK STAR

Erik Erikson

The psychoanalytic approach has also inspired a wealth of research on many aspects of emotional and social development, including infant–caregiver attachment, aggression, sibling relationships, child-rearing practices, morality, gender roles, and adolescent identity.

Despite its contributions, the psychoanalytic perspective is no longer in the mainstream of human development research. Psychoanalytic theorists were so strongly committed to in-depth study of individuals that they failed to consider other methods. In addition, many psychoanalytic ideas, such as psychosexual stages and ego functioning, are so vague that they are difficult or impossible to test empirically (Crain, 2005; Thomas, 2005). Nevertheless, Erikson's broad outline of lifespan change captures the essence of personality development during each major period, so we will return to it in later chapters.

Behaviorism and Social Learning Theory

As the psychoanalytic perspective gained in prominence, the study of development was also influenced by a very different perspective. According to **behaviorism,** directly observable events—stimuli and responses—are the appropriate focus of study. North American behaviorism began in the early twentieth century with the work of John Watson (1878–1958), who wanted to create an objective science of psychology.

Traditional Behaviorism. Watson was inspired by Russian physiologist Ivan Pavlov's studies of animal learning. Pavlov knew that dogs release saliva as an innate reflex when they are given food. But he noticed that his dogs were salivating before they tasted any food—when they saw the trainer who usually fed them. The dogs, Pavlov reasoned, must have learned to associate a neutral stimulus (the trainer) with another stimulus (food) that produces a reflexive response (salivation). Because of this association, the neutral stimulus alone could bring about a response resembling the reflex. Eager to test this idea, Pavlov successfully taught dogs to salivate at the sound of a bell by pairing it with the presentation of food. He had discovered *classical conditioning.*

In a historic experiment that applied classical conditioning to children's behavior, Watson taught an 11-month-old infant, Albert, to fear a neutral stimulus—a soft white rat—by presenting it several times with a sharp, loud sound, which naturally scared the baby. Little Albert, who at first had reached out eagerly to touch the furry rat, began to cry and turn his head away at the sight of it (Watson & Raynor, 1920). Watson concluded that environment is the supreme force in development and that adults can mold children's behavior by carefully controlling stimulus–response associations. He viewed development as a continuous process—a gradual increase with age in the number and strength of these associations.

Another form of behaviorism was B. F. Skinner's (1904–1990) *operant conditioning theory.* According to Skinner, the frequency of a behavior can be increased by following it with a wide variety of *reinforcers,* such as food, praise, or a friendly smile. It can also be decreased through *punishment,* such as disapproval or withdrawal of privileges. We will consider these conditioning techniques further in Chapter 4.

Social Learning Theory. Psychologists wondered whether behaviorism might offer a more direct and effective explanation of the development of social behavior than the less precise concepts of psychoanalytic theory. This sparked approaches that built on the principles of conditioning, offering expanded views of how children and adults acquire new responses.

Several kinds of **social learning theory** emerged. The most influential, devised by Albert Bandura (1925–), emphasizes *modeling,* also known as *imitation* or *observational learning,* as a powerful source of development. The baby who claps her hands after her mother does so and the child who angrily hits a playmate in the same way that he has been punished at home are displaying observational learning. In his early work, Bandura found that diverse factors affect children's motivation to imitate: their own history of reinforcement or punishment for the behavior, the promise of future reinforcement or punishment, and even observing the model being reinforced or punished.

Bandura's work continues to influence much research on social development. But today, his theory stresses the importance of *cognition,* or thinking. In fact, the most recent revision of Bandura's (1992, 2001) theory places such strong emphasis

Social learning theory recognizes that children acquire many skills through modeling. By observing and imitating her mother, this Vietnamese preschooler learns to use chopsticks.

on how we think about ourselves and other people that he calls it a *social-cognitive* rather than a social learning approach.

In Bandura's revised view, children gradually become more selective in what they imitate. From watching others engage in self-praise and self-blame and through feedback about the worth of their own actions, children develop *personal standards* for behavior and *a sense of self-efficacy*—the belief that their own abilities and characteristics will help them succeed. These cognitions guide responses in particular situations (Bandura, 1999, 2001). For example, imagine a parent who often remarks, "I'm glad I kept working on that task, even though it was hard," and who encourages persistence by saying, "I know you can do a good job on that homework!" Soon the child starts to view herself as hard-working and high-achieving and selects people with these characteristics as models. In this way, as individuals acquire attitudes, values, and convictions about themselves, they control their own learning and behavior.

Contributions and Limitations of Behaviorism and Social Learning Theory.
Behaviorism and social learning theory have been helpful in treating adjustment problems. **Behavior modification** consists of procedures that combine conditioning and modeling to eliminate undesirable behaviors and increase desirable responses. It has been used to relieve difficulties in children and adults, ranging from poor time management and unwanted habits to serious problems, such as language delays and persistent aggression (Martin & Pear, 2011).

Nevertheless, many theorists believe that behaviorism and social learning theory offer too narrow a view of important environmental influences, which extend beyond immediate reinforcement, punishment, and modeled behaviors to people's rich physical and social worlds. Behaviorism and social learning theory have also been criticized for underestimating people's contributions to their own development. Bandura, in emphasiz-

TABLE 1.3   Piaget's Stages of Cognitive Development

STAGE	PERIOD OF DEVELOPMENT	DESCRIPTION
Sensorimotor	Birth–2 years	Infants "think" by acting on the world with their eyes, ears, hands, and mouth. As a result, they invent ways of solving sensorimotor problems, such as pulling a lever to hear the sound of a music box, finding hidden toys, and putting objects into and taking them out of containers.
Preoperational	2–7 years	Preschool children use symbols to represent their earlier sensorimotor discoveries. Development of language and make-believe play takes place. However, thinking lacks the logic of the two remaining stages.
Concrete operational	7–11 years	Children's reasoning becomes logical. School-age children understand that a certain amount of lemonade or play dough remains the same even after its appearance changes. They also organize objects into hierarchies of classes and subclasses. However, children think in a logical, organized fashion only when dealing with concrete information they can perceive directly.
Formal operational	11 years on	The capacity for abstract, systematic thinking enables adolescents, when faced with a problem, to start with a hypothesis, deduce testable inferences, and isolate and combine variables to see which inferences are confirmed. Adolescents can also evaluate the logic of verbal statements without referring to real-world circumstances.

Jean Piaget

ing cognition, is unique among theorists whose work grew out of the behaviorist tradition in granting children and adults an active role in their own learning.

Piaget's Cognitive-Developmental Theory

If one individual has influenced research on child development more than any other, it is Swiss cognitive theorist Jean Piaget (1896–1980). North American investigators did not grant Piaget's work much attention until the 1960s, mainly because Piaget's ideas were at odds with behaviorism, which dominated North American psychology in the mid-twentieth century (Cairns & Cairns, 2006). Piaget did not believe that children's learning depends on reinforcers, such as rewards from adults. According to his **cognitive-developmental theory,** children actively construct knowledge as they manipulate and explore their world.

Piaget's Stages. Piaget's view of development was greatly influenced by his early training in biology. Central to his theory is the biological concept of *adaptation* (Piaget, 1971). Just as structures of the body are adapted to fit with the environment, so structures of the mind develop to better fit with, or represent, the external world. In infancy and early childhood, Piaget claimed, children's understanding is different from adults'. For example, he believed that young babies do not realize that an object hidden from view continues to exist. He also concluded that preschoolers' thinking is full of faulty logic. For example,

children younger than age 7 commonly say that the amount of a liquid changes when it is poured into a different-shaped container. According to Piaget, children eventually revise these incorrect ideas in their ongoing efforts to achieve an *equilibrium,* or balance, between internal structures and information they encounter in their everyday worlds.

In Piaget's theory, as the brain develops and children's experiences expand, they move through four broad stages, each characterized by qualitatively distinct ways of thinking. Table 1.3 provides a brief description of Piaget's stages.

In Piaget's concrete operational stage, school-age children think in an organized, logical fashion about concrete objects. This 7-year-old understands that the quantity of pie dough remains the same after he changes its shape from a ball to a flattened circle.

Piaget devised special methods for investigating how children think. Early in his career, he carefully observed his three infant children and presented them with everyday problems, such as an attractive object that could be grasped, mouthed, kicked, or searched for. From their responses, Piaget derived his ideas about cognitive changes during the first two years. To study childhood and adolescent thought, Piaget adapted the clinical method of psychoanalysis, conducting open-ended *clinical interviews* in which a child's initial response to a task served as the basis for Piaget's next question.

Contributions and Limitations of Piaget's Theory.

Piaget convinced the field that children are active learners whose minds consist of rich structures of knowledge. Besides investigating children's understanding of the physical world, Piaget explored their reasoning about the social world. His stages have sparked a wealth of research on children's conceptions of themselves, other people, and human relationships. In practical terms, Piaget's theory encouraged the development of educational philosophies and programs that emphasize discovery learning and direct contact with the environment.

Despite Piaget's overwhelming contributions, his theory has been challenged. Research indicates that Piaget underestimated the competencies of infants and preschoolers. When young children are given tasks scaled down in difficulty and relevant to their everyday experiences, their understanding appears closer to that of the older child and adult than Piaget assumed. Furthermore, many studies show that children's performance on Piagetian problems can be improved with training—findings that call into question Piaget's assumption that discovery learning rather than adult teaching is the best way to foster development (Siegler & Svetina, 2006). Critics also point out that Piaget's stagewise account pays insufficient attention to social and cultural influences on development. Finally, some lifespan theorists disagree with Piaget's conclusion that no major cognitive changes occur after adolescence. Several have proposed important transformations in adulthood (Labouvie-Vief, 2006; Moshman, 2011; Perry, 1970/1998).

ASK YOURSELF

REVIEW What aspect of behaviorism made it attractive to critics of the psychoanalytic perspective? How did Piaget's theory respond to a major limitation of behaviorism?

APPLY A 4-year-old becomes frightened of the dark and refuses to go to sleep at night. How would a psychoanalyst and a behaviorist differ in their views of how this problem developed?

REFLECT Describe a personal experience in which you received feedback from another person that strengthened your sense of self-efficacy—belief that your abilities and characteristics will help you succeed.

Recent Theoretical Perspectives

New ways of understanding development are constantly emerging—questioning, building on, and enhancing of earlier theories. Today, a burst of fresh approaches is broadening our insights into lifespan development.

Information Processing

In the 1970s and 1980s, researchers turned to the field of cognitive psychology for ways to understand the development of thinking. The design of digital computers that use mathematically specified steps to solve problems suggested to psychologists that the human mind might also be viewed as a symbol-manipulating system through which information flows—a perspective called **information processing** (Munakata, 2006). From the time information is presented to the senses at *input* until it emerges as a behavioral response at *output,* information is actively coded, transformed, and organized.

Information-processing researchers often design flowcharts to map the precise steps individuals use to solve problems and complete tasks. They seek to clarify how both task characteristics and cognitive limitations—for example, memory capacity or available knowledge—influence performance (Birney & Sternberg, 2011). To see the usefulness of this approach, let's look at an example.

In a study of problem solving, a researcher asked school-age children to build a bridge across a "river" too wide for any single block to span (Thornton, 1999). Whereas older children easily built successful bridges, only one 5-year-old did. Careful tracking of her efforts revealed that she repeatedly tried unsuccessful strategies, such as pushing two planks together and pressing down on their ends to hold them in place. But eventually, her experimentation triggered the idea of using the blocks as counterweights, as shown in Figure 1.4. Her mistaken procedures helped her understand why the counterweight approach worked.

Some information-processing models, like the one just considered, track children's mastery of one or a few tasks. Others describe the human cognitive system as a whole (Gopnik & Tenenbaum, 2007; Johnson & Mareschal, 2001; Westermann et al., 2006). These general models are used as guides for asking questions about broad changes in thinking: Does a child's ability to solve problems become more organized and "planful" with age? Are declines in memory during old age evident on all types of tasks or only some?

Like Piaget's theory, the information-processing approach regards people as active, sense-making beings (Munakata, 2006). But unlike Piaget's theory, it does not divide development into stages. Rather, most information-processing researchers regard the thought processes studied—perception, attention, memory, planning, categorization of information, and comprehension of written and spoken prose—as similar at all ages but

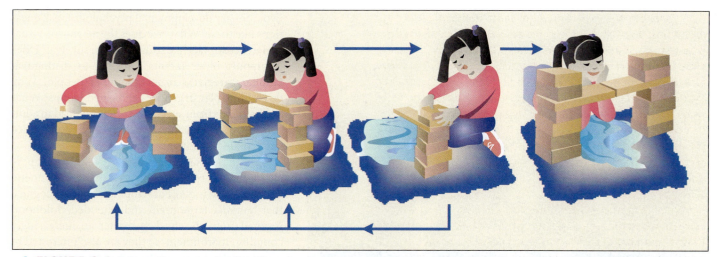

FIGURE 1.4 **Information-processing flowchart showing the steps that a 5-year-old used to solve a bridge-building problem.** Her task was to use blocks varying in size, shape, and weight, some of which were planklike, to construct a bridge across a "river" (painted on a floor mat) too wide for any single block to span. The child discovered how to counterweight and balance the bridge. The arrows reveal that, even after building a successful counterweight, she returned to earlier, unsuccessful strategies, which seemed to help her understand why the counterweight approach worked. (Adapted from Thornton, 1999.)

present to a lesser or greater extent. Their view of development is one of continuous change.

A great strength of the information-processing approach is its commitment to rigorous research methods. Because it has provided precise accounts of how children and adults tackle many cognitive tasks, its findings have important implications for education (Blumenfeld, Marx, & Harris, 2006; Siegler, 2009). But information processing has been better at analyzing thinking into its components than at putting them back together into a comprehensive theory. And it has little to say about aspects of cognition that are not linear and logical, such as imagination and creativity.

Developmental Cognitive Neuroscience

Over the past three decades, as information-processing research has expanded, a new area of investigation arose, called **developmental cognitive neuroscience.** It brings together researchers from psychology, biology, neuroscience, and medicine to study the relationship between changes in the brain and the developing person's cognitive processing and behavior patterns.

Improved methods for analyzing brain activity while children and adults perform various tasks have greatly enhanced knowledge of relationships between brain functioning, cognitive capacities, and behavior (Pennington, Snyder, & Roberts, 2007; Westermann et al., 2007). Armed with these brain-imaging techniques (which we will consider in Chapter 4), neuroscientists are tackling questions like these: How does genetic makeup combine with specific experiences to influence the growth and organization of the child's brain? What neurological changes are related to declines in various aspects of cognitive processing in old age?

During the first five years, the brain is highly plastic—especially open to growth as a result of experience. But it retains

considerable plasticity throughout life. Neuroscientists are identifying the types of experiences that support or undermine brain development at various ages. They are also clarifying the brain bases of many learning and behavior disorders and contributing to the design of effective interventions (Durston & Conrad, 2007; Luciana, 2007; Schlaggar & McCandliss, 2007).

An advantage of having many theories is that they encourage researchers to attend to previously neglected dimensions of people's lives. The final three perspectives we will discuss focus on *contexts* for development. The first of these views emphasizes that the development of many capacities is influenced by our long evolutionary history.

Ethology and Evolutionary Developmental Psychology

Ethology is concerned with the adaptive, or survival, value of behavior and its evolutionary history. Its roots can be traced to the work of Darwin. Two European zoologists, Konrad Lorenz and Niko Tinbergen, laid its modern foundations. Watching diverse animal species in their natural habitats, Lorenz and Tinbergen observed behavior patterns that promote survival. The best known of these is *imprinting,* the early following behavior of certain baby birds, such as geese, that ensures that the young will stay close to the mother and be fed and protected from danger. Imprinting takes place during an early, restricted period of development (Lorenz, 1952). If the mother goose is absent during this time but an object resembling her in important features is present, young goslings may imprint on it instead.

Observations of imprinting led to a major concept in human development: the *critical period.* It refers to a limited time span during which the individual is biologically prepared to acquire certain adaptive behaviors but needs the support of a stimulating environment. Many researchers have investigated whether

Ethology focuses on the adaptive, or survival, value of behavior and on similarities between human behavior and that of other species, especially our primate relatives. Observing this chimpanzee mother cuddling her infant helps us understand the human caregiver–infant relationship.

complex cognitive and social behaviors must be learned during certain time periods. For example, if children are deprived of adequate physical and social stimulation during their early years, will their intelligence be impaired? If language learning is impeded in childhood due to limited parent–child communication, is the capacity to acquire language later reduced?

In later chapters, we will see that the term *sensitive period* applies better to human development than the strict notion of a critical period (Bornstein, 1989). A **sensitive period** is a time that is optimal for certain capacities to emerge and in which the individual is especially responsive to environmental influences. However, its boundaries are less well-defined than those of a critical period. Development can occur later, but it is harder to induce.

Inspired by observations of imprinting, British psychoanalyst John Bowlby (1969) applied ethological theory to the understanding of the human infant–caregiver relationship. He argued that infant smiling, babbling, grasping, and crying are built-in social signals that encourage the caregiver to approach, care for, and interact with the baby. By keeping the parent near, these behaviors help ensure that the infant will be fed, protected from danger, and provided with stimulation and affection necessary for healthy growth. The development of attachment in humans is a lengthy process that leads the baby to form a deep affectionate tie with the caregiver (Thompson, 2006). Bowlby believed that this bond has lifelong consequences for human relationships. In later chapters, we will consider research that evaluates this assumption.

Recently, researchers have extended this effort in a new area of research called **evolutionary developmental psychology.** It seeks to understand the adaptive value of specieswide cognitive, emotional, and social competencies as those competencies change with age (Geary, 2006b; King & Bjorklund, 2010).

Evolutionary developmental psychologists ask questions like these: What role does the newborn's visual preference for facelike stimuli play in survival? Does it support older infants' capacity to distinguish familiar caregivers from unfamiliar people? Why do children play in gender-segregated groups? What do they learn from such play that might lead to adult gender-typed behaviors, such as male dominance and female investment in caregiving?

As these examples suggest, evolutionary psychologists are not just concerned with the genetic and biological roots of development. They recognize that humans' large brain and extended childhood resulted from the need to master an increasingly complex environment, so they are also interested in learning (Bjorklund, Causey, & Periss, 2009).

Recently, evolutionary psychologists have addressed the adaptiveness of human longevity—why adults live as much as one-fourth to one-third of their years after their children are grown (Greve & Bjorklund, 2009). The most common explanation involves the support that grandparents (especially grandmothers) offer in rearing young grandchildren. Another view emphasizes the adaptive value of aging adults' vast knowledge, experience, and sage advice—a rich resource for younger people as they tackle life's many challenges.

Vygotsky's Sociocultural Theory

The field of human development has recently seen a dramatic increase in studies addressing the cultural context of people's lives. Investigations that make comparisons across cultures, and between ethnic groups within cultures, provide insight into whether developmental pathways apply to all people or are limited to particular environmental conditions (Goodnow, 2010).

Today, much research is examining the relationship of *culturally specific beliefs and practices* to development. The contributions of Russian psychologist Lev Vygotsky (1896–1934) have played a major role in this trend. Vygotsky's (1934/1987) perspective, called **sociocultural theory,** focuses on how *culture*—the values, beliefs, customs, and skills of a social group—is transmitted to the next generation. According to Vygotsky, *social interaction*—in particular, cooperative dialogues with more knowledgeable members of society—is necessary for children to acquire the ways of thinking and behaving that make up a community's culture. Vygotsky believed that as adults and more expert peers help children master culturally meaningful activities, the communication between them becomes part of children's thinking. As children internalize the features of these dialogues, they can use the language within them to guide their own thought and actions and to acquire new skills (Winsler, Fernyhough, & Montero, 2009).

In Vygotsky's theory, children undergo certain stagewise changes. For example, when they acquire language, they gain

© ROGER HUTCHINGS/IN PICTURES/CORBIS

A Cambodian girl learns traditional dance forms from her grandmother. She acquires a culturally valued skill by interacting with an older, more experienced member of her culture.

in ability to participate in dialogues with others, and mastery of culturally valued competencies surges forward. When children enter school, they spend much time discussing language, literacy, and other academic concepts—experiences that encourage them to reflect on their own thinking (Bodrova & Leong, 2007). As a result, they advance dramatically in reasoning and problem solving.

At the same time, Vygotsky stressed that dialogues with experts lead to continuous changes in cognition that vary greatly from culture to culture. Consistent with this view, a major finding of cross-cultural research is that cultures select tasks for their members, and social interaction surrounding those tasks leads to competencies essential for success in a particular culture. For example, in industrialized nations, teachers help people learn to read, drive a car, or

use a computer. Among the Zinacanteco Indians of southern Mexico, adult experts guide young girls as they master complicated weaving techniques (Greenfield, 2004).

Research stimulated by Vygotsky's theory reveals that people in every culture develop unique strengths. But Vygotsky's emphasis on social experiences led him to neglect the biological side of development. Although he recognized the importance of heredity and brain growth, he said little about their role in cognitive change.

Ecological Systems Theory

Urie Bronfenbrenner (1917–2005) is responsible for an approach that has moved to the forefront of the field because it offers the most differentiated and complete account of contextual influences on development. **Ecological systems theory** views the person as developing within a complex *system* of relationships affected by multiple levels of the surrounding environment. Because the child's biologically influenced dispositions join with environmental forces to mold development, Bronfenbrenner characterized his perspective as a *bioecological model* (Bronfenbrenner & Morris, 2006).

Bronfenbrenner envisioned the environment as a series of nested structures, including but also extending beyond the home, school, neighborhood, and workplace settings in which people spend their everyday lives (see Figure 1.5). Each layer of the environment joins with the others to powerfully affect development.

FIGURE 1.5 Structure of the environment in ecological systems theory. The *microsystem* concerns relations between the developing person and the immediate environment; the *mesosystem,* connections among immediate settings; the *exosystem,* social settings that affect but do not contain the developing person; and the *macrosystem,* the values, laws, customs, and resources of the culture that affect activities and interactions at all inner layers. The *chronosystem* (not pictured) is not a specific context. Instead, it refers to the dynamic, ever-changing nature of the person's environment.

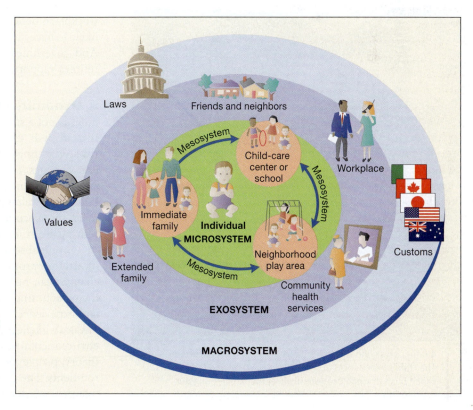

The Microsystem. The innermost level of the environment, the **microsystem,** consists of activities and interaction patterns in the person's immediate surroundings. Bronfenbrenner emphasized that to understand development at this level, we must keep in mind that all relationships are *bidirectional.* For example, adults affect children's behavior, but children's biologically and socially influenced characteristics—their physical attributes, personalities, and capacities—also affect adults' behavior. A friendly, attentive child is likely to evoke positive, patient reactions from parents, whereas an irritable or distractible child is more likely to receive impatience, restriction, and punishment (Crockenberg & Leerkes, 2003).

Third parties—other individuals in the microsystem—also affect the quality of any two-person relationship. If they are supportive, interaction is enhanced. For example, when parents encourage each other in their child-rearing roles, each engages in more effective parenting. In contrast, marital conflict is associated with inconsistent discipline and hostile reactions toward children, who often react with fear and anxiety or with anger and aggression (Caldera & Lindsey, 2006; Low & Stocker, 2012).

The Mesosystem. The second level of Bronfenbrenner's model, the **mesosystem,** encompasses connections between microsystems. For example, a child's academic progress depends not just on activities that take place in classrooms but also on parent involvement in school life and on the extent to which academic learning is carried over into the home (Jeynes, 2012). Among adults, how well a person functions as spouse and parent at home is affected by relationships in the workplace, and vice versa (Gottfried, Gottfried, & Bathurst, 2002).

The Exosystem. The **exosystem** consists of social settings that do not contain the developing person but nevertheless affect experiences in immediate settings. These can be formal organizations, such as the board of directors in the individual's workplace, religious institution, or community health and welfare services. Flexible work schedules, paid maternity and paternity leave, and sick leave for parents whose children are ill are examples of ways that work settings can help parents rear children and, indirectly, enhance the development of both adult and child. Exosystem supports can also be informal. Children are affected by their parents' social networks—friends and extended-family members who provide advice, companionship, and even financial assistance.

LOOK AND LISTEN

Ask a parent to explain his or her most worrisome child-rearing challenge. Cite one source of support at each level of Bronfenbrenner's model that could ease parental stress and promote child development. ●

The Macrosystem. The outermost level of Bronfenbrenner's model, the **macrosystem,** consists of cultural values, laws, customs, and resources. The priority that the macrosystem gives to the needs of children and adults affects the support they receive at inner levels of the environment. For example, in countries that set high standards for the quality of child care and workplace benefits for employed parents, children are more likely to have favorable experiences in their immediate settings. And governments that provide a generous pension plan for retirees support the well-being of older people.

A Dynamic, Ever-Changing System. The environment is not a static force that affects people in a uniform way. Instead, it is ever-changing. Whenever individuals alter the roles or settings in their lives, the breadth of their microsystems changes. These shifts in contexts—or *ecological transitions,* as Bronfenbrenner called them—are often important turning points in development. Starting school, entering the workforce, marrying, becoming a parent, getting divorced, moving, and retiring are examples.

Bronfenbrenner called the temporal dimension of his model the **chronosystem** (the prefix *chrono* means "time"). Life changes can be imposed externally or can arise from within the person, since individuals shape many of their own settings and experiences. How they do so depends on their age; their physical, intellectual, and personality characteristics; and their environmental opportunities. Therefore, in ecological systems theory, people are both products and producers of their environments: The person and the environment form a network of interdependent effects.

© ELLEN B. SENISI PHOTOGRAPHY

A father says good-bye to his daughter at the start of the school day. The child's experiences at school (microsystem) and the father's experiences at work (exosystem) affect the father–daughter relationship.

ASK YOURSELF

REVIEW Explain how each recent theoretical perspective regards children and adults as active contributors to their own development.

APPLY Mario wants to find out precisely how children of different ages recall stories. Anna is interested in how adult–child communication in different cultures influences children's storytelling. Which theoretical perspective has Mario probably chosen? How about Anna? Explain.

REFLECT To illustrate the chronosystem in ecological systems theory, select an important event from your childhood, such as a class with an inspiring teacher, or parental divorce. How did the event affect you? How might its impact have differed had you been five years younger? How about five years older?

Comparing Theories

In the preceding sections, we reviewed major theoretical perspectives in human development research. They differ in many respects. First, they focus on different domains of development. Some, such as the psychoanalytic perspective and ethology, emphasize emotional and social development. Others, such as Piaget's cognitive-developmental theory, information processing, and Vygotsky's sociocultural theory, stress changes in thinking. The remaining approaches—behaviorism, social learning theory, evolutionary developmental psychology, ecological systems theory, and the lifespan perspective—discuss many aspects of human functioning. Second, every theory contains a point of view about development. *TAKE A MOMENT...* As we conclude our review of theoretical perspectives, identify the stand each theory takes on the controversial issues presented at the beginning of this chapter. Then check your analysis against Table 1.4 on page 22.

Studying Development

In every science, research is usually based on a *hypothesis*—a prediction about behavior drawn from a theory. Theories and hypotheses, however, merely initiate the many activities that result in sound evidence on human development. Conducting research according to scientifically accepted procedures involves many steps and choices. Investigators must decide which participants, and how many, to include. Then they must figure out what the participants will be asked to do and when, where, and how many times each will be seen. Finally, they must examine and draw conclusions from their data.

In the following sections, we look at research strategies commonly used to study human development. We begin with common *research methods*—the specific activities of participants, such as taking tests, answering questionnaires, responding to interviews, or being observed. Then we turn to *research designs*—overall plans for research studies that permit the best possible test of the investigator's hypothesis. Finally, we discuss ethical issues involved in doing research with human participants.

Why learn about research strategies? Why not leave these matters to research specialists and concentrate, instead, on what is known about the developing person and how this knowledge can be applied? There are two reasons. First, each of us must be a wise and critical consumer of knowledge. Knowing the strengths and limitations of various research strategies is important in separating dependable information from misleading results. Second, individuals who work directly with children or adults may be in a unique position to build bridges between research and practice by conducting studies, either on their own or in partnership with experienced investigators. Community agencies such as schools, mental health facilities, and parks and recreation programs are increasingly collaborating with researchers in designing, implementing, and evaluating interventions aimed at enhancing development (Guerra, Graham, & Tolan, 2011). To broaden these efforts, a basic understanding of the research process is essential.

LOOK AND LISTEN

Ask a teacher, counselor, social worker, or nurse to describe a question about development he or she would like researchers to address. After reading the rest of this chapter, recommend research strategies best suited to answering that question, citing their strengths and limitations. ●

© ELLEN B. SENISI PHOTOGRAPHY

This preschool teacher is in a unique position to conduct research with important practical implications for young children's learning. To do so, she must be well versed in basic research strategies.

TABLE 1.4

Stances of Major Theories on Basic Issues in Human Development

THEORY	CONTINUOUS OR DISCONTINUOUS DEVELOPMENT?	ONE COURSE OF DEVELOPMENT OR MANY?	RELATIVE INFLUENCE OF NATURE AND NURTURE?
Psychoanalytic perspective	*Discontinuous:* Psychosexual and psychosocial development takes place in stages.	*One course:* Stages are assumed to be universal.	*Both nature and nurture:* Innate impulses are channeled and controlled through child-rearing experiences. *Early experiences* set the course of later development.
Behaviorism and social learning theory	*Continuous:* Development involves an increase in learned behaviors.	*Many possible courses:* Behaviors reinforced and modeled may vary from person to person.	*Emphasis on nurture:* Development is the result of conditioning and modeling. *Both early and later experiences* are important.
Piaget's cognitive-developmental theory	*Discontinuous:* Cognitive development takes place in stages.	*One course:* Stages are assumed to be universal.	*Both nature and nurture:* Development occurs as the brain grows and children exercise their innate drive to discover reality in a generally stimulating environment. *Both early and later experiences* are important.
Information processing	*Continuous:* Children and adults change gradually in perception, attention, memory, and problem-solving skills.	*One course:* Changes studied characterize most or all children and adults.	*Both nature and nurture:* Children and adults are active, sense-making beings who modify their thinking as the brain grows and they confront new environmental demands. *Both early and later experiences* are important.
Ethology and evolutionary developmental psychology	*Both continuous and discontinuous:* Children and adults gradually develop a wider range of adaptive behaviors. Sensitive periods occur in which qualitatively distinct capacities emerge fairly suddenly.	*One course:* Adaptive behaviors and sensitive periods apply to all members of a species.	*Both nature and nurture:* Evolution and heredity influence behavior, and learning lends greater flexibility and adaptiveness to it. In sensitive periods, *early experiences* set the course of later development.
Vygotsky's sociocultural theory	*Both continuous and discontinuous:* Language development and schooling lead to stagewise changes. Dialogues with more expert members of society also lead to continuous changes that vary from culture to culture.	*Many possible courses:* Socially mediated changes in thought and behavior vary from culture to culture.	*Both nature and nurture:* Heredity, brain growth, and dialogues with more expert members of society jointly contribute to development. *Both early and later experiences* are important.
Ecological systems theory	*Not specified.*	*Many possible courses:* Biologically influenced dispositions join with environmental forces at multiple levels to mold development in unique ways.	*Both nature and nurture:* The individual's characteristics and the reactions of others affect each other in a bidirectional fashion. *Both early and later experiences* are important.
Lifespan perspective	**Both continuous and discontinuous:** Continuous gains and declines and discontinuous, stagewise emergence of new skills occur.	**Many possible courses:** Development is influenced by multiple, interacting biological, psychological, and social forces, many of which vary from person to person, leading to diverse pathways of change.	**Both nature and nurture:** Development is multidimensional, affected by an intricate blend of hereditary and environmental factors. Emphasizes plasticity at all ages. **Both early and later experiences** are important.

Common Research Methods

How does a researcher choose a basic approach to gathering information? Common methods include systematic observation, self-reports (such as questionnaires and interviews), clinical or case studies of a single individual, and ethnographies of the life circumstances of a specific group of people. Table 1.5 summarizes the strengths and limitations of each of these methods.

Systematic Observation. Observations of behavior can be made in different ways. One approach is to go into the field, or natural environment, and record the behavior of interest—a method called **naturalistic observation.**

A study of preschoolers' responses to their peers' distress provides a good example (Farver & Branstetter, 1994). Observing 3- and 4-year-olds in child-care centers, the researchers recorded each instance of crying and the reactions of nearby

TABLE 1.5 **Strengths and Limitations of Common Research Methods**

METHOD	DESCRIPTION	STRENGTHS	LIMITATIONS
SYSTEMATIC OBSERVATION			
Naturalistic observation	Observation of behavior in natural contexts	Reflects participants' everyday lives.	Cannot control conditions under which participants are observed.
Structured observation	Observation of behavior in a laboratory, where conditions are the same for all participants	Grants each participant an equal opportunity to display the behavior of interest.	May not yield observations typical of participants' behavior in everyday life.
SELF-REPORTS			
Clinical interview	Flexible interviewing procedure in which the investigator obtains a complete account of the participant's thoughts	Comes as close as possible to the way participants think in everyday life. Great breadth and depth of information can be obtained in a short time.	May not result in accurate reporting of information. Flexible procedure makes comparing individuals' responses difficult.
Structured interview, questionnaires, and tests	Self-report instruments in which each participant is asked the same questions in the same way	Permits comparisons of participants' responses and efficient data collection. Researchers can specify answer alternatives that participants might not think of in an open-ended interview.	Does not yield the same depth of information as a clinical interview. Responses are still subject to inaccurate reporting.
CLINICAL, OR CASE STUDY, METHOD			
	A full picture of one individual's psychological functioning, obtained by combining interviews, observations, and test scores	Provides rich, descriptive insights into factors that affect development.	May be biased by researchers' theoretical preferences. Findings cannot be applied to individuals other than the participant.
ETHNOGRAPHY			
	Participant observation of a culture or distinct social group. By making extensive field notes, the researcher tries to capture the culture's unique values and social processes	Provides a more complete description than can be derived from a single observational visit, interview, or questionnaire.	May be biased by researchers' values and theoretical preferences. Findings cannot be applied to individuals and settings other than the ones studied.

children—whether they ignored, watched, commented on the child's unhappiness, scolded or teased, or shared, helped, or expressed sympathy. Caregiver behaviors—explaining why a child was crying, mediating conflict, or offering comfort—were noted to see if adult sensitivity was related to children's caring responses. A strong relationship emerged. The great strength of naturalistic observation is that investigators can see directly the everyday behaviors they hope to explain.

Naturalistic observation also has a major limitation: Not all individuals have the same opportunity to display a particular behavior in everyday life. In the study just described, some children might have witnessed a child crying more often than others or been exposed to more cues for positive social responses from caregivers. For these reasons, they might have displayed more compassion.

Researchers commonly deal with this difficulty by making **structured observations,** in which the investigator sets up a laboratory situation that evokes the behavior of interest so that every participant has equal opportunity to display the response. In one such study, 2-year-olds' emotional reactions to harm that

they thought they had caused were observed by asking each of them to take care of a rag doll that had been modified so its leg would fall off when the child picked it up. Researchers recorded children's facial expressions of sadness, efforts to help the doll, and body tension—responses indicating worry, remorse, and a desire to make amends for the mishap. In addition, mothers were asked to engage in brief conversations about emotions with their children (Garner, 2003). Toddlers whose mothers more often explained the causes and consequences of emotion were more likely to express concern for the injured doll.

Systematic observation provides invaluable information on how children and adults actually behave, but it tells us little about the reasoning behind their responses. For that information, researchers must turn to self-report techniques.

Self-Reports. Self-reports ask research participants to provide information on their perceptions, thoughts, abilities, feelings, attitudes, beliefs, and past experiences. They range from relatively unstructured interviews to highly structured interviews, questionnaires, and tests.

In a **clinical interview,** researchers use a flexible, conversational style to probe for the participant's point of view. In the following example, Piaget questioned a 5-year-old child about his understanding of dreams:

> *Where does the dream come from?*—I think you sleep so well that you dream.—*Does it come from us or from outside?*—From outside.—*When you are in bed and you dream, where is the dream?*—In my bed, under the blanket. I don't really know. If it was in my stomach, the bones would be in the way and I shouldn't see it.—*Is the dream there when you sleep?*—Yes, it is in the bed beside me. (Piaget, 1926/1930, pp. 97–98)

Although a researcher conducting clinical interviews with more than one participant would typically ask the same first question to establish a common task, individualized prompts are used to provide a fuller picture of each person's reasoning.

The clinical interview has two major strengths. First, it permits people to display their thoughts in terms that are as close as possible to the way they think in everyday life. Second, the clinical interview can provide a large amount of information in a fairly brief period. For example, in an hour-long session, we can obtain a wide range of information on child rearing from a parent or on life circumstances from an older adult—much more than we could capture by observing for the same amount of time.

A major limitation of the clinical interview has to do with accuracy. Some participants, wishing to please the interviewer, may make up answers that do not represent their actual thinking. When asked about past events, some may have trouble recalling exactly what happened. And because the clinical interview depends on verbal ability and expressiveness, it may underestimate the capacities of individuals who have difficulty putting their thoughts into words.

The clinical interview has also been criticized because of its flexibility. When questions are phrased differently for each participant, responses may reflect the manner of interviewing rather than real differences in the way people think about a topic. **Structured interviews** (including tests and questionnaires), in which each participant is asked the same set of questions in the same way, eliminate this problem. But structured interviews do not yield the same depth of information as clinical interviews. And they can still be affected by the problem of inaccurate reporting. Currently, more researchers are combining the two approaches to see if they yield consistent findings (Yoshikawa et al., 2008). And blending the two methods is likely to offer a clearer picture than either method can alone.

The Clinical, or Case Study, Method.

An outgrowth of psychoanalytic theory, the **clinical,** or **case study, method** brings together a wide range of information on one person, including interviews, observations, and test scores. The aim is to obtain as complete a picture as possible of that individual's psychological functioning and the experiences that led up to it.

The clinical method is well-suited to studying the development of certain types of individuals who are few in number but

Using the clinical, or case study, method, this researcher interacts with a 3-year-old during a home visit. Interviews and observations will contribute to an in-depth picture of this child's psychological functioning.

vary widely in characteristics. For example, the method has been used to find out what contributes to the accomplishments of *prodigies*—extremely gifted children who attain adult competence in a field before age 10. Consider Adam, a boy who read, wrote, and composed musical pieces before he was out of diapers. Clinical research indicates that such children rarely realize their extraordinary potential without nurturing, committed parents, and exceptional teachers who guide and encourage the child's special gift (Goldsmith, 2000; Moran & Gardner, 2006).

The clinical method yields richly detailed case narratives that offer valuable insights into the many factors influencing development. Nevertheless, because information often is collected unsystematically and subjectively, researchers' theoretical preferences may bias their observations and interpretations. In addition, investigators cannot assume that their conclusions apply, or generalize, to anyone other than the person studied (Stanovich, 2013). Even when patterns emerge across several cases, it is wise to confirm these with other research strategies.

Methods for Studying Culture.

To study the impact of culture, researchers adjust the methods just considered or tap procedures specially devised for cross-cultural and multicultural research (Triandis, 2007). Which approach investigators choose depends on their research goals.

Sometimes researchers are interested in characteristics that are believed to be universal but that vary in degree from one society to the next: Are parents warmer or more directive in some cultures than others? How strong are gender stereotypes in different nations? In each instance, several cultural groups will be compared, and all participants must be questioned or observed in the same way. Therefore, researchers draw on the observational and self-report procedures we have already considered, adapting them through translation so they can be understood in each cultural context. Still, investigators must be mindful of cultural differences in familiarity with being observed and responding to self-report instruments, which may bias their findings (Van de Vijver, Hofer, & Chasiotis, 2010).

At other times, researchers want to uncover the *cultural meanings* of children's and adults' behaviors by becoming as familiar as possible with their way of life. To achieve this goal, investigators rely on a method borrowed from the field of anthropology—**ethnography**. Like the clinical method, ethnographic research is a descriptive, qualitative technique. But instead of aiming to understand a single individual, it is directed toward understanding a culture or a distinct social group through *participant observation*. Typically, the researcher spends months, and sometimes years, in the cultural community, participating in its daily life. Extensive field notes are gathered, consisting of a mix of observations, self-reports from members of the culture, and careful interpretations by the investigator (Miller, Hengst, & Wang, 2003; Shweder et al., 2006). Later, these notes are put together into a description of the community that tries to capture its unique values and social processes.

In some ethnographies, investigators look at many aspects of experience, as one team of researchers did in describing what it is like to grow up in a small American town. Others focus on one or a few settings and issues—for example, barriers to effective parent–school communication in a Mexican-American community or African-Caribbean adults' reactions to a diagnosis of high blood pressure, signaling elevated risk for heart disease (Higginbottom, 2006; Peshkin, 1997; Valdés, 1998). Researchers may supplement traditional self-report and obser-

vational methods with ethnography if they suspect that unique meanings underlie cultural differences, as the Cultural Influences box on page 26 reveals.

Ethnographers strive to minimize their own influence on the culture they are studying by becoming part of it. Nevertheless, as with clinical studies, investigators' cultural values and theoretical commitments sometimes lead them to observe selectively or misinterpret what they see. In addition, the findings of ethnographic studies cannot be assumed to generalize beyond the people and settings in which the research was conducted.

ASK YOURSELF

REVIEW Why might a researcher choose structured observation over naturalistic observation? How about the reverse?

APPLY A researcher wants to study the thoughts and feelings of parents on active duty in the military and those of their school-age and adolescent children. Which method should she use? Why?

REFLECT Reread the description of nonnormative influences on page 9, and cite an example from your own life. Which method would be best-suited to studying the impact of such an event on development?

General Research Designs

In deciding on a research design, investigators choose a way of setting up a study that permits them to test their hypotheses with the greatest certainty possible. Two main types of designs are used in all research on human behavior: *correlational* and *experimental*.

Correlational Design. In a **correlational design**, researchers gather information on individuals, generally in natural life circumstances, without altering their experiences. Then they look at relationships between participants' characteristics and their behavior or development. Suppose we want to answer the following question: Do parents' styles of interacting with their children have any bearing on children's intelligence? In this and many other instances, the conditions of interest are difficult or impossible to arrange and control and must be studied as they currently exist.

Correlational studies have one major limitation: We cannot infer cause and effect. For example, if we were to find that parental interaction is related to children's intelligence, we would not know whether parents' behavior actually *causes* intellectual differences among children. In fact, the opposite is possible: The behaviors of highly intelligent children may be so attractive that they cause parents to interact more favorably. Or a third variable that we did not even consider, such as the amount of noise and distraction in the home, may cause changes in both parental interaction and children's intelligence.

This Western researcher spent months living among the Efe people of the Republic of Congo in an effort to understand their way of life. Here he observes young children sharing food.

© ED TRONICK/ANTHRO-PHOTO

Cultural Influences

Immigrant Youths: Adapting to a New Land

Over the past several decades, a rising tide of immigrants has come to North America, fleeing war and persecution in their homelands or seeking better life chances. Today, nearly one-fourth of U.S. children and adolescents have foreign-born parents, making them the fastest growing sector of the U.S. youth population. About 20 percent of these young people are foreign-born themselves, mostly from Latin America, the Caribbean, and Asia (Hernandez, Denton, & Macartney, 2008; Suárez-Orozco, Todorova, & Qin, 2006).

How well are immigrant youths adapting to their new country? To find out, researchers use multiple research methods—academic testing, questionnaires assessing psychological adjustment, and in-depth ethnographies.

Academic Achievement and Adjustment

Although educators and laypeople often assume that the transition to a new country has a negative impact on psychological well-being, evidence reveals that children of immigrant parents adapt well. Students who are first-generation (foreign-born) and second-generation (American-born, with immigrant parents) often achieve in school as well as or better than students of native-born parents (Fuligni, 2004; Hao & Woo, 2012; Hernandez, Denton, & Macartney, 2008). Findings on psychological adjustment are similar. Compared with their agemates, adolescents from immigrant families are less likely to commit delinquent and violent acts, to use drugs and alcohol, or to have early sex. They are also less likely to be obese or to have missed school because of illness. And they tend to report just as high, and at times higher, self-esteem as young people with native-born parents (Fuligni, 1998; Saucier et al., 2002; Supple & Small, 2006).

These outcomes are strongest for Chinese, Filipino, Japanese, Korean, and East Indian youths (Fuligni, 2004; Louie, 2001; Portes & Rumbaut, 2005). Variation in adjustment is greater among Mexican, Central American, and Southeast Asian (Hmong, Cambodian,

Laotian, Thai, and Vietnamese) young people, who show elevated rates of school dropout, delinquency, teenage parenthood, and drug use. Disparities in parental economic resources, education, English-language proficiency, and support of children contribute to these trends (García Coll & Marks, 2009; Pong & Landale, 2012).

Still, even youths whose parents face considerable financial hardship and who speak little English are successful (Hao & Woo, 2012; Hernandez, Denton, & Macartney, 2008). Factors other than income are responsible.

Family and Community Influences

Ethnographies reveal that immigrant parents view education as the surest way to improve life chances (García Coll & Marks, 2009; Goldenberg et al., 2001). They remind their children that, because educational opportunities were not available in their native countries, they themselves are often limited to menial jobs. And while preserving their culture's values, these parents also make certain adaptations—for example, supporting education for daughters even though their culture of origin endorses it only for sons.

Adolescents from these families internalize their parents' valuing of education, endorsing it more strongly than agemates with native-born parents (Fuligni, 2004; Su & Costigan, 2008). Because minority ethnicities usually stress allegiance to family and community over individual goals, first- and second-generation young people feel a strong sense of obligation to their parents. They view school success as both their own and their parents' success and as a way of repaying their parents for the hardships they have endured (Bacallao & Smokowski, 2007; Fuligni, Yip, & Tseng, 2002). Both family relationships and school achievement protect these youths from delinquency, early pregnancy and drug use, and other risky behav-

These Hmong boys perform in an ethnic festival in St. Paul, Minnesota, where many Hmong immigrants have settled. Cultural values that foster allegiance to family and community promote high achievement and protect many immigrant youths from involvement in risky behaviors.

iors (see the Biology and Environment box on resilience on page 8).

Immigrant parents of successful youths typically develop close ties to an ethnic community, which exerts additional control through a high consensus on values and constant monitoring of young people's activities. As one 16-year-old straight-A student remarked, "My parents know pretty much all the kids in the neighborhood. . . . Everybody here knows everybody else. It's hard to get away with much" (Zhou & Bankston, 1998, pp. 93, 130).

The experiences of well-adjusted immigrant youths are not problem-free. Chinese adolescents who had arrived in the United States within the previous year described their adjustment as very difficult because they were not proficient in English and, as a result, found many everyday tasks challenging and felt socially isolated (Yeh et al., 2008). Young immigrants also encounter racial and ethnic prejudices and experience tensions between family values and the new culture—challenges we will take up in Chapter 12. In the long term, however, family and community cohesion, supervision, and high expectations promote favorable outcomes.

Will the death of her husband affect this elderly widow's physical health and psychological well-being? A correlational design can be used to answer this question, but it does not permit researchers to determine the precise cause of their findings.

In correlational studies and in other types of research designs, investigators often examine relationships by using a **correlation coefficient**—a number that describes how two measures, or variables, are associated with each other. We will encounter the correlation coefficient in discussing research findings throughout this book, so let's look at what it is and how it is interpreted. A correlation coefficient can range in value from +1.00 to –1.00. The *magnitude, or size, of the number* shows the *strength of the relationship*. A zero correlation indicates no relationship; the closer the value is to +1.00 or –1.00, the stronger the relationship. For instance, a correlation of –.78 is high, –.52 is moderate, and –.18 is low. Note, however, that correlations of +.52 and –.52 are equally strong. The *sign of the number* (+ or –) refers to the *direction of the relationship*. A positive sign (+) means that as one variable *increases,* the other also *increases.* A negative sign (–) indicates that as one variable *increases,* the other *decreases.*

Let's look at some examples of how a correlation coefficient works. One researcher reported a +.55 correlation between a measure of maternal language stimulation and the size of children's vocabularies at 2 years of age (Hoff, 2003). This is a moderate correlation, which indicates that mothers who spoke more to their toddlers had children who were more advanced in language development. In two other studies, maternal sensitivity was modestly associated with children's cooperativeness in consistent ways. First, maternal warmth during play correlated positively with 2-year-olds' willingness to comply with their mother's directive to clean up toys, at +.34 (Feldman & Klein, 2003). Second, the extent to which mothers spoke harshly, interrupted, and controlled their 4-year-olds' play correlated negatively with children's compliance, at –.31 for boys and –.42 for girls (Smith et al., 2004).

TAKE A MOMENT... Are you tempted to conclude from these correlations that the maternal behaviors influenced children's responses? Although the researchers suspected this was so, they could not be sure of cause and effect. Can you think of other possible explanations? Finding a relationship in a corre-

lational study does suggest that tracking down its cause—using a more powerful experimental strategy, if possible—would be worthwhile.

Experimental Design. An **experimental design** permits inferences about cause and effect because researchers use an evenhanded procedure to assign people to two or more treatment conditions. In an experiment, the events and behaviors of interest are divided into two types: independent and dependent variables. The **independent variable** is the one the investigator expects to cause changes in another variable. The **dependent variable** is the one the investigator expects to be influenced by the independent variable. Cause-and-effect relationships can be detected because the researcher directly *controls* or *manipulates* changes in the independent variable by exposing participants to the treatment conditions. Then the researcher compares their performance on measures of the dependent variable.

In one *laboratory experiment,* investigators explored the impact of adults' angry interactions on children's adjustment (El-Sheikh, Cummings, & Reiter, 1996). They hypothesized that the way angry encounters end (independent variable) affects children's emotional reactions (dependent variable). Four- and 5-year-olds were brought to a laboratory one at a time, accompanied by their mothers. One group was exposed to an *unresolved-anger treatment,* in which two adult actors entered the room and argued but did not work out their disagreements. The other group witnessed a *resolved-anger treatment,* in which the adults ended their disputes by apologizing and compromising. When witnessing a follow-up adult conflict, children in the resolved-anger treatment showed fewer behavioral signs of distress, such as anxious facial expressions. The experiment revealed that anger resolution can reduce the stressful impact of adult conflict on children.

In experimental studies, investigators must control for participants' characteristics that could reduce the accuracy of their findings. In the study just described, if a greater number of children from homes high in parental conflict ended up in the unresolved-anger treatment, we could not tell what produced the results—the independent variable or the children's backgrounds. To protect against this problem, researchers engage in **random assignment** of participants to treatment conditions. By using an unbiased procedure, such as drawing numbers out of a hat or flipping a coin, investigators increase the chances that participants' characteristics will be equally distributed across treatment groups.

Modified Experimental Designs: Field and Natural Experiments. Most experiments are conducted in laboratories, where researchers can achieve the maximum possible control over treatment conditions. But, as we have already indicated, findings obtained in laboratories may not always apply to everyday situations. In *field experiments,* investigators assign participants randomly to treatment conditions in natural settings. In the experiment just described, we can conclude that the emotional climate established by adults affects

TABLE 1.6

Strengths and Limitations of Research Designs

DESIGN	DESCRIPTION	STRENGTHS	LIMITATIONS
GENERAL			
Correlational	The investigator obtains information on participants without altering their experiences.	Permits study of relationships between variables.	Does not permit inferences about cause-and-effect relationships.
Experimental	Through random assignment of participants to treatment conditions, the investigator manipulates an independent variable and examines its effect on a dependent variable. Can be conducted in the laboratory or the natural environment.	Permits inferences about cause-and-effect relationships.	When conducted in the laboratory, findings may not generalize to the real world. In *field experiments*, control over the treatment is usually weaker than in the laboratory. In *natural*, or *quasi-*, *experiments*, lack of random assignment substantially reduces the precision of research.
DEVELOPMENTAL			
Longitudinal	The investigator studies the same group of participants repeatedly at different ages.	Permits study of common patterns and individual differences in development and relationships between early and later events and behaviors.	Age-related changes may be distorted because of participant dropout, practice effects, and cohort effects.
Cross-sectional	The investigator studies groups of participants differing in age at the same point in time.	More efficient than the longitudinal design. Not plagued by such problems as participant dropout and practice effects.	Does not permit study of individual developmental trends. Age differences may be distorted because of cohort effects.
Sequential	The investigator conducts several similar cross-sectional or longitudinal studies (called sequences). These might study participants over the same ages but in different years, or they might study participants over different ages but during the same years.	When the design includes longitudinal sequences, permits both longitudinal and cross-sectional comparisons. Also reveals cohort effects. Permits tracking of age-related changes more efficiently than the longitudinal design.	May have the same problems as longitudinal and cross-sectional strategies, but the design itself helps identify difficulties.

children's behavior in the laboratory. But does it also do so in daily life?

Another study helps answer this question. Ethnically diverse, poverty-stricken families with a 2-year-old child were randomly assigned to either a brief intervention condition, called the Family Check-Up, or a no-intervention control group. The intervention consisted of three home-based sessions in which a consultant gave parents feedback about their child-rearing practices and their child's adjustment, explored parents' willingness to improve, and identified community services appropriate to each family's needs (Dishion et al., 2008). Findings showed that families assigned to the Family Check-Up (but not controls) gained in positive parenting, which predicted a reduction in child problem behaviors—sometimes still evident a year later.

When researchers cannot randomly assign participants and manipulate conditions in the real world, they can sometimes compromise by conducting *natural, or quasi-, experiments,* comparing treatments that already exist, such as different family environments, schools, workplaces, or retirement villages. These studies differ from correlational research only in that groups of participants are carefully chosen to ensure that their

characteristics are as much alike as possible. In this way, investigators do their best to rule out alternative explanations for their treatment effects, though they cannot achieve the precision and rigor of true experimental research.

Table 1.6 summarizes the strengths and limitations of correlational and experimental designs. It also includes an overview of designs for studying development, to which we turn next.

Designs for Studying Development

Scientists interested in human development require information about the way research participants change over time. To answer questions about development, they must extend correlational and experimental approaches to include measurements at different ages using longitudinal and cross-sectional designs.

The Longitudinal Design. In a **longitudinal design,** participants are studied repeatedly, and changes are noted as they get older. The time spanned may be relatively short (a few months to several years) or very long (a decade or even a lifetime). The longitudinal approach has two major strengths. First, because it tracks the performance of each person over time, researchers can identify common patterns as well as individual differences in development. Second, longitudinal studies permit investigators to examine relationships between early and later events and behaviors. Let's illustrate these ideas.

A group of researchers wondered whether children who display extreme personality styles—either angry and explosive or shy and withdrawn—retain the same dispositions when they become adults and, if so, the consequences for long-term adjustment. To answer these questions, the researchers delved into the archives of the Guidance Study, a well-known longitudinal investigation initiated in 1928 at the University of California, Berkeley, and continued for several decades (Caspi, Elder, & Bem, 1987, 1988).

Results revealed that the two personality styles were moderately stable. Between ages 8 and 30, a good number of individuals remained the same, whereas others changed substantially. When stability did occur, it appeared to be due to a "snowballing effect," in which children evoked responses from adults and peers that acted to maintain their dispositions. Explosive youngsters were likely to be treated with anger, whereas shy children were apt to be ignored. As a result, explosive children came to view others as hostile, while shy children regarded them as unfriendly (Caspi & Roberts, 2001). Together, these factors led explosive children to sustain or increase their unruliness and shy children to continue to withdraw—patterns that tended to persist into adulthood and to negatively affect adjustment to marriage, parenting, and work life. Shy women, however, were an exception. Because a withdrawn, unassertive style was socially acceptable for females at that time, they showed no special adjustment problems.

Problems in Conducting Longitudinal Research.
Despite their strengths, longitudinal investigations pose a number of problems. For example, participants may move away or drop out of the research for other reasons. This biases the sample so that it no longer represents the population to whom researchers would like to generalize their findings. Also, from repeated study, people may become more aware of their own thoughts, feelings, and actions and revise them in ways that have little to do with age-related change. In addition, they may become "test-wise." Their performance may improve as a result of *practice effects*—better test-taking skills and increased familiarity with the test—not because of factors commonly associated with development.

The most widely discussed threat to longitudinal findings is **cohort effects** (see page 9): Individuals born in the same time period are influenced by a particular set of historical and cultural conditions. Results based on one cohort may not apply to people developing at other times. For example, unlike the findings on female shyness described in the preceding section, which were gathered in the 1950s, today's shy adolescent girls and young women tend to be poorly adjusted—a difference that may be due to changes in gender roles in Western societies. Shy young people, whether male or female, feel more anxious, depressed, and lonely and may do less well in educational and

Cohort effects are particular historical and cultural conditions that affect individuals born in the same time period. Young people who witnessed Barack Obama and his family celebrating his election victory in 2008 and again in 2012 came away with a new sense of what is possible for members of America's ethnic minorities.

career attainment than their agemates (Karevold et al., 2012; Mounts et al., 2006). Similarly, a longitudinal study of lifespan development would probably result in quite different findings if it were carried out around the time of World War II versus in the second decade of the twenty-first century.

Cohort effects don't just operate broadly on an entire generation. They also occur when specific experiences influence some groups of individuals but not others in the same generation—for example, some children and adults more profoundly affected than others by an economic recession, a natural disaster, or a terrorist attack.

The Cross-Sectional Design.
The length of time it takes for many behaviors to change, even in limited longitudinal studies, has led researchers to turn toward a more efficient strategy for studying development. In the **cross-sectional design,** groups of people differing in age are studied at the same point in time. Because participants are measured only once, researchers need not be concerned about such difficulties as participant dropout or practice effects.

A study in which students in grades 3, 6, 9, and 12 filled out a questionnaire about their sibling relationships provides a good illustration (Buhrmester & Furman, 1990). Findings revealed that feelings of sibling companionship declined during adolescence. The researchers speculated that as adolescents move from psychological dependence on the family to greater involvement with peers, they may have less time and emotional need to invest in siblings. As we will see in Chapter 12, subsequent research has confirmed this age-related trend.

Problems in Conducting Cross-Sectional Research.

Despite its convenience, cross-sectional research does not provide evidence about development at the level at which it actually occurs: the individual. For example, in the cross-sectional study of sibling relationships just discussed, comparisons are limited to age-group averages. We cannot tell if important individual differences exist. Indeed, longitudinal findings reveal that adolescents vary considerably in the changing quality of their sibling relationships. Although many become more distant, others become more supportive and intimate, still others more rivalrous and antagonistic (Kim et al., 2006; Whiteman & Loken, 2006).

Cross-sectional studies—especially those that cover a wide age span—have another problem. Like longitudinal research, they can be threatened by cohort effects. For example, comparisons of 10-year-old cohorts, 20-year-old cohorts, and 30-year-old cohorts—groups born and reared in different years—may not really represent age-related changes. Instead, they may reflect unique experiences associated with the historical period in which the age groups were growing up.

Improving Developmental Designs.

Researchers have devised ways of building on the strengths and minimizing the weaknesses of longitudinal and cross-sectional approaches. Several modified developmental designs have resulted.

Sequential Designs.

To overcome some of the limitations of traditional developmental designs, investigators sometimes use **sequential designs,** in which they conduct several similar cross-sectional or longitudinal studies (called *sequences*). The sequences might study participants over the same ages but in different years, or they might study participants over different ages but during the same years. Figure 1.6 illustrates the first of these options. As it also reveals, some sequential designs combine longitudinal and cross-sectional strategies, an approach that has two advantages:

- We can find out whether cohort effects are operating by comparing participants of the same age who were born in different years. In the example in Figure 1.6, we can compare the three longitudinal samples at ages 20, 30, and 40. If they do not differ, we can rule out cohort effects.

- We can make longitudinal and cross-sectional comparisons. If outcomes are similar in both, then we can be especially confident about our findings.

In a study that used the design in Figure 1.6, researchers wanted to find out whether adult personality development progresses as Erikson's psychosocial theory predicts (Whitbourne et al., 1992). Questionnaires measuring Erikson's stages were given to three cohorts of 20-year-olds, each born a decade apart. The cohorts were reassessed at ten-year intervals. Consistent with Erikson's theory, longitudinal and cross-sectional gains in identity and intimacy occurred between ages 20 and 30—a trend unaffected by historical time period. But a powerful cohort effect emerged for the sense of industry: At age 20, Cohort 1 scored substantially below Cohorts 2 and 3. Notice that members of Cohort 1 reached age 20 in the mid-1960s. As college students, they were part of an era of political protest that reflected disenchantment with the work ethic. Once out of college, they caught up with the other cohorts in industry. Followed up in 2001 at age 54, Cohort 1 showed a decline in focus on identity issues and a gain in ego integrity—trends expected to continue through late adulthood (Sneed, Whitbourne, & Culang, 2006). Future tracking of Cohorts 2 and 3 will reveal whether they, too, follow this Erikson-predicted psychosocial path.

By uncovering cohort effects, sequential designs help explain diversity in development. Yet to date only a small number of sequential studies have been conducted.

Combining Experimental and Developmental Designs.

Perhaps you noticed that all the examples of longitudinal and cross-sectional research we have considered permit only correlational, not causal, inferences. Sometimes researchers can explore the causal link between experiences and development by experimentally manipulating the experiences. If, as a result, development improves, then we have strong evidence for a

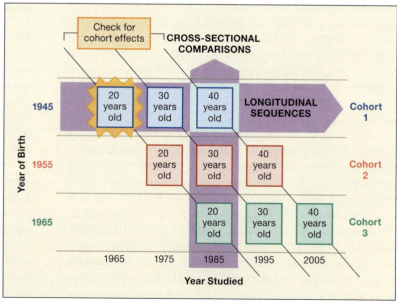

FIGURE 1.6 Example of a sequential design. Three cohorts, born in 1945 (blue), 1955 (pink), and 1965 (green), are followed longitudinally from 20 to 40 years of age. The design permits the researcher to check for cohort effects by comparing people of the same age who were born in different years. In a study that used this design, the 20-year-olds in Cohort 1 differed substantially from the 20-year-olds in Cohorts 2 and 3, indicating powerful cohort effects. This design also permits longitudinal and cross-sectional comparisons. Similar findings lend additional confidence in the results.

causal association. Today, research that combines an experimental strategy with either a longitudinal or a cross-sectional approach is becoming increasingly common.

ASK YOURSELF

REVIEW Explain how cohort effects can affect the findings of both longitudinal and cross-sectional studies. How do sequential designs reveal cohort effects?

APPLY A researcher compares older adults with chronic heart disease to those with no major health problems and finds that the first group scores lower on mental tests. Can the researcher conclude that heart disease causes a decline in intellectual functioning in late adulthood? Explain.

REFLECT Suppose a researcher asks you to enroll your baby in a 10-year longitudinal study. What factors would lead you to agree and stay involved? Do your answers shed light on why longitudinal studies often have biased samples?

Ethics in Lifespan Research

Research into human behavior creates ethical issues because, unfortunately, the quest for scientific knowledge can sometimes exploit people. For this reason, special guidelines for research have been developed by the federal government, by funding agencies, and by research-oriented associations, such as the American Psychological Association (2002) and the Society for Research in Child Development (2007). Table 1.7 presents a summary of basic research rights drawn from these guidelines. *TAKE A MOMENT…* After examining them, read about the following research situations, each of which poses a serious ethical dilemma. What precautions do you think should be taken in each instance?

● In a study of moral development, an investigator wants to assess children's ability to resist temptation by videotaping their behavior without their knowledge. She promises 7-year-olds a prize for solving difficult puzzles but tells them not to look at a classmate's correct solutions, which are deliberately placed at the back of the room. Informing children ahead of time that cheating is being studied or that their behavior is being monitored will destroy the purpose of the study.

● A researcher wants to study the impact of mild daily exercise on the physical and mental health of elderly patients in nursing homes. He consults each resident's doctor to make sure that the exercise routine will not be harmful. But when he seeks the residents' consent, he finds that many do not comprehend the purpose of the research. And some appear to agree simply to relieve feelings of loneliness.

As these examples indicate, when children or the aged take part in research, the ethical concerns are especially complex. Immaturity makes it difficult or impossible for children to evaluate for themselves what participation in research will mean. And because mental impairment rises with very advanced age, some older adults cannot make voluntary and informed choices (Dubois et al., 2011; Society for Research in Child Development, 2007). The life circumstances of others make them unusually vulnerable to pressure for participation.

TABLE 1.7 **Rights of Research Participants**

RESEARCH RIGHT	DESCRIPTION
Protection from harm	Participants have the right to be protected from physical or psychological harm in research. If in doubt about the harmful effects of research, investigators should seek the opinion of others. When harm seems possible, investigators should find other means for obtaining the desired information or abandon the research.
Informed consent	All participants, including children and aging adults, have the right to have explained to them, in language appropriate to their level of understanding, all aspects of the research that may affect their willingness to participate. When children are participants, informed consent of parents as well as of others who act on the child's behalf (such as school officials) should be obtained, preferably in writing. Older adults who are cognitively impaired should be asked to appoint a surrogate decision maker. If they cannot do so, then someone should be named by an institutional review board (IRB) after careful consultation with relatives and professionals who know the person well. All participants have the right to discontinue participation in the research at any time.
Privacy	Participants have the right to concealment of their identity on all information collected in the course of research. They also have this right with respect to written reports and any informal discussions about the research.
Knowledge of results	Participants have the right to be informed of the results of research in language that is appropriate to their level of understanding.
Beneficial treatments	If experimental treatments believed to be beneficial are under investigation, participants in control groups have the right to alternative beneficial treatments if they are available.

Sources: American Psychological Association, 2002; Society for Research in Child Development, 2007.

PIERRE ANDRIEU/AFP/GETTY IMAGES

This older adult requires only typical informed-consent procedures to participate in research. But some elders with cognitive impairments or chronic illnesses may need the assistance of a surrogate decision maker.

The ultimate responsibility for the ethical integrity of research lies with the investigator. But researchers are advised—and often required—to seek advice from others. Committees for this purpose, called *institutional review boards (IRBs),* exist in colleges, universities, and other institutions. If there are any risks to participants' safety and welfare that the research does not justify, then the IRB always favors the participants' interests.

The ethical principle of *informed consent* requires special interpretation when participants cannot fully appreciate the research goals and activities. Parental consent is meant to protect the safety of children, whose ability to decide is not yet mature. But as soon as children are old enough to appreciate the purpose of the research, and certainly by age 7, their own informed consent should be obtained in addition to parental consent. Around this age, changes in children's thinking permit them to better understand basic scientific principles and the needs of others. Researchers should respect and enhance these new capacities by giving school-age children a full explanation of research activities in language they can understand (Fisher, 1993). Extra care must be taken when telling children that the information they provide will be kept confidential and that they can end their participation at any time. Even adolescents may not understand, and sometimes do not believe, these promises (Bruzzese & Fisher, 2003; Ondrusek et al., 1998).

Most older adults require no more than the usual informed-consent procedures. Yet many investigators set upper age limits in studies relevant to the elderly, thereby excluding the oldest adults (Bayer & Tadd, 2000). Older adults should not be stereotyped as incompetent to decide about their own participation or to engage in research activities. Nevertheless, extra measures, such as the appointment of a surrogate decision maker to safeguard the older person's welfare, must be taken to protect those who are cognitively impaired or chronically ill.

Finally, all ethical guidelines advise that special precautions be taken in the use of deception and concealment, as occurs when researchers observe people from behind one-way mirrors, give them false feedback about their performance, or do not tell them the truth about the real purpose of the research. When these kinds of procedures are used, *debriefing,* in which the investigator provides a full account and justification of the activities, occurs after the research session is over. But young children often lack the cognitive skills to understand the reasons for deceptive procedures, and despite explanations, even older children may leave the research situation with their trust in adults undermined. Ethical standards permit deception if investigators satisfy IRBs that a study's potential benefits to society are great enough to justify infringing on participants' right to informed consent and risking other harm (Fisher, 2005). Nevertheless, because deception may have serious emotional consequences for some youngsters, many experts in research ethics believe that investigators should use it only if the risk of harm is minimal.

SUMMARY

A Scientific, Applied, and Interdisciplinary Field
(p. 3)

What is developmental science, and what factors stimulated expansion of the field?

- **Developmental science** is an interdisciplinary field devoted to understanding human constancy and change throughout the lifespan. Research on human development has been stimulated by both scientific curiosity and social pressures to improve people's lives.

Basic Issues (p. 3)

Identify three basic issues on which theories of human development take a stand.

- Each **theory** of human development takes a stand on three basic issues: (1) development as a **continuous** process or a series of **discontinuous stages;** (2) one course of development characterizing all individuals, or many possible courses, depending on **contexts;** (3) development determined primarily by genetic or environmental factors and either stable or characterized by substantial **plasticity.**

The Lifespan Perspective: A Balanced Point of View
(p. 5)

Describe the lifespan perspective on development.

- The **lifespan perspective** envisions development as a dynamic system and as lifelong, multidimensional (affected by biological, psychological, and social forces), multidirectional (a joint expression of growth and decline), and plastic (open to change through new experiences).

- Furthermore, in the lifespan perspective, three categories of influences shape the life course: (1) **age-graded influences,** which are predictable in timing and duration; (2) **history-graded influences,** unique to a particular historical era; and (3) **nonnormative influences,** unique to one or a few individuals.

Scientific Beginnings (p. 11)

Describe the major early influences on the scientific study of development.

- Darwin's theory of evolution influenced important developmental theories and inspired scientific child study. In the early twentieth century, Hall and Gesell introduced the **normative approach,** which produced a large body of descriptive facts about development.

- Binet and Simon constructed the first successful intelligence test, which sparked interest in individual differences in development and led to a heated **nature–nurture controversy.**

Mid-Twentieth-Century Theories (p. 12)

What theories influenced human development research in the mid-twentieth century?

- In the 1930s and 1940s, psychiatrists and social workers turned to the **psychoanalytic perspective** for help in treating people's emotional problems. In Freud's **psychosexual theory,** the individual moves through five stages, during which three portions of the personality—id, ego, and superego—become integrated. Erikson's **psychosocial theory** expands Freud's theory by emphasizing the development of culturally relevant attitudes and skills and the lifespan nature of development.

- As the psychoanalytic perspective gained in prominence, **behaviorism** and **social learning theory** emerged, emphasizing principles of conditioning and modeling and practical procedures of **behavior modification.**

- In contrast to behaviorism, Piaget's **cognitive-developmental theory** emphasizes children's active role in constructing knowledge as they manipulate and explore their world. According to Piaget, children move through four stages, from the baby's sensorimotor action patterns to the adolescent's capacity for abstract, systematic thinking.

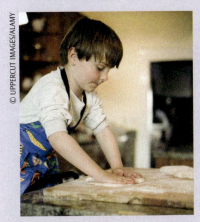

Recent Theoretical Perspectives (p. 16)

Describe recent theoretical perspectives on human development.

- **Information processing** views the mind as a complex symbol-manipulating system and development as undergoing continuous change. This approach provides precise accounts of how children and adults tackle cognitive tasks.

- Researchers in **developmental cognitive neuroscience** study the relationship between changes in the brain and the development of cognitive processing and behavior patterns. They are identifying the types of experiences to which the brain is sensitive at various ages and the brain bases of learning and behavior disorders.

- Three contemporary perspectives emphasize contexts of development. **Ethology** stresses the adaptive value of behavior and inspired the **sensitive period** concept. In **evolutionary developmental psychology,** which extends this emphasis, researchers seek to understand the adaptiveness of specieswide competencies as they change with age.

- Vygotsky's **sociocultural theory** focuses on how culture is transmitted from one generation to the next through social interaction. Through cooperative dialogues with more expert members of society, children acquire culturally relevant knowledge and skills.

- **Ecological systems theory** views the individual as developing within a complex system of relationships affected by multiple, nested layers of the surrounding environment—**microsystem, mesosystem, exosystem,** and **macrosystem.** The **chronosystem** represents the dynamic, ever-changing nature of individuals and their experiences.

Comparing Theories (p. 21)

Identify the stand taken by each major theory on the three basic issues of human development.

- Theories vary widely in their focus on different domains of development and in their view of how development occurs. (For a full summary, see Table 1.4 on page 22.)

Studying Development (p. 21)

Describe methods commonly used in research on human development.

- **Naturalistic observations,** gathered in everyday environments, permit researchers to see directly the everyday behaviors they hope to explain. In contrast, **structured observations,** which take place in laboratories, give every participant an equal opportunity to display the behaviors of interest.

- Self-report methods can be flexible and open-ended like the **clinical interview.** Alternatively, in **structured interviews** (including tests and questionnaires), each participant is asked the same questions in the same way. Investigators use the **clinical,** or **case study, method** to gain an in-depth understanding of a single individual.

- To understand the unique values and social processes of a culture or distinct social group, researchers rely on **ethnography,** engaging in participant observation.

Distinguish between correlational and experimental research designs, noting the strengths and limitations of each.

- The **correlational design** examines relationships between variables without altering people's experiences. The **correlation coefficient** is often used to measure the association between variables.

- An **experimental design** permits cause-and-effect inferences. Researchers manipulate an **independent variable** by exposing participants to two or more treatment conditions. Then they determine what effect this variable has on a **dependent variable. Random assignment** to treatment conditions reduces the chances that participant characteristics will affect the accuracy of experimental findings.

- Field and natural, or quasi-, experiments compare treatments in natural environments. However, these approaches are less rigorous than laboratory experiments.

Describe designs for studying development, noting the strengths and limitations of each.

- The **longitudinal design** permits researchers to identify common patterns and individual differences in development and to examine relationships between early and later events and behaviors. Longitudinal research poses several problems, including biased sampling, practice effects, and **cohort effects.**

AP IMAGES/CHRIS CARLSON

- The **cross-sectional design** is an efficient way to study age-related trends, but it is limited to comparisons of age-group averages. Cross-sectional studies, especially those that cover a wide age span, are also vulnerable to cohort effects.

- By comparing participants of the same age who were born in different years, investigators use **sequential designs** to discover whether cohort effects are operating. When researchers combine experimental and developmental designs, they can examine causal influences on development.

Ethics in Lifespan Research
(p. 31)

What special ethical concerns arise in research on human development?

- Because the quest for scientific knowledge has the potential to exploit people, the ethical principle of informed consent requires special safeguards for children and for elderly people who are cognitively impaired or chronically ill. The use of deception in research with children is especially risky because it may undermine their basic faith in the honesty of adults.

Important Terms and Concepts

Genetic and Environmental Foundations

© ELLEN B. SENISI PHOTOGRAPHY

Heredity and environment combine in intricate ways, making members of this large extended family both alike and different in physical characteristics and behavior.

chapter outline

"It's a girl!" announces the doctor, holding up the squalling newborn baby as her parents gaze with amazement at their miraculous creation.

"A girl! We've named her Sarah!" exclaims the proud father to eager relatives waiting for news of their new family member.

As we join these parents in thinking about how this wondrous being came into existence and imagining her future, we are struck by many questions. How could this baby, equipped with everything necessary for life outside the womb, have developed from the union of two tiny cells? What ensures that Sarah will, in due time, roll over, walk, talk, make friends, learn, imagine, and create—just like other typical children born before her? Why is she a girl and not a boy, dark-haired rather than blond, calm and cuddly instead of wiry and energetic? What difference will it make that Sarah is given a name and place in one family, community, nation, and culture rather than another?

To answer these questions, this chapter takes a close look at the foundations of development: heredity and environment. Because nature has prepared us for survival, all humans have features in common. Yet each of us is also unique. ***TAKE A MOMENT...*** Think about several of your friends, and jot down the most obvious physical and behavioral similarities between them and their parents. Did you find that one person shows combined features of both parents, another resembles just one parent, whereas a third is not like either parent? These directly observable characteristics are called **phenotypes.** They depend in part on the individual's **genotype**—the complex blend of genetic information that determines our species and influences all our unique characteristics. Yet phenotypes are also affected by each person's lifelong history of experiences.

We begin our discussion with a review of basic genetic principles that help explain similarities and differences among us in appearance and behavior. Then we turn to aspects of the environment that play powerful roles throughout the lifespan. Finally, we consider the question of how nature and nurture *work together* to shape the course of development. ●

Genetic Foundations

Each of us is made up of trillions of units called *cells*. Within every cell (except red blood cells) is a control center, or *nucleus,* containing rodlike structures called **chromosomes,** which store and transmit genetic information. Human chromosomes come in 23 matching pairs (an exception is the XY pair in males, which we will discuss shortly). Each member of a pair corresponds to the other in size, shape, and genetic functions, with one chromosome inherited from the mother and one from the father (see Figure 2.1).

The Genetic Code

Chromosomes are made up of a chemical substance called **deoxyribonucleic acid,** or **DNA.** As Figure 2.2 shows, DNA is a long, double-stranded molecule that looks like a twisted ladder. Each rung of the ladder consists of a specific pair of chemical substances called *bases,* joined together. It is this sequence of base pairs that provides genetic instructions. A **gene** is a segment of DNA along the length of the chromosome. Genes can be of different lengths—perhaps 100 to several thousand ladder rungs long. An estimated 20,000 to 25,000 genes lie along the human chromosomes (Human Genome Project, 2008).

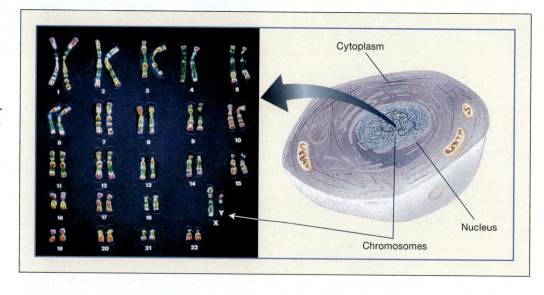

FIGURE 2.1 **A karyotype, or photograph, of human chromosomes.** The 46 chromosomes shown on the left were isolated from a human cell, stained, greatly magnified, and arranged in pairs according to decreasing size of the upper "arm" of each chromosome. The twenty-third pair, XY, reveals that the cell donor is a male. In a female, this pair would be XX. (© CNRI/ Science Photo Library/Photo Researchers, Inc.)

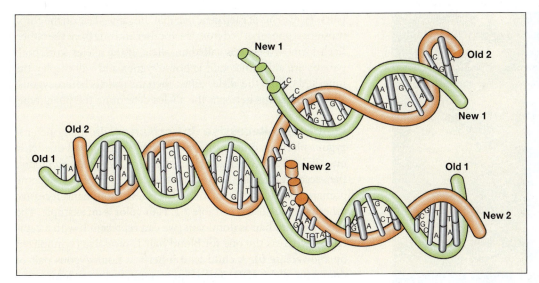

FIGURE 2.2 **DNA's ladder-like structure.** This figure shows that the pairings of bases across the rungs of the ladder are very specific: Adenine (A) always appears with thymine (T), and cytosine (C) always appears with guanine (G). Here, the DNA ladder duplicates by splitting down the middle of its ladder rungs. Each free base picks up a new complementary partner from the area surrounding the cell nucleus.

A unique feature of DNA is that it can duplicate itself through a process called **mitosis.** This special ability permits the one-celled fertilized ovum to develop into a complex human being composed of a great many cells. Refer again to Figure 2.2, and you will see that during mitosis, the chromosomes copy themselves. As a result, each new body cell contains the same number of chromosomes and genetic information.

Genes accomplish their task by sending instructions for making a rich assortment of proteins to the *cytoplasm,* the area surrounding the cell nucleus. Proteins, which trigger chemical reactions throughout the body, are the biological foundation on which our characteristics are built. How do humans, with far fewer genes than scientists once thought, develop into such complex beings? The answer lies in the proteins our genes make, which break up and reassemble in staggering variety—about 10 to 20 million altogether. Within the cell, wide-ranging environmental factors modify gene expression (Lashley, 2007). So even at this microscopic level, biological events are the result of *both* genetic and nongenetic forces.

The Sex Cells

New individuals are created when two special cells called **gametes,** or sex cells—the sperm and ovum—combine. A gamete contains only 23 chromosomes, half as many as a regular body cell. Gametes are formed through a cell division process called **meiosis,** which halves the number of chromosomes normally present in body cells. When sperm and ovum unite at conception, the resulting cell, called a **zygote,** will again have 46 chromosomes.

In meiosis, the chromosomes pair up and exchange segments, so that genes from one are replaced by genes from another. Then chance determines which member of each pair will gather with others and end up in the same gamete. These events make the likelihood extremely low—about 1 in 700 trillion—that nontwin siblings will be genetically identical (Gould & Keeton, 1996). The genetic variability produced by meiosis is adaptive:

It increases the chances that at least some members of a species will cope with ever-changing environments and will survive.

In the male, the cells from which sperm arise are produced continuously throughout life, so a healthy man can father a child at any age after sexual maturity. The female is born with a bank of ova already present in her ovaries, though new ova may arise from ovarian stem cells later on (White et al., 2012). Nevertheless, females can bear children for only three to four decades. Still, there are plenty of female sex cells: About 350 to 450 will mature during a woman's childbearing years (Moore, Persaud, & Torchia, 2013).

Boy or Girl?

Return to Figure 2.1 and note that 22 of the 23 pairs of chromosomes are matching pairs, called **autosomes** (meaning *not* sex chromosomes). The twenty-third pair consists of **sex chromosomes.** In females, this pair is called XX; in males, it is called XY. The X is a relatively large chromosome, whereas the Y is short and carries little genetic material. When gametes form in males, the X and Y chromosomes separate into different sperm cells. The gametes that form in females all carry an X chromosome. Therefore, the sex of the new organism is determined by whether an X-bearing or a Y-bearing sperm fertilizes the ovum.

Multiple Offspring

Ruth and Peter, a couple I know well, tried for several years to have a child, without success. Eventually, Ruth's doctor prescribed a fertility drug, and twins—Jeannie and Jason—were born. Jeannie and Jason are **fraternal,** or **dizygotic, twins,** the most common type of multiple offspring, resulting from the release and fertilization of two ova. Genetically, they are no more alike than ordinary siblings. Older maternal age, fertility drugs, and in vitro fertilization (to be discussed shortly) are major causes of the dramatic rise in fraternal twinning and

These identical, or monozygotic, twins were created when a duplicating zygote separated into two clusters of cells, which developed into two individuals with the same genetic makeup.

other multiple births in industrialized nations over the past several decades (Machin, 2005; Russell et al., 2003). Currently, fraternal twins account for 1 in about every 60 births in the United States (U.S. Department of Health and Human Services, 2010a).

Twins can also be created when a zygote that has started to duplicate separates into two clusters of cells that develop into two individuals. These are called **identical,** or **monozygotic, twins** because they have the same genetic makeup. The frequency of identical twins is the same around the world—about 1 in every 330 births (Hall, 2003). Animal research has uncovered environmental influences that prompt this type of twinning, including temperature changes, variation in oxygen levels, and late fertilization of the ovum. In a minority of cases, the identical twinning runs in families, suggesting a genetic influence (Lashley, 2007).

During their early years, children of single births often are healthier and develop more rapidly than twins. Jeannie and Jason, like most twins, were born several weeks early and required special care in the hospital. When the twins came home, Ruth and Peter had to divide time between them. Perhaps because neither received as much attention as the average single infant, Jeannie and Jason walked and talked several months later than most children their age, though both caught up by middle childhood (Lytton & Gallagher, 2002). Parental energies are further strained after the birth of triplets, whose early development is slower than that of twins (Feldman, Eidelman, & Rotenberg, 2004).

Patterns of Genetic Inheritance

Jeannie has her parents' dark, straight hair; Jason is curly-haired and blond. Patterns of genetic inheritance—the way genes from each parent interact—explain these outcomes. Recall that, except for the XY pair in males, all chromosomes come in matching

pairs. Two forms of each gene occur at the same place on the chromosomes, one inherited from the mother and one from the father. Each form of a gene is called an **allele.** If the alleles from both parents are alike, the child is **homozygous** and will display the inherited trait. If the alleles differ, then the child is **heterozygous,** and relationships between the alleles determine the phenotype.

Dominant–Recessive Inheritance. In many heterozygous pairings, **dominant–recessive inheritance** occurs: Only one allele affects the child's characteristics. It is called *dominant;* the second allele, which has no effect, is called *recessive.* Some human characteristics that follow the rules of dominant–recessive inheritance are listed in Table 2.1. Hair color is an example. The allele for dark hair is dominant (we can represent it with a capital *D*), whereas the one for blond hair is recessive (symbolized by a lowercase *b*). A child who inherits a homozygous pair of dominant alleles *(DD)* and a child who inherits a heterozygous pair *(Db)* will both be dark-haired, even though their genotypes differ. Blond hair (like Jason's) can result only from having two recessive alleles *(bb).* Still, heterozygous individuals with just one recessive allele *(Db)* can pass that trait to their children. Therefore, they are called **carriers** of the trait.

Many disabilities and diseases are the product of recessive alleles. One of the most frequently occurring is *phenylketonuria,* or *PKU,* which affects the way the body breaks down proteins contained in many foods. Infants born with two recessive alleles lack an enzyme that converts one of the basic amino acids that

TABLE 2.1 Examples of Dominant and Recessive Characteristics

DOMINANT	RECESSIVE
Dark hair	Blond hair
Normal hair	Pattern baldness
Curly hair	Straight hair
Nonred hair	Red hair
Facial dimples	No dimples
Normal hearing	Some forms of deafness
Normal vision	Nearsightedness
Farsightedness	Normal vision
Normal vision	Congenital eye cataracts
Normally pigmented skin	Albinism
Double-jointedness	Normal joints
Type A blood	Type O blood
Type B blood	Type O blood
Rh-positive blood	Rh-negative blood

Note: Many normal characteristics that were previously thought to be due to dominant–recessive inheritance, such as eye color, are now regarded as due to multiple genes. For the characteristics listed here, most experts agree that the simple dominant–recessive relationship holds.

Source: McKusick, 2011.

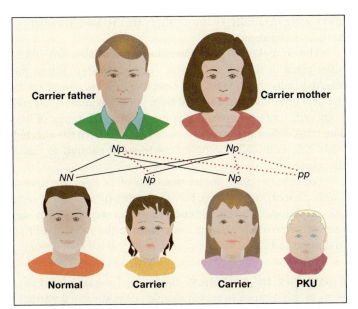

FIGURE 2.3 **Dominant–recessive mode of inheritance, as illustrated by PKU.** When both parents are heterozygous carriers of the recessive gene *(p)*, we can predict that 25 percent of their offspring are likely to be normal *(NN)*, 50 percent are likely to be carriers *(Np)*, and 25 percent are likely to inherit the disorder *(pp)*. Notice that the PKU-affected child, in contrast to his siblings, has light hair. The recessive gene for PKU also leads to fair coloring.

make up proteins (phenylalanine) into a byproduct essential for body functioning (tyrosine). Without this enzyme, phenylalanine quickly builds to toxic levels that damage the central nervous system, causing permanent mental retardation.

Despite its potentially damaging effects, PKU illustrates that inheriting unfavorable genes does not always lead to an untreatable condition. All U.S. states require that each newborn be given a blood test for PKU. If the disease is found, doctors place the baby on a diet low in phenylalanine. Children who receive this treatment nevertheless show mild deficits in memory, planning, decision making, and problem solving, because even small amounts of phenylalanine interfere with brain functioning (DeRoche & Welsh, 2008). But as long as dietary treatment begins early and continues, children with PKU usually attain an average level of intelligence and have a normal lifespan.

In dominant–recessive inheritance, if we know the genetic makeup of the parents, we can predict the percentage of children in a family who are likely to display or carry a trait. Figure 2.3 illustrates this for PKU. For a child to inherit the condition, each parent must have a recessive allele.

Incomplete Dominance.
In some heterozygous circumstances, the dominant–recessive relationship does not hold completely. Instead, we see **incomplete dominance**, a pattern of inheritance in which both alleles are expressed in the phenotype, resulting in a combined trait, or one that is intermediate between the two.

The *sickle cell trait,* a heterozygous condition present in many black Africans, provides an example. *Sickle cell anemia*

occurs in full form when a child inherits two recessive genes. They cause the usually round red blood cells to become sickle (crescent-moon) shaped, especially under low-oxygen conditions. The sickled cells clog the blood vessels and block the flow of blood, causing intense pain, swelling, and tissue damage. Despite medical advances that today allow 85 percent of affected children to survive to adulthood, North Americans with sickle cell anemia have an average life expectancy of only 55 years (Driscoll, 2007). Heterozygous individuals are protected from the disease under most circumstances. However, when they experience oxygen deprivation—for example, at high altitudes or after intense physical exercise—the single recessive allele asserts itself, and a temporary, mild form of the illness occurs.

X-Linked Inheritance.
Males and females have an equal chance of inheriting recessive disorders carried on the autosomes. But when a harmful allele is carried on the X chromosome, **X-linked inheritance** applies. Males are more likely to be affected because their sex chromosomes do not match. In females, any recessive allele on one X chromosome has a good chance of being suppressed by a dominant allele on the other X. But the Y chromosome is only about one-third as long and therefore lacks many corresponding genes to override those on the X. A well-known example is *hemophilia*, a disorder in which the blood fails to clot normally. Figure 2.4 shows its greater likelihood of inheritance by male children whose mothers carry the abnormal allele.

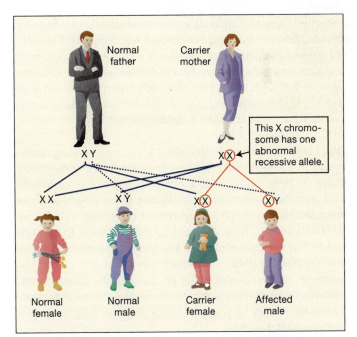

FIGURE 2.4 **X-linked inheritance.** In the example shown here, the allele on the father's X chromosome is normal. The mother has one normal and one abnormal recessive allele on her X chromosomes. By looking at the possible combinations of the parents' alleles, we can predict that 50 percent of these parents' male children are likely to have the disorder and 50 percent of their female children are likely to be carriers of it.

Besides X-linked disorders, many sex differences reveal the male to be at a disadvantage. Rates of miscarriage, infant and childhood deaths, birth defects, learning disabilities, behavior disorders, and mental retardation all are higher for boys (Butler & Meaney, 2005). It is possible that these sex differences can be traced to the genetic code. The female, with two X chromosomes, benefits from a greater variety of genes. Nature, however, seems to have adjusted for the male's disadvantage. Worldwide, about 106 boys are born for every 100 girls, and an even greater number of males are conceived (United Nations, 2011).

Genomic Imprinting. More than 1,000 human characteristics follow the rules of dominant–recessive and incomplete-dominance inheritance (McKusick, 2011). In these cases, whichever parent contributes a gene to the new individual, the gene responds in the same way. Geneticists, however, have identified some exceptions. In **genomic imprinting,** alleles are *imprinted,* or chemically *marked,* so that one pair member (either the mother's or the father's) is activated, regardless of its makeup (Hirasawa & Feil, 2010). The imprint is often temporary; it may be erased in the next generation, and it may not occur in all individuals.

Imprinting helps us understand certain puzzling genetic patterns. For example, children are more likely to develop diabetes if their father, rather than their mother, suffers from it. And people with asthma tend to have mothers, not fathers, with the illness. Genomic imprinting can also operate on the sex chromosomes, as *fragile X syndrome*—the most common inherited cause of mental retardation—reveals. In this disorder, which affects about 1 in 4,000 males and 1 in 6,000 females, an abnormal repetition of a sequence of DNA bases occurs on the X chromosome, damaging a particular gene. The defective gene at the fragile site is expressed only when it is passed from mother to child (Hagerman et al., 2009). Because the disorder is X-linked, males are more severely affected.

Mutation. Although less than 3 percent of pregnancies result in the birth of a baby with a hereditary abnormality, these children account for about 20 percent of infant deaths and contribute substantially to lifelong impaired physical and mental functioning (U.S. Department of Health and Human Services, 2010a). How are harmful genes created in the first place? The answer is **mutation,** a sudden but permanent change in a segment of DNA. A mutation may affect only one or two genes, or it may involve many genes, as in the chromosomal disorders we will discuss shortly. Some mutations occur spontaneously, simply by chance. Others are caused by hazardous environmental agents.

Ionizing (high-energy) radiation is an established cause of mutation. Women who receive repeated doses before conception are more likely to miscarry or to give birth to children with hereditary defects. The incidence of genetic abnormalities, such as physical malformations and childhood cancer, is also higher in children whose fathers are exposed to radiation in their occupation.

The examples just given illustrate *germline mutation,* which takes place in the cells that give rise to gametes. When the affected individual mates, the defective DNA is passed on to the next generation. In a second type, *somatic mutation,* normal body cells mutate, an event that can occur at any time of life. The DNA defect appears in every cell derived from the affected body cell, eventually becoming widespread enough to cause disease (such as cancer) or disability.

Somatic mutation shows that each of us does not have a single, permanent genotype. Rather, the genetic makeup of each cell can change over time. Somatic mutation increases with age, raising the possibility that it contributes to the age-related rise in disease and to the aging process itself (Salvioli et al., 2008).

Polygenic Inheritance. So far, we have discussed patterns of inheritance in which people either display a particular trait or do not. These cut-and-dried individual differences are much easier to trace to their genetic origins than are characteristics that vary on a continuum among people, such as height, weight, intelligence, and personality. These traits are due to **polygenic inheritance,** in which many genes influence the characteristic in question. Polygenic inheritance is complex, and much about it is still unknown. In the final section of this chapter, we will discuss how researchers infer the influence of heredity on human attributes when they do not know the precise patterns of inheritance.

Chromosomal Abnormalities

Besides harmful recessive alleles, abnormalities of the chromosomes are a major cause of serious developmental problems. Most chromosomal defects result from mistakes occurring during meiosis, when the ovum and sperm are formed. A chromosome pair does not separate properly, or part of a chromosome breaks off. Because these errors involve far more DNA than problems due to single genes, they usually produce many physical and mental symptoms.

Down Syndrome. The most common chromosomal disorder, occurring in 1 out of every 770 live births, is *Down syndrome.* In 95 percent of cases, it results from a failure of the twenty-first pair of chromosomes to separate during meiosis, so the new individual receives three of these chromosomes rather than the normal two. In other, less frequent forms, an extra broken piece of a twenty-first chromosome is attached to another chromosome (called *translocation* pattern). Or an error occurs during the early stages of mitosis, causing some but not all body cells to have the defective chromosomal makeup (called *mosaic* pattern) (U.S. Department of Health and Human Services, 2012a). Because the mosaic type involves less genetic material, symptoms may be less extreme.

ROBIN NELSON/PHOTOEDIT

Despite impaired development, this toddler with Down syndrome benefits from growing up in a stimulating, caring environment. As his physical therapist engages him in water play, he benefits intellectually, physically, and emotionally.

The consequences of Down syndrome include mental retardation, memory and speech problems, limited vocabulary, and slow motor development. Affected individuals also have distinct physical features—a short, stocky build, a flattened face, a protruding tongue, almond-shaped eyes, and (in 50 percent of cases) an unusual crease running across the palm of the hand. Infants with Down syndrome are often born with eye cataracts, hearing loss, and heart and intestinal defects (U.S. Department of Health and Human Services, 2012a). Because of medical advances, many individuals with Down syndrome survive into their fifties and a few into their sixties to eighties. However, more than half of affected individuals who live past age 40 show symptoms of *Alzheimer's disease,* the most common form of dementia (Wiseman et al., 2009). Genes on chromosome 21 are linked to this disorder.

The risk of bearing a baby with Down syndrome rises dramatically with maternal age. But exactly why older mothers are more likely to release ova with meiotic errors is not yet known (Martin, 2008). In about 5 to 10 percent of cases, the extra genetic material originates with the father (De Souza, Alberman, & Morris, 2009; Sherman et al., 2005).

Abnormalities of the Sex Chromosomes.
Other disorders of the autosomes other than Down syndrome usually disrupt development so severely that miscarriage occurs. When such babies are born, they rarely survive beyond early childhood. In contrast, sex chromosome disorders often are not recognized until adolescence when, in some deviations, puberty is delayed. The most common problems involve the presence of an extra chromosome (either X or Y) or the absence of one X in females.

Research has discredited a variety of myths about individuals with sex chromosome disorders. For example, males with *XYY syndrome* are not necessarily more aggressive and antisocial than XY males. And most children with sex chromosome disorders are not mentally retarded but, instead, have specific intellectual deficits. Verbal difficulties—for example, with reading and vocabulary—are common among girls with *triple X syndrome* and boys with *Klinefelter syndrome,* both of whom inherit an extra X chromosome. In contrast, girls with *Turner syndrome,* who are missing an X, have trouble with spatial relationships—for example, drawing pictures and following travel directions (Kesler, 2007). Brain-imaging evidence confirms that adding to or subtracting from the usual number of X chromosomes alters the development of certain brain structures, yielding particular intellectual deficits (Cutter et al., 2006; Itti et al., 2006).

ASK YOURSELF

REVIEW Cite evidence indicating that both heredity and environment contribute to the development of individuals with PKU and Down syndrome.

APPLY Gilbert's genetic makeup is homozygous for dark hair. Jan's is homozygous for blond hair. What proportion of their children are likely to be dark-haired? Explain.

REFLECT Select a genetic disorder discussed in the preceding sections, and imagine that you were the parent of an affected child. What factors, within and beyond the family, could help you support your child's development?

Reproductive Choices

Two years after they married, Ted and Marianne gave birth to their first child. Kendra appeared to be a healthy infant, but by 4 months her growth had slowed, and she was diagnosed with Tay-Sachs disease, a degenerative disorder of the central nervous system caused by inheritance of two recessive alleles. When Kendra died at 2 years of age, Ted and Marianne were devastated. Although they did not want to bring another infant into the world who would endure such suffering, they badly wanted to have a child.

In the past, many couples with genetic disorders in their families chose not to bear a child at all rather than risk the birth of an abnormal baby. Today, genetic counseling and prenatal diagnosis help people make informed decisions about conceiving, carrying a pregnancy to term, or adopting a child.

Social Issues: Health

The Pros and Cons of Reproductive Technologies

Some couples decide not to risk pregnancy because of a history of genetic disease. Many others—in fact, one-sixth of all couples who try to conceive—discover that they are infertile. And some never-married adults and gay and lesbian partners want to bear children. Today, increasing numbers of individuals are turning to alternative methods of conception—technologies that, although they fulfill the wish for parenthood, have become the subject of heated debate.

Donor Insemination and In Vitro Fertilization

For several decades, *donor insemination*—injection of sperm from an anonymous man into a woman—has been used to overcome male reproductive difficulties. In recent years, it has also permitted women without a male partner to become pregnant. Donor insemination is 70 to 80 percent successful, resulting in about 40,000 deliveries and 52,000 newborn babies in the United States each year (Wright et al., 2008).

In vitro fertilization is another reproductive technology that has become increasingly common. About 1 percent of all children in developed countries—60,000 babies in the United States—have been conceived through this technique annually (Centers for Disease Control and Prevention, 2011d). A woman is given hormones that stimulate the ripening of several ova. These are removed surgically and placed in a dish of nutrients, to which sperm are added. Once an ovum is fertilized and begins to duplicate into several cells, it is injected into the mother's uterus.

By mixing and matching gametes, pregnancies can be brought about when either or both partners have a reproductive problem. Usually, in vitro fertilization is used to treat women whose fallopian tubes are permanently damaged. But a recently developed technique permits a single sperm to be injected directly into an ovum, thereby overcoming most male fertility problems. And a "sex sorter" method helps ensure that couples who carry X-linked diseases (which usually affect males) have a daughter. Nevertheless, the success rate of in vitro fertilization declines steadily with age, from 40 percent in women younger than age 35 to 8 percent in women age 43 and older (Pauli et al., 2009).

Children conceived through these methods may be genetically unrelated to one or both of their parents. Does lack of genetic ties interfere with parent–child relationships? Perhaps because of a strong desire for parenthood, caregiving is actually somewhat warmer for young children conceived through donor insemination or in vitro fertilization. Also, in vitro children and adolescents are as well-adjusted as their naturally conceived counterparts (Golombok et al., 2004; Punamaki, 2006; Wagenaar et al., 2011).

Although reproductive technologies have many benefits, serious questions have arisen about their use. In many countries, including the United States, doctors are not required to keep records of donor characteristics, though information about the child's genetic background might be crucial in the case of serious disease (Adamson, 2005).

Furthermore, about 50 percent of in vitro procedures result in multiple births. Most are twins, but 9 percent are triplets and higher-order multiples. Consequently, among in vitro babies, the rate of low birth weight is nearly three times as high as in the general population (Wright et al., 2008). Risk of major birth defects also doubles because of many factors, including drugs used to induce ripening of ova and delays in fertilizing the ova outside the womb (Machin, 2005; Neri, Takeuchi, & Palermo, 2008).

Surrogate Motherhood

An even more controversial form of medically assisted conception is *surrogate motherhood.* In this procedure, in vitro fertilization may be used to impregnate a woman (called a surrogate) with a couple's fertilized ovum. Alternatively, sperm from a man whose partner is infertile may be used to inseminate the surrogate, who agrees to turn the baby over to the natural father. The child is then adopted by his partner.

Genetic Counseling and Prenatal Diagnosis

Genetic counseling is a communication process designed to help couples assess their chances of giving birth to a baby with a hereditary disorder and choose the best course of action in view of risks and family goals (Resta et al., 2006). Individuals likely to seek counseling are those who have had difficulties bearing children or who know that genetic problems exist in their families. In addition, women who delay childbearing are often candidates because, after age 35, the overall rate of chromosomal abnormalities rises sharply, from 1 in every 200 to 1 in every 20 pregnancies at age 45 (Schonberg & Tifft, 2007).

If a family history of mental retardation, psychological disorders, physical defects, or inherited diseases exists, the genetic counselor interviews the couple and prepares a *pedigree,* a picture of the family tree in which affected relatives are identified. The pedigree is used to estimate the likelihood of an abnormal child, using the genetic principles discussed earlier in this chapter. For many disorders, molecular genetic analyses (in which DNA is examined) can reveal whether the parent is a carrier of the harmful gene.

When all the relevant information is in, the genetic counselor helps people consider appropriate options. These include taking a chance and conceiving, choosing from among a variety of reproductive technologies (see the Social Issues: Health box above), or adopting a child.

Although most of these arrangements proceed smoothly, those that end up in court highlight serious risks for all concerned. In one case, both parties rejected the infant with severe disabilities who resulted from the pregnancy. In several others, the surrogate mother wanted to keep the baby, or the couple changed their mind during the pregnancy. These children came into the world in the midst of conflict that threatened to last for years. Furthermore, because surrogacy usually involves the wealthy as contractors for infants and the less economically advantaged as surrogates, it may promote exploitation of financially needy women.

New Reproductive Frontiers

Reproductive technologies are evolving faster than societies can weigh the ethics of these procedures. Doctors have used donor ova from younger women in combination with in vitro fertilization to help postmenopausal women become pregnant. Most recipients are in their forties, but several women in their fifties and sixties, and a few at age 70, have given birth. These cases raise questions about bringing children into the world whose parents may not live to see them reach adulthood.

Among other reproductive options at donor banks, customers can select ova or sperm on the basis of physical characteristics and even IQ. And scientists are devising ways to alter the DNA of human ova, sperm, and embryos to protect against hereditary disorders—techniques that could be used to

Fertility drugs and in vitro fertilization often result in multiple births. These quadruplets are healthy, but babies born with the aid of reproductive technologies are at high risk for low birth weight and major birth defects.

engineer other desired characteristics. Many worry that these practices are dangerous steps toward "designer babies"—controlling offspring characteristics by manipulating genetic makeup.

Although new reproductive technologies permit many barren couples to rear healthy newborn babies, laws are needed to regulate such practices. In the case of surrogate motherhood, the ethical problems are so complex that 11 U.S. states and the District of Columbia have sharply restricted the practice (Human Rights Campaign, 2008). Australia, Canada, and many European nations have banned it. Denmark, France, and Italy have prohibited in vitro fertilization for women past menopause. At present, little is known about the psychological consequences of being a product of these procedures. Research on how such children grow up, including later-appearing medical conditions and knowledge and feelings about their origins, is important for weighing the pros and cons of these techniques.

If couples who might bear an abnormal child decide to conceive, several **prenatal diagnostic methods**—medical procedures that permit detection of developmental problems before birth—are available (see Table 2.2 on page 44). Women of advanced maternal age are prime candidates for *amniocentesis* or *chorionic villus sampling.* Except for *maternal blood analysis,* however, prenatal diagnosis should not be used routinely because of injury risks to the developing organism.

Prenatal diagnosis has led to advances in fetal medicine. For example, by inserting a needle into the uterus, doctors can administer drugs to the fetus. Surgery has been performed to repair such problems as heart, lung, and diaphragm malformations, urinary tract obstructions, and neural defects. Fetuses

with blood disorders have been given blood transfusions. And those with immune deficiencies have received bone marrow transplants that succeeded in creating a normally functioning immune system (Deprest et al., 2010). Nevertheless, decisions to use these techniques are difficult because they frequently result in complications, the most common being premature labor and miscarriage (Schonberg & Tifft, 2007).

Advances in *genetic engineering* also offer hope for correcting hereditary defects. As part of the Human Genome Project—an ambitious international research program—thousands of genes have been identified, including those involved in hundreds of diseases, such as cystic fibrosis; Duchenne muscular dystrophy; Huntington disease; Marfan syndrome; heart, digestive, blood,

TABLE 2.2
Prenatal Diagnostic Methods

METHOD	DESCRIPTION
Amniocentesis	The most widely used technique. A hollow needle is inserted through the abdominal wall to obtain a sample of fluid in the uterus. Cells are examined for genetic defects. Can be performed by the 14th week after conception; 1 to 2 more weeks are required for test results. Small risk of miscarriage.
Chorionic villus sampling	A procedure that can be used if results are needed very early in pregnancy. A thin tube is inserted into the uterus through the vagina, or a hollow needle is inserted through the abdominal wall. A small plug of tissue is removed from the end of one or more chorionic villi, the hairlike projections on the chorion, the membrane surrounding the developing organism. Cells are examined for genetic defects. Can be performed at 9 weeks after conception; results are available within 24 hours. Entails a slightly greater risk of miscarriage than amniocentesis and is also associated with a small risk of limb deformities.
Fetoscopy	A small tube with a light source is inserted into the uterus to inspect the fetus for defects of the limbs and face. Also allows a sample of fetal blood to be obtained, permitting diagnosis of such disorders as hemophilia and sickle cell anemia, as well as neural defects (see below). Usually performed between 15 and 18 weeks after conception but can be done as early as 5 weeks. Entails some risk of miscarriage.
Ultrasound	High-frequency sound waves are beamed at the uterus; their reflection is translated into a picture on a video screen that reveals the size, shape, and placement of the fetus. Permits assessment of fetal age, detection of multiple pregnancies, and identification of gross physical defects. Also used to guide amniocentesis, chorionic villus sampling, and fetoscopy. Sometimes combined with magnetic resonance imaging (see page 95 in Chapter 4) to detect physical abnormalities with greater accuracy. When used five or more times, increases the chances of low birth weight.
Maternal blood analysis	By the second month of pregnancy, some of the developing organism's cells enter the maternal bloodstream. An elevated level of alpha-fetoprotein may indicate kidney disease, abnormal closure of the esophagus, or neural tube defects, such as anencephaly (absence of most of the brain) and spina bifida (bulging of the spinal cord from the spinal column). Isolated cells can be examined for genetic defects.
Ultrafast magnetic resonance imaging (MRI)	Sometimes used as a supplement to ultrasound, where brain or other abnormalities are detected and MRI can provide greater diagnostic accuracy. The ultrafast technique overcomes image blurring due to fetal movements. No evidence of adverse effects.
Preimplantation genetic diagnosis	After in vitro fertilization and duplication of the zygote into a cluster of cells, one or two cells are removed and examined for hereditary defects. Only if that sample is normal is the fertilized ovum implanted.

Sources: Hahn & Chitty, 2008; Jokhi & Whitby, 2011; Kumar & O'Brien, 2004; Moore, Persaud, & Torchia, 2013; Sermon, Van Steirteghem, & Liebaers, 2004.

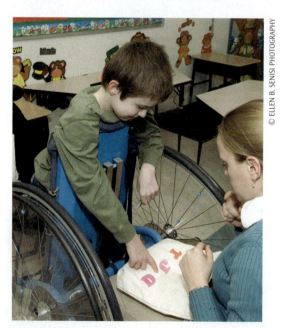

© ELLEN B. SENISI PHOTOGRAPHY

This child has Duchenne muscular dystrophy, a degenerative muscle disease caused by the inheritance of two recessive alleles. In the future, such children may benefit from gene-based treatments.

eye, and nervous system abnormalities; and many forms of cancer (National Institutes of Health, 2012). As a result, new treatments are being explored, such as *gene therapy*—correcting genetic abnormalities by delivering DNA carrying a functional gene to the cells. In recent experiments, gene therapy relieved symptoms in hemophilia patients and in patients with severe immune system dysfunction, though a few experienced serious side effects (Gillet et al., 2009). In another approach, called *proteomics,* scientists modify gene-specified proteins involved in biological aging and disease (Van Eyk & Dunn, 2008). But genetic treatments are still some distance away for most single-gene defects, and farther off for diseases involving multiple genes that combine in complex ways with each other and the environment.

Adoption

Adults who are infertile, who are likely to pass along a genetic disorder, or who are older and single but want a family are turning to adoption in increasing numbers. Because the availability of healthy babies has declined (fewer young unwed mothers give up their babies than in the past), more people in North

America and Western Europe are adopting from other countries or accepting children who are past infancy or who have known developmental problems (Schweiger & O'Brien, 2005).

Adopted children and adolescents tend to have more learning and emotional difficulties than other children, a difference that increases with the child's age at time of adoption (van den Dries et al., 2009; van IJzendoorn, Juffer, & Poelhuis, 2005; Verhulst, 2008). Various explanations exist for adoptees' more problematic childhoods. The biological mother may have been unable to care for the child because of problems believed to be partly genetic, such as alcoholism or severe depression, and may have passed this tendency to her offspring. Or perhaps she experienced stress, poor diet, or inadequate medical care during pregnancy—factors that can affect the child. Furthermore, children adopted after infancy often have a preadoptive history of conflict-ridden family relationships, including abuse and neglect, or deprived institutional rearing. Finally, adoptive parents and children, who are genetically unrelated, are less alike in intelligence and personality than are biological relatives—differences that may threaten family harmony.

Despite these risks, most adopted children fare well, and those with preexisting problems usually make rapid progress (Arcus & Chambers, 2008; Bimmel et al., 2003). In a study of internationally adopted children in the Netherlands, sensitive maternal care and secure attachment in infancy predicted cognitive and social competence at age 7 (Stams, Juffer, & van IJzendoorn, 2002). And children with troubled family histories who are adopted at older ages generally improve in feelings of trust and affection for their adoptive parents, as they come to feel loved and supported (Veríssimo & Salvaterra, 2006).

By adolescence, adoptees' lives are often complicated by unresolved curiosity about their roots. Some have difficulty accepting the possibility that they may never know their birth parents. Others worry about what they would do if their birth parents suddenly reappeared. Although these concerns are common, most adoptees appear well-adjusted as adults. When parents have been warm, open, and supportive in their communication about adoption, their children typically forge a positive sense of self (Brodzinsky, 2011). And as long as their parents took steps to help them learn about their heritage, young people adopted into a different ethnic group or culture generally develop identities that are healthy blends of their birth and rearing backgrounds (Nickman et al., 2005; Thomas & Tessler, 2007).

As we conclude our discussion of reproductive choices, perhaps you are wondering how things turned out for Ted and Marianne. Through genetic counseling, Marianne discovered a history of Tay-Sachs disease on her mother's side of the family. Ted had a distant cousin who died of the disorder. The genetic counselor explained that the chances of giving birth to another affected baby were 1 in 4. Ted and Marianne took the risk. Their son Douglas, now 12, is a carrier of the recessive allele but is a normal, healthy boy. In time, Ted and Marianne will explain to Douglas the importance of genetic counseling and testing before he has children of his own.

ASK YOURSELF

REVIEW Why is genetic counseling called a *communication process?* Who should seek it?

APPLY Imagine that you must counsel a couple considering in vitro fertilization using donor ova to overcome infertility. What medical and ethical risks would you raise?

REFLECT Suppose you are a carrier of fragile X syndrome and want to have children. Would you choose pregnancy, adoption, or surrogacy? If you became pregnant, would you opt for prenatal diagnosis? Explain your decisions.

Environmental Contexts for Development

Just as complex as genetic inheritance is the surrounding environment—a many-layered set of influences that combine to help or hinder physical and psychological well-being. **TAKE A MOMENT...** Think back to your childhood, and jot down a brief description of events and people that you believe significantly influenced your development. Next, do the same for your adult life. Do the items on your list resemble those of my students, who mostly mention experiences that involve their families? This emphasis is not surprising, since the family is the first and longest-lasting context for development. Other influences that make most students' top ten are friends, neighbors, school, workplace, and community and religious organizations.

Return to Bronfenbrenner's ecological systems theory, discussed in Chapter 1. It emphasizes that environments extending beyond the *microsystem*—the immediate settings just mentioned—powerfully affect development. Indeed, my students rarely mention one important context. Its impact is so pervasive that we seldom stop to think about it in our daily lives. This is the *macrosystem,* or broad social climate of society—its values and programs that support and protect human development. In the following sections, we take up these contexts. Because they affect every age and aspect of change, we will return to them in later chapters. For now, our discussion emphasizes that environments, as well as heredity, can enhance or create risks for development.

The Family

In power and breadth of influence, no other microsystem context equals the family. The family creates unique bonds among people. Attachments to parents and siblings are usually lifelong and serve as models for relationships in the wider world. Within the family, children learn the language, skills, and social and moral values of their culture. Warm, gratifying family ties predict physical and psychological health throughout development. In contrast, isolation or alienation from the family is often associated with developmental problems (Deković & Buist, 2005; Parke & Buriel, 2006).

Contemporary researchers view the family as a network of interdependent relationships (Bornstein & Sawyer, 2006; Bronfenbrenner & Morris, 2006). Recall from ecological systems theory that *bidirectional influences* exist in which the behaviors of each family member affect those of others. Indeed, the very term *system* implies that the responses of family members are related. These system influences operate both directly and indirectly.

Direct Influences. The next time you have a chance to observe family members interacting, watch carefully. You are likely to see that kind, patient communication evokes cooperative, harmonious responses, whereas harshness and impatience engender angry, resistive behavior. Each of these reactions, in turn, forges a new link in the interactive chain. In the first instance, a positive message tends to follow; in the second, a negative or avoidant one is likely.

These observations fit with a wealth of research on the family system. Studies of families of diverse ethnicities show that when parents are firm but warm, children tend to comply with their requests. And when children cooperate, their parents are

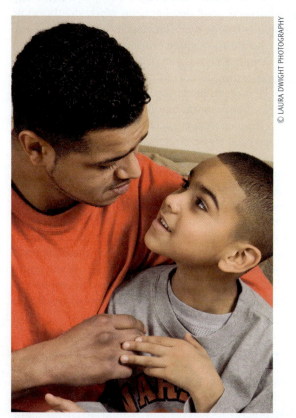

Family relationships are bidirectional, in that each member's behaviors affect those of others. This father's affectionate involvement evokes attentiveness and cooperation from his son, which promote further parental warmth and caring.

likely to be warm and gentle in the future. In contrast, children whose parents discipline harshly and impatiently are likely to refuse and rebel. And because children's misbehavior is stressful, parents may increase their use of punishment, leading to more unruliness by the child (Stormshak et al., 2000; Whiteside-Mansell et al., 2003). This principle also applies to other family relationships, such as siblings and marital partners. In each case, the behavior of one family member helps sustain a form of interaction in the other that either promotes or undermines psychological well-being.

LOOK AND LISTEN

Observe several parent–young child pairs in a context where parents are likely to place limits on children's behavior. How does quality of parent communication seem to influence the child's response? How does the child's response affect the parent's subsequent interaction? ●

Indirect Influences. The impact of family relationships on development becomes even more complicated when we consider that interaction between any two members is affected by others present in the setting. Recall from Chapter 1 that Bronfenbrenner calls these indirect influences the effect of *third parties*.

Third parties can serve as supports for or barriers to development. For example, when a marital relationship is warm and considerate, mothers and fathers are more likely to engage in effective **coparenting**, mutually supporting each other's parenting behaviors. Such parents are warmer, stimulate their children more, and scold them less. Effective coparenting, in turn, fosters a positive marital relationship (Morrill et al., 2010). In contrast, parents whose marriage is tense and hostile often interfere with one another's child-rearing efforts, are less responsive to children's needs, and are more likely to criticize, express anger, and punish (Caldera & Lindsey, 2006; McHale et al., 2002b).

Children chronically exposed to angry, unresolved parental conflict have serious emotional problems resulting from disrupted emotional security (Cummings & Merrilees, 2010; Schacht, Cummings, & Davies, 2009). These include both *internalizing difficulties* (especially among girls), such as feeling worried and fearful and trying to repair their parents' relationship; and *externalizing difficulties* (especially among boys), including anger and aggression (Cummings, Goeke-Morey, & Papp, 2004). These child problems can further disrupt parents' marital relationship.

Adapting to Change. Think back to the *chronosystem* in Bronfenbrenner's theory (see page 25 in Chapter 1). The interplay of forces within the family is dynamic and ever-changing. Important events, such as the birth of a baby or the addition to the household of an ill elderly parent, create challenges that modify existing relationships. The way such events affect family interaction depends on the support other family members provide and on the developmental status of each participant. For example, the arrival of a new baby prompts very different reactions in a toddler than in a school-age child. And caring for an ill elderly parent is more stressful for a middle-aged adult still rearing children than for one with no child-rearing responsibilities.

Historical time period also contributes to a dynamic family system. In recent decades, a declining birth rate, a high divorce rate, expansion of women's roles, and postponement of parenthood have led to a smaller family size. This, combined with a longer lifespan, means that more generations are alive, with fewer members in the youngest ones, leading to a "top-heavy" family structure. Young people today are more likely to have older relatives than at any time in history—a circumstance that can be enriching as well as a source of tension.

Nevertheless, some general patterns in family functioning do exist. In the United States and other industrialized nations, one important source of these consistencies is socioeconomic status.

Socioeconomic Status and Family Functioning

People in industrialized nations are stratified on the basis of what they do at work and how much they earn for doing it—factors that determine their social position and economic well-being. Researchers assess a family's standing on this continuum through an index called **socioeconomic status (SES)**, which combines three related, but not completely overlapping, variables: (1) years of education and (2) the prestige of one's job and the skill it requires, both of which measure social status; and (3) income, which measures economic status. As SES rises and falls, people face changing circumstances that profoundly affect family functioning.

SES is linked to timing of marriage and parenthood and to family size. People who work in skilled and semiskilled manual occupations (for example, construction workers and custodians) tend to marry and have children earlier as well as give birth to more children than people in professional and technical occupations. The two groups also differ in values and expectations. For example, when asked about personal qualities they desire for their children, lower-SES parents tend to emphasize external characteristics, such as obedience, politeness, and cleanliness. In contrast, higher-SES parents emphasize psychological traits, such as curiosity, happiness, and cognitive and social maturity (Duncan & Magnuson, 2003; Hoff, Laursen, & Tardif, 2002).

These differences are reflected in family interaction. Parents higher in SES talk to, read to, and otherwise stimulate their infants and preschoolers more. With older children and adolescents, they use more warmth, explanations, and verbal praise; set higher academic and other developmental goals; and allow their children to make more decisions. Commands ("You do that because I told you to"), criticism, and physical punishment all occur more often in low-SES households (Bush & Peterson, 2008; Mandara et al., 2009).

Education contributes substantially to these variations. Higher-SES parents' verbal stimulation and nurturing of inner

traits are supported by years of schooling, during which they learned to think about abstract, subjective ideas and, thus, to invest in their children's cognitive and social development (Mistry et al., 2008; Vernon-Feagins et al., 2008). At the same time, greater economic security enables parents to devote more time, energy, and material resources to fostering their children's psychological characteristics (Cheadle & Amato, 2011). In contrast, high levels of stress sparked by economic insecurity contribute to low-SES parents' reduced provision of stimulating interaction and activities as well as greater use of coercive discipline (Chin & Phillips, 2004; Conger & Donnellan, 2007). Because of limited education and low social status, many lower-SES parents feel a sense of powerlessness in their relationships beyond the home. At work, for example, they must obey rules of others in positions of authority (Greenberger, O'Neil, & Nagel, 1994). When they get home, their parent–child interaction seems to duplicate these experiences—but now they are in authority.

Poverty

When families slip into poverty, development is seriously threatened. Consider Zinnia Mae, who grew up in a close-knit black community located in a small southeastern American city (Heath, 1990). As unemployment struck and citizens moved away, 16-year-old Zinnia Mae caught a ride to Atlanta. Two years later, she was the mother of a daughter and twin boys, living in public housing.

Zinnia Mae worried constantly about scraping together enough money to put food on the table, freeing herself from rising debt, and finding the twins' father, who had stopped sending money. The children's play space was limited to the living room sofa and a mattress on the floor. Toys consisted of scraps of a blanket, spoons and food cartons, a small rubber ball, and a few plastic cars. At a researcher's request, Zinnia Mae agreed to tape record her interactions with her children. Cut off from family and community ties and overwhelmed by financial strain and feelings of helplessness, she found herself unable to join in activities with her children. In 500 hours of tape, she started a conversation with them only 18 times.

Today, about 15 percent—46 million Americans—live in poverty. Those hit hardest are parents under age 25 with young children and older adults who live alone. Poverty is also magnified among ethnic minorities and women. For example, more than 21 percent of U.S. children are poor, a rate that climbs to 32 percent for Hispanic children, 34 percent for Native-American children, and 38 percent for African-American children. For single mothers with preschool children and elderly women on their own, the poverty rate is close to 50 percent (DeNavas-Walt, Proctor, & Smith, 2011; U.S. Census Bureau, 2013).

As we will see later, inadequate government programs to meet family needs are responsible for these disheartening statistics. The poverty rate is higher among children than any other age group. And of all Western nations, the United States has the highest percentage of extremely poor children. Nearly

At a homeless shelter, a mother helps her 7-year-old with a homework assignment. But many homeless children suffer from developmental delays and emotional stress that interfere with school achievement.

10 percent of U.S. children live in deep poverty (at less than half the poverty threshold, the income level judged necessary for a minimum living standard). The earlier poverty begins, the deeper it is, and the longer it lasts, the more devastating are its effects. Children of poverty are more likely than other children to suffer from lifelong poor physical health, persistent deficits in cognitive development and academic achievement, high school dropout, mental illness, and antisocial behavior (Aber, Jones, & Raver, 2007; Morgan et al., 2009).

The constant stressors that accompany poverty weaken the family system. Poor families have many daily hassles—loss of welfare and unemployment payments, the car breaking down, something stolen from the house, to name just a few. When daily crises arise, family members become depressed, irritable, and distracted; and hostile interactions increase (Conger & Donnellan, 2007; Kohen et al., 2008).

Affluence

Despite their advanced education and great material wealth, affluent parents—those in prestigious and high-paying occupations—too often fail to engage in family interaction and parenting that promote favorable development. In several studies, researchers tracked the adjustment of youths growing up in high-SES suburbs (Luthar & Latendresse, 2005). By seventh grade, many showed serious problems that worsened in high school. Their school grades were poor, and they were more likely than low-SES youths to engage in alcohol and drug use and to report high levels of anxiety and depression (Luthar & Becker, 2002; Luthar & Goldstein, 2008).

Why are so many affluent youths troubled? Compared to their better-adjusted counterparts, poorly adjusted affluent young people report less emotional closeness and supervision from their parents, who lead professionally and socially demanding lives. As a group, wealthy parents are nearly as physically and emotionally unavailable to their youngsters as parents coping with serious financial strain. At the same time, these parents often make excessive demands for achievement (Luthar & Becker, 2002). Adolescents whose parents value their accomplishments more than their character are more likely to have academic and emotional problems.

Beyond the Family: Neighborhoods, Towns, and Cities

As the concepts of *mesosystem* and *exosystem* in ecological systems theory make clear, connections between family and community are vital for psychological well-being. From our discussion of poverty, perhaps you can see why: In poverty-stricken urban areas, community life is usually disrupted. Families move often, parks and playgrounds are in disarray, and community centers providing organized activities do not exist. Family violence, child abuse and neglect, child and youth internalizing and externalizing difficulties, adult criminal behavior, and elderly depression and declines in cognitive functioning are especially high (Aneshensel et al., 2007; Chen, Howard, & Brooks-Gunn, 2011; Dunn, Schaefer-McDaniel, & Ramsay, 2010; Lang et al., 2008). In contrast, strong family ties to the surrounding social context—as indicated by frequent contact with friends and relatives and regular church, synagogue, or mosque attendance—reduce stress and enhance adjustment.

Neighborhoods. Communities offer resources and social ties that play an important part in children's development. In several studies, low-SES families were randomly assigned vouchers to move out of public housing into neighborhoods varying widely in affluence. Compared with their peers who remained in poverty-stricken areas, children and youths who moved into low-poverty neighborhoods showed substantially better physical and mental health and school achievement (Goering, 2003; Leventhal & Brooks-Gunn, 2003).

Neighborhood resources have a greater impact on economically disadvantaged than well-to-do young people. Higher-SES families can afford to transport their children to lessons and entertainment and, if necessary, to better-quality schools. In low-income neighborhoods, in-school and after-school programs that substitute for lack of other resources by providing art, music, sports, scouting, and other enrichment activities predict favorable child and adolescent development, including increased self-confidence, school achievement, and educational aspirations (Barnes et al., 2007; Vandell, Reisner, & Pierce, 2007).

Yet in dangerous, disorganized neighborhoods, high-quality activities for children and adolescents are scarce. Even when they are available, crime and social disorder limit young people's access, and parents overwhelmed by stressors are less likely to encourage their children to participate (Dearing et al., 2009). Thus, the neediest children and youths are especially likely to miss out on these development-enhancing activities.

LOOK AND LISTEN

Ask several parents to list their school-age children's regular lessons and other enrichment activities. Then inquire about home and neighborhood factors that either encourage or impede their children's participation. ●

The Better Beginnings, Better Futures Project of Ontario, Canada, is a government-sponsored set of pilot programs aimed at preventing the dire consequences of neighborhood poverty. The most successful of these efforts provided children with in-class, before- and after-school, and summer enrichment activities. Project staff also met with each child's parents regularly, encouraging their involvement in the child's school and neighborhood life (Peters, 2005; Peters, Petrunka, & Arnold, 2003). Evaluations as children reached grades 3, 6, and 9 revealed wide-ranging benefits. Among these were improved family functioning, parenting, and parental community involvement, and gains in children's academic achievement and social adjustment, including a reduction in emotional and behavior problems.

As these outcomes suggest, neighborhoods also affect adults' well-being. An employed parent who can rely on a caring neighbor or community program for child-rearing assistance and who lives in a safe area gains access to valuable information and services, effective child-rearing role models, and peace of mind essential for productive work. In low-SES areas with high resident stability and social cohesion, where neighbors help and look after one another, adults report less stress, which in turn predicts substantially better physical health (Boardman, 2004; Feldman & Steptoe, 2004).

During late adulthood, neighborhoods become increasingly important because people spend more time in their homes. Despite the availability of planned housing for older adults, about 90 percent remain in regular housing, usually in the same neighborhood where they lived during their working lives (U.S. Census Bureau, 2013). In the absence of nearby family members, older adults mention neighbors and nearby friends as resources they rely on most for physical and social support (Hooyman & Kiyak, 2011).

Towns and Cities. Neighborhoods are embedded in towns and cities, which also mold children's and adults' daily lives. In rural areas and small towns, children and youths are more likely to be given important work tasks—caring for livestock, operating the snowplow, or playing in the town band. They usually perform these tasks alongside adults, who instill in them a strong sense of responsibility and teach them practical and social skills needed to sustain their community. Compared with large urban areas, small towns also offer stronger connections between settings that influence children's lives. For example, because most citizens know each

This 5-year-old enjoys working with volunteers at a community garden sponsored by the Boys & Girls Clubs of America. Neighborhood resources are especially important for the development of economically disadvantaged children and youths.

other and schools serve as centers of community life, contact between teachers and parents occurs often—an important factor in promoting children's academic achievement (Hill & Taylor, 2004).

Adults in small towns participate in more civic groups, such as school board or volunteer fire brigade. And they are more likely to occupy positions of leadership because a greater proportion of residents are needed to meet community needs (Elder & Conger, 2000). In late adulthood, people residing in small towns and suburbs have neighbors who are more willing to provide assistance. As a result, they form a greater number of warm relationships with nonrelatives.

Of course, small-town residents cannot visit museums, go to professional baseball games, or attend orchestra concerts on a regular basis. The variety of settings is not as great as in a large city. Small towns, however, are safer and more secure. Responsible adults are present in almost all settings to keep an eye on children and youths. And older adults feel safer—a strong contributor to how satisfied they are with their place of residence (Shields et al., 2002).

The Cultural Context

Our discussion in Chapter 1 emphasized that human development can be fully understood only when viewed in its larger cultural context. In the following sections, we expand on this theme by taking up the role of the *macrosystem* in development. First, we discuss ways that cultural values and practices affect environmental contexts for development. Second, we consider how healthy development depends on laws and government programs that shield people from harm and foster their well-being.

Cultural Values and Practices. Cultures shape family interaction and community settings beyond the home—in short, all aspects of daily life. Many of us remain blind to aspects of our own cultural heritage until we see them in relation to the practices of others.

TAKE A MOMENT... Consider the question, Who should be responsible for rearing young children? How would you answer it? Here are some typical responses from my students: "If parents decide to have a baby, then they should be ready to care for it." "Most people are not happy about others intruding into family life." These statements reflect a widely held opinion in the United States—that the care and rearing of children, and paying for that care, are the duty of parents, and only parents. This view has a long history—one in which independence, self-reliance, and the privacy of family life emerged as central American values (Halfon & McLearn, 2002). It is one reason, among others, that the public has been slow to endorse government-supported benefits for all families, such as high-quality child care and paid employment leave for meeting family needs. And it has also contributed to the large number of U.S. families who remain poor, even though family members are employed (Gruendel & Aber, 2007; UNICEF, 2007, 2010b).

Although the culture as a whole may value independence and privacy, not all citizens share the same values. Some belong to **subcultures**—groups of people with beliefs and customs that differ from those of the larger culture. Many ethnic minority groups in the United States have cooperative family structures, which help protect their members from the harmful effects of poverty. For example, the African-American tradition of **extended-family households,** in which three or more generations live together, is a vital feature of black family life that has enabled its members to survive, despite a long history of prejudice and economic deprivation. Within the extended family, grandparents play meaningful roles in guiding younger generations; adolescents and adults with employment, marital, or child-rearing difficulties receive assistance and emotional support; and caregiving is enhanced for children and the elderly. Active, involved extended families also characterize other minorities, such as Asian, Native-American, and Hispanic subcultures (Becker et al., 2003; Harwood et al., 2002).

Our discussion so far reflects a broad dimension on which cultures and subcultures differ: the extent to which *collectivism* versus *individualism* is emphasized. In **collectivist societies,** people define themselves as part of a group and stress group goals over individual goals. In **individualistic societies,** people think of themselves as separate entities and are largely concerned with their own personal needs (Triandis, 1995, 2005). As these definitions suggest, the two cultural patterns are associated with two distinct views of the self. Collectivist societies value an *interdependent self,* which stresses social harmony, obligations and responsibility to others, and collaborative endeavors. In contrast, individualistic societies value an *independent self,* which emphasizes personal exploration, discovery, achievement, and individual choice in relationships. Both interdependence and independence are part of the makeup of every person

(McAdams & Cox, 2010; Tamis-LeMonda et al., 2008). But societies vary greatly in the extent to which they emphasize each alternative.

Although individualism tends to increase as cultures become more complex, cross-national differences remain. The United States is strongly individualistic, whereas most Western European countries lean toward collectivism. As we will see next, collectivist versus individualistic values have a powerful impact on a nation's approach to protecting the well-being of its children, families, and aging citizens.

Public Policies and Lifespan Development.

When widespread social problems arise, such as poverty, homelessness, hunger, and disease, nations attempt to solve them through **public policies**—laws and government programs designed to improve current conditions. In the United States, public policies safeguarding children and youths have lagged behind policies for older adults. And both sets of policies have been especially slow to emerge relative to other industrialized nations.

Policies for Children, Youths, and Families. We have already seen that although many U.S. children fare well, a large number grow up in environments that threaten their development. As Table 2.3 reveals, the United States does not rank well on any key measure of children's health and well-being.

The problems of children and youths extend beyond the indicators in the table. Despite improved health-care provisions signed into law in 2010, the United States remains the only industrialized nation in the world without a universal, publicly funded health-care system. Approximately 10 percent

At this California resource center, low-income families learn about healthy eating and also receive food. U.S. public policies that support such programs lag behind those in other industrialized nations.

TABLE 2.3 How Does the United States Compare to Other Nations on Indicators of Children's Health and Well-Being?

INDICATOR	U.S. RANK[a]	SOME COUNTRIES THE UNITED STATES TRAILS
Childhood poverty (among 24 industrialized nations considered)	24th	Canada, Czech Republic, Germany, United Kingdom, Norway, Sweden, Poland, Spain
Infant deaths in the first year of life (worldwide)	28th	Canada, Hong Kong, Ireland, Singapore, Spain
Teenage birth rate (among 28 industrialized nations considered)	28th	Australia, Canada, Czech Republic, Denmark, Hungary, Iceland, Poland, Slovakia
Public expenditure on education as a percentage of gross domestic product[b] (among 22 industrialized nations considered)	12th	Belgium, France, Iceland, New Zealand, Portugal, Spain, Sweden
Public expenditure on health as a percentage of total health expenditure, public plus private (among 27 industrialized nations considered)	26th	Austria, Australia, Canada, France, Hungary, Iceland, Switzerland, New Zealand

[a]1 = highest, or best, rank.

[b]Gross domestic product is the value of all goods and services produced by a nation during a specified time period. It provides an overall measure of a nation's wealth.

Sources: Canada Campaign 2000, 2009; OECD, 2010a, 2010b; U.S. Census Bureau, 2013; U.S. Department of Education, 2012b.

of U.S. children—most in low-income families—have no health insurance (Kenney et al., 2010). Furthermore, the United States has been slow to move toward national standards and funding for child care. Affordable care is in short supply, and much of it is substandard in quality (Lamb & Ahnert, 2006; Muenchow & Marsland, 2007). In families affected by divorce, weak enforcement of child support payments heightens poverty in mother-headed households. And 8 percent of 16- to 24-year-olds who dropped out of high school have not returned to earn a diploma (U.S. Department of Education, 2012b).

Why have attempts to help children and youths been difficult to realize in the United States? Cultural values of self-reliance and privacy have made government hesitant to become involved in family matters. Furthermore, good social programs are expensive, and they must compete for a fair share of a country's economic resources. Children can easily remain unrecognized in this process because they cannot vote or speak out to protect their own interests (Ripple & Zigler, 2003). Instead, they must rely on the goodwill of others to become an important government priority.

Policies for Older Adults. Until well into the twentieth century, the United States had few policies in place to protect its aging population. For example, Social Security benefits were not awarded until the late 1930s. Yet most Western nations had social security systems in place a decade or more earlier (Karger & Stoesz, 2010). In the 1960s, U.S. federal spending on programs for older adults expanded rapidly. Medicare, a national health insurance program for older people, was initiated. But it requires participants to pay part of those costs, leaving about half of elderly health spending to be covered by supplemental private insurance, government health insurance for the poor, or out-of-pocket payments (U.S. Department of Health and Human Services, 2011g).

Social Security and Medicare consume 96 percent of the U.S. federal budget for the elderly; only 4 percent is devoted to other programs. Consequently, U.S. programs for the aged have been criticized for neglecting social services (Hooyman & Kiyak, 2011). To meet this need, approximately 630 Area Agencies on Aging have been established at regional and local levels to assess community needs and offer communal and home-delivered meals, self-care education, elder abuse prevention, and a wide range of other social services. But limited funding means that the Area Agencies help far too few people in need.

Many U.S. ethnic-minority older adults are poverty-stricken. This Native American, who lives in a remote Alaskan village, depends on an itinerant nurse for routine medical care.

Looking Toward the Future.

Despite the worrisome state of many children, families, and aging citizens, efforts are being made to improve their condition. Growing awareness of the gap between what we know and what we do to better people's lives has led experts in developmental science to join with concerned citizens as advocates for more effective policies. As a result, several influential interest groups devoted to the well-being of children or older adults have emerged.

In the United States, the Children's Defense Fund (CDF)—a private, nonprofit organization founded by Marian Wright Edelman in 1973—engages in public education, legal action, drafting of legislation, congressional testimony, and community organizing. To learn more about the Children's Defense Fund, visit its website at *www.childrensdefense.org*. Another energetic advocacy organization is the National Center for Children in Poverty, dedicated to advancing the health and welfare of U.S. children in low-income families by informing policy makers of relevant research. To explore its activities, visit *www.nccp.org*.

About half of Americans over age 50, both retired and employed, are members of AARP (originally known as the American Association of Retired Persons). Founded by Ethel Percy Andrus in 1958, AARP has a large and energetic lobbying staff that works for increased government benefits of all kinds for the aged. A description of AARP and its activities can be found at *www.aarp.org*.

Besides strong advocacy, public policies that enhance development depend on policy-relevant research that documents needs and evaluates programs to spark improvements. Today, more researchers are collaborating with community and government agencies to enhance the social relevance of their investigations. They are also doing a better job of disseminating their findings through reports to government officials, websites aimed at increasing public understanding, and collaborations with the media to ensure accurate and effective reporting in newspaper stories, magazine articles, and radio and television documentaries (Shonkoff & Bales, 2011). In these ways, researchers are helping to create the sense of immediacy about the condition of children, families, and the aged that is necessary to spur a society into action.

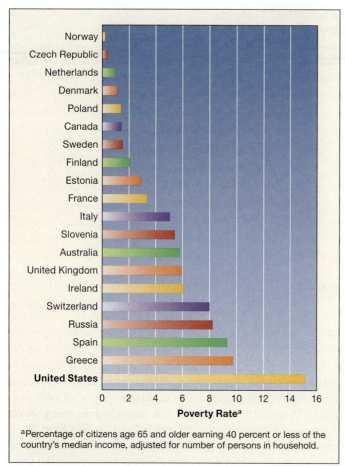

FIGURE 2.5 **Percentage of aging adults living in poverty in 20 industrialized nations.** Among the countries listed, the United States has the highest rate of aging adults living in poverty. Public expenditures on social security and other income guarantees for senior citizens are far greater in the highly ranked nations than in the United States. (Adapted from Luxembourg Income Study, 2011.)

[Chart: Poverty Rate[a], horizontal bars by country, x-axis 0 to 16]

Norway, Czech Republic, Netherlands, Denmark, Poland, Canada, Sweden, Finland, Estonia, France, Italy, Slovenia, Australia, United Kingdom, Ireland, Switzerland, Russia, Spain, Greece, **United States**

[a]Percentage of citizens age 65 and older earning 40 percent or less of the country's median income, adjusted for number of persons in household.

As noted earlier, many senior citizens—especially women, ethnic minorities, and those living alone—remain in dire economic straits. Although all Americans age 65 and older are guaranteed a minimum income, the guaranteed amount is below the poverty line—the amount judged necessary for bare subsistence by the federal government. Furthermore, Social Security benefits are rarely adequate as a sole source of retirement income. Therefore, U.S. older adults are more likely than other age groups to be among the "near poor" (U.S. Department of Health and Human Services, 2010b).

Nevertheless, the U.S. aging population is financially much better off now than in the past. Today, older adults are a large, powerful, well-organized constituency, far more likely than children or low-income families to attract the support of politicians. As a result, the number of aging poor has declined from 1 out of 3 people in 1960 to 1 out of 10 in the early twenty-first century (U.S. Census Bureau, 2013). Still, as Figure 2.5 shows, aging adults in the United States are less well off than those in many other Western nations, which provide more generous, government-funded income supplements to older adults.

ASK YOURSELF

REVIEW Links between family and community foster development throughout the lifespan. Provide examples from our discussion that support this idea.

APPLY Check your local newspaper or one or two national news magazines or news websites to see how often articles on the condition of children, families, and the aged appear. Why is it important for researchers to communicate with the general public about the well-being of these sectors of the population?

REFLECT Do you agree with the widespread American sentiment that government should not become involved in family life? Explain.

Understanding the Relationship Between Heredity and Environment

So far, we have discussed a wide variety of genetic and environmental influences, each of which has the power to alter the course of development. Yet people who are born into the same family (and who therefore share both genes and environments) are often quite different in characteristics. We also know that some individuals are affected more than others by their homes, neighborhoods, and communities. How do scientists explain the impact of heredity and environment when they seem to work in so many different ways?

Behavioral genetics is a field devoted to uncovering the contributions of nature and nurture to this diversity in human traits and abilities. Although scientists are making progress in identifying the multiple variations in DNA sequences associated with such complex traits as intelligence and personality, so far these genetic markers explain only a small amount of variation in human behavior, and a minority of cases of most psychological disorders (Plomin & Davis, 2009). For the most part, scientists are still limited to investigating the impact of genes on complex characteristics indirectly.

Some believe that it is useful and possible to answer the question of *how much each factor contributes* to differences among people. A growing consensus, however, regards that question as unanswerable. These investigators believe that heredity and environment are inseparable (Gottlieb, Wahlsten, & Lickliter, 2006; Lerner & Overton, 2008). The important question, they maintain, is *how nature and nurture work together*. Let's consider each position in turn.

The Question, "How Much?"

To infer the role of heredity in complex human characteristics, researchers use special methods, the most common being the *heritability estimate*. Let's look closely at the information this procedure yields, along with its limitations.

Heritability. Heritability estimates measure the extent to which individual differences in complex traits in a specific population are due to genetic factors. We will take a brief look at heritability findings on intelligence and personality here and will return to them in later chapters, when we consider these topics in greater detail. Heritability estimates are obtained from **kinship studies,** which compare the characteristics of family members. The most common type of kinship study compares identical twins, who share all their genes, with fraternal twins, who, on average, share only half. If people who are genetically more alike are also more similar in intelligence and personality, then the researcher assumes that heredity plays an important role.

Kinship studies of intelligence provide some of the most controversial findings in the field of developmental science. Some experts claim a strong genetic influence, whereas others believe that heredity is barely involved. Currently, most kinship findings support a moderate role for heredity. When many twin studies are examined, correlations between the scores of identical twins are consistently higher than those of fraternal twins. In a summary of more than 10,000 twin pairs, the correlation for intelligence was .86 for identical twins and .60 for fraternal twins (Plomin & Spinath, 2004).

Researchers use a complex statistical procedure to compare these correlations, arriving at a heritability estimate ranging from 0 to 1.00. The value for intelligence is about .50 for child and adolescent twin samples in Western industrialized nations. This suggests that differences in genetic makeup explain half the variation in intelligence. However, heritability increases through middle adulthood, with some estimates as high as .80 (Baird & Bergeman, 2011; Haworth et al., 2010). As we will see later, one explanation is that, compared to children, adults exert greater personal control over their intellectual experiences—for example, how much time they spend reading or solving challenging problems.

Heritability research also reveals that genetic factors are important in personality. For frequently studied traits, such as sociability, anxiety, agreeableness, and activity level, heritability estimates obtained on child, adolescent, and young adult twins are moderate, in the .40s and .50s (Caspi & Shiner, 2006; Rothbart & Bates, 2006; Wright et al., 2008). Unlike intelligence, however, heritability of personality does not increase over the lifespan (Loehlin et al., 2005).

Limitations of Heritability. The accuracy of heritability estimates depends on the extent to which the twin pairs studied reflect genetic and environmental variation in the population. Within a population in which all people have very similar home, school, and community experiences, individual differences in intelligence and personality would be largely genetic, and heritability estimates would be close to 1.00. Conversely, the more environments vary, the more likely they are to account for individual differences, yielding lower heritability estimates. In twin studies, most of the twin pairs are reared together under highly similar conditions. Even when separated twins are available for study, social service agencies have often placed them in advantaged homes that are alike in many ways (Rutter et al., 2001). Because the environments of most twin pairs are less diverse than those of the general population, heritability estimates are likely to exaggerate the role of heredity.

Heritability estimates are controversial measures because they can easily be misapplied. For example, high heritabilities have been used to suggest that ethnic differences in intelligence, such as the poorer performance of black children compared to white children, have a genetic basis (Jensen, 1969, 1998, 2001; Rushton & Jensen, 2005, 2006). Yet this line of reasoning is widely regarded as incorrect. Heritabilities computed on

© JACQUIE HEMMERDINGER/THE NEW YORK TIMES/REDUX

When Adriana and Tamara, identical twins separated at birth by adoption, met at age 20, they discovered many similarities, including academic achievement and love of dancing. Clearly, heredity contributes to psychological characteristics, but generalizing from twin evidence to the population is controversial.

mostly white twin samples do not tell us what causes test score differences between ethnic groups. We have already seen that large economic and cultural differences are involved. In Chapter 9, we will discuss research indicating that when black children are adopted into economically advantaged homes at an early age, their scores are well above average and substantially higher than those of children from impoverished families.

Perhaps the most serious criticism of heritability estimates has to do with their limited usefulness. Though interesting, these statistics give us no precise information on how intelligence and personality develop or how children might respond to environments designed to help them develop as far as possible (Baltes, Lindenberger, & Staudinger, 2006). Indeed, the heritability of children's intelligence increases as parental education and income increase—that is, as children grow up in conditions that allow them to make the most of their genetic endowment. In impoverished environments, children are prevented from realizing their potential. Consequently, enhancing experiences through interventions—such as increasing parent education and income and providing high-quality preschool or child care—has a greater impact on development (Bronfenbrenner & Morris, 2006).

In sum, heritability estimates confirm that heredity contributes to complex traits but tell us nothing about how environment can modify genetic influences. Still, scientists often rely on positive heritabilities before initiating more costly molecular analyses in search of specific genes that contribute to personality traits and disorders.

The Question, "How?"

Today, most researchers view development as the result of a dynamic interplay between heredity and environment. How do nature and nurture work together? Several concepts shed light on this question.

Gene–Environment Interaction. The first of these ideas is **gene–environment interaction,** which means that because of their genetic makeup, individuals differ in their responsiveness to qualities of the environment (Rutter, 2011). In other words, people have unique, genetically influenced reactions to particular experiences. Let's explore this idea in Figure 2.6. Gene–environment interaction can apply to any characteristic; here it is illustrated for intelligence. Notice that when environments vary from extremely unstimulating to highly enriched, Ben's intelligence increases steadily, Linda's rises sharply and then falls off, and Ron's begins to increase only after the environment becomes modestly stimulating.

Gene–environment interaction highlights two important points. First, it shows that because each of us has a unique genetic makeup, we respond differently to the same environment. Notice in Figure 2.6 how a poor environment results in similarly low scores for all three individuals. But when the environment provides a moderate level of stimulation, Linda is by far the best-performing child. And in a highly enriched environment, Ben does best, followed by Ron, both of whom now outperform Linda. Second, sometimes different gene–environment combi-

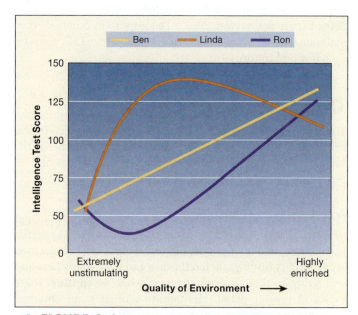

FIGURE 2.6 Gene–environment interaction, illustrated for intelligence by three children who differ in responsiveness to quality of the environment. As environments vary from extremely unstimulating to highly enriched, Ben's intelligence test score increases steadily, Linda's rises sharply and then falls off, and Ron's begins to increase only after the environment becomes modestly stimulating.

nations can make two people look the same! For example, if Linda is reared in a minimally stimulating environment, her score will be about 100—average for people in general. Ben and Ron can also obtain this score, but to do so, they must grow up in a fairly enriched home (Gottlieb, Wahlsten, & Lickliter, 2006).

Recently, researchers have made strides in identifying gene–environment interactions in personality development. In Chapter 6 we will see that young children with a gene that increases their risk of an emotionally reactive temperament respond especially strongly to variations in parenting quality (Pluess & Belsky, 2011). When parenting is favorable, they gain control over their emotions and adjust as well or better than other children. But when parenting is unfavorable, they become increasingly irritable, difficult, and poorly adjusted, more so than children not at genetic risk.

Gene–Environment Correlation. A major problem in trying to separate heredity and environment is that they are often correlated (Rutter, 2011; Scarr & McCartney, 1983). According to the concept of **gene–environment correlation,** our genes influence the environments to which we are exposed. The way this happens changes with age.

Passive and Evocative Correlation. At younger ages, two types of gene–environment correlation are common. The first is called *passive* correlation because the child has no control over it. Early on, parents provide environments influenced by their own heredity. For example, parents who are good athletes emphasize outdoor activities and enroll their children in swimming and gymnastics. Besides being exposed to an "athletic environment," the children may have inherited their parents' athletic ability. As a result, they are likely to become good athletes for both genetic and environmental reasons.

The second type of gene–environment correlation is *evocative.* Children evoke responses that are influenced by the child's heredity, and these responses strengthen the child's original style. For example, an active, friendly baby is likely to receive more social stimulation than a passive, quiet infant. And a cooperative, attentive child probably receives more patient and sensitive interactions from parents than an inattentive, distractible child. In support of this idea, the less genetically alike siblings are, the more their parents treat them differently, in both warmth and negativity. Thus, parents' treatment of identical twins is highly similar, whereas their treatment of fraternal twins and nontwin biological siblings is only moderately so. And little resemblance exists in parents' warm and negative interactions with unrelated stepsiblings (Reiss, 2003).

Active Correlation. At older ages, *active* gene–environment correlation becomes common. As children extend their experiences beyond the immediate family and are given the freedom to make more choices, they actively seek environments that fit with their genetic tendencies. The well-coordinated, muscular child spends more time at after-school sports, the musically talented

This mother shares her love of the piano with her daughter, who also may have inherited her mother's musical talent. When heredity and environment are correlated, the influence of one cannot be separated from the influence of the other.

child joins the school orchestra and practices his violin, and the intellectually curious child is a familiar patron at her local library.

This tendency to actively choose environments that complement our heredity is called **niche-picking** (Scarr & McCartney, 1983). Infants and young children cannot do much niche-picking because adults select environments for them. In contrast, older children, adolescents, and adults are increasingly in charge of their environments. Niche-picking explains why pairs of identical twins reared apart during childhood and later reunited may find, to their surprise, that they have similar hobbies, food preferences, and vocations—a trend that is especially marked when twins' environmental opportunities are similar (Plomin, 1994). Niche-picking also helps us understand why identical twins become somewhat more alike, and fraternal twins and adopted siblings less alike, in intelligence with age (Bouchard, 2004). And niche-picking sheds light on why adult identical twins, compared to fraternal twins and other adults, select more similar spouses and best friends—in height, weight, personality, political attitudes, and other characteristics (Rushton & Bons, 2005).

The influence of heredity and environment is not constant but changes over time. With age, genetic factors may become more important in influencing the environments we experience and choose for ourselves.

Environmental Influences on Gene Expression.

Notice how, in the concepts just considered, heredity is granted priority. In gene–environment interaction, it affects responsiveness to particular environments. Similarly, gene–environment correlation is viewed as driven by genetics, in that children's genetic makeup causes them to receive, evoke, or seek experiences that actualize their hereditary tendencies (Plomin, 2009; Rutter, 2011).

A growing number of researchers argue that heredity does not dictate children's experiences or development in a rigid way. In one study, boys with a genetic tendency toward antisocial behavior (based on the presence of a gene on the X chromosome known to predispose both animals and humans to aggression) were no more aggressive than boys without this gene, *unless* they also had a history of severe child abuse (Caspi et al., 2002). Boys with and without the gene did not differ in their experience of abuse, indicating that the "aggressive genotype" did not increase exposure to abuse. And in a large Finnish adoption study, children whose biological mothers had schizophrenia but who were being reared by healthy adoptive parents showed little mental illness. In contrast, schizophrenia and other psychological impairments piled up in adoptees whose biological and adoptive parents were both disturbed (Tienari, Wahlberg, & Wynne, 2006).

Furthermore, parents and other caring adults can *uncouple* unfavorable gene–environment correlations by providing children with positive experiences that modify the expression of heredity, yielding favorable outcomes. For example, in a study that tracked the development of 5-year-old identical twins, pair members tended to resemble each other in level of aggression. And the more aggression they displayed, the more maternal anger and criticism they received (a gene–environment correlation). Nevertheless, some mothers treated their twins differently. When followed up at age 7, twins who had been targets of more maternal negativity engaged in even more antisocial behavior. In contrast, their better-treated, genetically identical counterparts showed a reduction in disruptive acts (Caspi et al., 2004). Good parenting protected them from a spiraling, antisocial course of development.

Accumulating evidence reveals that the relationship between heredity and environment is not a one-way street, from genes to environment to behavior. Rather, like other system influences considered in this and the previous chapter, it is *bidirectional*: Genes affect people's behavior and experiences, but their experiences and behavior also affect gene expression (Diamond, 2009; Rutter, 2007). Researchers call this view of the relationship between heredity and environment the *epigenetic framework* (Gottlieb, 2007). It is depicted in Figure 2.7. **Epigenesis** means development resulting from ongoing, bidirectional exchanges between heredity and all levels of the environment. To illustrate, providing a baby with a healthy diet increases brain growth, leading to new connections between nerve cells, which transform gene expression. This opens the door to new gene–environment exchanges—for example, advanced exploration of objects and interaction with caregivers,

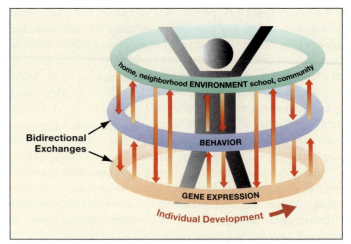

FIGURE 2.7 **The epigenetic framework.** Development takes place through ongoing, bidirectional exchanges between heredity and all levels of the environment. Genes affect behavior and experiences. Experiences and behavior also affect gene expression. (Adapted from Gottlieb, 2007.)

which further enhance brain growth and gene expression. These ongoing, bidirectional influences foster cognitive and social development. In contrast, harmful environments can negatively affect gene expression (see the Biology and Environment box on the following page for an example) (Blair & Raver, 2012). At times, the impact is so profound that later experiences can do little to change characteristics (such as intelligence and personality) that originally were flexible.

The concept of epigenesis reminds us that development is best understood as a series of complex exchanges between nature and nurture. Although people cannot be changed in any way we might desire, environments can modify genetic influences. The success of any attempt to improve development depends on the characteristics we want to change, the genetic makeup of the individual, and the type and timing of our intervention.

ASK YOURSELF

REVIEW Explain how each of the following concepts supports the conclusion that genetic influences on human characteristics are not constant but change over time: somatic mutation (page 40), niche-picking (page 55), and epigenesis (page 56).

APPLY Bianca's parents are accomplished musicians. At age 4, Bianca began taking piano lessons. By age 10, she was accompanying the school choir. At age 14, she asked to attend a special music high school. Explain how gene–environment correlation promoted Bianca's talent.

REFLECT What aspects of your own development—for example, interests, hobbies, college major, or vocational choice—are probably due to niche-picking? Explain.

Biology and Environment

A Case of Epigenesis: Smoking During Pregnancy Alters Gene Expression

A wealth of experimental research with animals confirms that environment can modify the genome in ways that have no impact on a gene's sequence of base pairs but nevertheless affect the operation of that gene (Zhang & Meaney, 2010). This epigenetic interplay, in which a gene's impact on the individual's phenotype depends on the gene's context, is now being vigorously investigated in humans.

Maternal smoking during pregnancy is among the risk factors for *attention-deficit hyperactivity disorder (ADHD)*—one of the most common disorders of childhood, which we will take up in greater detail in Chapter 9. ADHD symptoms—inattention, impulsivity, and overactivity—typically result in serious academic and social problems. Some studies report that individuals who are homozygous for a chromosome-5 gene (DD) containing a special repeat of base pairs are at increased risk for ADHD, though other research has not confirmed any role for this gene (Fisher et al., 2002; Gill et al., 1997; Waldman et al., 1998).

Animal evidence suggests that one reason for this inconsistency may be that environmental influences associated with ADHD—such as prenatal exposure to toxins—modify the gene's activity. To test this possibility, researchers recruited several hundred mothers

and their 6-month-old babies, obtaining infant blood samples for molecular genetic analysis and asking mothers whether they smoked regularly during pregnancy (Kahn et al., 2003). At a 5-year follow-up, parents responded to a widely used behavior rating scale that assesses children for ADHD symptoms.

Findings revealed that by itself, the DD genotype was unrelated to impulsivity, overactivity, or oppositional behavior. But children whose mothers had smoked during pregnancy scored higher in these behaviors than children of nonsmoking mothers. Furthermore, as Figure 2.8 shows, 5-year-olds with both prenatal nicotine exposure and the DD genotype obtained substantially higher impulsivity, overactivity, and oppositional scores than all other groups—outcomes that persisted even after a variety of other factors (quality of the home environment and maternal ethnicity, marital status, and post-birth smoking) had been controlled.

Another investigation following participants into adolescence yielded similar findings, suggesting that the epigenetic effect persists (Becker et al., 2008). What processes might account for it? In animal research,

Because his mother smoked during pregnancy, this baby may be at risk for attention-deficit hyperactivity disorder (ADHD). Prenatal nicotine exposure seems to alter expression of a chromosome-5 gene in ways that greatly heighten impulsivity, overactivity, and oppositional behavior.

tobacco smoke stimulates the DD genotype to release chemicals in the brain that that promote impulsivity and overactivity (Ernst, Moolchan, & Robinson, 2001). These behaviors, in turn, often evoke harsh, punitive parenting, which triggers defiance in children.

The DD genotype is widespread, present in more than 50 percent of people. Thus, the majority of children prenatally exposed to nicotine are at high risk for learning and behavior problems (refer to page 68 in Chapter 3). Growing evidence indicates that other genes, in epigenetic interplay with as yet unknown environmental factors, also contribute to ADHD symptoms (Hudziak & Rettew, 2009).

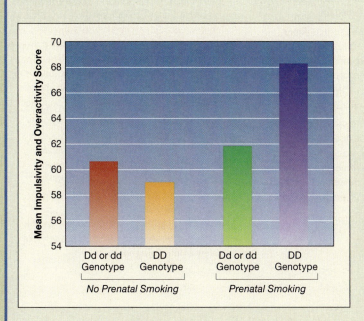

FIGURE 2.8 Combined influence of maternal prenatal smoking and genotype on impulsivity and overactivity at age 5. In the absence of prenatal smoking, 5-year-olds who were homozygous for a chromosome-5 gene (DD) showed no elevation in impulsivity and overactivity (orange bar) compared with children of other genotypes (Dd or dd) (red bar). Among children of all genotypes, prenatal smoking was associated with an increase in these behaviors (green and purple bars). And the combination of prenatal smoking and DD genotype greatly magnified impulsivity and overactivity (purple bar). Children's oppositional behavior followed a similar epigenetic pattern. (Adapted from Kahn et al., 2003.)

SUMMARY

Genetic Foundations (p. 36)

What are genes, and how are they transmitted from one generation to the next?

- Each individual's **phenotype,** or directly observable characteristics, is a product of both **genotype** and environment. **Chromosomes,** rodlike structures within the cell nucleus, contain our hereditary endowment. Along their length are **genes,** segments of **deoxyribonucleic acid (DNA)** that send instructions for making a rich assortment of proteins to the cell's cytoplasm.

- **Gametes,** or sex cells, result from a cell division process called **meiosis,** in which each individual receives a unique set of genes from each parent. Once sperm and ovum unite, the resulting **zygote** starts to develop into a complex human being through cell duplication, or **mitosis.**

- If the fertilizing sperm carries an X chromosome, the child will be a girl; if it contains a Y chromosome, a boy. **Fraternal,** or **dizygotic, twins** result when two ova are released from the mother's ovaries and each is fertilized. **Identical,** or **monozygotic, twins** develop when a zygote divides in two during the early stages of cell duplication.

Describe various patterns of genetic inheritance.

- Traits controlled by single genes follow **dominant–recessive** and **incomplete dominance** patterns of inheritance. **Homozygous** individuals have two identical **alleles,** or forms of a gene. **Heterozygous** individuals, with one dominant and one recessive allele, are **carriers** of the recessive trait.

- In **X-linked inheritance,** a harmful allele is carried on the X chromosome and, therefore, is more likely to affect males. In **genomic imprinting,** one parent's allele is activated, regardless of its makeup.

- Harmful genes arise from **mutation,** which can occur spontaneously or be caused by hazardous environmental agents. Germline mutation affects the cells that give rise to gametes; somatic mutation can occur in body cells at any time of life.

- Human traits that vary on a continuum, such as intelligence and personality, result from **polygenic inheritance**—the effects of many genes.

Describe major chromosomal abnormalities, and explain how they occur.

- Most chromosomal abnormalities result from errors during meiosis. The most common, Down syndrome, results in physical defects and mental retardation. **Sex chromosome** disorders are generally milder than defects of the **autosomes.**

Reproductive Choices (p. 41)

What procedures can assist prospective parents in having healthy children?

- **Genetic counseling** helps couples at risk for giving birth to children with genetic abnormalities decide whether or not to conceive. **Prenatal diagnostic methods** permit early detection of developmental problems.

- Reproductive technologies such as donor insemination, in vitro fertilization, surrogate motherhood, and postmenopausal-assisted childbirth enable individuals to become parents who otherwise would not, but they raise serious legal and ethical concerns.

- Many parents who are infertile or at high risk of transmitting a genetic disorder decide to adopt. Although adopted children have more learning and emotional problems than children in general, most fare well in the long run. Warm, sensitive parenting predicts favorable development.

Environmental Contexts for Development (p. 45)

Describe family functioning from the perspective of ecological systems theory, along with aspects of the environment that support family well-being and development.

- The first and foremost context for development is the family, a dynamic system characterized by bidirectional influences, in which each member's behaviors affect those of others. Both direct and indirect influences operate within the family system, which must continually adjust to new events and changes in its members.

- **Socioeconomic status (SES)** profoundly affects family functioning. Higher-SES families tend to be smaller, to emphasize psychological traits, and to engage in warm, verbally stimulating interaction with children. Lower-SES families often stress external characteristics and use more commands, criticism, and physical punishment. Many affluent parents are physically and emotionally unavailable, thereby impairing their children's adjustment. Poverty and homelessness can seriously undermine development.

- Connections between family and community are vital for psychological well-being. Stable, socially cohesive neighborhoods in which residents have access to social support and enrichment activities promote favorable development in both children and adults. Compared with urban environments, small towns foster greater community involvement, warm ties among nonrelatives, and a sense of safety among aging adults.

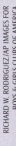

RICHARD W. RODRIGUEZ/AP IMAGES FOR BOYS & GIRLS CLUBS OF AMERICA

- The values and practices of cultures and **subcultures** affect all aspects of daily life. **Extended-family households,** which are common among many ethnic minorities, help protect family members from the negative effects of poverty and other stressful life conditions.

- **Collectivist societies,** which emphasize group needs and goals, and **individualistic societies,** which emphasize individual well-being, take different approaches to devising **public policies** to address social problems.

Understanding the Relationship Between Heredity and Environment
(p. 53)

Explain the various ways heredity and environment may combine to influence complex traits.

- **Behavioral genetics** is a field that examines the contributions of nature and nurture to diversity in human traits and abilities. Researchers use **kinship studies** to compute **heritability estimates,** which measure the extent to which genetic factors influence complex traits such as intelligence and personality. However, the accuracy and usefulness of heritability estimates have been challenged.

© LOU CYPHER/CORBIS

- **Gene–environment interaction, gene–environment correlation,** and **niche-picking** describe how genes affect the environments to which individuals are exposed. **Epigenesis** reminds us that development is best understood as a series of complex exchanges between heredity and all levels of the environment.

Important Terms and Concepts

allele (p. 38)
autosomes (p. 37)
behavioral genetics (p. 53)
carrier (p. 38)
chromosomes (p. 36)
collectivist societies (p. 50)
coparenting (p. 46)
deoxyribonucleic acid (DNA) (p. 36)
dominant–recessive inheritance (p. 38)
epigenesis (p. 56)
extended-family household (p. 50)
fraternal, or dizygotic, twins (p. 37)
gametes (p. 37)

gene (p. 36)
gene–environment correlation (p. 55)
gene–environment interaction (p. 54)
genetic counseling (p. 42)
genomic imprinting (p. 40)
genotype (p. 36)
heritability estimate (p. 53)
heterozygous (p. 38)
homozygous (p. 38)
identical, or monozygotic, twins (p. 38)
incomplete dominance (p. 39)
individualistic societies (p. 50)
kinship studies (p. 53)

meiosis (p. 37)
mitosis (p. 37)
mutation (p. 40)
niche-picking (p. 55)
phenotype (p. 36)
polygenic inheritance (p. 40)
prenatal diagnostic methods (p. 43)
public policies (p. 50)
sex chromosomes (p. 37)
socioeconomic status (SES) (p. 47)
subculture (p. 50)
X-linked inheritance (p. 39)
zygote (p. 37)

Prenatal Development, Birth, and the Newborn Baby

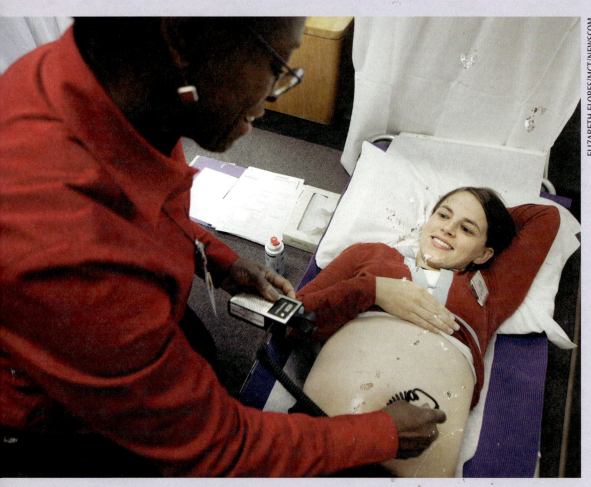

ELIZABETH FLORES/MCT/NEWSCOM

An expectant mother reacts with amazement on hearing the robust heartbeat of her nearly full-term fetus. High-quality prenatal care and preparation for the events of childbirth enable her to approach labor and delivery with confidence and excitement.

chapter outline

When I met Yolanda and Jay one fall in my child development class, Yolanda was just two months pregnant. After months of wondering if the time in their lives was right, they had decided to have a baby. Both were full of questions: "How does the baby grow before birth?" "When is each organ formed?" "Has its heart begun to beat?" "Can it hear, feel, or sense our presence?"

Yolanda and Jay wanted to do everything possible to make sure their baby would be born healthy. Yolanda started to wonder about her diet and whether she should keep up her daily aerobic workout. And she asked me whether an aspirin for a headache, a glass of wine at dinner, or a few daily cups of coffee might be harmful.

In this chapter, we answer Yolanda and Jay's questions, along with many more that scientists have asked about the events before birth. First, we trace prenatal development, paying special attention to environmental supports for healthy growth, as well as damaging influences that threaten the child's health and survival. Next, we turn to the events of childbirth, including the choices available to women in industrialized nations about where and how to give birth.

Yolanda and Jay's son Joshua was strong, alert, and healthy at birth. But the birth process does not always go smoothly. We will consider the pros and cons of medical interventions, such as pain-relieving drugs and surgical deliveries, designed to ease a difficult birth and protect the health of mother and baby. Our discussion also addresses the development of infants born underweight or too early. We conclude with a close look at the remarkable capacities of newborns. ●

Prenatal Development

The sperm and ovum that unite to form the new individual are uniquely suited for the task of reproduction. The ovum is a tiny sphere, measuring 1/175 inch in diameter—the size of the period at the end of this sentence. But in its microscopic world, it is a giant—the largest cell in the human body, making it a perfect target for the much smaller sperm, which measure only 1/500 inch.

occur, the corpus luteum shrinks, and the lining of the uterus is discarded two weeks later with menstruation.

The male produces sperm in vast numbers—an average of 300 million a day—in the *testes,* two glands located in the *scrotum,* sacs that lie just behind the penis. Each sperm develops a tail that permits it to swim long distances, upstream in the female reproductive tract, through the *cervix* (opening of the uterus) and into the fallopian tube, where fertilization usually takes place. The journey is difficult. Only 300 to 500 reach their

Conception

About once every 28 days, in the middle of a woman's menstrual cycle, an ovum bursts from one of her *ovaries,* two walnut-sized organs located deep inside her abdomen, and is drawn into one of two *fallopian tubes*—long, thin structures that lead to the hollow, soft-lined uterus (see Figure 3.1). While the ovum is traveling, the spot on the ovary from which it was released, now called the *corpus luteum,* secretes hormones that prepare the lining of the uterus to receive a fertilized ovum. If pregnancy does not

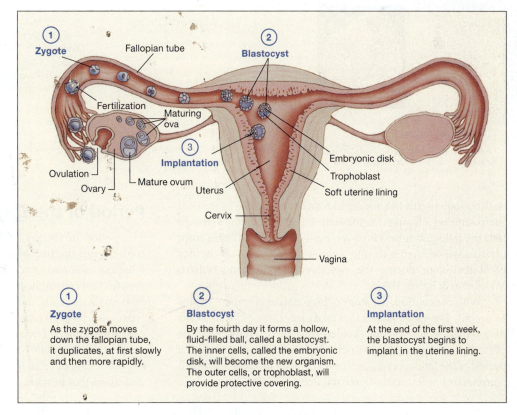

FIGURE 3.1 Female reproductive organs, showing fertilization, early cell duplication, and implantation. (From *Before We Are Born,* 6th ed., by K. L. Moore & T. V. N. Persaud, p. 87. Copyright © 2003, reprinted with permission from Elsevier, Inc.)

① Zygote
As the zygote moves down the fallopian tube, it duplicates, at first slowly and then more rapidly.

② Blastocyst
By the fourth day it forms a hollow, fluid-filled ball, called a blastocyst. The inner cells, called the embryonic disk, will become the new organism. The outer cells, or trophoblast, will provide protective covering.

③ Implantation
At the end of the first week, the blastocyst begins to implant in the uterine lining.

TABLE 3.1
Milestones of Prenatal Development

TRIMESTER	PERIOD		WEEKS	LENGTH AND WEIGHT	MAJOR EVENTS
First	Zygote		1		The one-celled zygote multiplies and forms a blastocyst.
			2		The blastocyst burrows into the uterine lining. Structures that feed and protect the developing organism begin to form—*amnion, chorion, yolk sac, placenta,* and *umbilical cord.*
	Embryo		3–4	¼ inch (6 mm)	A primitive brain and spinal cord appear. Heart, muscles, ribs, backbone, and digestive tract begin to develop.
			5–8	1 inch (2.5 cm); ½ ounce (4 g)	Many external body structures (face, arms, legs, toes, fingers) and internal organs form. The sense of touch begins to develop, and the embryo can move.
	Fetus		9–12	3 inches (7.6 cm); less than 1 ounce (28 g)	Rapid increase in size begins. Nervous system, organs, and muscles become organized and connected, and new behavioral capacities (kicking, thumb sucking, mouth opening, and rehearsal of breathing) appear. External genitals are well-formed, and the fetus's sex is evident.
Second			13–24	12 inches (30 cm); 1.8 pounds (820 g)	The fetus continues to enlarge rapidly. In the middle of this period, fetal movements can be felt by the mother. Vernix and lanugo keep the fetus's skin from chapping in the amniotic fluid. Most of the brain's neurons are in place by 24 weeks. Eyes are sensitive to light, and the fetus reacts to sound.
Third			25–38	20 inches (50 cm); 7.5 pounds (3,400 g)	The fetus has a good chance of survival if born during this time. Size increases. Lungs mature. Rapid brain development causes sensory and behavioral capacities to expand. In the middle of this period, a layer of fat is added under the skin. Antibodies are transmitted from mother to fetus to protect against disease. Most fetuses rotate into an upside-down position in preparation for birth.

Source: Moore, Persaud, & Torchia, 2013.

Photos (from top to bottom): © Claude Cortier/Photo Researchers, Inc.; © G. Moscoso/Photo Researchers, Inc.; © John Watney/Photo Researchers, Inc.; © James Stevenson/Photo Researchers, Inc.; © Lennart Nilsson, *A Child Is Born*/Scanpix.

destination. Sperm live for up to 6 days and can lie in wait for the ovum, which survives for only 1 day after being released into the fallopian tube. However, most conceptions result from intercourse occurring during a three-day period—on the day of ovulation or during the two days preceding it (Wilcox, Weinberg, & Baird, 1995).

With conception, the story of prenatal development begins to unfold. The vast changes that take place during the 38 weeks of pregnancy are usually divided into three phases: (1) the period of the zygote, (2) the period of the embryo, and (3) the period of the fetus. As we consider each, refer to Table 3.1, which summarizes milestones of prenatal development.

Period of the Zygote

The period of the zygote lasts about two weeks, from fertilization until the tiny mass of cells drifts down and out of the fallopian tube and attaches itself to the wall of the uterus. The zygote's first cell duplication is long and drawn out, taking about 30 hours. Gradually, new cells are added at a faster rate. By the fourth day, 60 to 70 cells exist that form a hollow, fluid-filled ball called a *blastocyst* (refer again to Figure 3.1). The cells on the inside, called the *embryonic disk,* will become the new organism; the outer ring of cells, termed the *trophoblast,* will become the structures that provide protective covering and nourishment.

Period of the zygote: seventh to ninth day. The fertilized ovum duplicates rapidly, forming a hollow ball of cells, or blastocyst, by the fourth day after fertilization. Here the blastocyst, magnified thousands of times, burrows into the uterine lining between the seventh and ninth day.

Implantation. Between the seventh and ninth days, **implantation** occurs: The blastocyst burrows deep into the uterine lining. Surrounded by the woman's nourishing blood, it starts to grow in earnest. At first, the trophoblast (protective outer layer) multiplies fastest. It forms a membrane, called the **amnion,** that encloses the developing organism in *amniotic fluid,* which helps keep the temperature of the prenatal world constant and provides a cushion against any jolts caused by the woman's movement. A *yolk sac* emerges that produces blood cells until the liver, spleen, and bone marrow are mature enough to take over this function (Moore, Persaud, & Torchia, 2013).

As many as 30 percent of zygotes do not survive this period. In some, the sperm and ovum do not join properly. In others, cell duplication never begins. By preventing implantation in these cases, nature eliminates most prenatal abnormalities (Sadler, 2010).

The Placenta and Umbilical Cord. By the end of the second week, cells of the trophoblast form another protective membrane—the **chorion,** which surrounds the amnion. From the chorion, tiny hairlike *villi,* or blood vessels, emerge.[1] As these villi burrow into the uterine wall, the *placenta* starts to develop. By bringing the embryo's and mother's blood close together, the **placenta** permits food and oxygen to reach the organism and waste products to be carried away.

[1]Recall from Table 2.2 on page 44 that *chorionic villus sampling* is the prenatal diagnostic method that can be performed earliest, at nine weeks after conception.

The placenta is connected to the developing organism by the **umbilical cord,** which contains one large vein that delivers blood loaded with nutrients and two arteries that remove waste products. The force of blood flowing through the cord keeps it firm, so it seldom tangles while the embryo, like a space-walking astronaut, floats freely in its fluid-filled chamber (Moore, Persaud, & Torchia, 2013).

Period of the Embryo

The period of the **embryo** lasts from implantation through the eighth week of pregnancy. During these brief six weeks, the groundwork is laid for all body structures and organs.

Last Half of the First Month. In the first week of this period, the embryonic disk forms three layers of cells: (1) the *ectoderm,* which will become the nervous system and skin; (2) the *mesoderm,* from which will develop the muscles, skeleton, circulatory system, and other internal organs; and (3) the *endoderm,* which will become the digestive system, lungs, urinary tract, and glands. These three layers give rise to all parts of the body.

At first, the nervous system develops fastest. The ectoderm folds over to form the **neural tube,** or primitive spinal cord. At 3½ weeks, the top swells to form the brain. While the nervous system is developing, the heart begins to pump blood, and the muscles, backbone, ribs, and digestive tract appear. At the end of the first month, the curled embryo—only ¼ inch long—consists of millions of organized groups of cells with specific functions.

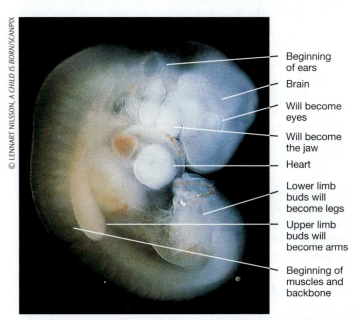

Period of the embryo: fourth week. This 4-week-old embryo is only ¼-inch long, but many body structures have begun to form. The primitive tail will disappear by the end of the embryonic period.

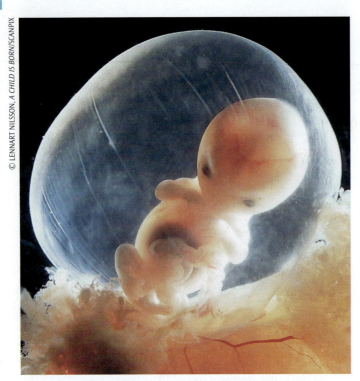

© LENNART NILSSON, A CHILD IS BORN/SCANPIX

Period of the embryo: seventh week. The embryo's posture is more upright. Body structures—eyes, nose, arms, legs, and internal organs—are more distinct. An embryo this age responds to touch. It can also move, although at less than one inch long and one ounce in weight, it is till too tiny to be felt by the mother.

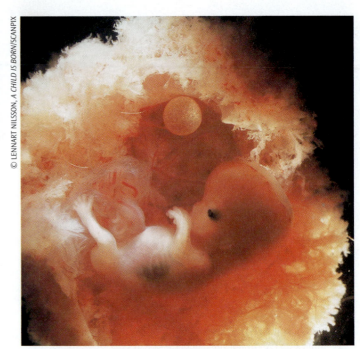

© LENNART NILSSON, A CHILD IS BORN/SCANPIX

Period of the fetus: eleventh week. The fetus grows rapidly. At 11 weeks, the brain and muscles are better connected. The fetus can kick, bend its arms, and open and close its hands and mouth, and suck its thumb. Notice the yolk sac, which shrinks as the internal organs take over its function of producing blood cells.

The Second Month. In the second month, growth continues rapidly. The eyes, ears, nose, jaw, and neck form. Tiny buds become arms, legs, fingers, and toes. Internal organs are more distinct: The intestines grow, the heart develops separate chambers, and the liver and spleen take over production of blood cells so that the yolk sac is no longer needed.

At 7 weeks, production of *neurons* (nerve cells that store and transmit information) begins deep inside the neural tube at the astounding pace of more than 250,000 per minute (Nelson, 2011). Once formed, neurons travel along tiny threads to their permanent locations, where they will form the major parts of the brain.

At the end of this period, the embryo—about 1 inch long and ½ ounce in weight—can already sense its world. It responds to touch, particularly in the mouth area and on the soles of the feet. And it can move, although its tiny flutters are still too light to be felt by the mother (Moore, Persaud, & Torchia, 2013).

Period of the Fetus

The period of the **fetus,** from the ninth week to the end of pregnancy, is the longest prenatal period. During this "growth and finishing" phase, the organism increases rapidly in size.

The Third Month. In the third month, the organs, muscles, and nervous system start to become organized and connected. When the brain signals, the fetus kicks, bends its arms, opens its mouth, and even sucks its thumb. The tiny lungs begin to expand and contract, rehearsing breathing movements. By the twelfth week, the external genitals are well-formed, and the sex of the fetus can be detected with ultrasound (Sadler, 2010). Other finishing touches appear, such as fingernails, toenails, tooth buds, and eyelids. The heartbeat can now be heard through a stethoscope.

Prenatal development is sometimes divided into **trimesters,** or three equal time periods. At the end of the third month, the *first trimester* is complete.

The Second Trimester. By the middle of the second trimester, between 17 and 20 weeks, the new being has grown large enough that the mother can feel its movements. A white, cheeselike substance called **vernix** protects its skin from chapping during the long months spent bathing in the amniotic fluid. White, downy hair called **lanugo** also appears over the entire body, helping the vernix stick to the skin.

At the end of the second trimester, many organs are well-developed, and most of the brain's billions of neurons are in place. However, *glial cells,* which support and feed the neurons, continue to increase rapidly throughout the remaining months of pregnancy, as well as after birth. Consequently, brain weight increases tenfold from the twentieth week until birth (Roelfsema et al., 2004). At the same time, neurons begin forming *synapses,* or connections, at a rapid pace.

Brain growth means new behavioral capacities. The 20-week-old fetus can be stimulated as well as irritated by sounds. And if a doctor looks inside the uterus using fetoscopy (see Table 2.2 on page 44), fetuses try to shield their eyes from the light with their hands, indicating that sight has begun to emerge (Moore, Persaud, & Torchia, 2013). Still, a fetus born at this time cannot survive. Its lungs are immature, and the brain cannot yet control breathing and body temperature.

The Third Trimester.
During the final trimester, a fetus born early has a chance for survival. The point at which the baby can first survive, called the **age of viability,** occurs sometime between 22 and 26 weeks (Moore, Persaud, & Torchia, 2013). A baby born between the seventh and eighth months, however, usually needs oxygen assistance to breathe. Although the brain's respiratory center is now mature, tiny air sacs in the lungs are not yet ready to inflate and exchange carbon dioxide for oxygen.

The brain continues to make great strides. The *cerebral cortex,* the seat of human intelligence, enlarges. As neural connectivity and organization improve, the fetus spends more time awake—about 11 percent at 28 weeks, a figure that rises to 16 percent just before birth (DiPietro et al., 1996). Between 30 and 34 weeks, fetuses display rhythmic alternations between sleep and wakefulness that gradually increase in organization (Rivkees, 2003). The fetus also shows signs of developing temperament. In one study, more active fetuses during the third trimester became 1-year-olds who could better handle frustration and 2-year-olds who were less fearful, in that they more readily interacted with toys and with an unfamiliar adult in a laboratory (DiPietro et al., 2002). Perhaps fetal activity is an indicator of healthy neurological development.

The third trimester brings greater responsiveness to stimulation. Between 23 and 30 weeks, connections form between the cerebral cortex and brain regions involved in pain sensitivity. By this time, painkillers should be used in any surgical procedures (Lee et al., 2005). Around 28 weeks, fetuses blink their eyes in reaction to nearby sounds (Kisilevsky & Low, 1998; Saffran, Werker, & Werner, 2006). And at 30 weeks, fetuses presented with a repeated auditory stimulus against the mother's abdomen

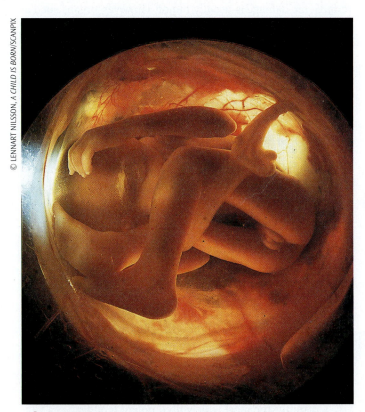

Period of the fetus: twenty-second week. This fetus is almost one foot long and weighs slightly more than one pound. Its movements can be felt easily by the mother and by other family members who place a hand on her abdomen. If born now, the fetus has a slim chance of surviving.

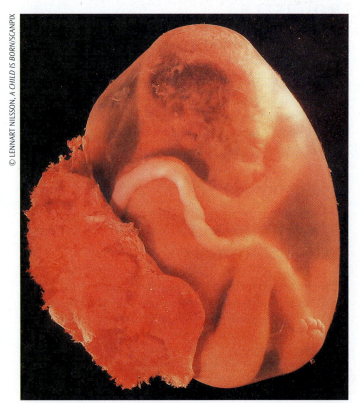

Period of the fetus: thirty-sixth week. This fetus fills the uterus. To nourish it, the umbilical cord and placenta have grown large. Notice the vernix (a cheeselike substance) on the skin, which protects it from chapping. The fetus has accumulated fat to aid temperature regulation after birth. In two more weeks, it will be full-term.

initially react with a rise in heart rate and body movements. But over the next 5 to 6 minutes, responsiveness gradually declines, indicating *habituation* (adaptation) to the sound. If the stimulus is reintroduced after a 10-minute delay, heart rate falls off far more quickly (Dirix et al., 2009). This suggests that fetuses can remember for at least a brief period.

Within the next six weeks, fetuses distinguish the tone and rhythm of different voices and sounds. They show systematic heart rate changes to a male versus a female speaker, to the mother's voice versus a stranger's, to a stranger speaking his or her native language (English) versus a foreign language (Mandarin Chinese), and to a simple familiar melody versus an unfamiliar melody (Granier-Deferre et al., 2003; Huotilainen et al., 2005; Kisilevsky et al., 2003, 2009; Lecanuet et al., 1993).

In the final three months, the fetus gains more than 5 pounds and grows 7 inches. In the eighth month, a layer of fat is added to assist with temperature regulation. The fetus also receives antibodies from the mother's blood that protect against illnesses, since the newborn's own immune system will not work well until several months after birth. In the last weeks, most fetuses assume an upside-down position.

ASK YOURSELF

REVIEW How is brain development related to fetal capacities and behavior?

APPLY Amy, two months pregnant, wonders how the embryo is being fed and what parts of the body have formed. "I don't look pregnant yet, so does that mean not much development has taken place?" she asks. How would you respond to Amy?

Prenatal Environmental Influences

Although the prenatal environment is far more constant than the world outside the womb, many factors can affect the embryo and fetus. Yolanda and Jay learned that parents—and society as a whole—can do a great deal to create a safe environment for development before birth.

Teratogens

The term **teratogen** refers to any environmental agent that causes damage during the prenatal period. The harm done by teratogens is not always simple and straightforward. It depends on the following factors:

- *Dose.* Larger doses over longer time periods usually have more negative effects.

- *Heredity.* The genetic makeup of the mother and the developing organism plays an important role. Some individuals are better able than others to withstand harmful environments.

- *Other negative influences.* The presence of several negative factors at once, such as additional teratogens, poor nutrition, and lack of medical care, can worsen the impact of a harmful agent.

- *Age.* The effects of teratogens vary with the age of the organism at time of exposure. To understand this last idea, think of the *sensitive period* concept introduced in Chapter 1. A sensitive period is a limited time span in which a part of the body or a behavior is biologically prepared to develop rapidly and is especially sensitive to its surroundings. If the environment is harmful, then damage occurs, and recovery is difficult and sometimes impossible.

Figure 3.2 summarizes prenatal sensitive periods. In the *period of the zygote,* before implantation, teratogens rarely have any impact. If they do, the tiny mass of cells is usually so damaged that it dies. The *embryonic period* is the time when serious defects are most likely to occur because the foundations for all body parts are being laid down. During the *fetal period,* teratogenic damage is usually minor. However, organs such as the brain, ears, eyes, teeth, and genitals can still be strongly affected.

Prescription and Nonprescription Drugs.
In the early 1960s, the world learned a tragic lesson about drugs and prenatal development. At that time, a sedative called *thalidomide* was widely available in Canada, Europe, and South America. When taken by mothers 4 to 6 weeks after conception, thalidomide produced gross deformities of the embryo's arms and legs and, less frequently, damage to the ears, heart, kidneys, and genitals. About 7,000 infants worldwide were affected (Moore, Persaud, & Torchia, 2013). As these children grew older, many scored below average in intelligence. Perhaps the drug damaged the central nervous system directly, or the child-rearing conditions of these severely deformed youngsters impaired their intellectual development.

Another medication, a synthetic hormone called *diethyl-stilbestrol (DES),* was widely prescribed between 1945 and 1970 to prevent miscarriages. As daughters of these mothers reached adolescence and young adulthood, they showed unusually high rates of cancer of the vagina, malformations of the uterus, and infertility. Similarly, young men were at increased risk of genital abnormalities and cancer of the testes (Goodman, Schorge, & Greene, 2011; Hammes & Laitman, 2003).

Currently, the most widely used potent teratogen is a vitamin A derivative called *Accutane* (known by the generic name *isotretinoin*), used to treat severe acne and taken by hundreds of thousands of women of childbearing age in industrialized nations. Exposure during the first trimester results in eye, ear, skull, brain, heart, and immune system abnormalities (Honein, Paulozzi, & Erickson, 2001). Accutane's packaging warns users

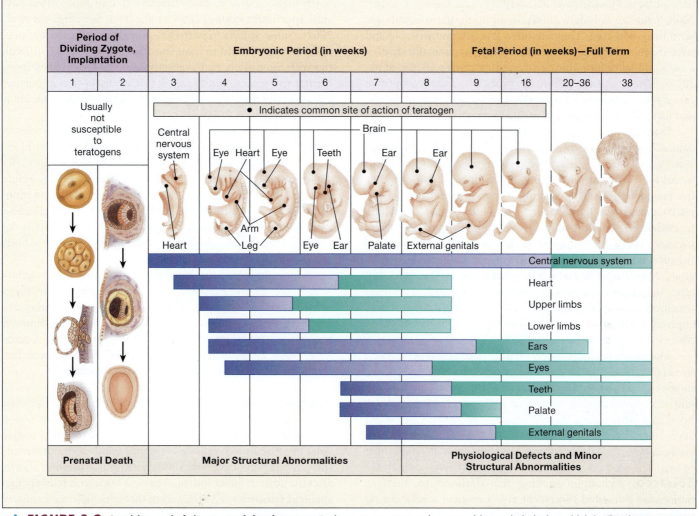

FIGURE 3.2 Sensitive periods in prenatal development. Each organ or structure has a sensitive period, during which its development may be disturbed. Blue horizontal bars indicate highly sensitive periods. Green horizontal bars indicate periods that are somewhat less sensitive to teratogens, although damage can occur. (Adapted from *Before We Are Born,* 7th ed., by K. L. Moore and T. V. N. Persaud, p. 313. Copyright © 2008, reprinted with permission from Elsevier, Inc.)

to avoid pregnancy by using two methods of birth control, but many women do not heed this advice (Garcia-Bournissen et al., 2008).

Indeed, any drug with a molecule small enough to penetrate the placental barrier can enter the embryonic or fetal bloodstream. Yet many pregnant women continue to take over-the-counter medications without consulting their doctors. Several studies suggest that regular aspirin use is linked to low birth weight, infant death around the time of birth, poorer motor development, and lower intelligence scores in early childhood, although other research fails to confirm these findings (Barr et al., 1990; Kozer et al., 2003; Streissguth et al., 1987). Coffee, tea, cola, and cocoa contain another frequently consumed drug, caffeine. High doses increase the risk of low birth weight (Brent, Christian, & Diener, 2011). And persistent intake of antidepressant medication is linked to premature delivery and birth complications, including respiratory distress, and to high blood pressure in infancy (Lund, Pedersen, & Henriksen, 2009; Roca et al., 2011; Udechuku et al., 2010).

Because children's lives are involved, we must take findings like these seriously. At the same time, we cannot be sure that these drugs actually cause the problems just mentioned. Often mothers take more than one drug. If the embryo or fetus is injured, it is hard to tell which drug might be responsible or whether other factors correlated with drug taking are at fault. Until we have more information, the safest course of action is the one Yolanda took: Avoid these drugs entirely.

Illegal Drugs. Nearly 4 percent of U.S. pregnant women use highly addictive mood-altering drugs, such as cocaine or heroin (Substance Abuse and Mental Health Services Administration, 2011). Babies born to users of these drugs are at risk for a wide variety of problems, including prematurity, low birth weight, physical defects, breathing difficulties, and death around the time of birth (Bandstra et al., 2010; Howell, Coles, & Kable, 2008; Schuetze & Eiden, 2006). In addition, these infants are born drug-addicted. They are often feverish and irritable and have trouble sleeping, and their cries are abnormally shrill—a common symptom among stressed newborns (Bauer et al., 2005). When mothers with many problems of their own must care for these babies, who are difficult to calm down, cuddle, and feed, behavior problems are likely to persist.

Evidence on cocaine suggests that some prenatally exposed babies develop lasting difficulties. Cocaine constricts the blood vessels, causing oxygen delivered to the developing organism to fall for 15 minutes following a high dose. It also can alter the production and functioning of neurons and the chemical balance in the fetus's brain. These effects may contribute to evidence in some studies of perceptual, motor, attention, memory, language, and impulse-control problems persist into the preschool and school years (Bandstra et al., 2011; Dennis et al., 2006; Lester & Lagasse, 2010; Linares et al., 2006). But other investigations reveal no major negative effects of prenatal cocaine exposure (Behnke et al., 2013; Hurt et al., 2009). These contradictory findings indicate how difficult it is to isolate the precise damage caused by illegal drugs.

Marijuana, the most widely used illegal drug, has been linked to smaller head size (a measure of brain growth); attention, memory, and academic achievement difficulties; impulsivity and overactivity; and depression as well as aggression in childhood and adolescence (Goldschmidt et al., 2004; Gray et al., 2005; Huizink & Mulder, 2006; Jutras-Aswad et al., 2009). As with cocaine, however, lasting consequences are not well-established.

Tobacco.
Although smoking has declined in Western nations, an estimated 14 percent of U.S. women smoke during their pregnancies (Tong et al., 2009). The best-known prenatal effect of smoking is low birth weight. But the likelihood of other serious consequences, such as miscarriage, prematurity, cleft lip and palate, blood vessel abnormalities, impaired heart rate and breathing during sleep, infant death, and asthma and cancer later in childhood, also increases (Geerts et al., 2012; Howell, Coles, & Kable, 2008; Mossey et al., 2009). The more cigarettes a mother smokes, the greater the chances that her baby will be affected. And if a pregnant woman stops smoking at any time, even during the third trimester, she reduces the likelihood that her infant will be born underweight and suffer from future problems (Klesges et al., 2001).

Newborns of smoking mothers also display slight behavioral abnormalities. They are less attentive to sounds, display more muscle tension, are more excitable when touched and visually stimulated, and more often have colic (persistent crying) (Law et al., 2003; Sondergaard et al., 2002). Some studies report that prenatally exposed children and adolescents tend to have shorter attention spans, difficulties with impulsivity and overactivity, poorer memories, lower mental test scores, and higher levels of disruptive, aggressive behavior (Espy et al., 2011; Fryer, Crocker, & Mattson, 2008; Lindblad & Hjern, 2010).

How does smoking harm the fetus? Nicotine, the addictive substance in tobacco, constricts blood vessels, lessens blood flow to the uterus, and causes the placenta to grow abnormally. This reduces the transfer of nutrients, so the fetus gains weight poorly. Also, nicotine raises the concentration of carbon monoxide in the bloodstreams of both mother and fetus. Because carbon monoxide displaces oxygen from red blood cells, it can cause damage to the central nervous system and slow body growth.

From one-third to one-half of nonsmoking pregnant women are "passive smokers" because their husbands, relatives, or co-workers use cigarettes. Passive smoking is also related to low birth weight, infant death, childhood respiratory illnesses, and possible long-term attention, learning, and behavior problems (Best, 2009; Pattenden et al., 2006). Clearly, expectant mothers should avoid smoke-filled environments.

Alcohol.
In his moving book *The Broken Cord,* Michael Dorris (1989), a Dartmouth College anthropology professor, described what it was like to rear his adopted son Abel (called Adam in the book), whose biological mother drank heavily throughout pregnancy and died of alcohol poisoning shortly after his birth. A Sioux Indian, Abel was born with **fetal alcohol spectrum disorder (FASD)**, a term that encompasses a range of

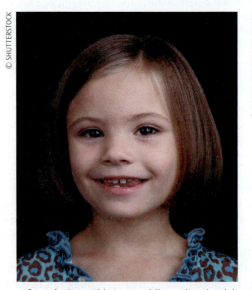

Left photo: This 5-year-old's mother drank heavily during pregnancy. Her widely spaced eyes, thin upper lip, and flattened philtrum are typical of fetal alcohol syndrome (FAS).
Right photo: This 12-year-old has the small head and facial abnormalities of FAS. She also shows the mental impairments and slow growth that accompany the disorder.

physical, mental, and behavioral outcomes caused by prenatal alcohol exposure. Children with FASD are given one of three diagnoses, which vary in severity:

1. **Fetal alcohol syndrome (FAS),** distinguished by (a) slow physical growth, (b) a pattern of three facial abnormalities (short eyelid openings; a thin upper lip; a smooth or flattened philtrum, or indentation running from the bottom of the nose to the center of the upper lip), and (c) brain injury, evident in a small head and impairment in at least three areas of functioning—for example, memory, language and communication, attention span and activity level (overactivity), planning and reasoning, motor coordination, or social skills. Other defects—of the eyes, ears, nose, throat, heart, genitals, urinary tract, or immune system—may also be present. Abel was diagnosed as having FAS. As is typical for this disorder, his mother drank heavily throughout pregnancy.

2. **Partial fetal alcohol syndrome (p-FAS),** characterized by (a) two of the three facial abnormalities just mentioned and (b) brain injury, again evident in at least three areas of impaired functioning. Mothers of children with p-FAS generally drank alcohol in smaller quantities, and children's defects vary with the timing and length of alcohol exposure. Furthermore, recent evidence suggests that paternal alcohol use around the time of conception can alter gene expression (see page 56 in Chapter 2), thereby contributing to symptoms (Ouko et al., 2009).

3. **Alcohol-related neurodevelopmental disorder (ARND),** in which at least three areas of mental functioning are impaired, despite typical physical growth and absence of facial abnormalities. Again, prenatal alcohol exposure, though confirmed, is less pervasive than in FAS (Chudley et al., 2005; Loock et al., 2005).

Even when provided with enriched diets, FAS babies fail to catch up in physical size during childhood. Mental impairment associated with all three FASD diagnoses is also permanent: In his teens and twenties, Abel Dorris had trouble concentrating and keeping a routine job, and he suffered from poor judgment. For example, he would buy something and not wait for change or would wander off in the middle of a task. He died at age 23, after being hit by a car. The more alcohol a pregnant woman consumes, the poorer the child's motor coordination, speed of information processing, reasoning, and intelligence and achievement test scores during the preschool and school years (Burden, Jacobson, & Jacobson, 2005; Mattson, Calarco, & Lang, 2006). In adolescence and early adulthood, FASD is associated with persisting attention and motor-coordination deficits, poor school performance, trouble with the law, inappropriate social and sexual behaviors, alcohol and drug abuse, depression, and high emotional reactivity to stress (Barr et al., 2006; Fryer, Crocker, & Mattson, 2008; Hellemans et al., 2010; Howell et al., 2006; Streissguth et al., 2004).

Alcohol produces its devastating effects by interfering with production and migration of neurons in the primitive neural tube. Brain-imaging research reveals reduced brain size, damage to many brain structures, and abnormalities in brain functioning, including transferring messages from one part of the brain to another (Coles et al., 2011; Haycock, 2009). Also, the body uses large quantities of oxygen to metabolize alcohol. A pregnant woman's heavy drinking draws away oxygen that the developing organism needs for cell growth.

About 25 percent of U.S. mothers report drinking at some time during their pregnancies. As with heroin and cocaine, alcohol abuse is higher in poverty-stricken women. On some Native-American reservations, the incidence of FAS is as high as 10 to 20 percent (Szlemko, Wood, & Thurman, 2006; Tong et al., 2009). Even mild drinking, less than one drink per day, is associated with reduced head size and body growth among children followed into adolescence (Jacobson et al., 2004; Martinez-Frias et al., 2004).

Radiation. Defects due to ionizing radiation were tragically apparent in children born to pregnant women who survived the bombings of Hiroshima and Nagasaki during World War II. Similar abnormalities surfaced in the nine months following the 1986 Chernobyl, Ukraine, nuclear power plant accident. After each disaster, the incidence of miscarriage and babies born with underdeveloped brains, physical deformities, and slow physical growth rose dramatically (Double et al., 2011; Schull, 2003).

© CAROLINE PENN/CORBIS

This child's deformities are linked to radiation exposure early in pregnancy, caused by the Chernobyl nuclear power plant disaster in 1986. She is also at risk for low intelligence and language and emotional disorders.

Even when a radiation-exposed baby seems normal, problems may appear later. For example, low-level radiation, resulting from industrial leakage or medical X-rays, can increase the risk of childhood cancer (Fattibene et al., 1999). In middle childhood, prenatally exposed Chernobyl children had abnormal brain-wave activity, lower intelligence test scores, and rates of language and emotional disorders two to three times greater than those of nonexposed Russian children (Loganovskaja & Loganovsky, 1999; Loganovsky et al., 2008).

Environmental Pollution. In industrialized nations, an astounding number of potentially dangerous chemicals are released into the environment. In the United States, more than 75,000 are in common use. When 10 newborns were randomly selected from U.S. hospitals for analysis of umbilical cord blood, researchers uncovered a startling array of industrial contaminants—287 in all (Houlihan et al., 2005). They concluded that many babies are "born polluted" by chemicals that not only impair prenatal development but increase the chances of health problems and life-threatening diseases later on.

Pregnant women are wise to avoid eating long-lived predatory fish, such as swordfish, albacore tuna, and shark, which are heavily contaminated with mercury. High levels of prenatal mercury exposure disrupt production and migration of neurons, causing widespread brain damage (Clarkson, Magos, & Myers, 2003; Hubbs-Tait et al., 2005). Prenatal mercury exposure from maternal seafood diets predicts deficits in speed of cognitive processing and motor, attention, and verbal test performance during the school years (Boucher et al., 2010; Debes et al., 2006).

For many years, *polychlorinated biphenyls (PCBs)* were used to insulate electrical equipment until research showed that, like mercury, they entered waterways and the food supply. Prenatal exposure to high levels of PCBs results in low birth weight, skin deformities, brain-wave abnormalities, and delayed cognitive development (Chen & Hsu, 1994; Chen et al., 1994). Even at low levels, PCBs are linked to reduced birth weights, smaller head size, persisting attention and memory difficulties, and lower intelligence test scores in childhood (Boucher, Muckle, & Bastien, 2009; Jacobson & Jacobson, 2003; Stewart et al., 2008).

Another teratogen, *lead,* is present in paint flaking off the walls of old buildings and in certain materials used in industrial occupations. High levels of prenatal lead exposure are related to prematurity, low birth weight, brain damage, and a wide variety of physical defects. Babies with low-level exposure show slightly poorer mental and motor development (Jedrychowski et al., 2009).

Finally, prenatal exposure to dioxins—toxic compounds resulting from incineration—is linked to brain, immune system, and thyroid damage in babies and to an increased incidence of breast and uterine cancers in women, perhaps through altering hormone levels (ten Tusscher & Koppe, 2004). Even tiny amounts of dioxin in the paternal bloodstream cause a dramatic change in sex ratio of offspring: Affected men father nearly twice as many girls as boys (Ishihara et al., 2007). Dioxin seems to impair the fertility of Y-bearing sperm prior to conception.

Infectious Disease. Most infectious diseases, such as the common cold, have no prenatal impact. Nevertheless, a few can cause extensive damage.

In the mid-1960s, a worldwide epidemic of *rubella* (three-day, or German, measles) led to the birth of more than 20,000 American babies with serious defects and to 13,000 fetal and newborn deaths. Consistent with the sensitive-period concept, more than 50 percent of infants whose mothers become ill during the embryonic period show deafness; eye cataracts; heart, genital, urinary, and intestinal defects; and mental retardation. Infection during the fetal period is less harmful, but low birth weight, hearing loss, and bone defects may still occur. The organ damage inflicted by prenatal rubella often leads to severe mental illness, diabetes, cardiovascular disease, and thyroid and immune-system dysfunction in adulthood (Brown, 2006; Duszak, 2009).

Routine vaccination in infancy and childhood has made new rubella outbreaks unlikely in industrialized nations. But an estimated 100,000 cases of prenatal infection continue to occur worldwide, primarily in developing countries in Africa and Asia with weak or absent immunization programs (Bale, 2009).

The *human immunodeficiency virus (HIV),* which can lead to *acquired immune deficiency syndrome (AIDS),* a disease that destroys the immune system, has infected increasing numbers of women over the past three decades. In developing countries, where 95 percent of new infections occur, more than half affect women. In South Africa, for example, nearly 30 percent of all pregnant women are HIV-positive (South African Department of Health, 2009). Untreated HIV-infected expectant mothers pass the deadly virus to the developing organism 20 to 30 percent of the time.

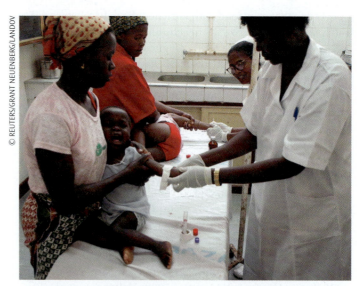

© REUTERS/GRANT NEUENBERG/LANDOV

Babies are tested for the HIV virus in a clinic in Mozambique, Africa. Prenatal treatment with antiretroviral drugs reduces transmission of AIDS from mother to child by as much as 95 percent.

AIDS progresses rapidly in infants, with most becoming ill by 6 months, and nearly half dying by 1 year of age, and 90 percent by age 3 (Devi et al., 2009). Antiretroviral drug therapy reduces prenatal AIDS transmission by as much as 95 percent, but even with increases in distribution, antiretroviral drugs are still not widely available in impoverished regions of the world (UNICEF, 2010a).

The developing organism is especially sensitive to the family of herpes viruses, for which no vaccine or treatment exists. Among these, *cytomegalovirus* (the most frequent prenatal infection, transmitted through respiratory or sexual contact) and *herpes simplex 2* (which is sexually transmitted) are especially dangerous. In both, the virus invades the mother's genital tract, infecting babies either during pregnancy or at birth.

Toxoplasmosis, caused by a parasite found in many animals, can affect pregnant women who eat raw or undercooked meat or from contact with the feces of infected cats. If it strikes during the first trimester, it is likely to cause eye and brain damage. Later infection is linked to mild visual and cognitive impairments (Jones, Lopez, & Wilson, 2003). Expectant mothers can avoid toxoplasmosis by making sure that the meat they eat is well-cooked, having pet cats checked for the disease, and turning over the care of litter boxes to other family members.

Other Maternal Factors

Besides avoiding teratogens, expectant parents can support the development of the embryo and fetus in other ways. In the following sections, we examine nutrition, emotional stress, blood type, age, and previous births.

Nutrition. During the prenatal period, when children are growing more rapidly than at any other time, they depend totally on the mother for nutrients. A healthy diet that results in a weight gain of 25 to 30 pounds (10 to 13.5 kilograms) helps ensure the health of mother and baby.

Prenatal malnutrition can cause serious damage to the central nervous system. The poorer the mother's diet, the greater the loss in brain weight, especially if malnutrition occurred during the last trimester, when the brain is increasing rapidly in size. An inadequate diet during pregnancy can also distort the structure of the liver, kidney, pancreas, and cardiovascular system, resulting in lifelong health problems (Barker, 2008; Whincup et al., 2008).

Many studies show that providing pregnant women with adequate food has a substantial impact on the health of their newborn babies. Vitamin–mineral enrichment is also crucial. For example, taking a folic acid supplement around the time of conception reduces by more than 70 percent abnormalities of the neural tube, such as *anencephaly* and *spina bifida* (see Table 2.2 on page 44). U.S. government guidelines recommend that all women of childbearing age consume 0.4 milligrams of folic acid per day. For women who have previously had a pregnancy affected by neural tube defect, the recommended amount is 4 to 5 milligrams (dosage must be carefully monitored, as exces-

sive intake can be harmful) (American Academy of Pediatrics, 2006). About half of U.S. pregnancies are unplanned, so government regulations mandate that bread, flour, rice, pasta, and other grain products be fortified with folic acid.

When poor nutrition persists throughout pregnancy, infants usually require more than dietary improvement. Successful interventions must also break the cycle of apathetic mother–baby interactions. Some do so by teaching parents how to interact effectively with their infants, while others focus on stimulating infants to promote active engagement with their physical and social surroundings (Grantham-McGregor et al., 1994; Grantham-McGregor, Schofield, & Powell, 1987).

Although prenatal malnutrition is highest in developing countries, it also occurs in the industrialized world. The U.S. Special Supplemental Food Program for Women, Infants, and Children (WIC), which provides food packages to low-income pregnant women, reaches about 90 percent of those who qualify (U.S. Department of Agriculture, 2011b). But many who need nutrition intervention are not eligible for WIC.

Emotional Stress. When women experience severe emotional stress during pregnancy, especially during the first two trimesters, their babies are at risk for a wide variety of difficulties, including miscarriage, prematurity, low birth weight, infant respiratory and digestive illnesses, colic (persistent infant crying), sleep disturbances, and irritability during the first three years (Field, 2011; Lazinski, Shea, & Steiner, 2008; van der Wal, van Eijsden, & Bonsel, 2007).

How can maternal stress affect the fetus? *TAKE A MOMENT...* To understand this process, list the changes you sensed in your own body the last time you were under stress. When we experience fear and anxiety, stress hormones released into our bloodstream—such as *epinephrine* (adrenaline) and *cortisol,* known as the "flight or fight" hormones—cause us to be "poised for action." Large amounts of blood are sent to parts of the body involved in the defensive response—the brain, heart, and muscles in the arms, legs, and trunk. Blood flow to other organs, including the uterus, is reduced, so the fetus is deprived of a full supply of oxygen and nutrients.

Maternal stress hormones also cross the placenta, causing a dramatic rise in fetal stress hormones and, therefore, in fetal heart rate, blood pressure, blood glucose, and activity level (Kinsella & Monk, 2009; Weinstock, 2008). Excessive fetal stress may permanently alter fetal neurological functioning, thereby heightening stress reactivity in later life. In several studies, infants and children of mothers who experienced severe prenatal anxiety displayed cortisol levels that were either abnormally high or abnormally low, both of which signal reduced physiological capacity to manage stress (Entringer et al., 2009; Van den Bergh et al., 2008). Furthermore, maternal emotional stress during pregnancy predicts childhood weakened immune system functioning and increased susceptibility to infectious disease (Huizink et al., 2008; Nielsen et al., 2011). It is also associated with diverse negative behavioral outcomes in childhood and adolescence, including anxiety, short attention span,

Social Issues: Health

The Nurse–Family Partnership: Reducing Maternal Stress and Enhancing Child Development Through Social Support

At age 17, Denise—an unemployed high-school dropout living with her disapproving parents—gave birth to Tara. Having no one to turn to for help during pregnancy and beyond, Denise felt overwhelmed and anxious much of the time. Tara was premature and cried uncontrollably, slept erratically, and suffered from frequent minor illnesses throughout her first year. When she reached school age, she had trouble keeping up academically, and her teachers described her as distractible, angry, and uncooperative.

The Nurse–Family Partnership, currently implemented in hundreds of counties across 42 U.S. states, is a voluntary home visiting program for first-time, low-income expectant mothers like Denise. Its goals are to reduce pregnancy and birth complications, promote competent early caregiving, and improve family conditions, thereby protecting children from lasting adjustment difficulties. A registered nurse visits the home weekly during the first month after enrollment, twice a month during the remainder of pregnancy and through the middle of the child's second year, and then monthly until age 2. In these sessions, the nurse provides the mother with intensive social support— a sympathetic ear; assistance in accessing health and other community services and the help of family members (especially fathers and grandmothers); and encouragement to finish high school, find work, and engage in future family planning.

To evaluate the program's effectiveness, researchers randomly assigned large samples of mothers at risk for high prenatal stress (due to teenage pregnancy, poverty, and other negative life conditions) to nurse-visiting or comparison conditions (just prenatal care, or prenatal care plus infant referral for developmental problems). Families were followed through their child's school-age years and, in one experiment, into adolescence (Kitzman et al., 2010; Olds et al., 2004, 2007; Rubin et al., 2011).

As kindergartners, Nurse–Family Partnership children obtained higher language and intelligence test scores. And at both ages 6 and 9, the children of home-visited mothers in the poorest mental health during pregnancy exceeded comparison children in academic achievement and displayed fewer behavior problems. Furthermore, from their baby's birth on, home-visited mothers were on a more favorable life course: They had fewer subsequent births, longer intervals between their first and second births, more frequent contact with the child's father, more stable intimate partnerships, less welfare dependence, and a greater sense of control over their lives. Perhaps for these reasons, 12-year-old children of home-visited mothers continued to be advantaged in academic achievement and reported less alcohol use and drug-taking than comparison-group agemates.

The Nurse–Family Partnership is highly cost-effective (Dawley, Loch, & Bindrich, 2007). For $1 spent, it saves more than $5 in public spending on pregnancy complications, preterm births, and child and youth learning and behavior problems.

COURTESY OF NURSE–FAMILY PARTNERSHIP

The Nurse–Family Partnership provides this first-time mother with regular home visits from a registered nurse. In follow-up research, children of home-visited mothers developed more favorably—cognitively, emotionally, and socially—than comparison children.

anger, aggression, overactivity, and lower mental test scores (de Weerth & Buitelaar, 2005; Gutteling et al., 2006; Lazinski, Shea, & Steiner, 2008; Loomans et al., 2011).

But stress-related prenatal complications are greatly reduced when mothers have partners, other family members, and friends who offer social support (Glover, Bergman, & O'Connor, 2008). The impact of social support is particularly strong for low-income women, who often lead highly stressful lives (see the Social Issues: Health box above).

Rh Factor Incompatibility. When inherited blood types of mother and fetus differ, serious problems sometimes result. The most common cause of these difficulties is **Rh factor incompatibility.** When the mother is Rh-negative (lacks the Rh blood protein) and the father is Rh-positive (has the protein), the baby may inherit the father's Rh-positive blood type. If even a little of a fetus's Rh-positive blood crosses the placenta into the Rh-negative mother's bloodstream, she begins to form antibodies to the foreign Rh protein. If these enter the fetus's system, they destroy red blood cells, reducing the oxygen supply to organs and tissues. Miscarriage, mental retardation, heart damage, and infant death can occur.

It takes time for the mother to produce Rh antibodies, so firstborn children are rarely affected. The danger increases with each additional pregnancy. Fortunately, Rh incompatibility can be prevented in most cases. After the birth of each Rh-positive baby, Rh-negative mothers are routinely given a vaccine to prevent the buildup of antibodies.

Maternal Age. In Chapter 2, we noted that women who delay childbearing until their thirties or forties face increased risk of infertility, miscarriage, and babies born with chromosomal defects. Are other pregnancy complications more common for older mothers? Research indicates that healthy women in their thirties have about the same rates as those in their twenties (Bianco et al., 1996; Dildy et al., 1996; Prysak, Lorenz, & Kisly, 1995). Thereafter, as Figure 3.3 reveals, complication rates increase, with a sharp rise among women age 50 to 55—an age at which because of menopause (end of menstruation) and aging reproductive organs, few women can conceive naturally (Salihu et al., 2003; Usta & Nassar, 2008).

In the case of teenage mothers, does physical immaturity cause prenatal complications? Infants born to teenagers have a higher rate of difficulties, but not directly because of maternal age. Most pregnant teenagers come from low-income backgrounds, where stress, poor nutrition, and health problems are common.

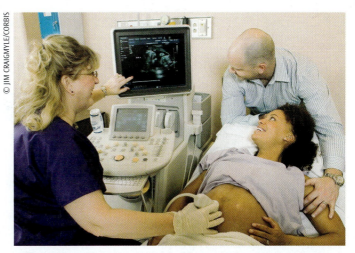

During a routine prenatal visit, this couple views an ultrasound image of their twins. All pregnant women need regular prenatal care to protect their health and that of their babies.

The Importance of Prenatal Health Care

Yolanda had her first prenatal appointment three weeks after missing her menstrual period. After that, she visited the doctor's office once a month until she was seven months pregnant, then twice during the eighth month, increasing her visits to once a week when birth grew near. The doctor kept track of her general health, her weight gain, the capacity of her uterus and cervix to support the fetus, and the fetus's growth.

Yolanda's pregnancy, like most others, was free of complications. But unexpected difficulties can arise, especially if mothers have health problems. For example, the 5 percent of pregnant women who have diabetes need careful monitoring. Extra glucose in the diabetic mother's bloodstream causes the fetus to grow larger than average, making pregnancy and birth problems more common. Maternal high blood glucose also compromises prenatal brain development: It is linked to poorer memory and learning in infancy and early childhood (deRegnier et al., 2007). Another complication, experienced by 5 to 10 percent of pregnant women, is *preeclampsia* (sometimes called *toxemia*), in which blood pressure increases sharply and the face, hands, and feet swell in the last half of pregnancy. If untreated, preeclampsia can cause convulsions in the mother and fetal death (Vidaeff, Carroll, & Ramin, 2005). Usually, hospitalization, bed rest, and drugs can lower blood pressure to a safe level.

Unfortunately, 6 percent of pregnant women in the United States wait until after the first trimester to seek prenatal care or receive none at all (Child Trends, 2012). Why do these mothers delay going to the doctor? One reason is a lack of health insurance. Although the poorest of these mothers are eligible for government-sponsored health services, many low-income women do not qualify.

Besides financial hardship, *situational barriers* (difficulty finding a doctor, getting an appointment, and arranging transportation) and *personal barriers* (psychological stress, the demands of taking care of other young children) prevent many

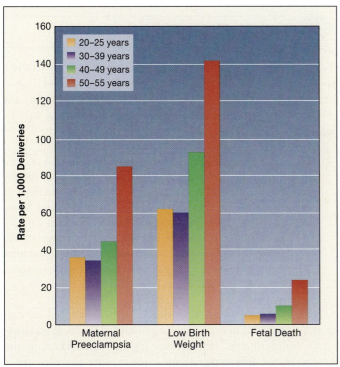

FIGURE 3.3 Relationship of maternal age to prenatal and birth complications. Complications increase after age 40, with a sharp rise between 50 and 55 years. (Adapted from Salihu et al., 2003.)

Applying **What We Know**

Do's and Don'ts for a Healthy Pregnancy

Do	Don't
Do make sure that you have been vaccinated against infectious diseases that are dangerous to the embryo and fetus, such as rubella, before you get pregnant. Most vaccinations are not safe during pregnancy.	Don't take any drugs without consulting your doctor.
Do see a doctor as soon as you suspect that you are pregnant, and continue to get regular medical checkups throughout pregnancy.	Don't smoke. If you have already smoked during part of your pregnancy, cut down or, better yet, quit. If other members of your family smoke, ask them to quit or to smoke outside.
Do eat a well-balanced diet and take vitamin–mineral supplements, as prescribed by your doctor, both prior to and during pregnancy. Gain 25 to 30 pounds gradually.	Don't drink alcohol from the time you decide to get pregnant or learn you are pregnant.
Do obtain literature from your doctor, library, or bookstore about prenatal development. Ask your doctor about anything that concerns you.	Don't engage in activities that might expose your embryo or fetus to environmental hazards, such as radiation or chemical pollutants. If you work in an occupation that involves these agents, ask for a safer assignment or a leave of absence.
Do keep physically fit through moderate exercise. If possible, join a special exercise class for expectant mothers.	Don't engage in activities that might expose your embryo or fetus to harmful infectious diseases, such as toxoplasmosis.
Do avoid emotional stress. If you are a single expectant mother, find a relative or friend on whom you can rely for emotional support.	Don't choose pregnancy as a time to go on a diet.
Do get plenty of rest. An overtired mother is at risk for pregnancy complications.	Don't gain too much weight during pregnancy. A very large weight gain is associated with complications.
Do enroll in a prenatal and childbirth education class with your partner or other companion. When parents know what to expect, the nine months before birth can be one of the most joyful times of life.	

mothers from seeking prenatal care. Many also engage in high-risk behaviors, such as smoking and drug abuse, which they do not want to reveal to health professionals (Daniels, Noe, & Mayberry, 2006; Maupin et al., 2004). These women, who receive little or no prenatal care, are among those who need it most!

Clearly, public education about the importance of early and sustained prenatal care for all pregnant women is badly needed. Refer to Applying What We Know above, which lists "do's and don'ts" for a healthy pregnancy, based on our discussion of the prenatal environment.

ASK YOURSELF

REVIEW Why is it difficult to determine the prenatal effects of many environmental agents, such as drugs and pollution?

APPLY Nora, pregnant for the first time, believes that a few cigarettes and a glass of wine a day won't be harmful. Provide Nora with research-based reasons for not smoking or drinking.

REFLECT If you had to choose five environmental influences to publicize in a campaign aimed at promoting healthy prenatal development, which ones would you choose, and why?

Childbirth

Yolanda and Jay agreed to return the following spring to share their experiences with my next class. Two-week-old Joshua came along as well. Their story revealed that the birth of a baby is one of the most dramatic and emotional events in human experience. Yolanda explained:

> By morning, we knew I was in labor. It was Thursday, so we went in for my usual weekly appointment. The doctor said, yes, the baby was on the way, but it would be a while. He told us to go home and relax and come to the hospital in three or four hours. We checked in at 3 in the afternoon; Joshua arrived at 2 o'clock the next morning. When, finally, I was ready to deliver, it went quickly; a half hour or so and some good hard pushes, and there he was! His face was red and puffy, and his head was misshapen, but I thought, "Our son! I can't believe he's really here."

Jay was also elated by Joshua's birth. "I wanted to support Yolanda and to experience as much as I could. It was awesome, indescribable," he said, holding Joshua and kissing him gently. In the following sections, we explore the experience of childbirth, from both the parents' and the baby's point of view.

The Stages of Childbirth

It is not surprising that childbirth is often referred to as labor. It is the hardest physical work a woman may ever do. A complex series of hormonal changes between mother and fetus initiates the process, which naturally divides into three stages (see Figure 3.4):

1. *Dilation and effacement of the cervix.* This is the longest stage of labor, lasting an average of 12 to 14 hours with a first birth and 4 to 6 hours with later births. Contractions of the uterus gradually become more frequent and powerful, causing the cervix, or uterine opening, to widen and thin to nothing, forming a clear channel from the uterus into the birth canal, or vagina.
2. *Delivery of the baby.* This stage is much shorter, lasting about 50 minutes for a first birth and 20 minutes in later births. Strong contractions of the uterus continue, but the mother also feels a natural urge to squeeze and push with her abdominal muscles. As she does so with each contraction, she forces the baby down and out.
3. *Delivery of the placenta.* Labor comes to an end with a few final contractions and pushes. These cause the placenta to separate from the wall of the uterus and be delivered in about 5 to 10 minutes.

The Baby's Adaptation to Labor and Delivery

At first glance, labor and delivery seem like a dangerous ordeal for the baby. The strong contractions exposed Joshua's head to a great deal of pressure, and they squeezed the placenta and the umbilical cord repeatedly. Each time, Joshua's supply of oxygen was temporarily reduced.

Fortunately, healthy babies are well-equipped to withstand these traumas. The force of the contractions causes the infant to produce high levels of stress hormones. Unlike during pregnancy, when excessive stress endangers the fetus, during childbirth high levels of infant cortisol and other stress hormones are adaptive. They help the baby withstand oxygen deprivation by sending a rich supply of blood to the brain and heart (Gluckman, Sizonenko, & Bassett, 1999). In addition, stress hormones prepare the baby to breathe by causing the lungs to absorb any remaining fluid and by expanding the bronchial tubes (passages leading to the lungs). Finally, stress hormones arouse the infant into alertness. Joshua was born wide awake, ready to interact with the surrounding world.

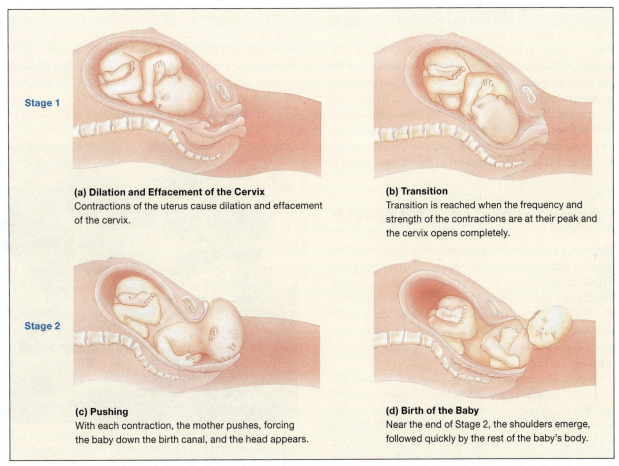

Stage 1

(a) Dilation and Effacement of the Cervix
Contractions of the uterus cause dilation and effacement of the cervix.

(b) Transition
Transition is reached when the frequency and strength of the contractions are at their peak and the cervix opens completely.

Stage 2

(c) Pushing
With each contraction, the mother pushes, forcing the baby down the birth canal, and the head appears.

(d) Birth of the Baby
Near the end of Stage 2, the shoulders emerge, followed quickly by the rest of the baby's body.

FIGURE 3.4 A Normal Birth. The first two stages of labor are depicted. In the third stage, the placenta is delivered.

TABLE 3.2   The Apgar Scale

SIGN[a]	RATING		
	0	1	2
Heart rate	No heartbeat	Under 100 beats per minute	100 to 140 beats per minute
Respiratory effort	No breathing for 60 seconds	Irregular, shallow breathing	Strong breathing and crying
Reflex irritability (sneezing, coughing, and grimacing)	No response	Weak reflexive response	Strong reflexive response
Muscle tone	Completely limp	Weak movements of arms and legs	Strong movements of arms and legs
Color[b]	Blue body, arms, and legs	Body pink with blue arms and legs	Body, arms, and legs completely pink

[a]To remember these signs, you may find it helpful to use a technique in which the original labels are reordered and renamed as follows: color = **A**ppearance; heart rate = **P**ulse; reflex irritability = **G**rimace; muscle tone = **A**ctivity; and respiratory effort = **R**espiration. Together, the first letters of the new labels spell **Apgar**.

[b]The skin tone of nonwhite babies makes it difficult to apply the "pink" color criterion. However, newborns of all races can be rated for pinkish glow resulting from the flow of oxygen through body tissues.

Source: Apgar, 1953.

Assessing the Newborn's Physical Condition: The Apgar Scale

Infants who have difficulty making the transition to life outside the uterus require special help at once. To assess the newborn's physical condition quickly, doctors and nurses use the **Apgar Scale.** As Table 3.2 shows, a rating of 0, 1, or 2 on each of five characteristics is made at 1 minute and again at 5 minutes after birth. A combined Apgar score of 7 or better indicates that the infant is in good physical condition. If the score is between 4 and 6, the baby needs assistance in establishing breathing and other vital signs. If the score is 3 or below, the infant is in serious danger and requires emergency medical attention. Two Apgar ratings are given because some babies have trouble adjusting at first but do quite well after a few minutes (Apgar, 1953).

 # Approaches to Childbirth

Childbirth practices, like other aspects of family life, are molded by the society of which mother and baby are a part. In many village and tribal cultures, expectant mothers are well-acquainted with the childbirth process. They also know they will be assisted. Among the Mayans of the Yucatán, for example, the mother leans against the body of a woman called the "head helper," who supports her weight and breathes with her during each contraction (Jordan, 1993).

In Western nations, childbirth has changed dramatically over the centuries. Before the late 1800s, birth usually took place at home and was a family-centered event. The industrial revolution brought greater crowding to cities, along with new health problems. As a result, childbirth moved from home to hospital, where the health of mothers and babies could be protected. Once doctors assumed responsibility for childbirth, women's

knowledge of it declined, and relatives and friends no longer participated (Borst, 1995).

By the 1950s and 1960s, women had begun to question the medical procedures that had come to be used routinely during labor and delivery. Many felt that routine use of strong drugs and delivery instruments had robbed them of a precious experience and was often neither necessary nor safe for the baby. Gradually, a natural childbirth movement arose in Europe and spread to North America. Its purpose was to make hospital birth as comfortable and rewarding for mothers as possible. Today, most hospitals offer birth centers that are family-centered and homelike and that encourage early contact between parents and baby.

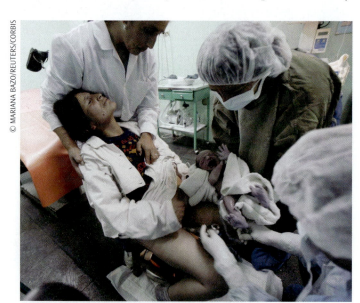

In this Peruvian health clinic, families are encouraged to incorporate practices of their village culture into the birth experience. Here, a familiar attendant soothes a new mother as her baby is delivered.

Natural, or Prepared, Childbirth

Yolanda and Jay chose **natural,** or **prepared, childbirth**—a group of techniques aimed at reducing pain and medical intervention and making childbirth a rewarding experience. Most natural childbirth programs draw on methods developed by Grantly Dick-Read (1959) in England and Fernand Lamaze (1958) in France. These physicians recognized that cultural attitudes had taught women to fear the birth experience. An anxious, frightened woman in labor tenses muscles, turning the mild pain that sometimes accompanies strong contractions into intense pain.

In a typical natural childbirth program, the expectant mother and a companion (a partner, relative, or friend) participate in three activities:

● *Classes.* Yolanda and Jay attended a series of classes in which they learned about the anatomy and physiology of labor and delivery. Knowledge about the birth process reduces a mother's fear.

● *Relaxation and breathing techniques.* During each class, Yolanda was taught relaxation and breathing exercises aimed at counteracting the pain of uterine contractions.

● *Labor coach.* Jay learned how to help Yolanda during childbirth by reminding her to relax and breathe, massaging her back, supporting her body, and offering encouragement and affection.

Social support is important to the success of natural childbirth techniques. In Guatemalan and American hospitals that routinely isolated patients during childbirth, some mothers were randomly assigned a *doula*—a Greek word referring to a trained lay attendant—who stayed with them throughout labor and delivery, talking to them, holding their hands, and rubbing their backs to promote relaxation. Doula support resulted in shorter labors, reduced use of pain-relieving medication, fewer birth complications, higher newborn Apgar scores, more positive mother–newborn interaction, and greater likelihood of breastfeeding (Campbell et al., 2006, 2007; Hodnet et al., 2003; McGrath & Kennell, 2008).

LOOK AND LISTEN

Talk to several mothers about social supports available to them during labor and delivery. From the mothers' perspectives, how did those supports (or lack of support) affect the birth experience? ●

Home Delivery

Home birth has always been popular in certain industrialized nations, such as England, the Netherlands, and Sweden. The number of American women choosing to have their babies at home rose during the 1970s and 1980s but remains small, at less than 1 percent (U.S. Department of Health and Human Services, 2011a). Although some home births are attended by

ANDERSEN ROSS/GETTY IMAGES/BRAND X PICTURES

After a home birth, the midwife and a lay attendant provide support to the new mother. For healthy women attended by a well-trained doctor or midwife, home birth is as safe as hospital birth.

doctors, many more are handled by *certified nurse–midwives,* who have degrees in nursing and additional training in childbirth management.

Is it just as safe to give birth at home as in a hospital? For healthy women who are assisted by a well-trained doctor or midwife, it seems so because complications rarely occur (Fullerton, Navarro, & Young, 2007; Wax, Pinette, & Cartin, 2010). However, if attendants are not carefully trained and prepared to handle emergencies, the rate of infant death is high (Mehlmadrona & Madrona, 1997). When mothers are at risk for any kind of complication, the appropriate place for labor and delivery is the hospital, where life-saving treatment is available.

Medical Interventions

Four-year-old Melinda walks with a halting, lumbering gait and has difficulty keeping her balance. She has *cerebral palsy,* a general term for a variety of impairments in muscle coordination caused by brain damage before, during, or just after birth. For about 10 percent of these children, including Melinda, brain damage was caused by **anoxia,** or inadequate oxygen supply, during labor and delivery (Bracci, Perrone, & Buonocore, 2006). Melinda was in **breech position,** turned so that the buttocks or feet would be delivered first, and the umbilical cord was wrapped around her neck. Had her mother come to the hospital earlier, doctors could have monitored Melinda's condition and delivered her surgically as soon as squeezing of the umbilical cord led to distress, thereby reducing the damage or preventing it entirely.

In cases like Melinda's, medical interventions are clearly justified. But in others, they can interfere with delivery and even pose new risks. In the following sections, we examine some commonly used medical procedures during childbirth.

Fetal Monitoring

Fetal monitors are electronic instruments that track the baby's heart rate during labor. An abnormal heartbeat may indicate that the baby is in distress due to anoxia and needs to be delivered immediately. Continuous fetal monitoring, which is required in most U.S. hospitals, is used in over 80 percent of American births (Natale & Dodman, 2003). The most popular type of monitor is strapped across the mother's abdomen throughout labor. A second, more accurate method involves threading a recording device through the cervix and placing it directly under the baby's scalp.

Fetal monitoring is a safe medical procedure that has saved the lives of many babies in high-risk situations. But in healthy pregnancies, it does not reduce the already low rates of infant brain damage and death (Haws et al., 2009). Furthermore, most infants have some heartbeat irregularities during labor, so critics worry that fetal monitors identify many babies as in danger who, in fact, are not. Monitoring is linked to an increase in the number of cesarean (surgical) deliveries, which we will discuss shortly (Thacker & Stroup, 2003). Still, fetal monitors will probably continue to be used routinely in the United States, even though they are not necessary in most cases. Doctors fear that they will be sued for malpractice if an infant dies or is born with problems and they cannot show that they did everything possible to protect the baby.

Labor and Delivery Medication

Some form of medication is used in more than 80 percent of U.S. births (Althaus & Wax, 2005). *Analgesics,* drugs used to relieve pain, may be given in mild doses during labor to help a mother relax. *Anesthetics* are a stronger type of painkiller that blocks sensation. Currently, the most common approach to controlling pain during labor is *epidural analgesia,* in which a regional pain-relieving drug is delivered continuously through a catheter into a small space in the lower spine. Because the mother retains the capacity to feel the pressure of the contractions and to move her trunk and legs, she is able to push during the second stage of labor.

Although pain-relieving drugs help women cope with childbirth and enable doctors to perform essential medical interventions, they also can cause problems. Epidural analgesia, for example, weakens uterine contractions. As a result, labor is prolonged, and the chances of cesarean (surgical) delivery increase (Nguyen et al., 2010). And because drugs rapidly cross the placenta, exposed newborns tend to be sleepy and withdrawn, to suck poorly during feedings, and to be irritable when awake (Caton et al., 2002; Eltzschig, Lieberman, & Camann, 2003).

Cesarean Delivery

A **cesarean delivery** is a surgical birth; the doctor makes an incision in the mother's abdomen and lifts the baby out of the uterus. Forty years ago, cesarean delivery was rare. Since then, cesarean rates have climbed internationally, reaching 16 percent in Finland, 23 percent in New Zealand, 26 percent in Canada, 30 percent in Australia, and 32 percent in the United States (OECD, 2011).

Cesareans have always been warranted by medical emergencies and in certain breech births, in which the baby risks head injury or anoxia (as in Melinda's case). But these factors do not explain the worldwide rise in cesarean deliveries. Instead, medical control over childbirth is largely responsible. Because many needless cesareans are performed, pregnant women should ask questions about the procedure before choosing a doctor. Although the operation itself is safe, mother and baby require more time for recovery. Anesthetic may have crossed the placenta, making cesarean newborns sleepy and unresponsive and at increased risk for breathing difficulties (McDonagh, Osterweil, & Guise, 2005).

ASK YOURSELF

REVIEW Describe the features and benefits of natural childbirth. What aspect contributes greatly to favorable outcomes, and why?

APPLY How might use of epidural analgesia negatively affect the parent–newborn relationship? Explain how your answer illustrates bidirectional influences between parent and child, emphasized in ecological systems theory.

REFLECT If you were an expectant parent, would you choose home birth? Why or why not?

Preterm and Low-Birth-Weight Infants

The average newborn weighs 7½ pounds (3,400 grams). Birth weight is the best available predictor of infant survival and healthy development. Many newborns who weigh less than 3½ pounds (1,500 grams) experience difficulties that are not overcome, an effect that becomes stronger as length of pregnancy and birth weight decrease (Baron & Rey-Casserly, 2010; Dombrowski, Noonan, & Martin, 2007). Brain abnormalities, frequent illness, inattention, overactivity, sensory impairments, poor motor coordination, language delays, low intelligence test scores, deficits in school learning, and emotional and behavior problems are some of the difficulties that persist through childhood and adolescence and into adulthood (Aarnoudse-Moens, Weiglas-Kuperus, & van Goudoever, 2009; Clark et al., 2008; Delobel-Ayoub et al., 2009; Nosarti et al., 2011).

About 1 in 13 American infants is born underweight. Although the problem can strike unexpectedly, it occurs especially often among poverty-stricken women (U.S. Department of Health and Human Services, 2011a). These mothers, as noted earlier, are more likely to be undernourished and to be exposed to other harmful environmental influences.

Preterm versus Small-for-Date Infants

Despite many obstacles to healthy development, most low-birth-weight infants go on to lead normal lives. About half of those born at 23 to 24 weeks gestation and weighing only a couple of pounds at birth have no disability. To better understand why some babies do better than others, researchers divide them into two groups. **Preterm infants** are those born several weeks or more before their due date. Although they are small, their weight may still be appropriate, based on time spent in the uterus. **Small-for-date infants** are below their expected weight considering length of the pregnancy. Some small-for-date infants are actually full-term. Others are preterm infants who are especially underweight.

Of the two types of babies, small-for-date infants usually have more serious problems. During the first year, they are more likely to die, catch infections, and show evidence of brain damage. By middle childhood, they have lower intelligence test scores, are less attentive, achieve more poorly in school, and are socially immature (Hediger et al., 2002; O'Keefe et al., 2003; Sullivan et al., 2008). Small-for-date infants probably experienced inadequate nutrition before birth. Perhaps their mothers did not eat properly, the placenta did not function normally, or the babies themselves had defects that prevented them from growing as they should.

Even among preterm newborns whose weight is appropriate for length of pregnancy, just seven more days—from 34 to 35 weeks—greatly reduces rates of illness, costly medical procedures, and lengthy hospital stays (Gladstone & Katz, 2004). And despite being relatively low-risk for disabilities, a substantial number of 34-week preterms are below average in physical growth and mildly to moderately delayed in cognitive development in early and middle childhood (Morse et al., 2009; Pietz et al., 2004; Stephens & Vohr, 2009). And in an investigation of over 120,000 New York City births, babies born even 1 or 2 weeks early showed slightly lower reading and math scores at a third-grade follow-up than children who experienced a full-length prenatal period (Noble et al., 2012). These outcomes persisted even after controlling for other factors linked to achievement, such as birth weight and SES. Yet doctors often induce births several weeks preterm, under the misconception that these babies are developmentally "mature."

Consequences for Caregiving

The appearance and behavior of preterm babies—scrawny and thin-skinned, sleepy and unresponsive, irritable when briefly awake—can lead parents to be less sensitive in caring for them.

Compared with full-term infants, preterm babies—especially those who are very ill at birth—are less often held close, touched, and talked to gently (Feldman, 2007). Distressed, emotionally reactive preterm infants are especially susceptible to the effects of parenting quality: Among a sample of preterm 9-month-olds, the combination of infant negativity and angry or intrusive parenting yielded the highest rates of behavior problems at 2 years of age. But with warm, sensitive parenting, distressed preterm babies' rates of behavior problems were the lowest (Poehlmann et al., 2011). When they are born to isolated, poverty-stricken mothers who cannot provide good nutrition, health care, and parenting, the likelihood of unfavorable outcomes increases. In contrast, parents with stable life circumstances and social supports usually can overcome the stresses of caring for a preterm infant (Ment et al., 2003).

These findings suggest that how well preterm infants develop has a great deal to do with the parent–child relationship. Consequently, interventions directed at supporting both sides of this tie are more likely to help these infants recover.

Interventions for Preterm Infants

A preterm baby is cared for in a special Plexiglas-enclosed bed called an *isolette*. Temperature is carefully controlled because these babies cannot yet regulate their own body temperature effectively. To help protect the baby from infection, air is filtered before it enters the isolette. When a preterm infant is fed through a stomach tube, breathes with the aid of a respirator, and receives medication through an intravenous needle, the isolette can be very isolating indeed!

Special Infant Stimulation. In proper doses, certain kinds of stimulation can help preterm infants develop. In some intensive care nurseries, preterm babies rock in suspended hammocks or are exposed to a tape recording of a heartbeat, soft

JOHN JAMES WOOD/GETTY IMAGES/PHOTOLIBRARY

This preterm infant is cared for in a Plexiglas-enclosed isolette. The fragile appearance and irritability of preterm newborns can lead parents—especially those who are poverty-stricken—to be less warm and sensitive in caregiving.

music, or the mother's voice. These experiences promote faster weight gain, more predictable sleep patterns, and greater alertness (Arnon et al., 2006; Marshall-Baker, Lickliter, & Cooper, 1998).

Touch is especially important. In baby animals, touching the skin releases certain brain chemicals that support physical growth—effects believed to occur in humans as well. When preterm infants were massaged several times each day in the hospital, they gained weight faster and, at the end of the first year, were advanced in mental and motor development over preterm babies not given this stimulation (Field, 2001; Field, Hernandez-Reif, & Freedman, 2004).

In developing countries where hospitalization is not always possible, skin-to-skin "kangaroo care" is the most readily available intervention for promoting the survival and recovery of

Top photo: A father in El Salvador uses skin-to-skin "kangaroo care" with his infant as part of a hospital program that teaches parents techniques for promoting survival and development in preterm and underweight babies. *Bottom photo:* Here, a U.S. mother uses kangaroo care with her fragile newborn.

preterm babies. It involves placing the infant in a vertical position between the mother's breasts or next to the father's chest (under the parent's clothing) so the parent's body functions as a human incubator. Kangaroo skin-to-skin contact fosters improved oxygenation of the baby's body, temperature regulation, sleep, breastfeeding, alertness, and infant survival (Conde-Agudelo, Belizan, & Diaz-Rossello, 2011; Lawn et al., 2010). Mothers and fathers practicing kangaroo care feel more confident about caring for their fragile babies and interact more sensitively and affectionately with them (Dodd, 2005; Feldman, 2007).

Together, these factors may explain why preterm babies given many hours of kangaroo care in their early weeks, compared to those given little or no such care, score higher on measures of mental and motor development during the first year (Charpak, Ruiz-Peláez, & Figueroa, 2005; Feldman, 2007). Because of its diverse benefits, more than 80 percent of U.S. hospitals now offer kangaroo care to preterm newborns (Field et al., 2006).

Training Parents in Infant Caregiving Skills.

Interventions that support parents of preterm infants generally teach them about the infant's characteristics and promote caregiving skills. For parents with adequate economic and personal resources to care for a preterm infant, just a few sessions of coaching in recognizing and responding to the baby's needs are linked to enhanced parent–infant interaction, reduced infant crying and improved sleep, more rapid language development in the second year, and steady gains in mental test scores that equal those of full-term children by middle childhood (Achenbach et al., 1990; Newnham, Milgrom, & Skouteris, 2009).

When preterm infants live in stressed, low-income households, long-term, intensive intervention is necessary. In the Infant Health and Development Program, preterm babies born into poverty received a comprehensive intervention that combined medical follow-up, weekly parent training sessions, and cognitively stimulating child care from 1 to 3 years of age. More than four times as many intervention children as controls (39 versus 9 percent) were within normal range at age 3 in intelligence, psychological adjustment, and physical growth (Bradley et al., 1994). In addition, mothers in the intervention group were more affectionate and more often encouraged play and cognitive mastery in their children—one reason their 3-year-olds may have been developing so favorably (McCarton, 1998). At ages 5 and 8, children who had attended the child-care program regularly—for more than 350 days over the three-year period—continued to show better intellectual functioning. In contrast, children who attended only sporadically gained little or even lost ground (Hill, Brooks-Gunn, & Waldfogel, 2003).

Nevertheless, even the best caregiving environments cannot "fix" the enormous biological risks associated with extremely low birth weight. A better course of action would be to prevent this serious threat to infant survival and development. The high rate of underweight babies in the United States—one of the worst in the industrialized world—could be greatly reduced by improving the health and social conditions described in the Social Issues: Health box on the following page.

Social Issues: Health

A Cross-National Perspective on Health Care and Other Policies for Parents and Newborn Babies

Infant mortality—the number of deaths in the first year of life per 1,000 live births—is an index used around the world to assess the overall health of a nation's children. Although the United States has the most up-to-date health-care technology in the world, it has made less progress in reducing infant deaths than many other countries. Over the past three decades, it has slipped in the international rankings, from seventh in the 1950s to twenty-eighth in 2012. At greatest risk are African-American and Native-American babies, who are nearly twice as likely as white infants to die in the first year of life (U.S. Census Bureau, 2013).

Neonatal mortality, the rate of death within the first month of life, accounts for 67 percent of the U.S. infant death rate. Two factors are largely responsible. The first is serious physical defects, most of which cannot be prevented. The percentage of babies born with physical defects is about the same in all ethnic and income groups. The second leading cause of neonatal mortality is low birth weight, which accounts for the increased risk of African-American and Native-American babies and is preventable (U.S. Census Bureau, 2013).

Widespread poverty and weak health-care programs for mothers and young children are largely responsible for these trends. Each country in Figure 3.5 that outranks the United States in infant survival provides all its citizens with government-sponsored health-care benefits. And each takes extra steps to make sure that pregnant mothers and babies have access to good nutrition, high-quality medical care, and social and economic supports that promote effective parenting.

For example, all Western European nations guarantee women a certain number of prenatal visits at very low or no cost. After a baby is born, a health professional routinely visits the home to provide counseling about infant care and to arrange continuing medical services. Paid, job-protected employment leave is another vital societal intervention for new parents. Canadian mothers are eligible for 15 weeks' maternity leave at 55 percent of prior earnings (up to a maximum of $485 per week), and Canadian mothers or fathers can take an additional 35 weeks of

parental leave at the same rate. Sweden has the most generous parental leave program in the world. Mothers can begin maternity leave 60 days prior to expected delivery, extending it to six weeks after birth; fathers are granted two weeks of birth leave. In addition, either parent can take full leave for 16 months at 80 percent of prior earnings, followed by an additional three months at a modest flat rate. Each parent is also entitled to another 18 months of unpaid leave (OECD, 2006; Waldfogel, 2001).

Yet in the United States, the federal government mandates *only 12 weeks of unpaid leave* for employees in businesses with at least 50 workers. Most women, however, work in smaller businesses, and many of those who work in large enough companies cannot afford to take unpaid leave (Hewlett, 2003). Similarly, though paternal leave predicts fathers' increased involvement in infant care at the end of the first year, many fathers take little or none at all (Nepomnyaschy & Waldfogel, 2007; OECD, 2006). In 2002, California became the first state to guarantee a mother or father paid leave—up to six weeks at half salary, regardless of the size of the company. Since then, Hawaii, New Jersey, New York, Rhode Island, and the territory of Puerto Rico have passed similar legislation.

Nevertheless, six weeks of childbirth leave (the norm in the United States) is not enough. When a family is stressed by a baby's arrival, leaves of six weeks or less are linked to increased maternal anxiety, depression, marital dissatisfaction, sense of role overload (conflict between work and family responsibilities), and negative interactions with the baby. A longer

leave (12 weeks or more) predicts favorable maternal mental health, supportive marital interaction, and sensitive caregiving (Feldman, Sussman, & Zigler, 2004; Hyde et al., 2001).

In countries with low infant mortality rates, expectant parents need not wonder how or where they will get health care and other resources to support their baby's development. The powerful impact of universal, high-quality health care, generous parental leave, and other social services on maternal and infant well-being provides strong justification for these policies.

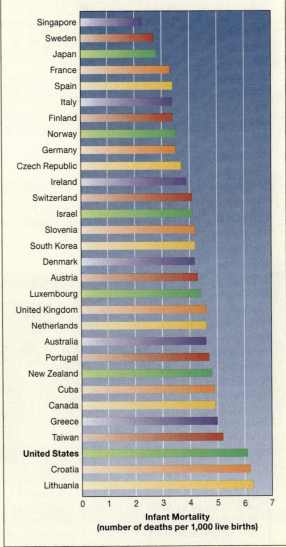

FIGURE 3.5 **Infant mortality in 30 nations.** Despite its advanced health-care technology, the United States ranks poorly. It is twenty-eighth in the world, with a death rate of 6.1 infants per 1,000 births. (Adapted from U.S. Census Bureau, 2012a.)

ASK YOURSELF

REVIEW Sensitive care can help preterm infants recover, but they are less likely than full-term newborns to receive such care. Explain why.

APPLY List factors discussed in this chapter that increase the chances that an infant will be born underweight. How many of these factors could be prevented by better health care for expectant mothers?

REFLECT Many people object to the use of extraordinary medical measures to save extremely low-birth-weight babies because of their high risk for serious developmental problems. Do you agree or disagree? Explain.

The Newborn Baby's Capacities

Newborn infants have a remarkable set of capacities that are crucial for survival and for evoking adult attention and care. In relating to the physical and social world, babies are active from the very start.

Reflexes

A **reflex** is an inborn, automatic response to a particular form of stimulation. Reflexes are the newborn baby's most obvious organized patterns of behavior. As Jay placed Joshua on a table in my classroom, we saw several. When Jay bumped the side of the table, Joshua reacted with the *Moro (or "embracing") reflex*, flinging his arms wide and bringing them back toward his body. As Yolanda stroked Joshua's cheek, he turned his head in her direction—a response called the *rooting reflex.*

Some reflexes have survival value. In our evolutionary past, when infants were carried about all day, the Moro reflex helped a baby who lost support to embrace and, along with the grasp reflex, regain its hold on the mother's body. The rooting reflex helps a breastfed baby find the mother's nipple. Babies display it only when hungry and touched by another person, not when they touch themselves (Rochat & Hespos, 1997). At birth, babies adjust their sucking pressure to how easily milk flows from the nipple (Craig & Lee, 1999). And if sucking were not automatic, our species would be unlikely to survive for a single generation!

A few reflexes form the basis for complex motor skills that will develop later. The stepping reflex looks like a primitive walking response. Unlike other reflexes, it appears in a wide range of situations—with the newborn's body in a sideways or upside-down position, with feet touching walls or ceilings, and even with legs dangling in the air (Adolph & Berger, 2006). When stepping is exercised regularly, babies are likely to walk several weeks earlier than if stepping is not practiced (Zelazo et al., 1993). However, there is no special need for infants to practice the stepping reflex because all normal babies walk in due time.

Reflexes help parents and infants establish gratifying interaction. A baby who searches for and successfully finds the nipple, sucks easily during feedings, and grasps when the hand is touched encourages parents to respond lovingly and feel

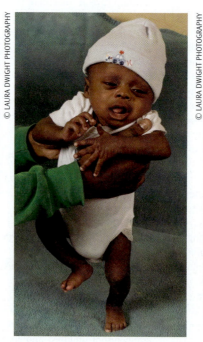

Left: In the Moro reflex, loss of support or a sudden loud sound causes the baby to extend the legs and throw the arms outward in an "embracing" motion. *Middle:* When held upright under the arms, newborns show a reflexive stepping response, which forms the basis for later walking. *Right:* The palmar grasp reflex is so strong during the first week after birth that many infants can use it to support their entire weight.

competent as caregivers. Caregivers can also make use of reflexes in comforting the baby. For example, on short trips with Joshua to the grocery store, Yolanda brought along a pacifier. If he became fussy, sucking helped quiet him until she could feed, change, or hold him.

Most newborn reflexes disappear during the first six months, due to a gradual increase in voluntary control over behavior as the cerebral cortex develops. Pediatricians test reflexes carefully because reflexes that are weak or absent, overly rigid or exaggerated, or evident beyond the point in development when they should normally disappear can signal brain damage (Schott & Rossor, 2003).

States

Throughout the day and night, newborn infants move in and out of five **states of arousal,** or degrees of sleep and wakefulness, described in Table 3.3 on page 84. Much to the relief of their fatigued parents, newborns spend the greatest amount of time asleep—about 16 to 18 hours a day. However, striking individual differences in daily rhythms exist that affect parents' attitudes toward and interactions with the baby. A few newborns sleep for long periods, increasing the energy their well-rested parents have for sensitive, responsive care. Other babies cry a great deal, and their parents must exert great effort to soothe them. If these parents do not succeed, they may feel less competent and less positive toward their infant. Babies who spend more time alert probably receive more social stimulation and opportunities to explore and, therefore, may have a slight advantage in mental development (Sadah et al., 2007; Smart & Hiscock, 2007).

As with adults, sleep enhances babies' learning and memory. In one study, eye-blink responses and brain-wave recordings revealed that sleeping newborns readily learned that a tone would be followed by a puff of air to the eye (Fifer et al., 2010). Because young infants spend so much time sleeping, the capacity to learn about external stimuli during sleep may be essential for adaptation to their surroundings.

Of the states listed in Table 3.3, the two extremes—sleep and crying—have been of greatest interest to researchers. Each tells us something about normal and abnormal early development.

Sleep. Observing Joshua as he slept, Yolanda and Jay wondered why his eyelids and body twitched and his rate of breathing varied. Sleep is made up of at least two states. During irregular, or **rapid-eye-movement (REM), sleep,** brain-wave activity is remarkably similar to that of the waking state. The eyes dart beneath the lids; heart rate, blood pressure, and breathing are uneven; and slight body movements occur. In contrast, during regular, or **non-rapid-eye-movement (NREM), sleep,** the body is almost motionless, and heart rate, breathing, and brain-wave activity are slow and even.

Like children and adults, newborns alternate between REM and NREM sleep, but they spend far more time in the REM state than they ever will again. REM sleep accounts for 50 percent of a newborn baby's sleep time. By 3 to 5 years, it has declined to an adultlike level of 20 percent (Louis et al., 1997). The stimulation of REM sleep is vital for growth of the central nervous system. Young infants seem to have a special need for this stimulation because they spend little time in an alert state, when they can get input from the environment. The percentage of REM sleep is especially great in the fetus and in preterm babies, who are even less able than full-term newborns to take advantage of external stimulation (de Weerd & van den Bossche, 2003; Peirano, Algarin, & Uauy, 2003).

Because newborns' normal sleep behavior is organized and patterned, observations of sleep states can help identify central nervous system abnormalities. In infants who are brain-damaged or who have experienced birth trauma, disturbed REM–NREM sleep cycles are often present. Babies with poor sleep organization are likely to be behaviorally disorganized and, therefore, to have difficulty learning and evoking caregiver

TABLE 3.3 **Infant States of Arousal**

STATE	DESCRIPTION	DAILY DURATION IN NEWBORN
Regular, or NREM, sleep	The infant is at full rest and shows little or no body activity. The eyelids are closed, no eye movements occur, the face is relaxed, and breathing is slow and regular.	8–9 hours
Irregular, or REM, sleep	Gentle limb movements, occasional stirring, and facial grimacing occur. Although the eyelids are closed, occasional rapid eye movements can be seen beneath them. Breathing is irregular.	8–9 hours
Drowsiness	The infant is either falling asleep or waking up. Body is less active than in irregular sleep but more active than in regular sleep. The eyes open and close; when open, they have a glazed look. Breathing is even but somewhat faster than in regular sleep.	Varies
Quiet alertness	The infant's body is relatively inactive, with eyes open and attentive. Breathing is even.	2–3 hours
Waking activity and crying	The infant shows frequent bursts of uncoordinated body activity. Breathing is very irregular. Face may be relaxed or tense and wrinkled. Crying may occur.	1–4 hours

Source: Wolff, 1966.

Biology and Environment

The Mysterious Tragedy of Sudden Infant Death Syndrome

Millie awoke with a start one morning and looked at the clock. It was 7:30, and Sasha had missed both her night waking and her early morning feeding. Wondering if she was all right, Millie and her husband Stuart tiptoed into the room. Sasha lay still, curled up under her blanket. She had died silently during her sleep.

Sasha was a victim of **sudden infant death syndrome (SIDS)**, the unexpected death, usually during the night, of an infant under 1 year of age that remains unexplained after thorough investigation. In industrialized nations, SIDS is the leading cause of infant mortality between 1 and 12 months, accounting for about 20 percent of these deaths in the United States (Mathews & MacDorman, 2008).

SIDS victims usually show physical problems from the beginning. Early medical records of SIDS babies reveal higher rates of prematurity and low birth weight, poor Apgar scores, and limp muscle tone. Abnormal heart rate and respiration and disturbances in sleep–wake activity and in REM–NREM cycles while asleep are also involved (Cornwell & Feigenbaum, 2006; Kato et al., 2003). At the time of death, many SIDS babies have a mild respiratory infection (Blood-Siegfried, 2009). This seems to increase the chances of respiratory failure in an already vulnerable baby.

Mounting evidence suggests that impaired brain functioning is a major contributor to SIDS. Between 2 and 4 months, when SIDS is most likely to occur, reflexes decline and are replaced by voluntary, learned responses. Neurological weaknesses may prevent SIDS babies from acquiring behaviors that replace defensive reflexes (Lipsitt, 2003). As a result, when breathing difficulties occur during sleep, infants do not wake up, shift their position, or cry out for help. Instead, they simply give in to oxygen deprivation and death. In support of this interpretation, autopsies reveal that the brains of SIDS babies contain unusually low levels of serotonin (a brain chemical that assists with arousal when survival is threatened) as well as other abnormalities in centers that control breathing and arousal (Duncan et al., 2010).

Several environmental factors are linked to SIDS. Maternal cigarette smoking, both during and after pregnancy, as well as smoking by other caregivers, doubles risk of the disorder. Babies exposed to cigarette smoke arouse less easily from sleep and have more respiratory infections (Richardson, Walker, & Horne, 2009; Shah, Sullivan, & Carter, 2006). Prenatal abuse of drugs that depress central nervous system functioning (alcohol, opiates, and barbiturates) increases the risk of SIDS as much as fifteenfold (Hunt & Hauck, 2006; Kinney, 2009).

SIDS babies are also more likely to sleep on their stomachs than on their backs and often are wrapped very warmly in clothing and blankets. Infants who sleep on their stomachs less often wake when their breathing is disturbed (Richardson, Walker, & Horne, 2008). In other cases, healthy babies sleeping face down on soft bedding may die from continually breathing their own exhaled breath.

Quitting smoking and drug taking, changing an infant's sleeping position, and removing a few bedclothes can reduce the incidence of SIDS. Public education cam-

Public education campaigns encouraging parents to put their infants down on their backs to sleep have helped reduce the incidence of SIDS by more than half in many Western nations.

paigns that encourage parents to put their infants down on their backs have cut the incidence of SIDS in half in many Western nations (Moon, Horne, & Hauck, 2007). Another protective measure is pacifier use: Sleeping babies who suck arouse more easily in response to breathing and heart-rate irregularities (Li et al., 2006).

When SIDS does occur, surviving family members require a great deal of help to overcome a sudden and unexpected death. As Millie commented six months after Sasha's death, "It's the worst crisis we've ever been through. What's helped us most are the comforting words of others who've experienced the same tragedy."

interactions that enhance their development. In the preschool years, they show delayed motor, cognitive, and language development (Feldman, 2006; Holditch-Davis, Belyea, & Edwards, 2005). And the brain-functioning problems that underlie newborn sleep irregularities may culminate in sudden infant death syndrome, a major cause of infant mortality (see the Biology and Environment box above).

Crying. Crying is the first way that babies communicate, letting parents know they need food, comfort, or stimulation. The baby's cry is a complex stimulus that varies in intensity, from a whimper to a message of all-out distress (Gustafson, Wood, & Green, 2000; Wood, 2009). Most of the time, the strength of the cry, combined with the experiences leading up to it, helps guide parents toward its cause.

Young infants usually cry because of physical needs, most commonly hunger, but babies may also cry in response to temperature change when undressed, a sudden noise, or a painful stimulus. Newborns (as well as older babies) often cry at the sound of another crying baby (Dondi, Simion, & Caltran, 1999; Geangu et al., 2010). Some researchers believe that this response reflects an inborn capacity to react to the suffering of others. Furthermore, crying typically increases during the early weeks, peaks at about 6 weeks, and then declines (Barr, 2001). Because this trend appears in many cultures with vastly different infant care practices, researchers believe that normal readjustments of the central nervous system underlie it.

Soothing Crying Infants. Although parents do not always interpret their baby's cry correctly, their accuracy improves with experience. At the same time, they vary widely in responsiveness. Parents who are high in empathy (ability to take the perspective of others in distress) and who hold "child-centered" attitudes toward infant care (for example, believe that babies cannot be spoiled by being picked up) are more likely to respond quickly and sensitively to a crying baby (Leerkes, 2010; Zeifman, 2003).

LOOK AND LISTEN

In a public setting, watch several parents soothe their crying babies. What techniques did the parents use, and how successful were they? ●

Fortunately, there are many ways to soothe a crying baby when feeding and diaper changing do not work. The technique that Western parents usually try first, lifting the baby to the shoulder and rocking or walking, is highly effective. Another common soothing method is swaddling—wrapping the baby snugly in a blanket. The Quechua, who live in the cold, high-altitude desert regions of Peru, dress young babies in layers of

Like the Quechua of Peru, the Mongol people of Central Asia heavily swaddle their babies, a practice that reduces crying and promotes sleep while also protecting infants from the region's harsh winters.

clothing and blankets that cover the head and body, a practice that reduces crying and promotes sleep (Tronick, Thomas, & Daltabuit, 1994). It also allows the baby to conserve energy for early growth in the harsh Peruvian highlands.

In many tribal and village societies and non-Western developed nations (such as Japan), babies are in physical contact with their caregivers almost continuously. Infants in these cultures show shorter bouts of crying than their American counterparts (Barr, 2001). When Western parents choose to practice "proximal care" by holding their babies extensively, amount of crying in the early months is reduced by about one-third (St James-Roberts et al., 2006).

Abnormal Crying. Like reflexes and sleep patterns, the infant's cry offers a clue to central nervous system distress. The cries of brain-damaged babies and those who have experienced prenatal and birth complications are often shrill, piercing, and shorter in duration than those of healthy infants (Boukydis & Lester, 1998; Green, Irwin, & Gustafson, 2000). Even newborns with a fairly common problem—*colic,* or persistent crying—tend to have high-pitched, harsh-sounding cries (Zeskind & Barr, 1997). Although the cause of colic is unknown, certain newborns, who react especially strongly to unpleasant stimuli, are susceptible. Colic generally subsides between 3 and 6 months (Barr et al., 2005; St James-Roberts et al., 2003).

Most parents try to respond to a crying baby with extra care and attention, but sometimes the cry is so unpleasant and persistent that parents become frustrated, resentful, and angry. Preterm and ill babies are more likely to be abused by highly stressed parents, who sometimes mention a high-pitched, grating cry as one factor that caused them to lose control (St James-Roberts, 2007). We will discuss a host of additional influences on child abuse in Chapter 8.

This father soothes his crying baby by lifting the baby to his shoulder and moving gently—a highly effective technique.

Sensory Capacities

On his visit to my class, Joshua looked wide-eyed at my bright pink blouse and turned to the sound of his mother's voice. During feedings, he lets Yolanda know through his sucking rhythm that he prefers the taste of breast milk to plain water. Clearly, Joshua has some well-developed sensory capacities. In the following sections, we explore the newborn's responsiveness to touch, taste, smell, sound, and visual stimulation.

Touch. In our discussion of preterm infants, we saw that touch helps stimulate early physical growth. As we will see in Chapter 6, it is vital for emotional development as well. Therefore, it is not surprising that sensitivity to touch is well-developed at birth. The newborn baby responds to touch, especially around the mouth, on the palms, and on the soles of the feet (Humphrey, 1978). Newborns even use touch to investigate their world. When small objects are placed in their palms, they can distinguish shape (prism versus cylinder) and texture (smooth versus rough), as indicated by their tendency to hold on longer to objects with an unfamiliar shape or texture (Sann & Streri, 2007, 2008).

At birth, infants are highly sensitive to pain. If male newborns are circumcised without anesthetic, they often respond with a high-pitched, stressful cry and a dramatic rise in heart rate, blood pressure, palm sweating, pupil dilation, and muscle tension (Lehr et al., 2007; Warnock & Sandrin, 2004). Brain-imaging research suggests that because of central nervous system immaturity, preterm babies, particularly males, feel the pain of a medical injection especially intensely (Bartocci et al., 2006).

Recent research establishing the safety of certain local anesthetics for newborns promises to ease the pain of these procedures. Offering a nipple that delivers a sweet liquid is also helpful in reducing crying and discomfort, with breast milk appearing to be especially effective (Nishitani et al., 2009). And combining sweet liquid with gentle holding by the parent lessens pain even more. Research on infant mammals indicates that physical touch releases *endorphins*—painkilling chemicals in the brain (Axelin, Salanterä, & Lehtonen, 2006; Gormally et al., 2001).

Allowing a baby to endure severe pain overwhelms the nervous system with stress hormones, which can disrupt the child's developing capacity to handle common, everyday stressors. The result is heightened pain sensitivity, sleep disturbances, feeding problems, and difficulty calming down when upset (Mitchell & Boss, 2002).

Taste and Smell. Newborns can distinguish several basic tastes. Like adults, they relax their facial muscles in response to sweetness, purse their lips when the taste is sour, and show a distinct archlike mouth opening when it is bitter (Steiner, 1979; Steiner et al., 2001). These reactions are important for survival: The food that best supports the infant's early growth is the

sweet-tasting milk of the mother's breast. Not until 4 months do babies prefer a salty taste to plain water, a change that may prepare them to accept solid foods (Mennella & Beauchamp, 1998).

As with taste, certain odor preferences are present at birth. The smell of bananas or chocolate causes a relaxed, pleasant facial expression, whereas the odor of rotten eggs makes the infant frown (Steiner, 1979). During pregnancy, the amniotic fluid is rich in tastes and smells that vary with the mother's diet—early experiences that influence newborns' preferences. In a study carried out in the Alsatian region of France, where anise is frequently used to flavor foods, researchers tested newborns for their reaction to the anise odor (Schaal, Marlier, & Soussignan, 2000). The mothers of some babies had regularly consumed anise during the last two weeks of pregnancy; the other mothers had never consumed it. When presented with the anise odor on the day of birth, the babies of non-anise-consuming mothers were far more likely to turn away with a negative facial expression (see Figure 3.6). These different reactions were still apparent four days later, even though all mothers had refrained from consuming anise during this time.

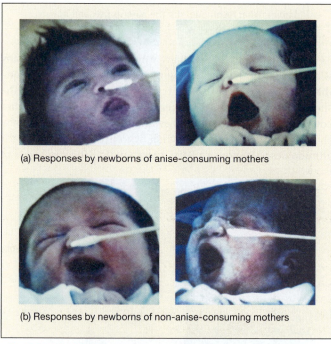

(a) Responses by newborns of anise-consuming mothers

(b) Responses by newborns of non-anise-consuming mothers

FIGURE 3.6 Examples of facial expressions of newborns exposed to the odor of anise whose mothers' diets differed in anise-flavored foods during late pregnancy. (a) Babies of anise-consuming mothers spent more time turning toward the odor and sucking, licking, and chewing. (b) Babies of non-anise-consuming mothers more often turned away with a negative facial expression. (From B. Schaal, L. Marlier, & R. Soussignan, 2000, "Human Foetuses Learn Odours from Their Pregnant Mother's Diet," *Chemical Senses,* 25, p. 731. © 2000 Oxford University Press. Reprinted by permission of Oxford University Press and Dr. Benoist Schaal.)

In many mammals, the sense of smell plays an important role in feeding and in protecting the young from predators by helping mothers and babies identify each other. Although smell is less well-developed in humans, traces of its survival value remain. If one breast is washed to remove its natural scent, most newborns grasp the unwashed breast, indicating that they are guided by smell (Varendi & Porter, 2001). At 4 days of age, breastfed babies prefer the smell of their own mother's breast to that of an unfamiliar lactating mother (Cernoch & Porter, 1985). And both breast- and bottle-fed 3- to 4-day-olds orient more to the smell of unfamiliar human milk than to formula milk, indicating that (even without prior exposure) the odor of human milk is more attractive to newborns (Marlier & Schaal, 2005). Newborns' dual attraction to the odor of their mother and to that of breast milk helps them locate an appropriate food source and, in the process, begin to distinguish their caregiver from other people.

Hearing. Newborn infants can hear a wide variety of sounds, and their sensitivity improves greatly over the first few months (Saffran, Werker, & Werner, 2006). At birth, infants prefer complex sounds, such as noises and voices, to pure tones. And babies only a few days old can tell the difference between diverse sound patterns: a series of tones arranged in ascending versus descending order; utterances with two versus three syllables; the stress patterns of words ("*ma-ma*" versus "*ma-ma*"); happy-sounding speech as opposed to speech with negative or neutral emotional qualities; and even two languages spoken by the same bilingual speaker, as long as those languages differ in their rhythmic features—for example, French versus Russian (Mastropieri & Turkewitz, 1999; Ramus, 2002; Sansavini, Bertoncini, & Giovanelli, 1997; Trehub, 2001; Winkler et al., 2009).

Young infants listen longer to human speech than structurally similar nonspeech sounds (Vouloumanos & Werker, 2004). And they make fine-grained distinctions among many speech sounds. Indeed, researchers have found only a few speech sounds that newborns cannot discriminate. These capacities reveal that the baby is marvelously prepared for the awesome task of acquiring language.

Immediately after birth, infants will suck more on a nipple to hear a recording of their mother's voice than that of an unfamiliar woman and to hear their native language as opposed to a foreign language—preferences may have developed from hearing the muffled sounds of the mother's voice before birth (Moon, Cooper, & Fifer, 1993; Spence & DeCasper, 1987).

Vision. Vision is the least-developed of the newborn baby's senses. Visual structures in both the eye and the brain are not yet fully formed. For example, cells in the *retina,* the membrane lining the inside of the eye that captures light and transforms it into messages that are sent to the brain, are not as mature or densely packed as they will be in several months. The optic nerve that relays these messages, and the visual centers in the brain that receive them, will not be adultlike for several years.

And the muscles of the *lens,* which permit us to adjust our visual focus to varying distances, are weak (Kellman & Arterberry, 2006).

As a result, newborns cannot focus their eyes well, and **visual acuity,** or fineness of discrimination, is limited. At birth, infants perceive objects at a distance of 20 feet about as clearly as adults do at 600 feet (Slater et al., 2010). In addition, unlike adults (who see nearby objects most clearly), newborn babies see unclearly across a wide range of distances (Banks, 1980; Hainline, 1998). Images such as the parent's face, even from close up, look quite blurred. Although newborns prefer to look at brightly colored rather than gray stimuli, they are not yet good at discriminating colors. It will take about four months for color vision to become adultlike (Kellman & Arterberry, 2006). Despite limited vision and slow, imprecise eye movements, newborns actively explore their visual world by scanning it for interesting sights and tracking moving objects.

Adjusting to the New Family Unit

Nature helps prepare expectant mothers and fathers for their new role. Toward the end of pregnancy, mothers begin producing the hormone oxytocin, which stimulates uterine contractions; causes the breasts to "let down" milk; induces a calm, relaxed mood; and promotes responsiveness to the baby (Russell, Douglas, & Ingram, 2001). And fathers show hormonal changes around the time of birth that are compatible with those of mothers—specifically, slight increases in *prolactin* (a hormone that stimulates milk production in females) and *estrogens* (sex hormones produced in larger quantities in females) and a drop in *androgens* (sex hormones produced in larger quantities in males) (Numan & Insel, 2003; Wynne-Edwards, 2001). These changes, which are induced by fathers' contact with the mother and baby, predict positive emotional reactions to infants and paternal caregiving (Feldman et al., 2010; Leuner, Glasper, & Gould, 2010).

Although birth-related hormones can facilitate caregiving, their release and effects may depend on experiences, such as a positive couple relationship. Furthermore, humans can parent effectively without experiencing birth-related hormonal changes, as successful adoption reveals. And as we have seen, a great many factors—from family functioning to social policies—are involved in good infant care.

Indeed, the early weeks after the baby's arrival are full of profound challenges. The mother needs to recuperate from childbirth. If she is breastfeeding, energies must be devoted to working out this intimate relationship. The father must become a part of this new threesome while supporting the mother in her recovery. At times, he may feel ambivalent about the baby, who constantly demands and gets the mother's attention. And as we will see in Chapter 6, siblings—especially those who are young and firstborn—understandably feel displaced. They sometimes react with jealousy and anger.

While all this is going on, the tiny infant demands to be fed, changed, and comforted at odd times of the day and night. The family schedule becomes irregular and uncertain. Yolanda spoke candidly about the changes she and Jay experienced:

> When we brought Joshua home, he seemed so small and helpless, and we worried about whether we would be able to take proper care of him. It took us 20 minutes to change the first diaper! I rarely feel rested because I'm up two to four times every night, and I spend a good part of my waking hours trying to anticipate Joshua's rhythms and needs. If Jay weren't so willing to help by holding and walking Joshua, I think I'd find it much harder.

How long does this time of adjustment to parenthood last? In Chapter 14, we will see that when marital relationships are positive, social support is available, and families have sufficient income, the stress caused by the birth of a baby remains man-

ageable. Nevertheless, new parenthood—with its ever-present demands, responsibilities, and concerns about the child's well-being—initiates a permanent change in parents' lives.

ASK YOURSELF

REVIEW What functions does REM sleep serve in young infants? Can sleep tell us anything about the health of the newborn's central nervous system? Explain.

APPLY How do the diverse capacities of newborn babies contribute to their first social relationships? Provide as many examples as you can.

REFLECT Are newborns more competent than you thought they were before you read this chapter? Which of their capacities most surprised you?

SUMMARY

Prenatal Development
(p. 61)

List the three periods of prenatal development, and describe the major milestones of each.

- The period of the zygote lasts about two weeks, from fertilization until **implantation** of the blastocyst in the uterine lining. During this time, structures that will support prenatal growth begin to form, including the **placenta** and the **umbilical cord.**

- During the period of the **embryo,** weeks 2 through 8, the groundwork is laid for all body structures. The **neural tube** forms and the nervous system starts to develop. Other organs follow rapidly. By the end of this period, the embryo responds to touch and can move.

- The period of the **fetus,** lasting until the end of pregnancy, involves dramatic increase in body size and completion of physical structures. At the end of the second **trimester,** most of the brain's neurons are in place.

- The fetus reaches the **age of viability** at the beginning of the third trimester, between 22 and 26 weeks. The brain continues to develop rapidly, and new sensory and behavioral capacities emerge. Gradually the lungs mature, the fetus fills the uterus, and birth is near.

Prenatal Environmental Influences (p. 66)

Cite factors that influence the impact of teratogens, noting agents that are known teratogens.

- The impact of **teratogens** varies with the amount and length of exposure, genetic makeup of mother and fetus, presence or absence of other harmful agents, and age of the organism at time of exposure. The developing organism is especially vulnerable during the embryonic period.

- The most widely used potent teratogen is Accutane, a drug used to treat severe acne. The prenatal impact of other commonly used medications, such as aspirin and caffeine, is hard to separate from other factors correlated with drug taking.

- Babies born to users of cocaine, heroin, or methadone are at risk for a wide variety of problems, including prematurity, low birth weight, physical defects, breathing difficulties, and death around the time of birth.

- Infants whose parents use tobacco are often born underweight, may have physical defects, and are at risk for long-term attention, learning, and behavior problems. Maternal alcohol consumption can lead to **fetal alcohol spectrum disorder (FASD). Fetal alcohol syndrome (FAS)** involves slow physical growth, facial abnormalities, and mental impairments. Milder forms—**partial fetal alcohol syndrome (p-FAS)** and **alcohol-related neurodevelopmental disorder (ARND)**—affect children whose mothers consumed smaller quantities of alcohol.

- Prenatal exposure to high levels of ionizing radiation, mercury, PCBs, lead, and dioxins leads to physical malformations and severe brain damage. Low-level exposure has been linked to cognitive deficits and emotional and behavioral disorders.

- Among infectious diseases, rubella causes a wide range of abnormalities. Babies with prenatally transmitted HIV rapidly develop AIDS, leading to brain damage and early death. Cytomegalovirus, herpes simplex 2, and toxoplasmosis can also be devastating to the embryo and fetus.

Describe the impact of additional maternal factors on prenatal development.

● Prenatal malnutrition can lead to low birth weight and organ damage. Vitamin–mineral enrichment, including folic acid, can prevent prenatal and birth complications.

● Severe emotional stress is linked to many pregnancy complications and may permanently alter fetal neurological functioning, thereby magnifying future stress reactivity. Its negative impact can be reduced by providing the mother with social support. **Rh factor incompatibility**—an Rh-negative mother carrying an Rh-positive fetus—can lead to oxygen deprivation, brain and heart damage, and infant death.

● Other than the risk of chromosomal abnormalities in older women, maternal age through the thirties is not a major cause of prenatal problems. Poor health and environmental risks associated with poverty are the strongest predictors of pregnancy complications.

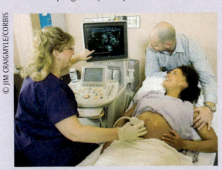

Why is early and regular health care vital during the prenatal period?

● Unexpected difficulties, such as preeclampsia, can arise, especially in mothers with preexisting health problems. Prenatal health care is especially critical for poverty-stricken women, who are at high risk for pregnancy complications.

Childbirth (p. 74)

Describe the three stages of childbirth and the baby's adaptation to labor and delivery.

● In the first stage of childbirth, contractions widen and thin the cervix. In the second stage, the mother feels an urge to push the baby through the birth canal. In the final stage, the placenta is delivered. During labor, infants produce high levels of stress hormones, which help them withstand oxygen deprivation, clear the lungs for breathing, and arouse them into alertness at birth.

● The **Apgar Scale** assesses the baby's physical condition at birth.

Approaches to Childbirth (p. 76)

Describe natural childbirth and home delivery, noting benefits and concerns associated with each.

● In **natural,** or **prepared, childbirth,** the expectant mother and a companion attend classes about labor and delivery, master relaxation and breathing techniques to counteract pain, and prepare for coaching during childbirth. Social support from a partner, relative, or doula reduces the length of labor and the incidence of birth complications.

● Home birth is safe for healthy mothers who are assisted by a well-trained doctor or midwife, but mothers at risk for complications are safer giving birth in a hospital.

Medical Interventions (p. 77)

List common medical interventions during childbirth, circumstances that justify their use, and any dangers associated with each.

● **Fetal monitors** help save the lives of many babies at risk for **anoxia** because of pregnancy and birth complications. When used routinely, however, they may identify infants as in danger who, in fact, are not.

● Use of analgesics and anesthetics to control pain, though necessary in complicated deliveries, can prolong labor and may have negative affects on the newborn's adjustment.

● **Cesarean deliveries** are warranted by medical emergency or serious maternal illness and for many babies who are in **breech position.** However, many unnecessary cesareans are performed.

Preterm and Low-Birth-Weight Infants (p. 78)

Describe risks associated with preterm birth and low birth weight, along with effective interventions.

● Low birth weight, most common in infants born to poverty-stricken women, is a major cause of neonatal and **infant mortality** and many developmental problems. Compared with **preterm infants,** whose weight is appropriate for time spent in the uterus, **small-for-date infants** usually have longer-lasting difficulties.

● Some interventions provide special stimulation in the intensive care nursery. Others teach parents how to care for and interact with their babies. Preterm infants in stressed, low-income households need long-term, intensive intervention.

The Newborn Baby's Capacities (p. 82)

Describe the newborn baby's reflexes and states of arousal, including sleep characteristics and ways to soothe a crying baby.

● **Reflexes** are the newborn baby's most obvious organized patterns of behavior. Some have survival value, others provide the foundation for voluntary motor skills, and still others help parents and infants establish gratifying interaction.

● Newborns move in and out of five **states of arousal** but spend most of their time asleep. Sleep includes at least two states, **rapid-eye-movement (REM) sleep** and **non-rapid-eye-movement (NREM) sleep.** Newborns spend about 50 percent of sleep time in REM sleep, which provides them with stimulation essential for central nervous system development.

- The intensity of the baby's cry and the experiences that led up to it help parents identify what is wrong. Once feeding and diaper changing have been tried, a highly effective soothing technique is lifting the baby to the shoulder and rocking and walking.

© KEVIN DODGE/CORBIS

Describe the newborn baby's sensory capacities.

- The senses of touch, taste, smell, and sound are well-developed at birth. Newborns use touch to investigate their world, are sensitive to pain, prefer sweet tastes and smells, and orient toward the odor of their own mother's lactating breast.

- Newborns can distinguish a variety of sound patterns and prefer complex sounds. They are especially responsive to human speech, can detect the sounds of any human language, and prefer their mother's voice.

- Vision is the least developed of the newborn's senses. At birth, focusing ability and **visual acuity** are limited. In exploring the visual field, newborn babies are attracted to bright objects but have difficulty discriminating colors.

Adjusting to the New Family Unit (p. 87)

Describe typical changes in the family after the birth of a new baby.

- The new baby's arrival is exciting but stressful, as the mother recuperates from childbirth and the family schedule becomes irregular and uncertain. When parents have a positive relationship as well as social support and adequate income, adjustment problems are usually temporary.

Important Terms and Concepts

age of viability (p. 65)
alcohol-related neurodevelopmental disorder (ARND) (p. 69)
amnion (p. 63)
anoxia (p. 77)
Apgar Scale (p. 76)
breech position (p. 77)
cesarean delivery (p. 78)
chorion (p. 63)
embryo (p. 63)
fetal alcohol spectrum disorder (FASD) (p. 68)
fetal alcohol syndrome (FAS) (p. 69)

fetal monitors (p. 78)
fetus (p. 64)
implantation (p. 63)
infant mortality (p. 81)
lanugo (p. 64)
natural, or prepared, childbirth (p. 77)
neural tube (p. 63)
non-rapid-eye-movement (NREM) sleep (p. 83)
partial fetal alcohol syndrome (p-FAS) (p. 69)
placenta (p. 63)
preterm infants (p. 79)
rapid-eye-movement (REM) sleep (p. 83)

reflex (p. 82)
Rh factor incompatibility (p. 72)
small-for-date infants (p. 79)
states of arousal (p. 83)
sudden infant death syndrome (SIDS) (p. 84)
teratogen (p. 66)
trimesters (p. 64)
umbilical cord (p. 63)
vernix (p. 64)
visual acuity (p. 87)

chapter

4

Physical Development in Infancy and Toddlerhood

© ELLEN B. SENISI PHOTOGRAPHY

Infants acquire new motor skills by building on previously acquired capacities. Eager to explore her world, this baby practices the art of crawling. Once she can fully move on her own, she will make dramatic strides in understanding her surroundings.

chapter outline

Body Growth
Changes in Body Size and Muscle–Fat Makeup • Individual and Group Differences • Changes in Body Proportions

Brain Development
Development of Neurons • Neurobiological Methods • Development of the Cerebral Cortex • Sensitive Periods in Brain Development • Changing States of Arousal

■ **CULTURAL INFLUENCES** Cultural Variation in Infant Sleeping Arrangements

Influences on Early Physical Growth
Heredity • Nutrition • Malnutrition

Learning Capacities
Classical Conditioning • Operant Conditioning • Habituation • Imitation

Motor Development
The Sequence of Motor Development • Motor Skills as Dynamic Systems • Fine-Motor Development: Reaching and Grasping

Perceptual Development
Hearing • Vision • Intermodal Perception • Understanding Perceptual Development

■ **BIOLOGY AND ENVIRONMENT** "Tuning In" to Familiar Speech, Faces, and Music: A Sensitive Period for Culture-Specific Learning

On a brilliant June morning, 16-month-old Caitlin emerged from her front door, ready for the short drive to the child-care home where she spent her weekdays while her mother, Carolyn, and her father, David, worked. Clutching a teddy bear in one hand and her mother's arm with the other, Caitlin descended the steps. "One! Two! Threeee!" Carolyn counted as she helped Caitlin down. "How much she's changed," Carolyn thought to herself, looking at the child who, not long ago, had been a newborn. With her first steps, Caitlin had passed from *infancy* to *toddlerhood*—a period spanning the second year of life. At first, Caitlin did, indeed, "toddle" with an awkward gait, tipping over frequently. But her face reflected the thrill of conquering a new skill.

As they walked toward the car, Carolyn and Caitlin spotted 3-year-old Eli and his father, Kevin, in the neighboring yard. Eli dashed toward them, waving a card. It read, "Announcing the arrival of Grace Ann. Born: Cambodia. Age: 16 months." Carolyn turned to Kevin and Eli. "That's wonderful news! When can we see her?"

"Let's wait a few days," Kevin suggested. "Monica's taken Grace to the doctor this morning. She's underweight and malnourished." Kevin described Monica's first night with Grace in a hotel room in Phnom Penh. Grace lay on the bed, withdrawn and fearful. Eventually she fell asleep, gripping crackers in both hands.

Carolyn felt Caitlin's impatient tug at her sleeve. Off they drove to child care, where Vanessa had just dropped off her 18-month-old son, Timmy. Within moments, Caitlin and Timmy were in the sandbox, shoveling sand into plastic cups with the help of their caregiver, Ginette.

A few weeks later, Grace joined Caitlin and Timmy at Ginette's child-care home. Although still tiny and unable to crawl or walk, she had grown taller and heavier, and her sad, vacant gaze had given way to an alert expression, a ready smile, and an enthusiastic desire to imitate and explore. When Caitlin headed for the sandbox, Grace stretched out her arms, asking Ginette to carry her there, too. Soon Grace was pulling herself up at every opportunity. Finally, at age 18 months, she walked!

This chapter traces physical growth during the first two years—one of the most remarkable and busiest times of development. We will see how rapid changes in the infant's body and brain support learning, motor skills, and perceptual capacities. Caitlin, Grace, and Timmy will join us along the way to illustrate individual differences and environmental influences on physical development. ●

HOANG DINH NAM/AFP/GETTY IMAGES

Body Growth

TAKE A MOMENT... The next time you're walking in your neighborhood park or at the mall, note the contrast between infants' and toddlers' physical capabilities. One reason for the vast changes in what children can do over the first two years is that their bodies change enormously—faster than at any other time after birth.

Changes in Body Size and Muscle–Fat Makeup

By the end of the first year, a typical infant's height is about 32 inches—more than 50 percent greater than at birth. By 2 years, it is 75 percent greater (36 inches). Similarly, by 5 months of age, birth weight has doubled, to about 15 pounds. At 1 year it has tripled, to 22 pounds, and at 2 years it has quadrupled, to about 30 pounds. Figure 4.1 illustrates this dramatic increase in body size.

One of the most obvious changes in infants' appearance is their transformation into round, plump babies by the middle of the first year. This early rise in "baby fat," which peaks at about 9 months, helps the small infant maintain a constant body temperature. In the second year, most toddlers slim down, a trend that continues into middle childhood (Fomon & Nelson, 2002). In contrast, muscle tissue increases very slowly during infancy and will not reach a peak until adolescence.

Individual and Group Differences

In infancy, girls are slightly shorter and lighter than boys, with a higher ratio of fat to muscle. These small sex differences persist throughout early and middle childhood and are greatly magnified at adolescence. Ethnic differences in body size are apparent as well. Grace was below the *growth norms* (height and weight averages for children her age). Early malnutrition contributed, but even after substantial catch-up, Grace—as is typical for Asian children—remained below North American norms. In contrast, Timmy is slightly above average, as African-American children tend to be (Bogin, 2001).

Children of the same age also differ in *rate* of physical growth; some make faster progress toward a mature body size than others. The best estimate of a child's physical maturity is *skeletal age*, a measure of bone development. It is determined by X-raying the long bones of the body to see the extent to which soft, pliable cartilage has hardened into bone, a gradual process that is completed in adolescence. When skeletal ages are examined, African-American children tend to be slightly ahead of Caucasian children at all ages, and girls are considerably ahead of boys (Tanner, Healy, & Cameron, 2001). Girls' greater physical maturity may contribute to their greater resistance to harmful environmental influences. As noted in Chapter 2, girls experience fewer developmental problems and have lower infant and childhood mortality rates.

FIGURE 4.1 Body growth during the first two years. These photos depict the dramatic changes in body size and proportions during infancy and toddlerhood in two individuals—a boy, Chris, and a girl, Mai. In the first year, the head is quite large in proportion to the rest of the body, and height and weight gain are especially rapid. During the second year, the lower portion of the body catches up. Notice, also, how both children added "baby fat" in the early months of life and then slimmed down, a trend that continues into middle childhood.

Changes in Body Proportions

As the child's overall size increases, different parts of the body grow at different rates. Two growth patterns describe these changes. The first is the **cephalocaudal trend**—from the Latin for "head to tail." During the prenatal period, the head develops more rapidly than the lower part of the body. At birth, the head takes up one-fourth of total body length, the legs only one-third. Notice how, in Figure 4.1, the lower portion of the body catches up. By age 2, the head accounts for only one-fifth and the legs for nearly one-half of total body length.

In the second pattern, the **proximodistal trend,** growth proceeds, literally, from "near to far"—from the center of the body outward. In the prenatal period, the head, chest, and trunk grow first, then the arms and legs, and finally the hands and feet. During infancy and childhood, the arms and legs continue to grow somewhat ahead of the hands and feet.

 ## Brain Development

At birth, the brain is nearer to its adult size than any other physical structure, and it continues to develop at an astounding pace throughout infancy and toddlerhood. We can best understand brain growth by looking at it from two vantage points: (1) the microscopic level of individual brain cells and (2) the larger level of the cerebral cortex, the most complex brain structure and the one responsible for the highly developed intelligence of our species.

Development of Neurons

The human brain has 100 to 200 billion **neurons,** or nerve cells that store and transmit information, many of which have thousands of direct connections with other neurons. Unlike other

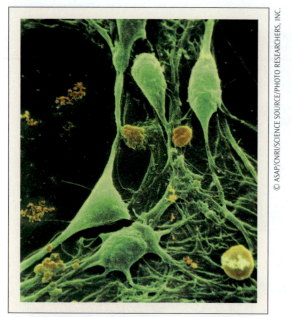

© ASAP/CNRI/SCIENCE SOURCE/PHOTO RESEARCHERS, INC.

FIGURE 4.2 Neurons and their connective fibers.
This photograph of several neurons, taken with the aid of a powerful microscope, shows the elaborate synaptic connections that form with neighboring cells.

body cells, neurons are not tightly packed together. Between them are tiny gaps, or **synapses,** where fibers from different neurons come close together but do not touch (see Figure 4.2). Neurons send messages to one another by releasing chemicals called **neurotransmitters,** which cross the synapse.

The basic story of brain growth concerns how neurons develop and form this elaborate communication system. In the prenatal period, neurons are produced in the embryo's primitive neural tube. From there, they migrate to form the major parts of the brain (see Chapter 3, page 64). Once neurons are in place, they differentiate, establishing their unique functions by extending their fibers to form synaptic connections with neighboring cells. During the first two years, neural fibers and synapses increase at an astounding pace (Huttenlocher, 2002; Moore, Persaud, & Torchia, 2013). A surprising aspect of brain growth is **programmed cell death,** which makes space for these connective structures: As synapses form, many surrounding neurons die—20 to 80 percent, depending on the brain region (de Haan & Johnson, 2003; Stiles, 2008). Fortunately, during the prenatal period, the neural tube produces far more neurons than the brain will ever need.

As neurons form connections, *stimulation* becomes vital to their survival. Neurons that are stimulated by input from the surrounding environment continue to establish synapses, forming increasingly elaborate systems of communication that support more complex abilities. At first, stimulation results in a massive overabundance of synapses, many of which serve identical functions, thereby ensuring that the child will acquire the motor, cognitive, and social skills that our species needs to survive. Neurons that are seldom stimulated soon lose their synapses, in a process called **synaptic pruning** that returns neurons not needed at the

moment to an uncommitted state so they can support future development. In all, about 40 percent of synapses are pruned during childhood and adolescence to reach the adult level (Webb, Monk, & Nelson, 2001). For this process to advance, appropriate stimulation of the child's brain is vital during periods in which the formation of synapses is at its peak (Bryk & Fisher, 2012).

If few new neurons are produced after the prenatal period, what causes the dramatic increase in brain size during the first two years? About half the brain's volume is made up of **glial cells,** which are responsible for **myelination,** the coating of neural fibers with an insulating fatty sheath (called *myelin*) that improves the efficiency of message transfer. Glial cells multiply rapidly from the fourth month of pregnancy through the second year of life—a process that continues at a slower pace through middle childhood and accelerates again in adolescence. Gains in neural fibers and myelination are responsible for the extraordinary gain in overall size of the brain—from nearly 30 percent of its adult weight at birth to 70 percent by age 2 (Johnson, 2011; Knickmeyer et al., 2008).

Brain development can be compared to molding a "living sculpture." First, neurons and synapses are overproduced. Then, cell death and synaptic pruning sculpt away excess building material to form the mature brain—a process jointly influenced by genetically programmed events and the child's experiences (Johnston et al., 2001). The resulting "sculpture" is a set of interconnected regions, each with specific functions—much like countries on a globe that communicate with one another.

Neurobiological Methods

This "geography" of the brain permits researchers to study its developing organization and the activity of its regions. To do so, scientists use *neurobiological methods* (see Table 4.1). The first two methods detect changes in *electrical activity* in the cerebral cortex. In an *electroencephalogram (EEG), brain-wave patterns* are examined for stability and organization—signs of mature cortical functioning. As the individual processes a particular stimulus, *event-related potentials (ERPs)* detect the general location of brain-wave activity—a technique often used to study preverbal infants' responsiveness to various stimuli and the impact of experience on specialization of cortical regions (DeBoer, Scott, & Nelson, 2007; deRegnier, 2005).

Neuroimaging techniques, which yield detailed, three-dimensional computerized pictures of the entire brain and its active areas, provide the most precise information about which brain regions are specialized for certain capacities and about abnormalities in brain functioning. The most promising of these methods is *functional magnetic resonance imaging (fMRI).* Unlike *positron emission tomography (PET),* fMRI does not depend on X-ray photography, which requires injection of a radioactive substance. Rather, when an individual is exposed to a stimulus, fMRI detects changes in blood flow and oxygen metabolism throughout the brain magnetically, yielding a colorful, moving picture of parts of the brain used to perform a given activity (see Figure 4.3a and b).

TABLE 4.1 **Methods for Measuring Brain Functioning**

METHOD	DESCRIPTION
Electroencephalogram (EEG)	Electrodes embedded in a head cap record electrical brain-wave activity in the brain's outer layers—the cerebral cortex.
Event-related potentials (ERPs)	Using the EEG, the frequency and amplitude of brain waves in response to particular stimuli (such as a picture, music, or speech) are recorded in multiple areas of the cerebral cortex. Enables identification of general regions of stimulus-induced activity.
Functional magnetic resonance imaging (fMRI)	While the person lies inside a tunnel-shaped apparatus that creates a magnetic field, a scanner magnetically detects increased blood flow and oxygen metabolism in areas of the brain as the individual processes particular stimuli. The result is a computerized moving picture of activity anywhere in the brain (not just its outer layers).
Positron emission tomography (PET)	After injection or inhalation of a radioactive substance, the person lies on an apparatus with a scanner that emits fine streams of X-rays, which detect increased blood flow and oxygen metabolism in areas of the brain as the person processes particular stimuli. As with fMRI, the result is a computerized image of "online" activity anywhere in the brain.
Near-infrared spectroscopy (NIRS)	Using thin, flexible optical fibers attached to the scalp through a head cap, infrared (invisible) light is beamed at the brain; its absorption by areas of the cerebral cortex varies with changes in blood flow and oxygen metabolism as the individual processes particular stimuli. The result is a computerized moving picture of active areas in the cerebral cortex. Unlike fMRI and PET, NIRS is appropriate for infants and young children, who can move within limited range.

Because PET and fMRI require that the participant lie as motionless as possible for an extended time, they are not suitable for infants and young children (Nelson, Thomas, & de Haan, 2006). A neuroimaging technique that works well in infancy and early childhood is *near-infrared spectroscopy (NIRS)*. Because the apparatus consists only of thin, flexible optical fibers attached to the scalp using a head cap, a baby can sit on the parent's lap and move during testing—as Figure 4.3c illustrates (Hespos et al., 2010). But unlike PET and fMRI, which map activity changes throughout the brain, NIRS examines only the functioning of the cerebral cortex.

Development of the Cerebral Cortex

The **cerebral cortex** surrounds the rest of the brain, resembling half of a shelled walnut. It accounts for 85 percent of the brain's weight and contains the greatest number of neurons and synapses. Because the cerebral cortex is the last part of the brain to stop growing, it is sensitive to environmental influences for a much longer period than any other part of the brain.

Regions of the Cerebral Cortex. Figure 4.4 on page 96 shows specific functions of regions of the cerebral cortex. The order in which cortical regions develop corresponds to the

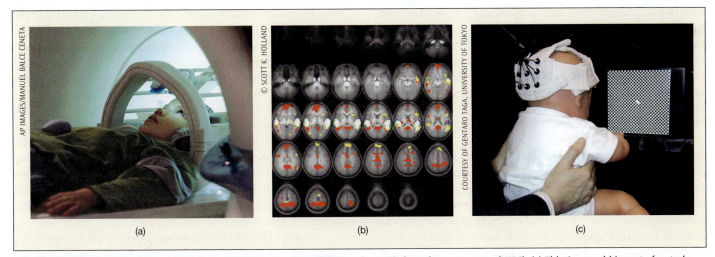

FIGURE 4.3 **Functional magnetic resonance imaging (fMRI) and near-infrared spectroscopy (NIRS).** (a) This 6-year-old is part of a study that uses fMRI to find out how his brain processes light and motion. (b) The fMRI image shows which areas of the child's brain are active while he views changing visual stimuli. (c) Here, NIRS is used to investigate a 2-month-old's response to a visual stimulus. During testing, the baby can move freely within a limited range. (Photo (c) from G. Taga, K. Asakawa, A. Maki, Y. Konishi, & H. Koisumi, 2003, "Brain Imaging in Awake Infants by Near-Infrared Optical Topography," *Proceedings of the National Academy of Sciences, 100*, p. 10723. Reprinted by permission.)

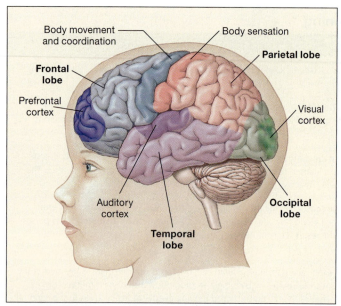

FIGURE 4.4 **The left side of the human brain, showing the cerebral cortex.** The cortex is divided into different lobes, each containing a variety of regions with specific functions. Some major regions are labeled here.

order in which various capacities emerge in the infant and growing child. For example, a burst of activity occurs in the auditory and visual cortexes and in areas responsible for body movement over the first year—a period of dramatic gains in auditory and visual perception and mastery of motor skills (Johnson, 2011). Language areas are especially active from late infancy through the preschool years, when language development flourishes (Pujol et al., 2006; Thompson, 2000).

The cortical regions with the most extended period of development are the *frontal lobes.* The **prefrontal cortex,** lying in front of areas controlling body movement, is responsible for thought—in particular, consciousness, inhibition of impulses, integration of information, and use of memory, reasoning, planning, and problem-solving strategies. From age 2 months on, the prefrontal cortex functions more effectively. But it undergoes especially rapid myelination and formation and pruning of synapses during the preschool and school years, followed by another period of accelerated growth in adolescence, when it reaches an adult level of synaptic connections (Nelson, 2002; Nelson, Thomas, & de Haan, 2006; Sowell et al., 2002).

Lateralization and Plasticity of the Cortex.

The cerebral cortex has two *hemispheres,* or sides, that differ in their functions. Some tasks are done mostly by the left hemisphere, others by the right. For example, each hemisphere receives sensory information from the side of the body opposite to it and controls only that side.[1] For most of us, the left hemisphere is largely responsible for verbal abilities (such as spoken and

[1]The eyes are an exception. Messages from the right half of each retina go to the right hemisphere; messages from the left half of each retina go to the left hemisphere. Thus, visual information from *both* eyes is received by *both* hemispheres.

written language) and positive emotion (such as joy). The right hemisphere handles spatial abilities (judging distances, reading maps, and recognizing geometric shapes) and negative emotion (such as distress) (Banish & Heller, 1998; Nelson & Bosquet, 2000). In left-handed people, this pattern may be reversed or, more commonly, the cerebral cortex may be less clearly specialized than in right-handers.

Why does this specialization of the two hemispheres, called **lateralization,** occur? Studies using fMRI reveal that the left hemisphere is better at processing information in a sequential, analytic (piece-by-piece) way, a good approach for dealing with communicative information—both verbal (language) and emotional (a joyful smile). In contrast, the right hemisphere is specialized for processing information in a holistic, integrative manner, ideal for making sense of spatial information and regulating negative emotion. A lateralized brain is certainly adaptive (Falk, 2005). It permits a wider array of functions to be carried out effectively than if both sides processed information exactly the same way.

Researchers study the timing of brain lateralization to learn more about **brain plasticity.** A highly plastic cerebral cortex, in which many areas are not yet committed to specific functions, has a high capacity for learning. And if a part of the cortex is damaged, other parts can take over tasks it would have handled. But once the hemispheres lateralize, damage to a specific region means that the abilities it controls cannot be recovered to the same extent or as easily as earlier.

At birth, the hemispheres have already begun to specialize. Most newborns show greater activation (detected with either ERP or NIRS) in the left hemisphere while listening to speech sounds or displaying a positive state of arousal. In contrast, the right hemisphere reacts more strongly to nonspeech sounds and to stimuli (such as a sour-tasting fluid) that evoke negative emotion (Fox & Davidson, 1986; Hespos et al., 2010).

Nevertheless, research on brain-damaged children and adults offers dramatic evidence for substantial plasticity in the young brain. Among preschoolers with brain injuries sustained in the first year of life, deficits in language and spatial abilities were milder than those observed in brain-injured adults (Akshoomoff et al., 2002; Stiles et al., 2005, 2008). As the children gained perceptual, motor, and cognitive experiences, other stimulated cortical structures compensated for the damaged areas, regardless of the site of injury. Still, mild deficits in complex skills, such as reading, math, and telling stories, were evident in the school years. When healthy brain regions take over the functions of damaged areas, multiple tasks must be done by a smaller-than-usual volume of brain tissue (Stiles, 2012). Consequently, the brain processes information less quickly and accurately than it would if it were intact.

Another illustration of how early experience greatly influences brain organization comes from studies of deaf adults who, as infants and children, learned sign language (a spatial skill). Compared with hearing adults, these individuals depend more on the right hemisphere for language processing (Neville & Bavelier, 2002). Also, toddlers who are advanced in language development show greater left-hemispheric specialization for language than their more slowly developing agemates (Luna et al., 2001; Mills et al., 2005). Apparently, the very process of acquiring language and other skills promotes lateralization.

In sum, the brain is more plastic during the first few years than it will ever be again. An overabundance of synaptic connections supports brain plasticity, ensuring that young children will acquire certain capacities even if some areas are damaged.

Sensitive Periods in Brain Development

Both animal and human studies reveal that early, extreme sensory deprivation results in permanent brain damage and loss of functions—findings that verify the existence of sensitive periods in brain development. For example, early, varied visual experiences must occur for the brain's visual centers to develop normally. If a 1-month-old kitten is deprived of light for just three or four days, these areas of the brain degenerate. If the kitten is kept in the dark during the fourth week of life and beyond, the damage is severe and permanent (Crair, Gillespie, & Stryker, 1998). And the general quality of the early environment affects overall brain growth. When animals reared from birth in physically and socially stimulating surroundings are compared with those reared under depleted conditions, the brains of the stimulated animals are larger and heavier and show much denser synaptic connections (Sale, Berardi, & Maffei, 2009).

Human Evidence: Victims of Deprived Early Environments.
For ethical reasons, we cannot deliberately deprive some infants of normal rearing experiences and observe the impact on their brains and competencies. Instead, we must turn to natural experiments, in which children were victims of deprived early environments that were later rectified. Such studies have revealed some parallels with the animal evidence just described.

In one investigation, researchers followed the progress of a large sample of children transferred between birth and 3½ years from extremely deprived Romanian orphanages to adoptive families in Great Britain (Beckett et al., 2006; O'Connor et al., 2000; Rutter et al., 1998, 2004, 2010). On arrival, most were impaired in all domains of development. Cognitive catch-up was impressive for children adopted before 6 months, who attained average mental test scores in childhood and adolescence, performing as well as a comparison group of early-adopted British-born children.

But Romanian children who had been institutionalized for more than the first six months showed serious intellectual deficits. Although they improved in test scores during middle childhood and adolescence, they remained substantially below average. And most displayed at least three serious mental health problems, such as inattention, overactivity, unruly behavior, and autistic-like symptoms (social disinterest, stereotyped behavior) (Kreppner et al., 2007, 2010).

Neurobiological findings indicate that early, prolonged institutionalization leads to a generalized decrease in activity in the cerebral cortex, especially the prefrontal cortex, which governs complex cognition and impulse control. Neural fibers

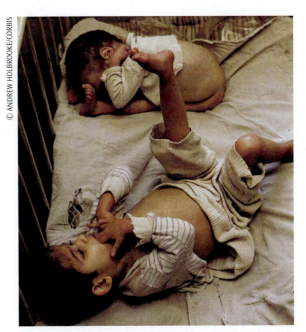

These children in an orphanage in Romania receive little adult contact or stimulation. The longer they remain in this barren environment, the more likely they are to display profound impairments in all domains of development.

connecting the prefrontal cortex with other brain structures involved in control of emotion are also reduced (Eluvathingal et al., 2006; Nelson, 2007b). And activation of the left cerebral hemisphere, governing positive emotion, is diminished relative to right cerebral activation, governing negative emotion (McLaughlin et al., 2011).

Additional evidence confirms that the chronic stress of early, deprived orphanage rearing disrupts the brain's capacity to manage stress, with long-term physical and psychological consequences. In another investigation, researchers followed the development of children who had spent their first eight months or more in Romanian institutions and were then adopted into Canadian homes (Gunnar et al., 2001; Gunnar & Cheatham, 2003). Compared with agemates adopted shortly after birth, these children showed extreme stress reactivity, as indicated by high concentrations of the stress hormone *cortisol* in their saliva—a physiological response linked to persistent illness and learning and behavior problems, including deficits in attention and control of anger and other impulses. The longer the children spent in orphanage care, the higher their cortisol levels—even 6½ years after adoption. In other investigations, orphanage children displayed abnormally low cortisol—a blunted physiological stress response that may be the central nervous system's adaptation to earlier, frequent cortisol elevations (Loman & Gunnar, 2010).

Appropriate Stimulation.
Unlike the orphanage children just described, Grace, whom Monica and Kevin had adopted in Cambodia at 16 months of age, showed favorable progress. Two years earlier, they had adopted Grace's older brother, Eli. When Eli was 2 years old, Monica and Kevin sent a letter and a photo of Eli to his biological mother, describing a bright, happy

child. The next day, the Cambodian mother tearfully asked an adoption agency to send her baby daughter to join Eli and his American family. Although Grace's early environment was very depleted, her biological mother's loving care—holding gently, speaking softly, playfully stimulating, and breastfeeding—may have prevented irreversible damage to her brain.

In the Bucharest Early Intervention Project, about 200 institutionalized Romanian babies were randomized into conditions of either care as usual or transfer to high-quality foster families between ages 5 and 30 months. Specially trained social workers provided foster parents with counseling and support. Follow-ups between 2½ and 4 years revealed that the foster-care group exceeded the institutional-care group in intelligence test scores, language skills, emotional responsiveness, and EEG and ERP assessments of brain activity (Nelson et al., 2007; Smyke et al., 2009). On all measures, the earlier the foster placement, the better the outcome. But consistent with an early sensitive period, the foster-care group remained behind never-institutionalized agemates living with Bucharest families.

In addition to impoverished environments, ones that overwhelm children with expectations beyond their current capacities interfere with the brain's potential. In recent years, expensive early learning centers have sprung up, in which infants are trained with letter and number flash cards and slightly older toddlers are given a full curriculum of reading, math, science, art, gym, and more. There is no evidence that these programs yield smarter "superbabies" (Hirsh-Pasek & Golinkoff, 2003). To the contrary, trying to prime infants with stimulation for which they are not ready can cause them to withdraw, thereby threatening their interest in learning and creating conditions much like stimulus deprivation!

How, then, can we characterize appropriate stimulation during the early years? To answer this question, researchers distinguish between two types of brain development. The first, **experience-expectant brain growth,** refers to the young brain's rapidly developing organization, which depends on ordinary experiences—opportunities to explore the environment, interact with people, and hear language and other sounds. As a result of millions of years of evolution, the brains of all infants, toddlers, and young children *expect* to encounter these experiences and, if they do, grow normally. The second type of brain development, **experience-dependent brain growth,** occurs throughout our lives. It consists of additional growth and refinement of established brain structures as a result of specific learning experiences that vary widely across individuals and cultures (Greenough & Black, 1992). Reading and writing, playing computer games, and practicing the violin are examples. The brain of a violinist differs in certain ways from the brain of a poet because each has exercised different brain regions for a long time.

Experience-expectant brain growth occurs early and naturally, as caregivers offer babies and preschoolers age-appropriate play materials and engage them in enjoyable daily routines—a shared meal, a game of peekaboo, a picture book to talk about, or a song to sing. The resulting growth provides the foundation for later-occurring, experience-dependent development (Huttenlocher, 2002; Shonkoff & Phillips, 2001). No evidence

Experience-expectant brain growth occurs naturally, through ordinary, stimulating experiences. This toddler exploring a mossy log enjoys the type of activity that best promotes brain development in the early years.

exists for a sensitive period in the first five or six years for mastering skills that depend on extensive training, such as reading, musical performance, or gymnastics. To the contrary, rushing early learning harms the brain by overwhelming its neural circuits, thereby reducing the brain's sensitivity to the everyday experiences it needs for a healthy start in life.

Changing States of Arousal

Rapid brain growth means that the organization of sleep and wakefulness changes substantially between birth and 2 years, and fussiness and crying also decline. The newborn baby takes round-the-clock naps that total about 16 to 18 hours (Davis, Parker & Montgomery, 2004). Total sleep time declines slowly; the average 2-year-old still needs 12 to 13 hours. But the sleep–wake pattern increasingly conforms to a night–day schedule. Most 6- to 9-month-olds take two daytime naps; by about 18 months, children generally need only one nap. Finally, between ages 3 and 5, napping subsides (Iglowstein et al., 2003).

LOOK AND LISTEN

Interview a parent of a baby about sleep challenges. What strategies has the parent tried to ease these difficulties? Are the techniques likely to be effective, in view of evidence on infant sleep development? ●

These changing arousal patterns are due to brain development, but they are also affected by cultural beliefs and practices and individual parents' needs (Super & Harkness, 2002). Dutch parents, for example, view sleep regularity as far more important than the U.S. parents do. And whereas U.S. parents regard a predictable sleep schedule as emerging naturally from

Cultural Influences

Cultural Variation in Infant Sleeping Arrangements

This Vietnamese mother and child sleep together—a practice common in their culture and around the globe. Hard wooden sleeping surfaces protect cosleeping children from entrapment in soft bedding.

Western child-rearing advice from experts strongly encourages nighttime separation of baby from parent. For example, the most recent edition of Benjamin Spock's *Baby and Child Care* recommends that babies sleep in their own room by 3 months of age, explaining, "By 6 months, a child who regularly sleeps in her parents' room may feel uneasy sleeping anywhere else" (Spock & Needlman, 2012, p. 62). And the American Academy of Pediatrics (2012) has issued a controversial warning that parent–infant bedsharing may increase the risk of sudden infant death syndrome (SIDS).

Yet parent–infant "cosleeping" is the norm for approximately 90 percent of the world's population, in cultures as diverse as the Japanese, the rural Guatemalan Maya, the Inuit of northwestern Canada, and the !Kung of Botswana. Japanese and Korean children usually lie next to their mothers in infancy and early childhood (Takahashi, 1990; Yang & Hahn, 2002). Among the Maya, mother–infant bedsharing is interrupted only by the birth of a new baby, when the older child is moved next to the father or to another bed in the same room (Morelli et al., 1992). Bedsharing is also common in U.S. subcultures, including African-American families and families of eastern Kentucky (Buswell & Spatz, 2007; McKenna & Volpe, 2007).

Cultural values—specifically, collectivism versus individualism (see Chapter 2)—strongly influence infant sleeping arrangements. In one study, researchers interviewed Guatemalan Mayan mothers and American middle-SES mothers about their sleeping practices. Mayan mothers stressed the importance of promoting an *interdependent self,* explaining that cosleeping builds a close parent–child bond, which is necessary for children to learn the ways of people around them. In contrast, American mothers emphasized an *independent self,* mentioning their desire to instill early autonomy and protect their own privacy (Morelli et al., 1992).

Over the past two decades, cosleeping has increased in Western nations. An estimated 13 percent of U.S. infants routinely bedshare, and an additional 30 to 35 percent sometimes do (Buswell & Spatz, 2007; Willinger et al., 2003). During the night, cosleeping babies breastfeed three times longer than infants who sleep alone. Because infants arouse to nurse more often when sleeping next to their mothers, some researchers believe that cosleeping may actually help safeguard babies at risk for SIDS (see page 84 in Chapter 3). Consistent with this view, SIDS is rare in Asian cultures where cosleeping is widespread, including Cambodia, China, Japan, Korea, Thailand, and Vietnam (McKenna, 2002; McKenna & McDade, 2005).

Infant sleeping practices affect other aspects of family life. For example, Mayan babies doze off in the midst of ongoing family activities and are carried to bed by their mothers. In contrast, for many American parents, bedtime often involves a lengthy, elaborate ritual. Perhaps bedtime struggles, so common in Western homes but rare elsewhere in the world, are related to the stress young children feel when they must fall asleep without assistance (Latz, Wolf, & Lozoff, 1999).

Critics warn that bedsharing will promote emotional problems, especially excessive dependency. Yet a study following children from the end of pregnancy through age 18 showed that young people who had bedshared in the early years were no different from others in any aspect of adjustment (Okami, Weisner, & Olmstead, 2002). Another concern is that infants might become trapped under the parent's body or in soft covers and suffocate. Parents who are obese or who use alcohol, tobacco, or illegal drugs do pose a serious risk to their sleeping babies, as does the use of quilts and comforters or an overly soft mattress (American Academy of Pediatrics, 2012).

But with appropriate precautions, parents and infants can cosleep safely (McKenna & Volpe, 2007). In cultures where cosleeping is widespread, parents and infants usually sleep with light covering on hard surfaces, such as firm mattresses, floor mats, and wooden planks, or infants sleep in a cradle or hammock next to the parents' bed (McKenna, 2001, 2002). And when sharing the same bed, infants typically lie on their back or side facing the mother—positions that promote frequent, easy communication between parent and baby and arousal if breathing is threatened.

within the child, Dutch parents believe that a schedule must be imposed, or the baby's development might suffer (Super & Harkness, 2010). At age 6 months, Dutch babies are put to bed earlier and sleep, on average, 2 hours more per day than their U.S. agemates.

Motivated by demanding work schedules and other needs, many Western parents try to get their babies to sleep through the night as early as 3 to 4 months by offering an evening feeding—a practice that may be at odds with young infants' neurological capacities. Not until the middle of the first year is the secretion of *melatonin,* a hormone within the brain that promotes drowsiness, much greater at night than during the day (Sadeh, 1997).

Furthermore, as the Cultural Influences box above reveals, isolating infants to promote sleep is rare elsewhere in the world.

When babies sleep with their parents, their average sleep period remains constant at three hours from 1 to 8 months of age. Only at the end of the first year, as REM sleep (the state that usually prompts waking) declines, do infants move in the direction of an adultlike sleep–waking schedule (Ficca et al., 1999).

ASK YOURSELF

REVIEW How do overproduction of synapses and synaptic pruning support infants' and children's ability to learn?

APPLY Which infant enrichment program would you choose: one that emphasizes gentle talking and touching and social games, or one that includes reading and number drills and classical music lessons? Explain.

REFLECT What is your attitude toward parent–infant cosleeping? Is it influenced by your cultural background? Explain.

Influences on Early Physical Growth

Physical growth, like other aspects of development, results from a complex interplay between genetic and environmental factors. Heredity, nutrition, and emotional well-being all affect early physical growth.

Heredity

Because identical twins are much more alike in body size than fraternal twins, we know that heredity is important in physical growth (Estourgie-van Burk et al., 2006; Touwslager et al., 2011). When diet and health are adequate, height and rate of physical growth are largely influenced by heredity. In fact, as long as negative environmental influences such as poor nutrition and illness are not severe, children and adolescents typically show *catch-up growth*—a return to a genetically influenced growth path once conditions improve. Still, the brain, the heart, the digestive system, and many other internal organs may be permanently compromised (Hales & Ozanne, 2003).

Genetic makeup also affects body weight: The weights of adopted children correlate more strongly with those of their biological than of their adoptive parents (Kinnunen, Pietilainen, & Rissanen, 2006). At the same time, environment—in particular, nutrition—plays a vital role.

Nutrition

Nutrition is especially crucial for development in the first two years because the baby's brain and body are growing so rapidly. Pound for pound, an infant's energy needs are twice those of an adult. Twenty-five percent of babies' total caloric intake is devoted to growth, and infants need extra calories to keep rapidly developing organs functioning properly (Meyer, 2009).

Breastfeeding versus Bottle-Feeding. Babies need not only enough food but also the right kind of food. In early infancy, breastfeeding is ideally suited to their needs, and bottled formulas try to imitate it. Applying What We Know on the following page summarizes major nutritional and health advantages of breastfeeding.

Because of these benefits, breastfed babies in poverty-stricken regions are much less likely to be malnourished and 6 to 14 times more likely to survive the first year of life. The World Health Organization recommends breastfeeding until age 2 years, with solid foods added at 6 months. These practices, if widely followed, would save the lives of more than a million infants annually (World Health Organization, 2012b). Even breastfeeding for just a few weeks offers some protection against respiratory and intestinal infections, which are devastating to young children in developing countries.

Yet many mothers in the developing world do not know about these benefits. In Africa, the Middle East, and Latin America, most babies get some breastfeeding, but fewer than 40 percent are exclusively breastfed for the first six months, and one-third are fully weaned from the breast before 1 year (UNICEF, 2009). In place of breast milk, mothers give their babies commercial formula or low-grade nutrients, such as highly diluted cow or goat milk. Contamination of these foods as a result of poor sanitation often leads to illness and infant death. The United Nations has encouraged all hospitals and maternity units in developing countries to promote breastfeed-

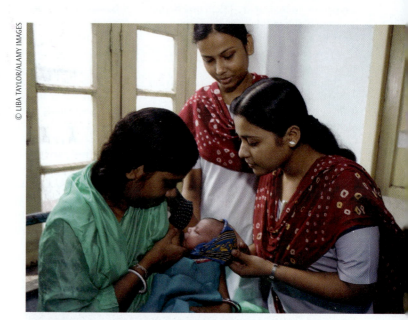

Midwives in India support a mother as she learns to breastfeed her infant. Breastfeeding is especially important in developing countries, where it helps protect babies against life-threatening infections and early death.

Applying What We Know

Reasons to Breastfeed

Nutritional and Health Advantages	Explanation
Provides the correct balance of fat and protein	Compared with the milk of other mammals, human milk is higher in fat and lower in protein. This balance, as well as the unique proteins and fats contained in human milk, is ideal for a rapidly myelinating nervous system.
Ensures nutritional completeness	A mother who breastfeeds need not add other foods to her infant's diet until the baby is 6 months old. The milks of all mammals are low in iron, but the iron contained in breast milk is much more easily absorbed by the baby's system. Consequently, bottle-fed infants need iron-fortified formula.
Helps ensure healthy physical growth	One-year-old breastfed babies are leaner (have a higher percentage of muscle to fat), a growth pattern that persists through the preschool years and that may help prevent later overweight and obesity.
Protects against many diseases	Breastfeeding transfers antibodies and other infection-fighting agents from mother to child and enhances functioning of the immune system. Compared with bottle-fed infants, breastfed babies have far fewer allergic reactions and respiratory and intestinal illnesses. Breast milk also has anti-inflammatory effects, which reduce the severity of illness symptoms. Breastfeeding in the first four months is linked to lower blood cholesterol levels in adulthood and, thereby, may help prevent cardiovascular disease.

Sources: American Academy of Pediatrics, 2005; Michels et al., 2007; Owen et al., 2008; Rosetta & Baldi, 2008.

ing as long as mothers do not have viral or bacterial infections (such as HIV or tuberculosis) that can be transmitted to the baby.

Partly as a result of the natural childbirth movement, breastfeeding has become more common in industrialized nations, especially among well-educated women. Today, 74 percent of American mothers breastfeed, but more than half stop by 6 months (Centers for Disease Control and Prevention, 2011a). Not surprisingly, mothers who return to work sooner wean their babies from the breast earlier (Kimbro, 2006). But mothers who cannot be with their infants all the time can still combine breast- and bottle-feeding. The U.S. Department of Health and Human Services (2010a) advises exclusive breastfeeding for the first 6 months and inclusion of breast milk in the baby's diet until at least 1 year.

Women who do not breastfeed sometimes worry that they are depriving their baby of an experience essential for healthy psychological development. Yet breastfed and bottle-fed infants in industrialized nations do not differ in quality of the mother–infant relationship or in later emotional adjustment (Fergusson & Woodward, 1999; Jansen, de Weerth, & Riksen-Walraven, 2008). Some studies report a slight advantage in intelligence test performance for children and adolescents who were breastfed, after controlling for many factors. Most, however, find no cognitive benefits (Der, Batty, & Deary, 2006).

Are Chubby Babies at Risk for Later Overweight and Obesity?
From early infancy, Timmy was an enthusiastic eater who gained weight quickly. Vanessa wondered: Was she overfeeding Timmy and increasing his chances of becoming overweight?

Most chubby babies with nutritious diets thin out during toddlerhood and early childhood, as weight gain slows and they become more active. But recent evidence does indicate a strengthening relationship between rapid weight gain in infancy and later obesity (Botton et al., 2008; Chomtho et al., 2008). The trend may be due to the rise in overweight adults, who promote unhealthy eating habits in their young children. Interviews with 1,500 U.S. parents of 4- to 24-month-olds revealed that many routinely served older infants and toddlers french fries, pizza, candy, sugary fruit drinks, and soda. On average, infants consumed 20 percent and toddlers 30 percent more calories than they needed. At the same time, one-fourth ate no fruits and one-third no vegetables (Siega-Riz et al., 2010).

How can parents prevent their infants from becoming overweight children and adults? One way is to breastfeed for the first six months, which is associated with slower early weight gain (Gunnarsdottir et al., 2010). Another is to avoid giving them foods loaded with sugar, salt, and saturated fats. Once toddlers learn to walk, climb, and run, parents can also provide plenty of opportunities for energetic play.

Malnutrition

In developing countries and war-torn areas where food resources are limited, malnutrition is widespread. Recent evidence indicates that about 27 percent of the world's children suffer from malnutrition before age 5 (World Health Organization, 2010). The 10 percent who are severely affected suffer from two dietary diseases. **Marasmus** is a wasted condition of the body caused by a diet low in all essential nutrients. It usually appears in the first year of life when a baby's mother is too malnourished to

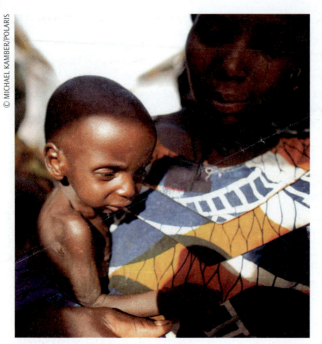

Left photo: This baby of Niger, Africa, has marasmus, a wasted condition caused by a diet low in all essential nutrients. *Right photo:* The swollen abdomen of this toddler, also of Niger, is a symptom of kwashiorkor, which results from a diet very low in protein. If these children survive, they are likely to be growth stunted and to suffer from lasting organ damage and serious cognitive and emotional impairments.

produce enough breast milk and bottle-feeding is also inadequate. Her starving baby becomes painfully thin and is in danger of dying. **Kwashiorkor** is caused by an unbalanced diet very low in protein. The disease usually strikes after weaning, between 1 and 3 years of age. It is common in regions where children get just enough calories from starchy foods but little protein. The child's body responds by breaking down its own protein reserves, which causes swelling of the abdomen and limbs, hair loss, skin rash, and irritable, listless behavior.

Children who survive these extreme forms of malnutrition grow to be smaller in all body dimensions and suffer from lasting damage to the brain, heart, liver, or other organs (Müller & Krawinkel, 2005). When their diets do improve, they tend to gain excessive weight (Uauy et al., 2008). A malnourished body protects itself by establishing a low basal metabolism rate, which may endure after nutrition improves. Also, malnutrition may disrupt appetite control centers in the brain, causing the child to overeat when food becomes plentiful.

Learning and behavior are also seriously affected. One long-term study of marasmic children revealed that an improved diet did not result in catch-up in head size, suggesting permanent loss in brain weight (Stoch et al., 1982). And animal evidence reveals that a deficient diet alters the production of neurotransmitters in the brain—an effect that can disrupt all aspects of development (Haller, 2005). These children score low on intelligence tests, show poor fine-motor coordination, and have difficulty paying attention (Galler et al., 1990; Liu et al., 2003). They also display a more intense stress response to fear-

arousing situations, perhaps caused by the constant, gnawing pain of hunger (Fernald & Grantham-McGregor, 1998).

Inadequate nutrition is not confined to developing countries. Because government-supported supplementary food programs do not reach all families in need, an estimated 21 percent of U.S. children suffer from *food insecurity*—uncertain access to enough food for a healthy, active life. Food insecurity is especially high among single-parent families and low-income ethnic minority families (U.S. Department of Agriculture, 2011a). Although few of these children have marasmus or kwashiorkor, their physical growth and ability to learn are still affected.

ASK YOURSELF

REVIEW Explain why breastfeeding can have lifelong consequences for the development of babies born in poverty-stricken regions of the world.

APPLY Eight-month-old Shaun is well below average in height and painfully thin. What serious growth disorder does he likely have, and what type of intervention, in addition to dietary enrichment, will help restore his development? (Hint: See page 71 in Chapter 3.)

REFLECT Imagine that you are the parent of a newborn baby. Describe feeding practices you would use, and ones you would avoid, to promote healthy development.

Learning Capacities

Learning refers to changes in behavior as the result of experience. Babies are capable of two basic forms of learning: classical and operant conditioning. They also learn through their natural preference for novel stimulation. Finally, shortly after birth, babies learn by observing others; they can imitate the facial expressions and gestures of adults.

Classical Conditioning

Newborn reflexes, discussed in Chapter 3, make **classical conditioning** possible in the young infant. In this form of learning, a neutral stimulus is paired with a stimulus that leads to a reflexive response. Once the baby's nervous system makes the connection between the two stimuli, the neutral stimulus produces the behavior by itself. Classical conditioning helps infants recognize which events usually occur together in the everyday world, so they can anticipate what is about to happen next. As a result, the environment becomes more orderly and predictable. Let's take a closer look at the steps of classical conditioning.

As Carolyn settled down in the rocking chair to nurse Caitlin, she often stroked Caitlin's forehead. Soon Carolyn noticed that each time she did this, Caitlin made sucking move-ments. Caitlin had been classically conditioned. Figure 4.5 shows how it happened:

1. Before learning takes place, an **unconditioned stimulus (UCS)** must consistently produce a reflexive, or **unconditioned, response (UCR)**. In Caitlin's case, sweet breast milk (UCS) resulted in sucking (UCR).

2. To produce learning, a *neutral stimulus* that does not lead to the reflex is presented just before, or at about the same time as, the UCS. Carolyn stroked Caitlin's forehead as each nursing period began. The stroking (neutral stimulus) was paired with the taste of milk (UCS).

3. If learning has occurred, the neutral stimulus by itself produces a response similar to the reflexive response. The neutral stimulus is then called a **conditioned stimulus (CS)**, and the response it elicits is called a **conditioned response (CR)**. We know that Caitlin has been classically conditioned because stroking her forehead outside the feeding situation (CS) results in sucking (CR).

If the CS is presented alone enough times, without being paired with the UCS, the CR will no longer occur, an outcome called *extinction*. In other words, if Carolyn repeatedly strokes Caitlin's forehead without feeding her, Caitlin will gradually stop sucking in response to stroking.

Young infants can be classically conditioned most easily when the association between two stimuli has survival value. In

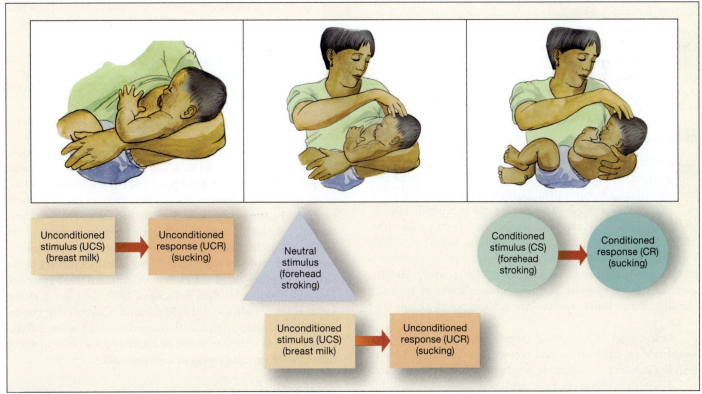

FIGURE 4.5 The steps of classical conditioning. This example shows how a mother classically conditioned her baby to make sucking movements by stroking the baby's forehead at the beginning of feedings.

the example just described, learning which stimuli regularly accompany feeding improves the infant's ability to get food and survive (Blass, Ganchrow, & Steiner, 1984).

In contrast, some responses, such as fear, are difficult to classically condition in young babies. Until infants have the motor skills to escape unpleasant events, they have no biological need to form these associations.

Operant Conditioning

In classical conditioning, babies build expectations about stimulus events in the environment, but their behavior does not influence the stimuli that occur. In **operant conditioning**, infants act, or *operate,* on the environment, and stimuli that follow their behavior change the probability that the behavior will occur again. A stimulus that increases the occurrence of a response is called a **reinforcer.** For example, sweet liquid *reinforces* the sucking response in newborns. Removing a desirable stimulus or presenting an unpleasant one to decrease the occurrence of a response is called **punishment.** A sour-tasting fluid *punishes* newborns' sucking response, causing them to purse their lips and stop sucking entirely.

Many stimuli besides food can serve as reinforcers of infant behavior. For example, newborns will suck faster on a nipple when their rate of sucking produces interesting sights and sounds, making operant conditioning a powerful tool for finding out what stimuli babies can perceive and which ones they prefer. Operant conditioning also plays a vital role in the formation of social relationships. As the baby gazes into the adult's eyes, the adult looks and smiles back, and then the infant looks and smiles again. As the behavior of each partner reinforces the other, both continue their pleasurable interaction. In Chapter 6, we will see that this contingent responsiveness contributes to the development of infant–caregiver attachment.

Habituation

At birth, the human brain is set up to be attracted to novelty. Infants tend to respond more strongly to a new element that has entered their environment. **Habituation** refers to a gradual reduction in the strength of a response due to repetitive stimulation. Looking, heart rate, and respiration rate may all decline, indicating a loss of interest. Once this has occurred, a new stimulus—a change in the environment—causes responsiveness to return to a high level, an increase called **recovery.** Habituation and recovery make learning more efficient by focusing our attention on those aspects of the environment we know least about.

Researchers investigating infants' understanding of the world rely on habituation and recovery more than any other learning capacity. For example, a baby who first *habituates* to a visual pattern (a photo of a baby) and then *recovers* to a new one (a photo of a bald man) appears to remember the first stimulus and perceive the second one as new and different from it. This method of studying infant perception and cognition, illustrated

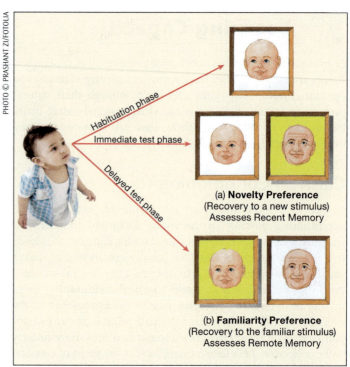

(a) Novelty Preference
(Recovery to a new stimulus)
Assesses Recent Memory

(b) Familiarity Preference
(Recovery to the familiar stimulus)
Assesses Remote Memory

FIGURE 4.6 Using habituation to study infant perception and cognition. In the habituation phase, infants view a photo of a baby until their looking declines. In the test phase, infants are again shown the baby photo, but this time it appears alongside a photo of a bald-headed man. (a) When the test phase occurs soon after the habituation phase (within minutes, hours, or days, depending on the age of the infants), participants who remember the baby face and distinguish it from the man's face show a *novelty preference;* they recover to (spend more time looking at) the new stimulus. (b) When the test phase is delayed for weeks or months, infants who continue to remember the baby face shift to a *familiarity preference;* they recover to the familiar baby face rather than to the novel man's face.

in Figure 4.6, can be used with newborns, including preterm infants (see pages 65–66 in Chapter 3).

Recovery to a new stimulus, or novelty preference, assesses infants' *recent memory.* **TAKE A MOMENT...** Think about what happens when you return to a place you have not seen for a long time. Instead of attending to novelty, you are likely to focus on aspects that are familiar: "I recognize that—I've been here before!" Like adults, infants shift from a novelty preference to a familiarity preference as more time intervenes between habituation and test phases in research. That is, babies recover to the familiar stimulus rather than to a novel stimulus (see Figure 4.6) (Bahrick, Hernandez-Reif, & Pickens, 1997; Courage & Howe, 1998; Flom & Bahrick, 2010; Richmond, Colombo, & Hayne, 2007). By focusing on that shift, researchers can also use habituation to assess *remote memory,* or memory for stimuli to which infants were exposed weeks or months earlier.

Imitation

Babies come into the world with a primitive ability to learn through **imitation**—by copying the behavior of another person.

For example, Figure 4.7 shows a human newborn imitating two adult facial expressions (Meltzoff & Moore, 1977). The newborn's capacity to imitate extends to certain gestures, such as head and index-finger movements, and has been demonstrated in many ethnic groups and cultures (Meltzoff & Kuhl, 1994; Nagy et al., 2005). Even newborn primates, including chimpanzees (our closest evolutionary relatives), imitate some behaviors (Ferrari et al., 2006; Myowa-Yamakoshi et al., 2004).

Although newborns' capacity to imitate is widely accepted, a few studies have failed to reproduce the human findings (see, for example, Anisfeld et al., 2001). And because newborn mouth and tongue movements occur with increased frequency to almost any arousing change in stimulation (such as lively music or flashing lights), some researchers argue that certain newborn "imitative" responses are actually mouthing—a common early exploratory response to interesting stimuli (Jones, 2009). Others claim that newborns—both primates and humans—imitate a variety of facial expressions and head movements with effort and determination, even after short delays—when the adult is no longer demonstrating the behavior (Meltzoff & Moore, 1999; Paukner, Ferrari, & Suomi, 2011).

According to Andrew Meltzoff, newborns imitate much as older children and adults do—by actively trying to match body movements they *see* with ones they *feel* themselves make (Meltzoff, 2007). Scientists have identified specialized cells in motor areas of the cerebral cortex in primates—called **mirror neurons**—that underlie these capacities (Ferrari & Coudé, 2011). Mirror neurons fire identically when a primate hears or sees an action and when it carries out that action on its own (Rizzolatti & Craighero, 2004). Human adults have especially elaborate systems of mirror neurons, which enable us to observe another's behavior (such as smiling or throwing a ball) while simulating the behavior in our own brain. Mirror neurons are believed to be the biological basis of a variety of interrelated, complex social abilities, including imitation, empathic sharing of emotions, and understanding others' intentions (Iacoboni, 2009; Schulte-Ruther et al., 2007).

Still, Meltzoff's view of newborn imitation as a flexible, voluntary capacity remains controversial. Mirror neurons, though possibly functional at birth, undergo an extended period of development (Bertenthal & Longo, 2007; Lepage & Théoret, 2007). Similarly, as we will see in Chapter 5, the capacity to imitate expands greatly over the first two years. But however limited it is at birth, imitation is a powerful means of learning. Using imitation, infants explore their social world, not only learning from other people but getting to know them by matching their behavioral states. As babies notice similarities between their own actions and those of others, they experience other people as "like me" and, thus, learn about themselves (Meltzoff, 2007). In this way, infant imitation may serve as the foundation for understanding others' thoughts and feelings. Finally, caregivers take great pleasure in a baby who imitates, which helps get the infant's relationship with parents off to a good start.

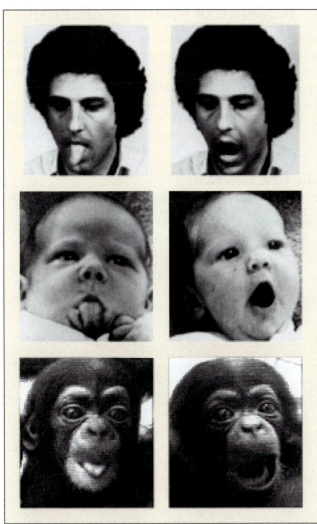

FIGURE 4.7 Imitation by human and chimpanzee newborns. The human infants in the middle row imitating (left) tongue protrusion and (right) mouth opening are 2 to 3 weeks old. The chimpanzee imitating both facial expressions is 2 weeks old. (From A. N. Meltzoff & M. K. Moore, 1977, "Imitation of Facial and Manual Gestures by Human Neonates," *Science, 198,* p. 75. Copyright © 1977 by AAAS. Reprinted with permission of the AAAS and A. N. Meltzoff. And from M. Myowa-Yamakoshi et al., 2004, "Imitation in Neonatal Chimpanzees [Pan Troglodytes]." *Developmental Science, 7,* p. 440. Copyright 2004 by Blackwell Publishing. Reproduced with permission of John Wiley & Sons Ltd.)

ASK YOURSELF

REVIEW Provide an example of classical conditioning, of operant conditioning, and of habituation/recovery in young infants. Why is each type of learning useful?

APPLY Nine-month-old Byron has a toy with large, colored push buttons on it. Each time he pushes a button, he hears a nursery tune. Which learning capacity is the manufacturer of this toy taking advantage of? What can Byron's play with the toy reveal about his perception of sound patterns?

Motor Development

Carolyn, Monica, and Vanessa each kept a baby book, filled with proud notations about when their children first held up their heads, reached for objects, sat by themselves, and walked alone. Parents are understandably excited about these new motor skills, which allow babies to master their bodies and the environment in new ways. For example, sitting upright gives infants a new perspective on the world. Reaching permits babies to find out about objects by acting on them. And when infants can move on their own, exploration multiplies.

Babies' motor achievements have a powerful effect on their social relationships. When Caitlin crawled at 7½ months, Carolyn and David began to restrict her movements. When she walked three days after her first birthday, the first "testing of wills" occurred (Biringen et al., 1995). Despite her mother's warnings, she sometimes pulled items from shelves that were off limits. "Don't do that!" Carolyn would say firmly, taking Caitlin's hand and redirecting her attention.

At the same time, newly walking babies more actively attend to and initiate social interaction (Clearfield, Osborn,

& Mullen, 2008; Karasik, Tamis-LeMonda, & Adolph, 2011). Caitlin frequently toddled over to her parents to express a greeting, give a hug, or show them objects of interest. Carolyn and David, in turn, increased their expressions of affection and playful activities. And when Caitlin encountered risky situations, such as a sloping walkway or a dangerous object, Carolyn and David intervened, combining emotional warnings with rich verbal and gestural information that helped Caitlin notice critical features of her surroundings and acquire language (Campos et al., 2000; Karasik et al., 2008). Motor, social, cognitive, and language competencies were developing together and supported one another.

The Sequence of Motor Development

Gross-motor development refers to control over actions that help infants get around in the environment, such as crawling, standing, and walking. *Fine-motor development* has to do with smaller movements, such as reaching and grasping. Table 4.2 shows the average age at which U.S. infants and toddlers achieve a variety of gross- and fine-motor skills. It also presents the age ranges during which most babies accomplish each skill, indicating large

TABLE 4.2
Gross- and Fine-Motor Development in the First Two Years

MOTOR SKILL	AVERAGE AGE ACHIEVED	AGE RANGE IN WHICH 90 PERCENT OF INFANTS ACHIEVE THE SKILL
When held upright, holds head erect and steady	6 weeks	3 weeks–4 months
When prone, lifts self by arms	2 months	3 weeks–4 months
Rolls from side to back	2 months	3 weeks–5 months
Grasps cube	3 months, 3 weeks	2–7 months
Rolls from back to side	4½ months	2–7 months
Sits alone	7 months	5–9 months
Crawls	7 months	5–11 months
Pulls to stand	8 months	5–12 months
Plays pat-a-cake	9 months, 3 weeks	7–15 months
Stands alone	11 months	9–16 months
Walks alone	11 months, 3 weeks	9–17 months
Builds tower of two cubes	11 months, 3 weeks	10–19 months
Scribbles vigorously	14 months	10–21 months
Walks up stairs with help	16 months	12–23 months
Jumps in place	23 months, 2 weeks	17–30 months
Walks on tiptoe	25 months	16–30 months

Note: These milestones represent overall age trends. Individual differences exist in the precise age at which each milestone is attained.
Sources: Bayley, 1969, 1993, 2005.
Photos: (top) © Laura Dwight Photography; (middle) © Laura Dwight Photography; (bottom) © Elizabeth Crews/The Image Works

individual differences in *rate* of motor progress. We would be concerned about a child's development only if many motor skills were seriously delayed.

Motor Skills as Dynamic Systems

According to **dynamic systems theory of motor development**, mastery of motor skills involves acquiring increasingly complex *systems of action*. When motor skills work as a system, separate abilities blend together, each cooperating with others to produce more effective ways of exploring and controlling the environment. For example, control of the head and upper chest combine into sitting with support. Kicking, rocking on all fours, and reaching combine to become crawling. Then crawling, standing, and stepping are united into walking (Adolph & Berger, 2006; Thelen & Smith, 1998).

Each new skill is a joint product of four factors: (1) central nervous system development, (2) the body's movement capacities, (3) the goals the child has in mind, and (4) environmental supports for the skill. Change in any element makes the system less stable, and the child starts to explore and select new, more effective motor patterns.

The broader physical environment also profoundly influences motor skills. Infants with stairs in their home learn to crawl up stairs at an earlier age and also more readily master a back-descent strategy—the safest but also the most challenging position because the baby must give up visual guidance of her goal and crawl backward (Berger, Theuring, & Adolph, 2007). And if children were reared on the moon, with its reduced gravity, they would prefer jumping to walking or running!

LOOK AND LISTEN

Spend an hour observing a newly crawling or walking baby. Note the goals that motivate the baby to move, along with the baby's effort and motor experimentation. Describe parenting behaviors and features of the environment that promote mastery of the skill. ●

When a skill is first acquired, infants must refine it. For example, in learning to walk, toddlers practice six or more hours a day, traveling the length of 29 football fields! Gradually their small, unsteady steps change to a longer stride, their feet move closer together, their toes point to the front, and their legs become symmetrically coordinated (Adolph, Vereijken, & Shrout, 2003). As movements are repeated thousands of times, they promote new synaptic connections in the brain that govern motor patterns.

Dynamic Motor Systems in Action. To find out how babies acquire motor capacities, some studies have tracked their first attempts at a skill until it became smooth and effortless. In one investigation, researchers held sounding toys alternately in front of infants' hands and feet, from the time they showed

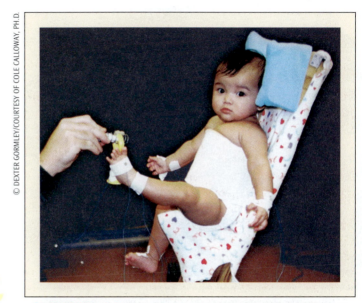

FIGURE 4.8 Reaching "feet first." When sounding toys were held in front of babies' hands and feet, they reached with their feet as early as 8 weeks of age, a month or more before they reached with their hands. This 2½-month-old skillfully explores an object with her foot.

interest until they engaged in well-coordinated reaching and grasping (Galloway & Thelen, 2004). As Figure 4.8 shows, the infants violated the normative sequence of arm and hand control preceding leg and foot control, shown in Table 4.2. They first reached for the toys with their feet—as early as 8 weeks of age, at least a month before reaching with their hands!

Why did babies reach "feet first"? Because the hip joint constrains the legs to move less freely than the shoulder constrains the arms, infants could more easily control their leg movements. Consequently, foot reaching required far less practice than hand reaching. As these findings confirm, rather than following a strict, predetermined pattern, the order in which motor skills develop depends on the anatomy of the body part being used, the surrounding environment, and the baby's efforts.

Cultural Variations in Motor Development. Cultural variations in infant-rearing practices affect motor development. *TAKE A MOMENT...* Take a quick survey of several parents you know: Should sitting, crawling, and walking be deliberately encouraged? Answers vary widely from culture to culture. Japanese mothers, for example, believe such efforts are unnecessary (Seymour, 1999). Among the Zinacanteco Indians of southern Mexico, rapid motor progress is actively discouraged (Greenfield, 1992). Babies who walk before they know enough to keep away from cooking fires and weaving looms are viewed as dangerous to themselves and disruptive to others.

In contrast, among the Kipsigis of Kenya and the West Indians of Jamaica, babies hold their heads up, sit alone, and walk considerably earlier than North American infants. In both societies, parents emphasize early motor maturity, practicing formal exercises to stimulate particular skills (Adolph, Karasik,

This West Indian mother of Jamaica "walks" her baby up her body in a deliberate effort to promote early mastery of walking.

& Tamis-LeMonda, 2010). In the first few months, babies are seated in holes dug in the ground, with rolled blankets to keep them upright. Walking is promoted by frequently bouncing babies on their feet (Hopkins & Westra, 1988; Super, 1981). As parents in these cultures support babies in upright postures and rarely put them down on the floor, their infants usually skip crawling—a motor skill regarded as crucial in Western nations!

Fine-Motor Development: Reaching and Grasping

Of all motor skills, reaching may play the greatest role in infant cognitive development. By grasping things, turning them over,

and seeing what happens when they are released, infants learn a great deal about the sights, sounds, and feel of objects.

Reaching and grasping, like many other motor skills, start out as gross, diffuse activity and move toward mastery of fine movements. Figure 4.9 illustrates some milestones of reaching over the first nine months. Newborns make poorly coordinated swipes, called *prereaching,* toward an object in front of them, but because of weak arm and hand control they rarely contact the object. Like newborn reflexes, prereaching drops out around 7 weeks of age. Yet these early behaviors suggest that babies are biologically prepared to coordinate hand with eye in the act of exploring (von Hofsten, 2004).

Around 3 to 4 months, as infants develop the necessary eye, head, and shoulder control, reaching reappears as purposeful, forward arm movements in the presence of a nearby toy and gradually improves in accuracy (Bhat, Heathcock, & Galloway, 2005; Spencer et al., 2000). By 5 to 6 months, infants reach for an object in a room that has been darkened during the reach by switching off the lights (McCarty & Ashmead, 1999). Early on, vision is freed from the basic act of reaching so it can focus on more complex adjustments. During the next few months, infants become better at reaching with one arm (rather than both) and reaching for moving objects (Fagard, Spelke, & von Hofsten, 2009; Wentworth, Benson, & Haith, 2000).

Once infants can reach, they modify their grasp. The newborn's grasp reflex is replaced by the *ulnar grasp,* a clumsy motion in which the fingers close against the palm. Still, even 4-month-olds adjust their grasp to the size and shape of an object—a capacity that improves over the first year (Barrett, Traupman, & Needham, 2008; Witherington, 2005). Around 4 to 5 months, when infants begin to sit up, both hands become coordinated in exploring objects (Rochat & Goubet, 1995). By the end of the first year, infants use the thumb and index finger opposably in a well-coordinated *pincer grasp.* Then the ability

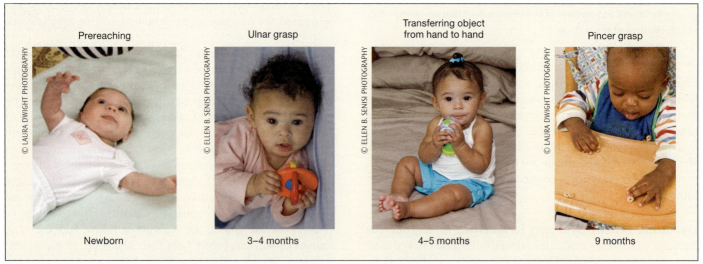

Prereaching — Newborn

Ulnar grasp — 3–4 months

Transferring object from hand to hand — 4–5 months

Pincer grasp — 9 months

FIGURE 4.9 **Some milestones of reaching and grasping.** The average age at which each skill is attained is given. (Ages from Bayley, 1969; Rochat, 1989.)

to manipulate objects greatly expands. The 1-year-old can pick up raisins and blades of grass, turn knobs, and open and close small boxes.

Finally, the capacity to reach for and manipulate an object increases infants' attention to the way an adult reaches for and plays with that same object (Hauf, Aschersleben, & Prinz, 2007). As babies watch what others do, they broaden their understanding of others' behaviors and of the range of actions that can be performed on various objects.

ASK YOURSELF

REVIEW Cite evidence that motor development is a joint product of biological, psychological, and environmental factors.

APPLY List everyday experiences that support mastery of reaching, grasping, sitting, and crawling. Why should caregivers place young infants in a variety of waking-time body positions?

REFLECT Do you favor early, systematic training of infants in motor skills such as crawling, walking, and stair climbing? Why or why not?

Perceptual Development

In Chapter 3, you learned that the senses of touch, taste, smell, and hearing—but not vision—are remarkably well-developed at birth. Now let's turn to a related question: How does perception change over the first year? Our discussion will address hearing and vision, the focus of almost all research. Recall that in Chapter 3, we used the word *sensation* to talk about these capacities. It suggests a fairly passive process—what the baby's receptors detect when exposed to stimulation. Now we use the word *perception,* which is active: When we perceive, we organize and interpret what we see. As we review the perceptual achievements of infancy, you may find it hard to tell where perception leaves off and thinking begins.

Hearing

On Timmy's first birthday, Vanessa bought several CDs of nursery songs, and she turned one on each afternoon at naptime. Soon Timmy let her know his favorite tune. If she put on "Twinkle, Twinkle," he stood up in his crib and whimpered until she replaced it with "Jack and Jill." Timmy's behavior illustrates the greatest change in hearing over the first year of life: Babies organize sounds into increasingly elaborate patterns.

Between 4 and 7 months, infants display a sense of musical phrasing: They prefer Mozart minuets with pauses between

phrases to those with awkward breaks (Krumhansl & Jusczyk, 1990). Around 6 to 7 months, they can distinguish musical tunes on the basis of variations in rhythmic patterns, including beat structure (duple or triple) and accent structure (emphasis on the first note of every beat unit or at other positions) (Hannon & Johnson, 2004). And by the end of the first year, infants recognize the same melody when it is played in different keys (Trehub, 2001). As we will see shortly, 6- to 12-month-olds make comparable discriminations in human speech.

Speech Perception. Recall from Chapter 3 that newborns can distinguish nearly all sounds in human languages and that they prefer listening to human speech over nonspeech sounds, and to their native tongue rather than a foreign language. As infants listen to people talking, they learn to focus on meaningful sound variations. ERP brain-wave recordings reveal that around 5 months, babies become sensitive to syllable stress patterns in their own language (Weber et al., 2004). Between 6 and 8 months, they start to "screen out" sounds not used in their native tongue (Anderson, Morgan, & White, 2003; Polka & Werker, 1994). As the Biology and Environment box on page 110 explains, this increased responsiveness to native-language sounds is part of a general "tuning" process in the second half of the first year—a possible sensitive period in which infants acquire a range of perceptual skills for picking up socially important information.

Soon after, infants focus on larger speech segments that are critical to figuring out meaning. They recognize familiar words in spoken passages and listen longer to speech with clear clause and phrase boundaries (Johnson & Seidl, 2008; Jusczyk & Hohne, 1997; Soderstrom et al., 2003). Around 7 to 9 months, infants extend this sensitivity to speech structure to individual words: They begin to divide the speech stream into wordlike units (Jusczyk, 2002; Saffran, Werker, & Werner, 2006).

How do infants make such rapid progress in perceiving the structure of language? Research shows that they have an impressive **statistical learning capacity.** By analyzing the speech stream for patterns—repeatedly occurring sequences of sounds—they acquire a stock of speech structures for which they will later learn meanings, long before they start to talk around age 12 months. For example, when presented with controlled sequences of nonsense syllables, babies listen for statistical regularities: They locate words by distinguishing syllables that often occur together (indicating they belong to the same word) from syllables that seldom occur together (indicating a word boundary) (Saffran, Aslin, & Newport, 1996; Saffran & Thiessen, 2003).

Once infants locate words, they focus on the words and, around 7 to 8 months, identify regular syllable-stress patterns—for example, in English and Dutch, that the onset of a strong syllable (*hap*-py, *rab*-bit) often signals a new word (Thiessen & Saffran, 2007). By 10 months, babies can detect words that start with weak syllables, such as "sur*prise*" (Kooijman, Hagoort, & Cutler, 2009).

Biology and Environment

"Tuning In" to Familiar Speech, Faces, and Music: A Sensitive Period for Culture-Specific Learning

To share experiences with members of their family and community, babies must become skilled at making perceptual discriminations that are meaningful in their culture. As we have seen, at first babies are sensitive to virtually all speech sounds, but around 6 months, they narrow their focus, limiting the distinctions they make to the language they hear and will soon learn.

The ability to perceive faces shows a similar **perceptual narrowing effect**— perceptual sensitivity that becomes increasingly attuned with age to information most often encountered. After habituating to one member of each pair of faces in Figure 4.10, 6-month-olds were shown the familiar and novel faces side-by-side. For both pairs, they recovered to (looked longer at) the novel face, indicating that they could discriminate individual faces of both humans and monkeys equally well (Pascalis, de Haan, & Nelson, 2002). But at 9 months, infants no longer showed a novelty preference when viewing the monkey pair. Like adults, they could distinguish only the human faces. Similar findings emerge with sheep faces: 4- to 6-months-olds easily distinguish them, but 9- to 11-month olds no longer do (Simpson et al., 2011).

The perceptual narrowing effect appears again in musical rhythm perception. Western adults are accustomed to the even-beat pattern of Western music—repetition of the same rhythmic structure in every measure of a tune—and easily notice rhythmic changes that disrupt this familiar beat. But present them with music that does not follow this typical Western rhythmic form— Baltic folk tunes, for example—and they fail to pick up on rhythmic-pattern deviations.

Six-month-olds, however, can detect such disruptions in both Western and non-Western melodies. But by 12 months, after added exposure to Western music, babies are no longer aware of deviations in foreign musical rhythms, although their sensitivity to Western rhythmic structure remains unchanged (Hannon & Trehub, 2005b).

Several weeks of regular interaction with a foreign-language speaker and of daily opportunities to listen to non-Western music fully restore 12-month-olds' sensitivity to wide-ranging speech sounds and music rhythms (Hannon & Trehub, 2005a; Kuhl, Tsao, & Liu, 2003). Similarly, 6-month-olds given three months of training in discriminating individual monkey faces, in which each image is labeled with a distinct name ("Carlos," "Iona") instead of the generic label "monkey," retain their ability to discriminate monkey faces at 9 months (Scott & Monesson, 2009). Adults given similar extensive experiences, by contrast, show little improvement in perceptual sensitivity.

Taken together, these findings suggest a heightened capacity—or sensitive period— in the second half of the first year, when babies are biologically prepared to "zero in" on socially meaningful perceptual distinctions. Notice how, between 6 and 12 months, learning is especially rapid across several domains (speech, faces, and music) and is easily modified by experience. This suggests a broad neurological change— perhaps a special time of experience-expectant brain growth (see page 98) in which babies analyze everyday stimulation of all kinds similarly, in ways that prepare them to participate in their cultural community.

FIGURE 4.10 Discrimination of human and monkey faces. Which of these pairs is easiest for you to tell apart? After habituating to one of the photos in each pair, infants were shown the familiar and the novel face side-by-side. For both pairs, 6-month-olds recovered to (looked longer at) the novel face, indicating that they could discriminate human and monkey faces equally well. By 12 months, babies lost their ability to distinguish the monkey faces. Like adults, they showed a novelty preference only to human stimuli. (From O. Pascalis et al., 2002, "Is Face Processing Species-Specific During the First Year of Life?" *Science, 296*, p. 1322. Copyright © 2002 by AAAS. Reprinted by permission from AAAS.)

Clearly, babies have a powerful ability to extract patterns from complex, continuous speech. Some researchers believe that infants are innately equipped with a general statistical learning capacity for detecting structure in the environment, which they also apply to nonspeech auditory information and to visual stimulation. Consistent with this idea, ERP recordings suggest that newborns perceive patterns in both sequences of speech syllables and sequences of tones (Kudo et al., 2011; Teinonen et al., 2009). And 2-month-olds detect regularities in sequences of visual stimuli (Kirkham, Slemmer, & Johnson, 2002).

Vision

For exploring the environment, humans depend on vision more than any other sense. Although at first a baby's visual world is fragmented, it undergoes extraordinary changes during the first 7 to 8 months.

Visual development is supported by rapid maturation of the eye and visual centers in the cerebral cortex. Around 2 months, infants can focus on objects about as well as adults can, and their color vision is adultlike by 4 months (Kellman & Arterberry, 2006). *Visual acuity* (fineness of discrimination) improves steadily, reaching 20/80 by 6 months and an adult level of about 20/20 by 4 years (Slater et al., 2010). Scanning the environment and tracking moving objects improve over the first half-year as infants better control their eye movements and build an organized perceptual world (Johnson, Slemmer, & Amso, 2004).

As babies explore their visual field, they figure out the characteristics of objects and how they are arranged in space. To understand how they do so, let's examine the development of depth and pattern perception.

Depth Perception.

Depth perception is the ability to judge the distance of objects from one another and from ourselves. It is important for understanding the layout of the environment and for guiding motor activity.

Figure 4.11 shows the *visual cliff,* designed by Eleanor Gibson and Richard Walk (1960) and used in the earliest studies of depth perception. It consists of a Plexiglas-covered table with a platform at the center, a "shallow" side with a checkerboard pattern just under the glass, and a "deep" side with a checkerboard several feet below the glass. The researchers found that crawling babies readily crossed the shallow side, but most reacted with fear to the deep side. They concluded that around the time infants crawl, most distinguish deep from shallow surfaces and avoid drop-offs.

The visual cliff shows that crawling and avoidance of drop-offs are linked, but not how they are related or when depth perception first appears. Subsequent research has looked at babies' ability to detect specific depth cues, using methods that do not require that they crawl.

Motion is the first depth cue to which infants are sensitive. Babies 3 to 4 weeks old blink their eyes defensively when an object moves toward their face as if it is going to hit (Nánez & Yonas, 1994). *Binocular depth cues* arise because our two eyes have slightly different views of the visual field. Sensitivity to binocular cues emerges between 2 and 3 months and improves rapidly over the first year (Brown & Miracle, 2003). Finally, beginning at 3 to 4 months and strengthening between 5 and 7 months, babies display sensitivity to *pictorial depth cues*—the ones artists often use to make a painting look three-dimensional. Examples include receding lines that create the illusion of perspective, changes in texture (nearby textures are more detailed than faraway ones), overlapping objects (an object partially hidden by another object is perceived to be more dis-

FIGURE 4.11 **The visual cliff.** Plexiglas covers the deep and shallow sides. By refusing to cross the deep side and showing a preference for the shallow side, this infant demonstrates the ability to perceive depth.

tant), and shadows cast on surfaces (indicating a separation in space between the object and the surface) (Kavšek, Yonas, & Granrud, 2012; Shuwairi, Albert, & Johnson, 2007).

Why does perception of depth cues emerge in the order just described? Researchers speculate that motor development is involved. For example, control of the head during the early weeks of life may help babies notice motion and binocular cues. Around the middle of the first year, the ability to turn, poke, and feel the surface of objects promotes sensitivity to pictorial cues as infants pick up information about size, texture, and three-dimensional shape (Bushnell & Boudreau, 1993; Soska, Adolph, & Johnson, 2010). And as we will see next, one aspect of motor progress—independent movement—plays a vital role in refinement of depth perception.

Independent Movement and Depth Perception.

At 6 months, Timmy started crawling. "He's fearless!" exclaimed Vanessa. "If I put him down in the middle of my bed, he crawls

Infants must learn to use depth cues to avoid falling in each new position—sitting, crawling, walking—and in various situations. As this 10-month-old takes her first steps, she uses vision to make postural adjustments, and her understanding of depth expands.

right over the edge. The same thing happens by the stairs." Will Timmy become wary of the side of the bed and the staircase as he becomes a more experienced crawler? Research suggests that he will. From extensive everyday experience, babies gradually figure out how to use depth cues in each body position (sitting, crawling, then walking) to detect the danger of falling (Adolph, 2008). For example, infants with more crawling experience (regardless of when they started to crawl) are far more likely to refuse to cross the deep side of the visual cliff. And with increased walking experience, toddlers figure out how to navigate slopes and uneven surfaces by making the necessary postural adjustments (Adolph et al., 2008; Joh & Adolph, 2006). As infants discover how to avoid falling in different postures and situations, their understanding of depth expands.

Independent movement promotes other aspects of three-dimensional understanding. Seasoned crawlers are better than their inexperienced agemates at remembering object locations and finding hidden objects (Campos et al., 2000). Why does crawling make such a difference? *TAKE A MOMENT...* Compare your own experience of the environment when you are driven from one place to another with what you experience when you walk or drive yourself. When you move on your own, you are much more aware of landmarks and routes of travel, and you take more careful note of what things look like from different points of view. The same is true for infants.

Pattern and Face Perception. Even newborns prefer to look at patterned rather than plain stimuli (Fantz, 1961). But because of their poor vision, very young babies cannot resolve the features in complex patterns, so they prefer, for example, to look at a checkerboard with large, bold squares than one with many small squares. Around 2 months, when detection of fine-grained detail has improved, infants spend more time looking at the more complex checkerboard (Gwiazda & Birch, 2001). With age, they prefer increasingly intricate patterns.

In the early weeks of life, infants respond to the separate parts of a pattern, staring at single, high-contrast features (Hunnius & Geuze, 2004a, 2004b). At 2 to 3 months, when vision improves and infants can better control their scanning, they thoroughly explore a pattern's features (Bronson, 1994).

Once babies take in all aspects of a pattern, they integrate the parts into a unified whole. Gradually, they become so good at detecting pattern organization that they perceive subjective boundaries that are not really present. For example, 9-month-olds look much longer at an organized series of blinking lights that resembles a human being walking than at an upside-down or scrambled version (Bertenthal, 1993). At 12 months, infants detect familiar objects represented by incomplete drawings, even when as much as two-thirds of the drawing is missing (see Figure 4.12) (Rose, Jankowski, & Senior, 1997). As these findings reveal, infants' increasing knowledge of objects and actions supports pattern perception.

Infants' tendency to search for structure in a patterned stimulus also applies to face perception. Newborns prefer to look at photos and simplified drawings of faces with features arranged naturally (upright) rather than unnaturally (upside-down or sideways) (see Figure 4.13) (Cassia, Turati, & Simion, 2004; Mondloch et al., 1999). They also track a facelike pattern moving across their visual field farther than they track other stimuli (Johnson, 1999). Yet another amazing capacity is newborns' tendency to look longer at both human and animal faces

FIGURE 4.12 Subjective boundaries in visual patterns. What does the image, missing two-thirds of its outline, look like to you? By 12 months, infants detect a motorcycle. After habituating to the incomplete motorcycle image, they were shown an intact motorcycle figure paired with a novel form. Twelve-month-olds recovered to (looked longer at) the novel figure, indicating that they recognized the motorcycle pattern on the basis of very little visual information. (Adapted from Rose, Jankowski, & Senior, 1997.)

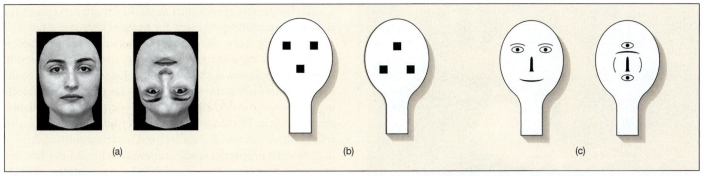

FIGURE 4.13 **Early face perception.** Newborns prefer to look at the photo of a face (a) and the simple pattern resembling a face (b) over the upside-down versions. (c) When the complex drawing of a face on the left and the equally complex, scrambled version on the right are moved across newborns' visual field, they follow the face longer. But if the two stimuli are stationary, infants show no preference for the face until around 2 months of age. (From Cassia, Turati, & Simion, 2004; Johnson, 1999; Mondloch et al., 1999.)

judged by adults as attractive—a preference that may be the origin of the widespread social bias favoring physically attractive people (Quinn et al., 2008; Slater et al., 2010).

Some researchers claim that these behaviors reflect a built-in capacity to orient toward members of one's own species, just as many newborn animals do (Slater et al., 2011). Others assert that newborns prefer any stimulus in which the most salient elements are arranged horizontally in the upper part of a pattern—like the "eyes" in Figure 4.13b (Turati, 2004). Another conjecture is that newborns are exposed to faces more often than to other stimuli—early experiences that might quickly "wire" the brain to detect faces and prefer attractive ones (Nelson, 2001).

Although newborns respond to facelike structures, they cannot discriminate a complex facial pattern from other, equally complex patterns (see Figure 4.13c). But from repeated exposures to their mother's face, they quickly learn to prefer her face to that of an unfamiliar woman, although they mostly attend to its broad outlines. Around 2 months, when they can combine pattern elements into an organized whole, babies prefer a complex drawing of the human face to other equally complex stimulus arrangements (Dannemiller & Stephens, 1988). And they clearly prefer their mother's detailed facial features to those of another woman (Bartrip, Morton, & de Schonen, 2001).

Around 3 months, infants make fine distinctions among the features of different faces—for example, between photographs of two strangers, even when the faces are moderately similar (Farroni et al., 2007). At 5 months—and strengthening over the second half-year—infants perceive emotional expressions as meaningful wholes. They treat positive faces (happy and surprised) as different from negative ones (sad and fearful) (Bornstein & Arterberry, 2003; Ludemann, 1991).

Experience influences face processing, leading babies to form group biases at a tender age. As early as 3 months, infants prefer and more easily discriminate among female faces than among male faces (Quinn et al., 2002; Ramsey-Rennels & Langlois, 2006). The greater time infants spend with female adults explains this effect, since babies with a male primary

caregiver prefer male faces. Furthermore, 3- to 6-month-olds exposed mostly to members of their own race prefer to look at the faces of members of that race and more easily detect differences among those faces (Bar-Haim et al., 2006; Kelly et al., 2007, 2009). This own-race face preference is absent in babies who have frequent contact with members of other races (Sangrigoli et al., 2005). ***TAKE A MOMENT...*** Notice how early experience promotes *perceptual narrowing* with respect to gender and racial information in faces, as occurs for species information, discussed in the Biology and Environment box on page 110.

Intermodal Perception

Our world provides rich, continuous *intermodal stimulation*—simultaneous input from more than one modality, or sensory system. In **intermodal perception,** we make sense of these running streams of light, sound, tactile, odor, and taste information, perceiving them as integrated wholes.

Babies perceive input from different sensory systems in a unified way by detecting *amodal sensory properties*—information that overlaps two or more sensory systems. Consider the sight and sound of a bouncing ball or the face and voice of a speaking person. In each event, visual and auditory information occur simultaneously and with the same rate, rhythm, duration, and intensity.

Even newborns are impressive perceivers of amodal properties. After touching an object placed in their palms, they recognize it visually, distinguishing it from a different-shaped object (Sann & Streri, 2007). And they require just one exposure to learn the association between the sight and sound of a toy, such as a rhythmically jangling rattle (Morrongiello, Fenwick, & Chance, 1998).

Within the first half-year, infants master a remarkable range of intermodal relationships. Three- to 4-month-olds can match faces with voices on the basis of lip–voice synchrony, emotional expression, and even age and gender of the speaker (Bahrick, Netto, & Hernandez-Reif, 1998). Between 4 and 6 months, infants can perceive and remember the unique face–

This baby exploring the surface of a guitar readily picks up amodal information, such as common rate, rhythm, duration, and temporal synchrony, in the visual appearance and sounds of its moving strings.

voice pairings of unfamiliar adults (Bahrick, Hernandez-Reif, & Flom, 2005).

How does intermodal perception develop so quickly? Young infants seem biologically primed to focus on amodal information. Their detection of amodal relations—for example, the common tempo and rhythm in sights and sounds—precedes and seems to provide the basis for detecting more specific inter-modal matches, such as the relation between a particular person's face and the sound of her voice or between an object and its verbal label (Bahrick, Hernandez-Reif, & Flom, 2005).

Intermodal sensitivity is crucial for perceptual development. In the first few months, when much stimulation is unfamiliar and confusing, it enables babies to notice meaningful correlations between sensory inputs and rapidly make sense of their surroundings (Bahrick, Lickliter, & Flom, 2004). And as the examples just reviewed suggest, intermodal perception also facilitates social and language processing.

Finally, early parent–infant interaction presents babies with a rich intermodal context consisting of many concurrent sights, sounds, and touches that helps them process information and learn faster (Bahrick, 2010). Intermodal perception is a fundamental capacity that fosters all aspects of psychological development.

Understanding Perceptual Development

Now that we have reviewed the development of infant perceptual capacities, how can we put together this diverse array of amazing achievements? Widely accepted answers come from the work of Eleanor and James Gibson. According to the Gibsons' **differentiation theory,** infants actively search for *invariant features* of the environment—those that remain stable—in a constantly changing perceptual world. In pattern perception, for example, young babies search for features that stand out and orient toward faces. Soon they thoroughly explore internal features, noticing *stable relationships* among them. As a result, they detect patterns, such as complex designs and faces. Similarly, infants analyze the speech stream for regularities, detecting words, word-order sequences, and—within words—syllable-stress patterns. The development of intermodal perception also reflects this principle. Babies seek out invariant relationships—first, amodal properties, such as common rate and rhythm in a voice and face, and later, more detailed associations, such as unique voice–face matches.

The Gibsons described their theory as *differentiation* (where *differentiate* means "analyze" or "break down") because over time, the baby detects finer and finer invariant features among stimuli. Thus, one way of understanding perceptual development is to think of it as a built-in tendency to seek order and consistency—a capacity that becomes increasingly fine-tuned with age (Gibson, 1970; Gibson, 1979).

Infants constantly look for ways in which the environment *affords possibilities for action* (Gibson, 2000, 2003). By exploring their surroundings, they figure out which things can be grasped, squeezed, bounced, or stroked and whether a surface is safe to cross or presents the possibility of falling (Adolph & Eppler, 1998, 1999). And from handling objects, babies become more aware of a variety of observable object properties (Perone et al., 2008). As a result, they differentiate the world in new ways and act more competently.

As we conclude this chapter, it is only fair to note that some researchers believe that babies do more than make sense of experience by searching for invariant features and action possibilities: They also *impose meaning on* what they perceive, constructing categories of objects and events in the surrounding environment. We have seen the glimmerings of this *cognitive* point of view in this chapter. For example, older babies *interpret* a familiar face as a source of pleasure and affection and a pattern of blinking lights as a moving human being. This cognitive perspective also has merit in understanding the achievements of infancy. In fact, many researchers combine these two positions, regarding infant development as proceeding from a perceptual to a cognitive emphasis over the first year of life.

ASK YOURSELF

REVIEW Using examples, explain why intermodal perception is vital for infants' developing understanding of their physical and social worlds.

APPLY After several weeks of crawling, Ben learned to avoid going headfirst down a steep incline. He has just started to walk. Can his parents trust him not to try walking down a steep surface? Explain.

SUMMARY

Body Growth (p. 92)

Describe major changes in body growth over the first two years.

- Height and weight gains are rapid during the first two years. Body fat is laid down quickly during the first nine months, whereas muscle development is slow and gradual. Body proportions change as growth follows the **cephalocaudal** and **proximodistal trends.**

Brain Development (p. 93)

Describe brain development during infancy and toddlerhood, including appropriate stimulation to support the brain's potential.

- Early in development, the brain grows faster than any other organ of the body. Once **neurons** are in place, they rapidly form **synapses.** To communicate, neurons release chemicals called **neurotransmitters,** which cross synapses. **Programmed cell death** makes space for neural fibers and synapses. Neurons that are seldom stimulated lose their synapses in a process called **synaptic pruning. Glial cells,** responsible for **myelination,** multiply rapidly through the second year, contributing to large gains in brain weight.

- The **cerebral cortex** is the largest, most complex brain structure and the last to stop growing. Its frontal lobes, which contain the **prefrontal cortex,** have the most extended period of development. Gradually, the hemispheres of the cerebral cortex specialize, a process called **lateralization.** But in the first few years of life, there is high **brain plasticity,** with many areas not yet committed to specific functions.

- Stimulation of the brain is essential during sensitive periods, when the brain is developing most rapidly. Prolonged early deprivation can impair functioning of the cerebral cortex, especially the prefrontal cortex, and interfere with the brain's capacity to manage stress, with long-term physical and psychological consequences.

- Early **experience-expectant brain growth** depends on ordinary experiences. No evidence exists for a sensitive period in the first few years for **experience-dependent brain growth,** which relies on specific learning experiences.

How does the organization of sleep and wakefulness change over the first two years?

- Infants' changing arousal patterns are primarily affected by brain growth, but the social environment also plays a role. Periods of sleep and wakefulness become fewer but longer, increasingly conforming to a night–day schedule. Parents in Western nations try to get their babies to sleep through the night much earlier than parents throughout most of the world, who are more likely to sleep with their babies.

Influences on Early Physical Growth (p. 100)

Cite evidence that heredity and nutrition both contribute to early physical growth.

- Twin and adoption studies reveal that heredity contributes to body size and rate of physical growth.

- Breast milk is ideally suited to infants' growth needs. Breastfeeding protects against disease and prevents malnutrition and infant death in poverty-stricken areas of the world. Because of unhealthy parental feeding practices, the relationship between rapid weight gain in infancy and later obesity is strengthening.

© LIBA TAYLOR/ALAMY IMAGES

- **Marasmus** and **kwashiorkor,** two dietary diseases caused by malnutrition, affect many children in developing countries. If prolonged, they can permanently stunt body growth and brain development.

Learning Capacities (p. 103)

Describe infant learning capacities, the conditions under which they occur, and the unique value of each.

- **Classical conditioning** is based on the infant's ability to associate events that usually occur together in the everyday world. Infants can be classically conditioned most easily when the pairing of an **unconditioned stimulus (UCS)** and a **conditioned stimulus (CS)** has survival value.

- In **operant conditioning,** infants act on the environment, and their behavior is followed by either **reinforcers,** which increase the occurrence of a preceding behavior, or **punishment,** which decreases the occurrence of a response. In young infants, interesting sights and sounds and pleasurable caregiver interaction serve as effective reinforcers.

- **Habituation** and **recovery** reveal that at birth, babies are attracted to novelty. Novelty preference (recovery to a novel stimulus) assesses recent memory, whereas familiarity preference (recovery to the familiar stimulus) assesses remote memory.

- Newborns have a primitive ability to imitate adults' facial expressions and gestures. **Imitation** is a powerful means of learning and contributes to the parent–infant bond. Specialized cells called **mirror neurons** underlie infants' capacity to imitate, but whether imitation is a voluntary capacity in newborns remains controversial.

Motor Development (p. 106)

Describe dynamic systems theory of motor development, along with factors that influence motor progress in the first two years.

- According to **dynamic systems theory of motor development,** children acquire new motor skills by combining existing skills into increasingly complex systems of action. Each new skill is a joint product of central nervous system development, the body's movement possibilities, the child's goals, and environmental supports for the skill. Cultural values and child-rearing customs also contribute to motor development.

- During the first year, infants perfect reaching and grasping. Reaching gradually becomes more accurate and flexible, and the clumsy ulnar grasp is transformed into a refined pincer grasp.

Perceptual Development
(p. 109)

What changes in hearing, depth and pattern perception, and intermodal perception take place during infancy?

- Infants organize sounds into increasingly complex patterns and, as part of the **perceptual narrowing effect,** begin to "screen out" sounds not used in their native tongue by the middle of the first year. An impressive **statistical learning capacity** enables babies to detect regular sound patterns in speech, for which they will later learn meanings.

- Rapid maturation of the eye and visual centers in the brain supports the development of focusing, color discrimination, and visual acuity during the first half-year. The ability to scan the environment and track moving objects also improves.

- Research on depth perception reveals that responsiveness to motion cues develops first, followed by sensitivity to binocular and then to pictorial cues. Experience in independent movement enhances depth perception and other aspects of three-dimensional understanding

- At first, babies stare at single, high-contrast features of a pattern. At 2 to 3 months, they thoroughly explore a pattern's features and start to detect pattern organization. Over time, they discriminate increasingly complex, meaningful patterns.

- Newborns prefer to look at and track simple, facelike stimuli, and they look longer at attractive faces. Around 2 months, they prefer their mother's facial features, and at 3 months, they distinguish the features of different faces. Starting at 5 months, they perceive emotional expressions as meaningful wholes.

- From the start, infants are capable of **intermodal perception.**

Explain differentiation theory of perceptual development.

- According to **differentiation theory,** perceptual development is a matter of detecting invariant features in a constantly changing perceptual world. Acting on the world plays a major role in perceptual differentiation. From a more cognitive perspective, infants also impose meaning on what they perceive. Many researchers combine these two ideas.

Important Terms and Concepts

brain plasticity (p. 96)
cephalocaudal trend (p. 93)
cerebral cortex (p. 95)
classical conditioning (p. 103)
conditioned response (CR) (p. 103)
conditioned stimulus (CS) (p. 103)
differentiation theory (p. 114)
dynamic systems theory of motor development (p. 107)
experience-dependent brain growth (p. 98)
experience-expectant brain growth (p. 98)
glial cells (p. 94)

habituation (p. 104)
imitation (p. 104)
intermodal perception (p. 113)
kwashiorkor (p. 102)
lateralization (p. 96)
marasmus (p. 101)
mirror neurons (p. 105)
myelination (p. 94)
neurons (p. 93)
neurotransmitters (p. 94)
operant conditioning (p. 104)
perceptual narrowing effect (p. 110)

prefrontal cortex (p. 96)
programmed cell death (p. 94)
proximodistal trend (p. 93)
punishment (p. 104)
recovery (p. 104)
reinforcer (p. 104)
statistical learning capacity (p. 109)
synapses (p. 94)
synaptic pruning (p. 94)
unconditioned response (UCR) (p. 103)
unconditioned stimulus (UCS) (p. 103)

chapter
5

Cognitive Development in Infancy and Toddlerhood

© KRISTIN DUVALL/GETTY IMAGES

A father encourages his child's curiosity and delight in discovery. With the sensitive support of caring adults, infants' and toddlers' cognition and language develop rapidly.

chapter outline

Piaget's Cognitive-Developmental Theory

Piaget's Ideas About Cognitive Change • The Sensorimotor Stage • Follow-Up Research on Infant Cognitive Development • Evaluation of the Sensorimotor Stage

■ **SOCIAL ISSUES: EDUCATION** Baby Learning from TV and Video: The Video Deficit Effect

Information Processing

A General Model of Information Processing • Attention • Memory • Categorization • Evaluation of Information-Processing Findings

■ **BIOLOGY AND ENVIRONMENT** Infantile Amnesia

The Social Context of Early Cognitive Development

■ **CULTURAL INFLUENCES** Social Origins of Make-Believe Play

Individual Differences in Early Mental Development

Infant and Toddler Intelligence Tests • Early Environment and Mental Development • Early Intervention for At-Risk Infants and Toddlers

Language Development

Theories of Language Development • Getting Ready to Talk • First Words • The Two-Word Utterance Phase • Individual and Cultural Differences • Supporting Early Language Development

When Caitlin, Grace, and Timmy, each nearly 18 months old, gathered at Ginette's child-care home, the playroom was alive with activity. Grace dropped shapes through holes in a plastic box that Ginette held and adjusted so the harder ones would fall smoothly into place. Once a few shapes were inside, Grace grabbed the box and shook it, squealing with delight as the lid fell open and the shapes scattered around her. The clatter attracted Timmy, who picked up a shape, carried it to the railing at the top of the basement steps, and dropped it overboard, then followed with a teddy bear, a ball, his shoe, and a spoon.

As the toddlers experimented, I could see the beginnings of spoken language—a whole new way of influencing the world. "All gone baw!" Caitlin exclaimed as Timmy tossed the bright red ball down the basement steps. Later that day, Grace revealed the beginnings of make-believe. "Night-night," she said, putting her head down and closing her eyes.

Over the first two years, the small, reflexive newborn baby becomes a self-assertive, purposeful being who solves simple prob-

lems and starts to master the most amazing human ability: language. Parents wonder, How does all this happen so quickly? This question has also captivated researchers, yielding a wealth of findings along with vigorous debate over how to explain the astonishing pace of infant and toddler cognition.

In this chapter, we take up three perspectives on early cognitive development: Piaget's *cognitive-developmental theory, information processing,* and Vygotsky's *sociocultural theory.* We also consider the usefulness of tests that measure infants' and toddlers' intellectual progress. Finally, we look at the beginnings of language. We will see how toddlers' first words build on early cognitive achievements and how, very soon, new words and expressions greatly increase the speed and flexibility of thinking. ●

Piaget's Cognitive-Developmental Theory

Swiss theorist Jean Piaget inspired a vision of children as busy, motivated explorers whose thinking develops as they act directly on the environment. According to Piaget, all aspects of cognition develop in an integrated fashion, changing in a similar way at about the same time as children move through four stages between infancy and adolescence.

Piaget's first stage, the **sensorimotor stage,** spans the first two years of life. Piaget believed that infants and toddlers "think" with their eyes, ears, hands, and other sensorimotor equipment. They cannot yet carry out many activities inside their heads. But by the end of toddlerhood, children can solve practical, everyday problems and represent their experiences in speech, gesture, and play.

Piaget's Ideas About Cognitive Change

According to Piaget, specific psychological structures—organized ways of making sense of experience called **schemes**—change with age. At first, schemes are sensorimotor action patterns. For example, at 6 months, Timmy dropped objects in a fairly rigid way, simply letting go of a rattle and watching with interest. By 18 months, his "dropping scheme" had become deliberate and creative. In tossing objects down the basement stairs, he threw some in the air, bounced others off walls, released some gently and others forcefully. Soon, instead of just acting on objects, he will show evidence of thinking before he acts. For Piaget, this change marks the transition from sensorimotor to preoperational thought.

In Piaget's theory, two processes, *adaptation* and *organization,* account for changes in schemes.

Adaptation. *TAKE A MOMENT...* The next time you have a chance, notice how infants and toddlers tirelessly repeat actions that lead to interesting effects. **Adaptation** involves building schemes through direct interaction with the environment. It consists of two complementary activities, *assimilation* and *accommodation.* During **assimilation,** we use our current schemes to interpret the external world. For example, when Timmy dropped objects, he was assimilating them to his senso-

In Piaget's theory, first schemes are sensorimotor action patterns. As this 11-month-old repeatedly experiments with her dropping scheme, her dropping behavior becomes more deliberate and varied.

rimotor "dropping scheme." In **accommodation,** we create new schemes or adjust old ones after noticing that our current ways of thinking do not capture the environment completely. When Timmy dropped objects in different ways, he modified his dropping scheme to take account of the varied properties of objects.

According to Piaget, the balance between assimilation and accommodation varies over time. When children are not changing much, they assimilate more than they accommodate—a steady, comfortable state that Piaget called cognitive *equilibrium*. During rapid cognitive change, however, children are in a state of *disequilibrium,* or cognitive discomfort. Realizing that new information does not match their current schemes, they shift from assimilation toward accommodation. After modifying their schemes, they move back toward assimilation, exercising their newly changed structures until they are ready to be modified again.

Each time this back-and-forth movement between equilibrium and disequilibrium occurs, more effective schemes are produced. Because the times of greatest accommodation are the earliest ones, the sensorimotor stage is Piaget's most complex period of development.

Organization.
Schemes also change through **organization,** a process that takes place internally, apart from direct contact with the environment. Once children form new schemes, they rearrange them, linking them with other schemes to create a strongly interconnected cognitive system. For example, eventually Timmy will relate "dropping" to "throwing" and to his developing understanding of "nearness" and "farness." According to Piaget, schemes truly reach equilibrium when they become part of a broad network of structures that can be jointly applied to the surrounding world (Piaget, 1936/1952).

In the following sections, we will first describe infant development as Piaget saw it, noting research that supports his observations. Then we will consider evidence demonstrating that, in some ways, babies' cognitive competence is more advanced than Piaget believed.

The Sensorimotor Stage

The difference between the newborn baby and the 2-year-old child is so vast that Piaget divided the sensorimotor stage into six substages, summarized in Table 5.1. Piaget based this sequence on a very small sample: observations of his son and two daughters as he presented them with everyday problems (such as hidden objects) that helped reveal their understanding of the world.

According to Piaget, at birth infants know so little that they cannot explore purposefully. The **circular reaction** provides a special means of adapting their first schemes. It involves stumbling onto a new experience caused by the baby's own motor activity. The reaction is "circular" because, as the infant tries to repeat the event again and again, a sensorimotor response that first occurred by chance strengthens into a new scheme. Consider Caitlin, who at age 2 months accidentally made a smacking noise after a feeding. Intrigued, she tried to repeat it until she became expert at smacking her lips. Infants' difficulty inhibiting new and interesting behaviors may underlie the circular reaction. This immaturity in inhibition seems to be adaptive, helping to ensure that new skills will not be interrupted before they strengthen (Carey & Markman, 1999). Piaget considered revisions in the circular reaction so important that, as Table 5.1 shows, he named the sensorimotor substages after them.

Repeating Chance Behaviors.
In Substage 1, babies suck, grasp, and look in much the same way, no matter what experiences they encounter. Around 1 month, as they enter Substage 2, infants start to gain voluntary control over their actions through the *primary circular reaction,* by repeating chance behaviors largely motivated by basic needs. This leads to some simple motor habits, such as sucking their fist or thumb. Babies also begin to vary their behavior in response to environmental demands. For example, they open their mouths differently for a nipple than for a spoon. And they start to anticipate events. When hungry, 3-month-old Timmy would stop

TABLE 5.1
Summary of Piaget's Sensorimotor Stage

SENSORIMOTOR SUBSTAGE	TYPICAL ADAPTIVE BEHAVIORS
1. Reflexive schemes (birth–1 month)	Newborn reflexes (see Chapter 3, pages 82–83)
2. Primary circular reactions (1–4 months)	Simple motor habits centered around the infant's own body; limited anticipation of events
3. Secondary circular reactions (4–8 months)	Actions aimed at repeating interesting effects in the surrounding world; imitation of familiar behaviors
4. Coordination of secondary circular reactions (8–12 months)	Intentional, or goal-directed, behavior; ability to find a hidden object in the first location in which it is hidden (object permanence); improved anticipation of events; imitation of behaviors slightly different from those the infant usually performs
5. Tertiary circular reactions (12–18 months)	Exploration of the properties of objects by acting on them in novel ways; imitation of novel behaviors; ability to search in several locations for a hidden object (accurate A–B search)
6. Mental representation (18 months–2 years)	Internal depictions of objects and events, as indicated by sudden solutions to problems; ability to find an object that has been moved while out of sight (invisible displacement); deferred imitation; and make-believe play

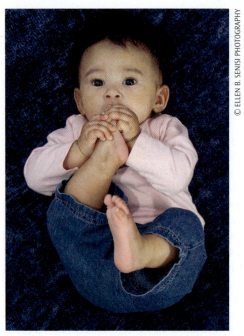

This 3-month-old tries to repeat a newly discovered action—sucking her toes—in a primary circular reaction that helps her gain voluntary control over her behavior.

crying as soon as Vanessa entered the room—a signal that feeding time was near.

During Substage 3, from 4 to 8 months, infants sit up and reach for and manipulate objects. These motor achievements strengthen the *secondary circular reaction,* through which babies try to repeat interesting events in the surrounding environment that are caused by their own actions. For example, 4-month-old Caitlin accidentally knocked a toy hung in front of her, producing a swinging motion. Over the next three days, Caitlin tried to repeat this effect, gradually forming a new "hitting" scheme.

Intentional Behavior.
In Substage 4, 8- to 12-month-olds combine schemes into new, more complex action sequences. As a result, actions that lead to new schemes no longer have a hit-or-miss quality—*accidentally* bringing the thumb to the mouth or *happening* to hit the toy. Instead, 8- to 12-month-olds can engage in **intentional, or goal-directed, behavior,** coordinating schemes deliberately to solve simple problems. Consider Piaget's famous object-hiding task, in which he shows the baby an attractive toy and then hides it behind his hand or under a cover. Infants of this substage can find the object by coordinating two schemes—"pushing" aside the obstacle and "grasping" the toy. Piaget regarded these *means–end action sequences* as the foundation for all problem solving.

Retrieving hidden objects reveals that infants have begun to master **object permanence,** the understanding that objects continue to exist when out of sight. But babies still make the *A-not-B search error:* If they reach several times for an object at a first hiding place (A), then see it moved to a second (B), they still search for it in the first hiding place (A).

Infants in Substage 4, who can better anticipate events, sometimes use their capacity for intentional behavior to try to change those events. At 10 months, Timmy crawled after Vanessa when she put on her coat, whimpering to keep her from leaving. Also, babies can now imitate behaviors slightly different from those they usually perform. After watching someone else, they try to stir with a spoon or push a toy car (Piaget, 1945/1951).

In Substage 5, from 12 to 18 months, the *tertiary circular reaction,* in which toddlers repeat behaviors with variation, emerges. Recall how Timmy dropped objects over the basement steps, trying first this action, then that, then another. This deliberately exploratory approach makes 12- to 18-month-olds better problem solvers. According to Piaget, this capacity to experiment leads toddlers to look for a hidden toy in several locations, displaying an accurate A–B search. Their more flexible action patterns also permit them to imitate many more behaviors.

Mental Representation.
Substage 6 brings the ability to create **mental representations**—internal depictions of information that the mind can manipulate. Our most powerful mental representations are of two kinds: (1) *images,* or mental pictures of objects, people, and spaces; and (2) *concepts,* or categories in which similar objects or events are grouped together. We use a mental image to retrace our steps when we've misplaced something or to imitate another's behavior long after observing it. By thinking in concepts and labeling them (for example, "ball" for all rounded, movable objects used in play), we can organize our diverse experiences into more manageable units.

Representation enables older toddlers to solve advanced object permanence problems involving *invisible displacement*—finding a toy moved while out of sight, such as into a small box

To find the toy hidden under the cloth, a 10-month-old engages in intentional, goal-directed behavior—the basis for all problem solving.

Through deferred imitation, toddlers greatly expand their sensorimotor schemes. While imitating, this 2-year-old encounters a problem faced by all cookie bakers at one time or another.

while under a cover. It permits **deferred imitation**—the ability to remember and copy the behavior of models who are not present. And it makes possible **make-believe play,** in which children act out everyday and imaginary activities. As the sensorimotor stage draws to a close, mental symbols have become major instruments of thinking.

Follow-Up Research on Infant Cognitive Development

Many studies suggest that infants display a wide array of understandings earlier than Piaget believed. Recall the operant conditioning research reviewed in Chapter 4, in which newborns sucked vigorously on a nipple to gain access to interesting sights and sounds. This behavior, which closely resembles Piaget's secondary circular reaction, shows that infants explore and control the external world long before 4 to 8 months. In fact, they do so as soon as they are born.

To discover what infants know about hidden objects and other aspects of physical reality, researchers often use the **violation-of-expectation method.** They may *habituate* babies to a physical event (expose them to the event until their looking declines) to familiarize them with a situation in which their knowledge will be tested. Or they may simply show babies an *expected event* (one that follows physical laws) and an *unexpected event* (a variation of the first event that violates physical laws). Heightened attention to the unexpected event suggests that the infant is "surprised" by a deviation from physical reality and, therefore, is aware of that aspect of the physical world.

The violation-of-expectation method is controversial. Some researchers believe that it indicates limited awareness of physical events—not the full-blown, conscious understanding that was Piaget's focus in requiring infants to act on their surroundings, as in searching for hidden objects (Campos et al., 2008; Munakata, 2001). Others maintain that the method reveals only babies' perceptual preference for novelty, not their knowledge of the physical world (Bremner, 2010; Cohen, 2010; Kagan, 2008b). Let's examine this debate in light of recent evidence.

Object Permanence. In a series of studies using the violation-of-expectation method, Renée Baillargeon and her collaborators claimed to have found evidence for object permanence in the first few months of life. Figure 5.1 explains and illustrates one of these studies (Aguiar & Baillargeon, 2002; Baillargeon & DeVos, 1991).

Additional violation-of-expectation studies yielded similar results, suggesting that infants look longer at a wide variety of unexpected events involving hidden objects (Wang, Baillargeon, & Paterson, 2005). And another type of looking behavior also suggests that young infants are aware that objects persist when out of view. Four- and 5-month-olds will track a ball's path of movement as it disappears and reappears from behind a barrier,

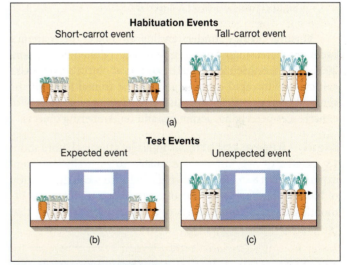

FIGURE 5.1 **Testing young infants for understanding of object permanence using the violation-of-expectation method.** (a) First, infants were habituated to two events: a short carrot and a tall carrot moving behind a yellow screen, on alternate trials. Next, the researchers presented two test events. The color of the screen was changed to help infants notice its window. (b) In the *expected event,* the carrot shorter than the window's lower edge moved behind the blue screen and reappeared on the other side. (c) In the *unexpected event,* the carrot taller than the window's lower edge moved behind the screen and did not appear in the window, but then emerged intact on the other side. Infants as young as 2½ to 3½ months looked longer at the *unexpected event,* suggesting that they had some understanding of object permanence. (Adapted from R. Baillargeon & J. DeVos, 1991, "Object Permanence in Young Infants: Further Evidence," *Child Development, 62,* p. 1230. © 1991, John Wiley and Sons. Reproduced with permission of John Wiley & Sons Ltd.)

even gazing ahead to where they expect it to emerge (Bertenthal, Longo, & Kenny, 2007; Rosander & von Hofsten, 2004). With age, babies are more likely to fixate on the predicted place of the ball's reappearance and wait for it—evidence of an increasingly secure grasp of object permanence.

Once 8- to 12-month-olds search for hidden objects, they make the A-not-B search error. Some research suggests that after finding the object several times at A, they do not attend closely when it is hidden at B (Ruffman & Langman, 2002). A more comprehensive explanation is that a dynamic system of factors—having built a habit of reaching toward A, continuing to look at A, having the hiding place at B appear similar to the one at A, and maintaining a constant body posture—increases the chances that the baby will make the A-not-B search error. Disrupting any one of these factors increases 10-month-olds' accurate searching at B (Thelen et al., 2001). In addition, older infants are still perfecting reaching and grasping (see Chapter 4) (Berger, 2010). If these motor skills are challenging, babies have little attention left to focus on inhibiting their habitual reach toward A.

LOOK AND LISTEN

Using an attractive toy and cloth, try several object-hiding tasks with 8- to 14-month-olds. Is their searching behavior consistent with research findings? ●

In sum, babies' understanding of object permanence becomes increasingly complex with age (Cohen & Cashon, 2006; Moore & Meltzoff, 2008). Success at object search tasks coincides with rapid development of the frontal lobes of the cerebral cortex (Bell, 1998). Also crucial are a wide variety of experiences perceiving, acting on, and remembering objects.

Mental Representation. In Piaget's theory, before about 18 months of age, infants are unable to mentally represent experience. Yet 8- to 10-month-olds' ability to recall the location of hidden objects after delays of more than a minute, and 14-month-olds' recall after delays of a day or more, indicate that

babies construct mental representations of objects and their whereabouts (McDonough, 1999; Moore & Meltzoff, 2004). And in studies of deferred imitation and problem solving, representational thought is evident even earlier.

Deferred and Inferred Imitation. Piaget studied deferred imitation by noting when his three children demonstrated it in their everyday behavior. But laboratory research suggests that it is present at 6 weeks of age! Infants who watched an unfamiliar adult's facial expression imitated it when exposed to the same adult the next day (Meltzoff & Moore, 1994). As motor capacities improve, infants copy actions with objects. In one study, an adult showed 6- and 9-month-olds a novel series of actions with a puppet: taking its glove off, shaking the glove to ring a bell inside, and replacing the glove. When tested a day later, infants who had seen the novel actions were far more likely to display them (see Figure 5.2) (Barr, Marrott, & Rovee-Collier, 2003).

Between 12 and 18 months, toddlers use deferred imitation skillfully to enrich their range of sensorimotor schemes. They retain modeled behaviors for at least several months, copy the actions of peers as well as adults, and imitate across a change in context—for example, enact at home a behavior seen at child care (Klein & Meltzoff, 1999; Meltzoff & Williamson, 2010). The ability to recall modeled behaviors in the order they occurred—evident as early as 6 months—also strengthens (Bauer, 2006; Rovee-Collier & Cuevas, 2009). And when toddlers imitate in correct sequence, they remember more behaviors (Knopf, Kraus, & Kressley-Mba, 2006).

Toddlers even imitate rationally, by *inferring* others' intentions! Fourteen-month-olds are more likely to imitate purposeful than accidental behaviors (Carpenter, Akhtar, & Tomasello, 1998). And they adapt their imitative acts to a model's goals. If 12-month-olds see an adult perform an unusual action for fun (make a toy dog enter a miniature house by jumping through the chimney, even though its door is wide open), they copy the behavior. But if the adult engages in the odd behavior because she *must* (she makes the dog go through the chimney only after

FIGURE 5.2 **Testing infants for deferred imitation.** After researchers performed a novel series of actions with a puppet, this 6-month-old imitated the actions a day later—at left, removing the glove; at right, shaking the glove to ring a bell inside. With age, gains in recall are evident in deferred imitation of others' behaviors over longer delays.

(a)   (b)

finding the door is locked), 12-month-olds typically imitate the more efficient action (putting the dog through the door) (Schwier et al., 2006).

Around 18 months, toddlers can imitate actions an adult *tries* to produce, even if these are not fully realized (Olineck & Poulin-Dubois, 2007, 2009). On one occasion, Ginette attempted to pour some raisins into a bag but missed, spilling them. A moment later, Grace began dropping the raisins into the bag, indicating that she had inferred Ginette's goal.

Problem Solving. As Piaget indicated, around 7 to 8 months, infants develop intentional means–end action sequences, which they use to solve simple problems, such as pulling on a cloth to obtain a toy resting on its far end (Willatts, 1999). Soon after, infants' representational skills permit more effective problem solving than Piaget's theory suggests.

By 10 to 12 months, infants can *solve problems by analogy*— apply a solution strategy from one problem to other relevant problems. In one study, 12-month-olds who were repeatedly presented with a spoon in the same orientation (handle to one side) readily adapted their motor actions when the spoon was presented with the handle to the other side, successfully transporting food to their mouths (McCarty & Keen, 2005). These findings reveal that at the end of the first year, infants have some ability to move beyond trial-and-error experimentation, represent a solution mentally, and use it in a new context.

Symbolic Understanding. One of the most momentous early attainments is the realization that words can be used to cue mental images of things not physically present—a symbolic capacity called **displaced reference** that emerges around the first birthday. It greatly expands toddlers' capacity to learn about the world through communicating with others. Observations of 12-month-olds reveal that they respond to the label of an absent toy by looking at and gesturing toward the spot where it usually

rests (Saylor, 2004). But at first, toddlers have difficulty using language to acquire new information about an absent object. In one study, an adult taught 19- and 22-month-olds a name for a stuffed animal—"Lucy" for a frog. Then, with the frog out of sight, the toddler was told that some water had spilled, so "Lucy's all wet!" Finally, the adult showed the toddler three stuffed animals—a wet frog, a dry frog, and a pig—and said, "Get Lucy!" (Ganea et al., 2007). Although all the children remembered that Lucy was a frog, only the 22-month-olds identified the wet frog as Lucy. This capacity to use language as a flexible symbolic tool—to modify and enrich existing mental representations—improves into the preschool years.

As long as pictures strongly resemble real objects, awareness of their symbolic function is evident by the middle of the second year. After hearing a novel label ("blicket") applied to a color photo of an unfamiliar object, most 15- to 24-month-olds—when presented with both the real object and its picture and asked to indicate the "blicket"—gave a symbolic response. They selected either the real object or both the object and its picture, not the picture alone (Ganea et al., 2009). Around this time, toddlers increasingly use pictures as vehicles for communicating with others and acquiring new knowledge (Ganea, Pickard, & DeLoache, 2008). They point to, name, and talk about pictures, and they can apply something learned from a book with realistic-looking pictures to real objects, and vice versa.

How do infants and toddlers interpret another ever-present, pictorial medium—video? Turn to the Social Issues: Education box on page 124 to find out.

Evaluation of the Sensorimotor Stage

Table 5.2 summarizes the remarkable cognitive attainments we have just considered. ***TAKE A MOMENT...*** Compare this table with Piaget's description of the sensorimotor substages in

TABLE 5.2

Some Cognitive Attainments of Infancy and Toddlerhood

AGE	COGNITIVE ATTAINMENTS
Birth–1 month	Secondary circular reactions using limited motor skills, such as sucking a nipple to gain access to interesting sights and sounds
1–4 months	Awareness of object permanence, object solidity, and gravity, as suggested by violation-of-expectation findings; deferred imitation of an adult's facial expression over a short delay (one day)
4–8 months	Improved knowledge of object properties and basic numerical knowledge, as suggested by violation-of-expectation findings; deferred imitation of an adult's novel actions on objects over a short delay (one to three days)
8–12 months	Ability to search for a hidden object when covered by a cloth; ability to solve simple problems by analogy to a previous problem
12–18 months	Ability to search in several locations for a hidden object, when a hand deposits it under a cloth, and when it is moved from one location to another (accurate A–B search); deferred imitation of an adult's novel actions on objects after long delays (at least several months) and across a change in situation (from child care to home); rational imitation, inferring the model's intentions; displaced reference of words
18 months–2 years	Ability to find an object moved while out of sight (invisible displacement); deferred imitation of actions an adult tries to produce, even if these are not fully realized; deferred imitation of everyday behaviors in make-believe play; beginning awareness of pictures and video as symbols of reality

TAKE A MOMENT... Which of the capacities listed in the table indicate that mental representation emerges earlier than Piaget believed?

Social Issues: Education

Baby Learning from TV and Video: The Video Deficit Effect

Children first become TV and video viewers in early infancy, as they are exposed to programs watched by parents and older siblings or to shows aimed at baby viewers, such as the Baby Einstein products. About 40 percent of U.S. 3-month-olds watch regularly, a figure that rises to 90 percent at age 2, a period during which average viewing time increases from just under an hour to 1½ hours a day (Zimmerman, Christakis, & Meltzoff, 2007). Although parents assume that babies learn from TV and videos, research indicates that they cannot take full advantage of them.

Initially, infants respond to videos of people as if viewing people directly—smiling, moving their arms and legs, and (by 6 months) imitating actions of a televised adult. But they confuse the images with the real thing (Barr, Muentener, & Garcia, 2007; Marian, Neisser, & Rochat, 1996). When shown videos of attractive toys, 9-month-olds manually explored the screen. By 19 months, touching had declined in favor of pointing at the images (Pierroutsakos & Troseth, 2003). Nevertheless, toddlers continue to have difficulty applying what they see on video to real situations.

In a series of studies, some 2-year-olds watched through a window while a live adult hid an object in an adjoining room, while others watched the same event on a video screen. Children in the direct viewing condition retrieved the toy easily; those in the video condition had difficulty (Troseth, 2003). This **video deficit effect**—poorer performance after a video than a live demonstration—has also been found for 2-year-olds' deferred imitation, word learning, and means–end problem solving (Deocampo, 2003; Hayne, Herbert, & Simcock, 2003; Krcmar, Grela, & Linn, 2007).

Toddlers seem to discount information on video as relevant to their everyday experiences because people do not look at and converse with them directly or establish a shared focus on objects, as their caregivers do. In one study, researchers gave some 2-year-olds an interactive video experience (using a two-way, closed-circuit video system). An adult on video interacted with the child for five minutes—calling the child by name, talking about the child's siblings and pets, waiting for the child to respond, and playing interactive games (Troseth, Saylor, & Archer, 2006). Compared with 2-year-olds who viewed the same adult in a noninteractive video, those in the interactive condition were far more likely to use a verbal cue from a person on video to retrieve a toy.

This baby thinks the child she sees on the TV screen is real. Not until she is about 2½ will she understand how onscreen images relate to real people and objects.

Around age 2½, the video deficit effect declines. Before this age, the American Academy of Pediatrics (2001) recommends against mass media exposure. In support of this advice, amount of TV viewing is negatively related to 8- to 18-month-olds' language progress (Tanimura et al., 2004; Zimmerman, Christakis, & Meltzoff, 2007). And 1- to 3-year-old heavy viewers tend to have attention, memory, and reading difficulties in the early school years (Christakis et al., 2004; Zimmerman & Christakis, 2005). When toddlers do watch TV and video, it is likely to work best as a teaching tool when it is rich in social cues—close-ups of characters who look directly at the camera, address questions to viewers, and pause to invite their response.

Table 5.1 on page 119. You will see that infants anticipate events, actively search for hidden objects, master the A–B object search, flexibly vary their sensorimotor schemes, engage in make-believe play, and treat pictures and video images symbolically within Piaget's time frame. Yet other capacities—including secondary circular reactions, understanding of object properties, first signs of object permanence, deferred imitation, problem solving by analogy, and displaced reference of words—emerge earlier than Piaget expected.

These findings show that the cognitive attainments of infancy do not develop together in the neat, stepwise fashion that Piaget assumed. They also reveal that infants comprehend a great deal before they are capable of the motor behaviors that Piaget assumed led to those understandings. How can we account for babies' amazing cognitive accomplishments?

Alternative Explanations. Unlike Piaget, who thought young babies constructed all mental representations out of sensorimotor activity, most researchers now believe that infants have some built-in cognitive equipment for making sense of experience. But intense disagreement exists over the extent of this initial understanding. Researchers who lack confidence in the violation-of-expectation method argue that babies' cognitive starting point is limited (Campos et al., 2008; Cohen, 2010; Cohen & Cashon, 2006; Kagan, 2008b). For example, some believe that newborns begin life with a set of biases for attending to certain information and with general-purpose learning procedures, such as powerful techniques for analyzing complex perceptual information. Together, these capacities enable infants to construct a wide variety of schemes (Bahrick, 2010; Quinn, 2008; Rakison, 2010).

Others, convinced by violation-of-expectation findings, believe that infants start out with impressive understandings. According to this **core knowledge perspective,** babies are born with a set of innate knowledge systems, or *core domains of thought.* Each of these prewired understandings permits a ready grasp of new, related information and therefore supports early, rapid development (Leslie, 2004; Spelke, 2004; Spelke & Kinzler, 2007). Core knowledge theorists argue that infants could not make sense of the complex stimulation around them without having been genetically "set up" in the course of evolution to comprehend its crucial aspects.

Researchers have conducted many studies of infants' *physical knowledge,* including object permanence, object solidity (that one object cannot move through another), and gravity (that an object will fall without support). Violation-of-expectation findings suggest that in the first few months, infants have some awareness of all these basic object properties and quickly build on this knowledge (Baillargeon, 2004; Hespos & Baillargeon, 2008; Luo & Baillargeon, 2005; Spelke, 2000). Core knowledge theorists also assume that an inherited foundation of *linguistic knowledge* enables swift language acquisition in early childhood—a possibility we will consider later in this chapter. Furthermore, these theorists argue, infants' early orientation toward people initiates rapid development of *psychological knowledge*—in particular, understanding of mental states, such as intentions, emotions, desires, and beliefs.

Research even suggests that infants have basic *numerical knowledge.* In the best-known study, 5-month-olds saw a screen raised to hide a single toy animal and then watched a hand place a second toy behind the screen. Finally the screen was removed to reveal either one or two toys. Infants looked longer at the unexpected, one-toy display, indicating that they kept track of the two objects and were able to add one object to another (Wynn, Bloom, & Chiang, 2002). Findings like these suggest that babies can discriminate quantities up to three and use that knowledge to perform simple arithmetic—both addition and subtraction (Kobayashi et al., 2004; Kobayashi, Hiraki, & Hasegawa, 2005).

Additional evidence suggests that 6-month-olds can distinguish among large sets of items, as long as the difference between those sets is very great—at least a factor of two. For example, they can tell the difference between 8 and 16 dots but not between 6 and 12 (Lipton & Spelke, 2004; Xu, Spelke, & Goddard, 2005). As a result, some researchers believe that infants can represent approximate large-number values, in addition to making small-number discriminations.

But babies' numerical capacities are controversial—not evident in all studies (Langer, Gillette, & Arriaga, 2003; Wakeley,

Did this toddler learn to build a block tower by repeatedly acting on objects, as Piaget assumed? Or did he begin life with innate knowledge that helps him understand objects and their relationships quickly, with little hands-on exploration?

Rivera, & Langer, 2000). These researchers point out that claims for infants' knowledge of number concepts are surprising, in view of other research indicating that before 14 to 16 months, toddlers have difficulty making less-than and greater-than comparisons between small sets. And not until the preschool years do children add and subtract small sets correctly.

The core knowledge perspective, while emphasizing native endowment, acknowledges that experience is essential for children to extend this initial knowledge. But so far, it has said little about which experiences are most important in each core domain of thought and how those experiences advance children's thinking. Despite these limitations, core knowledge research has sharpened the field's focus on specifying the starting point of human cognition and carefully tracking the changes that build on it.

Piaget's Legacy. Current research on infant cognition yields broad agreement on two issues. First, many cognitive changes of infancy are not abrupt and stagelike but gradual and continuous (Bjorklund, 2012; Courage & Howe, 2002). Second, rather than developing together, various aspects of infant cognition change unevenly because of the challenges posed by different types of tasks and infants' varying experience with them. These ideas serve as the basis for another major approach to cognitive development—*information processing.*

Before turning to this alternative point of view, let's recognize Piaget's enormous contributions. Piaget's work inspired a wealth of research on infant cognition, including studies that challenged his theory. His observations also have been of great practical value. Teachers and caregivers continue to look to the sensorimotor stage for guidelines on how to create developmentally appropriate environments for infants and toddlers.

Information Processing

Recall from Chapter 1 that the information-processing researchers are not satisfied with general concepts, such as assimilation and accommodation, to describe how children think. Instead, they want to know exactly what individuals of different ages do when faced with a task or problem (Birney & Sternberg, 2011; Miller, 2009).

A General Model of Information Processing

Most information-processing researchers assume that we hold information in three parts of the mental system for processing: the *sensory register,* the *short-term memory store,* and the *long-term memory store* (see Figure 5.3). As information flows through each, we can use *mental strategies* to operate on and transform it, increasing the chances that we will retain information, use it efficiently, and think flexibly, adapting the information to changing circumstances. To understand this more clearly, let's look at each component of the mental system.

First, information enters the **sensory register,** where sights and sounds are represented directly and stored briefly. *TAKE A MOMENT...* Look around you, and then close your eyes. An image of what you saw persists for a few seconds, but then it decays unless you use mental strategies to preserve it. For example, by *attending to* some information more carefully than to other information, you increase the chances that it will transfer to the next step of the information-processing system.

In the second part of the mind, the **short-term memory store,** we retain attended-to information briefly so we can actively "work" on it to reach our goals. One way of looking at the short-term store is in terms of its *basic capacity,* often referred to as

short-term memory: how many pieces of information can be held at once for a few seconds. But most researchers endorse a contemporary view of the short-term store, which offers a more meaningful indicator of its capacity, called **working memory—** the number of items that can be briefly held in mind while also engaging in some effort to monitor or manipulate those items. Working memory can be thought of as a "mental workspace." From childhood on, researchers assess its capacity by presenting individuals with lists of items (such as numerical digits or short sentences) and asking them to "work" on the items (for example, repeat the digits backward or remember the final word of each sentence in correct order).

The sensory register can take in a wide panorama of information. Short-term and working memory are far more restricted, though their capacity increases steadily from early childhood to early adulthood—on a verbatim digit-span task tapping short-term memory, from about 2 to 7 items; and on working-memory tasks, from about 2 to 5 items (Cowan & Alloway, 2009). Still, individual differences are evident at all ages. By engaging in a variety of basic cognitive procedures, such as focusing attention on relevant items and repeating (rehearsing) them rapidly, we increase the chances that information will be retained and accessible to ongoing thinking.

To manage the cognitive system's activities, the **central executive** directs the flow of information, implementing the basic procedures just mentioned and also engaging in more sophisticated activities that enable complex, flexible thinking. For example, the central executive coordinates incoming information with information already in the system, and it selects, applies, and monitors strategies that facilitate memory storage, comprehension, reasoning, and problem solving (Pressley & Hilden, 2006). The central executive is the conscious, reflective part of our mental system. It ensures that we think purposefully, to attain our goals.

The more effectively the central executive joins with working memory to process information, the better learned cognitive activities will be and the more *automatically* we can apply them. Consider the richness of your thinking while you automatically drive a car. **Automatic processes** are so well-learned that they require no space in working memory and, therefore, permit us to focus on other information while performing them. Furthermore, the more effectively we process information in working memory, the more likely it will transfer to the third, and largest, storage area—**long-term memory,** our permanent knowledge base, which is unlimited. In fact, we store so much in long-term memory that *retrieval*—getting information back from the system—can be problematic. To aid retrieval, we apply strategies, just as we do in working memory. Information in long-term memory is *categorized* by its contents, much like a library shelving system that enables us to retrieve items by following the same network of associations used to store them.

Information-processing research indicates that several aspects of the cognitive system improve during childhood and adolescence: (1) the *basic capacity* of its stores, especially work-

FIGURE 5.3 Model of the human information-processing system. Information flows through three parts of the mental system: the *sensory register*, the *short-term memory store*, and the *long-term memory store*. In each, mental strategies can be used to manipulate information, increasing the efficiency and flexibility of thinking and the chances that information will be retained. The *central executive* is the conscious, reflective part of the mental system. It coordinates incoming information with information already in the system, decides what to attend to, and oversees the use of strategies.

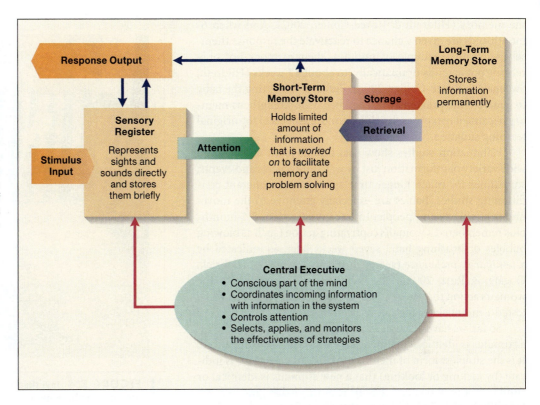

ing memory; (2) the *speed* with which information is worked on; and (3) the *functioning of the central executive*. Together, these changes make possible more complex forms of thinking with age (Case, 1998; Kail, 2003).

Gains in working-memory capacity are due in part to brain development, but greater processing speed also contributes. Fast, fluent thinking frees working-memory resources to support storage and manipulation of additional information. Furthermore, researchers have become increasingly interested in studying the development of **executive function**—the diverse cognitive operations and strategies that enable us to achieve our goals in cognitively challenging situations (Welsh, Friedman, & Spieker, 2008). These include controlling attention, suppressing impulses, coordinating information in working memory, and flexibly directing and monitoring thought and behavior. As we will see, gains in working memory capacity and aspects of executive function are under way in the first two years.

Attention

Recall from Chapter 4 that around 2 to 3 months of age, infants explore objects and patterns more thoroughly. Besides attending to more aspects of the environment, infants gradually take in information more quickly. Preterm and newborn babies require a long time—about 3 to 4 minutes—to habituate and recover to novel visual stimuli. But by 4 or 5 months, they need as little as 5 to 10 seconds to take in a complex visual stimulus and recognize it as different from a previous one (Rose, Feldman, & Jankowski, 2001; Slater et al., 1996).

Over the first year, infants attend to novel and eye-catching events. In the second year, as toddlers become increasingly capable of intentional behavior (refer back to Piaget's Substage 4), attraction to novelty declines (but does not disappear) and *sustained attention* improves. A toddler who engages even in simple goal-directed behavior, such as stacking blocks or putting them in a container, must sustain attention to reach the goal (Ruff & Capozzoli, 2003). As plans and activities gradually become more complex, the duration of attention increases.

Memory

Operant conditioning and habituation provide windows into early memory. Both methods show that retention of visual events increases dramatically over infancy and toddlerhood.

Using operant conditioning, researchers study infant memory by teaching 2- to 6-month-olds to move a mobile by kicking a foot tied to it with a long cord. Two-month-olds remember how to activate the mobile for 1 to 2 days after training, and 3-month-olds for one week. By 6 months, memory increases to two weeks (Rovee-Collier, 1999; Rovee-Collier & Bhatt, 1993). Around the middle of the first year, babies can manipulate switches or buttons to control stimulation. When 6- to 18-month-olds pressed a lever to make a toy train move around a track, duration of memory continued to increase with age; 13 weeks after training, 18-month-olds still remembered how to press the lever (Hartshorn et al., 1998).

Even after babies forget an operant response, they need only a brief prompt—an adult who shakes the mobile—to reinstate the memory (Hildreth & Rovee-Collier, 2002). And when 6-month-olds are given a chance to reactivate the response themselves for just a couple of minutes, their memory not only returns but extends dramatically, to about 17 weeks (Hildreth, Sweeney, & Rovee-Collier, 2003). Perhaps permitting the baby to generate the previously learned behavior strengthens memory because it reexposes the child to more aspects of the original learning situation.

Habituation studies show that infants learn and retain a wide variety of information just by watching objects and events, sometimes for much longer time spans than in operant conditioning studies. Babies are especially attentive to the movements of objects and people. In one investigation, 5½-month-olds remembered a woman's captivating action (such as blowing bubbles or brushing hair) seven weeks later, as indicated by a *familiarity preference* (see page 104 in Chapter 4) (Bahrick, Gogate, & Ruiz, 2002). The babies were so attentive to the woman's action that they did not remember her face, even when tested 1 minute later for a *novelty preference*.

So far, we have discussed only **recognition**—noticing when a stimulus is identical or similar to one previously experienced. It is the simplest form of memory: All babies have to do is indicate (by kicking or looking) that a new stimulus is identical or similar to a previous one. **Recall** is more challenging because it involves remembering something not present. But by the second half of the first year, infants are capable of recall, as indicated by their ability to find hidden objects and engage in deferred imitation. Recall, too, improves steadily with age.

Long-term recall depends on connections among multiple regions of the cerebral cortex, especially with the prefrontal cortex. During infancy and toddlerhood, these neural circuits develop rapidly (Nelson, Thomas, & de Haan, 2006). Yet a puzzling finding is that older children and adults no longer recall their earliest experiences! See the Biology and Environment box on the following page for a discussion of *infantile amnesia*.

Categorization

Categorization—grouping similar objects and events into a single representation—helps infants make sense of experience. It reduces the enormous amount of new information infants encounter so they can learn and remember (Rakison, 2010).

Creative variations of operant conditioning research with mobiles have been used to investigate infant categorization. One such study, of 3-month-olds, is described and illustrated in Figure 5.4. Similar investigations reveal that in the first few months, babies categorize stimuli on the basis of shape, size, and other physical properties (Wasserman & Rovee-Collier, 2001). By 6 months of age, they can categorize on the basis of two correlated features—for example, the shape and color of an alphabet letter (Bhatt et al., 2004). This ability to categorize using clusters of features prepares babies for acquiring many complex everyday categories.

Habituation has also been used to study infant categorization. Researchers show babies a series of pictures belonging to

COURTESY OF CAROLYN ROVEE-COLLIER

FIGURE 5.4 Investigating infant categorization using operant conditioning. Three-month-olds were taught to kick to move a mobile that was made of small blocks, all with the letter *A* on them. After a delay, kicking returned to a high level only if the babies were shown a mobile whose elements were labeled with the same form (the letter *A*). If the form was changed (from *A*s to *2*s), infants no longer kicked vigorously. While making the mobile move, the babies had grouped together its features. They associated the kicking response with the category *A* and, at later testing, distinguished it from the category *2*. (Bhatt, Rovee-Collier, & Weiner, 1994; Hayne, Rovee-Collier, & Perris, 1987.)

one category and then see whether they recover to (look longer at) a picture that is not a member of the category. Findings reveal that in the second half of the first year, infants group objects into an impressive array of categories—food items, furniture, land animals, air animals, sea animals, plants, vehicles, and spatial location ("above" and "below," "on" and "in") (Bornstein, Arterberry, & Mash, 2010; Casasola, Cohen, & Chiarello, 2003; Oakes, Coppage, & Dingel, 1997). Besides organizing the physical world, infants of this age categorize their emotional and social worlds. They sort people and their voices by gender and age, have begun to distinguish emotional expressions, and separate people's natural actions (walking) from other motions (see Chapter 4, page 112). Babies' earliest categories are based on similar overall appearance or prominent object part: legs for animals, wheels for vehicles. By the second half of the first year, more categories appear to be based on subtle sets of features (Mandler, 2004; Quinn, 2008). Older infants can even make categorical distinctions when the perceptual contrast between two categories is minimal (birds versus airplanes). Toddlers begin to categorize flexibly: When 14-month-olds are given four balls and four blocks, some made of soft rubber and some of rigid plastic, their sequence of object touching reveals

Biology and Environment

Infantile Amnesia

I f infants and toddlers recall many aspects of their everyday lives, how do we explain **infantile amnesia**—that most of us cannot retrieve events that happened to us before age 3? The reason cannot be merely the passage of time because we can recall many personally meaningful one-time events from both the recent and the distant past: the day a sibling was born or a move to a new house—recollections known as **autobiographical memory.**

Several accounts of infantile amnesia exist. One theory credits brain development, suggesting that vital changes in the prefrontal cortex pave the way for an *explicit* memory system—one in which children remember deliberately rather than *implicitly,* without conscious awareness (Nelson, 1995). But mounting evidence indicates that even young infants engage in conscious recall (Bauer, 2006; Rovee-Collier & Cuevas, 2009). Their memory processing is not fundamentally different from that of children and adults.

Another conjecture is that older children and adults often use verbal means for storing information, whereas infants' and toddlers' memory processing is largely nonverbal—an incompatibility that may prevent long-term retention of early experiences. To test this idea, researchers sent two adults to the homes of

2- to 4-year-olds with an unusual toy that the children were likely to remember: The Magic Shrinking Machine, shown in Figure 5.5. One adult showed the child how, after inserting an object in an opening on top of the machine and turning a crank that activated flashing lights and musical sounds, the child could retrieve a smaller, identical object (discretely dropped down a chute by the second adult) from behind a door on the front of the machine.

A day later, the researchers tested the children to see how well they recalled the event. Their nonverbal memory—based on acting out the "shrinking" event and recognizing the "shrunken" objects in photos—was excellent. But even when they had the vocabulary, children younger than age 3 had trouble describing features of the "shrinking" experience. Verbal recall increased sharply between ages 3 and 4—the period during which children "scramble over the amnesia barrier" (Simcock & Hayne, 2003, p. 813). In a second study, preschoolers could not translate their nonverbal memory for the game into language 6 months to 1 year later, when their language had improved dramatically. Their verbal reports were "frozen in time," reflecting their limited language skill at the age they played the game (Simcock & Hayne, 2002).

These findings help us reconcile infants' and toddlers' remarkable memory skills with infantile amnesia. During the first few years, children rely heavily on nonverbal memory techniques, such as visual images and motor actions. Only after age 3 do they often represent events verbally and participate in elaborate conversations with adults about them. As children encode autobiographical events in verbal form, they use language-based cues to retrieve them, increasing the accessibility of these memories at later ages (Peterson, Warren, & Short, 2011).

Other findings indicate that the advent of a clear self-image contributes to the end of infantile amnesia (Howe, Courage, & Rooksby, 2009). Toddlers who were advanced in development of a sense of self demonstrated better verbal memories a year later while conversing about past events with their mothers (Harley & Reese, 1999).

Very likely, both neurobiological change and social experience contribute to the decline of infantile amnesia. Brain development and adult–child interaction may jointly foster self-awareness, language, and improved memory, which enable children to talk with adults about significant past experiences (Bauer, 2007). As a result, preschoolers begin to construct a long-lasting autobiographical narrative of their lives and enter into the history of their family and community.

(a)

(b)

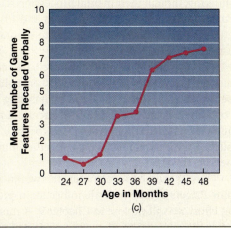

(c)

FIGURE 5.5 **The Magic Shrinking Machine, used to test young children's verbal and nonverbal memory of an unusual event.** After being shown how the machine worked, the child participated in selecting objects from a polka-dot bag, dropping them into the top of the machine (a), and turning a crank, which produced a "shrunken" object (b). When tested the next day, below 36 months, verbal recall was poor, based on the number of features recalled about the game (c). Recall improved between 36 and 48 months, the period during which infantile amnesia subsides. (From G. Simcock & H. Hayne, 2003, "Age-Related Changes in Verbal and Nonverbal Memory During Early Childhood," *Developmental Psychology, 39,* pp. 807, 809. Copyright © 2003 by the American Psychological Association. Reprinted with permission of the American Psychological Association. *Photos:* Ross Coombes/ Courtesy of Harlene Hayne.)

that after classifying by shape, they can switch to classifying by material (soft versus hard) (Ellis & Oakes, 2006).

Young toddlers' play behaviors reveal that they know certain actions (drinking) are appropriate only for animals, not inanimate objects (Mandler & McDonough, 1998). By the end of the second year, understanding of the animate–inanimate distinction expands. Nonlinear motions are typical of animates (a person or a dog jumping), linear motions of inanimates (a car or a table pushed along a surface). At 22 months, toddlers imitate a nonlinear motion only with toys in the animate category (a cat but not a bed) (Rakison, 2005, 2006). They seem to realize that whereas animates are self-propelled and therefore have varied paths of movement, inanimates move only when acted on, in restricted ways.

Researchers disagree on how toddlers gradually shift from categorizing on the basis of prominent perceptual features (things with flapping wings and feathers belong to one category; things with rigid wings and a smooth surface to another) to categorizing on a conceptual basis, grouping objects by their common function or behavior (birds versus airplanes, dogs versus cats) (Oakes et al., 2009; Rakison & Lupyan, 2008). But all acknowledge that exploration of objects and expanding knowledge of the world contribute. In addition, adult labeling ("Look at the car!" "Do you see the car?") calls babies' attention to commonalities among objects, fostering categorization as early as 3 to 4 months of age (Ferry, Hespos, & Waxman, 2010). Toddlers' vocabulary growth, in turn, fosters categorization (Cohen & Brunt, 2009).

Evaluation of Information-Processing Findings

The information-processing perspective underscores the continuity of human thinking from infancy into adult life. Infants and toddlers think in ways that are remarkably similar to adults' thinking, though their mental processing is far from proficient. And their capacity to recall events and to categorize stimuli attests, once again, to their ability to mentally represent their experiences.

Information-processing research has contributed greatly to our view of infants and toddlers as sophisticated cognitive beings. But its central strength—analyzing cognition into its components, such as perception, attention, memory, and categorization—is also its greatest drawback: It has had difficulty putting these components back together into a broad, comprehensive theory.

One approach to overcoming this weakness has been to combine Piaget's theory with the information-processing approach, an effort we will explore in Chapter 9. A more recent trend has been the application of a *dynamic systems view*. Researchers analyze each cognitive attainment to see how it results from a complex system of prior accomplishments and the child's current goals (Spencer & Perone, 2008; Thelen & Smith, 2006). Once these ideas are fully tested, they may move the field closer to a more powerful view of how the minds of infants and children develop.

The Social Context of Early Cognitive Development

Recall the description at the beginning of this chapter of Grace dropping shapes into a container. Notice that she learns about the toy with Ginette's support. According to Vygotsky's sociocultural theory, complex mental activities have their origins in social interaction (Bodrova & Leong, 2007; Rogoff, 2003). Through joint activities with more mature members of their society, children master activities and think in ways that have meaning in their culture.

A special Vygotskian concept explains how this happens. The **zone of proximal** (or potential) **development** refers to a range of tasks too difficult for the child to do alone but possible with the help of more skilled partners. To understand this idea, think about how a sensitive adult (such as Ginette) introduces a child to a new activity. The adult picks a task that the child can master but that is challenging enough that the child cannot do it by herself. As the adult guides and supports, the child joins in the interaction and picks up mental strategies. As her competence increases, the adult steps back, permitting the child to take more responsibility for the task.

A study by Barbara Rogoff and her collaborators (1984) illustrates this process. Placing a jack-in-the-box nearby, the researchers watched how several adults played with Rogoff's son and daughter over the first two years. In the early months, the adults tried to focus the baby's attention by working the toy and, as the bunny popped out, saying something like "My, what happened?" By the end of the first year, when the baby's cognitive

Using simple words and gestures, this mother brings a challenging task—rotating the plane's propeller—within her toddler's zone of proximal development. By adjusting her communication to suit the child's needs, she transfers mental strategies to him and promotes learning.

Cultural Influences

Social Origins of Make-Believe Play

One of the activities my husband, Ken, used to do with our two sons when they were young was to bake pineapple upside-down cake, a favorite treat. One Sunday afternoon as 4-year-old David stirred the batter, Ken poured some into a small bowl for 21-month-old Peter and handed him a spoon.

"Here's how you do it, Petey," instructed David, with a superior air. Peter watched as David stirred, then tried to copy his motion. When it was time to pour the batter, Ken helped Peter hold and tip the small bowl.

"Time to bake it," said Ken.

"Bake it, bake it," repeated Peter, watching Ken slip the pan into the oven.

Several hours later, we observed one of Peter's earliest instances of make-believe play. He got his pail from the sandbox and, after filling it with a handful of sand, carried it into the kitchen and put it down on the floor in front of the oven. "Bake it, bake it," Peter called to Ken. Together, father and son placed the pretend cake in the oven.

Vygotsky believed that society provides children with opportunities to represent culturally meaningful activities in play. Make-believe, he claimed, is first learned under the guidance of experts (Berk, Mann, & Ogan, 2006). In the example just described, Peter extended his capacity to represent daily events when Ken drew him into the baking task and helped him act it out in play.

Current evidence supports the idea that early make-believe is the combined result of children's readiness to engage in it and social experiences that promote it. In a study of U.S. middle-SES toddlers, 75 to 80 percent of make-believe involved mother–child interaction (Haight & Miller, 1993). At 12 months, almost all play episodes were initiated by mothers, but by the end of the second year, half of pretend episodes were initiated by each.

During make-believe, mothers offer toddlers a rich array of cues that they are pretending—looking and smiling at the child more, making more exaggerated movements, and using more "we" talk (acknowledging that pretending is a joint endeavor) than they do during the same real-life event (Lillard, 2007). When adults participate, toddlers' make-believe is more elaborate (Keren et al., 2005). And the more parents pretend with their toddlers, the more time their children devote to make-believe.

But in some cultures, such as those of Indonesia and Mexico, where sibling caregiving is common, make-believe is more frequent and complex with older siblings than with mothers. As early as age 3 to 4, children provide rich, challenging stimulation to their younger brothers and sisters, take these teaching responsibilities seriously, and, with age, become better at them (Zukow-Goldring, 2002). In a study of Zinacanteco Indian chil-

A Kenyan child guides his younger brother in pretend play. In cultures where sibling caregiving is common, make-believe play is more frequent and complex with older siblings than with mothers.

dren of southern Mexico, by age 8, sibling teachers were highly skilled at showing 2-year-olds how to play at everyday tasks, such as washing and cooking (Maynard, 2002). They often guided toddlers verbally and physically and provided feedback.

As we will see in Chapter 7, make-believe play is a major means through which children extend their cognitive skills and learn about important activities in their culture. Vygotsky's theory, and the findings that support it, tell us that providing a stimulating physical environment is not enough to promote early cognitive development. In addition, toddlers must be invited and encouraged by more skilled members of their culture to participate in the social world around them.

---

and motor skills had improved, interaction centered on how to use the toy. The adults guided the baby's hand in turning the crank and putting the bunny back in the box. During the second year, adults helped from a distance, using gestures and verbal prompts, such as making a turning motion with the hand near the crank. Research indicates that this fine-tuned support is related to advanced play, language, and problem solving in toddlerhood and early childhood (Bornstein et al., 1992; Charman et al., 2001; Tamis-LeMonda & Bornstein, 1989).

As early as the first year, cultural variations in social experiences affect mental strategies. In the jack-in-the-box example, adults and children focused their attention on a single activity—a strategy common in Western middle-SES infant and toddler play. In contrast, Guatemalan Mayan babies often attend to several events at once. For example, one 12-month-old skillfully put objects in a jar while watching a passing truck and blowing

into a toy whistle (Chavajay & Rogoff, 1999). Processing several competing events simultaneously may be vital in cultures where children largely learn through keen observation of others' ongoing activities. Children of Guatemalan Mayan, Mexican, and Native-American parents without extensive education continue to display this style of attention well into middle childhood (Correa-Chavez, Rogoff, & Mejía-Arauz, 2005).

Earlier we saw how infants and toddlers create new schemes by acting on the physical world (Piaget) and how certain skills become better developed as children represent their experiences more efficiently and meaningfully (information processing). Vygotsky adds a third dimension to our understanding by emphasizing that many aspects of cognitive development are socially mediated. The Cultural Influences box above presents additional evidence for this idea, and we will see even more in the next section.

Individual Differences in Early Mental Development

Because of Grace's deprived early environment, Kevin and Monica had a psychologist give her one of many tests available for assessing mental development in infants and toddlers. Worried about Timmy's progress, Vanessa also arranged for him to be tested. At age 22 months, he spoke only a handful of words, played in a less mature way than Caitlin and Grace, and seemed restless and overactive.

The cognitive theories we have just discussed try to explain the *process* of development—how children's thinking changes. Mental tests, in contrast, focus on cognitive *products*. Their goal is to measure behaviors that reflect development and to arrive at scores that *predict* future performance, such as later intelligence and school achievement.

Infant and Toddler Intelligence Tests

Accurately measuring infants' intelligence is a challenge because babies cannot answer questions or follow directions. As a result, most infant tests emphasize perceptual and motor responses. But new tests are being developed that also tap early language, cognition, and social behavior. One commonly used test, the *Bayley Scales of Infant and Toddler Development,* is suitable for children between 1 month and 3½ years. The most recent edition, the Bayley-III, has three main subtests: (1) the Cognitive Scale, which includes such items as attention to familiar and unfamiliar objects, looking for a fallen object, and pretend play; (2) the Language Scale, which assesses understanding and expression of language—for example, recognition of objects and people, following simple directions, and naming objects and pictures; and (3) the Motor Scale, which includes gross- and fine-motor skills, such as grasping, sitting, stacking blocks, and climbing stairs (Bayley, 2005).

Two additional Bayley-III scales depend on parental report: (4) the Social-Emotional Scale, which asks caregivers about such behaviors as ease of calming, social responsiveness, and imitation in play; and (5) the Adaptive Behavior Scale, which asks about adaptation to the demands of daily life, including communication, self-control, following rules, and getting along with others.

Computing Intelligence Test Scores. Intelligence tests for infants, children, and adults are scored in much the same way—by computing an **intelligence quotient (IQ),** which indicates the extent to which the raw score (number of items passed) deviates from the typical performance of same-age individuals. To make this comparison possible, test designers engage in **standardization**—giving the test to a large, representative sample and using the results as the *standard* for interpreting scores.

Within the standardization sample, performances at each age level form a **normal distribution,** in which most scores cluster around the mean, or average, with progressively fewer falling toward the extremes (see Figure 5.6). This *bell-shaped distribution* results whenever researchers measure individual differences in large samples. When intelligence tests are standardized, the mean IQ is set at 100. An individual's IQ is higher or lower than 100 by an amount that reflects how much his or her test performance deviates from the standardization-sample mean. In this way, the IQ indicates whether the individual is ahead, behind, or on time (average) in mental development in relation to others of the same age. The IQs of 96 percent of individuals fall between 70 and 130; only a few achieve higher or lower scores.

Predicting Later Performance from Infant Tests. Despite careful construction, most infant tests—including previous editions of the Bayley—predict later intelligence poorly. Infants and toddlers easily become distracted, fatigued, or bored

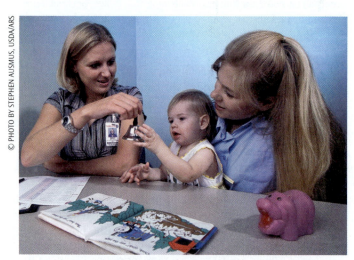

A trained examiner administers a test based on the Bayley Scales of Infant Development to a 1-year-old sitting in her mother's lap. This verbal item assesses the child's ability to name a common object.

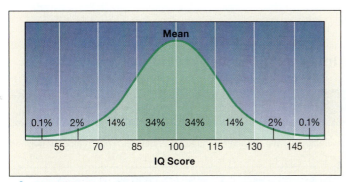

FIGURE 5.6 **Normal distribution of intelligence test scores.** To determine the percentage of same-age individuals in the population a person with a certain IQ outperformed, add the figures to the left of that IQ score. For example, an 8-year-old child with an IQ of 115 scored better than 84 percent of the population of 8-year-olds.

during testing, so their scores often do not reflect their true abilities. And infant perceptual and motor items differ from the tasks given to older children, which increasingly emphasize verbal, conceptual, and problem-solving skills. In contrast, the Bayley-III Cognitive and Language Scales, which better dovetail with childhood tests, are good predictors of preschool mental test performance (Albers & Grieve, 2007).

Most infant tests are better at making long-term predictions for extremely low-scoring babies. Today, they are largely used for *screening*—helping to identify for intervention babies who are likely to have developmental problems.

As an alternative to infant tests, some researchers have turned to information-processing measures, such as habituation, to assess early mental progress. Their findings show that speed of habituation and recovery to novel visual stimuli are among the best available infant predictors of IQ from early childhood through early adulthood (Fagan, Holland, & Wheeler, 2007; Kavšek, 2004; McCall & Carriger, 1993). Habituation and recovery seem to be an especially effective early index of intelligence because they assess memory as well as quickness and flexibility of thinking, which underlie intelligent behavior at all ages (Colombo, 2002; Colombo et al., 2004). The consistency of these findings has prompted designers of the Bayley-III to include items that tap such cognitive skills as habituation, object permanence, and categorization.

Early Environment and Mental Development

In Chapter 2, we indicated that intelligence is a complex blend of hereditary and environmental influences. As we consider evidence on the relationship of environmental factors to infant and toddler mental test scores, you will encounter findings that highlight the role of heredity as well.

Home Environment. The **Home Observation for Measurement of the Environment (HOME)** is a checklist for gathering information about the quality of children's home

lives through observation and parental interview (Caldwell & Bradley, 1994). Factors measured by HOME during the first three years include an organized, stimulating physical setting and parental affection, involvement, and encouragement. Regardless of SES and ethnicity, each predicts better language and IQ scores in toddlerhood and early childhood (Linver, Martin, & Brooks-Gunn, 2004; Tamis-LeMonda et al., 2004; Tong et al., 2007). The extent to which parents talk to infants and toddlers is particularly important. It contributes strongly to early language progress, which, in turn, predicts intelligence and academic achievement in elementary school (Hart & Risley, 1995).

Yet we must interpret these correlational findings cautiously. In all the studies, children were reared by their biological parents. Parents who are genetically more intelligent may provide better experiences while also giving birth to genetically brighter children, who evoke more stimulation from their parents. Research supports this hypothesis, which refers to *gene–environment correlation* (see Chapter 2, page 55) (Saudino & Plomin, 1997). But heredity does not account for the entire association between home environment and mental test scores. Family living conditions—both HOME scores and affluence of the surrounding neighborhood—continue to predict children's IQ beyond the contribution of parental IQ and education (Chase-Lansdale et al., 1997; Klebanov et al., 1998).

How can the research summarized so far help us understand Vanessa's concern about Timmy's development? Ben, the psychologist who tested Timmy, found that he scored only slightly below average. Ben talked with Vanessa about her child-rearing practices and watched her play with Timmy. A single parent who worked long hours, Vanessa had little energy for Timmy at the end of the day. Ben also noticed that Vanessa, anxious about Timmy's progress, tended to pressure him, dampening his active behavior and bombarding him with directions: "That's enough ball play. Stack these blocks."

Ben explained that when parents are intrusive in these ways, infants and toddlers are likely to be distractible, play immaturely, and do poorly on mental tests (Bono & Stifter, 2003; Stilson & Harding, 1997). He coached Vanessa in how to interact sensi-

A mother plays actively and affectionately with her baby. Parental warmth, attention, and verbal communication predict better language and IQ scores in toddlerhood and early childhood.

Applying What We Know

Signs of Developmentally Appropriate Infant and Toddler Child Care

Program Characteristics	Signs of Quality
Physical setting	Indoor environment is clean, in good repair, well-lighted, well-ventilated, and not overcrowded. Fenced outdoor play space is available.
Toys and equipment	Play materials are age-appropriate and placed on low shelves within easy reach. Cribs, highchairs, infant seats, and child-sized tables and chairs are available. Outdoor equipment includes riding toys, swings, slide, and sandbox.
Caregiver–child ratio	In child-care centers, caregiver–child ratio is no greater than 1 to 3 for infants and 1 to 6 for toddlers. Group size (number of children in one room) is no greater than 6 infants with 2 caregivers and 12 toddlers with 2 caregivers. In family child care, caregiver is responsible for no more than 6 children; within this group, no more than 2 are infants and toddlers.
Daily activities	Daily schedule includes times for active play, quiet play, naps, snacks, and meals. Atmosphere is warm and supportive, and children are never left unsupervised.
Interactions among adults and children	Caregivers respond promptly to infants' and toddlers' distress; hold, talk to, sing to, and read to them; and interact in a manner that respects each child's interests and tolerance for stimulation. Staffing is consistent, so infants and toddlers can form relationships with particular caregivers.
Caregiver qualifications	Caregiver has some training in child development, first aid, and safety.
Relationships with parents	Parents are welcome anytime. Caregivers talk frequently with parents about children's behavior and development.
Licensing and accreditation	Child-care setting is licensed by the state. In the United States, voluntary accreditation by the National Association for the Education of Young Children *(www.naeyc.org/academy)*, or the National Association for Family Child Care *(www.nafcc.org)* is evidence of an especially high-quality program.

Sources: Copple & Bredekamp, 2009.

tively with Timmy, while also assuring her warm, responsive parenting that builds on toddlers' current capacities is a much better indicator of how children will do later than an early mental test score.

Infant and Toddler Child Care. Today, more than 60 percent of U.S. mothers with a child under age 2 are employed (U.S. Census Bureau, 2013). Child care for infants and toddlers has become common, and its quality—though not as influential as parenting—affects mental development. Infants and young children exposed to poor-quality child care score lower on measures of cognitive and social skills (Belsky et al., 2007b; Hausfather et al., 1997; NICHD Early Child Care Research Network, 2000b, 2001, 2003b, 2006). In contrast, good child care can reduce the negative impact of a stressed, poverty-stricken home life, and it sustains the benefits of growing up in an economically advantaged family (Lamb & Ahnert, 2006; McCartney et al., 2007; NICHD Early Child Care Research Network, 2003b).

Unlike most European countries and Australia and New Zealand, where child care is nationally regulated and funded to ensure its quality, reports on U.S. child care raise serious concerns. Standards are set by the states and vary widely. In studies of quality, only 20 to 25 percent of U.S. child-care centers and family child-care homes provided infants and toddlers with sufficiently positive, stimulating experiences to promote healthy psychological development (NICHD Early Childhood Research Network, 2000a, 2004).

LOOK AND LISTEN

Ask several employed parents of infants or toddlers to describe what they sought in a child-care setting. Are the parents knowledgeable about the ingredients of high-quality care? ●

U.S. settings providing the very worst care tend to serve middle-SES families. These parents are especially likely to place their children in for-profit centers, where quality tends to be lowest. Low-SES children more often attend publicly subsidized, nonprofit centers, which have smaller group sizes and better teacher–child ratios (Lamb & Ahnert, 2006). Still, child-care quality for low-SES children varies widely. And probably because of greater access to adult stimulation, infants and toddlers in high-quality family child care score higher than those in center care in cognitive and language development (NICHD Early Child Care Research Network, 2000b).

See Applying What We Know above for signs of high-quality care for infants and toddlers, based on standards for

High-quality child care, with a generous caregiver–child ratio, well-trained caregivers, and developmentally appropriate activities, can be especially beneficial to children from low-SES homes.

developmentally appropriate practice. These standards, devised by the U.S. National Association for the Education of Young Children, specify program characteristics that serve young children's developmental and individual needs, based on both current research and consensus among experts.

Good child care is a cost-effective means of protecting children's well-being. And much like the programs we are about to consider, it can serve as effective early intervention for children whose development is at risk.

Early Intervention for At-Risk Infants and Toddlers

Children living in poverty are likely to show gradual declines in intelligence test scores and to achieve poorly when they reach school age—problems largely due to stressful home environments that undermine children's ability to learn and increase the likelihood that they will remain poor as adults (McLoyd, Aikens, & Burton, 2006). A variety of intervention programs have been developed to break this tragic cycle of poverty. Although most begin during the preschool years, a few start during infancy and continue through early childhood.

In center-based interventions, children attend an organized child-care or preschool program where they receive educational, nutritional, and health services, and their parents receive child-rearing and other social service supports. In home-based interventions, a skilled adult visits the home and works with parents, teaching them how to stimulate a very young child's development. In most programs of either type, participating children score higher than untreated controls on mental tests by age 2. The earlier intervention begins, the longer it lasts, and the greater its scope and intensity, the better participants' cognitive

and academic performance is throughout childhood and adolescence (Brooks-Gunn, 2004; Ramey, Ramey, & Lanzi, 2006).

The Carolina Abecedarian Project illustrates these favorable outcomes. In the 1970s, more than 100 infants from poverty-stricken families, ranging in age from 3 weeks to 3 months, were randomly assigned to either a treatment group or a control group. Treatment infants were enrolled in full-time, year-round child care through the preschool years. There they received stimulation aimed at promoting motor, cognitive, language, and social skills and, after age 3, literacy and math concepts. Special emphasis was placed on rich, responsive adult–child verbal communication. All children received nutrition and health services; the primary difference between treatment and controls was the intensive child-care experience.

As Figure 5.7 shows, treatment children sustained an IQ advantage from 12 months until last tested, at age 21. In addition, throughout their school years, treatment youths achieved considerably higher scores in reading and math. These gains translated into more years of schooling completed, higher rates of college enrollment and employment in skilled jobs, and lower rates of drug use and adolescent parenthood (Campbell et al., 2001, 2002; Campbell & Ramey, 2010).

Recognition of the power of intervening as early as possible led the U.S. Congress to provide limited funding for services directed at infants and toddlers who already have serious developmental problems or who are at risk for problems because of poverty. Early Head Start, begun in 1995, currently has 1,000 sites serving about 100,000 low-income children and their families (Early Head Start National Resource Center, 2013). A recent evaluation, conducted when children reached age 3, showed that intervention led to warmer, more stimulating parenting, a reduction in harsh discipline, gains in cognitive and language development, and lessening of child aggression (Love

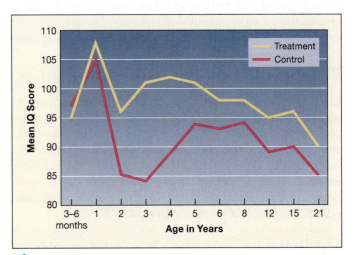

FIGURE 5.7 IQ scores of treatment and control children from infancy to 21 years in the Carolina Abecedarian Project. At 1 year, treatment children outperformed controls, an advantage consistently maintained through age 21. The IQ scores of both groups declined gradually during childhood and adolescence—a trend probably due to the damaging impact of poverty on mental development. (Adapted from Campbell et al., 2001.)

et al., 2005; Love, Chazan-Cohen, & Raikes, 2007; Raikes et al., 2010). The strongest effects occurred at sites mixing center- and home-based services. Though not yet plentiful enough to meet the need, such programs are a promising beginning.

ASK YOURSELF

REVIEW What probably accounts for the finding that speed of habituation and recovery to novel visual stimuli predicts later IQ better than most infant mental test scores?

APPLY Fifteen-month-old Joey scored 115 on an infant and toddler intelligence test. His mother wants to know exactly what this means and what she should do to support his mental development. How would you respond?

REFLECT Suppose you were seeking a child-care setting for your baby. What would you want it to be like, and why?

Language Development

Improvements in perception and cognition during infancy pave the way for an extraordinary human achievement—language. In Chapter 4, we saw that by the second half of the first year, infants make dramatic progress in distinguishing the basic sounds of their language and in segmenting the flow of speech into word and phrase units. They also start to comprehend some words and, around 12 months of age, say their first word. By age 6, children understand the meaning of about 10,000 words and speak in elaborate sentences.

How do infants and toddlers make such remarkable progress in launching these skills? To address this question, let's examine several prominent theories of language development.

Theories of Language Development

In the 1950s, researchers did not take seriously the idea that very young children might be able to figure out important properties of language. Children's regular and rapid attainment of language milestones suggested a process largely governed by maturation, inspiring the nativist perspective on language development. In recent years, new evidence has spawned the interactionist perspective, which emphasizes the joint roles of children's inner capacities and communicative experiences.

The Nativist Perspective. According to linguist Noam Chomsky's (1957) *nativist* theory, language is etched into the structure of the brain. Focusing on grammar, Chomsky reasoned that the rules of sentence organization are too complex to be directly taught to or discovered by even a cognitively sophisticated young child. Rather, he proposed that all children have a **language acquisition device (LAD),** an innate system that contains a *universal grammar,* or set of rules common to all languages. It enables children, no matter which language they hear, to understand and speak in a rule-oriented fashion as soon as they pick up enough words.

Are children biologically primed to acquire language? Recall from Chapter 4 that newborn babies are remarkably sensitive to speech sounds. And children everywhere reach major language milestones in a similar sequence. Furthermore, evidence that childhood is a *sensitive period* for language acquisition is consistent with Chomsky's idea of a biologically based language program. Researchers have examined the language competence of deaf adults who acquired their first language—American Sign Language (ASL), a gestural system used by the deaf—at different ages. The later learners, whose parents chose to educate them through speech and lip-reading, did not acquire spoken language because of their profound deafness. Consistent with the sensitive-period notion, those who learned ASL in adolescence or adulthood never became as proficient as those who learned in childhood (Mayberry, 2010; Newport, 1991; Singleton & Newport, 2004).

But challenges to Chomsky's theory suggest that it, too, provides only a partial account of language development. First, researchers have had great difficulty specifying Chomsky's universal grammar. Critics doubt that one set of rules can account for the extraordinary variation in grammatical forms among the world's 5,000 to 8,000 languages (Christiansen & Chater, 2008; Evans & Levinson, 2009). Second, children's progress in mastering many sentence constructions is gradual, with errors along the way, indicating more learning and discovery than Chomsky assumed (Tager-Flusbert & Zukowski, 2009).

The Interactionist Perspective. Recent ideas about language development emphasize *interactions* between inner capacities and environmental influences. One type of interactionist theory applies the information-processing perspective to language development. A second type emphasizes social interaction.

Some information-processing theorists assume that children make sense of their complex language environments by applying powerful cognitive capacities of a general kind (Bates, 2004; Munakata, 2006; Saffran, 2009). These theorists note that brain regions housing language also govern similar perceptual and cognitive abilities, such as the capacity to analyze musical and visual patterns (Saygin, Leech, & Dick, 2010).

Other theorists blend this information-processing view with Chomsky's nativist perspective. They argue that infants' capacity to analyze speech and other information is not sufficient to account for mastery of higher-level aspects of language, such as intricate grammatical structures (Aslin & Newport, 2009). They also point out that grammatical competence may depend more on specific brain structures than the other components of language. When 2- to 2½-year-olds and adults listened to short sentences—some grammatically correct, others with phrase-structure violations—both groups showed simi-

Infants communicate from the very beginning of life, as this interchange between a mother and her 1-month-old illustrates. How will this child become a fluent speaker of her native language within just a few years? Theorists disagree sharply on answers to this question.

larly distinct ERP brain-wave patterns for each sentence type in the left frontal and temporal lobes of the cerebral cortex (Oberecker & Friederici, 2006; Oberecker, Friedrich, & Friederici, 2005). This suggests that 2-year-olds process sentence structures using the same neural system as adults do.

Still other interactionists emphasize that social skills and language experiences are centrally involved in language development. In this *social-interactionist* view, an active child strives to communicate, cuing caregivers to provide appropriate language experiences, which help the child relate the content and structure of language to its social meanings (Bohannon & Bonvillian, 2009). Among social interactionists, disagreement continues over whether or not children are equipped with specialized language abilities (Lidz, 2007; Shatz, 2007; Tomasello, 2003, 2006). Nevertheless, as we chart the course of language development, we will encounter much support for their central premise—that children's social competencies and language experiences greatly affect their progress.

Getting Ready to Talk

Before babies say their first word, they make impressive language progress. They listen attentively to human speech, and they make speechlike sounds. As adults, we can hardly help but respond.

Cooing and Babbling. Around 2 months, babies begin to make vowel-like noises, called **cooing** because of their pleasant "oo" quality. Gradually, consonants are added, and around 6 months, **babbling** appears, in which infants repeat consonant-vowel combinations in long strings, such as "bababababa" or "nanananana."

Babies everywhere (even those who are deaf) start babbling at about the same age and produce a similar range of early sounds. But for babbling to develop further, infants must be able to hear human speech. In hearing-impaired babies, these speechlike sounds are greatly delayed. And a deaf infant not exposed to sign language will stop babbling entirely (Oller, 2000).

As infants listen to spoken language, babbling expands to a broader range of sounds. Around 7 months, it starts to include many sounds common in spoken languages (Goldstein & Schwade, 2008). By 10 months, babbling reflects the sound and intonation patterns of children's language community (Boysson-Bardies & Vihman, 1991).

Deaf infants exposed to sign language from birth and hearing babies of deaf, signing parents produce babblelike hand motions with the rhythmic patterns of natural sign languages (Petitto et al., 2001, 2004; Petitto & Marentette, 1991). This sensitivity to language rhythm—evident in both spoken and signed babbling—supports both discovery and production of meaningful language units.

Becoming a Communicator. At birth, infants are prepared for some aspects of conversational behavior. For example, newborns initiate interaction through eye contact and terminate it by looking away. By 3 to 4 months, infants start to gaze in the same general direction adults are looking—a skill that becomes more accurate at 10 to 11 months, as babies realize that others' focus offers information about their communicative intentions (Senju, Csibra, & Johnson, 2008). This **joint attention,** in which the child attends to the same object or event as the caregiver, contributes greatly to early language development. Infants and toddlers who frequently experience it sustain attention longer, comprehend more language, produce meaningful gestures and words earlier, and show faster vocabulary development (Brooks & Meltzoff, 2008; Flom & Pick, 2003; Silvén, 2001).

Between 4 and 6 months, interactions between caregivers and babies begin to include *give-and-take,* as in pat-a-cake and peekaboo games. At first, the parent starts the game and the baby is an amused observer. By 12 months, babies participate actively, practicing the turn-taking pattern of conversation. Infants' play maturity and vocalizations during games predict advanced language progress in the second year (Rome-Flanders & Cronk, 1995).

At the end of the first year, babies use *preverbal gestures* to direct adults' attention, to influence their behavior, and to convey helpful information (Tomasello, Carpenter, & Liszkowski, 2007). For example, Caitlin held up a toy to show it and pointed to the cupboard when she wanted a cookie. Carolyn responded to these gestures and also labeled them ("You want a cookie!"). In this way, toddlers learn that using language leads to desired results. Soon they integrate words with gestures, as in pointing

© LAURA DWIGHT PHOTOGRAPHY

This baby uses a preverbal gesture to draw his caregiver's attention to a picture. The caregiver's verbal response promotes the baby's transition to spoken language.

to a toy while saying "give." The earlier toddlers form word–gesture combinations, the faster their vocabulary growth, the sooner they produce two-word utterances at the end of the second year, and the more complex their sentences at age 3½ (Özçaliskan & Goldin-Meadow, 2005; Rowe & Goldin-Meadow, 2009).

First Words

In the second half of the first year, infants begin to understand word meanings. First spoken words, around 1 year, build on the sensorimotor foundations Piaget described and on categories children have formed. In a study tracking the first 10 words used by several hundred U.S. and Chinese (both Mandarin- and Cantonese-speaking) babies, important people ("Mama," "Dada"), common objects ("ball," "bread"), and sound effects ("woof-woof," "vroom") were mentioned most often. Action words ("hit," "grab," "hug") and social routines ("hi," "bye"), though also appearing in all three groups, were more often produced by Chinese than U.S. babies, and the Chinese babies also named more important people—differences we will consider shortly (Tardif et al., 2008).

When toddlers first learn words, they sometimes apply them too narrowly, an error called **underextension.** At 16 months, Caitlin used "bear" only to refer to the tattered bear she carried nearly constantly. As vocabulary expands, a more common error is **overextension**—applying a word to a wider collection of objects and events than is appropriate. For example, Grace used "car" for buses, trains, and trucks. Toddlers' overextensions reflect their sensitivity to categories (MacWhinney, 2005). They apply a new word to a group of similar experi-

ences, often overextending deliberately because they have difficulty recalling or have not acquired a suitable word.

Overextensions illustrate another important feature of language development: the distinction between language *production* (the words children use) and language *comprehension* (the words they understand). At all ages, comprehension develops ahead of production. Still, the two capacities are related. The speed and accuracy of toddlers' comprehension of spoken language, which increases dramatically over the second year, predicts words understood and produced at age 2 (Fernald, Perfors, & Marchman, 2006). Quick comprehension frees space in working memory for picking up new words and for the more demanding task of using them to communicate.

The Two-Word Utterance Phase

Young toddlers add to their spoken vocabularies at a rate of one to three words per week. Gradually, the number of words learned accelerates. Because gains in word production between 18 and 24 months are so impressive (one or two words per day), many researchers concluded that toddlers undergo a *spurt in vocabulary*—a transition from a slower to a faster learning phase. But recent evidence indicates that most children show a steady increase in rate of word learning that continues through the preschool years (Ganger & Brent, 2004).

Once toddlers produce 200 to 250 words, they start to combine two words: "Mommy shoe," "go car," "more cookie." These two-word utterances are called **telegraphic speech** because, like a telegram, they focus on high-content words, omitting smaller, less important ones. Children the world over use them to express an impressive variety of meanings.

Two-word speech consists largely of simple formulas ("more + X," "eat + X"), with different words inserted in the "X" position. Toddlers rarely make gross grammatical errors, such as saying "chair my" instead of "my chair." Rather than following grammatical rules, toddlers' word-order regularities are usually copies of adult word pairings, as when the parents says, "How about *more sandwich?*" (Tomasello, 2006; Tomasello & Brandt, 2009).

Individual and Cultural Differences

Although children typically produce their first word around their first birthday, the range is large, from 8 to 18 months—variation due to a complex blend of genetic and environmental influences. Earlier we saw that Timmy's spoken language was delayed, in part because of Vanessa's tense, directive communication with him. But Timmy is also a boy, and many studies show that girls are slightly ahead of boys in early vocabulary growth (Van Hulle, Goldsmith, & Lemery, 2004). The most common explanation is girls' faster rate of physical maturation, believed to promote earlier development of the left cerebral hemisphere.

Temperament matters, too. Shy toddlers often wait until they understand a great deal before trying to speak. Once they do speak, their vocabularies increase rapidly, although they remain slightly behind their agemates (Spere et al., 2004). Temperamentally negative toddlers also acquire language more slowly because their high emotional reactivity diverts them from processing linguistic information (Salley & Dixon, 2007).

The quantity of caregiver–child conversation and richness of adults' vocabularies also play a strong role (Zimmerman et al., 2009). Commonly used words for objects appear early in toddlers' speech, and the more often their caregivers use a particular noun, the sooner young children produce it (Goodman, Dale, & Li, 2008). Mothers talk more to toddler-age girls than to boys, and parents converse less often with shy than with sociable children (Leaper, Anderson, & Sanders, 1998; Patterson & Fisher, 2002).

Low-SES children, who receive less verbal stimulation in their homes than higher-SES children, usually have smaller vocabularies (Hoff, 2006). Limited parent–child book reading is a major factor. On average, a middle-SES child is read to for 1,000 hours between 1 and 5 years, a low-SES child for only 25 hours (Neuman, 2003). As a result, low-SES kindergartners have vocabularies only one-fourth as large as those of their higher SES agemates (Lee & Burkam, 2002). And low-income children are also behind in early literacy knowledge and later reading achievement, as we will see in Chapter 7.

Furthermore, 2-year-olds' spoken vocabularies vary substantially across languages—about 180 to 200 words for children acquiring Swedish, 250 to 300 words for children acquiring English, and 500 words for children acquiring Mandarin Chinese (Bleses et al., 2008; Tardif et al., 2009). In Swedish, a complicated system of speech sounds makes syllable and word boundaries challenging to discriminate and pronounce. In contrast, Mandarin Chinese has many short words with easy-to-pronounce initial consonants. Within Mandarin words, each syllable is given one of four distinct tones, aiding discrimination.

Supporting Early Language Development

Consistent with the interactionist view, a rich social environment builds on young children's natural readiness to acquire language. Adults in many cultures speak to babies in **infant-directed speech (IDS),** a form of communication made up of short sentences with high-pitched, exaggerated expression, clear pronunciation, distinct pauses between speech segments, and repetition of new words in a variety of contexts ("See the *ball*," "The *ball* bounced!") (Fernald et al., 1989; O'Neill et al., 2005). Deaf parents use a similar style of communication when signing to their deaf babies (Masataka, 1996). IDS builds on several

communicative strategies we have already considered: joint attention, turn-taking, and caregivers' sensitivity to toddlers' preverbal gestures. In this example, Carolyn uses IDS with 18-month-old Caitlin:

Caitlin: "Go car."

Carolyn: "Yes, time to go in the car. Where's your jacket?"

Caitlin: *[Looks around, walks to the closet.]* "Dacket!" *[Points to her jacket.]*

Carolyn: "There's that jacket! *[She helps Caitlin into the jacket.]* Now, say bye-bye to Grace and Timmy."

Caitlin: "Bye-bye, G-ace. Bye-bye, Te-te.

Carolyn: "Where's your bear?"

Caitlin: *[Looks around.]*

Carolyn: *[Pointing.]* "See? By the sofa."

From birth on, infants prefer IDS over other adult talk, and by 5 months they are more emotionally responsive to it (Aslin, Jusczyk, & Pisoni, 1998). Parents constantly fine-tune the length and content of their utterances to fit their children's needs—adjustments that foster word learning and enable toddlers to join in (Cameron-Faulkner, Lieven, & Tomasello, 2003; Rowe, 2008).

LOOK AND LISTEN

While observing a parent and toddler playing, describe how the parent adapts his or her language to the child's needs. Did the parent use IDS? ●

Do social experiences that promote language development remind you of those that strengthen cognitive development in general? IDS and parent–child conversation create a *zone of proximal development* in which children's language expands. In the next chapter, we will see that sensitivity to children's needs and capacities supports their emotional and social development as well.

ASK YOURSELF

REVIEW Describe evidence that supports the social interactionist perspective on language development.

APPLY Fran frequently corrects her 17-month-old son Jeremy's attempts to talk and—fearing that he won't use words—refuses to respond to his gestures. How might Fran be contributing to Jeremy's slow language progress?

REFLECT Find an opportunity to speak to an infant or toddler. Did you use IDS? What features of your speech are likely to promote early language development, and why?

SUMMARY

Piaget's Cognitive-Developmental Theory (p. 118)

According to Piaget, how do schemes change over the course of development?

- By acting on the environment, children move through four stages in which psychological structures, or **schemes,** achieve a better fit with external reality.

- Schemes change in two ways: through **adaptation,** which is made up of two complementary activities—**assimilation** and **accommodation**—and through **organization.**

Describe the major cognitive achievements of the sensorimotor stage.

- In the **sensorimotor stage,** the **circular reaction** provides a means of adapting first schemes, and the newborn's reflexes gradually transform into the flexible action patterns of the older infant. Eight- to 12-month-olds develop **intentional,** or **goal-directed, behavior** and begin to understand **object permanence.**

© LAURA DWIGHT PHOTOGRAPHY

- Between 18 and 24 months, **mental representation** is evident in mastery of object permanence problems involving invisible displacement, **deferred imitation,** and **make-believe play.**

What does follow-up research reveal about the accuracy of Piaget's sensorimotor stage?

- Many studies suggest that infants display certain understandings earlier than Piaget believed. Some awareness of object permanence, as revealed by the **violation-of-expectation method** and object-tracking research, may be evident in the first few months.

- Around the first birthday, babies understand **displaced reference** of words. By the middle of the second year, toddlers treat realistic-looking pictures symbolically; around 2½ years, they grasp the symbolic meaning of video.

- Today, researchers believe that newborns have more built-in equipment for making sense of their world than Piaget assumed, although they disagree on how much initial understanding infants have. According to the **core knowledge perspective,** infants are born with core domains of thought that support early, rapid cognitive development. Research suggests that infants have basic physical, linguistic, psychological, and numerical knowledge.

- Broad agreement exists that many cognitive changes of infancy are continuous rather than stagelike and that various aspects of cognition develop unevenly rather than in an integrated fashion.

Information Processing (p. 126)

Describe the information-processing view of cognitive development.

- Most information-processing researchers assume that we hold information in three parts of the mental system for processing: the **sensory register,** the **short-term memory store,** and **long-term memory.** The **central executive** joins with **working memory**—our "mental workspace"—to process information effectively, increasing the chances that it will transfer to our permanent knowledge base. Well-learned **automatic processes** require no space in working memory, permitting us to focus on other information while performing them.

- Gains in **executive function**—including attention, impulse control, and coordinating information in working memory—are under way in the first two years.

What changes in attention, memory, and categorization take place during the first two years?

- With age, infants attend to more aspects of the environment and take information in more quickly. In the second year, attention to novelty declines and sustained attention improves.

- Young infants are capable of **recognition** memory. By the second half of the first year, they also engage in **recall.**

- Infants group stimuli into increasingly complex categories, and toddlers' categorization gradually shifts from a perceptual to a conceptual basis. Understanding of the animate–inanimate distinction expands during toddlerhood.

Describe contributions and limitations of the information-processing approach to our understanding of early cognitive development.

- Information-processing findings reveal remarkable similarities between babies' and adults' thinking. But information processing has not yet provided a broad, comprehensive theory of children's thinking.

The Social Context of Early Cognitive Development (p. 130)

How does Vygotsky's concept of the zone of proximal development expand our understanding of early cognitive development?

- Vygotsky believed that infants master tasks within the **zone of proximal development**—ones just ahead of their current capacities—through the guidance of more skilled partners. As early as the first year, cultural variations in social experiences affect mental strategies.

© LAURA DWIGHT PHOTOGRAPHY

Individual Differences in Early Mental Development (p. 132)

Describe the mental testing approach and the extent to which infant tests predict later performance.

- The mental testing approach measures intellectual development in an effort to predict future performance. Scores are arrived at by computing an **intelligence quotient (IQ),** which compares an individual's test performance with that of a **standardization** sample of same-age individuals, whose scores form a **normal distribution.**

- Infant tests consisting largely of perceptual and motor responses predict later intelligence poorly. Speed of habituation and recovery to visual stimuli are better predictors of future performance.

Discuss environmental influences on early mental development and early intervention for at-risk infants and toddlers.

- Research with the **Home Observation for Measurement of the Environment (HOME)** shows that an organized, stimulating home environment and parental encouragement, involvement, and affection repeatedly predict early mental test scores. Although the HOME–IQ relationship is partly due to heredity, family living conditions also affect mental development.

- Quality of infant and toddler child care has a major impact on mental development. Standards for **developmentally appropriate practice** specify program characteristics that meet young children's developmental needs.

- Intensive intervention beginning in infancy and extending through early childhood can prevent the gradual declines in intelligence and poor academic performance of many poverty-stricken children.

Language Development
(p. 136)

Describe theories of language development, and indicate how much emphasis each places on innate abilities and environmental influences.

- Chomsky's *nativist* theory regards children as naturally endowed with a **language acquisition device (LAD).** Consistent with this perspective, mastery of a complex language system is unique to humans, and childhood is a sensitive period for language acquisition.

- Recent theories view language development as resulting from interactions between inner capacities and environmental influences. Some interactionists apply the information-processing perspective to language development. Others emphasize children's social skills and language experiences.

Describe major language milestones of the first two years, individual differences, and ways adults can support early language development.

- Infants begin **cooing** at 2 months and **babbling** at about 6 months. Around 10 to 11 months, their skill at establishing **joint attention** improves, and soon they use preverbal gestures. Adults can encourage language progress by responding to infants' coos and babbles, playing turn-taking games, establishing joint attention and labeling what babies see, and responding verbally to their preverbal gestures.

- Around 12 months, toddlers say their first word. Young children often make errors of **underextension** and **overextension.** Once vocabulary reaches 200 to 250 words, two-word utterances called **telegraphic speech** appear. At all ages, language comprehension is ahead of production.

- Girls show faster language progress than boys. Reserved, cautious toddlers may wait before trying to speak, and temperamentally negative toddlers also acquire language more slowly. Low-SES children, whose homes tend to be less verbally stimulating, typically have smaller vocabularies.

- Adults in many cultures speak to young children in **infant-directed speech (IDS),** a simplified form of language that is well suited to their learning needs. Parent–toddler conversation is a good predictor of language development and later reading success.

Important Terms and Concepts

accommodation (p. 119)
adaptation (p. 118)
assimilation (p. 118)
autobiographical memory (p. 129)
automatic processes (p. 126)
babbling (p. 137)
central executive (p. 126)
circular reaction (p. 119)
cooing (p. 137)
core knowledge perspective (p. 125)
deferred imitation (p. 121)
developmentally appropriate practice (p. 135)
displaced reference (p. 123)
executive function (p. 127)

Home Observation for Measurement of the
  Environment (HOME) (p. 133)
infant-directed speech (IDS) (p. 139)
infantile amnesia (p. 129)
intelligence quotient (IQ) (p. 132)
intentional, or goal-directed, behavior (p. 120)
joint attention (p. 137)
language acquisition device (LAD) (p. 136)
long-term memory (p. 126)
make-believe play (p. 121)
mental representation (p. 120)
normal distribution (p. 132)
object permanence (p. 120)
organization (p. 119)

overextension (p. 138)
recall (p. 128)
recognition (p. 128)
scheme (p. 118)
sensorimotor stage (p. 118)
sensory register (p. 126)
short-term memory store (p. 126)
standardization (p. 132)
telegraphic speech (p. 138)
underextension (p. 138)
video deficit effect (p. 124)
violation-of-expectation method (p. 121)
working memory (p. 126)
zone of proximal development (p. 130)

Emotional and Social Development in Infancy and Toddlerhood

© LAURA DWIGHT PHOTOGRAPHY

This father takes time to build a strong, affectionate bond with his infant daughter. His warmth and sensitivity engender a sense of security in the baby—a vital foundation for all aspects of early development.

chapter outline

Erikson's Theory of Infant and Toddler Personality

Basic Trust versus Mistrust • Autonomy versus Shame and Doubt

Emotional Development

Development of Basic Emotions • Understanding and Responding to the Emotions of Others • Emergence of Self-Conscious Emotions • Beginnings of Emotional Self-Regulation

■ **BIOLOGY AND ENVIRONMENT** Parental Depression and Child Development

Temperament and Development

The Structure of Temperament • Measuring Temperament • Stability of Temperament • Genetic and Environmental Influences • Temperament and Child Rearing: The Goodness-of-Fit Model

■ **BIOLOGY AND ENVIRONMENT** Development of Shyness and Sociability

Development of Attachment

Ethological Theory of Attachment • Measuring the Security of Attachment • Stability of Attachment • Cultural Variations • Factors That Affect Attachment Security • Multiple Attachments • Attachment and Later Development

■ **SOCIAL ISSUES: HEALTH** Does Child Care in Infancy Threaten Attachment Security and Later Adjustment?

Self-Development

Self-Awareness • Categorizing the Self • Self-Control

As Caitlin reached 8 months of age, her parents noticed that she had become more fearful. One evening, when Carolyn and David left her with a babysitter, she wailed as they headed for the door—an experience she had accepted easily a few weeks earlier. Caitlin and Timmy's caregiver Ginette also observed an increasing wariness of strangers. At the mail carrier's knock at the door, they clung to Ginette's legs, reaching out to be picked up.

At the same time, each baby seemed more willful. Removing an object from the hand produced little response at 5 months. But at 8 months, when Timmy's mother, Vanessa, took away a table knife he had managed to reach, Timmy burst into angry screams and could not be consoled or distracted.

All Monica and Kevin knew about Grace's first year was that she had been deeply loved by her destitute, homeless mother. Separation from her had left Grace in shock. At first she was extremely sad, turning away when Monica or Kevin picked her up. But as Grace's new parents held her close, spoke gently, and satisfied her craving for food, Grace returned their affection. Two weeks after her arrival, her despondency gave way to a sunny, easy-going disposition. As her second birthday approached, she pointed to herself, exclaiming "Gwace!" and laid claim to treasured possessions. "Gwace's teddy bear!"

Taken together, the children's reactions reflect two related aspects of personality development during the first two years: close ties to others and a sense of self. We begin with Erikson's psychosocial theory, which provides an overview of infant and toddler personality development. Then, as we chart the course of emotional development, we will discover why fear and anger became more apparent in Caitlin's and Timmy's range of emotions by the end of the first year. Our attention then turns to the origins and developmental consequences of individual differences in temperament.

Next, we take up attachment to the caregiver, the child's first affectionate tie. We will see how the feelings of security that grow out of this important bond support the child's sense of independence and expanding social relationships. Finally, we consider how cognitive advances combine with social experiences to foster early self-development and the beginnings of self-control in the second year. ●

Erikson's Theory of Infant and Toddler Personality

Our discussion in Chapter 1 revealed that the psychoanalytic perspective is no longer in the mainstream of human development research. But one of its lasting contributions is its ability to capture the essence of personality during each period of development. Recall that Sigmund Freud believed that psychological health and maladjustment could be traced to the quality of the child's relationships with parents during the early years. Although Freud came to be heavily criticized, the basic outlines of his theory were elaborated in several subsequent theories. The most influential is Erik Erikson's *psychosocial theory*, also introduced in Chapter 1.

Basic Trust versus Mistrust

Erikson accepted Freud's emphasis on the importance of the parent–infant relationship during feeding, but he expanded and enriched Freud's view. A healthy outcome during infancy, Erikson believed, depends on the *quality* of caregiving: relieving discomfort promptly and sensitively, waiting patiently until the baby has had enough milk, and weaning when the infant shows less interest in breast or bottle.

Erikson recognized that many factors affect parental responsiveness—personal happiness, current life conditions (for example, additional young children in the family), and culturally valued child-rearing practices. But when the *balance of care* is

sympathetic and loving, the psychological conflict of the first year—**basic trust versus mistrust**—is resolved on the positive side. The trusting infant expects the world to be good and gratifying, so he feels confident about venturing out and exploring it. The mistrustful baby cannot count on the kindness and compassion of others, so she protects herself by withdrawing from people and things around her.

Autonomy versus Shame and Doubt

With the transition to toddlerhood, Freud viewed the parents' manner of toilet training as decisive for psychological health. In Erikson' view, toilet training is only one of many influential experiences. The familiar refrains of newly walking, talking toddlers—"No!" "Do it myself!"—reveal a period of budding selfhood. The conflict of **autonomy versus shame and doubt** is resolved favorably when parents provide young children with suitable guidance and reasonable choices. A self-confident, secure 2-year-old has parents who do not criticize or attack him when he fails at new skills—using the toilet, eating with a spoon, or putting away toys. And they meet his assertions of independence with tolerance and understanding—for example, by giving him an extra five minutes to finish his play before leaving for the grocery store. In contrast, when parents are over- or undercontrolling, the outcome is a child who feels forced and shamed or who doubts his ability to control his impulses and act competently on his own.

In sum, basic trust and autonomy grow out of warm, sensitive parenting and reasonable expectations for impulse control

On a visit to a science museum, a 2-year-old insists on exploring a flight simulator. As the mother supports her toddler's desire to "do it myself," she fosters a healthy sense of autonomy.

starting in the second year. If children emerge from the first few years without sufficient trust in caregivers and without a healthy sense of individuality, the seeds are sown for adjustment problems.

Emotional Development

Researchers have conducted careful observations to find out how babies convey their emotions and interpret those of others. They have discovered that emotions play powerful roles in organizing the attainments that Erikson regarded as so important: social relationships, exploration of the environment, and discovery of the self (Halle, 2003; Saarni et al., 2006).

Development of Basic Emotions

Basic emotions—happiness, interest, surprise, fear, anger, sadness, and disgust—are universal in humans and other primates and have a long evolutionary history of promoting survival. Do newborns express basic emotions? Although signs of some emotions are present, babies' earliest emotional life consists of little more than two global arousal states: attraction to pleasant stimulation and withdrawal from unpleasant stimulation (Camras et al., 2003; Fox, 1991). Only gradually do emotions become clear, well-organized signals.

According to one view, sensitive, contingent caregiver communication, in which parents selectively mirror aspects of the baby's diffuse emotional behavior, helps infants construct emotional expressions that more closely resemble those of adults (Gergely & Watson, 1999). With age, face, voice, and posture form organized patterns that vary meaningfully with environmental events. For example, Caitlin typically responded to her parents' playful interaction with a joyful face, pleasant babbling, and a relaxed posture, as if to say, "This is fun!" In contrast, an

unresponsive parent often evokes a sad face, fussy sounds, and a drooping body (sending the message, "I'm despondent") or an angry face, crying, and "pick-me-up" gestures (as if to say, "Change this unpleasant event!") (Weinberg & Tronick, 1994; Yale et al., 1999).

Four basic emotions—happiness, anger, sadness, and fear—have received the most research attention. Let's see how they develop.

Happiness. Happiness—expressed first in blissful smiles and later through exuberant laughter—contributes to many aspects of development. When infants achieve new skills, they smile and laugh, displaying delight in motor and cognitive mastery. As the smile encourages caregivers to be affectionate and stimulating, the baby smiles even more (Aksan & Kochanska, 2004). Happiness binds parent and baby into a warm, supportive relationship that fosters the infant's developing competencies.

During the early weeks, newborn babies smile when full, during REM sleep, and in response to gentle stroking of the skin, rocking, and the mother's soft, high-pitched voice. By the end of the first month, infants smile at dynamic, eye-catching sights, such as a bright object jumping suddenly across their field of vision. Between 6 and 10 weeks, the parent's communication evokes a broad grin called the **social smile** (Lavelli & Fogel, 2005; Sroufe & Waters, 1976). These changes parallel the development of infant perceptual capacities—in particular, sensitivity to visual patterns, including the human face (see Chapter 4).

Laughter, which appears around 3 to 4 months, reflects faster processing of information than smiling. As with smiling, the first laughs occur in response to very active stimuli, such as the parent saying playfully, "I'm gonna get you!" and kissing the baby's tummy. As infants understand more about their world, they laugh at events with subtler elements of surprise, such as a silent game of peekaboo (Sroufe & Wunsch, 1972).

Around the middle of the first year, infants smile and laugh more when interacting with familiar people, a preference that strengthens the parent–child bond. Between 8 and 10 months, the smile becomes a deliberate social signal: Infants interrupt their play with an interesting toy to relay their delight to an attentive adult (Venezia et al., 2004).

Anger and Sadness. Newborn babies respond with generalized distress to a variety of unpleasant experiences, including hunger, changes in body temperature, and too much or too little stimulation. From 4 to 6 months into the second year, angry expressions increase in frequency and intensity (Braungart-Rieker, Hill-Soderlund, & Karrass, 2010). Older infants also react with anger in a wider range of situations—when an object is taken away, an expected pleasant event does not occur, the caregiver leaves for a brief time, or they are put down for a nap (Camras et al., 1992; Stenberg & Campos, 1990; Sullivan & Lewis, 2003).

Why do angry reactions increase with age? As infants become capable of intentional behavior (see Chapter 5), they

Biology and Environment

Parental Depression and Child Development

About 8 to 10 percent of women experience chronic depression—mild to severe feelings of sadness, distress, and withdrawal that continue for months or years. Sometimes, depression emerges or strengthens after childbirth and fails to subside. Julia experienced this type—called *postpartum depression.*

Although less recognized and studied, fathers, too, experience chronic depression. About 3 to 5 percent of fathers report symptoms after the birth of a child (Madsen & Juhl, 2007; Thombs, Roseman, & Arthurs, 2010). Parental depression can interfere with effective parenting and seriously impair children's development. Genetic makeup increases the risk of depressive illness, but social and cultural factors are also involved.

Maternal Depression

During Julia's pregnancy, her husband, Kyle, showed so little interest in the baby that Julia worried that having a child might be a mistake. Shortly after Lucy was born, Julia's mood plunged. She felt anxious and weepy, overwhelmed by Lucy's needs, and angry at loss of control over her own schedule. When Julia approached Kyle about her own fatigue and his unwillingness to help with the baby, he snapped that she was overreacting.

Julia's depressed mood quickly affected her baby. The more extreme the depression and the greater the number of stressors in a mother's life (such as marital discord, little or no social support, and poverty), the more the parent–child relationship suffers (Simpson et al., 2003). Julia rarely smiled at, comforted, or talked to Lucy, who responded to her mother's sad, vacant gaze by turning away, crying, and often looking sad or angry herself (Feldman et al., 2009; Field, 2011). By age 6 months, Lucy showed symptoms common

in babies of depressed mothers—delays in motor and mental development, an irritable mood, and attachment difficulties (Cornish et al., 2005; McMahon et al., 2006).

Depressed mothers use inconsistent discipline—sometimes lax, at other times too forceful. As we will see in later chapters, children who experience these maladaptive parenting practices often have serious adjustment problems. Some withdraw into a depressed mood themselves; others become impulsive and aggressive. In one study, infants born to mothers who had been depressed during pregnancy were four times more likely than babies of nondepressed mothers to engage in violent antisocial behavior by age 16, after other maternal stressors that could contribute to youth antisocial conduct had been controlled (Hay et al., 2010).

Paternal Depression

Paternal depression is also linked to dissatisfaction with marriage and family life after childbirth and to other life stressors, including job loss and divorce (Bielawska-Batorowicz & Kossakowska-Petrycka, 2006). Persistent paternal depression strongly predicts child behavior problems—especially overactivity, defiance, and aggression in boys (Ramchandani et al., 2008).

Paternal depression is linked to frequent father–child conflict as children grow older (Kane & Garber, 2004). Over time, children subjected to parental negativity develop a pessimistic world view—one in which they lack self-confidence and perceive their parents and other people as threatening. Children who constantly feel endangered are especially likely to become overly aroused in stressful situations, easily losing control in the face of cognitive and social challenges (Sturge-Apple et al., 2008).

This father appears completely disengaged from his wife and toddler. If his depression continues, disruptions in the parent–child relationship will likely lead to serious child behavior problems.

Interventions

Early treatment is vital to prevent parental depression from interfering with the parent–child relationship. Julia's doctor referred her to a therapist, who helped Julia and Kyle with their marital problems. At times, antidepressant medication is prescribed.

In addition to alleviating parental depression, therapy that encourages depressed mothers to engage in emotionally positive, responsive caregiving is vital for reducing young children's attachment and other developmental problems (Forman et al., 2007). When a depressed parent does not respond easily to treatment, a warm relationship with the other parent or another caregiver can safeguard children's development (Mezulis, Hyde, & Clark, 2004).

---

want to control their own actions. They are also more persistent about obtaining desired objects (Mascolo & Fischer, 2007). Furthermore, older infants are better at identifying who caused them pain or removed a toy. The rise in anger is also adaptive. New motor capacities enable an angry infant to defend herself or overcome an obstacle (Izard & Ackerman, 2000).

Although expressions of sadness also occur in response to pain, removal of an object, and brief separations, they are less frequent than anger (Alessandri, Sullivan, & Lewis, 1990). But when caregiver–infant communication is seriously disrupted, infant sadness is common—a condition that impairs all aspects of development (see the Biology and Environment box above).

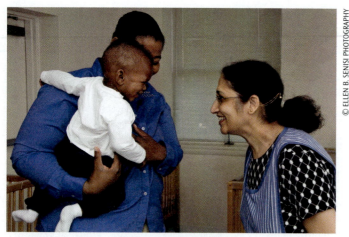

Stranger anxiety appears in many infants after 6 months of age. But this baby, safe in his mother's arms, also expresses curiosity, reaching out warily toward an unfamiliar adult who eases his fear by smiling and approaching slowly.

Fear. Like anger, fear rises from the second half of the first year into the second year (Braungart-Rieker, Hill-Soderland, & Karrass, 2010). Older infants hesitate before playing with a new toy, and newly crawling infants soon back away from heights (see Chapter 4). But the most frequent expression of fear is to unfamiliar adults, a response called **stranger anxiety.** Many infants and toddlers are quite wary of strangers, although the reaction varies with temperament (some babies are generally more fearful), past experiences with strangers, and the current situation. When an unfamiliar adult picks up the infant, stranger anxiety is likely. But if the adult sits still or acts warmly and playfully and a parent is nearby, infants often show positive and curious behavior (Horner, 1980).

Cross-cultural research reveals that infant-rearing practices can modify stranger anxiety. Among the Efe hunters and gatherers of the Republic of Congo, where the maternal death rate is high, infant survival is safeguarded by a collective caregiving system in which, starting at birth, Efe babies are passed from one adult to another. Consequently, Efe infants show little stranger anxiety (Tronick, Morelli, & Ivey, 1992).

LOOK AND LISTEN

While observing an 8- to 18-month-old with his or her parent, gently approach the baby, offering a toy. Does the baby respond with stranger anxiety? To better understand the baby's behavior, ask the parent to describe his or her temperament and past experiences with strangers. ●

The rise in fear after age 6 months keeps newly mobile babies' enthusiasm for exploration in check. Once wariness develops, babies use the familiar caregiver as a **secure base,** or point from which to explore, venturing into the environment and then returning for emotional support. As part of this adaptive system, encounters with strangers lead to two conflicting tendencies: approach (indicated by interest and friendliness)

and avoidance (indicated by fear). The infant's behavior is a balance between the two.

As toddlers learn to discriminate more effectively between threatening and nonthreatening people and situations, stranger anxiety and other fears of the first two years decline. Fear also wanes as toddlers acquire more strategies for coping with it, as you will see when we discuss emotional self-regulation.

Understanding and Responding to the Emotions of Others

Infants' emotional expressions are closely tied to their ability to interpret the emotional cues of others. We have seen that in the first few months, babies match the feeling tone of the caregiver in face-to-face communication. Perhaps infants respond in kind to others' emotions through a built-in, automatic process of *emotional contagion* (Stern, 1985). Alternatively, they may acquire these emotional contingencies through operant conditioning—for example, learning that a smile generally triggers pleasurable feedback and that distress prompts a comforting response (Saarni et al., 2006).

Around 3 to 4 months, infants become sensitive to the structure and timing of face-to-face interactions. When they gaze, smile, or vocalize, they now expect their social partner to respond in kind (Markova & Legerstee, 2006; Rochat, Striano, & Blatt, 2002). Recall from Chapter 4 (see page 105) that out of this early imitative communication, infants start to view others as "like me"—an awareness believed to lay the foundation for understanding others' thoughts and feelings (Meltzoff, 2007).

From 5 months on, infants perceive facial expressions as organized patterns (see Chapter 4). As skill at establishing joint attention improves, infants realize that an emotional expression not only has meaning but is also a meaningful reaction to a specific object or event (Moses et al., 2001; Tomasello, 1999).

Once these understandings are in place, beginning at 8 to 10 months, infants engage in **social referencing**—actively seeking emotional information from a trusted person in an uncertain situation (Mumme et al., 2007). Many studies show that the caregiver's emotional expression (happy, angry, or fearful) influences whether a 1-year-old will be wary of strangers, play with an unfamiliar toy, or cross the deep side of the visual cliff (see Chapter 4, page 111) (de Rosnay et al., 2006; Stenberg, 2003; Striano & Rochat, 2000).

Parents can take advantage of social referencing to teach their baby how to react to many everyday events. And around the middle of the second year, as toddlers begin to appreciate that others' emotional reactions may differ from their own, social referencing allows them to compare their own and others' assessments of events. In one study, an adult showed 14- and 18-month-olds broccoli and crackers and acted delighted with one food but disgusted with the other (Repacholi & Gopnik, 1997). When asked to share the food, 18-month-olds gave the adult whichever food she appeared to like, regardless of their own preferences.

In sum, in social referencing, toddlers move beyond simply reacting to others' emotional messages. They use those signals to evaluate the safety of their surroundings, to guide their own actions, and to gather information about others' intentions and preferences.

Emergence of Self-Conscious Emotions

Besides basic emotions, humans are capable of a second, higher-order set of feelings, including guilt, shame, embarrassment, envy, and pride. These are called **self-conscious emotions** because each involves injury to or enhancement of our sense of self. We feel guilt when we have harmed someone and want to correct the wrongdoing. When we are ashamed or embarrassed, we have negative feelings about our behavior, and we want to retreat so others will no longer notice our failings. In contrast, pride reflects delight in the self's achievements, and we are inclined to tell others what we have accomplished and to take on further challenges (Saarni et al., 2006).

Self-conscious emotions appear in the middle of the second year, as 18- to 24-month-olds become firmly aware of the self as a separate, unique individual. Toddlers show shame and embarrassment by lowering their eyes, hanging their heads, and hiding their faces with their hands. They show guiltlike reactions, too: One 22-month-old returned a toy she had grabbed and patted her upset playmate. Pride also emerges around this time, and envy by age 3 (Barrett, 2005; Garner, 2003; Lewis et al., 1989).

Besides self-awareness, self-conscious emotions require an additional ingredient: adult instruction in *when* to feel proud, ashamed, or guilty. Situations in which adults encourage these feelings vary from culture to culture. In Western individualistic nations, most children are taught to feel pride in personal achievement. But in collectivist cultures such as China and Japan, calling attention to individual success evokes embarrassment and self-effacement. And violating cultural standards by failing to show concern for others—a parent, a teacher, or an employer—sparks intense shame (Akimoto & Sanbonmatsu, 1999; Lewis, 1992).

Beginnings of Emotional Self-Regulation

Besides expressing a wider range of emotions, infants and toddlers begin to manage their emotional experiences. **Emotional self-regulation** refers to the strategies we use to adjust our emotional state to a comfortable level of intensity so we can accomplish our goals (Thompson & Goodvin, 2007). When you remind yourself that an anxiety-provoking event will be over soon, suppress your anger at a friend's behavior, or decide not to see a scary horror film, you are engaging in emotional self-regulation.

Emotional self-regulation requires voluntary, effortful management of emotions, a capacity that improves gradually, as a result of development of the prefrontal cortex and the assistance of caregivers (Fox & Calkins, 2003; Rothbart, Posner, & Kieras, 2006). A good start in regulating emotion during the first two years contributes greatly to autonomy and mastery of cognitive and social skills (Eisenberg et al., 2004; Lawson & Ruff, 2004).

In the early months, infants are easily overwhelmed by intense emotions. They depend on the soothing interventions of caregivers—being lifted to the shoulder, rocked, gently stroked, and talked to softly—for distraction and reorienting of attention. More effective functioning of the prefrontal cortex increases the baby's tolerance for stimulation. Between 2 and 4 months, caregivers build on this capacity by initiating face-to-face play and attention to objects. In these interactions, parents arouse pleasure in the baby while adjusting the pace of their behavior so the infant does not become distressed. As a result, the baby's tolerance for stimulation increases further (Kopp & Neufeld, 2003).

By 4 to 6 months, the ability to shift attention away from unpleasant events helps infants control emotion (Crockenberg & Leerkes, 2003). At the end of the first year, crawling and walking enable infants to regulate emotion more effectively by approaching or retreating from various situations.

Infants whose parents "read" and respond contingently and sympathetically to their emotional cues tend to be less fussy and fearful, to express more pleasurable emotion, to be more interested in exploration, and to be easier to soothe (Braungart-Rieker, Hill-Soderlund, & Karrass, 2010; Crockenberg & Leerkes, 2004; Volling et al., 2002). In contrast, parents who respond impatiently or angrily or who wait to intervene until the infant

© LAURA DWIGHT PHOTOGRAPHY

A mother praises her 2-year-old's success at tower-building. To experience self-conscious emotions, such as pride, young children need self-awareness as well as adult instruction.

has become extremely agitated reinforce the baby's rapid rise to intense distress. Consequently, brain structures that buffer stress may not develop properly, resulting in an anxious, reactive child who has a reduced capacity for managing emotional problems (Blair & Raver, 2012; Feldman, 2007).

Caregivers also provide lessons in socially approved ways of expressing feelings. As early as the first few months, parents encourage infants to suppress negative emotion by imitating their expressions of interest, happiness, and surprise more often than their expressions of anger and sadness. Boys get more of this training than girls, in part because boys have a harder time regulating negative emotion (Else-Quest et al., 2006; Malatesta et al., 1986). As a result, the well-known sex difference—females as emotionally expressive and males as emotionally controlled—is promoted at a tender age. Collectivist cultures place particular emphasis on socially appropriate emotional behavior. Compared with Americans, Japanese and Chinese adults discourage the expression of strong emotion in babies (Fogel, 1993; Kuchner, 1989). By the end of the first year, Chinese and Japanese infants smile and cry less than American infants (Camras et al., 1998; Gartstein et al., 2010).

Toward the end of the second year, a vocabulary for talking about feelings—"happy," "scary," "yucky"—develops rapidly, but toddlers are not yet good at using language to manage their emotions. Temper tantrums tend to occur when an adult rejects their demands, particularly when toddlers are fatigued or hungry (Mascolo & Fischer, 2007). Toddlers whose parents are emotionally sympathetic but set limits (by not giving in to tantrums), who distract the child by offering acceptable alternatives, and who later suggest better ways to handle adult refusals display more effective anger-regulation strategies and social skills during the preschool years (Lecuyer & Houck, 2006).

Patient, sensitive parents also encourage toddlers to describe their internal states. Then, when 2-year-olds feel distressed, they can guide caregivers in helping them (Cole, Armstrong, & Pemberton, 2010). For example, while listening to a story about monsters, Grace whimpered, "Mommy, scary." Monica put the book down and gave Grace a comforting hug.

ASK YOURSELF

REVIEW Why do many infants show stranger anxiety in the second half of the first year? What factors can increase or decrease wariness of strangers?

APPLY At age 14 months, Reggie built a block tower and gleefully knocked it down. But at age 2, he called to his mother and pointed proudly to his tall block tower. What explains this change in Reggie's emotional behavior?

REFLECT How do you typically manage negative emotion? How might your early experiences, gender, and cultural background have influenced your style of emotional self-regulation?

 # Temperament and Development

When we describe one person as cheerful and "upbeat," another as active and energetic, and still others as calm, cautious, persistent, or prone to angry outbursts, we are referring to **temperament**—early-appearing, stable individual differences in reactivity and self-regulation. *Reactivity* refers to quickness and intensity of emotional arousal, attention, and motor activity. *Self-regulation,* as we have seen, refers to strategies that modify that reactivity (Rothbart & Bates, 2006). The psychological traits that make up temperament are believed to form the cornerstone of the adult personality.

In 1956, Alexander Thomas and Stella Chess initiated the New York Longitudinal Study, a groundbreaking investigation of the development of temperament that followed 141 children from early infancy well into adulthood. Results showed that temperament can increase a child's chances of experiencing psychological problems or, alternatively, protect a child from the negative effects of a highly stressful home life. At the same time, Thomas and Chess (1977) discovered that parenting practices can modify children's temperaments considerably.

These findings stimulated a growing body of research on temperament. Let's begin with the structure, or makeup, of temperament and how it is measured.

The Structure of Temperament

Thomas and Chess's model of temperament inspired all others that followed. When detailed descriptions of infants' and children's behavior obtained from parent interviews were rated on nine dimensions of temperament, certain characteristics clustered together, yielding three types of children:

- The **easy child** (40 percent of the sample) quickly establishes regular routines in infancy, is generally cheerful, and adapts easily to new experiences.

- The **difficult child** (10 percent of the sample) is irregular in daily routines, is slow to accept new experiences, and tends to react negatively and intensely.

- The **slow-to-warm-up child** (15 percent of the sample) is inactive, shows mild, low-key reactions to environmental stimuli, is negative in mood, and adjusts slowly to new experiences.

Note that 35 percent of the children did not fit any of these categories. Instead, they showed unique blends of temperamental characteristics.

Difficult children are at high risk for adjustment problems—both anxious withdrawal and aggressive behavior in early and middle childhood (Bates, Wachs, & Emde, 1994; Ramos et al., 2005; Thomas, Chess, & Birch, 1968). Although slow-to-warm-up children present fewer problems, they tend to show excessive fearfulness and slow, constricted behavior in the late preschool and school years, when they are expected to respond actively

TABLE 6.1   Rothbart's Model of Temperament

DIMENSION	DESCRIPTION
REACTIVITY	
Activity level	Level of gross-motor activity
Attention span/persistence	Duration of orienting or interest
Fearful distress	Wariness and distress in response to intense or novel stimuli, including time to adjust to new situations
Irritable distress	Extent of fussing, crying, and distress when desires are frustrated
Positive affect	Frequency of expression of happiness and pleasure
SELF-REGULATION	
Effortful control	Capacity to voluntarily suppress a dominant, reactive response in order to plan and execute a more adaptive response

and quickly in classrooms and peer groups (Chess & Thomas, 1984; Schmitz et al., 1999).

Today, the most influential model of temperament is Mary Rothbart's, described in Table 6.1. It combines related traits proposed by Thomas and Chess and other researchers, yielding a concise list of six dimensions that represent the three underlying components included in the definition of temperament: (1) *emotion* ("fearful distress," "irritable distress," "positive affect," and "soothability"), (2) *attention* ("attention span/persistence"), and (3) *action* ("activity level"). According to Rothbart, individuals differ not only in their reactivity on each dimension but also in the self-regulatory dimension of temperament, **effortful control**—the capacity to voluntarily suppress a dominant response in order to plan and execute a more adaptive response (Rothbart, 2003; Rothbart & Bates, 2006). Variations in effortful control are evident in how effectively a child can focus and shift attention, inhibit impulses, and manage negative emotion.

Beginning in early childhood, effortful control predicts favorable development and adjustment in cultures as diverse as China and the United States (Zhou, Lengua, & Wang, 2009). Positive outcomes include persistence, task mastery, academic achievement, cooperation, moral maturity (such as concern about wrongdoing and willingness to apologize), and positive social behaviors of sharing and helpfulness (Eisenberg, 2010; Harris et al., 2007; Kochanska & Aksan, 2006; Posner & Rothbart, 2007; Valiente et al., 2010). *TAKE A MOMENT...* Turn back to page 127 in Chapter 5 to review the concept of executive function, and note its resemblance to effortful control. These converging concepts, which are associated with similar positive outcomes, reveal that the same mental activities lead to effective regulation in both the cognitive and emotional/social domains.

Measuring Temperament

Temperament is often assessed through interviews or questionnaires given to parents. Behavior ratings by pediatricians, teachers, and others familiar with the child and laboratory observations by researchers have also been used. Parental reports are convenient and take advantage of parents' depth of knowledge about their child across many situations (Gartstein & Rothbart, 2003). Although information from parents has been criticized as biased, parental reports are moderately related to researchers' observations of children's behavior (Majdandžić & van den Boom, 2007; Mangelsdorf, Schoppe, & Buur, 2000).

Observations by researchers avoid the subjectivity of parental reports but can lead to other inaccuracies. In homes, observers find it hard to capture rare but important events, such as infants' response to frustration. And in the unfamiliar lab setting, fearful children may become too upset to complete the session (Wachs & Bates, 2001). Still, researchers can better control children's experiences in the lab. And they can conveniently combine observations of behavior with neurobiological measures to gain insight into the biological bases of temperament.

Most neurobiological research has focused on children who fall at opposite extremes of the positive-affect and fearful-distress dimensions of temperament: **inhibited, or shy, children,** who react negatively to and withdraw from novel stimuli, and **uninhibited, or sociable, children,** who display positive emotion to and approach novel stimuli. As the Biology and Environment box on page 150 reveals, biologically based reactivity differentiates children with inhibited and uninhibited temperaments.

Stability of Temperament

Young children who score low or high on attention span, irritability, sociability, shyness, or effortful control tend to respond similarly when assessed again several months to a few years later and, occasionally, even into the adult years (Caspi et al., 2003; Kochanska & Knaack, 2003; Majdandžić & van den Boom, 2007; Rothbart, Ahadi, & Evans, 2000; van den Akker et al., 2010). However, the overall stability of temperament is low in infancy and toddlerhood and only moderate from the preschool years on (Putnam, Samson, & Rothbart, 2000).

A major reason is that temperament itself develops with age. To illustrate, let's look at irritability. Recall from Chapter 3 that most babies fuss and cry in the early months. As infants better regulate their attention and emotions with the help of patient, supportive parenting, many who initially seemed irritable become calm and content.

These discrepancies help us understand why long-term prediction from early temperament is best achieved after age 3, when styles of responding are better established (Roberts & DelVecchio, 2000). In line with this idea, between age 2½ and 3, children improve substantially on tasks requiring effortful control, such as waiting for a reward and selectively attending to one stimulus while ignoring competing stimuli (Kochanska,

Biology and Environment

Development of Shyness and Sociability

Two 4-month-old babies, Larry and Mitch, visited the laboratory of Jerome Kagan, who observed their reactions to various unfamiliar experiences. When exposed to new sights and sounds, such as a moving mobile decorated with colorful toys, Larry moved his arms and legs with agitation and cried. In contrast, Mitch remained relaxed and quiet, smiling and cooing.

As toddlers, Larry and Mitch returned to the lab, where they experienced several procedures designed to induce uncertainty. Electrodes were placed on their bodies and blood pressure cuffs on their arms to measure heart rate; toy robots, animals, and puppets moved before their eyes; and unfamiliar people behaved in unexpected ways. While Larry whimpered and quickly withdrew, Mitch watched with interest, laughed, and approached the toys and strangers.

On a third visit, at age 4½, Larry barely talked or smiled during an interview with an unfamiliar adult. In contrast, Mitch expressed pleasure at each new activity. In a playroom with two unfamiliar peers, Larry pulled back and watched, while Mitch quickly made friends.

In longitudinal research on several hundred children, Kagan found that about 20 percent of 4-month-old babies were, like Larry, easily upset by novelty; 40 percent, like Mitch, were comfortable, even delighted, with new experiences. About 20 to 30 percent of these groups retained their temperamental styles as they grew older (Kagan, 2003; Kagan & Saudino, 2001; Kagan et al., 2007). But most children's dispositions became less extreme over time. Biological makeup and child-rearing experiences jointly influenced stability and change in temperament.

Neurobiological Correlates of Shyness and Sociability

Individual differences in arousal of the *amygdala,* an inner brain structure devoted to processing emotional information, contrib-

ute to these contrasting temperaments. fMRI research reveals that in shy, inhibited children, novel stimuli easily excite the amygdala and its connections to the prefrontal cortex and the sympathetic nervous system, which prepares the body to act in the face of threat. In sociable, uninhibited children, the same level of stimulation evokes minimal neural excitation (Kagan & Fox, 2006). And the two emotional styles are distinguished by additional neurobiological responses known to be mediated by the amygdala:

- *Heart rate.* From the first few weeks of life, the heart rates of shy children are consistently higher than those of sociable children, and they speed up further in response to unfamiliar events (Schmidt et al., 2007; Snidman et al., 1995).

- *Cortisol.* Saliva concentrations of the stress hormone cortisol tend to be higher, and to rise more in response to a stressful event, in shy than in sociable children (Schmidt et al., 1997, 1999; Zimmermann & Stansbury, 2004).

- *Pupil dilation, blood pressure, and skin surface temperature.* Compared with sociable children, shy children show greater pupil dilation, rise in blood pressure, and cooling of the fingertips when faced with novelty (Kagan et al., 1999, 2007).

Furthermore, shy children show greater EEG activity in the right than in the left frontal lobe of the cerebral cortex, which is associated with negative emotional reactivity; sociable children show the opposite pattern (Fox et al., 2008; Kagan et al., 2007). Neural activity in the amygdala, which is transmitted to the frontal lobes, probably contributes to these differences.

Child-Rearing Practices

According to Kagan, extremely shy or sociable children inherit a physiology that biases them toward a particular temperamental style. Yet experience, too, has a powerful

A strong physiological response to uncertain situations prompts this toddler to cling to her father. With patient but insistent encouragement, her parents can help her overcome the urge to retreat.

impact. Warm, supportive parenting reduces shy infants' and preschoolers' intense reaction to novelty, whereas cold, intrusive parenting heightens anxiety (Coplan, Arbeau, & Armer, 2008; Hane et al., 2008). And if parents overprotect infants and young children who dislike novelty, they make it harder for their child to overcome an urge to retreat. Parents who make appropriate demands for their child to approach new experiences help shy youngsters overcome fear (Rubin & Burgess, 2002).

When inhibition persists, it leads to excessive cautiousness, low self-esteem, and loneliness and, in adolescence, increases the risk of severe anxiety, especially social phobia—intense fear of being humiliated in social situations (Kagan & Fox, 2006). To acquire effective social skills, inhibited children need parenting tailored to their temperaments—a theme we will encounter again in this and later chapters.

Murray, & Harlan, 2000; Li-Grining, 2007). Researchers believe that around this time, areas in the prefrontal cortex involved in suppressing impulses develop rapidly (Rothbart & Bates, 2006).

Nevertheless, the ease with which children manage their reactivity depends on the type and strength of the reactive emotion. Preschoolers who were highly fearful as toddlers score slightly better than their agemates in effortful control. In contrast, angry, irritable toddlers tend to be less effective at effortful control at later ages (Bridgett et al., 2009; Kochanska & Knaack, 2003).

In sum, many factors affect the extent to which a child's temperament remains stable, including development of the biological systems on which temperament is based, the child's capacity for effortful control, the success of her efforts (which depend on the quality and intensity of her emotional reactivity), and rearing experiences. With these ideas in mind, let's turn to genetic and environmental contributions to temperament and personality.

Genetic and Environmental Influences

Research indicates that identical twins are more similar than fraternal twins across a wide range of temperamental and personality traits (Bouchard, 2004; Bouchard & Loehlin, 2001; Caspi & Shiner, 2006; Goldsmith, Pollak, & Davidson, 2008). In Chapter 2, we noted that heritability estimates suggest a moderate role for heredity in personality: About half of individual differences have been attributed to differences in genetic makeup.

Although genetic influences are clear, environment is also powerful. For example, we have seen in early chapters that persistent nutritional and emotional deprivation profoundly alters temperament, resulting in maladaptive emotional reactivity. Other evidence shows that heredity and environment often jointly contribute to temperament, since a child's approach to the world affects the experiences to which she is exposed—an instance of gene–environment correlation (see page 55 in Chapter 2). To see how this works, let's look at ethnic and gender differences.

Ethnic and Gender Differences. Compared with American Caucasian infants, Chinese and Japanese babies tend to be less active, irritable, and vocal, more easily soothed when upset, and better at quieting themselves (Kagan et al., 1994; Lewis, Ramsay, & Kawakami, 1993). Chinese and Japanese babies are also more fearful and inhibited, remaining closer to their mothers in an unfamiliar playroom and displaying more anxiety when interacting with a stranger (Chen, Wang, & DeSouza, 2006).

These variations may have genetic roots, but they are supported by cultural beliefs and practices. Japanese mothers usually say that babies come into the world as independent beings who must learn to rely on their mothers through close physical contact. American mothers typically believe just the opposite—that they must wean babies away from dependency toward autonomy. And while Asian cultures tend to view calmness as an ideal emotional state, Americans highly value the arousal and excitement generated by new places and activities (Kagan, 2010). Consistent with these beliefs, Asian mothers interact gently, soothingly, and gesturally with their babies, whereas Caucasian mothers use a more active, stimulating, verbal approach (Rothbaum et al., 2000a). Also, recall from our discussion of emotional self-regulation that Chinese and Japanese adults discourage babies from expressing strong emotion, which contributes further to their infants' tranquility.

Similarly, gender differences in temperament are evident as early as the first year, suggesting a genetic foundation. Boys are more active and daring, more irritable when frustrated, and slightly more impulsive—factors that contribute to their higher injury rates throughout childhood and adolescence. And girls' large advantage in effortful control undoubtedly contributes to their greater compliance, better school performance, and lower incidence of behavior problems (Eisenberg et al., 2004; Else-Quest et al., 2006). At the same time, parents more often encourage their young sons to be physically active and their daughters to seek help and physical closeness—through the toys they provide (trucks and footballs for boys, dolls and tea sets for girls) and through more positive reactions when the child exhibits temperamental traits consistent with gender stereotypes (Bryan & Dix, 2009; Ruble, Martin, & Berenbaum, 2006).

Children's Unique Experiences. In families with several children, an additional influence on temperament is at work. *TAKE A MOMENT...* Ask several parents to describe each of their children's personalities. You will see that they often look for differences between siblings: "She's a lot more active," "He's more sociable," "She's far more persistent." As a result, parents often regard siblings as more distinct than other observers do (Saudino, 2003). Parents' tendency to emphasize each child's unique qualities affects their child-rearing practices. In an investigation of identical-twin toddlers, mothers' differential treatment predicted differences in psychological adjustment. The twin who received more warmth and less harshness was more positive in mood and social behavior (Deater-Deckard et al., 2001).

Besides different experiences within the family, siblings have distinct experiences with teachers, peers, and others in their community that affect personality development. And in middle childhood and adolescence, they often seek ways to differ from one another. For all these reasons, both identical and fraternal twins tend to become increasingly dissimilar in personality with age (Loehlin & Martin, 2001; McCartney, Harris, & Bernieri, 1990). In sum, temperament and personality can be understood only in terms of complex interdependencies between genetic and environmental factors.

Temperament and Child Rearing: The Goodness-of-Fit Model

If a child's disposition interferes with learning or getting along with others, adults must gently but consistently counteract the child's maladaptive style. Thomas and Chess (1977) proposed a **goodness-of-fit model** to describe how temperament and environment together can produce favorable outcomes. Goodness of fit involves creating child-rearing environments that recognize each child's temperament while encouraging more adaptive functioning.

Difficult children frequently experience parenting that fits poorly with their dispositions. By the second year, their parents tend to resort to angry, punitive discipline, which undermines the development of effortful control. As the child reacts with

A parent's firm but affectionate approach to discipline can help temperamentally difficult children gain in effortful control, managing negative emotion.

defiance and disobedience, parents become increasingly stressed (Bridgett et al., 2009; Paulussen-Hoogeboom et al., 2007). As a result, they continue their coercive tactics and also discipline inconsistently, at times rewarding the child's noncompliance by giving in to it—practices that sustain the child's conflict-ridden style (van Aken et al., 2007; Pesonen et al., 2008). In contrast, when parents are positive and sensitive, difficultness declines by age 2 or 3 (Feldman, Greenbaum, & Yirmiya, 1999). In toddlerhood and childhood, parental sensitivity, support, clear expectations, and limits foster effortful control, also reducing the likelihood that difficultness will persist (Cipriano & Stifter, 2010).

Recent evidence indicates that temperamentally difficult children function much worse than other children when exposed to inept parenting, yet benefit most from good parenting (Pluess & Belsky, 2011). Using molecular genetic analyses, researchers are investigating gene–environment interactions (see page 54 in Chapter 2) that explain this finding. In one study, 2-year-olds with a chromosome 17 gene that interferes with functioning of the neurotransmitter serotonin (involved in regulating negative mood) became increasingly irritable as their mothers' anxiety about parenting increased (Ivorra et al., 2010). Maternal anxiety had little impact on toddlers without this genetic marker. In another investigation, preschoolers with this gene benefited, especially, from positive parenting, displaying unusually large gains in effortful control (Kochanska, Philibert, & Barry, 2009).

The goodness-of-fit model reminds us that children have unique dispositions that adults must accept. Parents can neither take full credit for their children's virtues nor be blamed for all their faults. But parents can turn an environment that exaggerates a child's problems into one that builds on the child's strengths. As we will see, goodness of fit is also at the heart of infant–caregiver attachment. This first intimate relationship grows out of interaction between parent and baby, to which the emotional styles of both partners contribute.

ASK YOURSELF

REVIEW How do genetic and environmental factors work together to influence temperament? Cite several examples from research.

APPLY Mandy and Jeff are parents of 2-year-old inhibited Sam and 3-year-old difficult Maria. Explain the importance of effortful control to Mandy and Jeff, and suggest ways they can strengthen it in each of their children.

REFLECT How would you describe your temperament as a young child? Do you think your temperament has remained stable, or has it changed? What factors might be involved?

Development of Attachment

Attachment is the strong affectionate tie we have with special people in our lives that leads us to feel pleasure when we interact with them and to be comforted by their nearness in times of stress. By the second half of the first year, infants have become attached to familiar people who have responded to their needs. *TAKE A MOMENT...* Watch how babies of this age single out their parents for special attention. When the parent enters the room, the baby breaks into a broad, friendly smile. When she picks him up, he snuggles against her. When he feels anxious or afraid, he crawls into her lap and clings closely.

Attachment has also been the subject of intense theoretical debate. Recall that the *psychoanalytic perspective* regards feeding as the central context in which caregivers and babies build

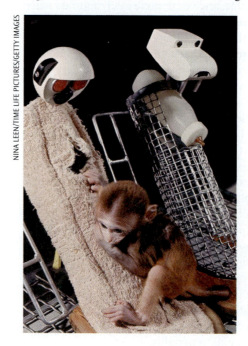

Baby monkeys reared with "surrogate mothers" preferred to cling to a soft terry-cloth "mother" over a wire-mesh "mother" holding a bottle—evidence that parent–infant attachment is based on more than satisfaction of hunger.

this close emotional bond. *Behaviorism,* too, emphasizes the importance of feeding, but for different reasons. According to a well-known behaviorist explanation, infants learn to prefer the mother's soft caresses, warm smiles, and tender words because these events are paired with tension relief as she satisfies the baby's hunger.

Although feeding is an important context for building a close relationship, attachment does not depend on hunger satisfaction. In the 1950s, a famous experiment showed that rhesus monkeys reared with terry-cloth and wire-mesh "surrogate mothers" clung to the soft terry-cloth substitute, even though the wire-mesh "mother" held the bottle and infants had to climb onto it to be fed (Harlow & Zimmerman, 1959). Human infants, too, become attached to family members who seldom feed them, including fathers, siblings, and grandparents. And toddlers in Western cultures who sleep alone and experience frequent daytime separations from their parents sometimes develop strong emotional ties to cuddly objects, such as blankets and teddy bears, that play no role in infant feeding!

Ethological Theory of Attachment

Today, **ethological theory of attachment,** which recognizes the infant's emotional tie to the caregiver as an evolved response that promotes survival, is the most widely accepted view. John Bowlby (1969), who first applied this idea to the infant–caregiver bond, was inspired by Konrad Lorenz's studies of imprinting (see Chapter 1). Bowlby believed that the human infant, like the young of other animal species, is endowed with a set of built-in behaviors that help keep the parent nearby to protect the infant from danger and to provide support for exploring and mastering the environment (Waters & Cummings, 2000).

The infant's relationship with the parent begins as a set of innate signals that call the adult to the baby's side. Over time, a true affectionate bond forms, supported by new cognitive and emotional capacities as well as by a history of warm, sensitive care. Attachment develops in four phases:

1. *Preattachment phase* (birth to 6 weeks). Built-in signals—grasping, smiling, crying, and gazing into the adult's eyes—help bring newborn babies into close contact with other humans, who comfort them.
2. *"Attachment-in-the-making" phase* (6 weeks to 6–8 months). During this phase, infants respond differently to a familiar caregiver than to a stranger. For example, at 4 months, Timmy smiled, laughed, and babbled more freely when interacting with his mother and quieted more quickly when she picked him up. As infants learn that their own actions affect the behavior of those around them, they begin to develop a *sense of trust*—the expectation that the caregiver will respond when signaled—but they still do not protest when separated from her.
3. *"Clear-cut" attachment phase* (6–8 months to 18 months–2 years). Babies display **separation anxiety,** becoming upset when their trusted caregiver leaves. Like stranger anxiety (see page 146), separation anxiety does not always occur; it depends on infant temperament and the current situation. But in many cultures, separation anxiety increases between 6 and 15 months. Besides protesting the parent's departure, older infants and toddlers approach, follow, and climb on her in preference to others. And they use the familiar caregiver as a secure base from which to explore.

LOOK AND LISTEN

Watch an 8- to 18-month-old at play for 20 to 30 minutes. Describe the baby's use of the parent or other familiar caregiver as a secure base from which to explore. ●

4. *Formation of a reciprocal relationship* (18 months to 2 years and on). Rapid growth in representation and language permits toddlers to understand some of the factors that influence the parent's coming and going and to predict her return. As a result, separation protest declines. Now children negotiate with the caregiver to alter her goals. At age 2, Caitlin asked Carolyn and David to read a story before leaving her with a babysitter. The extra time with her parents, along with a better understanding of when they would be back ("right after you go to sleep"), helped Caitlin withstand her parents' absence.

According to Bowlby (1980), out of their experiences during these four phases, children construct an enduring affectionate tie to the caregiver that they can use as a secure base in the parents' absence. This image serves as an **internal working model,** or set of expectations about the availability of attachment figures and their likelihood of providing support during times of stress. The internal working model becomes a vital part of personality, serving as a guide for all future close relationships (Bretherton & Munholland, 2008). With age, children continually revise and expand their internal working model as their cognitive, emotional, and social capacities increase and as they interact with parents and form other bonds with adults, siblings, and friends.

© ELLEN B. SENISI PHOTOGRAPHY

Because this 2-year-old has the language and representational skills to predict his mother's return, separation anxiety declines. He accepts his mother's departure.

Measuring the Security of Attachment

Although all family-reared babies become attached to a familiar caregiver, the quality of this relationship varies. A widely used laboratory procedure for assessing the quality of attachment between 1 and 2 years of age is the **Strange Situation.** Designed by Mary Ainsworth, it takes the baby through eight short episodes in which brief separations from and reunions with the parent occur in an unfamiliar playroom (see Table 6.2).

Observing infants' responses to these episodes, researchers identified a secure attachment pattern and three patterns of insecurity (Ainsworth et al., 1978; Barnett & Vondra, 1999; Main & Solomon, 1990; Thompson, 2006). *TAKE A MOMENT...* From the description at the beginning of this chapter, which pattern do you think Grace displayed after adjusting to her adoptive family?

- **Secure attachment.** These infants use the parent as a secure base. When separated, they may or may not cry, but if they do, it is because the parent is absent and they prefer her to the stranger. When the parent returns, they actively seek contact, and their crying is reduced immediately. About 60 percent of North American infants in middle-SES families show this pattern. (In low-SES families, a smaller proportion of babies are secure, with higher proportions falling into the insecure patterns.)

TABLE 6.2
Episodes in the Strange Situation

EPISODE	EVENTS	ATTACHMENT BEHAVIOR OBSERVED
1	Researcher introduces parent and baby to playroom and then leaves.	
2	Parent is seated while baby plays with toys.	Parent as a secure base
3	Stranger enters, is seated, and talks to parent.	Reaction to unfamiliar adult
4	Parent leaves room. Stranger responds to baby and offers comfort if baby is upset.	Separation anxiety
5	Parent returns, greets baby, and offers comfort if necessary. Stranger leaves room.	Reaction to reunion
6	Parent leaves room.	Separation anxiety
7	Stranger enters room and offers comfort.	Ability to be soothed by stranger
8	Parent returns, greets baby, offers comfort if necessary, and tries to reinterest baby in toys.	Reaction to reunion

Note: Episode 1 lasts about 30 seconds; each of the remaining episodes lasts about 3 minutes. Separation episodes are cut short if the baby becomes very upset. Reunion episodes are extended if the baby needs more time to calm down and return to play.
Source: Ainsworth et al., 1978.

- **Avoidant attachment.** These infants seem unresponsive to the parent when she is present. When she leaves, they usually are not distressed, and they react to the stranger in much the same way as to the parent. During reunion, they avoid or are slow to greet the parent, and when picked up, they often fail to cling. About 15 percent of North American infants in middle-SES families show this pattern.

- **Resistant attachment.** Before separation, these infants seek closeness to the parent and often fail to explore. When the parent leaves, they are usually distressed, and on her return they combine clinginess with angry, resistive behavior, sometimes hitting and pushing. Many continue to cry after being picked up and cannot be comforted easily. About 10 percent of North American infants in middle-SES families show this pattern.

- **Disorganized/disoriented attachment.** This pattern reflects the greatest insecurity. At reunion, these infants show confused, contradictory behaviors—for example, looking away while the parent is holding them or approaching the parent with flat, depressed emotion. About 15 percent of North American infants in middle-SES families show this pattern.

An alternative method, the **Attachment Q-Sort,** suitable for children between 1 and 4 years, depends on home observation (Waters et al., 1995). Either the parent or a highly trained observer sorts 90 behaviors ("Child greets mother with a big smile when she enters the room," "If mother moves very far, child follows along") into nine categories ranging from "highly descriptive" to "not at all descriptive" of the child. Then a score, ranging from high to low in security, is computed. The Q-Sort responses of expert observers correspond well with babies' secure-base behavior in the Strange Situation, but parents' Q-Sorts do not (van IJzendoorn et al., 2004). Parents of insecure children, especially, may have difficulty accurately reporting their child's attachment behaviors.

Stability of Attachment

Research on the stability of attachment patterns between 1 and 2 years of age yields a wide range of findings (Thompson, 2006). Quality of attachment is usually secure and stable for middle-SES babies experiencing favorable life conditions. And infants who move from insecurity to security typically have well-adjusted mothers with positive family and friendship ties. Perhaps many became parents before they were psychologically ready but, with social support, grew into the role. In contrast, in low-SES families with many daily stresses and little social support, attachment generally moves away from security or changes from one insecure pattern to another (Fish, 2004; Levendosky et al., 2011; Vondra et al., 2001).

These findings indicate that securely attached babies more often maintain their attachment status than insecure babies. The exception is disorganized/disoriented attachment, an insecure pattern that is either highly stable or that consistently predicts later insecurity of another type (Aikens, Howes, & Hamilton, 2009; Sroufe et al., 2005; Weinfield, Whaley, & Egeland, 2004).

As you will soon see, many disorganized/disoriented infants and children experience extremely negative caregiving, which may disrupt emotional self-regulation so severely that confused, ambivalent feelings toward parents often persist.

Cultural Variations

Cross-cultural evidence indicates that attachment patterns may have to be interpreted differently in certain cultures. For example, as Figure 6.1 reveals, German infants show considerably more avoidant attachment than American babies do. But German parents value independence and encourage their infants to be nonclingy (Grossmann et al., 1985). In contrast, a study of infants of the Dogon people of Mali, Africa, revealed that none showed avoidant attachment to their mothers (True, Pisani, & Oumar, 2001). Even when grandmothers are primary caregivers (as they are with firstborn sons), Dogon mothers remain available, holding their babies close and nursing promptly in response to hunger and distress.

Japanese infants, as well, rarely show avoidant attachment (refer again to Figure 6.1). Rather, many are resistantly attached, but this reaction may not represent true insecurity. Japanese mothers rarely leave their babies in others' care, so the Strange Situation probably induces greater stress in them than in infants who experience frequent maternal separations (Takahashi, 1990). Also, Japanese parents view the attention seeking that is part of resistant attachment as a normal indicator of infants' efforts to satisfy dependency and security needs (Rothbaum et al., 2007). Despite such cultural variations, the secure pattern is still the most common attachment quality in all societies studied (van IJzendoorn & Sagi-Schwartz, 2008).

Dogon mothers of Mali, West Africa, stay close to their babies and respond promptly and gently to infant hunger and distress. With their mothers consistently available, none of the Dogon babies show avoidant attachment.

Factors That Affect Attachment Security

What factors might influence attachment security? Researchers have looked closely at four important influences: (1) early availability of a consistent caregiver, (2) quality of caregiving, (3) the baby's characteristics, and (4) family context, including parents' internal working models.

Early Availability of a Consistent Caregiver.

Although adopted children who spent their first year or more in deprived Eastern European orphanages where they had no opportunity to establish a close tie to a caregiver are able to bond with their adoptive parents, they nevertheless show elevated rates of attachment insecurity (van den Dries et al., 2009; Smyke et al., 2010). They are also at high risk for emotional and social difficulties. Many are overly friendly to unfamiliar adults; others are sad, anxious, and withdrawn. These symptoms are associated with wide-ranging mental health problems in middle childhood and adolescence, including cognitive impairments, inattention and hyperactivity, depression, and either social avoidance or aggressive behavior (Kreppner et al., 2007, 2010; Rutter et al., 2007, 2010; Zeanah, 2000).

Furthermore, as early as 7 months, institutionalized children show reduced ERP brain waves in response to facial expressions of emotion and have trouble discriminating such expressions—outcomes that suggest disrupted formation of neural structures involved in "reading" emotions (Parker et al., 2005). Consistent with these findings, in adopted children with longer institutional stays, the volume of the *amygdala* (see page 150) is atypically large (Tottenham et al., 2011). The larger the amygdala, the worse adopted children perform on tasks assessing understanding of emotion and the poorer their emotional self-regulation. Overall, the evidence indicates that fully normal emotional development depends on establishing a close tie with a caregiver early in life.

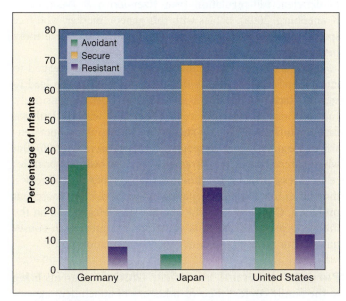

FIGURE 6.1 **A cross-cultural comparison of infants' reactions in the Strange Situation.** A high percentage of German babies seem avoidantly attached, whereas a substantial number of Japanese infants appear resistantly attached. Note that these responses may not reflect true insecurity. Instead, they are probably due to cultural differences in child-rearing practices. (Adapted from van IJzendoorn & Kroonenberg, 1988; van IJzendoorn & Sagi-Schwartz, 2008.)

Quality of Caregiving. Dozens of studies report that **sensitive caregiving**—responding promptly, consistently, and appropriately to infants and holding them tenderly and carefully—is moderately related to attachment security in diverse cultures and SES groups (Belsky & Fearon, 2008; De Wolff & van IJzendoorn, 1997; van IJzendoorn et al., 2004). In contrast, insecurely attached infants tend to have mothers who engage in less physical contact, handle them awkwardly or "routinely," and are resentful and rejecting, particularly in response to infant distress (Ainsworth et al., 1978; Isabella, 1993; McElwain & Booth-LaForce, 2006; Pederson & Moran, 1996).

Cultures, however, vary in their view of sensitivity toward infants. Among the Gusii people of Kenya, for example, mothers rarely cuddle, hug, or interact playfully with their babies, although they are very responsive to their infants' needs. Yet most Gusii infants appear securely attached (LeVine et al., 1994). This suggests that security depends on attentive caregiving, not necessarily on frequent physical affection or face-to-face interaction. Puerto Rican mothers, who highly value obedience and socially appropriate behavior, often physically direct and limit their babies' actions—a caregiving style linked to attachment security in Puerto Rican culture (Carlson & Harwood, 2003). Yet in many Western cultures, such physical control and restriction of exploration predict insecurity (Belsky & Fearon, 2008; Whipple, Bernier, & Mageau, 2011).

Compared with securely attached infants, avoidant babies tend to receive overstimulating, intrusive care. By avoiding the mother, these infants appear to be escaping from overwhelming interaction. Resistant infants often experience inconsistent care. Their mothers are unresponsive to infant signals. Yet when the baby begins to explore, these mothers interfere, shifting the infant's attention back to themselves. As a result, the baby is overly dependent as well as angry at the mother's lack of involvement (Cassidy & Berlin, 1994; Isabella & Belsky, 1991).

© JEFF GREENBERG/THE IMAGE WORKS

This father's sensitive, affectionate interaction contributes to his child's attachment security.

Highly inadequate caregiving is a powerful predictor of disruptions in attachment. Child abuse and neglect are associated with all three forms of attachment insecurity. Among maltreated infants, disorganized/disoriented attachment is especially high (van IJzendoorn, Schuengel, & Bakermans-Kranenburg, 1999). Persistently depressed mothers, mothers with very low marital satisfaction, and parents suffering from a traumatic event, such as loss of a loved one, also tend to promote the uncertain behaviors of this pattern (Campbell et al., 2004; Madigan et al., 2006; Moss et al., 2005). Some of these mothers display frightening, contradictory, and unpleasant behaviors—looking scared, teasing the baby, holding the baby stiffly at a distance, or seeking reassurance from the upset child (Abrams, Rifkin, & Hesse, 2006; Moran et al., 2008).

Infant Characteristics. Because attachment is the result of a *relationship* that builds between two partners, infant characteristics should affect how easily it is established. Babies whose temperament is emotionally reactive and difficult are more likely to develop later insecure attachments (van IJzendoorn et al., 2004; Vaughn, Bost, & van IJzendoorn, 2008). However, caregiving is also involved. In a study extending from birth to age 2, difficult infants more often had highly anxious mothers—a combination that, by the second year, often resulted in a "disharmonious relationship" characterized by both maternal insensitivity and attachment insecurity (Symons, 2001).

Other research on disorganized/disoriented attachment has uncovered gene–environment interactions (Gervai, 2009). In one investigation, mothers' experience of unresolved loss of a loved one or other trauma was associated with attachment disorganization only in infants with a chromosome-11 gene linked to deficient self-regulation (van IJzendoorn & Bakermans-Kranenburg, 2006). Babies with this genetic marker, who face special challenges in managing intense emotion, were more negatively affected by maternal adjustment problems.

Overall, infant characteristics are only weakly related to attachment quality because *many* child attributes can lead to secure attachment as long as the caregivers behave sensitively. Interventions that teach parents to interact with difficult-to-care-for infants are highly successful in enhancing both sensitive care and attachment security (Velderman et al., 2006). But when parents' capacity is strained—by their own personalities or by stressful living conditions—then infants with illnesses, disabilities, and difficult temperaments are at risk for attachment problems. Child care—as the Social Issues: Health box on the following page indicates—is yet another context with consequences for the infant–parent attachment relationship.

Parents' Internal Working Models. Parents bring to the family context their own history of attachment experiences, from which they construct internal working models that they apply to the bonds they establish with their children. Monica, who recalled her mother as tense and preoccupied, expressed regret that they had not had a closer relationship. Is her image of parenthood likely to affect Grace's attachment security?

Social Issues: Health

Does Child Care in Infancy Threaten Attachment Security and Later Adjustment?

Are infants who experience daily separation from their employed parents and early placement in child care at risk for attachment insecurity and development problems? Some researchers think so, but others disagree. Evidence from the National Institute of Child Health and Development (NICHD) Study of Early Child Care, the largest longitudinal investigation to date, including more than 1,300 infants and their families—reveals that nonparental care by itself does not affect attachment quality (NICHD Early Child Care Research Network, 1997, 2001). Rather, the relationship between child care and emotional well-being depends on both family and child-care experiences.

Family Circumstances

We have seen that family conditions affect children's attachment security and later adjustment. The NICHD Study confirmed that parenting quality, assessed using a combination of maternal sensitivity and HOME scores (see page 133 in Chapter 5), exerts a more powerful impact on children's adjustment than does exposure to child care (NICHD Early Childhood Research Network, 1998; Watamura et al., 2011).

For employed parents, balancing work and caregiving can be stressful. Mothers who feel overloaded by work and family pressures may respond less sensitively to their babies, thereby risking the infant's security. And as paternal involvement in caregiving has risen (see page 158), many more U.S. fathers in dual-earner families also report work–family life conflict (Galinsky, Aumann, & Bond, 2009).

Quality and Extent of Child Care

Nevertheless, poor-quality child care may contribute to a higher rate of insecure attachment. In the NICHD Study, when babies were exposed to combined home and child-care risk factors—insensitive caregiving at home

along with insensitive caregiving in child care, long hours in child care, or more than one child-care arrangement—the rate of attachment insecurity increased. Overall, mother–child interaction was more favorable when children attended higher-quality child care and also spent fewer hours in child care (NICHD Early Child Care Research Network, 1997, 1999).

Furthermore, when these children reached age 3, a history of higher-quality child care predicted better social skills (NICHD Early Child Care Research Network, 2002b). However, at age 4½ to 5, children averaging more than 30 child-care hours per week displayed more behavior problems, especially defiance, disobedience, and aggression (NICHD Early Child Care Research Network, 2003a, 2006).

This does not necessarily mean that child care causes behavior problems. Rather, heavy exposure to substandard care, which is widespread in the United States, may promote these difficulties, especially when combined with family risk factors. A closer look at the NICHD participants during the preschool years revealed that those in both poor-quality home and child-care environments fared worst in social skills and problem behaviors, whereas those in both high-quality home and child-child care environments fared best. In between were preschoolers in high-quality child care but poor-quality homes (Watamura et al., 2011). These children benefited from the *protective influence* of high-quality child care.

Evidence from other industrialized nations confirms that full-time child care need not harm children's development. In Australia, for example, infants who spend full days in government-funded, high-quality child-care centers have a higher rate of secure attachment than infants informally cared for by relatives, friends, or babysitters. And amount of time spent in child care is

© ELLEN B. SENISI PHOTOGRAPHY

High-quality child care, with generous caregiver–child ratios, small group sizes, and knowledgeable caregivers, can be part of a system that promotes all aspects of development, including attachment security.

unrelated to Australian children's behavior problems (Love et al., 2003).

Conclusions

Taken together, research suggests that some infants may be at risk for attachment insecurity and later adjustment problems due to inadequate child care, long hours in such care, and parental pressures of full-time employment and child rearing. But it is inappropriate to use these findings to justify a reduction in child-care services. When family incomes are limited or mothers who want to work are forced to stay at home, children's emotional security is not promoted.

Instead, it makes sense to increase the availability of high-quality child care and to relieve work–family-life conflict by providing parents with paid employment leave (see page 81 in Chapter 3) and opportunities for part-time work. In the NICHD study, part-time (as opposed to full-time) employment during the baby's first year was associated with greater maternal sensitivity and a higher-quality home environment, which yielded more favorable development in early childhood (Brooks-Gunn, Han, & Waldfogel, 2010).

To assess parents' internal working models, researchers ask them to evaluate childhood memories of attachment experiences (Main & Goldwyn, 1998). Parents who discuss their childhoods with objectivity and balance, regardless of whether their experiences were positive or negative, tend to have

securely attached children. In contrast, parents who dismiss the importance of early relationships or describe them in angry, confused ways usually have insecurely attached children and are less warm, sensitive, and encouraging of learning and mastery (Behrens, Hesse, & Main, 2007; Coyl, Newland,

& Freeman, 2010; Steele, Steele, & Fonagy, 1996; van IJzendoorn, 1995).

But we must not assume any direct transfer of parents' childhood experiences to quality of attachment with their own children. Internal working models are *reconstructed memories* affected by many factors, including relationship experiences over the life course, personality, and current life satisfaction. Longitudinal research reveals that negative life events can weaken the link between an individual's own attachment security in infancy and a secure internal working model in adulthood. And insecurely attached babies who become adults with insecure internal working models often have lives that, based on self-reports in adulthood, are filled with family crises (Waters et al., 2000; Weinfield, Sroufe, & Egeland, 2000).

In sum, our early rearing experiences do not destine us to become either sensitive or insensitive parents. Rather, the way we *view* our childhoods—our ability to come to terms with negative events, to integrate new information into our working models, and to look back on our own parents in an understanding, forgiving way—is far more influential in how we rear our children than the actual history of care we received (Bretherton & Munholland, 2008).

Multiple Attachments

Babies develop attachments to a variety of familiar people—not just mothers but also fathers, grandparents, siblings, and professional caregivers. Although Bowlby (1969) believed that infants are predisposed to direct their attachment behaviors to a single special person, especially when they are distressed, his theory allows for these multiple attachments.

Fathers. Fathers' sensitive caregiving with infants, like mothers', predicts attachment security (Lundy, 2003; van IJzendoorn et al., 2004). But in many cultures—Australia, Canada, Germany, India, Israel, Italy, Japan, and the United States—mothers and fathers tend to interact differently with their babies. Mothers devote more time to physical care and expressing affection, fathers to playful interaction (Freeman & Newland, 2010; Roopnarine et al., 1990).

Mothers and fathers also play differently. Mothers more often provide toys, talk to infants, and gently play conventional games like pat-a-cake. In contrast, fathers—especially with their infant sons—tend to engage in highly stimulating physical play with bursts of excitement (Feldman, 2003). As long as fathers are also sensitive, this stimulating, startling play style helps babies regulate emotion in intensely arousing situations, including novel physical environments and play with peers (Hazen et al., 2010; Paquette, 2004).

LOOK AND LISTEN

Observe parents at play with infants at home or a family gathering. Describe both similarities and differences in mothers' and fathers' behaviors. Are your observations consistent with research findings? ●

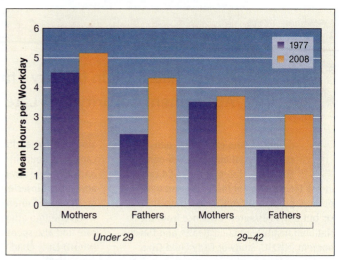

FIGURE 6.2 **Average amount of time per workday U.S. employed mothers and fathers reported spending with their children (age 12 and younger) in 1977 and 2008.** In national surveys of several thousand employed parents, mothers' time with children remained fairly stable from 1977 to 2008; fathers' time increased substantially. (Adapted from Galinsky, Aumann, & Bond, 2009.)

In cultures such as Japan, where long work hours prevent most fathers from sharing in infant caregiving, play is a vital context in which fathers build secure attachments (Hewlett, 2004; Newland, Coyl, & Freeman, 2008). In many Western nations, however, a strict division of parental roles—mother as caregiver, father as playmate—has changed over the past several decades in response to women's workforce participation.

Recent surveys indicated that U.S. fathers under age 29 devote about 85 percent as much time to children as mothers do—on average, just over 4 hours per workday, nearly double the hours young fathers reported three decades ago. Although fathers age 29 to 42 spend somewhat less time with children, their involvement has also increased substantially (see Figure 6.2). Today, nearly one-third of U.S. employed women say that their spouse or partner shares equally in or takes most responsibility for child-care tasks (Galinsky, Aumann, & Bond, 2009). Paternal availability to children is fairly similar across SES and ethnic groups, with one exception: Hispanic fathers spend more time engaged, probably because of the particularly high value that Hispanic cultures place on family involvement (Cabrera & García Coll, 2004; Parke et al., 2004).

A warm marital bond promotes both parents' sensitivity and involvement and children's attachment security, but it is particularly important for fathers (Brown et al., 2010; Sevigny & Loutzenhiser, 2010). And in studies carried out in many societies and ethnic groups, fathers' affectionate care of young children predicted later cognitive, emotional, and social competence as strongly as did mothers' warmth—and occasionally more strongly (Rohner & Veneziano, 2001; Veneziano, 2003).

Siblings. Despite declines in family size, 80 percent of North American and European children grow up with at least one sibling (Dunn, 2004). The arrival of a new baby is a difficult expe-

The arrival of a baby brother or sister is a difficult experience for most preschoolers. Maternal warmth toward both children assures the older sibling of continuing parental love and is related to positive sibling interaction.

rience for most preschoolers, who often become demanding, clingy, and deliberately naughty for a time. Attachment security also declines, especially for children over age 2 (old enough to feel threatened and displaced) and for those with mothers under stress (Baydar, Greek, & Brooks-Gunn, 1997; Teti et al., 1996).

Yet resentment is only one feature of a rich emotional relationship that soon develops between siblings. Older children also show affection and concern when the infant cries. By the end of the first year, babies are comforted by the presence of a preschool-age brother or sister during short parental absences. Throughout childhood, children continue to treat older siblings as attachment figures, turning to them for comfort in stressful situations when parents are unavailable (Seibert & Kerns, 2009).

Nevertheless, individual differences in sibling relationships emerge early. Certain temperamental traits—high emotional reactivity or activity level—increase the chances of sibling conflict (Brody, Stoneman, & McCoy, 1994; Dunn, 1994). And maternal warmth toward both children is related to positive sibling interaction and to preschoolers' support of a distressed younger sibling (Volling, 2001; Volling & Belsky, 1992). In contrast, maternal harshness and lack of involvement are linked to antagonistic sibling relationships (Howe, Aquan-Assee, & Bukowski, 2001).

Finally, a good marriage and effective coparenting are linked to preschool siblings' capacity to cope adaptively with jealousy and conflict (Volling, McElwain, & Miller, 2002). Perhaps good communication between parents serves as a model of effective problem solving. It may also foster a generally happy family environment, giving children less reason to feel jealous.

Attachment and Later Development

According to psychoanalytic and ethological theories, the inner feelings of affection and security that result from a healthy attachment relationship support all aspects of psychological development. Yet contrary evidence exists. In longitudinal research, secure infants generally fared better than insecure infants, but not always (Fearon et al., 2010; McCartney et al., 2004; Schneider, Atkinson, & Tardif, 2001; Stams, Juffer, & van IJzendoorn, 2002).

What accounts for this inconsistency? Mounting evidence indicates that *continuity of caregiving* determines whether attachment security is linked to later development (Lamb et al., 1985; Thompson, 2006). When a large sample of children were tracked from ages 1 to 3 years, those experiencing secure attachment followed by sensitive parenting scored highest in cognitive, emotional, and social outcomes. Those experiencing insecure attachment followed by parental insensitivity scored lowest, while those with mixed histories of attachment and maternal sensitivity scored in between (Belsky & Fearon, 2002a).

In sum, secure attachment in infancy launches the parent–child relationship on a positive path. An early warm, positive parent–child tie, sustained over time, predicts a more confident and complex self-concept, more advanced emotional understanding and social skills, a stronger sense of moral responsibility, and higher motivation to achieve in school (Thompson, 2006, 2008). But the effects of early attachment security are *conditional*—dependent on the quality of the baby's future relationships.

ASK YOURSELF

REVIEW What factors explain stability in attachment pattern for some children and change for others? Are these factors also involved in the link between attachment in infancy and later development? Explain.

APPLY Explain how the caregiving experiences of securely attached infants promote development of emotional self-regulation, described on page 147.

REFLECT How would you characterize your internal working model? What factors, in addition to your relationship with your parents, might have influenced it?

 ## Self-Development

Infancy is a rich formative period for the development of both physical and social understanding. In Chapter 5, you learned that infants develop an appreciation of the permanence of objects. In this chapter, we have seen that over the first year, infants recognize and respond appropriately to others' emotions and distinguish familiar from unfamiliar people. That both objects and people achieve an independent, stable existence for the infant implies that knowledge of the self as a separate, permanent entity is also emerging.

Self-Awareness

When Carolyn held Caitlin in front of a mirror, as early as the first few months Caitlin smiled and returned friendly behaviors to her image. At what age did she realize that the charming baby gazing and smiling back was herself?

Beginnings of Self-Awareness. Infants' remarkable capacity for *intermodal perception* (see page 113 in Chapter 4) supports the beginnings of self-awareness (Rochat, 2003). As they feel their own touch, feel and watch their limbs move, and feel and hear themselves cry, babies experience intermodal matches that differentiate their own body from surrounding bodies and objects.

Over the first few months, infants distinguish their own visual image from other stimuli. When shown two side-by-side video images of their kicking legs, one from their own perspective (camera behind the baby) and one from an observer's perspective (camera in front of the baby), 3-month-olds looked longer at the observer's view (Rochat, 1998). By 4 months, infants look and smile more at video images of others than at video images of themselves, indicating that they treat another person (as opposed to the self) as a social partner (Rochat & Striano, 2002).

Self-Recognition. During the second year, toddlers become consciously aware of the self's physical features. In several studies, 9- to 28-month-olds were placed in front of a mirror. Then, under the pretext of wiping the baby's face, each mother rubbed red dye on her child's nose or forehead. Toddlers older than 20 months touched or rubbed their noses or foreheads, indicating awareness of their unique appearance (Bard et al., 2006; Lewis & Brooks-Gunn, 1979). Around age 2, **self-recognition**—identification of the self as a physically unique being—is well under way. Children point to themselves in photos

This 20-month-old's response to her mirror image indicates that she recognizes her unique physical features and is aware of herself as a separate being, distinct from other people and objects.

and refer to themselves by name or with a personal pronoun ("I" or "me") (Lewis & Ramsay, 2004). Nevertheless, toddlers make **scale errors,** attempting to do things that their body size makes impossible. For example, they will try to put on dolls' clothes or walk through a doorway too narrow for them to pass through (Brownell, Zerwas, & Ramani, 2007; DeLoache, Uttal, & Rosengren, 2004). Possibly, toddlers lack an accurate understanding of their own body dimensions. Alternatively, they may simply be exploring the consequences of squeezing into restricted spaces, as they are far less likely to try when the risk of harming themselves is high (the too-narrow doorway is next to a ledge where they could fall) (Franchak & Adolph, 2012). Scale errors decline around age 2, but many 2½-year-olds still make them.

According to many theorists, self-awareness and self-recognition develop as infants and toddlers increasingly realize that their own actions cause objects and people to react in predictable ways (Nadel, Prepin, & Okanda, 2005). For example, batting a mobile and seeing it swing in a pattern different from the infant's own actions informs the baby about the relation between self and physical world. Smiling and vocalizing at a caregiver who smiles and vocalizes back helps clarify the relation between self and social world. The contrast between these experiences helps infants sense that they are separate from external reality.

Cultural variations exist in early self-development (Keller et al., 2004, 2005). Mothers of the Nso people of Cameroon, a collectivist farming society, engage in less face-to-face communication and object stimulation and more body contact and physical stimulation of their babies than do urban German and Greek mothers. Nso "proximal" parenting, which emphasizes interdependence, is associated with later attainment of self-recognition but earlier emergence of toddlers' compliance with adult requests.

Self-Awareness and Early Emotional and Social Development. Recall that self-conscious emotions depend on a strengthening sense of self. Self-awareness also leads to first efforts to appreciate others' perspectives. Toddlers express first signs of **empathy**—the ability to understand another's emotional state and *feel with* that person, or respond emotionally in a similar way. For example, they communicate concern when others are distressed and may offer what they themselves find comforting—a hug, a reassuring comment, or a favorite doll or blanket (Hoffman, 2000; Moreno, Klute, & Robinson, 2008).

At the same time, toddlers demonstrate clearer awareness of how to upset others. One 18-month-old heard her mother talking to another adult about an older sibling: "Anny is really frightened of spiders" (Dunn, 1989, p. 107). The innocent-looking toddler ran to the bedroom, returned with the toy spider, and pushed it in front of Anny's face!

Categorizing the Self

By the end of the second year, language becomes a powerful tool in self-development. Between 18 and 30 months, children develop a **categorical self** as they classify themselves and others on the basis of age ("baby," "boy," or "man"), sex ("boy" or "girl"), physical characteristics ("big," "strong"), and even goodness versus badness ("I a good girl." "Tommy mean!") and competencies ("Did it!" "I can't") (Stipek, Gralinski, & Kopp, 1990).

Toddlers use their limited understanding of these social categories to organize their own behavior. As early as 17 months, they select and play in a more involved way with toys that are stereotyped for their own gender—dolls and tea sets for girls, trucks and cars for boys. Their ability to label their own gender predicts a sharp rise in these play preferences over the next few months (Zosuls et al., 2009). Then parents encourage gender-typed behavior by responding more positively when toddlers display it (Ruble, Martin, & Berenbaum, 2006). As we will see in Chapter 8, gender typing increases dramatically in early childhood.

Self-Control

Self-awareness also contributes to strengthening of effortful control (see page 149). To behave in a self-controlled fashion, children must think of themselves as separate, autonomous beings who can direct their own actions. And they must have the representational and memory capacities to recall a caregiver's directive ("Caitlin, don't touch that light socket!") and apply it to their own behavior.

As these capacities emerge between 12 and 18 months, toddlers first become capable of **compliance.** They show clear awareness of caregivers' wishes and expectations and can obey simple requests and commands. And as every parent knows, they can also decide to do just the opposite! But for most, assertiveness and opposition occur alongside compliance with an eager, willing spirit, which suggests that the child is beginning to adopt the adult's directives as his own (Dix et al., 2007; Kochanska, Murray, & Harlan, 2000). Compliance quickly leads to toddlers' first consciencelike verbalizations—for example, correcting the self by saying "No!" before touching a delicate object or jumping on the sofa.

Researchers often study self-control by giving children tasks that, like the situations just mentioned, require **delay of gratification**—waiting for an appropriate time and place to engage in a tempting act. Between ages 1½ and 3, children show an increasing capacity to wait before eating a treat, opening a present, or playing with a toy (Vaughn, Kopp, & Krakow, 1984). Children who are advanced in development of attention and language tend to be better at delaying gratification (Else-Quest et al., 2006). These findings help explain why girls are typically more self-controlled than boys.

Like effortful control in general, young children's capacity to delay gratification is influenced by both biologically based temperament and quality of caregiving (Kochanska & Aksan, 2006; Kochanska & Knaack, 2003). Inhibited children find it easier to wait than angry, irritable children do. But toddlers who experience parental warmth and simple (as opposed to lengthy, detailed) statements that patiently redirect their behavior are more likely to be cooperative and resist temptation (Blandon

This toddler demonstrates compliance and the beginnings of self-control as she helps her father wash dishes. She eagerly joins in the task, suggesting that she is adopting the adult's directives as her own.

& Volling, 2008; Hakman & Sullivan, 2009). Recall that such parenting, which encourages and models patient, nonimpulsive behavior, is particularly important for emotionally reactive children (see page 152).

As self-control improves, parents gradually increase the range of rules they expect toddlers to follow, from safety and respect for property and people to family routines, manners, and simple chores (Gralinski & Kopp, 1993). Still, toddlers' control over their own actions depends on constant parental oversight and reminders. Several prompts ("Remember, we're going to go in just a minute") and gentle insistence were usually necessary to get Caitlin to stop playing so that she and her parents could go on an errand. Applying What We Know on page 162 summarizes ways to help toddlers develop compliance and self-control.

As the second year of life drew to a close, Carolyn, Monica, and Vanessa were delighted at their children's readiness to learn the rules of social life. As we will see in Chapter 8, advances in cognition and language, along with parental warmth and reasonable demands for maturity, lead preschoolers to make tremendous strides in this area.

ASK YOURSELF

REVIEW What type of early parenting fosters the development of emotional self-regulation, secure attachment, and self-control? Why, in each instance, is it effective?

APPLY Len, a caregiver of 1- and 2-year-olds, wonders whether toddlers recognize themselves. List signs of self-recognition in the second year that Len can observe.

REFLECT Do you think that "the terrible twos," a commonly used expression to characterize toddler behavior, is an apt description? Explain.

Applying What We Know

Helping Toddlers Develop Compliance and Self-Control

Suggestion	Rationale
Respond with sensitivity and encouragement.	Toddlers whose parents are sensitive and supportive actively resist at times, but they are also more compliant and self-controlled.
Provide advance notice when the toddler must stop an enjoyable activity.	Toddlers find it more difficult to stop a pleasant activity that is already under way than to wait before engaging in a desired action.
Offer many prompts and reminders.	Toddlers' ability to remember and comply with rules is limited; they need continuous adult oversight and patient assistance.
Respond to self-controlled behavior with verbal and physical approval.	Praise and hugs reinforce appropriate behavior, increasing the likelihood that it will occur again.
Encourage selective and sustained attention (see Chapter 5, page 127).	Development of attention is related to self-control. Children who can shift attention from a captivating stimulus and focus on a less attractive alternative are better at controlling their impulses.
Support language development (see Chapter 5, page 139).	In the second year, children begin to use language to remind themselves of adult expectations and to delay gratification.
Gradually increase rules in a manner consistent with the toddler's developing capacities.	As cognition and language improve, toddlers can follow more rules related to safety, respect for people and property, family routines, manners, and simple chores.

SUMMARY

Erikson's Theory of Infant and Toddler Personality (p. 143)

According to Erikson's psychosocial theory, how do infants and toddlers resolve the psychological conflicts of the first two years?

- Warm, responsive caregiving leads infants to resolve the psychological conflict of **basic trust versus mistrust** on the positive side. During toddlerhood, **autonomy versus shame and doubt** is resolved favorably when parents provide appropriate guidance and reasonable choices.

Emotional Development (p. 144)

Describe the development of basic emotions over the first year.

- During the first half-year, **basic emotions** gradually become clear, well-organized signals. The **social smile** appears between 6 and 10 weeks, laughter around 3 to 4 months. Happiness strengthens the parent–child bond and both reflects and supports physical and cognitive mastery.

- Anger and fear, especially in the form of **stranger anxiety,** increase in the second half-year as infants' cognitive and motor capacities improve. Newly mobile babies use the familiar caregiver as a **secure base** from which to explore.

Summarize changes during the first two years in understanding others' emotions, expression of self-conscious emotions, and emotional self-regulation.

- As infants' ability to detect the meaning of emotional expressions improves over the first year, **social referencing,** appears. By the middle of the second year, toddlers appreciate that others' emotional reactions may differ from their own.

- During toddlerhood, self-awareness and adult instruction provide the foundation for **self-conscious emotions. Emotional self-regulation** emerges as the prefrontal cortex functions more effectively and as caregivers build on the infants' increasing tolerance for stimulation. When caregivers are emotionally sympathetic but set limits, children develop more effective anger-regulation strategies in the preschool years.

Temperament and Development (p. 148)

What is temperament, and how is it measured?

- **Temperament** refers to early-appearing, stable individual differences in reactivity and self-regulation. The New York Longitudinal Study identified three patterns: the **easy child,** the **difficult child,** and the **slow-to-warm-up child.** Mary Rothbart's model of temperament includes **effortful control,** the ability to regulate one's reactivity.

- Temperament is assessed through parental reports, behavior ratings by others familiar with the child, and laboratory observations. Most neurobiological research has focused on distinguishing **inhibited,** or **shy, children** from **uninhibited,** or **sociable, children.**

What roles do heredity and environment play in the stability of temperament?

- Stability of temperament is generally low to moderate. Temperament has a genetic foundation, but child rearing and cultural beliefs and practices have much to do with maintaining or changing it.

© CORBIS

- According to the **goodness-of-fit model,** parenting practices that fit well with the child's temperament help children achieve more adaptive functioning.

Development of Attachment
(p. 152)

Describe the development of attachment during the first two years.

- **Ethological theory,** the most widely accepted perspective on **attachment**, recognizes the infant's emotional tie to the caregiver as an evolved response that promotes survival. In early infancy, a set of built-in behaviors encourages the parent to remain close to the baby.

- Around 6 to 8 months, **separation anxiety** and use of the caregiver as a secure base indicate that a true attachment bond has formed. As representation and language develop, separation protest declines. From early caregiving experiences, children construct an **internal working model** that guides future close relationships.

How do researchers measure attachment security, what factors affect it, and what are its implications for later development?

- Using the **Strange Situation,** a laboratory technique for assessing the quality of attachment between 1 and 2 years, researchers have identified four attachment patterns: **secure, avoidant, resistant,** and **disorganized/ disoriented.** The **Attachment Q-Sort,** a home observation method suitable for 1- to 4-year-olds, yields a score ranging from high to low in security.

- Securely attached babies more often maintain their attachment pattern than insecure babies, although the disorganized/disoriented pattern is highly stable. Cultural conditions must be considered in interpreting attachment patterns.

- Attachment quality is influenced by early availability of a consistent caregiver, **sensitive caregiving,** the fit between the baby's temperament and parenting practices, and family circumstances, including parents' internal working models.

- Continuity of caregiving is the crucial factor determining whether attachment security is linked to later development. If caregiving improves, children can recover from an insecure attachment history.

Describe infants' capacity for multiple attachments.

- Infants develop strong affectionate ties to fathers, who tend to engage in more exciting, physical play with babies than mothers do. Infants begin to build rich emotional relationships with siblings that mix affection and caring with rivalry and resentment. Individual differences in the quality of sibling relationships are influenced by temperament and parenting.

Self-Development (p. 159)

Describe the development of self-awareness in infancy and toddlerhood, along with the emotional and social capacities it supports.

- Babies' capacity for intermodal perception supports early self-awareness. Around age 2, **self-recognition**—identification of the self as a physically unique being—is well under way. However, toddlers make **scale errors,** attempting to do things that their body size makes impossible.

- Self-awareness leads to first signs of **empathy.** As language strengthens, toddlers develop a **categorical self** based on age, sex, physical characteristics, goodness versus badness, and competencies.

NATALIE KAUFFMAN/ FIRST LIGHT/GETTY IMAGES

- Self-awareness provides the foundation for the emergence of **compliance** between 12 and 18 months and gains in **delay of gratification** between 1½ and 3 years. Children who are advanced in development of attention and language and who have warm, encouraging parents tend to be more self-controlled.

Important Terms and Concepts

attachment (p. 152)
Attachment Q-Sort (p. 154)
autonomy versus shame and doubt (p. 143)
avoidant attachment (p. 154)
basic emotions (p. 144)
basic trust versus mistrust (p. 143)
categorical self (p. 160)
compliance (p. 161)
delay of gratification (p. 161)
difficult child (p. 148)
disorganized/disoriented attachment (p. 154)
easy child (p. 148)

effortful control (p. 149)
emotional self-regulation (p. 147)
empathy (p. 160)
ethological theory of attachment (p. 153)
goodness-of-fit model (p. 151)
inhibited, or shy, child (p. 149)
internal working model (p. 153)
resistant attachment (p. 154)
scale errors (p. 160)
secure attachment (p. 154)
secure base (p. 146)
self-conscious emotions (p. 147)

self-recognition (p. 160)
sensitive caregiving (p. 156)
separation anxiety (p. 153)
slow-to-warm-up child (p. 148)
social referencing (p. 146)
social smile (p. 144)
stranger anxiety (p. 146)
Strange Situation (p. 154)
temperament (p. 148)
uninhibited, or sociable, child (p. 149)

milestones

Development in Infancy and Toddlerhood

Birth–6 months

PHYSICAL

- Height and weight increase rapidly. (93)
- Newborn reflexes decline. (83)
- Distinguishes basic tastes and odors; shows preference for sweet-tasting foods. (86–87)
- Responses can be classically and operantly conditioned. (103–104)
- Habituates to unchanging stimuli; recovers to novel stimuli. (104)
- Sleep is increasingly organized into a night–day schedule. (98)
- Holds head up, rolls over, and grasps objects. (106, 108)
- Perceives auditory and visual stimuli as organized patterns. (109, 111, 112)
- Shows sensitivity to motion, then binocular, and finally pictorial depth cues. (111)
- Recognizes and prefers human facial pattern; recognizes features of mother's face. (112–113)
- Masters a wide range of intermodal (visual, auditory, and tactile) relationships. (113–114)

COGNITIVE

- Engages in immediate and deferred imitation of adults' facial expressions. (105, 122)
- Repeats chance behaviors that lead to pleasurable and interesting results. (119–120)

- Has some awareness of many physical properties (including object permanence) and basic numerical knowledge. (121, 125)
- Recognition memory for visual events improves. (127–128)
- Attention becomes more efficient and flexible. (127)
- Categorizes objects on the basis of similar physical features. (128)

LANGUAGE

- Coos and, by end of this period, babbles. (137)
- Begins to establish joint attention with caregiver, who labels objects and events. (137)

EMOTIONAL/SOCIAL

- Social smile and laughter emerge. (144)
- Matches feeling tone of caregiver in face-to-face communication; later, expects matched responses. (146)

- Emotional expressions become well-organized and meaningfully related to environmental events. (144)

- Regulates emotion by shifting attention and self-soothing. (147)
- Awareness of self as physically distinct from surroundings increases. (160)

7–12 months

PHYSICAL

- Approaches adultlike sleep–wake schedule. (98)
- Sits alone, crawls, and walks. (106)

- Reaching and grasping improve in flexibility and accuracy; shows refined pincer grasp. (108–109)
- Intermodal perception continues to improve. (113–114)

COGNITIVE

- Engages in intentional, or goal-directed, behavior. (120)
- Finds object hidden in an initial location. (120)
- Recall memory improves, as indicated by ability to find hidden objects and engage in deferred imitation. (122–123, 128)
- Solves simple problems by analogy to a previous problem. (123)
- Categorizes objects on the basis of subtle sets of features, even when the perceptual contrast between categories is minimal. (128)

Note: Numbers in parentheses indicate the page or pages on which each milestone is discussed.

LANGUAGE

- Babbling expands to include many sounds of spoken languages and patterns of the child's language community. (137)
- Joint attention with caregiver becomes more accurate. (137)
- Takes turns in games, such as pat-a-cake and peekaboo. (137)
- Comprehends some word meanings. (138)
- Uses preverbal gestures (showing, pointing) to influence others' behavior. (137)

- Around end of this period, understands displaced reference of words and says first words. (123, 138)

EMOTIONAL/SOCIAL

- Smiling and laughter increase in frequency and expressiveness. (144)
- Anger and fear increase in frequency and intensity. (144, 146)
- Stranger anxiety and separation anxiety appear. (146, 153)
- Uses caregiver as a secure base for exploration. (146)
- Shows "clear-cut" attachment to familiar caregivers. (153)
- Increasingly detects the meaning of others' emotional expressions and engages in social referencing. (146)
- Regulates emotion by approaching and retreating from stimulation. (147)

PHYSICAL

- Height and weight gain are rapid, but not as great as in first year. (93)
- Walking is better coordinated. (106, 107)
- Manipulates small objects with improved coordination. (108–109)

COGNITIVE

- Explores the properties of objects by acting on them in novel ways. (120)
- Searches in several locations for a hidden object. (120)
- Engages in deferred imitation of adults' actions with objects over longer delays and across a change in context—for example, from child care to home. (122–123)
- Sustained attention improves. (127)
- Recall memory improves further. (128)
- Sorts objects into categories. (128, 130)
- Realizes that pictures can symbolize real objects. (123)

LANGUAGE

- Steadily adds to vocabulary. (138)

EMOTIONAL/SOCIAL

- Joins in play with familiar adults and siblings. (158, 159)

- Realizes that others' emotional reactions may differ from one's own. (146)
- Complies with simple directives. (161)

PHYSICAL

- Jumps, walks on tiptoe, and runs. (106)
- Manipulates small objects with good coordination. (108–109)

COGNITIVE

- Solves simple problems using representation. (120)
- Finds a hidden object that has been moved while out of sight. (120)
- Engages in make-believe play, using simple actions experienced in everyday life. (121, 131)

- Engages in deferred imitation of actions an adult tries to produce, even if not fully realized. (123)
- Categorizes objects conceptually, on the basis of common function or behavior. (130)

LANGUAGE

- Produces 200 to 250 words. (138)
- Combines two words. (138)

EMOTIONAL/SOCIAL

- Self-conscious emotions (shame, embarrassment, guilt, envy, and pride) emerge. (147)
- Acquires a vocabulary for talking about feelings. (148)
- Begins to use language to assist with emotional self-regulation. (148)
- Begins to tolerate caregiver's absences more easily; separation anxiety declines. (154)
- Recognizes image of self and, by end of this period, uses own name or personal pronoun to refer to self. (160)
- Less often makes scale errors. (160)
- Shows signs of empathy. (160)
- Categorizes self and others on the basis of age, sex, physical characteristics, and goodness and badness. (160–161)
- Shows gender-stereotyped toy preferences. (161)
- Self-control, as indicated by delay of gratification, emerges. (161)

chapter
7

Physical and Cognitive Development in Early Childhood

Rich opportunities for playful exploration and peer cooperation contribute vitally to preschoolers' rapidly advancing cognitive and language skills.

© LAURA DWIGHT PHOTOGRAPHY

chapter outline

For more than a decade, my fourth-floor office window overlooked the preschool and kindergarten play yard of our university laboratory school. On mild fall and spring mornings, the doors of the classrooms swung open, and sand table, easels, and large blocks spilled out into a small courtyard. Alongside the building was a grassy area with jungle gyms, swings, a playhouse, and a flower garden planted by the children. Beyond it lay a circular path lined with tricycles and wagons. Each day, the setting was alive with activity.

The years from 2 to 6 are often called "the play years," since play blossoms during this time and supports every aspect of development. Our discussion opens with the physical attainments of early childhood—growth in body size and improvements in motor coordination. We look at genetic and environmental factors that support these changes and at their intimate connection with other domains of development.

Then we explore early childhood cognition, beginning with Piaget's preoperational stage. Recent research, along with Vygotsky's sociocultural theory and information processing, extends our understanding of preschoolers' cognitive competencies. Next, we address factors that contribute to early childhood mental development—the home environment, the quality of preschool and child care, and the many hours young children spend watching television and using computers. We conclude with the dramatic expansion of language in early childhood. ●

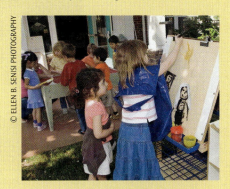

© ELLEN B. SENISI PHOTOGRAPHY

PHYSICAL DEVELOPMENT

A Changing Body and Brain

In early childhood, body growth tapers off from the rapid rate of the first two years. On average, children add 2 to 3 inches in height and about 5 pounds in weight each year. Boys continue to be slightly larger than girls. As "baby fat" drops off further, children gradually become thinner, although girls retain somewhat more body fat than boys, who are slightly more muscular. As Figure 7.1 on page 92 shows, by age 5 the top-heavy, bowlegged, potbellied toddler has become a more streamlined, flat-tummied, longer-legged child with body proportions similar to those of adults. Consequently, posture and balance improve—changes that support gains in motor coordination.

Individual differences in body size are even more apparent during early childhood than in infancy and toddlerhood. Speeding around the bike path in the play yard, 5-year-old Darryl—at 48 inches tall and 55 pounds—towered over his kindergarten classmates. (The average North American 5-year-old boy is 43 inches tall and weighs 42 pounds.) Priti, an Asian-Indian child, was unusually small because of genetic factors linked to her cultural ancestry. Hal, a Caucasian child from a poverty-stricken home, was well below average for reasons we will discuss shortly.

Skeletal Growth

The skeletal changes of infancy continue throughout early childhood. Between ages 2 and 6, approximately 45 new *epiphyses,* or growth centers in which cartilage hardens into bone, emerge in various parts of the skeleton. X-rays of these growth centers

enable doctors to estimate children's *skeletal age,* or progress toward physical maturity (see page 92 in Chapter 4).

By the end of the preschool years, children start to lose their primary, or "baby," teeth. Girls, who are ahead of boys in physical development, lose teeth earlier. Environmental influences also matter: Prolonged malnutrition delays the appearance of permanent teeth, whereas overweight and obesity accelerate it (Hilgers et al., 2006).

Diseased baby teeth can affect the health of permanent teeth, so preventing decay in primary teeth is essential—by brushing consistently, avoiding sugary foods, drinking fluoridated water, and getting topical fluoride treatments and sealants (plastic coatings that protect tooth surfaces). Another factor is exposure to tobacco smoke, which suppresses children's immune system, including the ability to fight bacteria responsible for tooth decay. Young children in homes with regular smokers are at increased risk for decayed teeth (Hanioka et al., 2011). Unfortunately, an estimated 28 percent of U.S. preschoolers have tooth decay, a figure that rises to 50 percent in middle childhood and 60 percent by age 18. About 30 percent of U.S. children living in poverty have untreated dental caries (National Institutes of Health, 2011).

Brain Development

Between ages 2 and 6, the brain increases from 70 percent of its adult weight to 90 percent. By age 4, many parts of the cerebral cortex have overproduced synapses, and fMRI evidence reveals that cerebral blood flow peaks, signifying a high energy need (Huttenlocher, 2002; Nelson, Thomas, & de Haan, 2006). *Synaptic pruning* follows: By age 8 to 10, energy consumption of most cortical regions diminishes to near-adult levels, and cognitive capacities increasingly localize in distinct neural systems, yielding a more fine-tuned, efficient neural organization (Tsujimoto, 2008).

PHOTOS OF CHRIS © BOB DAEMMRICH PHOTOGRAPHY. PHOTOS OF MARIEL © JIM WEST PHOTOGRAPHY

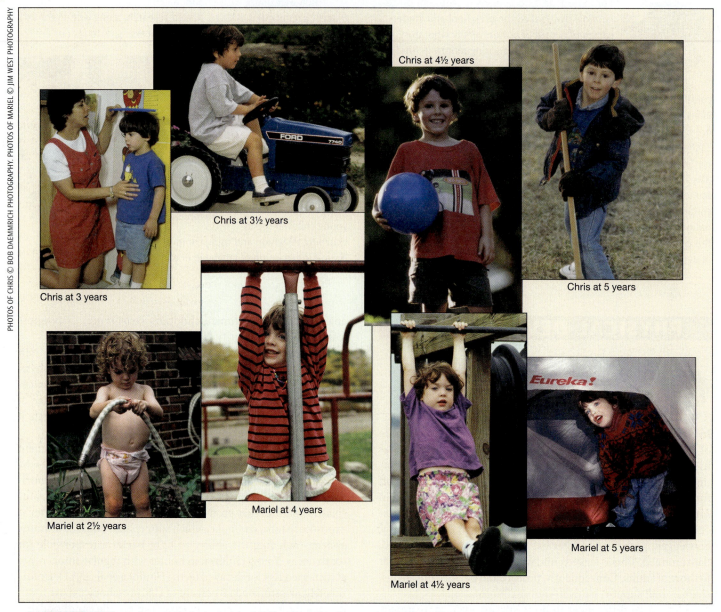

Chris at 4½ years

Chris at 3½ years

Chris at 3 years

Chris at 5 years

Mariel at 2½ years

Mariel at 4 years

Mariel at 4½ years

Mariel at 5 years

FIGURE 7.1 **Body growth during early childhood.** During the preschool years, children grow more slowly than in infancy and toddlerhood. Chris and Mariel's bodies became more streamlined, flat-tummied, and longer-legged. Boys continue to be slightly taller, heavier, and more muscular than girls. But generally, the two sexes are similar in body proportions and physical capacities.

EEG, NIRS, and fMRI measures of neural activity indicate especially rapid growth from early to middle childhood in areas of the prefrontal cortex devoted to executive function—inhibition of impulses, attention, memory, and planning and organizing behavior (Bunge & Wright, 2007; Durston & Casey, 2006). Furthermore, for most children, the left cerebral hemisphere is especially active between 3 and 6 years and then levels off. In contrast, activity in the right hemisphere increases steadily throughout early and middle childhood (Thatcher, Walker, & Giudice, 1987; Thompson et al., 2000).

In line with these developments, language skills (typically housed in the left hemisphere) increase at an astonishing pace. In contrast, spatial skills (usually located in the right hemi-sphere), such as giving directions, drawing pictures, and reading maps, develop gradually over childhood and adolescence.

Differences in development of the two hemispheres suggest that they are continuing to *lateralize* (specialize in cognitive functions). Let's take a closer look at brain lateralization in early childhood by focusing on handedness.

Handedness. Research on handedness, along with other evidence covered in Chapter 4, supports the joint contribution of nature and nurture to brain lateralization. By age 6 months, infants typically display a smoother, more efficient movement when reaching with their right than their left arm. This difference, believed to be biologically based, may contribute to

A 5-year-old illustrates gains in executive function, supported by rapid growth of the prefrontal cortex, as she engages in an activity that challenges her capacity to attend, remember, and plan.

the right-handed bias of most children by the end of the first year (Hinojosa, Sheu, & Michael, 2003; Rönnqvist & Domellöf, 2006). Gradually, handedness extends to additional skills.

Handedness reflects the greater capacity of one side of the brain—the individual's **dominant cerebral hemisphere**—to carry out skilled motor action. Other important abilities are generally located on the dominant side as well. For right-handed people—in Western nations, 90 percent of the population—language is housed in the left hemisphere with hand control. For the left-handed 10 percent, language is occasionally located in the right hemisphere or, more often, shared between the hemispheres (Szaflarski et al., 2012). This indicates that the brains of left-handers tend to be less strongly lateralized than those of right-handers.

Left-handed parents show only a weak tendency to have left-handed children (Vuoksimaa et al., 2009). One genetic theory proposes that most children inherit a gene that *biases* them for right-handedness and a left-dominant cerebral hemisphere. But that bias is not strong enough to overcome experiences that might sway children toward a left-hand preference (Annett, 2002). Even prenatal events may profoundly affect handedness. The orientation of most fetuses—facing toward the left—is believed to promote greater motor control on the body's right side (Previc, 1991).

Handedness also involves practice. It is strongest for complex skills requiring extensive training, such as eating with utensils, writing, and engaging in athletic activities. And wide cultural differences exist. For example, in tribal and village cultures, the rate of left-handedness is relatively high. But in one such society in New Guinea, individuals who had attended school in childhood were far more likely to be extremely right-handed, highlighting the role of experience (Geuze et al., 2012).

Most left-handers have no developmental problems. In fact, they are slightly advantaged in speed and flexibility of think-

ing and are more likely than their right-handed agemates to develop outstanding verbal and mathematical talents (Flannery & Liederman, 1995; Gunstad et al., 2007). More even distribution of cognitive functions across both brain hemispheres may be responsible.

Other Advances in Brain Development.
Besides the cerebral cortex, several other areas of the brain make strides during early childhood (see Figure 7.2). These changes involve establishing links between parts of the brain, increasing the coordinated functioning of the central nervous system.

At the rear and base of the brain is the **cerebellum,** a structure that aids in balance and control of body movement. Fibers linking the cerebellum to the cerebral cortex grow and myelinate from birth through the preschool years, contributing to dramatic gains in motor coordination. Connections between the cerebellum and cerebral cortex also support thinking: Children with damage to the cerebellum usually display both motor and cognitive deficits, including problems with memory, planning, and language (Noterdaeme et al., 2002; Riva & Giorgi, 2000).

The **reticular formation,** a structure in the brain stem that maintains alertness and consciousness, generates synapses and myelinates throughout childhood and into adolescence. Neurons in the reticular formation send out fibers to the prefrontal cortex, contributing to improvements in sustained, controlled attention.

An inner-brain structure called the **hippocampus,** which plays a vital role in memory and in images of space that help us find our way, undergoes rapid synapse formation and myelination in the second half of the first year, when recall memory and independent movement emerge. Over the preschool and

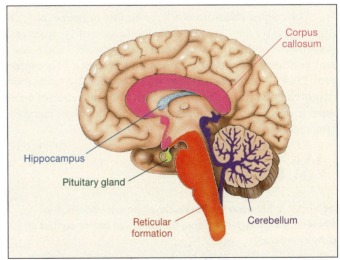

FIGURE 7.2 Cross-section of the human brain, showing the location of the cerebellum, the reticular formation, the hippocampus, and the corpus callosum. These structures undergo considerable development during early childhood. Also shown is the pituitary gland, which secretes hormones that control body growth (see page 170).

Growth and myelination of fibers linking the cerebellum to the cerebral cortex contribute to improved motor coordination and thinking, enabling this child to master a game that requires him to play hopscotch while also throwing a ball.

elementary school years, the hippocampus and surrounding areas of the cerebral cortex continue to develop swiftly, establishing connections with one another and with the prefrontal cortex (Nelson, Thomas, & de Haan, 2006). These changes support the dramatic gains in memory and spatial understanding of early and middle childhood.

The **corpus callosum** is a large bundle of fibers connecting the two cerebral hemispheres. Production of synapses and myelination of the corpus callosum peak between 3 and 6 years and continue more slowly through adolescence (Thompson et al., 2000). The corpus callosum supports smooth coordination of movements on both sides of the body and integration of many aspects of thinking, including perception, attention, memory, language, and problem solving.

ASK YOURSELF

REVIEW What aspects of brain development underlie the tremendous gains in language, thinking, and motor control of early childhood?

APPLY Dental checkups reveal a high incidence of untreated tooth decay in a U.S. preschool program serving low-income children. Using findings presented in this and previous chapters, list possible contributing factors.

Influences on Physical Growth and Health

As we consider factors affecting growth and health in early childhood, you will encounter some familiar themes. Heredity remains important, but environmental factors—good nutrition, relative freedom from disease, and physical safety—are also essential.

Heredity and Hormones

Children's physical size and rate of growth are related to those of their parents (Bogin, 2001). Genes influence growth by controlling the body's production of hormones. The **pituitary gland,** located at the base of the brain, plays a critical role by releasing two hormones that induce growth.

The first, **growth hormone (GH),** is necessary for development of all body tissues except the central nervous system and the genitals. Children who lack GH reach an average mature height of only 4 to 4½ feet. When treated early with injections of GH, such children show catch-up growth and then grow at a normal rate, becoming much taller than they would have without treatment (Bright, Mendoza, & Rosenfeld, 2009).

A second pituitary hormone, **thyroid-stimulating hormone (TSH),** prompts the thyroid gland in the neck to release *thyroxine,* which is necessary for brain development and for GH to have its full impact on body size. Infants born with a deficiency of thyroxine must receive it at once, or they will be mentally retarded. Once the most rapid period of brain development is complete, thyroxine deficiency no longer affects the central nervous system but still causes children to grow more slowly than average. With prompt treatment, such children catch up in body growth and eventually reach normal size (Salerno et al., 2001).

Nutrition

With the transition to early childhood, many children become unpredictable, picky eaters. Preschoolers' appetites decline because growth has slowed. Their wariness of new foods is also adaptive. In sticking to familiar foods, they are less likely to swallow dangerous substances when adults are not around to protect them (Birch & Fisher, 1995). Parents need not worry about variations in amount eaten from meal to meal. Preschoolers compensate for eating little at one meal by eating more at a later one (Hursti, 1999). Though they eat less, preschoolers require a high-quality diet, including the same foods adults need.

Children tend to imitate the food choices of people they admire, both adults and peers. Repeated, unpressured exposure to a new food also increases acceptance (Fuller et al., 2005). For example, serving broccoli or tofu increases children's liking for these healthy foods. In contrast, offering sweet fruit or soft drinks promotes "milk avoidance" (Black et al., 2002). Too much parental control limits children's opportunities to develop self-

Through repeated, unpressured exposure in a positive mealtime atmosphere, this 3-year-old learns to like foods that adults in his family and culture prefer.

control. Offering bribes ("Finish your vegetables, and you can have an extra cookie") causes children to like the healthy food less and the treat more (Birch, Fisher, & Davison, 2003).

LOOK AND LISTEN

Arrange to join a family with at least one preschooler for a meal, and closely observe parental mealtime practices. Are they likely to promote healthy eating habits? Explain. ●

As indicated in earlier chapters, many children in the United States and in developing countries lack access to sufficient high-quality food to support healthy development. Five-year-old Hal rode a bus from a poor neighborhood to our laboratory preschool. His mother's welfare check barely covered her rent, let alone food. Hal's diet was deficient in protein and in essential vitamins and minerals, and he was thin, pale, inattentive, and unruly. Throughout childhood and adolescence, a nutritionally deficient diet is associated with shorter stature, attention and memory difficulties, lower intelligence and achievement test scores, and hyperactivity and aggression—even after family factors that might account for these relationships are controlled (Cecil et al., 2005; Lukowski et al., 2010; Slack & Yoo, 2005).

Infectious Disease

One day, I noticed that Hal had been absent from the play yard for several weeks, so I asked Leslie, his preschool teacher, what was wrong. "Hal's been hospitalized with the measles," she explained. In well-nourished children, ordinary childhood illnesses have no effect on physical growth. But when children are undernourished, disease interacts with malnutrition in a vicious spiral, with potentially severe consequences.

Infectious Disease and Malnutrition. Hal's reaction to the measles is commonplace in developing nations, where many children live in poverty and do not receive routine immunizations. Poor diet depresses the body's immune system, making children far more susceptible to disease. Of the 7.5 million annual deaths of children under age 5 worldwide, 98 percent are in developing countries and 65 percent are due to infectious diseases (World Health Organization, 2012a).

Disease, in turn, reduces appetite and limits the body's ability to absorb foods, especially in children with intestinal infections. In developing countries, diarrhea, resulting from unsafe water and contaminated foods, leads to growth stunting and nearly 1 million childhood deaths each year (World Health Organization, 2012a). Studies carried out in Brazil and Peru reveal that the more persistent diarrhea is in early childhood, the shorter children are in height and the lower they score on mental tests during the school years (Checkley et al., 2003; Niehaus et al., 2002).

Most developmental impairments and deaths due to diarrhea can be prevented with nearly cost-free *oral rehydration therapy (ORT),* in which sick children are given a solution of glucose, salt, and water that quickly replaces fluids the body loses. Since 1990, public health workers have taught nearly half the families in the developing world how to administer ORT. Also, supplements of zinc (essential for immune system functioning) substantially reduce the incidence of severe diarrhea (Aggarwal, Sentz, & Miller, 2007).

Immunization. In industrialized nations, childhood diseases have declined dramatically during the past half-century, largely as a result of widespread immunization of infants and young children. Hal got the measles because, unlike his classmates from more economically advantaged homes, he did not receive a full program of immunizations. About 30 percent of U.S. preschoolers lack essential immunizations. The rate rises to 32 percent for poverty-stricken children, many of whom do not receive full protection until age 5 or 6, when it is required for school entry (U.S. Department of Health and Human Services, 2010e). In contrast, fewer than 10 percent of preschoolers lack immunizations in Denmark and Norway, and fewer than 7 percent in Canada, the Netherlands, Sweden, and the United Kingdom (World Health Organization, 2010).

Why does the United States lag behind in immunization? As noted in earlier chapters, many U.S. children do not have access to the health care they need. But inability to pay for vaccines is only one cause. Parents with stressful daily lives often fail to schedule vaccination appointments (Falagas & Zarkadoulia, 2008). Some parents have been influenced by media reports suggesting a link between a mercury-based preservative used for decades in vaccines and a rise in the number of children diagnosed with autism. But large-scale studies show no such association (Richler et al., 2006; Thompson et al., 2007). In areas where many parents have refused to immunize their children, disease outbreaks have occurred, with life-threatening consequences (Tuyen & Bisgard, 2003). Public

RED CHOPSTICKS/GETTY IMAGES

education programs directed at increasing parental knowledge about the importance and safety of timely immunizations are badly needed.

Childhood Injuries

Unintentional injuries are the leading cause of childhood mortality in industrialized nations. As Figure 7.3 reveals, the United States ranks poorly in these largely preventable events. About 20 percent of U.S. childhood deaths and 50 percent of adolescent deaths result from injuries (Centers for Disease Control and Prevention, 2012a). Among injured children and youths who survive, thousands suffer pain, brain damage, and permanent physical disabilities.

Auto and traffic accidents, drownings, and burns are the most common injuries during early and middle childhood (Safe Kids USA, 2011b). Motor vehicle collisions are by far the most frequent source of injury across all ages, ranking as the leading cause of death among children over 1 year old.

Childhood injury rates are especially high in developing countries with weak public safety measures. These Cambodian children play unsupervised in a poverty-stricken, rundown neighborhood near a former dump site.

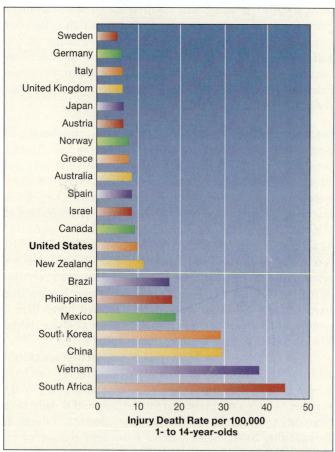

FIGURE 7.3 **International death rates due to unintentional injury among 1- to 14-year-olds.** Compared with other industrialized nations, the United States has a high injury death rate. Injury death rates are many times higher in developing nations, where poverty, rapid population growth, overcrowding in cities, and inadequate safety measures endanger children's lives. (Adapted from World Health Organization, 2008.)

Chart axis: Injury Death Rate per 100,000 1- to 14-year-olds

Factors Related to Childhood Injuries. The common view of childhood injuries as "accidental" suggests they are due to chance and cannot be prevented. In fact, they occur within a complex *ecological system* of individual, family, community, and societal influences—and we can do something about them.

Because of their higher activity level and greater impulsivity and risk taking, boys are 1.5 times more likely to be injured than girls (Safe Kids USA, 2008). Children with certain temperamental and personality characteristics—inattentiveness, overactivity, irritability, defiance, and aggression—are also at greater risk. Poverty, single parenthood, and low parental education are also strongly associated with injury (Dudani, Macpherson, & Tamim, 2010; Schwebel & Brezausek, 2007). Parents experiencing many daily stresses often have little energy to monitor the safety of their children. And their rundown homes and neighborhoods pose further risks (Dal Santo et al., 2004).

Childhood injury rates are high in the United States because of extensive poverty, shortages of high-quality child care (to supervise children in their parents' absence), and a high rate of births to teenagers, who are not ready for parenthood. But U.S. children from economically advantaged families are also at greater risk than children in Western Europe (World Health Organization, 2008). This indicates that besides reducing poverty and teenage pregnancy and upgrading the status of child care, additional steps are needed to ensure children's safety.

Preventing Childhood Injuries. Laws prevent many injuries by requiring car safety seats, child-resistant caps on medicine bottles, flameproof clothing, and fencing around backyard swimming pools. Communities can help by modifying their physical environments. Playgrounds, a common site of injury, can be covered with protective surfaces (Safe Kids USA, 2008). Free, easily installed window guards can be given to families in high-rise apartment buildings to prevent falls. And media campaigns can inform parents and children about safety issues.

But even though they know better, many parents and children behave in ways that compromise safety. About 27 percent of U.S. parents fail to place their preschoolers in car safety seats (Safe Kids USA, 2011a). Furthermore, many parents begin relying on children's knowledge of safety rules, rather than controlling access to hazards, as early as 2 or 3 years of age (Morrongiello, Ondejko, & Littlejohn, 2004). But even older preschoolers spontaneously recall only about half the safety rules their parents teach them. Even with well-learned rules, they need supervision to ensure they comply (Morrongiello, Midgett, & Shields, 2001). Parent interventions that highlight risk factors and that model and reinforce safety practices are effective in reducing childhood injuries (Kendrick et al., 2008). But attention must also be paid to relevant family conditions: relieving crowding in the home, providing social supports to ease parental stress, and teaching parents to use effective discipline—a topic we take up in Chapter 8.

ASK YOURSELF

REVIEW To effectively prevent childhood injury, why are diverse approaches essential? Cite examples at several levels of the *ecological system.*

APPLY One day, Leslie prepared a new snack to serve at preschool: celery stuffed with ricotta cheese. The first time she served it, few children touched it. How can Leslie encourage her students to accept the snack? What tactics should she avoid?

REFLECT Ask a parent or other family member whether, as a preschooler, you were a picky eater, suffered from many infectious diseases, or sustained any serious injuries. In each instance, what factors might have been responsible?

Motor Development

TAKE A MOMENT... Observe several 2- to 6-year-olds at play in a neighborhood park and you will see that an explosion of new motor skills occurs in early childhood. Preschoolers continue to integrate previously acquired skills into more complex, *dynamic systems.* Then they revise each new skill as their bodies grow larger and stronger, their central nervous systems develop, their environments present new challenges, and they set new goals.

As balance improves, preschoolers can combine upper- and lower-body skills into more refined actions, such as walking on stilts.

Gross-Motor Development

As children's bodies become more streamlined and less top-heavy, their center of gravity shifts downward, toward the trunk. As a result, balance improves greatly, paving the way for new gross-motor skills. By age 2, preschoolers' gaits become smooth and rhythmic—secure enough that soon they leave the ground, at first by running and later by jumping, hopping, galloping, and skipping.

As children become steadier on their feet, their arms and torsos are freed to experiment with new skills—throwing and catching balls, steering tricycles, and swinging on horizontal bars and rings. Then upper- and lower-body skills combine into more refined actions. Five- and 6-year-olds simultaneously steer and pedal a tricycle and flexibly move their whole body when throwing, catching, hopping, and jumping. By the end of the preschool years, all skills are performed with greater speed and endurance.

Fine-Motor Development

Fine-motor skills, too, take a giant leap forward. As control of the hands and fingers improves, young children put puzzles together, build with small blocks, cut and paste, and improve in self-help skills—dressing and undressing, using a fork adeptly, and (at the end of early childhood) cutting food with a knife and tying shoes. Fine-motor progress is also apparent in drawings and first efforts to write.

Drawing. A variety of cognitive factors combine with fine-motor control to influence changes in children's artful representations (Golomb, 2004). These include the realization that pictures can serve as symbols and improved planning and spatial understanding. Typically, drawing progresses through the following sequence:

1. *Scribbles.* At first, children's gestures rather than the resulting scribbles contain the intended representation. For example, one 18-month-old made her crayon hop and, as it produced a series of dots, explained, "Rabbit goes hop-hop" (Winner, 1986).

2. *First representational forms.* Around age 3, children's scribbles start to become pictures. Few 3-year-olds spontaneously draw so others can tell what their picture represents. But when adults draw with children and point out the resemblances between drawings and objects, preschoolers' pictures become more comprehensible and detailed (Braswell & Callanan, 2003).

   A major milestone in drawing occurs when children use lines to represent the boundaries of objects, enabling 3- and 4-year-olds to draw their first picture of a person. Fine-motor and cognitive limitations lead the preschooler to reduce the figure to the simplest form that still looks human: the universal "tadpole" image, a circular shape with lines attached, shown on the left in Figure 7.4.

3. *More realistic drawings.* Five- and 6-year-olds create more complex drawings, like the one on the right in Figure 7.4, containing more conventional human and animal figures, with the head and body differentiated. Older preschoolers' drawings still contain perceptual distortions because they have just begun to represent depth. This free depiction of reality makes their artwork look fanciful and inventive.

LOOK AND LISTEN

Visit a preschool or child-care center where artwork by 3- to 5-year-olds is plentiful. Note age differences in the complexity of children's drawings. ●

Early Printing. At first preschoolers do not distinguish writing from drawing. Around age 4, writing shows some distinctive features of print, such as separate forms arranged in a line on the page. But children often include picturelike devices—for example, a circular shape for "sun" (Ehri & Roberts, 2006). Only gradually, between ages 4 and 6, as they learn to name alphabet letters and link them with language sounds, do children realize that writing stands for language.

Preschoolers' first attempts to print often involve their name, generally using a single letter. "How do you make a *D*?" my older son, David, asked at age 3½. When I printed a large uppercase *D* for him to copy, he was quite satisfied with his backward, imperfect creation. By age 5, David printed his name clearly enough for others to read but, like many children, continued to reverse some letters until well into second grade. Until children start to read, they do not find it useful to distinguish between mirror-image forms, such as *b* and *d* and *p* and *q* (Bornstein & Arterberry, 1999).

Individual Differences in Motor Skills

Wide individual differences exist in the ages at which children reach motor milestones. A tall, muscular child tends to move more quickly and to acquire certain skills earlier than a short, stocky youngster. And as in other domains, parents and teachers probably provide more encouragement to children with biologically based motor-skill advantages.

Sex differences in motor skills are evident in early childhood. Boys are ahead of girls in skills that emphasize force and power. By age 5, they can broad-jump slightly farther, run slightly

FIGURE 7.4 Examples of young children's drawings. The universal tadpolelike shape that children use to draw their first picture of a person is shown on the left. The tadpole soon becomes an anchor for greater details that sprout from the basic shape. By the end of the preschool years, children produce more complex, differentiated pictures like the one on the right, drawn by a 6-year-old child. (*Left:* Reprinted by permission from *Artful Scribbles* by Howard Gardner. Available from Basic Books, an imprint of The Perseus Books Group. Copyright © 1982. *Right:* From E. Winner, "Where Pelicans Kiss Seals," *Psychology Today, 20*[8], August 1986, p. 35. Reprinted by permission from the collection of Ellen Winner.)

faster, and throw a ball about 5 feet farther. Girls have an edge in fine-motor skills and in certain gross-motor skills that depend on balance and agility, such as hopping and skipping (Fischman, Moore, & Steele, 1992; Haywood & Getchell, 2009). Boys' greater muscle mass and, in the case of throwing, slightly longer forearms contribute to their skill advantages. And girls' greater overall physical maturity may be partly responsible for their better balance and precision of movement.

From an early age, boys and girls are usually encouraged into different physical activities. For example, fathers are more likely to play catch with their sons than with their daughters. Sex differences in motor skills increase with age, but they remain small throughout childhood (Greendorfer, Lewko, & Rosengren, 1996). This suggests that greater social pressures for boys to be active and physically skilled exaggerate small, genetically based sex differences.

Children master the motor skills of early childhood during everyday play. Aside from throwing (where direct instruction is helpful), preschoolers exposed to gymnastics, tumbling, and other formal lessons do not make faster progress. And when parents and teachers criticize a child's performance, push specific motor skills, or promote a competitive attitude, they risk undermining children's self-confidence and, in turn, their motor progress (Berk, 2006). Adult involvement in young children's motor activities should focus on fun rather than on winning or perfecting the "correct" technique.

ASK YOURSELF

REVIEW Describe typical changes in children's drawings during early childhood, along with factors that contribute to those changes.

APPLY Mabel and Chad want to do everything they can to support their 3-year-old daughter's motor development. What advice would you give them?

COGNITIVE DEVELOPMENT

One rainy morning, as I observed in our laboratory preschool, Leslie, the children's teacher, joined me at the back of the room. "Preschoolers' minds are such a blend of logic, fantasy, and faulty reasoning," Leslie reflected. "Every day, I'm startled by the maturity and originality of what they say and do. Yet at other times, their thinking seems limited and inflexible."

Leslie's comments sum up the puzzling contradictions of early childhood cognition. Hearing a loud thunderclap outside, 3-year-old Sammy exclaimed, "A magic man turned on the thunder!" Even after Leslie explained that thunder is caused by lightning, not by a person turning it on, Sammy persisted: "Then a magic lady did it."

In other respects, Sammy's thinking was surprisingly advanced. At snack time, he accurately counted, "One, two,

three, four!" and then got four cartons of milk, one for each child at his table. But when his snack group included more than four children, Sammy's counting broke down. And after Priti dumped out her raisins, scattering them in front of her on the table, Sammy asked, "How come you got lots, and I only got this little bit?" He didn't realize that he had just as many raisins; his were simply all bunched up in a tiny red box.

To understand Sammy's reasoning, we turn first to Piaget's and Vygotsky's theories and evidence highlighting the strengths and limitations of each. Then we consider additional research on young children's cognition inspired by the information-processing perspective, address factors that contribute to individual differences in mental development, and look at the dramatic expansion of language in early childhood.

Piaget's Theory: The Preoperational Stage

As children move from the sensorimotor to the **preoperational stage,** which spans the years 2 to 7, the most obvious change is an extraordinary increase in representational, or symbolic, activity. Infants and toddlers' mental representations are impressive, but in early childhood, representational capacities blossom.

Advances in Mental Representation

Piaget acknowledged that language is our most flexible means of mental representation. Despite the power of language, however, Piaget did not regard it as a major ingredient in childhood cognitive change. Instead, he believed that sensorimotor activity leads to internal images of experience, which children then label with words (Piaget, 1936/1952). In support of Piaget's view, children's first words have a strong sensorimotor basis (see Chapter 5). In addition, infants and toddlers acquire an impressive range of categories long before they use words to label them (see page 128). But as we will see, Piaget underestimated the power of language to spur children's cognition.

Make-Believe Play

Make-believe play is another example of the development of representation in early childhood. Piaget believed that through pretending, young children practice and strengthen newly acquired representational schemes. Drawing on his ideas, investigators have traced changes in preschoolers' make-believe.

Development of Make-Believe. One day, Sammy's 20-month-old brother, Dwayne, visited the classroom. Dwayne wandered around, picked up a toy telephone receiver, said, "Hi, Mommy," and then dropped it. Next, he found a cup, pretended to drink, and then toddled off again. Meanwhile, Sammy joined Vance and Priti in the block area for a space shuttle launch.

"That can be our control tower," Sammy suggested, pointing to a corner by a bookshelf. "Countdown!" he announced,

© LAURA DWIGHT PHOTOGRAPHY

Make-believe play increases in sophistication during the preschool years. Children pretend with less realistic toys and increasingly coordinate make-believe roles, such as bus driver and passengers.

speaking into his "walkie-talkie"—a small wooden block. "Five, six, two, four, one, blastoff!" Priti made a doll push a pretend button, and the rocket was off!

Comparing Dwayne's pretend play with Sammy's, we see three important changes:

- *Play detaches from the real-life conditions associated with it.* In early pretending, toddlers use only realistic objects—a toy telephone to talk into or a cup to drink from. Their earliest pretend acts imitate adults' actions and are not yet flexible. Children younger than age 2, for example, will pretend to drink from a cup but refuse to pretend a cup is a hat (Rakoczy, Tomasello, & Striano, 2005). They have trouble using an object (cup) that already has an obvious use as a symbol of another object (hat).

  After age 2, children pretend with less realistic toys (a block for a telephone receiver). Gradually, they imagine objects and events without any support from the real world, as Sammy's imaginary control tower illustrates. And by age 3, they flexibly understand that an object (a yellow stick) may take on one fictional identity in one pretend game (a toothbrush) and another fictional identity (a carrot) in a different pretend game (Wyman, Rakoczy, & Tomasello, 2009).

- *Play becomes less self-centered.* At first, make-believe is directed toward the self—for example, Dwayne pretends to feed only himself. Soon, children direct pretend actions toward other objects, as when a child feeds a doll. Early in the third year, they become detached participants, making a doll feed itself or pushing a button to launch a rocket (McCune, 1993).

- *Play includes more complex combinations of schemes.* Dwayne can pretend to drink from a cup, but he does not yet combine pouring and drinking. Later, children combine schemes with those of peers in **sociodramatic play**, the make-believe with others that is under way by the end of the second year and increases rapidly in complexity during

early childhood (Kavanaugh, 2006). Already, Sammy and his classmates can create and coordinate several roles in an elaborate plot.

LOOK AND LISTEN

Observe the make-believe play of several 2- to 4-year-olds. Describe pretend acts that exemplify important developmental changes. ●

In sociodramatic play, children display awareness that make-believe is a representational activity—an understanding that strengthens over early childhood (Lillard, 2003; Rakoczy, Tomasello, & Striano, 2004; Sobel, 2006). *TAKE A MOMENT...* Listen closely to a group of preschoolers as they assign roles and negotiate make-believe plans: "You *pretend to be* the astronaut, I'll *act like* I'm operating the control tower!" In communicating about pretend, children think about their own and others' fanciful representations—evidence that they have begun to reason about people's mental activities.

Benefits of Make-Believe. Today, Piaget's view of make-believe as mere practice of representational schemes is regarded as too limited. Play not only reflects but also contributes to children's cognitive and social skills. Compared with social non-pretend activities (such as drawing or putting puzzles together), during sociodramatic play preschoolers' interactions last longer, show more involvement, draw more children into the activity, and are more cooperative (Creasey, Jarvis, & Berk, 1998).

It is not surprising, then, that preschoolers who spend more time at sociodramatic play are seen as more socially competent by their teachers (Connolly & Doyle, 1984). And many studies suggest that make-believe strengthens a wide variety of mental abilities, including sustained attention, memory, logical reasoning, language and literacy, imagination, creativity, and the ability to reflect on one's own thinking, regulate one's own emotions and behavior, and take another's perspective (Berk, Mann, & Ogan, 2006; Elias & Berk, 2002; Hirsh-Pasek et al., 2009; Ogan & Berk, 2009; Ruff & Capozzoli, 2003). We will return to the topic of early childhood play in this and the next chapter.

Symbol–Real-World Relations

To make believe and draw—and to understand other forms of representation, such as photographs, models, and maps—preschoolers must realize that each symbol corresponds to something specific in everyday life. In Chapter 5, we saw that by the middle of the second year, children grasp the symbolic function of realistic-looking photos, and around age 2½, of TV and video. When do children comprehend other challenging symbols—for example, three-dimensional models of real-world spaces?

In one study, 2½- and 3-year-olds watched an adult hide a small toy (Little Snoopy) in a scale model of a room and then were asked to retrieve it. Next, they had to find a larger toy (Big Snoopy) hidden in the room that the model represented. Not until age 3 could most children use the model as a guide to finding Big Snoopy in the real room (DeLoache, 1987). The

Preschoolers who experience a variety of symbols come to understand dual representation—for example, that this dollhouse is an object in its own right but can also stand for another, a full-sized house where people live.

2½-year-olds did not realize that the model could be both *a toy room* and *a symbol of another room.* They had trouble with **dual representation**—viewing a symbolic object as both an object in its own right and a symbol (DeLoache, 2000, 2002).

Recall, also, that in make-believe play, 1½- to 2-year-olds cannot use an object that has an obvious use (cup) to stand for another object (hat). Likewise, 2-year-olds do not yet grasp that a line drawing—an object in its own right—also represents real-world objects.

Similarly, when presented with objects disguised in various ways and asked what each "looks like" and what each "is really and truly," preschoolers have difficulty. When asked whether a stone painted to look like an egg "is really and truly" an egg, children younger than age 6 often responded "yes" (Flavell, Green, & Flavell, 1987). But simplify these appearance–reality tasks by permitting children to solve them nonverbally, by selecting from an array of objects the one that "really" has a particular identity, and most 3-year-olds perform well (Deák, Ray, & Brenneman, 2003). They realize that an object can be one thing (a stone) while symbolizing another (an egg).

How do children grasp the dual representation of symbolic objects? When adults point out similarities between models and real-world spaces, 2½-year-olds perform better on the find-Snoopy task (Peralta de Mendoza & Salsa, 2003). Also, insight into one type of symbol–real-world relation helps preschoolers master others. For example, children regard realistic-looking pictures as symbols early because a picture's primary purpose is to stand for something; it is not an interesting object in its own right (Simcock & DeLoache, 2006). And 3-year-olds who can use a model of a room to locate Big Snoopy readily transfer their understanding to a simple map (Marzolf & DeLoache, 1994). In sum, experiences with diverse symbols—photos, picture books, make-believe, and maps—help preschoolers appreciate that one object can stand for another.

Limitations of Preoperational Thought

Aside from gains in representation, Piaget described preschoolers in terms of what they *cannot* understand. As the term *preoperational* suggests, he compared them to older, more competent school-age children. According to Piaget, young children are not capable of *operations*—mental actions that obey logical rules. Rather, their thinking is rigid, limited to one aspect of a situation at a time, and strongly influenced by the way things appear at the moment.

Egocentrism. For Piaget, the most fundamental deficiency of preoperational thinking is **egocentrism**—failure to distinguish others' symbolic viewpoints from one's own. He believed that when children first mentally represent the world, they tend to focus on their own viewpoint and simply assume that others perceive, think, and feel the same way they do.

Piaget's most convincing demonstration of egocentrism involves his *three-mountains problem,* described in Figure 7.5. He also regarded egocentrism as responsible for preoperational children's *animistic thinking*—the belief that inanimate objects have lifelike qualities, such as thoughts, wishes, feelings, and intentions (Piaget, 1926/1930). Recall Sammy's firm insistence that someone must have turned on the thunder. According to Piaget, because young children egocentrically assign human purposes to physical events, magical thinking is common during the preschool years.

Piaget argued that preschoolers' egocentric bias prevents them from *accommodating,* or reflecting on and revising their faulty reasoning in response to their physical and social worlds. To understand this shortcoming, let's consider some additional tasks that Piaget gave to children.

FIGURE 7.5 Piaget's three-mountains problem. Each mountain is distinguished by its color and by its summit. One has a red cross, another a small house, and the third a snow-capped peak. Children at the preoperational stage respond egocentrically. They cannot select a picture that shows the mountains from the doll's perspective. Instead, they simply choose the photo that reflects their own vantage point.

FIGURE 7.6 Some Piagetian conservation tasks. Children at the preoperational stage cannot yet conserve. These tasks are mastered gradually over the concrete operational stage. Children in Western nations typically acquire conservation of number, mass, and liquid sometime between 6 and 7 years and of weight between 8 and 10 years.

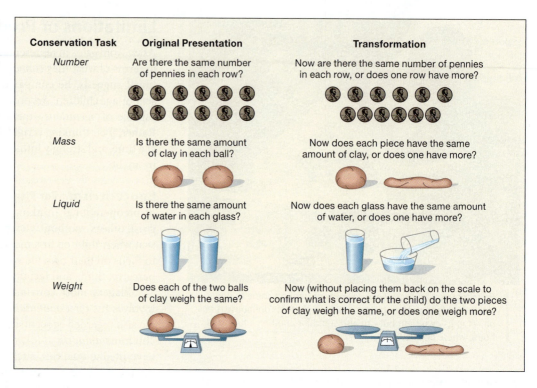

Conservation Task	Original Presentation	Transformation
Number	Are there the same number of pennies in each row?	Now are there the same number of pennies in each row, or does one row have more?
Mass	Is there the same amount of clay in each ball?	Now does each piece have the same amount of clay, or does one have more?
Liquid	Is there the same amount of water in each glass?	Now does each glass have the same amount of water, or does one have more?
Weight	Does each of the two balls of clay weigh the same?	Now (without placing them back on the scale to confirm what is correct for the child) do the two pieces of clay weigh the same, or does one weigh more?

Inability to Conserve. Piaget's famous conservation tasks reveal a variety of deficiencies of preoperational thinking. **Conservation** refers to the idea that certain physical characteristics of objects remain the same, even when their outward appearance changes. At snack time, Priti and Sammy had identical boxes of raisins, but when Priti spread her raisins out on the table, Sammy was convinced that she had more.

In another conservation task involving liquid, the child is shown two identical tall glasses of water and asked if they contain equal amounts. Once the child agrees, the water in one glass is poured into a short, wide container. Then the child is asked whether the amount of water has changed. Preoperational children think the quantity has changed. They explain, "There is less now because the water is way down here" (that is, its level is so low) or, "There is more now because it is all spread out." Figure 7.6 illustrates other conservation tasks that you can try with children.

The inability to conserve highlights several related aspects of preoperational children's thinking. First, their understanding is characterized by **centration.** They focus on one aspect of a situation, neglecting other important features. In conservation of liquid, the child *centers* on the height of the water, failing to realize that changes in width compensate for changes in height. Second, children are easily distracted by the *perceptual appearance* of objects. Third, children treat the initial and final states of the water as unrelated events, ignoring the *dynamic transformation* (pouring of water) between them.

The most important illogical feature of preoperational thought is its **irreversibility,** an inability to mentally go through a series of steps in a problem and then reverse direction, returning to the starting point. *Reversibility* is part of every logical operation. After Priti spills her raisins, Sammy cannot reverse by thinking, "I know that Priti doesn't have more raisins than I do. If we put them back in that little box, her raisins and my raisins would look just the same."

Lack of Hierarchical Classification. Preoperational children have difficulty with **hierarchical classification**—the organization of objects into classes and subclasses on the basis of similarities and differences. Piaget's famous *class inclusion problem,* illustrated in Figure 7.7, demonstrates this limitation. Preoperational children center on the overriding feature, red.

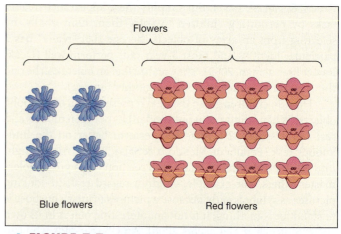

Flowers

Blue flowers   Red flowers

FIGURE 7.7 A Piagetian class inclusion problem. Children are shown 16 flowers, 4 of which are blue and 12 of which are red. Asked, "Are there more red flowers or flowers?" the preoperational child responds, "More red flowers," failing to realize that both red and blue flowers are included in the category "flowers."

They do not think reversibly by moving from the whole class (flowers) to the parts (red and blue) and back again.

Follow-Up Research on Preoperational Thought

Over the past three decades, researchers have challenged Piaget's view of preschoolers as cognitively deficient. Because many Piagetian problems contain unfamiliar elements or too many pieces of information for young children to handle at once, preschoolers' responses do not reflect their true abilities. Piaget also missed many naturally occurring instances of effective reasoning by preschoolers.

Egocentric, Animistic, and Magical Thinking.
When researchers use simplified tasks with familiar objects, 3-year-olds show clear awareness of others' vantage points, such as recognizing how something looks to another person who is looking at it through a color filter (Moll & Meltzoff, 2011). Even 2-year-olds realize that what they see sometimes differs from what another person sees. When asked to help an adult looking for a lost object, 24-month-olds—but not 18-month-olds—handed her a toy resting behind a bucket that was within the child's line of sight but not the adults' (Moll & Tomasello, 2006). Nonegocentric responses also appear in children's everyday interactions. In Chapter 5, we saw that toddlers have already begun to infer others' intentions (see pages 122–123).

In his later writings, Piaget (1945/1951) described preschoolers' egocentrism as a *tendency* rather than an inability. As we revisit the topic of perspective taking, we will see that it develops gradually throughout childhood and adolescence.

Piaget also overestimated preschoolers' animistic beliefs. By age 2½, children give psychological explanations ("he likes to" or "she wants to") for people and occasionally for animals, but rarely for objects (Hickling & Wellman, 2001). In addition, preschoolers rarely attribute biological properties (like eating and growing) to robots, indicating that they are well aware that even a self-moving robot with lifelike features is not alive. They often say that robots have perceptual and psychological capacities—for example, seeing, thinking, and remembering (Jipson & Gelman, 2007; Subrahmanyam, Gelman, & Lafosse, 2002). But these responses result from incomplete knowledge about certain objects, and they decline with age.

Similarly, preschoolers think that magic accounts for events they otherwise cannot explain—fairies, goblins, ghosts, and, for Sammy, thunder. Furthermore, older 3-year-olds and 4-year-olds think that violations of physical laws (walking through a wall) and mental laws (turning on the TV just by thinking about it) require magic more than violations of social conventions (taking a bath with shoes on) (Browne & Woolley, 2004). These responses indicate that preschoolers' notions of magic are flexible and appropriate.

Between ages 4 and 8, as children gain familiarity with physical events and principles, their magical beliefs decline. They figure out who is really behind Santa Claus and the Tooth Fairy, and they realize that the antics of magicians are due to trickery (Subbotsky, 2004). And increasingly, children say that characters and events in fantastical stories aren't real (Woolley & Cox, 2007). Still, because children entertain the possibility that something imaginary might materialize, they may react with anxiety to scary stories, TV shows, and nightmares.

Logical Thought.
When preschoolers are given tasks that are simplified and relevant to their everyday lives, they do not display the illogical characteristics that Piaget saw in the preoperational stage. For example, when a conservation-of-number task is scaled down to include only three items instead of six or seven, 3-year-olds perform well (Gelman, 1972). And when asked carefully worded questions about what happens to a substance (such as sugar) after it is dissolved in water, most 3- to 5-year-olds know that the substance is conserved—that it continues to exist, can be tasted, and makes the liquid heavier, even though it is invisible in the water (Au, Sidle, & Rollins, 1993; Rosen & Rozin, 1993).

Preschoolers' ability to reason about transformations is evident on other problems. They can engage in impressive *reasoning by analogy* about physical changes. Presented with the picture-matching problem "Play dough is to cut-up play dough as apple is to . . . ?," even 3-year-olds choose the correct answer (a cut-up apple) from a set of alternatives, several of which (a bitten apple, a cut-up loaf of bread) share physical features with the right choice (Goswami, 1996). Finally, without detailed biological or mechanical knowledge, preschoolers understand that the insides of animals are responsible for certain cause–effect sequences (such as willing oneself to move) that are impossible for nonliving things (Gelman, 2003; Keil & Lockhart, 1999). Preschoolers seem to use illogical reasoning only when grappling with unfamiliar topics, too much information, or contradictory facts that they cannot reconcile.

Categorization.
Despite their difficulty with Piagetian class inclusion tasks, preschoolers organize their everyday knowledge into nested categories at an early age. By the beginning of early childhood, children's categories include objects that go together because of their common function, behavior, or natural kind (animate versus inanimate), despite varying widely in perceptual features. Indeed, 2- to 5-year-olds readily draw appropriate inferences about nonobservable characteristics shared by category members (Gopnik & Nazzi, 2003). For example, after being told that a bird has warm blood and that a stegosaurus (dinosaur) has cold blood, preschoolers infer that a pterodactyl (labeled a dinosaur) has cold blood, even though it closely resembles a bird.

During the second and third years, and perhaps earlier, children's categories differentiate. They form many *basic-level categories*—ones that are at an intermediate level of generality, such as "chairs," "tables," and "beds." By the third year, children easily move back and forth between basic-level categories and *general categories*, such as "furniture." And they break down basic-level categories into *subcategories*, such as "rocking chairs" and "desk chairs."

These 4-year-olds understand that a category ("dinosaurs") can be based on underlying characteristics ("cold-blooded"), not just on perceptual features such as upright posture and scaly skin.

Preschoolers' rapidly expanding vocabularies and general knowledge support their impressive skill at categorizing. Also, adults label and explain categories to children, especially during picture-book reading (Gelman & Kalish, 2006). In conversing about books, parents provide information ("Penguins live at the South Pole, swim, catch fish, and have thick layers of fat and feathers that help them stay warm") that guides children's inferences about the structure of categories. Furthermore, as the Social Issues: Education box on the following page indicates, young children ask many questions about their world and usually get informative answers, which are well-suited to advancing their conceptual understanding.

In sum, although preschoolers' category systems are less complex than those of older children and adults, they already have the capacity to classify hierarchically and on the basis of nonobvious properties. And they use logical, causal reasoning to identify the interrelated features that form the basis of a category and to classify new members.

Evaluation of the Preoperational Stage

TAKE A MOMENT... Compare the cognitive attainments of early childhood, summarized in Table 7.1, with Piaget's description of the preoperational child on pages 175–178. The evidence as a whole indicates that Piaget was partly right and partly wrong about young children's cognitive capacities.

That preschoolers have some logical understanding suggests that they attain logical operations gradually, which poses yet another challenge to Piaget's stage concept of abrupt change toward logical reasoning around age 6 or 7. Does a preoperational stage really exist? Some no longer think so. Recall from Chapter 5 that according to the information-processing perspective, children work out their understanding of each type of task separately, and their thought processes are basically the same at all ages—just present to a greater or lesser extent.

Other experts think the stage concept is still valid, with modifications. For example, some *neo-Piagetian theorists* com-

TABLE 7.1 **Some Cognitive Attainments of Early Childhood**

APPROXIMATE AGE	COGNITIVE ATTAINMENTS
2–4 years	Shows a dramatic increase in representational activity, as reflected in language, make-believe play, drawing, understanding of symbol–real-world relations, and categorization
	Takes the perspective of others in simplified, familiar situations and in everyday, face-to-face communication
	Distinguishes animate beings from inanimate objects; denies that magic can alter everyday experiences
	Grasps conservation, notices transformations, reverses thinking, and understands many cause-and-effect relationships in familiar contexts
	Categorizes objects on the basis of common function, behavior, and natural kind, not just perceptual features. Uses logical, causal reasoning to identify interrelated features that form the basis of a category
	Sorts familiar objects into hierarchically organized categories
4–7 years	Becomes increasingly aware that make-believe (and other thought processes) are representational activities
	Replaces beliefs in magical creatures and events with plausible explanations

Social Issues: Education

Children's Questions: Catalyst for Cognitive Development

"Dad, what's that?" asked 4-year-old Emily as her father chopped vegetables for dinner.

"It's an onion," her father said.

"Is an onion a fruit?" Emily asked.

"It's a vegetable," her father replied. "A root vegetable because it grows underground."

Emily wrinkled her nose. "Why does it smell yucky?"

"I don't know," her father admitted. "But after dinner we can look it up online and find out."

When young children converse with adults, they ask, on average, more than one question per minute! An analysis of diaries that parents kept of their children's questions and of audio recordings of parent–child interactions revealed that at every age between 1 and 5 years, 70 to 90 percent of children's questions were information-seeking ("What's that [pointing to a crawfish]?") as opposed to non-information-seeking ("Can I have a cookie?") (Chouinard, 2007). And from age 2 on, children increasingly built on their fact-oriented questions with follow-up questions that asked for causes and explanations ("What do crawfish eat?" "Why does it have claws?"). By age 3½, these sets of "building questions" made up about half of children's questions,

confirming that preschoolers ask questions purposefully, to obtain clarifying information about things that puzzle them.

Unlike information obtained in other ways, answers to children's questions provide the precise knowledge they need at the precise moment they need it. And the content of children's questions is related to their cognitive development. At a time when vocabulary is advancing rapidly, about 60 percent of 1½- to 2-year-olds' questions ask for names of objects. With age, preschoolers increasingly ask about function ("What's it do?"), activity ("What's he doing?"), state ("Is she hungry?"), and theory of mind ("How does the pilot *know* where to fly?").

Most of the time, parents respond informatively. If they do not, preschoolers are amazingly persistent: They ask again until they get the information they want. Parents adjust the complexity of their answers to fit their children's maturity (Callanan & Oakes, 1992). To a question like "Why does the light

Preschoolers' questions are often purposeful efforts to understand things that puzzle them, making question-asking a powerful source of cognitive development.

come on?" 3-year-olds typically get simpler, "prior cause" explanations ("I turned on the switch"). Slightly older children frequently get "mechanism" explanations ("The switch allows electricity to reach the light bulb").

Clearly, asking questions is a major means through which children strive to attain adult-like understandings. Children's questions offer parents and teachers a fascinating window into their factual and conceptual knowledge, along with a wealth of opportunities to help them learn.

---

bine Piaget's stage approach with the information-processing emphasis on task-specific change (Case, 1998; Halford & Andrews, 2006). They believe that Piaget's strict stage definition must be transformed into a less tightly knit concept, one in which a related set of competencies develops over an extended period, depending on brain development and specific experiences. These investigators point to evidence that as long as the complexity of tasks and children's exposure to them are controlled, children approach those tasks in similar ways (Andrews & Halford, 2002; Case & Okamoto, 1996). For example, in drawing pictures, preschoolers depict objects separately, ignoring their spatial arrangement. In understanding stories, they grasp a single story line but have trouble with a main plot plus one or more subplots.

This flexible stage notion recognizes the unique qualities of early childhood thinking. At the same time, it provides a better account of why, as Leslie put it, "Preschoolers' minds are such a blend of logic, fantasy, and faulty reasoning."

ASK YOURSELF

REVIEW Select two of the following features of preoperational thought: egocentrism, a focus on perceptual appearances, difficulty reasoning about transformations, lack of hierarchical classification. Present evidence indicating that preschoolers are more capable thinkers than Piaget assumed.

APPLY Three-year-old Will understands that his tricycle isn't alive and can't feel or move on its own. But at the beach, while watching the sun dip below the horizon, Will exclaimed, "The sun is tired. It's going to sleep!" What explains this apparent contradiction in Will's reasoning?

REFLECT On the basis of what you have read, do you accept Piaget's claim for a preoperational stage of cognitive development? Explain.

Vygotsky's Sociocultural Theory

During early childhood, rapid growth of language broadens preschoolers' participation in social dialogues with more knowledgeable individuals, who encourage them to master culturally important tasks. According to Vygotsky's sociocultural theory, children start to communicate with themselves in much the same way they converse with others. This greatly enhances their thinking and ability to control their own behavior. Let's see how this happens.

Private Speech

TAKE A MOMENT... Watch preschoolers as they play and explore the environment, and you will see that they frequently talk out loud to themselves. For example, as Sammy worked a puzzle, he said, "Where's the red piece? Now, a blue one. No, it doesn't fit. Try it here."

Piaget (1923/1926) called these utterances *egocentric speech*, reflecting his belief that young children have difficulty taking the perspectives of others. Their talk, he said, is often "talk for self" in which they express thoughts in whatever form they happen to occur, regardless of whether a listener can understand. Piaget believed that cognitive development and certain social experiences eventually bring an end to egocentric speech. Specifically, through disagreements with peers, children see that others hold viewpoints different from their own.

Vygotsky (1934/1987) disagreed with Piaget's conclusions. Because language helps children think about their mental

A preschooler explores the possibilities of a handful of soap bubbles with the aid of private speech. Research supports Vygotsky's theory that children use private speech to guide their thinking and behavior.

activities and behavior and select courses of action, Vygotsky saw it as the foundation for all higher cognitive processes, including controlled attention, deliberate memorization and recall, categorization, planning, problem solving, and self-reflection. In Vygotsky's view, children speak to themselves for self-guidance. As they get older and find tasks easier, their self-directed speech is internalized as silent, *inner speech*—the internal verbal dialogues we carry on while thinking and acting in everyday situations.

Over the past three decades, almost all studies have supported Vygotsky's perspective (Berk & Harris, 2003; Winsler, 2009). As a result, children's self-directed speech is now called **private speech** instead of egocentric speech. Research shows that children use more of it when tasks are appropriately challenging (neither too easy nor too hard), after they make errors, or when they are confused about how to proceed. With age, as Vygotsky predicted, private speech goes underground, changing into whispers and silent lip movements. Furthermore, children who freely use private speech during a challenging activity are more attentive and involved and show better task performance than their less talkative agemates (Al-Namlah, Fernyhough, & Meins, 2006; Lidstone, Meins, & Fernyhough, 2010; Winsler, Naglieri, & Manfra, 2006).

Social Origins of Early Childhood Cognition

Where does private speech come from? Recall from Chapter 5 that Vygotsky believed that children's learning takes place within the *zone of proximal development*—a range of tasks too difficult for the child to do alone but possible with the help of adults and more skilled peers. Consider the joint activity of Sammy and his mother as she helps him put together a difficult puzzle:

Sammy: I can't get this one in. *[Tries to insert a piece in the wrong place.]*

Mother: Which piece might go down here? *[Points to the bottom of the puzzle.]*

Sammy: His shoes. *[Finds a piece that resembles the clown's shoes, tries it, and it fits; then attempts another piece and looks at his mother.]*

Mother: Try turning it just a little. *[Gestures to show him.]*

Sammy: There! *[Puts in several more pieces while his mother watches.]*

Sammy's mother keeps the puzzle at a manageable level of difficulty. To do so, she engages in **scaffolding**—adjusting the support offered during a teaching session to fit the child's current level of performance. When the child has little notion of how to proceed, the adult uses direct instruction, breaking the task into manageable units and suggesting strategies. As the child's competence increases, effective scaffolders gradually and sensitively withdraw support, turning over responsibility to the child. Then children take the language of these dialogues, make

© LAURA DWIGHT PHOTOGRAPHY

it part of their private speech, and use this speech to organize their independent efforts.

Consistent with Vygotsky's ideas, in several studies, children whose parents were effective scaffolders used more private speech, were more successful when attempting difficult tasks on their own, and were advanced in overall cognitive development (Berk & Spuhl, 1995; Conner & Cross, 2003; Mulvaney et al., 2006). Adult cognitive support—teaching in small steps and offering strategies—predicts gains in children's thinking. And among Caucasian-American parent–child pairs, adult emotional support—offering encouragement and allowing the child to take over the task—predicts children's effort (Neitzel & Stright, 2003).

Nevertheless, effective scaffolding varies among cultures. Unlike Caucasian-American parents, who emphasize independence by encouraging their children to think of ways to approach a task, Hmong immigrant parents from Southeast Asia—who highly value interdependence and child obedience—frequently tell their children what to do (for example, "Put this piece here, then that piece on top of it") (Stright, Herr, & Neitzel, 2009). Among Caucasian-American children, such directive scaffolding is associated with kindergartners' lack of self-control and behavior problems. Among Hmong children, however, it predicts greater rule following, organization, and task completion.

Finally, although children benefit from working on tasks with same-age peers, their planning and problem solving improve more when their partner is either an "expert" peer (especially capable at the task) or an adult. And peer disagreement (emphasized by Piaget) is less important in fostering cognitive development than the extent to which children resolve differences of opinion and cooperate (Kobayashi, 1994).

Vygotsky's View of Make-Believe Play

Vygotsky (1933/1978) saw make-believe play as the ideal social context for fostering cognitive development in early childhood. As children create imaginary situations, they learn to follow internal ideas and social rules rather than their immediate impulses. For example, a child pretending to go to sleep follows the rules of bedtime behavior. A child imagining himself as a father conforms to the rules of parental behavior. According to Vygotsky, make-believe play is a unique, broadly influential zone of proximal development in which children try out a wide variety of challenging activities and acquire many new competencies.

Turn back to page 176 to review findings that make-believe play enhances cognitive and social skills. Pretending is also rich in private speech—a finding that supports its role in helping children bring action under the control of thought (Meyers & Berk, 2014). And preschoolers who spend more time engaged in sociodramatic play are better at regulating emotion and at taking personal responsibility for following classroom rules (Berk, Mann, & Ogan, 2006). These findings support the role of make-believe in preschooler's increasing self-control.

In this Vygotsky-inspired classroom, 4- and 5-year-olds benefit from peer cooperation. As they jointly make music, their conductor ensures that each player stays on beat.

Evaluation of Vygotsky's Theory

In granting social experience a fundamental role in cognitive development, Vygotsky's theory underscores the vital impact of teaching and the wide cultural variation in children's cognitive skills. Nevertheless, his ideas have not gone unchallenged. Verbal communication may not be the only means through which children's thinking develops—or even, in some cultures, the most important means. When Western parents scaffold, their verbal communication resembles the teaching that takes place in school, where their children will spend years preparing for adult life. In cultures that place less emphasis on schooling and literacy, parents often expect children to acquire new skills through keen observation and participation in community activities (Paradise & Rogoff, 2009; Rogoff, 2003). (See the Cultural Influences box on page 184.)

To account for children's diverse ways of learning through involvement with others, Barbara Rogoff (1998, 2003) suggests the term **guided participation,** a broader concept than scaffolding. It refers to shared endeavors between more expert and less expert participants, without specifying the precise features of communication. Consequently, it allows for variations across situations and cultures.

Finally, Vygotsky's theory says little about how basic motor, perceptual, attention, memory, and problem-solving skills, discussed in Chapters 4 and 5, contribute to socially transmitted higher cognitive processes. For example, his theory does not address how these elementary capacities spark changes in children's social experiences, from which more advanced cognition springs (Miller, 2009). Piaget paid far more attention than Vygotsky to the development of basic cognitive processes. It is intriguing to speculate about the broader theory that might exist today if Piaget and Vygotsky—the two twentieth-century giants of cognitive development—had had a chance to meet and weave together their extraordinary accomplishments.

Cultural Influences

Children in Village and Tribal Cultures Observe and Participate in Adult Work

In Western societies, schools equip children with the skills they need to become competent workers. In early childhood, middle-SES parents focus on preparing their children by engaging in child-focused conversations and play that enhance language, literacy, and other academic knowledge. In village and tribal cultures, children receive little or no schooling, spend their days in contact with adult work, and assume mature responsibilities in early childhood (Rogoff et al., 2003). Consequently, parents have little need to rely on conversation and play to teach children.

A study comparing 2- and 3-year-olds' daily lives in four cultures—two U.S. middle-SES suburbs, the Efe hunters and gatherers of the Republic of Congo, and a Mayan agricultural town in Guatemala—documented these differences (Morelli, Rogoff, & Angelillo, 2003). In the U.S. communities, young children had little access to adult work and spent much time conversing and playing with adults. In contrast, the Efe and Mayan children spent their days close to—and frequently observing—adult work, which often took place in or near the Efe campsite or the Mayan family home.

An ethnography of a remote Mayan village in Yucatán, Mexico, shows that when young children are legitimate onlookers and participants in a daily life structured around adult work, their competencies differ from those of Western preschoolers (Gaskins, 1999; Gaskins, Haight, & Lancy, 2007). Yucatec Mayan adults are subsistence farmers. Men tend cornfields, aided by sons age 8 and older. Women prepare meals, wash clothes, and care for the livestock and garden, assisted by daughters and by sons too young to work in the fields. Children join in these activities from the second year on. When not participating, they are expected to be self-sufficient. Young children make many nonwork decisions for themselves—how much to sleep and eat, what to wear, and even when to start school. As a result, Yucatec Mayan preschoolers are highly competent at self-care. In contrast, their make-believe play is limited; when it occurs, they usually imitate adult work. Otherwise, they watch others—for hours each day.

Yucatec Mayan parents rarely converse or play with preschoolers or scaffold their learning. Rather, when children imitate adult tasks, parents conclude that they are ready for more responsibility. Then they assign chores, selecting tasks the child can do with little help so that adult work is not disturbed. If a child cannot do a task, the adult takes over and the child observes, reengaging when able to contribute.

A Mayan 3-year-old imitates her mother in balancing a basket of laundry on her head. Children in Guatemalan Mayan culture observe and participate in the work of their community from an early age.

Expected to be autonomous and helpful, Yucatec Mayan children seldom ask others for something interesting to do. From an early age, they can sit quietly for long periods—through a lengthy religious service or a ride to town. And when an adult directs them to do a chore, they respond eagerly to the type of command that Western children frequently avoid or resent. By age 5, Yucatec Mayan children spontaneously take responsibility for tasks beyond those assigned.

ASK YOURSELF

REVIEW Describe features of social interaction that support children's cognitive development. How does such interaction create a zone of proximal development?

APPLY Tanisha sees her 5-year-old son talking aloud to himself as he plays. She wonders whether she should discourage this behavior. How would you advise Tanisha?

REFLECT When do you use private speech? Does it serve a self-guiding function for you, as it does for children? Explain.

Information Processing

Recall from Chapter 5 that information processing focuses on cognitive operations and mental strategies that children use to transform stimuli flowing into their mental systems. As we have already seen, early childhood is a period of dramatic strides in mental representation. And the various components of *executive function* that enable children to succeed in cognitively challenging situations—including attention, impulse control, coordinating information in working memory, and planning—show impressive gains (Welsh, Friedman, & Spieker, 2008). Preschoolers also become more aware of their own mental life and begin to acquire academically relevant knowledge important for school success.

Attention

Although preschoolers are often easily distracted, sustained attention improves considerably in early childhood. A major reason is a steady gain in children's ability to inhibit impulses and keep their mind on a competing goal. Consider a task in which the child must say "night" to a picture of the sun and "day" to a picture of the moon with stars. Whereas 3- and 4-year-olds make many errors, by age 6 to 7, children find such tasks easy (Kirkham, Cruess, & Diamond, 2003). They can resist the "pull" of their attention toward a dominant stimulus—a skill that predicts social maturity and reading and math achievement from kindergarten through high school (Blair & Razza, 2007; Duncan et al., 2007; Rhoades, Greenberg, & Domitrovich, 2009).

During early childhood, children become better at *planning*—thinking out a sequence of acts ahead of time and allocating attention accordingly to reach a goal. As long as tasks are not too complex, 5-year-olds can generate and follow a plan, such as deciding in which of two locations to store a camera so an agemate, who wants to take a photo of a kangaroo, can retrieve the camera before arriving at the kangaroo's cage (McColgan & McCormack, 2008). Younger children have trouble reasoning about a sequence of future events they have never before experienced.

Children learn much from cultural tools that support planning—directions for playing games, patterns for construction, recipes for cooking—especially when they collaborate with more expert planners. When 4- to 7-year-olds were observed jointly constructing a toy with their mothers, the mothers provided basic information about the usefulness of plans and how to implement specific steps: "Do you want to look at the picture and see what goes where? What piece do you need first?" After working with their mothers, younger children more often referred to the plan when building on their own (Gauvain, 2004; Gauvain, de la Ossa, & Hurtado-Ortiz, 2001). When parents encourage planning in everyday activities, from loading the dishwasher to packing for a vacation, they help children plan more effectively.

Memory

Unlike infants and toddlers, preschoolers have the language skills to describe what they remember, and they can follow directions on memory tasks. As a result, memory becomes easier to study in early childhood.

Recognition and Recall. *TAKE A MOMENT...* Show a young child a set of 10 pictures or toys. Then mix them up with some unfamiliar items, and ask the child to point to the ones in the original set. You will find that preschoolers' *recognition* memory—ability to tell whether a stimulus is the same as or similar to one they have seen before—is remarkably good. In fact, 4- and 5-year-olds perform nearly perfectly. Now keep the items out of view, and ask the child to name the ones she saw. This more challenging task requires *recall*—that the child gener-

ate a mental image of an absent stimulus. Young children's recall is much poorer than their recognition. At age 2, they can recall no more than one or two items, at age 4 only about three or four (Perlmutter, 1984).

Improvement in recall in early childhood is strongly associated with language development, which greatly enhances long-lasting representations of past experiences (Melby-Lervag & Hulme, 2010). But even preschoolers with good language skills recall poorly because they are not skilled at using **memory strategies**—deliberate mental activities that improve our chances of remembering. Preschoolers do not yet *rehearse,* or repeat items over and over to remember. Nor do they *organize,* grouping together items that are alike (all the animals together, all the vehicles together) so they can easily retrieve them by thinking of their similar characteristics—even when they are trained to do so (Gathercole, Adams, & Hitch, 1994). Strategies tax the limited working memories of preschoolers, who have difficulty holding on to pieces of information and applying a strategy at the same time.

Memory for Everyday Experiences. Think about the difference between your recall of listlike information and your memory for everyday experiences—what researchers call **episodic memory.** In remembering lists, you recall isolated bits, reproducing them exactly as you originally learned them. In remembering everyday experiences, you recall complex, meaningful information. Between 3 and 6 years, children improve sharply in memory for relations among stimuli—for example, in a set of photos, remembering not only the animals they saw but their contexts, such as a bear emerging from a tunnel or a zebra tied to a tree (Lloyd, Doydum, & Newcombe, 2009). The capacity to bind together stimuli supports an increasingly rich episodic memory in early childhood.

Memory for Familiar Events. Like adults, preschoolers remember familiar, repeated events—what you do when you go to preschool or have dinner—in terms of **scripts,** general descriptions of what occurs and when it occurs in a particular situation. Young children's scripts begin as a structure of main acts. For example, when asked to tell what happens at a restaurant, a 3-year-old might say, "You go in, get the food, eat, and then pay." Although first scripts contain only a few acts, they are almost always recalled in correct sequence (Bauer, 2002, 2006). With age, scripts become more elaborate, as in this 5-year-old's account of going to a restaurant: "You go in. You can sit in a booth or at a table. Then you tell the waitress what you want. You eat. If you want dessert, you can have some. Then you pay and go home" (Hudson, Fivush, & Kuebli, 1992).

Scripts help children (and adults) organize and interpret everyday experiences. Once formed, they can be used to predict what will happen in the future. Children rely on scripts in make-believe play and when listening to and telling stories. Scripts also support children's earliest efforts at planning as they represent sequences of actions that lead to desired goals (Hudson & Mayhew, 2009).

As this toddler talks with his mother about past experiences, she responds in an elaborative style, asking varied questions and contributing her own recollections. Through such conversations, she enriches his autobiographical memory.

Memory for One-Time Events. In Chapter 5, we considered a second type of episodic memory—*autobiographical memory,* or representations of personally meaningful, one-time events. As preschoolers' cognitive and conversational skills improve, their descriptions of special events become better organized in time and more detailed.

Adults use two styles to elicit children's autobiographical narratives. In the *elaborative style,* they follow the child's lead, ask varied questions, add information to the child's statements, and volunteer their own recollections and evaluations of events. For example, after a trip to the zoo, the parent might say, "Where did we go first? Why weren't the parrots in their cages? I thought the lion was scary. What did you think?" In contrast, adults who use the *repetitive style* provide little information and keep repeating the same questions regardless of the child's interest: "Do you remember the zoo? What did we do at the zoo?" Preschoolers who experience the elaborative style recall more information about past events, and they also produce more organized and detailed personal stories when followed up one to two years later (Cleveland & Reese, 2005; Farrant & Reese, 2000).

As children talk with adults about the past, they create a shared history that strengthens close relationships and self-understanding. Parents and preschoolers with secure attachment bonds engage in more elaborate reminiscing (Bost et al., 2006). And 5- and 6-year-olds of elaborative-style parents describe themselves in clearer, more consistent ways (Bird & Reese, 2006).

The Young Child's Theory of Mind

As representation of the world, memory, and problem solving improve, children reflect on their own thought processes. They begin to construct a *theory of mind,* or coherent set of ideas about mental activities. This understanding is also called **metacognition,** or "thinking about thought" (the prefix *meta-* means "beyond" or "higher"). As adults, we have a complex appreciation of our inner mental worlds, which we use to inter-

pret our own and others' behavior and to improve our performance on various tasks. How early are children aware of their mental lives, and how complete and accurate is their knowledge?

Awareness of Mental Life. At the end of the first year, babies view people as intentional beings who can share and influence one another's mental states, a milestone that opens the door to new forms of communication—joint attention, social referencing, preverbal gestures, and spoken language. As 2-year-olds' vocabularies expand, their first verbs include such mental-state words as *want, remember,* and *pretend* (Wellman, 2002). By age 3, children realize that thinking takes place inside their heads and that a person can think about something without seeing, touching, or talking about it (Flavell, Green, & Flavell, 1995). But 2- to 3-year-olds' verbal responses indicate that they think people always behave in ways consistent with their *desires;* they do not understand that less obvious, more interpretive mental states, such as *beliefs,* also affect behavior.

Between ages 3 and 4, children increasingly refer to their own and others' thoughts and beliefs (Wellman, 2011). And from age 4 on, they say that both *beliefs* and *desires* determine behavior. Dramatic evidence comes from games that test whether preschoolers realize that *false beliefs*—ones that do not represent reality accurately—can guide people's actions. ***TAKE A MOMENT...*** For example, show a child two small closed boxes—a familiar Band-Aid box and a plain, unmarked box. Then say, "Pick the box you think has the Band-Aids in it." Children usually pick the marked container. Next, open the boxes and show the child that, contrary to her own belief, the marked one is empty and the unmarked one contains the Band-Aids. Finally, introduce the child to a hand puppet and explain, "Pam has a cut, see? Where do you think she'll look for Band-Aids? Why would she look in there? Before you looked inside, did you think that the plain box contained Band-Aids? Why?" (Bartsch & Wellman, 1995). Only a handful of 3-year-olds can explain Pam's—and their own—false beliefs, but many 4-year-olds can.

Nevertheless, growing evidence indicates that toddlers may have an *implicit* grasp of false belief, revealed by their nonverbal behaviors. Most 18-month-olds—after witnessing an object moved from one box to another while an adult was not looking—helped the adult, when he tried to open the original box, locate the object in the new box (Buttelmann, Carpenter, & Tomasello, 2009). And 15- to 18-month-olds' looking behaviors—toward the location they expect an adult to reach for an object—yield similar findings (Baillargeon, Scott, & He, 2010; Senju et al., 2011). Performance on these implicit false-belief tasks predicts later *explicit* understanding, evident in older preschoolers' verbal explanations (San Juan & Astington, 2012; Thoermer et al., 2012). Still, investigators disagree sharply on the depth of toddlers' insights.

Explicit false-belief understanding strengthens after age 3½, becoming more secure between ages 4 and 6 (Amsterlaw & Wellman, 2006; Flynn, 2006). During that time, it becomes a powerful tool for understanding oneself and others and a good predictor of social skills (Harwood & Farrar, 2006; Hughes, Ensor, & Marks, 2010).

Factors Contributing to Preschoolers' Theory of Mind.

How do children develop a theory of mind at such a young age? Language, executive function, make-believe play, and social experiences all contribute.

Many studies indicate that language ability strongly predicts preschoolers' false-belief understanding (Milligan, Astington, & Dack, 2007). Children who spontaneously use, or who are trained to use, mental-state words in conversation are especially likely to pass false-belief tasks (Hale & Tager-Flusberg, 2003; San Juan & Astington, 2012). Among the Quechua people of the Peruvian highlands, whose language lacks mental-state terms, children have difficulty with false-belief tasks for years after children in industrialized nations have mastered them (Vinden, 1996). In contrast, Chinese languages have verb markers that can label the word *believe* as decidedly false. When adults use those markers in false-belief tasks, Chinese preschoolers perform better (Tardif, Wellman, & Cheung, 2004).

Several aspects of preschoolers' executive function—the ability to inhibit inappropriate responses, think flexibly, and plan—predict mastery of false belief (Drayton, Turley-Ames, & Guajardo, 2011; Hughes & Ensor, 2007; Müller et al., 2012). Gains in inhibition are strongly related to mastery of false belief, perhaps because children must suppress an irrelevant response— the tendency to assume that others share their own knowledge and beliefs.

Social experience also promotes understanding of the mind. In longitudinal research, mothers of securely attached babies were more likely to comment appropriately on their infants' mental states: "Do you *remember* Grandma?" "You really *like* that swing!" These mothers continued to describe their children, when they reached preschool age, in terms of mental characteristics: "She's got a mind of her own!" This maternal "mind-mindedness" was positively associated with later performance on false-belief and other theory-of-mind tasks (Meins et al., 1998, 2003; Ruffman et al., 2006).

Also, preschoolers with siblings who are children (but not infants)—especially older siblings or two or more siblings— tend to be more aware of false belief because they are exposed to more family talk about others' perspectives (McAlister & Peterson, 2006, 2007). Similarly, preschool friends who often engage in mental-state talk—as children do during make-believe play—are ahead in false-belief understanding (de Rosnay & Hughes, 2006).

Style of adult–child interaction contributes, too. Well-connected discourse, in which each speaker's remark is related to the other's previous remark, predicts preschoolers' theory-of-mind progress (Ontai & Thompson, 2010). These exchanges offer children extra opportunities to talk about inner states, receive feedback, and become increasingly aware of their own and others' mental activities.

Core knowledge theorists (see Chapter 5, page 159) believe that to profit from the social experiences just described, children must be biologically prepared to develop a theory of mind. They claim that children with *autism,* for whom mastery of false belief is either greatly delayed or absent, are deficient in the brain mechanism enabling humans to detect mental states. See the Biology and Environment box on page 188 to find out more about the biological basis of reasoning about the mind.

Limitations of Preschoolers' Understanding of Mental Life.

Though surprisingly advanced, preschoolers' awareness of mental activities is far from complete. For example, children younger than age 5 pay little attention to the *process* of thinking. When asked about subtle distinctions between mental states, such as *know* and *guess,* they express confusion (Lyon & Flavell, 1994). And they believe that all events must be directly observed to be known. They do not understand that *mental inferences* can be a source of knowledge (Miller, Hardin, & Montgomery, 2003).

These findings suggest that preschoolers view the mind as a passive container of information. As they move into middle childhood, they will increasingly see it as an active, constructive agent—a change we will consider further in Chapter 9.

Early Childhood Literacy

One week, Leslie's students created a make-believe grocery store. They placed empty food boxes on shelves in the classroom, labeled items with prices, and made paper money for use at the cash register. A sign at the entrance announced the daily specials: "APLS BNS 5¢" ("apples bananas 5¢").

As such play reveals, preschoolers understand a great deal about written language long before they learn to read or write in conventional ways. This is not surprising: Children in industrialized nations live in a world filled with written symbols. Their active efforts to construct literacy knowledge through informal experiences are called **emergent literacy.**

Young preschoolers search for units of written language as they "read" memorized versions of stories and recognize familiar signs, such as "PIZZA." But they do not yet understand the symbolic function of the elements of print (Bialystok & Martin, 2003). Many preschoolers think that a single letter stands for a

Preschoolers acquire literacy knowledge informally through participating in everyday activities involving written symbols. Here a young chef "jots down" a phone order for a take-out meal.

Biology and Environment

"Mindblindness" and Autism

Michael stood at the water table in Leslie's classroom, repeatedly filling a plastic cup and dumping out its contents—dip–splash, dip–splash—until Leslie came over and redirected his actions. Without looking at Leslie's face, Michael moved to a new repetitive pursuit: pouring water from one cup into another and back again. As other children entered the play space and conversed, Michael hardly noticed.

Michael has *autism* (a term that means "absorbed in the self"), the most severe behavior disorder of childhood. Like other children with autism, by age 3 he displayed deficits in three core areas of functioning. First, he had only limited ability to engage in nonverbal behaviors required for successful social interaction, such as eye contact, facial expressions, gestures, imitation, and give-and-take. Second, his language was delayed and stereotyped. He used words to echo what others said and to get things he wanted, not to exchange ideas. Third, he engaged in much less make-believe play than other children (Frith, 2003; Walenski, Tager-Flusberg, & Ullman, 2006). And Michael showed another typical feature of autism: His interests were narrow and overly intense. For example, one day he sat for more than an hour spinning a toy Ferris wheel.

Researchers agree that autism stems from abnormal brain functioning, usually due to genetic or prenatal environmental causes. Beginning in the first year, children with the disorder have larger-than-average brains, perhaps due to massive overgrowth of synapses and lack of synaptic pruning (Courchesne, Carper, & Akshoomoff, 2003). Furthermore, the amygdala, devoted to emotion processing (see page 150 in Chapter 6), grows especially large in childhood, followed by a greater than average reduction in size in adolescence and adulthood. fMRI evidence indicates weaker connections between the amygdala and areas of the cerebral cortex involved in processing emotional information. These deviant growth patterns are believed to contribute to the deficits in emotional responsiveness and social interaction involved in the disorder (Monk et al., 2010; Schumann et al., 2009; Schumann & Amaral, 2010).

Mounting evidence reveals that children with autism have a deficient theory of mind. Long after they reach the intellectual level of an average 4-year-old, they have great difficulty with false belief. Most find it hard to attribute mental states to themselves or others (Steele, Joseph, & Tager-Flusberg, 2003).

As early as the second year, children with autism show deficits in capacities believed to contribute to an understanding of mental life. Compared with other children, they have difficulty distinguishing facial expressions and less often establish joint attention, engage in social referencing, or imitate an adult's novel behaviors (Chawarska & Shic, 2009; Mundy & Stella, 2000; Vivanti et al., 2008).

Do these findings indicate that autism is due to impairment in an innate, core brain function, which leaves the child "mindblind" and therefore unable to engage in human sociability? Some researchers think so (Baron-Cohen & Belmonte, 2005; Scholl & Leslie, 2000). But others point out that individuals with mental retardation but not autism also

This child, who has autism, is barely aware of his teacher and classmates. His "mindblindness" might be due to a core deficit in social awareness. Alternatively, it might stem from a general impairment in executive function.

do poorly on tasks assessing mental understanding (Yirmiya et al., 1998). This suggests that some kind of general intellectual impairment may be involved.

One conjecture is that children with autism are impaired in executive function. This leaves them deficient in skills involved in flexible, goal-oriented thinking, including shifting attention to relevant aspects of a situation, inhibiting irrelevant responses, applying strategies to hold information in working memory, and generating plans (Joseph & Tager-Flusberg, 2004; Robinson et al., 2009). An inability to think flexibly would interfere with understanding the social world because social interaction requires quick integration of information from various sources and evaluation of alternative possibilities.

It is not clear which of these hypotheses is correct. Perhaps several biologically based deficits underlie the tragic social isolation of children like Michael.

---

whole word or that each letter in a person's signature represents a separate name. Children revise these ideas as their cognitive capacities improve, as they encounter writing in many contexts, and as adults help them with written communication.

Eventually, children figure out that letters are parts of words and are linked to sounds in systematic ways, as 5- to 7-year-olds' invented spellings illustrate. At first, children rely on sounds in the names of letters, as in "ADE LAFWTS KRMD NTU A LAVATR" ("eighty elephants crammed into a[n] elevator"). Soon they grasp sound–letter correspondences (McGee & Richgels, 2012).

Literacy development builds on a broad foundation of spoken language and knowledge about the world (Dickinson, Golinkoff, & Hirsh-Pasek, 2010). Over time, children's language and literacy progress facilitate each other. **Phonological awareness**—the ability to reflect on and manipulate the sound

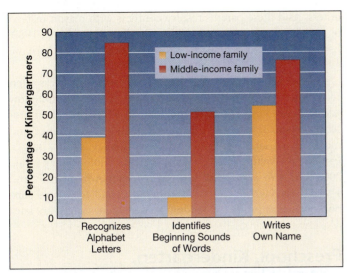

FIGURE 7.8 Some kindergarten reading readiness skills by family income. The gap in emergent literacy development between entering-kindergarten students from low-income and middle-income families is large. (Adapted from Lee & Burkam, 2002.)

structure of spoken language, as indicated by sensitivity to changes in sounds within words, to rhyming, and to incorrect pronunciation—is a strong predictor of emergent literacy knowledge (Paris & Paris, 2006). When combined with sound–letter knowledge, it enables children to isolate speech segments and link them with their written symbols. Vocabulary and grammatical skills are also influential.

The more informal literacy-related experiences young children have, the better their language and emergent literacy development and their later reading skills (Dickinson & McCabe, 2001; Speece et al., 2004). Pointing out letter–sound correspondences and playing language–sound games enhance children's awareness of the sound structure of language and how it is represented in print (Ehri & Roberts, 2006). *Interactive reading,* in which adults discuss storybook content with preschoolers, promotes many aspects of language and literacy development.

Preschoolers from low-income families have fewer home and preschool language and literacy learning opportunities—a gap that translates into large differences in skills vital for reading readiness at kindergarten entry (see Figure 7.8) and into widening disparities in reading achievement during the school years (Hoff, 2013; Turnbull et al., 2009). Providing child-care centers and parents with children's books, along with guidance in how to stimulate literacy learning, greatly enhances low-income preschoolers' emergent literacy skills (High et al., 2000; Huebner & Payne, 2010).

Early Childhood Mathematical Reasoning

Mathematical reasoning, like literacy, builds on informally acquired knowledge. Between 14 and 16 months, toddlers display a beginning grasp of **ordinality,** or order relationships

between quantities—for example, that 3 is more than 2, and 2 is more than 1. And 2-year-olds often indicate without counting that a set of items has "lots," "many," or "little" in relation to others (Ginsburg, Lee, & Boyd, 2008). By the time children turn 3, most can count rows of about five objects, although they do not yet know exactly what the words mean. But 2½- to 3½-year-olds understand that when a number label changes (for example, from *five* to *six*), the number of items should also change (Sarnecka & Gelman, 2004).

By age 3½ to 4, most children grasp the meaning of numbers up to 10, count correctly, and grasp the vital principle of **cardinality**—that the last number in a counting sequence indicates the quantity of items in a set (Geary, 2006a). Mastery of cardinality increases the efficiency of children's counting.

Around age 4, children use counting to solve arithmetic problems. At first, their strategies are tied to the order of numbers as presented; to add 2 + 4, they count on from 2 (Bryant & Nunes, 2002). But soon they experiment with other strategies and eventually arrive at the most efficient, accurate approach— in this example, beginning with the higher digit. Around this time, children realize that subtraction cancels out addition. Knowing, for example, that 4 + 3 = 7, they can infer without counting that 7 – 3 = 4 (Rasmussen, Ho, & Bisanz, 2003). Grasping basic arithmetic rules facilitates rapid computation, and with enough practice, children recall answers automatically.

When adults provide many occasions for counting, comparing quantities, and talking about number concepts, children acquire these understandings sooner (Ginsburg, Lee, & Boyd, 2008). Math proficiency at kindergarten entry predicts math achievement years later, in elementary and secondary school (Duncan et al., 2007; Romano et al., 2010).

This board game helps preschoolers acquire basic math knowledge by affording many opportunities to count, compare quantities, and talk about number concepts.

ASK YOURSELF

REVIEW Describe a typical 4-year-old's understanding of mental activities, noting both strengths and limitations.

APPLY Lena wonders why her son's preschool teacher provides extensive playtime in learning centers instead of teaching formal lessons. Explain to Lena why adult-supported play is the best way for preschoolers to develop academically.

REFLECT Describe informal experiences while you were growing up that may have contributed to your literacy and math development.

Individual Differences in Mental Development

Five-year-old Hal sat in a testing room while Sarah gave him an intelligence test. Some of Sarah's questions were *verbal.* For example, she showed him a picture of a shovel and said, "Tell me what this is"—an item measuring vocabulary. She tested his memory by asking him to repeat sentences and lists of numbers back to her. To assess Hal's spatial reasoning, Sarah used *nonverbal* tasks: Hal copied designs with special blocks, figured out the pattern in a series of shapes, and indicated what a piece of paper folded and cut would look like when unfolded (Roid, 2003; Wechsler, 2002).

The questions Sarah asked Hal tap knowledge and skills that not all children have equal opportunity to learn. In Chapter 9, we will take up the hotly debated issue of *cultural bias* in mental testing. For now, keep in mind that intelligence tests do not sample all human abilities, and performance is affected by cultural and situational factors (Sternberg, 2005). Nevertheless, test scores remain important: By age 6 to 7, they are good predictors of later IQ and academic achievement, which are related to vocational success. Let's see how the environments in which preschoolers spend their days—home, preschool, and child care—affect mental test performance.

Home Environment and Mental Development

A special version of the *Home Observation for Measurement of the Environment (HOME),* covered in Chapter 5, assesses aspects of 3- to 6-year-olds' home lives that support mental development. Preschoolers who develop well intellectually have homes rich in educational toys and books. Their parents are warm and affectionate, stimulate language and academic knowledge, and arrange interesting outings. They also make reasonable demands for socially mature behavior—for example, that the child perform simple chores and behave courteously toward others. And these parents resolve conflicts with reason instead of physical force and punishment (Bradley & Caldwell, 1982; Espy, Molfese, & DiLalla, 2001; Roberts, Burchinal, & Durham, 1999).

As we saw in Chapter 2, these characteristics are less often seen in low-SES families. When parents manage, despite low education and income, to obtain high HOME scores, their preschoolers do substantially better on tests of intelligence and measures of language and emergent literacy skills (Berger, Paxson, & Waldfogel, 2009; Foster et al., 2005; Mistry et al., 2008). And in a study of low-SES African-American 3- and 4-year-olds, HOME cognitive stimulation and emotional support subscales predicted reading achievement four years later (Zaslow et al., 2006).

Preschool, Kindergarten, and Child Care

Largely because of the rise in maternal employment, over the past several decades the number of young children enrolled in preschool or child care has steadily increased to more than 60 percent in the United States (U.S. Census Bureau, 2013). The line between preschool and child care is fuzzy. In response to the needs of employed parents, many U.S. preschools, as well as most public school kindergartens, have increased their hours from half to full days (U.S. Department of Education, 2012b). At the same time, good child care should provide the same high-quality educational experiences that an effective preschool does.

Types of Preschool and Kindergarten. Preschool and kindergarten programs range along a continuum from child-centered to teacher-directed. In **child-centered programs,** teachers provide a variety of activities from which children select, and much learning takes place through play. In contrast, in **academic programs,** teachers structure children's learning, teaching letters, numbers, colors, shapes, and other academic skills through formal lessons, often using repetition and drill.

Despite evidence that formal academic training in early childhood undermines motivation and emotional well-being, preschool and kindergarten teachers have felt increased pressure to take this approach. Young children who spend much time passively sitting and completing worksheets display more stress behaviors (such as wiggling and rocking), have less confidence in their abilities, prefer less challenging tasks, and are less advanced in motor, academic, language, and social skills at the end of the school year (Marcon, 1999a; Stipek et al., 1995). Follow-ups reveal lasting effects through elementary school in poorer study habits and achievement (Burts et al., 1992; Hart et al., 1998, 2003). These outcomes are strongest for low-SES children.

A special type of child-centered approach is *Montessori education,* devised a century ago by Italian physician Maria Montessori, who originally applied her method to poverty-stricken children. Features of Montessori schooling include materials specially designed to promote exploration and discovery, child-chosen activities, and equal emphasis on academic and social development (Lillard, 2007). In an evaluation of public preschools serving mostly urban minority children in Milwaukee, researchers compared students randomly assigned to either Montessori or other classrooms (Lillard & Else-Quest, 2006). Five-year-olds who had completed two years of Montessori education outperformed controls in literacy and math skills, false-belief understanding, concern with fairness in solving conflicts with peers, and cooperative play with classmates.

Early Intervention for At-Risk Preschoolers.

In the 1960s, as part of the "War on Poverty" in the United States, many intervention programs for economically disadvantaged preschoolers were initiated in an effort to address learning problems before formal schooling begins. The most extensive of these federal programs, **Project Head Start,** began in 1965. A typical Head Start center provides children with a year or two of preschool, along with nutritional and health services. Parent involvement is central to the Head Start philosophy. Parents serve on policy councils, contribute to program planning, work directly with children in classrooms, attend special programs on parenting and child development, and receive services directed at their own emotional, social, and vocational needs. Currently, Head Start serves about 904,000 children and their families across the nation (Head Start Bureau, 2010).

Several decades of research have established the long-term benefits of preschool intervention. The most extensive of these studies combined data from seven interventions implemented by universities or research foundations. Results showed that poverty-stricken children who attended programs scored higher in IQ and achievement than controls during the first two to three years of elementary school. After that, differences declined

Project Head Start provides children from poverty-stricken families with preschool education and nutritional and health services. High-quality early educational intervention has benefits lasting into adulthood.

© ELLEN B. SENISI PHOTOGRAPHY

(Lazar & Darlington, 1982). But on real-life measures of school adjustment, children and adolescents who had received intervention remained ahead. They were less likely to be placed in special education or retained in grade, and a greater number graduated from high school.

A separate report on one program—the High/Scope Perry Preschool Project—revealed benefits lasting well into adulthood. Two years' exposure to cognitively enriching preschool was associated with increased employment and reduced pregnancy and delinquency rates in adolescence. At age 27, those who had attended preschool were more likely than no-preschool controls to have graduated from high school and college, have higher earnings, be married, and own their own home—and less likely to have been involved with the criminal justice system. In the most recent follow-up, at age 40, the intervention group sustained its advantage on all measures of life success, including education, income, family life, and law-abiding behavior (Schweinhart, 2010; Schweinhart et al., 2005).

Do effects on school adjustment of these well-designed and well-delivered programs generalize to Head Start and other community-based preschool interventions? Findings are similar, though not as strong, because quality of services often does not equal that of model university-based programs (Barnett, 2011). But interventions of high quality are associated with diverse, long-lasting favorable outcomes, including higher rates of high school graduation and college enrollment and lower rates of adolescent drug use and delinquency (Garces, Thomas, & Currie, 2002; Love et al., 2006; Mashburn, 2008).

A consistent finding is that gains in IQ and achievement test scores from attending Head Start and other interventions quickly dissolve. In the Head Start Impact Study, a nationally representative sample of 5,000 Head Start 3- and 4-year-olds was randomly assigned to one year of Head Start or to a control group that could attend other types of preschool programs (U.S. Department of Health and Human Services, 2010d). By year's end, Head Start 3-year-olds exceeded controls in vocabulary, emergent literacy, and math skills; 4-year-olds in vocabulary, emergent literacy, and color identification. But except for language skills, academic advantages were no longer evident by end of first grade.

What explains these disappointing results? Head Start children typically enter inferior public schools in poverty-stricken neighborhoods, which undermine the benefits of preschool education (Brooks-Gunn, 2003; Ramey, Ramey, & Lanzi, 2006). Still, the improved school adjustment that results from attending a one- or two-year Head Start program is impressive. Program effects on parents may contribute: The more involved parents are in Head Start, the better their child-rearing practices and the more stimulating their home learning environments—factors positively related to preschoolers' task persistence and year-end academic, language, and social skills (Marcon, 1999b; McLoyd, Aikens, & Burton, 2006; Parker et al., 1999).

Head Start is highly cost-effective when compared with the cost of providing special education, treating criminal behavior, and supporting unemployed adults. Economists estimate a

Applying What We Know

Signs of Developmentally Appropriate Early Childhood Programs

Program Characteristics	Signs of Quality
Physical setting	Classroom space is divided into richly equipped activity areas, including make-believe play, blocks, science, math, games and puzzles, books, art, and music. Fenced outdoor play space is equipped with swings, climbing equipment, tricycles, and sandbox.
Group size	In preschools and child-care centers, group size is no greater than 18 to 20 children with two teachers.
Caregiver–child ratio	In preschools and child-care centers, teacher is responsible for no more than 8 to 10 children. In family child-care, caregiver is responsible for no more than 6 children.
Daily activities	Children select many of their own activities and learn through experiences relevant to their own lives, mainly in small groups or individually. Teachers facilitate children's involvement and adjust expectations to children's developing capacities.
Interactions between adults and children	Teachers move among groups and individuals, asking questions, offering suggestions, and adding more complex ideas. Teachers use positive guidance techniques, such as modeling and encouraging expected behavior and redirecting children to more acceptable activities.
Teacher qualifications	Teachers have college-level specialized preparation in early childhood development, early childhood education, or a related field.
Relationships with parents	Parents are encouraged to observe and participate. Teachers talk frequently with parents about children's behavior and development.
Licensing and accreditation	Child-care setting, whether a center or a home, is licensed by the state. Voluntary accreditation by the National Association for the Education of Young Children (www.naeyc.org/academy) or the National Association for Family Child Care (www.nafcc.org) is evidence of an especially high-quality program.

Source: Copple & Bredekamp, 2009.

lifetime return to society of $300,000 to $500,000 on an investment of about $17,000 per preschool child—a potential total savings of many billions of dollars if every poverty-stricken preschooler in the United States were enrolled (Heckman et al., 2010). Because of limited funding, however, only 60 percent of poverty-stricken 3- and 4-year-olds attend some type of preschool program, with Head Start serving just half of these children (Magnuson & Shager, 2010).

Child Care. We have seen that high-quality early intervention can enhance the development of economically disadvantaged children. As noted in Chapter 5, however, much U.S. child care lacks quality. Preschoolers exposed to substandard child care, especially for long hours, score lower in cognitive and social skills and higher in behavior problems (Belsky, 2006; Lamb & Ahnert, 2006; NICHD Early Child Care Research Network, 2003b, 2006). Externalizing difficulties are especially likely to endure into adolescence after extensive exposure to mediocre care (Belsky et al., 2007b; Vandell et al., 2010). In contrast, good child care enhances cognitive, language, and social development, especially for low-SES children—effects that persist into elementary school and, for academic achievement, adolescence (Belsky et al., 2007b; Burchinal, Vandergrift, & Pianta, 2010; NICHD Early Child Care Research Network, 2006; Vandell et al., 2010).

Applying What We Know above summarizes characteristics of high-quality early childhood programs, based on standards for developmentally appropriate practice devised by the U.S. National Association for the Education of Young Children.

Educational Media

Besides home and preschool, young children spend much time in another learning environment: electronic media, including both television and computers. In the industrialized world, nearly all homes have at least one television set, and most have two or more. And more than 90 percent of U.S. children live in homes with one or more computers (Rideout, Foehr, & Roberts, 2010; U.S. Census Bureau, 2012b).

Educational Television. Sammy's favorite TV program, *Sesame Street*, uses lively visual and sound effects to stress basic literacy and number concepts and puppet and human characters to teach general knowledge, emotional and social understanding, and social skills. Today, *Sesame Street* is broadcast in more than 140 countries, making it the most widely viewed children's program in the world (Sesame Workshop, 2009).

Time devoted to watching children's educational programs is associated with gains in early literacy and math skills and academic progress in elementary school (Ennemoser & Schneider,

2007; Linebarger et al., 2004; Wright et al., 2001). Consistent with these findings, one study reported a link between preschool viewing of *Sesame Street* and other similar educational programs and getting higher grades, reading more books, and placing more value on achievement in high school (Anderson et al., 2001).

Sesame Street has modified its previous rapid-paced format in favor of more leisurely episodes with a clear story line. Children's programs with slow-paced action and easy-to-follow narratives lead to greater recall of program content and gains in vocabulary and reading skills in the early school grades than programs that simply provide information (Linebarger & Piotrowski, 2010; Singer & Singer, 2005). Narratively structured educational TV eases processing demands, freeing up space in working memory for applying program content to real-life situations.

Despite the spread of computers, television remains the dominant form of youth media. The average U.S. 2- to 6-year-old watches TV and videos from 1½ to 2⅔ hours a day. In middle childhood, viewing time increases to an average of 3½ hours a day, before declining slightly in adolescence (Rideout, Foehr, & Roberts, 2010; Rideout & Hamel, 2006). Low-SES, African-American, and Hispanic children are more frequent viewers, perhaps because few alternative forms of entertainment are available in their neighborhoods or affordable for their parents. Also, parents with limited education are more likely to engage in practices that heighten TV viewing, including leaving the TV on all day and eating family meals in front of it (Rideout, Foehr, & Roberts, 2010). About one-third of U.S. preschoolers and 70 percent of school-age children and adolescents have a TV set in their bedroom; these children spend from 40 to 90 more minutes per day watching than agemates without one (Rideout & Hamel, 2006).

Does extensive TV viewing take children away from worthwhile activities? The more preschool and school-age children watch prime-time shows and cartoons, the less time they spend reading and interacting with others and the poorer their academic skills (Ennemoser & Schneider, 2007; Wright et al., 2001). Whereas educational programs can be beneficial, watching entertainment TV—especially heavy viewing—detracts from children's school success and social experiences.

Learning with Computers. More than one-fourth of 4- to 6-year-olds use a computer regularly, with preschoolers of higher-SES parents having greater computer access (Calvert et al., 2005). And because computers can have rich educational benefits, many early childhood classrooms include computer learning centers. Kindergartners who use computers to draw or write produce more elaborate pictures and text, make fewer writing errors, and edit their work much as older children do. And combining everyday and computer experiences with math manipulatives is especially effective in promoting math concepts and skills (Clements & Sarama, 2003).

Simplified computer languages that children can use to make designs or build structures introduce them to programming skills. As long as adults support children's efforts, com-

puter programming promotes improved problem solving and metacognition because children must plan and reflect on their thinking to get their programs to work (Nastasi & Clements, 1994; Resnick & Silverman, 2005).

As with television, children spend much time using computers for entertainment purposes, especially game playing. Both media are rife with gender stereotypes and violence. We will consider their impact on emotional and social development in the next chapter.

ASK YOURSELF

REVIEW What findings indicate that child-centered rather than academic preschools and kindergartens are better suited to fostering academic development?

APPLY Your senator has heard that IQ gains resulting from Head Start do not last, so he plans to vote against additional funding. Write a letter explaining why he should support Head Start.

REFLECT How much and what kinds of TV viewing and computer use did you engage in as a child? How do you think your home media environment influenced your development?

 # Language Development

Language is intimately related to virtually all cognitive changes discussed in this chapter. Between ages 2 and 6, children make momentous advances.

Vocabulary

At age 2, Sammy had a spoken vocabulary of about 250 words. Buy age 6 he will have acquired around 10,000 words (Bloom, 1998). To accomplish this feat, Sammy learned about five new words each day. How do children build their vocabularies so quickly? Research shows that they can connect new words with their underlying concepts after only a brief encounter, a process called **fast-mapping**.

Types of Words. Children in many Western and non-Western language communities fast-map labels for objects especially rapidly because these refer to concepts that are easy to perceive. Soon children add verbs (*go, run, broke),* which require understandings of relationships between objects and actions. Children learning Chinese, Japanese, and Korean—languages in which nouns are often omitted from adult sentences, while verbs are stressed—acquire verbs especially quickly (Kim, McGregor, & Thompson, 2000; Tardif, 2006). Gradually, preschoolers add modifiers (*red, round, sad).*

To fill in for words they have not yet learned, children as young as age 3 coin new words using ones they already know—for example, "plant-man," for a gardener, "crayoner" for a child using crayons. Preschoolers also extend language meanings through metaphor—like the 3-year-old who described a stomachache as a "fire engine in my tummy" (Winner, 1988). Young preschoolers' metaphors involve concrete sensory comparisons: "Clouds are pillows," "Leaves are dancers." Once vocabulary and general knowledge expand, children also appreciate nonsensory comparisons: "Friends are like magnets," "Time flies by" (Keil, 1986; Özçaliskan, 2005).

Strategies for Word Learning.

Preschoolers figure out the meanings of new words by contrasting them with words they already know. How do they discover which concept each word picks out? One speculation is that early in vocabulary growth, children adopt a *mutual exclusivity bias*—the assumption that words refer to entirely separate (nonoverlapping) categories (Markman, 1992). Consistent with this idea, when 2-year-olds hear the labels for two distinct novel objects (for example, *clip* and *horn*), they assign each word correctly, to the whole object and not just a part of it (Waxman & Senghas, 1992). Indeed, children's first several hundred nouns refer mostly to objects well-organized by shape. And learning of nouns based on the perceptual property of shape heightens young children's attention to the distinctive shapes of other objects (Smith et al., 2002; Yoshida & Smith, 2003). This *shape bias* helps preschoolers master additional names of objects, and vocabulary accelerates. Once the name of a whole object is familiar, on hearing a new name for the object, 2- and 3-year-olds set aside the mutual exclusivity bias. For example, if the object (bottle) has a distinctively shaped part (spout), children readily apply the new label to it (Hansen & Markman, 2009).

Still, mutual exclusivity and object shape cannot account for preschoolers' remarkably flexible responses when objects have more than one name. Children often call on other components of language in these instances. According to one proposal, preschoolers figure out many word meanings by observing how words are used in the structure of sentences (Gleitman et al., 2005; Naigles & Swenson, 2007). Consider an adult who says, "This is a *citron* one," while showing the child a yellow car. Two- and 3-year-olds conclude that a new word used as an adjective for a familiar object (car) refers to a property of that object (Imai & Haryu, 2004).

Young children also take advantage of rich social information that adults frequently provide when introducing new words. In one study, an adult performed an action on an object and then used a new label while looking back and forth between the child and the object, as if inviting the child to play. Two-year-olds concluded that the label referred to the action, not the object (Tomasello & Akhtar, 1995). By age 3, children can even use a speaker's recently expressed desire ("I really want to play with the *riff*") to figure out a word's meaning (Saylor & Troseth, 2006).

While making a bird feeder, this preschooler attends to a variety of perceptual, social, and linguistic cues to grasp the meanings of unfamiliar words, such as *pine cone, spread, dip,* and *seeds.*

According to a recent theory of early vocabulary development, children draw on a *coalition* of cues—perceptual, social, and linguistic—which shift in importance with age (Golinkoff & Hirsh-Pasek, 2006, 2008). Infants rely solely on perceptual features. Toddlers and young preschoolers, while still sensitive to perceptual features (such as object shape), increasingly attend to social cues—the speaker's direction of gaze, gestures, and expressions of desire and intention (Hollich, Hirsh-Pasek, & Golinkoff, 2000; Pruden et al., 2006). And as language develops further, linguistic cues—sentence structure and intonation (stress, pitch, and loudness)—play larger roles.

Preschoolers are most successful at figuring out new word meanings when several kinds of information are available (Saylor, Baldwin, & Sabbagh, 2005). Researchers have just begun to study the multiple cues that children use for different kinds of words and how their combined strategies change with development.

Grammar

Between ages 2 and 3, English-speaking children use simple sentences that follow a subject–verb–object word order. Children learning other languages adopt the word orders of the adult speech to which they are exposed.

Basic Rules.

Studies of children acquiring diverse languages reveal that their first use of grammatical rules is piecemeal—limited to just a few verbs. As children listen for familiar verbs in adults' speech, they expand their own utterances containing those verbs, relying on adult speech as their model (Gathercole,

© ELLEN B. SENISI PHOTOGRAPHY

Sebastián, & Soto, 1999; Lieven, Pine, & Baldwin, 1997). Sammy, for example, added the preposition *with* to the verb *open* ("You open with scissors") because he often heard his parents say, "open with." But he failed to add *with* to the verb *hit* ("He hit me stick").

To test preschoolers' ability to generate novel sentences that conform to basic English grammar, researchers had them use a new verb in the subject–verb–object form after hearing it in a different construction, such as passive: "Ernie is getting *gorped* by the dog." The percentage of children who, when asked what the dog was doing, could respond, "He's *gorping* Ernie," rose steadily with age. But not until age 3½ to 4 could the majority of children apply the subject–verb–object structure broadly, to newly acquired verbs (Chan et al., 2010; Tomasello, 2006, 2011).

Once children form three-word sentences, they make small additions and changes to words that enable them to express meanings flexibly and efficiently. For example, they add *-s* for plural (*cats*), use prepositions (*in* and *on*), and form various tenses of the verb *to be* (*is, are, were, has been, will*). English-speaking children master these grammatical markers in a regular sequence, starting with those that involve the simplest meanings and structures (Brown, 1973; de Villiers & de Villiers, 1973).

When preschoolers acquire these markers, they sometimes overextend the rules to words that are exceptions—a type of error called **overregularization.** "My toy car *breaked*" and "We each have two *foots*" are expressions that appear between ages 2 and 3 (Maratsos, 2000; Marcus, 1995).

Complex Structures. Gradually, preschoolers master more complex grammatical structures, although they do make mistakes. In first creating questions, 2- to 3-year-olds use many formulas: "Where's *X*?" "Can I *X*?" (Dabrowska, 2000; Tomasello, 2003). Question asking remains variable for the next couple of years. An analysis of one child's questions revealed that he inverted the subject and verb when asking certain questions but not others ("What she will do?" "Why he can go?") The correct expressions were the ones he heard most often in his mother's speech (Rowland & Pine, 2000). And sometimes children produce errors in subject–verb agreement ("Where does the dogs play?") and in subject case ("Where can me sit?") (Rowland, 2007).

Similarly, children have trouble with some passive sentences. When told, "The car was pushed by the truck," young preschoolers often make a toy car push a truck. By age 5, they understand such expressions, but full mastery of the passive form is not complete until the end of middle childhood (Lempert, 1990; Tomasello, 2006).

Nevertheless, 4- to 5-year-olds form embedded sentences ("I think *he will come*"), tag questions ("Dad's going to be home soon, *isn't he?*"), and indirect objects ("He showed *his friend* the present") (Tager-Flusberg & Zukowski, 2009). As the preschool years draw to a close, children use most of the grammatical constructions of their language competently.

Conversation

Besides acquiring vocabulary and grammar, children must learn to engage in effective and appropriate communication. This practical, social side of language is called **pragmatics,** and preschoolers make considerable headway in mastering it.

As early as age 2, children are skilled conversationalists. In face-to-face interaction, they take turns and respond appropriately to their partners' remarks (Pan & Snow, 1999). With age, the number of turns over which children can sustain interaction and their ability to maintain a topic over time increase. By age 4, children adjust their speech to fit the age, sex, and social status of their listeners. For example, in acting out roles with hand puppets, they use more commands when playing socially dominant and male roles (teacher, doctor, father) but speak more politely and use more indirect requests when playing less dominant and female roles (student, patient, mother) (Anderson, 2000).

Preschoolers' conversational skills occasionally do break down—for example, when talking on the phone. Here is an excerpt from one 4-year-old's phone conversation with his grandfather:

> *Grandfather:*   How old will you be?
> *John:*   Dis many. [*Holding up four fingers.*]
> *Grandfather:*   Huh?
> *John:*   Dis many. [*Again holding up four fingers.*] (Warren & Tate, 1992, pp. 259–260)

Young children's conversations appear less mature in highly demanding situations in which they cannot see their listeners' reactions or rely on typical conversational aids, such as gestures and objects to talk about. But when asked to tell a listener how to solve a simple puzzle, 3- to 6-year-olds give more specific directions over the phone than in person, indicating that they realize the need for more verbal description on the phone (Cameron & Lee, 1997). Between ages 4 and 8, both conversing and giving directions over the phone improve greatly. Telephone talk provides yet another example of how preschoolers' competencies depend on the demands of the situation.

Supporting Language Development in Early Childhood

How can adults foster preschoolers' language development? As in toddlerhood, conversational give-and-take with adults, either at home or in preschool, is consistently related to language progress (Hart & Risley, 1995; NICHD Early Child Care Research Network, 2000b).

Sensitive, caring adults use additional techniques that promote early language skills. When children use words incorrectly or communicate unclearly, they give explicit feedback, such as, "I can't tell which ball you want. Do you mean the large red one?" But they do not overcorrect, especially when children make grammatical mistakes. Criticism discourages children from freely using language in ways that lead to new skills.

Responding to his 3-year-old child, this father expands her brief sentences and recasts them into accurate form—techniques that inform children about correct grammar.

Instead, adults often provide indirect feedback about grammar by using two strategies, often in combination: **recasts**—restructuring inaccurate speech into correct form, and **expansions**—elaborating on children's speech, increasing its complexity (Bohannon & Stanowicz, 1988; Chouinard & Clark, 2003). For example, if a child says, "I gotted new red shoes," the parent might respond, "Yes, you got a pair of new red shoes." But these techniques do not consistently affect children's usage (Strapp & Federico, 2000; Valian, 1999). Rather than eliminating errors, perhaps expansions and recasts model grammatical alternatives and encourage children to experiment with them.

LOOK AND LISTEN

In a 30- to 60-minute observation of a 2- to 4-year-old and his or her parent, note grammatical errors the child makes and adult feedback. How often does the parent reformulate child errors or ask clarifying questions? How does the child respond? ●

Do the findings just described remind you once again of Vygotsky's theory? In language, as in other aspects of intellectual growth, parents and teachers gently prompt children to take the next step forward. Children strive to master language because they want to connect with other people. Adults, in turn, respond to children's desire to become competent speakers by listening attentively, elaborating on what children say, modeling correct usage, and stimulating children to talk further. In the next chapter, we will see that this combination of warmth and encouragement of mature behavior is at the heart of early childhood emotional and social development as well.

ASK YOURSELF

REVIEW Explain how children's strategies for word learning support the interactionist perspective on language development, described on pages 136–137 in Chapter 5.

APPLY Sammy's mother explained to him that the family would take a vacation in Miami. The next morning, Sammy announced, "I gotted my bags packed. When are we going to Your-ami?" What explains Sammy's errors?

SUMMARY

PHYSICAL DEVELOPMENT

A Changing Body and Brain (p. 167)

Describe body growth and brain development during early childhood.

- Children grow more slowly in early childhood than they did in the first two years, and they become longer and leaner. New growth centers emerge in the skeleton, and by the end of early childhood, children start to lose their primary teeth.

- Areas of the prefrontal cortex devoted to various aspects of executive function develop rapidly. The left cerebral hemisphere is especially active, supporting preschoolers' expanding language skills and improved executive function.

- Hand preference, reflecting an individual's **dominant cerebral hemisphere,** strengthens during early childhood. Research on handedness supports the joint contribution of nature and nurture to brain lateralization.

- In early childhood, fibers linking the **cerebellum** to the cerebral cortex grow and myelinate, enhancing motor coordination and thinking. The **reticular formation,** responsible for alertness and consciousness; the **hippocampus,** which plays a vital role in memory and spatial orientation; and the **corpus callosum,** connecting the two cerebral hemispheres, also develop rapidly.

Influences on Physical Growth and Health (p. 170)

Describe the effects of heredity, nutrition, and infectious disease on physical growth in early childhood.

- Heredity controls production and release of two hormones from the **pituitary gland:** Two hormones are especially influential: **growth hormone (GH)** and **thyroid-stimulating hormone (TSH).**

- As growth rate slows, preschoolers' appetites decline, and many become picky eaters. Repeated, unpressured exposure to new foods promotes healthy, varied eating.

- Dietary deficiencies can affect growth and are associated with attention and memory difficulties, academic and behavior problems, and greater susceptibility to infectious diseases. Disease—especially intestinal infections—also contribute to malnutrition.

What factors increase the risk of unintentional injuries, and how can childhood injuries be prevented?

- Unintentional injuries are the leading cause of childhood mortality in industrialized nations. Victims are more likely to be boys; to be temperamentally inattentive, overactive, irritable, defiant, and aggressive; and to be growing up in stressed, poverty-stricken families.

- Effective injury prevention includes passing laws that promote child safety; creating safer home, travel, and play environments; improving public education; changing parent and child behaviors; and providing social supports to ease parental stress.

Motor Development (p. 173)

Cite major milestones of gross- and fine-motor development in early childhood, and describe individual differences.

- As the child's center of gravity shifts toward the trunk, balance improves, paving the way for many gross-motor achievements, including running, jumping, hopping, skipping, and ball skills.

- Improved control of the hands and fingers leads to dramatic gains in fine-motor skills. Preschoolers gradually become self-sufficient at dressing and feeding.

- By age 3, children's scribbles become pictures. With age, their drawings increase in complexity and realism, influenced by their culture's artistic traditions. Preschoolers also try to print alphabet letters and, later, words.

- Body build and opportunity for physical play affect motor development. Sex differences that favor boys in force and power and girls in balance and fine movements are partly genetic, but environmental pressures exaggerate them.

COGNITIVE DEVELOPMENT

Piaget's Theory: The Preoperational Stage (p. 175)

Describe cognitive advances and limitations during the preoperational stage.

- Rapid advances in mental representation mark the beginning of Piaget's **preoperational stage.** Make-believe, which supports many aspects of development, becomes increasingly complex, evolving into **sociodramatic play** with peers. Gradually, children become capable of **dual representation**—viewing a symbolic object as both an object in its own right and a symbol.

- **Egocentrism**—inability to imagine others' perspectives—contributes to preoperational children's **centration,** focus on perceptual appearances, and **irreversibility.** As a result, preschoolers fail **conservation** and **hierarchical classification** tasks.

What does follow-up research reveal about the accuracy of Piaget's preoperational stage?

- When given simplified tasks relevant to their everyday lives, preschoolers recognize others' perspectives, distinguish animate from inanimate objects, reason by analogy about physical transformations, understand cause-and-effect relationships, and organize knowledge into hierarchical categories.

- Evidence that operational thinking develops gradually over the preschool years challenges Piaget's stage concept. Some theorists propose a more flexible view of stages.

Vygotsky's Sociocultural Theory (p. 182)

Explain Vygotsky's perspective on children's private speech and make-believe play.

- Unlike Piaget, Vygotsky regarded language as the foundation for all higher cognitive processes. According to Vygotsky, **private speech,** or language used for self-guidance, emerges out of social communication as adults and more skilled peers help children master appropriately challenging tasks. Private speech is eventually internalized as silent, inner speech.

- **Scaffolding**—adjusting teaching support to fit children's current needs and suggesting strategies—promotes gains in children's thinking. Make-believe play is a vital zone of proximal development that promotes many competencies.

- **Guided participation,** a broader concept than scaffolding, recognizes cultural and situational variations in shared endeavors between more expert and less expert participants.

Information Processing (p. 184)

How do attention and memory change during early childhood?

- Preschoolers' attention gradually becomes more sustained, and planning improves.

- Preschoolers' recognition memory is remarkably good, but their recall for listlike information is poor because they are not skilled at using **memory strategies.**

- **Episodic memory**—memory for everyday experiences—improves greatly in early childhood. Like adults, preschoolers remember recurring events as **scripts,** which become increasingly elaborate with age. When adults use an elaborative style of conversing about the past, children's autobiographical memory becomes more organized and detailed.

Describe the young child's theory of mind.

- Preschoolers begin to construct a theory of mind, evidence of their capacity for **metacognition.** Language, executive function, and social experiences all contribute. Toddlers' nonverbal behaviors suggest an implicit awareness that people can hold false beliefs; around age 4, children's understanding becomes explicit.

- Preschoolers regard the mind as a passive container of information rather than as an active, constructive agent.

Summarize children's literacy and mathematical knowledge during early childhood.

- Children's active efforts to figure out how written symbols convey meaning are known as **emergent literacy.** Preschoolers revise these ideas as their cognitive capacities improve, as they encounter writing in many contexts, and as adults help them with written communication. **Phonological awareness** is a strong predictor of emergent literacy knowledge.

- Toddlers display a beginning grasp of **ordinality.** By age 4, preschoolers understand **cardinality** and experiment with counting to solve arithmetic problems, eventually arriving at the most efficient, accurate approach. Adults promote children's mathematical knowledge by providing many occasions for counting, comparing quantities, and talking about number concepts.

Individual Differences in Mental Development (p. 190)

Discuss the impact of home, educational programs, child care, and media on preschoolers' mental development.

- By age 6 to 7, intelligence test scores are good predictors of later IQ and academic achievement. Children growing up in warm, stimulating homes with parents who make reasonable demands for mature behavior develop well intellectually.

- Preschool and kindergarten programs include both **child-centered programs,** in which much learning takes place through play, and **academic programs,** in which teachers train children in academic skills. Emphasizing formal academic instruction undermines young children's motivation and negatively influences later achievement.

- **Project Head Start** is the most extensive U.S. federally funded preschool program for low-income children. High-quality preschool intervention results in immediate IQ and achievement gains and long-term improvements in school adjustment. Good child care enhances cognitive, language, and social development, especially for low-SES children.

- Children pick up many cognitive skills from educational television programs. Programs with slow-paced action and easy-to-follow story lines foster vocabulary and reading skills. Heavy exposure to entertainment TV is associated with poorer academic skills.

- Computers can have rich educational benefits when young children use them to draw or write, combine computer experiences with math manipulatives, or learn programming skills.

Language Development (p. 193)

Trace the development of vocabulary, grammar, and conversational skills in early childhood.

- Supported by **fast-mapping,** preschoolers' vocabularies increase dramatically. Initially, they rely heavily on the perceptual cue of object shape to expand their vocabulary. With age, they increasingly draw on social and linguistic cues.

- Between ages 2 and 3, children adopt the basic word order of their language. As preschoolers gradually master grammatical rules, they sometimes overextend them in a type of error called **overregularization.** By the end of early childhood, children have acquired complex grammatical forms.

- **Pragmatics** is the practical, social side of language. Two-year-olds are already skilled conversationalists in face-to-face interaction. By age 4, children adapt their speech to their listener's age, sex, and social status.

Cite factors that support language learning in early childhood.

- Conversational give-and-take with more skilled speakers fosters language progress. Adults provide explicit feedback on the clarity of children's language and indirect feedback about grammar through **recasts** and **expansions.**

Important Terms and Concepts

chapter
8

Emotional and Social Development in Early Childhood

During the preschool years, children make great strides in understanding the thoughts and feelings of others, and they build on these skills as they form first friendships—special relationships marked by attachment and common interests.

© ELLEN B. SENISI PHOTOGRAPHY

chapter outline

Erikson's Theory: Initiative versus Guilt

Self-Understanding

Foundations of Self-Concept • Emergence of Self-Esteem

Emotional Development

Understanding Emotion • Emotional Self-Regulation • Self-Conscious Emotions • Empathy and Sympathy

Peer Relations

Advances in Peer Sociability • First Friendships • Peer Relations and School Readiness • Parental Influences on Early Peer Relations

Foundations of Morality

The Psychoanalytic Perspective • Social Learning Theory • The Cognitive-Developmental Perspective • The Other Side of Morality: Development of Aggression

■ **CULTURAL INFLUENCES** Ethnic Differences in the Consequences of Physical Punishment

Gender Typing

Gender-Stereotyped Beliefs and Behavior • Biological Influences on Gender Typing • Environmental Influences on Gender Typing • Gender Identity • Reducing Gender Stereotyping in Young Children

■ **SOCIAL ISSUES: EDUCATION** Young Children Learn About Gender Through Mother–Child Conversations

Child Rearing and Emotional and Social Development

Styles of Child Rearing • What Makes Authoritative Child Rearing Effective? • Cultural Variations • Child Maltreatment

As the children in Leslie's classroom moved through the preschool years, their personalities took on clearer definition. By age 3, they voiced firm likes and dislikes as well as new ideas about themselves. "See, I'm great at this game," Sammy announced with confidence, as he aimed a beanbag toward the mouth of a large clown face—an attitude that kept him trying, even though he missed most of the throws.

The children's conversations also revealed early notions about morality. Often they combined adults' statements about right and wrong with forceful attempts to defend their own desires. "You're 'posed to share," stated Mark, grabbing the beanbag out of Sammy's hand.

"I was here first! Gimme it back," demanded Sammy, pushing Mark. The two boys struggled until Leslie intervened, provided an extra set of beanbags, and showed them how they could both play.

As the interaction between Sammy and Mark reveals, preschoolers quickly become complex social beings. Young children argue, grab, and push, but cooperative exchanges are far more frequent. Between ages 2 and 6, first friendships form, in which children converse, act out complementary roles, and learn that their own desires for companionship and toys are best met when they consider others' needs and interests.

The children's developing understanding of their social world was especially apparent in their growing attention to gender roles. While Priti and Karen cared for a sick baby doll in the housekeeping area, Sammy, Vance, and Mark transformed the block corner into a busy intersection. "Green light, go!" shouted police officer Sammy as Vance and Mark pushed large wooden cars and trucks across the floor. Already, the children preferred peers of their own gender, and their play themes mirrored their culture's gender stereotypes.

This chapter is devoted to the many facets of early childhood emotional and social development. We begin with Erik Erikson's view of personality change in the preschool years. Then we consider children's concepts of themselves, their insights into their social and moral worlds, their gender typing, and their increasing ability to manage their emotional and social behaviors. Finally, we ask, What is effective child rearing? And we discuss the complex conditions that support good parenting or lead it to break down. ●

Erikson's Theory: Initiative versus Guilt

According to Erikson (1950), once children have a sense of autonomy, they become less contrary than they were as toddlers. Their energies are freed for tackling the psychological conflict of the preschool years: **initiative versus guilt.** As the word *initiative* suggests, young children have a new sense of purposefulness. They are eager to tackle new tasks, join in activities with peers, and discover what they can do with the help of adults. They also make strides in conscience development.

Erikson regarded play as a means through which young children learn about themselves and their social world. Play creates a small social organization of children who try out culturally meaningful roles and skills and who cooperate to achieve common goals. Around the world, children act out family scenes and highly visible occupations—police officer, doctor, and nurse in Western societies, hut builder and spear maker among the Baka of West Africa (Göncü, Patt, & Kouba, 2004).

Through patient, reasonable adult guidance and play experiences with peers, preschoolers also acquire both the moral and gender-role standards of their society. For Erikson, the negative outcome of early childhood is an overly strict conscience, or superego (see Chapter 1, page 12) that causes children to feel too much guilt because they have been threatened, criticized, and punished excessively by adults. When this happens, preschoolers' exuberant play and bold efforts to master new tasks break down.

As we will see, Erikson's image of initiative captures the diverse changes in young children's emotional and social lives. Early childhood is, indeed, a time when children develop a confident self-image, more effective control over their emotions, new social skills, the foundations of morality, and a sense of themselves as boy or girl.

A Guatemalan 3-year-old pretends to shell corn. By acting out family scenes and highly visible occupations, young children around the world develop a sense of initiative, gaining insight into what they can do and become in their culture.

Self-Understanding

In Chapter 7, we noted that young children acquire a vocabulary for talking about their inner mental lives and gain in understanding of mental states. As self-awareness strengthens, preschoolers focus more intently on qualities that make the self unique. They begin to develop a **self-concept**, the set of attributes, abilities, attitudes, and values that an individual believes defines who he or she is.

Foundations of Self-Concept

Ask a 3- to 5-year-old to tell you about himself, and you are likely to hear something like this: "I'm Tommy. See, I got this new red T-shirt. I'm 4 years old. I have a new Tinkertoy set, and I made this big, big tower." Preschoolers' self-concepts consist largely of observable characteristics, such as their name, physical appearance, possessions, and everyday behaviors (Harter, 2006; Watson, 1990).

By age 3½, children also describe themselves in terms of typical emotions and attitudes—"I'm happy when I play with my friends"; "I don't like scary TV programs"; "I usually do what Mommy says"—suggesting a beginning understanding of their unique psychological characteristics (Eder & Mangelsdorf, 1997). And by age 5, children's degree of agreement with such statements coincides with maternal reports of their personality traits, indicating that older preschoolers have a sense of their own timidity, agreeableness, and positive or negative affect (Brown et al., 2008). But preschoolers do not yet say, "I'm helpful" or "I'm shy." Direct references to personality traits must wait for greater cognitive maturity.

A warm, sensitive parent–child relationship seems to foster a more positive, coherent early self-concept. In one study, 4-year-olds with a secure attachment to their mothers were more likely than their insecurely attached agemates to describe themselves in favorable terms at age 5—with statements that reflect agreeableness and positive affect (Goodvin et al., 2008). Also recall from Chapter 7 that securely attached preschoolers participate in more elaborative parent–child conversations about personally experienced events, which help them understand themselves (see page 186).

As early as age 2, parents use narratives of past events to impart rules, standards for behavior, and evaluative information about the child: "You added the milk when we made the mashed potatoes. That's a very important job!" (Nelson, 2003). These self-evaluative narratives are a major means through which caregivers imbue the young child's self-concept with cultural values. In observational research on Irish-American families in Chicago and Chinese families in Taiwan, Chinese parents frequently told their preschoolers long stories about the child's misdeeds. In a warm, caring tone, they stressed the impact of the child's misbehavior on others ("You made Mama lose face."). Irish-American parents, in contrast, rarely dwelt on children's transgressions and, when they did, interpreted these acts positively ("He's got a lot of spunk!") (Miller et al., 1997, 2002, 2012).

Consistent with these narrative differences, the Chinese child's self-image emphasizes obligations to others, whereas the American child's is more autonomous.

Emergence of Self-Esteem

Another aspect of self-concept emerges in early childhood: **self-esteem,** the judgments we make about our own worth and the feelings associated with those judgments. **TAKE A MOMENT...** Make a list of your own self-judgments. Notice that, besides a global appraisal of your worth as a person, you have a variety of separate self-evaluations concerning how well you perform at different activities. These evaluations are among the most important aspects of self-development because they affect our emotional experiences, future behavior, and long-term psychological adjustment.

By age 4, preschoolers have several self-judgments—for example, about learning things in school, making friends, getting along with parents, and treating others kindly (Marsh, Ellis, & Craven, 2002). But because they have difficulty distinguishing between their desired and their actual competence, they usually rate their own ability as extremely high and underestimate task difficulty, as when Sammy asserted, despite his many misses, that he was great at beanbag throwing (Harter, 2006).

High self-esteem contributes greatly to preschoolers' initiative. By age 3, children whose parents criticize their worth and performance give up easily when faced with a challenge and express shame and despondency after failing (Kelley, Brownell, & Campbell, 2000). Adults can avoid promoting these self-defeating reactions by adjusting their expectations to children's capacities, scaffolding children's attempts at difficult tasks (see Chapter 7, page 182), and pointing out effort and improvement in children's behavior.

© ELLEN B. SENISI PHOTOGRAPHY

After creating a "camera" and "flash," this preschooler pretends to take pictures. Her high self-esteem contributes greatly to her initiative in mastering many new skills.

Emotional Development

Gains in representation, language, and self-concept support emotional development in early childhood. Between ages 2 and 6, children achieve a better understanding of their own and others' feelings, and *emotional self-regulation* improves. In addition, preschoolers more often experience *self-conscious emotions* and *empathy,* which contribute to their developing sense of morality.

Understanding Emotion

Early in the preschool years, children refer to causes, consequences, and behavioral signs of emotion, and over time their understanding becomes more accurate and complex (Stein & Levine, 1999). By age 4 to 5, children correctly judge the causes of many basic emotions ("He's happy because he's swinging very high"; "He's sad because he misses his mother"). Preschoolers' explanations tend to emphasize external factors over internal states, a balance that changes with age (Levine, 1995). After age 4, children appreciate that both desires and beliefs motivate behavior (Chapter 7). Then their grasp of how internal factors can trigger emotion expands.

Preschoolers can also predict what a playmate expressing a certain emotion might do next. Four-year-olds know that an angry child might hit someone and that a happy child is more likely to share (Russell, 1990). And they realize that thinking and feeling are interconnected—that a person reminded of a previous sad experience is likely to feel sad (Lagattuta, Wellman, & Flavell, 1997). Furthermore, they come up with effective ways to relieve others' negative feelings, such as hugging to reduce sadness (Fabes et al., 1988).

The more parents label emotions, explain them, and express warmth and enthusiasm when conversing with preschoolers, the more "emotion words" children use and the better developed their emotional understanding (Fivush & Haden, 2005). Furthermore, 3- to 5-year-olds who are securely attached to their mothers better understand emotion, likely because attachment security is related to parent–child narratives that more often highlight the emotional significance of events (Laible, 2004; Laible & Song, 2006; Raikes & Thompson, 2006).

As preschoolers learn about emotion from interacting with adults, they engage in more emotion talk with siblings and friends, especially during make-believe play (Hughes & Dunn, 1998). Make-believe, in turn, contributes to emotional understanding, especially when children play with siblings (Youngblade & Dunn, 1995). The intense nature of the sibling relationship, combined with frequent acting out of feelings, makes pretending an excellent context for learning about emotions.

As early as 3 to 5 years of age, knowledge about emotions is linked to children's friendly, considerate behavior, willingness to make amends after harming another, and constructive responses to disputes with agemates (Dunn, Brown, & Maguire, 1995; Garner & Estep, 2001; Hughes & Ensor, 2010). Also, the more preschoolers refer to feelings when interacting with playmates, the better liked they are by their peers (Fabes et al., 2001). Children seem to recognize that acknowledging others' emotions and explaining their own enhance the quality of relationships.

Emotional Self-Regulation

Language also contributes to preschoolers' improved *emotional self-regulation* (Cole, Armstrong, & Pemberton, 2010). By age 3 to 4, children verbalize a variety of strategies for adjusting their emotional arousal to a more comfortable level. For example, they know they can blunt emotions by restricting sensory input (covering their eyes or ears to block out an unpleasant sight or sound), talking to themselves ("Mommy said she'll be back soon"), or changing their goals (deciding that they don't want to play anyway after being excluded from a game) (Thompson & Goodvin, 2007). As children use these strategies, emotional outbursts decline. *Effortful control*—in particular, inhibiting impulses and shifting attention—also continues to be vital in managing emotion. Three-year-olds who can distract themselves when frustrated tend to become cooperative school-age children with few problem behaviors (Gilliom et al., 2002).

Warm, patient parents who explain strategies for controlling feelings strengthen children's capacity to handle stress (Colman et al., 2006; Morris et al., 2011). In contrast, when parents rarely express positive emotion, dismiss children's feelings as unimportant, and have difficulty controlling their own anger, children have continuing problems in managing emotion (Thompson & Goodman, 2010; Thompson & Meyer, 2007).

As with infants and toddlers, preschoolers who experience negative emotion intensely find it harder to shift attention away from disturbing events. They are more likely to be anxious and fearful, respond with irritation to others' distress, react angrily or aggressively when frustrated, and get along poorly with teachers and peers (Chang et al., 2003; Eisenberg et al., 2005a; Raikes et al., 2007).

Self-Conscious Emotions

One morning in Leslie's classroom, a group of children crowded around for a bread-baking activity. Leslie asked them to wait patiently while she got a baking pan. But Sammy reached over to feel the dough, and the bowl tumbled off the table. When Leslie returned, Sammy looked at her, then covered his eyes with his hands. He felt ashamed and guilty.

As their self-concepts develop, preschoolers become increasingly sensitive to praise and blame or to the possibility of such feedback. They more often experience *self-conscious emotions*—feelings that involve injury to or enhancement of their sense of self (see Chapter 6). By age 3, self-conscious emotions are clearly linked to self-evaluation (Lewis, 1995; Thompson, Meyer, & McGinley, 2006). But because preschoolers are still developing standards of excellence and conduct, they depend on the messages of parents, teachers, and others who matter to them to know *when* to feel proud, ashamed, or guilty (Thompson, Meyer, & McGinley, 2006).

When parents repeatedly comment on the worth of the child and her performance ("That's a bad job! I thought you were a good girl!"), children experience self-conscious emotions intensely—more shame after failure, more pride after success. In contrast, parents who focus on how to improve performance ("You did it this way; now try it that way") induce moderate, more adaptive levels of shame and pride and greater persistence on difficult tasks (Kelley, Brownell, & Campbell, 2000; Lewis, 1998).

Among Western children, intense shame is associated with feelings of personal inadequacy ("I'm stupid"; "I'm a terrible person") and with maladjustment—withdrawal and depression as well as intense anger and aggression toward those who shamed them (Lindsay-Hartz, de Rivera, & Mascolo, 1995; Mills, 2005). In contrast, guilt—when it occurs in appropriate circumstances and is not accompanied by shame—is related to good adjustment. Guilt helps children resist harmful impulses, and it motivates a misbehaving child to repair the damage and behave more considerately (Mascolo & Fischer, 2007; Tangney, Stuewig, & Mashek, 2007). But overwhelming guilt—involving such high emotional distress that the child cannot make amends—is linked to depressive symptoms as early as age 3 (Luby et al., 2009).

The consequences of shame for children's adjustment, however, may vary across cultures. As Chinese parents' narratives about their child's misdeeds illustrate (see page 201), adults in Asian collectivist societies more often induce shame in children, viewing it as an adaptive reminder of the importance of others' judgments (Bedford, 2004).

Empathy and Sympathy

Another emotional capacity, *empathy,* serves as an important motivator of **prosocial,** or **altruistic, behavior**—actions that benefit another person without any expected reward for the self (Spinrad & Eisenberg, 2009). Compared with toddlers, preschoolers rely more on words to communicate empathic feelings. And as the ability to take another's perspective improves, empathic responding increases.

Yet in some children, empathy—*feeling with* another person and responding emotionally in a similar way—does not yield acts of kindness and helpfulness but, instead, escalates into personal distress. In trying to reduce these feelings, the child focuses on his own anxiety rather than the person in need. As a result, empathy does not lead to **sympathy**—feelings of concern or sorrow for another's plight.

Temperament plays a role in whether empathy prompts sympathetic, prosocial behavior or self-focused personal distress. Children who are sociable, assertive, and good at regulating emotion are more likely to help, share, and comfort others in distress (Bengtsson, 2005; Eisenberg et al., 1998; Valiente et al., 2004). But poor emotion regulators, who are often over-

As children's language skills and capacity to take the perspective of others improve, empathy also increases, motivating prosocial, or altruistic, behavior.

whelmed by their feelings, less often display sympathetic concern and prosocial behavior.

As with other aspects of emotional development, parenting affects empathy and sympathy. When parents show sensitive, empathic concern for their preschoolers' feelings, children are likely to react in a concerned way to the distress of others—relationships that persist into adolescence and early adulthood (Koestner, Franz, & Weinberger, 1990; Michalik et al., 2007). Besides modeling sympathy, parents can teach children the importance of kindness and can intervene when they display inappropriate emotion—strategies that predict high levels of sympathetic responding (Eisenberg, 2003).

Peer Relations

As children become increasingly self-aware and better at communicating and understanding others' thoughts and feelings, their skill at interacting with peers improves rapidly. Peers provide young children with learning experiences they can get in no other way. Because peers interact on an equal footing, children must keep a conversation going, cooperate, and set goals in play. With peers, children form friendships—special relationships marked by attachment and common interests.

Advances in Peer Sociability

Mildred Parten (1932), one of the first to study peer sociability among 2- to 5-year-olds, noticed a dramatic rise with age in joint, interactive play. She concluded that social development proceeds in a three-step sequence. It begins with **nonsocial activity**—unoccupied, onlooker behavior and solitary play.

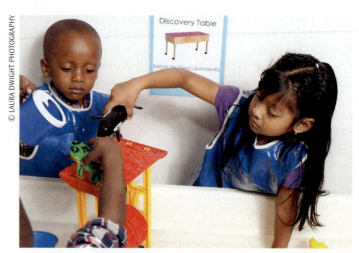

These 4-year-olds (left) engage in parallel play. Cooperative play (right) develops later than parallel play, but preschool children continue to move back and forth between the two types of sociability, using parallel play as a respite from the complex demands of cooperation.

Then it shifts to **parallel play,** in which a child plays near other children with similar materials but does not try to influence their behavior. At the highest level are two forms of true social interaction. In **associative play,** children engage in separate activities but exchange toys and comment on one another's behavior. Finally, in **cooperative play,** a more advanced type of interaction, children orient toward a common goal, such as acting out a make-believe theme.

Follow-Up Research on Peer Sociability.
Longitudinal evidence indicates that these play forms emerge in the order suggested by Parten but that later-appearing ones do not replace earlier ones (Rubin, Bukowski, & Parker, 2006). Rather, all types coexist in early childhood.

TAKE A MOMENT... Watch children move from one type of play to another in a play group or preschool classroom, and you will see that they often transition from onlooker to parallel to cooperative play and back again (Robinson et al., 2003). Preschoolers seem to use parallel play as a way station—a respite from the demands of complex social interaction and a crossroad to new activities. Also, both solitary and parallel play remain fairly stable from 3 to 6 years, accounting for as much of the child's play as cooperative interaction (Rubin, Fein, & Vandenberg, 1983).

We now understand that the *type,* not the amount, of solitary and parallel play changes in early childhood. In studies of preschoolers' play in Taiwan and the United States, researchers rated the *cognitive maturity* of nonsocial, parallel, and cooperative play, using the categories shown in Table 8.1. Within each play type, older children displayed more cognitively mature behavior than younger children (Pan, 1994; Rubin, Watson, & Jambor, 1978).

Often parents wonder whether a preschooler who spends much time playing alone is developing normally. But only *certain types* of nonsocial activity—aimless wandering, hovering near peers, and functional play involving repetitive motor action—are cause for concern. Children who watch peers without playing are usually temperamentally inhibited—high in social fearfulness (Coplan et al., 2004). And preschoolers who engage in solitary, repetitive behavior (banging blocks, making a doll jump up and down) tend to be immature, impulsive children who find it difficult to regulate anger and aggression (Coplan et al., 2001). In the classroom, both reticent and impulsive children tend to experience peer ostracism (Coplan & Arbeau, 2008). But most preschoolers with low rates of peer interaction simply like to play alone, and their solitary activities are positive and constructive. When they do play with peers, they show socially skilled behavior (Coplan & Armer, 2007).

TABLE 8.1

Developmental Sequence of Cognitive Play Categories

PLAY CATEGORY	DESCRIPTION	EXAMPLES
Functional play	Simple, repetitive motor movements with or without objects, especially common during the first two years	Running around a room, rolling a car back and forth, kneading clay with no intent to make something
Constructive play	Creating or constructing something, especially common between 3 and 6 years	Making a house out of toy blocks, drawing a picture, putting together a puzzle
Make-believe play	Acting out everyday and imaginary roles, especially common between 2 and 6 years	Playing house, school, or police officer; acting out storybook or television characters

Source: Rubin, Fein, & Vandenberg, 1983.

Agta village children in the Philippines play a tug-of-war game. Large-group, highly cooperative play is typical of peer sociability in collectivist societies.

© JACOB MAENTZ/CORBIS

Cultural Variations.

Peer sociability in collectivist societies, which stress group harmony, takes different forms than in individualistic cultures (Chen & French, 2008). For example, children in India generally play in large groups, which require high levels of cooperation. Much of their behavior is imitative, occurs in unison, and involves close physical contact. In a game called Bhatto Bhatto, children act out a script about a trip to the market, touching one another's elbows and hands as they pretend to cut and share a tasty vegetable (Roopnarine et al., 1994).

Cultural beliefs about the importance of play also affect early peer associations. Caregivers who view play as mere entertainment are less likely to provide props or to encourage pretend than those who value its cognitive and social benefits (Gaskins, 2000). Preschoolers of Korean-American parents, who emphasize task persistence as vital for learning, spend less time than Caucasian-American children in joint make-believe and more time unoccupied and in parallel play (Farver, Kim, & Lee, 1995).

First Friendships

As preschoolers interact, first friendships form that serve as important contexts for emotional and social development. Preschoolers understand that a friend is someone "who likes you," with whom you spend a lot of time playing, and with whom you share toys. But friendship does not yet have a long-term, enduring quality based on mutual trust (Damon, 1988a; Hartup, 2006). "Mark's my best friend," Sammy would declare on days when the boys got along well. But when a dispute arose, he would reverse himself: "Mark, you're not my friend!"

Nevertheless, interactions between young friends are unique. Preschool friends are more cooperative and emotionally expressive—talking, laughing, and looking at each other more often than nonfriends do (Hartup, 2006). Furthermore, children who begin kindergarten with friends in their class or readily make

new friends adjust to school more favorably (Ladd, Birch, & Buhs, 1999; Ladd & Price, 1987). The company of friends seems to serve as a secure base from which to develop new relationships, enhancing children's feelings of comfort in the new classroom.

Peer Relations and School Readiness

The ease with which kindergartners are accepted by their classmates predicts cooperative participation in classroom activities and self-directed completion of learning tasks—behaviors linked to gains in achievement (Ladd, Birch, & Buhs, 1999; Ladd, Buhs, & Seid, 2000). Positive peer relationships enable kindergartners to integrate themselves into classroom environments in ways that foster both academic and social competence. In one study, 4-year-olds of average intelligence but with above-average social skills fared better in academic achievement in first grade than children of equal mental ability who were socially below average (Konold & Pianta, 2005).

Because social maturity in early childhood contributes to later academic performance, a growing number of experts propose that kindergarten readiness be assessed in terms of not just academic skills but also social skills (Ladd, Herald, & Kochel, 2006; Thompson & Raikes, 2007). Preschool programs, too, should attend to these vital social prerequisites. Warm, responsive teacher–child interaction is vital. In studies involving several thousand 4-year-olds in public preschools in six states, teacher sensitivity and emotional support were strong predictors of children's social competence, both during preschool and after kindergarten entry (Curby et al., 2009; Mashburn et al., 2008).

Parental Influences on Early Peer Relations

Children first acquire skills for interacting with peers within the family. Parents influence children's peer sociability both *directly,* through attempts to influence children's peer relations, and *indirectly,* through their child-rearing practices and play behaviors (Ladd & Pettit, 2002; Rubin et al., 2005).

Direct Parental Influences. Preschoolers whose parents frequently arrange informal peer play activities tend to have larger peer networks and to be more socially skilled (Ladd, LeSieur, & Profilet, 1993). In providing play opportunities, parents show children how to initiate peer contacts. And parents' skillful suggestions for managing conflict, discouraging teasing, and entering a play group are associated with preschoolers' social competence and peer acceptance (Mize & Pettit, 2010; Parke et al., 2004).

Indirect Parental Influences. Many parenting behaviors not directly aimed at promoting peer sociability nevertheless influence it. For example, secure attachments to parents are linked to more responsive, harmonious peer interaction, larger peer networks, and warmer, more supportive friendships during the preschool and school years (Laible, 2007; Lucas-Thompson

Through involved, emotionally positive play, this father promotes his child's capacity to engage in harmonious, supportive peer interaction.

& Clarke-Stewart, 2007; Wood, Emmerson, & Cowan, 2004). The sensitive, emotionally expressive communication that contributes to attachment security may be responsible. In several studies, involved, emotionally positive parent–child conversations and play predicted preschoolers' prosocial behavior and positive peer relations (Clark & Ladd, 2000; Lindsey & Mize, 2000).

As we have seen, some preschoolers already have great difficulty with peer relations. In Leslie's classroom, Robbie was one of them. Wherever he happened to be, comments like "Robbie ruined our block tower" and "Robbie hit me for no reason" could be heard. As we take up moral development in the next section, you will learn more about how parenting contributed to Robbie's peer problems.

ASK YOURSELF

REVIEW Among children who spend much time playing alone, what factors distinguish those who are likely to have adjustment difficulties from those who are well-adjusted and socially skilled?

APPLY Three-year-old Ben lives in the country, with no other preschoolers nearby. His parents wonder whether it is worth driving Ben into town once a week to participate in a peer play group. What advice would you give Ben's parents, and why?

REFLECT What did your parents do, directly and indirectly, that might have influenced your earliest peer relationships?

 # Foundations of Morality

Children's conversations and behavior provide many examples of their developing moral sense. By age 2, they use words to evaluate behavior as "good" or "bad" and react with distress to aggressive or otherwise harmful acts (Kochanska, Casey, & Fukumoto, 1995).

Adults everywhere take note of this budding capacity to distinguish right from wrong. Some cultures have special terms for it. The Utku Indians of Hudson Bay say the child develops *ihuma* (reason). The Fijians believe that *vakayalo* (sense) appears. In response, parents hold children more responsible for their behavior (Dunn, 2005). By the end of early childhood, children can state many moral rules: "Don't take someone's things without asking!" "Tell the truth!" In addition, they argue over matters of justice: "It's not fair. He got more!"

All theories of moral development recognize that conscience begins to take shape in early childhood. And most agree that at first, the child's morality is *externally controlled* by adults. Gradually, it becomes regulated by *inner standards*. Truly moral individuals do not do the right thing just to conform to others' expectations. Rather, they have developed compassionate concerns and principles of good conduct, which they follow in many situations.

Each major theory emphasizes a different aspect of morality. Psychoanalytic theory stresses the *emotional side* of conscience development—in particular, identification and guilt as motivators of good conduct. Social learning theory focuses on how *moral behavior* is learned through reinforcement and modeling. Finally, the cognitive-developmental perspective emphasizes *thinking*—children's ability to reason about justice and fairness.

The Psychoanalytic Perspective

Recall from Chapter 1 that according to Freud, young children form a *superego*, or conscience, by adopting the same-sex parent's moral standards. Children obey the superego to avoid *guilt*, a painful emotion that arises each time they are tempted to misbehave. Moral development, Freud believed, is largely complete by 5 to 6 years of age.

Today, most researchers disagree with Freud's view of conscience development. In his theory, fear of punishment and loss of parental love motivate conscience formation and moral behavior. Yet children whose parents frequently use threats, commands, or physical force tend to violate standards often and feel little guilt, whereas parental warmth and responsiveness predict greater guilt following transgressions (Kochanska et al., 2005, 2008). And if a parent withdraws love after misbehavior—for example, refuses to speak to or states a dislike for the child—children often respond with high levels of self-blame, thinking "I'm no good." Eventually, to protect themselves from overwhelming guilt, these children may deny the emotion and, as a result, also develop a weak conscience (Kochanska, 1991).

A teacher uses inductive discipline to explain to a child the impact of her transgression on others, pointing out classmates' feelings. Induction encourages empathy, sympathy, and commitment to moral standards.

Inductive Discipline.

In contrast, conscience formation is promoted by a type of discipline called **induction,** in which an adult helps the child notice feelings by pointing out the effects of the child's misbehavior on others. For example, a parent might say, "She's crying because you won't give back her doll" (Hoffman, 2000). Preschoolers with warm parents who use induction are more likely to refrain from wrongdoing, confess and repair damage after misdeeds, and display prosocial behavior (Kerr et al., 2004; Volling, Mahoney, & Rauer, 2009; Zahn-Waxler, Radke-Yarrow, & King, 1979).

The success of induction may lie in its power to motivate children's active commitment to moral standards. By emphasizing the impact of the child's actions on others, it encourages empathy and sympathy (Krevans & Gibbs, 1996). And giving children reasons for changing their behavior encourages them to adopt moral standards because they make sense.

The Child's Contribution.

Although good discipline is crucial, children's characteristics also affect the success of parenting techniques. Twin studies suggest a modest genetic contribution to empathy (Knafo et al., 2009). A highly empathic child is more responsive to induction.

Temperament is also influential. Mild, patient tactics—requests, suggestions, and explanations—are sufficient to prompt guilt reactions in anxious, fearful preschoolers (Kochanska et al., 2002). But with fearless, impulsive children, gentle discipline has little impact. Power assertion also works poorly. It undermines the child's capacity for effortful control, which strongly predicts good conduct, empathy, sympathy, and prosocial behavior (Kochanska & Aksan, 2006; Kochanska & Knaack, 2003). Parents of impulsive children can foster conscience development by ensuring a secure attachment relationship and combining firm correction with induction (Kochanska, Aksan, & Joy, 2007). When children are so low in anxiety that parental disapproval causes them little discomfort, a close parent–child bond motivates them to listen to parents as a means of preserving an affectionate, supportive relationship.

The Role of Guilt.

Although little support exists for Freudian ideas about conscience development, Freud was correct that guilt is an important motivator of moral action. Inducing *empathy-based guilt* (expressions of personal responsibility and regret, such as "I'm sorry I hurt him") by explaining that the child is harming someone and has disappointed the parent is a means of influencing children without using coercion. Empathy-based guilt reactions are associated with stopping harmful actions, repairing damage caused by misdeeds, and engaging in future prosocial behavior (Baumeister, 1998; Eisenberg, Eggum, & Edwards, 2010).

But contrary to what Freud believed, guilt is not the only force that compels us to act morally. Nor is moral development complete by the end of early childhood. Rather, it is a gradual process, extending into adulthood.

Social Learning Theory

According to social learning theory, moral behavior is acquired just like any other set of responses: through reinforcement and modeling.

Importance of Modeling.

Operant conditioning—reinforcement for good behavior with approval, affection, and other rewards—is not enough for children to acquire moral responses. For a behavior to be reinforced, it must first occur spontaneously. Yet many prosocial acts, such as sharing, helping, or comforting an unhappy playmate, occur so rarely at first that reinforcement cannot explain their rapid development in early childhood. Rather, social learning theorists believe that children learn to behave morally largely through *modeling*—observing and imitating people who demonstrate appropriate behavior (Bandura, 1977; Grusec, 1988). Once children acquire a moral response, reinforcement in the form of praise increases its frequency (Mills & Grusec, 1989).

Many studies show that having helpful or generous models increases young children's prosocial responses. Models are most

As this preschooler imitates his father's laundry folding, he internalizes a family prosocial rule: everyone helps with household chores.

influential in the early years. In one study, toddlers' eager, willing imitation of their mothers' behavior predicted moral conduct (not cheating in a game) and guilt following transgressions at age 3 (Forman, Aksan, & Kochanska, 2004). At the end of early childhood, children who have had consistent exposure to caring adults have internalized prosocial rules and follow them whether or not a model is present (Mussen & Eisenberg-Berg, 1977).

Effects of Punishment.

A sharp reprimand or physical force to restrain or move a child is justified when immediate obedience is necessary—for example, when a 3-year-old is about to run into the street. In fact, parents are most likely to use forceful methods under these conditions. But to foster long-term goals, such as acting kindly toward others, they tend to rely on warmth and reasoning (Kuczynski, 1984). And in response to very serious transgressions, such as lying and stealing, they often combine power assertion with reasoning (Grusec, 2006).

Frequent punishment, however, promotes only momentary compliance. For example, Robbie's parents often punished by hitting, criticizing, and shouting at him. But as soon as they were out of sight, Robbie usually engaged in the unacceptable behavior again. The more harsh threats, angry physical control, and physical punishment children experience, the more likely they are to develop serious, lasting mental health problems. These include weak internalization of moral rules; depression, aggression, antisocial behavior, and poor academic performance in childhood and adolescence; and depression, alcohol abuse, criminality, and partner and child abuse in adulthood (Afifi et al., 2006; Bender et al., 2007; Gershoff, 2002a; Kochanska, Aksan, & Nichols, 2003; Lynch et al., 2006).

Repeated harsh punishment has wide-ranging, undesirable side effects:

- It models aggression.
- It induces a chronic sense of being personally threatened, which prompts children to focus on their own distress rather than respond sympathetically to others.
- It causes children to avoid the punishing adult, who, as a result, has little opportunity to teach desirable behaviors.
- By stopping children's misbehavior temporarily, it offers immediate relief to adults, who may then punish more often—a course of action that can spiral into serious abuse.
- Adults whose parents used corporal punishment—the use of physical force to inflict pain but not injury—are more accepting of it (Deater-Deckard et al., 2003; Vitrup & Holden, 2010). In this way, use of physical punishment may transfer to the next generation.

Although corporal punishment spans the SES spectrum, its frequency and harshness are elevated among less educated, economically disadvantaged parents (Lansford et al., 2004, 2009). And consistently, parents with conflict-ridden marriages and with mental health problems are more likely to be punitive and also to have hard-to-manage children (Berlin et al., 2009; Erath et al., 2006; Taylor et al., 2010). These parent–child similarities

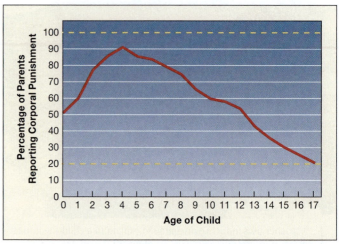

FIGURE 8.1 **Prevalence of corporal punishment by children's age.** Estimates are based on the percentage of parents in a nationally representative U.S. sample of nearly 1,000 reporting one or more instances of spanking, slapping, pinching, shaking, or hitting with a hard object in the past year. Physical punishment increases sharply during early childhood and then declines, but it is high at all ages. (From M. A. Straus & J. H. Stewart, 1999, "Corporal Punishment by American Parents: National Data on Prevalence, Chronicity, Severity, and Duration, in Relation to Child and Family Characteristics," *Clinical Child and Family Psychology Review, 2,* p. 59. Adapted with kind permission from Springer Science+Business Media and Murray A. Straus.)

suggest that heredity contributes to the link between punitive discipline and children's adjustment difficulties.

But heredity is not a complete explanation. Return to page 56 in Chapter 2 to review findings indicating that good parenting can shield children who are genetically at risk for aggression and antisocial activity from developing those behaviors. Furthermore, longitudinal studies reveal that parental harshness and corporal punishment predict child and adolescent emotional and behavior problems, even after child, parenting, and family characteristics that might otherwise account for the relationship were controlled (Berlin et al., 2009; Lansford et al., 2009, 2011; Taylor et al., 2010).

Surveys of nationally representative samples of U.S. families reveal that although corporal punishment increases from infancy to age 5 and then declines, it is high at all ages (see Figure 8.1) (Gershoff et al., 2012; Straus & Stewart, 1999). And more than one-fourth of physically punishing parents report having used a hard object, such as a brush or a belt (Gershoff, 2002b).

A prevailing American belief is that corporal punishment, if implemented by caring parents, is harmless, perhaps even beneficial. But as the Cultural Influences box on the following page reveals, this assumption is valid only under conditions of limited use in certain social contexts.

Alternatives to Harsh Punishment.

Alternatives to criticism, slaps, and spankings can reduce the side effects of punishment. A technique called **time out** involves removing children from the immediate setting—for example, by sending them to their rooms—until they are ready to act appropriately. When a child is out of control, a few minutes in time out can

Cultural Influences

Ethnic Differences in the Consequences of Physical Punishment

In an African-American community, six elders, who had volunteered to serve as mentors for parents facing child-rearing challenges, met to discuss parenting issues at a social service agency. Their attitudes toward discipline were strikingly different from those of the white social workers who had brought them together. Each elder argued that successful child rearing required appropriate physical tactics. At the same time, they voiced strong disapproval of screaming or cursing at children, calling such out-of-control parental behavior "abusive." Ruth, the oldest and most respected member of the group, characterized good parenting as a complex combination of warmth, teaching, talking nicely, and disciplining physically. She related how an older neighbor advised her to handle her own children when she was a young parent:

> She said to me says, don't scream . . . you talk to them real nice and sweet and when they do something ugly . . . she say you get a nice little switch and you won't have any trouble with them and from that day that's the way I raised 'em. (Mosby et al., 1999, pp. 511–512)

In several studies, corporal punishment predicted externalizing problems similarly among white, black, Hispanic, and Asian children (Gershoff et al., 2012; Pardini, Fite, & Burke, 2008). But other investigations point to ethnic variations.

In one, researchers followed several hundred families for 12 years, collecting information on disciplinary strategies and problem behaviors (Lansford et al., 2004). Even after many child and family characteristics were controlled, the findings were striking: In Caucasian-American families, physical punishment was positively associated with adolescent aggression and antisocial behavior. In African-American families, by contrast, the more mothers had disciplined physically in childhood, the less their teenagers displayed angry, acting-out behavior and got in trouble at school and with the police.

African-American and Caucasian-American parents seem to mete out physical punishment differently. In black families, such discipline is typically culturally approved and often mild, delivered in a context of parental warmth, and aimed at helping children become responsible adults. White parents, in contrast, consider physical punishment to be wrong, so when they resort to it, they are usually highly agitated and rejecting of the child (Dodge, McLoyd, & Lansford, 2006). As a result, many black children may view spanking as a practice carried out with their best interests in mind, whereas white children may regard it as an "act of personal aggression" (Gunnoe & Mariner, 1997, p. 768).

In support of this view, when several thousand ethnically diverse children were followed from the preschool through the early

In African-American families, discipline often includes mild physical punishment. Because the practice is culturally approved and delivered in a context of parental warmth, children may view it as an effort to encourage maturity, not as an act of aggression.

school years, spanking was associated with a rise in behavior problems if parents were cold and rejecting, but not if they were warm and supportive (McLoyd & Smith, 2002). And in another study, spanking predicted depressive symptoms only among African-American children whose mothers disapproved of the practice and, as a result, tended to use it when they were highly angry and frustrated (McLoyd et al., 2007).

These findings are not an endorsement of physical punishment. Other forms of discipline, including the positive strategies listed on page 210, are far more effective. But it is noteworthy that the meaning and impact of physical discipline vary sharply with its intensity level, context of warmth and support, and cultural approval.

---

be enough to change behavior while also giving angry parents a cooling-off period (Morawska & Sanders, 2011). Another approach is *withdrawal of privileges,* such as watching a favorite TV program. When parents do decide to use these forms of punishment, they can increase their effectiveness in three ways:

- *Consistency.* Permitting children to act inappropriately on some occasions confuses them, and the unacceptable act persists (Acker & O'Leary, 1996).

- *A warm parent–child relationship.* Children of involved, caring parents find the interruption in parental affection that accompanies punishment especially unpleasant. They want to regain parental warmth and approval as quickly as possible.

- *Explanations.* Providing reasons for mild punishment helps children relate the misdeed to expectations for future behavior, resulting in far greater reduction in misbehavior than using punishment alone (Larzelere et al., 1996).

Positive Relationships, Positive Parenting. The most effective forms of discipline encourage good conduct—by building a mutually respectful bond with the child, letting the child know ahead of time how to act, and praising mature behavior. When sensitivity, cooperation, and shared positive emotion are evident in joint activities between parents and preschoolers, children show firmer conscience development—expressing empathy after transgressions, playing fairly in games, and considering others' welfare (Kochanska et al., 2005, 2008).

Applying What We Know

Positive Parenting

Strategy	Explanation
Use transgressions as opportunities to teach.	When a child engages in harmful or unsafe behavior, intervene firmly, and then use induction, which motivates children to make amends and behave prosocially.
Reduce opportunities for misbehavior.	On a long car trip, bring back-seat activities that relieve children's restlessness. At the supermarket, converse with children and let them help with shopping. As a result, children learn to occupy themselves constructively when options are limited.
Provide reasons for rules.	When children appreciate that rules are rational, not arbitrary, they are more likely to strive to follow the rules.
Arrange for children to participate in family routines and duties.	By joining with adults in preparing a meal, washing dishes, or raking leaves, children develop a sense of responsible participation in family and community life and acquire many practical skills.
When children are obstinate, try compromising and problem solving.	When a child refuses to obey, express understanding of the child's feelings, suggest a compromise, and help the child think of ways to avoid the problem in the future. Responding firmly but kindly and respectfully increases the likelihood of willing cooperation.
Encourage mature behavior.	Express confidence in children's capacity to learn and appreciation for effort and cooperation: "You gave that your best!" Adult encouragement fosters pride and satisfaction in succeeding, thereby inspiring children to improve further.

Sources: Berk, 2001; Grusec, 2006.

Consult Applying What We Know above for ways to parent positively. Parents who use these strategies focus on long-term social and life skills—cooperation, problem solving, and consideration for others. This greatly reduces the need for punishment.

The Cognitive-Developmental Perspective

The psychoanalytic and behaviorist approaches to morality focus on how children acquire ready-made standards of good conduct from adults. In contrast, the cognitive-developmental perspective regards children as *active thinkers* about social rules. As early as the preschool years, children make moral judgments, deciding what is right or wrong on the basis of concepts they construct about justice and fairness (Gibbs, 2010a; Turiel, 2006).

Young children have some well-developed ideas about morality. As long as researchers emphasize people's intentions, 3-year-olds say that a person with bad intentions—someone who deliberately frightens, embarrasses, or otherwise hurts another—is more deserving of punishment than a well-intentioned person (Helwig, Zelazo, & Wilson, 2001). Around age 4, children know that a person who expresses an insincere intention—saying, "I'll come over and help you rake leaves," while not intending to do so—is lying (Maas, 2008). And 4-year-olds approve of telling the truth and disapprove of lying, even when a lie remains undetected (Bussey, 1992).

Furthermore, preschoolers distinguish **moral imperatives,** which protect people's rights and welfare, from two other types of rules and expectations: **social conventions,** customs determined solely by consensus, such as table manners and politeness rituals (saying "hello," "please," "thank you"); and **matters of personal choice,** such as friends, hairstyle, and leisure activities, which do not violate rights and are up to the individual (Killen, Margie, & Sinno, 2006; Nucci, 1996; Smetana, 2006). Interviews with 3- and 4-year-olds reveal that they judge moral violations (stealing an apple) as more wrong than violations of social conventions (eating ice cream with your fingers). And preschoolers' concern with personal choice, conveyed through statements like "I'm gonna wear *this* shirt," serves as the springboard for moral concepts of individual rights (Nucci, 2005).

Within the moral domain, however, preschool and young school-age children tend to reason *rigidly,* making judgments based on salient features and consequences while neglecting other important information. For example, they are more likely than older children to claim that stealing and lying are always wrong, even when a person has a morally sound reason for engaging in these acts (Lourenco, 2003). Their explanations for why hitting others is wrong, even in the absence of rules against hitting, are simplistic and centered on physical harm: "When you get hit, it hurts, and you start to cry" (Nucci, 2008). And their focus on outcomes means that they fail to realize that a promise is still a promise, even if it is unfulfilled (Maas, 2008; Maas & Abbeduto, 2001).

Cognition and language support preschoolers' moral understanding, but social experiences are vital. Disputes with siblings and peers over rights, possessions, and property allow preschoolers to negotiate, compromise, and work out their first ideas about justice and fairness. Children also learn from warm, sensitive parental communication and from observing the way adults handle rule violations to protect the welfare of others (Turiel & Killen, 2010). Children who are advanced in moral thinking tend to have parents who adapt their communications about fighting, honesty, and ownership to what their children can understand, tell stories with moral implications, encourage prosocial behavior, and gently stimulate the child to think further, without being hostile or critical (Janssens & Deković, 1997; Walker & Taylor, 1991a).

Preschoolers who verbally and physically assault others, often without provocation, are already delayed in moral reasoning (Helwig & Turiel, 2004; Sanderson & Siegal, 1988). Without special help, such children show long-term disruptions in moral development.

The Other Side of Morality: Development of Aggression

Beginning in late infancy, all children display aggression at times. As interactions with siblings and peers increase, so do aggressive outbursts. By the second year, aggressive acts with two distinct purposes emerge. Initially, the most common is **proactive** (or *instrumental*) **aggression,** in which children act to fulfill a need or desire—obtain an object, privilege, space, or social reward, such as adult or peer attention—and unemotionally attack a person to achieve their goal. The other type, **reactive** (or *hostile*) **aggression,** is an angry, defensive response to provocation or a blocked goal and is meant to hurt another person (Dodge, Coie, & Lynam, 2006; Little et al., 2003).

Proactive and reactive aggression come in three forms:

- **Physical aggression** harms others through physical injury—pushing, hitting, kicking, or punching others or destroying another's property.
- **Verbal aggression** harms others through threats of physical aggression, name-calling, or hostile teasing.
- **Relational aggression** damages another's peer relationships through social exclusion, malicious gossip, or friendship manipulation.

In early childhood, verbal aggression gradually replaces physical aggression (Alink et al., 2006; Tremblay et al., 1999). And proactive aggression declines as preschoolers' improved capacity to delay gratification enables them to avoid grabbing others' possessions. But reactive aggression in verbal and relational forms tends to rise over early and middle childhood (Côté et al., 2007; Tremblay, 2000). Older children are better able to recognize malicious intentions and, as a result, more often respond in hostile ways.

By age 17 months, boys are more physically aggressive than girls—a difference found throughout childhood in many cultures (Baillargeon et al., 2007; Card et al., 2008). The sex difference is due in part to biology—in particular, to male sex hormones

These preschoolers display proactive aggression, pushing and grabbing as they argue over a game. As children learn to compromise and share, and as their capacity to delay gratification improves, proactive aggression declines.

(androgens) and temperamental traits (activity level, irritability, impulsivity) on which boys exceed girls. Gender-role conformity is also important. As soon as preschoolers are aware of gender stereotypes—that males and females are expected to behave differently—physical aggression drops off more sharply for girls than for boys (Fagot & Leinbach, 1989).

Although girls have a reputation for being both more verbally and relationally aggressive than boys, the sex difference is small (Crick et al., 2004, 2006; Crick, Ostrov, & Werner, 2006). Beginning in the preschool years, girls concentrate most of their aggressive acts in the relational category. Boys inflict harm in more variable ways and, therefore, display overall rates of aggression that are much higher than girls'.

At the same time, girls more often use indirect relational tactics that—in disrupting intimate bonds especially important to girls—can be particularly mean. Whereas physical attacks are usually brief, acts of indirect relational aggression may extend for hours, weeks, or even months (Nelson, Robinson, & Hart, 2005; Underwood, 2003). In one instance, a 6-year-old girl formed a "pretty-girls club" and—for nearly an entire school year—convinced its members to exclude several classmates by saying they were "ugly and smelly."

An occasional aggressive exchange between preschoolers is normal. But children who are emotionally negative, impulsive, and disobedient are prone to early, high rates of physical or relational aggression (or both) that often persist, placing them at risk for internalizing and externalizing difficulties, social skills deficits, and antisocial activity in middle childhood and adolescence (Campbell et al., 2006; Côté et al., 2007). These negative outcomes, however, depend on child-rearing conditions.

The Family as Training Ground for Aggressive Behavior. "I can't control him, he's impossible," Robbie's mother, Nadine, complained to Leslie one day. When Leslie

asked if Robbie might be troubled by something happening at home, she discovered that his parents fought constantly and resorted to harsh, inconsistent discipline. The same child-rearing practices that undermine moral internalization— love withdrawal, power assertion, critical remarks, physical punishment, and inconsistent discipline—are linked to aggression from early childhood through adolescence in diverse cultures, with most of these practices predicting both physical and relational forms (Bradford et al., 2003; Casas et al., 2006; Côté et al., 2007; Gershoff et al., 2010; Kuppens et al., 2009; Nelson et al., 2006a).

In families like Robbie's, anger and punitiveness quickly create a conflict-ridden family atmosphere and an "out-of-control" child. The pattern begins with forceful discipline, which occurs more often with stressful life experiences, a parent with an unstable personality, or a difficult child (Dodge, Coie, & Lynam, 2006). Typically, the parent threatens, criticizes, and punishes, and the child angrily resists until the parent "gives in." As these cycles become more frequent, they generate anxiety and irritability among other family members, including siblings, who soon join in the hostile interactions. Destructive sibling conflict, in turn, quickly spreads to peer relationships, contributing to poor impulse control and antisocial behavior (Garcia et al., 2000; Ostrov, Crick, & Stauffacher, 2006).

Boys are more likely than girls to be targets of harsh, inconsistent discipline because they are more active and impulsive and therefore harder to control. When children who are extreme in these characteristics are exposed to emotionally negative, inept parenting, their capacity for emotional self-regulation, empathic responding, and guilt after transgressions is disrupted (Eisenberg, Eggum, & Edwards, 2010). Consequently, they lash out when disappointed, frustrated, or faced with a sad or fearful victim.

Children subjected to these family processes acquire a distorted view of the social world, often seeing hostile intent where it does not exist and, as a result, making many unprovoked attacks (Lochman & Dodge, 1998; Orbio de Castro et al., 2002). And some, who conclude that aggression "works" to access rewards and control others, callously use it to advance their own goals and are unconcerned about causing suffering in others—an aggressive style associated with later more severe conduct problems, violent behavior, and delinquency (Marsee & Frick, 2010).

Violent Media and Aggression.
In the United States, 57 percent of TV programs between 6 A.M. and 11 P.M. contain violent scenes, often portraying repeated aggressive acts that go unpunished. Victims of TV violence are rarely shown experiencing serious harm, and few programs condemn violence or depict other ways of solving problems (Center for Communication and Social Policy, 1998). Verbally and relationally aggressive acts are particularly frequent in reality TV shows (Coyne, Robinson, & Nelson, 2010). And violent content is 9 percent above average in children's programming, with cartoons being the most violent.

Reviewers of thousands of studies have concluded that TV violence increases the likelihood of hostile thoughts and emotions and of verbally, physically, and relationally aggressive behavior (Ostrov, Gentile, & Crick, 2006; Scharrer, 2013). And a growing number of studies confirm that playing violent video games has similar effects (Anderson et al., 2008; Hofferth, 2010).

LOOK AND LISTEN

Watch a half-hour of Saturday morning cartoons and a prime-time movie on TV, and tally the number of violent acts, including those that go unpunished. How often did violence occur in each type of program? What do young viewers learn about the consequences of violence? ●

Violent programming not only creates short-term difficulties in parent and peer relations but also has lasting negative consequences. In longitudinal research, time spent watching TV in childhood and adolescence predicted aggressive behavior in adulthood, after other factors linked to TV viewing (such as prior child and parent aggression, IQ, parent education, family income, and neighborhood crime) were controlled (Graber et al., 2006; Huesmann, 1986; Huesmann et al., 2003; Johnson et al., 2002). Aggressive children and adolescents have a greater appetite for violent TV and computer games. And boys devote more time to violent media than girls, in part because of male-oriented themes of conquest and adventure. But even in nonaggressive children, violent TV sparks hostile thoughts and behavior; its impact is simply less intense (Bushman & Huesmann, 2001).

The ease with which television and video games can manipulate children's attitudes and behavior has led to strong public pressure to improve media content. In the United States, the First Amendment right to free speech has hampered efforts to regulate TV broadcasting. Instead, all programs must be rated for violent and sexual content, and all new TV sets are required to contain the V-chip, which allows parents to block undesired material. In general, parents bear most responsibility for regulating their children's exposure to media violence and other inappropriate content. As with the V-chip for TV, parents can control children's Internet access by using filters or programs that monitor website visits. Yet surveys of U.S. parents indicate that 20 to 30 percent of preschoolers and about half of school-age children experience no limits on TV or computer use at home (Rideout, Foehr, & Roberts, 2010; Rideout & Hamel, 2006; Varnhagen, 2007). Besides regulating media exposure, parents are best off participating in children's TV and computer use— expressing disapproval of onscreen violent acts and encouraging discussion, with the aim of helping children understand and critique media content.

Helping Children and Parents Control Aggression.
Treatment for aggressive children is best begun early, before their antisocial behavior becomes well-practiced and difficult to change. Breaking the cycle of hostilities between family members and promoting effective ways of relating to others are crucial.

Leslie suggested that Robbie's parents enroll in a parent training program aimed at improving the parenting of children with conduct problems. In one approach, called *Incredible Years*, parents complete 18 weekly group sessions facilitated by two professionals, who teach positive parenting techniques for promoting preschool and school-age children's academic, emotional, and social skills and for managing disruptive behaviors (Webster-Stratton & Reid, 2010b). A complementary six-day training program for teachers, aimed at improving classroom management strategies and strengthening children's social skills, is also available. And a 22-week program intervenes directly with children, teaching appropriate classroom behavior, self-control, and social skills.

Evaluations in which families with aggressive children were randomly assigned to either Incredible Years or control groups reveal that the program improves parenting and reduces child behavior problems. Combining parent training with teacher and/or child intervention strengthens child outcomes (Webster-Stratton & Herman, 2010). And effects of parent training endure. In one long-term follow-up, 75 percent of young children with serious conduct problems whose parents participated in Incredible Years were well-adjusted as teenagers (Webster-Stratton & Reid, 2010a; Webster-Stratton, Rinaldi, & Reid, 2011).

Other interventions focus on modifying aggressive children's distorted social perspectives, by encouraging them to attend to nonhostile social cues, seek additional information before acting, and take the perspective of others, which promotes empathy and sympathetic concern for others. Another approach is to teach effective conflict-resolution skills. At preschool, Robbie participated in a social problem-solving intervention. Over several months, he met with Leslie and a small group of classmates to act out common conflicts using puppets, discuss alternatives for settling disputes, and practice successful strategies. Children who receive such training show gains in social competence still present several months later (Bierman & Powers, 2009; Shure & Aberson, 2005).

Finally, Robbie's parents sought counseling for their marital problems. When parents receive help in coping with stressors in their own lives, interventions aimed at reducing children's aggression are even more effective (Kazdin & Whitley, 2003).

ASK YOURSELF

REVIEW What must parents do to foster conscience development in fearless, impulsive children? How does this illustrate the concept of goodness of fit (see page 151 in Chapter 6)?

APPLY Alice and Wayne want their two children to become morally mature, caring individuals. List some parenting practices they should use and some they should avoid.

REFLECT Which types of punishment for a misbehaving preschooler do you endorse, and which types do you reject? Why?

As these preschoolers' imaginative play reveals, they have already acquired the gender-stereotyped belief that cooking is a "feminine" activity.

Gender Typing

Gender typing refers to any association of objects, activities, roles, or traits with one sex or the other in ways that conform to cultural stereotypes (Liben & Bigler, 2002). Already, the children in Leslie's classroom had acquired many gender-linked beliefs and preferences and tended to play with peers of their own sex.

Social learning theory, with its emphasis on modeling and reinforcement, and *cognitive-developmental theory,* with its focus on children as active thinkers about their social world, offer contemporary explanations of children's gender typing. As we will see, neither is adequate by itself. *Gender schema theory,* a third perspective that combines elements of both, has gained favor. In the following sections, we consider the early development of gender typing.

Gender-Stereotyped Beliefs and Behavior

Recall from Chapter 6 that around age 2, children use such words as *boy, girl, lady,* and *man* appropriately. As soon as gender categories are established, children sort out what they mean in terms of activities and behavior. Preschoolers associate toys, articles of clothing, tools, household items, games, occupations, colors (blue and pink), and behaviors (physical and relational aggression) with one sex or the other (Banse et al., 2010; Giles & Heyman, 2005; Poulin-Dubois et al., 2002). And their actions reflect their beliefs, not only in play preferences but in personality traits as well. As we have seen, boys tend to be more active, impulsive, assertive, and physically aggressive. Girls tend to be more fearful, dependent, emotionally sensitive, compliant, advanced in effortful control, and skilled at understanding self-conscious emotions and at inflicting indirect relational aggression (Bosacki & Moore, 2004; Else-Quest et al., 2006; Underwood, 2003).

During early childhood, gender-stereotyped beliefs strengthen—so much so that many children apply them as blanket rules rather than as flexible guidelines. When children were asked whether gender stereotypes could be violated, half or more of 3- and 4-year-olds answered "no" to clothing, hairstyle, and play with certain toys (Barbie dolls and G.I. Joes) (Blakemore, 2003). Furthermore, most 3- to 6-year-olds are firm about not wanting to be friends with a child who violates a gender stereotype (a boy who wears nail polish, a girl who plays with trucks) or to attend a school where such violations are allowed (Ruble et al., 2007). These one-sided judgments are a joint product of gender stereotyping in the environment and young children's cognitive limitations (Trautner et al., 2005). Most preschoolers do not yet realize that characteristics *associated with* being male or female—activities, toys, occupations, hairstyle, and clothing—do not *determine* a person's sex.

Biological Influences on Gender Typing

The sex differences just described appear in many cultures around the world (Munroe & Romney, 2006). Certain ones—male activity level and physical aggression, female emotional sensitivity, and preference for same-sex playmates—are widespread among mammalian species (de Waal, 1993, 2001). According to an evolutionary perspective, the adult life of our male ancestors was largely oriented toward competing for mates, that of our female ancestors toward rearing children. Therefore, males became genetically primed for dominance and females for intimacy, responsiveness, and cooperativeness (Konner, 2010; Maccoby, 2002).

Experiments with animals reveal that prenatally administered androgens increase active play and aggression and suppress maternal caregiving in both male and female mammals (Sato et al., 2004). Eleanor Maccoby (1998) argues that sex hormones also affect human play styles, leading to rough, noisy movements among boys and calm, gentle actions among girls. Then, as children interact with peers, they choose partners whose interests and behaviors are compatible with their own. Preschool girls increasingly seek out other girls and like to play in pairs because they share a preference for quieter activities involving cooperative roles. Boys come to prefer larger-group play with other boys, who share a desire to run, climb, play-fight, and compete (Fabes, Martin, & Hanish, 2003). By age 6, children spend 11 times as much time with same-sex as with other-sex playmates (Martin & Fabes, 2001).

Even stronger support for the role of biology in human gender typing comes from research on girls exposed prenatally to high levels of androgens. These girls showed more "masculine" behavior—a preference for trucks and blocks over dolls, for active over quiet play, and for boys as playmates—even when

parents encouraged them to engage in gender-typical play (Cohen-Bendahan, van de Beek, & Berenbaum, 2005; Pasterski et al., 2005).

Research on boys with low early androgen exposure, either because production by the testes is reduced or because body cells are androgen-insensitive, also yields consistent findings (Jürgensen et al., 2007). The greater the degree of impairment, the more these boys display "feminine" behaviors, including toy choices and preference for girl playmates.

Environmental Influences on Gender Typing

A wealth of evidence reveals that environmental forces—at home, at school, and in the community—build on genetic influences to promote vigorous gender typing in early childhood.

Parents. Beginning at birth, parents have different expectations of sons than of daughters. Many describe achievement, competition, and control of emotion as important for sons and warmth, "ladylike" behavior, and closely supervised activities as important for daughters (Brody, 1999; Turner & Gervai, 1995).

Parenting practices reflect these beliefs. Parents typically give their sons toys that stress action and competition (cars, tools, footballs) and their daughters toys that emphasize nurturance, cooperation, and physical attractiveness (dolls, tea sets, jewelry) (Leaper, 1994; Leaper & Friedman, 2007). Parents also actively reinforce independence in boys and closeness and dependency in girls. For example, parents react more positively when a son plays with cars and trucks, demands attention, runs and climbs, or tries to take toys from others. When interacting with daughters, parents more often direct play activities, provide help, encourage participation in household tasks, refer to emo-

Of the two sexes, boys are more gender-typed. Fathers, especially, promote "masculine" behavior in their preschool sons through activities that stress action and competition.

tions, and express approval and agreement (Clearfield & Nelson, 2006; Fagot & Hagan, 1991; Kuebli, Butler, & Fivush, 1995).

Language is a powerful indirect means for teaching children about gender stereotypes. Even parents who believe strongly in gender equality unconsciously use language that highlights gender distinctions and informs children about traditional gender roles (see the Social Issues: Education box on page 216).

LOOK AND LISTEN

> Observe a parent discussing a picture book with a 3- to 6-year-old. How many times did the parent make generic statements about gender? How about the child? Did the parent accept or correct the child's generic utterances? ●

Of the two sexes, boys are more gender-typed, and fathers, especially, insist that boys conform to gender roles. They place more pressure to achieve on sons than on daughters and are less tolerant of "cross-gender" behavior in sons—more concerned when a boy acts like a "sissy" than when a girl acts like a "tomboy" (Wood, Desmarais, & Gugula, 2002). But parents who hold nonstereotyped values and consciously avoid behaving in these ways have children who are less gender-typed (Tenenbaum & Leaper, 2002).

Teachers. Like parents, preschool teachers give girls more encouragement to participate in adult-structured activities. Girls frequently cluster around the teacher, following directions, whereas boys are attracted to play areas where teachers are minimally involved (Campbell, Shirley, & Candy, 2004; Powlishta, Serbin, & Moller, 1993). As a result, boys and girls practice different social behaviors. Compliance and bids for help occur more often in adult-structured contexts; assertiveness, leadership, and creative use of materials in unstructured pursuits.

Furthermore, as early as kindergarten, teachers give more overall attention (both positive and negative) to boys than to girls—a difference evident in diverse countries, including China, England, and the United States. They tend to praise boys more for their academic knowledge, perhaps as a means of motivating them because boys' school performance is behind that of girls. Teachers also use more disapproval and controlling discipline with boys (Chen & Rao, 2011; Davies, 2008; Swinson & Harrop, 2009). They seem to expect boys to misbehave more often—a belief based partly on boys' actual behavior and partly on gender stereotypes.

Peers. Children's same-sex peer association make the peer context a potent source of gender-role learning (Martin & Fabes, 2001). By age 3, same-sex peers positively reinforce one another for gender-typed play by praising, imitating, or joining in. In contrast, when preschoolers engage in "cross-gender" activities—for example, when boys play with dolls or girls with cars and trucks—peers criticize them. Boys are especially intolerant of cross-gender play in other boys (Thorne, 1993).

Children also develop different styles of social influence in gender-segregated peer groups. To get their way in large-group play, boys often rely on commands, threats, and physical force. Girls' preference for playing in pairs leads to greater concern with a partner's needs, evident in polite requests, persuasion, and acceptance. Girls soon find that these tactics succeed with other girls but not with boys, who ignore their courteous overtures (Leaper, 1994; Leaper, Tenenbaum, & Shaffer, 1999). Boys' unresponsiveness gives girls another reason to stop interacting with them.

As boys and girls separate, *in-group favoritism*—more positive evaluations of members of one's own gender—becomes another factor that sustains the separate social worlds of boys and girls. As a result, "two distinct subcultures" of knowledge, beliefs, interests, and behaviors form (Maccoby, 2002).

Gender Identity

As adults, each of us has a **gender identity**—an image of oneself as relatively masculine or feminine in characteristics. By middle childhood, researchers can measure gender identity by asking children to rate themselves on personality traits. A child or adult with a "masculine" identity scores high on traditionally masculine items (such as *ambitious, competitive,* and *self-sufficient*) and low on traditionally feminine items (such as *affectionate, cheerful,* and *soft-spoken*). Someone with a "feminine" identity does the reverse. And a substantial minority (especially females) have a gender identity called **androgyny,** scoring high on both masculine and feminine personality characteristics.

"Masculine" and androgynous children and adults have higher self-esteem than "feminine" individuals (Boldizar, 1991; DiDonato & Berenbaum, 2011; Harter, 2006). Also, androgynous individuals are more adaptable—able to show masculine independence or feminine sensitivity, depending on the situation (Huyck, 1996; Taylor & Hall, 1982). The existence of an androgynous identity demonstrates that children can acquire a mixture of positive qualities traditionally associated with each gender—an orientation that may best help them realize their potential.

Emergence of Gender Identity. How do children develop a gender identity? According to *social learning theory,* behavior comes before self-perceptions. Preschoolers first acquire gender-typed responses through modeling and reinforcement and only later organize these behaviors into gender-linked ideas about themselves. In contrast, *cognitive-developmental theory* maintains that self-perceptions come before behavior. Over the preschool years, children acquire a cognitive appreciation of the permanence of their sex. They develop **gender constancy**—a full understanding of the biologically based permanence of their gender, including the realization that sex remains the same even if clothing, hairstyle, and play activities change. Then children use this knowledge to guide their behavior.

Children younger than age 6 who watch an adult dress a doll in "other-gender" clothing typically insist that the doll's

Social Issues: Education

Young Children Learn About Gender Through Mother–Child Conversations

In an investigation of the power of language to shape preschoolers' beliefs about gender, mothers were asked to converse with their 2- to 6-year-olds about picture books containing images both consistent and inconsistent with gender stereotypes (Gelman, Taylor, & Nguyen, 2004). Each picture was accompanied by the question, "Who can X?" where X was the activity on the page.

Analyses of picture-book conversations revealed that mothers' directly expressed gender attitudes were neutral, largely because they mostly posed questions to their children, such as, "Who's driving that boat?" "Who can be a sailor? Boys and girls?" But by age 4, children often voiced stereotypes ("No, only boys can do that!"), and nearly one-third of the time, mothers affirmed them ("OK, only boys"). Rarely—just 2 percent of the time—did they explicitly counter a child's stereotype, and usually only when the book itself included stereotype-inconsistent pictures.

Although the mothers were not asked to discuss gender, they called attention to it even when they did not need to do so. In English, many nouns referring to people convey age-related information (*kid, baby, 2-year-old, preschooler, teenager, grownup, senior*), whereas only a few encode gender (*male, female, sister, brother, aunt, uncle*). Yet when referring to persons, mothers

called attention to gender more than half the time, even though the people shown in the books varied as much in age as in gender. Referring often to gender encourages young children to sort the social world into gender categories.

Furthermore, both mothers and children frequently expressed *generic utterances*—ones that were broad in scope, referring to many, or nearly all, males and females: "Boys can be sailors." "Most girls don't like trucks." Even generics that were gender-neutral ("Lots of girls in this book") or that denied a stereotype ("Boys can be ballet dancers") prompted children to view individuals of the same gender as alike and to ignore exceptions.

Mothers' and children's use of generics increased with age. At age 2, mothers introduced these generalizations nearly three times as often as children. But by age 6 children were producing generics more often than mothers. Generics were especially common in speech to and from boys, likely contributing to boys' stronger gender typing.

Even though these mothers overwhelmingly believed in gender equality, in conversing with their children, they provided a wealth of implicit cues that foster gender-stereotyping. Adults can combat children's gender stereotyped beliefs by refraining from

While reading, this mother may unconsciously teach her child to see the world in gender-linked terms—by referring to gender unnecessarily or by making generic gender statements ("Most girls prefer X"; "Boys usually don't like X").

labeling gender unnecessarily (substituting *friend* for *boy* or *girl*), using references to individuals ("That person wants to be fire-fighter") or qualifiers ("Some boys and some girls want to be firefighters"), countering children's stereotypical claims, and asking children to avoid using gender labels and generics.

---

sex has also changed (Chauhan, Shastri, & Mohite, 2005; Fagot, 1985). Attainment of gender constancy is strongly related to ability to pass verbal appearance–reality tasks (see page 177 in Chapter 7) (Trautner, Gervai, & Nemeth, 2003). Indeed, gender constancy tasks can be considered a type of appearance–reality problem, in that children must distinguish what a person looks like from who he or she really is.

Is cognitive-developmental theory correct that gender constancy is responsible for children's gender-typed behavior? Evidence for this assumption is weak. "Gender-appropriate" behavior appears so early in the preschool years that its initial appearance must result from modeling and reinforcement, as social learning theory suggests. Although outcomes are not entirely consistent, some evidence suggests that gender con-

stancy actually contributes to more flexible gender-role attitudes during the school years (Ruble et al., 2007). But overall, the impact of gender constancy on gender typing is not great. As research in the following section reveals, gender-role adoption is more powerfully affected by children's beliefs about how close the connection must be between their own gender and their behavior.

Gender Schema Theory. **Gender schema theory** is an information-processing approach that combines social learning and cognitive-developmental features. It explains how environmental pressures and children's cognitions work together to shape gender-role development (Martin & Halverson, 1987; Martin, Ruble, & Szkrybalo, 2002). At an early age, children pick up gender-typed preferences and behaviors from others. At the same time, they organize their experiences into *gender schemas,* or masculine and feminine categories, that they use to interpret their world. As soon as preschoolers can label their own gender, they select gender schemas consistent with it ("Only boys can be doctors" or "Cooking is a girl's job") and apply those categories to themselves. Their self-perceptions then become gender-typed and serve as additional schemas that children use to process information and guide their own behavior.

We have seen that individual differences exist in the extent to which children endorse gender-typed views. Children who acquire rigid gender schemas use them to filter their experiences (Liben & Bigler, 2002). When such children see others behaving in "gender-inconsistent" ways, they often cannot remember the information or distort it to make it "gender-consistent." For example, when shown a picture of a male nurse, they may remember him as a doctor (Martin & Ruble, 2004). And because gender-schematic preschoolers typically conclude, "What I like, children of my own sex will also like," they often use their own preferences to add to their gender biases. For example, a girl who dislikes oysters may conclude that only boys like oysters even though she has never actually been given information promoting such a stereotype. At least partly for this reason, young children's gender schemas contain both culturally standard and nonstandard ideas (Tenenbaum et al., 2010). Not until well into the school years do children's gender schemas fully resemble those of adults.

Reducing Gender Stereotyping in Young Children

How can we help young children avoid developing gender schemas? No easy recipe exists. Biology clearly affects children's gender typing, channeling boys toward active, competitive play and girls toward quieter, more intimate interaction. But most aspects of gender typing are not built into human nature (Ruble, Martin, & Berenbaum, 2006).

Because young children's cognitive limitations lead them to assume that cultural practices determine gender, adults are wise to try to delay preschoolers' exposure to gender-stereotyped messages. Parents and teachers can begin by limiting traditional gender roles in their own behavior and by providing children with nontraditional alternatives—for example, giving boys and girls both trucks and dolls, avoiding use of language that conveys gender stereotypes, and shielding children from media presentations that do the same.

Once children notice the vast array of gender stereotypes in their society, parents and teachers can point out exceptions. For example, they can arrange for children to see men and women pursuing nontraditional careers and can explain that interests and skills, not sex, should determine a person's occupation. Research shows that such reasoning is highly effective in reducing children's tendency to view the world in a gender-biased fashion. By middle childhood, children who hold flexible beliefs about what boys and girls can do are more likely to notice instances of gender discrimination (Brown & Bigler, 2004). And as we will see next, a rational approach to child rearing promotes healthy, adaptable functioning in many other areas as well.

ASK YOURSELF

REVIEW Explain how the social environment and young children's cognitive limitations jointly contribute to rigid gender stereotyping in early childhood.

APPLY List findings indicating that language and communication—between parents and children, between teachers and children, and between peers—powerfully affect children's gender typing. What recommendations would you make to counteract these influences?

REFLECT Would you describe your own gender identity as "masculine," "feminine," or androgynous? What biological and social factors might have influenced your gender identity?

Child Rearing and Emotional and Social Development

In this and previous chapters, we have seen how parents can foster children's competence—by building a parent–child relationship based on affection and cooperation, by serving as models and reinforcers of mature behavior, by using reasoning and inductive discipline, and by guiding and encouraging children's mastery of new skills. Now let's put these practices together into an overall view of effective parenting.

Styles of Child Rearing

Child-rearing styles are combinations of parenting behaviors that occur over a wide range of situations, creating an enduring child-rearing climate. In a landmark series of studies, Diana Baumrind (1971) gathered information on child rearing by watching parents interact with their preschoolers. Her findings, and those of others who have extended her work, reveal three features that consistently differentiate an effective style from less effective ones: (1) acceptance and involvement, (2) control, and (3) autonomy granting (Gray & Steinberg, 1999; Hart, Newell, & Olsen, 2003). Table 8.2 on page 218 shows how child-rearing styles differ in these features.

Authoritative Child Rearing. The **authoritative child-rearing style**—the most successful approach—involves high acceptance and involvement, adaptive control techniques, and

TABLE 8.2 **Features of Child-Rearing Styles**

CHILD-REARING STYLE	ACCEPTANCE AND INVOLVEMENT	CONTROL	AUTONOMY GRANTING
Authoritative	Is warm, responsive, attentive, patient, and sensitive to the child's needs	Makes reasonable demands for maturity and consistently enforces and explains them	Permits the child to make decisions in accord with readiness Encourages the child to express thoughts, feelings, and desires When parent and child disagree, engages in joint decision making when possible
Authoritarian	Is cold and rejecting and frequently degrades the child	Makes many demands coercively, using force and punishment Often uses psychological control, withdrawing love and intruding on the child's individuality	Makes decisions for the child Rarely listens to the child's point of view
Permissive	Is warm but overindulgent or inattentive	Makes few or no demands for maturity	Permits the child to make many decisions before the child is ready
Uninvolved	Is emotionally detached and withdrawn	Makes few or no demands for maturity	Is indifferent to the child's decision making and point of view

appropriate autonomy granting. Authoritative parents are warm, attentive, and sensitive, establishing an enjoyable, emotionally fulfilling parent–child relationship that draws the child into close connection. At the same time, authoritative parents exercise firm, reasonable control. They insist on appropriate maturity and give reasons for their expectations. Finally, authoritative parents engage in gradual, appropriate autonomy granting, allowing the child to make decisions in areas where he is ready to do so (Kuczynski & Lollis, 2002; Russell, Mize, & Bissaker, 2004).

Throughout childhood and adolescence, authoritative parenting is linked to many aspects of competence—an upbeat mood, self-control, task persistence, cooperativeness, high self-esteem, social and moral maturity, and favorable school performance (Amato & Fowler, 2002; Aunola, Stattin, & Nurmi, 2000; Gonzalez & Wolters, 2006; Mackey, Arnold, & Pratt, 2001; Milevsky et al., 2007; Steinberg, Darling, & Fletcher, 1995).

Authoritarian Child Rearing. The **authoritarian child-rearing style** is low in acceptance and involvement, high in coercive control, and low in autonomy granting. Authoritarian parents appear cold and rejecting. To exert control, they yell, command, criticize, and threaten, demanding unquestioning obedience. If the child resists, authoritarian parents resort to force and punishment.

Children of authoritarian parents are likely to be anxious, unhappy, and low in self-esteem and self-reliance. When frustrated, they tend to react with hostility and, like their parents, resort to force when they do not get their way. Boys, especially, show high rates of anger and defiance. Although girls also engage in acting-out behavior, they are more likely to be dependent and overwhelmed by challenging tasks (Hart, Newell, Olsen, 2003; Kakihara et al., 2010; Thompson, Hollis, & ...ds, 2003). Children and adolescents exposed to the

authoritarian style typically do poorly in school, but because of their parents' concern with control, they tend to achieve better than peers with undemanding parents—that is, whose parents use one of the styles we will consider next (Steinberg, Blatt-Eisengart, & Cauffman, 2006).

In addition to unwarranted direct control, authoritarian parents engage in a more subtle type called **psychological control**—behaviors that intrude on and manipulate children's verbal expression, individuality, and attachments to parents. In an attempt to decide virtually everything for the child, these parents frequently interrupt or put down the child's ideas, decisions, and choice of friends. When they are dissatisfied, they withdraw love, making their affection or attention contingent on the child's compliance. They also hold excessively high expectations that do not fit the child's developing capacities. Children subjected to psychological control exhibit adjustment problems involving both anxious, withdrawn behavior and defiance and aggression—especially the relational form, which (like parental psychological control) damages relationships through manipulation and exclusion (Barber et al., 2005; Kuppens et al., 2009; Nelson et al., 2006b; Silk et al., 2003).

Permissive Child Rearing. The **permissive child-rearing style** is warm and accepting but uninvolved. Permissive parents are either overindulgent or inattentive and, thus, engage in little control. Instead of gradually granting autonomy, they allow children to make many of their own decisions at an age when they are not yet capable of doing so. Their children can eat meals and go to bed whenever they wish and can watch as much television as they want. They do not have to learn good manners or do any household chores. Although some permissive parents truly believe in this approach, many others simply lack confidence in their ability to influence their child's behavior (Oyserman et al., 2005).

Children of permissive parents tend to be impulsive, disobedient, and rebellious. Compared with children whose parents exert more control, they are also overly demanding and dependent on adults, and they show less persistence on tasks, poorer school achievement, and more antisocial behavior (Barber & Olsen, 1997; Baumrind, 1971; Steinberg, Blatt-Eisengart, & Cauffman, 2006).

Uninvolved Child Rearing. The **uninvolved child-rearing style** combines low acceptance and involvement with little control and general indifference to issues of autonomy. Often these parents are emotionally detached and depressed and so overwhelmed by life stress that they have little time and energy for children. At its extreme, uninvolved parenting is a form of child maltreatment called *neglect*. Especially when it begins early, it disrupts virtually all aspects of development (see Chapter 6, page 145). Even with less extreme parental disengagement, children and adolescents display many problems—poor emotional self-regulation, school achievement difficulties, depression, anger, and antisocial behavior (Aunola, Stattin, & Nurmi, 2000; Kurdek & Fine, 1994; Schroeder et al., 2010).

What Makes Authoritative Child Rearing Effective?

Like all correlational findings, the relationship between the authoritative style and children's competence is open to interpretation. Perhaps parents of well-adjusted children are authoritative because their youngsters have especially cooperative dispositions. But although temperamentally fearless, impulsive children and emotionally negative, difficult children are more likely to evoke coercive, inconsistent discipline, extra warmth and firm control succeed in modifying these children's maladaptive styles (Cipriano & Stifter, 2010; Kochanska, Philibert, & Barry, 2009; Pettit et al., 2007). Furthermore, a variant of authoritativeness in which parents exert strong control—becoming directive but not coercive—yields just as favorable long-term outcomes as a more democratic approach (Baumrind, Larzelere, & Owens, 2010). Indeed, some children, because of their dispositions, require "heavier doses" of certain authoritative features.

In sum, authoritative child rearing seems to create a positive emotional context for parental influence in the following ways:

- Warm, involved parents who are secure in the standards they hold for their children provide models of caring concern as well as confident, self-controlled behavior.

- Children are far more likely to comply with and internalize control that appears fair and reasonable, not arbitrary.

- Authoritative parents appropriately make demands and grant autonomy. By conveying a sense of competence to their children, parents foster favorable self-esteem and cognitive and social maturity.

- Supportive aspects of the authoritative style are a powerful source of *resilience*, protecting children from the negative effects of family stress and poverty (Beyers et al., 2003).

LOOK AND LISTEN

Ask several parents to explain their style of child rearing, inquiring about acceptance and involvement, control, and autonomy granting. Look, especially, for variations in authoritativeness—more or less control over the child's behavior—along with parents' rationales. ●

Cultural Variations

Although authoritative parenting is broadly advantageous, parents of different ethnicities often have distinct child-rearing beliefs and practices that reflect cultural values. Let's take some examples.

Compared with Western parents, Chinese parents describe their parenting as more controlling. They are more directive in teaching and scheduling their children's time, as a way of fostering self-control and high achievement. Chinese parents may appear less warm than Western parents because they withhold praise, which they believe results in self-satisfied, poorly motivated children (Chao, 1994; Chen et al., 2001). Chinese parents report expressing affection and using induction and other reasoning-oriented discipline as much as American parents do (Cheah et al., 2009; Shwalb et al., 2004; Wu et al., 2002). When Chinese parents engage in psychological or coercive control, Chinese children display the same negative outcomes as Western children: poor academic achievement, anxiety, depression, and aggressive behavior (Chan, 2010; Nelson et al., 2006b; Pong, Johnston, & Chen, 2010).

In Hispanic families, Asian Pacific Island families, and Caribbean families of African and East Indian origins, firm insistence on respect for parental authority is paired with high parental warmth—a combination suited to promoting cognitive and social competence and family loyalty (Halgunseth, Ispa, & Rudy, 2006; Roopnarine & Evans, 2007). Hispanic fathers often spend much time with their children and are warm and sensitive (Cabrera & Bradley, 2012). In Caribbean families that have immigrated to the United States, fathers' authoritativeness—but not mothers'—predicted preschoolers' literacy and math skills, probably because Caribbean fathers take a larger role in guiding their children's academic progress (Roopnarine et al., 2006).

In low-SES African-American families, parents tend to expect immediate obedience, regarding strictness as fostering self-control and a watchful attitude in risky surroundings. Consistent with these beliefs, African-American parents who use more controlling strategies tend to have more cognitively and socially competent children (Brody & Flor, 1998). Recall, also, that a history of physical punishment is associated with a reduction in antisocial behavior among African-American youths but with an increase among Caucasian Americans (see page 209). Most African-American parents who use strict, "no-nonsense"

In Caribbean families of African origin, respect for parental authority is paired with high parental warmth—a combination that promotes competence and family loyalty.

discipline use physical punishment sparingly and combine it with warmth and reasoning.

These cultural variations remind us that child-rearing styles must be viewed in their larger context. As we have seen, many factors contribute to good parenting: personal characteristics of child and parent, SES, access to extended family and community supports, cultural values and practices, and public policies. As we turn to the topic of child maltreatment, our discussion will underscore, once again, that effective child rearing is sustained not just by the desire of mothers and fathers to be good parents. Almost all want to be. Unfortunately, when vital supports for parenting break down, children—as well as parents—can suffer terribly.

Child Maltreatment

Child maltreatment is as old as human history, but only recently has the problem been widely acknowledged and research aimed at understanding it. Perhaps public concern has increased because child maltreatment is especially common in large industrialized nations. In the most recently reported year, about 700,000 U.S. children (9 out of every 1,000) were identified as victims (U.S. Department of Health and Human Services, 2011b). Most cases go unreported, so the true figures are much higher.

Child maltreatment takes the following forms:

- *Physical abuse:* Assaults, such as kicking, biting, shaking, punching, or stabbing, that inflict physical injury

- *Sexual abuse:* Fondling, intercourse, exhibitionism, commercial exploitation through prostitution or production of pornography, and other forms of exploitation

- *Neglect:* Failure to meet a child's basic needs for food, clothing, medical attention, education, or supervision

- *Emotional abuse:* Acts that could cause serious mental or behavioral disorders, including social isolation, repeated unreasonable demands, ridicule, humiliation, intimidation, or terrorizing

Parents commit more than 80 percent of abusive incidents. Other relatives account for about 7 percent. The remainder are perpetrated by parents' unmarried partners, school officials, camp counselors, and other adults. Maternal and paternal rates of physical and emotional abuse are fairly similar. Infants and young preschoolers are at greatest risk for neglect; preschool and school-age children for physical, emotional, and sexual abuse (Trocmé & Wolfe, 2002; U.S. Department of Health and Human Services, 2011b). Because most sexual abuse victims are identified in middle childhood, we will pay special attention to this form of maltreatment in Chapter 10.

Origins of Child Maltreatment. For help in understanding child maltreatment, researchers turned to *ecological systems theory* (see Chapters 1 and 2). They discovered that many interacting variables—at the family, community, and cultural levels—contribute.

The Family. Within the family, children whose characteristics make them more challenging to rear are more likely to become targets of abuse. These include premature or very sick babies and children who are temperamentally difficult, are inattentive and overactive, or have other developmental problems. Child factors, however, only slightly increase the risk (Jaudes & Mackey-Bilaver, 2008; Sidebotham et al., 2003). Whether such children are maltreated largely depends on parents' characteristics.

Maltreating parents are less skillful than other parents in handling discipline confrontations. They also suffer from biased thinking about their child. For example, they often attribute their baby's crying or their child's misdeeds to a stubborn or bad disposition, evaluate child transgressions as worse than they are, and feel powerless in parenting—perspectives that lead them to move quickly toward physical force (Bugental & Happaney, 2004; Crouch et al., 2008).

Most parents have enough self-control not to respond with abuse to their child's misbehavior or developmental problems. Other factors combine with these conditions to prompt an extreme response. Abusive parents react to stressful situations with high emotional arousal. And low income, low education (less than a high school diploma), unemployment, alcohol and drug use, marital conflict, overcrowded living conditions, frequent moves, and extreme household disorganization are common in abusive homes (Wekerle et al., 2007; Wulczyn, 2009).

Each year, fourth to sixth graders across Los Angeles County enter a poster contest to celebrate National Child Abuse Prevention Month. This 2012 winner expresses a heartfelt appeal: "Don't Let Our Children Live in Fear." (Gillian Lih Bautista, 6th Grade, St. Genevieve Elementary, Panorama City, CA. Courtesy ICAN Associates, Los Angeles County Inter-Agency Council on Child Abuse and Neglect, ican4kids.org.)

These conditions increase the chances that parents will be too overwhelmed to meet basic child-rearing responsibilities or will vent their frustrations by lashing out at their children.

The Community. The majority of abusive and neglectful parents are isolated from both formal and informal social supports. Because of their life histories, many have learned to mistrust and avoid others and are poorly skilled at establishing and maintaining positive relationships. Also, maltreating parents are more likely to live in unstable, rundown neighborhoods that provide few links between family and community, such as preschool programs, recreation centers, and religious institutions (Coulton et al., 2007; Guterman et al., 2009). They lack "lifelines" to others and have no one to turn to for help during stressful times.

The Larger Culture. Cultural values, laws, and customs profoundly affect the chances that child maltreatment will occur when parents feel overburdened. Although the United States has laws to protect children from maltreatment, widespread support exists for use of physical force with children (refer back to page 208). Many countries—including Austria, Croatia, Cyprus, Denmark, Finland, Germany, Israel, Italy, Latvia, Norway, Sweden, and Uruguay—have outlawed corporal punishment, a measure that dampens both physical discipline and abuse (Zolotor & Puzia, 2010). Furthermore, all industrialized nations except the United States and France now prohibit corporal punishment in schools. The U.S. Supreme Court has twice upheld the right of school officials to use corporal punishment. Fortunately, 31 U.S. states and the District of Columbia have passed laws that ban it.

Consequences of Child Maltreatment. The family circumstances of maltreated children impair the development of emotional self-regulation, empathy and sympathy, self-concept, social skills, and academic motivation. Over time, these youngsters show serious adjustment problems—cognitive deficits (including impaired working memory and executive function), severe depression, aggressive behavior, peer difficulties, substance abuse, and violent crime—that persist into adulthood (Gould et al., 2010; Kaplow & Widom, 2007; Sanchez & Pollak, 2009).

How do these damaging consequences occur? Think back to our earlier discussion of hostile cycles of parent–child interaction. For abused children, these are especially severe. Also, a family characteristic strongly associated with child abuse is partner abuse (Graham-Bermann & Howell, 2011). Clearly, the home lives of abused children overflow with experiences that evoke profound distress and with opportunities to learn to use aggression to solve problems.

Furthermore, the trauma of repeated abuse is associated with central nervous system damage, including abnormal EEG brain-wave activity; fMRI-detected reduced size and impaired functioning of the cerebral cortex, corpus callosum, and cerebellum; and atypical production of the stress hormone cortisol—initially too high but, after months of abuse, often too low. Over time, the massive trauma of persistent abuse seems to blunt children's normal physiological response to stress (Cicchetti, 2007; Hart & Rubia, 2012). These effects increase the chances that cognitive and emotional problems will endure.

Preventing Child Maltreatment. Because child maltreatment is embedded in families, communities, and society as a whole, efforts to prevent it must be directed at each of these levels. Many approaches have been suggested, from teaching high-risk parents effective child-rearing strategies to developing broad social programs aimed at improving community services and economic conditions.

Providing social supports to families eases parental stress, sharply reducing child maltreatment. Parents Anonymous, a U.S. organization with affiliate programs around the world, helps child-abusing parents learn constructive parenting practices, largely through social supports. Its local chapters offer self-help group meetings, daily phone calls, and regular home visits to relieve social isolation and teach child-rearing skills.

Early intervention aimed at strengthening both child and parent competencies can reduce child maltreatment. Healthy Families America, a program that began in Hawaii and has spread to 440 sites across the United States and Canada, identifies at-risk families during pregnancy or at birth. Each receives three years of home visitation, in which a trained worker helps parents manage crises, encourages effective child rearing, and puts parents in touch with community services (Healthy Families America, 2011). In an evaluation of its effectiveness, Healthy Families home visitation alone reduced only neglect, not abuse (Duggan et al., 2004). But adding a *cognitive component* dramatically increased its impact. When home visitors helped parents change negative appraisals of their children, physical punishment and abuse dropped sharply after one year of intervention (Bugental et al., 2002).

Child maltreatment is a sad note on which to end our discussion of a period of childhood that is so full of excitement, awakening, and discovery. But there is reason to be optimistic. Great strides have been made over the past several decades in understanding and preventing child maltreatment.

ASK YOURSELF

REVIEW Is the concept of authoritative parenting useful for understanding effective parenting across cultures? Explain.

APPLY Chandra heard a news report about 10 severely neglected children, living in squalor in an inner-city tenement. She wondered, "Why would parents so mistreat their children?" How would you answer Chandra?

REFLECT How would you classify your parents' child-rearing styles? What factors might have influenced their approach to parenting?

SUMMARY

Erikson's Theory: Initiative versus Guilt (p. 200)

What personality changes take place during Erikson's stage of initiative versus guilt?

- Preschoolers develop a new sense of purposefulness as they grapple with Erikson's psychological conflict of **initiative versus guilt.** A healthy sense of initiative depends on exploring the social world through play, forming a conscience, and experiencing supportive parenting.

Self-Understanding (p. 201)

Describe preschoolers' self-concepts and the development of self-esteem.

- As preschoolers think more intently about themselves, they construct a **self-concept** consisting largely of observable characteristics and typical emotions and attitudes. A warm, sensitive parent–child relationship seems to foster a more positive, coherent early self-concept.

- During early childhood, high **self-esteem** contributes to a mastery-oriented approach to the environment. But even a little adult disapproval can undermine a young child's self-esteem and enthusiasm for learning.

Emotional Development (p. 202)

Identify changes in understanding and expressing emotion during early childhood, citing factors that influence those changes.

- Preschoolers' impressive understanding of the causes, consequences, and behavioral signs of basic emotions is supported by cognitive and language development, secure attachment, and conversations about feelings. By age 3 to 4, children are aware of various strategies for emotional self-regulation. Temperament and parental communication about coping strategies influence preschoolers' capacity to handle stress and negative emotion.

- As their self-concepts develop, preschoolers more often experience self-conscious emotions. They depend on feedback from parents and other adults to know when to feel each of these emotions.

- Empathy also becomes more common. Temperament and parenting influence the extent to which empathy leads to **sympathy** and results in **prosocial, or altruistic, behavior.**

Peer Relations (p. 203)

Describe peer sociability and friendship in early childhood, along with parental influences on early peer relations.

- During early childhood, peer interaction increases as children move from **nonsocial activity** to **parallel play,** then to **associative** and **cooperative play.** Nevertheless, both solitary and parallel play remain common.

- Preschoolers understand something about the uniqueness of friendship, but their friendships do not yet have an enduring quality. Children's social maturity contributes to later academic performance. Parents affect peer sociability both directly, through attempts to influence their child's peer relations, and indirectly, through their child-rearing practices.

Foundations of Morality (p. 206)

What are the central features of psychoanalytic, social learning, and cognitive-developmental approaches to moral development?

- Psychoanalytic theory emphasizes the emotional side of moral development, especially identification and guilt as motivators of good conduct. Contrary to Freud's theory, conscience formation is promoted not by fear of punishment and loss of parental love but by **induction,** in which an adult points out the effects of the child's misbehavior on others.

© AGE FOTOSTOCK/ROBERT HARDING

- Social learning theory focuses on how moral behavior is learned through reinforcement and modeling. Effective adult models of prosocial responses are warm and powerful, and they practice what they preach.

- Alternatives to harsh punishment such as **time out** and withdrawal of privileges can help parents avoid undesirable side effects of punishment. Parents can increase the effectiveness of punishment by being consistent, maintaining a warm parent–child relationship, and offering explanations.

- The cognitive-developmental perspective views children as active thinkers about social rules. By age 4, children consider intentions in making moral judgments. Preschoolers also distinguish **moral imperatives** from **social conventions** and **matters of personal choice.** However, they tend to reason rigidly about morality, focusing on outcomes and on physical harm.

Describe the development of aggression in early childhood, including family and media influences and effective approaches to reducing aggressive behavior.

- During early childhood, **proactive aggression** declines while **reactive aggression** increases. Proactive and reactive aggression come in three forms: **physical aggression** (more common in boys), **verbal aggression,** and **relational aggression.**

- Ineffective discipline and a conflict-ridden family atmosphere promote children's aggression, as does media violence. Effective approaches to reducing aggressive behavior include training parents in effective child-rearing practices, teaching children conflict-resolution skills, helping parents cope with stressors in their own lives, and shielding children from violent media.

Gender Typing (p. 213)

Discuss genetic and environmental influences on preschoolers' gender-stereotyped beliefs and behavior.

- **Gender typing** is well under way in the preschool years. Preschoolers acquire a wide range of gender-stereotyped beliefs, often applying them rigidly.

- Prenatal sex hormones contribute to boys' higher activity level and rougher play and to children's preference for same-sex playmates. But parents, teachers, peers, and the broader social environment also encourage many gender-typed responses.

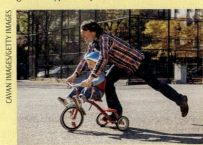

CAVAN IMAGES/GETTY IMAGES

Describe and evaluate theories that explain the emergence of gender identity.

- Although most people have a traditional **gender identity,** some are **androgynous,** combining both masculine and feminine characteristics. Masculine and androgynous identities are linked to better psychological adjustment.

- According to social learning theory, preschoolers first acquire gender-typed responses through modeling and reinforcement and then organize these behaviors into gender-linked ideas about themselves. Cognitive-developmental theory maintains that children must master **gender constancy** before they develop gender-typed behavior.

- **Gender schema theory** combines features of social learning and cognitive-developmental perspectives. As children acquire gender-typed preferences and behaviors, they form masculine and feminine categories, or gender schemas, that they apply to themselves and their world.

Child Rearing and Emotional and Social Development (p. 217)

Describe the impact of child-rearing styles on children's development, and note cultural variations in child rearing.

- Three features distinguish **child-rearing styles:** (1) acceptance and involvement, (2) control, and (3) autonomy granting. In contrast to the **authoritarian, permissive, and uninvolved** styles, the **authoritative style** promotes cognitive, emotional, and social competence. Warmth, explanations, and reasonable demands for mature behavior account for the effectiveness of this style. **Psychological control,** associated with authoritarian parenting, contributes to adjustment problems.

- Certain ethnic groups, including Chinese, Hispanic, Asian Pacific Island, and African-American, combine parental warmth with high levels of control. But when control becomes harsh and excessive, it impairs academic and social competence.

Discuss the multiple origins of child maltreatment, its consequences for development, and effective prevention.

- Maltreating parents use ineffective discipline, hold a negatively biased view of their child, and feel powerless in parenting. Unmanageable parental stress and social isolation greatly increase the likelihood of abuse and neglect. Societal approval of physical force as a means of solving problems promotes child abuse.

- Maltreated children are impaired in emotional self-regulation, empathy and sympathy, self-concept, social skills, and academic motivation. The trauma of repeated abuse is associated with central nervous system damage and serious, lasting adjustment problems. Successful prevention requires efforts at the family, community, and societal levels.

Important Terms and Concepts

milestones

Development in Early Childhood

PHYSICAL

- Running, jumping, hopping, throwing, and catching become better coordinated. (173)
- Pedals and steers tricycle. (173)

© LAURA DWIGHT PHOTOGRAPHY

- Galloping and one-foot skipping appear. (173)
- Fastens and unfastens large buttons. (173)
- Uses scissors. (173)
- Uses fork effectively. (173)
- Draws first picture of a person, using tadpole image. (174)

COGNITIVE

- Understands the symbolic function of drawings and of models of real-world spaces. (174, 176–177)
- Distinguishes appearance from reality. (177)
- Grasps conservation, reasons about transformations, reverses thinking, and understands cause–effect sequences in familiar contexts. (178)
- Sorts familiar objects into hierarchically organized categories. (178)
- Uses private speech to guide behavior during challenging tasks. (182)
- Improves in sustained attention. (185)
- Uses scripts to recall familiar events. (185)
- Understands that both beliefs and desires determine behavior. (186)
- Knows the meaning of numbers up to 10, counts correctly, and grasps cardinality. (189)

© ELLEN B. SENISI PHOTOGRAPHY

- Takes the perspective of others in simplified, familiar situations and in face-to-face communication. (179)
- Recognition memory is well-developed. (185)
- Shows awareness of the distinction between inner mental and outer physical events. (186)
- Begins to count. (189)

LANGUAGE

- Vocabulary increases rapidly. (193)
- Uses a coalition of cues—perceptual and, increasingly, social and linguistic—to figure out word meanings. (194)
- Speaks in simple sentences that follow basic word order of native language, gradually adding grammatical markers. (194–195)
- Displays effective conversational skills. (195)

EMOTIONAL/SOCIAL

- Understands causes, consequences, and behavioral signs of basic emotions. (202)
- Begins to develop self-concept and self-esteem. (201)
- Shows early signs of developing moral sense—verbal evaluations of own and others' actions and distress at harmful behaviors. (206)
- May display proactive (instrumental) aggression. (211)
- Gender-stereotyped beliefs and behavior increase. (213)

© ELLEN B. SENISI PHOTOGRAPHY

2 years

PHYSICAL

- Throughout early childhood, height and weight increase more slowly than in toddlerhood. (167)
- Balance improves; walks more rhythmically; hurried walk changes to run. (173)
- Jumps, hops, throws, and catches with rigid upper body. (173)
- Puts on and removes simple items of clothing. (173)
- Uses spoon effectively. (173)
- First drawings are gestural scribbles. (174)

COGNITIVE

- Make-believe becomes less dependent on realistic objects, less self-centered, and more complex; sociodramatic play increases. (175–176)
- Understands the symbolic function of photos and realistic-looking pictures. (176–177)

Note: Numbers in parentheses indicate the page or pages on which each milestone is discussed.

LANGUAGE

- Aware of some meaningful features of written language. (187–188)
- Coins new words based on known words; extends language meanings through metaphor. (194)
- Masters increasingly complex grammatical structures, occasionally overextending grammatical rules to exceptions. (195)
- Adjusts speech to fit the age, sex, and social status of listeners. (195)

EMOTIONAL/SOCIAL

- Describes self in terms of observable characteristics and typical emotions and attitudes. (201)
- Has several self-esteems, such as learning things in school, making friends, getting along with parents, and treating others kindly. (201)
- Emotional self-regulation improves. (202)
- Experiences self-conscious emotions more often. (202)
- Relies more on language to express empathy. (203)

- Engages in associative and cooperative play with peers, in addition to parallel play. (204)
- Forms first friendships, based on pleasurable play and sharing of toys. (205)
- Distinguishes truthfulness from lying. (210)
- Distinguishes moral imperatives from social conventions and matters of personal choice. (210)
- Proactive aggression declines, while reactive aggression (verbal and relational) increases. (211)
- Preference for same-sex playmates strengthens. (214)

5–6 years

PHYSICAL

- Starts to lose primary teeth. (167)
- Increases running speed, gallops more smoothly, and engages in true skipping. (173)
- Displays mature, flexible throwing and catching patterns. (173)
- Uses knife to cut soft foods. (173)
- Ties shoes. (173–174)

- Draws more complex pictures. (174)
- Copies some numbers and simple words; prints name. (174)

COGNITIVE

- Magical beliefs decline. (179)
- Improves in ability to distinguish appearance from reality. (177)

- Improves in sustained attention and planning. (185)
- Recognition, recall, scripted memory, and autobiographical memory improve. (185–186)

- Understanding of false belief strengthens. (186)

LANGUAGE

- Understands that letters and sounds are linked in systematic ways. (188)
- Uses invented spellings. (188)
- By age 6, vocabulary reaches about 10,000 words. (193)
- Uses most grammatical constructions competently. (195)

EMOTIONAL/SOCIAL

- Improves in emotional understanding (ability to interpret, predict, and influence others' emotional reactions). (202)

- Has acquired many morally relevant rules and behaviors. (207)
- Gender-stereotyped beliefs and behavior and preference for same-sex playmates continue to strengthen. (214)
- Understands gender constancy. (215–216)

225

Physical and Cognitive Development in Middle Childhood

© ELLEN B. SENISI PHOTOGRAPHY

During a science lesson, sixth graders use a map to chart catastrophic weather events around the world. An improved capacity to remember, reason, and reflect on one's own thinking makes middle childhood a time of dramatic advances in academic learning and problem solving.

chapter outline

"I'm on my way, Mom!" hollered 10-year-old Joey as he stuffed the last bite of toast into his mouth, slung his book bag over his shoulder, dashed out the door, jumped on his bike, and headed down the street for school. Joey's 8-year-old sister Lizzie followed, pedaling furiously until she caught up with Joey.

"They're branching out," Rena, the children's mother and one of my colleagues at the university, told me over lunch that day as she described the children's expanding activities and relationships. Homework, household chores, soccer teams, music lessons, scouting, friends at school and in the neighborhood, and Joey's new paper route were all part of the children's routine. "It seems the basics are all there. Being a parent is still challenging, but it's more a matter of refinements—helping them become independent, competent, and productive."

Joey and Lizzie have entered middle childhood—the years from 6 to 11. Around the world, children of this age are assigned new responsibilities. For children in industrialized nations, middle childhood is often called the "school years" because its onset is marked by the start of formal schooling. In village and tribal cultures, the school may be a field or a jungle. But universally in this period, children are guided by mature members of society toward real-world tasks that increasingly resemble those they will perform as adults.

By age 6, the brain has reached 90 percent of its adult weight, and the body continues to grow slowly. In this way, nature gives school-age children the mental powers to master challenging tasks as well as added time to acquire the knowledge and skills essential for life in a complex social world.

We begin by reviewing typical growth trends, gains in motor skills, and health concerns. Then we return to Piaget's theory and the information-processing approach for an overview of cognitive changes. Next, we examine genetic and environmental contributions to IQ scores and the further blossoming of language. Finally, we turn to the importance of schools in children's learning and development. ●

PHYSICAL DEVELOPMENT

Body Growth

Physical growth during the school years continues at the slow, regular pace of early childhood. At age 6, the average North American child weighs about 45 pounds and is 3½ feet tall. Over the next few years, children add about 2 to 3 inches in height and 5 pounds in weight each year (see Figure 9.1 on page 228). Between ages 6 and 8, girls are slightly shorter and lighter than boys. By age 9, this trend reverses as girls approach the dramatic adolescent growth spurt, which occurs two years earlier in girls than in boys.

Because the lower portion of the body is growing fastest, Joey and Lizzie appeared longer-legged than they had in early childhood. Girls continue to have slightly more body fat and boys more muscle. After age 8, girls begin accumulating fat at a faster rate, and they will add even more during adolescence (Siervogel et al., 2000).

During middle childhood, the bones of the body lengthen and broaden. But ligaments are not yet firmly attached to bones; this, combined with increasing muscle strength, gives children the unusual flexibility needed to perform cartwheels and handstands. As their bodies become stronger, many children experience a greater desire for physical exercise. Nighttime "growing pains"—stiffness and aches in the legs—are common as muscles adapt to an enlarging skeleton (Evans, 2008).

Between ages 6 and 12, all 20 primary teeth are lost and replaced by permanent ones, with girls losing their teeth slightly earlier than boys. For a while, the permanent teeth seem much too large. Gradually, growth of facial bones, especially the jaw and chin, causes the child's face to lengthen and mouth to widen, accommodating the newly erupting teeth.

Health Issues

Children from economically advantaged homes, like Joey and Lizzie, are at their healthiest in middle childhood, full of energy and play. The cumulative effects of good nutrition, combined with rapid development of the body's immune system, offer greater protection against disease. At the same time, growth in lung size permits more air to be exchanged with each breath, so children are better able to exercise vigorously without tiring.

Not surprisingly, poverty continues to be a powerful predictor of ill health during the school years. Because economically disadvantaged U.S. families often lack health insurance, many children do not have regular access to a doctor. A substantial number also lack such basic necessities as regular meals.

Nutrition

School-age children need a well-balanced, plentiful diet to provide energy for learning and increased physical activity. With their increasing focus on friendships and new activities, many children spend little time at the table, and the percentage who eat dinner with their families drops sharply between ages 9 and 14. Yet eating an evening meal with parents leads to a diet higher in fruits, vegetables, grains, and milk products and lower in soft drinks and fast foods (Burgess-Champoux et al., 2009; Fiese & Schwartz, 2008).

PHOTOS COURTESY OF PATRICIA SELFE

Andy at 8 years

Andy at 6 years

Andy at 10½ years

Andy at 9 years

Amy at 8 years

Amy at 6 years

Amy at 9 years

Amy at 10½ years

FIGURE 9.1 **Body growth during middle childhood.** School-age children continue the slow, regular pattern of growth they showed in early childhood. But around age 9, girls begin to grow at a faster rate than boys. At age 10½, Amy was taller, heavier, and more mature-looking than Andy.

As we saw in earlier chapters, many poverty-stricken children in developing countries and in the United States suffer from serious and prolonged malnutrition. Unfortunately, malnutrition that persists from infancy or early childhood into the school years usually leads to permanent physical and mental damage (Grantham-McGregor, Walker, & Chang, 2000; Liu et al., 2003). Government-sponsored supplementary food programs from the early years through adolescence can prevent these effects.

Overweight and Obesity

Mona, a very heavy child in Lizzie's class, often watched from the sidelines during recess. When she did join in games, she was slow and clumsy. Most afternoons, she walked home from school alone while the other children gathered in groups, talking, laughing, and chasing. At home, Mona sought comfort in high-calorie snacks.

Mona suffers from **obesity,** a greater-than-20-percent increase over healthy weight, based on *body mass index (BMI)*— a ratio of weight to height associated with body fat. (A BMI above the 85th percentile for a child's age and sex is considered *overweight,* a BMI above the 95th percentile *obese.*) During the past several decades, a rise in overweight and obesity has occurred

in many Western nations. Today, 32 percent of U.S. children and adolescents are overweight, more than half of them extremely so: 17 percent are obese—trends that are worsening (Ogden et al., 2010; World Health Organization, 2012c, 2013a).

Obesity rates are also increasing rapidly in developing countries, as urbanization shifts the population toward sedentary lifestyles and diets high in meats and energy-dense refined foods (World Health Organization, 2012c, 2013a). In China, for example, 20 percent of children are overweight and 7 percent obese—a nearly fivefold increase over the past 25 years, with boys affected more than girls (Ding, 2008). In addition to lifestyle changes, a prevailing belief in Chinese culture that excess body fat signifies prosperity and health—carried over from a half-century ago, when famine caused millions of deaths—has contributed to this alarming upsurge. High valuing of sons may induce Chinese parents to offer boys especially generous portions of energy-dense foods.

Overweight increases with age, from 21 percent among U.S. preschoolers to 35 percent among school-age children and adolescents. An estimated 70 percent of affected teenagers become overweight adults (U.S. Department of Health and Human Services, 2011e). High blood pressure, high cholesterol levels, respiratory abnormalities, and insulin resistance are powerful

© OCEAN/CORBIS

Parental unhealthy feeding practices—frequent take-out meals consisting of foods high in calories and fat—and a physically inactive lifestyle play major roles in these siblings' excessive weight gain.

predictors of heart disease, circulatory difficulties, type 2 diabetes, gallbladder disease, sleep and digestive disorders, many forms of cancer, and early death (Krishnamoorthy, Hart, & Jelalian, 2006; World Cancer Research Fund, 2007). Furthermore, obesity has caused a dramatic rise in cases of diabetes in children, sometimes leading to early, severe complications, including stroke, kidney failure, and circulatory problems that heighten the risk of blindness and leg amputation (Hannon, Rao, & Arslanian, 2005).

Causes of Obesity. Overweight children tend to have overweight parents, and identical twins are more likely to share the disorder than fraternal twins. But heredity accounts for only a *tendency* to gain weight (Kral & Faith, 2009). The importance of environment is apparent in the consistent relationship of low SES to overweight and obesity in industrialized nations, especially among ethnic minorities—in the United States, African-American, Hispanic, and Native-American children and adults (Anand et al., 2001; Ogden et al., [...] ctors responsible include lack of knowledge about hea[...], a tendency to buy high-fat, low-cost foods; and famil[...] which can prompt overeating. Recall, also, that childre[...] ere undernourished in their early years are at risk for l[...] sive weight gain (see page 102 in Chapter 4).

Parental feeding practices [...] a role. Some parents anxiously overfeed, interpreting [...] ll their child's discomforts as a desire for food. Others [...] sure their children to eat, a practice common among immigrant parents and grandparents who, as children themselves, survived periods of food deprivation. Still other parents are overly controlling, restricting when, what, and how much their child eats and constantly worrying about weight gain (Moens, Braet, & Soetens, 2007). In each case, parents fail to help children learn to regulate their own food

intake. Also, parents of overweight children often use high-fat, sugary foods to reinforce other behaviors, leading children to attach great value to treats (Sherry et al., 2004). Because of these experiences, obese children develop maladaptive eating habits. They are more responsive than normal-weight individuals to external stimuli associated with food—taste, sight, smell, time of day, and food-related words—and less responsive to internal hunger cues (Jansen et al., 2003; Temple et al., 2007).

Another factor consistently associated with weight gain is insufficient sleep (Nielsen, Danielsen, & Sørensen, 2011). Reduced sleep may increase time available for eating, leave children too fatigued for physical activity, or disrupt the brain's regulation of hunger and metabolism.

Overweight children are less physically active than their normal-weight peers, which is both cause and consequence of excessive weight gain. Research reveals that the rise in childhood obesity is due in part to the many hours U.S. children spend watching television. In a study that tracked children's TV viewing from ages 4 to 11, the more TV children watched, the more body fat they added (Proctor et al., 2003). Watching TV reduces time spent in physical exercise, and TV ads encourage children to eat fattening, unhealthy snacks. Children permitted to have a TV in their bedroom—a practice linked to especially high TV viewing—are at even further risk for overweight (Adachi-Mejia et al., 2007).

Finally, the broader food environment affects the incidence of obesity. Over the past three decades, the number of families who frequently eat meals outside the home has risen dramatically. Eating in restaurants or at relatives', neighbors', or friends' homes, as opposed to at home, substantially increases children's overall food consumption, including high-calorie drinks, fast foods, and snacks, and their risk of weight gain (Ayala et al., 2008; Poti & Popkin, 2011).

Psychological Consequences of Obesity. Unfortunately, physical attractiveness is a powerful predictor of social acceptance. In Western societies, both children and adults stereotype obese youngsters as lazy, sloppy, ugly, stupid, self-doubting, and deceitful (Kilpatrick & Sanders, 1978; Penny & Haddock, 2007; Tiggemann & Anesbury, 2000). In school, obese children and adolescents are often socially isolated. They report more emotional, social, and school difficulties, including peer teasing and consequent low self-esteem, depression, and (among obese teenagers) suicidal thoughts and suicide attempts. Persistent obesity from childhood into adolescence predicts serious disorders, including defiance, aggression, and severe depression (Puhl & Latner, 2007; Young-Hyman et al., 2006). These psychological consequences combine with continuing discrimination to result in reduced life chances in close relationships and employment.

Treating Obesity. The most effective interventions are family-based and focus on changing behaviors (Oude et al., 2009). In Mona's case, the school nurse suggested that Mona and her obese mother enter a weight-loss program together. But

Mona's mother, unhappily married for many years, had her own reasons for overeating and rejected this idea. In one program, both parent and child revised eating patterns, exercised daily, and reinforced each other with praise and points for progress, which they exchanged for special activities and times together. The more weight parents lost, the more their children lost (Wrotniak et al., 2004). Follow-ups after five and ten years showed that children maintained their weight loss more effectively than adults—a finding that underscores the importance of early intervention (Epstein, Roemmich, & Raynor, 2001). But diet and lifestyle interventions work best when parents' and children's weight problems are not severe (Nemet et al., 2005).

Because obesity is expected to rise further without broad prevention strategies, many U.S. states and cities have passed obesity-reduction legislation (Levi et al., 2009). Among measures taken are weight-related school screenings for all children, improved school nutrition standards, additional school recess time and physical education, school-based obesity awareness and weight-reduction programs, and menu nutrition labeling (including calorie counts) in chain and fast-food restaurants.

LOOK AND LISTEN

Contact your state government to find out about its childhood obesity prevention legislation. Can its policies be improved? ●

Illnesses

Children experience a somewhat higher rate of illness during the first two years of elementary school than later because of exposure to sick children and an immune system that is still developing. About 15 to 20 percent of U.S. children have chronic diseases and conditions (including physical disabilities) (Van Cleave, Gortmaker, & Perrin, 2010). By far the most common—accounting for about one-third of childhood chronic illness and the most frequent cause of school absence and childhood hospitalization—is *asthma,* in which the bronchial tubes (passages that connect the throat and lungs) are highly sensitive (Bonilla et al., 2005). In response to a variety of stimuli, such as cold weather, infection, exercise, allergies, and emotional stress, they fill with mucus and contract, leading to coughing, wheezing, and serious breathing difficulties.

From 1980 to 1997, the prevalence of asthma among U.S. children more than doubled and then stabilized at 9 percent (Akinbami et al., 2009). Although heredity contributes to asthma, environmental factors seem necessary to spark the illness. Boys, African-American children, and children who were born underweight, whose parents smoke, or who live in poverty are at greatest risk (Federico & Liu, 2003; Pearlman et al., 2006). For African-American and poverty-stricken children, pollution in inner-city areas (which triggers allergic reactions), stressful home lives, and lack of access to good health care are implicated. Childhood obesity is also related to asthma, perhaps due to high levels of blood-circulating inflammatory substances associated with body fat (Story, 2007).

About 2 percent of U.S. children have more severe chronic illnesses, such as sickle cell anemia, diabetes, arthritis, cancer, and AIDS. Painful medical treatments, physical discomfort, and changes in appearance often disrupt the sick child's daily life, making it difficult to concentrate in school and separating the child from peers. As the illness worsens, family stress increases (LeBlanc, Goldsmith, & Patel, 2003). For these reasons, chronically ill children are at risk for academic, emotional, and social difficulties.

A strong link exists between good family functioning and child well-being for chronically ill children, just as it does for physically healthy children (Drotar et al., 2006). Interventions that foster positive family relationships help parent and child cope with the disease and improve children's adjustment. These include health education, counseling, parent and peer support groups, and disease-specific summer camps, which teach children self-help skills and give parents time off from the demands of caring for an ill youngster.

 # Motor Development and Play

TAKE A MOMENT... Visit a park on a pleasant weekend afternoon, and watch several preschool and school-age children at play. You will see that gains in body size and muscle strength support improved motor coordination in middle childhood. And greater cognitive and social maturity enables older children to use their new motor skills in more complex ways.

Gross-Motor Development

During the school years, running, jumping, hopping, and ball skills become more refined. Third to sixth graders burst into sprints as they race across the playground, jump quickly over rotating ropes, engage in intricate hopscotch patterns, kick and dribble soccer balls, bat at balls pitched by their classmates, and balance adeptly as they walk heel-to-toe across narrow ledges. These diverse skills reflect gains in four basic motor capacities:

- *Flexibility.* Compared with preschoolers, school-age children are physically more pliable and elastic, a difference evident as they swing bats, kick balls, jump over hurdles, and execute tumbling routines.

- *Balance.* Improved balance supports many athletic skills, including running, skipping, throwing, kicking, and the rapid changes of direction required in team sports.

- *Agility.* Quicker and more accurate movements are evident in the fancy footwork of dance and cheerleading and in the forward, backward, and sideways motions used to dodge opponents in tag and soccer.

- *Force.* Older youngsters can throw and kick a ball harder and propel themselves farther off the ground when running and jumping (Haywood & Getchell, 2009).

Improved physical flexibility, balance, agility, and force, along with more efficient information processing, are evident in these 8-year-olds' soccer skills.

Along with body growth, more efficient information processing contributes greatly to improved motor performance. During middle childhood, the capacity to react only to relevant information increases. And steady gains in reaction time occur, with 11-year-olds responding twice as quickly as 5-year-olds (Kail, 2003; Largo et al., 2001). Because 6- and 7-year-olds are seldom successful at batting a thrown ball, T-ball is more appropriate for them than baseball. Similarly, handball, four-square, and kickball should precede instruction in tennis, basketball, and football.

Fine-Motor Development

Fine-motor development also improves over the school years. By age 6, most children can print the alphabet, their first and last names, and the numbers from 1 to 10 with reasonable clarity. Their writing is large, however, because they make strokes with the entire arm rather than just the wrist and fingers. Children usually master uppercase letters first because their horizontal and vertical motions are easier to control than the small curves of the lowercase alphabet. Legibility of writing gradually increases as children produce more accurate letters with uniform height and spacing. These improvements prepare children for mastering cursive writing by third grade.

By the end of the preschool years, children can accurately copy many two-dimensional shapes, and they integrate these into their drawings. Some depth cues have also begun to appear, such as making distant objects smaller than near ones (Braine et al., 1993). Around 9 to 10 years, the third dimension is clearly evident through overlapping objects, diagonal placement, and converging lines. Furthermore, as Figure 9.2 shows, school-age children not only depict objects in considerable detail but also relate them to one another as part of an organized whole (Case, 1998).

Sex Differences

Sex differences in motor skills extend into middle childhood and, in some instances, become more pronounced. Girls have an edge in fine-motor skills of handwriting and drawing and in gross-motor capacities that depend on balance and agility, such as hopping and skipping. But boys outperform girls on all other gross-motor skills, especially throwing and kicking (Cratty, 1986; Haywood & Getchell, 2009).

School-age boys' genetic advantage in muscle mass is not large enough to account for their gross-motor superiority. Rather, social experiences play a larger role. Parents hold higher expectations for boys' athletic performance, and children readily absorb these messages. From first through twelfth grades, girls are less positive than boys about the value of sports and their own sports ability (Fredricks & Eccles, 2002). The more

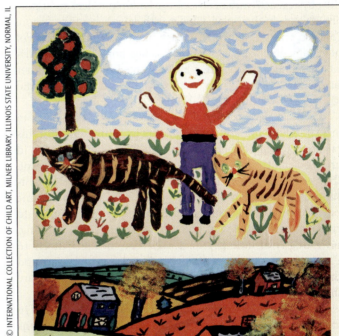

FIGURE 9.2 Organization, detail, and depth in school-age children's drawings. In the drawing by an 8-year-old on the top, notice how all parts are depicted in relation to one another and with greater detail. Integration of depth cues increases dramatically over the school years, as shown in the drawing on the bottom, by an 11-year-old. Here, the third dimension is indicated by overlapping objects and diagonal lines, as well as by making distant objects appear smaller than near ones.

strongly girls believe that females are incompetent at sports (such as hockey or soccer), the lower they judge their own ability and the poorer they actually perform (Belcher et al., 2003; Chalabaev, Sarrazin & Fontayne, 2009).

Educating parents about the minimal differences between school-age boys' and girls' physical capacities and sensitizing them to unfair biases against promotion of girls' athletic ability may help increase girls' self-confidence and participation in athletics. And greater emphasis on skill training for girls, along with increased attention to their athletic achievements, is also likely to help. As a positive sign, compared with a generation ago, many more girls now participate in individual and team sports such as gymnastics and soccer (National Council of Youth Sports, 2008; Sabo & Veliz, 2011).

Games with Rules

The physical activities of school-age children reflect an important advance in their play: Games with rules become common. Children around the world engage in an enormous variety of informally organized games, such as tag, hopscotch, and variants of popular sports. They have invented hundreds of other games, including red rover, statues, leapfrog, kick the can, and prisoner's base (Kirchner, 2000).

Gains in perspective taking—in particular, the ability to understand the roles of several players in a game—permit this transition to rule-oriented games. These play experiences, in turn, contribute greatly to emotional and social development. Child-invented games usually rely on simple physical skills and a sizable element of luck. As a result, they rarely become contests of individual ability. Instead, they permit children to try out different styles of cooperating, competing, winning, and losing with little personal risk. Also, in their efforts to organize a game, children discover why rules are necessary and which ones work well—experiences that foster more mature concepts of fairness and justice.

School-age children today spend less time engaged in informal outdoor play—a change that reflects parental concerns about neighborhood safety as well as competition for children's time from TV, video games, and the Internet. Another factor is the rise in adult-organized sports, such as Little League baseball and soccer and hockey leagues, which fill many hours that children used to devote to spontaneous play. About half of U.S. children—60 percent of boys and 37 percent of girls—participate in organized sports at some time between ages 5 and 18 (National Council of Youth Sports, 2008).

For most children, joining community athletic teams is associated with increased self-esteem and social skills (Daniels & Leaper, 2006; Fletcher, Nickerson, & Wright, 2003). Among shy children, sports participation seems to foster self-confidence and a decline in social anxiety (Findlay & Coplan, 2008). And children who view themselves as good at sports are more likely to continue playing on teams in adolescence, which predicts greater participation in sports and other physical fitness activities in early adulthood (Kjønniksen, Anderssen, & Wold, 2009; Marsh et al., 2007). In some cases, though, youth

With their coach's encouragement, these young softball players are likely to view themselves as good at sports and to continue playing.

sports overemphasize competition and adult control. Coaches and parents who criticize rather than encourage can prompt intense anxiety in some children, setting the stage for emotional difficulties and early athletic dropout (Tofler, Knapp, & Drell, 1998; Wall & Côté, 2007). By permitting children to select an appropriate sport on the basis of their interests, encouraging them to contribute to rules and strategies, and emphasizing effort, skill gains, and teamwork rather than winning, adults can ensure that athletic leagues provide positive learning experiences.

LOOK AND LISTEN

Observe a youth athletic league game, such as soccer, baseball, or hockey. Do coaches and parents encourage children's effort and skill gains, or are they overly focused on winning? Cite examples of adult and child behaviors. ●

Shadows of Our Evolutionary Past

TAKE A MOMENT... While watching children in your neighborhood park, notice how they sometimes wrestle, roll, hit, and run after one another, alternating roles while smiling and laughing. This friendly chasing and play-fighting is called **rough-and-tumble play.** It emerges in the preschool years and peaks in middle childhood, and children in many cultures engage in it with peers whom they like especially well (Pellegrini, 2004).

Children's rough-and-tumble play resembles the social behavior of many other young mammals. It is more common among boys, probably because prenatal exposure to androgens (male sex hormones) predisposes boys toward active play (see Chapter 8). In our evolutionary past, rough-and-tumble play may have been important for developing fighting skill. Children seem to use play-fighting as a safe context to assess the strength of peers so they can refrain from challenging agemates with whom they are not well-matched physically (Pellegrini & Smith, 1998; Roseth et al., 2007).

Social Issues: Education

School Recess—A Time to Play, a Time to Learn

When 7-year-old Whitney's family moved to a new city, she left a school with three daily recess periods for one with just a single 15-minute break per day, which her second-grade teacher cancelled if any child misbehaved. Whitney, who had previously enjoyed school, complained daily of headaches and an upset stomach. Her mother, Jill, thought, "My child is stressing out because she can't move all day!" After Jill and other parents successfully appealed to the school board to add a second recess period, Whitney's symptoms vanished (Rauber, 2006).

In recent years, recess—with its rich opportunities for child-organized play and peer interaction—has diminished or disappeared in many U.S. elementary schools (Ginsburg, 2007; Pellegrini & Holmes, 2006). Under the assumption that extra time for academics will translate into achievement gains, 7 percent of U.S. schools no longer provide recess to students as young as second grade. And over half of schools that do have recess now schedule it just once a day (U.S. Department of Education, 2012b).

Yet rather than subtracting from classroom learning, recess periods boost it!

Research dating back more than a century confirms that distributing cognitively demanding tasks over a longer time by introducing regular breaks enhances attention and performance at all ages. Such breaks are particularly important for children. In a series of studies, elementary school students were more attentive in the classroom after recess than before it—an effect that was greater for second than fourth graders (Pellegrini, Huberty, & Jones, 1995). Teacher ratings of classroom disruptive behavior also decline for children who have more than 15 minutes of recess a day (Barros, Silver, & Stein, 2009).

In other research, kindergartners' and first graders' engagement in peer conversation and games during recess positively predicted academic achievement, even after other factors that might explain the relationship (such

Recess offers rich opportunities for child-organized play and games that provide practice in social skills while also promoting physical and academic competence.

as previous achievement) were controlled (Pellegrini, 1992; Pellegrini et al., 2002). Recall from Chapter 8 that children's social maturity contributes substantially to academic competence. Recess is one of the few remaining contexts devoted to child-organized games that provide practice in vital social skills—cooperation, leadership, followership, and inhibition of aggression—under adult supervision rather than adult direction. As children transfer these skills to the classroom, they may participate in discussions, collaborate, follow rules, and enjoy academic pursuits more—factors that enhance motivation and achievement.

In our evolutionary past, rough-and-tumble play—which can be distinguished from aggression by its friendly quality—may have been important for developing fighting skill.

As children reach puberty, individual differences in strength become apparent, and rough-and-tumble play declines. When it does occur, its meaning changes: Adolescent boys' rough-and-tumble is linked to aggression (Pellegrini, 2003). Unlike children, teenage rough-and-tumble players "cheat," hurting their opponent. In explanation, boys often say that they are retaliating, apparently to reestablish dominance. Thus, a play behavior that limits aggression in childhood becomes a context for hostility in adolescence.

Physical Education

Physical activity supports many aspects of children's development—health, sense of self-worth, and the cognitive and social skills necessary for getting along with others. Yet to devote more time to academic instruction, U.S. elementary schools have cut back on recess, despite its contribution to all domains of development (see the Social Issues: Education box above). Similarly, only six U.S. states require physical education in every grade, and only one mandates at least 30 minutes per school day in elementary school and 45 minutes in middle and high school. Not surprisingly, fewer than one-third of 6- to 17-year-olds engage in at least moderate-intensity activity for 60 minutes per day and vigorous activity (involving breathing hard and sweating) for 20 minutes, recommended for good health (National Association for Sport and Physical Education, 2010).

Many experts also recommend changing the content of these physical education classes. Training in competitive sports, often a high priority, is unlikely to reach the least physically fit youngsters. Instead, programs should emphasize enjoyable, informal games and individual exercise—pursuits most likely to endure.

Physically fit children tend to become active adults who reap many benefits (Kjønniksen, Torsheim, & Wold, 2008; Tammelin et al., 2003). These include greater physical strength, resistance to many illnesses, enhanced psychological well-being, and a longer life.

ASK YOURSELF

REVIEW Select either obesity or asthma, and explain how both genetic and environmental factors contribute to this common health problem of middle childhood.

APPLY Nine-year-old Allison thinks she isn't good at sports, and she doesn't like physical education class. Suggest strategies her teacher can use to improve her pleasure and involvement in physical activity.

REFLECT Did you participate in adult-organized sports as a child? If so, what kind of climate for learning did coaches and parents create?

COGNITIVE DEVELOPMENT

"Finally!" 6-year-old Lizzie exclaimed the day she entered first grade. "Now I get to go to real school, just like Joey!" Lizzie walked into her classroom confidently, pencils, crayons, and writing pad in hand, ready for a more disciplined approach to learning. In a single morning, she and her classmates wrote in journals, met in reading groups, worked on addition and subtraction, and sorted leaves gathered for a science project. As Lizzie and Joey moved through the elementary school grades, they tackled increasingly complex tasks and became more accomplished at reading, writing, math skills, and general knowledge of the world. To understand the cognitive attainments of middle childhood, we turn to research inspired by Piaget's theory and the information-processing perspective. And we look at expanding definitions of intelligence that help us appreciate individual differences.

Piaget's Theory: The Concrete Operational Stage

When Lizzie visited my child development class as a 4-year-old, Piaget's conservation problems confused her (see Chapter 7, page 178). But when she returned at age 8, she found these tasks easy. "Of course it's the same!" she exclaimed. "The water's shorter, but it's also wider. Pour it back," she instructed the college student who was interviewing her. "You'll see, it's the same amount!"

Concrete Operational Thought

Lizzie has entered Piaget's **concrete operational stage,** which extends from about 7 to 11 years. Compared with early childhood, thought is far more logical, flexible, and organized.

Conservation. The ability to pass *conservation tasks* provides clear evidence of *operations*—mental actions that obey logical rules. Notice how Lizzie is capable of *decentration*, focusing on several aspects of a problem and relating them, rather than centering on just one. She also demonstrates **reversibility,** the capacity to think through a series of steps and then mentally reverse direction, returning to the starting point. Recall from Chapter 7 that reversibility is part of every logical operation. It is solidly achieved in middle childhood.

Classification. Between ages 7 and 10, children pass Piaget's *class inclusion problem* (see page 178). This indicates that they are more aware of classification hierarchies and can focus on relations between a general category and two specific categories at the same time—that is, on three relations at once (Hodges & French, 1988; Ni, 1998). Collections—stamps, coins, baseball cards, rocks, bottle caps—become common in middle childhood. At age 10, Joey spent hours sorting and resorting his baseball cards, grouping them first by league and team, then by playing position and batting average. He could separate the players into a variety of classes and subclasses and easily rearrange them.

Seriation. The ability to order items along a quantitative dimension, such as length or weight, is called **seriation.** To test for it, Piaget asked children to arrange sticks of different lengths from shortest to longest. Older preschoolers can put the sticks in a row, but they do so haphazardly, making many errors. In contrast, 6- to 7-year-olds create the series efficiently, moving in an orderly sequence from the smallest stick, to the next largest, and so on.

The concrete operational child can also seriate mentally, an ability called **transitive inference.** In a well-known transitive inference problem, Piaget showed children pairings of sticks of

An improved ability to categorize underlies children's interest in collecting objects during middle childhood. This 9-year-old sorts and classifies her extensive shell collection.

different colors. From observing that Stick *A* is longer than Stick *B* and Stick *B* is longer than Stick *C,* children must infer that *A* is longer than *C.* Like Piaget's class inclusion task, transitive inference requires children to integrate three relations at once—in this instance, *A–B, B–C,* and *A–C.* When researchers take steps to ensure that children remember the premises (*A–B* and *B–C*), 7-year-olds can grasp transitive inference (Andrews & Halford, 1998; Wright, 2006).

Spatial Reasoning. Piaget found that school-age children's understanding of space is more accurate than that of preschoolers. Let's consider children's **cognitive maps**—mental representations of familiar large-scale spaces, such as their neighborhood or school. Drawing a map of a large-scale space requires considerable perspective-taking skill. Because the entire space cannot be seen at once, children must infer its overall layout by relating its separate parts.

Preschoolers and young school-age children include *landmarks* on the maps they draw, but their arrangement is not always accurate. They do better when asked to place stickers showing the location of desks and people on a map of their classroom. But if the map is rotated to a position other than the orientation of the classroom, they have difficulty (Liben & Downs, 1993).

Around age 8 to 10, children's maps become better organized, showing landmarks along an *organized route of travel.* By the end of middle childhood, children combine landmarks and routes into an *overall view of a large-scale space.* And they readily draw and read maps of extended outdoor environments, even when the orientation of the map and the space it represents do not match (Liben, 2009). Ten- to 12-year-olds also grasp the notion of *scale*—the proportional relation between a space and its representation on a map (Liben, 2006).

LOOK AND LISTEN

Ask a 6- to 8-year-old and a 9- to 12-year-old to draw a neighborhood map showing important landmarks, such as the school, a friend's house, or a shopping area. In what ways do the children's maps differ? ●

Limitations of Concrete Operational Thought

Concrete operational thinking suffers from one important limitation: Children think in an organized, logical fashion only when dealing with concrete information they can perceive directly. Their mental operations work poorly with abstract ideas—ones not apparent in the real world. Consider children's solutions to transitive inference problems. When shown pairs of sticks of unequal length, Lizzie easily engaged in transitive inference. But she had difficulty with a hypothetical version of this task: "Susan is taller than Sally, and Sally is taller than Mary. Who is the tallest?" Not until age 11 or 12 can children solve this problem.

That logical thought is at first tied to immediate situations helps account for a special feature of concrete operational reasoning: Children master concrete operational tasks step by step. For example, they usually grasp conservation of number first, followed by conservation of length, liquid, and mass, and then weight. This *continuum of acquisition* (or gradual mastery) of logical concepts is another indication of the limitations of concrete operational thinking. Rather than coming up with general logical principles that they apply to all relevant situations, school-age children seem to work out the logic of each problem separately.

Follow-Up Research on Concrete Operational Thought

According to Piaget, brain development combined with experience in a rich and varied external world should lead children everywhere to reach the concrete operational stage at about the same time. Yet recent evidence indicates that specific cultural and school practices have much to do with mastery of Piagetian tasks (Rogoff, 2003). And information-processing research helps explain the gradual mastery of logical concepts in middle childhood.

The Impact of Culture and Schooling. In tribal and village societies, conservation is often delayed. Among the Hausa of Nigeria, who live in small agricultural settlements and rarely send their children to school, even basic conservation tasks—number, length, and liquid—are not understood until age 11 or later (Fahrmeier, 1978). This suggests that participating in relevant everyday activities helps children master conservation and other Piagetian problems.

© LAUREN GREENFIELD/INSTITUTE

This Zinacanteco Indian girl learns the centuries-old practice of backstrap weaving. Although Zinacanteco children might do poorly on Piaget's tasks, they are adept at complex mental transformations required to master intricate weaving techniques.

The very experience of going to school seems to promote mastery of Piagetian tasks. When children of the same age are tested, those who have been in school longer do better on transitive inference problems (Artman & Cahan, 1993). Opportunities to seriate objects, to learn about order relations, and to remember the parts of complex problems are probably responsible. Yet certain informal nonschool experiences can also foster operational thought. Around age 7 to 8, Zinacanteco Indian girls of southern Mexico, who learn to weave elaborately designed fabrics as an alternative to schooling, engage in mental transformations to figure out how a warp strung on a loom will turn out as woven cloth—reasoning expected at the concrete operational stage. American children of the same age, who do much better than Zinacanteco children on Piagetian tasks, have great difficulty with these weaving problems (Maynard & Greenfield, 2003).

On the basis of such findings, some investigators have concluded that the forms of logic required by Piagetian tasks do not emerge spontaneously but, rather, are heavily influenced by training, context, and cultural conditions. Does this view remind you of Vygotsky's sociocultural theory, discussed in earlier chapters?

An Information-Processing View of Concrete Operational Thought.

The gradual mastery of logical concepts in middle childhood raises a familiar question about Piaget's theory: Is an abrupt stagewise transition to logical thought the best way to describe cognitive development in middle childhood?

Some *neo-Piagetian theorists* argue that the development of operational thinking can best be understood in terms of gains in information-processing speed rather than a sudden shift to a new stage (Halford & Andrews, 2006). For example, Robbie Case (1996, 1998) proposed that, with practice, cognitive schemes demand less attention and become more automatic. This frees up space in *working memory* so children can focus on combin-

ing old schemes and generating new ones. For instance, the child who sees water poured from one container to another recognizes that the height of the liquid changes. As this understanding becomes routine, the child notices that the width of the water changes as well. Soon children coordinate these observations, and they grasp conservation of liquid. Then, as this logical idea becomes well-practiced, the child transfers it to more demanding situations.

Once the schemes of a Piagetian stage are sufficiently automatic, enough working memory is available to integrate them into an improved representation. As a result, children acquire *central conceptual structures*—networks of concepts and relations that permit them to think more effectively about a wide range of situations (Case, 1996, 1998). The central conceptual structures that emerge from integrating concrete operational schemes are broadly applicable principles that result in increasingly complex, systematic reasoning, which we will discuss in Chapter 11 in the context of formal operational thought.

Case and his colleagues—along with other information-processing researchers—have examined children's performance on a wide variety of tasks: solving arithmetic word problems, understanding stories, drawing pictures, and interpreting social situations. In each task, preschoolers typically focus on only one dimension. In understanding stories, for example, they grasp only a single story line. By the early school years, they combine two story lines into a single plot. Around 9 to 11 years, children integrate multiple dimensions (Case, 1998; Halford & Andrews, 2006). They tell coherent stories with a main plot and several subplots.

Case's theory helps explain why many understandings appear in specific situations at different times rather than being mastered all at once. First, different forms of the same logical insight, such as the various conservation tasks, vary in their processing demands, with those acquired later requiring more space in working memory. Second, children's experiences vary widely. A child who often listens to and tells stories but rarely draws pictures displays more advanced thinking in storytelling. Compared with Piaget's, Case's theory better accounts for unevenness in cognitive development.

Evaluation of the Concrete Operational Stage

Piaget was correct that school-age children approach many problems in more organized, rational ways than preschoolers. But disagreement continues over whether this difference occurs because of *continuous* improvement in logical skills or *discontinuous* restructuring of children's thinking (as Piaget's stage idea assumes). Many researchers think that both types of change may be involved (Case, 1998; Demetriou et al., 2002; Fischer & Bidell, 2006; Halford & Andrews, 2006). During the school years, children apply logical schemes to many more tasks. In the process, their thought seems to change qualitatively—toward a more comprehensive grasp of the underlying principles of logical thought.

ASK YOURSELF

REVIEW Children's performance on conservation tasks illustrates a continuum of acquisition of logical concepts. Review the preceding sections, and list additional examples of gradual development of operational reasoning.

APPLY Nine-year-old Adrienne spends many hours helping her father build furniture in his woodworking shop. How might this experience facilitate Adrienne's advanced performance on Piagetian seriation problems?

REFLECT Which aspects of Piaget's description of the concrete operational child do you accept? Which do you doubt? Explain, citing research evidence.

Information Processing

In contrast to Piaget's focus on overall cognitive change, the information-processing perspective examines separate aspects of thinking. Working-memory capacity, as noted in our discussion of Case's theory, continues to increase in middle childhood. And school-age children make great strides in executive function, yielding significant advances in attention, planning, memory, and self-regulation. Each contributes vitally to academic learning.

Working-Memory Capacity

Improved performance on working-memory tasks (see pages 126–127 in Chapter 5) is supported by brain development. And working memory—as we have seen in our discussion of Case's theory—benefits from enhanced speed of thinking. Time needed to process information on a wide variety of cognitive tasks declines rapidly between ages 6 and 12, likely due to myelination and synaptic pruning in the cerebral cortex (Kail, 1993, 1997). A faster thinker can hold on to and operate on more information in working memory (Luna et al., 2004; Nettelbeck & Burns, 2010). Still, individual differences exist in working-memory capacity, which predicts intelligence test scores and academic achievement in diverse subjects (Colom et al., 2007; Gathercole et al., 2005).

Observations of elementary school children with limited working memories revealed that they often failed at school assignments that made heavy memory demands (Alloway, 2009; Gathercole, Lamont, & Alloway, 2006). They could not follow complex instructions, lost their place in tasks with multiple steps, and frequently gave up before finishing their work.

Children from poverty-stricken families are especially likely to score low on working-memory tasks—a strong contributor to their generally poorer academic achievement (Farah et al., 2006; Noble, McCandliss, & Farah, 2007). In one study,

years of childhood spent in poverty predicted reduced working-memory capacity in early adulthood (Evans & Schamberg, 2009). Childhood neurobiological measures of stress—elevated blood pressure and stress hormone levels, including cortisol—largely explained this poverty–working-memory association. Chronic stress, as we saw in Chapter 4, can impair brain structure and function, especially in the prefrontal cortex and its connections with the hippocampus, which govern working-memory capacity.

Interventions are needed that reduce memory loads so children with limited working memories can learn. Effective approaches include communicating in short sentences, repeating task instructions, breaking complex tasks into manageable parts, and encouraging use of external memory aids (such as lists of useful spellings when writing or number lines when doing math) (Gathercole & Alloway, 2008). Do these techniques remind you of *scaffolding*, a style of teaching introduced in Chapter 7 known to promote cognitive development?

Executive Function

During the school years, a time of continued development of the prefrontal cortex, executive function undergoes its most energetic period of development (Luciana, 2003; Welsh, 2002). Children handle increasingly difficult tasks that require the integration of working memory, inhibition, planning, flexible use of strategies, and self-monitoring and self-correction of behavior.

Heritability evidence suggests substantial genetic influence on various aspects of executive function, including combining information in working memory, controlling attention, and inhibiting inappropriate responses (Hansell et al., 2001; Polderman et al., 2009; Young et al., 2009). But environmental

Middle childhood is a period of dramatic gains in executive function. This map-making project requires fourth graders to coordinate relevant information in working memory, inhibit inappropriate responses, and flexibly implement strategies.

contexts also contribute importantly. In Chapter 3, we reviewed evidence indicating that prenatal teratogens can impair impulse control, attention, planning, and other executive processes. And as with working memory, poverty and stressful living conditions can undermine executive function, with powerfully negative consequences for academic achievement and social adjustment (Blair & Raver, 2012). As we turn now to the development of an array of executive processes, our discussion will confirm that supportive home and school experiences are essential.

Attention

In middle childhood, attention becomes more selective, adaptable, and planful. First, children become better at deliberately attending to just those aspects of a situation that are relevant to their goals. When researchers introduce irrelevant stimuli into a task and see how well children attend to its central elements, performance improves sharply between ages 6 and 10 (Tabibi & Pfeffer, 2007; Vakil et al., 2009).

Second, older children are better at flexibly adapting their attention to task requirements. When asked to sort cards with pictures that vary in both color and shape, children age 5 and older readily switch their basis of sorting from color to shape; younger children typically persist in sorting in just one way (Brooks et al., 2003; Zelazo, Carlson, & Kesek, 2008).

Finally, planning improves greatly in middle childhood (Gauvain, 2004; Scholnick, 1995). On tasks with many parts, school-age children make decisions about what to do first and what to do next in an orderly fashion.

The attentional strategies just considered are crucial for success in school. Unfortunately, some children have grave difficulties paying attention. See the Biology and Environment box on the following page for a discussion of the serious learning and behavior problems of children with attention-deficit hyperactivity disorder.

Memory Strategies

As attention improves, so do *memory strategies,* deliberate mental activities we use to store and retain information. When Lizzie had a list of things to learn—for example, the state capitals of the United States—she immediately used **rehearsal**—repeating the information to herself. This memory strategy first appears in the early grade school years. Soon after, a second strategy becomes common: **organization**—grouping related items together (for example, all state capitals in the same part of the country) (Schneider, 2002).

Perfecting memory strategies requires time and effort. Eight-year-old Lizzie rehearsed in a piecemeal fashion. After being given the word *cat* in a list of items, she said, "Cat, cat, cat." But 10-year-old Joey used a more effective approach: He combined previous words with each new item, saying, "Desk, man, yard, cat, cat." This more active rehearsal approach, in which neighboring words create contexts for one another that trigger recall, yields much better memory (Lehman & Hasselhorn, 2007, 2010). Furthermore, whereas Lizzy organized by everyday association (hat–head, carrot–rabbit), Joey grouped items *taxonomically,* based on common properties (clothing, food, animals) and, thus, into fewer categories—an efficient procedure yielding dramatic memory gains (Bjorklund et al., 1994). And Joey used organization in a wide range of memory tasks, whereas Lizzie used it only when categorical relations among items were obvious.

Furthermore, Joey often combined several strategies—for example, organizing items, then stating the category names, and finally rehearsing. The more strategies children apply simultaneously and consistently, the better they remember (DeMarie et al., 2004; Schwenck, Bjorklund, & Schneider, 2007). Younger school-age children often try out various memory strategies but use them less systematically and successfully than older children. Still, their tendency to experiment allows them to discover which strategies work best and how to combine them effectively (Siegler, 1996, 2007).

By the end of middle childhood, children start to use **elaboration**—creating a relationship, or shared meaning, between two or more pieces of information that do not belong to the same category. For example, to learn the words *fish* and *pipe,* you might generate the verbal statement or mental image, "The fish is smoking a pipe." This highly effective memory technique, which requires considerable effort and space in working memory, becomes increasingly common in adolescence and early adulthood (Schneider & Pressley, 1997). Because organization and elaboration combine items into *meaningful chunks,* they permit children to hold onto much more information and also to *retrieve* it easily by thinking of other items associated with it.

Knowledge and Memory

During middle childhood, the long-term knowledge base grows larger and becomes organized into increasingly elaborate, hierarchically structured networks. This rapid growth of knowledge helps children use strategies and remember (Schneider, 2002). In other words, knowing more about a topic makes new information more meaningful and familiar so it is easier to store and retrieve.

To test this idea, researchers classified fourth graders as either experts or novices in knowledge of soccer and then gave both groups lists of soccer and nonsoccer items to learn. Experts remembered far more items on the soccer list (but not on the nonsoccer list) than novices. And during recall, experts' listing of items was better organized, as indicated by clustering of items into categories (Schneider & Bjorklund, 1992). This superior organization at retrieval suggests that highly knowledgeable children organize information in their area of expertise with little or no effort. Consequently, experts can devote more working-memory resources to using recalled information for reasoning and problem solving.

Biology and Environment

Children with Attention-Deficit Hyperactivity Disorder

While the other fifth graders worked quietly at their desks, Calvin squirmed, dropped his pencil, looked out the window, and fiddled with his shoelaces. "Hey Joey," he yelled across the room, "wanna play ball after school?" But the other children weren't eager to play with Calvin, who was physically awkward and failed to follow the rules of the game. He had trouble taking turns at bat and, in the outfield, looked elsewhere when the ball came his way. Calvin's desk was a chaotic mess. He often lost pencils, books, and other school materials and forgot to do his assignments.

Symptoms of ADHD

Calvin is one of 3 to 7 percent of U.S. school-age children with **attention-deficit hyperactivity disorder** (**ADHD**), which involves inattention, impulsivity, and excessive motor activity resulting in academic and social problems (American Psychiatric Association, 2013). Boys are diagnosed about four times as often as girls. However, many girls with ADHD seem to be overlooked, either because their symptoms are less flagrant or because of a gender bias: A difficult, disruptive boy is more likely to be referred for treatment (Biederman et al., 2005).

Children with ADHD cannot stay focused on a task that requires mental effort for more than a few minutes. They often act impulsively, lashing out with hostility when frustrated. Many, though not all, are *hyperactive*, exhausting parents and teachers and irritating other children with their excessive motor activity. For a child to be diagnosed with ADHD, these symptoms must have appeared before age 7 as a persistent problem.

Because of their difficulty concentrating, children with ADHD score 7 to 15 points lower than other children on intelligence tests (Barkley, 2002). Researchers agree that executive function deficiencies underlie ADHD symptoms. According to one view, children with ADHD are impaired in capacity to inhibit action in favor of thought—a basic difficulty resulting in wide-ranging inadequacies in executive processing and, therefore, in impulsive, disorganized behavior (Barkley, 2003a). Another hypothesis is that ADHD is

the direct result of a cluster of executive processing problems that interfere with ability to guide one's own actions (Brown, 2006). Research confirms that children with ADHD do poorly on tasks requiring sustained attention; find it hard to ignore irrelevant information; have difficulty with memory, planning, reasoning, and problem solving; and often fail to manage frustration and intense emotion (Barkley, 2003b, 2006).

This child frequently engages in disruptive behavior at school. Children with ADHD have great difficulty staying on task and often act impulsively, ignoring social rules.

Origins of ADHD

ADHD runs in families and is highly heritable: Identical twins share it more often than fraternal twins (Freitag et al., 2010; Rasmussen et al., 2004). Children with ADHD show abnormal brain functioning, including reduced electrical and blood-flow activity and structural abnormalities in the prefrontal cortex (Mackie et al., 2007; Sowell et al., 2003). Also, the brains of children with ADHD grow more slowly and are about 3 percent smaller in overall volume, with a thinner cerebral cortex, than those of unaffected agemates (Narr et al., 2009; Shaw et al., 2007). Several genes that disrupt functioning of neurotransmitters involved in inhibition and cognitive processing have been implicated in the disorder (Bobb et al., 2006; Faraone & Mick, 2010).

At the same time, ADHD is associated with environmental factors. Exposure to prenatal teratogens—such as tobacco, alcohol, and environmental pollutants—are linked to inattention and hyperactivity. And they can combine with certain genotypes to greatly increase risk of the disorder (see page 57 in Chapter 2). Furthermore, children with ADHD are more likely to come from homes in which marriages are unhappy and family stress is high (Bernier & Siegel, 1994). But a stressful home life rarely causes ADHD. Rather, these children's behaviors can contribute to family problems, which intensify the child's preexisting difficulties.

Treating ADHD

Calvin's doctor eventually prescribed stimulant medication, the most common treatment for ADHD. As long as dosage is carefully regulated, these drugs reduce activity level and improve attention, academic performance, and peer relations for about 70 percent of children who take them (Greenhill, Halperin, & Abikoff, 1999). Stimulant medication seems to increase activity in the prefrontal cortex, thereby improving the child's capacity to sustain attention and to inhibit off-task behavior.

Nevertheless, drug treatment cannot teach children to compensate for inattention and impulsivity. The most effective treatment approach combines medication with interventions that model and reinforce appropriate academic and social behavior (Smith, Barkley, & Shapiro, 2006). Family intervention is also important. Inattentive, overactive children strain the patience of parents, who are likely to react punitively and inconsistently—a child-rearing style that strengthens defiant, aggressive behavior. In fact, in 50 to 75 percent of cases, these two sets of behavior problems occur together (Goldstein, 2011).

ADHD is usually a lifelong disorder. Adults with ADHD continue to need help in structuring their environments, regulating negative emotion, selecting appropriate careers, and understanding their condition as a biological deficit rather than a character flaw.

By the end of the school years, extensive knowledge and use of memory strategies support one another. Children who are expert in an area are usually highly motivated. As a result, they not only acquire knowledge more quickly, but also *actively use what they know* to add more. In contrast, academically unsuccessful children fail to ask how previously stored information can clarify new material (Schneider & Bjorklund, 1998). This, in turn, interferes with the development of a broad knowledge base.

Culture and Memory Strategies

A repeated finding is that people in non-Western cultures who lack formal schooling rarely use or benefit from instruction in memory strategies (Rogoff & Chavajay, 1995). Tasks that require children to recall isolated bits of information, which are common in school, strongly motivate use of memory strategies. In fact, Western children get so much practice with this type of learning that they do not refine techniques that rely on cues available in everyday life, such as spatial location and arrangement of objects. For example, Guatemalan Mayan 9-year-olds do slightly better than their U.S. agemates when told to remember the placement of 40 familiar objects in a play scene. U.S. children often rehearse object names when it would be more effective to keep track of spatial relations (Rogoff & Wadell, 1982). The development of memory strategies, then, is not just a product of a more competent information-processing system. It also depends on task demands and cultural circumstances.

An 8-year-old Ethiopian child winds cotton onto a bobbin for weaving. Despite his keen memory for the complex steps of this task, he might have difficulty recalling the isolated bits of information that school tasks often require.

NIGEL PAVITT/AWL IMAGES RM/GETTY IMAGES

The School-Age Child's Theory of Mind

During middle childhood, children's *theory of mind,* or set of ideas about mental activities, becomes more elaborate and refined. Recall from Chapter 7 that this awareness of thought is often called *metacognition.* School-age children's improved ability to reflect on their own mental life is another reason that their thinking advances.

Unlike preschoolers, who view the mind as a passive container of information, older children regard it as an active, constructive agent that selects and transforms information. Consequently, they have a much better understanding of cognitive processes and their impact on performance. For example, with age, school-age children become increasingly aware of effective memory strategies and why they work (Alexander et al., 2003). They also grasp relationships between mental activities—for example, that remembering is crucial for understanding and that understanding strengthens memory (Schwanenflugel, Henderson, & Fabricius, 1998).

Furthermore, school-age children's understanding of sources of knowledge expands. They realize that people can extend their knowledge not just by directly observing events and talking to others but also by making *mental inferences* (Miller, Hardin, & Montgomery, 2003). This grasp of inference enables knowledge of *false belief* to expand. By age 7, children are aware that people form beliefs about other people's beliefs ("Joe thinks Andy thinks the kitten is lost") and that these second-order beliefs can be wrong! Appreciation of *second-order false belief* enables children to pinpoint the reasons that another person arrived at a certain belief (Astington, Pelletier, & Homer, 2002; Miller, 2009; Naito & Seki, 2009). This assists them greatly in understanding others' perspectives.

Besides more complex thinking and language, experiences that foster awareness of mental activities contribute to school-age children's more reflective, process-oriented view of the mind. In a study of rural children of Cameroon, Africa, those who attended school performed much better on theory-of-mind tasks (Vinden, 2002). In school, teachers often call attention to the workings of the mind by asking children to remember mental steps, share points of view with peers, and evaluate their own and others' reasoning.

Cognitive Self-Regulation

Although metacognition expands, school-age children often have difficulty putting what they know about thinking into action. They are not yet good at **cognitive self-regulation,** the process of continuously monitoring progress toward a goal, checking outcomes, and redirecting unsuccessful efforts. For example, Lizzie knows that she should group items when memorizing and reread a complicated paragraph to make sure she understands. But she does not always engage in these activities.

Why does cognitive self-regulation develop gradually? Monitoring and controlling task outcomes is cognitively demanding, requiring constant evaluation of effort and progress. Throughout elementary and secondary school, self-regulation predicts academic success (Valiente et al., 2008; Zimmerman & Cleary, 2009). In one study, researchers observed parents helping their children with problem solving during the summer before third grade. Parents who patiently pointed out important features of the task and suggested strategies had children who, in the classroom, more often discussed ways to approach problems and monitored their own performance (Stright et al., 2002). Explaining the effectiveness of strategies is particularly helpful because it provides a rationale for future action.

Children who acquire effective self-regulatory skills develop a sense of *academic self-efficacy*—confidence in their own ability, which supports future self-regulation (Zimmerman & Moylan, 2009). Unfortunately, some children receive messages from parents and teachers that seriously undermine their academic self-esteem and self-regulatory skills. We will consider these *learned-helpless* children in Chapter 10.

Applications of Information Processing to Academic Learning

Fundamental discoveries about the development of information processing have been applied to children's learning of reading and mathematics. Researchers are identifying the cognitive ingredients of skilled performance, tracing their development, and pinpointing differences in cognitive skills between good and poor learners. They hope, as a result, to design teaching methods that will improve children's learning.

Reading. Reading makes use of many skills at once, taxing all aspects of our information-processing system. Joey and Lizzie must perceive single letters and letter combinations, translate them into speech sounds, recognize the visual appearance of many common words, hold chunks of text in working memory while interpreting their meaning, and combine the meanings of various parts of a text passage into an understandable whole. If one or more of these skills are poorly developed, they will compete for space in our limited working memories, and reading performance will decline.

As children make the transition from emergent literacy to conventional reading, *phonological awareness* (see pages 188–189 in Chapter 7) continues to predict reading (and spelling) progress. Other information-processing skills also contribute. Gains in processing speed foster children's rapid conversion of visual symbols into sounds (McBride-Chang & Kail, 2002). Visual scanning and discrimination play important roles and improve with reading experience (Rayner, Pollatsek, & Starr, 2003). Performing all these skills efficiently releases working memory for higher-level activities involved in comprehending the text's meaning.

Until recently, researchers were involved in an intense debate over how to teach beginning reading. Those who took a **whole-language approach** argued that from the beginning, children should be exposed to text in its complete form—stories, poems, letters, posters, and lists—so that they can appreciate the communicative function of written language. Other experts advocated a **phonics approach,** believing that children should first be coached on *phonics*—the basic rules for translating written symbols into sounds. Only after mastering these skills should they get complex reading material.

Many studies show that children learn best with a mixture of both approaches. In kindergarten and first and second grades, teaching that includes phonics boosts reading scores, especially for children who lag behind in reading progress (Stahl & Miller, 2006; Xue & Meisels, 2004). And when teachers combine real reading and writing with teaching of phonics and engage in other excellent teaching practices—encouraging children to tackle reading challenges and integrating reading into all school subjects—first graders show far greater literacy progress (Pressley et al., 2002).

Why might combining phonics with whole language work best? Learning relationships between letters and sounds enables children to *decode,* or decipher, words they have never seen before. Children who enter school low in phonological awareness make far better reading progress when given training in phonics (Casalis & Cole, 2009). Yet too much emphasis on basic skills may cause children to lose sight of the goal of reading: understanding. Children who read aloud fluently without registering meaning know little about effective metacognitive reading strategies—for example, that they must read more carefully if they will be tested than if they are reading for pleasure. Providing instruction aimed at increasing knowledge and use of reading strategies enhances reading performance from third grade on (McKeown & Beck, 2009; Paris & Paris, 2006).

Mathematics. Mathematics teaching in elementary school builds on and greatly enriches children's informal knowledge of number concepts and counting. Written notation systems and formal computational procedures enhance children's ability to represent numbers and compute. Over the early elementary school years, children acquire basic math facts through a combination of frequent practice, experimentation with diverse

By using manipulative materials to understand number and place value, these first graders gain conceptual knowledge that helps them become more effective math problem solvers.

computational procedures (through which they discover faster, more accurate techniques), reasoning about number concepts, and teaching that conveys effective strategies. Eventually children retrieve answers automatically and apply this knowledge to more complex problems.

Arguments about how to teach mathematics resemble those in reading, pitting drill in computing against "number sense," or understanding. Again, a blend of both approaches is most beneficial (Fuson, 2009). In learning basic math, poorly performing students use cumbersome techniques or try to retrieve answers from memory too soon. They have not sufficiently experimented with strategies to see which are most effective and to reorganize their observations in logical, efficient ways—for example, noticing that multiplication problems involving 2 (2 × 8) are equivalent to addition doubles (8 + 8) (Canobi, 2004; Canobi, Reeve, & Pattison, 2003). This suggests that encouraging students to apply strategies and making sure they understand why certain strategies work well are essential for solid mastery of basic math. In one study, second graders taught in these ways not only mastered correct procedures but even invented their own successful strategies, some of which were superior to standard, school-taught methods (Fuson & Burghard, 2003).

In Asian countries, students receive a variety of supports for acquiring mathematical knowledge and often excel at both math reasoning and computation. Use of the metric system helps Asian children grasp place value. The consistent structure of number words in Asian languages (*ten-two* for 12, *ten-three* for 13) also makes this idea clear (Miura & Okamoto, 2003). And because Asian number words are shorter and more quickly pronounced, more digits can be held in working memory at once, increasing the speed of thinking. Furthermore, Chinese parents provide their preschoolers with extensive practice in counting and adding—experiences that contribute to the superiority of Chinese over U.S. children's math knowledge even before school entry (Siegler & Mu, 2008; Zhou et al., 2006). Finally, as we will see later in this chapter, compared with lessons in the United States, those in Asian classrooms devote more time to exploring math concepts and strategies and less to drill and repetition.

ASK YOURSELF

REVIEW Explain why gains in working-memory capacity and executive-function skills are vital for mastery of reading and math in middle childhood.

APPLY After viewing a slide show on endangered species, second and fifth graders were asked to remember as many animals as they could. Explain why fifth graders recalled much more than second graders.

REFLECT In your own elementary school math education, how much emphasis was placed on computational drill and how much on understanding of concepts? How do you think that balance affected your interest and performance in math?

Individual Differences in Mental Development

Around age 6, IQ becomes more stable than it was at earlier ages, and it correlates moderately well with academic achievement, typically around .50 to .60. And children with higher IQs are more likely when they grow up to attain higher levels of education and enter more prestigious occupations (Brody, 1997; Deary et al., 2007). Because IQ predicts school performance and educational attainment, it often enters into educational decisions. Do intelligence tests accurately assess the school-age child's ability to profit from academic instruction? Let's look closely at this controversial issue.

Defining and Measuring Intelligence

Virtually all intelligence tests provide an overall score (the IQ), which represents *general intelligence,* or reasoning ability, along with an array of separate scores measuring specific mental abilities. But intelligence is a collection of many capacities, not all of which are included on currently available tests (Carroll, 2005; Sternberg, 2005). See Figure 9.3 for items typically included in intelligence tests for children.

The intelligence tests given from time to time in classrooms are *group-administered tests.* They permit large numbers of students to be tested at once and are useful for identifying children who require more extensive evaluation with *individually administered tests,* which demand considerable training and experience to give well. The examiner not only considers the child's answers but also observes the child's behavior, noting such reactions as attention to and interest in the tasks and wariness of the adult. These observations provide insight into whether the test results accurately reflect the child's abilities. Two individual tests—the Stanford-Binet and the Wechsler—are often used to identify highly intelligent children and to diagnose children with learning problems.

The contemporary descendant of Alfred Binet's first successful intelligence test is the *Stanford-Binet Intelligence Scales,* Fifth Edition, for individuals from age 2 to adulthood. In addition to general intelligence, it assesses five intellectual factors, each of which includes a verbal mode and a nonverbal mode of testing (Roid, 2003). The nonverbal mode is useful when assessing individuals with limited English or communication disorders. Knowledge and quantitative reasoning factors emphasize culturally loaded, fact-oriented information, such as vocabulary and arithmetic problems. In contrast, the visual–spatial processing, working-memory, and basic information-processing factors are assumed to be less culturally biased (see the spatial visualization item in Figure 9.3).

The *Wechsler Intelligence Scale for Children (WISC-IV)* is the fourth edition of a widely used test for 6- through 16-year-olds (Wechsler, 2003). It measures general intelligence and four

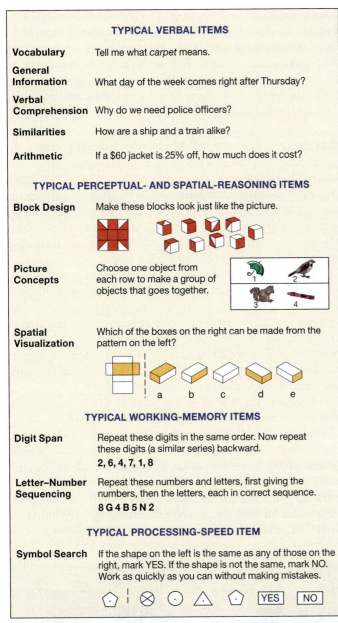

FIGURE 9.3 Test items like those on commonly used intelligence tests for children. The verbal items emphasize culturally loaded, fact-oriented information. The perceptual- and spatial-reasoning, working-memory, and processing-speed items emphasize aspects of information processing and are assumed to assess more biologically based skills.

broad factors: verbal reasoning, perceptual (or visual–spatial) reasoning, working memory, and processing speed. The WISC-IV was designed to downplay culturally dependent knowledge, which is emphasized on only one factor (verbal reasoning). According to the test designers, the result is the most "culture-fair" intelligence test available (Williams, Weis, & Rolfhus, 2003). The WISC was also the first test to be standardized on children representing the total population of the United States, including ethnic minorities.

Recent Efforts to Define Intelligence

As we have seen, mental tests now tap important aspects of information processing. In line with this trend, some researchers combine the mental testing approach to defining intelligence with the information-processing approach. They believe that once we identify the processing skills that separate individuals who test well from those who test poorly, we will know more about how to intervene to improve performance. These investigators conduct *componential analyses* of children's test scores. This means that they look for relationships between aspects (or components) of information processing and children's intelligence test scores.

Processing speed, assessed in terms of reaction time on diverse cognitive tasks, is moderately related to IQ (Deary, 2001; Li et al., 2004). Individuals whose nervous systems function more efficiently, permitting them to take in information and manipulate it quickly, appear to have an edge in intellectual skills.

But flexible attention, memory, and reasoning strategies are as important as efficient thinking in predicting IQ, and they explain some of the association between response speed and good test performance (Lohman, 2000; Miller & Vernon, 1992). Children who apply strategies effectively acquire more knowledge and can retrieve it rapidly. Similarly, available space in working memory depends in part on effective inhibition (the ability to keep one's mind from straying to irrelevant thoughts). Inhibition and sustained and selective attention are among a wide array of attentional skills that are good predictors of IQ (Schweizer, Moosbrugger, & Goldhammer, 2006).

The componential approach has one major shortcoming: It regards intelligence as entirely due to causes within the child. Throughout this book, we have seen how cultural and situational factors affect children's thinking. Robert Sternberg has expanded componential approach into a comprehensive theory that regards intelligence as a product of inner and outer forces.

Sternberg's Triarchic Theory. As Figure 9.4 on page 244 shows, Sternberg's (2001, 2005, 2008) **triarchic theory of successful intelligence** identifies three broad, interacting intelligences: (1) *analytical intelligence,* or information-processing skills; (2) *creative intelligence,* the capacity to solve novel problems; and (3) *practical intelligence,* application of intellectual skills in everyday situations. Intelligent behavior involves balancing all three to succeed in life according to one's personal goals and the requirements of one's cultural community.

Analytical Intelligence. *Analytical intelligence* consists of the information-processing components that underlie all intelligent acts: applying strategies, acquiring task-relevant and metacognitive knowledge, and engaging in self-regulation. But on mental tests, processing skills are used in only a few of their potential ways, resulting in far too narrow a view of intelligent behavior.

Creative Intelligence. In any context, success depends not only on processing familiar information but also on generating useful solutions to new problems. People who are *creative* think

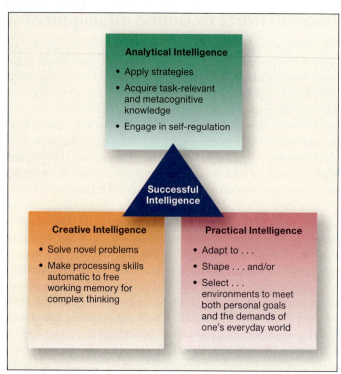

FIGURE 9.4 Sternberg's triarchic theory of successful intelligence. People who behave intelligently balance three interrelated intelligences—analytical, creative, and practical—to achieve success in life, defined by their personal goals and the requirements of their cultural communities.

more skillfully than others when faced with novelty. Given a new task, they apply their information-processing skills in exceptionally effective ways, rapidly making these skills automatic so that working memory is freed for more complex aspects of the situation.

Practical Intelligence. Finally, intelligence is a *practical,* goal-oriented activity aimed at *adapting to, shaping,* or *selecting environments.* Intelligent people skillfully *adapt* their thinking to fit with both their desires and the demands of their everyday worlds. When they cannot adapt to a situation, they try to *shape,* or change, it to meet their needs. If they cannot shape it, they *select* new contexts that better match their skills, values, or goals. Practical intelligence reminds us that children with certain life histories do well on intelligence tests and adapt easily to the testing conditions. Others, with different backgrounds, may misinterpret or reject the testing context. Yet such children often display sophisticated abilities in daily life—for example, engaging in complex artistic activities or interacting skillfully with other people.

The triarchic theory highlights the limitations of current intelligence tests in assessing the complexity of intelligent behavior. For example, out-of-school, practical forms of intelligence are vital for life success and help explain why cultures vary widely in the behaviors they regard as intelligent (Sternberg et al., 2000). When researchers asked ethnically diverse parents to describe an intelligent first grader, Caucasian Americans

mentioned cognitive traits. In contrast, ethnic minorities (Cambodian, Filipino, Vietnamese, and Mexican immigrants) identified noncognitive capacities—motivation, self-management, and social skills (Okagaki & Sternberg, 1993). According to Sternberg, mental tests can easily underestimate, and even overlook, the intellectual strengths of some children, especially ethnic minorities.

Gardner's Theory of Multiple Intelligences. In yet another view of how information-processing skills underlie intelligent behavior, Howard Gardner's (1983, 1993, 2000) **theory of multiple intelligences** defines intelligence in terms of distinct sets of processing operations that permit individuals to engage in a wide range of culturally valued activities. Dismissing the idea of general intelligence, Gardner proposes at least eight independent intelligences (see Table 9.1).

Gardner believes that each intelligence has a unique biological basis, a distinct course of development, and different expert, or "end-state," performances. At the same time, he emphasizes that a lengthy process of education is required to transform any raw potential into a mature social role (Connell, Sheridan, & Gardner, 2003). Cultural values and learning opportunities affect the extent to which a child's intellectual strengths are realized and the ways they are expressed.

Gardner's list of abilities has yet to be firmly grounded in research. Neurological evidence for the independence of his abilities is weak. Some exceptionally gifted individuals have abilities that are broad rather than limited to a particular domain (Piirto, 2007). Nevertheless, Gardner calls attention to several intelligences not tapped by IQ scores. For example, his interpersonal and intrapersonal intelligences include a set of capacities for dealing with people and understanding oneself that are vital for a satisfying, successful life.

According to Gardner, people are capable of at least eight distinct intelligences. Through a project aimed at improving sea turtle nesting habitats, these children expand and enrich their naturalist intelligence.

TABLE 9.1 Gardner's Multiple Intelligences

INTELLIGENCE	PROCESSING OPERATIONS	END-STATE PERFORMANCE POSSIBILITIES
Linguistic	Sensitivity to the sounds, rhythms, and meaning of words and the functions of language	Poet, journalist
Logico-mathematical	Sensitivity to, and capacity to detect, logical or numerical patterns; ability to handle long chains of logical reasoning	Mathematician
Musical	Ability to produce and appreciate pitch, rhythm (or melody), and aesthetic quality of the forms of musical expressiveness	Instrumentalist, composer
Spatial	Ability to perceive the visual–spatial world accurately, to perform transformations on those perceptions, and to re-create aspects of visual experience in the absence of relevant stimuli	Sculptor, navigator
Bodily-kinesthetic	Ability to use the body skillfully for expressive as well as goal-directed purposes; ability to handle objects skillfully	Dancer, athlete
Naturalist	Ability to recognize and classify all varieties of animals, minerals, and plants	Biologist
Interpersonal	Ability to detect and respond appropriately to the moods, temperaments, motivations, and intentions of others	Therapist, salesperson
Intrapersonal	Ability to discriminate complex inner feelings and to use them to guide one's own behavior; knowledge of one's own strengths, weaknesses, desires, and intelligences	Person with detailed, accurate self-knowledge

Sources: Gardner, 1993, 1998, 2000.

Explaining Individual and Group Differences in IQ

When we compare individuals in terms of academic achievement, years of education, and occupational status, it quickly becomes clear that certain sectors of the population are advantaged over others. In trying to explain these differences, researchers have compared the IQ scores of ethnic and SES groups. American black children and adolescents score, on average, 10 to 12 IQ points below American white children, although the difference has been shrinking over the past several decades (Edwards & Oakland, 2006; Flynn, 2007; Nisbett, 2009). Hispanic children fall midway between black and white children, and Asian Americans score slightly higher than their white counterparts—about 3 points (Ceci, Rosenblum, & Kumpf, 1998).

The gap between middle- and low-SES children—about 9 points—accounts for some of the ethnic differences in IQ, but not all. Matching black and white children on parental education and income reduces the black–white IQ gap by a third to a half (Brooks-Gunn et al., 2003). Of course, IQ varies greatly *within* each ethnic and SES group. Still, these group differences are large enough and of serious enough consequence that they cannot be ignored.

In the 1970s, the IQ nature–nurture controversy escalated after psychologist Arthur Jensen (1969) published a controversial monograph entitled, "How Much Can We Boost IQ and Scholastic Achievement?" Jensen claimed—and still maintains—that heredity is largely responsible for individual, ethnic, and SES variations in intelligence (Jensen, 1998, 2001; Rushton & Jensen, 2006, 2010). His work sparked an outpouring of research

and responses, including ethical challenges reflecting deep concern that his conclusions would fuel social prejudices. Richard Herrnstein and Charles Murray rekindled the controversy with *The Bell Curve* (1994). Like Jensen, they argued that heredity contributes substantially to individual and SES differences (and possibly to ethnic differences) in IQ. Let's look closely at some important evidence.

Nature versus Nurture. In Chapter 2, we introduced the *heritability estimate*. The most powerful evidence on the heritability of IQ involves twin comparisons. The IQ scores of identical twins (who share all their genes) are more similar than those of fraternal twins (who are genetically no more alike than ordinary siblings). On the basis of this and other kinship evidence, researchers estimate that about half the differences in IQ among children can be traced to their genetic makeup.

But heritabilities risk overestimating genetic influences and underestimating environmental influences (see page 53). And heritability estimates do not reveal the complex processes through which genes and experiences influence intelligence as children develop.

Adoption studies offer a wider range of information. When young children are adopted into caring, stimulating homes, their IQs rise substantially compared with the IQs of nonadopted children who remain in economically deprived families (van IJzendoorn, Juffer, & Poelhuis, 2005). But adopted children benefit to varying degrees. In one investigation, children of two extreme groups of biological mothers—those with IQs below 95 and those with IQs above 120—were adopted at birth by parents who were well above average in income and education.

During the school years, the children of the low-IQ biological mothers scored above average in IQ. But they did not do as well as children of high-IQ biological mothers placed in similar adoptive families (Loehlin, Horn, & Willerman, 1997). Adoption research confirms that heredity and environment contribute jointly to IQ.

Adoption research also sheds light on the black–white IQ gap. In two studies, African-American children adopted into economically well-off white homes during the first year of life scored high on intelligence tests, attaining mean IQs of 110 and 117 by middle childhood (Moore, 1986; Scarr & Weinberg, 1983). The IQ gains of black children "reared in the culture of the tests and schools" are consistent with a wealth of evidence that poverty severely depresses the intelligence of ethnic minority children (Nisbett, 2009).

Furthermore, a dramatic *secular trend* in mental test performance—a generational rise in average IQ in both industrialized nations and the developing world—supports the role of environmental factors. The greatest gains have occurred on tests of spatial reasoning—tasks often assumed to be "culture fair" and, therefore, more genetically based (Flynn, 2007). The existence of a large, environmentally induced secular trend that exceeds the black–white IQ gap presents another major challenge to the assumption that ethnic variations in IQ are mostly genetic.

Cultural Influences.
A controversial question raised about ethnic differences in IQ has to do with whether they result from *test bias*. If a test samples knowledge and skills that not all groups of children have had equal opportunity to learn, or if the testing situation impairs the performance of some groups but not others, then the resulting score is a biased, or unfair, measure (Ceci & Williams, 1997; Sternberg, 2005).

Communication Styles. Ethnic minority families often foster unique language skills. An observational study carried out in low-SES African-American homes in a southeastern U.S. city revealed that the black parents rarely asked their children knowledge-training questions ("What color is it?" "What's this story about?"), which are typical of middle-SES white parents and of tests and classrooms. Instead, the black parents asked analogy questions ("What's that like?") or story-starter questions ("Did you hear Sally this morning?") that called for elaborate responses and had no "right" answer. Black children with these home experiences may be confused by the "objective" questions they encounter on tests and in classrooms.

Furthermore, many ethnic minority parents without extensive schooling prefer a *collaborative style of communication* when completing tasks with children. They work together in a coordinated, fluid way, each focused on the same aspect of the problem—a pattern observed in Native-American, Canadian Inuit, Hispanic, and Guatemalan Mayan cultures (Chavajay & Rogoff, 2002; Crago, Annahatak, & Ningiuruvik, 1993; Paradise & Rogoff, 2009). With increasing education, parents establish a *hierarchical style of communication,* like that of classrooms and

tests. The parent directs each child to carry out an aspect of the task, and children work independently (Greenfield, Suzuki, & Rothstein-Fish, 2006). This sharp discontinuity between home and school practices may contribute to low-SES minority children's lower IQs and school performance.

Knowledge. Many researchers argue that IQ scores are affected by specific information acquired as part of majority-culture upbringing. Consistent with this view, low-SES African-American children often miss vocabulary words on mental tests that have alternative meanings in their cultural community—for example, interpreting the word *frame* as "physique" and *wrapping* as "rapping," referring to the style of music (Champion, 2003a). Even nonverbal test items, such as spatial reasoning, depend on learning opportunities. For example, using small blocks to duplicate designs and playing video games requiring mental rotation of visual images increase success on spatial tasks (Dirks, 1982; Maynard, Subrahmanyam, & Greenfield, 2005). Low-income minority children, who often grow up in more "people-oriented" than "object-oriented" homes, may lack toys and games that promote certain intellectual skills.

Furthermore, the sheer amount of time a child spends in school predicts IQ. When children of the same age enrolled in different grades are compared, those who have been in school longer score higher on intelligence tests (Ceci, 1991, 1999). Taken together, these findings indicate that children's exposure to the knowledge and ways of thinking valued in classrooms has a sizable impact on their intelligence test performance.

Stereotypes. Imagine trying to succeed at an activity when the prevailing attitude is that members of your group are incompetent. **Stereotype threat**—the fear of being judged on the basis of a negative stereotype—can trigger anxiety that interferes with performance. Mounting evidence confirms that stereotype

Fear of being judged on the basis of a negative ethnic stereotype may be behind this child's reluctance to try a new task in school.

© ELLEN B. SENISI PHOTOGRAPHY

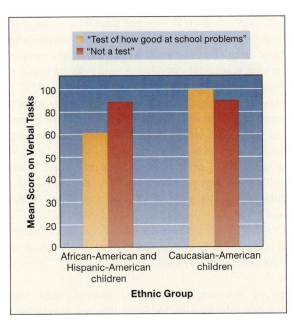

FIGURE 9.5 Effect of stereotype threat on test performance. Among African-American and Hispanic-American children who were aware of ethnic stereotypes, being told that verbal tasks were a "test of how good children are at school problems" led to far worse performance than being told the tasks were "not a test." These statements had little impact on the performance of Caucasian-American children. (Adapted from McKown & Weinstein, 2003.)

threat undermines test taking in children and adults (McKown & Strambler, 2009; Steele, 1997). For example, researchers gave African-American, Hispanic, and Caucasian 6- to 10-year-olds verbal tasks. Some children were told that the tasks were "not a test." Others were told they were "a test of how good children are at school problems" (McKown & Weinstein, 2003). Among children who were aware of ethnic stereotypes (such as "black people aren't smart"), African Americans and Hispanics performed far worse in the "test" condition than in the "not a test" condition. Caucasian children, in contrast, performed similarly in both conditions (see Figure 9.5).

Over middle childhood, children become increasingly conscious of ethnic stereotypes, and those from stigmatized groups are especially mindful of them. By early adolescence, many low-SES minority students start to say that doing well in school is not important to them (Cooper & Huh, 2008). Self-protective disengagement, sparked by stereotype threat, may be responsible. This weakening of motivation can have serious, long-term consequences. Research shows that self-discipline—effort and delay of gratification—predicts school performance at least as well as, and sometimes better than, IQ does (Duckworth & Seligman, 2005).

Reducing Cultural Bias in Testing. Although not all experts agree, many acknowledge that IQ scores can underestimate the intelligence of children from ethnic minority groups. A special concern exists about incorrectly labeling minority children as slow learners and assigning them to remedial classes, which are far less stimulating than regular school experiences.

To avoid this danger, test scores need to be combined with assessments of children's adaptive behavior—their ability to cope with the demands of their everyday environments. The child who does poorly on an intelligence test yet plays a complex game on the playground or figures out how to rewire a broken TV is unlikely to be mentally deficient.

In addition, culturally relevant testing procedures enhance minority children's test performance. In an approach called **dynamic assessment,** an innovation consistent with Vygotsky's zone of proximal development, an adult introduces purposeful teaching into the testing situation to find out what the child can attain with social support. Research shows that children's receptivity to teaching and their capacity to transfer what they have learned to novel problems contribute substantially to gains in test performance (Haywood & Lidz, 2007; Sternberg & Grigorenko, 2002). In one study, Ethiopian 6- and 7-year-olds who had recently immigrated to Israel scored well below their Israeli-born agemates on spatial reasoning tasks. The Ethiopian children had little experience with this type of thinking. After several dynamic assessment sessions in which the adult suggested effective strategies, the Ethiopian children's scores rose sharply, nearly equaling those of the Israeli-born children (Tzuriel & Kaufman, 1999). They also transferred their learning to new test items.

In view of its many problems, should intelligence testing in schools be suspended? Most experts reject this solution. Without testing, important educational decisions would be based only on subjective impressions, perhaps increasing discriminatory placement of minority children. Intelligence tests are useful when interpreted carefully by psychologists and educators who are sensitive to cultural influences on test performance. And despite their limitations, IQ scores continue to be fairly accurate measures of school learning potential for the majority of Western children.

This teacher uses dynamic assessment, tailoring instruction to students' individual needs—an approach that reveals what each child can learn with social support.

ASK YOURSELF

REVIEW Using Sternberg's triarchic theory and Gardner's theory of multiple intelligences, explain the limitations of current intelligence tests in assessing the diversity of human intelligence.

APPLY Josefina, a Hispanic fourth grader, does well on homework assignments. But when her teacher announces, "It's time for a test to see how much you've learned," Josefina usually does poorly. How might stereotype threat explain this inconsistency?

REFLECT Do you think that intelligence tests are culturally biased? What observations and evidence influenced your conclusions?

Language Development

Vocabulary, grammar, and pragmatics continue to develop in middle childhood, though less obviously than at earlier ages. In addition, children's attitude toward language undergoes a fundamental shift: They develop language awareness.

Schooling contributes greatly to these language competencies. Reflecting on language is extremely common during reading instruction. And fluent reading is a major new source of language learning (Ravid & Tolchinsky, 2002). As we will see, an improved ability to reflect on language grows out of literacy and supports many complex language skills.

Vocabulary and Grammar

During the elementary school years, vocabulary increases fourfold, eventually exceeding comprehension of 40,000 words, a rate of growth greater than in early childhood. In addition to the word-learning strategies discussed in Chapter 7, school-age children add to their vocabularies by analyzing the structure of complex words. From *happy* and *decide,* they quickly derive the meanings of *happiness* and *decision* (Larsen & Nippold, 2007). They also figure out many more word meanings from context (Nagy & Scott, 2000).

As at earlier ages, children benefit from conversation with more expert speakers (Weizman & Snow, 2001). But because written language contains a far more diverse and complex vocabulary than spoken language, reading contributes enormously to vocabulary growth.

As their knowledge expands and becomes better organized, older school-age children think about and use words more precisely: In addition to the verb *fall,* for example, they also use *topple, tumble,* and *plummet* (Berman, 2007). Word definitions also illustrate this change. Five- and 6-year-olds offer concrete descriptions referring to functions or appearance—*knife:* "when

you're cutting carrots"; *bicycle:* "it's got wheels, a chain, and handlebars." By the end of elementary school, synonyms and explanations of categorical relationships appear—for example, *knife:* "something you could cut with. A saw is like a knife. It could also be a weapon" (Wehren, De Lisi, & Arnold, 1981).

School-age children's more reflective, analytical approach to language permits them to appreciate the multiple meanings of words—to recognize, for example, that many words, such as *cool* or *neat,* have psychological as well as physical meanings: "What a cool shirt!" or "That movie was really neat!" This grasp of double meanings permits 8- to 10-year-olds to comprehend subtle metaphors, such as "sharp as a tack" and "spilling the beans" (Nippold, Taylor, & Baker, 1996; Wellman & Hickling, 1994). It also leads to a change in children's humor. Riddles and puns that alternate between different meanings of a key word are common: "Hey, did you take a bath?" "Why, is one missing?"

Mastery of complex grammatical constructions also improves. For example, English-speaking children use the passive voice more frequently, and they more often extend it from an abbreviated form ("It broke") into full statements ("The glass was broken by Mary") (Israel, Johnson, & Brooks, 2000; Tomasello, 2006). Although the passive form is challenging, language input makes a difference. When adults speak a language that emphasizes full passives, such as Inuktitut (spoken by the Inuit people of Arctic Canada), children produce them earlier (Allen & Crago, 1996).

Another grammatical achievement of middle childhood is advanced understanding of infinitive phrases—the difference between "John is eager to please" and "John is easy to please" (Berman, 2007; Chomsky, 1969). Like gains in vocabulary, appreciation of these subtle grammatical distinctions is supported by an improved ability to analyze and reflect on language.

Pragmatics

Improvements in *pragmatics,* the communicative side of language, also occur. Conversational strategies become more refined. For example, school-age children are better at phrasing things to get their way. When an adult refuses to hand over a desired object, 9-year-olds, but not 5-year-olds, state their second requests more politely (Axia & Baroni, 1985).

Furthermore, as a result of improved memory and ability to take the perspective of listeners, children's narratives increase in organization, detail, and expressiveness. A typical 4- or 5-year-old's narrative states what happened: "We went to the lake. We fished and waited. Paul caught a huge catfish." Six- and 7-year-olds add orienting information (time, place, participants) and connectives ("next," "then," "so," "finally") that lend coherence to the story. Gradually, narratives lengthen into a *classic form* in which events not only build to a high point but resolve: "After Paul reeled in the catfish, Dad cleaned and cooked it. Then we ate it all up!" And evaluative comments rise dramatically, becoming common by age 8 to 9: "The catfish tasted great. Paul was so proud!" (Melzi & Ely, 2009; Ukrainetz et al., 2005).

In families who regularly eat meals together, children are advanced in language and literacy development. Mealtimes offer many opportunities to relate complex, extended personal stories.

Because children pick up the narrative styles of significant adults in their lives, their narrative forms vary widely across cultures. For example, instead of the *topic-focused style* of most Caucasian-American school-age children, who describe an experience from beginning to end, African-American children often use a *topic-associating style* in which they blend several similar anecdotes. One 9-year-old related having a tooth pulled, then described seeing her sister's tooth pulled, next told how she had removed one of her baby teeth, and concluded, "I'm a pullin-teeth expert . . . call me, and I'll be over" (McCabe, 1997, p. 164). As a result, African-American children's narratives are usually longer and more complex than those of white children (Champion, 2003b).

The ability to generate clear oral narratives enhances reading comprehension and prepares children for producing longer, more explicit written narratives. In families who regularly eat meals together, children are advanced in language and literacy development (Snow & Beals, 2006). Mealtimes offer many opportunities to relate personal stories.

Learning Two Languages

Throughout the world, many children grow up *bilingual,* learning two languages and sometimes more than two. An estimated 20 percent of U.S. children—10 million in all—speak a language other than English at home (U.S. Census Bureau, 2013).

Bilingual Development. Children can become bilingual in two ways: (1) by acquiring both languages at the same time in early childhood or (2) by learning a second language after mastering the first. Children of bilingual parents who teach them both languages in infancy and early childhood separate the language systems early on and attain early language milestones according to a typical timetable (Conboy & Thal, 2006; Genesee & Nicoladis, 2007; Weikum et al., 2007). When school-age children acquire a second language after they already speak a first language, they generally take five to seven years to attain

speaking and writing skills on a par with those of native-speaking agemates (Paradis, 2007).

As with first-language development, a *sensitive period* for second-language development exists. Mastery must begin sometime in childhood for most second-language learners to attain full proficiency (Hakuta, Bialystok, & Wiley, 2003). But a precise age cutoff for a decline in second-language learning has not been established. Rather, a continuous age-related decrease from childhood to adulthood occurs.

A large body of research shows that bilingualism has positive consequences for development. Children who are fluent in two languages outperform others on tests of selective attention, inhibition of irrelevant information, analytical reasoning, concept formation, and cognitive flexibility (Bialystok et al., 2009; Carlson & Meltzoff, 2008). They are also advanced in certain aspects of language awareness, such as detection of errors in grammar and meaning. And children readily transfer their phonological awareness skills in one language to the other, especially if the two languages share phonological features, as Spanish and English do (Siegal, Iozzi, & Surian, 2009; Snow & Kang, 2006). These capacities, as noted earlier, enhance reading achievement.

Bilingual Education. The advantages of bilingualism provide strong justification for bilingual education programs in schools. In Canada, about 7 percent of elementary school students are enrolled in *language immersion programs,* in which English-speaking children are taught entirely in French for several years. This strategy succeeds in developing children who are proficient in both languages and who, by grade 6, achieve as well in reading, writing, and math as their counterparts in the regular English program (Harley & Jean, 1999; Holobow, Genesee, & Lambert, 1991; Turnbull, Hart, & Lapkin, 2003).

The child on the left, a native Spanish speaker, benefits from an English–Spanish bilingual classroom, which sustains her native language while she masters English. And her native-English-speaking classmate has the opportunity to begin learning Spanish!

In the United States, fierce disagreement exists over the question of how best to educate ethnic minority children with limited English proficiency. Some believe that time spent communicating in the child's native tongue detracts from English-language learning. Other educators, committed to developing minority children's native language while fostering mastery of English, note that providing instruction in the native tongue lets minority children know that their heritage is respected. It also prevents inadequate proficiency in both languages. Minority children who gradually lose the first language as a result of being taught the second end up limited in both languages for a time (Ovando & Collier, 1998). This circumstance leads to serious academic difficulties and is believed to contribute to high rates of school failure and dropout among low-SES Hispanic young people, who make up nearly 50 percent of the U.S. language-minority population.

At present, public opinion and educational practice favor English-only instruction. Many U.S. states have passed laws declaring English to be their official language, creating conditions in which schools have no obligation to teach minority students in languages other than English. Yet in classrooms where both languages are integrated into the curriculum, minority children are more involved in learning and acquire the second language more easily—gains that predict better academic achievement (Guglielmi, 2008). In contrast, when teachers speak only in a language children can barely understand, minority children display frustration, boredom, and escalating academic difficulties (Kieffer, 2008). Supporters of U.S. English-only education often point to the success of Canadian language immersion programs, in which classroom lessons are conducted in the second language. But Canadian parents enroll their children in immersion classrooms voluntarily, and both French and English are majority languages that are equally valued in Canada. For U.S. non-English-speaking minority children, whose native languages are not valued by the larger society, a different strategy seems necessary: one that promotes children's native-language skills while they learn English.

ASK YOURSELF

REVIEW Cite examples of how language awareness fosters language progress.

APPLY Ten-year-old Shana arrived home from soccer practice and remarked, "I'm wiped out!" Megan, her 5-year-old sister, looked puzzled. "What did'ya wipe out, Shana?" Megan asked. Explain Shana's and Megan's different understandings of this expression.

REFLECT Did you acquire a second language at home or study one in school? If so, when did you begin, and how proficient are you? What changes would you make in your second-language learning, and why?

Learning in School

Evidence cited throughout this chapter indicates that schools are vital forces in children's cognitive development. How do schools exert such a powerful influence? Research looking at schools as complex social systems—educational philosophies, teacher–student relationships, and larger cultural context—provides important insights. As you read about these topics, refer to Applying What We Know on the following page, which summarizes characteristics of high-quality education in elementary school.

Educational Philosophies

Teachers' educational philosophies play a major role in children's learning. Two philosophical approaches have received most research attention. They differ in what children are taught, the way they are believed to learn, and how their progress is evaluated.

Traditional versus Constructivist Classrooms.
In a **traditional classroom**, the teacher is the sole authority for knowledge, rules, and decision making. Students are relatively passive—listening, responding when called on, and completing teacher-assigned tasks. Their progress is evaluated by how well they keep pace with a uniform set of standards for their grade.

A **constructivist classroom**, in contrast, encourages students to *construct* their own knowledge. Although constructivist approaches vary, many are grounded in Piaget's theory, which views children as active agents who reflect on and coordinate their own thoughts rather than absorbing those of others. A glance inside a constructivist classroom reveals richly equipped learning centers, small groups and individuals solving self-chosen problems, and a teacher who guides and supports in response to children's needs. Students are evaluated by considering their progress in relation to their own prior development.

In the United States, the pendulum has swung back and forth between these two views. In the 1960s and early 1970s, constructivist classrooms gained in popularity. Then, as concern arose over the academic progress of children and youths, a "back-to-basics" movement arose, and classrooms returned to traditional instruction. This style, still prevalent today, has become increasingly pronounced as a result of the U.S. No Child Left Behind Act, signed into law in 2001 (Darling-Hammond, 2010; Ravitch, 2010). Because it places heavy pressure on teachers and school administrators to improve achievement test scores, it has narrowed the curricular focus in many schools to preparing students to take such tests.

Although older elementary school children in traditional classrooms have a slight edge in achievement test scores, constructivist settings are associated with many other benefits—gains in critical thinking, greater social and moral maturity, and more positive attitudes toward school (DeVries, 2001; Rathunde & Csikszentmihalyi, 2005; Walberg, 1986). And as noted in Chapter 7, when teacher-directed instruction is

Applying What We Know

Signs of High-Quality Education in Elementary School

Classroom Characteristics	Signs of Quality
Class size	Optimum class size is no larger than 18 children.
Physical setting	Space is divided into richly equipped activity centers—for reading, writing, playing math or language games, exploring science, using computers, and other academic pursuits. Spaces are used flexibly for individual and small-group activities and whole-class gatherings.
Curriculum	The curriculum helps children both achieve academic standards and make sense of their learning. Subjects are integrated so that children apply knowledge in one area to others. Learning activities are responsive to children's interests, ideas, and everyday lives, including their cultural backgrounds.
Interactions between teachers and children	Teachers foster each child's progress and use intellectually engaging strategies, including posing problems, asking thought-provoking questions, discussing ideas, and adding complexity to tasks. They also demonstrate, explain, coach, and assist in other ways, depending on each child's learning needs.
Evaluations of progress	Teachers regularly evaluate children's progress through written observations and work samples, which they use to enhance and individualize teaching. They help children reflect on their work and decide how to improve it. They also seek information and perspectives from parents on how well children are learning and include parents' views in evaluations.
Relationship with parents	Teachers forge partnerships with parents. They hold periodic conferences and encourage parents to visit the classroom anytime, to observe and volunteer.

Source: Copple & Bredekamp, 2009.

emphasized in preschool and kindergarten, it actually undermines academic motivation and achievement, especially in low-SES children.

Recent Philosophical Directions.

Recent approaches to education, grounded in Vygotsky's sociocultural theory, capitalize on the rich social context of the classroom to spur children's learning. In these **social-constructivist classrooms,** children participate in a wide range of challenging activities with teachers and peers, with whom they jointly construct understandings. As children acquire knowledge and strategies through working together, they become competent, contributing members of their classroom community and advance in cognitive and social development (Bodrova & Leong, 2007; Palincsar, 2003). Vygotsky's emphasis on the social origins of higher cognitive processes has inspired the following educational themes:

● *Teachers and children as partners in learning.* A classroom rich in both teacher–child and child–child collaboration transfers culturally valued ways of thinking to children.

● *Experiences with many types of symbolic communication in meaningful activities.* As children master reading, writing, and mathematics, they become aware of their culture's communication systems, reflect on their own thinking, and bring it under voluntary control.

● *Teaching adapted to each child's zone of proximal development.* Assistance that both responds to current understandings and encourages children to take the next step helps ensure that each child makes the best progress possible.

According to Vygotsky, besides teachers, more expert peers can spur children's learning, as long as they adjust the help they provide to fit the less mature child's zone of proximal development. Consistent with this idea, mounting evidence confirms that peer collaboration promotes development only under certain conditions. A crucial factor is **cooperative learning,** in which small groups of classmates work toward common goals—by resolving differences of opinion, sharing responsibilities, and providing one another with sufficient explanations to correct misunderstandings. And when more expert students cooperate with less expert students, both benefit in achievement and self-esteem (Ginsburg-Block, Rohrbeck, & Fantuzzo, 2006).

LOOK AND LISTEN

Ask an elementary school teacher to sum up his or her educational philosophy. Is it closest to a traditional, constructivist, or social-constructivist view? Has the teacher encountered any obstacles to implementing that philosophy? Explain. ●

Because Western cultural-majority children regard competition and independent work as natural, they typically require extensive guidance to succeed at cooperative learning. In several studies, groups of students trained in collaborative processes displayed more cooperative behavior, gave clearer explanations, enjoyed learning more, and made greater academic progress in diverse school subjects than did untrained groups (Gillies, 2000, 2003; Terwel et al., 2001; Webb et al., 2008).

These children attending a rural school in Laos cooperate easily while completing a writing assignment. Their Western cultural-majority agemates, in contrast, typically require extensive guidance to succeed at cooperative learning.

Teacher–Student Interaction

Elementary school students describe good teachers as caring, helpful, and stimulating—behaviors associated with gains in motivation, achievement, and positive peer relations (Hughes & Kwok, 2006, 2007; O'Connor & McCartney, 2007). But too many U.S. teachers emphasize repetitive drill over higher-level thinking, such as grappling with ideas and applying knowledge to new situations (Sacks, 2005).

Of course, teachers do not interact in the same way with all children. Well-behaved, high-achieving students typically get more encouragement and praise, whereas unruly students have more conflicts with teachers and receive more criticism (Henricsson & Rydell, 2004). Overall, higher-SES students—who tend to be higher-achieving and to have fewer discipline problems—have more supportive relationships with teachers (Jerome, Hamre, & Pianta, 2009).

Unfortunately, once teachers' attitudes toward students are established, they can become more extreme than is warranted by students' behavior. Of special concern are **educational self-fulfilling prophecies:** Children may adopt teachers' positive or negative views and start to live up to them. This effect is especially strong when teachers emphasize competition and publicly compare children, regularly favoring the best students (Kuklinski & Weinstein, 2001; Weinstein, 2002).

Teacher expectations have a greater impact on low-achieving than high-achieving students (Madon, Jussim, & Eccles, 1997). When a teacher is critical, high achievers can fall back on their history of success. Low-achieving students' sensitivity to self-fulfilling prophecies can be beneficial when teachers believe in them. But biased teacher judgments are usually slanted in a negative direction. In one study, African-American and Hispanic elementary school students taught by high-bias teachers (who expected them to do poorly) showed substantially lower end-of-year achievement than their counterparts taught by low-bias teachers (McKown & Weinstein, 2008). Recall our discussion of *stereotype threat.* A child in the position of confirming a negative

stereotype may respond with anxiety and reduced motivation, amplifying a negative self-fulfilling prophecy.

In many schools, students are assigned to *homogeneous* groups or classes in which children of similar ability levels are taught together. Homogeneous grouping can be a potent source of self-fulfilling prophecies. Low-group students—who are more likely to be low-SES, minority, and male—get more drill on basic facts and skills, engage in less discussion, and progress at a slower pace. Gradually, they decline in self-esteem and motivation and fall further behind in achievement (Lleras & Rangel, 2009; Worthy, Hungerford-Kresser, & Hampton, 2009). Unfortunately, widespread SES and ethnic segregation in U.S. schools consigns large numbers of low-SES minority students to a form of schoolwide homogeneous grouping. Refer to the Social Issues: Education box on the following page to find out how magnet schools foster heterogeneous learning contexts, thereby reducing achievement differences between SES and ethnic minority groups.

Teaching Children with Special Needs

We have seen that effective teachers flexibly adjust their teaching strategies to accommodate students with a wide range of characteristics. These adjustments are especially challenging at the very low and high ends of the ability distribution. How do schools serve children with special learning needs?

Children with Learning Difficulties. U.S. legislation mandates that schools place children who require special supports for learning in the "least restrictive" (as close to normal as possible) environments that meet their educational needs. In **inclusive classrooms,** students with learning difficulties learn alongside typical students in the regular educational setting for all or part of the school day—a practice designed to prepare them for participation in society and to combat prejudices against individuals with disabilities (Kugelmass & Ainscow,

In this inclusive first-grade classroom, a teacher encourages special-needs students' active participation. They are likely to do well if they also receive support from a special education teacher.

Social Issues: Education

Magnet Schools: Equal Access to High-Quality Education

Each school-day morning, Emma leaves her affluent suburban neighborhood, riding a school bus to a magnet school in an impoverished, mostly Hispanic inner-city community. In her sixth-grade class, she settles into a science project with her friend, Maricela, who lives in the local neighborhood. The girls use a thermometer, ice water, and a stopwatch to determine which of several materials is the best insulator, recording and graphing their data. Throughout the school, which specializes in innovative math and science teaching, students diverse in SES and ethnicity learn side-by-side.

Despite the 1954 U.S. Supreme Court *Brown v. Board of Education* decision ordering schools to desegregate, school integration has receded since the late 1980s, as federal courts canceled their integration orders and returned this authority to states and cities. Today, the racial divide in American education is deepening (Frankenburg & Orfield, 2007). African-American children are just as likely to attend a school that serves a mostly black population as they were in the 1960s; Hispanic children are even more segregated. And when minority students attend ethnically mixed schools, they typically do so with other minorities.

U.S. schools in low-income neighborhoods are vastly disadvantaged in funding and therefore in educational opportunities

(Darling-Hammond, 2010). Consequently, dilapidated school buildings, inexperienced teachers, and poor-quality educational resources are widespread in inner-city neighborhoods (Kozol, 2005). The negative impact on student achievement is severe.

Magnet schools offer a solution. In addition to the usual curriculum, they emphasize a specific area of interest—such as performing arts, math and science, or technology. Families outside the school neighborhood are attracted to magnet schools (hence the name) by their rich academic offerings. Often magnets are located in low-income minority areas, where they serve the neighborhood student population. Other students, who apply and are admitted by lottery, are bussed in—many from well-to-do city and suburban neighborhoods. In another model, all students—including those in the surrounding neighborhood—must apply. In either case, magnet schools are voluntarily desegregated.

Research confirms that less segregated education enhances minority student achievement (Linn & Welner, 2007). Is this

Third graders at a fine-arts magnet school jointly create a painting. The ethnically diverse learning environments of many magnet schools enhance academic achievement, especially among low-SES minority students.

© ELLEN B. SENISI PHOTOGRAPHY

so for magnet schools? A Connecticut study comparing seventh to tenth graders enrolled in magnet schools with those whose lottery numbers were not drawn and who therefore attended other city schools confirmed that magnet students showed greater gains in reading and math achievement over a two-year period (Bifulco, Cobb, & Bell, 2009). These outcomes were strongest for low-SES, ethnic minority students.

By high school, the higher-achieving peer environments of ethnically diverse schools encourage more students to pursue higher education (Franklin, 2012). In sum, magnet schools are a promising approach to overcoming the negative forces of SES and ethnic isolation in American schools.

2004). Largely as the result of parental pressures, an increasing number of students experience *full inclusion*—full-time placement in regular classrooms.

Some students in inclusive classrooms have *mild mental retardation:* Their IQs fall between 55 and 70, and they also show problems in adaptive behavior, or skills of everyday living (American Psychiatric Association, 2013). But the largest number—5 to 10 percent of school-age children—have **learning disabilities,** great difficulty with one or more aspects of learning, usually reading. As a result, their achievement is considerably behind what would be expected on the basis of their IQ. Sometimes deficits express themselves in other ways—for example, as severe inattention, which depresses both IQ and achievement (recall our discussion of ADHD on page 239). The problems of students with learning disabilities cannot be traced to any obvious physical or emotional difficulty or to environ-

mental disadvantage. Instead, deficits in brain functioning are involved (Waber, 2010). In many instances, the cause is unknown.

Although some students benefit academically from inclusion, many do not. Achievement gains depend on both the severity of the disability and the support services available (Downing, 2010). Furthermore, children with disabilities are often rejected by regular-classroom peers. Students with mental retardation are overwhelmed by the social skills of their classmates; they cannot interact adeptly in a conversation or game. And the processing deficits of some students with learning disabilities lead to problems in social awareness and responsiveness (Kelly & Norwich, 2004; Lohrmann & Bambara, 2006).

Does this mean that students with special needs cannot be served in regular classrooms? Not necessarily. Often these children do best when they receive instruction in a resource room for part of the day and in the regular classroom for the remainder

(Weiner & Tardif, 2004). In the resource room, a special education teacher works with students on an individual and small-group basis. Then, depending on their progress, children join regular classmates for different subjects and amounts of time.

Special steps must to be taken to promote peer relations in inclusive classrooms. Cooperative learning and peer-tutoring experiences in which teachers guide children with learning difficulties and their classmates in working together lead to friendly interaction, improved peer acceptance, and achievement gains (Fuchs et al., 2002a, 2002b).

Gifted Children.   In Joey and Lizzie's school, some children are **gifted,** displaying exceptional intellectual strengths. One or two students in every grade have IQ scores above 130, the standard definition of giftedness based on intelligence test performance. High-IQ children, as we have seen, have keen memories and an exceptional capacity to solve challenging academic problems. Yet recognition that intelligence tests do not sample the entire range of human mental skills has led to an expanded conception of giftedness.

Creativity and Talent.   **Creativity** is the ability to produce work that is original yet appropriate—something others have not thought of that is useful in some way (Kaufman & Sternberg, 2007; Sternberg, 2003). Tests of creative capacity tap **divergent thinking**—the generation of multiple and unusual possibilities when faced with a task or problem. Divergent thinking contrasts with **convergent thinking,** which involves arriving at a single correct answer and is emphasized on intelligence tests (Guilford, 1985).

Because highly creative children (like high-IQ children) are often better at some tasks than others, a variety of tests of divergent thinking are available (Runco, 1992; Torrance, 1988). A verbal measure might ask children to name uses for common objects (such as a newspaper). A figural measure might ask them to create drawings based on a circular motif (see Figure 9.6). A "real-world problem" measure requires students to suggest solutions to everyday problems. Responses can be scored for the number of ideas generated and their originality.

Yet critics point out that these measures tap only one of the complex cognitive contributions to creative accomplishment in everyday life (Plucker & Makel, 2010). Also involved are defining new and important problems, evaluating divergent ideas, choosing the most promising, and calling on relevant knowledge to understand and solve problems (Sternberg, 2003; Lubart, Georgsdottir, & Besançon, 2009).

Consider these ingredients, and you will see why people usually demonstrate creativity in only one or a few related areas. Partly for this reason, definitions of giftedness have been extended to include **talent**—outstanding performance in a specific field. Case studies reveal that excellence in creative writing, mathematics, science, music, visual arts, athletics, or leadership has roots in specialized interests and skills that first appear in childhood (Moran & Gardner, 2006). Highly talented children are biologically prepared to master their domain of interest, and they display a passion for doing so.

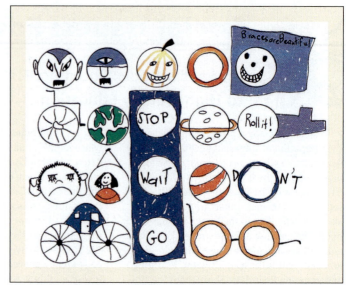

FIGURE 9.6 **Responses of an 8-year-old who scored high on a figural measure of divergent thinking.** This child was asked to make as many pictures as she could from the circles on the page. The titles she gave her drawings, from left to right, are as follows: "Dracula," "one-eyed monster," "pumpkin," "Hula-Hoop," "poster," "wheelchair," "earth," "stop-light," "planet," "movie camera," "sad face," "picture," "beach ball," "the letter *O*," "car," "glasses." Tests of divergent thinking tap only one of the complex cognitive contributions to creativity. (Reprinted by permission of Laura E. Berk.)

But talent must be nurtured. Studies of the backgrounds of talented children and highly accomplished adults often reveal warm, sensitive parents who provide a stimulating home life, are devoted to developing their child's abilities, and provide models of hard work. These parents are reasonably demanding but not driving or overambitious (Winner, 2000, 2003). They arrange for caring teachers while the child is young and for more rigorous master teachers as the talent develops.

Many gifted children and adolescents are socially isolated, partly because their nonconforming, independent styles leave them out of step with peers and partly because they enjoy solitude, which is necessary to develop their talents. Still, gifted children desire gratifying peer relationships, and some—more often girls than boys—try to become better-liked by hiding their abilities. Compared with their typical agemates, gifted youths, especially girls, report more emotional and social difficulties, including low self-esteem and depression (Reis, 2004; Winner, 2000).

Finally, whereas many talented youths become experts in their fields, few become highly creative. Rapidly mastering an existing field requires different skills than innovating in that field (Moran & Gardner, 2006). The world, however, needs both experts and creators.

Educating the Gifted.   Debate about the effectiveness of school programs for the gifted typically focuses on factors irrelevant to giftedness—whether to provide enrichment in regular classrooms, pull children out for special instruction (the most common practice), or advance brighter students to a higher grade. Overall, gifted children fare well academically and socially within each of these models, as long as the special activities provided do not reinforce convergent thinking to the detriment of problem solving, critical thinking, and creativity (Guignard & Lubart, 2007).

Gardner's theory of multiple intelligences has inspired several model programs that provide enrichment to all students in diverse disciplines. Meaningful activities, each tapping a specific intelligence or set of intelligences, serve as contexts for assessing strengths and weaknesses and, on that basis, teaching new knowledge and original thinking (Gardner, 2000; Hoerr, 2004). For example, linguistic intelligence might be fostered through storytelling or playwriting; spatial intelligence through drawing, sculpting, or taking apart and reassembling objects; and kinesthetic intelligence through dance or pantomime.

Evidence is still needed on how well these programs nurture children's talents and creativity. But they have already succeeded in one way—by highlighting the strengths of some students who previously had been considered unexceptional or even at risk for school failure (Kornhaber, 2004). Consequently, they may be especially useful in identifying talented low-SES, ethnic minority children, who are underrepresented in school programs for the gifted (McBee, 2006).

How Well-Educated Are U.S. Children?

Our discussion of schooling has largely focused on how teachers can support the education of children. Yet many factors—both within and outside schools—affect children's learning. Societal values, school resources, quality of teaching, and parental encouragement all play important roles. These multiple influences are especially apparent than when schooling is examined in cross-cultural perspective.

In international studies of reading, mathematics, and science achievement, young people in China, Korea, and Japan are consistently top performers. Among Western nations, Australia, Canada, Finland, the Netherlands, and Switzerland are also in the top tier. But U.S. students typically perform at or below the international averages (see Figure 9.7) (Programme for International Student Assessment, 2009).

Why do U.S. students fall behind in academic accomplishment? According to international comparisons, instruction in the United States is less challenging, more focused on absorbing facts, and less focused on high-level reasoning and critical thinking than in other countries. Furthermore, compared with top-achieving countries, the United States is far less equitable in the quality of education it provides to its low-income and ethnic minority students. And U.S. teachers vary much more in training, salaries, and teaching conditions.

Finland is a case in point. Its nationally mandated curricula, teaching practices, and assessments are aimed at cultivating initiative, problem solving, and creativity—vital abilities needed for success in the twenty-first century. Finnish teachers are highly trained: They must complete several years of graduate-level education at government expense (Sahlberg, 2010). And Finnish education is grounded in equal opportunity for all—a policy that has nearly eliminated SES variations in achievement.

Country	Average Math Achievement Score
High-Performing Nations	
China (Shanghai)	600
Singapore	562
China (Hong Kong)	555
Korea	546
Taiwan	543
Finland	541
Switzerland	534
Japan	529
Canada	527
Netherlands	526
China (Macao)	525
New Zealand	519
Belgium	515
Australia	514
Germany	513
Intermediate-Performing Nations	
Iceland	507
Denmark	503
Norway	498
France	497
Austria	496
International Average = 496	
Poland	495
Sweden	494
Czech Republic	493
United Kingdom	492
Hungary	490
Luxembourg	489
United States	**487**
Ireland	487
Portugal	487
Italy	483
Spain	483
Low-Performing Nations	
Russian Federation	468
Greece	466
Turkey	445
Bulgaria	428

FIGURE 9.7 Average mathematics scores of 15-year-olds by country. The Programme for International Student Assessment measured achievement in many nations around the world. In its most recent comparison of countries' performance, the United States performed below the international average in math; in reading and science, its performance was about average. (Adapted from Programme for International Student Assessment, 2009.)

In-depth research on learning environments in Asian nations, such as Japan, Korea, and Taiwan, also highlights social forces that foster strong student learning. Among these is cultural valuing of effort. Whereas American parents and teachers tend to regard native ability as the key to academic success, Japanese, Korean, and Taiwanese parents and teachers believe that all children can succeed academically with enough effort. Asian parents devote many more hours to helping their children with homework (Stevenson, Lee, & Mu, 2000). And Asian children, influenced by collectivist values, typically view striving to achieve as a moral obligation—part of their responsibility to family and community (Hau & Ho, 2010).

As in Finland, all students in Japan, Korea, and Taiwan receive the same nationally mandated, high-quality curriculum that encourages high-level thinking, delivered by teachers who

© ANNA DAMMERT

Finnish students explain the results of a static electricity experiment. Their country's education system—designed to cultivate initiative, problem solving, and creativity in all students—has nearly eliminated SES variations in achievement.

- strengthening teacher education
- supporting parents in creating stimulating home learning environments and monitoring their children's academic progress
- investing in high-quality preschool education, so every child arrives at school ready to learn
- vigorously pursuing school improvements that reduce the large inequities in quality of education between SES and ethnic groups (Economic Policy Institute, 2010).

are well-prepared and highly respected in their society (Kang & Hong, 2008; U.S. Department of Education, 2012a).

The Finnish and Asian examples underscore the need for American families, schools, and the larger society to work together to upgrade education. Recommended strategies, verified by research, include:

- providing intellectually challenging, relevant instruction with real-world applications

ASK YOURSELF

REVIEW List some teaching practices that foster children's achievement and some that undermine it. Provide a brief explanation of each practice.

APPLY Sandy would like her daughter Morgan, who has a learning disability, to be fully included in a regular classroom. What supports will Morgan need to ensure the success of full inclusion, and why?

REFLECT What teaching philosophy characterized most of your elementary education—traditional, constructivist, or social constructivist? What impact do you think that approach had on your motivation and achievement?

SUMMARY

PHYSICAL DEVELOPMENT

Body Growth (p. 227)

Describe major trends in body growth during middle childhood.

- During middle childhood, physical growth continues at a slow, regular pace. Bones lengthen and broaden, and permanent teeth replace the primary teeth. By age 9, girls overtake boys in physical size.

Health Issues (p. 227)

Describe the causes and consequences of serious nutritional problems in middle childhood, giving special attention to obesity.

- Many poverty-stricken children in developing countries and in the United States continue to suffer from serious and prolonged malnutrition, which can permanently impair physical and mental development.

- Overweight and **obesity** have increased dramatically in both industrialized and developing nations, especially in the United States. Although heredity contributes to obesity, parental feeding practices, maladaptive eating habits, reduced sleep, lack of exercise, and diets high in meats and energy-dense refined foods play powerful roles.

© OCEAN/CORBIS

- Obese children are rated as less likable by peers and adults and have serious adjustment problems. The most effective interventions are family-based and focus on changing parents' and children's eating patterns and lifestyles.

What factors contribute to illness during the school years, and how can these health problems be reduced?

- Children experience more illnesses during the first two years of elementary school than later because of exposure to sick children and an immature immune system.

- The most common cause of school absence and childhood hospitalization is asthma. Although heredity contributes to asthma, environmental factors—pollution, stressful home lives, lack of access to good health care, and the rise in childhood obesity—have led to an increase in the disease, especially among African-American and poverty-stricken children.

- Children with severe chronic illnesses are at risk for academic, emotional, and social difficulties, but positive family relationships improve adjustment.

Motor Development and Play (p. 230)

Cite major changes in motor development and play during middle childhood.

- Gains in flexibility, balance, agility, and force, along with more efficient information processing, contribute to school-age children's improved gross-motor performance.

- Fine-motor development also improves. Children's writing becomes more legible, and their drawings increase in organization, detail, and depth cues.

- Although girls outperform boys in fine-motor skills, boys outperform girls in all gross-motor skills except those requiring balance and agility. Parents' higher expectations for boys' athletic performance play a large role.

- Games with rules become common during the school years, contributing to emotional and social development. Children, especially boys, also engage in **rough-and-tumble play,** through which they safely assess the strength of peers to avoid challenging stronger agemates.

- Most U.S. school-age children are not active enough for good health, in part because of cutbacks in recess and physical education.

COGNITIVE DEVELOPMENT

Piaget's Theory: The Concrete Operational Stage (p. 234)

What are the major characteristics of concrete operational thought?

- In the **concrete operational stage,** children's thought becomes more logical, flexible, and organized. Mastery of conservation demonstrates decentration and **reversibility** in thinking.

- School-age children are also better at hierarchical classification and **seriation,** including **transitive inference.** Their spatial reasoning improves, evident in their ability to create **cognitive maps** representing familiar large-scale spaces.

- Concrete operational thought is limited in that children do not come up with general logical principles. They master concrete operational tasks step by step.

Discuss follow-up research on concrete operational thought.

- Specific cultural practices, especially those associated with schooling, promote children's mastery of Piagetian tasks.

- Some researchers attribute the gradual development of operational thought to gains in information-processing speed. Case's neo-Piagetian theory proposes that with practice, cognitive schemes become more automatic, freeing up space in working memory for combining old schemes and generating new ones. Eventually, children consolidate schemes into central conceptual structures, which enable them to coordinate and integrate multiple dimensions.

Information Processing (p. 237)

Describe gains in working-memory capacity and executive function, along with the development of attention and memory in middle childhood.

- Brain development contributes to increases in processing speed and working-memory capacity, which predicts intelligence test scores and academic achievement. As the prefrontal cortex continues to develop, children make great strides in executive function.

- Attention becomes more selective, adaptable, and planful, and memory strategies also improve. **Rehearsal** appears first, followed by **organization** and then **elaboration.** With age, children combine memory strategies.

- Development of the long-term knowledge base makes new information easier to store and retrieve. Children's motivation to use what they know also contributes to memory development. Memory strategies are promoted by learning activities in school.

Describe the school-age child's theory of mind and capacity to engage in self-regulation.

- School-age children regard the mind as an active, constructive agent, yielding a better understanding of cognitive processes, including effective memory strategies, mental inference, and second-order false belief. **Cognitive self-regulation** develops gradually, improving with adult instruction in strategy use.

Discuss current controversies in teaching reading and mathematics to elementary school children.

- Skilled reading draws on all aspects of the information-processing system. A combination of **whole language** and **phonics** is most effective for teaching beginning reading. Teaching that blends practice in basic skills with conceptual understanding also is best in mathematics.

Individual Differences in Mental Development (p. 242)

Describe major approaches to defining and measuring intelligence.

- Most intelligence tests yield an overall score as well as scores for separate intellectual factors. During the school years, IQ becomes more stable and correlates moderately with academic achievement.

- Componential analyses identify information-processing skills that contribute to mental test performance. Processing speed and flexible attention, memory, and reasoning strategies are positively related to IQ.

- Sternberg's **triarchic theory of successful intelligence** identifies three broad, interacting intelligences: analytical intelligence (information-processing skills), creative intelligence (capacity to solve novel problems), and practical intelligence (application of intellectual skills in everyday situations).

- Gardner's **theory of multiple intelligences** identifies at least eight distinct mental abilities. The theory has helped draw attention to children's unique intellectual strengths, though it has yet to be verified by research.

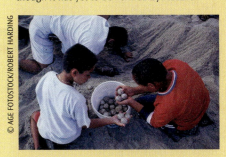

Describe evidence indicating that both heredity and environment contribute to intelligence.

- Heritability estimates and adoption research indicate that intelligence is a product of both heredity and environment. Adoption studies indicate that environmental factors underlie the black–white IQ gap.

- IQ scores are affected ... ...influenced communication styles and knowledge. **Stereotype threat** triggers anxiety that interferes with test performance. **Dynamic assessment** helps many minority children perform more competently on mental tests.

Language Development

(p. 248)

Describe changes in school-age children's vocabulary, grammar, and pragmatics, and cite the advantages of bilingualism for development.

- Language awareness contributes to school-age children's language progress. They have a more precise and flexible understanding of word meanings and use more complex grammatical constructions and conversational strategies. Their narratives increase in organization, detail, and expressiveness.

- Mastery of a second language must begin in childhood for full proficiency to occur. Bilingualism has positive consequences for cognitive development and aspects of language awareness. In Canada, language immersion programs succeed in developing children who are proficient in both English and French. In the United States, bilingual education that combines instruction in the native tongue and in English supports ethnic minority children's academic learning.

Learning in School (p. 250)

Describe the impact of class size and educational philosophies on children's motivation and academic achievement.

- Smaller classes in the early elementary grades promote lasting gains in academic achievement. Older elementary school students in **traditional classrooms** have a slight edge in achievement test scores over those in **constructivist classrooms,** who gain in critical thinking, social and moral maturity, and positive attitudes toward school.

- Students in **social-constructivist classrooms** benefit from working collaboratively in meaningful activities and from teaching adapted to each child's zone of proximal development. **Cooperative learning** promotes achievement and self-esteem.

© AGE FOTOSTOCK/ROBERT HARDING

Discuss the role of teacher–student interaction in academic achievement.

- Caring, helpful, and stimulating teaching fosters children's motivation, achievement, and peer relations. **Educational self-fulfilling prophecies** have a greater impact on low than high achievers and are especially likely to occur in classrooms that emphasize competition and public evaluation.

Under what conditions is placement of children with learning difficulties in regular classrooms successful?

- The success of **inclusive classrooms** for students with mild mental retardation and **learning disabilities** depends on meeting individual learning needs and promoting positive peer relations.

Describe the characteristics of gifted children and current efforts to meet their educational needs.

- **Giftedness** includes high IQ, **creativity,** and **talent.** Tests of creativity that tap **divergent** rather than **convergent thinking** focus on only one of the ingredients of creativity. Highly talented children generally have parents and teachers who nurture their exceptional abilities. Gifted children benefit from educational programs that build on their special strengths.

How well-educated are U.S. children compared with children in other industrialized nations?

- In international studies, young people in Asian nations are consistently top performers, whereas U.S. students typically perform at or below international averages. Compared with top-achieving countries, education in the United States is more focused on absorbing facts, less focused on high-level reasoning and critical thinking, and less equitable across SES groups.

Important Terms and Concepts

chapter

10

Emotional and Social Development in Middle Childhood

© ELLEN B. SENISI PHOTOGRAPHY

Social understanding expands greatly in middle childhood. Like others their age around the world, these third graders choose friends based on personal qualities, and they count on those friends for understanding and emotional support.

chapter outline

Late one afternoon, Rena heard her son Joey burst through the front door, run upstairs, and phone his best friend. "Terry, gotta talk to you," Joey pleaded breathlessly. "Everything was going great until I got that word—*porcupine*," Joey went on, referring to the fifth-grade spelling bee at school that day. "Just my luck! *P-o-r-k,* that's how I spelled it! I can't believe it. Maybe I'm not so good at social studies," Joey confided, "but I *know* I'm better at spelling than that stuck-up Belinda Brown. I knocked myself out studying those spelling lists. Then *she* got all the easy words. If I *had* to lose, why couldn't it be to a nice person?"

Joey's conversation reflects new emotional and social capacities. By entering the spelling bee, he shows *industriousness,* the energetic pursuit of meaningful achievement in his culture. Joey's social understanding has also expanded: He can size up strengths, weaknesses, and personality characteristics. Furthermore, friendship means something different than it did earlier—Joey counts on his best friend, Terry, for understanding and emotional support.

For an overview of the personality changes of middle childhood, we return to Erikson's theory. Then we look at children's views of themselves and of others, their moral understanding, and their peer relationships. Each increases in complexity as children reason more effectively and spend more time in school and with agemates.

Despite changing parent–child relationships, the family remains powerfully influential in middle childhood. Today, family lifestyles are more diverse than ever before. Through Joey and his younger sister Lizzie's experiences with parental divorce, we will see that family functioning is far more important than family structure in ensuring children's well-being. Finally, we look at some common emotional problems of middle childhood. ●

Erikson's Theory: Industry versus Inferiority

According to Erikson (1950), children whose previous experiences have been positive enter middle childhood prepared to redirect their energies toward realistic accomplishment. Erikson believed that the combination of adult expectations and children's drive toward mastery sets the stage for the psychological conflict of middle childhood, **industry versus inferiority,** which is resolved positively when children develop a sense of competence at useful skills and tasks.

In industrialized nations and increasingly in developing regions of the world, the beginning of formal schooling marks the transition to middle childhood. In school, children discover their own and others' unique capacities, learn the value of division of labor, and develop a sense of moral commitment and responsibility. The danger at this stage is *inferiority,* reflected in the pessimism of children who lack confidence in their ability to do things well. This sense of inadequacy can develop when family life has not prepared children for school life or when teachers and peers destroy children's self-confidence with negative responses.

Erikson's sense of industry combines several developments of middle childhood: a positive but realistic self-concept, pride in accomplishment, moral responsibility, and cooperative participation with agemates. How do these aspects of self and social relationships change over the school years?

Self-Understanding

In middle childhood, children begin to describe themselves in terms of psychological traits, compare their own characteris-

tics with those of their peers, and speculate about the causes of their strengths and weaknesses. These transformations in self-understanding have a major impact on self-esteem.

Self-Concept

During the school years, children refine their self-concept, organizing their observations of behaviors and internal states into general dispositions. A major change takes place between ages 8 and 11, as the following self-description by an 11-year-old illustrates:

> My name is A. I'm a human being. I'm a girl. I'm a truthful person. I'm not pretty. I do so-so in my studies. I'm a very good cellist. . . . I try to be helpful. I'm always ready to be friends with anybody. Mostly I'm good, but I lose my temper. (Montemayor & Eisen, 1977, pp. 317–318)

Instead of specific behaviors, this child emphasizes competencies: "I'm a very good cellist" (Damon & Hart, 1988). She also describes her personality, mentioning both positive and negative traits: "truthful" but short-tempered. Older school-age children are far less likely than younger children to describe themselves in extreme, all-or-none ways. These qualified, trait-based self-descriptions result from cognitive advances—specifically, the ability to combine typical experiences and behaviors into psychological dispositions. Children also become better at *perspective taking*—inferring others' attitudes toward the child—and incorporating those attitudes into their self-definitions. These cognitive capacities, combined with more experiences in which children are evaluated against agemates, prompt **social comparisons**—judgments of one's own appearance, abilities, and behavior in relation to those of others. For example, Joey observed that he was better than his peers at spelling but not so good at social studies (Harter, 2006). As children internalize others' expectations and make social comparisons, they form an *ideal self* that they use to evaluate their *real self*. As we will see, a large discrepancy between the two can undermine self-esteem, leading to sadness, hopelessness, and depression.

In middle childhood, children look to more people beyond the family for information about themselves as they enter a wider range of settings in school and community. And self-descriptions now include frequent reference to social groups: "I'm a Boy Scout, a paper boy, and a Prairie City soccer player," said Joey. As children move into adolescence, although parents and other adults remain influential, self-concept is increasingly vested in feedback from close friends (Oosterwegel & Oppenheimer, 1993).

But recall that the makeup of self-concept varies from culture to culture. In earlier chapters, we noted that Asian parents stress harmonious interdependence, whereas Western parents stress independence and self-assertion. When asked to recall personally significant past experiences (their last birthday, a time their parent scolded them), U.S. school-age children gave longer accounts including more personal preferences, interests, skills, and opinions. Chinese children, in contrast, more often referred to social interactions and to others. Similarly, in their self-descriptions, U.S. children listed more personal attributes ("I'm smart," "I like hockey"), Chinese children more attributes involving group membership and relationships ("I'm in second grade," "My friends are crazy about me") (Wang, 2006; Wang, Shao, & Li, 2010).

Finally, although school-age children from diverse cultures view themselves as more knowledgeable about their own inner attributes than significant adults, Japanese children credit their parents and teachers with considerably more knowledge than Western children do (Mitchell et al., 2010, p. 249). Perhaps because of their more interdependent self, Japanese children assume that their inner states are more transparent to others.

Self-Esteem

Recall that most preschoolers have extremely high self-esteem. But as children enter school and receive more feedback about how well they perform compared with their peers, self-esteem differentiates and also adjusts to a more realistic level.

Researchers have asked children to indicate the extent to which statements such as "I am good at reading" or "I'm usually the one chosen for games" are true of themselves. By age 6 to 7, children have formed at least four broad self-evaluations: academic competence, social competence, physical/athletic competence, and physical appearance. Within these are more refined categories that become increasingly distinct with age (Marsh, 1990; Marsh & Ayotte, 2003; Van den Bergh & De Rycke, 2003). Furthermore, the capacity to view the self in terms of stable dispositions permits school-age children to combine their separate self-evaluations into a general psychological image of themselves—an overall sense of self-esteem (Harter, 2003, 2006). As a result, self-esteem takes on the hierarchical structure shown in Figure 10.1 on page 262.

Children attach greater importance to certain self-evaluations than to others. Although individual differences exist, during childhood and adolescence, perceived physical appearance correlates more strongly with overall self-worth than any other self-esteem factor (Klomsten, Skaalvik, & Espnes, 2004; Shapka & Keating, 2005). Emphasis on appearance—in the media, by parents and peers, and in society—has major implications for young people's overall satisfaction with themselves.

Over the first few years of elementary school, level of self-esteem declines as children evaluate themselves in various areas (Marsh, Craven, & Debus, 1998; Wigfield et al., 1997). Typically, the drop is not great enough to be harmful. Most (but not all) children appraise their characteristics and competencies realistically while maintaining an attitude of self-respect. Then, from fourth grade on, self-esteem rises for the majority of young people, who feel especially good about their peer relationships and athletic capabilities (Impett et al., 2008; Twenge & Campbell, 2001).

Influences on Self-Esteem

From middle childhood on, individual differences in self-esteem become increasingly stable (Trzesniewski, Donnellan, & Robins, 2003). And positive relationships among self-esteem, valuing of various activities, and success at those activities emerge and strengthen (Denissen, Zarrett, & Eccles, 2007; Valentine, DuBois, & Cooper, 2004; Whitesell et al., 2009). What social influences might lead self-esteem to be high for some children and low for others?

Culture. An especially strong emphasis on social comparison in school may explain why Chinese and Japanese children, despite their higher academic achievement, score lower than U.S. children in self-esteem (Harter, 2006; Hawkins, 1994; Twenge & Crocker, 2002). And because their culture values

In response to feedback from classmates and teachers, the self-esteem of these schoolchildren in India gradually adjusts to a more realistic level.

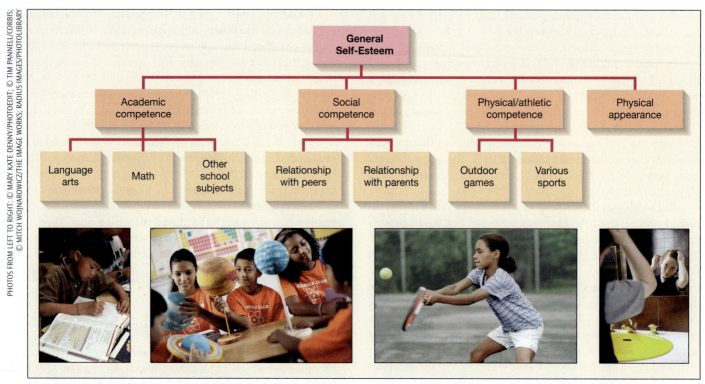

FIGURE 10.1 Hierarchical structure of self-esteem in the mid-elementary school years. From their experiences in different settings, children form at least four separate self-esteems: academic competence, social competence, physical/athletic competence, and physical appearance. These differentiate into additional self-evaluations and combine to form a general sense of self-esteem.

social harmony, Asian children tend to be reserved about judging themselves positively but generous in their praise of others (Falbo et al., 1997).

Gender-stereotyped expectations also affect self-esteem. In one study, the more 5- to 8-year-old girls talked with friends about the way people look, watched TV shows focusing on physical appearance, and perceived their friends as valuing thinness, the greater their dissatisfaction with their physical

An 11-year-old performs a traditional African dance at a community Kwanzaa celebration. A stronger sense of ethnic pride may be partly responsible for African-American children's higher self-esteem relative to their Caucasian agemates.

self and the lower their overall self-esteem a year later (Dohnt & Tiggemann, 2006). In academic self-judgments, girls score higher in language arts self-esteem, whereas boys have higher math, science, and physical/athletic self-esteem—even when children of equal skill levels are compared (Fredricks & Eccles, 2002; Jacobs et al., 2002; Kurtz-Costes et al., 2008). At the same time, girls exceed boys in self-esteem dimensions of close friendship and social acceptance. And despite a widely held assumption that boys' overall self-worth is much higher than girls', the difference is slight (Marsh & Ayotte, 2003; Young & Mroczek, 2003). Girls may think less well of themselves because they internalize this negative cultural message.

Compared with their Caucasian agemates, African-American children tend to have slightly higher self-esteem, possibly because of warm extended families and a stronger sense of ethnic pride (Gray-Little & Hafdahl, 2000). Finally, children and adolescents who attend schools or live in neighborhoods where their SES and ethnic groups are well-represented feel a stronger sense of belonging and have fewer self-esteem problems (Gray-Little & Carels, 1997).

Child-Rearing Practices. Children whose parents use an *authoritative* child-rearing style (see Chapter 8) feel especially good about themselves (Lindsey et al., 2008; Wilkinson, 2004). Warm, positive parenting lets children know that they are accepted as competent and worthwhile. And firm but appropriate expectations, backed up with explanations, help them evaluate their own behavior against reasonable standards.

Controlling parents—~~too often~~ help or make decisions for their child—communicate a sense of inadequacy to children. Having parents who are repeatedly disapproving is also linked to low self-esteem (Kernis, 2002; Pomerantz & Eaton, 2000). Children subjected to such parenting need constant reassurance, and many rely heavily on peers to affirm their self-worth—a risk factor for adjustment difficulties, including aggression and antisocial behavior (Donnellan et al., 2005). In contrast, indulgent parenting is correlated with unrealistically high self-esteem. These children tend to lash out at challenges to their overblown self-images and, thus, are also likely to be hostile and aggressive (Hughes, Cavell, & Grossman, 1997; Thomaes et al., 2008).

The best way to foster a positive, secure self-image is to encourage children to strive for worthwhile goals. Over time, achievement fosters self-esteem, which contributes to further effort and gains in performance (Gest, Domitrovich, & Welsh, 2005; Marsh et al., 2005). What can adults do to promote, and to avoid undermining, this mutually supportive relationship between motivation and self-esteem? Some answers come from research on the precise content of adults' messages to children in achievement situations.

Achievement-Related Attributions. *Attributions* are our common, everyday explanations for the causes of behavior—our answers to the question, "Why did I or another person do that?" Notice how Joey, in talking about the spelling bee at the beginning of this chapter, attributes his disappointing performance to *luck* (Belinda got all the easy words) and his usual success to *ability* (he *knows* he's a better speller than Belinda). Joey also appreciates that *effort* matters: "I knocked myself out studying those spelling lists."

Cognitive development permits school-age children to separate all these variables in explaining performance (Dweck, 2002). Those who are high in academic self-esteem and motivation make **mastery-oriented attributions,** crediting their successes to ability—a characteristic they can improve through trying hard and can count on when facing new challenges. And they attribute failure to factors that can be changed or controlled, such as insufficient effort or a very difficult task (Heyman & Dweck, 1998). Whether these children succeed or fail, they take an industrious, persistent approach to learning.

In contrast, children who develop **learned helplessness** attribute their failures, not their successes, to ability. When they succeed, they conclude that external factors, such as luck, are responsible. Unlike their mastery-oriented counterparts, they believe that ability is fixed and cannot be improved by trying hard (Cain & Dweck, 1995). When a task is difficult, these children experience an anxious loss of control—in Erikson's terms, a pervasive sense of inferiority. They give up without really trying.

Children's attributions affect their goals. Mastery-oriented children seek information on how best to increase their ability through effort. Hence, their performance improves over time (Blackwell, Trzesniewski, & Dweck, 2007). In contrast, learned-

A 7-year-old in a woodworking class seeks additional information on how to assemble a jewelry box. Using this mastery-oriented, effortful approach to overcoming obstacles, his performance will improve over time.

helpless children focus on obtaining positive and avoiding negative evaluations of their fragile sense of ability. Over time, their ability no longer predicts how well they do (Pomerantz & Saxon, 2001). Because they fail to connect effort with success, learned-helpless children do not develop the metacognitive and self-regulatory skills necessary for high achievement (see Chapter 9). Lack of effective learning strategies, reduced persistence, and a sense of loss of control sustain one another in a vicious cycle (Chan & Moore, 2006).

Influences on Achievement-Related Attributions. Adult communication plays a key role in the different attributions of mastery-oriented and learned-helplessness children (Pomerantz & Dong, 2006). Children with a learned-helpless style often have parents who believe that their child is not very capable. When the child fails, the parent might say, "You can't do that, can you? It's OK if you quit." When the child succeeds, the parent might offer feedback that evaluates the child's traits ("You're so smart"). Such trait statements—even when positive—encourage children to adopt a fixed view of ability (Mueller & Dweck, 1998). This leads them to question their competence in the face of challenges.

LOOK AND LISTEN

Observe a school-age child working on a challenging homework assignment under the guidance of a parent or other adult. What features of the adult's communication likely foster mastery-oriented attributions? How about learned helplessness? Explain. ●

Despite their higher achievement, girls more often than boys blame poor performance on lack of ability. When girls do not do well, they tend to receive messages from teachers and parents that their ability is at fault, and negative stereotypes (for example, that girls are weak at math) undermine their interest and effort (Bleeker & Jacobs, 2004; Cole et al., 1999). And as

Chapter 9 revealed, low-SES ethnic minority students often receive less favorable feedback from teachers—conditions that result in a drop in academic self-esteem and achievement (Harris & Graham, 2007).

Finally, cultural values affect the likelihood that children will develop learned helplessness. Asian parents and teachers are more likely than their American counterparts to view effort as key to success and as a moral responsibility—messages they transmit to children (Mok, Kennedy, & Moore, 2011; Pomerantz, Ng, & Wang, 2008). Asians also attend more to failure than to success because failure indicates where corrective action is needed. Americans, in contrast, focus more on success because it enhances self-esteem. Observations of U.S. and Chinese mothers' responses to their fourth and fifth graders' puzzle solutions revealed that the U.S. mothers offered more praise after success, whereas the Chinese mothers more often pointed out the child's inadequate performance. And Chinese mothers made more task-relevant statements aimed at ensuring that children exerted sufficient effort ("You concentrated on it": "You got only 6 out of 12") (Ng, Pomerantz, & Lam, 2007). When children continued with the task after mothers left the room, the Chinese children showed greater gains in performance.

Fostering a Mastery-Oriented Approach. Attribution research suggests that well-intended messages from adults sometimes undermine children's competence. An intervention called *attribution retraining* encourages learned-helpless children to believe that they can overcome failure by exerting more effort. Children are given tasks difficult enough that they will experience some failure, followed by repeated feedback that helps them revise their attributions: "You can do it if you try harder." After they succeed, children receive additional feedback—"You're really good at this" or "You really tried hard on that one"—so that they attribute their success to both ability and effort, not chance. Another approach is to encourage low-effort students to focus less on grades and more on mastering a task for individual improvement (Hilt, 2004; Yeh, 2010). Instruction in effective strategies and self-regulation is also vital, to compensate for development lost in this area and to ensure that renewed effort pays off (Wigfield et al., 2006).

ASK YOURSELF

REVIEW How does level of self-esteem change in middle childhood, and what accounts for these changes?

APPLY Should parents promote children's self-esteem by telling them they're "smart" or "wonderful"? Are children harmed if they do not feel good about everything they do? Why or why not?

REFLECT Recall your own attributions for academic successes and failures when you were in elementary school. What are those attributions like now? What messages from others may have contributed to your attributions?

Emotional Development

Greater self-awareness and social sensitivity support gains in emotional competence in middle childhood. Changes take place in experience of self-conscious emotions, emotional understanding, and emotional self-regulation.

Self-Conscious Emotions

In middle childhood, the self-conscious emotions of pride and guilt become clearly governed by personal responsibility. Children experience pride in a new accomplishment and guilt over a transgression, even when no adult is present (Harter & Whitesell, 1989).

Pride motivates children to take on further challenges, whereas guilt prompts them to make amends and to strive for self-improvement. But in Chapter 8 we noted that excessive guilt is linked to depressive symptoms. And harsh, insensitive reprimands from adults ("Everyone else can do it! Why can't you?") can lead to intense shame, which is particularly destructive, yielding both internalizing and externalizing problems (see page 203).

Emotional Understanding

School-age children's understanding of mental activity means that, unlike preschoolers, they are likely to explain emotion by referring to internal states, such as happy or sad thoughts (Flavell, Flavell, & Green, 2001). Also, between ages 6 and 12, children become more aware of circumstances likely to spark mixed emotions, each of which may be positive or negative and may differ in intensity (Larsen, To, & Fireman, 2007; Pons et al., 2003). For example, Joey reflected, "I was very happy that I got a birthday present from my grandma but a little sad that I didn't get just what I wanted."

Appreciating mixed emotions helps children realize that people's expressions may not reflect their true feelings (Misailidi, 2006). It also fosters awareness of self-conscious emotions. For example, between ages 6 and 7, children improve sharply in ability to distinguish pride from happiness and surprise (Tracy, Robins, & Lagattuta, 2005). And 8- and 9-year-olds understand that pride combines two sources of happiness—joy in accomplishment and joy that a significant person recognized that accomplishment (Harter, 1999).

As with self-understanding, gains in emotional understanding are supported by cognitive development and social experiences, especially adults' sensitivity to children's feelings and willingness to discuss emotions. Together, these factors lead to a rise in empathy as well. As children move closer to adolescence, advances in perspective taking permit an empathic response not just to people's immediate distress but also to their general life condition (Hoffman, 2000). As Joey and Lizzie imagined how people who are chronically ill or hungry feel and evoked those emotions in themselves, they gave part of their allowance to charity and joined in school and scouting fundraising projects.

Detroit-area schoolchildren prepare meal packages for families in need. Gains in emotional understanding and perspective taking enable children to expand their empathic responding to include people's general life condition.

Emotional Self-Regulation

Rapid gains in emotional self-regulation occur in middle childhood. As children engage in social comparison and care more about peer approval, they must learn to manage negative emotion that threatens their self-esteem.

By age 10, most children shift adaptively between two general strategies for managing emotion. In **problem-centered coping,** they appraise the situation as changeable, identify the difficulty, and decide what to do about it. If problem solving does not work, they engage in **emotion-centered coping,** which is internal, private, and aimed at controlling distress when little can be done about an outcome (Kliewer, Fearnow, & Miller, 1996; Lazarus & Lazarus, 1994). For example, when faced with an anxiety-provoking test or an angry friend, older school-age children view problem solving and seeking social support as the best strategies. But when outcomes are beyond their control—for example, after receiving a bad grade—they opt for distraction or try to redefine the situation: "Things could be worse. There'll be another test." School-age children's improved ability to appraise situations and reflect on thoughts and feelings means that, compared with preschoolers, they more often use these internal strategies to manage emotion (Brenner & Salovey, 1997).

When emotional self-regulation has developed well, school-age children acquire a sense of *emotional self-efficacy*—a feeling of being in control of their emotional experience (Saarni, 2000; Thompson & Goodman, 2010). This fosters a favorable self-image and an optimistic outlook, which further help children face emotional challenges. As at younger ages, school-age children whose parents respond sensitively and helpfully when the child is distressed are emotionally well-regulated—generally upbeat in mood and also empathic and prosocial. In contrast, poorly regulated children often experience hostile, dismissive parental reactions to distress (Davidov & Grusec, 2006; Zeman, Shipman, & Suveg, 2002). These children are overwhelmed by negative emotion, a response that interferes with empathy and prosocial behavior.

 ## Moral Development

Recall from Chapter 8 that preschoolers pick up many morally relevant behaviors through modeling and reinforcement. By middle childhood, they have had time to internalize rules for good conduct: "It's good to help others in trouble" or "It's wrong to take something that doesn't belong to you." This change leads children to become considerably more independent and trustworthy.

In Chapter 8, we also saw that children do not just copy their morality from others but actively think about right and wrong. An expanding social world, the capacity to consider more information when reasoning, and perspective taking lead moral understanding to advance greatly in middle childhood.

Moral and Social-Conventional Understanding

During the school years, children construct a flexible appreciation of moral rules. By age 7 to 8, they no longer say truth telling is always good and lying is always bad but also consider prosocial and antisocial intentions. They evaluate certain types of truthfulness very negatively—for example, blunt statements, particularly when made in public contexts where they are especially likely to have negative social consequences (telling a classmate that you don't like her drawing) (Bussey, 1999; Ma et al., 2011).

As children's ideas about justice take into account an increasing number of variables, they clarify and link moral imperatives and social conventions. School-age children, for example, distinguish social conventions with a clear *purpose* (not running in school hallways to prevent injuries) from ones with no obvious justification (crossing a "forbidden" line on the playground). They regard violations of purposeful social conventions as closer to moral transgressions (Buchanan-Barrow & Barrett, 1998). With age, they also realize that people's *intentions* and the *contexts* of their actions affect the moral implications of violating a social convention. In one study, 8- to 10-year-olds

This 10-year-old understands the moral implications of observing social conventions, such as expressing respect for his country's flag. He also grasps that flag burning is sometimes justifiable as a form of freedom of expression.

stated that because of a flag's symbolic value, burning it to express disapproval of a country or to start a cooking fire is worse than burning it accidentally. But they recognized that flag burning is a form of freedom of expression, and most agreed that it would be acceptable in a country that treated its citizens unfairly (Helwig & Prencipe, 1999).

Children in Western and non-Western cultures reason similarly about moral and social-conventional concerns (Neff & Helwig, 2002; Nucci, 2005, 2008). When a directive is fair and caring, such as telling children to stop fighting or to share candy, school-age children view it as right, regardless of who states it—a principal, a teacher, or a child with no authority. In contrast, even in Korean culture, which places a high value on deference to authority, 7- to 11-year-olds evaluate negatively a teacher's or principal's order to engage in immoral acts, such as stealing or refusing to share (Kim, 1998; Kim & Turiel, 1996). In sum, children everywhere seem to realize that higher principles, independent of rule and authority, must prevail when people's personal rights and welfare are at stake.

Understanding Individual Rights

When children challenge adult authority, they typically do so within the personal domain. As their grasp of moral imperatives and social conventions strengthens, so does their conviction that certain choices, such as hairstyle, friends, and leisure activities, are up to the individual.

Notions of personal choice, in turn, enhance children's moral understanding. As early as age 6, children view freedom of speech and religion as individual rights, even if laws exist that deny those rights (Helwig, 2006). And they regard laws that discriminate against individuals—for example, denying certain people access to medical care or education—as wrong and worthy of violating (Helwig & Jasiobedzka, 2001). In justifying their responses, children appeal to personal privileges and, by the end of middle childhood, to the importance of individual rights for maintaining a fair society.

At the same time, older school-age children place limits on individual choice, depending on circumstances. Fourth graders faced with conflicting moral and personal concerns—such as whether or not to befriend a classmate of a different race or gender—typically decide in favor of kindness and fairness (Killen et al., 2002). Partly for this reason, as we will see next, prejudice usually declines during middle childhood.

Understanding Diversity and Inequality

By the early school years, children associate power and privilege with white people and poverty and inferior status with people of color. They do not necessarily acquire these views directly from parents or friends, whose attitudes often differ from their own (Aboud & Doyle, 1996). Rather, children seem to pick up prevailing societal attitudes from social contexts that present a world sorted into groups, such as racial and ethnic segregation in schools and communities.

In-Group and Out-Group Biases: Development of Prejudice. Studies in diverse Western nations confirm that by age 5 to 6, white children generally evaluate their own racial group favorably and other racial groups less favorably or negatively. *In-group favoritism* emerges first; children simply prefer their own group, generalizing from self to similar others (Bennett et al., 2004; Nesdale et al., 2004). And the ease with which a trivial group label supplied by an adult can induce in-group favoritism is striking. In one study, Caucasian-American 5-year-olds were told that they were members of a group based on T-shirt color. Although no information was provided about group status and the children never met any group members, they still displayed vigorous in-group favoritism (Dunham, Baron, & Carey, 2011). When shown photos of unfamiliar agemates wearing either an in-group or an out-group shirt, the children claimed to like members of their own group better, gave them more resources, and engaged in positively biased recall of group members' behavior.

Out-group prejudice requires a more challenging social comparison between in-group and out-group. But it does not take long for white children to acquire negative attitudes toward ethnic minority out-groups when such attitudes are encouraged by their environments. When white Canadian 4- to 7-year-olds living in a white community and attending nearly all-white schools sorted positive and negative adjectives into boxes labeled as belonging to a white child and a black child, out-group prejudice emerged at age 5. Unfortunately, many minority children show a reverse pattern: *out-group favoritism,* in which they assign positive characteristics to the privileged white majority and negative characteristics to their own group (Averhart & Bigler, 1997; Corenblum, 2003).

But recall that with age, children pay more attention to inner traits. The capacity to classify the social world in multiple ways enables school-age children to understand that people who look different need not think, feel, or act differently (Aboud, 2008). Consequently, voicing of negative attitudes toward minorities declines. After age 7 to 8, both majority and minority children express in-group favoritism, and white children's openly expressed prejudice against out-group members often weakens (Nesdale et al., 2005; Ruble et al., 2004). Yet even in children aware of the injustice of discrimination, prejudice can operate automatically without awareness—through subtle negative emotional reactions toward the out-group—as it does in many white adults (Degner & Wentura, 2010; Dunham, Baron, & Banaji, 2006). At least to some degree, then, older school-age children's desire to present themselves in a socially acceptable light may contribute to reduced overt expressions of prejudice with age.

The extent to which children hold racial and ethnic biases varies, depending on the following personal and situational factors:

- *A fixed view of personality traits.* Children who believe that people's personality traits are fixed rather than changeable readily form prejudices on the basis of limited information.

For example, they might infer that "a new child at school who tells a lie to get other kids to like her" is simply a bad kid (Levy & Dweck, 1999).

- *Overly high self-esteem.* Children (and adults) with very high self-esteem are more likely to hold racial and ethnic prejudices (Baumeister et al., 2003; Bigler, Brown, & Markell, 2001). These individuals seem to belittle disadvantaged people or groups to justify their own extremely favorable, yet insecure, self-evaluations.

- *A social world in which people are sorted into groups.* The more adults highlight group distinctions and the less interracial contact children experience, the more likely white children will express out-group prejudice (Killen et al., 2010).

Reducing Prejudice. Research confirms that an effective way to reduce prejudice is through intergroup contact, in which racially and ethnically different children have equal status, work toward common goals, and become personally acquainted. Children assigned to cooperative learning groups with peers of diverse backgrounds show low levels of prejudice in their expressions of likability and in their behavior. For example, they form more cross-race friendships (Pettigrew & Tropp, 2006). Sharing thoughts and feelings with close, cross-race friends, in turn, reduces even subtle, unintentional prejudices (Turner, Hewstone, & Voci, 2007). But these positive effects seem not to generalize to out-group members who are not part of these learning teams.

Long-term contact and collaboration among neighborhood, school, and community groups may be the best way to reduce prejudice (Rutland, Killen, & Abrams, 2010). Classrooms that expose children to ethnic diversity, teach them to value those differences, directly address the damage caused by preju-dice, and encourage perspective taking and empathy both prevent children from forming negative biases and reduce already acquired biases (Dweck, 2009).

Finally, inducing children to view others' traits as changeable, by discussing with them the many possible influences on those traits, is helpful. The more children believe that people can change their personalities, the more they report liking and perceiving themselves as similar to members of disadvantaged out-groups. Furthermore, children who believe in the changeability of human attributes spend more time volunteering to help the needy (Karafantis & Levy, 2004). Volunteering may, in turn, promote a changeable view of others by helping children appreciate the social conditions that lead to disadvantage.

ASK YOURSELF

REVIEW How does emotional self-regulation improve in middle childhood? What implications do these changes have for children's self-esteem?

APPLY Seven-year-old Tracy heard her parents discussing an older cousin's fiancé. "Molly can marry whomever she wants," Tracy chimed in. "That's *her* choice." How is Tracy's reasoning contributing to her moral understanding?

REFLECT Did you attend an integrated elementary school? Why is school integration vital for reducing racial and ethnic prejudice?

Peer Relations

In middle childhood, the society of peers becomes an increasingly important context for development. Peer contact, as we have seen, contributes to perspective taking and understanding of self and others. These developments, in turn, enhance peer interaction. Compared with preschoolers, school-age children resolve conflicts more effectively, using persuasion and compromise (Mayeux & Cillessen, 2003). Sharing, helping, and other prosocial acts also increase. In line with these changes, aggression declines. But the drop is greatest for physical attacks (Côté et al., 2007). As we will see, verbal and relational aggression continue as children form peer groups.

Peer Groups

TAKE A MOMENT... Watch children in the schoolyard or neighborhood, and notice how often they gather in groups of three to a dozen or more. In what ways are members of the same group noticeably alike? By the end of middle childhood, children display a strong desire for group belonging. They form **peer groups,** collectives that generate unique values and standards for behavior and a social structure of leaders and

Third graders perform a traditional Chinese dance at their culturally diverse school. Long-term contact and collaboration with members of other ethnic groups reduces prejudice.

followers. Peer groups organize on the basis of proximity (being in the same classroom) and similarity in sex, ethnicity, academic achievement, popularity, and aggression (Rubin, Bukowski, & Parker, 2006).

The practices of these informal groups lead to a "peer culture" that typically involves a specialized vocabulary, dress code, and place to "hang out." These customs bind peers together, creating a sense of group identity. Within the group, children acquire many social skills—cooperation, leadership, follower-ship, and loyalty to collective goals.

Most school-age children believe a group is wrong to exclude a peer (Killen, Crystal, & Watanabe, 2002). Neverthe-less, children do exclude, often using relationally aggressive tactics. Peer groups—at the instigation of their leaders, who can be skillfully aggressive—frequently oust no longer "respected" children. Some of these castouts, whose own previous behavior toward outsiders reduces their chances of being included else-where, turn to other low-status peers with poor social skills (Farmer et al., 2010; Werner & Crick, 2004). Socially anxious children, when ousted, often become increasingly peer-avoidant and thus more isolated (Buhs, Ladd, & Herald-Brown, 2010). In either case, opportunities to acquire socially competent behav-ior diminish.

School-age children's desire for group membership can also be satisfied through formal group ties such as scouting, 4-H, and religious youth groups. Adult involvement holds in check the negative behaviors associated with children's informal peer groups.

These boys have probably established a peer-group structure of leaders and followers as they gather for joint activities. Their relaxed body language and similar way of dressing suggest a strong sense of group belonging.

Friendships

Whereas peer groups provide children with insight into larger social structures, friendships contribute to the development of trust and sensitivity. During the school years, friendship becomes more complex and psychologically based. Consider the follow-ing 8-year-old's ideas:

> *How come you like Shelly better than anyone else?* She's done the most for me. She never disagrees, she never eats in front of me, she never walks away when I'm crying, and she helps me with my homework. . . . *How do you get someone to like you?* . . . If you're nice to [your friends], they'll be nice to you. (Damon, 1988b, pp. 80–81)

As these responses show, friendship has become a mutually agreed-on relationship in which children like each other's per-sonal qualities and respond to one another's needs and desires. And once a friendship forms, *trust* becomes its defining feature. Consequently, older children regard violations of trust, such as not helping when others need help, breaking promises, and gos-siping behind the other's back, as serious breaches of friendship (Hartup & Abecassis, 2004).

LOOK AND LISTEN

Ask an 8- to 11-year-old to tell you what he or she looks for in a best friend. Is *trust* centrally important? Does the child mention personality traits, just as school-age children do in describing themselves? ●

Because of these features, school-age children's friendships are more selective. Whereas preschoolers say they have lots of friends, by age 8 or 9, children name only a handful of good friends, and their friendships last longer—sometimes for sev-eral years. Girls, who demand greater closeness than boys, are more exclusive in their friendships (Markovits, Benenson, & Dolensky, 2001).

In addition, children tend to select friends similar to them-selves in age, sex, ethnicity, and SES. Friends also resemble one another in personality (sociability, inattention/hyperactiv-ity, aggression, depression), popularity, academic achievement, prosocial behavior, and judgments (including biased percep-tions) of other people (Hartup, 2006; Mariano & Harton, 2005). But friendship opportunities offered by children's environments also affect their choices. As noted earlier, in integrated class-rooms with mixed-race collaborative learning groups, students form more cross-race friendships.

Through friendship, children come to realize that close relationships can survive disagreements if friends are secure in their liking for each other (Hartup, 2006). In this way, friendship provides an important context in which children learn to toler-ate criticism and resolve disputes.

Yet the impact of friendships on development depends on the nature of those friends. Children who bring kindness and compassion to their friendships strengthen each other's pro-social tendencies and form more lasting ties. When aggressive children make friends, the relationship is often riddled with

DAVID ROTH/TAXI/GETTY IMAGES

Cross-race friendships are common in integrated classrooms with rich opportunities for collaborative learning.

hostile interaction and is at risk for breakup, especially when just one member of the pair is aggressive (Ellis & Zarbatany, 2007). Aggressive girls' friendships are full of jealousy, conflict, and betrayal. Aggressive boys' friendships involve frequent expressions of anger, coercive statements, physical attacks, and enticements to rule-breaking behavior (Bagwell & Coie, 2004; Crick & Nelson, 2002; Werner & Crick, 2004). These findings indicate that the social problems of aggressive children operate within their closest peer ties.

Peer Acceptance

Peer acceptance refers to likability—the extent to which a child is viewed by a group of agemates, such as classmates, as a worthy social partner. Unlike friendship, likability is not a mutual relationship but a one-sided perspective, involving the group's view of an individual. Nevertheless, certain social skills that contribute to friendship also enhance peer acceptance. Better-accepted children tend to have more friends and more positive relationships with them (Lansford et al., 2006).

To assess peer acceptance, researchers usually use self-reports that measure *social preferences*—for example, asking children to identify classmates whom they "like very much" or "like very little" (Hymel et al., 2004). Another approach assesses *social prominence*—children's judgments of the peers most of their classmates admire. Only moderate correspondence exists between the classmates children identify as prominent (looked up to by many others) and those they say they personally prefer (Prinstein & Cillessen, 2003).

Children's self-reports yield four general categories of peer acceptance:

- **Popular children,** who get many positive votes (are well-liked)
- **Rejected children,** who get many negative votes (are disliked)

- **Controversial children,** who get a large number of positive and negative votes (are both liked and disliked)
- **Neglected children,** who are seldom mentioned, either positively or negatively

About two-thirds of students in a typical elementary school classroom fit one of these categories (Coie, Dodge, & Coppotelli, 1982). The remaining one-third, who do not receive extreme scores, are *average* in peer acceptance.

Peer acceptance is a powerful predictor of psychological adjustment. Rejected children, especially, are anxious, unhappy, disruptive, and low in self-esteem. Both teachers and parents rate them as having a wide range of emotional and social problems. Peer rejection in middle childhood is also strongly associated with poor school performance, absenteeism, dropping out, substance use, depression, antisocial behavior, and delinquency in adolescence and with criminality in early adulthood (Ladd, 2005; Laird et al., 2001; Rubin, Bukowski, & Parker, 2006).

However, earlier influences—children's characteristics combined with parenting practices—may largely explain the link between peer acceptance and adjustment. School-age children with peer-relationship problems are more likely to have weak emotion regulation skills and to have experienced family stress due to low income, insensitive child rearing, and coercive discipline (Cowan & Cowan, 2004; Trentacosta & Shaw, 2009). Nevertheless, peer rejection adds to the risk of maladjustment, beyond rejected children's maladaptive behavioral styles (Sturaro et al., 2011).

Determinants of Peer Acceptance. Why is one child liked while another is rejected? A wealth of research reveals that social behavior plays a powerful role.

Popular Children. Two subtypes of popular children exist. The majority are **popular-prosocial children,** who combine academic and social competence, performing well in school and communicating with peers in sensitive, friendly, and cooperative ways (Cillessen & Bellmore, 2004). A smaller number are admired for their socially adept yet belligerent behavior. These **popular-antisocial children** include "tough" boys—athletically skilled but poor students who cause trouble and defy adult authority—and relationally aggressive boys and girls who enhance their own status by ignoring, excluding, and spreading rumors about other children (Rodkin et al., 2000; Rose, Swenson, & Waller, 2004; Vaillancourt & Hymel, 2006). With age, peers like these high-status, aggressive youths less and less and may eventually reject them.

Rejected Children. Rejected children display a wide range of negative social behaviors. The largest subtype, **rejected-aggressive children,** show high rates of conflict, physical and relational aggression, and hyperactive, inattentive, and impulsive behavior. They are even more belligerent than popular-aggressive children and are also deficient in perspective taking and emotion regulation (Dodge, Coie, & Lynam, 2006; Hoza et al., 2005). In contrast, **rejected-withdrawn children** are passive

Biology and Environment

Bullies and Their Victims

Follow the activities of aggressive children over a school day, and you will see that they reserve their hostilities for certain peers. A particularly destructive form of interaction is **peer victimization**, in which certain children become targets of verbal and physical attacks or other forms of abuse. What sustains these repeated assault–retreat cycles?

About 20 percent of children are bullies, while 25 percent are repeatedly victimized. Most bullies are boys who use both physically, verbally, and relationally aggressive tactics, but a considerable number of girls bombard vulnerable classmates with verbal and relational hostility (Cook et al., 2010). As bullies move into adolescence, gender harassment increases—powerful youths (more often boys) delivering insults of a sexual nature against weaker agemates, and heterosexual youths targeting sexual minority peers (Pepler et al., 2006). Furthermore, many youths amplify their attacks through electronic means. About 20 to 40 percent of youths have experienced "cyberbullying" through text messages, e-mail, chat rooms, or other electronic tools (Tokunaga, 2010). They often do not report it to parents or adults at school.

Many bullies are disliked because of their cruelty. But a substantial number are socially prominent youngsters, who are broadly admired for their physical attractiveness, leadership, or athletic abilities (Vaillancourt et al., 2010c). To preserve their high social status, bullies often target already peer-rejected children, whom classmates are unlikely to defend (Veenstra et al., 2010). This helps explain why peers rarely intervene to help victims, and why 20 to 30 per-

cent of onlookers actually encourage bullies, even joining in (Salmivalli & Voeten, 2004).

Chronic victims tend to be passive when active behavior is expected. On the playground, they hang around chatting or wander on their own. When bullied, they give in, cry, and assume defensive postures (Boulton, 1999). Biologically based traits—an inhibited temperament and a frail physical appearance—contribute to victimization. But victims also have histories of resistant attachment, overly controlling child rearing, and maternal overprotection—parenting that prompts anxiety, low self-esteem, and dependency, resulting in a fearful demeanor that marks these children as vulnerable (Snyder et al., 2003). Victims' adjustment problems include depression, loneliness, poor school performance, unruly behavior, and school avoidance (Paul & Cillessen, 2003). And like persistent child abuse, victimization is linked to impaired production of cortisol, suggesting a disrupted physiological response to stress (Vaillancourt et al., 2010b).

Interventions that change victimized children's negative opinions of themselves and that teach them to respond in nonreinforcing ways to their attackers are helpful. Another way to assist victimized children is to help them form and maintain a gratifying friendship (Fox & Boulton, 2006). When children have a close friend to whom they can turn for help, bullying episodes usually end quickly.

Although modifying victimized children's behavior can help, this does not mean they

Some bullies are high-status youngsters, but many are disliked, or become so, because of their cruelty. And chronic victims are often easy targets—physically weak, passive, and inhibited.

are to blame. The best way to reduce bullying is to promote prosocial attitudes and behaviors. Effective approaches include developing school and community codes against bullying; teaching child bystanders to intervene; strengthening adult supervision of high-bullying areas in schools, such as hallways and schoolyard; enlisting parents' assistance in changing bullies' behaviors; and (if necessary) moving socially prominent bullies to another class or school (Kiriakidis & Kavoura, 2010; Vaillancourt et al., 2010a).

and socially awkward. These timid children are overwhelmed by social anxiety, hold negative expectations for treatment by peers, and worry about being scorned and attacked (see the Biology and Environment box above) (Hart et al., 2000; Rubin, Bowker, & Gazelle, 2010; Troop-Gordon & Asher, 2005). As rejected children are excluded, their classroom participation declines, their feelings of loneliness rise, their academic achievement falters, and they want to avoid school (Buhs, Ladd, & Herald-Brown, 2010; Gooren et al., 2011). Most have few friends, and some have none—a circumstance that predicts severe adjustment difficulties (Ladd et al., 2011).

LOOK AND LISTEN

Contact a nearby elementary school or a school district to find out what practices are in place to prevent bullying. Inquire about a written antibullying policy, and request a copy. ●

Controversial and Neglected Children. Consistent with the mixed peer opinion they engender, controversial children display a blend of positive and negative social behaviors. They are hostile and disruptive, but they also engage in positive, prosocial acts (de Bruyn & Cillessen, 2006; Newcomb, Bukowski, & Pattee, 1993). But like their popular-antisocial and rejected-aggressive counterparts, they often bully others and engage in calculated relational aggression to sustain their dominance (DeRosier & Thomas, 2003; Putallaz et al., 2007).

Perhaps the most surprising finding is that neglected children, once thought to be in need of treatment, are usually well-adjusted. Although they engage in low rates of interaction, most are just as socially skilled as average children. They do not report feeling lonely or unhappy, and when they want to, they can break away from their usual pattern of playing alone, cooperating well with peers and forming positive, stable friendships (Ladd & Burgess, 1999; Ladd et al., 2011). Neglected, socially competent children remind us that an outgoing, gregarious personality style is not the only path to emotional well-being.

Helping Rejected Children. A variety of interventions exist to improve the peer relations and psychological adjustment of rejected children. Most involve coaching, modeling, and reinforcing positive social skills, such as how to initiate interaction with a peer, cooperate in play, and respond to another child with friendly emotion and approval. Several of these programs have produced lasting gains in social competence and peer acceptance (Asher & Rose, 1997; DeRosier, 2007).

Still another approach focuses on training in perspective taking and in solving social problems. But many rejected-aggressive children are unaware of their poor social skills and do not take responsibility for their social failures (Mrug, Hoza, & Gerdes, 2001). Rejected-withdrawn children, in contrast, are likely to develop a *learned-helpless* approach to peer difficulties—concluding, after repeated rebuffs, that they will never be liked (Wichmann, Coplan, & Daniels, 2004). Both types of children need help attributing their peer difficulties to internal, changeable causes.

As rejected children gain in social skills, teachers must encourage peers to alter their negative opinions. Accepted children often selectively recall rejected classmates' negative acts while overlooking their positive ones (Mikami, Lerner, & Lun, 2010; Peets et al., 2007). Consequently, even in the face of contrary evidence, rejected children's negative reputations tend to persist. Teachers' praise and expressions of liking can modify peer judgments.

Finally, because rejected children's social incompetence often originates in harsh, authoritarian parenting, interventions focusing on the child alone may not be sufficient (Bierman & Powers, 2009). If the parent–child interaction does not change, children may soon return to their old behavior patterns.

Gender Typing

Children's understanding of gender roles broadens in middle childhood, and their gender identities (views of themselves as relatively masculine or feminine) change as well. We will see that development differs for boys and girls.

Gender-Stereotyped Beliefs

Research in many countries reveals that stereotyping of personality traits increases steadily in middle childhood, becoming adultlike around age 11 (Best, 2001; Heyman & Legare, 2004). For example, children regard "tough," "aggressive," "rational," and "dominant" as masculine and "gentle," "sympathetic," and "dependent" as feminine (Serbin, Powlishta, & Gulko, 1993).

Children derive these distinctions from observing sex differences in behavior as well as from adult treatment. When helping a child with a task, for example, parents (especially fathers) behave in a more mastery-oriented fashion with sons, setting higher standards, explaining concepts, and pointing out important features of tasks—particularly during gender-typed pursuits, such as science activities (Tenenbaum & Leaper, 2003; Tenenbaum et al., 2005). Furthermore, parents less often encourage girls to make their own decisions. And both parents and teachers more often praise boys for knowledge and accomplishment, girls for obedience (Good & Brophy, 2003; Leaper, Anderson, & Sanders, 1998; Pomerantz & Ruble, 1998).

Also in line with adult stereotypes, school-age children quickly figure out which academic subjects and skill areas are "masculine" and which are "feminine." They often regard reading, spelling, art, and music as more for girls and mathematics, athletics, and mechanical skills as more for boys (Cvencek, Meltzoff, & Greenwald, 2011; Eccles, Jacobs, & Harold, 1990). These attitudes influence children's preferences and sense of competence. As we saw earlier (page 262), boys tend to feel more competent at math, science, and athletics, whereas girls feel more competent at language arts—gender differences still evident after controlling for actual performance.

An encouraging sign is that in several recent investigations carried out in Canada, France, and the United States, a majority of elementary and secondary students disagreed with the idea that math is a "masculine" subject (Martinot & Désert, 2007; Plante, Théoret, & Favreau, 2009; Rowley et al. 2007). And although school-age children are aware of many stereotypes, they also develop a more open-minded view of what males and females *can do* (Trautner et al., 2005). The ability to classify flexibly contributes to this change. School-age children realize that a person's sex is not a certain predictor of his or her personality traits, activities, and behavior. Similarly, by the end of middle childhood, most children regard gender typing as socially rather than biologically influenced (Taylor, Rholdes, & Gelman, 2009).

Nevertheless, acknowledging that people *can* cross gender lines does not mean that children always *approve* of doing so. In one longitudinal study, between ages 7 and 13, children of both genders became more open-minded about girls being offered the same opportunities as boys. This increasing flexibility, however, was less pronounced among boys (Crouter et al., 2007). Furthermore, many children take a harsh view of certain violations—boys playing with dolls and wearing girls' clothing, girls acting noisily and roughly. They are especially intolerant when boys engage in these "cross-gender" acts (Blakemore, 2003).

Gender Identity and Behavior

From third to sixth grade, boys tend to strengthen their identification with "masculine" personality traits, whereas girls' identification with "feminine" traits declines. Girls are more *androgynous,* often describing themselves as having some "other-gender" characteristics (Serbin, Powlishta, & Gulko, 1993). And whereas boys usually stick to "masculine" activities, many girls experiment with a wider range of options—from cooking and sewing to sports and science fairs—and consider traditionally male future work roles (Liben & Bigler, 2002).

These changes are due to a mixture of cognitive and social forces. School-age children of both sexes are aware that society attaches greater prestige to "masculine" characteristics. For example, they rate "masculine" occupations as having higher status than "feminine" occupations (Liben, Bigler, & Krogh, 2001; Weisgram, Bigler, & Liben, 2010). Messages from adults and peers are also influential. In Chapter 8, we saw that parents (especially fathers) are far less tolerant when sons, as opposed to daughters, cross gender lines. Similarly, a tomboyish girl can make her way into boys' activities without losing the approval of her female peers, but a boy who engages in "feminine" pursuits is likely to be ridiculed and rejected.

As school-age children make social comparisons and characterize themselves in terms of stable dispositions, their gender identity expands to include the following self-evaluations, which greatly affect their adjustment:

- *Gender typicality*—the degree to which the child feels he or she "fits in" with others of the same gender (Egan & Perry, 2001).

- *Gender contentedness*—the degree to which the child feels comfortable with his or her gender assignment.
- *Felt pressure to conform to gender roles*—the degree to which the child feels parents and peers disapprove of his or her gender-related traits.

In a longitudinal study of third through seventh graders, *gender-typical* and *gender-contented* children gained in self-esteem over the following year. In contrast, children who were *gender-atypical* and *gender-discontented* declined in self-worth. Furthermore, gender-atypical children who reported *intense pressure to conform to gender roles* experienced serious difficulties—withdrawal, sadness, disappointment, and anxiety (Yunger, Carver, & Perry, 2004). Intervening with parents and peers to help them become more accepting of children's gender-atypical interests and behaviors can protect gender-atypical children's well-being (Bigler, 2007; Conway, 2007; Crawford, 2003).

ASK YOURSELF

REVIEW Why are girls more androgynous than boys in middle childhood?

APPLY What changes in parent–child relationships are probably necessary to help rejected children?

REFLECT As a school-age child, did you have classmates you would classify as popular-aggressive? What were they like, and why do you think peers admired them?

An 8-year-old launches the rocket she made in her school's Young Astronaut Club. Whereas school-age boys usually stick to "masculine" pursuits, girls experiment with a wider range of options.

© TAMPA BAY TIMES/CHRIS ZUPPA/THE IMAGE WORKS

 # Family Influences

As children move into school, peer, and community contexts, the parent–child relationship changes. At the same time, children's well-being continues to depend on the quality of family interaction. In the following sections, we will see that contemporary diversity in family life—divorce, remarriage, maternal employment, and dual-earner families—can have positive as well as negative effects on children. In later chapters, we take up other family structures, including gay and lesbian families, never-married single-parent families, and the increasing numbers of grandparents rearing grandchildren.

Parent–Child Relationships

In middle childhood, the amount of time children spend with parents declines dramatically. Children's growing independence means that parents must deal with new issues. "I've struggled with how many chores to assign, how much allowance to give, whether their friends are good influences, and what to do about problems at school," Rena remarked. "And then there's the challenge of keeping track of them when they're out—or even when they're home and I'm not there to see what's going on."

Despite these new concerns, child rearing becomes easier for those parents who established an authoritative style during the early years. Reasoning is more effective with school-age children because of their greater capacity for logical thinking and their increased respect for parents' expert knowledge (Collins, Madsen, & Susman-Stillman, 2002).

As children demonstrate that they can manage daily activities and responsibilities, effective parents engage in **coregulation,** a form of supervision in which parents exercise general oversight while letting children take charge of moment-by-moment decision making. Coregulation grows out of a warm, cooperative relationship between parent and child based on give-and-take. Parents must guide and monitor from a distance and effectively communicate expectations when they are with their children. And children must inform parents of their whereabouts, activities, and problems so parents can intervene when necessary (Maccoby, 1984).

As at younger ages, mothers tend to spend more time than fathers with school-age children. Still, many fathers are highly involved (Galinsky, Aumann, & Bond, 2009). Each parent, however, tends to devote more time to children of his or her own sex (Lamb & Lewis, 2004; Tucker, McHale, & Crouter, 2003). And parents are more vigilant about monitoring the activities of same-sex children while their children are away from home.

Siblings

Sibling rivalry tends to increase in middle childhood. As children participate in a wider range of activities, parents often compare siblings' traits and accomplishments (Dunn, 2004; Tamrouti-Makkink et al., 2004). The child who gets less parental affection, more disapproval, or fewer material resources is likely to be resentful and show poorer adjustment.

For same-sex siblings who are close in age, parental comparisons are more frequent, resulting in more antagonism. This effect is particularly strong when parents are under stress as a result of financial worries, marital conflict, single parenthood, or child negativity (Jenkins, Rasbash, & O'Connor, 2003). Parents whose energies are drained become less careful about being fair.

To reduce this rivalry, siblings often strive to be different from one another. For example, two brothers I know deliberately selected different athletic pursuits and musical instruments. Parents can limit the effects of rivalry by making an effort not to compare children, but some feedback about their competencies is inevitable. As siblings strive to win recognition for their own uniqueness, they shape important aspects of each other's development.

Although conflict rises, school-age siblings continue to rely on each other for companionship and support (Seibert & Kerns, 2009; Tucker, McHale, & Crouter, 2001). But for siblings to reap these benefits, parental encouragement of warm, considerate sibling ties is vital. The more positive their relationship, the

Although sibling rivalry tends to increase in middle childhood, siblings also provide each other with emotional support and help with difficult tasks.

more siblings resolve disagreements constructively, provide each other with various forms of assistance, and contribute to resilience in the face of major stressors, such as parental divorce (Conger, Stocker, & McGuire, 2009; Soli, McHale, & Feinberg, 2009).

When siblings get along well, the older sibling's academic and social competence tends to "rub off on" the younger sibling, fostering more favorable achievement and peer relations (Brody & Murry, 2001; Lamarche et al., 2006). But destructive sibling conflict in middle childhood is associated with negative outcomes, including conflict-ridden peer relationships, anxiety, depressed mood, and later substance use and delinquency, even after other family relationship factors are controlled (Criss & Shaw, 2005; Kim et al., 2007; Stocker, Burwell, & Briggs, 2002).

Only Children

Although sibling relationships bring many benefits, they are not essential for healthy development. Contrary to popular belief, only children are not spoiled, and in some respects, they are advantaged. U.S. children growing up in one-child and multichild families do not differ in self-rated personality traits (Mottus, Indus, & Allik, 2008). And compared to children with siblings, only children are higher in self-esteem, do better in school, and attain higher levels of education. One reason may be that only children have somewhat closer relationships with parents, who may exert more pressure for mastery and accomplishment (Falbo, 1992). However, only children tend to be less well-accepted in the peer group, perhaps because they have not

WANG ZHAO/AFP/GETTY IMAGES

Limiting family size has been a national policy in China for more than three decades. In urban areas, the majority of couples have no more than one child.

had opportunities to learn effective conflict-resolution strategies through sibling interactions (Kitzmann, Cohen, & Lockwood, 2002).

Favorable development also characterizes only children in China, where a one-child family policy has been enforced in urban areas for more than three decades to control population growth (Yang, 2008). Compared with agemates who have siblings, Chinese only children are advanced in cognitive development and academic achievement. They also feel more emotionally secure, perhaps because government disapproval promotes tension in families with more than one child (Falbo & Poston, 1993; Jiao, Ji, & Jing, 1996; Yang et al., 1995).

China's birth rate, at 1.5 overall and 0.7 in its largest cities, is now lower than that of many developed nations. As a result, its elderly population is rapidly increasing while its working-age population has leveled off—an imbalance that threatens the country's economic progress. And because sons are more highly valued than daughters, the policy has resulted in an epidemic of abortions of female fetuses and abandonment of girl babies, yielding a vastly skewed population sex ratio (130 male births for every 100 female births) that jeopardizes social stability (Zhu & Hesketh, 2009). Consequently, China is considering relaxing the one-child policy, but it is now so culturally ingrained that couples typically say they would not have a second child, even if offered the opportunity (LaFraniere, 2011).

Divorce

Children's interactions with parents and siblings are affected by other aspects of family life. Joey and Lizzie's relationship, Rena told me, had been particularly negative only a few years before. Joey pushed, hit, and taunted Lizzie and called her names—fighting that coincided with Rena and her husband's growing

marital unhappiness. When Joey was 8 and Lizzie 5, their father, Drake, moved out.

Between 1960 and 1985, divorce rates in Western nations rose dramatically before stabilizing in most countries. The United States has experienced a decline in divorces over the past decade, largely due to a rise in age at first marriage (Amato & Dorius, 2010). Nevertheless, the United States continues to have the highest divorce rate in the world (see Figure 10.2). Of the 45 percent of American marriages that end in divorce, half involve children. At any given time, one-fourth of U.S. children live in single-parent households. Although most reside with their mothers, the percentage in father-headed households has increased steadily, to about 12 percent (Federal Interagency Forum on Child and Family Statistics, 2011).

Children of divorce spend an average of five years in a single-parent home. About two-thirds of divorced parents marry again. Half of their children eventually experience a third major change—the end of a parent's second marriage (Hetherington & Kelly, 2002).

These figures reveal that divorce is a transition that leads to a variety of new living arrangements, accompanied by changes in housing, income, and family roles and responsibilities. Since the 1960s, many studies have reported that marital breakup is stressful for children. But how well children fare depends on

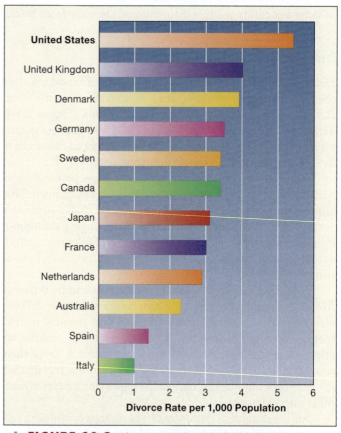

FIGURE 10.2 Divorce rates in 12 industrialized nations. The U.S. divorce rate is the highest in the industrialized world, far exceeding divorce rates in other countries. (Adapted from U.S. Census Bureau, 2013.)

many factors: the custodial parent's psychological health, the child's characteristics, and social supports within the family and surrounding community (Fine, Ganong, & Demo, 2010).

Immediate Consequences.

"Things were worst during the period Drake and I decided to separate," Rena reflected. "We fought over division of our belongings and custody of the children, and the kids suffered. Sobbing, Lizzie told me she was 'sorry she made Daddy go away.' Joey kicked and threw things at home and didn't do his work at school. In the midst of everything, I could hardly deal with their problems. We had to sell the house, and I needed a better-paying job."

Family conflict often rises around the time of divorce as parents try to settle disputes over children and possessions. Once one parent moves out, additional events threaten supportive interactions between parents and children. Many mother-headed households experience a sharp drop in income. In the United States, 27 percent of divorced mothers with young children live in poverty, and more are low-income, getting less than the full amount of child support from the absent father or none at all (Grall, 2011).

The transition from marriage to divorce typically leads to high maternal stress, depression, and anxiety and to a disorganized family situation. Declines in well-being are greatest for mothers of young children (Williams & Dunne-Bryant, 2006). "Meals and bedtimes were at all hours, and I stopped taking Joey and Lizzie on weekend outings," said Rena. As children react with distress and anger to their less secure home lives, discipline may become harsh and inconsistent. Contact with noncustodial fathers often decreases over time (Hetherington & Kelly, 2002). Fathers who see their children only occasionally are inclined to be permissive and indulgent, making the mother's task of managing the child even more difficult.

The more parents argue and fail to provide children with warmth, involvement, and consistent guidance, the poorer children's adjustment. About 20 to 25 percent of children in divorced families display severe problems, compared with about 10 percent in nondivorced families (Lansford, 2009; Noller et al., 2008). At the same time, reactions vary with children's age, temperament, and sex.

Children's Age.

Preschool and young school-age children often blame themselves for a marital breakup (as Lizzie did) and fear that both parents may abandon them. And although older children have the cognitive maturity to understand that they are not responsible for their parents' divorce, many react strongly, declining in school performance, becoming unruly, and escaping into undesirable peer activities, especially when family conflict is high (D'Onofrio et al., 2006; Lansford et al., 2006). Some older children—especially the oldest child in the family—display more mature behavior, willingly taking on extra household tasks as well as emotional support of a depressed, anxious mother. But if these demands are too great, these children may eventually become resentful and engage in angry, acting-out behavior (Hetherington, 1999).

Children's Temperament and Sex.

Exposure to stressful life events and inadequate parenting magnifies the problems of temperamentally difficult children (Lengua et al., 2000). In contrast, easy children are less often targets of parental anger and also cope more effectively with adversity.

These findings help explain sex differences in response to divorce. Girls sometimes respond as Lizzie did, with internalizing reactions such as crying, self-criticism, and withdrawal. More often, children of both sexes show demanding, attention-getting behavior. But in mother-custody families, boys are at slightly greater risk for serious adjustment problems (Amato, 2010). Recall from Chapter 8 that boys are more active and noncompliant—behaviors that increase with exposure to parental conflict and inconsistent discipline.

Long-Term Consequences.

Rena eventually found better-paying work and gained control over the daily operation of the household. And after several meetings with a counselor, Rena and Drake realized the harmful impact of their quarreling on Joey and Lizzie. Drake visited regularly and handled Joey's unruliness with firmness and consistency. Soon Joey's school performance improved, his behavior problems subsided, and both children seemed calmer and happier.

Most children show improved adjustment by two years after divorce. Yet overall, children and adolescents of divorced parents continue to score slightly lower than children of continuously married parents in academic achievement, self-esteem, social competence, and emotional and behavior problems (Lansford, 2009). And divorce is linked to problems with adolescent sexuality and development of intimate ties. Young people who experienced parental divorce—especially more than once—display higher rates of early sexual activity and adolescent parenthood. Some experience other lasting difficulties—reduced educational attainment, troubled romantic relationships and marriages, and divorce in adulthood (Amato, 2006, 2010).

The overriding factor in positive adjustment following divorce is effective parenting—shielding the child from family conflict and using authoritative child rearing (Leon, 2003; Wolchik et al., 2000). Where the custodial parent is the mother, contact with fathers is important. In the United States, paternal contact has risen over the past three decades, with about one-third of children today experiencing at least weekly visits (Amato & Dorius, 2010).

The more paternal contact and the warmer the father–child relationship, the less children react with defiance and aggression (Dunn et al., 2004). For girls, a good father–child relationship protects against early sexual activity and unhappy romantic involvements. For boys, it seems to affect overall psychological well-being. In fact, several studies indicate that outcomes for sons are better when the father is the custodial parent (Clarke-Stewart & Hayward, 1996; McLanahan, 1999). Fathers' greater economic security and image of authority seem to help them engage in effective parenting with sons.

Although divorce is painful for children, remaining in an intact but high-conflict family is much worse than making the

Applying What We Know

Helping Children Adjust to Their Parents' Divorce

Suggestion	Explanation
Shield children from conflict.	Witnessing intense parental conflict is very damaging to children. If one parent insists on expressing hostility, children fare better if the other parent does not respond in kind.
Provide children with as much continuity, familiarity, and predictability as possible.	Children adjust better during the period surrounding divorce when their lives have some stability—for example, the same school, bedroom, babysitter, playmates, and daily schedule.
Explain the divorce, and tell children what to expect.	Children are more likely to develop fears of abandonment if they are not prepared for their parents' separation. They should be told that their parents will not be living together anymore, which parent will be moving out, and when they will be able to see that parent. Parents should provide a reason that each child can understand and assuring children that they are not to blame.
Emphasize the permanence of the divorce.	Fantasies of parents getting back together can prevent children from accepting the reality of their current life. Children should be told that the divorce is final and that they cannot change this fact.
Respond sympathetically to children's feelings.	For children to adjust well, their painful emotions must be acknowledged, not denied or avoided.
Engage in authoritative parenting.	Parents who engage in authoritative parenting—providing affection and acceptance, reasonable demands for mature behavior, and consistent, rational discipline—greatly reduce their children's risk of maladjustment.
Promote a continuing relationship with both parents.	When parents disentangle their lingering hostility toward the former spouse from the child's need for a continuing relationship with the other parent, children adjust well. Grandparents and other extended-family members can help by not taking sides.

Source: Teyber, 2001.

transition to a low-conflict, single-parent household (Greene et al., 2003; Strohschein, 2005). However, more parents today are divorcing because they are moderately (rather than extremely) dissatisfied with their relationship. Research suggests that children in these low-discord homes are especially puzzled and upset. Perhaps these youngsters' inability to understand the marital breakup and grief over the loss of a seemingly happy home life explain why the adjustment problems of children of divorce have intensified over time (Amato, 2001; Lansford, 2009). Regardless of the extent of their friction, divorcing parents who manage to engage in *coparenting* (see page 46 in Chapter 2), supporting each other in their child-rearing roles, greatly improve the chances of favorable child outcomes.

Divorce Mediation, Joint Custody, and Child Support. Community-based services aimed at helping divorcing families include *divorce mediation,* a series of meetings between divorcing adults and a trained professional aimed at reducing family conflict, including legal battles over property division and child custody. Research reveals that mediation increases out-of-court settlements, cooperation and involvement of both parents in child rearing, and parents' and children's feelings of well-being (Emery, Sbarra, & Grover, 2005).

Joint custody, which grants parents equal say in important decisions about the child's upbringing, is becoming increasingly common. Children usually reside with one parent and see the other on a fixed schedule, similar to the typical sole-custody

situation. In other cases, parents share physical custody, and children move between homes—transitions that can be especially hard on some children. Joint-custody parents report little conflict—fortunately so, since the success of the arrangement depends on effective coparenting. And their children tend to be better-adjusted than children in sole-maternal-custody homes (Bauserman, 2002).

Finally, many single-parent families depend on child support from the noncustodial parent to relieve financial strain. All U.S. states have procedures for withholding wages from parents who fail to make these payments. Noncustodial fathers who have generous visitation schedules and who often see their children are more likely to pay child support regularly (Amato & Sobolewski, 2004). Applying What We Know above summarizes ways to help children adjust to their parents' divorce.

Blended Families

"If you get married to Wendell, and Daddy gets married to Carol," Lizzie wondered aloud to Rena, "then I'll have two sisters and one more brother. And let's see, how many grandmothers and grandfathers? A lot!" exclaimed Lizzie.

About 60 percent of divorced parents remarry within a few years. Others *cohabit,* or share a sexual relationship and a residence with a partner outside of marriage. Parent, stepparent, and children form a new family structure called the **blended, or reconstituted, family.** For some children, this expanded family network is positive, bringing greater adult attention. But children in blended families usually have more adjustment problems than children in stable, first-marriage families (Jeynes, 2007; Nicholson et al., 2008). Switching to stepparents' new rules and expectations can be stressful, and children often view steprelatives as intruders. How well they adapt is, again, related to the quality of family functioning (Hetherington & Kelly, 2002). This depends on which parent forms a new relationship, the child's age and sex, and the complexity of blended-family relationships. As we will see, older children and girls seem to have the hardest time.

Mother–Stepfather Families.

Because mothers generally retain custody of children, the most common form of blended family is a mother–stepfather arrangement. Boys tend to adjust quickly, welcoming a stepfather who is warm and who refrains from exerting his authority too quickly. Mothers' friction with sons also declines as a result of greater economic security, another adult to share household tasks, and an end to loneliness (Visher, Visher, & Pasley, 2003). Girls, however, often react with sulky, resistant behavior when a new stepfather disrupts the close ties they have established with their mothers (Bray, 1999; Ganong, Coleman, & Jamison, 2011).

But age affects these findings. Older school-age children and adolescents of both sexes display more irresponsible, acting-out behavior than their peers not in stepfamilies (Hetherington & Stanley-Hagan, 2000; Robertson, 2008). If parents are warmer and more involved with their biological children than with their stepchildren, older children are more likely to notice and challenge unfair treatment. And adolescents often view the new stepparent as a threat to their freedom. But when teenagers have affectionate, cooperative relationships with their mothers, many eventually develop good relations with their stepfathers—a circumstance linked to better adjustment (King, 2009; Yuan & Hamilton, 2006).

To help these teenagers adapt to life in a complex blended family, both father and stepmother must avoid favoring their much younger children, born after remarriage.

Father–Stepmother Families.

Remarriage of noncustodial fathers often leads to reduced contact with their biological children, especially when fathers remarry quickly, before they have established postdivorce parent–child routines (Dunn, 2002; Juby et al., 2007). When fathers have custody, children typically react negatively to remarriage. One reason is that children living with fathers often start out with more problems. Perhaps the biological mother could no longer handle the difficult child (usually a boy), so the father and his new partner are faced with a youngster who has behavior problems. In other instances, the father has custody because of a very close relationship with the child, and his remarriage disrupts this bond (Buchanan, Maccoby, & Dornbusch, 1996).

Girls, especially, have a hard time getting along with their stepmothers, either because the remarriage threatens the girl's bond with her father or because she becomes entangled in loyalty conflicts between the two mother figures. But the longer girls live in father–stepmother households, the more positive their interaction with stepmothers becomes (King, 2007). Eventually, most girls benefit from the support of a second mother figure.

Support for Blended Families.

Parenting education and couples counseling can help parents and children adapt to the complexities of blended families. Effective approaches encourage stepparents to move into their new roles gradually by first building a warm relationship with the child (Nicholson et al., 2008). Counselors can offer couples guidance in coparenting to limit loyalty conflicts and provide consistency in child rearing.

Unfortunately, the divorce rate for second marriages is even higher than for first marriages. Parents with antisocial tendencies and poor child-rearing skills are particularly likely to have several divorces and remarriages, and their children have greater adjustment difficulties (Amato, 2010). These families usually require prolonged, intensive therapy.

Maternal Employment and Dual-Earner Families

Today, more than three-fourths of mothers, whether single or married, with school-age children are employed (U.S. Census Bureau, 2013). In previous chapters, we saw that the impact of maternal employment on early development depends on the quality of child care and the continuing parent–child relationship. The same is true in middle childhood.

Maternal Employment and Child Development.

When mothers enjoy their work and remain committed to parenting, children show favorable adjustment—higher self-esteem, more positive family and peer relations, less gender-stereotyped beliefs, and better grades in school. Girls, especially, profit from the image of female competence. Regardless of SES, daughters of employed mothers are more achievement- and career-oriented (Hoffman, 2000).

Parenting practices contribute to these benefits. Employed mothers who value their parenting role are more likely to use authoritative child rearing and coregulation. And maternal employment leads fathers—especially those who believe in the importance of the paternal role and who feel successful at parenting—to take on greater child-care responsibilities (Gottfried, Gottfried, & Bathurst, 2002; Jacobs & Kelley, 2006). Paternal involvement is associated in childhood and adolescence with higher intelligence and achievement, more mature social behavior, and a flexible view of gender roles (Pleck & Masciadrelli, 2004).

But when employment places heavy demands on a mother's or a father's schedule or is stressful for other reasons, children are at risk for ineffective parenting—reduced parental sensitivity, fewer joint parent–child activities, and poorer cognitive development throughout childhood and adolescence (Brooks-Gunn, Han, & Waldfogel, 2002; Bumpus, Crouter, & McHale, 2006; Strazdins et al., 2006). In contrast, part-time employment and flexible work schedules, which help parents meet children's needs, are associated with sensitive, involved parenting and good child adjustment (Buehler & O'Brien, 2011).

Child Care for School-Age Children. High-quality child care is vital for children's well-being, even in middle childhood. An estimated 5 million 5- to 14-year-olds in the United States are **self-care children** who regularly look after themselves for some period of time after school (Afterschool Alliance, 2009). Self-care increases with age and also with SES, perhaps because of the greater safety of higher-income neighborhoods. But when lower-SES parents lack alternatives, their children spend more hours on their own (Casper & Smith, 2002).

Younger school-age children who spend many hours alone have emotional and social difficulties (Vandell & Posner, 1999). As children become old enough to look after themselves, those who have a history of authoritative child rearing, are monitored by parental telephone calls, and have regular after-school chores appear responsible and well-adjusted. In contrast, children left to their own devices are more likely to bend to peer pressures and engage in antisocial behavior (Coley, Morris, & Hernandez, 2004; Vandell et al., 2006).

Before age 8 or 9, most children need supervision because they are not yet competent to handle emergencies (Galambos & Maggs, 1991). Also, throughout middle childhood, attending high-quality after-school programs with stimulating activities is linked to good school performance and emotional and social adjustment (Durlak & Weissberg, 2007; Granger, 2008). Low-SES children who participate in "after-care" programs offering academic assistance and enrichment activities (scouting, music and art lessons, clubs) show special benefits. They exceed their self-care counterparts in classroom work habits, academic achievement, and prosocial behavior and display fewer behavior problems (Lauer et al., 2006; Vandell et al., 2006).

Unfortunately, good after care is in especially short supply in low-income neighborhoods (Afterschool Alliance, 2009;

High-quality after-school programs with enrichment activities yield academic and social benefits for low-SES children.

Dearing et al., 2009). A special need exists for well-planned programs in these areas—ones that provide safe environments, warm relationships with adults, and enjoyable, goal-oriented activities.

ASK YOURSELF

REVIEW Describe and explain changes in sibling relationships during middle childhood.

APPLY Steve and Marissa are in the midst of an acrimonious divorce. Their 9-year-old son Dennis has become hostile and defiant. How can Steve and Marissa help Dennis adjust?

REFLECT What after-school child-care arrangements did you experience in elementary school? How do you think they influenced your development?

Some Common Problems of Development

We have considered a variety of stressful experiences that place children at risk for future problems. Next, we address two more areas of concern: school-age children's fears and anxieties and the consequences of child sexual abuse. Finally, we sum up factors that help children cope effectively with stress.

Fears and Anxieties

Although fears of the dark, thunder and lightning, and supernatural beings persist into middle childhood, older children's anxieties are also directed toward new concerns. Common fears of the school years include poor academic performance, peer rejection, the possibility of personal harm (being robbed or shot), threats to parents' health, and media events (Gullone, 2000; Weems & Costa, 2005).

Children's fears are shaped in part by their culture. Children in Western nations mention exposure to negative information in the media as the most frequent source of their fears, followed by direct exposure to frightening events (Muris et al., 2001). Nevertheless, as we saw in Chapter 8, many parents have no rules about their children's TV viewing or computer use, including Internet access.

Most children handle fears constructively, and they decline with age (Gullone, 2000). But about 5 percent of school-age children develop an intense, unmanageable fear called a **phobia.** Children with inhibited temperaments are at high risk (Ollendick, King, & Muris, 2002).

For example, in *school phobia,* children feel severe apprehension about attending school, often accompanied by physical complaints (dizziness, nausea, and stomachaches). About one-third of children with school phobia are 5- to 7-year-olds for whom the real fear is maternal separation. Family therapy helps these children, whose difficulty can often be traced to parental overprotection (Elliott, 1999).

Most cases of school phobia appear around age 11 to 13, in children who usually find a particular aspect of school frightening—an overcritical teacher, a school bully, or too much parental pressure to achieve. A change in school environment or parenting practices may be needed (Silverman & Pina, 2008). Firm insistence that the child return to school, along with training in how to cope with difficult situations, is also helpful.

Severe childhood anxieties may arise from harsh living conditions. In inner-city ghettos and in war-torn areas of the world, children live in the midst of constant danger and deprivation. As the Cultural Influences box on page 280 reveals, these youngsters are at risk for long-term difficulties. Finally, as we saw in our discussion of child abuse in Chapter 8, too often violence and other destructive acts become part of adult–child relationships. During middle childhood, child sexual abuse increases.

Child Sexual Abuse

Until recently, child sexual abuse was considered rare, and adults often dismissed children's claims of abuse. In the 1970s, efforts by professionals and media attention led to recognition of child sexual abuse as a serious and widespread problem. About 65,000 cases in the United States were confirmed in the most recently reported year (U.S. Department of Health and Human Services, 2011b).

Characteristics of Abusers and Victims. Sexual abuse is committed against children of both sexes, but more often against girls. Most cases are reported in middle childhood, but for some victims, abuse begins early in life and continues for many years (Hoch-Espada, Ryan, & Deblinger, 2006; Goodyear-Brown, Fath, & Myers, 2012).

Typically, the abuser is male, either a parent or someone the parent knows well—a father, stepfather, or live-in boyfriend, somewhat less often an uncle or older brother. But in about 25 percent of cases, mothers are the offenders, more often with sons (Boroughs, 2004). If the abuser is a nonrelative, the person is usually someone the child has come to know and trust. However, the Internet and mobile phones have become avenues through which other adults commit sexual abuse—for example, by exposing children and adolescents to pornography and online sexual advances as a way of "grooming" them for sexual acts offline (Wolak et al., 2008).

Many offenders blame the abuse on the willing participation of a seductive youngster. Yet children are not capable of making a deliberate, informed decision to enter into a sexual relationship! Even adolescents are not free to say yes or no. Rather, the responsibility lies with abusers, who tend to have characteristics that predispose them toward sexual exploitation of children. They have great difficulty controlling their impulses and may suffer from psychological disorders, including alcohol and drug abuse. Often they pick out children who are unlikely to defend themselves or to be believed—those who are physically weak, emotionally deprived, socially isolated, or affected by disabilities (Bolen, 2001).

Reported cases of child sexual abuse are linked to poverty and marital instability. Children who live in homes with a constantly changing cast of characters—repeated marriages, separations, and new partners—are especially vulnerable (Goodyear-Brown, Fath, & Myers, 2012). But children in economically advantaged, stable families are also victims, although their abuse is more likely to escape detection.

Consequences. The adjustment problems of child sexual abuse victims—including anxiety, depression, low self-esteem,

Children in Hyderabad, India, participate in a "Stay Safe" campaign against child abuse and sexual exploitation—part of a global effort to prevent all forms of abuse.

Cultural Influences

Impact of Ethnic and Political Violence on Children

Around the world, many children live with armed conflict, terrorism, and other acts of violence stemming from ethnic and political tensions. Some children may participate in fighting, either because they are forced or because they want to please adults. Others are kidnapped, assaulted, and tortured. Those who are bystanders often come under direct fire and may be killed or physically maimed. And many watch in horror as family members, friends, and neighbors flee, are wounded, or die. In the past decade, wars have left 6 million children physically disabled, 20 million homeless, and more than 1 million separated from their parents (UNICEF, 2011).

When war and social crises are temporary, most children do not show long-term emotional difficulties. But chronic danger can seriously impair their psychological functioning. Many children of war lose their sense of safety, become desensitized to violence, are haunted by terrifying intrusive memories, display immature moral reasoning, and hold a pessimistic view of the future. Anxiety and depression increase, as do aggression and antisocial behavior (Eisenberg & Silver, 2011; Klingman, 2006). These outcomes appear to be culturally universal, observed in children in every war zone studied—from Bosnia, Angola, Rwanda, and the Sudan to the West Bank, Gaza, Afghanistan, and Iraq (Barenbaum, Ruchkin, & Schwab-Stone, 2004).

Parental affection and reassurance are the best protection against lasting problems. When parents offer security, discuss traumatic experiences sympathetically, and serve as role models of calm emotional strength, most children can withstand even extreme war-related violence (Gewirtz, Forgatch, & Wieling, 2008). Children who are separated from parents must rely on help from their communities. Orphans in Eritrea who were placed in residential settings where they could form a close emotional tie with an adult showed less emotional stress five years later than orphans placed in impersonal settings (Wolff & Fesseha, 1999). Education and recreation programs are powerful safeguards, too, providing children with consistency in their lives along with teacher and peer supports.

With the September 11, 2001, terrorist attacks on the World Trade Center, some U.S. children experienced extreme wartime violence firsthand. Most children, however, learned about the attacks indirectly—from the media or from caregivers or peers. Although both direct and indirect exposure triggered child and adolescent distress, extended exposure—having a family member affected or repeatedly witnessing the attacks on TV—resulted in more severe symptoms (Agronick et al., 2007; Otto et al., 2007; Rosen & Cohen, 2010). During the following months, distress reactions declined, though more slowly for children with conflict-ridden parent–child relationships or preexisting adjustment problems.

At a refugee camp in Jordan, Syrian children wearing facemasks to protect against blowing sand play games with a caring adult. Most have witnessed violent atrocities and lost family members in Syria's civil war. Sensitive adult support can help them regain a sense of safety.

Unlike many war-traumatized children in the developing world, students in New York's Public School 31, who watched from their classroom windows as the towers collapsed, received immediate intervention—a "trauma curriculum" in which they expressed their emotions through writing, drawing, and discussion and participated in experiences aimed at restoring trust and tolerance (Lagnado, 2001). Older children learned about the feelings of their Muslim classmates, the dire condition of children in Afghanistan, and ways to help victims as a means of overcoming a sense of helplessness.

When wartime drains families and communities of resources, international organizations must step in and help children. Efforts to preserve children's physical, psychological, and educational well-being may be the best way to stop transmission of violence to the next generation.

mistrust of adults, and anger and hostility—are often severe and can persist for years after the abusive episodes. Younger children frequently react with sleep difficulties, loss of appetite, and generalized fearfulness. Adolescents may run away and show suicidal reactions, eating disorders, substance abuse, and delinquency (Hornor, 2010; Wolfe, 2006). And repeated sexual abuse, like physical abuse, is associated with central nervous system damage (Gaskill & Perry, 2012).

Sexually abused children frequently display precocious sexual knowledge and behavior. In adolescence, abused young people often become promiscuous, and as adults, they show increased arrest rates for sex crimes (mostly against children) and prostitution (Salter et al., 2003; Whipple, 2006). Furthermore, women who were sexually abused are likely to choose partners who abuse them and their children, and they often engage in child abuse and neglect themselves (Pianta, Egeland, & Erickson, 1989). In all these ways, the harmful impact of sexual abuse is transmitted to the next generation.

Prevention and Treatment. Because sexual abuse typically appears in the midst of other serious family problems, long-term therapy with both children and parents is often needed

(Saunders, 2012). The best way to reduce the suffering of victims is to prevent sexual abuse from continuing. Today, courts are prosecuting abusers more vigorously and taking children's testimony more seriously.

Educational programs that teach children to recognize inappropriate sexual advances and identify sources of help reduce the risk of abuse (Finkelhor, 2009). Yet because of controversies over educating children about sexual abuse, few schools offer these interventions. New Zealand is the only country with a national, school-based prevention program targeting sexual abuse. In Keeping Ourselves Safe, children and adolescents learn that abusers are rarely strangers. Parent involvement ensures that home and school collaborate in teaching children self-protection skills. Evaluations reveal that virtually all New Zealand parents and children support the program and that it has helped many children avoid or report abuse (Sanders, 2006).

Fostering Resilience in Middle Childhood

Throughout middle childhood—and other periods of development—children encounter challenging and sometimes threatening situations that require them to cope with psychological stress. In this and the previous chapter, we have considered such topics as chronic illness, learning disabilities, achievement expectations, divorce, harsh living conditions and wartime trauma, and sexual abuse. Each taxes children's coping resources, creating serious risks for development.

Nevertheless, only a modest relationship exists between stressful life experiences and psychological disturbance in childhood (Masten & Reed, 2002). Recall from Chapter 1 that four broad factors protect against maladjustment: (1) the child's personal characteristics, including an easy temperament and a mastery-oriented approach to new situations; (2) a warm parental relationship; (3) an adult outside the immediate family who offers a support system; and (4) community resources, such as

good schools, social services, and youth organizations and recreation centers (Commission on Children at Risk, 2008; Wright & Masten, 2005).

Often just one or a few of these ingredients account for why one child is "stress-resilient" and another is not. Usually, however, personal and environmental factors are interconnected: Each resource favoring resilience strengthens others. For example, safe, stable neighborhoods with family-friendly community services reduce parents' daily hassles and stress, thereby promoting good parenting (Chen, Howard, & Brooks-Gunn, 2011). In contrast, unfavorable home and neighborhood experiences increase the chances that children will act in ways that expose them to further hardship.

Rather than a preexisting attribute, *resilience* is a capacity that develops, enabling children to use internal and external resources to cope with adversity (Dessel, 2010; Riley & Masten, 2004). As the next two chapters will reveal, young people whose childhood experiences helped them learn to control impulses, overcome obstacles, strive for self-direction, and respond considerately and sympathetically to others meet the challenges of the next period—adolescence—quite well.

ASK YOURSELF

REVIEW Describe adjustment problems of victims of child sexual abuse. How can the harmful consequences of sexual abuse carry over to the next generation?

APPLY Claire told her 6-year-old daughter never to talk to or take candy from strangers. Why will Claire's warning not protect her daughter from sexual abuse?

REFLECT Describe a challenging time during your childhood. What aspects of the experience increased stress? What resources helped you cope with adversity?

SUMMARY

Erikson's Theory: Industry versus Inferiority (p. 260)

What personality changes take place during Erikson's stage of industry versus inferiority?

- According to Erikson, children who successfully resolve the psychological conflict of **industry versus inferiority** develop a sense of competence at useful skills and tasks, learn the value of division of labor, and develop a sense of moral commitment and responsibility.

Self-Understanding (p. 260)

Describe school-age children's self-concept and self-esteem, and discuss factors that affect their achievement-related attributions.

- During middle childhood, children's self-concepts include personality traits, competencies, and **social comparisons.**

- Self-esteem differentiates further, becoming hierarchically organized and more realistic. Authoritative parenting is linked to favorable self-esteem.

- Children who hold **mastery-oriented attributions** believe ability can be improved by trying hard and attribute failure to controllable factors, such as insufficient effort. In contrast, children who receive negative feedback about their ability are likely to develop **learned helplessness,** attributing success to external factors, such as luck, and failure to low ability.

Emotional Development (p. 264)

Cite changes in self-conscious emotions, emotional understanding, and management of emotion in middle childhood.

- Self-conscious emotions of pride and guilt become clearly governed by personal responsibility. Intense shame is particularly destructive, yielding both internalizing and externalizing problems.

- School-age children develop an appreciation of mixed emotions. Empathy increases and includes sensitivity to both people's immediate distress and their general life condition.

- By age 10, most children shift adaptively between **problem-centered** and **emotion-centered coping** to regulate emotion. Children who acquire a sense of emotional self-efficacy are upbeat, empathic, and prosocial.

Moral Development (p. 265)

Describe changes in moral understanding during middle childhood, including children's understanding of diversity and inequality.

- By middle childhood, children have internalized rules for good conduct. They clarify and link moral imperatives and social conventions and develop a better understanding of personal choice and individual rights.

- Children of all races pick up prevailing societal attitudes about race and ethnicity. With age, voicing of prejudice typically declines though automatic prejudice may persist. Children most likely to hold biases are those who believe that personality traits are fixed, who have inflated self-esteem, and who live in a social world that highlights group differences. Long-term intergroup contact is most effective at reducing prejudice.

Peer Relations (p. 267)

How do peer sociability and friendship change in middle childhood?

- Peer interaction becomes more prosocial, and physical aggression declines. By the end of middle childhood, children organize themselves into **peer groups.**

- Friendships develop into mutual relationships based on trust. Children tend to select friends similar to themselves in many ways.

Describe categories of peer acceptance and ways to help rejected children.

- On measures of **peer acceptance, popular children** are well-liked by many agemates; **rejected children** are actively disliked; **controversial children** are both liked and disliked; and **neglected children** arouse little response, either positive or negative.

- **Popular-prosocial children** combine academic and social competence, while **popular-antisocial children** are aggressive but admired. **Rejected-aggressive children** are especially high in conflict and hostility; in contrast, **rejected-withdrawn children** are passive, socially awkward, and frequent targets of **peer victimization.**

- Coaching in social skills, academic tutoring, and training in perspective taking and in solving social problems have been used to help rejected children gain in social competence and peer acceptance. Intervening to improve the quality of parent–child interaction is often necessary.

Gender Typing (p. 271)

What changes in gender-stereotyped beliefs and gender identity occur during middle childhood?

- School-age children extend their awareness of gender stereotypes to personality traits and academic subjects. But they also develop a more open-minded view of what males and females can do.

- Boys strengthen their identification with masculine traits, whereas girls more often experiment with "other-gender" activities. Gender identity includes self-evaluations of gender typicality, contentedness, and felt pressure to conform to gender roles—each of which affects adjustment.

Family Influences (p. 272)

How do parent–child communication and sibling relationships change in middle childhood?

- Despite declines in time spent with parents, **coregulation** allows parents to exercise general oversight over children, who increasingly make their own decisions.

- Sibling rivalry tends to increase with participation in a wider range of activities and more frequent parental comparisons. Compared to children with siblings, only children are higher in self-esteem, school performance, and educational attainment.

What factors influence children's adjustment to divorce and blended family arrangements?

- Marital breakup is often quite stressful for children. Individual differences are affected by parental psychological health, child characteristics (age, temperament, and sex), and social supports. Children with difficult temperaments are at greater risk for adjustment problems. Divorce is linked to early sexual activity, adolescent parenthood, and long-term relationship difficulties.

- The overriding factor in positive adjustment following divorce is effective parenting. Positive father–child relationships are protective, as are supports from extended-family members, teachers, siblings, and friends. Divorce mediation can reduce parental conflict in the period surrounding divorce. The success of joint custody depends on effective coparenting.

- When divorced parents enter new relationships and form **blended,** or **reconstituted, families,** girls, older children, and children in father–stepmother families tend to have more adjustment problems. Stepparents who move into their roles gradually help children adjust.

How do maternal employment and life in dual-earner families affect school-age children?

- When employed mothers enjoy their work and remain committed to parenting, their children benefit from higher self-esteem, more positive family and peer relations, less gender-stereotyped beliefs, and better school grades. In dual-earner families, the father's willingness to share responsibilities is a crucial factor. Workplace supports help parents in their child-rearing roles.

- Authoritative child rearing, parental monitoring, and regular after-school chores lead **self-care children** to be responsible and well-adjusted. Good "after-care" programs also aid school performance and emotional and social adjustment, especially for low-SES children.

Some Common Problems of Development (p. 278)

Cite common fears and anxieties in middle childhood.

- School-age children's fears are directed toward new concerns, including poor academic performance, peer rejection, physical harm, parents' health, and medial events. Children with inhibited temperaments are at higher risk of developing **phobias.** Harsh living conditions can also cause severe anxiety.

Discuss factors related to child sexual abuse and its consequences for children's development.

- Child sexual abuse is typically committed by male family members, more often against girls than boys. Abusers have characteristics that predispose them toward sexual exploitation of children. Reported cases are strongly associated with poverty and marital instability. Abused children often have severe adjustment problems.

NOAH SEELAM/AFP/GETTY IMAGES

Cite factors that foster resilience in middle childhood.

- Only a modest relationship exists between stressful life experiences and psychological disturbance in childhood. Children's personal characteristics, a warm family life, authoritative parenting, and school, community, and societal resources predict resilience.

Important Terms and Concepts

blended, or reconstituted, families (p. 276)
controversial children (p. 269)
coregulation (p. 273)
emotion-centered coping (p. 265)
industry versus inferiority (p. 260)
learned helplessness (p. 263)
mastery-oriented attributions (p. 263)

neglected children (p. 269)
peer acceptance (p. 269)
peer group (p. 267)
peer victimization (p. 270)
phobia (p. 279)
popular-antisocial children (p. 269)
popular children (p. 269)

popular-prosocial children (p. 269)
problem-centered coping (p. 265)
rejected-aggressive children (p. 269)
rejected children (p. 269)
rejected-withdrawn children (p. 269)
self-care children (p. 278)
social comparisons (p. 260)

milestones

Development in Middle Childhood

- Self-concept begins to include personality traits, competencies, and social comparisons. (260)
- Self-esteem differentiates, becomes hierarchically organized, and declines to a more realistic level. (261)
- Self-conscious emotions of pride and guilt are governed by personal responsibility. (264)
- Recognizes that individuals can experience more than one emotion at a time and that people's expressions may not reflect their true feelings. (264)

- Awareness of memory strategies and the impact of psychological factors, such as mental inferences, on performance improves. (240)
- Appreciates second-order false beliefs. (240)
- Uses informal knowledge of number concepts and counting to master increasingly complex mathematical skills. (241–242)

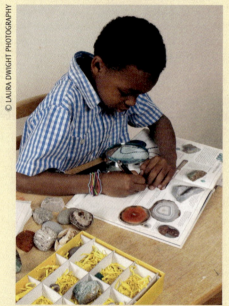

- Empathy increases. (264)
- Becomes more independent and trustworthy. (265)
- Constructs a flexible appreciation of moral rules, taking prosocial and antisocial intentions into account. (265)
- Physical aggression declines; verbal and relational aggression continue. (267)
- Resolves conflicts more effectively. (267)

6–8 years

PHYSICAL

- Slow gains in height and weight continue until adolescent growth spurt. (227)
- Permanent teeth gradually replace primary teeth. (227)
- Legibility of writing increases, preparing children to master cursive writing. (231)
- Drawings become more organized and detailed and include some depth cues. (231)
- Games with rules and rough-and-tumble play become common. (232)

COGNITIVE

- Thought becomes more logical, as shown by the ability to pass Piagetian conservation, class inclusion, and seriation problems. (234)
- Attention becomes more selective, adaptable, and planful. (238)
- Uses memory strategies of rehearsal and then organization. (238)
- Views the mind as an active, constructive agent, capable of transforming information. (240)

LANGUAGE

- Vocabulary increases rapidly throughout middle childhood, eventually exceeding comprehension of 40,000 words. (248)
- Word definitions are concrete, referring to functions and appearance. (248)
- Narratives increase in organization, detail, and expressiveness. (248)
- Transitions from emergent literacy to conventional reading. (241)
- Language awareness improves. (248)
- Conversational strategies become more refined. (248)

9–11 years

PHYSICAL

- Adolescent growth spurt begins two years earlier in girls than in boys. (227)

Note: Numbers in parentheses indicate the page or pages on which each milestone is discussed.

- Executes gross-motor skills of running, jumping, throwing, catching, kicking, batting, and dribbling more quickly and with better coordination. (230)
- Steady gains in attention and reaction time contribute to improved motor performance. (231)
- Representation of depth in drawings expands. (231)

COGNITIVE

- Continues to master Piagetian tasks in a step-by-step fashion. (235)
- Spatial reasoning improves; readily draws and reads maps of large-scale spaces, and grasps the notion of scale. (235)

- Selective attention and planning improve further. (238)
- Uses memory strategies of rehearsal and organization more effectively. (238)
- Applies several memory strategies simultaneously; begins to use elaboration. (238)
- Long-term knowledge base grows larger and becomes better organized. (238)
- Theory of mind becomes more elaborate and refined. (240)
- Cognitive self-regulation improves. (240–241)

LANGUAGE

- Thinks about and uses words more precisely; word definitions emphasize synonyms and categorical relations. (248)

- Grasps double meanings of words, as reflected in comprehension of metaphors and humor. (248)
- Continues to master complex grammatical constructions. (248)
- Continues to refine conversational strategies. (248)
- Narratives lengthen, become more coherent, and include more evaluative comments. (248)

EMOTIONAL/SOCIAL

- Self-esteem tends to rise. (261)
- Distinguishes ability, effort, and external factors (such as luck) in attributions for success and failure. (263)
- Empathic responding extends to general life conditions. (264)

- Shifts adaptively between problem-centered and emotion-centered strategies in regulating emotion. (265)

- Clarifies and links moral rules and social conventions. (265)
- Convictions about matters of personal choice strengthen, and understanding of individual rights expands. (266)
- Overt expressions of outgroup prejudice decline. (266)
- Friendships become more selective and are based on mutual trust. (268)
- Peer groups emerge. (267–268)

- Becomes aware of more gender stereotypes, including personality traits and achievement, but has a flexible appreciation of what males and females can do. (271)
- Gender identity expands to include self-evaluations of typicality, contentedness, and felt pressure to conform. (272)
- Sibling rivalry tends to increase. (273)

chapter

11

Physical and Cognitive Development in Adolescence

© TIM PANNELL/CORBIS

The dramatic physical and cognitive changes of adolescence make it both an exhilarating and apprehensive period of development. Although their bodies are full-grown and sexually mature, these exuberant teenagers have many skills to acquire and hurdles to surmount before they are ready for full assumption of adult roles.

chapter outline

On Sabrina's eleventh birthday, her friend Joyce gave her a surprise party, but Sabrina seemed somber during the celebration. Although Sabrina and Joyce had been close friends since third grade, their relationship was faltering. Sabrina was a head taller and some 20 pounds heavier than most girls in her sixth-grade class. Her breasts were well-developed, her hips and thighs had broadened, and she had begun to menstruate. In contrast, Joyce still had the short, lean, flat-chested body of a school-age child.

Ducking into the bathroom while the other girls put candles on the cake, Sabrina frowned at her image in the mirror. "I'm so big and heavy," she whispered. At church youth group on Sunday, Sabrina broke away from Joyce and joined the eighth-grade girls. Around them, she didn't feel so large and awkward.

Once a month, parents gathered at Sabrina's and Joyce's school to discuss child-rearing concerns. Sabrina's parents, Franca and Antonio, attended whenever they could. "How you know they are becoming teenagers is this," volunteered Antonio. "The bedroom door is closed, and they want to be alone. Also, they contradict and disagree. I tell Sabrina, 'You have to go to Aunt Gina's on Saturday for dinner with the family.' The next thing I know, she's arguing with me."

Sabrina has entered **adolescence**, the transition between childhood and adulthood. In industrialized societies, the skills young people must master are so complex and the choices confronting them so diverse that adolescence is greatly extended. But around the world, the basic tasks of this period are much the same. Sabrina must accept her full-grown body, acquire adult ways of thinking, attain greater independence from her family, develop more mature ways of relating to peers of both sexes, and begin to construct an identity—a secure sense of who she is in terms of sexual, vocational, moral, ethnic, religious, and other life values and goals.

The beginning of adolescence is marked by **puberty**, a flood of biological events leading to an adult-sized body and sexual maturity. As Sabrina's reactions suggest, entry into adolescence can be an especially trying time for some young people. In this chapter, we trace the events of puberty and take up a variety of health concerns—physical exercise, nutrition, sexual activity, substance abuse, and other challenges that many teenagers encounter on the path to maturity.

© DANIEL GRILL/TETRA IMAGES/CORBIS

Adolescence also brings with it vastly expanded powers of reasoning. Teenagers can grasp complex scientific and mathematical principles, grapple with social and political issues, and delve into the meaning of a poem or story. The second part of this chapter traces these extraordinary changes from both Piaget's and the information-processing perspective. Next, we examine sex differences in mental abilities. Finally, we turn to the main setting in which adolescent thought takes shape: the school. ●

PHYSICAL DEVELOPMENT

Conceptions of Adolescence

Why is Sabrina self-conscious, argumentative, and in retreat from family activities? Historically, theorists explained the impact of puberty on psychological development by resorting to extremes—either a biological or a social explanation.

In the early twentieth century, major theorists viewed adolescence from a "storm-and-stress" perspective. The most influential, G. Stanley Hall, based his ideas on Darwin's theory of evolution. Hall (1904) described adolescence as a period so turbulent that it resembled the era in which humans evolved from savages into civilized beings. Similarly, Anna Freud (1969), who expanded the focus on adolescence of her father Sigmund Freud's theory, viewed the teenage years as a biologically based "developmental disturbance."

Contemporary research shows that the storm-and-stress notion of adolescence is exaggerated. Certain problems, such as eating disorders, depression, suicide, and lawbreaking, do occur more often than earlier (Farrington, 2009; Graber, 2004). But the overall rate of serious psychological disturbance rises only slightly from childhood to adolescence, reaching 15 to 20 percent (Merikangas et al., 2010). Though much greater than the adulthood rate (about 6 percent), emotional turbulence is not a routine feature of the teenage years.

The first researcher to point out the wide variability in adolescent adjustment was anthropologist Margaret Mead (1928). Returning from the Pacific islands of Samoa, she concluded that because of the culture's relaxed social relationships and openness toward sexuality, adolescence "is perhaps the pleasantest time the Samoan girl (or boy) will ever know" (p. 308). Mead offered an alternative view in which the social environment is entirely responsible for the range of teenage experiences, from erratic and agitated to calm and stress-free. Later researchers found that Samoan adolescence was not as untroubled as Mead had assumed (Freeman, 1983).

Today we know that biological, psychological, and social forces combine to influence adolescent development (Susman & Dorn, 2009). Biological changes are universal—found in all primates and all cultures. These internal stresses and the social expectations accompanying them—that the young person give up childish ways, develop new interpersonal relationships, and take on greater responsibility—are likely to prompt moments of uncertainty, self-doubt, and disappointment in all teenagers. Adolescents' prior and current experiences affect their success in surmounting these challenges.

At the same time, the length of adolescence and its demands and pressures vary substantially among cultures. Most tribal and village societies have only a brief intervening phase between childhood and full assumption of adult roles (Weisfield, 1997). In industrialized nations, young people face prolonged dependence on parents and postponement of sexual gratification while they prepare for a productive work life. As a result, adolescence is greatly extended.

The more the social environment supports young people in achieving adult responsibilities, the better they adjust. For all the biological tensions and uncertainties about the future that teenagers feel, most negotiate this period successfully.

Puberty: The Physical Transition to Adulthood

The changes of puberty are dramatic: Within a few years, the body of the school-age child is transformed into that of a full-grown adult. Genetically influenced hormonal processes regulate pubertal growth. Girls, who have been advanced in physical maturity since the prenatal period, reach puberty, on average, two years earlier than boys.

Hormonal Changes

The complex hormonal changes that underlie puberty occur gradually and are under way by age 8 or 9. Secretions of *growth hormone (GH)* and *thyroxine* (see Chapter 7, page 170) increase, leading to tremendous gains in body size and to attainment of skeletal maturity.

Sexual maturation is controlled by the sex hormones. Although we think of *estrogens* as female hormones and *androgens* as male hormones, both types are present in each sex but in different amounts. The boy's testes release large quantities of the androgen *testosterone*, which leads to muscle growth, body and facial hair, and other male sex characteristics. Androgens (especially testosterone for boys) exert a GH-enhancing effect, contributing to gains in body size. The testes secrete small amounts of estrogen as well. In both sexes, estrogens also increase GH secretion, adding to the growth spurt and, in combination with androgens, stimulating gains in bone density, which continue into early adulthood (Cooper, Sayer, & Dennison, 2006; Styne, 2003).

Estrogens released by girls' ovaries cause the breasts, uterus, and vagina to mature, the body to take on feminine proportions, and fat to accumulate. Estrogens also contribute to regulation of the menstrual cycle. *Adrenal androgens,* released from the adrenal glands on top of each kidney, influence girls' height spurt and stimulate growth of underarm and pubic hair. They have little impact on boys, whose physical characteristics are influenced mainly by androgen and estrogen secretions from the testes.

As you can see, pubertal changes are of two broad types: (1) overall body growth and (2) maturation of sexual characteristics. Boys and girls differ in both aspects. In fact, puberty is the time of greatest sexual differentiation since prenatal life.

Body Growth

The first outward sign of puberty is the rapid gain in height and weight known as the **growth spurt**. On average, it is under way for North American girls shortly after age 10, for boys around age 12½. Because estrogens trigger and then restrain GH secretion more readily than androgens, the typical girl is taller and heavier during early adolescence (Archibald, Graber, & Brooks-Gunn, 2006; Bogin, 2001). At age 14, she is surpassed by the typical boy, whose adolescent growth spurt has now started, whereas hers is almost finished. Growth in body size is complete for most girls by age 16 and for boys by age 17½, when the epiphyses at the ends of the long bones close completely (see Chapter 7, page 167). Altogether, adolescents add 10 to 11 inches in height and 50 to 75 pounds—nearly 50 percent of adult body weight. Figure 11.1 illustrates pubertal changes in general body growth.

Body Proportions and Muscle–Fat Makeup. During puberty, the cephalocaudal growth trend of infancy and childhood reverses. The hands, legs, and feet accelerate first, followed by the torso, which accounts for most of the adolescent height gain. This pattern helps explain why early adolescents often appear awkward and out of proportion—long-legged, with giant feet and hands.

Large sex differences in body proportions also appear, caused by the action of sex hormones on the skeleton. Boys' shoulders broaden relative to the hips, whereas girls' hips broaden relative to the shoulders and waist. Of course, boys also end up larger than girls, and their legs are longer in relation to the rest of the body—mainly because boys have two extra years of preadolescent growth, when the legs are growing the fastest.

Sex differences in pubertal growth are obvious among these 11-year-olds. Compared with the boys, the girls are taller and more mature-looking.

FIGURE 11.1 Body growth during adolescence. Because the pubertal growth spurt takes place earlier for girls than for boys, Kate reached her adult body size earlier than Steven. Rapid pubertal growth is accompanied by large sex differences in body proportions.

Around age 8, girls start to add fat on their arms, legs, and trunk, a trend that accelerates between ages 11 and 16. In contrast, arm and leg fat decreases in adolescent boys (Rogol, Roemmich, & Clark, 2002). Although both sexes gain in muscle, this increase is much greater in boys, who develop larger skeletal muscles, hearts, and lung capacity—trends that contribute greatly to teenage boys' superior strength and athletic performance (Ramos et al., 1998).

Motor Development and Physical Activity

Puberty brings steady improvements in gross-motor performance, but changes differ for boys and girls. Girls' gains are slow and gradual, leveling off by age 14. In contrast, boys show a dramatic spurt in strength, speed, and endurance that continues through the teenage years. By midadolescence, few girls perform as well as the average boy in running speed, broad jump, or throwing distance (Haywood & Getchell, 2005; Malina & Bouchard, 1991).

Among boys, athletic competence is strongly related to peer admiration and self-esteem. Some adolescents become so obsessed with physical prowess that they turn to performance-enhancing drugs. About 8 percent of U.S. high school seniors, mostly boys, report having used creatine, an over-the-counter substance that enhances short-term muscle power but carries a risk of serious side effects, including muscle tissue disease, brain seizures, and heart irregularities (Castillo & Comstock, 2007). And 2 percent of seniors, again mostly boys, have taken anabolic steroids or a related substance, androstenedione—powerful prescription medications that boost muscle mass and strength (Johnston et al., 2012). Teenagers usually obtain steroids illegally, ignoring side effects, which range from acne, excess body hair, and high blood pressure to mood swings, aggressive behavior, and damage to the liver, circulatory system, and reproductive organs (Casavant et al., 2007). Coaches and health professionals should inform teenagers of the dangers of these performance-enhancing substances.

Besides improving motor performance, sports and exercise influence cognition and social development, providing lessons in teamwork, problem solving, assertiveness, and competition. And regular, sustained physical activity—which required physical education can ensure—is associated with lasting physical and mental health benefits and enjoyment of sports and exercise

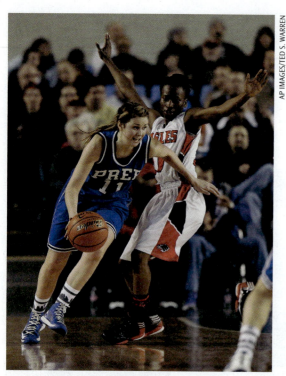

AP IMAGES/TED S. WARREN

High school girls' participation in sports has increased but still falls far short of boys'. Yet athletic participation yields many benefits—not just gains in motor skills but important lessons in teamwork, problem solving, assertiveness, and competition.

(Brand et al., 2010). Yet physical activity among U.S. adolescents declines dramatically with age. By age 15, less than one-third meet the U.S. government recommendation of at least 60 minutes of moderate to strenuous physical activity per day (Nader et al., 2008). In high school, only 57 percent of U.S. boys and 47 percent of girls are enrolled in any physical education, with 31 percent of all students experiencing a daily physical education class (U.S. Department of Health and Human Services, 2012f).

Sexual Maturation

Accompanying rapid body growth are changes in physical features related to sexual functioning. Some, called **primary sexual characteristics**, involve the reproductive organs (ovaries, uterus, and vagina in females; penis, scrotum, and testes in males). Others, called **secondary sexual characteristics**, are visible on the outside of the body and serve as additional signs of sexual maturity (for example, breast development in females and the appearance of underarm and pubic hair in both sexes). As Table 11.1 shows, these characteristics develop in a fairly standard sequence, although the ages at which each begins and is completed vary greatly. Typically, pubertal development takes about four years, but some adolescents complete it in two years, whereas others take five to six years.

Sexual Maturation in Girls. Female puberty usually begins with the budding of the breasts and the growth spurt. **Menarche**, or first menstruation, typically occurs around age

12½ for North American girls, 13 for Western Europeans. But the age range is wide, from 10½ to 15½ years. Following menarche, breast and pubic hair growth are completed, and underarm hair appears. Notice in Table 11.1 that nature delays sexual maturity until the girl's body is large enough for childbearing; menarche takes place after the peak of the height spurt.

Sexual Maturation in Boys. The first sign of puberty in boys is the enlargement of the testes (glands that manufacture sperm), accompanied by changes in the texture and color of the scrotum. Pubic hair emerges soon after, about the same time the penis begins to enlarge (Rogol, Roemmich, & Clark, 2002).

As Table 11.1 reveals, the growth spurt occurs much later in the sequence of pubertal events for boys than for girls. When it reaches its peak around age 14, enlargement of the testes and penis is nearly complete, and underarm hair appears. So do facial and body hair, which increase gradually for several years. Another landmark of male physical maturity is the deepening of the voice as the larynx enlarges and the vocal cords lengthen. (Girls' voices also deepen slightly.) Voice change usually takes place at the peak of the male growth spurt and is often not complete until puberty is over (Archibald, Graber, & Brooks-Gunn, 2006).

While the penis is growing, the prostate gland and seminal vesicles (which together produce semen, the fluid containing sperm) enlarge. Then, around age 13½, **spermarche, or first ejaculation,** occurs (Rogol, Roemmich, & Clark, 2002).

Individual Differences in Pubertal Growth

Heredity contributes substantially to the timing of pubertal changes. Identical twins are more similar than fraternal twins in attainment of most pubertal milestones (Eaves et al., 2004; Mustanski et al., 2004). Nutrition and exercise also make a difference. In females, a sharp rise in body weight and fat may trigger sexual maturation. Fat cells release a protein called *leptin*, which is believed to signal the brain that the girl's energy stores are sufficient for puberty—a likely reason that breast and pubic hair growth and menarche occur earlier for heavier and, especially, obese girls. In contrast, girls who begin rigorous athletic training at an early age or who eat very little (both of which reduce the percentage of body fat) usually experience later puberty (Kaplowitz, 2007; Lee et al., 2007; Rubin et al., 2009). Few studies, however, report a link between body fat and puberty in boys.

In poverty-stricken regions where malnutrition and infectious disease are common, menarche is greatly delayed, occurring as late as age 14 to 16 in many parts of Africa. Within developing countries, girls from higher-income families reach menarche 6 to 18 months earlier than those living in economically disadvantaged homes (Parent et al., 2003).

Early family experiences may also affect pubertal timing. One theory suggests that humans have evolved to be sensitive to the emotional quality of their childhood environments. When children's safety and security are at risk, it is adaptive for

TABLE 11.1   ### Pubertal Development in North American Girls and Boys

GIRLS	AVERAGE AGE ATTAINED	AGE RANGE	BOYS	AVERAGE AGE ATTAINED	AGE RANGE
Breasts begin to "bud"	10	8–13	Testes begin to enlarge	11.5	9.5–13.5
Height spurt begins	10	8–13	Pubic hair appears	12	10–15
Pubic hair appears	10.5	8–14	Penis begins to enlarge	12	10.5–14.5
Peak strength spurt	11.6	9.5–14	Height spurt begins	12.5	10.5–16
Peak height spurt	11.7	10–13.5	Spermarche (first ejaculation) occurs	13.5	12–16
Menarche (first menstruation) occurs	12.5	10.5–14	Peak height spurt	14	12.5–15.5
Peak weight spurt	12.7	10–14	Peak weight spurt	14	12.5–15.5
Adult stature reached	13	10–16	Facial hair begins to grow	14	12.5–15.5
Pubic hair growth completed	14.5	14–15	Voice begins to deepen	14	12.5–15.5
Breast growth completed	15	10–17	Penis and testes growth completed	14.5	12.5–16
			Peak strength spurt	15.3	13–17
			Adult stature reached	15.5	13.5–17.5
			Pubic hair growth completed	15.5	14–17

Sources: Chumlea et al., 2003; Herman-Giddens, 2006; Rogol, Roemmich, & Clark, 2002; Rubin et al., 2009; Wu, Mendola, & Buck, 2002.

Photos: (left) © Laura Dwight Photography; (right) Rob Melnychuk/Taxi/Getty Images.

them to reproduce early. Research indicates that girls and (less consistently) boys with a history of family conflict, harsh parenting, or parental separation tend to reach puberty early. In contrast, those with warm, stable family ties reach puberty relatively late (Belsky et al., 2007; Bogaert, 2005; Ellis, 2004; Ellis & Essex, 2007; Mustanski et al., 2004; Tremblay & Frigon, 2005). Two longitudinal studies confirm the following chain of influence among girls: from adverse family environments in childhood to earlier pubertal timing to increased sexual risk taking (Belsky et al., 2010; James et al., 2012).

In the research we have considered, threats to emotional health accelerate puberty, whereas threats to physical health delay it. A **secular trend**, or generational change, in pubertal timing lends added support to the role of physical well-being in pubertal development. In industrialized nations, age of menarche declined steadily—by about 3 to 4 months per decade—from 1900 to 1970, a period in which nutrition, health care, sanitation, and control of infectious disease improved greatly. Boys, too, have reached puberty earlier in recent decades (Herman-Giddens et al., 2012). In the United States and a few European countries, soaring rates of overweight and obesity are responsible for a modest, continuing trend toward earlier menarche (Kaplowitz, 2006). A worrisome consequence is that girls who reach sexual maturity at age 10 or 11 will experience pressure for unfavorable peer involvements, including sexual activity.

Brain Development

The physical transformations of adolescence include major changes in the brain. Brain-imaging research reveals continued pruning of unused synapses in the cerebral cortex, especially in the prefrontal cortex. In addition, linkages between the two cerebral hemispheres through the corpus callosum, and between the prefrontal cortex and other areas in the cerebral cortex and the inner brain (including the amygdala), expand, myelinate, and attain rapid communication. As a result, the prefrontal cortex becomes a more effective "executive"—managing the integrated functioning of various areas, yielding more complex, flexible, and adaptive thinking and behavior (Blakemore & Choudhury, 2006; Lenroot & Giedd, 2006). Consequently, adolescents gain in diverse cognitive skills, including processing speed and executive function.

But these advances occur gradually over the teenage years. fMRI evidence reveals that adolescents recruit the prefrontal cortex's network of connections with other brain areas less effectively than adults do. Because the *prefrontal cognitive-control network* still requires fine-tuning, teenagers' performance on executive function tasks requiring inhibition, planning, and future orientation (rejecting a smaller immediate reward in favor of a larger delayed reward) is not yet fully mature (McClure et al., 2004; Smith, Xiao, & Bechara, 2012; Steinberg et al., 2009).

Adding to these self-regulation difficulties are changes in the brain's *emotional/social network*. In humans and other mammals, neurons become more responsive to excitatory neurotransmitters during puberty. As a result, adolescents react more strongly to stressful events and experience pleasurable stimuli more intensely. But because the cognitive control network is not yet functioning optimally, most teenagers find it hard to manage these powerful feelings (Ernst & Spear, 2009; Steinberg et al., 2008). This imbalance contributes to teenagers' drive for novel experiences, including drug taking, reckless driving, unprotected sex, and delinquent activity (Pharo et al., 2011). In a longitudinal study of a nationally representative sample of 7,600 U.S. youths, researchers tracked changes in self-reported impulsivity and sensation seeking between ages 12 and 24 (Harden & Tucker-Drob, 2011). As Figure 11.2 shows, impulsivity declined steadily with age—evidence for gradual improvement of the cognitive-control network. But sensation seeking increased from 12 to 16, followed by a more gradual decline through age 24, reflecting the challenge posed by the emotional/social network.

In sum, changes in the adolescent brain's emotional/social network outpace development of the cognitive-control network. Only over time are young people able to effectively manage their emotions and reward-seeking behavior (Pharo et al., 2011). Of course, wide individual differences exist in the extent to which teenagers manifest this rise in risk-taking in the form of careless, dangerous acts—some not at all, and others extremely so.

At puberty, revisions also occur in brain regulation of sleep, perhaps because of increased neural sensitivity to evening light. As a result, adolescents go to bed much later than they did as children. Yet they need almost as much sleep as they did in middle childhood—about nine hours. When the school day begins early, their sleep needs are not satisfied (Jenni, Achermann, & Carskadon, 2005). Sleep-deprived adolescents

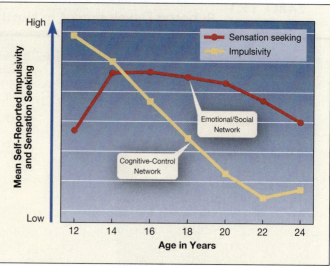

FIGURE 11.2 Development of impulsivity and sensation seeking from 12 to 24 years. In this longitudinal study of a large, nationally representative U.S. sample, impulsivity declined steadily, while sensation seeking increased in early adolescence and then diminished more gradually. Findings confirm the challenge posed by the emotional/social network to the cognitive control network. (From K. P. Harden and E. M. Tucker-Drob, 2011, "Individual Differences in the Development of Sensation Seeking and Impulsivity During Adolescence: Further Evidence for a Dual Systems Model," *Developmental Psychology, 47*, p. 742. Copyright © 2011 by the American Psychological Association. Adapted with permission of the American Psychological Association.)

display declines in executive function, performing especially poorly on cognitive tasks during morning hours. And they are more likely to achieve less well in school, suffer from anxiety and depressed mood, and engage in high-risk behaviors (Dahl & Lewin, 2002; Hansen et al., 2005; Talbot et al., 2010). Delayed school start times, while helpful, do not fully solve the problem.

In adolescence, changes in the brain's emotional/social network outpace development of the cognitive-control network. As a result, teenagers do not yet have the capacity to control their powerful drive for new—and sometimes risky—experiences.

The Psychological Impact of Pubertal Events

TAKE A MOMENT... Think back to your late elementary and middle school days. As you reached puberty, how did your feelings about yourself and your relationships with others change? Research reveals that pubertal events affect adolescents' self-image, mood, and interaction with parents and peers. Some outcomes are a response to dramatic physical change, whenever it occurs. Others have to do with pubertal timing.

Reactions to Pubertal Changes

Girls commonly react to menarche with "surprise," undoubtedly due to the sudden onset of the event. Otherwise, they typically report a mixture of positive and negative emotions (DeRose & Brooks-Gunn, 2006). Yet wide individual differences exist that depend on prior knowledge and support from family members.

For girls who have no advance information, menarche can be shocking and disturbing. Unlike 50 to 60 years ago, today few girls are uninformed, a shift that is probably due to parents' greater willingness to discuss sexual matters and to the spread of health education classes (Omar, McElderry, & Zakharia, 2003). Almost all girls get some information from their mothers. And some evidence suggests that compared with Caucasian-American families, African-American families may treat menarche as an important milestone and express less conflict over girls reaching sexual maturity—factors that lead African-American girls to react more favorably (Martin, 1996).

Like girls' reactions to menarche, boys' responses to spermarche reflect mixed feelings. Virtually all boys know about ejaculation ahead of time, but many say that no one spoke to them before or during puberty about physical changes (Omar, McElderry, & Zakharia, 2003). Usually they get their information from reading material or websites. As with girls, boys who feel better prepared tend to react more positively (Stein & Reiser, 1994). But whereas almost all girls eventually tell a friend that they are menstruating, far fewer boys tell anyone about spermarche (DeRose & Brooks-Gunn, 2006). Overall, boys get less social support than girls for the physical changes of puberty.

Many tribal and village societies celebrate the onset of puberty with an *initiation ceremony,* a ritualized announcement to the community that marks an important change in privilege and responsibility. Consequently, young people know that reaching puberty is valued in their culture. In contrast, Western societies grant little formal recognition to movement from childhood to adolescence or from adolescence to adulthood. Ceremonies such as the Jewish bar or bat mitzvah and the *quinceañera* in Hispanic communities (celebrating a 15-year-old girl's sexual maturity and marriage availability), resemble initiation ceremonies, but only within the ethnic or religious subculture. They do not mark a significant change in social status in the larger society.

Instead, Western adolescents are granted partial adult status at many different ages—for example, an age for starting employment, for driving, for leaving high school, for voting, and for drinking. The absence of a widely accepted marker of physical and social maturity makes the process of becoming an adult more confusing.

Pubertal Change, Emotion, and Social Behavior

A common belief is that puberty has something to do with adolescent moodiness and the desire for greater physical and psychological separation from parents. Let's see what research says about these relationships.

Adolescent Moodiness. Higher pubertal hormone levels are linked to greater moodiness, but only modestly so (Buchanan, Eccles, & Becker, 1992; Graber, Brooks-Gunn, & Warren, 2006). What other factors might contribute?

In several studies, the moods of school-age children, adolescents, and adults were monitored by having them carry electronic pagers that beeped at random intervals, signaling them to write down what they were doing, whom they were with, and how they felt. As expected, adolescents' moods were the least favorable (Larson et al., 2002; Larson & Lampman-Petraitis, 1989). But their negative moods were linked to an increase in negative life events, such as conflicts with parents, disciplinary actions at school, and breaking up with a boyfriend or girlfriend.

Furthermore, compared with the moods of older adolescents and adults, those of younger adolescents (ages 12 to 16) were less stable and strongly related to situational changes. Low points tended to occur in adult-structured settings—class, job, and religious services. High points were times spent with peers and coincided with Friday and Saturday evenings, especially in high school. Going out with friends and romantic partners increases so dramatically during adolescence that it becomes a "cultural script" for what is *supposed* to happen (Larson & Richards, 1998). Consequently, teenagers who spend weekend evenings at home often feel profoundly lonely.

Fortunately, frequent reports of negative mood level off in late adolescence (Natsuaki, Biehl, & Ge, 2009). And overall, teenagers with supportive family and peer relationships less often report negative moods than their agemates with few social supports (Weinstein et al., 2006). Poorly adjusted young people with low self-esteem and conduct difficulties often express intense negative emotion to unpleasant daily experiences, which compounds their adjustment problems (Schneiders et al., 2006).

This 13-year-old's bat mitzvah ceremony recognizes her as an adult with moral and religious responsibilities in the Jewish community. In the larger society, however, she will experience no change in status.

© ISRAEL IMAGES/ALAMY

Parent–Child Relationships. Sabrina's father noticed that as his children entered adolescence, they kept their bedroom doors closed, resisted spending time with the family, and became more argumentative. Sabrina and her mother squabbled over Sabrina's messy room ("It's *my* room, Mom. You don't have to live in it!"). And Sabrina protested the family's weekly visit to Aunt Gina's ("Why do I *always* have to go?"). Research in cultures as diverse as the United States and Turkey shows that puberty is related to a rise in intensity of parent–child conflict, which persists into middle adolescence (Gure, Ucanok, & Sayil, 2006; McGue et al., 2005).

Why should a youngster's more adultlike appearance trigger these disputes? The association may have adaptive value. Among nonhuman primates, the young typically leave the family group around the time of puberty. The same is true in many nonindustrialized cultures (Schlegel & Barry, 1991). Departure of young people discourages sexual relations between close blood relatives. But adolescents in industrialized nations, who are still economically dependent on parents, cannot leave the family. Consequently, a substitute seems to have emerged: psychological distancing.

As children become physically mature, they demand to be treated in adultlike ways. And as we will see, adolescents' new powers of reasoning may also contribute to a rise in family tensions. Parent–adolescent disagreements focus largely on everyday matters such as driving, dating partners, and curfews (Adams & Laursen, 2001). But beneath these disputes lie serious concerns: parental efforts to protect teenagers from harm.

Parent–daughter conflict tends to be more intense than conflict with sons, perhaps because parents place more restrictions on girls (Allison & Schultz, 2004). But most disputes are mild and diminish by late adolescence. Parents and teenagers display both conflict and affection, and they usually agree on important values, such as honesty and the importance of education. As the teenage years conclude, parent–adolescent interactions are less hierarchical, setting the stage for mutually supportive relationships in adulthood (Laursen & Collins, 2009).

LOOK AND LISTEN

Interview several parents and/or their 12- to 14-year-olds about recent changes in parent–child relationships. Has conflict increased? Over what topics? ●

Pubertal Timing

"All our children were early maturers," said Franca during the parents' discussion group. "The boys were tall by age 13, but it was easier for them. They felt big and important. Sabrina was skinny as a little girl, but now she says she's too fat and needs to diet. She thinks about boys and doesn't concentrate on her schoolwork."

Findings of several studies match the experiences of Sabrina and her brothers. Both adults and peers viewed early-maturing boys as relaxed, independent, self-confident, and physically attractive. Popular with agemates, they tended to hold leadership positions in school and to be athletic stars. In contrast, late-maturing boys expressed more anxiety and depressed mood than their on-time counterparts (Brooks-Gunn, 1988; Huddleston & Ge, 2003). But early-maturing boys, though viewed as well-adjusted, reported more psychological stress, depressed mood, and problem behaviors than both their on-time and later-maturing agemates (Ge, Conger, & Elder, 2001; Natsuaki, Biehl, & Ge, 2009; Susman & Dorn, 2009).

In contrast, early-maturing girls were unpopular, withdrawn, lacking in self-confidence, anxious (especially about others' negative evaluations), and prone to depression, and they held few leadership positions (Blumenthal et al., 2011; Ge, Conger, & Elder, 1996; Graber, Brooks-Gunn, & Warren, 2006; Jones & Mussen, 1958). And like early-maturing boys, they were more involved in deviant behavior (smoking, drinking, sexual activity) (Caspi et al., 1993; Dick et al., 2000; Ge et al., 2006). Their later-maturing counterparts, however, were regarded as physically attractive, lively, sociable, and leaders at school.

Two factors largely account for these trends: (1) how closely the adolescent's body matches cultural ideals of physical attractiveness, and (2) how well young people fit in physically with their peers.

The Role of Physical Attractiveness. *TAKE A MOMENT...* Flip through your favorite popular magazine. You will see evidence of our society's view of an attractive female as thin and long-legged and of a good-looking male as tall, broad-shouldered, and muscular. The female image is a girlish shape that favors the late developer. The male image fits the early-maturing boy.

Consistent with these preferences, early-maturing Caucasian girls tend to report a less positive **body image**—conception

Perhaps because their families and friends tend to welcome menarche, African-American early-maturing girls are more likely to report a positive body image than their Caucasian counterparts.

© JEFF GREENBERG/THE IMAGE WORKS

of and attitude toward their physical appearance—than their on-time and late-maturing agemates. Compared with African-American and Hispanic girls, Caucasian girls are more likely to have internalized the cultural ideal of female attractiveness. Most want to be thinner (Rosen, 2003; Stice, Presnell, & Bearman, 2001; Williams & Currie, 2000). Although boys are less consistent, early, rapid maturers are more likely to be satisfied with their physical characteristics (Alsaker, 1995; Sinkkonen, Anttila, & Siimes, 1998).

Body image is a strong predictor of young people's self-esteem (Harter, 2006). But the negative effects of pubertal timing on body image and—as we will see next—emotional adjustment are greatly amplified when accompanied by other stressors (Stice, 2003).

The Importance of Fitting in with Peers.

Physical status in relation to peers also explains differences in adjustment between early and late maturers. From this perspective, early-maturing girls and late-maturing boys have difficulty because they fall at the extremes of physical development and feel out of place when with their agemates. Not surprisingly, adolescents feel most comfortable with peers who match their own level of biological maturity (Stattin & Magnusson, 1990).

Because few agemates of the same pubertal status are available, early-maturing adolescents of both sexes seek out older companions, who often encourage them into activities they are not ready to handle emotionally. And hormonal influences on the brain's emotional/social network are stronger for early maturers, further magnifying their receptiveness to sexual activity, drug and alcohol use, and delinquent acts (Steinberg, 2008). Perhaps as a result, early maturers of both sexes more often report feeling stressed and show declines in academic performance (Mendle, Turkheimer, & Emery, 2007; Natsuaki, Biehl, & Ge, 2009).

At the same time, the young person's context greatly increases the likelihood that early pubertal timing will lead to negative outcomes. Early maturers in economically disadvantaged neighborhoods are especially vulnerable to establishing ties with deviant peers. And because families in such neighborhoods tend to be exposed to chronic, severe stressors and to have few social supports, these early maturers are also more likely to experience harsh, inconsistent parenting (Ge et al., 2002, 2011). Such parenting, in turn, predicts both deviant peer associations and antisocial behavior.

Long-Term Consequences.

Follow-ups reveal that early-maturing girls, especially, are prone to lasting difficulties. In one study, which followed young people from ages 14 to 24, early-maturing boys showed good adjustment. But early-maturing girls reported poorer-quality relationships with family and friends, smaller social networks, and lower life satisfaction into early adulthood than their on-time counterparts (Graber et al., 2004).

Recall that childhood family conflict and harsh parenting are linked to earlier pubertal timing, more so for girls than for boys (see page 291). Perhaps many early-maturing girls enter adolescence with emotional and social difficulties. As the stresses of puberty interfere with school performance and lead to unfavorable peer pressures, poor adjustment deepens (Graber, 2003). Clearly, interventions that target at-risk early-maturing youths are needed. These include educating parents and teachers and providing adolescents with counseling and social supports.

ASK YOURSELF

REVIEW Summarize the impact of pubertal timing on adolescent development.

APPLY As a school-age child, Chloe enjoyed leisure activities with her parents. Now, at age 14, she spends hours in her room and resists going on weekend family excursions. Explain Chloe's behavior.

REFLECT Recall your own reactions to the physical changes of puberty. Are they consistent with research findings? Explain.

Health Issues

The arrival of puberty brings new health issues related to the young person's efforts to meet physical and psychological needs. As adolescents attain greater autonomy, their personal decision making becomes important, in health as well as other areas. Yet none of the health concerns we are about to discuss can be traced to a single cause. Rather, biological, psychological, family, peer, and cultural factors jointly contribute.

Nutritional Needs

Puberty leads to a dramatic increase in nutritional requirements, at a time when the diets of many young people are the poorest. Of all age groups, adolescents are the most likely to skip breakfast (a practice linked to obesity), eat on the run, and consume empty calories (Ritchie et al., 2007; Striegel-Moore & Franko, 2006). Fast-food restaurants, where teenagers often gather, have begun to offer some healthy menu options. But adolescents need guidance in choosing these alternatives. Eating fast foods is strongly associated with excess fat and sugar consumption, indicating that teenagers often make unhealthy food choices (Bowman et al., 2004; Kubik et al., 2003).

As with school-age children, frequency of family meals is strongly associated with healthy eating in teenagers (Burgess-Champoux et al., 2009; Fiese & Schwartz, 2008). But families with adolescents eat fewer meals together.

Eating Disorders

Sabrina's desire to lose weight worried Franca. She explained to her daughter that her build was really quite average for an adolescent girl and reminded her that her Italian ancestors had considered a plump female body more beautiful than a thin one. Girls who reach puberty early, who are very dissatisfied with their body image, and who grow up in homes where concern with weight and thinness is high are at risk for eating problems. Severe dieting is the strongest predictor of the onset of an eating disorder in adolescence (Lock & Kirz, 2008). The two most serious are anorexia nervosa and bulimia nervosa.

Anorexia Nervosa. **Anorexia nervosa** is a tragic eating disorder in which young people starve themselves because of a compulsive fear of getting fat. It affects about 1 percent of North American and Western European teenage girls. During the past half-century, cases have increased sharply, fueled by cultural admiration of female thinness. Anorexia nervosa is equally common in all SES groups, but Asian-American, Caucasian-American, and Hispanic girls are at greater risk than African-American girls, who tend to be more satisfied with their size and shape (Granillo, Jones-Rodriguez, & Carvajal, 2005; Ozer & Irwin, 2009; Steinhausen, 2006). Boys account for 10 to 15 percent of anorexia cases; about half of these are gay or bisexual young people who are uncomfortable with a strong, muscular appearance (Raevuori et al., 2009; Robb & Dadson, 2002).

Individuals with anorexia have an extremely distorted body image. Even after they have become severely underweight, they see themselves as too heavy. Most go on self-imposed diets so strict that they struggle to avoid eating in response to hunger. To enhance weight loss, they exercise strenuously.

Aiva, a 16-year-old anorexia nervosa patient, is shown at left on the day she entered treatment—weighing just 77 pounds—and, at right, after a 10-week treatment program. Less than 50 percent of young people with anorexia recover fully.

© LAUREN GREENFIELD/INSTITUTE

In their attempt to reach "perfect" slimness, individuals with anorexia lose between 25 and 50 percent of their body weight. Because a normal menstrual cycle requires about 15 percent body fat, either menarche does not occur or menstrual periods stop. Malnutrition causes pale skin, brittle discolored nails, fine dark hairs all over the body, and extreme sensitivity to cold. If it continues, the heart muscle can shrink, the kidneys can fail, and irreversible brain damage and loss of bone mass can occur. About 6 percent of individuals with anorexia die of the disorder (Katzman, 2005).

Forces within the person, the family, and the larger culture give rise to anorexia nervosa. Identical twins share the disorder more often than fraternal twins, indicating a genetic influence. Abnormalities in neurotransmitters in the brain, linked to anxiety and impulse control, may make some individuals more susceptible (Kaye, 2008; Lock & Kirz, 2008). Many young people with anorexia have unrealistically high standards for their own behavior and performance, are emotionally inhibited, and avoid intimate ties outside the family. Consequently, they are often excellent students who are responsible and well-behaved. But as we have also seen, the societal image of "thin is beautiful" contributes to the poor body image of many girls—especially early-maturing girls, who are at greatest risk for anorexia nervosa (Hogan & Strasburger, 2008).

In addition, parent–adolescent interactions reveal problems related to adolescent autonomy. Often the mothers of these girls have high expectations for physical appearance, achievement, and social acceptance and are overprotective and controlling. Fathers tend to be emotionally distant. These parental attributes may contribute to affected girls' persistent anxiety and fierce pursuit of perfection in achievement, respectable behavior, and thinness (Kaye, 2008). Nevertheless, it remains unclear whether maladaptive parent–child relationships precede the disorder, emerge in response to it, or both.

Because individuals with anorexia typically deny or minimize the seriousness of their disorder, treating it is difficult (Couturier & Lock, 2006). Hospitalization is often necessary to prevent life-threatening malnutrition. The most successful treatment is family therapy plus medication to reduce anxiety and neurotransmitter imbalances (Robin & Le Grange, 2010; Treasure & Schmidt, 2005). Still, less than 50 percent of young people with anorexia recover fully.

Bulimia Nervosa. In **bulimia nervosa**, young people (again, mainly girls, but gay and bisexual boys are also vulnerable) engage in strict dieting and excessive exercise accompanied by binge eating, often followed by deliberate vomiting and purging with laxatives (Herzog, Eddy, & Beresin, 2006; Wichstrøm, 2006). Bulimia typically appears in late adolescence and is more common than anorexia nervosa, affecting about 2 to 4 percent of teenage girls, only 5 percent of whom previously suffered from anorexia.

Twin studies show that bulimia, like anorexia, is influenced by heredity (Klump, Kaye, & Strober, 2001). Overweight and early menarche increase the risk. Some adolescents with bulimia, like those with anorexia, are perfectionists. But most are impulsive, sensation-seeking young people who lack self-control in many areas, engaging in petty shoplifting, alcohol abuse, and other risky behaviors (Kaye, 2008). And although girls with bulimia, like those with anorexia, are pathologically anxious about gaining weight, they may have experienced their parents as disengaged and emotionally unavailable rather than controlling (Fairburn & Harrison, 2003).

In contrast to young people with anorexia, those with bulimia usually feel depressed and guilty about their abnormal eating habits. As a result, bulimia is usually easier to treat than anorexia, through support groups, nutrition education, training in changing eating habits, and anti-anxiety, antidepressant, and appetite-control medication (Hay & Bacaltchuk, 2004).

Sexuality

Sabrina's 16-year-old brother Louis and his girlfriend Cassie hadn't planned to have intercourse—it "just happened." But before and after, a lot of things passed through their minds. After they had dated for three months, Cassie began to wonder, "Will Louis think I'm normal if I don't have sex with him? If he wants to and I say no, will I lose him?" Both young people knew their parents wouldn't approve. But that Friday evening, Louis and Cassie's feelings for each other seemed overwhelming. "If I don't make a move," Louis thought, "will she think I'm a wimp?"

With the arrival of puberty, hormonal changes—in particular, the production of androgens in young people of both sexes—lead to an increase in sex drive (Halpern, Udry, & Suchindran, 1997). In response, adolescents become very concerned about managing sexuality in social relationships. New cognitive capacities involving perspective taking and self-reflection affect their efforts to do so. Yet like the eating behaviors we have just discussed, adolescent sexuality is heavily influenced by the young person's social context.

The Impact of Culture. **TAKE A MOMENT...** When did you first learn the "facts of life"—and how? Was sex discussed openly in your family, or was it treated with secrecy? Exposure to sex, education about it, and efforts to limit the sexual curiosity of children and adolescents vary widely around the world.

Despite the prevailing image of sexually free adolescents, sexual attitudes in North America are relatively restrictive. Typically, parents provide little or no information about sex, discourage sex play, and rarely talk about sex in children's presence. When young people become interested in sex, only about half report getting information from parents about intercourse, pregnancy prevention, and sexually transmitted disease. Many parents avoid meaningful discussions about sex out of fear of embarrassment or concern that the adolescent will not take them seriously (Wilson et al., 2010). Yet warm, open give-and-take is associated with teenagers' adoption of parents' views and with reduced sexual risk taking (Jaccard, Dodge, & Dittus, 2003; Usher-Seriki, Bynum, & Callands, 2008).

Adolescents who do not get information about sex from their parents are likely to learn from friends, books, magazines, movies, TV, and the Internet (Jaccard, Dodge, & Dittus, 2002;

Cultural attitudes will profoundly affect the way these young teenagers, who are just beginning to explore their sexual attraction to each other, learn to manage sexuality in social relationships.

Sutton et al., 2002). On prime-time TV shows, which adolescents watch more than other TV offerings, 80 percent of programs contain sexual content. Most depict partners as spontaneous and passionate, taking no steps to avoid pregnancy or sexually transmitted disease, and experiencing no negative consequences (Roberts, Henriksen, & Foehr, 2004). In several studies, teenagers' media exposure to sexual content predicted subsequent sexual activity, pregnancies, and sexual harassment behaviors (offensive name-calling or touching, pressuring a peer for a date) even after many other relevant factors were controlled (Brown & L'Engle, 2009; Chandra et al., 2008; Roberts, Henriksen, & Foehr, 2009).

Not surprisingly, adolescents who are prone to early sexual activity choose to consume more sexualized media (Steinberg & Monahan, 2011). The Internet is an especially hazardous "sex educator." In a survey of a large sample of U.S. 10- to 17-year-old Web users, 42 percent said they had viewed online pornographic websites (images of naked people or people having sex) while surfing the Internet in the past 12 months. Of these, 66 percent indicated they had encountered the images accidentally and did not want to view them (Wolak, Mitchell, & Finkelhor, 2007). Youths who felt depressed, had been bullied by peers, or were involved in delinquent activities had more encounters with Internet pornography, which may have intensified their adjustment problems.

Consider the contradictory messages young people receive. On one hand, adults express disapproval of sex at a young age and outside of marriage. On the other hand, the social environment extols sexual excitement, experimentation, and promiscuity. American teenagers are left bewildered, poorly informed

TOBY BURROWS/PHOTODISC/GETTY IMAGES

about sexual facts, and with little sound advice on how to conduct their sex lives responsibly.

Characteristics of Sexually Active Adolescents.

Overall, teenage sexual activity rates are similar in the United States and other Western countries: Nearly half of adolescents have had intercourse. But quality of sexual experiences differs. U.S. youths become sexually active earlier than their Canadian and European counterparts (Boyce et al., 2006; U.S. Department of Health and Human Services, 2012f). As Figure 11.3 illustrates, a substantial percentage of U.S. young people are sexually active quite early, by ninth grade (age 14 to 15). Males tend to have their first intercourse earlier than females. And about 18 percent of U.S. adolescent boys and 13 percent of girls—more than in other Western nations—have had sexual relations with four or more partners in the past year. Most teenagers, however, have had only one or two sexual partners by the end of high school.

Early and frequent teenage sexual activity is linked to personal, family, peer, and educational characteristics. These include childhood impulsivity, weak sense of personal control over life events, early pubertal timing, parental divorce, single-parent and stepfamily homes, large family size, little or no religious involvement, weak parental monitoring, disrupted parent–child communication, sexually active friends and older siblings, poor school performance, lower educational aspirations, and tendency to engage in norm-violating acts, including alcohol and drug use and delinquency (Coley, Votruba-Drzal, & Schindler, 2009; Crockett, Raffaelli, & Shen, 2006;

Siebenbruner, Zimmer-Gembeck, & Egeland, 2007; Zimmer-Gembeck & Helfand, 2008).

Notice that many of these factors are associated with growing up in an economically disadvantaged home. Living in a neighborhood high in physical deterioration, crime, and violence also increases the likelihood that teenagers will be sexually active (Ge et al., 2002). In such neighborhoods, social ties are weak, adults exert little oversight and control over adolescents' activities, and negative peer influences are widespread. In fact, the high rate of sexual activity among African-American teenagers—60 percent report having had sexual intercourse, compared with 47 percent of all U.S. young people—is largely accounted for by widespread poverty in the black population (Darroch, Frost, & Singh, 2001; U.S. Department of Health & Human Services, 2012f).

Contraceptive Use.

Although adolescent contraceptive use has increased in recent years, about 20 percent of sexually active teenagers in the United States are at risk for unintended pregnancy because they do not use contraception consistently (Fortenberry, 2010). Why do so many fail to take precautions? Typically, teenagers respond, "I was waiting until I had a steady boyfriend," or "I wasn't planning to have sex." As we will see when we take up adolescent cognitive development, although adolescents can consider multiple possibilities when faced with a problem, they often fail to apply this advanced reasoning to everyday situations.

The social environment also contributes to teenagers' reluctance to use contraception. Those without the rewards of meaningful education and work are especially likely to engage in irresponsible sex, sometimes within relationships characterized by exploitation. About 12 percent of U.S. girls and 5 percent of boys say they were pressured to have intercourse when they were unwilling (U.S. Department of Health and Human Services, 2012f).

In contrast, teenagers who report good relationships with parents and who talk openly with them about sex and contraception are more likely to use birth control (Henrich et al., 2006; Kirby, 2002a). But few adolescents believe their parents would be understanding and supportive. School sex education classes, as well, often leave teenagers with incomplete or incorrect knowledge. Some do not know where to get birth control counseling and devices. And those engaged in high-risk sexual behaviors are especially likely to worry that a doctor or family planning clinic might not keep their visits confidential (Lehrer et al., 2007). Most of these young people forgo essential health care but continue to have sex without contraception.

Sexual Orientation.

So far, we have focused only on heterosexual behavior. About 4 percent of U.S. 15- to 44-year-olds identify as lesbian, gay, or bisexual (Mosher, Chandra, & Jones, 2005). An unknown number experience same-sex attraction but have not come out to friends or family (see the Social Issues: Health box on the following page).

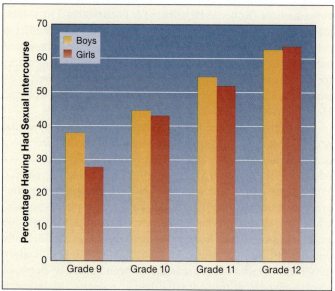

FIGURE 11.3 U.S. adolescents who report ever having had sexual intercourse. Many young adolescents are sexually active—more than in other Western nations. Boys tend to have their first intercourse earlier than girls. By the end of high school, rates of boys and girls having had sexual intercourse are similar. (From U.S. Department of Health and Human Services, 2012f.)

Social Issues: Health

Lesbian, Gay, and Bisexual Youths: Coming Out to Oneself and Others

Cultures vary as much in their acceptance of homosexuality as in their approval of extramarital sex. In the United States, homosexuals are stigmatized. This makes forming a sexual identity especially challenging for lesbian, gay, and bisexual youths.

Wide variations in sexual identity formation exist, depending on personal, family, and community factors. Yet interviews with gay and lesbian adolescents and adults reveal that many move through a three-phase sequence in coming out to themselves and others.

Feeling Different

Typically, first sense of a biologically determined gay or lesbian orientation appears between ages 6 and 12, in play interests more like those of the other gender (Rahman & Wilson, 2003). Boys may find that they are less interested in sports, more drawn to quieter activities, and more emotionally sensitive than other boys; girls that they are more athletic and active than other girls.

By age 10, many of these children start to engage in *sexual questioning*—wondering why the typical heterosexual orientation does not apply to them. Often, they experience their sense of being different as deeply distressing. Compared with children who are confident of their homosexuality, sexual-questioning children report greater anxiety about peer relationships and greater dissatisfaction with their biological gender over time (Carver, Egan, & Perry, 2004).

Confusion

With the arrival of puberty, feeling different clearly encompasses feeling sexually different. Awareness of a same-sex physical attraction occurs, on average, between ages 11 and 12 for boys and 14 and 15 for girls, perhaps because adolescent social pressures toward heterosexuality are particularly intense for girls (D'Augelli, 2006; Diamond, 1998).

Realizing that homosexuality has personal relevance sparks additional confusion. A few adolescents resolve their discomfort by crystallizing a gay, lesbian, or bisexual identity quickly, with a flash of insight into their

sense of being different. But most experience an inner struggle that is intensified by lack of role models and social support (D'Augelli, 2002; Safren & Pantalone, 2006).

Some throw themselves into activities they associate with heterosexuality. Boys may go out for athletic teams; girls may drop softball and basketball in favor of dance. And many homosexual youths (more females than males) try heterosexual dating (D'Augelli, 2006; Dubé, Savin-Williams, & Diamond, 2001). Those who are extremely troubled and guilt-ridden may escape into alcohol, drugs, and suicidal thinking. Suicide attempts are unusually high among lesbian, gay, and bisexual young people (Morrow, 2006; Teasdale & Bradley-Engen, 2010).

Self-Acceptance

By the end of adolescence, the majority of gay, lesbian, and bisexual teenagers accept their sexual identity. But they face another crossroad: whether to tell others. Powerful stigma against their sexual orientation leads some to decide that disclosure is impossible: While self-defining as gay, they otherwise "pass" as heterosexual (Savin-Williams, 2001). When homosexual youths do come out, they often face intense hostility, including verbal abuse and physical attacks, because of their sexual orientation. These experiences trigger intense emotional distress, depression, suicidal thoughts, school truancy, and drug use in victims (Almeida et al., 2009; Birkett, Espelage, & Koenig, 2009).

Nevertheless, many eventually acknowledge their sexual orientation publicly, usually by telling trusted friends first. Once teenagers establish a same-sex sexual or romantic relationship, many come out to parents. Although few parents respond with severe rejection, lesbian, gay, and bisexual young people report lower levels of family

support than their heterosexual agemates (Needham & Austin, 2010; Savin-Williams & Ream, 2003). Parental understanding is the strongest predictor of favorable adjustment (D'Augelli, Grossman, & Starks, 2008).

When people react positively, coming out strengthens the young person's view of homosexuality as a valid, meaningful, and fulfilling identity. Contact with other gays and lesbians is important for reaching this phase, and changes in society permit many adolescents in urban areas to attain it earlier than their counterparts did a decade or two ago. Gay and lesbian communities exist in large cities, along with specialized interest groups, social clubs, religious groups, newspapers, and periodicals. But teenagers in small towns and rural areas may have difficulty finding a supportive environment. These adolescents have a special need for caring adults and peers who can help them find self- and social acceptance.

Lesbian, gay, and bisexual teenagers who succeed in coming out to themselves and others integrate their sexual orientation into a broader sense of identity, a process we will address in Chapter 12. As a result, energy is freed for other aspects of psychological growth. In sum, coming out can foster many facets of adolescent development, including self-esteem, psychological well-being, and relationships with family and friends.

Lesbian, gay, bisexual, and transgender high school students and their allies participate in an annual Youth Pride Festival and March. When peers react with acceptance, coming out strengthens the young person's view of homosexuality as a valid and fulfilling identity.

Heredity makes an important contribution to homosexuality: Identical twins of both sexes are much more likely than fraternal twins to share a homosexual orientation; so are biological (as opposed to adoptive) relatives (Kendler et al., 2000; Kirk et al., 2000). Furthermore, male homosexuality tends to be more common on the maternal than on the paternal side of families, suggesting that it may be X-linked (see Chapter 2) (Hamer et al., 1993).

How might heredity lead to homosexuality? According to some researchers, certain genes affect the level or impact of prenatal sex hormones, which modify brain structures in ways that induce homosexual feelings and behavior (Bailey et al., 1995; LeVay, 1993). Keep in mind, however, that environmental factors can also alter prenatal hormones. Girls exposed prenatally to very high levels of androgens or estrogens—either because of a genetic defect or from drugs given to the mother to prevent miscarriage—are more likely to become lesbian or bisexual (Meyer-Bahlburg et al., 1995). Furthermore, gay men tend to be later in birth order and to have a higher-than-average number of older brothers (Blanchard & Bogaert, 2004). One possibility is that mothers with several male children sometimes produce antibodies to androgens, reducing the prenatal impact of male sex hormones on the brains of later-born boys.

Stereotypes and misconceptions about homosexuality persist. For example, most homosexual adolescents are not "gender-deviant" in dress or behavior. And attraction to members of the same sex is not limited to lesbian, gay, and bisexual teenagers. About 50 to 60 percent of adolescents who report having engaged in homosexual acts identify as heterosexual (Savin-Williams & Diamond, 2004). And in a study of lesbian, bisexual, and "unlabeled" young women over a 10-year period, most reported stable proportions of same-sex versus other-sex attractions over time, providing evidence that bisexuality is not, as often assumed, a transient state (Diamond, 2008).

Sexually Transmitted Diseases

Sexually active adolescents, both homosexual and heterosexual, are at risk for sexually transmitted diseases (STDs). Adolescents have the highest rates of STDs of all age groups. Despite a recent decline in STDs in the United States, one out of five to six sexually active teenagers contracts one of these illnesses each year—a rate three or more times as high as that of Canada and Western Europe (Centers for Disease Control and Prevention, 2011c). Left untreated, STDs can lead to sterility and life-threatening complications.

By far the most serious STD is AIDS. In contrast to other Western nations, where the incidence of AIDS among people under age 30 is low, about 15 percent of U.S. AIDS cases occur in young people between ages 20 and 29. Because AIDS symptoms typically do not emerge until 8 to 10 years after infection with the HIV virus, nearly all these cases originated in adolescence. Drug-abusing teenagers who share needles and male adolescents who have sex with HIV-positive same-sex partners account for most cases, but heterosexual spread of the disease remains high. It is at least twice as easy for a male to infect a female with any STD, including HIV, as for a female to infect a male. Currently, females account for about 25 percent of new U.S. HIV cases (Centers for Disease Control and Prevention, 2011b).

As a result of school courses and media campaigns, most adolescents are aware of basic facts about AIDS. But they have limited understanding of other STDs and are poorly informed about how to protect themselves (Centers for Disease Control and Prevention, 2007a; Copen, Chandra, & Martinez, 2012; Ethier et al., 2003). Furthermore, high school students report engaging in oral sex about as often as intercourse. But few report consistently using STD protection during oral sex, which is a significant mode of transmission of several STDs (Copen, Chandra, & Martinez, 2012). Concerted efforts are needed to educate young people about the full range of STDs and risky sexual behaviors.

Adolescent Pregnancy and Parenthood

Cassie didn't get pregnant after having sex with Louis, but some of her classmates were less fortunate. About 727,000 U.S. teenage girls (12,000 of them younger than age 15) became pregnant in the most recently reported year. Despite a decline of almost one-half since 1990, the U.S. adolescent pregnancy rate remains higher than that of most other industrialized countries (see Figure 11.4) (Ventura, Curtin, & Abma, 2012). Three factors heighten the incidence of adolescent pregnancy: (1) Effective sex education reaches too few teenagers; (2) convenient,

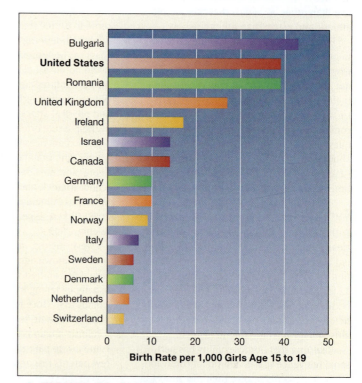

FIGURE 11.4 Birth rates among 15- to 19-year-olds in 15 industrialized nations. The U.S. adolescent birth rate greatly exceeds that of most other industrialized nations. (From Centers for Disease Control and Prevention, 2011b.)

low-cost contraceptive services for adolescents are scarce; and (3) many families live in poverty, which encourages young people to take risks.

Because about one-fourth of U.S. adolescent pregnancies end in abortion, the number of American teenage births is considerably lower than it was 50 years ago (Ventura, Curtin, & Abma, 2012). But teenage parenthood is a much greater problem today because adolescents are far less likely to marry before childbirth. In 1960, only 15 percent of teenage births were to unmarried females, compared with 87 percent today (Child Trends, 2011). Increased social acceptance of single motherhood, along with the belief of many teenage girls that a baby might fill a void in their lives, means that very few girls give up their infants for adoption.

Correlates and Consequences of Adolescent Parenthood.
Teenage parents have both life conditions and personal attributes that interfere with their capacity to parent effectively. Their backgrounds often include low parental warmth and involvement, poverty, domestic violence and child abuse, repeated parental divorce and remarriage, adult models of unmarried parenthood, and residence in neighborhoods where other adolescents also display these risks. Girls at risk for early pregnancy do poorly in school, engage in alcohol and drug use, have a childhood history of aggressive and antisocial behavior, associate with deviant peers, and experience high rates of depression (Elfenbein & Felice, 2003; Hillis et al., 2004; Luster & Haddow, 2005). Many turn to early parenthood as a way to move into adulthood when educational and career avenues are unavailable.

After a baby is born, the lives of expectant teenagers tend to worsen in several respects:

- *Educational attainment.* Parenthood before age 18 reduces the likelihood of finishing high school. Only about 70 percent of U.S. adolescent mothers graduate, compared with 95 percent of girls who wait to become parents (National Women's Law Center, 2007).

- *Marital patterns.* Teenage motherhood reduces the chances of marriage and, for those who do marry, increases the likelihood of divorce (Moore & Brooks-Gunn, 2002). Consequently, teenage mothers spend more of their parenting years as single parents. About 35 percent become pregnant again within two years. Of these, about half go on to deliver a second child (Child Trends, 2011).

- *Economic circumstances.* Many teenage mothers are on welfare or work in unsatisfying, low-paid jobs. Adolescent fathers, too, are generally unemployed or earn too little to provide their children with basic necessities (Bunting & McAuley, 2004). And for both mothers and fathers, reduced educational and occupational attainment often persists well into adulthood (Taylor, 2009).

Because many pregnant teenage girls do not receive early prenatal care, their babies often experience pregnancy and birth complications—especially preterm and low birth weight

(Khashan, Baker, & Kenny, 2010). And compared with adult mothers, adolescent mothers know less about child development, perceive their babies as more difficult, interact less effectively with them, and more often engage in child abuse (Moore & Florsheim, 2001; Pomerleau, Scuccimarri, & Malcuit, 2003; Sieger & Renk, 2007). Their children tend to score low on intelligence tests, achieve poorly in school, and engage in disruptive social behavior.

Furthermore, adolescent parenthood frequently is repeated in the next generation (Meade, Kershaw, & Ickovics, 2008). Even when children born to teenage mothers do not become early childbearers, their development is often compromised, in terms of likelihood of high school graduation, financial independence in adulthood, and long-term physical and mental health (Pogarsky, Thornberry, & Lizotte, 2006). Still, outcomes vary widely. If a teenage parent finishes high school, secures gainful employment, avoids additional births, and finds a stable partner, long-term disruptions in her child's development will be less severe.

Prevention Strategies.
Preventing teenage pregnancy means addressing the many factors underlying early sexual activity and lack of contraceptive use. Sex education courses typically improve awareness of sexual facts—knowledge necessary for responsible sexual behavior. Knowledge, however, is not enough: Sex education must also help teenagers build a bridge between what they know and what they do. Effective sex education programs include several key elements:

- They teach techniques for handling sexual situations through role-playing and other activities.

- They deliver clear, accurate messages that are appropriate in view of participating adolescents' culture and sexual experiences.

- They last long enough to have an impact.

- They provide specific information about contraceptives and ready access to them.

Many studies show that these components can delay the initiation of sexual activity, reduce the frequency of sex and the number of sexual partners, increase contraceptive use, change attitudes (for example, strengthen future orientation), and reduce pregnancy rates (Kirby, 2002b; Kirby & Laris, 2009; Thomas & Dimitrov, 2007).

LOOK AND LISTEN

Contact a nearby public school district for information about its sex education curriculum. Considering research findings, do you think it is likely to be effective in delaying initiation of sexual activity and reducing adolescent pregnancy rates? ●

Proposals to increase access to contraceptives are the most controversial aspect of U.S. adolescent pregnancy prevention efforts. Yet sex education programs encouraging abstinence without encouraging contraceptive use have little or no impact on delaying teenage sexual activity or preventing pregnancy (Rosenbaum, 2009; Underhill, Montgomery, & Operario, 2007). In Canada and Western Europe, where community- and school-based clinics offer adolescents contraceptives and where universal health insurance helps pay for them, teenage sexual activity is no higher than in the United States—but pregnancy, childbirth, and abortion rates are much lower (Schalet, 2007).

Efforts to prevent adolescent pregnancy and parenthood must go beyond improving sex education and access to contraception to build academic and social competence (Allen, Seitz, & Apfel, 2007). In one intervention, at-risk high school students took a community service class, in which they spent at least 20 hours per week in volunteer work tailored to their interests and in discussions focused on enhancing coping with everyday challenges. At the end of the school year, rates of pregnancy, school failure, and school suspension were substantially lower among intervention participants than among high-risk students with regular classroom experiences (Allen et al., 1997).

Finally, teenagers who look forward to a promising future are far less likely to engage in early and irresponsible sex. By expanding educational, vocational, and employment opportunities, society can give young people good reasons to postpone childbearing.

Intervening with Adolescent Parents. The most difficult and costly way to deal with adolescent parenthood is to wait until it happens. Young parents need health care, encouragement to stay in school, job training, instruction in parenting and life-management skills, and high-quality, affordable child care. Schools that provide these services reduce the incidence of low-birth-weight babies, increase educational success, and prevent additional childbearing (Key et al., 2008; Seitz & Apfel, 2005).

Early parenthood imposes lasting hardships on adolescent parents and their newborn babies. But the involvement of a caring father and a stable partnership between the parents can improve outcomes for young families.

Adolescent mothers also benefit from relationships with family members and other adults who are sensitive to their developmental needs. In one study, teenage mothers who had a long-term "mentor" relationship—an aunt, neighbor, or teacher who provided emotional support and guidance—were far more likely than those without a mentor to stay in school and graduate (Klaw, Rhodes, & Fitzgerald, 2003). Home visiting programs are also effective. Return to page 72 in Chapter 3 to review the Nurse–Family Partnership, which helps launch teenage mothers and their babies on a favorable life course.

Although nearly half of young fathers visit their children during the first few years, contact usually diminishes. As with teenage mothers, support from family members helps fathers stay involved (Bunting & McAuley, 2004). Teenage mothers who receive financial and child-care assistance and emotional support from their child's father are less distressed and more likely to sustain a relationship with him (Cutrona et al., 1998; Gee & Rhodes, 2003). And infants with lasting ties to their teenage fathers show better long-term adjustment (Florsheim & Smith, 2005; Furstenberg & Harris, 1993).

Substance Use and Abuse

At age 14, Louis waited until he was alone at home, took some cigarettes from his uncle's pack, and smoked. At an unchaperoned party, he and Cassie drank several cans of beer and lit up marijuana joints. Louis got little physical charge out of these experiences. A good student, who was well-liked by peers and got along well with his parents, he did not need drugs as an escape valve. But he knew of other teenagers who started with alcohol and cigarettes, moved on to harder substances, and eventually were hooked.

According to the most recent nationally representative survey of U.S. high school students, by tenth grade, 33 percent of U.S. young people have tried cigarette smoking, 58 percent drinking, and 37 percent at least one illegal drug (usually marijuana). At the end of high school, 11 percent smoke cigarettes regularly, and 27 percent have engaged in heavy drinking during the past month. About 25 percent have tried at least one highly addictive and toxic substance, such as amphetamines, cocaine, phencyclidine (PCP), Ecstasy (MDMA), inhalants, heroin, sedatives (including barbiturates), or OxyContin (a narcotic painkiller) (Johnston et al., 2011).

These figures represent a substantial decline since the mid-1990s, probably resulting from greater parent, school, and media focus on the hazards of drug use. But use of marijuana, inhalants, sedatives, and OxyContin has risen slightly in recent years (Johnston et al., 2011). Other drugs, such as LSD, PCP, and Ecstasy, have made a comeback as adolescents' knowledge of their risks faded. In part, drug taking reflects the sensation seeking of the teenage years. But adolescents also live in drug-dependent cultural contexts. They see adults relying on caffeine to stay alert, alcohol and cigarettes to cope with daily hassles, and other remedies to relieve stress, depression, and physical discomfort. And compared to a decade or two ago, today doctors more often prescribe—and parents frequently seek—

medication to treat children's problems (Olfman & Robbins, 2012). In adolescence, these young people may readily "self-medicate" when stressed.

Most teenagers who dabble in alcohol, tobacco, and marijuana are not headed for a life of addiction. These *minimal experimenters* are usually psychologically healthy, sociable, curious young people (Shedler & Block, 1990). Poverty is linked to family and peer contexts that promote illegal drug use. At the same time, use of diverse drugs is lower among African Americans than among Hispanic and Caucasian Americans; Native-American youths rank highest in drug taking (Johnston et al., 2011). Researchers have yet to explain these variations.

Adolescent experimentation with any drug should not be taken lightly. Because most drugs impair perception and thought processes, a single heavy dose can lead to permanent injury or death. And a worrisome minority of teenagers move from substance *use* to *abuse*—taking drugs regularly, requiring increasing amounts to achieve the same effect, moving on to harder substances, and using enough to interfere with their ability to meet daily responsibilities.

Correlates and Consequences of Adolescent Substance Abuse.

Unlike experimenters, drug abusers are seriously troubled young people. Their impulsive, disruptive, hostile style is often evident in early childhood. Compared with other young people, their drug taking starts earlier and may have genetic roots (Dick, Prescott, & McGue, 2008; Tarter, Vanyukov, & Kirisci, 2008). But environmental factors also contribute. These include low SES, family mental health problems, parental and older sibling drug abuse, lack of parental warmth and involvement, physical and sexual abuse, and poor school performance. Especially among teenagers with family difficulties, encouragement from friends who use and provide drugs increases substance abuse (Ohannessian & Hesselbrock, 2008; U.S. Department of Health and Human Services, 2010c).

Introducing drugs while the adolescent brain is still a work-in-progress can have profound, lasting consequences, impairing neurons and their connective networks. At the same time, teenagers who use substances to deal with daily stresses fail to learn responsible decision-making skills and alternative coping techniques. They show serious adjustment problems, including chronic anxiety, depression, and antisocial behavior, that are both cause and consequence of heavy drug taking (Kassel et al., 2005; U.S. Department of Health and Human Services, 2010c). And they often enter into marriage, childbearing, and the work world prematurely and fail at them—painful outcomes that further promote addictive behavior.

Prevention and Treatment.

School and community programs that reduce drug experimentation typically teach skills for resisting peer pressure, emphasize health and safety risks of drug-taking, and get adolescents to commit to not using drugs (Stephens et al., 2009). But given that adolescent drug taking is widespread, interventions that prevent teenagers from harming themselves and others when they do experiment are essential. Many communities offer weekend on-call transporta-

Teenagers enjoy a community party sponsored by Drug Free Youth in Town (DFYIT), a substance abuse prevention program. DFYIT trains high school students as peer educators, who teach middle school students life skills and strategies for resisting peer pressure.

tion services that any young person can contact for a safe ride home, with no questions asked.

Different strategies are required to prevent drug use. One approach is to work with parents early, reducing family adversity and improving parenting skills (Velleman, Templeton, & Copello, 2005). Programs that teach at-risk teenagers effective strategies for handling life stressors and that build competence through community service reduce alcohol and drug abuse, just as they reduce teenage pregnancy.

When an adolescent becomes a drug abuser, family and individual therapy are generally needed to treat maladaptive parent–child relationships, impulsivity, low self-esteem, anxiety, and depression. Academic and vocational training to improve life success also helps. But even comprehensive programs have alarmingly high relapse rates—from 35 to 85 percent (Brown & Ramo, 2005; Sussman, Skara, & Ames, 2008). One recommendation is to start treatment gradually, through support-group sessions that focus on reducing drug taking (Myers et al., 2001). Modest improvements may increase young people's motivation to make longer-lasting changes through intensive treatment.

ASK YOURSELF

REVIEW Compare risk factors for anorexia nervosa and bulimia nervosa. How do treatments and outcomes differ for the two disorders?

APPLY After 17-year-old Veronica gave birth to Ben, her parents told her they didn't have room for the baby. Veronica dropped out of school and moved in with her boyfriend, who soon left. Why are Veronica and Ben likely to experience long-term hardships?

REFLECT Describe your experiences with peer pressure to experiment with alcohol and drugs. What factors influenced your response?

COGNITIVE DEVELOPMENT

One mid-December evening, a knock at the front door announced the arrival of Franca and Antonio's oldest son, Jules, home for vacation after the fall semester of his sophomore year at college. The family gathered around the kitchen table. "How did it all go, Jules?" asked Antonio.

"Well, physics and philosophy were awesome," Jules responded with enthusiasm. "The last few weeks, our physics prof introduced us to Einstein's theory of relativity. Boggles my mind, it's so incredibly counterintuitive."

"Counter-what?" asked 11-year-old Sabrina.

"Counterintuitive. Unlike what you'd normally expect," explained Jules. "Imagine you're on a train, going unbelievably fast, like 160,000 miles a second. The faster you go, approaching the speed of light, the slower time passes and the denser and heavier things get relative to on the ground. The theory revolutionized the way we think about time, space, matter—the entire universe."

Sabrina wrinkled her forehead, baffled by Jules's otherworldly reasoning. "Time slows down when I'm bored, like right now, not on a train when I'm going somewhere exciting," Sabrina announced.

Sixteen-year-old Louis reacted differently. "Totally cool, Jules. So what'd you do in philosophy?"

"We studied the ethics of futuristic methods in human reproduction. For example, we argued the pros and cons of a world in which all embryos develop in artificial wombs."

"What do you mean?" asked Louis. "You order your kid at the lab?"

"That's right. I wrote my term paper on it. I had to evaluate it in terms of principles of justice and freedom. . . ."

As this conversation illustrates, adolescence brings with it vastly expanded powers of reasoning. At age 11, Sabrina finds it difficult to move beyond her firsthand experiences to a world of possibilities. Over the next few years, her thinking will acquire the complex qualities that characterize the cognition of her older brothers. Jules and Louis consider multiple variables simultaneously and think about situations that are not easily detected in the real world or that do not exist at all. As a result, they can grasp advanced scientific and mathematical principles and grapple with social and political issues. Compared with school-age children's thinking, adolescent thought is more enlightened, imaginative, and rational.

Systematic research on adolescent cognitive development began with testing of Piaget's ideas (Kuhn, 2009). Recently, information-processing research has greatly enhanced our understanding.

Piaget's Theory: The Formal Operational Stage

According to Piaget, around age 11 young people enter the **formal operational stage**, in which they develop the capacity for abstract, systematic, scientific thinking. Whereas concrete operational children can "operate on reality," formal operational adolescents can "operate on operations." They no longer require concrete things or events as objects of thought. Instead, they can come up with new, more general logical rules through internal reflection (Inhelder & Piaget, 1955/1958). Let's look at two major features of the formal operational stage.

Hypothetico-Deductive Reasoning

Piaget believed that at adolescence, young people first become capable of **hypothetico-deductive reasoning**. When faced with a problem, they start with a *hypothesis*, or prediction about variables that might affect an outcome, from which they *deduce* logical, testable inferences. Then they systematically isolate and combine variables to see which of these inferences are confirmed in the real world. Notice how this form of problem solving begins with possibility and proceeds to reality. In contrast, concrete operational children start with reality—with the most obvious predictions about a situation. If these are not confirmed, they usually cannot think of alternatives and fail to solve the problem.

Adolescents' performance on Piaget's famous *pendulum problem* illustrates this approach. Suppose we present several school-age children and adolescents with strings of different lengths, objects of different weights to attach to the strings, and a bar from which to hang the strings (see Figure 11.5). Then we ask each of them to figure out what influences the speed with which a pendulum swings through its arc.

Formal operational adolescents hypothesize that four variables might be influential: (1) the length of the string, (2) the

FIGURE 11.5 Piaget's pendulum problem. Adolescents who engage in hypothetico-deductive reasoning think of variables that might possibly affect the speed with which a pendulum swings through its arc. Then they isolate and test each variable, as well as testing the variables in combination. Eventually they deduce that the weight of the object, the height from which it is released, and how forcefully it is pushed have no effect. Only string length makes a difference.

weight of the object hung on it, (3) how high the object is raised before it is released, and (4) how forcefully the object is pushed. By varying one factor at a time while holding the other three constant, they test each variable separately and, if necessary, also in combination. Eventually they discover that only string length makes a difference.

In contrast, concrete operational children cannot separate the effects of each variable. They may test for the effect of string length without holding weight constant—comparing, for example, a short, light pendulum with a long, heavy one. Also, they typically fail to notice variables that are not immediately suggested by the concrete materials of the task—for example, how high the object is raised or how forcefully it is released.

Propositional Thought

A second important characteristic of Piaget's formal operational stage is **propositional thought**—adolescents' ability to evaluate the logic of propositions (verbal statements) without referring to real-world circumstances. In contrast, children can evaluate the logic of statements only by considering them against concrete evidence in the real world.

In a study of propositional reasoning, a researcher showed children and adolescents a pile of poker chips and asked whether statements about the chips were true, false, or uncertain (Osherson & Markman, 1975). In one condition, the researcher hid a chip in her hand and presented the following propositions:

"*Either* the chip in my hand is green or it is not green."
"The chip in my hand is green *and* it is not green."

In another condition, the experimenter made the same statements while holding either a red or a green chip in full view.

School-age children focused on the concrete properties of the poker chips. When the chip was hidden, they replied that they were uncertain about both statements. When it was visible, they judged both statements to be true if the chip was green and false if it was red. In contrast, adolescents analyzed the logic of

As these students discuss problems in a social studies class, they reason logically from premises that do not refer to real-world circumstances. They are far better at propositional thought than they were as children.

© CINDY CHARLES/PHOTOEDIT

the statements. They understood that the "either-or" statement is always true and the "and" statement is always false, regardless of the poker chip's color.

Although Piaget did not view language as playing a central role in children's cognitive development (see Chapter 7), he acknowledged its importance in adolescence. Formal operations require language-based and other symbolic systems that do not stand for real things, such as those in higher mathematics. Secondary school students use such systems in algebra and geometry. Formal operational thought also involves verbal reasoning about abstract concepts. Jules was thinking in this way when he pondered relationships among time, space, and matter in physics and wondered about justice and freedom in philosophy.

Follow-Up Research on Formal Operational Thought

Research on formal operational thought poses questions similar to those we discussed with respect to Piaget's earlier stages: Does formal operational thinking appear earlier than Piaget expected? Do all individuals reach formal operations during their teenage years?

Are Children Capable of Hypothetico-Deductive and Propositional Thinking? School-age children show the glimmerings of hypothetico-deductive reasoning, although they are less competent at it than adolescents. In simplified situations involving no more than two possible causal variables, 6-year-olds understand that hypotheses must be confirmed by appropriate evidence (Ruffman et al., 1993). But school-age children cannot sort out evidence that bears on three or more variables at once. And children have difficulty explaining why a pattern of observations supports a hypothesis, even when they recognize the connection between the two.

With respect to propositional thought, when a simple set of premises defies real-world knowledge ("All cats bark. Rex is a cat. Does Rex bark?"), 4- to 6-year-olds can reason logically in make-believe play. To justify their answer, they are likely to say, "We can pretend cats bark!" (Dias & Harris, 1988, 1990). But in an entirely verbal mode, children have great difficulty reasoning from premises that contradict reality or their own beliefs.

Consider this set of statements: "If dogs are bigger than elephants and elephants are bigger than mice, then dogs are bigger than mice." Children younger than 10 judge this reasoning to be false because some of the relations specified do not occur in real life (Moshman & Franks, 1986; Pillow, 2002). They have more difficulty than adolescents inhibiting activation of well-learned knowledge ("Elephants are larger than dogs") that impedes effective reasoning (Klaczynski, Schuneman, & Daniel, 2004; Simoneau & Markovits, 2003). Partly for this reason, they fail to grasp the *logical necessity* of propositional reasoning—that the accuracy of conclusions drawn from premises rests on the rules of logic, not on real-world confirmation.

As with hypothetico-deductive reasoning, in early adolescence, young people become better at analyzing the *logic* of propositions irrespective of their *content*. And as they get older, they handle problems requiring increasingly complex mental operations. In justifying their reasoning, they more often explain the logical rules on which it is based (Müller, Overton, & Reese, 2001; Venet & Markovits, 2001). But these capacities do not appear suddenly at puberty. Rather, gains occur gradually from childhood on—findings that call into question the emergence of a new stage of cognitive development at adolescence (Kuhn, 2009; Moshman, 2005).

Do All Individuals Reach the Formal Operational Stage? *TAKE A MOMENT...* Try giving one or two of the formal operational tasks just described to your friends. How well do they do? Even well-educated adults often have difficulty (Kuhn, 2009; Markovits & Vachon, 1990). One reason is that people are most likely to think abstractly and systematically on tasks in which they have had extensive guidance and practice in using such reasoning. This conclusion is supported by evidence that taking college courses leads to improvements in formal reasoning related to course content. Math and science prompt gains in propositional thought, social science in methodological and statistical reasoning (Lehman & Nisbett, 1990).

Individuals in tribal and village societies rarely do well on tasks typically used to assess formal operational reasoning (Cole, 1990). Piaget acknowledged that without the opportunity to solve hypothetical problems, people in some societies might not display formal operations. Still, researchers ask, Does formal operational thought largely result from children's and adolescents' independent efforts to make sense of their world, as Piaget claimed? Or is it a culturally transmitted way of thinking that is specific to literate societies and taught in school? In an Israeli study, after controlling for participants' age, researchers found that years of schooling fully accounted for early adolescent gains in propositional thought (Artman, Cahan, & Avni-Babad, 2006). School tasks, the investigators speculated, provide crucial experiences in setting aside the "if . . . then" logic of everyday conversations that is often used to convey intentions, promises, and threats ("If you don't do your chores, then you won't get your allowance") but that conflicts with the logic of academic reasoning. In school, then, adolescents encounter rich opportunities to realize their neurological potential to think more effectively.

An Information-Processing View of Adolescent Cognitive Development

Information-processing theorists refer to a variety of specific mechanisms, including diverse aspects of executive function, as underlying cognitive gains in adolescence. Each was discussed

in previous chapters (Kuhn, 2009; Kuhn & Franklin, 2006; Luna et al., 2004). Now let's draw them together:

- *Attention* becomes more selective (focused on relevant information) and better-adapted to the changing demands of tasks.
- *Inhibition*—both of irrelevant stimuli and of well-learned responses in situations where they are inappropriate—improves, supporting gains in attention and reasoning.
- *Strategies* become more effective, improving storage, representation, and retrieval of information.
- *Knowledge* increases, easing strategy use.
- *Metacognition* (awareness of thought) expands, leading to new insights into effective strategies for acquiring information and solving problems.
- *Cognitive self-regulation* improves, yielding better moment-by-moment monitoring, evaluation, and redirection of thinking.
- *Speed of thinking* and *processing capacity* increase. As a result, more information can be held at once in working memory and combined into increasingly complex, efficient representations, "opening possibilities for growth" in the capacities just listed and also improving as a result of gains in those capacities (Demetriou et al., 2002, p. 97).

As we look at influential findings from an information-processing perspective, we will see some of these mechanisms of change in action. And we will discover that researchers regard one of them—*metacognition*—as central to adolescent cognitive development.

Scientific Reasoning: Coordinating Theory with Evidence

During a free moment in physical education class, Sabrina wondered why more of her tennis serves and returns passed the net and dropped into her opponent's court when she used a particular brand of balls. "Is it something about their color or size?" she asked herself. "Hmm . . . or maybe it's their surface texture that might affect their bounce."

The heart of scientific reasoning is coordinating theories with evidence. Deanna Kuhn (2002) has conducted extensive research into the development of scientific reasoning, using problems that, like Piaget's tasks, involve several variables that might affect an outcome. In one series of studies, third, sixth, and ninth graders and adults were first given evidence—sometimes consistent and sometimes conflicting with theories—and then questioned about the accuracy of each theory.

For example, participants were given a problem much like Sabrina's: to theorize about which of several features of sports balls—size (large or small), color (light or dark), texture (rough or smooth), or presence or absence of ridges on the surface—influences the quality of a player's serve. Next, they were told about the theory of Mr. (or Ms.) S, who believes that the

FIGURE 11.6 Which features of these sports balls—size, color, surface texture, or presence or absence of ridges—influence the quality of a player's serve? This set of evidence suggests that color might be important, since light-colored balls are largely in the good-serve basket and dark-colored balls in the bad-serve basket. But the same is true for texture! The good-serve basket has mostly smooth balls; the bad-serve basket, rough balls. Since all light-colored balls are smooth and all dark-colored balls are rough, we cannot tell whether color or texture makes a difference. But we can conclude that size and presence or absence of ridges are not important, since these features are equally represented in the good-serve and bad-serve baskets. (Adapted from Kuhn, Amsel, & O'Loughlin, 1988.)

ball's size is important, and the theory of Mr. (or Ms.) C, who thinks color matters. Finally, the interviewer presented evidence by placing balls with certain characteristics in two baskets, labeled "good serve" and "bad serve" (see Figure 11.6).

The youngest participants often discounted obviously causal variables, ignored evidence conflicting with their own initial judgments, and distorted evidence in ways consistent with their preferred theory. These findings, and others like them, suggest that on complex, multivariable tasks, children—instead of viewing evidence as separate from and bearing on a theory—often blend the two into a single representation of "the way things are." Children are especially likely to overlook evidence that does not match their prior beliefs when a causal variable is implausible (like color affecting the performance of a sports ball) and when task demands (number of variables to be evaluated) are high (Yang & Tsai, 2010; Zimmerman, 2007). The ability to distinguish theory from evidence and use logical rules to examine their relationship improves steadily from childhood into adolescence, continuing into adulthood (Kuhn & Dean, 2004).

How Scientific Reasoning Develops

What factors support skill at coordinating theory with evidence? Greater working-memory capacity, permitting a theory and the effects of several variables to be compared at once, is vital. Adolescents also benefit from exposure to increasingly complex problems and to teaching that highlights critical features of scientific reasoning—for example, why a scientist's

expectations in a particular situation are inconsistent with everyday beliefs and experiences (Chinn & Malhotra, 2002). This explains why scientific reasoning is strongly influenced by years of schooling, whether individuals grapple with traditional scientific tasks (like the sports-ball problem) or engage in informal reasoning—for example, justifying a theory about what causes children to fail in school (Amsel & Brock, 1996).

Researchers believe that sophisticated *metacognitive understanding* is vital for scientific reasoning (Kuhn, 2009; Kuhn & Pease, 2006). When adolescents regularly pit theory against evidence over many weeks, they experiment with various strategies, reflect on and revise them, and become aware of the nature of logic. Then they apply their appreciation of logic to an increasingly wide variety of situations. The ability to *think about* theories, *deliberately isolate* variables, *consider all influential* variables, and *actively seek* disconfirming evidence is rarely present before adolescence (Kuhn, 2000; Kuhn et al., 2008; Moshman, 1998).

But adolescents and adults vary widely in scientific reasoning skills. Many continue to show a self-serving bias, applying logic more effectively to ideas they doubt than to ideas they favor (Klaczynski & Narasimham, 1998). Reasoning scientifically requires the metacognitive capacity to evaluate one's objectivity—to be fair-minded rather than self-serving (Moshman, 2005). As we will see in Chapter 12, this flexible, open-minded approach is both a cognitive attainment and a personality trait—one that assists teenagers greatly in forming an identity and developing morally. Information-processing findings confirm that scientific reasoning is not the result of an abrupt, stagewise change. Instead, it develops out of many specific experiences that require children and adolescents to match theories against evidence and reflect on and evaluate their thinking.

LOOK AND LISTEN

Describe one or more memorable experiences from your high school classes that helped you advance in scientific reasoning—pit theory against evidence and become receptive to disconfirming evidence even for theories you favored. ●

Consequences of Adolescent Cognitive Changes

The development of increasingly complex, effective thinking leads to dramatic revisions in the way adolescents see themselves and others. But just as adolescents are occasionally awkward in using their transformed bodies, so they initially falter in their abstract thinking. As we will see, teenagers' self-concern, idealism, criticism, and faulty decision making, though perplexing to adults, are usually beneficial in the long run.

Self-Consciousness and Self-Focusing

Adolescents' ability to reflect on their own thoughts, combined with physical and psychological changes, leads them to think more about themselves. Piaget's followers identified two distorted images of the relation between self and other that commonly appear.

The first is called the **imaginary audience**, adolescents' belief that they are the focus of everyone else's attention and concern (Elkind & Bowen, 1979). As a result, they become extremely self-conscious. The imaginary audience helps explain why adolescents spend long hours inspecting every detail of their appearance and why they are so sensitive to public criticism. To teenagers, who believe that everyone is monitoring their performance, a critical remark from a parent or teacher can be mortifying.

A second cognitive distortion is the **personal fable**. Certain that others are observing and thinking about them, teenagers develop an inflated opinion of their own importance—a feeling that they are special and unique. Many adolescents view themselves as reaching great heights of omnipotence and also sinking to unusual depths of despair—experiences that others cannot possibly understand (Elkind, 1994). One teenager wrote in her diary, "My parents' lives are so ordinary, so stuck in a rut. Mine will be different. I'll realize my hopes and ambitions."

Imaginary-audience and personal-fable ideation are partly an outgrowth of advances in perspective taking, which cause young teenagers to be more concerned with what others think (Steinberg, 2008; Vartanian & Powlishta, 1996). When asked why they worry about the opinions of others, adolescents responded that others' evaluations have important *real* consequences—for self-esteem, peer acceptance, and social support (Bell & Bromnick, 2003). With respect to the personal fable, in one study, sense of omnipotence predicted favorable self-esteem and overall positive adjustment. Viewing the self as highly capable and influential helps young people cope with challenges of

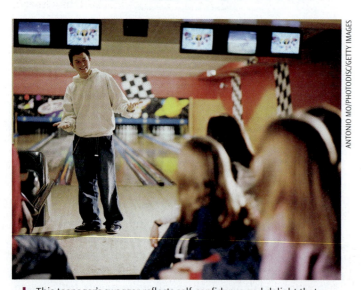

This teenager's swagger reflects self-confidence and delight that all eyes are on him. When the personal fable engenders a view of oneself as highly capable and influential, it may help young people cope with the challenges of adolescence.

adolescence. In contrast, sense of personal uniqueness was associated with depression and suicidal thinking (Aalsma, Lapsley, & Flannery, 2006). Focusing on the distinctiveness of one's own experiences may interfere with forming close, rewarding relationships, which provide social support in stressful times.

Idealism and Criticism

Adolescents' capacity to think about possibilities opens up the world of the ideal. Teenagers can imagine alternative family, religious, political, and moral systems, and they want to explore them. They often construct grand visions of a world with no injustice, discrimination, or tasteless behavior. The disparity between teenagers' idealism and adults' greater realism creates tension between parent and child. Envisioning a perfect family against which their parents and siblings fall short, adolescents become fault-finding critics.

Overall, however, teenage idealism and criticism are advantageous. Once adolescents come to see other people as having both strengths and weaknesses, they have a much greater capacity to work constructively for social change and to form positive, lasting relationships (Elkind, 1994).

Decision Making

Recall that changes in the brain's emotional/social network outpace development of the prefrontal cortex's cognitive-control network. Consequently, teenagers often perform less well than adults in decision making, where they must inhibit emotion and impulses in favor of thinking rationally.

Good decision making involves: (1) identifying the pros and cons of each alternative, (2) assessing the likelihood of various outcomes, (3) evaluating one's choice in terms of whether goals were met and, if not, (4) learning from the mistake and making a better future decision. When researchers modified a card game to trigger strong emotion by introducing immediate feedback about gains and losses after each choice, teenagers behaved more irrationally, taking far greater risks than adults in their twenties (Figner et al., 2009). They were more influenced by the possibility of immediate reward (see page 291).

Nevertheless, teenagers are less effective than adults at decision making even under "cool," unemotional conditions (Huizenga, Crone, & Jansen, 2007). They less often carefully evaluate alternatives, instead falling back on well-learned intuitive judgments (Jacobs & Klaczynski, 2002). Consider a hypothetical problem requiring a choice, on the basis of two arguments, between taking a traditional lecture class and taking a computer-based class. One argument contains large-sample information: course evaluations from 150 students, 85 percent of whom liked the computer class. The other argument contains small-sample personal reports: complaints of two honor-roll students who both hated the computer class and enjoyed the traditional class. Most adolescents, even those who knew that selecting the large-sample argument was "more intelligent," based their choice on the small-sample argument, which resembled the informal opinions they depend on in everyday life (Klaczynski, 2001).

These high school students attending a college fair will face many choices over the next few years. But in making decisions, teenagers are less likely than adults to carefully weigh the pros and cons of each alternative.

Earlier we noted that processing skills governed by the prefrontal cortex's cognitive-control system, such as decision making, develop gradually. But like other aspects of brain development, the cognitive-control system is affected by experience (Kuhn, 2009). As "first-timers" in many situations, adolescents do not have sufficient knowledge to consider pros and cons and predict likely outcomes. And after engaging in risky behavior without negative consequences, teenagers rate its benefits higher and its risks lower than peers who have not tried it—judgments that increase the chances of continued risk-taking (Halpern-Felsher et al., 2004).

Over time, young people learn from their successes and failures, gather information from others about factors that affect decision making, and reflect on the decision-making process (Byrnes, 2003; Reyna & Farley, 2006). But because taking risks without experiencing harm can heighten adolescents' sense of invulnerability, they need supervision and protection from high-risk experiences until their decision making improves.

ASK YOURSELF

REVIEW How does evidence on adolescent decision making help us understand teenagers' risk taking in sexual activity and drug use?

APPLY Clarissa, age 14, is convinced that no one appreciates how hurt she feels at not being invited to the homecoming dance. Meanwhile, 15-year-old Justine, alone in her room, pantomimes being sworn in as student body president with her awestruck parents looking on. Which aspect of the personal fable is each girl displaying? Which girl is more likely to be well-adjusted, which poorly adjusted? Explain.

REFLECT Cite examples of your own idealistic thinking or poor decision making as a teenager. How has your thinking changed?

 # Learning in School

In complex societies, adolescence coincides with entry into secondary school. Most young people move into either a middle or a junior high school and then into a high school. With each change, academic achievement increasingly determines higher education options and job opportunities. In the following sections, we take up various aspects of secondary school life.

School Transitions

When Sabrina started middle school, she left a small, intimate, self-contained sixth-grade classroom for a much larger school. "I don't know most of the kids in my classes, and my teachers don't know me," Sabrina complained to her mother at the end of the first week. "Besides, there's too much homework. I get assignments in all my classes at once. I can't do all this!" she shouted, bursting into tears.

Impact of School Transitions. As Sabrina's reactions suggest, school transitions can create adjustment problems. With each school change—from elementary to middle or junior high and then to high school—adolescents' grades decline. The drop is partly due to tighter academic standards. At the same time, the transition to secondary school often means less personal attention, more whole-class instruction, and less chance to participate in classroom decision making (Seidman, Aber, & French, 2004).

It is not surprising, then, that students rate their middle- and high school learning experiences less favorably than their elementary-school experiences, stating that their teachers care less about them, grade less fairly, and stress competition more (Wigfield & Eccles, 1994). Consequently, many young people feel less academically competent and decline in motivation (Barber & Olsen, 2004; Gutman & Midgley, 2000; Otis, Grouzet, & Pelletier, 2005).

On the first day of school, a teacher's caring attention helps this sixth grader deal with the stress of moving from a small, self-contained elementary school classroom to a large middle school.

Inevitably, students must readjust their feelings of self-confidence and self-worth as they encounter revised academic expectations and a more complex social world. But adolescents who face added strains—family disruption, poverty, low parental involvement, or learned helplessness on academic tasks—are at greatest risk for self-esteem and academic difficulties (de Bruyn, 2005; Rudolph et al., 2001; Seidman et al., 2003). Furthermore, high-school transition is especially challenging for African-American and Hispanic students who move to a new school with substantially fewer peers of the same ethnicity (Benner & Graham, 2009). Under these conditions, minority adolescents report decreased feelings of belonging and school liking, and they show steeper declines in grades.

Distressed youths whose school performance either remains low or drops sharply after school transition often show a persisting pattern of poor self-esteem, motivation, and achievement. In one investigation, researchers compared "multiple-problem" youths (those with both academic and mental health problems), youths with difficulties in just one area (either academic or mental health), and well-adjusted youths (those doing well in both areas) across the transition to high school. Although all groups declined in grade point average, well-adjusted students continued to get high marks and multiple-problem youths low marks, with the others falling in between. And as Figure 11.7 shows, the multiple-problem youths showed a far greater rise in truancy and out-of-school problem behaviors (Roeser, Eccles, & Freedman-Doan, 1999). For some, school transition initiates a downward spiral in academic performance and school involvement that leads to dropping out.

Helping Adolescents Adjust to School Transitions. As these findings reveal, school transitions often lead to environmental changes that fit poorly with adolescents' developmental needs (Eccles & Roeser, 2009). They disrupt close relationships with teachers at a time when adolescents need adult support. They emphasize competition during a period of heightened self-focusing. They reduce decision making and choice as the desire for autonomy is increasing. And they interfere with peer networks as young people become more concerned with peer acceptance.

Support from parents, teachers, and peers can ease these strains. Parental involvement, monitoring, gradual autonomy granting, and emphasis on mastery rather than merely good grades are associated with better adjustment (Grolnick et al., 2000; Gutman, 2006). Adolescents with close friends are more likely to sustain these friendships across the transition, which increases social integration and academic motivation in the new school (Aikens, Bierman, & Parker, 2005). Forming smaller units within larger schools promotes closer relationships with both teachers and peers and greater extracurricular involvement (Seidman, Aber, & French, 2004). And a "critical mass" of same-ethnicity peers—according to one suggestion, at least 15 percent of the student body—helps teenagers feel socially accepted and reduces fear of out-group hostility (National Research Council, 2007).

LOOK AND LISTEN

Ask several secondary school students to describe their experiences after school transition. What supports for easing the stress of transition did their teachers and school provide?

Other, less extensive changes are also effective. In the first year after a school transition, homerooms can be provided in which teachers offer academic and personal counseling. Assigning students to classes with several familiar peers or a constant group of new peers strengthens emotional security and social support. In schools that took these steps, students were less likely to decline in academic performance or display other adjustment problems (Felner et al., 2002).

Academic Achievement

Adolescent achievement is the result of a long history of cumulative effects. Early on, positive educational environments, both family and school, lead to personal traits that support achievement—intelligence, confidence in one's own abilities, the desire to succeed, and high educational aspirations. Nevertheless, improving an unfavorable environment can foster resilience among poorly performing young people.

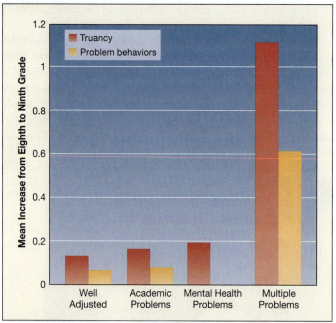

FIGURE 11.7 **Increase in truancy and out-of-school problem behaviors across the transition to high school in four groups of students.** Well-adjusted students, students with only academic problems, and students with only mental health problems showed little change. (Good students with mental health problems actually declined in problem behaviors, so no orange bar is shown for them.) In contrast, multiple-problem students—with both academic and mental health difficulties—increased sharply in truancy and problem behaviors after changing schools from eighth to ninth grade. (Adapted from Roeser, Eccles, & Freedman-Doan, 1999.)

Child-Rearing Styles. As in childhood, authoritative parenting is linked to higher grades among adolescents varying widely in SES, just as it predicts mastery-oriented behavior in childhood. In contrast, authoritarian and permissive styles are associated with lower grades (Collins & Steinberg, 2006; Vazsonyi, Hibbert, & Snider, 2003). Uninvolved parenting predicts the poorest grades and worsening school performance over time (Glasgow et al., 1997; Kaisa, Stattin, & Nurmi, 2000).

Adolescents whose parents engage in joint decision making, gradually permitting more autonomy with age, achieve especially well (Spera, 2005; Wang, Pomerantz, & Chen, 2007). Warmth, open discussion, firmness, and monitoring of the adolescents' whereabouts and activities make young people feel cared about and valued, encourage reflective thinking and self-regulation, and increase awareness of the importance of doing well in school. These factors, in turn, are related to mastery-oriented attributions, effort, achievement, and high educational aspirations (Aunola, Stattin, & Nurmi, 2000; Gregory & Weinstein, 2004; Trusty, 1999).

Parent–School Partnerships. High-achieving students typically have parents who keep tabs on their child's progress, communicate with teachers, and make sure their child is enrolled in challenging, well-taught classes (Hill & Taylor, 2004). In a nationally representative sample of U.S. adolescents, parents' school involvement in eighth grade strongly predicted students' grade point average in tenth grade, beyond the influence of SES and previous academic achievement (Keith et al., 1998). Parents who are in frequent contact with the school send a message to their child about the value of education, model constructive solutions to academic problems, and promote wise educational decisions.

The daily stresses of living in low-income, high-risk neighborhoods reduce parents' energy for school involvement (Bowen, Bowen, & Ware, 2002). Yet stronger home–school links could relieve some of this stress. Schools can build parent–school partnerships by strengthening personal relationships between

By attending parent–teacher conferences and keeping tabs on her daughter's academic progress, this mother sends her child a message about the importance of education.

teachers and parents, tapping parents' talents to improve the quality of school programs, and including parents in school governance so they remain invested in school goals.

Peer Influences. Peers play an important role in adolescent achievement, in a way that relates to both family and school. Teenagers whose parents value achievement generally choose friends who share those values (Kiuru et al., 2009; Woolley, Kol, & Bowen, 2009). For example, when Sabrina began to make new friends in middle school, she often studied with her girlfriends. Each wanted to do well and reinforced this desire in the others.

Peer support for high achievement also depends on the overall climate of the peer culture, which, for ethnic minority youths, is powerfully affected by the surrounding social order. In one study, integration into the school peer network predicted higher grades among Caucasians and Hispanics but not among Asians and African Americans (Faircloth & Hamm, 2005). Asian cultural values stress respect for family and teacher expectations over close peer ties (Chao & Tseng, 2002; Chen, 2005). African-American minority adolescents may observe that their ethnic group is worse off than the white majority in educational attainment, jobs, income, and housing. And discriminatory treatment by teachers and peers, often resulting from stereotypes that they are "not intelligent," triggers anger, anxiety, self-doubt, declines in achievement, association with peers who are not interested in school, and increases in problem behaviors (Wong, Eccles, & Sameroff, 2003).

Schools that build close networks of support between teachers and peers can prevent these negative outcomes. One high school with a largely low-income ethnic minority student body (65 percent African American) reorganized into "career academies"—learning communities within the school, each offering a different career-related curriculum (for example, one focusing on health, medicine, and life sciences, another on computer technology). The smaller-school climate and common theme helped create caring teacher–student relationships and a peer culture focused on valuing academic success (Conchas, 2006). High school graduation and college enrollment rates rose from a small minority to over 90 percent.

Finally, teenagers' use of text messaging and e-mail to remain continuously in touch with peers—even during class and while working on homework—is an aspect of contemporary peer-group life that poses risks to achievement. Turn to the Social Issues: Education box on page 312 to find out about the impact of "media multitasking" on attention and learning.

Classroom Learning Experiences. Adolescents need school environments that are responsive to their expanding powers of reasoning and their emotional and social needs. Without appropriate learning experiences, their cognitive potential is unlikely to be realized.

As noted earlier, in large, departmentalized secondary schools, many adolescents report that their classes lack warmth and supportiveness, which dampens their motivation. Of course,

Social Issues: Education

Media Multitasking Disrupts Attention and Learning

"Mom, I'm going to study for my biology test now," called 16-year-old Cassie while shutting her bedroom door. Sitting down at her desk, she accessed a popular social-networking website on her laptop, donned headphones and began listening to a favorite song on her MP3 player, and placed her cell phone next to her elbow so she could hear it chime if any text messages arrived. Only then did she open her textbook and begin to read.

In a survey of a nationally representative sample of U.S. 8- to 18-year-olds, more than two-thirds reported engaging in two or more media activities at once, some or most of the time (Rideout, Foehr, & Roberts, 2010). Their most frequent type of media multitasking is listening to music while doing homework, but many also report watching TV or using the Internet while studying (Jeong & Fishbein, 2007). The presence of a television or computer in the young person's bedroom is a strong predictor of this behavior (Foehr, 2006). And it extends into classrooms, where students can be seen text-messaging under their desks or surfing the Internet on cell phones.

Research confirms that media multitasking greatly reduces learning. In one experiment, participants were given two tasks: learning to predict the weather in two dif-

ferent cities using colored shapes as cues and keeping a mental tally of how many high-pitched beeps they heard through headphones. Half the sample performed the tasks simultaneously, the other half separately (Foerde, Knowlton, & Poldrack, 2006). Both groups learned to predict the weather in the two-city situation, but the multitaskers were unable to apply their learning to new weather problems.

fMRI evidence revealed that the participants working only on the weather task activated the hippocampus, which plays a vital role in *explicit memory*—conscious, strategic recall, which enables new information to be used flexibly and adaptively in contexts outside the original learning situation. In contrast, the multitaskers activated subcortical areas involved in *implicit memory*—a shallower, automatic form of learning that takes place unconsciously.

As early as 1980, studies linked heavy media use with executive-function difficulties (Nunez-Smith et al., 2008). Frequent media multitaskers, who are accustomed to con-

Media multitasking while doing homework fragments attention, yielding superficial learning. Frequent multitaskers are likely to have trouble filtering out irrelevant stimuli even when they are not multitasking.

tinuously shifting their attention between tasks, have a harder time filtering out irrelevant stimuli when they are not multitasking (Ophir, Nass, & Wagner, 2009).

Beyond superficial preparation for her biology test, Cassie is likely to have trouble concentrating and strategically processing new information after turning off her computer and MP3 player. Experienced teachers often complain that compared to students of a generation ago, today's teenagers are more easily distracted and learn less thoroughly. One teacher reflected, "It's the way they've grown up—working short times on many different things at one time" (Clay, 2009, p. 40).

---

an important benefit of separate classes in each subject is that adolescents can be taught by experts, who are more likely to encourage high-level thinking and emphasize content relevant to students' experiences—factors that contribute to interest, effort, and achievement (Eccles, 2004). But many classrooms do not consistently provide stimulating, challenging teaching.

Because of the uneven quality of instruction, many seniors graduate from high school deficient in basic academic skills. Although the achievement gap separating African-American, Hispanic, and Native-American students from white students has declined since the 1970s, mastery of reading, writing, mathematics, and science by low-SES ethnic minority students remains disappointing (U.S. Department of Education, 2007, 2009, 2010). Too often these young people attend underfunded schools with rundown buildings, outdated equipment, and textbook shortages. In some, crime and discipline problems receive more attention than teaching and learning.

By middle school, many low-SES minority students have been placed in low academic tracks, compounding their learning difficulties. Longitudinal research following thousands of U.S. students from eighth to twelfth grade reveals that assignment to a college preparatory track accelerates academic progress, whereas assignment to a vocational or general education track decelerates it (Hallinan & Kubitschek, 1999). Even in secondary schools with no formal tracking program, low-SES minority students tend to be assigned to lower course levels in most or all academic subjects, resulting in *de facto* (unofficial) *tracking* (Lucas & Behrends, 2002). Compared to students in higher tracks, those in low tracks exert substantially less effort—a difference due in part to less stimulating classroom experiences (Worthy, Hungerford-Kresser, & Hampton, 2009).

High school students are separated into academic and vocational tracks in virtually all industrialized nations. In China, Japan, and most Western European countries, students'

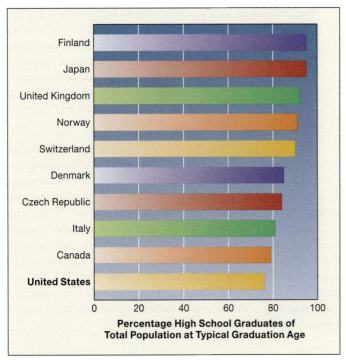

FIGURE 11.8 High school graduation rates in 10 industrialized nations. The United States ranks below many other developed countries. (From OECD, 2011a.)

placement in high school is determined by a national exam, which usually establishes the young person's future possibilities. In the United States, students who are not assigned to a college preparatory track or who do poorly in high school can still attend college. Ultimately, however, many young people do not benefit from the more open U.S. system. By adolescence, SES differences in quality of education and academic achievement are greater in the United States than in most other industrialized countries (Marks, Cresswell, & Ainley, 2006). And the United States has a higher percentage of young people who see themselves as educational failures and drop out of high school (see Figure 11.8).

Dropping Out

Across the aisle from Louis in math class sat Norman, who daydreamed, crumpled his notes into his pocket after class, and rarely did his homework. On test days, he twirled a rabbit's foot for good luck but left most questions blank. To Louis, who was quick at schoolwork, Norman seemed to live in another world. Once or twice a week, Norman cut class; one spring day, he stopped coming altogether.

Norman is one of about 8 percent of U.S. 16- to 24-year-olds who dropped out of high school and remain without a diploma or a GED (U.S. Department of Education, 2012f). The dropout rate is higher among boys than girls and is particularly high among low-SES ethnic minority youths, especially Native-American and Hispanic teenagers (15 and 18 percent, respectively). The decision to leave school has dire consequences.

Youths without upper secondary education have much lower literacy scores than high school graduates; they lack the skills employers value in today's knowledge-based economy. Consequently, dropouts have much lower employment rates than high school graduates. Even when employed, dropouts are far more likely to remain in menial, low-paying jobs.

Factors Related to Dropping Out. Although many dropouts achieve poorly and show high rates of norm-violating acts, a substantial number, like Norman, have few behavior problems, experience academic difficulties, and quietly disengage from school (Janosz et al., 2000; Newcomb et al., 2002). The pathway to dropping out starts early. Risk factors in first grade predict dropout nearly as well as risk factors in secondary school (Entwisle, Alexander, & Olson, 2005).

Norman had a long history of marginal-to-failing school grades and low academic self-esteem. Faced with a challenging task, he gave up, relying on luck—his rabbit's foot—to get by. As Norman got older, he attended class less regularly, paid little attention when he was there, and rarely did his homework. He didn't join school clubs or participate in sports. As a result, few teachers or students knew him well. By the day he left, Norman felt alienated from all aspects of school life.

As with other dropouts, Norman's family background contributed to his problems. Compared with other students, even those with the same grade profile, dropouts are more likely to have parents who are uninvolved in their teenager's education and engage in little monitoring of their youngster's daily activities (Englund, Egeland, & Collins, 2008; Pagani et al., 2008). Many are single parents, never finished high school themselves, and are unemployed.

Students who drop out often have school experiences that undermine their chances for success: grade retention, which marks them as academic failures; large, impersonal secondary schools; and classes with unsupportive teachers and few opportunities for active participation (Brown & Rodriguez, 2009). Students in general education and vocational tracks are three times as likely to drop out as those in a college preparatory track (U.S. Department of Education, 2012b).

Prevention Strategies. Among the diverse strategies available for helping teenagers at risk of dropping out, several common themes are related to success:

- *Remedial instruction and counseling that offer personalized attention.* Most potential dropouts need academic assistance combined with social support (Christenson & Thurlow, 2004). In one successful approach, at-risk students are matched with retired adults, who serve as tutors, mentors, and role models in addressing academic and vocational needs (Prevatt, 2003).

- *High-quality vocational training.* For many marginal students, the real-life nature of vocational education is more comfortable and effective than purely academic work (Harvey, 2001). To work well, vocational education must

St. Paul, Minnesota, police chief Thomas Smith warmly greets one of his student mentees following a high school fundraising event for a charitable organization. Support from a caring adult and extracurricular involvement are effective ways to prevent school dropout.

carefully integrate academic and job-related instruction so students see the relevance of classroom experiences to their future goals.

- *Efforts to address the many factors in students' lives related to leaving school early.* Programs that strengthen parent involvement, offer flexible work–study arrangements, and provide on-site child care for teenage parents can make staying in school easier for at-risk adolescents.

- *Participation in extracurricular activities.* Another way of helping marginal students is to draw them into the community life of the school. In small high schools (500 to 700 students or fewer), at-risk youths are more likely to be

needed to help staff activities and to feel attached to their school (Feldman & Matjasko, 2007). Creation of smaller "schools within schools" has the same effect. Participation in arts, community service, or vocational development activities promotes improved academic performance, reduced antisocial behavior, more favorable self-esteem and initiative, and increased peer acceptance (Fredricks, 2012; Fredricks & Eccles, 2006).

As we conclude our discussion of academic achievement, let's place the school dropout problem in historical perspective. Over the second half of the twentieth century, the percentage of U.S. young people completing high school by age 24 increased steadily, from less than 50 percent to just over 90 percent. Although many dropouts get caught in a vicious cycle in which their lack of self-confidence and skills prevents them from seeking further education and training, about one-third return to finish their secondary education within a few years (U.S. Department of Education, 2012b). And some extend their schooling further as they come to realize how essential education is for a rewarding job and a satisfying adult life.

ASK YOURSELF

REVIEW List ways that parents can promote their adolescent's academic achievement. Explain why each is effective.

APPLY Tanisha is finishing sixth grade. She can either continue in her current school through eighth grade or switch to a much larger seventh- to ninth-grade middle school. Which choice would you suggest, and why?

REFLECT Describe your own experiences in making the transition to middle or junior high school and then to high school. What did you find stressful? What helped you adjust?

SUMMARY

PHYSICAL DEVELOPMENT

Conceptions of Adolescence
(p. 287)

How have conceptions of adolescence changed over the past century?

- **Adolescence** is the transition between childhood and adulthood. Early theorists viewed adolescence as either a biologically determined period of storm and stress or entirely influenced by the social environment. Contemporary researchers view adolescence as a joint product of biological, psychological, and social forces.

Puberty: The Physical Transition to Adulthood
(p. 288)

Describe body growth, motor performance, and sexual maturation during puberty.

- Hormonal changes under way in middle childhood initiate **puberty**, on average, two years earlier for girls than for boys. The first outward sign is the **growth spurt**. As the body enlarges, girls' hips and boys' shoulders broaden. Girls add more fat, boys more muscle.

- Puberty brings slow, gradual improvements in gross-motor performance for girls, dramatic gains for boys. Nevertheless, participation in regular physical activity declines sharply with age.

- At puberty, changes in **primary** and **secondary sexual characteristics** accompany rapid body growth. **Menarche** occurs late in the girl's sequence of pubertal events, after the growth spurt peaks. In boys, the peak in growth occurs later, preceded by enlargement of the sex organs and **spermarche**.

What factors influence the timing of puberty?

● Heredity, nutrition, exercise, and overall physical health influence the timing of puberty. The emotional quality of family experiences may play a role.

● A **secular trend** toward earlier puberty has occurred in industrialized nations as physical well-being increased. In some countries, rising obesity rates have extended this trend.

What changes in the brain take place during adolescence?

● Pruning of unused synapses in the cerebral cortex continues, and linkages between areas of the brain expand and myelinate. As the prefrontal cortex becomes a more effective "executive," adolescents gradually gain in processing speed and executive function.

● During puberty, neurons become more responsive to excitatory neurotransmitters, heightening emotional reactivity and reward-seeking. Changes in the brain's emotional/social network outpace development of the cognitive-control network, resulting in self-regulation difficulties.

● Revisions also occur in brain regulation of sleep timing, leading to a sleep "phase delay." Sleep deprivation contributes to poorer achievement, depressed mood, and high-risk behaviors.

The Psychological Impact of Pubertal Events (p. 292)

Explain adolescents' reactions to the physical changes of puberty.

● Girls typically react to menarche with mixed emotions, although those who receive advance information and support from family members respond more positively. Boys, who receive little social support for pubertal changes, react to spermarche with mixed feelings.

● Besides higher hormone levels, negative life events and adult-structured situations are associated with adolescents' negative moods. Psychological distancing between parent and child at puberty may be a modern substitute for physical departure from the family.

Describe the impact of pubertal timing on adolescent adjustment, noting sex differences.

● Early-maturing boys and late-maturing girls have a more positive **body image** and usually adjust well. In contrast, early-maturing girls and late-maturing boys tend to experience emotional and social difficulties, which—for girls—persist into early adulthood.

Health Issues (p. 295)

Describe nutritional needs during adolescence, and cite factors related to eating disorders.

● Nutritional requirements increase with rapid body growth, and vitamin and mineral deficiencies may result from poor eating habits. Frequency of family meals is associated with healthy eating.

● Early puberty, certain personality traits, maladaptive family interactions, and societal emphasis on thinness heighten risk of eating disorders such as **anorexia nervosa** and **bulimia nervosa**. Heredity also plays a role.

Discuss social and cultural influences on adolescent sexual attitudes and behavior.

● North American attitudes toward adolescent sex remain relatively restrictive, and parents and the mass media deliver contradictory messages.

● Early, frequent sexual activity is linked to factors associated with economic disadvantage. Adolescent cognitive processes and weak social supports for responsible sexual behavior underlie the failure of many sexually active teenagers to practice contraception consistently.

Cite factors involved in the development of homosexuality.

● Biological factors, including heredity and prenatal hormone levels, play an important role in homosexuality. Lesbian, gay, and bisexual teenagers face special challenges in establishing a positive sexual identity.

Discuss factors related to sexually transmitted disease and teenage pregnancy and parenthood, noting prevention and intervention strategies.

● Early sexual activity, combined with inconsistent contraceptive use, results in high rates of sexually transmitted diseases (STDs) among U.S. adolescents.

● Life conditions linked to poverty and personal attributes jointly contribute to adolescent childbearing. Teenage parenthood is associated with school dropout, reduced chances of marriage, greater likelihood of divorce, and long-term economic disadvantage.

● Effective sex education, access to contraceptives, and programs that build academic and social competence help prevent early pregnancy. Adolescent mothers need school programs that provide job training, instruction in life-management skills, and child care. When teenage fathers stay involved, children develop more favorably.

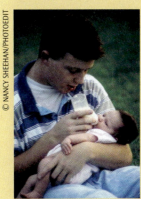

What personal and social factors are related to adolescent substance use and abuse?

● Drug taking reflects adolescent sensation seeking and drug-dependent cultural contexts. The minority who move to substance abuse tend to start using drugs early and have serious personal, family, school, and peer problems. Effective prevention programs work with parents early to reduce family adversity, strengthen parenting skills, and build teenagers' competence.

COGNITIVE DEVELOPMENT

Piaget's Theory: The Formal Operational Stage (p. 304)

What are the major characteristics of formal operational thought?

● In Piaget's **formal operational stage**, adolescents become capable of **hypothetico-deductive reasoning**. To solve problems, they start with a hypothesis; deduce logical, testable inferences; and systematically isolate and combine variables to see which inferences are confirmed.

● Adolescents also develop **propositional thought**—the ability to evaluate the logic of verbal statements without referring to real-world circumstances.

Discuss follow-up research on formal operational thought and its implications for the accuracy of Piaget's formal operational stage.

- Adolescents, like adults, are most likely to think abstractly and systematically in situations in which they have had extensive guidance and practice in using such reasoning. Individuals in tribal and village societies rarely do well on tasks typically used to assess formal operational reasoning. Learning activities in school provide adolescents with rich opportunities to acquire formal operations.

An Information-Processing View of Adolescent Cognitive Development (p. 306)

How do information-processing researchers account for cognitive changes in adolescence?

- Information-processing researchers believe that a variety of specific mechanisms underlie cognitive gains in adolescence: improved attention, inhibition, strategies, knowledge, metacognition, cognitive self-regulation, speed of thinking, and processing capacity.

- The ability to coordinate theory with evidence improves as adolescents solve increasingly complex problems and acquire more sophisticated metacognitive understanding.

Consequences of Adolescent Cognitive Changes (p. 307)

Describe typical reactions of adolescents that result from their advancing cognition.

- As adolescents reflect on their own thoughts, two distorted images of the relation between self and other appear—the **imaginary audience** and the **personal fable**. Both result from heightened social sensitivity and gains in perspective taking.

ANTONIO MO/PHOTODISC/GETTY IMAGES

- Teenagers' capacity to think about possibilities prompts idealistic visions at odds with reality, and they often become fault-finding critics.

- Adolescents are less effective than adults at decision making. They take greater risks in emotionally charged situations, less often weigh alternatives, and more often fall back on intuitive judgments.

Learning in School (p. 309)

Discuss the impact of school transitions on adolescent adjustment.

- School transitions bring larger, more impersonal school environments, in which grades and feelings of competence decline. Teenagers coping with added stressors are at greatest risk for self-esteem and academic problems.

Discuss family, peer, and school influences on academic achievement during adolescence.

- Authoritative parenting and parents' school involvement promote high achievement. Teenagers whose parents value achievement generally choose friends who share those values. Schools can help by promoting a peer culture that values academic success.

- Warm, supportive classroom environments that encourage student interaction and high-level thinking enable adolescents to reach their academic potential.

- By high school, separate educational tracks that dovetail with students' future plans are necessary. However, U.S. high school tracking usually extends the educational inequalities of earlier years.

What factors increase the risk of high school dropout?

- Factors contributing to the high U.S. dropout rate include lack of parental support for achievement, a history of poor school performance, large impersonal secondary schools, and unsupportive teachers.

Important Terms and Concepts

adolescence (p. 287)
anorexia nervosa (p. 296)
body image (p. 294)
bulimia nervosa (p. 296)
formal operational stage (p. 304)
growth spurt (p. 288)

hypothetico-deductive reasoning (p. 304)
imaginary audience (p. 308)
menarche (p. 290)
personal fable (p. 308)
primary sexual characteristics (p. 290)
propositional thought (p. 305)

puberty (p. 287)
secondary sexual characteristics (p. 290)
secular trend (p. 291)
spermarche (p. 290)

chapter 12

Emotional and Social Development in Adolescence

JOHN GIUSTINA/ICONICA/GETTY IMAGES

As adolescents spend less time with family members, peer groups become more tightly knit into cliques. Mixed-sex cliques prepare teenagers for dating by providing models of how to interact and opportunities to do so without having to be intimate.

chapter outline

Louis sat on the grassy hillside overlooking the high school, waiting for his best friend, Darryl, to arrive from his fourth-period class. Watching as hundreds of students poured onto the school grounds, Louis reflected on what he had learned in government class that day. "Suppose I *had* been born in the People's Republic of China. I'd be sitting here, speaking a different language, being called by a different name, and thinking about the world in different ways. Wow," Louis pondered. "I am who I am through some quirk of fate."

Louis awoke from his thoughts with a start to see Darryl standing in front of him. "Hey, dreamer! I've been shouting and waving from the bottom of the hill for five minutes. How come you're so spaced out lately, Louis?"

"Oh, just wondering about stuff—what I want, what I believe in. You ever feel that way?"

"Yeah, a lot," Darryl admitted, looking at Louis seriously. "I wonder, what am I really like? Who will I become?"

Louis and Darryl's introspective remarks are signs of a major reorganization of the self at adolescence: the development of identity. Both young people are attempting to formulate who

they are—their personal values and the directions they will pursue in life.

We begin this chapter with Erikson's account of identity development and the research it has stimulated on teenagers' thoughts and feelings about themselves. The quest for identity extends to many aspects of development. We will see how a sense of cultural belonging, moral understanding, and masculine and feminine self-images are refined during adolescence. And as parent–child relationships are revised and young people become increasingly independent of the family, friendships and peer networks become crucial contexts for bridging the gap between childhood and adulthood. Our chapter concludes with a discussion of several serious adjustment problems of adolescence: depression, suicide, and delinquency. ●

© MARY KATE DENNY/ALAMY

Erikson's Theory: Identity versus Role Confusion

Erikson (1950, 1968) was the first to recognize **identity** as the major personality achievement of adolescence and as a crucial step toward becoming a productive, content adult. Constructing an identity involves defining who you are, what you value, and the directions you choose to pursue in life. One expert described it as an explicit theory of oneself as a rational agent—one who acts on the basis of reason, takes responsibility for those actions, and can explain them (Moshman, 2005). This search for what is true and real about the self drives many choices—vocation, interpersonal relationships, community involvement, ethnic-group membership, and expression of one's sexual orientation, as well as moral, political, and religious ideals.

Although the seeds of identity formation are planted early, not until late adolescence and early adulthood do young people become absorbed in this task. According to Erikson, in complex societies, teenagers experience an *identity crisis*—a temporary period of distress as they experiment with alternatives before settling on values and goals. They go through a process of inner soul-searching, sifting through characteristics that defined the self in childhood and combining them with emerging traits, capacities, and commitments. Then they mold these into a solid inner core that provides a mature identity—a sense of self-continuity as they move through various roles in daily life. Once formed, identity continues to be refined in adulthood as people reevaluate earlier commitments and choices.

Erikson called the psychological conflict of adolescence **identity versus role confusion.** If young people's earlier conflicts were resolved negatively or if society limits their choices

to ones that do not match their abilities and desires, they may appear shallow, directionless, and unprepared for the challenges of adulthood.

Current theorists agree with Erikson that questioning of values, plans, and priorities is necessary for a mature identity, but they no longer describe this process as a "crisis" (Côté, 2009; Kroger, 2007). For most young people, identity development is not traumatic and disturbing but, rather, a process of *exploration* followed by *commitment*. As young people try out life possibilities, they gather important information about themselves and their environment and move toward making enduring decisions. In doing so, they forge an organized self-structure (Arnett, 2000, 2006; Moshman, 2005). In the following sections, we will see that adolescents go about the task of defining the self in ways that closely match Erikson's description.

Self-Understanding

During adolescence, the young person's vision of the self becomes more complex, well-organized, and consistent. Compared with younger children, adolescents evaluate an increasing variety of aspects of the self. Over time, they construct a balanced, integrated representation of their strengths and limitations.

Changes in Self-Concept

In describing themselves, adolescents unify separate traits ("smart" and "curious") into more abstract descriptors ("intelligent"). But at first, their generalizations are not interconnected and are often contradictory. For example, 12- to 14-year-olds might mention opposing traits—"intelligent" and "dork," "extrovert" and "introvert." These disparities result from the expansion of adolescents' social world, which creates pressure to display different selves in different relationships. As adolescents' awareness of these inconsistencies grows, they frequently agonize over "which is the real me" (Harter, 2003, 2006).

Gradually, cognitive changes enable teenagers to combine their traits into an organized system. Their use of qualifiers ("I have a *fairly* quick temper," "I'm not *thoroughly* honest") reveals an increasing awareness that psychological qualities can vary from one situation to the next. Older adolescents also add integrating principles that make sense of formerly troublesome contradictions. "I'm very adaptable," said one young person. "When I'm around my friends, who think what I say is important, I'm talkative; but around my family I'm quiet because they're never interested enough to really listen to me" (Damon, 1990, p. 88).

Compared with school-age children, teenagers place more emphasis on social virtues, such as being friendly, considerate, kind, and cooperative. Among older adolescents, personal and moral values also appear as key themes as young people revise their views of themselves to include enduring beliefs and plans.

Changes in Self-Esteem

Self-esteem, the evaluative side of self-concept, continues to differentiate in adolescence. Teenagers add several new dimensions of self-evaluation—close friendship, romantic appeal, and job competence—to those of middle childhood (see Chapter 10, pages 261–262) (Harter, 2003, 2006).

Level of self-esteem also changes. Though some adolescents experience temporary or persisting declines after school transitions (see Chapter 11, pages 309–310), self-esteem rises for most young people (Impett et al., 2008; Twenge & Campbell, 2001). Teenagers often assert that they have become more mature, capable, personable, and attractive. In longitudinal research on a nationally representative sample of U.S. youths, an increasing sense of mastery—feeling competent and in control of one's life—strongly predicted this age-related rise in self-esteem (Erol & Orth, 2011).

In adolescence, authoritative parenting continues to predict high self-esteem, as does encouragement from teachers (Lindsey et al., 2008; McKinney, Donnelly, & Renk, 2008; Wilkinson, 2004). In contrast, feedback that is negative, inconsistent, or not contingent on performance triggers, at best, uncertainty about the self's capacities and, at worst, a sense of being incompetent and unloved. Teenagers who experience such parenting tend to rely only on peers, not on adults, to affirm their self-esteem—a risk factor for adjustment difficulties (DuBois et al., 1999, 2002).

Paths to Identity

Adolescents' well-organized self-descriptions and differentiated sense of self-esteem provide the cognitive foundation for forming an identity. Through interviews or questionnaires,

DON TREMAIN/PHOTODISC/GETTY IMAGES

During adolescence, self-esteem rises for most young people, who feel especially good about their peer relationships and athletic capabilities.

researchers commonly evaluate progress in identity development on two key criteria derived from Erikson's theory: *exploration* and *commitment*. Their various combinations yield four *identity statuses,* summarized in Table 12.1 on page 320: **identity achievement,** commitment to values, beliefs, and goals following a period of exploration; **identity moratorium,** exploration without having reached commitment; **identity foreclosure,** commitment in the absence of exploration; and **identity diffusion,** an apathetic state characterized by lack of both exploration and commitment.

Identity development follows many paths. Some young people remain in one status, whereas others experience many status transitions. And the pattern often varies across *identity domains,* such as sexual orientation, vocation, and religious and political values. Most young people change from "lower" statuses (foreclosure or diffusion) to higher ones (moratorium or achievement) between their mid-teens and mid-twenties, but as many remain stable, and some move in the reverse direction (Kroger, 2007; Kroger, Martinussen, & Marcia, 2010; Meeus et al., 2012).

Because attending college provides opportunities to explore values, career options, and lifestyles, college students make more identity progress than they did in high school (Klimstra et al., 2010; Montgomery & Côté, 2003). After college, they often sample a broad range of life experiences before choosing a life course. Those who go to work immediately after high school graduation often settle on a self-definition earlier. But if they encounter obstacles to realizing their occupational goals because of lack of training or vocational choices, they are at risk for identity foreclosure or diffusion (Cohen et al., 2003; Eccles et al., 2003).

TABLE 12.1   **The Four Identity Statuses**

IDENTITY STATUS	DESCRIPTION	EXAMPLE
Identity achievement	Having already explored alternatives, identity-achieved individuals are committed to a clearly formulated set of self-chosen values and goals. They feel a sense of psychological well-being, of sameness through time, and of knowing where they are going.	When asked how willing she would be to give up going into her chosen occupation if something better came along, Lauren responded, "Well, I might, but I doubt it. I've thought long and hard about law as a career. I'm pretty certain it's for me."
Identity moratorium	*Moratorium* means "delay or holding pattern." These individuals have not yet made definite commitments. They are in the process of exploring—gathering information and trying out activities, with the desire to find values and goals to guide their lives.	When asked whether he had ever had doubts about his religious beliefs, Ramón said, "Yes, I guess I'm going through that right now. I just don't see how there can be a God and yet so much evil in the world."
Identity foreclosure	Identity-foreclosed individuals have committed themselves to values and goals without exploring alternatives. They accept a ready-made identity chosen for them by authority figures—usually parents but sometimes teachers, religious leaders, or romantic partners.	When asked if she had ever reconsidered her political beliefs, Emily answered, "No, not really, our family is pretty much in agreement on these things."
Identity diffusion	Identity-diffused individuals lack clear direction. They are not committed to values and goals, nor are they actively trying to reach them. They may never have explored alternatives or may have found the task too threatening and overwhelming.	When asked about his attitude toward nontraditional gender roles, Justin responded, "Oh, I don't know. It doesn't make much difference to me. I can take it or leave it."

Identity Status and Psychological Well-Being

A wealth of research verifies that both identity achievement and moratorium are psychologically healthy routes to a mature self-definition. Long-term foreclosure and diffusion, in contrast, are maladaptive.

Adolescents in moratorium resemble identity-achieved individuals in using an active, *information-gathering cognitive style* to make personal decisions and solve problems: They seek out relevant information, evaluate it carefully, and critically reflect on and revise their views (Berzonsky, 2003, 2011). Young people who are identity-achieved or exploring have higher self-esteem, feel more in control of their lives, are more likely to view school and work as feasible avenues for realizing their aspirations, and are more advanced in moral reasoning (Berzonsky et al., 2011; Kroger, 2007; Serafini & Adams, 2002).

Adolescents stuck in either foreclosure or diffusion are passive in the face of identity concerns and have adjustment difficulties. Foreclosed individuals display a *dogmatic, inflexible cognitive style,* internalizing the values and beliefs of parents and others without deliberate evaluation and resisting information that threatens their position (Berzonsky & Kuk, 2000; Berzonsky et al., 2011). Most fear rejection by people on whom they depend for affection and self-esteem.

Long-term diffused individuals are the least mature in identity development. They typically use a *diffuse-avoidant cognitive style* in which they avoid dealing with personal decisions and problems and, instead, allow current situational pressures to dictate their reactions (Berzonsky & Kuk, 2000; Krettenauer, 2005). Taking an "I don't care" attitude, they entrust themselves to luck or fate, tend to go along with the crowd, and are focused on short-term personal pleasures. As a result, they

experience time management and academic difficulties and, of all young people, are most likely to commit antisocial acts and to use and abuse drugs (Berzonsky et al., 2011; Schwartz et al., 2005). Often at the heart of their apathy is a sense of hopelessness about the future.

Factors Affecting Identity Development

Adolescent identity formation begins a lifelong, dynamic process in which a change in either the individual or the context opens up the possibility of reformulating identity (Kunnen & Bosma, 2003). A wide variety of factors influence identity development.

© KATHY MCLAUGHLIN/THE IMAGE WORKS

An internship in a veterinary office enables this teenager to explore a real-world career related to her love of animals, thereby fostering identity development.

Applying **What We Know**

Supporting Healthy Identity Development

Strategy	Explanation
Engage in warm, open communication.	Provides both emotional support and freedom to explore values and goals.
Initiate discussions that promote high-level thinking at home and at school.	Encourages rational and deliberate selection among beliefs and values.
Provide opportunities to participate in extracurricular activities and vocational training programs.	Permits young people to explore the real world of adult work.
Provide opportunities to talk with adults and peers who have worked through identity questions.	Offers models of identity achievement and advice on how to resolve identity concerns.
Provide opportunities to explore ethnic heritage and learn about other cultures in an atmosphere of respect.	Fosters identity achievement in all areas and ethnic tolerance, which supports the identity explorations of others.

Identity status, as we have just seen, is both cause and consequence of personality characteristics. Adolescents who assume that absolute truth is always attainable tend to be foreclosed, while those who doubt that they will ever feel certain about anything are more often identity-diffused. Young people who appreciate that they can use rational criteria to choose among alternatives are likely to be exploring or identity achieved (Berzonsky & Kuk, 2000; Berzonsky et al., 2011).

Parenting practices are associated with identity statuses. Adolescents who feel attached to their parents but also free to voice their own opinions tend to be in a state of moratorium or identity achievement (Berzonsky, 2004; Luyckx, Goossens, & Soenens, 2006; Schwartz et al., 2005). Foreclosed teenagers usually have close bonds with parents but lack opportunities for healthy separation. And diffused young people report the lowest levels of parental support and of warm, open communication (Reis & Youniss, 2004; Zimmerman & Becker-Stoll, 2002).

Interaction with diverse peers through school and community activities encourages adolescents to explore values and role possibilities (Barber et al., 2005). In one study, 15-year-olds with warm, trusting peer ties were more involved in exploring relationship issues—for example, thinking about what they valued in close friends and in a life partner (Meeus, Oosterwegel, & Vollebergh, 2002). In another study, young people's attachment to friends predicted progress in choosing a career (Felsman & Blustein, 1999).

Schools and communities can help by offering rich and varied opportunities for exploration. Supportive experiences include classrooms that promote high-level thinking, teachers and counselors who encourage low-SES students to go to college, extracurricular activities that offer teenagers responsible roles consistent with their interests and talents, and vocational training that immerses adolescents in the real world of adult work (Coatsworth et al., 2005; Hardy et al., 2011; McIntosh, Metz, & Youniss, 2005).

Finally, societal forces also are responsible for the special challenges faced by gay, lesbian, and bisexual youths (see Chapter 11) and by ethnic minority adolescents in forming a secure identity (see the Cultural Influences box on page 322). Applying What We Know above summarizes ways that adults can support adolescents in their quest for identity.

ASK YOURSELF

REVIEW List personal and contextual factors that promote identity development.

APPLY Return to the conversation between Louis and Darryl in the opening of this chapter. Which identity status best characterizes each of the two boys, and why?

REFLECT Does your identity status vary across the domains of sexuality, close relationships, vocation, religious beliefs, and political values? Describe factors that may have influenced your identity development in an important domain.

Moral Development

Eleven-year-old Sabrina sat at the kitchen table reading the Sunday newspaper, her eyes wide with interest. "Look at this!" she said to 16-year-old Louis, who was munching cereal. Sabrina held up a page of large photos showing a 70-year-old woman standing in her home. The floor and furniture were piled with stacks of newspapers, cardboard boxes, tin cans, glass containers, food, and clothing. The accompanying article described crumbling plaster on the walls, frozen pipes, and nonfunctioning sinks, toilet, and furnace. The headline read: "Loretta Perry: My Life Is None of Their Business."

"Look what they're trying to do to this poor lady," exclaimed Sabrina. "They wanna throw her out of her house and tear it down! Those city inspectors must not care about anyone. Here it says, 'Mrs. Perry has devoted much of her life to doing favors for people.' Why doesn't someone help *her*?"

Cultural Influences

Identity Development Among Ethnic Minority Adolescents

Most adolescents are aware of their cultural ancestry but relatively unconcerned about it. However, for teenagers who are members of minority groups, **ethnic identity**—a sense of ethnic group membership and attitudes and feelings associated with that membership—is central to the quest for identity. As they develop cognitively and become more sensitive to feedback from the social environment, minority youths become painfully aware that they are targets of prejudice and discrimination. This discovery complicates their efforts to develop a sense of cultural belonging and a set of personally meaningful goals.

In many immigrant families from collectivist cultures, adolescents' commitment to obeying their parents and fulfilling family obligations lessens the longer the family has been in the immigrant-receiving country—a circumstance that induces **acculturative stress,** psychological distress resulting from conflict between the minority and the host culture (Phinney, Ong, & Madden, 2000). When immigrant parents tightly restrict their teenagers through fear that assimilation into the larger society will undermine their cultural traditions, their youngsters often rebel, rejecting aspects of their ethnic background.

At the same time, discrimination can interfere with the formation of a positive ethnic identity. In one study, Mexican-American youths who had experienced more discrimination were less likely to explore their ethnicity and to report feeling good about it (Romero & Roberts, 2003). Those with low ethnic pride showed a sharp drop in self-esteem in the face of discrimination.

With age, many minority young people strengthen their ethnic identity. But because the process of forging an ethnic identity can be painful and confusing, others show no change, and still others regress (Huang & Stormshak, 2011). Young people with parents of different ethnicities face extra challenges. In a large survey of high school students, part-black biracial teenagers reported as much discrimination as their monoracial black counterparts, yet they felt less positively about their ethnicity. And compared with monoracial minorities, many biracial young people—including black–white, black–Asian, white–Asian, black–Hispanic, and white–Hispanic—regarded ethnicity as less central to their identities (Herman, 2004). Perhaps these adolescents encountered fewer opportunities in their homes and communities to forge a strong sense of belonging to either culture.

Adolescents whose family members encourage them to disprove ethnic stereotypes of low achievement or antisocial behavior typically surmount the threat that discrimination poses to a favorable ethnic identity. These young people manage experiences of unfair treatment effectively, by seeking social support and engaging in direct problem solving (Phinney & Chavira, 1995; Scott, 2003). Also, adolescents whose families taught them the history, traditions, values, and language of their ethnic group and who frequently interact with same-ethnicity peers are more likely to forge a favorable ethnic identity (Hughes et al., 2006; McHale et al., 2006).

How can society help minority adolescents resolve identity conflicts constructively? Here are some relevant approaches:

- Promote effective parenting, in which children and adolescents benefit from family ethnic pride yet are encouraged to explore the meaning of ethnicity in their own lives.

- Ensure that schools respect minority youths' native languages, unique learning styles, and right to high-quality education.

- Foster contact with peers of the same ethnicity, along with respect between ethnic groups (García Coll & Magnuson, 1997).

Stilt walkers celebrate their heritage at a Caribbean youth festival. Minority youths whose culture is respected in their community are more likely to incorporate ethnic values and customs into their identity.

A strong, secure ethnic identity is associated with higher self-esteem, optimism, and sense of mastery over the environment (St. Louis & Liem, 2005; Umana-Taylor & Updegraff, 2007; Worrell & Gardner-Kitt, 2006). For these reasons, adolescents with a positive connection to their ethnic group cope more effectively with stress, show higher achievement in school, and have fewer emotional and behavior problems than agemates who identify only weakly with their ethnicity (Ghavami et al., 2011; Greene, Way, & Pahl, 2006; Seaton, Scottham, & Sellers, 2006; Umana-Taylor & Alfaro, 2006).

Forming a **bicultural identity**—by exploring and adopting values from both the adolescent's subculture and the dominant culture—offers added benefits. Biculturally identified adolescents tend to be achieved in other areas of identity as well and to have especially favorable relations with members of other ethnic groups (Phinney, 2007; Phinney et al., 2001). In sum, achievement of ethnic identity enhances many aspects of emotional and social development.

"Sabrina, you're missing the point," Louis responded. "Mrs. Perry is violating the law—30 building code standards! And she's not just a threat to herself—she's a danger to her neighbors, too. Suppose her house caught on fire. You can't live around other people and say your life is nobody's business."

"You don't just knock someone's home down," Sabrina replied angrily. "Why aren't her friends and neighbors over there fixing up that house? You're just like those building inspectors, Louis. You've got no feelings!"

As Louis and Sabrina's disagreement over Loretta Perry's plight illustrates, cognitive development and expanding social experiences permit adolescents to better understand larger social structures—societal institutions and law-making systems—that govern moral responsibilities. As their grasp of social arrangements expands, adolescents construct new ideas about what should be done when the needs and desires of people conflict. As a result, they move toward increasingly just, fair, and balanced solutions to moral problems.

Kohlberg's Theory of Moral Development

Early work by Piaget on the moral judgment of the child inspired Lawrence Kohlberg's more comprehensive cognitive-developmental theory of moral understanding. Kohlberg used a clinical interviewing procedure in which he presented a sample of 10- to 16-year-old boys with hypothetical *moral dilemmas*—stories involving a conflict between two moral values—and asked them what the main actor should do and why. Then he followed the participants longitudinally, reinterviewing them at 3- to 4-year intervals over the next 20 years. The best known of Kohlberg's dilemmas, the "Heinz dilemma," pits the value of obeying the law (not stealing) against the value of human life (saving a dying person):

> In Europe a woman was near death from cancer. There was one drug the doctors thought might save her. A druggist in the same town had discovered it, but he was charging ten times what the drug cost him to make. The sick woman's husband, Heinz, went to everyone he knew to borrow the money, but he could only get together half of what it cost. The druggist refused to sell the drug for less or let Heinz pay later. So Heinz became desperate and broke into the man's store to steal the drug for his wife. Should Heinz have done that? Why or why not? (paraphrased from Colby et al., 1983, p. 77)

Kohlberg emphasized that it is *the way an individual reasons about the dilemma,* not *the content of the response* (whether or not to steal), that determines moral maturity. Individuals who believe Heinz should take the drug and those who think he should not can be found at each of Kohlberg's first four stages. Only at the two highest stages do moral reasoning and content come together in a coherent ethical system (Kohlberg, Levine, & Hewer, 1983). Given a choice between obeying the law and preserving individual rights, the most advanced moral thinkers support individual rights (in the Heinz dilemma, stealing the drug to save a life).

Kohlberg's Stages. Kohlberg organized moral development into three levels, each with two stages, yielding six stages in all. He believed that moral understanding is promoted by the same factors Piaget thought were important for cognitive development: (1) actively grappling with moral issues and noticing weaknesses in one's current reasoning and (2) gains in perspective taking, which permit individuals to resolve moral conflicts in more effective ways. *TAKE A MOMENT...* As we examine Kohlberg's developmental sequence and illustrate it with responses to the Heinz dilemma, look for changes in perspective taking that each stage assumes.

The Preconventional Level. At the **preconventional level,** morality is externally controlled. Children accept the rules of authority figures and judge actions by their consequences. Behaviors that result in punishment are viewed as bad, those that lead to rewards as good.

- *Stage 1: The punishment and obedience orientation.* Children at this stage find it difficult to consider two points of view in a moral dilemma. As a result, they overlook people's intentions. Instead, they focus on fear of authority and avoidance of punishment as reasons for behaving morally.

    Prostealing: "If you let your wife die, you will . . . be blamed for not spending the money to help her and there'll be an investigation of you and the druggist for your wife's death." (Kohlberg, 1969, p. 381)

    Antistealing: "You shouldn't steal the drug because you'll be caught and sent to jail if you do. If you do get away, [you'd be scared that] the police would catch up with you any minute." (Kohlberg, 1969, p. 381)

- *Stage 2: The instrumental purpose orientation.* Children become aware that people can have different perspectives in a moral dilemma, but at first this understanding is

If the child on the right expects a favor in return for helping her friend, she is at Kohlberg's preconventional level. If she is motivated by ideal reciprocity, as in the Golden Rule, she has advanced to the conventional level.

concrete. They view right action as flowing from self-interest and understand reciprocity as equal exchange of favors: "You do this for me and I'll do that for you."

> *Prostealing*: "[I]f Heinz decides to risk jail to save his wife, it's his life he's risking; he can do what he wants with it. And the same goes for the druggist; it's up to him to decide what he wants to do." (Rest, 1979, p. 26)
>
> *Antistealing*: "[Heinz] is running more risk than it's worth [to save a wife who is near death]." (Rest, 1979, p. 27)

The Conventional Level. At the **conventional level,** individuals continue to regard conformity to social rules as important, but not for reasons of self-interest. Rather, they believe that actively maintaining the current social system ensures positive relationships and societal order.

- **Stage 3: The "good boy–good girl" orientation, or the morality of interpersonal cooperation.** The desire to obey rules because they promote social harmony first appears in the context of close personal ties. Stage 3 individuals want to maintain the affection and approval of friends and relatives by being a "good person"—trustworthy, loyal, respectful, helpful, and nice. The capacity to view a two-person relationship from the vantage point of an impartial, outside observer supports this new approach to morality. At this stage, individuals understand *ideal reciprocity*: They express the same concern for the welfare of another as they do for themselves—a standard of fairness summed up by the Golden Rule: "Do unto others as you would have them do unto you."

  > *Prostealing*: "No one will think you're bad if you steal the drug, but your family will think you're an inhuman husband if you don't. If you let your wife die, you'll never be able to look anyone in the face again." (Kohlberg, 1969, p. 381)
  >
  > *Antistealing*: "It isn't just the druggist who will think you're a criminal, everyone else will too. . . . [Y]ou'll feel bad thinking how you've brought dishonor on your family and yourself." (Kohlberg, 1969, p. 381)

- **Stage 4: The social-order-maintaining orientation.** At this stage, the individual takes into account a larger perspective—that of societal laws. Moral choices no longer depend on close ties to others. Instead, rules must be enforced in the same evenhanded fashion for everyone, and each member of society has a personal duty to uphold them. The Stage 4 individual believes that laws should never be disobeyed because they are vital for ensuring societal order and cooperation between people.

  > *Prostealing*: "Heinz has a duty to protect his wife's life; it's a vow he took in marriage. But it's wrong to steal, so he would have to take the drug with the idea of paying the druggist for it and accepting the penalty for breaking the law later."
  >
  > *Antistealing*: "Even if his wife is dying, it's still [Heinz's] duty as a citizen to obey the law. . . . If everyone starts breaking the law in a jam, there'd be no civilization, just crime and violence." (Rest, 1979, p. 30)

The Postconventional or Principled Level. Individuals at the **postconventional level** move beyond unquestioning support for their own society's rules and laws. They define morality in terms of abstract principles and values that apply to all situations and societies.

- **Stage 5: The social contract orientation.** At Stage 5, individuals regard laws and rules as flexible instruments for furthering human purposes. They can imagine alternatives to their own social order, and they emphasize fair procedures for interpreting and changing the law. When laws are consistent with individual rights and the interests of the majority, each person follows them because of a *social contract orientation*—free and willing participation in the system because it brings about more good for people than if it did not exist.

  > *Prostealing*: "Although there is a law against stealing, the law wasn't meant to violate a person's right to life. . . . If Heinz is prosecuted for stealing, the law needs to be reinterpreted to take into account situations in which it goes against people's natural right to keep on living."
  >
  > *Antistealing*: At this stage, there are no antistealing responses.

- **Stage 6: The universal ethical principle orientation.** At this highest stage, right action is defined by self-chosen ethical principles of conscience that are valid for all people, regardless of law and social agreement. Stage 6 individuals typically mention such abstract principles as respect for the worth and dignity of each person.

  > *Prostealing*: "It doesn't make sense to put respect for property above respect for life itself. [People] could live together without private property at all. Respect for human life and personality is absolute and accordingly [people] have a mutual duty to save one another from dying." (Rest, 1979, p. 37)
  >
  > *Antistealing*: At this stage, there are no antistealing responses.

Research on Kohlberg's Stage Sequence. Kohlberg's original research and other longitudinal studies provide the most convincing evidence for his stage sequence. With few exceptions, individuals move through the first four stages in the predicted order (Boom, Wouters, & Keller, 2007; Dawson, 2002; Walker & Taylor, 1991b). Moral development is slow and gradual: Reasoning at Stages 1 and 2 decreases in early adolescence, while Stage 3 increases through midadolescence and then declines. Stage 4 reasoning rises over the teenage years until, among college-educated young adults, it is the typical response.

Few people move beyond Stage 4. In fact, postconventional morality is so rare that no clear evidence exists that Kohlberg's Stage 6 actually follows Stage 5. This poses a key challenge to Kohlberg's theory: If people must reach Stages 5 and 6 to be considered truly morally mature, few individuals anywhere would measure up! According to one reexamination of Kohlberg's stages, moral maturity can be found in a revised understanding of Stages 3 and 4 (Gibbs, 2014). These stages are not "conventional"—based on social conformity—as Kohlberg assumed. Rather, they require profound moral constructions—an understanding of ideal reciprocity as the basis for relationships (Stage 3) and for widely accepted moral standards, set forth in rules and laws (Stage 4). In this view, "postconventional" morality is a highly reflective endeavor limited to a handful of people who have attained advanced education, usually in philosophy.

TAKE A MOMENT... Think of an actual moral dilemma you faced recently. How did you solve it? Did your reasoning fall at the same stage as your thinking about Heinz? Real-life conflicts often elicit moral reasoning below a person's actual capacity because they involve practical considerations and mix cognition with intense emotion (Walker, 2004).

The influence of situational factors on moral judgments indicates that like Piaget's cognitive stages, Kohlberg's moral stages are loosely organized and overlapping. Rather than developing in a neat, stepwise fashion, people draw on a range of moral responses that vary with context. With age, this range shifts upward as less mature moral reasoning is gradually replaced by more advanced moral thought.

Are There Sex Differences in Moral Reasoning?

In the discussion at the beginning of this section, notice how Sabrina's moral argument focuses on caring and commitment to others. Carol Gilligan (1982) is the best-known of those who have argued that Kohlberg's theory does not adequately represent the morality of girls and women. Gilligan believes that feminine morality emphasizes an "ethic of care" that Kohlberg's system devalues. Sabrina's reasoning falls at Stage 3 because it is based on mutual trust and affection, whereas Louis's is at Stage 4 because he emphasizes following the law. According to Gilligan, a concern for others is a *different* but no less valid basis for moral judgment than a focus on impersonal rights.

Most studies, however, do not support the claim that Kohlberg's approach underestimates the moral maturity of females (Turiel, 2006; Walker, 2006). On hypothetical dilemmas as well as everyday moral problems, adolescent and adult females display reasoning at the same stage as their male agemates and often at a higher stage. And themes of justice and caring appear in the responses of both sexes (Jadack et al., 1995; Walker, 1995).

Nevertheless, some evidence indicates that although the morality of males and females taps both orientations, females tend to emphasize care, whereas males either stress justice or focus equally on justice and care (Jaffee & Hyde, 2000; Wark & Krebs, 1996; Weisz & Black, 2002). This difference in emphasis, which appears more often in real-life dilemmas than in hypothetical ones, may reflect women's greater involvement in daily activities involving care and concern for others.

Coordinating Moral, Social-Conventional, and Personal Concerns

Adolescents' moral advances are also evident in their reasoning about situations that raise competing moral, social-conventional, and personal issues. In diverse Western and non-Western cul-

tures, concern with matters of personal choice strengthens during the teenage years—a reflection of adolescents' quest for identity and increasing independence (Neff & Helwig, 2002; Nucci, 2002). As young people firmly insist that parents not encroach on the personal arena (dress, hairstyle, diary records, friendships), disputes over these issues increase (Hasebe, Nucci, & Nucci, 2004).

As they enlarge the range of issues they regard as personal, adolescents think more intently about conflicts between personal choice and community obligations—for example, whether, and under what conditions, it is permissible to restrict speech, religion, marriage, childbearing, group membership, and other individual rights (Wainryb, 1997). When asked if it is OK to exclude a child from a peer group on the basis of race or gender, fourth graders usually say exclusion is always unfair. But by tenth grade, young people, though increasingly mindful of fairness, indicate that under certain conditions—in intimate relationships (friendship) and private contexts (at home or in a small club), and on the basis of gender more often than race—exclusion is OK (Killen et al., 2002, 2007; Rutland, Killen, & Abrams, 2010). In explaining, they mention the right to personal choice as well as concerns about effective group functioning.

As adolescents integrate personal rights with ideal reciprocity, they demand that the protections they want for themselves extend to others. For example, with age, they are more likely to defend the government's right to limit the individual freedom to engage in risky health behaviors such as smoking and drinking, in the interest of the larger public good (Flanagan, Stout, & Gallay, 2008). Similarly, they eventually realize that violating strongly held conventions in favor of asserting personal choices—showing up at a wedding in a T-shirt, talking out of turn at a student council meeting—can harm others, either by inducing distress or by undermining fair treatment (Nucci, 2001). As their grasp of fairness deepens, young people realize that many social conventions have moral implications: They are

These teenagers participate in a demonstration in favor of gun control. Adolescent moral development involves thinking intently about conflicts between personal choice and community obligation—for example, whether, and under what conditions, individuals' right to bear arms should be restricted.

vital for maintaining a just and peaceful society. Notice how this understanding is central to Kohlberg's Stage 4, which is typically attained as adolescence draws to a close.

Influences on Moral Reasoning

Many factors influence moral understanding, including child-rearing practices, schooling, peer interaction, and culture. Growing evidence suggests that, as Kohlberg believed, these experiences work by presenting young people with cognitive challenges, which stimulate them to think about moral problems in more complex ways.

Child-Rearing Practices.
Adolescents who gain most in moral understanding have parents who engage in moral discussions, encourage prosocial behavior, and create a supportive atmosphere by listening sensitively, asking clarifying questions, and presenting higher-level reasoning (Carlo et al., 2011; Pratt, Skoe, & Arnold, 2004; Wyatt & Carlo, 2002). In one study, 11-year-olds were asked what they thought an adult would say to justify a moral rule, such as not lying, stealing, or breaking a promise. Those with warm, demanding, communicative parents were far more likely than their agemates to point to the importance of ideal reciprocity: "You wouldn't like it if I did it to you" (Leman, 2005). In contrast, when parents lecture, use threats, or make sarcastic remarks, adolescents show little or no change in moral reasoning over time (Walker & Taylor, 1991a).

Schooling.
Years of schooling is a powerful predictor of movement to Kohlberg's Stage 4 or higher (Dawson et al., 2003; Gibbs et al., 2007). Higher education introduces young people to social issues that extend beyond personal relationships to entire political or cultural groups. Consistent with this idea, college students who report more perspective-taking opportunities (for example, classes that emphasize open discussion of opinions, friendships with others of different cultural backgrounds) and who indicate that they have become more aware of social diversity tend to be advanced in moral reasoning (Comunian & Gielen, 2006; Mason & Gibbs, 1993a, 1993b).

Peer Interaction.
Interaction among peers who present differing viewpoints promotes moral understanding. When young people negotiate and compromise, they realize that social life can be based on cooperation between equals rather than authority relations (Killen & Nucci, 1995). Furthermore, recall from Chapter 10 that intergroup contact—cross-race friendships and interactions in schools and communities—reduces racial and ethnic prejudice. It also affects young people morally, strengthening their conviction that race-based and other forms of peer exclusion are wrong (Crystal, Killen, & Ruck, 2008).

Peer discussions of moral problems have provided the basis for interventions aimed at improving high school and college students' moral understanding. But for these to be effective, young people must be highly engaged—confronting and critiquing one another's viewpoints, as Sabrina and Louis did when they argued over Mrs. Perry's plight (Berkowitz & Gibbs, 1983;

Comunian & Gielen, 2006). And because moral development occurs gradually, many peer interaction sessions over weeks or months are needed to produce moral change.

Culture.
Individuals in industrialized nations move through Kohlberg's stages more quickly and advance to a higher level than individuals in village societies, who rarely move beyond Stage 3. One explanation is that in village societies, moral cooperation is based on direct relations between people and does not allow for the development of advanced moral understanding (Stages 4 to 6), which depends on appreciating the role of larger social structures, such as laws and government institutions (Gibbs et al., 2007).

A second possible reason for cultural variation is that responses to moral dilemmas in collectivist cultures (including village societies) are often more other-directed than in Western Europe and North America (Miller, 2006). In both village and industrialized cultures that highly value interdependency, statements portraying the individual as vitally connected to the social group are common. In one study, Japanese adolescents, who almost always integrated care- and justice-based reasoning, placed greater weight on care, which they regarded as a communal responsibility (Shimizu, 2001). Similarly, in research conducted in India, even highly educated people (expected to have attained Kohlberg's Stages 4 and 5) viewed solutions to moral dilemmas as the responsibility of the entire society, not of a single person (Miller & Bersoff, 1995).

These findings raise the question of whether Kohlberg's highest level represents a culturally specific way of thinking—one limited to Western societies that emphasize individualism and an appeal to an inner, private conscience. At the same time, a review of over 100 studies confirmed an age-related trend consistent with Kohlberg's Stages 1 to 4 across diverse societies (Gibbs et al., 2007). A common justice morality is clearly evident in the dilemma responses of people from vastly different cultures.

Members of this small village community in Mozambique experience moral cooperation as based on direct relations between people. Consequently, their moral reasoning is unlikely to advance beyond Kohlberg's Stage 3.

Moral Reasoning and Behavior

A central assumption of the cognitive-developmental perspective is that moral understanding should affect moral action. According to Kohlberg, mature moral thinkers realize that behaving in line with their beliefs is vital for creating and maintaining a just social world (Gibbs, 2014). Consistent with this idea, higher-stage adolescents more often act prosocially by helping, sharing, and defending victims of injustice and by volunteering in their communities (Carlo et al., 1996, 2011; Comunian & Gielen, 2000, 2006). Also, they less often engage in cheating, aggression, and other antisocial behaviors (Gregg, Gibbs, & Fuller, 1994; Raaijmakers, Engels, & van Hoof, 2005; Stams et al., 2006).

Yet the connection between mature moral reasoning and action is only modest. As we have seen, moral behavior is influenced by many factors besides cognition, including the emotions of empathy, sympathy, and guilt; individual differences in temperament; and a long history of cultural experiences and intuitive beliefs that affect moral decision making (Haidt & Kesebir, 2010). **Moral identity**—the degree to which morality is central to self-concept—also affects moral behavior (Hardy & Carlo, 2011). In a study of low-SES African-American and Hispanic teenagers, those who emphasized moral traits and goals in their self-descriptions displayed exceptional levels of community service (Hart & Fegley, 1995). But they did not differ from their agemates in moral reasoning.

Researchers have begun to identify factors that strengthen moral identity. Certain parenting practices—inductive discipline (see page 207 in Chapter 8) and clearly conveyed moral expectations—augment adolescents' moral identity (Patrick & Gibbs, 2011). And *just educational environments*—in which teachers guide students in democratic decision making and rule setting, resolving disputes civilly, and taking responsibility for others' welfare—are influential (Atkins, Hart, & Donnelly, 2004). In one study, tenth graders who reported fair teacher treatment were more likely than those who had experienced unjust treatment (an unfair detention or a lower grade than they deserved) to regard excluding a peer on the basis of race as a moral transgression (Crystal, Killen, & Ruck, 2010).

LOOK AND LISTEN

Would you characterize your high school as a *just educational environment?* Cite specific features and experiences that may have contributed to students' moral development and civic engagement. ●

Religious Involvement and Moral Development

Religion is especially important in U.S. family life. In recent national polls, nearly two-thirds of Americans reported actively practicing religion, compared with one-half of those in Canada, one-third of those in Great Britain and Italy, and even fewer elsewhere in Europe (CIA, 2012; Gallup News Service, 2006;

Playing in a brass quartet at church gives these adolescents a sense of connection to their faith. Religious involvement promotes teenagers' moral development, encouraging responsible academic work and community service.

Jones, 2003). As adolescents search for a personally meaningful identity, formal religious involvement tends to decline (Kerestes & Youniss, 2003; Pew Research Center, 2010b). Nevertheless, teenagers who remain part of a religious community are advantaged in moral values and behavior. Compared with nonaffiliated youths, they are more involved in community service activities aimed at helping the less fortunate (Kerestes, Youniss, & Metz, 2004). And religious involvement promotes responsible academic and social behavior and discourages misconduct (Dowling et al., 2004).

A variety of factors probably contribute to these favorable outcomes. In a study of inner-city high school students, religiously involved young people were more likely to report trusting relationships with parents, adults, and friends who hold similar worldviews. The more activities they shared with this network, the higher they scored in empathy and prosocial behavior (King & Furrow, 2004). Furthermore, religious education and youth activities directly teach concern for others and provide opportunities for moral discussions and civic engagement. And adolescents who feel connected to a higher being may develop certain inner strengths, including prosocial values and a strong moral identity, that help them translate their thinking into action (Hardy & Carlo, 2005; Sherrod & Spiewak, 2008). An exception is evident in religious cults, where rigid indoctrination into the group's beliefs, suppression of individuality, and estrangement from society all work against moral maturity (Scarlett & Warren, 2010).

Further Challenges to Kohlberg's Theory

Although much evidence is consistent with the cognitive-developmental approach to morality, Kohlberg's has faced major challenges. The most radical opposition comes from researchers who—referring to wide variability in moral reasoning across situations—claim that Kohlberg's stage sequence inadequately accounts for morality in everyday life (Krebs and Denton, 2005). These investigators favor abandoning Kohlberg's stages for a *pragmatic approach to morality.* They assert that everyday moral judgments—rather than being efforts to arrive at just solutions—are practical tools that people use to achieve their goals. To benefit personally, they often must advocate cooperation with others. But people often act first and then invoke moral judgments to rationalize their actions, regardless of whether their behavior is self-centered or prosocial (Haidt, 2001; Haidt & Kesebir, 2010).

Is the pragmatic approach correct that people strive to resolve moral conflicts fairly only when they themselves have nothing to lose? Supporters of the cognitive-developmental perspective point out that people frequently rise above self-interest to defend others' rights. For example, moral leaders in business—rather than resorting to Stage 2 reasoning—endorse trust, integrity, good faith, and just laws and codes of conduct (Damon, 2004; Gibbs, 2006). Also, adolescents and adults are well aware of the greater adequacy of higher-stage moral reasoning, which some people act on despite highly corrupt environments. And individuals who engage in sudden altruistic action may have previously considered relevant moral issues so thoroughly that their moral judgment activates automatically, triggering an immediate response (Gibbs et al., 2009; Pizarro & Bloom, 2003). In these instances, people who appear to be engaging in after-the-fact moral justification are actually behaving with great forethought.

In sum, the cognitive-developmental approach to morality has done much to clarify our profound moral potential. And despite opposition, Kohlberg's central assumption—that with age, humans everywhere construct a deeper understanding of fairness and justice that guides moral action—remains powerfully influential.

Gender Typing

As Sabrina entered adolescence, she began to worry about walking, talking, eating, dressing, laughing, and competing in ways consistent with a feminine gender role. According to one hypothesis, the arrival of adolescence is typically accompanied by **gender intensification**—increased gender stereotyping of attitudes and behavior, and movement toward a more traditional gender identity. Research on gender intensification, however, is mixed, with some studies finding evidence for it and others reporting few instances (Basow & Rubin, 1999; Galambos, Almeida, & Petersen, 1990; Huston & Alvarez, 1990; Priess, Lindberg, & Hyde, 2009). When gender intensification is evident, it seems to be stronger for adolescent girls. Although girls continue to be less gender-typed than boys, some may feel less free to experiment with "other-gender" activities and behaviors than they did in middle childhood.

In young people who do exhibit gender intensification, biological, social, and cognitive factors likely are involved. As puberty magnifies sex differences in appearance, teenagers may

For some young people, early adolescence is a time of gender intensification. Pubertal changes in appearance, traditional gender-role expectations of parents, and increased concern with what others think can prompt a move toward a more traditional gender identity.

spend more time thinking about themselves in gender-linked ways. Pubertal changes might also prompt gender-typed pressures from others. Parents with traditional gender-role beliefs may encourage "gender-appropriate" activities and behavior more than they did earlier (Shanahan et al., 2007). And when adolescents start to date, they may become more gender-typed as a way of increasing their attractiveness. Finally, cognitive changes—in particular, greater concern with what others think—might make young teenagers more responsive to gender-role expectations.

Gender intensification declines by late adolescence, but not all affected young people move beyond it to the same degree. Teenagers who are encouraged to explore non-gender-typed options and to question the value of gender stereotypes for themselves and society are more likely to build an androgynous gender identity (see Chapter 8, page 215). Overall, androgynous adolescents, especially girls, tend to be psychologically healthier—more self-confident, more willing to speak their own mind, better-liked by peers, and identity-achieved (Bronstein, 2006; Dusek, 1987; Harter, 2006).

ASK YOURSELF

REVIEW How does an understanding of ideal reciprocity contribute to moral development? Why are Kohlberg's Stages 3 and 4 morally mature?

APPLY Tam grew up in a small village culture, Lydia in a large industrial city. At age 15, Tam reasons at Kohlberg's Stage 3, Lydia at Stage 4. What factors might account for the difference?

REFLECT Do you favor a cognitive-developmental or a pragmatic approach to morality, or both? Explain, drawing on research evidence and personal experiences.

The Family

Franca and Antonio remember their son Louis's freshman year of high school as a difficult time. Because of a demanding project at work, Franca was away from home many evenings and weekends. In her absence, Antonio took over, but when business declined and he had to cut costs at his hardware store, he, too, had less time for the family. That year, Louis and two friends used their computer know-how to gain entry to their classmates' systems to pirate video game software. Louis's grades fell, and he often left the house without saying where he was going. When Franca and Antonio noticed the video-game icons covering Louis's computer desktop, they knew they had cause for concern.

During adolescence, striving for **autonomy**—a sense of oneself as a separate, self-governing individual—becomes a salient task. Teenagers strive to rely more on themselves and less on parents for decision making (Collins & Laursen, 2004; Steinberg & Silk, 2002). Nevertheless, parent–child relationships remain vital for helping adolescents become autonomous, responsible individuals.

Parent–Child Relationships

A variety of changes within the adolescent support autonomy. In Chapter 11, we saw that puberty triggers psychological distancing from parents. In addition, as young people look more mature, parents give them more independence and responsibility (McElhaney et al., 2009). Gradually, adolescents solve problems and make decisions more effectively. And an improved ability to reason about social relationships leads teenagers to *deidealize* their parents, viewing them as "just people." Consequently, they no longer bend as easily to parental authority as they did when younger.

Parent–child relationships are vital for helping adolescents attain autonomy. Though teenagers benefit from freedom to explore ideas and make their own decisions, they need guidance and protection from dangerous situations.

Yet as Franca and Antonio's episode with Louis illustrates, teenagers still need guidance and protection from dangerous situations. In diverse ethnic groups and cultures, warm, supportive parenting that grants young people freedom to explore while making appropriate demands for maturity fosters autonomy, predicting high self-reliance, effortful control, academic achievement, positive work orientation, favorable self-esteem, and ease of separation in the transition to college (Bean, Barber, & Crane, 2007; Eisenberg et al., 2005b; Supple et al., 2009; Wang, Pomerantz, & Chen, 2007).

Conversely, parents who are coercive or psychologically controlling interfere with the development of autonomy. These tactics are linked to low self-esteem, depression, drug and alcohol use, and antisocial behavior—outcomes that often persist into early adulthood (Barber, Stolz, & Olsen, 2005; Bronte-Tinkew, Moore, & Carrano, 2006; Wissink, Deković, & Meijer, 2006).

In Chapter 2, we described the family as a *system* that must adapt to changes in its members. The rapid physical and psychological changes of adolescence trigger conflicting expectations in parent–child relationships. Parents and teenagers—especially young teenagers—differ sharply on the appropriate age for granting certain privileges, such as control over clothing, school choices, going out with friends, and dating (Smetana, 2002). Consistent parental monitoring of the young person's daily activities, through a cooperative relationship in which the adolescent willingly discloses information, is linked to a variety of positive outcomes—prevention of delinquency, reduction in sexual activity, improved school performance, and positive psychological well-being (Crouter & Head, 2002; Jacobson & Crockett, 2000).

LOOK AND LISTEN

Ask an early adolescent and his or her parent for their views on when the young person is mature enough to begin dating, own a cell phone, create a Facebook page, and be given other privileges. Do adolescent and parent perspectives differ? ●

Immigrant parents from cultures that highly value family closeness and obedience to authority have greater difficulty adapting to their teenagers' push for autonomy, often reacting more strongly to adolescent disagreement. And as adolescents acquire the host culture's language and are increasingly exposed to its individualistic values, immigrant parents may become even more critical, causing teenagers to rely less on the family network for social support (Yau, Tasopoulos-Chan, & Smetana, 2009). The resulting *acculturative stress* is associated with a decline in self-esteem and a rise in anxiety, depressive symptoms, and deviant behavior, including alcohol use and delinquency (Park, 2009; Suarez-Morales & Lopez, 2009; Warner et al., 2006).

Throughout adolescence, the quality of the parent–child relationship is the single most consistent predictor of mental health. In well-functioning families, teenagers remain attached to parents and seek their advice, but they do so in a context of greater freedom (Collins & Steinberg, 2006). The mild conflict that typically arises facilitates adolescent identity and autonomy by helping family members express and tolerate disagreement. Conflicts also inform parents of teenagers' changing needs and expectations, signaling a need for adjustments in the parent–child relationship. By middle to late adolescence, most parents and children achieve this mature, mutual relationship, and harmonious interaction is on the rise.

Family Circumstances

As Franca and Antonio's experience with Louis reminds us, adult life stress can interfere with warm, involved parenting and, in turn, with children's adjustment at any period of development. But parents who are financially secure, not overloaded with job pressures, and content with their marriages usually find it easier to grant teenagers appropriate autonomy and experience less conflict with them (Cowan & Cowan, 2002; Crouter & Bumpus, 2001). When Franca and Antonio's work stress eased and they recognized Louis's need for more involvement and guidance, his problems subsided.

Among the minority of families with seriously troubled parent–adolescent relationships, most difficulties began in childhood (Collins & Laursen, 2004). Teenagers who develop well despite family stress continue to benefit from factors that fostered resilience in earlier years: an appealing, easy-going disposition; a parent who combines warmth with high expectations; and (especially if parental supports are lacking) bonds with prosocial adults outside the family who care deeply about the adolescent's well-being (Masten, 2001; Masten & Shaffer, 2006).

Siblings

Like parent–child relationships, sibling interactions adapt to development at adolescence. As younger siblings become more self-sufficient, they accept less direction from their older brothers and sisters, and sibling influence declines. Also, as teenagers become more involved in friendships and romantic relationships, they invest less time and energy in siblings, who are part of the family from which they are trying to establish autonomy (Hetherington, Henderson, & Reiss, 1999; Kim et al., 2006). As a result, sibling relationships often become less intense, in both positive and negative feelings.

Nevertheless, attachment between siblings remains strong for most young people. Overall, siblings who established a positive bond in early childhood continue to display greater affection and caring, which contribute to more favorable adolescent adjustment (Kim et al., 2007; Samek & Rueter, 2011). Culture also influences quality of sibling relationships. In one study, Mexican-American adolescents who expressed a strong Mexican cultural orientation resolved sibling conflicts more cooperatively than did those more oriented toward U.S. individualistic values (Killoren, Thayer, & Updegraff, 2008).

Finally, mild sibling differences in perceived parental affection no longer trigger jealousy but, instead, predict greater sibling warmth (Feinberg et al., 2003). Perhaps adolescents interpret a unique relationship with parents, as long as it is generally accepting, as a gratifying sign of their own individuality.

Peer Relations

As adolescents spend less time with family members, peers become increasingly important. In industrialized nations, young people spend most of each weekday with agemates in school. Teenagers also spend much out-of-class time together, more in some cultures than others. For example, U.S. young people have about 50 hours of free time per week, Europeans about 45 hours, and East Asians about 33 hours (Larson, 2001). A shorter school year and less demanding academic standards, which lead American youths to devote much less time to schoolwork, account for this difference.

In the following sections, we will see that adolescent peer relations can be both positive and negative. At their best, peers serve as critical bridges between the family and adult social roles.

Friendships

Number of best friends declines from about four to six in early adolescence to one or two in adulthood (Hartup & Stevens, 1999). At the same time, the nature of the relationship changes.

Characteristics of Adolescent Friendships.
When asked about the meaning of friendship, teenagers stress three characteristics. The most important is *intimacy,* or psychological closeness, which is supported by *mutual understanding* of each other's values, beliefs, and feelings. In addition, more than younger children, teenagers want their friends to be *loyal*—to stick up for them and not leave them for somebody else (Collins & Madsen, 2006).

As frankness and faithfulness increase, *self-disclosure* (sharing of private thoughts and feelings) between friends rises over the adolescent years (see Figure 12.1). As a result, teenage friends get to know each other better as personalities. In addition to the many characteristics that school-age friends share (see page 268 in Chapter 10), adolescent friends tend to be alike in identity status, educational aspirations, political beliefs, and willingness to try drugs and engage in lawbreaking acts (Berndt & Murphy, 2002; Selfhout, Branje, & Meeus, 2008). Occasionally, however, teenagers choose friends with differing attitudes and values, which permits them to explore new perspectives within the security of a compatible relationship.

During adolescence, cooperation and mutual affirmation between friends increase—changes that reflect greater skill at preserving the relationship and sensitivity to a friend's needs and desires (De Goede, Branje, & Meeus, 2009). Adolescents also are less possessive of their friends than they were in childhood (Parker et al., 2005). Desiring a certain degree of autonomy for themselves, they recognize that friends need this, too.

Sex Differences in Friendships. *TAKE A MOMENT...*
Ask several adolescents to describe their close friendships. You are likely to find a consistent sex difference: Emotional closeness is more common between girls than between boys (Markovits, Benenson, & Dolensky, 2001). Girls frequently get together to

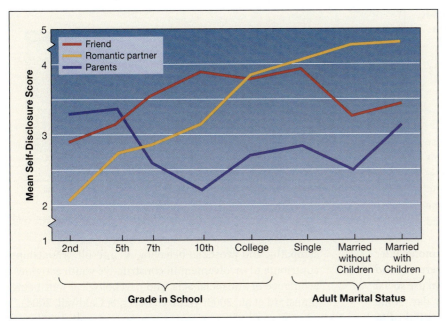

FIGURE 12.1 **Age changes in reported self-disclosure to parents and peers, based on findings of several studies.** Self-disclosure to friends increases steadily during adolescence, reflecting intimacy as a major basis of friendship. Self-disclosure to romantic partners also rises, but it does not surpass intimacy with friends until the college years. Self-disclosure to parents declines in early adolescence, a time of mild parent–child conflict. As family relationships readjust to the young person's increasing autonomy, self-disclosure to parents rises. (From D. Buhrmester, 1996, "Need Fulfillment, Interpersonal Competence, and the Developmental Contexts of Early Adolescent Friendship," in W. M. Bukowski, A. F. Newcomb, & W. W. Hartup [Eds.], *The Company They Keep: Friendship in Childhood and Adolescence,* New York: Cambridge University Press, p. 168. Reprinted with permission of Cambridge University Press.)

"just talk," and their interactions contain more self-disclosure and supportive statements. In contrast, boys more often gather for an activity—usually sports and competitive games. Boys' discussions usually focus on accomplishments and involve more competition and conflict (Brendgen et al., 2001; Rubin, Bukowski, & Parker, 2006).

Friendship closeness has costs as well as benefits. When friends focus on deeper thoughts and feelings, they tend to *coruminate,* or repeatedly mull over problems and negative

Compared to boys, adolescent girls place a higher value on emotional closeness, engaging in more self-disclosure and supportive statements with friends.

emotions—an activity that, while contributing to high friendship quality, also triggers anxiety and depression, symptoms more common among girls (Hankin, Stone, & Wright, 2010; Rose, Carlson, & Waller, 2007). And when conflict arises between intimate friends, more potential exists for one party to harm the other through relational aggression—for example, by divulging sensitive personal information to outsiders. Partly for this reason, girls' closest same-sex friendships tend to be of shorter duration than boys' (Benenson & Christakos, 2003).

Friendships on the Internet. Teenagers frequently use cell phones and the Internet to communicate with friends. About 75 percent of U.S. 12- to 17-year-olds own a cell phone, a rate that has nearly doubled during the past decade. Cell-phone texting has become the preferred means of electronic interaction between teenage friends, with cell calling second, followed by social networking sites and instant messaging (see Figure 12.2 on page 332). Girls use cell phones to text and call their friends considerably more often than boys (Lenhart et al., 2010). These forms of online interaction seem to support friendship closeness. In several studies, as amount of online messaging between preexisting friends increased, so did young people's perceptions of intimacy in the relationship and feelings of well-being (Reich, Subrahmanyam, & Espinoza, 2012; Valkenburg & Peter, 2007a, 2007b, 2009). The effect is largely due to friends' online disclosure of personal information, such as worries, secrets, and romantic feelings.

Although mostly communicating with friends they know, teenagers are also drawn to meeting new people over the Internet. Social networking sites such as Facebook and MySpace (used by nearly three-fourths of U.S. teenagers) along with blogs, message boards, and chat rooms open up vast alternatives beyond their families, schools, and communities (Lenhart et al., 2010). Through these online ties, young people explore central adolescent issues—sexuality, challenges in parent and peer relationships, and identity issues, including attitudes and values—in contexts that may feel less threatening than similar everyday conversations (Subrahmanyam, Smahel, & Greenfield, 2006; Valkenburg & Peter, 2011). Online interactions with strangers also offer some teenagers vital social support. Young people suffering from depression, eating disorders, and other problems can access message boards where participants provide mutual assistance (Whitlock, Powers, & Eckenrode, 2006).

But online communication also poses dangers. In unmonitored chat rooms, teenagers are likely to encounter degrading racial and ethnic slurs and sexually obscene and harassing remarks (Subrahmanyam & Greenfield, 2008). Furthermore, in a survey of a nationally representative sample of U.S. 10- to 17-year-olds, 14 percent reported having formed online close

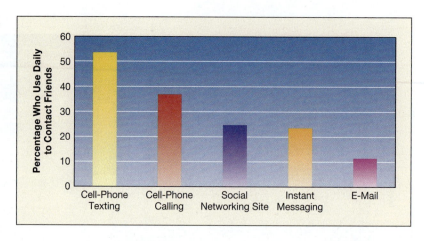

FIGURE 12.2 **Percentage of U.S. 12- to 17-year-olds who use various communication channels daily to contact friends.** A nationally representative sample of 800 U.S. 12- to 17-year-olds responded to a survey about their communication strategies with friends. Cell-phone texting emerged as the preferred channel, with over half of teenagers reporting that they used it daily. (Adapted from Lenhart et al., 2010.)

friendships or romances. Although some of these youths were well-adjusted, many reported high levels of conflict with parents, peer victimization, depression, and delinquency (Wolak, Mitchell, & Finkelhor, 2003). They also more often had been asked by online friends for face-to-face meetings and had attended those meetings—without telling their parents.

Finally, time devoted to social media is rising among older children and adolescents. For example, nearly 45 percent send more than 50 texts per day, and more than 70 percent use social networking sites for an average of 37 minutes per day. Some evidence suggests that very high social media use is linked to unsatisfying face-to-face social experiences, boredom, unhappiness, and Internet addiction (obsessive Internet use) (Pea et al., 2012; Rideout, Foehr, & Roberts, 2010; Smahel, Brown, & Blinka, 2012). Furthermore, high Internet consumers often engage in "face-to-face multitasking," such as texting at the dinner table or web surfing while chatting with friends (Abelson, Ledeen, & Lewis, 2008). These behaviors detract from high-quality face-to-face communication.

In sum, the Internet's value for enabling convenient and satisfying interaction among teenage friends must be weighed against its potential for facilitating harmful social consequences. Parents are wise to point out the risks of Internet communication, including excessive use, harassment, and exploitation, and to insist that teenagers follow Internet safety rules (see www.safeteens.com).

Friendship and Adjustment. As long as adolescent friendships are high in trust, intimate sharing, and support and not characterized by relational aggression or attraction to antisocial behavior, they contribute to many aspects of psychological health and competence into early adulthood (Bukowski, 2001; Waldrip, 2008), for several reasons:

- *Close friendships provide opportunities to explore the self and develop a deep understanding of another.* Through open, honest communication, friends become sensitive to each other's strengths and weaknesses, needs and desires—a process that supports the development of self-concept, perspective taking, and identity.

- *Close friendships provide a foundation for future intimate relationships.* Conversations with teenage friends about sexuality and romance, along with the intimacy of friendship itself, may help adolescents establish and work out problems in romantic partnerships (Connolly & Goldberg, 1999).

- *Close friendships help young people deal with the stresses of adolescence.* Supportive friendships promote empathy,

sympathy, and prosocial behavior. As a result, friendships contribute to involvement in constructive youth activities, avoidance of antisocial acts, and psychological well-being (Lansford et al., 2003; Wentzel, Barry, & Caldwell, 2004).

- *Close friendships can improve attitudes toward and involvement in school.* Close friendships promote good school adjustment, academically and socially (Wentzel, Barry, & Caldwell, 2004). When teenagers enjoy interacting with friends at school, they may begin to view all aspects of school life more positively.

LOOK AND LISTEN

Interview several adolescents about qualities they value most in their best friends. Ask how friendships have helped them cope with stress and resulted in other personal benefits. •

Cliques and Crowds

In early adolescence, *peer groups* (see Chapter 10) become increasingly common and tightly knit. They are organized into **cliques,** groups of about five to seven members who are friends and, therefore, usually resemble one another in family background, attitudes, and values (Brown & Dietz, 2009). At first, cliques are limited to same-sex members. Among girls but not boys, being in a clique predicts academic and social competence. Clique membership is more important to girls, who use it as a context for expressing emotional closeness (Henrich et al., 2000). By midadolescence, mixed-sex cliques are common.

Among Western adolescents attending high schools with complex social structures, often several cliques with similar values form a larger, more loosely organized group called a **crowd.** Unlike the more intimate clique, membership in a crowd is based on reputation and stereotype, granting the adolescent an identity within the larger social structure of the school. Prominent crowds in a typical high school might include "brains" (nonathletes who enjoy academics), "jocks" (who are very involved in sports), "populars" (class leaders who are highly social and involved in activities), "partyers" (who value social-

These high school drama club members form a crowd, establishing relationships on the basis of shared abilities and interests. Crowd membership grants them an identity within the larger social structure of the school.

izing but care little about schoolwork), "nonconformists" (who like unconventional clothing and music), "druggies" (who frequently use substances, engage in sexual risk-taking, and otherwise get into trouble), and "normals" (average to good students who get along with most other peers) (Kinney, 1999; Stone & Brown, 1999).

What influences the sorting of teenagers into cliques and crowds? Crowd affiliations are linked to strengths in adolescents' self-concepts, which reflect their abilities and interests (Prinstein & La Greca, 2002). Ethnicity also plays a role. Minority teenagers who associate with an ethnically defined crowd, as opposed to a crowd reflecting their abilities and interests, may be motivated by discrimination in their school or neighborhood. Alternatively, they may be expressing a strong ethnic identity (Brown et al., 2008). Family factors are important, too. In a study of 8,000 ninth to twelfth graders, adolescents who described their parents as authoritative were members of "brain," "jock," and "popular" groups that accepted both adult and peer reward systems. In contrast, boys with permissive parents aligned themselves with the "partyers" and "druggies," suggesting lack of identification with adult reward systems (Durbin et al., 1993).

As interest in dating increases, boys' and girls' cliques come together. Mixed-sex cliques provide boys and girls with models of how to interact and a chance to do so without having to be intimate (Connolly et al., 2004). By late adolescence, when boys and girls feel comfortable enough about approaching each other directly, the mixed-sex cliques disappear (Connolly & Goldberg, 1999).

Crowds also decline in importance. As adolescents settle on personal values and goals, they no longer feel a need to broadcast, through dress, language, and activities, who they are. From tenth to twelfth grade, about half of young people switch crowds, mostly in favorable directions (Strouse, 1999). "Brains" and "normal" crowds grow and deviant crowds lose members as teenagers focus more on their future.

Dating

The hormonal changes of puberty increase sexual interest, but cultural expectations determine when and how dating begins. Asian youths start dating later and have fewer dating partners than young people in Western societies, which tolerate and even encourage romantic involvements from middle school on. At age 12 to 14, these relationships are usually casual, lasting only briefly. But by age 16, they continue, on average, for nearly two years (Carver, Joyner, & Udry, 2003). Early adolescents tend to mention recreation and achieving peer status as reasons for dating. By late adolescence, as young people are ready for greater psychological intimacy, they seek dating partners who offer personal compatibility, companionship, affection, and social support (Collins & van Dulmen, 2006b; Meier & Allen, 2009).

The achievement of intimacy between dating partners typically lags behind that between friends. And recall from Chapter 6 that according to ethological theory, early attachment bonds lead to an *internal working model,* or set of expectations about attachment figures, that guides later close relationships. Consistent with this idea, secure attachment to parents in infancy and childhood—together with recollections of that security in adolescence—predicts quality of teenagers' friendship and romantic ties (Collins & van Dulmen, 2006a; Collins, Welsh, & Furman, 2009).

Perhaps because early adolescent dating relationships are shallow and stereotyped, early dating is related to drug use, delinquency, and poor academic achievement (Eaton et al., 2007; Miller et al., 2009). These factors, along with a history of uninvolved parenting and aggression in family and peer relationships, increase the likelihood of dating violence. About 10 to 20 percent of adolescents are physically or sexually abused by dating partners, with boys and girls equally likely to report being victims, and violence by one partner often returned by the other (Cyr, McDuff, & Wright, 2006; Williams et al., 2008). Mental health consequences are severe, including increased

For this young couple out shopping together, dating extends the benefits of adolescent friendships, promoting sensitivity, empathy, self-esteem, and identity development.

anxiety, depression, suicide attempts, and risky sexual behavior (Wekerle & Avgoustis, 2003). Young teenagers are better off sticking with group activities, such as parties and dances, before becoming involved with a steady boyfriend or girlfriend.

Gay and lesbian youths face special challenges in initiating and maintaining visible romances. Their first dating relationships seem to be short-lived and to involve little emotional commitment, but for reasons different from those of heterosexuals: They fear peer harassment and rejection (Diamond & Lucas, 2004). In addition, many have difficulty finding a same-sex partner because their gay and lesbian peers have not yet come out. Often their first contacts with other sexual-minority youths occur in support groups, where they are free to date publicly (Diamond, 2003).

As long as it does not begin too soon, dating promotes sensitivity, empathy, self-esteem, social support, compromise, and identity development, thereby enhancing the quality of other peer relationships (Collins, Welsh, & Furman, 2009). Still, about half of first romances do not survive high school graduation, and those that do usually become less satisfying (Shaver, Furman, & Buhrmester, 1985). Because young people are still forming their identities, high school couples often find that they have little in common after graduation. Nevertheless, warm, caring romantic ties in adolescence can have long-term implications. They are positively related to gratifying, committed relationships in early adulthood (Meier & Allen, 2009).

ASK YOURSELF

REVIEW Describe the distinct positive functions of friendships, cliques, and crowds in adolescence. What factors lead some friendships and peer-group ties to be harmful?

APPLY Thirteen-year-old Mattie's parents are warm, firm in their expectations, and consistent in monitoring her activities. At school, Mattie met some girls who want her to tell her parents she's going to a friend's house but, instead, join them at the beach for a party. Is Mattie likely to comply? Explain.

REFLECT How did family experiences influence your crowd membership in high school? How did your crowd membership influence your behavior?

Problems of Development

Most young people move through adolescence with little disturbance. But as we have seen, some encounter major disruptions in development, such as early parenthood, substance abuse, and school failure. In each instance, biological and psychological changes, families, schools, peers, communities, and culture combine to yield particular outcomes. Serious difficulties rarely occur in isolation but are usually interrelated—as is apparent in three additional problems of the teenage years: depression, suicide, and delinquency.

Depression

Depression—feeling sad, frustrated, and hopeless about life, accompanied by loss of pleasure in most activities and disturbances in sleep, appetite, concentration, and energy—is the most common psychological problem of adolescence. About 15 to 20 percent of teenagers have had one or more major depressive episodes, a rate comparable to that of adults. From 2 to 8 percent are chronically depressed—gloomy and self-critical for many months and sometimes years (Graber & Sontag, 2009; Rushton, Forcier, & Schectman, 2002).

Serious depression affects only 1 to 2 percent of children, many of whom (especially girls) remain depressed in adolescence. In addition, depression increases sharply from ages 12 to 16 in industrialized nations, with many more girls than boys displaying adolescent onset. Teenage girls are twice as likely as boys to report persistent depressed mood—a difference sustained throughout the lifespan (Dekker et al., 2007; Hankin & Abela, 2005; Nolen-Hoeksema, 2006).

Factors Related to Depression. Kinship studies reveal that heredity plays an important role in depression (Glowinski et al., 2003). Genes can induce depression by affecting the balance of neurotransmitters in the brain, the development of brain regions involved in inhibiting negative emotion, or the body's hormonal response to stress.

But experience can also promote these biological changes. In earlier chapters we saw that depressed or otherwise stressed parents often engage in maladaptive parenting. As a result, their child's emotional self-regulation, attachment, and self-esteem may be impaired, with serious consequences for many cognitive and social skills (Abela et al., 2005; Yap, Allen, & Ladouceur, 2008). In a vulnerable young person, numerous events can spark depression—for example, failing at something important, parental divorce, or the end of a close friendship or romantic partnership.

Sex Differences. Why are girls more prone to depression than boys? Biological changes associated with puberty cannot be responsible because in many developing countries, rates of depression are similar for males and females and occasionally higher in males (Culbertson, 1997). And in industrialized nations, the extent to which females exceed males in depression varies widely.

Instead, gender-typed coping styles seem to be responsible. Early-maturing girls are especially prone to depression (see Chapter 11). Adolescent gender intensification may strengthen girls' passivity, dependency, and tendency to ruminate on their anxieties and problems—maladaptive approaches to tasks expected of teenagers in complex cultures. Consistent with this explanation, adolescents who identify strongly with "feminine" traits ruminate more and are more depressed, regardless of their sex (Lopez, Driscoll, & Kistner, 2009; Papadakis et al., 2006). And having friends with depressive symptoms is linked to a rise in teenagers' own depressive symptoms, perhaps because corumination is high in such relationships (Conway et al., 2011).

In industrialized nations, stressful life events and gender-typed coping styles—passivity, dependency, and rumination—make adolescent girls more prone to depression than boys.

Girls who repeatedly feel troubled and insecure develop an overly reactive physiological stress response and cope more poorly with future challenges (Hyde, Mezulis, & Abramson, 2008; Nolen-Hoeksema, 2006). In this way, stressful experiences and stress reactivity feed on one another, sustaining depression. Profound depression can lead to suicidal thoughts, which all too often are translated into action.

Suicide

The suicide rate increases from childhood to old age, but it jumps sharply at adolescence. Currently, suicide is the third-leading cause of death among American youths, after motor vehicle collisions and homicides. At the same time, rates of adolescent suicide vary widely among industrialized nations—low in Greece, Italy, the Netherlands, and Spain; intermediate in Australia, Canada, Japan, and the United States; and high in Finland, New Zealand, and Singapore (Bridge, Goldstein, & Brent, 2006). These international differences remain unexplained.

Factors Related to Adolescent Suicide. Despite girls' higher rates of depression, the number of boys who kill themselves exceeds the number of girls by a ratio of 3 or 4 to 1. Girls make more unsuccessful suicide attempts and use methods from which they are more likely to be revived, such as a sleeping pill overdose. In contrast, boys tend to choose techniques that lead to instant death, such as firearms (Langhinrichsen-Rohling, Friend, & Powell, 2009). Gender-role expectations may contribute; less tolerance exists for feelings of helplessness and failed efforts in males.

Possibly due to greater extended-family support, African Americans and Hispanics have lower suicide rates than Caucasian Americans. Recently, however, suicide has risen among African-American adolescent males; the current rate approaches that of Caucasian-American males. And Native-American youths commit suicide at rates two to six times national averages (Balis & Postolache, 2008; U.S. Census Bureau, 2013). High rates of profound family poverty, school failure, alcohol and drug use, and depression probably underlie these trends. Gay, lesbian, and bisexual youths are also at high risk, attempting suicide three times as often as other adolescents. Those who have tried to kill themselves report more family conflict over their gender-atypical behavior, inner turmoil about their sexuality, and peer victimization (D'Augelli et al., 2005).

Suicide tends to occur in two types of young people. The first group includes adolescents who are highly intelligent but solitary, withdrawn, and unable to meet their own standards or those of important people in their lives. Members of the second, larger group show antisocial tendencies (Evans, Hawton, & Rodham, 2004). Besides being hostile and destructive, they turn their anger and disappointment inward.

Suicidal adolescents often have a family history of emotional and antisocial disorders. In addition, they are likely to have experienced multiple stressful life events, including economic disadvantage, parental divorce, frequent parent–child conflict, and abuse and neglect (Beautrais, 2003; Kaminski et al., 2010). Triggering events include parental blaming of the teenager for family problems, the breakup of an important peer relationship, or the humiliation of having been caught engaging in antisocial acts.

Why does suicide increase in adolescence? One factor seems to be teenagers' improved ability to plan ahead. Although some act impulsively, many young people take purposeful steps toward killing themselves. Other cognitive changes also contribute. Belief in the personal fable (see Chapter 11) leads many depressed young people to conclude that no one could possibly understand their intense pain.

Prevention and Treatment. To prevent suicides, parents and teachers must be trained to pick up on the signals that a troubled teenager sends (see Table 12.2 on page 336). Schools and community settings, such as recreational and religious organizations, can help by providing counseling and support (Goldston et al., 2008; Miller, 2011). Once a teenager takes steps toward suicide, staying with the young person, listening, and expressing compassion and concern until professional help can be obtained are essential.

Treatments for depressed and suicidal adolescents range from antidepressant medication to individual, family, and group therapy. On a broader scale, gun-control legislation that limits adolescents' access to the most frequent and deadly suicide method in the United States would greatly reduce both the number of suicides and the high teenage homicide rate (Commission on Adolescent Suicide Prevention, 2005).

Teenage suicides often occur in clusters, with one death increasing the likelihood of others among depressed peers who knew the young person (Bearman & Moody, 2004; Feigelman & Gorman, 2008). In view of this trend, an especially watchful eye must be kept on vulnerable adolescents after a suicide happens.

TABLE 12.2

Warning Signs of Suicide

Efforts to put personal affairs in order—smoothing over troubled relationships, giving away treasured possessions

Verbal cues—saying goodbye to family members and friends, making direct or indirect references to suicide ("I won't have to worry about these problems much longer"; "I wish I were dead")

Feelings of sadness, despondency, "not caring" anymore

Extreme fatigue, lack of energy, boredom

No desire to socialize; withdrawal from friends

Easily frustrated

Emotional outbursts—spells of crying or laughing, bursts of energy

Inability to concentrate, distractible

Decline in grades, absence from school, discipline problems

Neglect of personal appearance

Sleep change—loss of sleep or excessive sleepiness

Appetite change—eating more or less than usual

Physical complaints—stomachaches, backaches, headaches

Delinquency

Juvenile delinquents are children or adolescents who engage in illegal acts. Although youth crime has declined in the United States since the mid-1990s, 12- to 17-year-olds account for about 14 percent of police arrests, although they constitute only 8 percent of the population (U.S. Department of Justice, 2010). When asked directly and confidentially about lawbreaking, almost all teenagers admit to having committed some sort of offense—usually a minor crime, such as petty stealing or disorderly conduct (Flannery et al., 2003).

Both police arrests and self-reports show that delinquency rises over early and middle adolescence and then declines (Farrington, 2009; U.S. Department of Justice, 2010). Antisocial behavior increases among teenagers as a result of heightened reward seeking and desire for peer approval. Over time, peers become less influential; decision making, emotional self-regulation, and moral reasoning improve; and young people enter social contexts (such as higher education, work, marriage, and career) that are less conducive to lawbreaking.

For most adolescents, a brush with the law does not forecast long-term antisocial behavior. But repeated arrests are cause for concern. Teenagers are responsible for 15 percent of violent offenses in the United States (U.S. Department of Justice, 2010). A small percentage become recurrent offenders, who commit most of these crimes, and some enter a life of crime.

Factors Related to Delinquency. In adolescence, the gender gap in physical aggression widens. Although girls account for about one in five adolescent arrests for violence,

their offenses are largely limited to simple assault (such as pushing or spitting). Serious violent crime is mostly the domain of boys (Dahlberg & Simon, 2006). SES and ethnicity are strong predictors of arrests but only mildly related to teenagers' self-reports of antisocial acts. The difference is due to the tendency to arrest, charge, and punish low-SES ethnic minority youths more often than their higher-SES white and Asian counterparts (Farrington, 2009; U.S. Department of Justice, 2010).

Difficult temperament, low intelligence, poor school performance, peer rejection in childhood, and association with antisocial peers are linked to chronic delinquency (Laird et al., 2005). How do these factors fit together? One of the most consistent findings about delinquent youths is that their families are low in warmth, high in conflict, and characterized by harsh, inconsistent discipline and low monitoring (Barnes et al., 2006; Capaldi et al., 2002). Our discussion on page 212 in Chapter 8 explained how ineffective parenting can promote and sustain children's aggression, with boys—who are more active and impulsive—more often targets of parental anger, physical punishment, and inconsistency. When these child temperamental traits combine with emotionally negative, inept parenting, aggression rises sharply during childhood, leads to violent offenses in adolescence, and persists into adulthood (see the Biology and Environment box on the following page).

Teenagers commit more crimes in poverty-stricken neighborhoods with limited recreational and employment opportunities and high adult criminality (Leventhal, Duprere, & Brooks-Gunn, 2009). In such neighborhoods, adolescents have easy access to deviant peers, drugs, and firearms and are likely to be recruited into antisocial gangs, whose members commit the vast majority of violent delinquent acts. Furthermore, schools in these locales typically fail to meet students' developmental needs (Chung, Mulvey, & Steinberg, 2011; Flannery et al., 2003). Large classes, weak instruction, rigid rules, and reduced academic

© CHROMORANGE/PICTURE-ALLIANCE/NEWSCOM

Delinquency—usually petty stealing and disorderly conduct—rises over early and middle adolescence and then declines. But a small percentage of young people engage in repeated, serious offenses and are at risk for a life of crime.

Biology and Environment

Two Routes to Adolescent Delinquency

Persistent adolescent delinquency follows two paths, one involving a small number of youths with an onset of conduct problems in childhood, the second a larger number with an onset in adolescence. The early-onset type is far more likely to lead to a life-course pattern of aggression and criminality (Moffitt, 2007). The late-onset type usually does not persist beyond the transition to early adulthood.

Why does antisocial activity more often continue and escalate into violence in the first group? Longitudinal studies yield similar answers to this question. Most research has focused on boys, but several investigations report that girls who were physically aggressive in childhood are also at risk for later problems—occasionally violent delinquency but more often other norm-violating behaviors and psychological disorders (Broidy et al., 2003; Chamberlain, 2003). Early relational aggression is linked to adolescent conduct problems as well.

Early-Onset Type

Early-onset youngsters seem to inherit traits that predispose them to aggressiveness. Violence-prone boys are emotionally negative, restless, willful, and physically aggressive as early as age 2. They also show subtle deficits in cognitive functioning that seem to contribute to disruptions in the development of language, memory, and cognitive and

emotional self-regulation (Moffitt, 2007; Shaw et al., 2003). Some have attention-deficit hyperactivity disorder (ADHD), which compounds their learning and self-control problems (see Chapter 9, page 239).

Yet these biological risks are not sufficient to sustain antisocial behavior: Most early-onset boys decline in aggression over time. Among those who follow the life-course path, inept parenting transforms their undercontrolled style into defiance and persistent aggression (Brame, Nagin, & Tremblay, 2001; Broidy et al., 2003). As they fail academically and are rejected by peers, they befriend other deviant youths, who facilitate one another's violent behavior (see Figure 12.3) (Hughes, 2010; Lacourse et al., 2003). Limited cognitive and social skills result in high rates of school dropout and unemployment, contributing further to antisocial involvements (Patterson & Yoerger, 2002).

Preschoolers high in relational aggression also tend to be hyperactive and frequently in conflict with peers and adults. As these behaviors trigger peer rejection, relationally aggressive girls befriend other girls high in relational hostility, and their relational aggression rises (Werner & Crick, 2004). Adolescents high in relational aggression are often angry, vengeful, and defiant of adult rules. Among teenagers who combine physical and relational hostility, these oppositional reactions intensify, increasing

the likelihood of serious antisocial activity (Harachi et al., 2006; Prinstein, Boergers, & Vernberg, 2001).

Late-Onset Type

Other youths first display antisocial behavior around the time of puberty, gradually increasing their involvement. Their conduct problems arise from the peer context, not from biological deficits and a history of unfavorable development. For some, quality of parenting may decline for a time, perhaps due to family stresses or the challenges of disciplining an unruly teenager (Moffitt, 2007). When age brings gratifying adult privileges, these youths draw on prosocial skills mastered before adolescence and abandon their antisocial ways.

A few late-onset youths do continue to engage in antisocial acts. The seriousness of their adolescent offenses seems to trap them in situations that close off opportunities for responsible behavior. Being employed or in school and forming positive, close relationships predict an end to criminal offending by age 20 to 25 (Clingempeel & Henggeler, 2003; Stouthamer-Loeber et al., 2004). In contrast, the longer antisocial young people spend in prison, the more likely they are to sustain a life of crime.

These findings suggest a need for a fresh look at policies aimed at stopping youth crime. Keeping youth offenders locked up for many years disrupts their vocational lives and access to social support during a crucial period of development, condemning them to a bleak future.

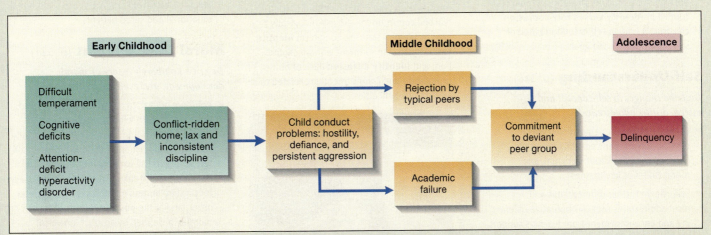

FIGURE 12.3 Path to chronic delinquency for adolescents with childhood-onset antisocial behavior. Difficult temperament and cognitive deficits characterize many of these youths in early childhood; some have attention-deficit hyperactivity disorder. Inept parenting transforms biologically based self-control difficulties into hostility and defiance.

expectations and opportunities are associated with higher rates of lawbreaking, even after other influences are controlled.

Prevention and Treatment.

Because delinquency has roots in childhood and results from events in several contexts, prevention must start early and take place at multiple levels (Frey et al., 2009). Positive family relationships, authoritative parenting, high-quality teaching in schools, and communities with healthy economic and social conditions go a long way toward reducing adolescent antisocial acts.

Lacking resources for effective prevention, many U.S. schools have implemented *zero tolerance policies,* which punish all disruptive and threatening behavior, usually with suspension or expulsion. Yet often these policies are implemented inconsistently: Low-SES minority students are two to three times as likely to be punished, especially for minor misbehaviors (Goode & Goode, 2007; Reppucci, Meyer, & Kostelnik, 2011). No evidence exists that zero tolerance reduces youth misconduct (Stinchcomb, Bazemore, & Riestenberg, 2006). To the contrary, some studies find that these policies heighten high school dropout and antisocial behavior.

Treating serious offenders requires an intensive, often lengthy approach, also directed at the multiple determinants of delinquency. In a program called *multisystemic therapy,* counselors combined family intervention with integrating violent youths into positive school, work, and leisure activities and disengaging them from deviant peers. Compared with conventional services or individual therapy, the intervention led to greater improvement in parent–adolescent relationships and school performance and a dramatic drop in number of arrests. Multisystemic therapy also helped limit family instability once youth offenders reached adulthood, as measured by involvement in civil suits over divorce, paternity, or child support (Borduin, 2007; Henggeler et al., 2009; Sawyer & Borduin, 2011). Efforts to create nonaggressive environments—at the family, community, and cultural levels—are needed to help delinquent youths and to foster healthy development of all young people.

ASK YOURSELF

REVIEW Why are adolescent girls at greater risk for depression and adolescent boys at greater risk for suicide?

APPLY Zeke had been well-behaved in elementary school, but at age 13 he started spending time with the "wrong crowd." At 16, he was arrested for property damage. Is Zeke likely to become a long-term offender? Why or why not?

SUMMARY

Erikson's Theory: Identity versus Role Confusion (p. 318)

According to Erikson, what is the major personality achievement of adolescence?

● Erikson viewed **identity** as the major personality achievement of adolescence. Young people who successfully resolve the psychological conflict of **identity versus role confusion** construct a unified self-definition based on self-chosen values and goals.

Self-Understanding (p. 318)

Describe changes in self-concept and self-esteem during adolescence.

● Cognitive changes enable adolescents to develop more organized, consistent self-descriptions, with social, personal, and moral values as key themes.

● Self-esteem further differentiates and, for most adolescents, rises. Authoritative parenting and encouragement from teachers support positive self-esteem.

Describe the four identity statuses, along with factors that promote identity development.

● Researchers evaluate progress in identity development on two key criteria: exploration and commitment. **Identity achievement** (exploration followed by commitment to values, beliefs, and goals) and **identity moratorium** (exploration without having reached commitment) are psychologically healthy identity statuses. Long-term **identity foreclosure** (commitment without exploration) and **identity diffusion** (lack of both exploration and commitment) are related to adjustment difficulties.

● An information-gathering cognitive style, healthy parental attachment, interaction with diverse peers, and schools and communities offering rich and varied opportunities promote healthy identity development. To forge a strong, secure **ethnic identity,** minority adolescents often must overcome **acculturative stress.** A **bicultural identity** offers additional emotional and social benefits.

Moral Development (p. 321)

Describe Kohlberg's theory of moral development, and evaluate its accuracy.

● Kohlberg organized moral development into three levels, each with two stages. At the **preconventional level,** morality is externally controlled and actions are judged by their consequences; at the **conventional level,** conformity to laws and rules is regarded as necessary for positive human relationships and societal order; and at the **postconventional level,** morality is defined by abstract, universal principles.

- A reexamination of Kohlberg's stages suggests that moral maturity can be found at Stages 3 and 4; few people attain the postconventional level. Because situational factors influence moral judgments, Kohlberg's stages are best viewed as loosely organized and overlapping.

- Contrary to Gilligan's claim, Kohlberg's theory does not underestimate the moral maturity of females but instead taps both justice and caring orientations.

- Compared with children, teenagers display more subtle reasoning about conflicts between personal choice and community obligation and are increasingly aware of the moral implications of following social conventions.

Describe influences on moral reasoning and its relationship to moral behavior.

- Factors contributing to moral maturity include warm, rational child-rearing practices, education level, and peer discussions of moral issues. In village societies, moral reasoning rarely moves beyond Kohlberg's Stage 3. In collectivist cultures, moral dilemma responses are more other-directed than in Western societies.

- Maturity of moral reasoning is only modestly related to moral behavior. Moral action is also influenced by empathy and guilt, temperament, history of morally relevant experiences, and **moral identity.** Although formal religious involvement declines in adolescence, most religiously affiliated teenagers are advantaged in moral values and behavior.

- Researchers favoring a pragmatic approach to morality assert that moral maturity varies depending on context and motivations.

Gender Typing (p. 328)

How does gender typing change in adolescence?

- Some research suggests that adolescence is a time of **gender intensification,** in which gender stereotyping of attitudes and behavior increases, though evidence is mixed.

The Family (p. 329)

Discuss changes in parent–child and sibling relationships during adolescence.

- In their quest for **autonomy,** adolescents rely more on themselves and less on parents for decision making. Teenagers deidealize their parents, often questioning parental authority. Warm, supportive parenting, appropriate demands for maturity, and consistent monitoring predict favorable outcomes.

- Sibling influence declines as adolescents separate from the family and turn toward peers. Still, attachment to siblings remains strong for most young people.

Peer Relations (p. 330)

Describe adolescent friendships, peer groups, and dating relationships and their consequences for development.

- Adolescent friendships are based on intimacy, mutual understanding, and loyalty and contain more self-disclosure. Girls place greater emphasis on emotional closeness, boys on shared activities and accomplishments.

- Online communication supports closeness with existing friends. Though online communication with strangers provides some teenagers with vital social support, it also poses risks. High social media use is linked to unsatisfying face-to-face social experiences.

- Adolescent friendships—when not characterized by relational aggression or attraction to antisocial behavior—promote self-concept, perspective taking, identity, and the capacity for intimate relationships. They also help young people deal with stress and can foster improved attitudes toward and involvement in school.

- Adolescent peer groups are organized into **cliques,** particularly important to girls, and **crowds,** which grant teenagers an identity within the larger social structure of the school. With interest in dating, mixed-sex cliques increase in importance. Both cliques and crowds diminish as teenagers settle on personal values and goals.

- Intimacy in dating relationships lags behind that between friends. Positive relationships with parents and friends contribute to secure romantic ties.

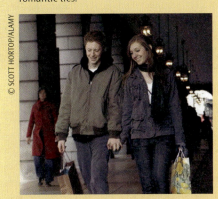

© SCOTT HORTOP/ALAMY

Problems of Development (p. 334)

Describe factors related to adolescent depression and suicide.

- Depression is the most common psychological problem of adolescence, with girls at greater risk in industrialized nations. Combinations of biological and environmental factors are implicated, including heredity, maladaptive parenting, and negative life events.

- The suicide rate increases sharply at adolescence. Although teenage girls make more unsuccessful suicide attempts, boys account for more deaths. Teenagers at risk for suicide may be withdrawn but more often are antisocial. Family turmoil is common in the backgrounds of suicidal adolescents.

Discuss factors related to delinquency.

- Delinquency rises over early and middle adolescence and then declines. But only a few teenagers are serious repeat offenders—usually boys with a childhood history of conduct problems.

- A family environment low in warmth, high in conflict, and characterized by inconsistent discipline and low monitoring is consistently related to delinquency, as are poverty-stricken neighborhoods with high crime rates and ineffective schools.

Important Terms and Concepts

milestones

Development in Adolescence

© RUDY VON BRIEL/PHOTOEDIT

© BOB DAEMMRICH/PHOTOEDIT

- Becomes more self-conscious and self-focused. (308)
- Becomes more idealistic and critical. (308)
- Metacognition and self-regulation continue to improve. (291, 306)

EMOTIONAL/SOCIAL

- Self-concept includes abstract descriptors unifying separate personality traits, but these are not interconnected and often contradictory. (318–319)
- In striving for autonomy, spends less time with parents and siblings, more time with peers. (330)
- Friendships decline in number and are based on intimacy, mutual understanding, and loyalty. (330)
- Peer groups become organized around same-sex cliques. (332)
- In high schools with complex social structures, cliques with similar values form crowds. (332)

© CINDY CHARLES/PHOTOEDIT

Early Adolescence: 11–14

PHYSICAL

- If a girl, reaches peak of growth spurt. (288)
- If a girl, adds more body fat than muscle. (289)
- If a girl, starts to menstruate. (290)
- If a boy, begins growth spurt. (288)
- If a boy, starts to ejaculate seminal fluid. (290)
- Is likely to be aware of sexual orientation. (299)
- If a girl, motor performance increases gradually, leveling off by age 14. (289)
- Reacts more strongly to stressful events; shows heightened sensation-seeking and risk-taking behavior. (292)

COGNITIVE

- Gains in hypothetico-deductive reasoning and propositional thought. (304–305)
- Gains in scientific reasoning—coordinating theory with evidence—on complex, multivariable tasks. (307)

Middle Adolescence: 14–16

PHYSICAL

- If a girl, completes growth spurt. (288)
- If a boy, reaches peak of growth spurt. (288)
- If a boy, voice deepens. (290)
- If a boy, adds muscle while body fat declines. (289)
- If a boy, motor performance improves dramatically. (289)
- May have had sexual intercourse. (298)

COGNITIVE

- Continues to improve in hypothetico-deductive reasoning and propositional thought. (304–305)
- Continues to improve in scientific reasoning. (307)

© BOB DAEMMRICH/PHOTOEDIT

Note: Numbers in parentheses indicate the page or pages on which each milestone is discussed.

- Becomes less self-conscious and self-focused. (308)
- Improves in decision making. (308–309)

EMOTIONAL/SOCIAL

- Combines features of the self into an organized self-concept. (319)
- Self-esteem differentiates further and tends to rise. (319)
- In most cases, begins to move from "lower" to "higher" identity statuses. (319)
- Increasingly emphasizes ideal reciprocity and societal laws as the basis for resolving moral dilemmas. (324)
- Engages in more subtle reasoning about conflicts between moral, social-conventional, and personal-choice issues. (325)

- Mixed-sex cliques become common. (332)
- Has probably started dating. (333)

Late Adolescence: 16–18

PHYSICAL

- If a boy, completes growth spurt. (288)
- If a boy, gains in motor performance continue. (289)

COGNITIVE

- Continues to improve in metacognition, scientific reasoning, and decision making. (306–309)

EMOTIONAL/SOCIAL

- Self-concept emphasizes personal and moral values. (319)
- Continues to construct an identity, typically moving to higher identity statuses. (319)
- Continues to advance in maturity of moral reasoning. (324)
- Cliques and crowds decline in importance. (333)
- Seeks psychological intimacy in romantic ties, which last longer. (333–334)

Physical and Cognitive Development in Early Adulthood

© CEZARO DE LUCA/EPA/CORBIS

Early adulthood brings momentous changes—among them, choosing a vocation, starting full-time work, and attaining economic independence. This Argentinean forensic anthropologist, who recently completed her higher education, has joined a team identifying people who went missing several decades ago, during a dark period of her country's history.

chapter outline

The back seat and trunk piled high with belongings, 23-year-old Sharese hugged her mother and brother goodbye, jumped in the car, and headed toward the interstate with a sense of newfound freedom mixed with apprehension.

Three months earlier, the family had watched proudly as Sharese received her bachelor's degree in chemistry from a small university 40 miles from her home. Her college years had been a time of gradual release from economic and psychological dependency on her family. She returned home periodically on weekends and lived there during the summer months. Her mother supplemented Sharese's loans with a monthly allowance. But this day marked a turning point. She was moving to her own apartment in a city 800 miles away, with plans to work on a master's degree. With a teaching assistantship and a student loan, Sharese felt more "on her own" than at any previous time.

During her college years, Sharese made lifestyle changes and settled on a vocational direction. Overweight throughout high school, she lost 20 pounds in her sophomore year, revised her diet, and began an exercise regimen by joining the university's Ultimate Frisbee team, eventually becoming its captain. A summer spent as a counselor at a camp for chronically ill children helped convince Sharese to apply her background in science to a career in public health.

Still, two weeks before she was to leave, Sharese confided in her mother that she had doubts about her decision. "Sharese," her mother advised, "we never know if our life choices are going to suit us just right, and most times they aren't perfect. It's what we make of them—how we view and mold them—that turns them into successes." So Sharese embarked on her journey and found herself face-to-face with a multitude of exciting challenges and opportunities.

In this chapter, we take up the physical and cognitive sides of early adulthood, which extends from about age 18 to 40. As noted in Chapter 1, the adult years are difficult to divide into discrete periods because the timing of important milestones varies greatly among individuals. But for most people, early adulthood involves a common set of tasks: leaving home, completing education, beginning full-time work, attaining economic independence, establishing a long-term sexually and emotionally intimate relationship, and starting a family. These are energetic decades filled with momentous decisions that, more than any other time of life, offer the potential for living to the fullest. ●

PHYSICAL DEVELOPMENT

We have seen that throughout childhood and adolescence, the body grows larger and stronger, coordination improves, and sensory systems gather information more effectively. Once body structures reach maximum capacity and efficiency, **biological aging**, or **senescence**, begins—genetically influenced declines in the functioning of organs and systems that are universal in all members of our species. Like physical growth, however, biological aging varies widely across parts of the body, and individual differences are great—variation that the *lifespan perspective* helps us understand. A host of contextual factors—including each person's genetic makeup, lifestyle, living environment, and historical period—influence biological aging, each of which can accelerate or slow age-related declines (Arking, 2006). As a result, the physical changes of the adult years are, indeed, *multidimensional* and *multidirectional* (see page 6 in Chapter 1).

In the following sections, we examine the process of biological aging. Then we turn to physical and motor changes already under way in early adulthood. As you will see, biological aging can be modified substantially through behavioral and environmental interventions. During the twentieth century, improved nutrition, medical treatment, sanitation, and safety added 25 to 30 years to *average life expectancy* in industrialized nations, a trend that is continuing (see Chapter 1, page 5).

Biological Aging Is Under Way in Early Adulthood

In her early twenties, Sharese is at her peak in strength, endurance, sensory acuteness, and immune system responsiveness. Yet over the next two decades, she will age and, as she moves into middle and late adulthood, will show more noticeable declines.

This whitewater kayaker, in his early twenties, is at his peak in strength, endurance, and sensory acuteness.

Biological aging is the combined result of many causes, some operating at the level of DNA, others at the level of cells, and still others at the level of tissues, organs, and the whole organism (Arking, 2006). Hundreds of theories exist, indicating that our understanding is incomplete.

Aging at the Level of DNA and Body Cells

Current explanations of biological aging at the level of DNA and body cells are of two types: (1) those that emphasize the *programmed effects of specific genes* and (2) those that emphasize the *cumulative effects of random events* that damage genetic and cellular material. Support for both views exists, and a combination may eventually prove to be correct.

Genetically programmed aging receives some support from kinship studies indicating that longevity is a family trait. People whose parents had long lives tend to live longer themselves. And greater similarity exists in the lifespans of identical than fraternal twins. But the heritability of longevity is modest, ranging from .15 to .35 for age at death and from .27 to .57 for various measures of current biological age, such as strength of hand grip, respiratory capacity, blood pressure, and bone density (Cevenini et al., 2008; Dutta et al., 2011; Gögele et al., 2011). Rather than inheriting longevity directly, people probably inherit risk and protective factors, which influence their chances of dying earlier or later.

One "genetic programming" theory proposes the existence of "aging genes" that control certain biological changes, such as menopause, gray hair, and deterioration of body cells. The strongest evidence for this view comes from research showing that human cells allowed to divide in the laboratory have a lifespan of 50 divisions, plus or minus 10 (Hayflick, 1998). With

each duplication, a special type of DNA called **telomeres**—located at the ends of chromosomes, serving as a "cap" to protect the ends from destruction—shortens. Eventually, so little remains that the cells no longer duplicate at all. Telomere shortening acts as a brake against somatic mutations (such as those involved in cancer), which become more likely as cells duplicate (Shay & Wright, 2011). But an increase in the number of senescent cells (ones with short telomeres) also contributes to age-related disease, loss of function, and earlier mortality (Epel et al., 2009; Shin et al., 2006). As the Biology and Environment box on the following page reveals, researchers have begun to identify health behaviors and psychological states that accelerate telomere shortening—powerful biological evidence that certain life circumstances compromise longevity.

According to an alternative, "random events" theory, DNA in body cells is gradually damaged through spontaneous or externally caused mutations. As these accumulate, cell repair and replacement become less efficient, and abnormal cancerous cells are often produced. Animal studies confirm an increase in DNA breaks and deletions and damage to other cellular material with age (Freitas & Magalhães, 2011). Similar evidence is accruing for humans.

One hypothesized cause of age-related DNA and cellular abnormalities is the release of **free radicals**—naturally occurring, highly reactive chemicals that form in the presence of oxygen. (Radiation and certain pollutants and drugs can trigger similar effects.) When oxygen molecules break down within the cell, the reaction strips away an electron, creating a free radical. As it seeks a replacement from its surroundings, it destroys nearby cellular material, including DNA, proteins, and fats essential for cell functioning. Free radicals are thought to be involved in more than 60 disorders of aging, including cardiovascular disease, neurological disorders, cancer, cataracts, and arthritis (Cutler & Mattson, 2006; Stohs, 2011). Although our bodies produce substances that neutralize free radicals, some harm occurs, and it accumulates over time.

Some researchers believe that genes for longevity work by defending against free radicals. In support of this view, animal species with longer life expectancies tend to display slower rates of free-radical damage to DNA (Sanz, Pamplona, & Barja, 2006). But contrary evidence also exists. For example, experimental manipulation of the mouse genome, by either augmenting or deleting antioxidant genes, has no impact on longevity (Speakman & Selman, 2011).

Research suggests that foods low in saturated fat and rich in vitamins can forestall free-radical damage (Bullo, Lamuela-Raventos, & Salas-Salvadó, 2011). Nevertheless, the role of free radicals in aging is controversial.

Aging at the Level of Tissues and Organs

What consequences might age-related DNA and cellular deterioration have for the overall structure and functioning of organs and tissues? There are many possibilities. Among those

Kinship studies indicate that longevity is a family trait. In addition to favorable heredity, these grandsons will likely benefit from the model of a fit, active grandfather who buffers stress by enjoying life.

RONNIE KAUFMAN/LARRY HIRSHOWITZ/BLEND IMAGES/GETTY IMAGES

Biology and Environment

Telomere Length: A Marker of the Impact of Life Circumstances on Biological Aging

In the not-too-distant future, your annual physical exam may include an assessment of the length of your *telomeres*—DNA at the ends of chromosomes, which safeguard the stability of your cells. Telomeres shorten with each cell duplication; when they drop below a critical length, the cell can no longer divide and becomes senescent (see Figure 13.1). Although telomeres shorten with age, the rate at which they do so varies greatly. An enzyme called *telomerase* prevents shortening and can even reverse the trend, causing telomeres to lengthen and, thus, protecting the aging cell.

Over the past decade, research examining the influence of life circumstances on telomere length has exploded. A well-established finding is that chronic illnesses, such as cardiovascular disease and cancer, hasten telomere shortening in white blood cells, which play a vital role in the immune response (see page 348). Telomere shortening, in turn, predicts more rapid disease progression and earlier death (Fuster & Andres, 2006).

Accelerated telomere shortening has been linked to a variety of unhealthy behaviors, including cigarette smoking and the physical inactivity and overeating that lead to obesity and to insulin resistance, which often precedes type 2 diabetes (Epel et al., 2006; Gardner et al., 2005). Unfavorable health conditions may alter telomere length as early as the prenatal period, with possible long-term negative consequences for biological aging. In research on rats, poor maternal nutrition during pregnancy resulted in low birth weight and development of shorter telomeres in kidney and heart tissue (Jennings et al., 1999; Tarry-Adkins et al., 2008). In a human

investigation, preschoolers who had been low-birth-weight as infants had shorter telomeres in their white blood cells than did their normal-birth-weight agemates (Raqib et al., 2007).

Persistent psychological stress—in childhood, abuse or bullying; in adulthood, parenting a child with a chronic illness or caring for an elder with dementia—is linked to reduced telomerase activity and telomere shortness in white blood cells (Damjanovic et al., 2007; McEwen, 2007; Shalev, 2012; Simon et al., 2006). Can stress actually modify telomeres? In a laboratory experiment, researchers exposed human white blood cells to the stress hormone cortisol. The cells responded by decreasing production of telomerase (Choi, Fauce, & Effros, 2008).

Fortunately, when adults make positive lifestyle changes, telomeres seem to respond accordingly. In a study of obese women, those who responded to a lifestyle intervention with reduced psychological stress and healthier eating behaviors also displayed gains in telomerase activity (Daubenmier et al., 2012). In another investigation of men varying widely in age, greater maximum vital capacity of the lungs (a measure of physical fitness) was associated with reduced age-

related accumulation of senescent white blood cells (Spielmann et al., 2011).

Currently, researchers are working on identifying sensitive periods of telomere change—times when telomeres are most susceptible to modification. Early intervention—for example, enhanced prenatal care and interventions to reduce obesity in childhood—may be particularly powerful. But telomeres are changeable well into late adulthood (Epel et al., 2009). As our understanding of predictors and consequences of telomere length expands, it may become an important index of health and aging throughout life.

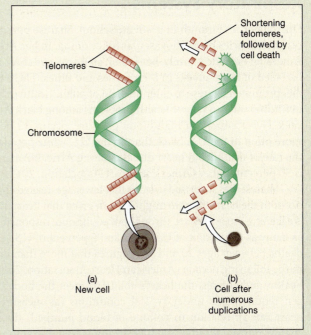

FIGURE 13.1 Telomeres at the ends of chromosomes. (a) Telomeres in a newly created cell. (b) With each cell duplication, telomeres shorten; when too short, they expose DNA to damage, and the cell dies.

with clear support is the **cross-linkage theory of aging.** Over time, protein fibers that make up the body's connective tissue form bonds, or links, with one another. When these normally separate fibers cross-link, tissue becomes less elastic, leading to many negative outcomes, including loss of flexibility in the skin and other organs, clouding of the lens of the eye, clogging of arteries, and damage to the kidneys. Like other aspects of aging, cross-linking can be reduced by external factors, including regular exercise and a healthy diet (Kragstrup, Kjaer, & Mackey, 2011; Wickens, 2001).

Gradual failure of the endocrine system, which produces and regulates hormones, is yet another route to aging. An obvious example is decreased estrogen production in women, which culminates in menopause. Because hormones affect many body functions, disruptions in the endocrine system can have widespread effects on health and survival. For example, a gradual drop in growth hormone (GH) is associated with loss of muscle and bone mass, addition of body fat, thinning of the skin, and decline in cardiovascular functioning. Again, a healthy diet and physical activity can limit these aspects of biological aging.

Finally, declines in immune system functioning contribute to many conditions of aging, including increased susceptibility to infectious disease and cancer and changes in blood vessel walls associated with cardiovascular disease. Decreased vigor of the immune response seems to be genetically programmed, but other aging processes we have considered (such as weakening of the endocrine system) can intensify it (Alonso-Férnandez & De la Fuente, 2011; Hawkley & Cacioppo, 2004).

Physical Changes

The physical changes of aging are summarized in Table 13.1. During the twenties and thirties, they are so gradual that most are hardly noticeable. We will examine several in detail here and take up others in later chapters.

Cardiovascular and Respiratory Systems

During her first month in graduate school, Sharese pored over research articles on cardiovascular functioning. In her African-American extended family, her father, an uncle, and three aunts had died of heart attacks in their forties and fifties. These tragedies prompted Sharese to enter the field of public health in hopes of finding ways to relieve health problems among black Americans. *Hypertension,* or high blood pressure, occurs 12 percent more often in the U.S. black than in the U.S. white population; the rate of death from heart disease among African Americans is 30 percent higher (American Heart Association, 2012).

Sharese was surprised to learn that fewer age-related changes occur in the heart than we might expect, given that heart disease is a leading cause of death throughout adulthood, responsible for as many as 10 percent of U.S. male and 5 percent of U.S. female deaths between ages 20 and 34—figures that more than double in the following decade (American Heart Association, 2012). In healthy individuals, the heart's ability to meet the body's oxygen requirements under typical conditions (as measured by heart rate in relation to volume of blood pumped) does not change during adulthood. Only during stressful exercise does heart performance decline with age—a change due to a decrease in maximum heart rate and greater rigidity of the heart muscle (Arking, 2006).

One of the most serious diseases of the cardiovascular system is *atherosclerosis,* in which heavy deposits of plaque containing cholesterol and fats collect on the walls of the main arteries. If present, it usually begins early in life, progresses during middle adulthood, and culminates in serious illness. Atherosclerosis is multiply determined, making it hard to separate the contributions of biological aging from individual genetic and environmental influences. The complexity of causes is illustrated by research indicating that before puberty, a high-fat diet produces only fatty streaks on the artery walls (Oliveira, Patin, & Escrivao, 2010). In sexually mature adults, however, it leads to serious plaque deposits, suggesting that sex hormones may heighten the insults of a high-fat diet.

Heart disease has decreased considerably since the mid-twentieth century, with a larger drop in the last 25 years due to a decline in cigarette smoking, to improved diet and exercise among at-risk individuals, and to better medical detection and treatment of high blood pressure and cholesterol (American Heart Association, 2012; Liu et al., 2012). Later, when we consider health and fitness, we will see why heart attacks were so common in Sharese's family—and why they occur at especially high rates in the African-American population.

Like the heart, lung capacity decreases during physical exertion. Maximum vital capacity (amount of air that can be forced in and out of the lungs) declines by 10 percent per decade after age 25 (Mahanran et al., 1999; Wilkie et al., 2012). Connective tissue in the lungs, chest muscles, and ribs stiffens with age, making it more difficult for the lungs to expand to full volume (Smith & Cotter, 2008). Fortunately, under normal conditions, we use less than half our vital capacity. Nevertheless, aging of the lungs contributes to older adults' difficulty in meeting the body's oxygen needs while exercising.

Motor Performance

Declines in heart and lung functioning under conditions of exertion, combined with gradual muscle loss, lead to changes in motor performance. In most people, the impact of biological aging on motor skills is difficult to separate from decreases in motivation and practice. Therefore, researchers study competitive athletes, who try to attain their very best performance in real life (Tanaka & Seals, 2003).

In several investigations, the mean ages for best performance of Olympic and professional athletes in a variety of sports

AP IMAGES/ALAN DIAZ

Performance on athletic tasks such as tennis usually peak in the early twenties. But with improved training methods, tennis champion Serena Williams—in her early thirties—recently became the oldest player to be ranked World No. 1.

TABLE 13.1 **Physical Changes of Aging**

ORGAN OR SYSTEM	TIMING OF CHANGE	DESCRIPTION
Sensory		
Vision	From age 30	As the lens stiffens and thickens, ability to focus on close objects declines. Yellowing of the lens, weakening of muscles controlling the pupil, and clouding of the vitreous (gelatin-like substance that fills the eye) reduce light reaching the retina, impairing color discrimination and night vision. Visual acuity, or fineness of discrimination, decreases, with a sharp drop between ages 70 and 80.
Hearing	From age 30	Sensitivity to sound declines, especially at high frequencies but gradually extending to all frequencies. Change is more than twice as rapid for men as for women.
Taste	From age 60	Sensitivity to the four basic tastes—sweet, salty, sour, and bitter—is reduced. This may be due to factors other than aging, since number and distribution of taste buds do not change.
Smell	From age 60	Loss of smell receptors reduces ability to detect and identify odors.
Touch	Gradual	Loss of touch receptors reduces sensitivity on the hands, particularly the fingertips.
Cardiovascular	Gradual	As the heart muscle becomes more rigid, maximum heart rate decreases, reducing the heart's ability to meet the body's oxygen requirements when stressed by exercise. As artery walls stiffen and accumulate plaque, blood flow to body cells is reduced.
Respiratory	Gradual	Under physical exertion, respiratory capacity decreases and breathing rate increases. Stiffening of connective tissue in the lungs and chest muscles makes it more difficult for the lungs to expand to full volume.
Immune	Gradual	Shrinking of the thymus limits maturation of T cells and disease-fighting capacity of B cells, impairing the immune response.
Muscular	Gradual	As nerves stimulating them die, fast-twitch muscle fibers (responsible for speed and explosive strength) decline in number and size to a greater extent than slow-twitch fibers (which support endurance). Tendons and ligaments (which transmit muscle action) stiffen, reducing speed and flexibility of movement.
Skeletal	Begins in the late thirties, accelerates in the fifties, slows in the seventies	Cartilage in the joints thins and cracks, leading bone ends beneath it to erode. New cells continue to be deposited on the outer layer of the bones, and mineral content of bone declines. The resulting broader but more porous bones weaken the skeleton and make it more vulnerable to fracture. Change is more rapid in women than in men.
Reproductive	In women, accelerates after age 35; in men, begins after age 40	Fertility problems (including difficulty conceiving and carrying a pregnancy to term) and risk of having a baby with a chromosomal disorder increase.
Nervous	From age 50	Brain weight declines as neurons lose water content and die, mostly in the cerebral cortex, and as ventricles (spaces) within the brain enlarge. Development of new synapses and limited generation of new neurons can, in part, compensate for these declines.
Skin	Gradual	Epidermis (outer layer) is held less tightly to the dermis (middle layer); fibers in the dermis and hypodermis (inner layer) thin; fat cells in the hypodermis decline. As a result, the skin becomes looser, less elastic, and wrinkled. Change is more rapid in women than in men.
Hair	From age 35	Grays and thins.
Height	From age 50	Loss of bone strength leads to collapse of disks in the spinal column, leading to a height loss of as much as 2 inches by the seventies and eighties.
Weight	Increases to age 50; declines from age 60	Weight change reflects a rise in fat and a decline in muscle and bone mineral. Since muscle and bone are heavier than fat, the resulting pattern is weight gain followed by loss. Body fat accumulates on the torso and decreases on the extremities.

Sources: Arking, 2006; Lemaitre et al., 2012; Whitbourne, 1996.

were charted over time. Absolute performance in most events improved during the past century. Athletes continually set new world records, suggesting improved training methods. But ages of best performance remained relatively constant. Athletic tasks that require speed of limb movement, explosive strength, and gross-motor coordination—sprinting, jumping, and tennis—typically peak in the early twenties. Those that depend on endurance, arm–hand steadiness, and aiming—long-distance running, baseball, and golf—usually peak in the late twenties and early thirties (Bradbury, 2009; Schulz & Curnow, 1988).

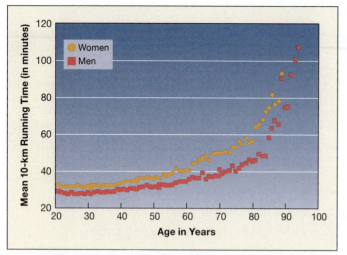

FIGURE 13.2 Ten-kilometer running times with advancing age, based on longitudinal performances of hundreds of master athletes. Runners maintain their speed into the mid-thirties, followed by modest increases in running times into the sixties, with a progressively steeper increase thereafter. (From H. Tanaka & D. R. Seals, 2003, "Dynamic Exercise Performance in Masters Athletes: Insight into the Effects of Primary Human Aging on Physiological Functional Capacity," *Journal of Applied Physiology, 5,* p. 2153. © The American Physiological Society (APS). All rights reserved. Adapted with permission.)

Because these skills require either stamina or precise motor control, they take longer to perfect.

These findings tell us that the upper biological limit of motor capacity is reached in the first part of early adulthood. How quickly do athletic skills weaken in later years? Longitudinal research on master runners reveals that as long as practice continues, speed drops only slightly from the mid-thirties into the sixties, when performance falls off at an accelerating pace (see Figure 13.2) (Tanaka & Seals, 2003; Trappe, 2007). Indeed, sustained training leads to adaptations in body structures that minimize motor declines. In a study of hundreds of thousands of amateur marathon competitors, 25 percent of the 65- to 69-year-old runners were faster than 50 percent of the 20- to 54-year-old runners (Leyk et al., 2010). Yet many of the older runners had begun systematic marathon training only in the past five years.

In sum, before late adulthood, biological aging accounts for only a small part of age-related declines. Lower levels of performance by healthy people into their sixties and seventies largely reflect reduced capacities resulting from a less physically demanding lifestyle.

Immune System

The immune response is the combined work of specialized cells that neutralize or destroy antigens (foreign substances) in the body. Two types of white blood cells play vital roles. *T cells,* which originate in the bone marrow and mature in the thymus (a small gland located in the upper part of the chest), attack antigens directly. *B cells,* manufactured in the bone marrow, secrete antibodies into the bloodstream that multiply, capture antigens, and permit the blood system to destroy them. Because receptors on their surfaces recognize only a single antigen, T and B cells come in great variety. They join with additional cells to produce immunity.

The capacity of the immune system to offer protection against disease increases through adolescence and declines after age 20. The trend is partly due to changes in the thymus, which is largest during the teenage years, then shrinks until it is barely detectable by age 50. As a result, production of thymic hormones is reduced, and the thymus is less able to promote full maturity of T cells (Fülöp et al., 2011). Because B cells release far more antibodies when T cells are present, the immune response is compromised further.

Withering of the thymus is not the only reason that the body gradually becomes less effective in warding off illness. The immune system interacts with the nervous and endocrine systems. For example, psychological stress can weaken the immune response. During final exams, for example, Sharese was less resistant to colds. Conflict-ridden relationships, caring for an ill aging parent, sleep deprivation, and chronic depression can also reduce immunity (Fagundes et al., 2011; Robles & Carroll, 2011). And physical stress—from pollution, allergens, poor nutrition, and rundown housing—undermines immune functioning throughout adulthood (Friedman & Lawrence, 2002). When physical and psychological stressors combine, the risk of illness is magnified.

Reproductive Capacity

Many people believe that pregnancy during the twenties is ideal, not only because of lower risk of miscarriage and chromosomal disorders (see Chapter 2) but also because younger parents have more energy to keep up with active children. Nevertheless, first births to women in their thirties have increased greatly over the past three decades. Many people are delaying childbearing until their education is complete and their careers are well-established.

Nevertheless, between ages 15 and 29, 11 percent of U.S. married childless women report fertility problems, a figure that rises to 14 percent among 30- to 34-year-olds and to over 40 percent among 35- to 44-year-olds, when the success of reproductive technologies drops sharply (see page 42 in Chapter 2) (U.S. Department of Health and Human Services, 2012b). Because the uterus shows no consistent changes from the late thirties through the forties, the decline in female fertility is largely due to reduced number and quality of ova. In many mammals, including humans, a certain level of reserve ova in the ovaries is necessary for conception (Balasch, 2010; Djahanbakhch, Ezzati, & Zosmer, 2007). Some women have normal menstrual cycles but do not conceive because their reserve of ova is too low.

In males, semen volume, sperm motility, and percentage of normal sperm decrease gradually after age 35, contributing to reduced fertility rates in older men (Lambert, Masson, & Fisch, 2006).

ASK YOURSELF

REVIEW How do life conditions that accelerate telomere shortening illustrate the concept of epigenesis, discussed in Chapter 2 (see page 56)?

APPLY Penny is a long-distance runner for her college track team. What factors will affect Penny's running performance 30 years from now?

REFLECT Before reading this chapter, had you thought of early adulthood as a period of aging? Why is it important for young adults to be aware of influences on biological aging?

Health and Fitness

Figure 13.3 displays leading causes of death in early adulthood in the United States. Death rates for all causes exceed those of other industrialized nations—a difference likely due to a combination of factors, including higher rates of poverty and extreme obesity, more lenient gun-control policies, and historical lack of universal health insurance in the United States (OECD, 2012b). But, as we have noted, wide individual and group differences in physical changes are linked to environmental risks and health-related behaviors.

SES variations in health over the lifespan reflect these influences. Income, education, and occupational status show strong relationships with almost every disease and health indicator (Braveman et al., 2010; Smith & Infurna, 2011). Furthermore,

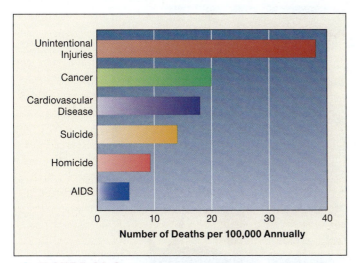

FIGURE 13.3 Leading causes of death between 25 and 44 years of age in the United States. Nearly half of unintentional injuries are motor vehicle accidents. As later chapters will reveal, unintentional injuries remain a leading cause of death at older ages, rising sharply in late adulthood. Rates of cancer and cardiovascular disease rise steadily during middle and late adulthood. (Adapted from U.S. Department of Health and Human Services, 2011b.)

SES variations in health in the United States are in part due to lack of access to affordable health care. This Los Angeles free clinic offers preventive services to over 1,200 patients per day.

SES largely accounts for the sizable health advantage of white over ethnic minority adults in the United States (Phuong, Frank, & Finch, 2012). Consequently, improving socioeconomic conditions is essential for closing ethnic gaps in health.

SES variations in health and mortality larger in the United States than in other industrialized nations. Besides lack of universal health insurance, low-income and poverty-stricken U.S. families are financially less well-off than families classified in these ways in other countries (Wilkinson & Pickett, 2006). In addition, SES groups are more likely to be segregated by neighborhood in the United States, resulting in greater inequalities in environmental factors that affect health, such as housing, pollution, education, and community services.

These findings reveal, once again, that the living conditions that nations and communities provide combine with those that people create for themselves to affect physical aging. Because the incidence of health problems is much lower during the twenties and thirties than later on, early adulthood is an excellent time to prevent later problems. In the following sections, we take up a variety of major health concerns—nutrition, exercise, substance abuse, sexuality, and psychological stress.

Nutrition

Bombarded with advertising claims and an extraordinary variety of food choices, adults find it increasingly difficult to make wise dietary decisions. An abundance of food, combined with a heavily scheduled life, means that most Americans eat because they feel like it or because it is time to do so rather than to maintain the body's functions (Donatelle, 2012). Overweight and obesity and a high-fat diet are widespread nutritional problems with long-term consequences for adult health.

Overweight and Obesity.

In Chapter 9, we noted that obesity (a greater than 20 percent increase over average body weight, based on age, sex, and physical build) has increased dramatically in many Western nations, and it is on the rise in the developing world as well. Among adults, a body mass index (BMI) of 25 to 29 constitutes overweight, a BMI of 30 or greater (amounting to 30 or more excess pounds) constitutes obesity. Today, 36 percent of U.S. adults are obese. The rate rises to 38 percent among Hispanics, 39 percent among Native Americans, and 50 percent among African Americans (Flegal et al., 2012). The overall prevalence of obesity is similar among men and women.

Overweight—a less extreme but nevertheless unhealthy condition—affects an additional 33 percent of Americans. Combine the rates of overweight and obesity and the total, 69 percent, makes Americans the heaviest people in the world. ***TAKE A MOMENT...*** Notice in these figures that the U.S. obesity rate now exceeds its rate of overweight, a blatant indicator of the growing severity of the problem.

Recall from Chapter 9 that overweight teenagers are very likely to become overweight adults. But a substantial number of people show large weight gains in adulthood, most often between ages 25 and 40. And young adults who were already overweight or obese typically get heavier, leading obesity rates to rise steadily between ages 20 and 65 (Flegel et al., 2012).

Causes and Consequences.

As noted in Chapter 9, heredity makes some people more vulnerable to obesity than others. But environmental pressures underlie the rising rates of obesity in industrialized nations: With the decline in need for physical labor in the home and workplace, our lives have become more sedentary. Meanwhile, the average number of calories and amount of sugar and fat consumed by Americans rose over most of the twentieth and early twenty-first century, with a sharp increase after 1970.

Adding some weight between ages 25 and 50 is a normal part of aging because **basal metabolic rate (BMR), the amount of energy the body uses at complete rest,** gradually declines as the number of active muscle cells (which create the greatest energy demand) drops off. But excess weight is strongly associated with serious health problems (see pages 228–229 in Chapter 9)—including type 2 diabetes, heart disease, and many forms of cancer—and with early death.

Furthermore, overweight adults suffer enormous social discrimination. Compared with their normal-weight agemates, they are less likely to find mates, be rented apartments, receive financial aid for college, or be offered jobs. And they report frequent mistreatment by family members, peers, co-workers, and health professionals (Ickes, 2011; Puhl, Heuer, & Brownell, 2010). Since the mid-1990s, discrimination experienced by overweight Americans has risen, with serious physical and

mental health consequences that increase the chances that unhealthy eating behaviors will persist and even worsen (Puhl & Heuer, 2010). The widespread but incorrect belief that obesity is a personal choice promotes negative stereotyping of obese persons.

Treatment.

Because obesity climbs in early and middle adulthood, treatment for adults should begin as soon as possible. Even moderate weight loss reduces health problems substantially (Poobalan et al., 2010). But most adults who start a weight-loss program return to their original weight, and often to a higher weight, within two years (Vogels, Diepvens, & Westerterp-Plantenga, 2005). The high rate of failure is partly due to limited evidence on just how obesity disrupts the complex neural, hormonal, and metabolic factors that maintain a normal body-weight set point. Until more information is available, researchers are examining the features of treatments and participants associated with greater success. The following elements promote lasting behavior change:

- *A lifestyle change to a nutritious diet lower in calories, sugar, and fat, plus regular exercise.* To lose weight, Sharese dramatically altered her diet and physical activity in these ways. Although most people believe that only temporary lifestyle changes are needed, research confirms that permanent modifications are essential (MacLean et al., 2011).

- *Training participants to keep an accurate record of food intake and body weight.* About 30 to 35 percent of obese people sincerely believe they eat less than they do. And although they have continued to gain weight, American adults generally report weight losses—suggesting that they are in denial about the seriousness of their weight condition (Wetmore

A permanent lifestyle change that includes an increase in physical activity is essential for treating obesity.

& Mokdad, 2012). As Sharese recognized how often she ate when not actually hungry and regularly recorded her weight, she was better able to limit food intake.

- *Social support.* Group or individual counseling and encouragement from friends and relatives help sustain weight-loss efforts by fostering self-esteem and self-efficacy (Poobalan et al., 2010). Once Sharese decided to act, with the support of her family and a weight-loss counselor, she felt better about herself even before the first pounds were shed.

- *Teaching problem-solving skills.* Most overweight adults do not realize that because their body has adapted to overweight, difficult periods requiring high self-control and patience are inevitable in successful weight loss (MacLean et al., 2011). Weight-loss maintainers are more likely than individuals who relapse to be conscious of their behavior, to use social support, and to confront problems directly.

- *Extended intervention.* Longer treatments (from 25 to 40 weeks) that include the components listed here grant people time to develop new habits.

Dietary Fat. U.S. national dietary recommendations include reducing fat to 30 percent of total caloric intake, with no more than 7 percent made up of saturated fat, which generally comes from meat and dairy products and is solid at room temperature (U.S. Department of Agriculture, 2011a). Many researchers believe that dietary fat plays a role in the age-related rise in breast cancer and (when it includes large amounts of red meat) is linked to colon cancer (Ferguson, 2010; Turner, 2011). But the main reasons for limiting dietary fat are the strong connection of total fat with obesity and of saturated fat with cardiovascular disease (Hooper et al., 2012). Nevertheless, despite a slight drop in fat consumption, most American adults eat too much.

Moderate fat consumption is essential for normal body functioning. But when we consume too much, some is converted to cholesterol, which accumulates as plaque on the arterial walls in atherosclerosis. Earlier in this chapter, we noted that atherosclerosis is determined by multiple biological and environmental factors. But excess fat consumption (along with other societal conditions) is an important contributor to the high rate of heart disease in the U.S. black population. When researchers compared Africans in West Africa, the Caribbean, and the United States (the historic path of the slave trade), dietary fat consumption increased across the three regions, and so did high blood pressure and heart disease (Luke et al., 2001).

The best rule of thumb is to eat less fat of all kinds, replacing saturated fat with unsaturated fat (which is derived from vegetables or fish and is liquid at room temperature) and with complex carbohydrates (whole grains, fruits, and vegetables), which are beneficial to cardiovascular health and protective against colon cancer (Kaczmarczyk, Miller, & Freund, 2012). Furthermore, regular exercise can reduce the harmful influence of saturated fat because it creates chemical byproducts that help eliminate cholesterol from the body.

Exercise

Three times a week, over the noon hour, Sharese delighted in running, making her way to a wooded trail that cut through a picturesque area of the city. Regular exercise kept her fit and slim, and she noticed that she caught fewer respiratory illnesses than in previous years, when she had been sedentary and overweight. As Sharese explained to a friend, "Exercise gives me a positive outlook and calms me down. Afterward, I feel a burst of energy that gets me through the day."

Although most Americans are aware of the health benefits of exercise, over half of Americans are inactive, with no regular brief sessions of even light activity (U.S. Department of Health and Human Services, 2011c). More women than men are inactive. And inactivity is greater among low-SES adults, who live in less safe neighborhoods, have more health problems, experience less social support for exercising regularly, and feel less personal control over their health.

LOOK AND LISTEN

Contact your local parks and recreation department to find out what community supports and services exist to increase adult physical activity. Are any special efforts made to reach low-SES adults? ●

Besides reducing body fat and building muscle, exercise fosters resistance to disease. Frequent bouts of moderate-intensity exercise enhance the immune response, lowering the risk of colds or flu and promoting faster recovery from these illnesses (Donatelle, 2012). Furthermore, animal and human evidence indicates that physical activity is linked to reduced incidence of several types of cancer, with the strongest findings for breast and colon cancer (Anzuini, Battistella, & Izzotti, 2011). Physically active people are also less likely to develop diabetes and cardiovascular disease (Bassuk & Manson, 2005). If they do, these illnesses typically occur later and are less severe than among their inactive agemates.

How does exercise help prevent these serious illnesses? First, it reduces the incidence of obesity—a risk factor for heart disease, diabetes, and cancer. In addition, people who exercise probably adopt other healthful behaviors, thereby lowering the risk of diseases associated with high-fat diets, alcohol consumption, and smoking. Exercise also promotes cardiovascular functioning by strengthening the heart muscle, decreasing blood pressure, and producing a form of "good cholesterol" (high-density lipoproteins, or HDLs) that helps remove "bad cholesterol" (low-density lipoproteins, or LDLs) from the artery walls (Donatelle, 2012).

Yet another way that exercise guards against illness is through its mental health benefits. Physical activity reduces anxiety and depression and improves mood, alertness, and energy. Furthermore, EEG and fMRI evidence indicates that exercise enhances neural activity in the cerebral cortex, and it improves overall cognitive functioning (Carek, Laibstain, & Carek, 2011; Etnier & Labban, 2012). The stress-reducing

LORI ADAMSKI PEEK/STONE/GETTY IMAGES

Regular exercise of at least moderate intensity predicts a healthier, longer life. Participants in this kickboxing class reap both physical and mental health benefits.

properties of exercise undoubtedly strengthen immunity to disease. And as physical activity enhances cognitive functioning and psychological well-being, it promotes on-the-job productivity, self-esteem, ability to cope with stress, and life satisfaction.

How much exercise is recommended for a healthier, happier, and longer life? Moderately intense physical activity—for example, 30 minutes of brisk walking—on most days leads to health benefits for previously inactive people. Adults who exercise at greater intensity—enough to build up a sweat—derive even greater protection (American College of Sports Medicine, 2011). Regular, vigorous exercisers show large reductions in risk of cardiovascular disease, diabetes, colon cancer, and obesity.

Substance Abuse

Eager to try a wide range of experiences before settling down to the responsibilities of adulthood, U.S. 19- to 25-year-olds are more likely than younger or older individuals to smoke cigarettes, chew tobacco, use marijuana, and take stimulants to enhance cognitive or physical performance (U.S. Department of Health and Human Services, 2011d). Binge drinking, driving under the influence, and experimentation with prescription drugs (such as OxyContin, a highly addictive painkiller) and "party drugs" (such as LSD and MDMA, or Ecstasy) also increase, at times with tragic consequences. Risks include brain damage, lasting impairments in mental functioning, and unintentional injury and death (Montoya et al., 2002; National Institute on Drug Abuse, 2012).

Furthermore, when alcohol and drug taking become chronic, they intensify the psychological problems that underlie addiction. As many as 12 percent of 19- to 25-year-old men and 6 percent of women are substance abusers (U.S. Department of Health and Human Services, 2011d). The same personal and situational conditions are predictive in the adult years. Cigarette smoking and alcohol consumption are the most common substance disorders.

Cigarette Smoking. Dissemination of information on the harmful effects of cigarette smoking has helped reduce its prevalence among U.S. adults from 40 percent in 1965 to 19 percent in 2010 (Centers for Disease Control and Prevention, 2012b). Still, smoking has declined very slowly, and most of the drop is among college graduates. Although more men than women smoke, the gender gap is much smaller today than in the past, reflecting a sharp increase in smoking among young women who did not finish high school. Smoking among college students has also risen (U.S. Department of Health and Human Services, 2011d). The earlier people start smoking, the greater their daily cigarette consumption and likelihood of continuing, an important reason that preventive efforts with adolescents and young adults are vital.

The ingredients of cigarette smoke—nicotine, tar, carbon monoxide, and other chemicals—leave their damaging mark throughout the body, in deterioration of the retina of the eye; constriction of blood vessels leading to painful vascular disease; skin abnormalities, including premature aging, poor wound healing, and hair loss; decline in bone mass; decrease in reserve ova, uterine abnormalities, and earlier menopause in women; and reduced sperm count and higher rate of sexual impotence in men (Dechanet et al., 2011; Thornton et al., 2005). Other deadly outcomes include increased risk of heart attack, stroke, acute leukemia, melanoma, and cancer of the mouth, throat, larynx, esophagus, lungs, stomach, pancreas, kidneys, and bladder.

Cigarette smoking is the single most important preventable cause of death in industrialized nations. One out of every three young people who become regular smokers will die from a smoking-related disease, and the vast majority will suffer from at least one serious illness (Adhikari et al., 2009). Benefits of quitting include return of most disease risks to nonsmoker levels within one to ten years. In a study of 1.2 million British women, those who had been regular smokers but stopped before they reached age 45 avoided 90 percent of the elevated risk of premature death from cigarettes (Pirie et al., 2012). And those who quit before age 35 avoided 97 percent of the added risk. Unfortunately, most who try to stop fail (Aveyard & Raw, 2012). Too few treatments last long enough, effectively combine counseling with medications that reduce nicotine withdrawal symptoms, and teach skills for avoiding relapse.

Alcohol. National surveys reveal that about 10 percent of men and 3 percent of women in the United States are heavy drinkers (U.S. Department of Health and Human Services, 2011d). About one-third of them are *alcoholics*—people who cannot limit their alcohol use. In men, alcoholism usually begins in the teens and early twenties and worsens over the following decade. In women, its onset is typically later, in the twenties and thirties, and its course is more variable.

Twin and adoption studies support a genetic contribution to alcoholism. Genes moderating alcohol metabolism and those influencing impulsivity and sensation seeking (temperamental traits linked to alcohol addiction) are involved (Buscemi & Turchi, 2011). But whether a person comes to deal with life's problems through drinking is greatly affected by environment: Half of alcoholics have no family history of problem drinking. Alcoholism crosses SES and ethnic lines but is higher in some groups than others (Schuckit, 2009). In cultures where alcohol is a traditional part of religious or ceremonial activities, people are less likely to abuse it. Where access to alcohol is carefully controlled and viewed as a sign of adulthood, dependency is more likely—factors that may, in part, explain why college students drink more heavily than young people not enrolled in college (Slutske et al., 2004). Poverty, hopelessness, and a history of physical or sexual abuse in childhood are among factors that sharply increase the risk of excessive drinking (Donatelle, 2012; Lown et al., 2011; U.S. Department of Health and Human Services, 2011d).

Alcohol acts as a depressant, impairing the brain's ability to control thought and action. In a heavy drinker, it relieves anxiety at first but then induces it as the effects wear off, so the alcoholic drinks again. The best-known complication of chronic alcohol use is liver disease, but it is also linked to cardiovascular disease, inflammation of the pancreas, irritation of the intestinal tract, bone marrow problems, disorders of the blood and joints, and some forms of cancer. Over time, alcohol causes brain damage, leading to confusion, apathy, inability to learn, and impaired memory (O'Connor, 2012). The costs to society are enormous. About 30 percent of fatal motor vehicle crashes in the United States involve drivers who have been drinking (U.S. Department of Transportation, 2012). About half of police activities in large cities involve alcohol-related offenses (McKim & Hancock, 2013). Alcohol frequently plays a part in sexual coercion, including date rape, and in domestic violence.

The most successful treatments combine personal and family counseling, group support, and aversion therapy (use of

medication that produces a physically unpleasant reaction to alcohol). Nevertheless, breaking an addiction that has dominated a person's life is difficult; about half of alcoholics relapse within a few months (Kirshenbaum, Olsen, & Bickel, 2009).

Sexuality

At the end of high school, about 65 percent of U.S. young people have had sexual intercourse; by age 25, nearly all have done so, and the gender and SES differences that were apparent in adolescence (see page 298 in Chapter 11) have diminished (U.S. Department of Health and Human Services, 2012f). Compared with earlier generations, contemporary adults display a wider range of sexual choices and lifestyles, including cohabitation, marriage, extramarital experiences, and orientation toward a heterosexual or homosexual partner. In this chapter, we explore the attitudes, behaviors, and health concerns that arise as sexual activity becomes a regular event in young people's lives. In Chapter 14, we focus on the emotional side of close relationships.

Heterosexual Attitudes and Behavior. One Friday evening, Sharese accompanied her roommate Heather to a young singles bar, where two young men soon joined them. Faithful to her boyfriend, Ernie, whom she had met in college and who worked in another city, Sharese remained aloof for the next hour. In contrast, Heather was talkative and gave one of the men, Rich, her phone number. The next weekend, Heather went out with Rich. On the second date, they had intercourse, but the romance lasted only a few weeks. Aware of Heather's more adventurous sex life, Sharese wondered whether her own was normal. Only after several months of dating exclusively had she and Ernie slept together.

What are the sexual attitudes and behaviors of contemporary adults? Answers were difficult to find until the National Health and Social Life Survey, the first in-depth study of U.S. adults' sex lives based on a nationally representative sample, was carried out in the early 1990s. Nearly four out of five randomly chosen 18- to 59-year-olds agreed to participate—3,400 in all. Findings were remarkably similar to those of surveys conducted at about the same time in France, Great Britain, and Finland, and to a more recent U.S. survey (Langer, 2004; Laumann et al., 1994; Michael et al., 1994).

Although their sexual practices are diverse, adults in Western nations are far less sexually active than we have come to believe on the basis of widespread display of sexuality in the media. Monogamous, emotionally committed couples like Sharese and Ernie are more typical (and more satisfied) than couples like Heather and Rich.

Sexual partners, whether dating, cohabiting, or married, tend to be similar in age (within five years), education, ethnicity, and (to a lesser extent) religion. In addition, people who establish lasting relationships often meet in conventional ways—through friends or family members, or at school or social events where people similar to themselves congregate. Sustaining an intimate relationship is easier when adults share interests and values and people they know approve of the match.

In cultures where alcohol is a traditional part of religious or ceremonial activities, people are less likely to abuse it. For Jewish families, holiday celebrations, such as this Passover Seder, include blessing and drinking wine.

PHOTO RESEARCHERS/GETTY IMAGES

The Internet is an increasingly popular way to initiate romantic relationships. Here, young people attend a "speed dating" event, organized online, where they have brief conversations with potential partners.

Over the past decade, the Internet has become an increasingly popular way to initiate relationships: In a survey of a nationally representative sample of 4,000 Americans, most of whom were married or in a romantic relationship, 22 percent said they had met on the Internet, making it the second most common way to meet a partner, just behind meeting through friends (Finkel et al., 2012).

Nevertheless, the services of online dating sites sometimes undermine, rather than enhance, the chances of forming a successful romantic relationship. Especially when computer-mediated communication persists for a long time (six weeks or more), people form idealized impressions that often lead to disappointment at face-to-face meetings (Finkel et al., 2012; Ramirez & Zhang, 2007). Furthermore, having a large pool of potential partners from which to choose can promote a persistent "shopping mentality," which reduces online daters' willingness to make a commitment (Heino, Ellison, & Gibbs, 2010). Finally, the techniques that matching sites claim to use to pair partners—sophisticated analyses of information daters provide—have not demonstrated any greater success than conventional off-line means of introducing people.

Consistent with popular belief, Americans today have more sexual partners over their lifetimes than they did a generation ago. For example, one-third of adults over age 50 have had five or more partners, whereas half of 30- to 50-year-olds have accumulated that many in much less time. And although women are more opposed to casual sex then men, after excluding a small number of men (less than 3 percent) with a great many sexual partners, contemporary men and women differ little in average number of lifetime sexual partners (Langer, 2004). Why is this so? From an evolutionary perspective, effective contraception has permitted sexual activity with little risk of pregnancy, enabling women to have as many partners as men without risking the welfare of their offspring.

But when adults of any age are asked how many partners they have had in the past year, the usual reply (for about 70 percent) is one. What explains the trend toward more relationships in the context of sexual commitment? In the past, dating several partners was followed by marriage. Today, dating more often gives way to cohabitation, which leads either to marriage or to breakup. In addition, people are marrying later, and the divorce rate remains high. Together, these factors create more opportunities for new partners. Still, survey evidence indicates that most U.S. 18- to 29-year-olds want to settle down with a mutually exclusive lifetime sexual partner eventually (Arnett, 2012). In line with this goal, most people spend the majority of their lives with one partner.

How often do Americans have sex? Not nearly as frequently as the media suggest. One-third of 18- to 59-year-olds have intercourse as often as twice a week, another third have it a few times a month, and the remaining third have it a few times a year or not at all. Three factors affect frequency of sexual activity: age, whether people are cohabiting or married, and how long the couple has been together. Single people have more partners, but this does not translate into more sex! Sexual activity increases through the twenties and (for men) the thirties as people either cohabit or marry (Herbenick et al., 2010; Langer, 2004). Then it declines, as the demands of daily life—working, commuting, taking care of home and children—intensify.

Most adults say they are happy with their sex lives. For those in committed relationships, more than 80 percent report feeling "extremely physically and emotionally satisfied," a figure that rises to 88 percent for married couples. In contrast, as number of sex partners increases, satisfaction declines sharply. These findings challenge two stereotypes—that marriage is sexually dull and that people who engage in casual dating have the "hottest" sex (Paik, 2010). In actuality, individuals prone to unsatisfying relationships are more likely to prefer "hookups" or "friends with benefits."

A minority of U.S. adults—women more often than men—report persistent sexual problems. For women, the two most frequent difficulties are lack of interest in sex (39 percent) and inability to achieve orgasm (20 percent) (Shifren et al., 2008). Most often mentioned by men are climaxing too early (29 percent) and anxiety about performance (16 percent). Sexual difficulties are linked to low SES and psychological stress and are more common among people who are not married, have had more than five partners, and have experienced sexual abuse during childhood or (for women) sexual coercion in adulthood (Laumann, Paik, & Rosen, 1999). As these findings suggest, a history of unfavorable relationships and sexual experiences increases the risk of sexual dysfunction.

But overall, a completely untroubled physical experience is not essential for sexual happiness. Surveys of adults repeatedly show that satisfying sex involves more than technique; it is attained in the context of love, affection, and fidelity (Bancroft, 2002; Santtila et al., 2008).

Homosexual Attitudes and Behavior. The majority of Americans support civil liberties and equal employment opportunities for gay men, lesbians, and bisexuals. And attitudes toward sex and romantic relationships between adults of

Gay and lesbian romantic partners, like heterosexual partners, tend to be similar in education and background. With greater openness and political activism, attitudes toward same-sex relationships have become more accepting.

the same sex have gradually become more accepting: Nearly half of U.S. adults say same-sex sexual relations are "not wrong at all" or only "sometimes wrong" and support same-sex marriage, and three-fourths favor same-sex civil unions (Pew Research Center, 2013; Smith, 2011b). But the United States lags behind Western Europe in positive attitudes. Nations with greatest acceptance tend to have a greater proportion of highly educated, economically well-off citizens who are low in religiosity (Smith, 2011a).

An estimated 3.5 percent of U.S. men and women—more than 8 million adults—identify as lesbian, gay, or bisexual. Estimates from national surveys conducted in Australia, Canada, and Western Europe tend to be lower, at 1.5 to 2 percent (Gates, 2011). But many people who are gay, lesbian, or bisexual do not report themselves as such in survey research. This unwillingness to answer questions, engendered by a climate of persecution, has limited researchers' access to information about the sex lives of gay men and lesbians. The little evidence available indicates that homosexual sex follows many of the same rules as heterosexual sex: People tend to seek out partners similar in education and background to themselves; partners in committed relationships have sex more often and are more satisfied; and the overall frequency of sex is modest (Laumann et al., 1994; Michael et al., 1994).

Homosexuals tend to live in or near large cities, where many others share their sexual orientation, or in college towns, where attitudes are more accepting. Living in small communities where prejudice is intense and no social network exists through which to find compatible homosexual partners is isolating, lonely, and predictive of mental health problems (Meyer, 2003).

Sexual Coercion. After a long day of classes, Sharese flipped on the TV and caught a talk show on sex without consent. Karen, a 25-year-old woman, described her husband Mike pushing, slapping, verbally insulting, and forcing her to have sex. "It was a control thing," Karen explained tearfully. "He

complained that I wouldn't always do what he wanted. I was confused and blamed myself. I didn't leave because I was sure he'd come after me and get more violent."

One day, as Karen was speaking long distance to her mother on the phone, Mike grabbed the receiver and shouted, "She's not the woman I married! I'll kill her if she doesn't shape up!" Alarmed, Karen's parents arrived by plane the next day to rescue her and helped her start divorce proceedings and get treatment.

An estimated 18 percent of U.S. women, sometime in their lives, have endured *rape,* legally defined as intercourse by force, by threat of harm, or when the victim is incapable of giving consent (because of mental illness, mental retardation, or alcohol consumption). About 45 percent of women have experienced other forms of sexual aggression. The majority of victims (eight out of ten) are under age 30 (Black et al., 2011; Schewe, 2007). Women are vulnerable to partners, acquaintances, and strangers, but in most instances their abusers are men they know well. Sexual coercion crosses SES and ethnic lines; people of all walks of life are offenders and victims.

Personal characteristics of the man with whom a woman is involved are far better predictors of her chances of becoming a victim than her own characteristics. Men who engage in sexual assault tend to be manipulative of others, lack empathy and remorse, pursue casual sexual relationships rather than emotional intimacy, approve of violence against women, and accept rape myths (such as "Women really want to be raped"). Perpetrators also tend to interpret women's social behaviors inaccurately, viewing friendliness as seductiveness, assertiveness as hostility, and resistance as desire (Abbey & Jacques-Tiura, 2011; Abbey & McAuslan, 2004). Furthermore, sexual abuse in childhood, promiscuity in adolescence, and alcohol abuse in adulthood are associated with sexual coercion. Approximately half of all sexual assaults take place while people are intoxicated (Black et al., 2011).

LOOK AND LISTEN

Obtain from your campus student services or police department the number of sexual assaults reported by students during the most recent year. What percentage involved alcohol? What prevention and intervention services does your college offer? ●

Cultural forces also contribute. When men are taught from an early age to be dominant, competitive, and aggressive and women to be submissive and cooperative, the themes of rape are reinforced. Societal acceptance of violence also sets the stage for rape, which typically occurs in relationships in which other forms of aggression are commonplace.

About 7 percent of men have been victims of coercive sexual behavior. Although rape victims report mostly male perpetrators, women are largely responsible for other forms of sexual coercion against men (Black et al, 2011). Victimized men often say that women who committed these acts used threats of physical force or actual force, encouraged them to get drunk, or threatened to end the relationship unless they complied (Anderson & Savage, 2005). Unfortunately, authorities rarely recognize female-initiated forced sex as illegal, and few men report these crimes.

© HARISH TYAGI/EPA/CORBIS

In 2012, in New Delhi, India, the brutal gang rape of a 23-year-old student who died from her injuries prompted protests throughout the country. Participants demanded increased government and police action to prevent sexual violence against women.

Consequences. Psychological reactions to rape resemble those of survivors of extreme trauma. Immediate responses—shock, confusion, withdrawal, and psychological numbing—eventually give way to chronic fatigue, tension, disturbed sleep, depression, substance abuse, social anxiety, and suicidal thoughts (Black et al., 2011; Schewe, 2007). Victims of ongoing sexual coercion may fall into a pattern of extreme passivity and fear.

One-third to one-half of female rape victims are physically injured. From 4 to 30 percent contract sexually transmitted diseases, and pregnancy results in about 5 percent of cases. Furthermore, victims of rape (and other sexual crimes) report more symptoms of illness across almost all body systems. And they are more likely to engage in negative health behaviors, including smoking and alcohol use (McFarlane et al., 2005; Schewe, 2007).

Prevention and Treatment. A variety of community services, including safe houses, crisis hotlines, support groups, and legal assistance, exist to help women take refuge from abusive partners, but most are underfunded and cannot reach out to everyone in need. Practically no services are available for victimized men, who are often too embarrassed to come forward.

The trauma induced by rape is severe enough that therapy is important—both individual treatment to reduce anxiety and depression and group sessions where contact with other survivors helps counter isolation and self-blame (Street, Bell, & Ready, 2011). Other critical features that foster recovery include

- *Routine screening for victimization* during health-care visits to ensure referral to community services and protection from future harm

- *Validation of the experience,* by acknowledging that many others have been physically and sexually assaulted by intimate partners; that such assaults lead to a wide range of persisting symptoms, are illegal and inappropriate, and should not be tolerated; and that the trauma can be overcome

- *Safety planning,* even when the abuser is no longer present, to prevent recontact and reassault.

Finally, many steps can be taken at the level of the individual, the community, and society to prevent sexual coercion. Some are listed in Applying What We Know on the following page.

Psychological Stress

A final health concern, threaded throughout previous sections, has such a broad impact that it merits a comment of its own. Psychological stress, measured in terms of adverse social conditions, traumatic experiences, negative life events, or daily hassles, is related to a wide variety of unfavorable health outcomes—both unhealthy behaviors and clear physical consequences. And recall from earlier chapters that intense, persistent stress, from the prenatal period on, disrupts the brain's inherent ability to manage stress, with long-term consequences.

As SES decreases, exposure to diverse stressors rises—an association that likely plays an important role in the strong connection between low SES and poor health (see page 349) (Chandola & Marmot, 2011). Chronic stress is linked to overweight and obesity, diabetes, hypertension, and atherosclerosis. And in susceptible individuals, acute stress can trigger cardiac events, including heart-beat rhythm abnormalities and heart attacks (Bekkouche et al., 2011; Brooks, McCabe, & Schneiderman, 2011). These relationships contribute to the high incidence of heart disease in low-income groups, especially African Americans. Compared with higher-SES individuals, low-SES adults show a stronger cardiovascular response to stress, perhaps because they more often perceive stressors as unsolvable (Almeida et al., 2005; Carroll et al., 2007). Earlier we mentioned that stress interferes with immune system functioning, a link that may underlie its relationship to cancer. And by reducing digestive activity as blood flows to the brain, heart, and extremities, stress can cause gastrointestinal difficulties, including constipation, diarrhea, colitis, and ulcers (Donatelle, 2012).

The many challenging tasks of early adulthood make it a particularly stressful time of life. Young adults more often report depressive feelings than middle-aged people, many of whom have attained vocational success and financial security and are enjoying more free time as parenting responsibilities decline (Nolen-Hoeksema & Aldao, 2011). Also, as we will see in Chapters 15 and 16, middle-aged and older adults are better than young adults at coping with stress (Blanchard-Fields, Mienaltowski, & Baldi, 2007).

In previous chapters, we repeatedly noted the stress-buffering effect of social support, which continues throughout

Applying **What We Know**

Preventing Sexual Coercion

Suggestion	Description
Reduce gender stereotyping and gender inequalities.	The roots of men's sexual coercion of women lie in the historically subordinate status of women. Unequal educational and employment opportunities keep women economically dependent on men and therefore poorly equipped to avoid partner violence. At the same time, increased public awareness that women sometimes commit sexually aggressive acts is needed.
Mandate treatment for men and women who physically or sexually assault their partners.	Ingredients of effective intervention include combating rape myths and inducing personal responsibility for violent behavior; teaching social awareness, social skills, and anger management; and developing a support system to prevent future attacks.
Expand interventions for children and adolescents who have witnessed violence between their parents.	Although most child witnesses to parental violence do not become involved in abusive relationships as adults, they are at increased risk.
Teach both men and women to take precautions that lower the risk of sexual assault.	Risk of sexual assault can be reduced by communicating sexual limits clearly to a date; developing supportive ties to neighbors; increasing the safety of the immediate environment (for example, installing deadbolt locks, checking the back seat of the car before entering); avoiding deserted areas; not walking alone after dark; and leaving parties where alcohol use is high.
Broaden definitions of rape to be gender-neutral.	In some U.S. states, where the definition of rape is limited to vaginal or anal penetration, a woman legally cannot rape a man. A broader definition is needed to encompass women as both victims and perpetrators of sexual aggression.

Sources: Anderson & Savage, 2005; Schewe, 2007.

life. Helping stressed young adults establish and maintain satisfying, caring social ties is as important a health intervention as any we have mentioned.

ASK YOURSELF

REVIEW Why are people in committed relationships likely to be more sexually active and satisfied than those who are dating several partners?

APPLY Tom had been going to a health club three days a week after work, but job pressures convinced him that he no longer had time for regular exercise. Explain to Tom why he should keep up his exercise regimen, and suggest ways to fit it into his busy life.

REFLECT List three strategies that you can implement now to enhance your health in future decades, noting research that supports the importance of each change in your behavior.

COGNITIVE DEVELOPMENT

The cognitive changes of early adulthood are supported by further development of the prefrontal cortex and its connections with other brain regions. Pruning of synapses along with growth and myelination of stimulated neural fibers continue,

though at a slower pace than in adolescence (Nelson, Thomas, & De Haan, 2006; Zelazo & Lee, 2010). These changes result in continued fine-tuning of the *prefrontal cognitive-control network* (see page 291 in Chapter 11). Consequently, planning, reasoning, and decision making improve, supported by major life events of this period—including attaining higher education, establishing a career, and grappling with the demands of marriage and child rearing. Furthermore, fMRI evidence reveals that as young adults become increasingly proficient in a chosen field of endeavor, regions of the cerebral cortex specialized for those activities undergo further *experience-dependent brain growth* (see page 98 in Chapter 4). Besides more efficient functioning, structural changes occur as greater knowledge and refinement of skills result in more cortical tissue devoted to the task and, at times, reorganization of brain areas governing the activity (Hill & Schneider, 2006; Lenroot & Giedd, 2006).

How does cognition change in early adulthood? Lifespan theorists have examined this question from three familiar vantage points. First, they have proposed transformations in the structure of thought—new, qualitatively distinct ways of thinking that extend the cognitive-developmental changes of adolescence. Second, adulthood is a time of acquiring advanced knowledge in a particular area, an accomplishment that has important implications for information processing and creativity. Finally, researchers have been interested in the extent to which the diverse mental abilities assessed by intelligence tests remain stable or change during the adult years—a topic addressed in Chapter 15.

Changes in the Structure of Thought

Sharese described her first year in graduate school as a "cognitive turning point." As part of her internship in a public health clinic, she observed firsthand the many factors that affect human health-related behaviors. For a time, the realization that everyday dilemmas did not have clear-cut solutions made her intensely uncomfortable. "Working in this messy reality is so different from the problem solving I did in my undergraduate classes," she told her mother over the phone one day.

Piaget (1967) recognized that important advances in thinking follow the attainment of formal operations. He observed that adolescents prefer an idealistic, internally consistent perspective on the world to one that is vague, contradictory, and adapted to particular circumstances (see Chapter 11, page 308). Sharese's reflections fit the observations of researchers who have studied **postformal thought**—cognitive development beyond Piaget's formal operational stage. To clarify how thinking is restructured in adulthood, let's look at some influential theories, along with supportive research. Together, they show how personal effort and social experiences spark increasingly rational, flexible, and practical ways of thinking that accept uncertainties and vary across situations.

Perry's Theory: Epistemic Cognition

The work of William Perry (1981, 1970/1998) provided the starting point for an expanding research literature on the development of *epistemic cognition. Epistemic* means "of or about knowledge," and **epistemic cognition** refers to our reflections on how we arrived at facts, beliefs, and ideas. When mature, rational thinkers reach conclusions that differ from those of others, they consider the justifiability of their conclusions. When they cannot justify their approach, they revise it, seeking a more balanced, adequate route to acquiring knowledge.

Development of Epistemic Cognition. Perry interviewed Harvard University undergraduates at the end of each of their four years, asking "what stood out" during the previous year. Responses indicated that students' reflections on knowing changed as they experienced the complexities of university life and moved closer to adult roles—findings confirmed in many subsequent studies (King & Kitchener, 1994, 2002; Magolda, Abes, & Torres, 2009; Moore, 2002).

Younger students regarded knowledge as made up of separate units (beliefs and propositions), whose truth could be determined by comparing them to objective standards—standards that exist apart from the thinking person and his or her situation. As a result, they engaged in **dualistic thinking,** dividing information, values, and authority into right and wrong, good and bad, we and they. As one college freshman put it, "When I went to my first lecture, what the man said was just like God's word. I believe everything he said because he is a

professor . . . and this is a respected position" (Perry, 1981, p. 81). And when asked, "If two people disagree on the interpretation of a poem, how would you decide which one is right?" a sophomore replied, "You'd have to ask the poet. It's his poem" (Clinchy, 2002, p. 67).

Older students, in contrast, had moved toward **relativistic thinking,** viewing all knowledge as embedded in a framework of thought. Aware of a diversity of opinions on many topics, they gave up the possibility of absolute truth in favor of multiple truths, each relative to its context. As a result, their thinking became more flexible and tolerant. As one college senior put it, "Just seeing how [famous philosophers] fell short of an all-encompassing answer, [you realize] that ideas are really individualized. And you begin to have respect for how great their thought could be, without its being absolute" (Perry, 1970/1998, p. 90).

Eventually, the most mature individuals progress to **commitment within relativistic thinking.** Instead of choosing between opposing views, they try to formulate a more personally satisfying perspective that synthesizes contradictions. When considering which of two theories studied in a college course is better, or which of several movies most deserves an Oscar, the individual moves beyond the stance that everything is a matter of opinion and generates rational criteria against which options can be evaluated (Moshman, 2003, 2005). By the end of the college years, some students reach this extension of relativism. Adults who attain it generally display a more sophisticated approach to learning, in which they actively seek differing perspectives to deepen their knowledge and understanding and to clarify the basis for their own perspective.

Importance of Peer Interaction and Reflection. Advances in epistemic cognition depend on further gains in metacognition, which are likely to occur in situations that challenge young peoples' perspectives and induce them to consider

When college students challenge one another's reasoning while tackling realistic, ambiguous problems, they are likely to gain in epistemic cognition.

the rationality of their thought processes (Magolda, Abes, & Torres, 2009). In a study of the college learning experiences of seniors scoring low and high in epistemic cognition, high-scoring students frequently reported activities that encouraged them to struggle with realistic but ambiguous problems in a supportive environment, in which faculty offered encouragement and guidance. For example, an engineering major, describing an airplane-design project that required advanced epistemic cognition, noted his discovery that "you can design 30 different airplanes and each one's going to have its benefits and there's going to be problems with each one" (Marra & Palmer, 2004, p. 116). Low-scoring students rarely mentioned such experiences.

In tackling challenging, ill-structured problems, interaction among individuals who are roughly equal in knowledge and authority is beneficial because it prevents acceptance of another's reasoning simply because of greater power or expertise. When college students were asked to devise the most effective solution to a difficult logical problem, only 3 out of 32 students (9 percent) in a "work alone" condition succeeded. But in an "interactive" condition, 15 out of 20 small groups (75 percent) arrived at the correct solution following extensive discussion (Moshman & Geil, 1998). Most groups engaged in a process of "collective rationality" in which members challenged one another to justify their reasoning and collaborated in working out the most defensible strategy.

Of course, reflection on one's own thinking can also occur individually. But peer interaction fosters the necessary type of individual reflection: arguing with oneself over competing ideas and strategies and coordinating opposing perspectives into a new, more effective structure. *TAKE A MOMENT...* Return to page 251 in Chapter 9 to review how peer collaboration fosters cognitive development in childhood. It remains a highly effective basis for education in early adulthood.

LOOK AND LISTEN

Describe learning experiences in one of your college courses that advanced your epistemic cognition. How did your thinking change? ●

Labouvie-Vief's Theory: Pragmatic Thought and Cognitive-Affective Complexity

Gisella Labouvie-Vief's (1980, 1985) portrait of adult cognition echoes features of Perry's theory. Adolescents, she points out, operate within a world of possibility. Adulthood involves movement from hypothetical to **pragmatic thought**, a structural advance in which logic becomes a tool for solving real-world problems.

According to Labouvie-Vief, the need to specialize motivates this change. As adults select one path out of many alternatives, they become more aware of the constraints of everyday life. And in the course of balancing various roles, they accept contradictions as part of existence and develop ways of thinking that thrive on imperfection and compromise. Sharese's friend

Christy, a married graduate student and parent of her first child at age 26, illustrates:

> I've always been a feminist, and I wanted to remain true to my beliefs in family and career. But this is Gary's first year of teaching high school, and he's saddled with four preparations and coaching the school's basketball team. At least for now, I've had to settle for "give-and-take feminism"—going to school part-time and shouldering most of the child-care responsibilities while he gets used to his new job. Otherwise, we'd never make it financially.

Labouvie-Vief (2003, 2006) also points out that young adults' enhanced reflective capacities alter the dynamics of their emotional lives: They become more adept at integrating cognition with emotion and, in doing so, again make sense of discrepancies. Examining the self-descriptions of 10- to 80-year-olds diverse in SES, Labouvie-Vief found that from adolescence through middle adulthood, people gained in **cognitive-affective complexity**—awareness of conflicting positive and negative feelings and coordination of them into a complex, organized structure that recognizes the uniqueness of individual experiences (see Figure 13.4) (Labouvie-Vief, 2008; Labouvie-Vief et al., 1995, 2007). For example, one 34-year-old combined roles, traits, and diverse emotions into this coherent self-description: "With the recent birth of our first child, I find myself more fulfilled than ever, yet struggling in some ways. My elation is tempered by my gnawing concern over meeting all my responsibilities in a satisfying way while remaining an individualized person with needs and desires."

Cognitive-affective complexity promotes greater awareness of one's own and others' perspectives and motivations. As

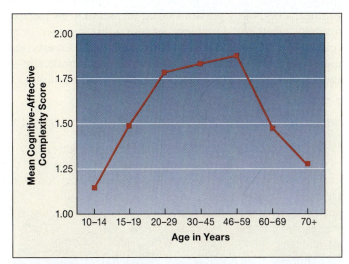

FIGURE 13.4 Changes in cognitive-affective complexity from adolescence to late adulthood. Performance, based on responses of several hundred 10- to 80-year-olds' descriptions of their roles, traits, and emotions, increased steadily from adolescence through early adulthood, peaked in middle age, and fell off in late adulthood when (as we will see in later chapters) basic information-processing skills decline. (From G. Labouvie-Vief, 2003, "Dynamic Integration: Affect, Cognition, and the Self in Adulthood," *Current Directions in Psychological Science, 12,* p. 203, copyright © 2003, Sage Publications. Reprinted by permission of SAGE Publications.)

Labouvie-Vief (2003) notes, it is valuable in solving many pragmatic problems. Individuals high in cognitive-affective complexity view events and people in a tolerant, open-minded fashion. And because cognitive-affective complexity involves accepting and making sense of both positive and negative feelings, it helps people regulate intense emotion and, therefore, think rationally about real-world dilemmas (Labouvie-Vief, Grühn, & Studer, 2010). As we will see next, adults' increasingly specialized and context-bound thought, although it closes off certain options, opens new doors to higher levels of competence.

Expertise and Creativity

In Chapter 9, we noted that children's expanding knowledge improves their ability to remember new information related to what they already know. For young adults, **expertise—acquisition of extensive knowledge in a field or endeavor—**is supported by the specialization that begins with selecting a college major or an occupation, since it takes many years to master any complex domain. Once attained, expertise has a profound impact on information processing.

Compared with novices, experts remember and reason more quickly and effectively. The expert knows more domain-specific concepts and represents them in richer ways—at a deeper and more abstract level and as having more features that can be linked to other concepts. As a result, unlike novices, whose understanding is superficial, experts approach problems with underlying principles in mind. For example, a highly trained physicist notices when several problems deal with conservation of energy and can therefore be solved similarly. In contrast, a beginning physics student focuses only on surface features—whether the problem contains a disk, a pulley, or a coiled spring (Chi, 2006; Chi, Glaser, & Farr, 1988). Experts can use what they know to arrive at many solutions automatically—through quick and easy remembering. And when a problem is

A sculptor works on a statue to honor those who died in the Asian tsunami of 2004. The creative products of adulthood often are not just original but also directed at a social or aesthetic need.

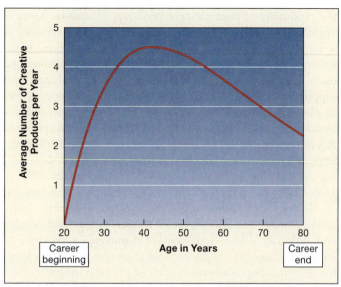

FIGURE 13.5 **Changes in creative productivity during adulthood.** Productivity typically rises over early adulthood and then declines, though creative older adults continue to produce more than adults just starting their careers. (Adapted from Simonton, 2012.)

challenging, they tend to plan ahead, systematically analyzing and categorizing elements and selecting the best from many possibilities, while the novice proceeds more by trial and error.

Expertise is necessary for creativity (Weissberg, 2006). Mature creativity requires a unique cognitive capacity—the ability to formulate new, culturally meaningful problems and to ask significant questions that have not been posed before. Case studies support the 10-year rule in development of master-level creativity—a decade between initial exposure to a field and sufficient expertise to produce a creative work (Simonton, 2000; Winner, 2003). Furthermore, a century of research reveals that creative productivity typically rises in early adulthood, peaks in the late thirties or early forties, and gradually declines, though creative individuals near the end of their careers are usually more productive than those just starting their careers (see Figure 13.5) (Simonton, 2012). But exceptions exist. Those who get an early start in creativity tend to peak and drop off sooner, whereas "late bloomers" reach their full stride at older ages. This suggests that creativity is more a function of "career age" than of chronological age.

The course of creativity also varies across disciplines (Simonton, 2006, 2012). For example, poets, visual artists, and musicians typically show an early rise in creativity, perhaps because they do not need extensive formal education before they begin to produce. Academic scholars and scientists, who must earn higher academic degrees and spend years doing research to make worthwhile contributions, tend to display their achievements later and over a longer time.

Though creativity is rooted in expertise, it also requires other qualities. A vital ingredient is an innovative thinking style. In one study, college students who preferred to think intuitively (rely on "first impression") were told to solve a real-world problem using a rational approach (be as "analytical" as possible)

(Dane et al., 2011). Compared to controls who used their natural style, students required to use a style that differed sharply from their typical approach—who thought "outside the box"—generated many more creative ideas. Creative individuals are also tolerant of ambiguity, open to new experiences, persistent and driven to succeed, and willing to try again after failure (Lubart, 2003; Zhang & Sternberg, 2011). Finally, creativity demands time and energy. For women especially, it may be postponed or disrupted by child rearing, divorce, or an unsupportive partner (Vaillant & Vaillant, 1990).

In sum, creativity is multiply determined. When personal and situational factors jointly promote it, creativity can continue for many decades, well into old age.

ASK YOURSELF

REVIEW How does expertise affect information processing? Why is expertise necessary for, but not the same as, creativity?

APPLY For her human development course, Marcia wrote a paper discussing the differing implications of Piaget's and Vygotsky's theories for education. Next, she reasoned that combining the two perspectives is more effective than relying on either position by itself. Explain how Marcia's reasoning illustrates advanced epistemic cognition.

REFLECT Describe a classroom experience or assignment in one of your college courses that promoted relativistic thinking.

 ## The College Experience

Looking back at the trajectory of their lives, many people view the college years as formative—more influential than any other period of adulthood. This is not surprising. College serves as a "developmental testing ground," a time for devoting full attention to exploring alternative values, roles, and behaviors. To facilitate this exploration, college exposes students to a form of "culture shock"—encounters with new ideas and beliefs, new freedoms and opportunities, and new academic and social demands. More than 70 percent of U.S. high school graduates enroll in an institution of higher education (U.S. Department of Education, 2012b). Besides offering a route to a high-status career and its personal and monetary rewards, colleges and universities have a transforming impact on young people.

Psychological Impact of Attending College

Thousands of studies reveal broad psychological changes from the freshman to the senior year of college (Montgomery & Côté, 2003; Pascarella & Terenzini, 1991, 2005). As research inspired by Perry's theory indicates, students become better at reasoning about problems that have no clear solution, identifying the

Community college students join in a Peace Week activity, keeping pace with the beat of a drum circle. The more students interact with diverse peers in academic and extracurricular settings, the more they benefit cognitively from attending college.

strengths and weaknesses of opposing sides of complex issues, and reflecting on the quality of their thinking. Their attitudes and values also broaden. They show increased interest in literature, the performing arts, and philosophical and historical issues and greater tolerance for racial and ethnic diversity. Also, as noted in Chapter 12, college leaves its mark on moral reasoning by fostering concern with individual rights and human welfare, sometimes expressed in political activism. Finally, exposure to multiple worldviews encourages young people to look more closely at themselves. During the college years, students develop greater self-understanding, enhanced self-esteem, and a firmer sense of identity.

The more students interact with diverse peers in academic and extracurricular settings, the more they benefit cognitively—in grasping the complex causes of events, thinking critically, and generating effective problem solutions (Bowman, 2011a). Also, interacting with racially and ethnically mixed peers—both in courses exploring diversity issues and in out-of-class settings—predicts gains in civic engagement. And students who connect their community service experiences with their classroom learning show large cognitive gains (Bowman, 2011b). These findings underscore the importance of programs that integrate commuting students into out-of-class campus life.

Dropping Out

Completing a college education has enduring effects on people's cognitive development, worldview, and postcollege opportunities. In the 1970s, the United States ranked first in the world in percentage of young adults with college degrees; today it is sixteenth, with just 41 percent of 25- to 34-year-olds having graduated. It lags far behind such countries as Canada, Japan, and South Korea, the global leader—where the rate is 63 percent (OECD, 2012a). Major contributing factors are the high U.S. child poverty rate, poor-quality elementary and secondary schools in low-income neighborhoods, and the high rate of high school dropout

© ST. PETERSBURG TIMES/BRENDAN FITTERER/THE IMAGE WORKS

among teenagers. College leaving is also influential: 44 percent of U.S. students at two-year institutions and 32 percent of students at four-year institutions drop out, most within the first year and many within the first six weeks (ACT, 2010). Dropout rates are higher in colleges with less selective admission requirements. And ethnic minority students from low-SES families are, once again, at increased risk of dropping out.

Both personal and institutional factors contribute to college leaving. First-year students who have trouble adapting—because of lack of motivation, poor study skills, financial pressures, or emotional dependence on parents—quickly develop negative attitudes toward the college environment. Often these exit-prone students do not meet with their advisers or professors. At the same time, colleges that do little to help high-risk students, through developmental courses and other support services, have a higher percentage of dropouts (Moxley, Najor-Durack, & Dumbrigue, 2001).

Reaching out to students, especially during the early weeks and throughout the first year, is crucial. Programs that forge bonds between teachers and students and that provide academic support, part-time work opportunities, and meaningful extracurricular roles increase retention. Membership in campus-based social and religious organizations is especially helpful in strengthening minority students' sense of belonging (Chen, 2012). Young people who feel that their college community is concerned about them as individuals are far more likely to graduate.

Vocational Choice

Young adults, college-bound or not, face a major life decision: the choice of a suitable work role. What influences young people's decisions about careers? What is the transition from school to work like, and what factors make it easy or difficult?

Selecting a Vocation

In societies with an abundance of career possibilities, occupational choice is a gradual process that begins early. Major theorists view the young person as moving through several periods of vocational development (Gottfredson, 2005; Super, 1990, 1994):

1. The **fantasy period:** In early and middle childhood, children gain insight into career options by fantasizing about them (Howard & Walsh, 2010). Their preferences, guided largely by familiarity and excitement, bear little relation to the decisions they will eventually make.
2. The **tentative period:** Between ages 11 and 16, adolescents think about careers in more complex ways, at first in terms of their *interests,* and soon—as they become more aware of personal and educational requirements for different vocations—in terms of their *abilities* and *values.* "I like science and the process of discovery," Sharese thought as she

neared high school graduation. "But I'm also good with people, and I'd like to do something to help others. So maybe teaching or medicine would suit my needs."

3. The **realistic period:** By the late teens and early twenties, with the economic and practical realities of adulthood just around the corner, young people start to narrow their options. A first step is often further *exploration*—gathering more information about possibilities that blend with their personal characteristics. In the final phase, *crystallization,* they focus on a general vocational category and experiment for a time before settling on a single occupation (Stringer, Kerpelman, & Skorikov, 2011). As a college sophomore, Sharese pursued her interest in science, but she had not yet selected a major. Once she decided on chemistry, she considered whether to pursue teaching, medicine, or public health.

Factors Influencing Vocational Choice

Most, but not all, young people follow this pattern of vocational development. A few know from an early age just what they want to be and follow a direct path to a career goal. Some decide and later change their minds, and still others remain undecided for an extended period. College students are granted added time to explore various options. In contrast, the life conditions of many low-SES youths restrict their range of choices.

Making an occupational choice is not simply a rational process in which young people weigh abilities, interests, and values against career options. Like other developmental milestones, it is the result of a dynamic interaction between person and environment (Gottfredson & Duffy, 2008).

Personality. People are attracted to occupations that complement their personalities. John Holland (1985, 1997) identified six personality types that affect vocational choice:

- The *investigative person,* who enjoys working with ideas, is likely to select a scientific occupation (for example, anthropologist, physicist, or engineer).
- The *social person,* who likes interacting with people, gravitates toward human services (counseling, social work, or teaching).
- The *realistic person,* who prefers real-world problems and working with objects, tends to choose a mechanical occupation (construction, plumbing, or surveying).
- The *artistic person,* who is emotional and high in need for individual expression, looks toward an artistic field (writing, music, or the visual arts).
- The *conventional person,* who likes well-structured tasks and values material possessions and social status, has traits well-suited to certain business fields (accounting, banking, or quality control).
- The *enterprising person,* who is adventurous, persuasive, and a strong leader, is drawn to sales and supervisory positions or to politics.

These lab technicians, who entered the workforce during the late-2000s recession, prepare DNA samples for analysis. They chose a career with greater employment opportunities than in many other professions.

TAKE A MOMENT... Does one of these personality types describe you? Or do you have aspects of more than one type? Research confirms a relationship between personality and vocational choice in diverse cultures, but it is only moderate. Many people are blends of several personality types and can do well at more than one kind of occupation (Holland, 1997; Spokane & Cruza-Guet, 2005).

Furthermore, career decisions are made in the context of family influences, financial resources, educational and job opportunities, and current life circumstances. For example, Sharese's friend Christy scored high on Holland's investigative dimension. But after she married, had her first child, and faced increasing financial pressures, she postponed her dream of becoming a college professor and chose a human services career that required fewer years of education. During the late-2000s recession, which substantially increased unemployment among new college graduates, increasing numbers of U.S. college students chose to major in business, physical or biological sciences, health professions, or computer science, where the chances of securing a job—particularly a better-paying one—were greatest (U.S. Department of Education, 2012b).

Family Influences. Individuals who grew up in higher-SES homes are more likely to select high-status, white-collar occupations, such as doctor, lawyer, scientist, or engineer. In contrast, those with lower-SES backgrounds tend to choose less prestigious, blue-collar careers—for example, plumber, construction worker, food service employee, or office worker. Parent–child vocational similarity is partly a function of similarity in personality, intellectual abilities, and—especially—educational attainment (Ellis & Bonin, 2003; Schoon & Parsons, 2002). Years of schooling completed powerfully predict occupational status.

Other factors also promote family resemblance in occupational choice. Higher-SES parents are more likely to give their children important information about the worlds of education and work and to have connections with people who can help the young person obtain a high-status position (Kalil, Levine, & Ziol-Guest, 2005). Parenting practices also shape work-related preferences. Recall from Chapter 2 that higher-SES parents tend to promote curiosity and self-direction, which are required in many high-status careers. Still, all parents can foster higher aspirations. Parental guidance, pressure to do well in school, and encouragement toward high-status occupations predict career attainment beyond SES (Bryant, Zvonkovic, & Reynolds, 2006; Stringer & Kerpelman, 2010).

Teachers. Young adults preparing for or engaged in careers requiring extensive education often report that teachers influenced their choice (Bright et al., 2005; Reddin, 1997). College-bound high school students tend to have closer relationships with teachers than do other students—relationships that are especially likely to foster high career aspirations in young women (Wigfield et al., 2002). These findings provide yet another reason to promote positive teacher–student relations, especially for high school students from low-SES families. Teachers who offer encouragement and act as role models can serve as an important source of resilience for these young people.

Gender Stereotypes. Over the past four decades, young women have expressed increasing interest in occupations largely held by men (Gottfredson, 2005). Changes in gender-role attitudes, along with a dramatic rise in numbers of employed mothers who serve as career-oriented models for their daughters, are common explanations for women's attraction to nontraditional careers.

But women's progress in entering and excelling at male-dominated professions has been slow. As Table 13.2 on page 364 shows, although the percentage of women engineers, lawyers, doctors, and business executives has increased in the United States over the past quarter-century, it still falls far short of equal representation. Women remain concentrated in less-well-paid, traditionally feminine professions such as writing, social work, education, and nursing (U.S. Census Bureau, 2013). In virtually all fields, their achievements lag behind those of men, who write more books, make more discoveries, hold more positions of leadership, and produce more works of art.

Ability cannot account for these dramatic sex differences. In elementary and secondary school, girls are advantaged in reading and writing achievement, and the gender gap favoring boys in math is small (Halpern, 2004; Halpern, Wai, & Saw, 2005). Rather, gender-stereotyped messages play a key role. Although girls earn higher grades than boys, they reach secondary school less confident of their abilities, more likely to underestimate their achievement, and less likely to express interest in STEM careers (Ceci & Williams, 2010; Parker et al., 2012).

In college, the career aspirations of many women decline further as they question their capacity and opportunities to succeed in male-dominated fields and worry about combining a highly demanding career with family responsibilities (Chhin,

TABLE 13.2 Percentage of Women in Various Professions in the United States, 1983 and 2011

PROFESSION	1983	2011
Architect or engineer	5.8	12.9
Lawyer	15.8	31.5
Doctor	15.8	32.3
Business executive	32.4	38.2[a]
Author, artist, entertainer	42.7	46.2
Social worker	64.3	80.8
Elementary or middle school teacher	93.5	81.8
Secondary school teacher	62.2	57.0
College or university professor	36.3	45.9
Librarian	84.4	82.8
Registered nurse	95.8	91.1
Psychologist	57.1	66.7

Source: U.S. Census Bureau, 2013.

[a]This percentage includes executives and managers at all levels. As of 2011, women made up only 4 percent of chief executive officers at Fortune 500 companies, although that figure represents more than 2½ times as many as in 2003.

Bleeker, & Jacobs, 2008; Wigfield et al., 2006). In a recent study, science professors at a broad sample of U.S. universities were sent an undergraduate student's application for a lab manager position. For half, the application bore a male name; for the other half, a female name (Moss-Racusin et al., 2012). Professors of both genders viewed the female student as less competent, less deserving of mentoring, and meriting a lower salary, though her accomplishments were identical to those of the male! In line with these findings, many mathematically talented college women settle on nonscience majors. And those who remain in the sciences more often choose medicine or another health profession and less often choose engineering or a math or physical science career than their male counterparts (Robertson et al., 2010).

These findings reveal a pressing need for programs that sensitize educators to the special problems women face in developing and maintaining high vocational aspirations and selecting nontraditional careers. Supportive relationships with women scientists and engineers enhance female students' interest in and expectancies for success in STEM fields (Holdren & Lander, 2012). And such mentoring may help them see how altruistic values—which are particularly important to females—can be fulfilled within STEM occupations.

Compared to women, men have changed little in their interest in nontraditional occupations. See the Social Issues: Education box on the following page for research on the motivations and experiences of men who do choose female-dominated careers.

Vocational Preparation of Non-College-Bound Young Adults

Sharese's younger brother Leon graduated from high school in a vocational track. Like approximately one-third of U.S. young people with a high school diploma, he had no current plans to go to college. He hoped to work in data processing after graduation, but six months later he was still a part-time sales clerk at a candy store. Although Leon had filled out many job applications, he got no interviews or offers.

Leon's inability to find a job other than the one he held as a student is typical for U.S. non-college-bound high school graduates. Although they are more likely to find employment than youths who drop out, they have fewer work opportunities than high school graduates of several decades ago. With rising unemployment during the late-2000s recession, these conditions worsened as entry-level positions went to the large pool of available college graduates. About 30 percent of recent U.S. high school graduates who do not continue their education are unemployed (Shierholz, Sabadish, & Wething, 2012). When they do find work, most hold low-paid, unskilled jobs. In addition, they have few alternatives for vocational counseling and job placement as they transition from school to work.

American employers regard recent high school graduates as unprepared for skilled business and industrial occupations and manual trades. And there is some truth to this impression. Unlike European nations, the United States has no widespread training system for non-college-bound youths. As a result, most graduate without work-related skills and experience a "floundering period" that lasts for several years.

In Germany, young people who do not go to a Gymnasium (college-preparatory high school) have access to one of the most successful work–study apprenticeship systems in the world for entering business and industry. About two-thirds of German youths participate. After completing full-time schooling at age 15 or 16, they spend the remaining two years of compulsory education in the Berufsschule, combining part-time vocational courses with an apprenticeship that is jointly planned by educators and employers (Deissinger, 2007). Apprentices who complete the program and pass a qualifying examination are certified as skilled workers and earn union-set wages. Businesses provide financial support because they know that the program guarantees a competent, dedicated work force (Kerckhoff, 2002). Many apprentices are hired into well-paid jobs by the firms that train them.

The success of the German system—and of similar systems in Austria, Denmark, Switzerland, and several East European countries—suggests that a national apprenticeship program would improve the transition from high school to work for U.S. young people. The many benefits of bringing together the worlds of schooling and work include helping non-college-bound young people establish productive lives right after uation, motivating at-risk youths to stay in school, and c ing to the nation's economic growth. Nevertheless, i an apprenticeship system poses major challe

Social Issues: Education

Masculinity at Work: Men Who Choose Nontraditional Careers

Ross majored in engineering through his sophomore year of college, when he startled his family and friends by switching to nursing. "I've never looked back," Ross said. "I love the work." He noted some benefits of being a male in a female work world, including rapid advancement and the high regard of women colleagues. "But as soon as they learn what I do," Ross remarked with disappointment, "guys on the outside question my abilities and masculinity."

What factors influence the slowly increasing number of men who, like Ross, enter careers dominated by women? Compared to their traditional-career counterparts, these men are more liberal in their social attitudes, less gender-typed, less focused on the social status of their work, and more interested in working with people (Dodson & Borders, 2006; Jome, Surething, & Taylor, 2005). Perhaps their gender-stereotype flexibility allows them to choose occupations they find satisfying, even if those jobs are not typically regarded as appropriate for men. In one investigation, 40 men who were primary school teachers, nurses, airline stewards, or librarians, when asked how they arrived at their choice, described diverse pathways (Simpson, 2005). Some actively sought the career, others happened on it while exploring possibilities, and still others first spent time in another occupation (usu-

ally male-dominated), found it unsatisfying, and then settled into their current career.

The men also confirmed Ross's observations: Because of their male minority status, co-workers often assumed they were more knowledgeable than they actually were. They also had opportunities to move quickly into supervisory positions, although many did not seek advancement (Simpson, 2004). As one teacher commented, "I just want to be a good classroom teacher. What's wrong with that?" Furthermore, while in training and on the job, virtually all the men reported feeling socially accepted—relaxed and comfortable working with women.

But when asked to reflect on how others reacted to their choice, many men expressed anxiety about being stigmatized by other men. To reduce these feelings, the men frequently described their job in ways that minimized its feminine image. Several librarians emphasized technical requirements by referring to their title as "information scientist" or "researcher." The nurses sometimes distanced themselves from a feminine work identity by specializing in "adrenaline-charged" areas such as accident or emergency.

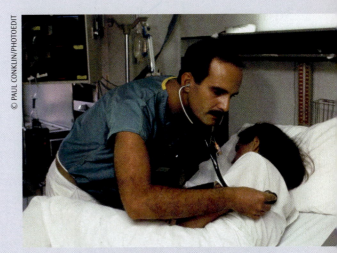

This nurse exemplifies the increasing number of men entering careers dominated by women. Compared with his traditional-career counterparts, he is likely to be less gender-typed and more interested in working with people.

Like their female counterparts, men face certain barriers in preparing for nontraditional careers. For example, male students in college nursing programs often mention lack of male mentors and a "cooler" educational climate, which they attribute to subtle gender discrimination and unsupportive behaviors of women nurse educators (Bell-Scriber, 2008; Meadus & Twomey, 2011). To facilitate entry into nontraditional careers, men, too, would benefit from supportive relationships with same-gender role models and an end to faculty gender-biased beliefs and behaviors.

the reluctance of employers to assume part of the responsibility for vocational training, ensuring cooperation between schools and businesses, and preventing low-SES youths from being concentrated in the lowest-skilled apprenticeship placements, an obstacle that Germany itself has not yet fully overcome (Lang, 2010). Currently, small-scale school-to-work projects in the United States are attempting to solve these problems and build bridges between learning and working.

Although vocational development is a lifelong process, adolescence and early adulthood are crucial periods for defining occupational goals and launching a career. The support of families, schools, businesses, communities, and society as a whole can contribute greatly to a positive outcome. In Chapter 14, we will take up the challenges of establishing a career and integrating it with other life tasks.

ASK YOURSELF

REVIEW What student and college-environment characteristics contribute to favorable psychological changes during the college years?

APPLY Diane, a college freshman, knows that she wants to "work with people" but doesn't yet have a specific career in mind. Diane's father is a chemistry professor, her mother a social worker. What steps can Diane's parents take to help her focus on an occupational goal?

REFLECT Describe personal and environmental influences on your progress in choosing a vocation.

SUMMARY

PHYSICAL DEVELOPMENT

Biological Aging Is Under Way in Early Adulthood (p. 343)

Describe current theories of biological aging, both at the level of DNA and body cells and at the level of tissues and organs.

- Once body structures reach maximum capacity and efficiency in the teens and twenties, **biological aging,** or **senescence,** begins.

- The programmed effects of specific genes may control certain age-related biological changes. For example, **telomere** shortening results in senescent cells, which contribute to disease and loss of function.

- DNA may also be damaged as random mutations accumulate, leading to less efficient cell repair and replacement and to abnormal cancerous cells. Release of **free radicals** is a possible cause of age-related DNA and cellular damage.

- The **cross-linkage theory of aging** suggests that over time, protein fibers form links and become less elastic, producing negative changes in many organs. Declines in the endocrine and immune systems may also contribute to aging.

Physical Changes (p. 346)

Describe the physical changes of aging, paying special attention to the cardiovascular and respiratory systems, motor performance, the immune system, and reproductive capacity.

- Gradual physical changes take place in early adulthood and later accelerate. Declines in heart and lung performance are evident during exercise. Heart disease is a leading cause of death in adults, although it has decreased since the mid-twentieth century.

- Athletic skills requiring speed, strength, and gross-motor coordination peak in the early twenties; those requiring endurance, arm–hand steadiness, and aiming peak in the late twenties and early thirties. Less active lifestyles rather than biological aging are largely responsible for age-related declines in motor performance.

- The immune response declines after age 20 because of shrinkage of the thymus gland and increased difficulty coping with physical and psychological stress.

- Women's reproductive capacity declines with age due to reduced quality and quantity of ova. In men, semen volume and sperm quality decrease gradually after age 35.

Health and Fitness (p. 349)

Describe the impact of SES, nutrition, and exercise on health, and discuss obesity in adulthood.

- SES is strongly related to almost every health indicator. Diverse health-related circumstances and habits are responsible.

- Today, Americans are the heaviest people in the world. Some weight gain in adulthood reflects a decrease in **basal metabolic rate (BMR),** but many young adults show large increases because of sedentary lifestyles and diets high in sugar and fat.

- Regular exercise reduces body fat, builds muscle, helps prevent disease, and enhances psychological well-being. Health benefits increase with greater intensity of exercise.

What are the two most commonly abused substances, and what health risks do they pose?

- Cigarette smoking and alcohol consumption are the two most common substance abuses. Smokers, most of whom began before age 21, are at increased risk for many health problems, including decline in bone mass, heart attack, stroke, and numerous cancers.

- About one-third of heavy drinkers suffer from alcoholism, to which both heredity and environment contribute. Alcohol is implicated in liver and cardiovascular disease, certain cancers and other physical disorders, highway fatalities, crime, and sexual coercion.

Describe sexual attitudes and behavior of young adults, and discuss sexually transmitted diseases and sexual coercion.

- Most adults are less sexually active than media images suggest, but they display a wider range of sexual choices and lifestyles and have had more sexual partners than earlier generations. The Internet has become a popular way to initiate relationships.

- Adults in committed relationships report high satisfaction with their sex lives. Only a minority report persistent sexual problems—difficulties linked to low SES and psychological stress.

- Attitudes toward same-sex couples have become more accepting. Homosexual relationships, like heterosexual relationships, are characterized by similarity between partners in education and background, greater satisfaction in committed relationships, and modest frequency of sexual activity.

- Most rape victims have been harmed by men they know well. Men who commit sexual assault typically support traditional gender roles, approve of violence against women, accept rape myths, and misinterpret women's social behaviors. Female-initiated coercive sexual behavior also occurs but is less often reported and recognized by authorities.

How does psychological stress affect health?

- Chronic psychological stress induces physical responses that contribute to heart disease, several types of cancer, and gastrointestinal problems. Because the challenges of early adulthood make it a highly stressful time of life, interventions that help stressed young people form supportive social ties are especially important.

COGNITIVE DEVELOPMENT

Changes in the Structure of Thought (p. 358)

Explain how thinking changes in early adulthood.

- Development of the cerebral cortex in early adulthood results in continued fine-tuning of the prefrontal cognitive-control network, contributing to improvements in planning, reasoning, and decision making.

- Cognitive development beyond Piaget's formal operations is known as **postformal thought.** In Perry's theory of **epistemic cognition,** college students move from **dualistic thinking,** dividing information into right and wrong, to **relativistic thinking,** awareness of multiple truths. The most mature individuals progress to **commitment within relativistic thinking,** which synthesizes contradictions.

- Advances in epistemic cognition depend on gains in metacognition. Peer collaboration on challenging, ill-structured problems is especially beneficial.

- In Labouvie-Vief's theory, the need to specialize motivates adults to move from hypothetical to **pragmatic thought,** which uses logic as a tool for solving real-world problems. Adults' enhanced reflective capacities permit gains in **cognitive-affective complexity**— coordination of positive and negative feelings into a complex, organized structure.

Expertise and Creativity (p. 360)

What roles do expertise and creativity play in adult thought?

- Specialization in college and in an occupation leads to **expertise,** which is necessary for both problem solving and creativity. Although creativity tends to rise in early adulthood and to peak in the late thirties or early forties, its development varies across disciplines and individuals. Diverse personal and situational factors jointly promote creativity.

© BORDERLANDS/ALAMY

The College Experience (p. 361)

Describe the impact of a college education on young people's lives, and discuss the problem of dropping out.

- College students' explorations, both academic and nonacademic, yield gains in knowledge and reasoning ability, broadening of attitudes and values, enhanced self-understanding and self-esteem, and a firmer sense of identity.

- Personal and institutional factors contribute to college dropout, which is more common in less selective colleges and among ethnic minority students from low-SES families. High-risk students benefit from interventions that show concern for them as individuals.

Vocational Choice (p. 362)

Trace the development of vocational choice, and cite factors that influence it.

- Vocational choice moves through a **fantasy period,** in which children explore career options by fantasizing about them; a **tentative period,** in which teenagers evaluate careers in terms of their interests, abilities, and values; and a **realistic period,** in which young people settle on a vocational category and then a specific occupation.

- Vocational choice is influenced by personality; parents' provision of educational opportunities, vocational information, and encouragement; and close relationships with teachers.

- Women's progress in male-dominated professions has been slow, and their achievements lag behind those of men in virtually all fields. Gender-stereotyped messages play a key role.

What problems do U.S. non-college-bound young people face in preparing for a vocation?

- Most U.S. non-college-bound high school graduates are limited to low-paid, unskilled jobs, and too many are unemployed. Work–study apprenticeships, like those widely available in European countries, would improve the transition from school to work for these young people.

Important Terms and Concepts

basal metabolic rate (BMR) (p. 350)
biological aging, or senescence (p. 343)
cognitive-affective complexity (p. 359)
commitment within relativistic thinking (p. 358)
cross-linkage theory of aging (p. 345)
dualistic thinking (p. 358)

epistemic cognition (p. 358)
expertise (p. 360)
fantasy period (p. 362)
free radicals (p. 344)
postformal thought (p. 358)
pragmatic thought (p. 359)

realistic period (p. 362)
relativistic thinking (p. 358)
telomeres (p. 344)
tentative period (p. 362)

Emotional and Social Development in Early Adulthood

THE WASHINGTON POST/
GETTY IMAGES

This college student, a volunteer for a nonprofit organization called FoodCorps, helps children in economically disadvantaged communities plant a school garden, teaching them about healthy foods and how they grow. For many young people in industrialized nations, the transition to early adulthood is a time of prolonged exploration of attitudes, values, and life possibilities.

chapter outline

After completing her master's degree at age 26, Sharese returned to her hometown, where she and Ernie would soon be married. During their year-long engagement, Sharese had vacillated about whether to follow through. At times, she looked with envy at Heather, still unattached and free to choose from an array of options before her. After graduating from college, Heather accepted a Peace Corps assignment in a remote region of Ghana, forged a romance with another Peace Corps volunteer that she ended at the conclusion of her tour of duty, and then traveled for eight months before returning to the United States to contemplate next steps.

Sharese also pondered the life circumstances of Christy and her husband, Gary—married and first-time parents by their mid-twenties. Despite his good teaching performance, Gary's relationship with the high school principal deteriorated, and he quit his job at the end of his first year. A tight job market impeded Gary's efforts to find another teaching position, and financial pressures and parenthood put Christy's education and career plans on hold. Sharese wondered whether it was really possible to combine family and career.

As her wedding approached, Sharese's ambivalence intensified, and she admitted to Ernie that she didn't feel ready to marry. But Ernie reassured her of his love. His career had been under way for two years, and at age 28, he looked forward to marriage and starting a family. Uncertain and conflicted, Sharese felt swept toward the altar as relatives and friends arrived. On the appointed day, she walked down the aisle.

In this chapter, we take up the emotional and social sides of early adulthood. Notice that Sharese, Ernie, and Heather moved toward adult roles slowly, at times vacillating along the way. Not until their mid- to late twenties did they make lasting career and romantic choices and attain full economic independence—markers of adulthood that young people of previous generations reached considerably earlier. Each received financial and other forms of support from parents and other family members, which enabled them to postpone taking on adult roles. We consider whether prolonged exploration of life options has become so widespread that it merits a new developmental period—*emerging adulthood*—to describe and understand it.

Recall from Chapter 12 that identity development continues to be a central focus from the late teens into the mid-twenties (see page 319). As they achieve a secure identity and independence from parents, young adults seek close, affectionate ties. Yet the decade of the twenties is accompanied by a rise in feelings of personal control over events in their lives—in fact, a stronger sense of control than they will ever experience again (Grob, Krings, & Bangerter, 2001). Perhaps for this reason, like Sharese, young people often fear losing their freedom. Once this struggle is resolved, early adulthood leads to new family units and parenthood, accomplished in the context of diverse lifestyles. At the same time, young adults must master the tasks of their chosen career.

Our discussion will reveal that identity, love, and work are intertwined. In negotiating these arenas, young adults do more choosing, planning, and changing course than any other age group. When their decisions are in tune with themselves and their social and cultural worlds, they acquire many new competencies, and life is full and rewarding. ●

A Gradual Transition: Emerging Adulthood

TAKE A MOMENT... Think about your own development. Do you consider yourself to have reached adulthood? When a large sample of American 18- to 25-year-olds was asked this question, the majority gave an ambiguous answer: "yes and no." Only after reaching their late twenties and early thirties did most feel that they were truly adult—findings evident in a wide range of industrialized nations (Arnett, 2001, 2003, 2007a; Buhl & Lanz, 2007; Macek, Bejĉek, & Vaníĉková, 2007; Nelson, 2009; Sirsch et al., 2009). The life pursuits and subjective judgments of many contemporary young people indicate that the transition to adult roles has become so delayed and prolonged that it has spawned a new transitional period extending from the late teens to the mid- to late-twenties, called **emerging adulthood.**

Unprecedented Exploration

Psychologist Jeffrey Arnett is the leader of a movement that regards emerging adulthood as a distinct period of life. As Arnett explains, emerging adults have left adolescence but are still a considerable distance from taking on adult responsibilities. Their parents agree: In a survey of parents of a large sample of ethnically and religiously diverse U.S. undergraduate and graduate students, most viewed their children as not yet fully adult (Nelson et al., 2007). Rather, young people who have the economic resources to do so explore alternatives in education, work, and personal values and behavior more intensely than they did as teenagers.

Not yet immersed in adult roles, many emerging adults can engage in activities of the widest possible scope. Because so little is normative, or socially expected, routes to adult responsibilities are highly diverse in timing and order across individuals (Côté, 2006). For example, more college students than in past generations pursue their education in a drawn-out, nonlinear way—changing majors as they explore career options, taking courses while working part-time, or interrupting school to work, travel, or participate in national or international service programs. About one-third of U.S. college graduates enter graduate school, taking still more years to settle into their desired career track (U.S. Department of Education, 2012b).

As a result of these experiences, young people's interests, attitudes, and values broaden (see page 361 in Chapter 13). Exposure to multiple viewpoints also encourages development of a more complex self-concept that includes awareness of their own changing traits and values over time, along with enhanced self-esteem rises (Labouvie-Vief, 2006; Orth, Robins, & Widaman, 2012). Together, these changes contribute to advances in identity.

Identity Development. During the college years, young people refine their approach to constructing an identity. Besides exploring in *breadth* (weighing multiple possibilities), they also explore in *depth*—evaluating existing commitments (Luyckx et al., 2006). For example, if you have not yet selected your major, you may be taking classes in a broad array of disciplines. Once you choose a major, you are likely to embark on an in-depth evaluation of your choice—reflecting on your interest, motivation, and performance and on your career prospects as you take additional classes in that field. Depending on the outcome of your evaluation, either your commitment to your major strengthens, or you return to a broad exploration of options.

In a longitudinal study extending over the first two years of college, most students cycled between making commitments and evaluating commitments in various identity domains. Fluctuations in students' certainty about their commitments sparked movement between these two states (Luyckx, Goossens, & Soenens, 2006). *TAKE A MOMENT...* Consider your own identity progress. Does it fit this *dual-cycle model,* in which identity formation is a lengthy process of feedback loops? Notice how

the model helps explain the movement between identity statuses displayed by many young people, described in Chapter 12. College students who move toward exploration in depth and certainty of commitment are higher in self-esteem, psychological well-being, and academic, emotional, and social adjustment. Those who spend much time exploring in breadth without making commitments, or who are identity diffused (engaging in no exploration), tend to be poorly adjusted—anxious, depressed, and higher in alcohol and drug use, casual and unprotected sex, and other health-compromising behaviors (Kunnen et al., 2008; Schwartz et al., 2011).

Many aspects of the life course that were once socially structured—marriage, parenthood, religious beliefs, and career paths—are increasingly left to individual decision. As a result, emerging adults are required to "individualize" their identities—a process that requires a sense of self-efficacy, purpose, determination to overcome obstacles, and responsibility for outcomes. Among young people of diverse ethnicities and SES levels, this set of qualities, termed *personal agency,* is positively related to an information-gathering cognitive style and identity exploration followed by commitment (Schwartz, Côté, & Arnett, 2005; Stringer & Kerpelman, 2010).

Religion and Worldview. Most emerging adults say that constructing a worldview, or a set of beliefs and values to live by, is essential for attaining adult status—even more important than finishing their education and settling into a career and marriage (Arnett, 2006, 2007b). During the late teens and twenties, attendance at religious services drops to its lowest level throughout the lifespan as young people continue to question the beliefs they acquired in their families (Kunnen et al., 2008; Schwartz et al., 2011). About one-fourth of U.S. 18- to 29-year-olds are unaffiliated with a particular faith—considerably more than in their parents' generation at the same age (see Figure 14.1).

Nevertheless, religion is more important in the lives of U.S. young people than it is for their agemates in other developed countries. More than one-third of those who are religiously affiliated say they are "strong" members of their faith—equivalent to same-age individuals who said so a decade earlier (Pew Forum on Religion and Public Life, 2010). Women are more religious than men, a difference evident in other Western nations and throughout the lifespan. Also among the more religious are immigrants and certain ethnic minorities, including African Americans and Hispanics (Barry et al., 2010). And whether or not they are involved in organized religion, many young people begin to construct their own individualized faith and, if attending college, frequently discuss religious beliefs and experiences with friends (Montgomery-Goodnough & Gallagher, 2007; Stoppa & Lefkowitz, 2010). Often they weave together beliefs and practices from diverse sources, including Eastern and Western religious traditions, science, and popular culture.

As with adolescents, U.S. emerging adults who are religious or spiritual tend to be better-adjusted. They are higher in self-esteem, less likely to commit antisocial acts, and more likely to engage in community service (Barry & Nelson, 2008; Knox, Langehough, & Walters, 1998; White et al., 2006).

© SYRACUSE NEWSPAPERS/PETER CHEN/THE IMAGE WORKS

Volunteers with Habitat for Humanity help low-income home owners with major repairs. Despite a widespread view of today's young adults as self-centered, many emerging adults are committed to improving their communities, nation, and world.

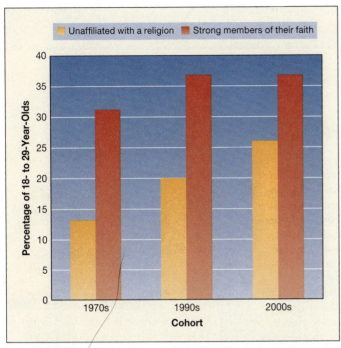

FIGURE 14.1 U.S. 18- to 29-year-olds' religiosity across generations. The percentage of unaffiliated young people rose substantially from the 1970s to 2000s. At the same time, among those in the 2000s cohort who are religiously affiliated, about one-third say they are strong members of their faith—similar to the 1990s cohort. (Adapted from Pew Forum on Religion and Public Life, 2010.)

Perhaps because emerging adults are so focused on exploring and "finding themselves," a widespread opinion is that that they forge self-centered worldviews, as the descriptor "generation me" suggests (Arnett, 2010). This issue has generated heated controversy. Analyses of large, nationally representative samples of U.S. young people, collected repeatedly over several decades, suggest that compared to past generations, the Millennial generation reports greater narcissism (egotistical self-admiration) and materialism—valuing of money and leisure and reduced empathy for the less fortunate (Gentile, Twenge, & Campbell, 2010; O'Brien, Hsing, & Konrath, 2010; Twenge, Campbell, & Freeman, 2012).

But other researchers claim that generational changes in egotism and other traits are too small to be meaningful (Trzesniewski & Donnellan, 2009, 2010). And gradual, age-related gains in self-esteem extending from adolescence through emerging adulthood and into mid-life are similar across generations, with average self-esteem of today's young people no higher than that of past cohorts (Orth, Robins, & Widaman, 2012; Orth, Trzesniewski, & Robins, 2010). Over these years, adults derive a greater sense of competence from making identity commitments, entering and succeeding at their careers, and becoming involved in their communities.

Additional evidence supports the view that many emerging adults are committed to improving their communities, nation, and world. In a survey of several hundred thousand first-year students enrolled in nearly 300 U.S. colleges and universities, a record number—nearly 30 percent—said that there is "a very

good chance" they will participate in community service—nearly double the number two decades earlier (Pryor et al., 2009). An additional 41 percent expressed "some chance" of participating, and only 6 percent said they would not volunteer. Among college students who expect to volunteer, the overwhelming majority actually do so within their first year (DeAngelo, Hurtado, & Pryor, 2010).

LOOK AND LISTEN

Ask 10 to 15 of your college classmates to answer the following question: What would you do if you had a million dollars? How often do respondents mention prosocial as opposed to self-centered acts? ●

Finally, compared to previous generations, contemporary 18- to 29-year-olds have been labeled "apathetic no shows" when it comes to voting. But in the 2012 U.S. presidential election, they made up more of the total electorate (19 percent) than did citizens over age 65 (16 percent), who traditionally have been the highest participants. In this respect, emerging adults' civic involvement appears to have strengthened.

Cultural Change, Cultural Variation, and Emerging Adulthood

Rapid cultural change explains the recent appearance of emerging adulthood. First, entry-level positions in many fields require more education than in the past, prompting young adults to seek higher education in record numbers and thus delaying financial independence and career commitment. Second, wealthy nations with longer-lived populations have no pressing need for young people's labor, freeing those who are financially able for extended exploration.

Indeed, emerging adulthood is limited to cultures that postpone entry into adult roles until the twenties. In developing nations such as Brazil, China, India, and Mexico, only a privileged few—usually those from wealthier families who are admitted to universities—experience it, often for a shorter time than their Western counterparts (Arnett, 2011; Nelson & Chen, 2007). Furthermore, the overwhelming majority of young people in traditional non-Western countries—those who have few economic resources or who remain in the rural regions where they grew up—have no emerging adulthood (UNICEF, 2010b). With limited education, they typically enter marriage, parenthood, and lifelong work early.

In industrialized countries, many young people experience these transitional years. Typically, their families are sufficiently well-off to provide them with financial support, without which few could advance their education, explore career possibilities, and travel to—as one emerging adult put it—"experience as much as possible." And although most emerging adults are pursuing higher education or have earned an advanced degree, some non-college-bound young people also benefit from this extended transition (Tanner, Arnett, & Leis, 2009). But they may do so by trying out different types of work rather than college majors or travel.

Cultural Influences

Is Emerging Adulthood Really a Distinct Period of Development?

Although broad consensus exists that cultural change has prolonged the transition to adult roles for many young people, disagreement persists over whether these years of "emergence" merit the creation of a new developmental period (Hendry & Kloep, 2007, 2010). Critics of the concept of emerging adulthood offer the following arguments.

First, burgeoning higher education enrollment, delayed career entry, and later marriage and parenthood are cultural trends that began as early as the 1970s in industrialized nations, only gradually becoming more conspicuous. At no time has adulthood in complex societies been attained at a distinct moment (Côté & Bynner, 2008). Rather, young people in the past reached adult status earlier in some domains and later in others, just as they do today. They also may reverse direction—for example, move back to the parental home to get their bearings after finishing college or being laid off from a job. In accord with the lifespan perspective, development is multidimensional and multidirectional, for 18- to 29-year-olds as it is for adults of all ages. Transitions occur during all periods of adult life, with societal conditions heavily influencing their timing, length, and complexity.

Second, the term *emerging adulthood* fails to describe the experiences of the majority of the world's youths (Galambos & Martinez, 2007). In most developing countries, young people—particularly women—are limited in education and marry and have children early. According to one estimate, over 1 billion individuals—nearly 70 percent of young people—follow this traditional route to adulthood (World Health Organization, 2011).

Third, research on emerging adulthood largely emphasizes its personal and societal benefits. But the extended exploration that defines this period can be risky for those who have not developed the personal agency to make good choices and acquire adult skills. These young people may remain uncommitted for too long—an outcome that impedes the focused learning required for a successful work life. A favorable emerging adulthood, then, depends on whether it is used to acquire competencies essential for contemporary living.

Finally, the financial upheaval of the late 2000s has left large numbers of bachelor's degree holders under age 25 with restricted options. In 2011, over 9 percent were unemployed and 20 percent underemployed—in low-paid jobs not requiring a college degree and, thus, without experiences necessary for advancing their skills (Shierholz, Sabadish, & Wething, 2012). Rather than a period of unparalleled opportunities, these graduates' delayed leap into adult roles is filled with anxiety and frustration. One young person, who might have been high in personal agency in a stable economy, remarked, "It has been tough finding a job that keeps me wanting to stick with something" (Kotkin, 2012).

Proponents of emerging adulthood as a distinct developmental period respond that, though not universal, it applies to most young people in industrialized societies and is spreading in developing nations that play major roles in our global economy (Tanner & Arnett, 2011). But skeptics counter that

© ELLEN B. SENISI PHOTOGRAPHY

This young woman in Burma cares for her baby while working as a food vendor. Like most young people in developing countries, she has no emerging adulthood.

emerging adulthood is unlikely to become a prominent period of life in developing countries with high concentrations of poverty or, in industrialized countries, among low-income youths or those not involved in higher education (Côté & Bynner, 2008; Kloep & Hendry, 2011). And for college graduates, societal conditions can readily restrict the prospects and rewards of this period.

Critics also emphasize that in developed nations, age-graded influences have declined in favor of nonnormative influences throughout contemporary adulthood (see page 9 in Chapter 1 to review) (Hendry & Kloep, 2010). In their view, rather than being unique, emerging adults are part of a general trend toward blurring of age-related expectations, yielding multiple transitions and increased diversity in development across the adult years.

Nevertheless, for the large numbers of U.S. low-SES young people who are burdened by early parenthood, do not finish high school, are otherwise academically unprepared for college, or do not have access to vocational training, emerging adulthood is limited or nonexistent (see Chapters 11 and 13). Because of its strong association with SES and higher education, some researchers reject the notion of emerging adulthood as a distinct period of development (see the Cultural Influences box above). Others disagree, predicting that emerging adulthood will become increasingly common as *globaliza-*

tion—the exchange of ideas, information, trade, and immigration among nations—accelerates. As globalization proceeds, gains in higher education and the formation of a common "global identity" among young people may lead to the spread of emerging adulthood (Arnett, 2007a; Nelson & Chen, 2007). But, as the Cultural Influences box above points out, the recession's weak labor market has also left many college graduates with limited options. In sum, societal conditions enabling an emerging adulthood abundant in opportunity have recently contracted.

Applying What We Know

Resources That Foster Resilience in Emerging Adulthood

Type of Resource	Description
Cognitive attributes	Effective planning and decision making
	Information-gathering cognitive style and mature epistemic cognition
	Good school performance
	Knowledge of vocational options and necessary skills
Emotional and social attributes	Positive self-esteem
	Good emotional self-regulation and flexible coping strategies
	Good conflict-resolution skills
	Confidence in one's ability to reach one's goals
	Sense of personal responsibility for outcomes
	Persistence and effective use of time
	Healthy identity development—movement toward exploration in depth and commitment certainty
	Strong moral character
	Sense of meaning and purpose in life, engendered by religion, spirituality, or other sources
	Desire to contribute meaningfully to one's community
Social supports	Positive relationships with parents, peers, teachers, and mentors
	Financial assistance from parents or others
	Sense of connection to social institutions, such as school, church, workplace, and community center

Sources: Benson et al., 2006; Eccles and Gootman, 2002.

Risk and Resilience in Emerging Adulthood

In grappling with momentous choices and acquiring the skills to succeed in demanding life roles, emerging adults often encounter disappointments in love and work that require them to adjust, and sometimes radically change, their life path. Their vigorous explorations also extend earlier risks, including unprotected sexual activity, substance use, and hazardous driving behavior (see Chapter 13). And feelings of loneliness are higher at this time than at any other time of life (Rokach, 2003). As emerging adults move through school and employment settings, they must constantly separate from friends and forge new relationships.

Longitudinal research shows that the personal attributes and social supports listed in Applying What We Know above foster successful passage through these years, as indicated by completing a college education, forging a warm, stable intimate relationship, finding and keeping a well-paying job, and volunteering in one's community (Benson et al., 2006; Eccles & Gootman, 2002). Notice how the resources in the table overlap with ones discussed in previous chapters that promote development through *resilience,* the capacity to overcome challenge and adversity.

Relationships with parents have an especially wide-ranging influence. A secure, affectionate parent–emerging adult bond that extends the balance of connection and separation estab-

lished in adolescence—an empathic approach in which parents recognize the weighty challenges the young person faces and encourage personally valued choices—predicts many aspects of adaptive functioning: favorable self-esteem, identity progress, successful transition to college life, higher academic achievement, more rewarding friendships and romantic ties, and positive psychological well-being (Aquilino, 2006, p. 201).

In contrast, excessive parental rule-setting and regulation of the young person's daily life (including taking over when the young person encounters challenges) and psychological control (invalidating the young person's thoughts and feelings) are linked to poor adjustment, including low self-esteem, inability to make commitments in identity formation, and increased anxiety, depression, and alcohol use (Luyckz et al., 2007; Nelson et al., 2011; Patock-Peckam & Morgan-Lopez, 2009). In another form of parenting—called *helicopter parenting* in popular culture—warm, well-intentioned parents "hover" over the emerging adult out of excessive concern for his or her well-being. They might, for example, take the child to college but refuse to leave and contact professors to discuss the child's grades. Perhaps because helicopter parenting is motivated by strong parental affection and involvement, it is not associated with the negative outcomes just noted. But it is related to reduced school engagement (going to class, completing assignments) (Padilla-Walker & Nelson, 2012). And it likely interferes with emerging adults' ability to acquire the skills they need to act on their own.

Although well-intentioned, these hovering "helicopter" parents make it harder for their daughter to acquire the skills she needs to manage the challenges of college life on her own.

Finally, exposure to multiple negative life events—family conflict, abusive intimate relationships, repeated romantic breakups, academic or employment difficulties, and financial strain—undermines development, even in emerging adults whose childhood and adolescence prepared them well for this transition (Masten et al., 2004). In sum, supportive family, school, and community environments are crucial, just as they were at earlier ages. The overwhelming majority of young people with access to these resources are optimistic about their future and likely to transition successfully to adult roles (Arnett, 2006). Now let's turn to theories of psychosocial development in early adulthood.

ASK YOURSELF

REVIEW What cultural changes have led to the appearance of emerging adulthood?

APPLY List supports that your college environment offers emerging adults in its health and counseling services, academic advising, residential living, and extracurricular activities. How does each help young people transition to adult roles?

REFLECT Should emerging adulthood be considered a distinct developmental period? Why or why not?

Erikson's Theory: Intimacy versus Isolation

Erikson's vision has influenced all contemporary theories of adult personality development. His psychological conflict of early adulthood is **intimacy versus isolation,** reflected in the young person's thoughts and feelings about making a permanent commitment to an intimate partner.

As Sharese discovered, establishing a mutually gratifying close relationship is challenging. Intimacy requires that young people redefine their identity to include both partners' values and interests. Those in their late teens and early twenties frequently say they don't feel ready for a lasting tie (Carroll et al., 2009). During their first year of marriage, Sharese separated from Ernie twice as she tried to reconcile her desire for self-determination with her desire for intimacy. Maturity involves balancing these forces. Without intimacy, young adults face the negative outcome of Erikson's early adulthood stage: loneliness and self-absorption. Ernie's patience and stability helped Sharese realize that committed love requires generosity and compromise but not total surrender of the self.

Research confirms that—as Erikson emphasized—a secure identity fosters attainment of intimacy. Commitment to personally meaningful values and goals prepares young adults for interpersonal commitments, which increase as early adulthood progresses. Among large samples of college students, identity achievement was positively correlated with fidelity (loyalty in relationships) and love, for both men and women. In contrast, identity moratorium—a state of searching prior to commitment—was negatively associated with fidelity and love (Markstrom et al., 1997; Markstrom & Kalmanir, 2001). Other studies show that advanced identity development strongly predicts involvement in a deep, committed love partnership or readiness to establish such a partnership (Beyers & Seiffge-Krenke, 2010; Montgomery, 2005). Still, the coordination of identity and intimacy is more complex for women, who are more likely than men to consider the impact of their personal goals on important relationships (Archer, 2002).

Erikson believed that successful resolution of intimacy versus isolation prepares the individual for the middle adulthood stage, which focuses on *generativity*—caring for the next generation and helping to improve society. But childbearing and child rearing, as well as contributions to society through work and community service, are under way in the twenties and thirties. Still, in line with Erikson's ideas, high friendship or romantic intimacy in early adulthood does predict a stronger generative orientation (Mackinnon et al., 2011).

In sum, identity, intimacy, and generativity are concerns of early adulthood, with shifts in emphasis that differ among individuals. Recognizing that Erikson's theory provides only a broad sketch of adult personality development, other theorists have expanded his stage approach, adding detail.

Other Theories of Adult Psychosocial Development

In the 1970s, growing interest in adult development led to several widely read books on the topic. Daniel Levinson's *The Seasons of a Man's Life* (1978) and *The Seasons of a Woman's Life* (1996), and George Vaillant's *Adaptation to Life* (1977) and *Aging Well* (2002), present psychosocial theories in the tradition of Erikson.

Levinson's Seasons of Life

On the basis of in-depth biographical interviews with 35- to 45-year-old men—and, later, similar interviews with women in the same age range—Levinson (1978, 1996) depicted adult development as a sequence of qualitatively distinct eras (or "seasons") coinciding with Erikson's stages and separated by *transitions*. The *life structure*, a key concept in Levinson's theory, is the underlying design of a person's life, consisting of relationships with significant others—individuals, groups, and institutions. Of its many components, usually only a few, relating to family, close friendships, and occupation, are central. But wide individual differences exist in the weights of central and peripheral components.

Levinson found that during the transition to early adulthood, most young people constructed a *dream*—an image of themselves in the adult world that guides their decision making. For men, the dream usually emphasized achievement in a career, whereas most career-oriented women had "split dreams" involving both marriage and career. Young adults also formed a relationship with a *mentor* who facilitated realization of their dream—often a senior colleague at work but occasionally a more experienced friend, neighbor, or relative.

Around age 30, a second transition occurred: Young people who had been preoccupied with career and were single usually focused on finding a life partner, while women who had emphasized marriage and family often developed more individualistic goals. For example, Christy, who had dreamed of becoming a professor, finally earned her doctoral degree in her mid-thirties and secured a college teaching position. For young people without a satisfying intimate tie or a vocational direction, this can be a time of crisis.

To create an early adulthood culminating life structure, men usually "settled down" by focusing on certain relationships and aspirations, in an effort to establish a niche in society consistent with their values, whether those be wealth, prestige, artistic or scientific achievement, or forms of family or community participation. In his late thirties, Ernie became a partner in his firm, coached his son's soccer team, and was elected treasurer of his church. He paid less attention to golf, travel, and playing the guitar than previously.

Many women, however, remained unsettled in their thirties, often because they added an occupational or relationship commitment. When her two children were born, Sharese felt torn between her research position in the state health department and her family. She took three months off after the arrival of each baby. When she returned to work, she did not pursue attractive administrative openings that required travel and time away from home. And shortly after Christy began teaching, she and Gary divorced. Becoming a single parent while starting her professional life introduced new strains. Not until middle age did many women reach career maturity and take on more authority in the community.

Vaillant's Adaptation to Life

Vaillant (1977) followed the development of nearly 250 men born in the 1920s, selected for study while they were students at a competitive liberal arts college. Participants were interviewed extensively while in college and answered lengthy questionnaires during each succeeding decade. Then Vaillant (2002) interviewed them at ages 47, 60, and 70 about work, family, and physical and mental health.

Looking at how the men altered themselves and their social world to adapt to life, Vaillant—like Levinson—confirmed Erikson's stages but filled gaps between them. After focusing on intimacy concerns in their twenties, the men turned to career consolidation in their thirties. During their forties, they became more generative. In their fifties and sixties, they extended that generativity; they became "keepers of meaning," or guardians of their culture, expressing a deep need to preserve and pass on cultural traditions by teaching others what they had learned from life experience (Vaillant & Koury, 1994). Finally, in their seventies, the men became more spiritual and reflective. In a later lifelong study of a sample of well-educated women, Vaillant (2002) identified a similar series of changes.

Nevertheless, the developmental patterns Vaillant and Levinson described are based largely on interviews with people born in the first few decades of the twentieth century. As our discussion of emerging adulthood illustrates, development is far more variable today—so much so that some researchers doubt that adult psychosocial changes can be organized into distinct stages (Newton & Stewart, 2010). Rather, people may assemble the themes and dilemmas identified by these theorists into individualized arrangements, in a *dynamic system* of interacting biological, psychological, and social forces. Studies of new generations—both men and women of diverse backgrounds—are needed to shed light on the extent of commonality and variation among young people in psychosocial development.

© PETER HVIZDAK/THE IMAGE WORKS

A digital archives specialist shows an apprentice librarian how to scan text. For young people starting out in a career, an effective mentor can serve as a role model and guide in overcoming challenges.

The Social Clock

As we have seen, changes in society from one generation to the next can affect the life course. Bernice Neugarten (1968a, 1979) identified an important cultural and generational influence on adult development: the **social clock**—age-graded expectations for major life events, such as beginning a first job, getting married, birth of the first child, buying a home, and retiring. All societies have such timetables. Research of two to three decades ago revealed that conformity to or departure from the social clock can be a major source of adult personality change, affecting self-esteem, independence, responsibility, and other attributes because adults (like children and adolescents) make social comparisons, measuring their progress against that of agemates (Helson, 1992; Vandewater & Stewart, 1997).

Among economically better-off young people, finishing one's education, marrying, and having children occur much later in the lifespan than they did a generation or two ago. Furthermore, departures from social-clock life events have become increasingly common. As we will see later, a growing number of women, mostly of lower income, are not marrying and, instead, rearing children as single mothers, turning not to a spouse but rather to their extended families for assistance (Furstenberg, 2010).

LOOK AND LISTEN

Describe your social clock, listing major life events along with the age you expect to attain each. Then ask a parent and/or grandparent to recall his or her own early adulthood social clock. Analyze generational differences. ●

These conditions can create intergenerational tensions when parents expect their young-adult children to attain adult milestones on an outdated schedule, at odds with their children's current opportunities and desires. Young adults may also feel distressed because their own timing of major milestones is not widely shared by their contemporaries or supported by current public policies, thereby weakening both informal and formal social supports (Settersten, 2007). And while rendering greater flexibility and freedom to young people's lives, an ill-defined social clock likely causes them to feel inadequately grounded—unsure of what others expect and of what to expect of themselves.

In sum, following a social clock of some kind seems to foster confidence and social stability because it guarantees that young people will develop skills, engage in productive work, and gain in understanding of self and others (Hendry & Kloep, 2007). In contrast, "crafting a life of one's own," whether self-chosen or the result of circumstances, is risky—more prone to breakdown (Settersten, 2007, p. 244). With this in mind, let's take a closer look at how men and women traverse major tasks of young adulthood.

ASK YOURSELF

REVIEW Return to page 319 in Chapter 12, and review the contributions of exploration and commitment to a mature identity. Using the two criteria, explain why identity achievement is positively related to attainment of intimacy (fidelity and love), whereas identity moratorium is negatively predictive.

APPLY In view of contemporary changes in the social clock, explain Sharese's conflicted feelings about marrying Ernie.

REFLECT Describe your early adulthood dream. Then ask a friend or classmate of the other gender to describe his or her dream, and compare the two. Are they consistent with Levinson's findings?

Close Relationships

To establish an intimate tie to another person, people must find a partner and build an emotional bond that they sustain over time. Although young adults are especially concerned with romantic love, the need for intimacy can also be satisfied through other relationships involving mutual commitment—with friends, siblings, and co-workers.

Romantic Love

Finding a life partner is a major milestone of early adult development, with profound consequences for self-concept and psychological well-being (Meeus et al., 2007). As Sharese and Ernie's relationship reveals, it is also a complex process that unfolds over time and is affected by a variety of events.

Because the social clock has become increasingly flexible, this 30-year-old attorney, committed to her challenging, demanding career, may not feel pressure to conform to a strict timetable for major life events such as marriage and parenthood.

Selecting a Mate. Recall from Chapter 13 that intimate partners generally meet in places where they are likely to find people of their own age, ethnicity, SES, and religion, or they connect through dating websites. People usually select partners who resemble themselves in other ways—attitudes, personality, educational plans, intelligence, physical attractiveness, and even height (Keith & Schafer, 1991; Simpson & Harris, 1994). Romantic partners sometimes have complementary personality traits—one self-assured and dominant, the other hesitant and submissive. Because this difference permits each to sustain their preferred style of behavior, it contributes to compatibility (Sadler, Ethier, & Woody, 2011). But overall, little support exists for the idea that "opposites attract." Rather, partners who are similar in personality and other attributes tend to be more satisfied with their relationship and more likely to stay together (Furnham, 2009; Markey & Markey, 2007).

Nevertheless, men and women differ in the importance they place on certain characteristics. In diverse industrialized and developing countries, women assign greater weight to intelligence, ambition, financial status, and moral character, whereas men place more emphasis on physical attractiveness and domestic skills. In addition, women prefer a same-age or slightly older partner, men a younger partner (Buunk, 2002; Cramer, Schaefer, & Reid, 2003; Stewart, Stinnett, & Rosenfeld, 2000).

According to an evolutionary perspective, because their capacity to reproduce is limited, women seek a mate with traits, such as earning power and emotional commitment, that help ensure children's survival and well-being. In contrast, men look for a mate with traits that signal youth, health, sexual pleasure, and ability to give birth to and care for offspring. As further evidence for this difference, men often want a relationship to move quickly toward physical intimacy, whereas women typically prefer to take the time to achieve psychological intimacy first (Buss, 2012).

In an alternative, social learning view, gender roles profoundly influence criteria for mate selection. Beginning in childhood, men learn to be assertive and independent—behaviors needed for success in the work world. Women acquire nurturant behaviors, which facilitate caregiving. Then each sex learns to value traits in the other that fit with this traditional division of labor (Eagly & Wood, 2012). In support of this theory, in cultures and in younger generations experiencing greater gender equity, men and women are more alike in their mate preferences. For example, compared with men in China and Japan, American men place more emphasis on their mate's financial prospects, less on her domestic skills. And both sexes care somewhat less about their mate's age relative to their own. Rather, they place a high value on relationship satisfaction (Buss et al., 2001; Toro-Morn & Sprecher, 2003).

As the Social Issues: Health box on page 378 reveals, young people's choice of an intimate partner and the quality of their relationship also are affected by memories of their early parent–child bond. Finally, for romance to lead to a lasting partnership, it must happen at the right time. If one or both do not feel ready to marry, the relationship is likely to dissolve.

The warmth and intimacy of this couple's communication form the basis for mutual affection, caring, acceptance, and respect, which are vital for a satisfying, enduring bond.

The Components of Love. How do we know that we are in love? Robert Sternberg's (1988, 2000, 2006) **triangular theory of love** identifies three components—intimacy, passion, and commitment—that shift in emphasis as romantic relationships develop. *Intimacy,* the emotional component, involves warm, tender communication, expressions of concern about the other's well-being, and a desire for the partner to reciprocate. *Passion,* the desire for sexual activity and romance, is the physical- and psychological-arousal component. *Commitment* is the cognitive component, leading partners to decide that they are in love and to maintain that love.

At the beginning of a relationship, **passionate love**—intense sexual attraction—is strong. Gradually, passion declines in favor of intimacy and commitment, which form the basis for **companionate love**—warm, trusting affection and caregiving (Acker & Davis, 1992; Fehr, 1994). Each aspect of love, however, helps sustain the relationship. Early passionate love is a strong predictor of whether partners keep dating. But without the quiet intimacy, predictability, and shared attitudes and values of companionate love, most romances eventually break up (Hendrick & Hendrick, 2002).

Couples whose relationships endure generally report that they love each other more than they did earlier (Sprecher, 1999). In the transformation of romantic involvements from passionate to companionate, *commitment* may be the aspect of love that determines whether a relationship survives. Communicating that commitment in ways that strengthen *intimacy*—through warmth, attentiveness, empathy, caring, acceptance, and respect—strongly predicts relationship maintenance and satisfaction (Neff & Karney, 2008; Lavner & Bradbury, 2012). For example, Sharese's doubts about getting married subsided largely because of Ernie's warm expressions of commitment.

Partners who consistently express their commitment report higher-quality and longer-lasting relationships (Fitzpatrick &

Social Issues: Health

Childhood Attachment Patterns and Adult Romantic Relationships

In Bowlby's ethological theory of attachment, the early attachment bond leads to construction of an *internal working model,* or set of expectations about attachment figures, that serves as a guide for close relationships throughout life. Adults' evaluations of their early attachment experiences are related to their parenting behaviors—specifically, to the quality of attachments they build with their children (see pages 156–158 in Chapter 6). Additional evidence indicates that recollections of childhood attachment patterns predict romantic relationships in adulthood.

In studies carried out in Australia, Israel, and the United States, researchers asked people about their early parental bonds (attachment history), their attitudes toward intimate relationships (internal working model), and their actual experiences with romantic partners. In a few studies, investigators also observed couples' behaviors. Consistent with Bowlby's theory, adults' memories and interpretations of childhood attachment patterns were good indicators of internal working models and relationship experiences. (To review patterns of attachment, see Chapter 6, page 154.)

Secure Attachment

Adults who described their attachment history as secure (warm, loving, and supportive parents) had internal working models that reflected this security. They viewed themselves as likable, were comfortable with intimacy, and rarely worried about abandonment. They characterized their most important love relationship in terms of trust, happiness, and friendship (Cassidy, 2001). Their behaviors toward their partner were empathic and supportive and their conflict resolution strategies constructive. They were also at ease in turning to their partner for comfort and assistance (Collins et al., 2006; Creasey & Jarvis, 2009; Roisman et al., 2002).

Avoidant Attachment

Adults who reported an avoidant attachment history (demanding, disrespectful, and critical parents) displayed internal working models that stressed independence, mistrust of love partners, and anxiety about people getting too close. They were convinced that others disliked them and that romantic love is hard to find and rarely lasts. Jealousy, emotional distance, lack of support in response to their partner's distress, and little enjoyment of physical contact pervaded their most important love relationship (Collins et al., 2006). They endorsed many unrealistic beliefs about relationships—for example, that partners cannot change, that males' and females' needs differ, and that "mind reading" is expected (Stackert & Bursik, 2003).

Resistant Attachment

Adults recalling a resistant attachment history (parents who responded unpredictably and unfairly) presented internal working models in which they sought to merge completely with another person and fall in love quickly (Cassidy, 2001). At the same time, they worried that their intense feelings would overwhelm others, who really did not love them and would not want to stay with them. Their most important love relationship was riddled with jealousy, emotional highs and lows, and desperation about whether the partner would return their affection (Feeney, 1999). Resistant adults, though offering support, do so in ways that fit poorly with their partner's needs (Collins et al., 2006).

Are adults' descriptions of their childhood attachment experiences accurate? In several longitudinal studies, quality of parent–child interactions, observed or assessed through family interviews 5 to 23 years earlier, were good predictors of internal working models and romantic-relationship quality in early adulthood (Donnellan, Larsen-Rife, & Conger, 2005; Ogawa et al., 1997; Roisman et al., 2001). However, attributes of the current

Did the internal working model constructed by this baby influence the relationship he later forged with his wife? Research indicates that early attachment is associated with the quality of later intimate ties.

partner also influence internal working models and intimate ties. When generally insecure individuals manage to form a secure representation of their partner, they report stronger feelings of affection and concern and reduced relationship conflict and anxiety (Sibley & Overall, 2010; Sprecher & Fehr, 2011).

In sum, negative parent–child experiences can be carried forward into adult close relationships. At the same time, internal working models are continuously "updated." When adults with a history of unhappy love lives have a chance to form a satisfying intimate tie, they may revise their internal working model.

Sollie, 1999; Madey & Rodgers, 2009). An important feature of their communication is constructive conflict resolution—directly expressing wishes and needs, listening patiently, asking for clarification, compromising, accepting responsibility, forgiving their partner, and avoiding the escalation of negative interaction sparked by criticism, contempt, defensiveness, and stonewalling (Johnson et al., 2005; Schneewind & Gerhard, 2002). In a longitudinal study, newlyweds' negativity during problem solving predicted marital dissatisfaction and divorce over the following decade (Sullivan et al., 2010). Those who displayed little warmth and caring often resorted to anger and contempt when dealing with problems. These findings reveal that deficits in intimacy foreshadow poor conflict-resolution skills and eventual weakening of the marital tie.

Compared with women, men are less skilled at communicating in ways that foster intimacy, offering less comfort and helpful support in their close relationships. Men also tend to be less effective at negotiating conflict, frequently avoiding discussion (Burleson & Kunkel, 2006; Wood, 2009).

Finally, for gay and lesbian couples, widespread social stigma complicates the process of forging a satisfying, committed bond. Those who worry most about being stigmatized, who try to conceal their romance, or who harbor negative attitudes toward their own sexual orientation report lower-quality and less enduring love relationships (Mohr & Daly, 2008; Mohr & Fassinger, 2006).

Culture and the Experience of Love. Passion and intimacy, which form the basis for romantic love, became the dominant basis for marriage in twentieth-century Western nations as the value of individualism strengthened. From this vantage point, mature love is based on autonomy, appreciation of the partner's unique qualities, and intense emotion (Hatfield, Rapson, & Martel, 2007). Trying to satisfy dependency needs through an intimate bond is regarded as immature.

This Western view contrasts sharply with the perspectives of Eastern cultures, such as China and Japan, where lifelong dependency is accepted and viewed positively and the self is defined through role relationships—son or daughter, brother or sister, husband or wife. Furthermore, in choosing a mate, Chinese and Japanese young people are expected to consider obligations to others, especially parents. College students of Asian

heritage are less likely than those of American or European descent to endorse a view of love based solely on physical attraction and deep emotion (Hatfield, Rapson, & Martel, 2007; Hatfield & Sprecher, 1995). Instead, compared to Westerners, they place greater weight on companionship and practical matters—similarity of background, career promise, and likelihood of being a good parent.

Still, even in countries where arranged marriages are still fairly common (including China, India, and Japan), parents and prospective brides and grooms consult one another before moving forward (Goodwin & Pillay, 2006). If parents try to force their children into an unappealing marriage, sympathetic extended family members may come to children's defense. And in developing countries, women who attain higher education—and who therefore have acquired more of an autonomous identity—are more likely to insist on actively participating in an arranged marriage (Bhopal, 2011). In sum, today young people in many countries consider love to be a prerequisite for marriage, though Westerners assign greater importance to love—especially, its passionate component.

Friendships

Like romantic partners and childhood friends, adult friends are usually similar in age, sex, and SES. As in earlier years, friends in adulthood enhance self-esteem and psychological well-being through affirmation, acceptance, autonomy support (permitting disagreement and choice), and support in times of stress (Collins & Madsen, 2006; Deci et al., 2006). Friends also make life more interesting by expanding social opportunities and access to knowledge and points of view.

Trust, intimacy, and loyalty, along with shared interests and values and enjoyment of each other's company, continue to be important in adult friendships, as they were in adolescence (Blieszner & Roberto, 2012). Sharing thoughts and feelings is sometimes greater in friendship than in marriage, although commitment is less strong as friends come and go over the life course. Even so, some adult friendships continue for many years, at times throughout life. Female friends get together more than male friends do, which contributes to greater friendship continuity for women (Sherman, de Vries, & Lansford, 2000).

But because of the dramatic rise in social media use, today's friendships are no longer as constrained by physical proximity. Nearly three-fourths of 18- to 29-year-olds who access the Internet use social networking sites; Facebook reports more than 500 million active users worldwide. Consequently, networks of "friends" have expanded. Do social networking sites lead young adults to form a large number of acquaintances at the expense of intimate friendships? Research reveals that people with 500 or more Facebook friends actually interact individually—by "liking" posts, leaving comments on walls, or engaging in Facebook chats—with far fewer. Among these large-network Facebook users, men engaged in one-on-one communication with an average of just 10 friends, women with just 16 (Henig & Henig, 2012). Facebook led passive tracking of casual relationships to rise while core friendships remained limited.

© ELLEN B. SENISI PHOTOGRAPHY

Although arranged marriages are still common in parts of Southeast Asia, young couples increasingly expect love to be a prerequisite for marriage, and their parents are likely to acquiesce.

Ask your Facebook friends to indicate the size of their Facebook network along with the number of friends they interacted with individually during the past month. Do large-network users have only a limited number of core friendships? ●

Same-Sex Friendships. Extending a pattern evident in childhood and adolescence, women have more intimate same-sex friendships than men (see Chapter 12, pages 330–331). Barriers to intimacy between male friends include competitiveness, which may make men unwilling to disclose weaknesses, and concern that if they tell about themselves, their friends will not reciprocate (Reid & Fine, 1992). Because of greater intimacy and give-and-take, women generally evaluate their same-sex friendships more positively than men do. But they also have higher expectations of friends (Blieszner & Roberto, 2012). Thus, they are more disapproving if friends do not meet their expectations.

Of course, individual differences in friendship quality exist. The longer-lasting men's friendships are, the closer they become and the more they include disclosure of personal information (Sherman, de Vries, & Lansford, 2000). And gay and lesbian romantic relationships often develop out of close same-sex friendships, with lesbians, especially, forging compatible friendships before becoming involved romantically (Diamond, 2006).

As they develop romantic ties and marry, young adults—especially men—direct more of their disclosures toward their partners (Kito, 2005). Still, friendships continue to be vital contexts for personal sharing throughout adulthood. A best friendship can augment well-being when a marriage is not fully satisfying (but not when the marriage is low in quality) (Birditt & Antonucci, 2007). Turn back to Figure 12.1 on page 331 to view developmental trends in self-disclosure to romantic partners and friends.

ROB LANG/GETTY IMAGES

Men often experience barriers to friendship intimacy due to competitiveness. But the longer-lasting men's friendships are, the more intimate they become, increasingly including disclosure of personal information.

Other-Sex Friendships. From the college years through career exploration and settling into work roles, other-sex friendships increase. After marriage, they decline for men but continue to rise for women, who more often form them in the workplace. Highly educated, employed women have the largest number of other-sex friends. Through these relationships, young adults often gain in companionship and self-esteem and learn about masculine and feminine styles of intimacy (Bleske & Buss, 2000). Because men confide especially easily in their female friends, such friendships offer them a unique opportunity to broaden their expressive capacity. And women sometimes say male friends offer objective points of view on problems and situations—perspectives not available from female friends (Monsour, 2002).

Many people try to keep other-sex friendships platonic to safeguard their integrity (Messman, Canary, & Hause, 2000). But sometimes the relationship changes into a romantic bond. When a solid other-sex friendship does evolve into a romance, it may be more stable and enduring than a romantic relationship formed without a foundation in friendship. And emerging adults, especially, are flexible about people they include in their friendship networks (Barry & Madsen, 2010). After a breakup, they may even keep a former romantic partner on as a friend.

Siblings as Friends. As young people marry and invest less time in developing a romantic partnership, siblings—especially sisters whose earlier bond was positive—become more frequent companions (Birditt & Antonucci, 2007). A childhood history of intense parental favoritism and sibling rivalry can disrupt sibling bonds in adulthood (Panish & Stricker, 2002). But when family experiences have been positive, relationships between adult siblings can be especially close and are important sources of psychological well-being (Sherman, Lansford, & Volling, 2006).

In families with five to ten siblings, common in industrialized nations in the past and still widespread in some cultures, close sibling bonds may replace friendships (Fuller-Iglesias, 2010). One 35-year-old with five siblings, who all—with their partners and children—resided in the same small city, remarked, "With a family like this, who needs friends?"

ASK YOURSELF

REVIEW Describe gender differences in traits usually desired in a long-term partner. What findings indicate that both biological and social forces contribute to those differences?

APPLY After dating for two years, Mindy and Graham reported greater love and relationship satisfaction than during their first few months of dating. What features of communication probably deepened their bond, and why is it likely to endure?

REFLECT Do you have a nonromantic, close other-sex friendship? If so, how has it enhanced your emotional and social development?

The Family Life Cycle

For most young people, the life course takes shape within the **family life cycle**—a series of phases characterizing the development of most families around the world. In early adulthood, people typically live on their own, marry, and bear and rear children. In middle age, as their children leave home, their parenting responsibilities diminish. Late adulthood brings retirement, growing old, and (more often for women) death of one's spouse (McGoldrick & Shibusawa, 2012). Stress tends to be greatest during transitions between phases, as family members redefine and reorganize their relationships.

But today, wide variations exist in the sequence and timing of family life-cycle phases—high rates of out-of-wedlock births, delayed marriage and childbearing, divorce, and remarriage, among others. And some people, voluntarily or involuntarily, do not experience all phases. Still, the family life-cycle model offers an organized way of thinking about how the family system changes over time and the impact of each phase on the family unit and its members.

Leaving Home

Departure from the parental home is a major step toward assuming adult responsibilities. The average age of leaving has risen since the 1960s; today, it resembles the departure age at the beginning of the twentieth century. But reasons for coresidence have changed: Early twentieth-century young adults resided with parents so they could contribute to the family economy. Twenty-first-century young adults living at home are typically financially dependent on their parents. This trend toward later home-leaving is evident in most industrialized nations, though substantial variation in timing exists. Because government support is available, young adults in the Scandinavian countries move out relatively early (Furstenberg, 2010). In contrast, cultural traditions in Mediterranean countries promote lengthy coresidence, extending for men into the mid-thirties.

Departures for education tend to occur at earlier ages, those for full-time work and marriage later. Because the majority of U.S. young adults enroll in higher education, many leave home around age 18. Those from divorced, single-parent homes tend to be early leavers, perhaps because of family stress (Cooney & Mortimer, 1999). Compared with the previous generation, fewer North American and Western European young people leave home to marry; more do so just to be "independent"—to express their adult status.

Slightly over half of U.S. 18- to 25-year-olds return to their parents' home for brief periods after first leaving (U.S. Census Bureau, 2013). Usually, role transitions, such as the end of college or military service, bring young people back. But tight job markets, high housing costs, or failures in work or love can also prompt a temporary return home.

The extent to which young people live on their own before marriage varies with SES and ethnicity. Those who are economi-

A father helps his son move belongings back into the parental home after graduation. Parents usually respond to their children's return with generous support, doing everything possible to help them move into adult roles.

cally well-off are more likely to establish their own residence. Among African-American, Hispanic, and Native-American groups, poverty and a cultural tradition of extended-family living lead to lower rates of leaving home, even among young people in college or working (De Marco & Berzin, 2008; Fussell & Furstenberg, 2005). Unmarried Asian young adults also tend to live with their parents. But the longer Asian families have lived in the United States, where they are exposed to individualistic values, the more likely young people are to move out before marriage (Lou, Lalonde, & Giguère, 2012).

Parents of young adults living at home are usually highly committed to helping their children move into adult roles. Many provide wide-ranging assistance—not just financial support, but material resources, advice, companionship, and emotional support as well (Fingerman et al., 2009, 2012b). Still, in homes where parents and young adults live together, conflict over personal and moral values related to the young person's future tends to rise (Rodríguez & López, 2011). But when young adults feel securely attached to parents and well-prepared for independence, departure from the home is linked to more satisfying parent–child interaction and successful transition to adult roles, even among ethnic minorities that strongly emphasize family loyalty and obligations (Smetana, Metzger, & Campione-Barr, 2004; Whiteman, McHale, & Crouter, 2010). And regardless of living arrangements, young people doing well typically have close, enjoyable relationships with their parents, who offer help because they see it as key to their child's future success (Fingerman et al., 2012c).

In contrast, leaving home very early because of a lack of parental financial and emotional support is associated with less successful educational, marriage, and work lives. U.S. poverty-stricken young people are more likely than their nonpoor counterparts to leave home by age 18 (Berzin & De Marco, 2010). But if still at home beyond that age, they often remain there well into their thirties—a trend that may reflect the steep challenges they face in attaining self-sufficiency and exiting poverty.

Joining of Families in Marriage

The average age of first marriage in the United States has risen from about 20 for women and 23 for men in 1960 to 26½ for women and 29 for men today. Consequently, just 20 percent of contemporary U.S. 18- to 29-year-olds are married, compared to 60 percent a half-century ago (U.S. Census Bureau, 2012b). Postponement of marriage is even more marked in Western Europe—to the early thirties for men and the late twenties for women.

The number of first and second marriages has declined over the last few decades as more people stay single, cohabit, or do not remarry after divorce. In 1960, 85 percent of Americans had been married at least once; today, the figure is 70 percent. At present, 51 percent of U.S. adults, only a slight majority, live together as married couples (U.S. Census Bureau, 2012b). In one recent survey, 4 out of 10 American adults agreed that "marriage is becoming obsolete." Nevertheless, marriage remains a central life goal for young people (Pew Forum on Religion and Public Life, 2010; Smith & Snell, 2009). Irrespective of SES and ethnicity, most U.S. 18- to 23-year-olds say they want to marry and have children.

Same-sex marriages are recognized nationwide in Argentina, Belgium, Brazil, Canada, Denmark, France, Iceland, the Netherlands, New Zealand, Norway, Portugal, South Africa, Spain, Sweden, and Uruguay. In the United States, 14 states—California, Connecticut, Delaware, Iowa, Maine, Maryland, Massachusetts, Minnesota, New Hampshire, New Jersey, New York, Rhode Island, Vermont, and Washington—and the District of Columbia have legalized same-sex marriage. Several other states either grant people in same-sex unions the same legal status as married couples or extend nearly all spousal rights to same-sex partnerships. Because legalization is so recent, research on same-sex couples in the context of marriage is scant. But evidence on cohabiting same-sex couples suggests that the same factors that contribute to happiness in other-sex marriages do so in same-sex unions (Diamond, 2006).

Marriage is more than the joining of two individuals. It also requires that two systems—the spouses' families—adapt and overlap to create a new subsystem. Consequently, marriage presents complex challenges.

Marital Roles.   Their honeymoon over, Sharese and Ernie turned to a multitude of issues they had previously decided individually or their families of origin had prescribed—from everyday matters (when and how to eat, sleep, talk, work, relax, have sex, and spend money) to family traditions and rituals (which to retain, which to work out for themselves). And as they related to their social world as a couple, they modified relationships with parents, siblings, extended family, friends, and co-workers.

Contemporary alterations in the context of marriage, including changing gender roles and living farther from family members, mean that couples must work harder than in the past to define their relationships. Although partners are usually similar in religious and ethnic background, "mixed" marriages are increasingly common today. Among new marriages in the United States, 15 percent are between partners of a different race or ethnicity, more than double the rate in 1980 (Taylor et al., 2012). Because of increased opportunities for interracial contact in colleges, workplaces, and neighborhoods and more positive attitudes toward intermarriage, highly educated young adults are more likely than their less educated counterparts to marry partners of another race or ethnicity (Qian & Lichter, 2011). Nevertheless, couples whose backgrounds differ face extra challenges in transitioning to married life.

Age of marriage is the most consistent predictor of marital stability. Young people who marry in their teens to mid-twenties are more likely to divorce than those who marry later (Lehrer & Chen, 2011). Both early marriage followed by childbirth and childbirth before marriage are more common among low-SES adults (U.S. Census Bureau, 2012b). This acceleration of family formation complicates adjustment to life as a couple.

Despite progress in the area of women's rights, **traditional marriages,** involving a clear division of roles—husband as head of household responsible for family economic well-being, wife as caregiver and homemaker—still exist in Western nations. In recent decades, however, these marriages have changed, with many women who focused on motherhood while their children were young returning to the work force later.

In **egalitarian marriages,** partners relate as equals, sharing power and authority. Both try to balance the time and energy they devote to their occupations, their children, and their relationship. Most well-educated, career-oriented women expect this form of marriage. And college-student couples who eventually intend to marry often plan in advance how they will coor-

© ARIEL SKELLEY/BLEND IMAGES/CORBIS

Arms laden with her toddler, a briefcase, and a bag of groceries, an employed mother heads home to prepare dinner. In industrialized nations, women in dual-earner marriages continue to shoulder most housework responsibilities.

dinate work and family roles, especially if the woman intends to enter a male-dominated career (Peake & Harris, 2002).

In Western nations, men in dual-earner marriages participate much more in child care than in the past. U.S. fathers in such marriages put in 85 percent as much time as mothers do. But housework—cleaning, cooking, laundry, and picking up clutter—reveals a different story. Recent surveys indicate that women in the United States and most Western European nations spend nearly twice as much time as men on housework, and women in Australia spend four times as much (Sayer, 2010). In Sweden, which places a high value on gender equality, men do more than in other nations. In contrast, men typically do little housework or child care in Japan, where corporate jobs demand long work hours and traditional marriages are common (Geist, 2010; Shwalb et al., 2004).

Women's housework hours do decline as their employment hours increase. But a close look at gender differences in most industrialized countries reveals that men fail to compensate (Cooke, 2010; Lippe, 2010). As Figure 14.2 shows for Australia, the United Kingdom, and the United States, men spend the same amount of time at housework, irrespective of their partners' employment schedules. Therefore, employed women's reduced housework hours are made possible by either purchase of time-saving services (cleaning help, prepackaged meals) or greater tolerance for unkempt homes, or both (Lachance-Grzela & Bouchard, 2010). In sum, true equality in marriage is still rare, and couples who strive for it usually attain a form of marriage in between traditional and egalitarian.

Marital Satisfaction. Despite its rocky beginnings, Sharese and Ernie's marriage grew to be especially happy. In contrast, Christy and Gary became increasingly discontented. Differences between these two couples mirror the findings of a large body of research on personal and contextual factors, summarized in Table 14.1.

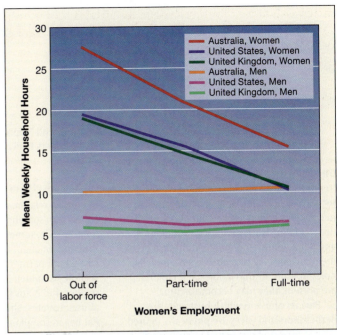

FIGURE 14.2 **Women's and men's housework hours by women's employment for couples in Australia, the United Kingdom, and the United States.** In each nation, as women's employment hours increase, they devote less time to housework. Men's contribution to housework is substantially less than women's. And women's level of employment has no influence on men's housework hours. (From L. P. Cooke, 2010, "The Politics of Housework," in J. Treas & S. Drobnic, [Eds.], *Dividing the Domestic: Men, Women, and Household Work in Cross-National Perspective,* p. 70. Copyright © 2010 by the Board of Trustees of the Leland Stanford Jr. University. Adapted with the permission of Stanford University Press, www.sup.org.)

Christy and Gary had children early and struggled financially. Gary's negative, critical personality led him to get along poorly with Christy's parents and to feel threatened when he and Christy disagreed. Christy tried to offer Gary encouragement

TABLE 14.1 **Factors Related to Marital Satisfaction**

FACTOR	HAPPY MARRIAGE	UNHAPPY MARRIAGE
Family backgrounds	Partners similar in SES, education, religion, and age	Partners very different in SES, education, religion, and age
Age at marriage	After mid-20s	Before mid-20s
Timing of first pregnancy	After first year of marriage	Before or within first year of marriage
Relationship to extended family	Warm and positive	Negative; wish to maintain distance
Marital patterns in extended family	Stable	Unstable; frequent separations and divorces
Financial and employment status	Secure	Insecure
Family responsibilities	Shared; perception of fairness	Largely the woman's responsibility; perception of unfairness
Personality characteristics and behavior	Emotionally positive; common interests; good conflict-resolution skills	Emotionally negative and impulsive; lack of common interests; poor conflict-resolution skills

Note: The more factors present, the greater the likelihood of marital happiness or unhappiness.

Sources: Diamond, Fagundes, & Butterworth, 2010; Gere et al., 2011; Johnson et al., 2005.

Social Issues: Health

Partner Abuse

Violence in families is a widespread health and human rights issue, occurring in all cultures and SES groups. Often one form of domestic violence is linked to others. Recall the story of Karen in Chapter 13. Her husband, Mike, not only assaulted her sexually and physically but also abused her psychologically—isolating, humiliating, and demeaning her. Violent adults also break their partner's favorite possessions, punch holes in walls, or throw objects. If children are present, they may become victims.

Partner abuse in which husbands are perpetrators and wives are physically injured is most likely to be reported to authorities. But many acts of family violence are not reported. When researchers ask American couples about fights that led to acts of hostility, men and women report similar rates of assault (Dutton, 2007). Women victims are more often physically injured, but sex differences in severity of abuse are small (Dutton, 2012; Ehrensaft, Moffitt, & Caspi, 2004). Partner abuse occurs at about the same rate in same-sex relationships as in heterosexual relationships (Schwartz & Waldo, 2004). "Getting my partner's attention," "gaining

control," and "expressing anger" are reasons that partners typically give for abusing each other.

Factors Related to Partner Abuse

In abusive relationships, dominance–submission sometimes proceeds from husband to wife, sometimes from wife to husband. In about one-third to one-half of cases, both partners are violent (Dutton, Nicholls, & Spidel, 2005). Marvin and Pat's relationship helps us understand how partner abuse escalates. Shortly after their wedding, Pat began complaining about the demands of Marvin's work and insisted that he come home early to spend time with her. When he resisted, she hurled epithets, threw objects, and slapped him. One evening, Marvin became so angry at Pat's hostilities that he smashed a dish against the wall, threw his wedding ring at her, and left the house. The next morning, Pat apologized and promised not to attack again. But her outbursts became more frequent and desperate.

These violence–remorse cycles, in which aggression escalates, characterize many abusive relationships. Personality and devel-

opmental history, family circumstances, and cultural factors combine to make partner abuse more likely (Diamond, Fagundes, & Butterworth, 2010).

Many abusers are overly dependent emotionally on their spouses as well as jealous, possessive, and controlling. For example, the thought of Karen ever leaving induced such high anxiety in Mike that he monitored all her activities. And because they have great difficulty managing anger, trivial events—such as an unwashed shirt or a late meal—can trigger abusive episodes. When asked to explain their offenses, they attribute greater blame to their partner than to themselves (Henning, Jones, & Holdford, 2005).

A high proportion of spouse abusers grew up in homes where parents engaged in hostile interactions, used coercive discipline, and were abusive toward their children (Ehrensaft, 2009). Perhaps this explains why conduct problems in childhood and violent delinquency in adolescence also predict partner abuse (Dutton, 2007). Stressful life events, such as job loss or financial difficulties, increase the likelihood of partner abuse. Because of widespread poverty, African Americans and Native Americans report high rates of partner violence (Hoff, 2001). Alcohol abuse is another related factor.

---

and support, but her own needs for nurturance and individuality were not being met. Gary was uncomfortable with Christy's career aspirations. As she came closer to attaining them, the couple grew further apart. In contrast, Sharese and Ernie married later, after their educations were complete. They postponed having children until their careers were under way and they had built a sense of togetherness that allowed each to thrive as an individual. Patience, caring, common values and interests, humor, affection, sharing of personal experiences through conversation, cooperating in household responsibilities, and good conflict-resolution skills contributed to their compatibility.

Although quality of the marital relationship predicts mental health similarly for both genders, men tend to report feeling slightly happier with their marriages than women do (Howard, Galambos, & Krahn, 2010; Kurdek, 2005). Women feel particularly dissatisfied when the demands of husband, children, housework, and career are overwhelming (Forry, Leslie, & Letiecq, 2007; Saginak & Saginak, 2005). Equal power in the relationship and sharing of family responsibilities usually enhance both partners' satisfaction, largely

by strengthening marital harmony (Amato & Booth, 1995; Xu & Lai, 2004).

Of course, from time to time, individuals are bound to say or do something upsetting to their partner. When this happens, the partner's attributions, or explanations for the behavior, make a difference. For example, a wife who interprets her husband's critical remark about her weight as unintentional ("He just isn't aware I'm sensitive about that") is far more likely to express both current and long-term marital satisfaction than a wife who views such comments as malicious ("He's trying to hurt my feelings") (Barelds & Dijkstra, 2011; Fincham & Bradbury, 2004). In fact, partners who hold overly positive (but still realistic) biases concerning each other's attributes are happier with their relationships (Claxton et al., 2011). As they turn to each other for feedback about themselves, these "positive illusions" enhance self-esteem and psychological well-being.

In contrast, people who feel devalued by their partner tend to react with anxiety and insecurity—more so when they are low in self-esteem, which heightens fear of rejection. To protect themselves, they often mete out criticism and contempt in kind,

At a societal level, cultural norms that endorse male dominance and female submissiveness promote partner abuse (Kaya & Cook, 2010). As Figure 14.3 shows, in economically distressed countries that also sanction gender inequality, partner violence against women is especially high, affecting nearly half or more of the female population.

Victims are chronically anxious and depressed and experience frequent panic attacks (Warshaw, Brashler, & Gil, 2009). Yet a variety of situational factors discourage them from leaving these destructive relationships. A victimized wife may depend on her husband's earning power or fear even worse harm to herself or her children. Extreme assaults, including homicide, tend to occur after partner separation (Campbell & Glass, 2009). And victims of both sexes, but especially men, are deterred by the embarrassment of going to the police.

Intervention and Treatment

Community services available to battered women include crisis telephone lines that provide anonymous counseling and social support and shelters that offer safety and treatment (see page 356). Because many women return to their abusive partners several times before making their final move, community agencies usually offer therapy to male batterers (Whitaker, Baker, & Arias, 2007). Most rely on several months to a year of group sessions that confront rigid gender stereotyping; teach communication, problem solving, and anger control; and use social support to motivate behavior change.

Although existing treatments are better than none, most are not effective at dealing with relationship difficulties or alcohol abuse. Consequently, many treated perpetrators repeat their violent behavior with the same or a new partner (Hamberger et al., 2009). At present, few interventions acknowledge that men also are victims. Yet ignoring their needs perpetuates domestic violence. When victims do not want to separate from a violent partner, a whole-family treatment approach that focuses on changing partner interaction and reducing high life stress is crucial.

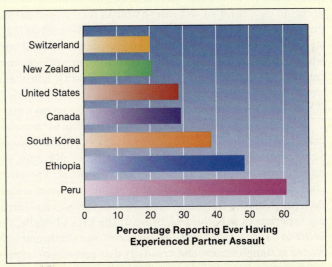

FIGURE 14.3 **Assaults by intimate partners against women in seven nations.** In each country, samples of women were asked to indicate whether they had ever experienced partner physical abuse. The incidence, always underreported, is high in all nations. It is especially high in countries that endorse traditional gender roles and suffer from widespread poverty. (From Kaya & Cook, 2010; World Health Organization, 2000, 2005.)

setting in motion hostile, defensive exchanges that create the very rejection they fear (Murray, 2008). Alternatively, individuals may disengage emotionally, suppressing negative feelings so as not to poison the relationship (Driver et al., 2012). In the process, shared positive emotion also declines, and intimacy erodes.

At their worst, marital relationships can become contexts for intense opposition, dominance–submission, and emotional and physical violence. As the Social Issues: Health box above explains, although women are more often targets of severe partner abuse, both men and women play both roles: perpetrator and victim.

High school and college courses in family life education can promote better mate selection and teach communication skills that contribute to gratifying romantic partnerships and marriages. And counseling aimed at helping couples listen to each other with understanding and empathy, focus on positive traits and memories, and use effective conflict-resolution strategies can cultivate the self-esteem, affection, and respect needed for the relationship to be resilient and enduring (Gottman, 2011).

Parenthood

In the past, the issue of whether to have children was, for many adults, a biological given or a compelling social expectation. Today, in Western industrialized nations, it is a matter of true individual choice. Effective birth control techniques enable adults to avoid having children in most instances. And changing cultural values allow people to remain childless with far less fear of social criticism.

In 1950, 78 percent of American married couples were parents. Today, 70 percent bear children, and they tend to be older when they have their first child. Consistent with this pattern of delayed childbearing and with the decision of most women to divide their energies between family and work, family size in industrialized nations has declined. In 1950, the average number of children per woman was 3.1. Currently, it is 2.1 in the United States, 1.9 in the United Kingdom, 1.7 in Sweden, 1.6 in Canada, 1.4 in Germany, and 1.3 in Italy and Japan (U.S. Census Bureau, 2012a, 2013). Nevertheless, the vast majority of married people continue to embrace parenthood as one of life's most meaningful experiences.

The Decision to Have Children.

The choice of parenthood is affected by a complex array of factors, including financial circumstances, personal and religious values, and health conditions. Women with traditional gender identities usually decide to have children. Whether a woman is employed has less impact on childbearing than her occupation. Women in high-status, demanding careers less often choose parenthood and, when they do, more often delay it than women with less consuming jobs. Parenthood typically reduces work hours and slows career progress among career-oriented women (Abele & Spurk, 2011). In contrast, it generally has no impact on men.

When Americans are asked about their desire to have children, they mention a variety of advantages and disadvantages. Some ethnic and regional differences exist, but in all groups, the most important reasons for having children include the warm, affectionate relationship and the stimulation and fun that children provide. Also frequently mentioned are growth and learning experiences that children bring to the lives of adults, the desire to have someone carry on after one's own death, and feelings of accomplishment and creativity that come from helping children grow (Cowan & Cowan, 2000; O'Laughlin & Anderson, 2001).

Among disadvantages of parenthood, Americans cite loss of freedom most often, followed by concerns about role overload (not enough time for both family and work responsibilities) and about the financial strains. According to a conservative estimate, today's new parents in the United States will spend about $280,000 to rear a child from birth to age 18, and many will incur substantial additional expense for higher education and financial dependency during emerging adulthood (U.S. Department of Agriculture, 2012).

Transition to Parenthood.

The early weeks after a baby enters the family are full of profound changes: constant caregiving, added financial responsibilities, and less time for the couple's relationship. In response, gender roles of husband and wife usually become more traditional—even for couples like Sharese and Ernie who are strongly committed to gender equality (Katz-Wise, Priess, & Hyde, 2010; Lawrence et al., 2010).

For most new parents, however, the arrival of a baby—though often associated with mild declines in relationship satisfaction and communication quality—does not cause significant marital strain. Marriages that are gratifying and supportive tend to remain so (Doss et al., 2009; Feeney et al., 2001). But troubled marriages usually become even more distressed after childbirth (Houts et al., 2008; Kluwer & Johnson, 2007). And when expectant mothers anticipate lack of partner support in parenting, their prediction generally becomes reality, yielding an especially difficult postbirth adjustment (Driver et al., 2012; McHale & Rotman, 2007).

Violated expectations about division of labor in the home powerfully affect new parents' well-being. In dual-earner marriages, the larger the difference in men's and women's caregiving responsibilities, the greater the decline in marital satisfaction after childbirth, especially for women—with negative consequences for parent–infant interaction. In contrast, sharing

Compared to a first birth, a second birth typically requires that fathers become more actively involved in parenting, sharing in the high demands of tending to both a baby and a young child.

caregiving predicts greater parental happiness and sensitivity to the baby (McHale et al., 2004; Moller, Hwang, & Wickberg, 2008).

Postponing childbearing until the late twenties or thirties, as more couples do today, eases the transition to parenthood. Waiting permits couples to pursue occupational goals, gain life experience, and strengthen their relationship. Under these circumstances, men are more enthusiastic about becoming fathers and therefore more willing to participate. And women whose careers are well under way and whose marriages are happy are more likely to encourage their husbands to share housework and child care, which fosters fathers' involvement (Lee & Doherty, 2007; Schoppe-Sullivan et al., 2008).

A second birth typically requires that fathers take an even more active role in parenting—by caring for the firstborn while the mother is recuperating and by sharing in the high demands of tending to both a baby and a young child. Consequently, well-functioning families with a newborn second child typically pull back from the traditional division of responsibilities that occurred after the first birth. Fathers' willingness to place greater emphasis on the parenting role is strongly linked to mothers' adjustment after the arrival of a second baby (Stewart, 1990).

Generous, paid employment leave—widely available in industrialized nations but not in the United States—is crucial for parents of newborns (see Chapter 3, page 81). But financial pressures mean that many new mothers who are eligible for unpaid work leave take far less than they are guaranteed by U.S. federal law, while new fathers take little or none. When favorable workplace policies exist and parents take advantage of them, couples are more likely to support each other and experience family life as gratifying (Feldman, Sussman, & Zigler, 2004). As a result, the stress caused by the birth of a baby stays at manageable levels.

Families with Young Children.

In today's complex world, men and women are less certain about how to rear children than in previous generations. Clarifying child-rearing values and implementing them in warm, involved, and appropriately demanding ways are crucial for the welfare of the next generation and society. Yet cultures do not always place a high priority on parenting, as indicated by lack of many societal supports for children and families (see Chapter 2, pages 50–51). Furthermore, changing family forms mean that the lives of today's parents differ substantially from those of past generations.

In previous chapters, we discussed a wide variety of influences on child-rearing styles, including personal characteristics of children and parents, SES, and ethnicity. The couple's relationship is also vital. Parents who engage in effective coparenting, collaborating and showing solidarity and respect for each other in parenting roles, are more likely to gain in warm marital interaction, feel competent as parents, use effective child-rearing practices, and have children who are developing well (McHale et al., 2002a; Schoppe-Sullivan et al., 2004).

For employed parents, a major struggle is finding good child care and, when their child is ill or otherwise in need of emergency care, taking time off from work or making other urgent arrangements. The younger the child, the greater parents' sense of risk and difficulty—especially low-income parents, who must work longer hours to pay bills; who often, in the United States, have no workplace benefits (health insurance or paid sick leave); who typically cannot afford the cost of child care; and who experience more immediate concerns about their children's safety (Halpern, 2005b; Nomaguchi & Brown, 2011). When competent, convenient child care is not available, the woman usually faces added pressures. She must either curtail or give up her work, with profound financial consequences in low-income families, or endure unhappy children, missed workdays, and constant searches for new arrangements.

Despite its challenges, rearing young children is a powerful source of adult development. Parents report that it expands their emotional capacities, enriches their lives, and enhances psychological well-being (Nomaguchi & Milkie, 2003; Schindler, 2010). For example, involved parents say that parenthood helped them tune in to others' feelings and needs, required that they become more tolerant, self-confident, and responsible, and broadened their extended family, friendship, and community ties. In a survey of a large, nationally representative sample of U.S. fathers, engagement with children predicted greater community service and assistance of extended family members in middle adulthood (Eggebeen, Dew, & Knoester, 2010).

Families with Adolescents.

Adolescence brings sharp changes in parental roles. In Chapters 11 and 12, we noted that parents must establish a revised relationship with their adolescent children—blending guidance with freedom and gradually loosening control. As adolescents gain in autonomy and explore values and goals in their search for identity, parents often complain that their teenager is too focused on peers and no longer cares about being with the family. Heightened parent–child bickering over everyday issues takes a toll, especially on mothers, who do most of the negotiating with teenagers.

Overall, children seem to navigate the challenges of adolescence more easily than parents, many of whom report a dip in marital and life satisfaction. More people seek family therapy during this period of the family life cycle than during any other (Steinberg & Silk, 2002).

Parent Education.

In the past, family life changed little from one generation to the next, and adults learned what they needed to know about parenting through modeling and direct experience. Today's world confronts adults with a host of factors that impinge on their ability to succeed as parents.

Contemporary parents eagerly seek information on child rearing. In addition to popular parenting books, magazines, and websites, new mothers access knowledge about parenting through social media, including chat rooms and blogs. They also reach out to networks of other women for knowledge and assistance. Fathers, by contrast, rarely have social networks through which they can learn about child care and child rearing. Consequently, they frequently turn to mothers to figure out how to relate to their child, especially if they have a close, confiding marriage (Lamb & Lewis, 2004; McHale, Kuersten-Hogan, & Rao, 2004). Recall from Chapter 6 that marital harmony fosters both parents' positive engagement with babies, but it is especially important for fathers.

Parent education courses exist to help parents clarify child-rearing values, improve family communication, understand how children develop, and apply more effective parenting strategies. A variety of programs yield positive outcomes, including enhanced knowledge of effective parenting practices, improved parent–child interaction, and heightened awareness by parents of their role as educators of their children (Bert, Farris, & Borkowski, 2008; Smith, Perou, & Lesesne, 2002). Another benefit is social support—opportunities to discuss concerns with experts and other dedicated parents.

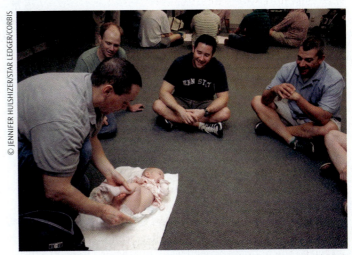

© JENNIFER HULSHIZER/STAR LEDGER/CORBIS

Men are less likely than women to learn about child rearing through informal social networks. Fathers especially may benefit from parent education programs that help them clarify child-rearing values, learn about child development, and parent effectively.

ASK YOURSELF

REVIEW What strategies can couples use to ease the transition to parenthood?

APPLY After her wedding, Sharese was convinced she had made a mistake. Cite factors that sustained her marriage and led it to become especially happy.

REFLECT Do you live with your parents or on your own? Describe factors that contributed to your current living arrangements. How would you characterize the quality of your relationship with your parents? Do your responses match the findings of research?

The Diversity of Adult Lifestyles

The current array of adult lifestyles dates back to the 1960s, when young people began to question the conventional wisdom of previous generations and to ask, "What kinds of commitments should I make to live a full and rewarding life?" As the public became more accepting of diverse lifestyles, choices such as staying single, cohabiting, remaining childless, and divorcing seemed more available.

Today, nontraditional family options have penetrated the American mainstream. As we will see, some adults make a deliberate decision to adopt a lifestyle, whereas others drift into it. The lifestyle may be imposed by society, as is the case for cohabiting same-sex couples in the United States, who cannot marry legally in most states. Or people may choose a certain lifestyle because they feel pushed away from another, such as a marriage gone sour. In sum, the adoption of a lifestyle can be within or beyond the person's control.

Singlehood

On finishing her education, Heather joined the Peace Corps and spent four years in Ghana. Though open to a long-term relationship, she had only fleeting romances. After she returned to the United States, she went from one temporary job to another until, at age 30, she finally found steady employment in a large international travel company as a tour director. A few years later, she advanced into a management position. At age 35, over lunch with Sharese, she reflected on her life: "I was open to marriage, but after I got my career going, it would have interfered. Now I'm so used to independence that I question whether I could adjust to living with another person. I like being able to pick up and go where I want, when I want. But there's a tradeoff: I sleep alone, eat most of my meals alone, and spend a lot of my leisure time alone."

Singlehood—not living with an intimate partner—has increased in recent years, especially among young adults. For example, the rate of never-married Americans in their twenties has nearly tripled since 1960, to 75 percent of young people. As they move into their thirties, more people marry: By 30 to 34 years of age, about 32 percent remain single. More people marry later or not at all, and divorce has added to the numbers of single adults—slightly more than half when adults of all ages are considered. In view of these trends, it is likely that most Americans will spend a substantial part of their adult lives single, and a growing minority—about 8 to 10 percent—will stay that way (Pew Research Center, 2010a; U.S. Census Bureau, 2013).

Because they marry later, more young-adult men than women are single. But women are far more likely than men to remain single for many years or their entire life. With age, fewer men are available with characteristics that most women seek in a mate—the same age or older, equally or better educated, and professionally successful. In contrast, men can choose partners from a large pool of younger unmarried women. Because of the tendency for women to "marry up" and men to "marry down," men with a high school diploma or less and highly educated women in prestigious careers are overrepresented among singles after age 30.

Ethnic differences also exist. For example, the percentage of never-married African Americans is nearly twice as great as that of Caucasian Americans in early adulthood (U.S. Census Bureau, 2013). As we will see later, high unemployment among black men interferes with marriage. Many African Americans eventually marry in their late thirties and forties, a period in which black and white marriage rates come closer together.

The most commonly mentioned advantages of singlehood are freedom and mobility. But singles also recognize drawbacks—loneliness, the dating grind, limited sexual and social life, reduced sense of security, and feelings of exclusion from the

Compared with single men, single women more easily come to terms with their lifestyle, in part because of the greater social support available to women through intimate same-sex friendships.

world of married couples. Single men have more physical and mental health problems than single women, who more easily come to terms with their lifestyle, in part because of the greater social support available to women through intimate same-sex friendships (Pinquart, 2003). But overall, people over age 35 who have always been single are content with their lives (DePaulo & Morris, 2005; Lucas et al., 2003). Though not quite as happy as married people, they report feeling considerably happier than people recently widowed or divorced.

Nevertheless, many single people go through a stressful period in their late twenties or early thirties, when most of their friends have married. Widespread veneration of marriage, along with negative stereotyping of singles as socially immature and self-centered, contributes (Morris et al., 2008). The mid-thirties is another trying time for women, as the biological deadline for pregnancy approaches (Sharp & Ganong, 2011). A few decide to become parents through artificial insemination or a love affair. And an increasing number are adopting, often from overseas countries.

Cohabitation

Cohabitation refers to the lifestyle of unmarried couples who have a sexually intimate relationship and who share a residence. Until the 1960s, cohabitation in Western nations was largely limited to low-SES adults. Since then, it has increased in all groups, with an especially dramatic rise among well-educated, economically advantaged young people. Today's young adults are much more likely than those of a generation ago to form their first conjugal union through cohabitation. Among American young people, cohabitation is now the preferred mode of entry into a committed intimate partnership, chosen by over 60 percent of couples (U.S. Census Bureau, 2013). Cohabitation rates are even higher among adults with failed marriages.

Although Americans are more open to cohabitation than in the past, their attitudes are not as positive as those of Western Europeans. In the Netherlands, Norway, and Sweden, cohabitation is thoroughly integrated into society, with cohabiters having many of the same legal rights and responsibilities as married couples. Consequently, they are nearly as committed to each other as married people (Fussell & Gauthier, 2005; Perelli-Harris & Gassen, 2012). Compared with those in Western Europe, U.S. cohabiting unions are far more likely to dissolve within two years. Furthermore, U.S. couples who cohabit before they are engaged to be married are more prone to divorce than couples who wait to live together until after they have made a commitment to each other. But this association is less strong or absent in Western European nations (Jose, O'Leary, & Moyer, 2010; Rhoades, Stanley, & Markman, 2006). U.S. young people who cohabit prior to engagement tend to have less conventional

Among U.S. couples, making a long-term commitment by becoming engaged before cohabiting predicts an enduring marriage. U.S. young people who cohabit prior to engagement are at increased risk for divorce.

values. They have had more sexual partners and are more politically liberal, less religious, and more androgynous. In addition, a larger number have parents who divorced (Kurdek, 2006).

These personal characteristics may contribute to the negative outcomes associated with U.S. cohabitation. But the cohabitation experience itself also plays a role. U.S. cohabiters have poorer-quality relationships (Kline et al., 2004). Perhaps the open-ended nature of the cohabiting relationship reduces motivation to develop effective conflict-resolution skills. When cohabiters carry negative communication into marriage, it undermines marital satisfaction.

Certain couples, however, are exceptions to the trends just described. People who cohabit after separation or divorce often test a new relationship carefully to prevent another failure, especially when children are involved. As a result, they cohabit longer and are less likely to move toward marriage. Similarly, cohabitation is often an alternative to marriage among low-SES couples (Pew Research Center, 2010a). Many regard their earning power as too uncertain for marriage and continue living together, sometimes giving birth to children and marrying when their financial status improves.

Finally, U.S. cohabiting gay and lesbian couples report strong relationship commitment (Kurdek, 2006). When their relationships become difficult, they end more often than those of heterosexual cohabiters and married couples because of fewer barriers to separating. For example, in 36 U.S. states, same-sex cohabiters cannot legalize their relationship because of laws or constitutional provisions that limit marriage to a man and a woman. Furthermore, same-sex cohabiters are less likely to have children in common and more likely to have extended family members who are unsupportive (Lau, 2012; Rothblum, Balsam, & Solomon, 2011). In a study in which same-sex couples in Vermont were followed over three years, cohabiters were more likely than couples in civil unions to have ended their relationships (Balsam et al., 2008). Civil unions were as stable as heterosexual marriages.

Childlessness

At work, Sharese got to know Beatrice and Daniel. Married for seven years and in their mid-thirties, they did not have children and were not planning any. To Sharese, their relationship seemed especially caring and affectionate. "At first, we were open to becoming parents," Beatrice explained, "but eventually we decided to focus on our marriage."

Childlessness in the United States has increased steadily, from 9 percent of women between ages 20 and 44 in 1975 to about 20 percent today, with similar trends occurring in other Western nations (Livingston & Cohn, 2010). Some people are *involuntarily childless* because they did not find a partner with whom to share parenthood or their efforts at fertility treatments did not succeed. Beatrice and Daniel are in another category—men and women who are *voluntarily childless*. But voluntary childlessness is not always a permanent condition. A few people decide early that they do not want to be parents and stick to their plans. But most, like Beatrice and Daniel, make their decision after they are married and have developed a lifestyle they do not want to give up. Later, some change their minds.

Besides marital satisfaction and freedom from child-care responsibilities, common reasons for not having children include the woman's career and economic security (Amba & Martinez, 2006; Kemkes-Grottenhaler, 2003). Consistent with these motives, the voluntarily childless are usually college-educated, have prestigious occupations, and are highly committed to their work.

Voluntarily childless adults are just as content with their lives as parents who have warm relationships with their children. But adults who cannot overcome infertility are likely to be dissatisfied—some profoundly disappointed, others more ambivalent, depending on compensations in other areas of their lives (Letherby, 2002; Nichols & Pace-Nichols, 2000). Childlessness seems to interfere with adjustment and life satisfaction only when it is beyond a person's control.

Divorce and Remarriage

Divorce rates have stabilized since the mid-1980s, partly because of rising age of marriage, which is linked to greater financial stability and marital satisfaction. In addition, the increase in cohabitation has curtailed divorce: Many relationships that once would have been marriages now break up before marriage. Still, 45 percent of U.S. marriages dissolve (U.S. Census Bureau, 2013). Because most divorces occur within seven years of marriage, many involve young children. Divorces are also common during the transition to midlife, when people have adolescent children—a period (as noted earlier) of reduced marital satisfaction.

Factors Related to Divorce. Why do so many marriages fail? As Christy and Gary's divorce illustrates, the most obvious reason is a disrupted husband–wife relationship. Christy and Gary did not argue more than Sharese and Ernie.

But their problem-solving style was ineffective. When Christy raised concerns, Gary reacted with contempt, resentment, defensiveness, and retreat. This demand–withdraw pattern is found in many partners who split up, with women more often insisting on change and men more often retreating (Birditt et al., 2010; Haltzman, Holstein, & Moss, 2007). Another typical style involves little conflict, but partners increasingly lead separate lives because they have different expectations of family life and few shared interests, activities, or friends (Gottman & Levenson, 2000).

What problems underlie these maladaptive communication patterns? In a nine-year longitudinal study, researchers asked a U.S. national sample of 2,000 married people about marital problems and followed up three, six, and nine years later to find out who had separated or divorced (Amato & Rogers, 1997). Wives reported more problems than husbands, with the gender difference largely involving the wife's emotions, such as anger and hurt feelings. Husbands seemed to have difficulty sensing their wife's distress, which contributed to her view of the marriage as unhappy. Regardless of which spouse reported the problem or was judged responsible for it, the strongest predictors of divorce during the following decade were infidelity, spending money foolishly, drinking or using drugs, expressing jealousy, engaging in irritating habits, and moodiness.

Background factors that increase the chances of divorce are younger age at marriage, not attending religious services, being previously divorced, and having parents who had divorced. Low religious involvement subtracts an influential context for instilling positive marital attitudes and behaviors. And research following families over two decades reveals that parental divorce elevates risk of divorce in at least two succeeding generations, in part because it promotes child adjustment problems and reduces commitment to the norm of lifelong marriage (Amato & Cheadle, 2005; Wolfinger, 2005).

An ineffective problem-solving style can lead to divorce. Partners who split up often follow a pattern in which one partner raises concerns, and the other reacts with resentment, anger, and retreat.

Poorly educated, economically disadvantaged couples who suffer multiple life stresses are especially likely to split up (Clarke-Stewart & Brentano, 2006). But Christy's case represents another trend—rising marital breakup among well-educated, career-oriented, economically independent women. When a woman's workplace status and income exceed her husband's, the risk of divorce increases—an association explained by differing gender-role beliefs between the spouses. A husband's lack of support for his wife's career can greatly heighten her unhappiness and, therefore, the chances that she will end the marriage. Overall, women are twice as likely as men to initiate divorce proceedings.

In addition to the relationship factors just described, American individualism—which includes the belief that each person has the right to pursue self-expression and personal happiness—contributes to the unusually high U.S. divorce rate (see page 276 in Chapter 10) (Cherlin, 2009). Whether cohabiting or married, Americans partner, split up, and repartner more often than anywhere else in the industrialized world.

Consequences of Divorce.

Divorce involves the loss of a way of life and therefore a part of the self sustained by that way of life. As a result, it provides opportunities for both positive and negative change. Immediately after separation, both men and women experience disrupted social networks, a decline in social support, and increased anxiety, depression, and impulsivity (Amato, 2000). For most, these reactions subside within two years. Nonworking women who organized their identities around their husbands have an especially hard time (Coleman, Ganong, & Leon, 2006). And some noncustodial fathers feel disoriented and rootless as a result of decreased contact with their children.

Finding a new partner contributes most to the life satisfaction of divorced adults (Forste & Heaton, 2004; Wang & Amato, 2000). But it is more crucial for men, who adjust less well than women to living on their own. Despite loneliness and a drop in income (see Chapter 10), women tend to bounce back more easily from divorce. However, a few women—especially those who are anxious and fearful, who remain strongly attached to their ex-spouses, or who lack education and job skills—experience a drop in self-esteem and persistent depression (Amato, 2000; Coleman, Ganong, & Leon, 2006). Job training, continued education, career advancement, and social support from family and friends play vital roles in the economic and psychological well-being of many divorced women.

Remarriage.

On average, people remarry within four years of divorce, men somewhat faster than women. Remarriages are especially vulnerable to breakup for several reasons. First, practical matters—financial security, help in rearing children, relief from loneliness, and social acceptance—figure more heavily into a second marriage. Second, some people transfer the negative patterns of interaction learned in their first marriage to the second. Third, people with a failed marriage behind them are

more likely to view divorce as an acceptable solution when marital difficulties resurface. Finally, remarried couples experience more stress from stepfamily situations (Coleman, Ganong, & Leon, 2006). As we will see, stepparent–stepchild ties are powerful predictors of marital happiness.

Blended families generally take three to five years to develop the connectedness and comfort of intact biological families. Family life education, couples counseling, and group therapy can help divorced and remarried adults adapt to the complexities of their new circumstances.

Varied Styles of Parenthood

Diverse family forms result in varied styles of parenthood. Each type of family—blended, never-married, gay or lesbian, among others—presents unique challenges to parenting competence and adult psychological well-being.

Stepparents.

Whether stepchildren live in the household or visit only occasionally, stepparents are in a difficult position. Stepparents enter the family as outsiders and, too often, move into their new parental role too quickly. Lacking a warm attachment bond to build on, their discipline is usually ineffective (Ganong & Coleman, 2004). Compared with first-marriage parents, remarried parents typically report higher levels of tension and disagreement, most centering on child-rearing issues. When both adults have children from prior marriages, rather than only one, more opportunities for conflict exist.

Stepmothers are especially likely to experience conflict. Those who have not previously been married and had children may have an idealized image of family life, which is quickly shattered. Expected to be in charge of family relationships, stepmothers quickly find that stepparent–stepchild ties do not develop instantly. After divorce, biological mothers are frequently jealous, uncooperative, and possessive of their children. Even when their husbands do not have custody, stepmothers feel stressed (Church, 2004; MacDonald & DeMaris, 1996). As stepchildren go in and out of the home, stepmothers find life easier without resistant children and then may feel guilty about their "unmaternal" feelings.

Stepfathers with children of their own tend to establish positive bonds with stepchildren relatively quickly, perhaps because they are experienced in building warm parent–child ties and feel less pressure than stepmothers to plunge into parenting (Ganong et al., 1999). But stepfathers without biological children (like their stepmother counterparts) can have unrealistic expectations. Or their wives may push them into the father role, sparking negativity from children.

In interviews in which young-adult stepchildren provided retrospective accounts of their stepparent relationships, the quality of these ties varied widely. A caring husband–wife bond, sensitive relationship-building behaviors by the stepparent, cooperation from the biological parent, and supportive extended family members all affected stepparent–stepchild ties. Over time, many couples built a coparenting partnership that improved interactions with stepchildren (Ganong, Coleman, & Jamison, 2011). But because stepparent–stepchild bonds are hard to establish, the divorce rate is higher for remarried couples with stepchildren than for those without them.

Never-Married Single Parents.

Today, about 40 percent of U.S. births are to single mothers, more than double the percentage in 1980. Whereas teenage parenthood has declined (see page 300 in Chapter 11), unwed parenthood among mothers in their twenties and older has risen. About 11 percent of U.S. children live with a single mother who has never married (U.S.Census Bureau, 2013).

In the United States, African-American young women make up the largest group of never-married parents. About 64 percent of births to black mothers in their twenties are to women without a partner, compared with 28 percent of births to white women (U.S. Census Bureau, 2013). African-American women postpone marriage more and childbirth less than women in other U.S. ethnic groups. Job loss, persisting unemployment, and consequent inability of many black men to support a family have contributed to the number of African-American never-married, single-mother families.

Never-married African-American mothers tap the extended family, especially their own mothers and sometimes male relatives, for help in rearing their children (Gasden, 1999; Jayakody & Kalil, 2002). For about one-third, marriage—not necessarily to the child's biological father—occurs within a decade after birth of the first child (Wu, Bumpass, & Musick, 2001). These couples function much like other first-marriage parents. Their children are often unaware that the father is a stepfather, and parents do not report the child-rearing difficulties typical of blended families (Ganong & Coleman, 1994).

Still, for low-SES women, never-married parenthood generally increases financial hardship; about half live in poverty (Mather, 2010). Nearly 50 percent of white mothers and 60 percent of black mothers have a second child while unmarried. And children of never-married mothers who lack father involvement achieve less well in school and display more antisocial behavior than children in low-SES, first-marriage families—problems that make life more difficult for mothers (Waldfogel, Craigie, & Brooks-Gunn, 2010). But marriage to the child's biological father benefits children only when the father is a reliable source of economic and emotional support. For example, adolescents who feel close to their nonresident father fare better in school performance and emotional and social adjustment than do those in two-parent homes where a close father tie is lacking (Booth, Scott, & King, 2010). Unfortunately, most unwed fathers—who usually are doing poorly financially—gradually spend less and less time with their children (Lerman,

2010). Strengthening parenting skills, social support, education, and employment opportunities for low-SES parents would greatly enhance the well-being of unmarried mothers and their children.

Gay and Lesbian Parents.

About 20 to 35 percent of lesbian couples and 5 to 15 percent of gay couples are parents, most through previous heterosexual marriages, some through adoption, and a growing number through reproductive technologies (Gates et al., 2007; Goldberg, 2010; Patterson & Riskind, 2010). In the past, because of laws assuming that homosexuals could not be adequate parents, those who divorced a heterosexual partner lost custody of their children. Today, some U.S. states hold that sexual orientation by itself is irrelevant to custody. A few U.S. states, however, ban gay and lesbian couples from adopting children. Among other countries, gay and lesbian adoptions are legal in Argentina, Belgium, Brazil, Canada, Iceland, Mexico, the Netherlands, Norway, South Africa, Spain, Sweden, the United Kingdom, and Uruguay.

Most research on homosexual parents and children is limited to volunteer samples. Findings indicate that gay and lesbian parents are as committed to and effective at child rearing as heterosexual parents and sometimes more so (Bos, van Balen, & van den Boom, 2007; Tasker, 2005). Also, whether born to or adopted by their parents or conceived through donor insemination, children in gay and lesbian families did not differ from the children of heterosexuals in mental health, peer relations, gender-role behavior, or sexual orientation (Allen & Burrell, 1996; Bos & Sandfort, 2010; Farr, Forssell, & Patterson, 2010; Goldberg, 2010). Three additional studies, which surmounted the potential bias associated with volunteer participants by including representative samples of lesbian-mother

© MARILYN HUMPHRIES/THE IMAGE WORKS

Gay and lesbian parents are as committed to and effective at child rearing as heterosexual parents. Overall, families headed by same-sex partners are distinguishable only by issues related to a nonsupportive society.

families, also reported that children were developing favorably (Brewaeys et al., 1997; Chan, Raboy, & Patterson, 1998; Golombok et al., 2003).

When extended-family members withhold acceptance, homosexual mothers and fathers often build "families of choice" through friends, who assume the roles of relatives. Usually, however, parents of gays and lesbians cannot endure a permanent rift (Fisher, Easterly, & Lazear, 2008). With time, interactions between homosexual parents and their families of origin become more positive and supportive.

A major concern of gay and lesbian parents is that their children will be stigmatized by their parents' sexual orientation. Most studies indicate that incidents of teasing or bullying are rare because parents and children carefully manage the information they reveal to others (Tasker, 2005). Overall, families headed by homosexuals can be distinguished from other families only by issues related to living in a nonsupportive society.

Career Development

Besides family life, vocational life is a vital domain of social development in early adulthood. Young people must learn how to perform work tasks well, get along with co-workers, respond to authority, and protect their own interests. When work experiences go well, adults develop new competencies, feel a sense of personal accomplishment, make new friends, and become financially independent and secure. And as we have seen, aspirations and accomplishments in the workplace and the family are interwoven.

Establishing a Career

Our discussion earlier in this chapter highlighted diverse paths and timetables for career development. *TAKE A MOMENT...*

Consider, once again, the wide variations among Sharese, Ernie, Christy, and Gary. Notice that Sharese and Christy, like many women, had *discontinuous* career paths—ones that were interrupted or deferred by child rearing and other family needs (Huang & Sverke, 2007; Moen & Roehling, 2005). Furthermore, not all people embark on the vocation of their dreams. As noted in our consideration of emerging adulthood, the late-2000s recession greatly increased the number of young people in jobs that do not match their educational preparation.

Even for those who enter their chosen field, initial experiences can be discouraging. At the health department, Sharese discovered that paperwork consumed much of her day. Because each project had a deadline, the pressure of productivity weighed heavily on her. Adjusting to unanticipated disappointments in salary, supervisors, and co-workers is difficult. As workers in their twenties become aware of the gap between their expectations and reality, they change jobs often.

Recall from our discussion of Levinson's theory that career progress often depends on the quality of a mentoring relationship. Access to an effective mentor is jointly affected by the availability of willing people and the individual's capacity to select an appropriate individual (Ramaswami & Dreher, 2007). The best mentors are seldom top executives, who tend to be preoccupied and therefore less helpful and sympathetic. Usually, young adults fare better with mentors who are just above them in experience and advancement or who are members of their professional associations (Allen & Finkelstein, 2003). Furthermore, mentoring early in a worker's career increases the likelihood of mentoring later on (Bozionelos et al., 2011). The professional and personal benefits of mentoring induce employees to provide it to others and to seek it again for themselves.

Women and Ethnic Minorities

Women and ethnic minorities have penetrated nearly all professions, but their talents often are not developed to the fullest. Women, especially those who are members of economically disadvantaged minorities, remain concentrated in occupations that offer little opportunity for advancement, and they are underrepresented in executive and managerial roles (see Chapter 13, pages 363–364). And although the overall difference between men's and women's earnings is smaller today than 30 years ago, it remains considerable in all industrialized countries (Rampell, 2010). U.S. government surveys following 9,000 U.S. college-educated workers for a decade revealed that a year after receiving their bachelor's degrees, women working full time earned just 80 percent as much as men. The difference was largely (but not entirely) due to gender differences in college majors: Women more often chose education and service fields, men higher-paying scientific and technical fields. Ten years after graduation, the gender pay gap had widened: Women's pay was only 69 percent of men's, and in no profession did women's earnings equal men's (Dey & Hill, 2007). Gender disparities in career development accounted for about 90 percent of the gap, with the remaining 10 percent attributed to on-the-job discrimination.

Especially for women in traditionally feminine occupations, career planning is often short-term and subject to change. Many women enter and exit the labor market several times, or reduce their work hours from full-time to part-time as they give birth to and rear children (Furchtgott-Roth, 2009; Lips, 2013). Time away from a career greatly hinders advancement—a major reason that women in prestigious, male-dominated careers tend to delay or avoid childbearing (Blair-Loy & DeHart, 2003).

In addition, low self-efficacy with respect to male-dominated fields limits women's career progress. Women who pursue nontraditional careers usually have "masculine" traits—high achievement orientation, self-reliance, and belief that their efforts will result in success. But even those with high self-efficacy are less certain than their male counterparts that they can overcome barriers to career success. In a study of women scientists on university faculties, those reporting a sexist work climate (sexual harassment or discrimination in salary, promotion, or resources) were less satisfied with their jobs and less productive (Settles et al., 2006).

Gender-stereotyped images of women as followers rather than leaders slow advancement into top-level management positions. And because men dominate high-status fields, they must be willing to mentor women into leadership positions and take time from their work responsibilities to do so. Mentoring by a senior-male executive predicts progress into management roles and pay gains more strongly for women in male-dominated industries than for men (Ramaswami et al., 2010). When a powerful male leader *sponsors* the advancement of a talented woman, designating her as having the qualities to succeed, senior-level decision makers are far more likely to take notice.

Despite laws guaranteeing equality of opportunity, racial and ethnic bias in career opportunities remains strong (Smith, Brief, & Colella, 2010). In one study, researchers recruited two three-member teams consisting of a white, a black, and a Hispanic male job applicant, each 22 to 26 years old and matched on verbal and interpersonal skills and physical attractiveness. The applicants were assigned identical fictitious résumés (with the exception that the résumé of the white member of the second team disclosed a criminal record) and sent out to apply for 170 entry-level jobs in New York City (Pager, Western, & Bonikowski, 2009). The white applicant received callbacks or job offers from employers slightly more often than the Hispanic applicant, with the black applicant trailing far behind. When the experiment was repeated with the second team, the white felon remained slightly preferred over both minority applicants, despite their clean records. In line with these findings, African Americans spend more time searching for work, experience less stable employment, and acquire less work experience than Caucasian Americans with equivalent job qualifications (Pager & Shepherd, 2008).

Ethnic minority women often must surmount combined gender and racial discrimination to realize their career poten-

Women in male-dominated fields, such as this scientist, usually have "masculine" traits, such as high achievement orientation and self-reliance. Nevertheless, many encounter workplace barriers to career success.

tial. Those who succeed frequently display an unusually high sense of self-efficacy, attacking problems head-on despite repeated obstacles to achievement. In interviews with African-American women who had become leaders in diverse fields, all reported intense persistence, fueled by supportive relationships with other women, including teachers and peers. Many described their mothers as inspiring role models who had set high standards for them (Richie et al., 1997). Others felt empowered by a deep sense of connection to their African-American communities.

Combining Work and Family

The majority of women with children are in the work force (see page 277 in Chapter 10), most in dual-earner marriages or cohabiting relationships. More women than men report moderate to high levels of stress in trying to meet both work and family responsibilities (Higgins, Duxbury, & Lyons, 2010; Zhao, Settles, & Sheng, 2011).

TAKE A MOMENT... Think about a dual-earner family you know well. What are the main sources of strain? When Sharese returned to her job after her children were born, she felt a sense of *role overload,* or conflict between the demands of work and family responsibilities. In addition to a challenging career, she also (like most employed women) shouldered more household and child-care tasks. And both Sharese and Ernie felt torn between the desire to excel at their jobs and the desire to spend more time with each other, their children, and their friends and relatives. Role overload is linked to increased psychological stress, physical health problems, poorer marital relations, less effective parenting, child behavior problems, and poorer job performance (Perry-Jenkins, Repetti, & Crouter, 2000; Saginak & Saginak, 2005; ten Brummelhuis et al., 2012).

Applying What We Know

Strategies That Help Dual-Earner Couples Combine Work and Family Roles

Strategy	Description
Devise a plan for sharing household tasks.	As soon as possible in the relationship, discuss relative commitment to work and family and division of household responsibilities. Decide who does a particular chore on the basis of who has the needed skill and time, not on the basis of gender. Schedule regular times to rediscuss your plan.
Begin sharing child care right after the baby's arrival.	For fathers, strive to spend equal time with the baby early. For mothers, refrain from imposing your standards on your partner. Instead, share the role of "child-rearing expert" by discussing parenting values and concerns often. Attend a parent education course together.
Talk over conflicts about decision making and responsibilities.	Face conflict through communication. Clarify your feelings and needs and express them to your partner. Listen and try to understand your partner's point of view. Then be willing to negotiate and compromise.
Establish a balance between work and family.	Critically evaluate the time you devote to work in view of your family values and priorities. If it is too much, cut back.
Press for workplace and public policies that assist dual-earner-family roles.	Encourage your employer to provide benefits that help combine work and family, such as flexible work hours, parental leave with pay, and on-site high-quality, affordable child care. Communicate with lawmakers and other citizens about improving public policies for children and families.

Workplace supports can greatly reduce role overload, yielding substantial payoffs for employers. Among a large, nationally representative sample of U.S. working adults, the greater the number of time-flexible policies available in their work settings (for example, time off to care for a sick child, choice in start and stop times, and opportunities to work from home), the better their work performance (Halpern, 2005a). Employees with several time-flexible options missed fewer days of work, less often arrived at work late or left early, felt more committed to their employer, and worked harder. They also reported fewer stress-related health symptoms.

THINKSTOCK IMAGES/GETTY IMAGES

Time-flexible policies enabling employees to work from home help parents adjust work roles to meet family needs. As a result, employees work harder, take less time off, and feel more committed to their jobs.

LOOK AND LISTEN

Talk with one or more dual-earner couples about workplace supports for good parenting. Which policies are available? Which additional ones would they find especially helpful? ●

Effectively balancing work and family brings many benefits—a better standard of living, improved work productivity, enhanced psychological well-being, greater self-fulfillment, and happier marriages. Ernie took great pride in Sharese's dedication to both family life and career. And the skills, maturity, and self-esteem each derived from coping successfully with challenges at home strengthened their capacity to surmount difficulties at work (Graves, Ohlott, & Ruderman, 2007). Applying What We Know above lists strategies that help dual-earner couples attain mastery and pleasure in both spheres of life.

ASK YOURSELF

REVIEW Why do professionally accomplished women, especially those who are members of economically disadvantaged minorities, typically display high self-efficacy?

APPLY Write an essay aimed at convincing a company executive that family-friendly policies are "win-win" situations for both workers and employers.

REFLECT Ask someone who has succeeded in a career of interest to you to describe mentoring relationships that aided his or her progress.

SUMMARY

A Gradual Transition: Emerging Adulthood (p. 369)

What is emerging adulthood, and how has cultural change contributed to it?

- In **emerging adulthood,** young people from the late teens to the mid- to late-twenties have not yet taken on adult responsibilities. Instead, those with economic resources engage in extended exploration of alternatives in education, work, and personal values. Identity development extends into the college years, with young people exploring possibilities in breadth and depth.

- During the late teens and early twenties, religious attendance drops to its lowest level. Regardless of whether they participate in organized religion, many emerging adults begin to construct an individualized faith. They are also committed to improving their world, often engaging in community service.

- Increased education required for entry-level positions in many fields, gains in economic prosperity, and reduced need for young people's labor in industrialized nations have prompted the appearance of emerging adulthood. But because of its strong association with SES and higher education, some researchers do not view emerging adulthood as a distinct period of development.

- In exploring possibilities, emerging adults must adjust to disappointments in love and work, and their explorations may extend risky behaviors of adolescence. A wide array of personal attributes and social supports foster resilience. Relationships with parents are especially influential.

Erikson's Theory: Intimacy versus Isolation (p. 374)

According to Erikson, what personality changes take place during early adulthood?

- In Erikson's theory, young adults must resolve the conflict of **intimacy versus isolation** as they form a close relationship with a partner. The negative outcome is loneliness and self-absorption.

- Young people also focus on aspects of generativity, including parenting and contributions to society through work and community service.

Other Theories of Adult Psychosocial Development (p. 374)

Describe and evaluate Levinson's and Vaillant's psychosocial theories of adult personality development.

- Expanding Erikson's stage approach, Levinson described a series of eras in which people revise their life structure. Young adults usually construct a dream, typically involving career for men and both marriage and career for women, and form a relationship with a mentor. In their thirties, men tend to settle down, whereas many women remain unsettled into middle adulthood.

- Also in the tradition of Erikson, Vaillant portrayed the twenties as devoted to intimacy, the thirties to career consolidation, the forties to generativity, and the fifties and sixties to passing on cultural values.

- Young adults' development is far more variable today than Levinson's and Vaillant's theories depict.

What is the social clock, and how does it affect personality in adulthood?

- Following a **social clock**—age-graded expectations for major life events—grants confidence to young adults. Deviating from it can bring psychological distress.

- As age-graded expectations for appropriate behavior have become increasingly flexible, departures from social-clock life events are common and can create intergenerational tensions.

Close Relationships (p. 376)

Describe factors affecting mate selection and the role of romantic love in the young adult's quest for intimacy.

- Romantic partners tend to resemble each other in age, education level, ethnicity, religion, and various personal and physical attributes.

- According to an evolutionary perspective, women seek a mate with traits that help ensure children's survival, while men look for characteristics signaling sexual pleasure and ability to bear offspring. From a social learning perspective, gender roles profoundly influence criteria for mate selection. Research suggests that both biological and social forces are involved.

- According to Sternberg's **triangular theory of love,** the balance among intimacy, passion, and commitment changes as romantic relationships move from **passionate love** toward **companionate love.** The Western emphasis on romantic love in mate selection does not characterize all cultures.

Describe adult friendships and sibling relationships.

- Adult friendships, like earlier friendships, are based on trust, intimacy, and loyalty. Women's same-sex friendships tend to be more intimate than men's. After marriage, other-sex friendships decline with age for men but increase for women, who tend to form them in the workplace. When family experiences have been positive, adult sibling relationships often resemble friendships

The Family Life Cycle (p. 381)

Trace phases of the family life cycle that are prominent in early adulthood, and cite factors that influence these phases today.

- Wide variations exist in the sequence and timing of the **family life cycle.** A trend toward later home-leaving has occurred in most industrialized nations. Departures generally occur earlier for education than for full-time work or marriage; role transitions may prompt a move back. Parents of young adults living at home are usually highly committed to helping their children move into adult roles.

- The average age of first marriage in the United States and Western Europe has risen. Many countries and a growing number of U.S. states recognize same-sex marriages.

VSTOCK LLC/TANYA CONSTANTINE/GETTY IMAGES

● Both **traditional marriages** and **egalitarian marriages** are affected by women's participation in the work force. Women in Western nations spend nearly twice as much time as men on housework, although men participate much more in child care than in the past. Women feel particularly dissatisfied when the combined demands of work and family roles are overwhelming. Partners who hold overly positive (but still realistic) biases concerning each other's attributes express greater relationship satisfaction.

● Although most couples in industrialized nations become parents, they do so later and have fewer children than in the past. The arrival of a child brings increased responsibilities, often prompting a shift to more traditional roles. After the birth of a second child, this may reverse. Shared caregiving predicts greater parental happiness and positive parent–infant interaction.

● Couples with young children face challenges of clarifying and implementing child-rearing values. Those who engage in effective coparenting are more likely to gain in warm marital interaction, use effective child-rearing practices, and have children who are developing well.

● Parents of adolescents must establish revised relationships with their increasingly autonomous teenagers, blending guidance with freedom and gradually loosening control. Marital satisfaction often declines in this phase.

The Diversity of Adult Lifestyles (p. 388)

Discuss the diversity of adult lifestyles, focusing on singlehood, cohabitation, and childlessness.

● Postponement of marriage and a high divorce rate have contributed to a rise in singlehood. Despite an array of drawbacks, singles typically appreciate their freedom and mobility.

● **Cohabitation** among U.S. couples has increased, becoming the preferred mode of entry into a committed intimate partnership. Compared with their Western European counterparts, Americans who cohabit before marriage tend to be less conventional in values and less committed to their partner, and their subsequent marriages are more likely to fail. But gay and lesbian couples who cohabit because they cannot legally marry report commitment equal to that of married couples.

● Voluntarily childless adults tend to be college-educated, career-oriented, and content with their lives. But involuntary childlessness interferes with adjustment and life satisfaction.

Cite factors that contribute to today's high rates of divorce and remarriage.

● Almost half of U.S. marriages dissolve. Although nearly two-thirds of divorced people remarry, many divorce again. Maladaptive communication patterns, younger ages at marriage, a family history of divorce, poverty, the changing status of women, and American individualism all contribute to divorce.

● Remarriages are especially vulnerable to breakup. Reasons include the prominence of practical concerns in the decision to remarry, the persistence of negative styles of communication, the acceptance of divorce as a solution to marital difficulties, and problems adjusting to a stepfamily.

Discuss challenges associated with varied styles of parenthood, including stepparents, never-married parents, and gay and lesbian parents.

● Establishing stepparent–stepchild ties is difficult, especially for stepmothers and for stepfathers without children of their own. A caring husband–wife bond that includes a coparenting partnership, cooperation from the biological parent, and extended-family support promote positive stepparent–stepchild ties.

● Never-married single parenthood is especially high among African-American women in their twenties. Even with help from extended family members, these mothers find it difficult to overcome poverty.

● Gay and lesbian parents are as effective at child rearing as heterosexual parents, and their children are as well-adjusted as those reared by heterosexual parents.

Career Development (p. 393)

Discuss patterns of career development, and cite difficulties faced by women, ethnic minorities, and couples seeking to combine work and family.

● Men's career paths are usually continuous, whereas women's are often interrupted by family needs. Once young adults settle into an occupation, their progress is affected by opportunities and access to an effective mentor.

● Women and ethnic minorities have penetrated most professions, but their career advancement has been hampered by time away from the labor market, low self-efficacy, lack of mentoring, and gender stereotypes. Racial and ethnic bias remains strong. Ethnic minority women who succeed display an unusually high sense of self-efficacy.

● Couples in dual-earner marriages often experience role overload. Effectively balancing work and family enhances standard of living, work productivity, psychological well-being, and marital happiness.

Important Terms and Concepts

cohabitation (p. 389)
companionate love (p. 377)
egalitarian marriage (p. 382)
emerging adulthood (p. 369)

family life cycle (p. 381)
intimacy versus isolation (p. 374)
passionate love (p. 377)
social clock (p. 376)

traditional marriage (p. 382)
triangular theory of love (p. 377)

milestones

Development in Early Adulthood

- Gains in cognitive–affective complexity. (359)
- Develops expertise in a field of endeavor, which enhances problem solving. (360)
- May increase in creativity. (360–361)

DANIEL LECLAIR/REUTERS/CORBIS

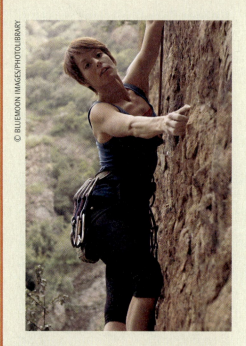

© BLUEMOON IMAGES/PHOTOLIBRARY

- As basal metabolic rate declines, gradual weight gain begins in the middle of this decade and continues through middle adulthood. (350)
- Sexual activity increases. (353–354)

© TROY HOUSE/CORBIS

COGNITIVE

- If college educated, dualistic thinking declines in favor of relativistic thinking. (358)
- Moves from hypothetical to pragmatic thought. (359)
- Narrows vocational options and settles on a specific career. (362)

EMOTIONAL/SOCIAL

- In the first half of this decade, if life circumstances permit, may engage in the extended exploration that characterizes emerging adulthood. (369–370)
- Forms a more complex self-concept that includes awareness of own changing traits and values. (370)
- Is likely to achieve a personally meaningful identity. (370)
- Leaves the parental home permanently. (381)
- Strives to make a permanent commitment to an intimate partner. (374, 376–377)

© ROLF BRUDERER/CORBIS

- Usually constructs a dream—an image of the self in the adult world that guides decision making. (375)

18–30 years

PHYSICAL

- Athletic skills that require speed of limb movement, explosive strength, and gross motor coordination peak early in this decade, then decline. (347–348)
- Athletic skills that depend on endurance, arm–hand steadiness, and aiming peak at the end of this decade, then decline. (347–348)
- Declines in touch sensitivity, cardiovascular and respiratory capacity, immune system functioning, and skin elasticity begin and continue throughout adulthood. (346–347)

© MYRLEEN FERGUSON CATE/PHOTOEDIT

Note: Numbers in parentheses indicate the page or pages on which each milestone is discussed.

- Typically forms a relationship with a mentor. (375)
- If in a high-status career, acquires professional skills, values, and credentials. (375)
- Develops mutually gratifying adult friendships and work ties. (379–380)
- May cohabit, marry, and bear children. (382, 385–386, 389)
- Sibling relationships become more companionate. (380)

HUMMER/DIGITAL VISION/GETTY IMAGES

30–40 years

PHYSICAL

- Declines in vision, hearing, and the skeletal system begin and continue throughout adulthood. (347)
- In women, reproductive capacity declines, and fertility problems increase sharply after the middle of this decade. (348)

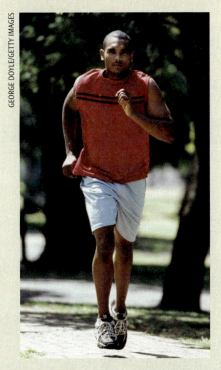

GEORGE DOYLE/GETTY IMAGES

- In men, semen volume, sperm motility, and percentage of normal sperm decrease gradually in the second half of this decade. (348)
- Hair begins to gray and thin in the middle of this decade. (347)
- Sexual activity declines, probably as a result of the demands of daily life. (353–354)

COGNITIVE

- May develop commitment within relativistic thinking. (358)
- Creative accomplishment often peaks in the second half of this decade, although this varies across disciplines. (360)

ANDREW BROOKES, NATIONAL PHYSICAL LABORATORY/SCIENCE SOURCE

EMOTIONAL/SOCIAL

- May cohabit, marry, and bear children. (382, 385–386, 389)

© ST. PETERSBURG TIMES/DIRK SHADD/THE IMAGE WORKS

- Increasingly establishes a stable niche in society through family, occupation, and community activities. (375)

© BIG CHEESE PHOTO LLC/ALAMY

chapter
15

Physical and Cognitive Development in Middle Adulthood

© RIA NOVOSTI/ALAMY

A principal dancer at the Grand Opera of Paris teaches a master class for young professional dancers, transferring knowledge, skill, and passion for his art to a new generation. In middle adulthood, expertise reaches its height.

chapter outline

On a snowy December evening, Devin and Trisha sat down to read the holiday cards piled high on the kitchen counter. Devin's 55th birthday had just passed; Trisha would turn 48 in a few weeks. During the past year, they had celebrated their 24th wedding anniversary. These milestones, along with annual updates they received from friends, brought the changes of midlife into bold relief.

Instead of new births, children starting school, or a first promotion at work, holiday cards and letters sounded new themes. Jewel's recap of the past year reflected growing awareness of a finite lifespan, one in which time had become more precious. She wrote:

My mood has been lighter ever since my birthday. There was some burden I laid down by turning 49. My mother passed away when she was 48, so it all feels like a gift now. Blessed be!

George and Anya reported on their son's graduation from law school and their daughter Michelle's first year of university:

Anya is filling the gap created by the children's departure by returning to college for a nursing degree. After enrolling this fall, she was surprised to find herself in the same psychology class as Michelle. At first, Anya worried about handling the academic work, but after a semester of success, she's feeling more confident.

Tim's message reflected continuing robust health, acceptance of physical changes, and a new burden: caring for aging parents—a firm reminder of the limits of the lifespan:

I used to be a good basketball player in college, but recently I noticed that my 20-year-old nephew, Brent, can dribble and shoot circles around me. It must be my age! But I ran our city marathon in September and came in seventh in the over-50 division. Brent ran, too, but he opted out a few miles short of the finish line to get some pizza while I pressed on. That must be my age, too!

The saddest news is that my dad had a bad stroke. His mind is clear, but his body is partially paralyzed. It's really upsetting because he was getting to enjoy the computer I gave him, and it was so upbeat to talk with him about it in the months before the stroke.

Middle adulthood, which begins around age 40 and ends at about 65, is marked by narrowing life options and a shrinking future as children leave home and career paths become more determined. In other ways, middle age is hard to define because wide variations in attitudes and behaviors exist. Some individuals seem physically and mentally young at age 65—active and optimistic, with a sense of serenity and stability. Others feel old at age 40—as if their lives had peaked and were on a downhill course.

In this chapter, we trace physical and cognitive development in midlife. In both domains, we will encounter not just progressive declines but also sustained performance and compensating gains. As in earlier chapters, we will see that change occurs in manifold ways. Besides heredity and biological aging, our personal approach to passing years combines with family, community, and cultural contexts to affect the way we age. ●

PHYSICAL DEVELOPMENT

Physical development in middle adulthood is a continuation of the gradual changes under way in early adulthood. Even the most vigorous adults notice an older body when looking in the mirror or at family photos. Hair grays and thins, new lines appear on the face, and a fuller, less youthful body shape is evident. During midlife, most individuals begin to experience life-threatening health episodes—if not in themselves, then in their partners and friends. And a change in time orientation, from "years since birth" to "years left to live," adds to consciousness of aging (Neugarten, 1968b).

These factors lead to a revised physical self-image, with somewhat less emphasis on hoped-for gains and more on feared declines (Bybee & Wells, 2003; Frazier, Barreto, & Newman, 2012). Prominent concerns of 40- to 65-year-olds include getting a fatal disease, being too ill to maintain independence, and losing mental capacities. Unfortunately, many middle-aged adults fail to embrace realistic alternatives. People can do much to promote physical vigor and good health in midlife.

Physical Changes

As she dressed for work one morning, Trisha remarked jokingly to Devin, "I think I'll leave the dust on the mirror so I can't see the wrinkles and gray hairs." Catching sight of her image, she continued in a more serious tone. "And look at this fat—it just doesn't want to go! I need to fit some regular exercise into my life." In response, Devin glanced soberly at his own enlarged midriff.

At breakfast, Devin took his glasses on and off and squinted while reading the paper. "Trish—what's the eye doctor's phone number? I've got to get these bifocals adjusted again." As they conversed between the kitchen and the adjoining den, Devin sometimes asked Trisha to repeat herself. And he kept turning up the radio and TV volume. "Does it need to be that loud?" Trisha would ask.

In the following sections, we look closely at the major physical changes of midlife. As we do so, you may find it helpful to refer back to Table 13.1 on page 347, which provides a summary.

Vision

By the forties, difficulty reading small print is common, due to thickening of the lens combined with weakening of the muscle that enables the eye to *accommodate* (adjust its focus) to nearby objects. As new fibers appear on the surface of the lens, they compress older fibers toward the center, creating a thicker, denser, less pliable structure that eventually cannot be transformed at all. By age 50, the accommodative ability of the lens is one-sixth of what it was at age 20. Around age 60, the lens loses its capacity to adjust to objects at varying distances entirely, a condition called **presbyopia** (literally, "old eyes"). As the lens enlarges, the eye rapidly becomes more farsighted between ages 40 and 60 (Charman, 2008). Corrective lenses—or, for nearsighted people, bifocals—ease reading problems.

A second set of changes limits ability to see in dim light, which declines at twice the rate of daylight vision (Jackson & Owsley, 2000). Throughout adulthood, the size of the pupil shrinks and the lens yellows. In addition, starting at age 40, the *vitreous* (transparent gelatin-like substance that fills the eye) develops opaque areas, reducing the amount of light reaching the retina. Changes in the lens and vitreous also cause light to scatter within the eye, increasing sensitivity to glare. While driving at night, Devin sometimes had trouble making out signs and moving objects (Owsley, 2011). And his vision was more disrupted by bright light sources, such as headlights of oncoming cars. Yellowing of the lens and increasing density of the vitreous also limit color discrimination, especially at the green–blue–violet end of the spectrum (Paramei, 2012). Occasionally, Devin had to ask whether his sport coat, tie, and socks matched.

Besides structural changes in the eye, neural changes in the visual system occur. Gradual loss of rods and cones (light- and color-receptor cells) in the retina and of neurons in the optic nerve (the pathway between the retina and the cerebral cortex) contributes to visual declines (Owsley, 2011).

Middle-aged adults are at increased risk of **glaucoma**, a disease in which poor fluid drainage leads to a buildup of pressure within the eye, damaging the optic nerve. Glaucoma affects nearly 2 percent of people over age 40, more often women than men. It typically progresses without noticeable symptoms and is a leading cause of blindness. Heredity contributes to glaucoma, which runs in families: Siblings of people with the disease have a tenfold increased risk, and it occurs three to four times as often in African Americans and Hispanics as in Caucasians (Guedes, Tsai, & Loewen, 2011; Kwon et al., 2009). Starting in midlife, eye exams should include a glaucoma test. Drugs that promote release of fluid and surgery to open blocked drainage channels prevent vision loss.

Hearing

An estimated 14 percent of Americans between ages 45 and 64 suffer from hearing loss, often resulting from adult-onset hearing impairments (Center for Hearing and Communication, 2012). Although some conditions run in families and may be

THOMAS BARWICK/STONE/GETTY IMAGES

A worker uses a grinder to smooth a metal surface in a steel manufacturing facility. Men's hearing declines more rapidly than women's, a difference associated with several factors, including intense noise in some male-dominated occupations.

hereditary, most are age-related, a condition called **presbycusis** ("old hearing").

As we age, inner-ear structures that transform mechanical sound waves into neural impulses deteriorate through natural cell death or reduced blood supply caused by atherosclerosis. Processing of neural messages in the auditory cortex also declines. Age-related cognitive changes—in processing speed, attention, and memory—that we will take up shortly are also associated with hearing loss (Lin et al., 2011). The first sign, around age 50, is a noticeable decline in sensitivity to high-frequency sounds, which gradually extends to all frequencies. Late in life, human speech becomes more difficult to make out, especially rapid speech and speech against a background of voices (Humes et al., 2012). Still, throughout middle adulthood, most people hear reasonably well across a wide frequency range. And African tribal peoples display little age-related hearing loss (Jarvis & van Heerden, 1967; Rosen, Bergman, & Plester, 1962). These findings suggest factors other than biological aging are involved.

Men's hearing tends to decline earlier and more rapidly than women's, a difference associated with cigarette smoking, intense noise and chemical pollutants in some male-dominated occupations, and (at older ages) high blood pressure and cerebrovascular disease, or strokes that damage brain tissue (Heltzner et al., 2005; Van Eyken, Van Camp, & Van Laer, 2007). Most middle-aged and elderly people with hearing difficulties benefit from sound amplification with hearing aids.

Skin

Our skin consists of three layers: (1) the *epidermis,* or outer protective layer, where new skin cells are constantly produced; (2) the *dermis,* or middle supportive layer, consisting of connective tissue that stretches and bounces back, giving the skin flexibility; and (3) the *hypodermis,* an inner fatty layer that adds to the soft lines and shape of the skin. As we age, the epidermis becomes less firmly attached to the dermis, fibers in the dermis thin, cells in both the epidermis and dermis decline in water content, and fat in the hypodermis diminishes, leading the skin to wrinkle, loosen, and feel dry.

In the thirties, lines develop on the forehead as a result of smiling, furrowing the brow, and other facial expressions. In the forties, these become more pronounced, and "crow's-feet" appear around the eyes. Gradually, the skin loses elasticity and begins to sag, especially on the face, arms, and legs (Khavkin & Ellis, 2011). After age 50, "age spots," collections of pigment under the skin, increase. Blood vessels in the skin become more visible as the fatty layer thins.

Because sun exposure hastens wrinkling and spotting, individuals who have spent much time outdoors without proper skin protection look older than their contemporaries. And partly because the dermis of women is not as thick as that of men, women's skin ages more quickly (Makrantonaki & Xouboulis, 2007).

Muscle–Fat Makeup

As Trisha and Devin make clear, weight gain—"middle-age spread"—is a concern for both men and women. A common pattern of change is an increase in body fat and a loss of lean body mass (muscle and bone). The rise in fat largely affects the torso and occurs as fatty deposits within the body cavity; as noted earlier, fat beneath the skin on the limbs declines. On average, size of the abdomen increases 7 to 14 percent. Although a large portion is due to weight gain, age-related changes in muscle–fat makeup also contribute (Stevens, Katz, & Huxley, 2010). In addition, sex differences in fat distribution appear. Men accumulate more on the back and upper abdomen, women around the waist and upper arms (Sowers et al., 2007). Muscle mass declines very gradually in the forties and fifties, largely due to atrophy of fast-twitch fibers, responsible for speed and explosive strength.

Yet, as indicated in Chapter 13, large weight gain and loss of muscle power are not inevitable. With age, people must gradually reduce caloric intake to adjust for the age-related decline in basal metabolic rate (see page 350). In a longitudinal study of nearly 30,000 U.S. 50- to 79-year-old women diverse in SES and ethnicity, a healthy low-fat diet was associated with greater initial weight loss and success at maintaining that loss over a seven-year period (Howard et al., 2006). In nonhuman animals, dietary restraint dramatically increases longevity while sustaining health and vitality. Currently, researchers are identifying the biological mechanisms involved and studying their relevance to humans (see the Biology and Environment box on page 404).

Furthermore, weight-bearing exercise that includes resistance training (placing a moderately stressful load on the muscles) can offset both excess weight and muscle loss (Macaluso & De Vito, 2004; Rivlin, 2007). Consider Devin's 57-year-old friend Tim, who for years has ridden his bike to and from work and jogged on weekends, averaging an hour of vigorous activity per day. Like many endurance athletes, he maintained the same weight and muscular physique throughout early and middle adulthood.

Skeleton

As new cells accumulate on their outer layers, the bones broaden, but their mineral content declines, so they become more porous. This leads to a gradual loss in bone density that begins around age 40 and accelerates in the fifties, especially among women (Clarke & Khosla, 2010). Women's reserve of bone minerals is lower than men's to begin with. And following menopause, the favorable impact of estrogen on bone mineral absorption is lost. Reduction in bone density during adulthood is substantial—about 8 to 12 percent in men and 20 to 30 percent in women (Seeman, 2008).

Loss of bone strength causes the disks in the spinal column to collapse. Consequently, height may drop by as much as 1 inch by age 60, a change that will hasten thereafter. In addition, the weakened bones cannot support as much load: They fracture more easily and heal more slowly. A healthy lifestyle—including weight-bearing exercise, adequate calcium and vitamin D intake, and avoidance of smoking and heavy alcohol consumption—can slow bone loss in postmenopausal women by as much as 30 to 50 percent (Cooper et al., 2009).

When bone loss is very great, it leads to a debilitating disorder called *osteoporosis*. We will take up this condition shortly when we consider illness and disability.

Reproductive System

The midlife transition in which fertility declines is called the **climacteric.** In women, it brings an end to reproductive capacity; in men, by contrast, fertility diminishes but is retained.

Reproductive Changes in Women. The changes involved in women's climacteric occur gradually over a 10-year period, during which the production of estrogen drops. As a result, the number of days in a woman's monthly cycle shortens from about 28 in her twenties and thirties to perhaps 23 by her late forties, and her cycles become more irregular. In some, ova are not released; when they are, more are defective (see Chapter 2, page 42). The climacteric concludes with **menopause, the end of menstruation and reproductive capacity.** This occurs, on average, in the early fifties among North American, European, and East Asian women, although the age range extends from the late thirties to the late fifties (Avis, Crawford, & Johannes, 2002; Rossi, 2005). Women who smoke or who have not borne children tend to reach menopause earlier.

Following menopause, estrogen declines further, causing the reproductive organs to shrink in size, the genitals to be less easily stimulated, and the vagina to lubricate more slowly during arousal. As a result, complaints about sexual functioning increase, with about 35 to 40 percent of women reporting difficulties, especially among those with health problems or whose partners have sexual performance difficulties (Lindau et al., 2007; Walsh & Berman, 2004). The drop in estrogen also contributes to decreased elasticity of the skin and loss of bone mass. Also lost is estrogen's ability to help protect against

Biology and Environment

Anti-Aging Effects of Dietary Calorie Restriction

For nearly 70 years, scientists have known that dietary calorie restriction in nonprimate animals slows aging while maintaining good health and body functions. Rats and mice fed 30 to 40 percent fewer calories than they would freely eat beginning in early life show various physiological health benefits, lower incidence of chronic diseases, and a 60 percent increase in length of life (Fontana, 2009). Mild to moderate calorie restriction begun after rodents reach physical maturity also slows aging and extends longevity, though to a lesser extent. Other studies reveal similar dietary-restriction effects in mice, fleas, spiders, worms, fish, and yeast.

Nonhuman Primate Research

Would primates, especially humans, also benefit from a restricted diet? Researchers have been tracking health indicators in rhesus monkeys after placing some on regimens of 30 percent reduced calories at young, middle, and older ages. More than two decades of longitudinal findings revealed that, compared with freely eating controls, dietary-restricted monkeys were smaller but not overly thin. They accumulated body fat differently—less on the torso, a type of fat distribution that reduces middle-aged humans' risk of heart disease.

Calorie-restricted monkeys also had a lower body temperature and basal metabolic rate—changes that suggest they shifted physiological processes away from growth to life-maintaining functions. Consequently, like calorie-restricted rodents, they seemed better able to withstand severe physical stress, such as surgery and infectious disease (Weindruch et al., 2001).

Among physiological processes mediating these benefits, two seem most powerful. First, calorie restriction inhibited production of free radicals, thereby limiting cellular deterioration, which contributes to many diseases of aging (see page 344 in Chapter 13) (Carter et al., 2007; Yu, 2006). Second, calorie restriction reduced blood glucose and improved insulin sensitivity, offering protection against diabetes and cardiovascular disease. Lower blood pressure and cho-

lesterol and a high ratio of "good" to "bad" cholesterol in calorie-restricted primates strengthened these effects (Fontana, 2008).

Nevertheless, long-term tracking of the monkeys' age of death revealed no difference in length of survival between the calorie-restricted and control groups, regardless of the age at which restriction began. Limiting food intake delayed the onset of age-related diseases, including cancer, cardiovascular disease, and arthritis, but it did not extend the monkeys' longevity (Mattison et al., 2012). In sum, the calorie-restricted monkeys benefited from more years of healthy life, not from an extended lifespan.

Human Research

Prior to World War II, residents of the island of Okinawa consumed an average of 20 percent fewer calories (while maintaining a healthy diet) than mainland Japanese citizens. Their restricted diet was associated with a 60 to 70 percent reduction in incidence of deaths due to cancer and cardiovascular disease, leading many more Okinawan seniors to live to age 100 than in other regions of Japan. Recent generations of Okinawans no longer show these health and longevity advantages (Gavrilova & Gavrilov, 2012). The reason, some researchers speculate, is the introduction of Westernized food, including fast food, to Okinawa.

Similarly, normal-weight and overweight people who have engaged in self-imposed calorie restriction for 1 to 12 years display health benefits—reduced blood glucose, cholesterol, and blood pressure and a stronger immune-system response than individuals eating a typical Western diet (Fontana et al., 2004, 2010; Redman et al., 2008). Furthermore, in the first experiment involving random assignment of human participants to calorie-restricted and nonrestricted conditions, the restricted group again displayed improved cardiovascular and other health indicators, suggesting reduced risk

An Okinawan grandfather and grandson enjoy an afternoon of kite flying. Before World War II, residents of Okinawa consumed a restricted diet that was associated with health benefits and longer life. Recent generations no longer show these advantages, possibly due to the introduction of Westernized food to Okinawa.

of age-related disease (Redman & Ravussin, 2011).

Because nonhuman primates (unlike nonprimate animals) show no gains in length of life, researchers believe that calorie restriction is also unlikely to prolong human longevity. But the health benefits that accrue from limiting calorie intake are now well-established. They seem to result from a physiological response to food scarcity that evolved to increase the body's capacity to survive adversity.

Nevertheless, very few people would be willing to maintain a substantially reduced diet for most of their lifespan. As a result, scientists have begun to explore *calorie-restriction mimetics*—agents such as natural food substances, herbs, and vigorous exercise regimens—that might yield the same health effects as calorie restriction, without dieting (Rizvi & Jha, 2011). These investigations are still in their early stages.

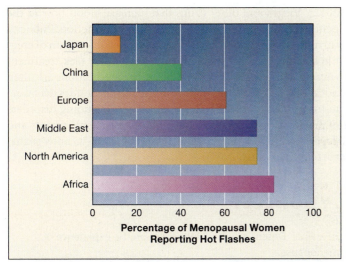

FIGURE 15.1 **Percentage of menopausal women in different regions of the world reporting hot flashes.** Findings are derived from interviews with large samples in each region. Women in Asian nations, especially Japanese women, are less likely to suffer from hot flashes. (Adapted from Obermeyer, 2000; Shea, 2006.)

accumulation of plaque on the walls of the arteries, by boosting "good cholesterol" (high-density lipoprotein).

The period leading up to and following menopause is often accompanied by emotional and physical symptoms, including mood fluctuations and *hot flashes*—sensations of warmth accompanied by a rise in body temperature and redness in the face, neck, and chest, followed by sweating. Hot flashes—which may occur during the day and also, as *night sweats,* during sleep—affect more than 50 percent of women in Western industrialized nations (Nelson, 2008). Typically, they are not severe: Only about 1 in 12 women experiences them every day.

Although menopausal women tend to report increased irritability and less satisfying sleep, research using EEG and other neurobiological measures finds no links between menopause and changes in quantity or quality of sleep (Lamberg, 2007; Young et al., 2002). Also, most studies reveal no association between menopause and depression in the general population (Soares, 2007; Vesco et al., 2007; Woods et al., 2008). Rather, women who have a previous history of depression, are physically inactive, or are experiencing highly stressful life events are more likely to experience depressive episodes during the climacteric. In view of these findings, sleep difficulties or depression should not be dismissed as temporary byproducts of menopause: These problems merit serious evaluation and treatment.

As Figure 15.1 illustrates, compared with North American, European, African, and Middle Eastern women, Asian women report fewer menopausal complaints, including hot flashes (Obermeyer, 2000). Asian diets, which are low in fat and high in soy-based foods (a rich source of plant estrogen) may be involved.

Hormone Therapy. To reduce the physical discomforts of menopause, doctors may prescribe **hormone therapy,** or low daily doses of estrogen. Hormone therapy comes in two types:

(1) estrogen alone, or *estrogen replacement therapy (ERT),* for women who have had hysterectomies (surgical removal of the uterus); and (2) estrogen plus progesterone, or *hormone replacement therapy (HRT),* for other women. Combining estrogen with progesterone lessens the risk of cancer of the endometrium (lining of the uterus), which has long been known as a serious side effect of hormone therapy.

Hormone therapy is highly successful at counteracting hot flashes and vaginal dryness. It also offers some protection against bone deterioration. Nevertheless, more than 20 experiments, in which nearly 43,000 peri- or postmenopausal women had been randomly assigned to take hormone therapy (ERT or HRT) or a sugar pill for at least one year and were followed for an average of seven years, revealed an array of negative consequences. Hormone therapy was associated with an increase in heart attack, stroke, blood clots, breast cancer, gallbladder disease, and deaths from lung cancer. ERT, when compared with HRT, intensified the risk of blood clots, stroke, and gallbladder disease. And women age 65 and older taking HRT showed an elevated risk of Alzheimer's disease and other dementias (Marjoribanks et al., 2012).

Fortunately, the number of alternative treatments for menopausal symptoms is increasing. A relatively safe migraine-headache medication, gabapentin, substantially reduces hot flashes, perhaps by acting on the brain's temperature regulation center. Several antidepressant drugs and black cohosh, an herbal medication, are helpful as well (Guttuso, 2012; Thacker, 2011). Alternative medications are also available to protect the bones, although their long-term safety is not yet clear.

Women's Psychological Reactions to Menopause. How do women react to menopause—a clear-cut signal that their childbearing years are over? The answer lies in how they interpret the event in relation to their past and future lives.

For Jewel, who had wanted marriage and family but never attained these goals, menopause was traumatic. Her sense of physical competence was still bound up with the ability to have children. Physical symptoms can also make menopause a difficult time (Elavsky & McAuley, 2007). And in a society that values a youthful appearance, some women respond to the climacteric with disappointment about a loss of sex appeal (Howell & Beth, 2002).

Many women, however, find menopause to be little or no trouble, regard it as a new beginning, and report improved quality of life (George, 2002; Mishra & Kuh, 2006). When more than 2,000 U.S. women were asked what their feelings were about no longer menstruating, nearly 50 percent of those currently experiencing changes in their menstrual cycles, and 60 percent of those whose periods had ceased, said they felt relieved (Rossi, 2005). Most do not want more children and are thankful to be freed from worry about birth control. And highly educated women usually have more positive attitudes toward menopause than those with less education (Pitkin, 2010).

Other research suggests that African-American and Mexican-American women hold especially favorable views. In several studies, African-American women experienced less

African-American women, who generally view menopause as normal, inevitable, even welcome, experience less irritability and moodiness during this transition than Caucasian-American women.

irritability and moodiness than Caucasian Americans (Melby, Lock, & Kaufert, 2005). They rarely spoke of menopause in terms of physical aging but, instead, regarded it as normal, inevitable, and even welcome (Sampselle et al., 2002, p. 359). Several African Americans expressed exasperation at society's readiness to label as "crazy" middle-aged women's authentic reactions to work- or family-based stressors that often coincide with menopause. Among Mexican-American women who have not yet adopted the language (and perhaps certain beliefs) of the larger society, attitudes toward menopause are especially positive (Bell, 1995).

The wide variation in physical symptoms and attitudes indicates that menopause is not just a hormonal event. It is also affected by cultural beliefs and practices.

Reproductive Changes in Men. Although men also experience a climacteric, no male counterpart to menopause exists. Both quantity and motility of sperm decrease from the twenties on, and quantity of semen diminishes after age 40, negatively affecting fertility in middle age (Sloter et al., 2006). Still, sperm production continues throughout life, and men in their nineties have fathered children. Testosterone production also declines with age, but the change is minimal in healthy men who continue to engage in sexual activity, which stimulates cells that release testosterone.

Nevertheless, because of reduced blood flow to and changes in connective tissue in the penis, more stimulation is required for an erection, and it may be harder to maintain. Difficulty attaining an erection becomes more common in midlife, affecting about 34 percent of U.S. men by age 60 (Shaeer & Shaeer,

2012). Viagra and other drugs that increase blood flow to the penis offer temporary relief from erectile dysfunction. Publicity surrounding these drugs has prompted open discussion of erectile dysfunction and encouraged more men to seek treatment (Berner et al., 2008). But those taking the medications are often not adequately screened for the host of factors besides declining testosterone that contribute to impotence, including disorders of the nervous, circulatory, and endocrine systems; anxiety and depression; pelvic injury; and loss of interest in one's sexual partner (Montorsi, 2005).

ASK YOURSELF

REVIEW Describe cultural influences on the experience of menopause.

APPLY Between ages 40 and 50, Nancy gained 20 pounds. She also began to have trouble opening tightly closed jars, and her calf muscles ached after climbing a flight of stairs. "Exchanging muscle for fat must be an inevitable part of aging," Nancy thought. Is she correct? Why or why not?

REFLECT In view of the benefits and risks of hormone therapy, what factors would you consider, or advise others to consider, before taking such medication?

Health and Fitness

In midlife, nearly 85 percent of Americans rate their health as either "excellent" or "good"—still a large majority, but lower than the 95 percent figure in early adulthood (U.S. Department of Health and Human Services, 2012c). Whereas younger people usually attribute health complaints to temporary infections, middle-aged adults more often point to chronic diseases. As we will see, among those who rate their health unfavorably, men are more likely to suffer from fatal illnesses, women from nonfatal, limiting health problems.

In addition to typical negative indicators—major diseases and disabling conditions—our discussion takes up sexuality as a positive indicator of health. Before we begin, it is important to note that our understanding of health in middle and late adulthood is limited by insufficient research on women and ethnic minorities. Fortunately, this situation is changing. For example, the Women's Health Initiative (WHI)—a commitment by the U.S. federal government, extending from 1993 to 2005, to study the impact of various lifestyle and medical prevention strategies on the health of nearly 162,000 postmenopausal women of all ethnic groups and SES levels—has led to important findings, including health risks associated with hormone therapy, discussed earlier. Two five-year extensions, involving annual health updates from 115,000 WHI participants in 2005–2010, and 94,000 participants in 2010–2015, continue to yield vital information.

Sexuality

Frequency of sexual activity among married couples tends to decline in middle adulthood, but for most, the drop is slight. In the National Social Life, Health, and Aging Project, a nationally representative sample of 3,000 U.S. middle-aged and older adults was surveyed about their sex lives. Even in the latter years of midlife (ages 57 to 64), the overwhelming majority of married and cohabiting adults were sexually active (90 percent of men and 80 percent of women) (Waite et al., 2009). About two-thirds reported having sex several times a month, one-third once or twice a week.

Longitudinal research reveals that stability of sexual activity is far more typical than dramatic change. Couples who have sex often in early adulthood continue to do so in midlife (Dennerstein & Lehert, 2004; Walsh & Berman, 2004). And the best predictor of sexual frequency is marital happiness, an association that is probably bidirectional (DeLamater, 2012). Sex is more likely to occur in the context of a good marriage, and couples who have sex often probably view their relationship more positively.

Nevertheless, *intensity* of sexual response diminishes in midlife due to physical changes of the climacteric. Both men and women take longer to feel aroused and to reach orgasm (Bartlik & Goldstein, 2001; Walsh & Berman, 2004). Yet in the context of a positive outlook, sexual activity can become more satisfying. For example, with greater freedom from the demands of work and family, Devin and Trisha's sex life became more spontaneous. And most couples over age 50 find ways to overcome difficulties with sexual functioning. One happily married 52-year-old woman commented, "We know what we are doing, we've had plenty of practice (laughs), and I would never have believed that it gets better as you get older, but it does" (Gott & Hinchliff, 2003, p. 1625; Kingsberg, 2002).

Illness and Disability

As Figure 15.2 shows, cancer and cardiovascular disease are the leading causes of U.S. deaths in middle age. Unintentional injuries, though still a major health threat, occur at a lower rate than in early adulthood, largely because motor vehicle collisions decline. But falls resulting in bone fractures and death nearly double from early to middle adulthood (U.S. Census Bureau, 2013).

As in earlier decades, economic disadvantage is a strong predictor of poor health and premature death, with SES differences widening in midlife (Smith & Infurna, 2011). And largely because of more severe poverty and lack of universal health insurance, the United States continues to exceed most other industrialized nations in death rates from major causes (OECD, 2012b). Furthermore, men are more vulnerable than women to most health problems. Among middle-aged men, cancer deaths exceed cardiovascular disease deaths by a small margin; among women, cancer is by far the leading cause of death (refer again to Figure 15.2). Finally, as we take a closer look at illness and disability in the following sections, we will encounter yet

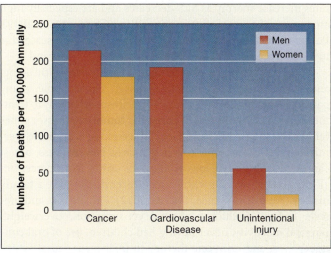

FIGURE 15.2 **Leading causes of death among people age 45 to 64 in the United States.** Men are more vulnerable than women to each leading cause of death. Cancer is the leading killer of both sexes, by a far smaller margin over cardiovascular disease for men than for women. (Adapted from U.S. Census Bureau, 2012b.)

another familiar theme: the close connection between psychological and physical well-being. Personality traits that magnify stress—especially hostility and anger—are serious threats to health in midlife.

Cancer. The incidence of many types of cancer is currently leveling off or declining. But from early to middle adulthood, the cancer death rate multiplies tenfold, accounting for about one-third of all midlife deaths in the United States. Lung cancer is the most common cause of cancer deaths in both genders, worldwide. In the past two decades, its incidence dropped in men; 50 percent fewer smoke today than in the 1950s. In contrast, lung cancer has just begun to decrease in women after a long period of increase, due to large numbers of women taking up smoking in the decades after World War II (American Cancer Society, 2012).

Cancer occurs when a cell's genetic program is disrupted, leading to uncontrolled growth and spread of abnormal cells that crowd out normal tissues and organs. Cancer-causing mutations can be either *germline* (due to an inherited predisposition) or *somatic* (occurring in a single cell, which then multiplies) (see page 40 in Chapter 2 to review). Recall from Chapter 13 that according to one theory, error in DNA duplication increases with age, either occurring spontaneously or resulting from the release of free radicals or breakdown of the immune system. Environmental toxins may initiate or intensify this process.

For cancers that affect both sexes, men are generally more vulnerable than women. The difference may be due to genetic makeup, exposure to cancer-causing agents as a result of lifestyle or occupation, and men's greater tendency to delay going to the doctor. Although the relationship of SES to cancer varies with site (for example, lung and stomach cancers are linked to lower SES, breast and prostate cancers to higher SES), cancer death rates increase sharply as SES decreases and are especially high among low-income ethnic minorities (Clegg et al., 2009). Poorer medical care and reduced ability to fight the disease, due to inadequate diet and high life stress, underlie this trend.

Overall, a complex interaction of heredity, biological aging, and environment contributes to cancer. For example, many patients with familial breast cancer who respond poorly to treatment have defective forms of particular tumor-suppressor genes (either BRCA1 or BRCA2). Genetic screening is available, permitting prevention efforts to begin early. Nevertheless, breast cancer susceptibility genes account for only 5 to 10 percent of all cases; most women with breast cancer do not have a family history (American Cancer Society, 2012). Other genes and lifestyle factors—including alcohol consumption, overweight, physical inactivity, never having had children, use of oral contraceptives, and hormone therapy to treat menopausal symptoms—heighten women's risk.

People often fear cancer because they believe it is incurable. Yet nearly 60 percent of affected individuals are cured—free of the disease for five years or longer. Survival rates, however, vary widely with type of cancer (Siegel, Naishadham, & Jemal, 2012). For example, they are relatively high for breast and prostate cancers, intermediate for cervical and colon cancers, and low for lung and pancreatic cancers.

Breast cancer is the leading malignancy for women, prostate cancer for men. Lung cancer ranks second for both sexes, causing more deaths (due to smoking) than any other cancer type. It is followed closely by colon and rectal cancer. Scheduling annual medical checkups and learning warning signs—a change in bowel or bladder habits, a sore that does not heal, unusual bleeding or discharge, thickening or lump in a breast or elsewhere in your body, indigestion or swallowing difficulty, change in a wart or mole, nagging cough or hoarseness—can reduce cancer death rates considerably.

Surviving cancer is a triumph, but it also brings emotional challenges. Unfortunately, stigmas associated with cancer exist (Daher, 2012). Friends, family, and co-workers may need reminders that cancer is not contagious and that with patience and support from supervisors and co-workers, cancer survivors regain their on-the-job productivity.

Cardiovascular Disease.

Each year about 25 percent of middle-aged American deaths are caused by cardiovascular disease (U.S. Department of Health and Human Services, 2012c). We associate cardiovascular disease with heart attacks, but Devin, like many middle-aged and older adults, learned of the condition during an annual checkup. His doctor detected high blood pressure, high blood cholesterol, and *atherosclerosis*—a buildup of plaque in his coronary arteries, which encircle the heart and provide its muscles with oxygen and nutrients. These indicators of cardiovascular disease are known as "silent killers" because they often have no symptoms.

When symptoms *are* evident, they take different forms. The most extreme is a *heart attack*—blockage of normal blood supply to an area of the heart, usually brought on by a blood clot in one or more plaque-filled coronary arteries. Intense pain results as muscle in the affected region dies. A heart attack is a medical emergency; over 50 percent of victims die before reaching the hospital, another 15 percent during treatment, and an additional 15 percent over the next few years (Go et al., 2013). Among other, less extreme symptoms of cardiovascular disease are *arrhythmia,* or irregular heartbeat. When it persists, it can prevent the heart from pumping enough blood and result in faintness. It can also allow clots to form within the heart's chambers, which may break loose and travel to the brain. In some individuals, indigestion-like pain or crushing chest pain, called *angina pectoris,* reveals an oxygen-deprived heart.

Today, cardiovascular disease can be treated in many ways—including coronary bypass surgery, medication, and pacemakers to regulate heart rhythm. To relieve arterial blockage, Devin had *angioplasty,* a procedure in which a surgeon threaded a needle-thin catheter into his arteries and inflated a balloon at its tip, which flattened fatty deposits to allow blood to flow more freely. Unless Devin took other measures to reduce his risk, his doctor warned, the arteries would clog again within a year.

Some risks, such as heredity, advanced age, and being male, cannot be changed. But cardiovascular disease is so disabling and deadly that people must be alert for it where they least expect it—for example, in women. Because men account for over 70 percent of cases in middle adulthood, doctors often view a heart condition as a "male problem" and frequently overlook women's symptoms, which tend to be milder, more often taking the form of angina than a heart attack (Go et al., 2013). In follow-ups of victims of heart attacks, women—especially African-American women, who are at increased risk—were less likely to be offered drugs to treat blood clots and costly, invasive therapies, such as angioplasty and bypass surgery (Lawton, 2011; Mosca, Barrett-Conner, & Wenger, 2012; Poon et al., 2012). As a result, treatment outcomes—including recurrence and death—tend to be worse for women, particularly black women.

Osteoporosis.

When age-related bone loss is severe, a condition called **osteoporosis** develops. The disorder, affecting about 10 million U.S. adults, 80 percent of whom are women, greatly magnifies the risk of bone fractures. An estimated 55 percent of people over age 50 are at risk for osteoporosis because they have bone density levels low enough to be of concern, and 12 percent have been diagnosed with it (American Academy of Orthopaedic Surgeons, 2009). After age 70, osteoporosis affects the majority of people of both sexes. Although we associate it with a "dowager's hump" in the upper back, this extreme is rare. Because the bones gradually become more porous over many years, osteoporosis may not be evident until fractures—typically in the spine, hips, and wrist—occur or are discovered through X-rays.

A major factor related to osteoporosis is the decline in estrogen associated with menopause. In middle and late adulthood, women lose about 50 percent of their bone mass, about half of it in the first 10 years following menopause—a decline that, by the late sixties, is two to five times greater than in men (Bonnick, 2008). In men, the age-related decrease in testosterone—though much more gradual than estrogen loss in women—

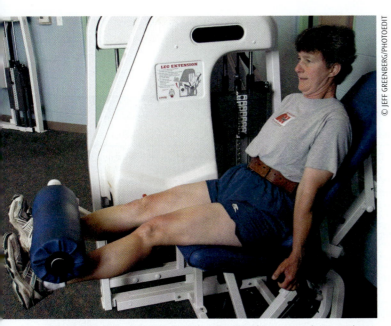

Physical inactivity increases the chances of osteoporosis. More than half of people over age 50, mostly women, are at risk. Weight-bearing exercise and strength training are recommended for both prevention and treatment.

contributes to bone loss because the body converts some to estrogen.

Heredity plays an important role. A family history of osteoporosis increases risk, with identical twins more likely than fraternal twins to share the disorder (Ralston & Uitterlinden, 2010). People with thin, small-framed bodies are more likely to be affected because they typically attain a lower peak bone mass in adolescence. In contrast, higher bone density makes African Americans less susceptible than Asian Americans, Caucasians, Hispanics, and Native Americans (Cauley, 2011). An unhealthy lifestyle also contributes: A diet deficient in calcium and vitamin D (essential for calcium absorption), excess intake of sodium and caffeine, and physical inactivity reduce bone mass. Cigarette smoking and alcohol consumption are also harmful because they interfere with replacement of bone cells (Body et al., 2011; Langsetmo et al., 2012).

When major bone fractures (such as the hip) occur, 10 to 20 percent of patients die within a year (Marks, 2010). Because osteoporosis has become known as a "women's disease," men are far less likely to be screened and treated for it, even after a hip fracture. And compared with women, men with hip fractures tend to be older. Probably for these reasons, the one-year mortality rate after hip fracture is nearly twice as great for men as for women—a gap that widens with age (Haentjens et al., 2010).

To treat osteoporosis, doctors recommend a diet enriched with calcium and vitamin D, weight-bearing exercise (walking rather than swimming), resistance training, and bone-strengthening medications (American Academy of Orthopaedic Surgeons, 2009). A better way to reduce lifelong risk is through early prevention: maximizing peak bone density by increasing calcium and vitamin D intake and engaging in regular exercise in childhood, adolescence, and early adulthood.

Hostility and Anger

Whenever Trisha's sister Dottie called, she seemed like a powder keg ready to explode. Dottie was critical of her boss at work and dissatisfied with the way Trisha, a lawyer, had handled the family's affairs after their father died. Inevitably, Dottie's anger surfaced, exploding in hurtful remarks: "Any lawyer knows that, Trisha. How could you be so stupid! I should have called a *real* lawyer."

After listening as long as she could bear, Trisha would warn, "Dottie, if you continue, I'm going to hang up!"

At age 53, Dottie had high blood pressure, difficulty sleeping, and back pain. In the past five years, she had been hospitalized five times—twice for treatment of digestive problems, twice for an irregular heartbeat, and once for a benign tumor on her thyroid gland. Trisha often wondered whether Dottie's personal style was partly responsible for her health problems.

That hostility and anger might have negative effects on health is a centuries-old idea. Several decades ago, researchers first tested this notion by identifying 35- to 59-year-old men who displayed the **Type A behavior pattern**—extreme competitiveness, ambition, impatience, hostility, angry outbursts, and a sense of time pressure. They found that within the next eight years, Type As were more than twice as likely as Type Bs (people with a more relaxed disposition) to develop heart disease (Rosenman et al., 1975).

Later studies, however, often failed to confirm these results. Type A is actually a mix of behaviors, only one or two of which affect health. Current evidence pinpoints hostility as a "toxic" ingredient of Type A, since isolating it from global Type A consistently predicts heart disease and other health problems in both men and women (Eaker et al., 2004; Matthews et al., 2004; Smith et al., 2004). *Expressed hostility* in particular—angry outbursts; rude, disagreeable behavior; critical and condescending nonverbal cues during social interaction, including glares; and expressions of contempt and disgust—is associated with greater cardiovascular arousal, coronary artery plaque buildup, and heart disease (Haukkala et al., 2010; Julkunen & Ahlström, 2006; Smith & Cundiff, 2011; Smith et al., 2012). As people get angry, heart rate, blood pressure, and stress hormones escalate until the body's response is extreme.

Can Dottie preserve her health by bottling up her hostility instead of expressing it? Repeatedly suppressing overt anger or ruminating about past anger-provoking events is also associated with high blood pressure and heart disease (Eaker et al., 2007; Hogan & Linden, 2004). A better alternative, as we will see, is to develop effective ways of handling stress and conflict.

 ## Adapting to the Physical Challenges of Midlife

Middle adulthood is often a productive time of life, when people attain their greatest accomplishments and satisfactions. Nevertheless, it takes considerable stamina to cope with the full array of changes this period can bring. Devin responded to his

Applying **What We Know**

Managing Stress

Strategy	Description
Reevaluate the situation.	Learn to differentiate normal reactions from those based on irrational beliefs.
Focus on events you can control.	Don't worry about things you cannot change or that may never happen; focus on strategies for handling events under your control.
View life as fluid.	Expect change and accept it as inevitable; then many unanticipated changes will have less emotional impact.
Consider alternatives.	Don't rush into action; think before you act.
Set reasonable goals for yourself.	Aim high, but be realistic about your capacities, motivation, and the situation.
Exercise regularly.	A physically fit person can better handle stress, both physically and emotionally.
Master relaxation techniques.	Relaxation helps refocus energies and reduce the physical discomfort of stress. Classes and self-help books teach these techniques.
Use constructive approaches to anger reduction.	Delay responding ("Let me check into that and get back to you"); use mentally distracting behaviors (counting to 10 backwards) and self-instruction (a covert "Stop!") to control anger arousal; then engage in calm, self-controlled problem solving ("I should call him rather than confront him personally").
Seek social support.	Friends, family members, co-workers, and organized support groups can offer information, assistance, and suggestions for coping with stressful situations.

expanding waistline and cardiovascular symptoms by leaving his desk twice a week to attend a low-impact aerobics class and by reducing job-related stress through daily 10-minute meditation sessions. And Trisha's generally optimistic outlook enabled her to cope successfully with the physical changes of midlife, the pressures of her legal career, and Devin's chronic illness.

Stress Management

TAKE A MOMENT... Turn back to Chapter 13, pages 348 and 356, and review the negative consequences of psychological stress on the cardiovascular, immune, and gastrointestinal systems. Stress management is important at any age, but in middle adulthood it can limit the age-related rise in illness and, when disease strikes, reduce its severity.

Applying What We Know above summarizes effective ways to reduce stress. Even when stressors cannot be eliminated, people can change how they handle some and view others. At work, Trisha focused on problems she could control—not on her boss's irritability but on ways to delegate routine tasks to her staff so she could focus on challenges that required her knowledge and skills. When Dottie phoned, Trisha learned to distinguish normal emotional reactions from unreasonable self-blame. Instead of interpreting Dottie's anger as a sign of her own incompetence, she reminded herself of Dottie's difficult temperament and hard life. And greater life experience helped her accept change as inevitable, so she was better-equipped to deal with the jolt of sudden events, such as Devin's hospitalization for treatment of arterial blockage.

Notice how Trisha called on two general strategies for coping with stress, discussed in Chapter 10: (1) *problem-centered coping,* in which she appraised the situation as changeable, identified the difficulty, and decided what to do about it; and (2) *emotion-centered coping,* which is internal, private, and aimed at controlling distress when little can be done about a situation. Longitudinal research shows that adults who effectively reduce stress move flexibly between problem-centered and emotion-centered techniques, depending on the situation

© JOHNER IMAGES/ALAMY

Stress management in middle adulthood helps limit the age-related rise in illness. This midlifer reduces stress by periodically leaving her high-pressure office environment to work in a tranquil, picturesque setting.

(Zakowski et al., 2001). Their approach is deliberate, thoughtful, and respectful of both themselves and others.

Notice, also, that problem-focused and emotion-focused coping, though they have different immediate goals, facilitate each other. Effective problem-focused coping reduces emotional distress, while effective emotion-focused coping helps people face problems more calmly and, thus, generate better solutions. Ineffective coping, in contrast, is largely emotion-centered and self-blaming, impulsive, or escapist.

As noted in Chapter 13, people tend to cope with stress more effectively as they move from early to middle adulthood. They may become more realistic about their ability to change situations and more skilled at anticipating stressful events and at preparing to manage them (Aldwin, Yancura, & Boeninger, 2010). Furthermore, when middle-aged adults surmount a highly stressful experience, they often report lasting personal benefits as they look back with amazement at what they were able to accomplish under extremely trying conditions. Interpreting trauma as growth-promoting is related to more effective coping with current stressors and with increased physical and mental health years later (Aldwin & Yancura, 2011; Carver, 2011). In this way, managing intense stress can serve as a context for positive development.

LOOK AND LISTEN

Interview a middle-aged adult who has overcome a highly stressful experience, such as a serious illness, about how he or she coped. Inquire about any resulting changes in outlook on life. Do the adult's responses fit with research findings? ●

Exercise

Regular exercise, as noted in Chapter 13, has a range of physical and psychological benefits—among them, equipping adults to handle stress more effectively and reducing the risk of many diseases. Heading for his first aerobics class, Devin wondered, Can starting to exercise at age 50 counteract years of physical inactivity? His question is important: Nearly 70 percent of U.S. middle-aged adults are sedentary, and half of those who begin an exercise program discontinue it within the first six months (U.S. Department of Health and Human Services, 2011c).

A person beginning to exercise in midlife must overcome initial barriers and ongoing obstacles—lack of time and energy, inconvenience, work conflicts, and health factors (such as overweight). *Self-efficacy* is just as vital in adopting, maintaining, and exerting oneself in an exercise regimen as it is in career progress (see Chapter 14). An important outcome of starting an exercise program is that sedentary adults gain in self-efficacy, which further promotes physical activity (McAuley & Elavsky, 2008; Wilbur et al., 2005). Enhanced physical fitness, in turn, prompts middle-aged adults to feel better about their physical selves. Over time, their physical self-esteem—sense of body conditioning and attractiveness—rises (Elavsky & McAuley, 2007; Gothe et al., 2011).

In cities across the United States, barriers to physical activity are being overcome through the creation of attractive, safe parks and trails. But low-SES adults need greater access to convenient, pleasant exercise environments.

The exercise format that works best depends on the beginning exerciser's characteristics. Normal-weight adults are more likely to stick with group classes than are overweight adults, who may feel embarrassed and struggle to keep up with the pace. Overweight people do better with an individualized, home-based routine planned by a consultant (King, 2001). However, adults with highly stressful lives are more likely to persist in group classes, which offer a regular schedule and the face-to-face support of others (King et al., 1997).

Accessible, attractive, and safe exercise environments— parks, walking and biking trails, and community recreation centers—and frequent opportunities to observe others using them also promote physical activity. Besides health problems and daily stressors, low-SES adults often mention inconvenient access to facilities, expense, unsafe neighborhoods, and unclean streets as barriers to exercise—important reasons that activity level declines sharply with SES (Taylor et al., 2007; Wilbur et al., 2003).

An Optimistic Outlook

What type of individual is likely to cope adaptively with stress brought on by the inevitable changes of life? Researchers interested in this question have identified a set of three personal qualities—control, commitment, and challenge—that, together, they call **hardiness** (Maddi, 2005, 2007, 2011).

Trisha fit the pattern of a hardy individual. First, she regarded most experiences as *controllable*. "You can't stop all bad things from happening," she advised Jewel after hearing about her menopausal symptoms, "but you can try to do something about them." Second, Trisha displayed a *committed,* involved approach to daily activities, finding interest and meaning in almost all of them. Finally, she viewed change as a *challenge*—a normal, welcome, even exciting part of life.

Hardiness influences the extent to which people appraise stressful situations as manageable. These optimistic appraisals, in turn, predict health-promoting behaviors, tendency to seek social support, reduced physiological arousal to stress, and fewer physical and emotional symptoms (Maddi, 2006; Maruta et al., 2002; Räikkönen et al., 1999; Smith, Young, & Lee, 2004). Furthermore, high-hardy individuals are likely to use active, problem-centered coping strategies in situations they can control. In contrast, low-hardy people more often use emotion-centered and avoidant coping strategies—for example, saying, "I wish I could change how I feel," denying that the stressful event occurred, or eating and drinking to forget about it (Maddi, 2007; Soderstrom et al., 2000).

In this and previous chapters, we have seen that many factors act as stress-resistant resources—among them heredity, diet, exercise, social support, and coping strategies. Research on hardiness adds yet another ingredient: a generally optimistic outlook and zest for life.

Gender and Aging: A Double Standard

Negative stereotypes of aging, which lead many middle-aged adults to fear physical changes, are more likely to be applied to women than to men, yielding a double standard (Antonucci, Blieszner, & Denmark, 2010). Though many women in midlife say they have "hit their stride"—feel assertive, confident, versatile, and capable of resolving life's problems—people often rate them as less attractive and as having more negative personality characteristics than middle-aged men (Denmark & Klara, 2007; Kite et al., 2005).

These effects appear more often when people rate photos as opposed to verbal descriptions of men and women. The ideal of a sexually attractive woman—smooth skin, good muscle tone, lustrous hair—may be at the heart of the double standard of aging. Some evidence suggests that the end of a woman's ability to bear children contributes to negative judgments of physical appearance, especially by men (Marcus-Newhall, Thompson, & Thomas, 2001). Yet societal forces exaggerate this view. For example, middle-aged people in media ads are usually male executives, fathers, and grandfathers—handsome images of competence and security. And many more cosmetic products designed to hide signs of aging are offered for women than for men.

Fortunately, recent surveys suggest that the double standard is declining—that more people are viewing middle age as a potentially upbeat, satisfying time for both genders (Menon, 2001; Narayan, 2008). Models of older women with lives full of intimacy, accomplishment, hope, and imagination are promoting acceptance of physical aging and a new vision of growing older—one that emphasizes gracefulness, fulfillment, and inner strength.

COGNITIVE DEVELOPMENT

In middle adulthood, the cognitive demands of everyday life extend to new and sometimes more challenging situations. Consider a typical day in the lives of Devin and Trisha. Recently appointed dean of faculty at a small college, Devin was at his desk by 7:00 A.M. In between strategic-planning meetings, he reviewed files of applicants for new positions and worked on the coming year's budget. Meanwhile, Trisha prepared for a civil trial, participated in jury selection, and then joined the other top lawyers at her firm for a conference about management issues. That evening, Trisha and Devin advised their 20-year-old son, Mark, who had dropped by to discuss his uncertainty over whether to change his college major. By 7:30 P.M., Trisha was off to an evening meeting of the local school board. And Devin left for a biweekly gathering of an amateur quartet in which he played the cello.

Middle adulthood is a time of expanding responsibilities—on the job, in the community, and at home. To juggle diverse roles effectively, Devin and Trisha called on a wide array of intellectual abilities, including accumulated knowledge, verbal fluency, memory, rapid analysis of information, reasoning, problem solving, and expertise in their areas of specialization. What changes in thinking take place in middle adulthood, and what factors influence those changes? And what can be done to support the rising tide of adults who are returning to higher education in hopes of enhancing their knowledge and quality of life?

Changes in Mental Abilities

At age 50, when he occasionally couldn't recall a name or had to pause in the middle of a lecture or speech to think about what to say next, Devin wondered, Are these signs of an aging mind? Twenty years earlier, he had taken little notice of the same events. His questioning stems from widely held stereotypes of older adults as forgetful and confused. Most cognitive aging research has focused on deficits while neglecting cognitive stability and gains.

As we examine changes in thinking in middle adulthood, we will revisit the theme of diversity in development. Although declines occur in some areas, most people display cognitive competence, especially in familiar contexts, and some attain outstanding accomplishment. Overall, the evidence supports a positive view of adult cognitive potential.

The research we are about to consider illustrates core assumptions of the lifespan perspective: development as *multidimensional,* or the combined result of biological, psychological, and social forces; development as *multidirectional,* or the joint expression of growth and decline, with the precise mix varying across abilities and individuals; and development as *plastic,* or open to change, depending on how a person's biological and environmental history combines with current life conditions. You may find it helpful to return to pages 6–7 in Chapter 1 to review these ideas.

Cohort Effects

Research using intelligence tests sheds light on the widely held belief that intelligence inevitably declines in middle and late adulthood as the brain deteriorates. Many early cross-sectional studies showed this pattern—a peak in performance at age 35 followed by a steep drop into old age. But widespread testing of college students and soldiers in the 1920s provided a convenient opportunity to conduct longitudinal research, retesting participants in middle adulthood. These findings revealed an age-related increase! To explain this contradiction, K. Warner Schaie (1998, 2005) used a sequential design, combining longitudinal and cross-sectional approaches (see page 30 in Chapter 1) in the Seattle Longitudinal Study.

In 1956, people ranging in age from 22 to 70 were tested cross-sectionally. Then, at regular intervals, longitudinal follow-ups were conducted and new samples added, yielding a total of 5,000 participants, five cross-sectional comparisons, and longitudinal data spanning more than 60 years. Findings on five mental abilities showed the typical cross-sectional drop after the mid-thirties. But longitudinal trends for those abilities revealed modest gains in midlife, sustained into the fifties and the early sixties, after which performance decreased gradually.

Cohort effects are largely responsible for this difference. In cross-sectional research, each new generation experienced better health and education than the one before it (Schaie, 2011). Also, the tests given may tap abilities less often used by older individuals, whose lives no longer require that they learn information for its own sake but, instead, skillfully solve real-world problems.

Crystallized and Fluid Intelligence

A close look at diverse mental abilities shows that only certain ones follow the longitudinal pattern just described. To appreci-

Don Clarke, who flew attack helicopters in the U.S. army, fulfilled a long-held dream when he became an emergency medical service helicopter pilot. Flying search-and-rescue missions requires Clarke, now in his early sixties, to make use of complex mental abilities that are at their peak in midlife.

ate this variation, let's consider two broad mental abilities, each of which includes an array of specific intellectual factors.

The first of these broad abilities, **crystallized intelligence**, refers to skills that depend on accumulated knowledge and experience, good judgment, and mastery of social conventions—abilities acquired because they are valued by the individual's culture. Devin made use of crystallized intelligence when he expressed himself articulately at the alumni luncheon and suggested effective ways to save money in budget planning. On intelligence tests, vocabulary, general information, verbal comprehension, and logical reasoning items measure crystallized intelligence.

In contrast, **fluid intelligence** depends more heavily on basic information-processing skills—ability to detect relationships among visual stimuli, speed of analyzing information, and capacity of working memory. Though fluid intelligence often combines with crystallized intelligence to support effective reasoning and problem solving, it is believed to be influenced less by culture than by conditions in the brain and by learning unique to the individual (Horn & Noll, 1997). Intelligence test items reflecting fluid abilities include spatial visualization, digit span, letter–number sequencing, and symbol search. (Refer to page 243 in Chapter 9 for examples.)

Many cross-sectional studies show that crystallized intelligence increases steadily through middle adulthood, whereas fluid intelligence begins to decline in the twenties. These trends have been found repeatedly in investigations in which younger and older participants had similar education and general health status, largely correcting for cohort effects (Horn, Donaldson, & Engstrom, 1981; Kaufman & Horn, 1996; Park et al., 2002). In one such investigation, including nearly 2,500 mentally and physically healthy 16- to 85-year-olds, verbal (crystallized) IQ peaked between ages 45 and 54 and did not decline until the eighties! Nonverbal (fluid) IQ, in contrast, dropped steadily over the entire age range (Kaufman, 2001).

The midlife rise in crystallized abilities makes sense because adults are constantly adding to their knowledge and skills at work, at home, and in leisure activities. In addition, many crystallized skills are practiced almost daily. But does longitudinal evidence confirm the progressive falloff in fluid intelligence?

Schaie's Seattle Longitudinal Study. Figure 15.3 shows Schaie's longitudinal findings in detail. The five factors that gained in early and middle adulthood—verbal ability, inductive reasoning, verbal memory, spatial orientation, and numeric ability—include both crystallized and fluid skills. Their paths of change confirm that midlife is a time when some of the most complex mental abilities are at their peak (Willis & Schaie, 1999). According to these findings, middle-aged adults are intellectually "in their prime," not—as stereotypes would have it— "over the hill."

Figure 15.3 also shows a sixth ability, *perceptual speed*— a fluid skill in which participants must, for example, identify within a time limit which of five shapes is identical to a model or whether pairs of multidigit numbers are the same or different. Perceptual speed decreased from the twenties to the late eighties—a pattern that fits with a wealth of research indicating

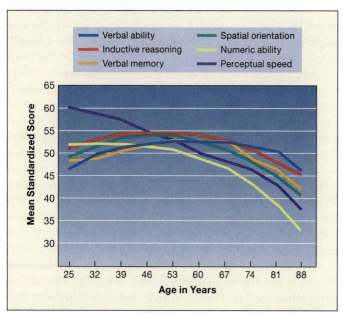

FIGURE 15.3 **Longitudinal trends in six mental abilities, from the Seattle Longitudinal Study.** In five abilities, modest gains occurred into the fifties and early sixties, followed by gradual declines. The sixth ability—perceptual speed—decreased steadily from the twenties to the late eighties. And late in life, fluid factors (spatial orientation, numeric ability, and perceptual speed) showed greater decrements than crystallized factors (verbal ability, inductive reasoning, and verbal memory). (From K. W. Schaie, 1994, "The Course of Adult Intellectual Development," *American Psychologist, 49,* p. 308. Copyright © 1994 by the American Psychological Association. Reprinted with permission of American Psychological Association.)

that cognitive processing slows as people get older (Schaie, 1998, 2005). Also notice in Figure 15.3 how, late in life, fluid factors (spatial orientation, numeric ability, and perceptual speed) show greater decrements than crystallized factors (verbal ability, inductive reasoning, and verbal memory).

Explaining Changes in Mental Abilities. Some theorists believe that a general slowing of central nervous system functioning underlies nearly all age-related declines in cognitive performance (Salthouse, 1996, 2006). Many studies offer at least partial support for this idea. Researchers have also identified other important changes in information processing, some of which may be triggered by declines in speed.

Before we turn to this evidence, let's clarify why research reveals gains followed by stability in crystallized abilities, despite a much earlier decline in fluid intelligence, or basic information-processing skills. First, the decrease in basic processing, while substantial after age 45, may not be great enough to affect many well-practiced performances until quite late in life. Second, as we will see, adults often compensate for cognitive limitations by drawing on their cognitive strengths. Finally, as people discover that they are no longer as good as they once were at certain tasks, they accommodate, shifting to activities that depend less on cognitive efficiency and more on accumulated knowledge. Thus, the basketball player becomes a coach, the once quick-witted salesperson a manager.

Still, mental abilities, including fluid skills, remain plastic. In the Seattle Longitudinal Study, baby boomers, now mostly middle-aged, were compared with the previous generation at the same age, revealing cohort effects. On verbal memory, inductive reasoning, and spatial orientation, baby boomers performed substantially better, reflecting advances in education, technology, environmental stimulation, and health care (Schaie, 2011; Willis & Schaie, 1999). These gains are expected to continue: Today's children, adolescents, and adults of all ages attain substantially higher mental test scores than same-age individuals born just a decade or two earlier—differences that are largest for fluid-ability tasks (Flynn, 2007, 2011; Zelinski & Kennison, 2007).

Information Processing

Many studies confirm that as processing speed slows, certain basic aspects of executive function, including attention and working memory, decline. Yet midlife is also a time of great expansion in cognitive competence as adults apply their vast knowledge and life experience to problem solving in the everyday world.

Speed of Processing

Devin watched with fascination as his 20-year-old son, Mark, played a computer game, responding to multiple on-screen cues in rapid-fire fashion. When Devin tried it, though he practiced over several days, his performance remained well behind Mark's.

Similarly, on a family holiday in Australia, Mark adjusted quickly to driving on the left side of the road, but after a week, Trisha and Devin still felt confused at intersections, where rapid responses were needed.

These real-life experiences fit with laboratory findings. On both simple reaction-time tasks (pushing a button in response to a light) and complex ones (pushing a left-hand button to a blue light, a right-hand button to a yellow light), response time increases steadily from the early twenties into the nineties. The more complex the situation, the more disadvantaged older adults are. Although the decline in speed is gradual and quite small—less than 1 second in most studies—it is nevertheless of practical significance (Der & Deary, 2006; Dykiert et al., 2012).

Researchers agree that changes in the brain are responsible but disagree on the precise explanation (Hartley, 2006; Salthouse & Caja, 2000). According to the **neural network view,** as neurons in the brain die, breaks in neural networks occur. The brain adapts by forming bypasses—new synaptic connections that go around the breaks but are less efficient (Cerella, 1990). Another hypothesis, the **information-loss view,** suggests that older adults experience greater loss of information as it moves through the cognitive system. As a result, the whole system must slow down to inspect and interpret the information. Imagine making a photocopy, then using it to make another copy. Each subsequent copy is less clear. Similarly, with each step of thinking, information degrades. The older the adult, the more exaggerated this effect (Myerson et al., 1990). Complex tasks, which have more processing steps, are more affected by information loss.

At present, researchers are not sure whether just one or two neural changes, or multiple neural changes that vary across individuals, underlie declines in processing speed (Hartley, 2006; Salthouse, 2011). What is clear is that processing speed predicts adults' performance on many tests of complex abilities. The slower their reaction time, the lower people's scores on tests of memory, reasoning, and problem solving, with relationships greater for fluid- than crystallized-ability items (Finkel et al., 2007; Salthouse, 2006). This suggests that processing speed contributes broadly to declines in cognitive functioning (Li et al., 2004).

Yet processing speed correlates only moderately with older adults' performances, including fluid-ability tasks. And it is not the only major predictor of age-related cognitive changes. Other factors—declines in vision and hearing and in attentional resources, inhibition, working-memory capacity, and use of memory strategies—also predict diverse age-related cognitive performances (Hartley, 2006; Luo & Craik, 2008). Consequently, disagreement persists over whether age-related cognitive changes have just one common cause, best represented by processing speed, or multiple independent causes, which include an array of perceptual and cognitive skills in addition to processing speed.

Furthermore, processing speed is a weak predictor of the skill with which older adults perform complex, familiar tasks in everyday life, which they continue to do with considerable proficiency. Devin, for example, played a Mozart quartet on his cello with great speed and dexterity, keeping up with three other players 10 years his junior. How did he manage? Compared with the others, he more often looked ahead in the score (Krampe & Charness, 2007). Using this compensatory approach, he could prepare a response in advance, thereby minimizing the importance of speed. Knowledge and experience can also compensate for impairments in processing speed. Devin's many years of playing the cello undoubtedly supported his ability to play swiftly and fluidly.

Because older adults find ways to compensate for cognitive slowing on familiar tasks, their reaction time is considerably better on verbal items (indicating as quickly as possible whether a string of letters forms a word) than on nonverbal items (responding to a light or other signal) (Hultsch, MacDonald, & Dixon, 2002; Verhaeghen & Cerella, 2008). Finally, as we will see in Chapter 17, older adults' processing speed can be improved through training, though age differences remain.

Attention

Studies of attention focus on how much information adults can take into their mental systems at once; the extent to which they can attend selectively, ignoring irrelevant information; and the ease with which they can adapt their attention, switching from one task to another as the situation demands. Trisha sometimes tried to prepare dinner or check her e-mail inbox while talking on the phone. But with age, she found it harder to engage in the two activities simultaneously.

Consistent with Trisha's experience, laboratory research reveals that sustaining two tasks at once, when at least one of the tasks is complex, becomes more challenging with age. Older adults have difficulty even when they have recently engaged in extensive practice of one of the activities and it is therefore expected to be automatic (Maquestiaux et al., 2010). An age-related decrement also occurs in the ability to switch back and forth between mental operations, such as judging one of a pair of numbers as "odd or even" on some trials, "more or less" on others (Kramer & Kray, 2006; Verhaeghen & Cerella, 2008). These declines in attention might be due to the slowdown in information processing described earlier, which limits the amount of information a person can focus on at once (Allen, Ruthruff, & Lien, 2007; Verhaeghen, 2012).

As adults get older, *inhibition*—resistance to interference from irrelevant information—is also harder (Gazzaley et al., 2005; Hasher, Lustig, & Zacks, 2007). On *continuous performance tasks,* in which participants are shown a series of stimuli on a computer screen and asked to press the space bar only after a particular sequence occurs (for example, the letter *K* immediately followed by the letter *A*), performance declines steadily from the thirties into old age, with older adults making more errors of commission (pressing the space bar in response to incorrect letter sequences). And when extraneous noise is introduced, errors of omission (not pressing the space bar after a *K–A* sequence) also rise with age (Mani, Bedwell, & Miller, 2005). In everyday life, inhibitory difficulties cause older adults to appear

Conductors and teachers must focus on relevant information within a complex field of stimulation and divide their attention among competing tasks—well-practiced skills that may help slow age-related declines in attention.

distractible—inappropriately diverted from the task at hand by a thought or a feature of the environment.

Again, adults can compensate for these changes. People highly experienced in attending to critical information and performing several tasks at once, such as air traffic controllers and pilots, know exactly what to look for. As a result, they show smaller age-related attentional declines (Tsang & Shaner, 1998). Similarly, older adults focus on relevant information and handle two tasks proficiently when they have extensively practiced those activities over their lifetimes (Kramer & Madden, 2008). Furthermore, practice can improve the ability to divide attention between two tasks, selectively focus on relevant information, and switch back and forth between mental operations. When older adults receive training in these skills, their performance improves as much as that of younger adults, although training does not close the gap between age groups (Bherer et al., 2006; Erickson et al., 2007; Kramer, Hahn, & Gopher, 1998).

Memory

From the twenties into the sixties, the amount of information people can retain in working memory diminishes. Whether given lists of words or digits (verbal tasks) or serial location stimuli (spatial tasks involving retaining each location on a screen of a series of stimuli), middle-aged and older adults recall less than young adults, although verbal memory suffers much less than spatial memory (Hale et al., 2011; Old & Naveh-Benjamin, 2008). Verbal memory may be better preserved because the older adults tested have previously formed and often used verbal representations of the to-be-learned information (Kalpouzos & Nyberg, 2012). The necessary spatial representations, in contrast, are far less familiar.

These changes are affected by a decline in use of memory strategies. Older individuals rehearse less than younger individuals—a difference believed to be due to a slower rate of thinking (Salthouse, 1996). Older people cannot repeat new information

to themselves as quickly as younger people. Reduced working-memory capacity is another influence, leading to difficulties in retaining to-be-remembered items and processing them at the same time (Basak & Verhaeghen, 2011).

Memory strategies of organization and elaboration, which require people to link incoming information with already stored information, are also applied less often and less effectively with age (Dunlosky & Hertzog, 2001; Troyer et al., 2006). An additional reason older adults are less likely to use these techniques is that they find it harder to retrieve information from long-term memory that would help them recall. For example, given a list of words containing *parrot* and *blue jay,* they don't immediately access the category "bird," even though they know it well (Hultsch et al., 1998). Greater difficulty keeping one's attention on relevant information seems to be involved (Hasher, Lustig, & Zacks, 2007). As irrelevant stimuli take up space in working memory, less is available for the memory task at hand.

But keep in mind that the memory tasks given by researchers require strategies that many adults seldom use and may not be motivated to use, since most are not in school (see Chapter 9, page 240). When given training in strategic memorizing, middle-aged and older people use strategies willingly, and they show improved performance over long periods, though age differences remain (Derwinger, Neely, & Bäckman, 2005).

Furthermore, tasks can be designed to help older people compensate for age-related declines in working memory—for example, by slowing the pace at which information is presented. In one study, adults ranging in age from 19 to 68 were shown a video and immediately tested on its content (a pressured, classroomlike condition). Then they were given a packet of information on the same topic as the video to study at their leisure and told to return three days later to be tested (a self-paced condition) (Beier & Ackerman, 2005). Performance declined with age only in the pressured condition, not in the self-paced condition. And although topic-relevant knowledge predicted better recall in both conditions, it did so more strongly in the self-paced condition, which granted participants ample time to retrieve and apply what they already knew.

As these findings illustrate, assessing older adults in highly structured, constrained conditions substantially underestimates what they can remember when given opportunities to pace and direct their own learning. (Refer to the Social Issues: Education box on the following page for a "dramatic" illustration.) When we consider the variety of memory skills we call on in daily life, the decrements just described are limited in scope. General *factual knowledge* (such as historical events), *procedural knowledge* (such as how to drive a car or solve a math problem), and knowledge related to one's occupation either remain unchanged or increase into midlife.

Finally, middle-aged people who have trouble recalling something often draw on decades of accumulated *metacognitive knowledge* about how to maximize memory—reviewing major points before an important presentation, organizing notes and files so information can be found quickly, and parking the car in the same area of the parking lot each day. Research confirms that aging has little impact on metacognitive knowledge and the

Social Issues: Education

The Art of Acting Improves Memory in Older Adults

Actors face a daunting task: They must memorize massive quantities of dialogue and then reproduce it accurately and spontaneously, as if they genuinely mean what they say. No wonder the most common question asked of actors is, "How did you learn all those lines?"

Interviews with professional actors reveal that most don't memorize lines by rote, rehearsing them many times. Instead, they focus on the meaning of the words, an approach that produces much better recall. First, they analyze the script for the character's intentions, breaking it down into what they call "beats"—small, goal-directed chunks of dialogue. Then they represent the role as a sequence of goals, one leading to the next. When actors recall this chain of goals, lines become easier to remember (Noice & Noice, 2006). For example, one actor divided a half-page of dialogue into three beats: "to put [the other character] at ease," "to start a conversation with him," "to flatter/draw him out."

To create a beat sequence, actors engage in extensive elaboration of dialogue segments. For example, to the line, "Perhaps he's in love with me but doesn't know it," an actor might create a visual image of an uncertain lover, relate the material to a past love affair of her own, and match her own mood to feeling tone of the statement. Deep elaborative processing of the dialogue segment, along with analysis of its beat goal, yields substantial verbatim recall without rote memorization.

Actors' script learning is so successful that on stage, they are free to "live in the moment," focusing on communicating authentic meaning through action, emotion, and utterance while speaking the lines. This intermodal integration of spoken word with facial expression, tone of voice, and body language contributes further to script retention.

Can aging adults benefit from exercises that teach the essence of acting? To find out, researchers gave middle-aged and older adults nine 90-minute cognitively demanding group sessions of theater training over a month's time. Each session required them to analyze the goals of brief scenes so they could become fully engrossed in acting out their meaning (Noice, Noice, & Staines, 2004). Compared with no-intervention controls, theater-training participants showed greater gains on tests of working-memory capacity, word recall, and problem solving—improvements still evident four months after the intervention ended.

fMRI research indicates that deeply processing verbal meanings strongly activates

© JESSE FOLKS

These community-theater actors master their lines through deep, elaborate processing of goal-oriented segments of dialogue. Teaching these script-learning techniques to aging adults yields lasting gains in memory performance.

certain areas in the frontal lobes of the cerebral cortex in middle-aged adults, restoring them to patterns close to those of young adults (Park, 2002). These findings lend neurobiological support to the power of acting, with its challenging intermodal processing of meaning, to enhance human memory.

---

ability to apply such knowledge to improve learning (Hertzog & Dunlosky 2011).

LOOK AND LISTEN

Ask several adults in their fifties or early sixties to list their top three everyday memory challenges and to explain what they do to enhance recall. How knowledgeable are these midlifers about effective memory strategies? •

In sum, age-related changes in memory vary widely across tasks and individuals as people use their cognitive capacities to meet the requirements of their everyday worlds. **TAKE A MOMENT...** Does this remind you of Sternberg's *theory of successful intelligence,* described in Chapter 9—in particular, his notion of *practical intelligence* (see page 244)? To understand memory development (and other aspects of cognition) in adulthood, we must view it in context. As we turn to problem solving, expertise, and creativity, we will encounter this theme again.

Practical Problem Solving and Expertise

One evening, as Devin and Trisha sat in the balcony of the Chicago Opera House awaiting curtain time, the announcement came that 67-year-old Ardis Krainik, the opera company's general director and "life force," had died. After a shocked hush, members of the audience began turning to one another, asking about the woman who had made the opera company into one of the world's greatest.

Starting as a chorus singer and clerk typist, Ardis rose rapidly through the ranks, becoming assistant to the director and developing a reputation for tireless work and unmatched organizational skill. When the opera company fell deeply in debt, Ardis—now the newly appointed general director—erased the deficit within a year and restored the company's sagging reputation. She charmed donors into making large contributions, attracted world-class singers, and filled the house to near capacity.

Ardis's story is a dramatic one, but all middle-aged adults encounter opportunities to display continued cognitive growth in the realm of **practical problem solving**, which requires people to size up real-world situations and analyze how best to achieve goals that have a high degree of uncertainty. Gains in *expertise*—an extensive, highly organized, and integrated knowledge base that can be used to support a high level of performance—help us understand why practical problem solving takes this leap forward.

The development of expertise is under way in early adulthood and reaches its height in midlife, leading to highly efficient and effective approaches to solving problems. This rapid, implicit application of knowledge is the result of years of learning, experience, and effortful practice (Birney & Sternberg, 2006; Krampe & Charness, 2007). It cannot be assessed by laboratory tasks or mental tests that do not call on this knowledge.

Expertise is not just the province of the highly educated and of those who rise to the top of administrative ladders. In a study of food service workers, researchers identified the diverse ingredients of expert performance in terms of physical skills (strength and dexterity); technical knowledge (of menu items, ordering, and food presentation); organizational skills (setting priorities, anticipating customer needs); and social skills (confident presentation and a pleasant, polished manner). Next, 20- to 60-year-olds with fewer than two to more than ten years of experience were evaluated on these qualities. Although physical strength and dexterity declined with age, job knowledge and organizational and social skills increased (Perlmutter, Kaplan, & Nyquist, 1990). Compared to younger adults with similar years of experience, middle-aged employees performed more competently, serving customers in especially adept, attentive ways.

Age-related advantages are also evident in solutions to everyday problems—for example, how to resolve a disagreement between two friends, or whether to make a costly repair to one's home (Denney, 1990; Denney & Pearce, 1989). From middle age on, adults place greater emphasis on thinking through a practical problem with multiple potential solutions—trying to understand it better, interpreting it from different perspectives, and solving it through logical analysis (Kim & Hasher, 2005; Mienaltowski, 2011). Perhaps for this reason, they are more rational decision makers—less likely than young adults to select attractive-looking options that, on further reflection, are not the best.

Creativity

As noted in Chapter 13, creative accomplishment tends to peak in the late thirties or early forties and then decline, but with considerable variation across individuals and disciplines. Some people produce highly creative works in later decades: In her early sixties, Martha Graham choreographed *Clytemnestra*, recognized as one of the great full-length modern-dance dramas. Igor Stravinsky composed his last major musical work at age 84. Charles Darwin finished *On the Origin of Species* at age 50 and wrote additional groundbreaking books and papers in his sixties and seventies. Harold Gregor, who painted the dazzling image

on the cover of this book, continues to invent new styles and to be a highly productive artist at age 83. And as with problem solving, the *quality* of creativity may change with advancing age—in at least three ways.

First, youthful creativity in literature and the arts is often spontaneous and intensely emotional, while creative works produced after age 40 often appear more deliberately thoughtful (Lubart & Sternberg, 1998). Perhaps for this reason, poets produce their most frequently cited works at younger ages than do authors of fiction and nonfiction (Cohen-Shalev, 1986). Poetry depends more on language play and "hot" expression of feelings, whereas story- and book-length works require extensive planning and molding.

Second, with age, many creators shift from generating unusual products to combining extensive knowledge and experience into unique ways of thinking. Creative works by older adults more often sum up or integrate ideas. Mature academics typically devote less energy to new discoveries in favor of writing memoirs, histories of their field, and other reflective works. And in older creators' novels, scholarly writings, and commentaries about their paintings and musical compositions, learning from life experience and living with old age are common themes (Beckerman, 1990; Lindauer, Orwoll, & Kelley, 1997; Sternberg & Lubart, 2001).

Finally, creativity in middle adulthood frequently reflects a transition from a largely egocentric concern with self-expression to more altruistic goals (Tahir & Gruber, 2003). As the middle-aged person overcomes the youthful illusion that life is eternal, the desire to give to humanity and enrich the lives of others increases.

Taken together, these changes may contribute to an overall decline in creative output in later decades. In reality, however, creativity takes new forms.

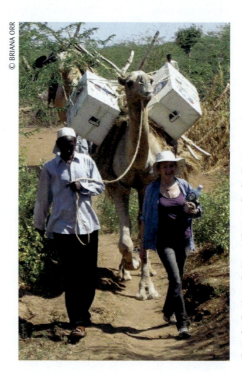

© BRIANA ORR

In midlife, creativity often shifts to more altruistic goals. Author Masha Hamilton's travels to northeastern Kenya to research her novel, *The Camel Bookmobile,* led her to help organize the Camel Book Drive. It has funded the purchase of camels, books, and equipment for nomadic schools in the area.

ASK YOURSELF

REVIEW How do slowing of cognitive processing, reduced working-memory capacity, and difficulties with inhibition affect memory in midlife? What can older adults do to compensate for these declines?

APPLY Asked about hiring middle-aged sales personnel, a department store manager replied, "They're my best employees!" Why does this manager find older employees desirable, despite age-related declines in processing speed, attention, and working memory?

This 50-year-old, a full-time undergraduate at Mount Holyoke College, is one of many nontraditional students in U.S. colleges and universities. Appropriate academic advising and encouragement from family members, friends, and faculty help middle-aged learners succeed.

Adult Learners: Becoming a Student in Midlife

Adults are returning to undergraduate and graduate study in record numbers. During the past three decades, students age 25 and older in U.S. colleges and universities increased from 27 to 39 percent of total enrollment, with an especially sharp rise in those over age 35 (U.S. Department of Education, 2012b). Life transitions often trigger a return to formal education, as with Devin and Trisha's friend Anya, who entered a nursing program after her last child left home. Divorce, widowhood, a job layoff, a family move, a youngest child reaching school age, older children entering college, and rapid changes in the job market are other events that commonly precede reentry (Hostetler, Sweet, & Moen, 2007). Among a sample of African-American women, additional motivations included serving as a role model for children and enriching their ethnic community as a whole (Coker, 2003).

Characteristics of Returning Students

About 60 percent of adult learners are women (U.S. Department of Education, 2012b). They often report feeling especially self-conscious, inadequate, and hesitant to talk in class (Compton, Cox, & Laanan, 2006). Their anxiety stems partly from not having practiced academic learning for many years and partly from negative aging, gender, and (for minority students) ethnic stereotypes about ability to learn.

Role demands outside of school—from children, spouses, other family members, friends, and employers—pull many returning women in conflicting directions. Those reporting high psychological stress typically are single parents with limited financial resources, or married women with high career aspirations, young children, and nonsupportive partners (Deutsch & Schmertz, 2011). When couples fail to rework divisions of household and child-care responsibilities to accommodate the woman's return to school, marital satisfaction declines (Sweet & Moen, 2007). As a classmate remarked to Anya, "I tried keeping the book open and reading, cooking, and talking to the kids. It didn't work. They felt I was ignoring them."

Because of multiple demands on their time, mature-age women tend to take fewer credits, experience more interruptions in their academic programs, and progress at a slower pace than mature-age men. Role overload is the most common reason for not completing their degrees (Jacobs & King, 2002). But many express high motivation to work through those difficulties, referring to the excitement of learning, to the fulfillment academic success brings, and to their hope that a college education will improve both their work and family lives (Kinser & Deitchman, 2007).

LOOK AND LISTEN

Interview a nontraditional student on your campus about the personal challenges and rewards of working toward a degree at a later age. ●

Supporting Returning Students

As these findings suggest, social supports for returning students can make the difference between continuing in school and dropping out. Adult students need family members and friends who encourage their efforts and enable them to find time for uninterrupted study. Anya's classmate explained, "My doubts subsided when one day, Bill volunteered, 'You take your books and do what you need to do. I can cook dinner and do the laundry.'" Institutional services for returning students are also essential. Personal relationships with faculty, peer networks enabling adult students to get to know one another, conveniently scheduled evening and Saturday classes, online courses, and financial aid for part-time students increase the chances of academic success.

Although nontraditional students rarely require assistance in settling on career goals, they report a strong desire for help in choosing the most appropriate courses and for small, discussion-based classes that meet their learning and relationship needs. Academic advising and professional internship opportunities are vital. Students from low-SES backgrounds often need special assistance, such as academic tutoring, sessions in confidence building and assertiveness, and—in the case of ethnic minorities—help adjusting to styles of learning that are at odds with their cultural background.

When support systems are in place, most returning students gain in self-efficacy and do well academically (Chao & Good, 2004). After finishing her degree, Anya secured a position as a parish nurse with creative opportunities to counsel members of a large congregation about health concerns. Education granted her new life options, financial rewards, and increased self-esteem as she reevaluated her own competencies. Sometimes (though not in Anya's case) revised values and greater self-reliance can spark other changes, such as a divorce or a new intimate partnership (Sweet & Moen, 2007). In middle adulthood as in earlier years, education transforms development, often profoundly reshaping the life course.

ASK YOURSELF

REVIEW In view of the impact of education and other experiences on midlife cognitive development, evaluate the saying "You can't teach an old dog new tricks."

APPLY Marcella completed one year of college in her twenties. Now, at age 42, she has returned to earn a degree. Plan a set of experiences for Marcella's first semester that will increase her chances of success.

REFLECT What range of services does your institution offer to support returning students? What additional supports would you recommend?

SUMMARY

PHYSICAL DEVELOPMENT

Physical Changes (p. 401)

Describe the physical changes of middle adulthood, paying special attention to vision, hearing, the skin, muscle–fat makeup, and the skeleton.

- The gradual physical changes begun in early adulthood continue in midlife, contributing to a revised physical self-image, with less emphasis on hoped-for gains and more on feared declines.

- Vision is affected by **presbyopia** (loss of the accommodative ability of the lens), reduced vision in dim light, increased sensitivity to glare, and diminished color discrimination. After age 40, risk of **glaucoma**, a buildup of pressure in the eye that damages the optic nerve, increases.

- Age-related hearing loss, or **presbycusis**, begins with a decline in detection of high frequencies and then spreads to other tones. Eventually, human speech becomes harder to decipher.

- The skin wrinkles, loosens, dries, and starts to develop age spots. Muscle mass declines and fat deposits increase. A low-fat diet and regular exercise, including resistance training, can offset both excess weight and muscle loss.

- Bone density declines, especially in women after menopause. Height loss and bone fractures can result.

Describe reproductive changes in both sexes during middle adulthood.

- The **climacteric** in women, which occurs gradually as estrogen production drops, concludes with **menopause**, often accompanied by emotional and physical symptoms.

- **Hormone therapy** can reduce the discomforts of menopause, but its use increases the risk of cardiovascular disease, certain cancers, and cognitive declines.

- Although sperm production continues throughout life, quantity of semen diminishes and erections become harder to attain and maintain. Drugs are available to combat impotence.

Health and Fitness (p. 406)

Discuss sexuality in middle adulthood and its association with psychological well-being.

- Frequency of sexual activity among married couples declines only slightly in middle adulthood. Intensity of sexual response diminishes due to physical changes of the climacteric. Most married people over age 50 find ways to overcome difficulties with sexual functioning.

Discuss cancer, cardiovascular disease, and osteoporosis, noting risk factors and interventions.

- The death rate from cancer multiplies tenfold from early to middle adulthood. A complex interaction of heredity, biological aging, and environment contributes to cancer. Regular screenings and various preventive steps can reduce the incidence of cancer and cancer deaths.

- Despite a decline in recent decades, cardiovascular disease remains a major cause of death in middle adulthood, especially among men. Symptoms include high blood pressure, high blood cholesterol, atherosclerosis, heart attack, arrhythmia, and angina pectoris. Quitting smoking, reducing blood cholesterol, exercising, and reducing stress can decrease risk and aid in treatment.

- **Osteoporosis** affects 12 percent of people over age 50; most are postmenopausal women. Adequate calcium and vitamin D, weight-bearing exercise, resistance training, and bone-strengthening medications can help prevent and treat osteoporosis.

Discuss the association of hostility and anger with heart disease and other health problems.

- Expressed hostility, a component of the **Type A behavior pattern**, predicts heart disease and other health problems, largely due to physiological arousal associated with anger. Anger suppression is also related to health problems; a better alternative is to develop effective ways of handling stress and conflict.

Adapting to the Physical Challenges of Midlife (p. 409)

Discuss the benefits of stress management, exercise, and an optimistic outlook in dealing effectively with the physical challenges of midlife.

- Effective stress management includes both problem-centered and emotion-centered coping, depending on the situation. In middle adulthood, people tend to cope with stress more effectively, often reporting lasting personal benefits.

- Regular exercise offers physical and psychological advantages, making it worthwhile for sedentary middle-aged people to begin exercising. Developing a sense of self-efficacy, choosing an appropriate exercise format, and having access to accessible, attractive, and safe exercise environments promote physical activity.

- **Hardiness** is made up of three personal qualities: control, commitment, and challenge. By inducing a generally optimistic outlook, hardiness helps people cope with stress adaptively.

Explain the double standard of aging.

- Although negative stereotypes of aging discourage both men and women, middle-aged women are more likely to be viewed unfavorably. Recent surveys suggest that this double standard is declining.

COGNITIVE DEVELOPMENT

Changes in Mental Abilities (p. 412)

Describe cohort effects on intelligence revealed by Schaie's Seattle Longitudinal Study.

- Early cross-sectional research showed a peak in intelligence test performance at age 35 followed by a steep decline, whereas longitudinal evidence revealed modest gains in midlife. Using a sequential design, Schaie found that the cross-sectional, steep drop-off largely resulted from cohort effects, as each new generation experienced better health and education.

Describe changes in crystallized and fluid intelligence in middle adulthood.

- **Crystallized intelligence**, which depends on accumulated knowledge and experience, gains steadily through middle adulthood. In contrast, **fluid intelligence**, which depends more on basic information-processing skills, begins to decline in the twenties.

AP IMAGES/THE ARIZONA DAILY SUN, JAKE BACON

- In the Seattle Longitudinal Study, perceptual speed shows steady, continuous decline. But other fluid skills, in addition to crystallized abilities, increase through middle adulthood, confirming that midlife is a time of peak performance on a variety of complex abilities. Furthermore, mental abilities—including fluid skills—remain plastic, as illustrated by gains in certain intellectual skills by the baby boomers relative to the previous generation.

Information Processing (p. 414)

How does information processing change in midlife?

- Speed of cognitive processing slows with age. According to the **neural network view**, as neuronal connections deteriorate, the brain adapts by forming new, less efficient synaptic connections. The **information-loss view** states that older adults experience greater loss of information as it moves through the cognitive system, resulting in slower processing to interpret the information.

- As processing speed slows, people perform less well on memory, reasoning, and problem-solving tasks, especially fluid-ability items. But other factors also predict age-related cognitive performances.

- Middle-aged people show declines in ability to divide their attention, focus on relevant stimuli, and switch from one task to another as the situation demands. Inhibition becomes harder, at times prompting distractibility.

- Adults in midlife retain less information in working memory, largely due to a decline in use of memory strategies. But training, improved design of tasks, and metacognitive knowledge enable older adults to compensate for age-related decrements.

Discuss the development of practical problem solving, expertise, and creativity in middle adulthood.

- Middle-aged adults display continued growth in **practical problem solving**, largely due to gains in expertise. Creativity becomes more deliberately thoughtful, and it often shifts from generating unusual products to integrating ideas and from concern with self-expression to more altruistic goals.

Adult Learners: Becoming a Student in Midlife (p. 419)

Discuss the challenges that adults face in returning to college, ways to support returning students, and benefits of earning a degree in midlife.

- Adults are returning to college and graduate school in record numbers. The majority are women, often motivated by life transitions. Returning students must cope with a lack of recent practice at academic work; negative aging, gender, and ethnic stereotypes; and demands of multiple roles.

AP IMAGES/NANCY PALMIERI

- Social support from family and friends and institutional services suited to their needs can help returning students succeed. Further education results in enhanced competencies and reshaped life paths.

Important Terms and Concepts

climacteric (p. 403)
crystallized intelligence (p. 413)
fluid intelligence (p. 413)
glaucoma (p. 402)
hardiness (p. 411)

hormone therapy (p. 405)
information-loss view (p. 415)
menopause (p. 403)
neural network view (p. 415)
osteoporosis (p. 408)

practical problem solving (p. 418)
presbycusis (p. 402)
presbyopia (p. 402)
Type A behavior pattern (p. 409)

Emotional and Social Development in Middle Adulthood

HAGEN HOPKINS/GETTY IMAGES FOR NZOC

Midlife is a time of increased generativity—giving to and guiding younger generations. Charles Callis, director of New Zealand's Olympic Museum, shows visiting schoolchildren how to throw a discus. His enthusiastic demonstration conveys the deep sense of satisfaction he derives from generative activities.

chapter outline

One weekend when Devin, Trisha, and their 24-year-old son, Mark, were vacationing together, the two middle-aged parents knocked on Mark's hotel room door. "Your dad and I are going off to see a crafts exhibit," Trisha explained.

"Feel free to stay behind," she offered, recalling Mark's antipathy toward attending such events as an adolescent.

"That exhibit sounds great!" Mark replied. "I'll meet you in the lobby."

"Sometimes I forget he's an adult!" exclaimed Trisha as she and Devin returned to their room to grab their coats. "It's been great to have Mark with us—like spending time with a good friend."

In their forties and fifties, Trisha and Devin built on earlier strengths and intensified their commitment to leaving a legacy for those who would come after them. When Mark faced a difficult job market after graduating from college, he returned home to live with Trisha and Devin and remained there for several years. With their support, he took graduate courses while working part-time, found steady employment in his late twenties, and married in his mid-thirties. With each milestone, Trisha and Devin felt a sense of pride at having escorted a member of the next generation into responsible adult roles. Family activities, which had declined during Mark's adolescent and college years, increased as Trisha and Devin related to their son as an enjoyable adult companion. Challenging careers and more time for community involvement, leisure pursuits, and each other contributed to a richly diverse and gratifying time of life.

The midlife years were not as smooth for two of Trisha and Devin's friends. Fearing that she might grow old alone, Jewel frantically pursued her quest for an intimate partner. She attended singles events, registered with dating services, and traveled in hopes of meeting a like-minded companion. "I can't stand the thought of turning 50," she lamented in a letter to Trisha. Jewel also had compensating satisfactions—friendships that had grown more meaningful, a warm relationship with a nephew and niece, and a successful consulting business.

Tim, Devin's best friend from graduate school, had been divorced for over five years. Recently, he had met Elena and had come to love her deeply. But in addition to her own divorce, Elena was dealing with a troubled daughter, a new career, and other life changes. Whereas Tim had reached the peak of his career and was ready to enjoy life, Elena wanted to recapture much of what she had missed in earlier decades, including opportunities to realize her talents. "I don't know where I fit into Elena's plans," Tim wondered aloud on the phone with Trisha.

Increasing awareness of limited time ahead prompts adults to reevaluate the meaning of their lives, refine and strengthen their identities, and reach out to future generations. Most make modest adjustments in their outlook, goals, and daily lives. But a few experience profound inner turbulence and initiate major changes, often in an effort to make up for lost time. Together with advancing years, family and work transitions contribute greatly to emotional and social development.

More midlifers are addressing these tasks than ever before, now that the baby boomers have reached their forties, fifties, and sixties (see page 10 in Chapter 1 to review how baby boomers have reshaped the life course). As our discussion will reveal, they have brought increased self-confidence, social consciousness, and vitality—along with great developmental diversity—to this period of the lifespan.

A monumental survey called *Midlife Development in the United States (MIDUS),* conducted in the mid-1990s, has contributed enormously to our understanding of midlife emotional and social development.

Its nationally representative sample included over 7,000 U.S. 25- to 75-year-olds, enabling those in the middle years to be compared with younger and older individuals. Through telephone interviews and self-administered questionnaires, participants responded to over 1,100 items addressing wide-ranging psychological, health, and background factors, yielding unprecedented breadth of information in a single study (Brim, Ryff, & Kessler, 2005). The research endeavor also included "satellite" studies, in which subsamples of respondents were questioned in greater depth on key topics. And it has been extended longitudinally, with 75 percent of the sample recontacted at first follow-up, in the mid-2000s (Radler & Ryff, 2010).

MIDUS has greatly expanded our knowledge of the *multidimensional* and *multidirectional* nature of midlife change. Hence, our discussion repeatedly draws on MIDUS, at times delving into its findings, at other times citing them alongside those of other investigations. Let's turn now to Erikson's theory and related research, to which MIDUS has contributed. ⬤

Erikson's Theory: Generativity versus Stagnation

Erikson's psychological conflict of midlife is called **generativity versus stagnation.** Generativity involves reaching out to others in ways that give to and guide the next generation. It is under way in early adulthood through work, community service, and childbearing and child rearing. Generativity expands greatly in midlife, when adults focus more intently on extending commitments beyond oneself and one's life partner to a larger group—family, community, or society (McAdams & Logan, 2004). The generative adult combines the need for self-expression with the need for communion, integrating personal goals with the welfare of the larger social world.

Erikson (1950) selected the term *generativity* to encompass everything generated that can outlive the self and ensure society's continuity and improvement: children, ideas, products,

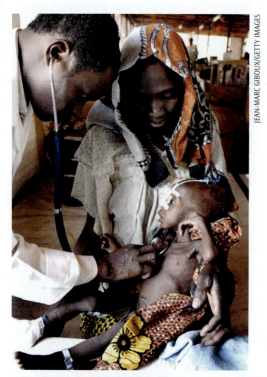

Through his work with severely malnourished children in Niger, this nurse, affiliated with the Nobel Prize–winning organization Doctors Without Borders, integrates personal goals with a broader concern for society.

works of art. Although parenting is a major means of realizing generativity, it is not the only means: Adults can be generative in other family relationships (as Jewel was with her nephew and niece), as mentors in the workplace, in volunteer endeavors, and through many forms of productivity and creativity.

Notice, from what we have said so far, that generativity brings together personal desires and cultural demands. On the personal side, middle-aged adults feel a need to be needed—to attain symbolic immortality by making a contribution that will survive their death (Kotre, 1999; McAdams, Hart, & Maruna, 1998). This desire may stem from a deep-seated evolutionary urge to protect and advance the next generation. On the cultural side, society imposes a social clock for generativity in midlife, requiring adults to take responsibility for the next generation through their roles as parents, teachers, mentors, leaders, and coordinators (McAdams & Logan, 2004). And according to Erikson, a culture's "belief in the species"—the conviction that life is good and worthwhile, even in the face of human destructiveness and deprivation—is a major motivator of generative action, which has improving humanity as its goal.

The negative outcome of this stage is stagnation: Once people attain certain life goals, such as marriage, children, and career success, they may become self-centered and self-indulgent. Adults may express a sense of stagnation in many ways—through lack of interest in young people (including their own children), through a focus on what they can get from others rather than what they can give, and through taking little interest in being productive at work, developing their talents, or bettering the world in other ways.

Much research indicates that generativity tends to increase in midlife. For example, in longitudinal and cross-sectional studies of college-educated women, and in an investigation of middle-aged adults diverse in SES, self-rated generativity rose throughout middle adulthood (see Figure 16.1). At the same time, participants expressed greater concern about aging, increased security with their identities, and a stronger sense of competence (Miner-Rubino, Winter, & Stewart, 2004; Newton & Stewart, 2010; Stewart, Ostrove, & Helson, 2001; Zucker, Ostrove, & Stewart, 2002).

Just as Erikson's theory suggests, highly generative people appear especially well-adjusted—low in anxiety and depression; high in autonomy, self-acceptance, and life satisfaction; and more likely to have successful marriages and close friends (Ackerman, Zuroff, & Moskowitz, 2000; An & Cooney, 2006; Grossbaum & Bates, 2002; Westermeyer, 2004). They are also more open to differing viewpoints, possess leadership qualities, desire more from work than financial rewards, and care greatly about the welfare of their children, their partner, their aging parents, and the wider society (Peterson, 2002; Peterson, Smirles, & Wentworth, 1997). Furthermore, generativity is associated with more effective child rearing—higher valuing of trust, open communication, transmission of generative values to children, and an authoritative style (Peterson, 2006; Peterson & Duncan, 2007; Pratt et al., 2008).

Although these findings characterize adults of all backgrounds, individual differences in contexts for generativity exist. Having children seems to foster generative development in both men and women. In several studies, including the MIDUS survey, fathers scored higher in generativity than childless men (Marks, Bumpass, & Jun, 2004; McAdams & de St. Aubin, 1992; Snarey et al., 1987). Similarly, in an investigation of well-educated women from ages 43 to 63, those with family commit-

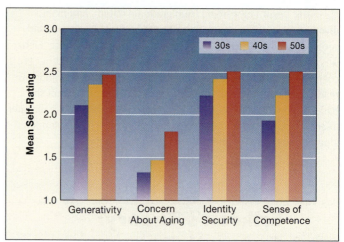

FIGURE 16.1 **Age-related changes in self-rated generativity, concern about aging, identity security, and sense of competence.** In a longitudinal study of over 300 college-educated women, self-rated generativity increased from the thirties to the fifties, as did concern about aging. The rise in generativity was accompanied by other indicators of psychological health—greater security with one's identity and sense of competence. (Adapted from Stewart, Ostrove, & Helson, 2001.)

ments (with or without a career) expressed greater generative concerns than childless women who were solely focused on their careers (Newton & Stewart, 2010). Parenting seems to spur especially tender, caring attitudes toward succeeding generations.

For low-SES men with troubled pasts, fatherhood can provide a context for highly generative, positive life change (Roy & Lucas, 2006). As one former gang member, who earned an associate's degree and struggled to keep his teenage sons off the streets, explained, "I came through the depths of hell to try to be a father. I let my sons know, 'You're never without a daddy, don't you let anybody tell you that.' I tell them that if me and your mother separate, I make sure that wherever I go, I build something for you to come to" (p. 153).

Finally, compared with Caucasians, African Americans more often engage in certain types of generativity. They are more involved in religious groups and activities, offer more social support to members of their community, and are more likely to view themselves as role models and sources of wisdom for their children (Hart et al., 2001). A life history of strong support from church and extended family may strengthen these generative values and actions. Among Caucasian Americans, religiosity and spirituality are also linked to greater generative activity (Dillon & Wink, 2004; Son & Wilson, 2011; Wink & Dillon, 2008). Highly generative middle-aged adults often indicate that as children and adolescents, they internalized moral values rooted in a religious tradition and sustained their commitment to those values, which provided lifelong encouragement for generative action (McAdams, 2006). Especially in individualistic societies, belonging to a religious community or believing in a higher being may help preserve generative commitments.

Other Theories of Psychosocial Development in Midlife

Erikson's broad sketch of psychosocial change in midlife has been extended by Levinson and Vaillant. Let's revisit their theories, which were introduced in Chapter 14.

Levinson's Seasons of Life

Return to page 375 to review Levinson's eras (seasons of life). His interviews with adults revealed that middle adulthood begins with a transition, during which people evaluate their success in meeting early adulthood goals. Realizing that from now on, more time will lie behind than ahead, they regard the remaining years as increasingly precious. Consequently, some make drastic revisions in their life structure: divorcing, remarrying, changing careers, or displaying enhanced creativity. Others make smaller changes in the context of marital and occupational stability.

Whether these years bring a gust of wind or a storm, most people turn inward for a time, focusing on personally meaning-

ful living (Neugarten, 1968b). According to Levinson, to reassess and rebuild their life structure, middle-aged adults must confront four developmental tasks. Each requires the individual to reconcile two opposing tendencies within the self, attaining greater internal harmony.

- *Young–old:* The middle-age person must seek new ways of being both young and old. This means giving up certain youthful qualities, transforming others, and finding positive meaning in being older. Perhaps because of the double standard of aging (see page 412 in Chapter 15), most middle-aged women express concern about appearing less attractive as they grow older (Rossi, 2005). But middle-aged men—particularly non-college-educated men, who often hold blue-collar jobs requiring physical strength and stamina—are also highly sensitive to physical aging (Miner-Rubino, Winter, & Stewart, 2004).

  Compared with previous midlife cohorts, U.S. baby boomers are especially interested in controlling physical changes—a desire that has helped energize a huge industry of anti-aging cosmetic products and medical procedures (Jones, Whitbourne, & Skultety, 2006; Lachman, 2004). And sustaining a youthful *subjective age* (feeling younger than one's actual age) is more strongly related to self-esteem and psychological well-being among American than Western-European middle-aged and older adults (Westerhof & Barrett, 2005; Westerhof, Whitbourne, & Freeman, 2012). In the more individualistic U.S. context, a youthful self-image seems more important for viewing oneself as self-reliant and capable of planning for an active, fulfilling late adulthood.

- *Destruction–creation:* With greater awareness of mortality, the middle-aged person focuses on ways he or she has acted destructively. Past hurtful acts toward parents, intimate partners, children, friends, and co-workers are countered by a strong desire to participate in activities that advance human welfare and leave a legacy for future generations. The image of a legacy can be satisfied in many ways—through charitable gifts, creative products, volunteer service, or mentoring young people.

- *Masculinity–femininity:* The middle-aged person must create a better balance between "masculine" and "feminine" parts of the self. For men, this means greater acceptance of traits of nurturance and caring, which enhance close relationships and compassionate exercise of authority in the workplace. For women, it generally means being more open to characteristics of autonomy and assertiveness. Recall from Chapter 8 that people who combine masculine and feminine traits have an androgynous gender identity. Later we will see that androgyny is associated with favorable adjustment.

- *Engagement–separateness:* The middle-aged person must forge a better balance between engagement with the external world and separateness. For many men, and for women who have had successful careers, this may mean reducing concern with ambition and achievement and attending more fully to oneself. But women who have been devoted to child rearing or an unfulfilling job often feel compelled to move in the other direction (Levinson, 1996). At age 48, Elena left her position as a reporter for a small-town newspaper, pursued an advanced degree in creative writing, accepted a college teaching position, and began writing a novel. Tim, in contrast, recognized his overwhelming desire for a gratifying romantic partnership. By scaling back his own career, he realized he could grant Elena the time and space she needed to build a rewarding work life.

People who flexibly modify their identities in response to age-related changes yet maintain a sense of self-continuity are more aware of their own thoughts and feelings and are higher in self-esteem and life satisfaction (Jones, Whitbourne, & Skultety, 2006; Sneed et al., 2012). But when poverty, unemployment, and lack of a respected place in society dominate the life course, energies are directed toward survival rather than realistically approaching age-related changes. And even adults whose jobs are secure and who live in pleasant neighborhoods may find that employment conditions restrict possibilities for growth by placing too much emphasis on productivity and profit and too little on the meaning of work. In her early forties, Trisha left a large law firm, where she felt constant pressure to bring in high-fee clients and received little acknowledgment of her efforts, for a small practice.

Opportunities for advancement ease the transition to middle adulthood. Yet these are far less available to women than to men. Individuals of both sexes in blue-collar jobs also have few possibilities for promotion (Christensen & Larsen, 2008). Many men find compensating rewards in moving to the senior generation of their families.

Vaillant's Adaptation to Life

Whereas Levinson interviewed 35- to 45-year-olds, Vaillant (1977, 2002)—in his longitudinal research on well-educated men and women—followed participants past the half-century mark. Recall from Chapter 14 how adults in their late fifties and sixties extend their generativity, becoming "keepers of meaning," or guardians of their culture (see page 375). "Passing the torch"—concern that the positive aspects of their culture survive—became a major preoccupation.

In societies around the world, older people are guardians of traditions, laws, and cultural values. This stabilizing force holds in check too-rapid change sparked by the questioning and challenging of adolescents and young adults. As people approach the end of middle age, they focus on longer-term, less-personal goals, such as the state of human relations in their society. And they become more philosophical, accepting the fact that not all problems can be solved in their lifetime.

Is There a Midlife Crisis?

Levinson (1978, 1996) reported that most men and women in his samples experienced substantial inner turmoil during the transition to middle adulthood. Yet Vaillant (1977, 2002) saw few examples of crisis but, rather, slow and steady change. These contrasting findings raise the question of how much personal upheaval actually accompanies entry to midlife. Are self-doubt and stress especially great during the forties, and do they prompt major restructuring of the personality, as the term **midlife crisis** implies?

Consider the reactions of Trisha, Devin, Jewel, Tim, and Elena to middle adulthood. Trisha and Devin moved easily into this period, whereas Jewel, Tim, and Elena sought alternative life paths. Clearly, wide individual differences exist in response to midlife. **TAKE A MOMENT...** Now ask several individuals in their twenties and thirties whether they expect to encounter a midlife crisis between ages 40 and 50. You are likely to find that Americans often anticipate it, perhaps because of culturally induced apprehension of aging (Wethington, Kessler, & Pixley, 2004). Yet little evidence supports this view of middle age as a turbulent time.

When MIDUS participants were asked to describe "turning points" (major changes in the way they felt about an important aspect of their lives) that had occurred during the past five years, most of the ones reported concerned work. Women's work-related turning points peaked in early adulthood, when many adjusted their work lives to accommodate marriage and childrearing (see Chapter 14). The peak for men, in contrast, came at midlife, a time of increased career responsibility and advancement. Other common turning points in early and middle adulthood were positive: They involved fulfilling a dream and learning something good about oneself (Wethington, Kessler, & Pixley, 2004). Overall, turning points rarely resembled midlife crises. Even negative work-related turning points generally led to personal growth—for example, a layoff that

Like many midlifers, elementary school teacher Jaime Malwitz modified his career in ways that resemble a turning point, not a crisis. He designed a scientist-in-residence program for elementary schools. Here he serves as a resident physicist, discussing a density experiment with a fifth grader.

AP IMAGES/THE REPORTER, KEITH VANDERVORT

sparked a positive career change or a shift in energy from career to personal life.

Asked directly if they had ever experienced something they would consider a midlife crisis, only one-fourth of the MIDUS respondents said yes. And they defined such events much more loosely than researchers do. Some reported a crisis well before age 40, others well after age 50. And most attributed it not to age but rather to challenging life events (Wethington, 2000).

Another way of exploring midlife questioning is to ask adults about life regrets—attractive opportunities for career or other life-changing activities they did not pursue or lifestyle changes they did not make. In two investigations of women in their early forties, those who acknowledged regret without making life changes, compared to those who modified their lives, reported less favorable psychological well-being and poorer physical health over time (Landman et al., 1995; Stewart & Vandewater, 1999).

By late midlife, with less time ahead to make life changes, people's interpretation of regrets plays a major role in their well-being. Mature, contented adults acknowledge a past characterized by some losses but are able to disengage from them, investing in current, personally rewarding goals (King & Hicks, 2007). Among a sample of several hundred 60- to 65-year-olds diverse in SES, about half expressed at least one regret. Compared to those who had not resolved their disappointments, those who had come to terms with them (accepted and identified some eventual benefits) or had "put the best face on things" (identified benefits but still had some lingering regret) reported better physical health and greater life satisfaction (Torges, Stewart, & Miner-Rubino, 2005).

In sum, life evaluation is common during middle age. Most people make changes that are best described as turning points rather than drastic alterations of their lives. Those who cannot modify their life paths often look for the "silver lining" in life's difficulties (King & Hicks, 2007; Wethington, Kessler, & Pixley, 2004). The few midlifers who are in crisis typically have had early adulthoods in which gender roles, family pressures, or low income and poverty severely limited their ability to fulfill personal needs and goals, at home or in the wider world.

ASK YOURSELF

REVIEW What personal and cultural forces motivate generativity? Why does it increase and contribute vitally to favorable adjustment in midlife?

APPLY After years of experiencing little personal growth at work, 42-year-old Mel looked for a new job and received an attractive offer in another city. Although he was distressed at moving away from extended family and close friends, after several weeks of soul searching, he took the new job. Was Mel's dilemma a midlife crisis? Why or why not?

REFLECT Think of a middle-aged adult whom you admire. Describe the various ways that individual expresses generativity.

Stability and Change in Self-Concept and Personality

Midlife changes in self-concept and personality reflect growing awareness of a finite lifespan, longer life experience, and generative concerns. Yet certain aspects of personality remain stable, revealing the persistence of individual differences established during earlier periods.

Possible Selves

On a business trip, Jewel found a spare afternoon to visit Trisha. Sitting in a coffee shop, the two women reminisced about the past and thought aloud about the future. "It's been tough living on my own and building the business," Jewel said. "What I hope for is to become better at my work, to be more community-oriented, and to stay healthy and available to my friends. Of course, I would rather not grow old alone, but if I don't find that special person, I suppose I can take comfort in the fact that I'll never have to face divorce or widowhood."

Jewel is discussing **possible selves,** future-oriented representations of what one hopes to become and what one is afraid of becoming. Possible selves are the temporal dimension of self-concept—what the individual is striving for and attempting to avoid. To lifespan researchers, these hopes and fears are just as vital in explaining behavior as people's views of their current characteristics. Indeed, possible selves may be an especially strong motivator of action in midlife, as adults attach increased meaning to time (Frazier & Hooker, 2006). As we age, we may rely less on social comparisons in judging our self-worth and more on temporal comparisons—how well we are doing in relation to what we had planned.

Throughout adulthood, the personality traits people assign to their current selves show considerable stability. A 30-year-old who says he is cooperative, competent, outgoing, or successful is likely to report a similar picture at a later age. But reports of possible selves change greatly. Adults in their early twenties mention many possible selves, and their visions are lofty and idealistic—being "perfectly happy," "rich and famous," "healthy throughout life," and not being "a person who does nothing important." With age, possible selves become fewer in number and more modest and concrete. They are largely concerned with performance of roles and responsibilities already begun—"being competent at work," "being a good husband and father," "putting my children through college," "staying healthy," and not being "a burden to my family" (Bybee & Wells, 2003; Cross & Markus, 1991; Ryff, 1991).

What explains these shifts in possible selves? Because the future no longer holds limitless opportunities, adults preserve mental health by adjusting their hopes and fears. To stay motivated, they must maintain a sense of unachieved possibility, yet they must still manage to feel good about themselves and their lives despite disappointments (Bolkan & Hooker, 2012). For example, although Jewel feared loneliness in old age, she reminded herself that marriage can lead to equally negative outcomes, such as divorce and widowhood—possibilities that made not having attained an important interpersonal goal easier to bear.

Self-Acceptance, Autonomy, and Environmental Mastery

An evolving mix of competencies and experiences leads to changes in certain aspects of personality during middle adulthood. In Chapter 15, we noted that midlife brings gains in expertise and practical problem solving. Middle-aged adults also offer more complex, integrated descriptions of themselves than do younger and older individuals (Labouvie-Vief, 2003). Furthermore, midlife is typically a period in which the number of social roles peaks—spouse, parent, worker, and engaged community member. And status at work and in the community typically rises, as adults take advantage of opportunities for leadership and other complex responsibilities (Helson, Soto, & Cate, 2006).

These changes in cognition and breadth of roles undoubtedly contribute to other gains in personal functioning. In research on adults ranging in age from the late teens into the seventies, and in cultures as distinct as the United States and Japan, three qualities increased from early to middle adulthood:

- *Self-acceptance:* More than young adults, middle-aged people acknowledged and accepted both their good and bad qualities and felt positively about themselves and life.

- *Autonomy:* Middle-aged adults saw themselves as less concerned about others' expectations and evaluations and more concerned with following self-chosen standards.

- *Environmental mastery:* Middle-aged people saw themselves as capable of managing a complex array of tasks easily and effectively (Karasawa et al., 2011; Ryff & Keyes, 1995).

As these findings indicate, midlife is generally a time of increased comfort with the self, independence, assertiveness, commitment to personal values, and life satisfaction (Helson, Jones, & Kwan, 2002; Keyes, Shmotkin, & Ryff, 2002; Stone et al., 2010). Perhaps because of this rise in overall psychological well-being, middle age is sometimes referred to as "the prime of life."

At the same time, factors contributing to psychological well-being differ substantially among cohorts, as self-reports gathered from 25- to 65-year-old MIDUS survey respondents reveal (Carr, 2004). Among women who were born during the baby-boom years or later, and who thus benefited from the women's movement, balancing career with family predicted greater self-acceptance and environmental mastery. But also consider that women born before or during World War II who sacrificed career to focus on child rearing—expected of young mothers in the 1950s and 1960s—were similarly advantaged in

self-acceptance. Likewise, men who were in step with prevailing social expectations scored higher in well-being. Baby-boom and younger men who modified their work schedules to make room for family responsibilities—who fit their cohort's image of the "good father"—were more self-accepting. But older men who made this accommodation scored much lower in self-acceptance than those who focused on work and thus conformed to the "good provider" ideal of their times. (See the Biology and Environment box on the following page for additional influences on midlife psychological well-being.)

Coping with Daily Stressors

In a MIDUS satellite study in which more than 1,000 participants were interviewed on eight consecutive evenings, researchers found an early- to mid-adulthood plateau in frequency of daily stressors, followed by a decline as work and family responsibilities ease and leisure time increases (Almeida & Horn, 2004). Compared with older people, young and midlife adults also perceived their stressors as more disruptive and unpleasant, perhaps because they often experienced several at once, and many involved financial risks and children.

But recall from Chapter 15 that midlife brings an increase in effective coping strategies. Middle-aged individuals are more likely to identify the positive side of difficult situations, postpone action to permit evaluation of alternatives, anticipate and plan ways to handle future discomforts, and use humor to express ideas and feelings without offending others (Diehl, Coyle, & Labouvie-Vief, 1996). Notice how these efforts flexibly draw on both problem-centered and emotion-centered strategies.

Why might effective coping increase in middle adulthood? Other personality changes seem to support it. Complex, integrated self-descriptions—which increase in midlife, indicating an improved ability to blend strengths and weaknesses into an organized picture—predict a stronger sense of personal control over outcomes and good coping strategies (Hay & Diehl, 2010; Labouvie-Vief & Diehl, 2000). Midlife gains in emotional stability and confidence in handling life's problems may also contribute (Roberts et al., 2007; Roberts & Mroczek, 2008). These attributes predict work and relationship effectiveness—outcomes that reflect the sophisticated, flexible coping of middle age.

Gender Identity

In her forties and early fifties, Trisha appeared more assertive at work, taking on leadership roles and speaking out freely. She was also more dominant in family relationships, expressing her opinions to her husband and son more readily than she had 10 or 15 years earlier. In contrast, Devin's sense of empathy and caring became more apparent, and he was less assertive and more accommodating to Trisha's wishes.

Many studies report an increase in "masculine" traits in women and "feminine" traits in men across middle age (Huyck, 1990; James et al., 1995). Women become more confident, self-sufficient, and forceful, men more emotionally sensitive, caring,

Biology and Environment

What Factors Promote Psychological Well-Being in Midlife?

What factors contribute to individual differences in psychological well-being at midlife? Consistent with the lifespan perspective, biological, psychological, and social forces are involved, and their effects are interwoven.

Good Health and Exercise

Good health affects energy and zest for life at any age. But during middle and late adulthood, taking steps to improve health and prevent disability becomes a better predictor of psychological well-being. Many studies confirm that engaging in regular exercise—walking, dancing, jogging, or swimming—is more strongly associated with self-rated health and a positive outlook in older than in younger adults (Bherer, 2012). Middle-aged people who maintain an exercise regimen are likely to perceive themselves as particularly active for their age and, therefore, to feel a special sense of accomplishment (Netz et al., 2005). In addition, physical activity enhances self-efficacy and effective stress management (see page 411 in Chapter 15).

Sense of Control and Personal Life Investment

Middle-aged adults who report a high sense of control over events in various aspects of their lives—health, family, and work—also report more favorable psychological well-being. Sense of control contributes further to self-efficacy. It also predicts use of more effective coping strategies, including seeking of social support, and thereby helps sustain a positive outlook in the face of health, family, and work difficulties (Lachman, Neupert, & Agrigoroaei, 2011).

Personal life investment—firm commitment to goals and involvement in pursuit of those goals—also adds to mental health and life satisfaction (Staudinger & Bowen, 2010). According to Mihaly Csikszentmihalyi, a vital wellspring of happiness is *flow*—the psychological state of being so engrossed in a demanding, meaningful activity that one loses all sense of time and self-awareness.

People describe flow as the height of enjoyment, even as an ecstatic state. The more people experience flow, the more they judge their lives to be gratifying (Nakamura & Csikszentmihalyi, 2009). Flow depends on perseverance and skill at complex endeavors that offer potential for growth. These qualities are well-developed in middle adulthood.

These yoga students express a sense of purpose and accomplishment. Maintaining an exercise regimen contributes greatly to midlife psychological well-being.

Close Friendships and a Good Marriage

Supportive friendships improve mental health by promoting positive emotions and protecting against stress (Fiori, Antonucci, & Cortina, 2006; Powdthavee, 2008). In a survey of college alumni, those who preferred occupational prestige and high income to close friends were twice as likely as other respondents to describe themselves as "fairly" or "very" unhappy (Perkins, 1991, as cited by Myers, 2000).

A good marriage boosts psychological well-being even more. When interviews with over 13,000 U.S. adults were repeated five years later, people who remained married reported greater happiness than those who remained single. Those who separated or divorced became less happy, reporting considerable depression (Marks & Lambert, 1998). The role of marriage in mental health increases with age, becoming a powerful predictor by late midlife (Marks, Bumpass, & Jun, 2004; Marks & Greenfield, 2009).

Although not everyone is better off married, the link between marriage and well-being is similar in many nations, suggesting that marriage changes people's behavior in ways that make them better off (Diener et al., 2000; Lansford et al., 2005). Married partners monitor each other's health and offer care in times of illness. They also earn and save more money than single people,

and higher income is modestly linked to psychological well-being (Myers, 2000). Furthermore, sexual satisfaction predicts mental health, and married couples have more satisfying sex lives than singles (see Chapter 13).

Mastery of Multiple Roles

Success in handling multiple roles—spouse, parent, worker, community volunteer—is linked to psychological well-being. In the MIDUS survey, as role involvement increased, both men and women reported greater environmental mastery, more rewarding social relationships, heightened sense of purpose in life, and more positive emotion. Furthermore, adults who occupied multiple roles and who also reported high control (suggesting effective role management) scored especially high in well-being—an outcome that was stronger for less-educated adults (Ahrens & Ryff, 2006). Control over roles may be vital for individuals with lower educational attainment, whose role combinations may be particularly stressful and who have fewer economic resources.

Finally, among nonfamily roles, community volunteering in the latter part of midlife contributes uniquely to psychological well-being (Choi & Kim, 2011; Ryff et al., 2012). It may do so by strengthening self-efficacy, generativity, and altruism.

RAMIRO OLACIREGUI/GETTY IMAGES

In middle age, gender identity becomes more androgynous for both sexes. Men tend to show an increase in "feminine" traits, becoming more emotionally sensitive, caring, considerate, and dependent.

considerate, and dependent. These trends appear in not just Western industrialized nations but also village societies such as the Maya of Guatemala, the Navajo of the United States, and the Druze of the Middle East (Fry, 1985; Gutmann, 1977; Turner, 1982). Consistent with Levinson's theory, gender identity in midlife becomes more androgynous—a mixture of "masculine" and "feminine" characteristics.

Although the existence of these changes is well-accepted, explanations for them are controversial. A well-known evolutionary view, **parental imperative theory,** holds that identification with traditional gender roles is maintained during the active parenting years to help ensure the survival of children. Men become more goal-oriented, while women emphasize nurturance (Gutmann & Huyck, 1994). After children reach adulthood, parents are free to express the "other-gender" side of their personalities.

But this biological account has been criticized. As discussed in earlier chapters, parents need both warmth and assertiveness (in the form of firmness and consistency) to rear children effectively. And although children's departure from the home is related to men's openness to the "feminine" side of their personalities, the link to a rise in "masculine" traits among women is less apparent (Huyck, 1996, 1998). In longitudinal research, college-educated women in the labor force became more independent by their early forties, regardless of whether they had children (Helson & Picano, 1990; Wink & Helson, 1993). Furthermore, cohort effects can contribute to this trend: In one study, middle-aged women of the baby-boom generation—who experienced new career opportunities as a result of the women's movement—more often described themselves as having masculine and androgynous traits than did older women (Strough et al., 2007).

Additional demands of midlife may prompt a more androgynous orientation. For example, among men, a need to enrich a marital relationship after children have departed, along with reduced chances for career advancement, may be involved in the awakening of emotionally sensitive traits. Women are far more likely than men to face economic and social disadvantages. A greater number remain divorced, are widowed, and encounter discrimination in the workplace. Self-reliance and assertiveness are vital for coping with these circumstances.

In adulthood, androgyny is associated with cognitive flexibility, creativity, advanced moral reasoning, and psychosocial maturity (Prager & Bailey, 1985; Runco, Cramond, & Pagnani, 2010; Waterman & Whitbourne, 1982). People who integrate the masculine and feminine sides of their personalities tend to be psychologically healthier, perhaps because they are able to adapt more easily to the challenges of aging.

Individual Differences in Personality Traits

Although Trisha and Jewel both became more self-assured and assertive in midlife, in other respects they differed. Trisha had always been more organized and hard-working, Jewel more gregarious and fun-loving. Once, the two women traveled together. At the end of each day, Trisha was disappointed if she had not kept to a schedule and visited every tourist attraction. Jewel liked to "play it by ear"—wandering through streets and stopping to talk with shopkeepers and residents.

In previous sections, we considered personality changes common to many middle-aged adults, but stable individual differences also exist. The hundreds of personality traits on which people differ have been reduced to five basic factors, often referred to as the **"big five" personality traits:** neuroticism, extroversion, openness to experience, agreeableness, and conscientiousness. Table 16.1 provides a description of each. Notice that Trisha is high in conscientiousness, whereas Jewel is high in extroversion.

Longitudinal and cross-sectional studies of U.S. men and women in many countries reveal that agreeableness and conscientiousness increase from the teenage years through middle age, whereas neuroticism declines, and extroversion and openness to experience do not change or decrease slightly—changes that reflect "settling down" and greater maturity (McCrae & Costa, 2006; Roberts, Walton, & Viechtbauer, 2006; Schmitt et al., 2007; Soto et al., 2011; Srivastava et al., 2003). The consistency of these cross-cultural findings has led some researchers to conclude that adult personality change is genetically influenced. They note that individual differences in the "big five" traits are large and highly stable: A person who scores high or low at one age is likely to do the same at another, over intervals ranging from 3 to 30 years (McCrae & Costa, 2006).

How can there be high stability in personality traits, yet significant changes in aspects of personality discussed earlier? Theorists concerned with change due to experience focus on how personal needs and life events induce new strategies and goals; their interest is in "the human being as a complex adaptive system" (Block, 2011, p. 19). In contrast, those who emphasize stability due to heredity measure personality traits on which individuals can easily be compared and that are present at any time of life.

TABLE 16.1 The "Big Five" Personality Traits

TRAIT	DESCRIPTION
Neuroticism	Individuals who are high on this trait are worrying, temperamental, self-pitying, self-conscious, emotional, and vulnerable. Individuals who are low are calm, even-tempered, self-content, comfortable, unemotional, and hardy.
Extroversion	Individuals who are high on this trait are affectionate, talkative, active, fun-loving, and passionate. Individuals who are low are reserved, quiet, passive, sober, and emotionally unreactive.
Openness to experience	Individuals who are high on this trait are imaginative, creative, original, curious, and liberal. Individuals who are low are down-to-earth, uncreative, conventional, uncurious, and conservative.
Agreeableness	Individuals who are high on this trait are soft-hearted, trusting, generous, acquiescent, lenient, and good-natured. Individuals who are low are ruthless, suspicious, stingy, antagonistic, critical, and irritable.
Conscientiousness	Individuals who are high on this trait are conscientious, hard-working, well-organized, punctual, ambitious, and persevering. Individuals who are low are negligent, lazy, disorganized, late, aimless, and nonpersistent.

Source: McCrae, 2011; McCrae & Costa, 2006.

To resolve this apparent contradiction, we can think of adults as changing in overall organization and integration of personality but doing so on a foundation of basic, enduring dispositions that support a coherent sense of self as people adapt to changing life circumstances. When more than 2,000 individuals in their forties were asked to reflect on their personalities during the previous six years, 52 percent said they had "stayed the same," 39 percent said they had "changed a little," and 9 percent said they had "changed a lot" (Herbst et al., 2000). Again, these findings contradict a view of middle adulthood as a period of great turmoil and change. But they also underscore that personality remains an "open system," responsive to the pressures of life experiences. Indeed, certain midlife personality changes may strengthen trait consistency! Improved self-understanding, self-acceptance, and skill at handling challenging situations can result in less need to modify basic personality dispositions over time.

ASK YOURSELF

REVIEW Summarize personality changes at midlife. How can these changes be reconciled with increasing stability of the "big five" personality traits?

APPLY Jeff, age 46, suggested to his wife, Julia, that they set aside time once a year to discuss their relationship—both positive aspects and ways to improve. Julia was surprised because Jeff had never before expressed interest in working on their marriage. What midlife developments probably fostered this new concern?

REFLECT List your hoped-for and feared possible selves. Then ask family members in early and middle adulthood to do the same. Are their reports consistent with age-related research findings? Explain.

 # Relationships at Midlife

The emotional and social changes of midlife take place within a complex web of family relationships and friendships. Although some middle-aged people live alone, the vast majority—87 percent in the United States—live in families, most with a spouse (U.S. Census Bureau, 2013). Partly because they have ties to older and younger generations in their families and partly because their friendships are well-established, people tend to have a larger number of close relationships during midlife than at any other period (Antonucci, Akiyama, & Takahashi, 2004).

The middle adulthood phase of the family life cycle is often referred to as "launching children and moving on." In the past, it was called the "empty nest," but this phrase implies a negative transition, especially for women who have devoted themselves entirely to their children and for whom the end of active parenting can trigger feelings of emptiness and regret. But for most people, middle adulthood is a liberating time, offering a sense of completion and opportunities to strengthen social ties and rekindle interests.

As our discussion in Chapter 14 revealed, increasing numbers of young adults are living at home because of tight job markets and financial challenges, yielding launch–return–relaunch patterns for many middle-aged parents. As adult children depart and marry, middle-aged parents must adapt to new roles of parent-in-law and grandparent. At the same time, they must establish a different type of relationship with their aging parents, who may become ill or infirm and die.

Middle adulthood is marked by the greatest number of exits and entries of family members. Let's see how ties within and beyond the family change during this period of life.

Marriage and Divorce

Although not all couples are financially comfortable, middle-aged households are well-off compared with other age groups.

For many middle-aged couples, having forged a relationship that permits satisfaction of both family and individual needs results in deep feelings of love.

Americans between 45 and 54 have the highest average annual income. And the baby boomers—more of whom have earned college and postgraduate degrees and live in dual-earner families—are financially better off than previous midlife generations (Eggebeen & Sturgeon, 2006; U.S. Census Bureau, 2013). Partly because of increased education and financial security, the contemporary social view of marriage in midlife is one of expansion and new horizons.

These forces strengthen the need to review and adjust the marital relationship. For Devin and Trisha, this shift was gradual. By middle age, their marriage had permitted satisfaction of family and individual needs, endured many changes, and culminated in deeper feelings of love. Elena's marriage, in contrast, became more conflict-ridden as her teenage daughter's problems introduced added strains and as departure of children made marital difficulties more obvious. Tim's failed marriage revealed yet another pattern. With passing years, the number of problems declined, but so did the love expressed (Rokach, Cohen, & Dreman, 2004). As less happened in the relationship, good or bad, the couple had little to keep them together.

As the Biology and Environment box on page 429 revealed, marital satisfaction is a strong predictor of midlife psychological well-being. As in early adulthood, divorce is one way of resolving an unsatisfactory marriage. The divorce rate of U.S. 50- to 65-year-olds has doubled over the past two decades (Brown & Lin, 2012). Divorce at any age takes a heavy psychological toll, but midlifers seem to adapt more easily than younger people (Marks & Lambert, 1998). Midlife gains in practical problem solving and effective coping strategies may reduce the stressful impact of divorce.

Nevertheless, for many women, marital breakup—especially when it is repeated—severely reduces standard of living (see page 275 in Chapter 10). For this reason, in midlife and earlier, it is a strong contributor to the **feminization of poverty**—a trend in which women who support themselves or their families have become the majority of the adult population living in poverty, regardless of age and ethnic group. Because of weak public policies safeguarding families (see Chapter 2), the gender gap in poverty is higher in the United States than in other Western industrialized nations (U.S. Census Bureau, 2013).

Longitudinal evidence reveals that middle-aged women who weather divorce successfully tend to become more tolerant, comfortable with uncertainty, nonconforming, and self-reliant in personality—factors believed to be fostered by divorce-forced independence. And both men and women reevaluate what they consider important in a healthy relationship, placing greater weight on equal friendship and less on passionate love than they had the first time (Baum, Rahav, & Sharon, 2005; Schneller & Arditti, 2004). Little is known about long-term adjustment following divorce among middle-aged men, perhaps because most enter new relationships and remarry within a short time.

Changing Parent–Child Relationships

Parents' positive relationships with their grown children are the result of a gradual process of "letting go," starting in childhood, gaining momentum in adolescence, and culminating in children's independent living. As mentioned earlier, most middle-aged parents adjust well to the launching phase of the family life cycle (Mitchell & Lovegreen, 2009). Investment in nonparental relationships and roles, children's characteristics, parents' marital and economic circumstances, and cultural forces affect the extent to which this transition is expansive and rewarding or sad and distressing.

After their son Mark secured a career-entry job and moved out of the family home permanently, Devin and Trisha felt a twinge of nostalgia. Beyond this, they returned to rewarding careers and community participation and delighted in having more time for each other.

Wide cultural variations exist in the social clock for children's departure. Recall from Chapter 13 that many young people from low-SES homes and with cultural traditions of extended-family living do not leave home early. In the southern European countries of Greece, Italy, and Spain, parents often actively delay their children's leaving. In Italy, for example, parents believe that moving out without a "justified" reason signifies that something is wrong in the family. Hence, many more Italian young adults reside with their parents until marriage than in other Western nations. At the same time, Italian parent–adult-child relationships are usually positive, making shared living attractive (Rusconi, 2004).

With the end of parent–child coresidence, parental authority declines sharply. But continued positive communication is important to middle-aged adults. Departure of children is a relatively minor event as long as parent–child contact and affection are sustained (Mitchell & Lovegreen, 2009). When it results in little or no communication or persistent conflict, parents' psychological well-being declines.

Whether or not they reside with parents, adolescent and young-adult children who are "off-time" in development— who deviate from parental expectations about how the path to adult responsibilities should unfold—can prompt parental strain (Fingerman et al., 2012a; Settersten, 2003). Consider Elena, whose daughter was doing poorly in her college courses and in danger of not graduating. The need for extensive parental guidance, at a time when she expected her daughter to be more responsible and independent, caused anxiety and unhappiness for Elena.

Throughout middle adulthood, parents continue to give more assistance to children than they receive, especially while children are unmarried or when they face difficulties, such as marital breakup or unemployment. Support in Western countries typically flows "downstream": Although ethnic variations exist, most middle-aged parents provide more financial, practical, emotional, and social support to their offspring than to their aging parents, unless a parent has an urgent need (declining health or other crises) (Fingerman & Birditt, 2011; Fingerman et al., 2011a). In explaining their generous support of adult children, parents usually mention the importance of the relationship. And providing adult children with assistance enhances midlife psychological well-being (Marks & Greenfield, 2009). Clearly, middle-aged adults remain invested in their adult children's development and continue to reap deep personal rewards from the parental role.

When children marry, parents must adjust to an enlarged family network that includes in-laws. Difficulties occur when parents do not approve of their child's partner or when the young couple adopts a way of life inconsistent with parents' values. Parents who take steps to forge a positive tie with a future daughter- or son-in-law generally experience a closer relationship after the couple marries (Fingerman et al., 2012b). And when warm, supportive relationships endure, intimacy between parents and children increases over the adult years, with great benefits for parents' life satisfaction (Ryff, Singer, & Seltzer, 2002). Members of the middle generation, especially mothers, usually take on the role of **kinkeeper,** gathering the family for celebrations and making sure everyone stays in touch.

Grandparenthood

Two years after Mark married, Devin and Trisha were thrilled to learn that a granddaughter was on the way. Although the stereotypical image of grandparents as elderly persists, today the average age of becoming a grandparent is 50 years for American women, 52 for American men (Legacy Project, 2012). A longer life expectancy means that many adults will spend one-third or more of their lifespan in the grandparent role.

Meanings of Grandparenthood. Middle-aged adults typically rate grandparenthood as highly important, following closely behind the roles of parent and spouse but ahead of worker, son or daughter, and sibling (Reitzes & Mutran, 2002).

Why did Trisha and Devin, like many others their age, greet the announcement of a grandchild with such enthusiasm? Most people experience grandparenthood as a significant milestone, mentioning one or more of the following gratifications:

● *Valued elder*—being perceived as a wise, helpful person

● *Immortality through descendants*—leaving behind not just one but two generations after death

● *Reinvolvement with personal past*—being able to pass family history and values to a new generation

● *Indulgence*—having fun with children without major child-rearing responsibilities (AARP, 2002; Hebblethwaite & Norris, 2011)

Grandparent–Grandchild Relationships. Grandparents' styles of relating to grandchildren vary as widely as the meanings they derive from their new role. The grandparent's and grandchild's age and sex make a difference. When their granddaughter was young, Trisha and Devin enjoyed an affectionate, playful relationship with her. As she got older, she looked to them for information and advice in addition to warmth and caring. By the time their granddaughter reached adolescence, Trisha and Devin had become role models, family historians, and conveyers of social, vocational, and religious values.

Living nearby is the strongest predictor of frequent, face-to-face interaction with young grandchildren. Most grandparents in Western nations live close enough to at least one grandchild to enable regular visits, but because time and resources are limited, number of "grandchild sets" (households with grandchildren) reduces contact (Uhlenberg & Hammill, 1998). As grandchildren get older, distance becomes less influential and relationship quality more so: The extent to which adolescent or young-adult grandchildren believe their grandparent values contact is a good predictor of a close bond (Brussoni & Boon, 1998).

© BLUE JEAN IMAGES/ALAMY

Many grandparents derive great joy from an affectionate, playful relationship with young grandchildren. As this grandchild gets older, he may look to his grandfather for advice, as a role model, and for family history in addition to warmth and caring.

Maternal grandmothers report more frequent visits with grandchildren than do paternal grandmothers, who are slightly advantaged over both maternal and paternal grandfathers (Uhlenberg & Hammill, 1998). Typically, relationships are closer between grandparents and grandchildren of the same sex and, especially, between maternal grandmothers and granddaughters—a pattern found in many countries (Brown & Rodin, 2004). Grandmothers also report higher satisfaction with the grandparent role than grandfathers, perhaps because grandmothers are more likely to participate in recreational, religious, and family activities with grandchildren (Reitzes & Mutran, 2004; Silverstein & Marenco, 2001). The grandparent role may be a vital means through which women satisfy their kinkeeping function.

SES and ethnicity also influence grandparent–grandchild ties. In low-income families, grandparents are more likely to perform essential activities. For example, many single parents live with their families of origin and depend on grandparents' financial and caregiving assistance to reduce the impact of poverty. Compared with grandchildren in intact families, grandchildren in single-parent and stepparent families report engaging in more diverse, higher-quality activities with their grandparents (Kennedy & Kennedy, 1993).

In some cultures, grandparents are absorbed into an extended-family household and become actively involved in child rearing. When a Chinese, Korean, or Mexican-American maternal grandmother is a homemaker, she is the preferred caregiver while parents of young children are at work (Kamo, 1998; Williams & Torrez, 1998). Similarly, involvement in child care is high among Native-American grandparents. In the absence of a biological grandparent, an unrelated aging adult may be integrated into the family to serve as a mentor and disciplinarian for children (Werner, 1991).

Increasingly, grandparents have stepped in as primary caregivers in the face of serious family problems. As the Social Issues: Health box on the following page reveals, a rising number of American children live apart from their parents in grandparent-headed households. Despite their willingness to help and their competence at child rearing, grandparents who take full responsibility for young children experience considerable emotional and financial strain. They need more assistance from community and government agencies than is currently available.

Because parents usually serve as gatekeepers of grandparents' contact with grandchildren, relationships between grandparents and their daughter-in-law or son-in-law strongly affect the closeness of grandparent–grandchild ties. A positive bond with a daughter-in-law seems particularly important in the relationship between grandparents and their son's children (Fingerman, 2004). And after a marital breakup, grandparents who are related to the custodial parent (typically the mother) have more frequent contact with grandchildren.

When family relationships are positive, grandparenthood provides an important means of fulfilling personal and societal needs in midlife and beyond. Grandparents are a frequent source of pleasure, support, and knowledge for grandchildren,

while providing them with firsthand experience in how older people think and function. In return, grandchildren become deeply attached to grandparents and keep them abreast of social change.

Middle-Aged Children and Their Aging Parents

The percentage of middle-aged Americans with living parents has risen dramatically—from 10 percent in 1900 to over 50 percent in the first decade of the twenty-first century (U.S. Census Bureau, 2013). A longer life expectancy means that adult children and their parents are increasingly likely to grow old together.

Frequency and Quality of Contact.
Approximately two-thirds of older adults in the United States live close to at least one of their children, and frequency of contact is high through both visits and telephone calls (U.S. Census Bureau, 2013). Proximity increases with age: Aging adults who move usually do so in the direction of kin, and younger people tend to move in the direction of their aging parents.

Middle age is a time when adults reassess relationships with their parents, just as they rethink other close ties. Many adult children become more appreciative of their parents' strengths and generosity and mention positive changes in the quality of the relationship, even after parents show physical declines. A warm, enjoyable relationship contributes to both parent and adult-child well-being (Fingerman et al., 2007, 2008; Pudrovska,

In midlife, many adults develop warmer, more supportive relationships with their aging parents. At a birthday party for her mother, this daughter expresses love and appreciation for her mother's strengths and generosity.

Social Issues: Health

Grandparents Rearing Grandchildren: The Skipped-Generation Family

Nearly 2.4 million U.S. children—4 to 5 percent of the child population—live with grandparents but apart from parents, in **skipped-generation families** (U.S. Census Bureau, 2013). The number of grandparents rearing grandchildren has increased over the past two decades. The arrangement occurs in all ethnic groups, though more often in African-American, Hispanic, and Native-American families than in Caucasian families. Although grandparent caregivers are more likely to be women than men, many grandfathers participate (Fuller-Thomson & Minkler, 2005, 2007; Minkler & Fuller-Thomson, 2005). Grandparents generally step in when parents' troubled lives—as a result of substance abuse, child abuse and neglect, family violence, or physical or mental illness—threaten children's well-being (Langosch, 2012). Often these families take in two or more children.

As a result, grandparents usually assume the parenting role under highly stressful life circumstances. Unfavorable child-rearing experiences have left their mark on the children, who show high rates of learning difficulties, depression, and antisocial behavior. Absent parents' adjustment difficulties strain family relationships. These children also introduce financial burdens into households that often are already low-income (Mills, Gomez-Smith, & De Leon, 2005; Williamson, Softas-Nall, & Miller, 2003). All these factors heighten grandparents' emotional distress.

Grandparent caregivers, at a time when they anticipated having more time for spouses, friends, and leisure, instead have less. Many report feeling emotionally drained, depressed, and worried about what will happen to the children if their own health fails (Hayslip & Kaminski, 2005; Langosch, 2012). Some families are extremely burdened. Native-American caregiving grandparents are especially likely to be unemployed, to have a disability, to be caring for several grandchildren, and to be living in extreme poverty (Fuller-Thomson & Minkler, 2005).

Despite great hardship, these grandparents seem to realize their widespread image as "silent saviors," often forging close emotional bonds with their grandchildren and using effective child-rearing practices (Fuller-Thomson & Minkler, 2000; Gibson, 2005). Compared with children in divorced, single-parent families, blended families, or foster families, children reared by grandparents fare better in adjustment (Rubin et al., 2008; Solomon & Marx, 1995).

Skipped-generation families have a tremendous need for social and financial support and intervention services for troubled children. Custodial grandparents describe support groups—both for themselves and for their grandchildren—as especially helpful, yet few make use of such interventions (Smith, Rodriguez, & Palmieri, 2010). This suggests that grandparents need special help

A custodial grandmother helps her 8-year-old granddaughter with homework. Although grandparents usually assume the parenting role under highly stressful circumstances, most find compensating rewards in rearing grandchildren.

in finding out about and accessing support services.

Although their everyday lives are often stressful, caregiving grandparents—even those rearing children with serious problems—report as much fulfillment in the grandparent role as typical grandparents do. The warmer the grandparent–grandchild bond, the greater grandparents' long-term life satisfaction (Goodman, 2012). Many grandparents mention joy from sharing children's lives and feelings of pride at children's progress, which help compensate for difficult circumstances. And some grandparents view the rearing of grandchildren as a "second chance"—an opportunity to make up for earlier, unfavorable parenting experiences and "do it right" (Dolbin-MacNab, 2006).

2009). Trisha, for example, felt closer to her parents and often asked them to tell her more about their earlier lives.

Research indicates that middle-aged daughters forge closer, more supportive relationships with aging parents, especially mothers, than do middle-aged sons (Fingerman, 2003). But this gender difference may be declining. Sons report closer ties and greater assistance to aging parents in recent than in previous studies (Fingerman et al., 2007, 2008). Changing gender roles are likely responsible. Because the majority of contemporary middle-aged women are employed, they face many competing demands on their time and energy. Consequently, men are

becoming more involved in family responsibilities, including with aging parents (Fingerman & Birditt, 2011). Despite this shift, women's investment continues to exceed men's.

In collectivist cultures, older adults most often live with their married children. For example, traditionally, Chinese, Japanese, and Korean seniors moved in with a son and his wife and children; today, many live with a daughter and her family, too. This tradition of coresidence, however, is declining in some parts of Asia and in the United States, as more Asian and Asian-American aging adults choose to live on their own (Davey & Takagi, 2013; Zhan & Montgomery, 2003; Zhang, 2004). In

African-American and Hispanic families as well, coresidence is common. Regardless of whether coresidence and daily contact are typical, relationship quality usually reflects patterns established earlier: Positive parent–child ties generally remain so, as do conflict-ridden interactions.

The more positive the history of the parent–child tie, the more help given and received. Also, aging parents give more help to unmarried adult children and to those with disabilities. Similarly, adult children give more to elderly parents who are widowed or in poor health—usually emotional support and practical help, less often financial assistance. At the same time, middle-aged adults do what they can to maximize the overall quantity of help offered, as needed: While continuing to provide generous assistance to their young-adult children, they augment the aid they give to elderly parents as parental health problems increase (Kunemund, Motel-Klingebiel, & Kohli, 2005; Stephens et al., 2009).

Even when parent–child relationships have been emotionally distant, adult children offer more support as parents age, out of a sense of altruism and family duty (Silverstein et al., 2002). And although the baby-boom generation is often described as self-absorbed, baby-boom midlifers actually express a stronger commitment to caring for their aging parents than the preceding middle-aged generation (Gans & Silverstein, 2006).

In sum, as long as multiple roles are manageable and the experiences within each are high in quality, midlife intergenerational assistance as family members (aging parents) have increased needs is best characterized as *resource expansion* rather than as merely conflicting demands that inevitably drain energy and detract from psychological well-being (Grundy & Henretta, 2006; Stephens et al., 2009). Recall from the Biology and Environment box on page 429 that midlifers derive great personal benefits from successfully managing multiple roles. Their enhanced self-esteem, mastery, and sense of meaning and purpose expand their motivation and energy to handle added family-role demands, from which they reap additional personal rewards.

Caring for Aging Parents. About 25 percent of U.S. adult children provide unpaid care to an aging adult (MetLife, 2011). The burden of caring for aging parents can be great. In Chapter 2, we noted that as birthrates have declined, the family structure has become increasingly "top-heavy," with more generations alive but fewer younger members. Consequently, more than one older family member is likely to need assistance, with fewer younger adults available to provide it.

The term **sandwich generation** is widely used to refer to the idea that middle-aged adults must care for multiple generations above and below them at the same time (Riley & Bowen, 2005). Although only a minority of contemporary middle-aged adults who care for aging parents have children younger than age 18 at home, many are providing assistance to young-adult children and to grandchildren—obligations that, when combined with work and community responsibilities, can lead middle-aged caregivers to feel "sandwiched," or squeezed, between the pressures of older and younger generations. As more baby

Caring for an aging parent with a chronic illness or disability is highly stressful. But social support reduces physical and emotional strain, enabling adult children to find satisfactions and rewards in tending to parents' needs.

boomers move into late adulthood, the number of sandwiched midlifers will increase.

Middle-aged adults living far from aging parents who are in poor health often substitute financial help for direct care, if they have the means. But when parents live nearby and have no spouse to meet their needs, adult children usually engage in direct care. Regardless of family income level, African-American, Asian-American, and Hispanic adults give aging parents more direct care and financial help than Caucasian-American adults do (Shuey & Hardy, 2003). Compared with their white counterparts, African Americans and Hispanics express a stronger sense of obligation, and find it more personally rewarding, to support their aging parents (Fingerman et al., 2011b; Swartz, 2009). And African Americans often draw on close, family-like relationships with friends and neighbors for caregiving assistance.

In all ethnic groups, responsibility for providing care to aging parents falls more on daughters than on sons. Families turn to the person who seems most available—living nearby and with fewer commitments that might interfere with the ability to assist. These unstated rules, in addition to parents' preference for same-sex caregivers (aging mothers live longer), lead more women to fill the role (see Figure 16.2). Daughters also feel more obligated than sons to care for aging parents (Gans & Silverstein, 2006; Stein, 2009).

As Figure 16.2 shows, nearly one-fourth of American working women are caregivers; others quit their jobs to provide care. And the time they devote to caring for a disabled aging parent

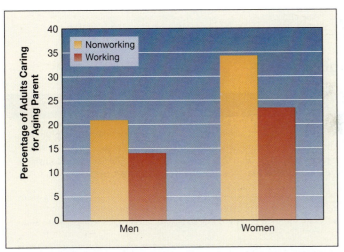

FIGURE 16.2 Baby boomers, by work status and gender, who provide basic personal care to an aging parent in poor health. A survey of a nationally representative sample of 1,100 U.S. men and women over age 50 with at least one parent living revealed that more nonworking than working adults engaged in basic personal care (assistance with such activities as dressing, feeding, and bathing). Regardless of work status, many more women than men were caregivers. (Adapted from *The MetLife Study of Caregiving Costs to Working Caregivers: Double Jeopardy for Baby Boomers Caring for Their Parents*, June 2011, Figure 3. Reprinted by permission of The MetLife Mature Market Institute, New York, NY.)

is substantial, averaging 10 to 20 hours per week (Metlife, 2011; Takamura & Williams, 2002). Nevertheless, men—although doing less than women—do contribute. In one investigation, employed men spent an average of 7½ hours per week caring for parents or parents-in-law (Neal & Hammer, 2007). Tim, for example, looked in on his father, a recent stroke victim, every evening, reading to him, running errands, making household repairs, and taking care of finances. His sister, however, provided more hands-on care—cooking, feeding, bathing, managing medication, and doing laundry. The care sons and daughters provide tends to be divided along gender-role lines (Pinquart & Sörensen, 2006).

As adults move from early to later middle age, the sex difference in parental caregiving declines. Perhaps as men reduce their vocational commitments and feel less need to conform to a "masculine" gender role, they grow more able and willing to provide basic care (Marks, 1996; MetLife, 2011). At the same time, parental caregiving may contribute to men's greater openness to the "feminine" side of their personalities. A man who cared for his mother, severely impaired by Alzheimer's disease, commented on how the experience altered his outlook: "It was so difficult to do these tasks; things a man, a son, is not supposed to do. I have definitely modified my views on conventional expectations" (Hirsch, 1996, p. 112).

Although most adult children help willingly, caring for a chronically ill or disabled parent is highly stressful. Over time, the parent usually gets worse, and the caregiving task escalates. As Tim explained to Devin and Trisha, "One of the hardest aspects is the emotional strain of seeing my father's physical and mental decline up close."

Caregivers who share a household with ill parents—about 23 percent of U.S. adult children—experience the most stress. When a parent and child who have lived separately for years must move in together, conflicts generally arise over routines and lifestyles. But the greatest source of stress is problem behavior, especially for caregivers of parents who have deteriorated mentally (Alzheimer's Association, 2012b). Tim's sister reported that their father would wake during the night, ask repetitive questions, follow her around the house, and become agitated and combative.

Parental caregiving often has emotional, physical, and financial consequences. It leads to role overload, high job absenteeism, exhaustion, inability to concentrate, feelings of hostility, anxiety about aging, and high rates of depression, with women more profoundly affected than men (Neal & Hammer, 2007; Pinquart & Sörensen, 2006). Despite having more time to care for an ill parent, women who quit work fare especially poorly in adjustment, probably because of social isolation and financial strain (Bookman & Kimbrel, 2011). Positive experiences at work can actually reduce the stress of parental care as caregivers bring a favorable self-evaluation and a positive mood home with them.

In cultures and subcultures where adult children feel an especially strong sense of obligation to care for aging parents, the emotional toll is also high (Knight & Sayegh, 2010). In research on Korean, Korean-American, and Caucasian-American caregivers of parents with mental disabilities, the Koreans and Korean Americans reported higher levels of family obligation and care burden—and also higher levels of anxiety and depression—than the Caucasian Americans (Lee & Farran, 2004; Youn et al., 1999). And among African-American caregivers, women who strongly endorsed cultural reasons for providing care ("It's what my people have always done") fared less well in mental health two years later than women who moderately endorsed cultural reasons (Dilworth-Anderson, Goodwin, & Williams, 2004).

LOOK AND LISTEN

Ask a middle-aged adult caring for an aging parent in declining health to describe both the stressful and rewarding aspects of caregiving. What strategies does he or she use to reduce stress? ●

Social support is highly effective in reducing caregiver stress. In Denmark, Sweden, and Japan, a government-sponsored home helper system eases the burden of parental care by making specially trained nonfamily caregivers available, based on seniors' needs (Saito, Auestad, & Waerness, 2010). In the United States, in-home care by a nonfamily caregiver is too costly for most families; only 10 to 20 percent arrange it (Family Caregiver Alliance, 2009). And unless they must, few people want to place their parents in formal care, such as nursing homes, which also are expensive. Applying What We Know on page 438 summarizes ways to relieve the stress of caring for an aging parent—at the individual, family, community, and societal levels. We will address additional care options, along with interventions for caregivers, in Chapter 17.

Applying What We Know

Relieving the Stress of Caring for an Aging Parent

Strategy	Description
Use effective coping strategies.	Use problem-centered coping to manage the parent's behavior and caregiving tasks. Delegate responsibilities to other family members, seek assistance from friends and neighbors, and recognize the parent's limits while calling on capacities the parent does have. Use emotion-centered coping to reinterpret the situation positively, such as emphasizing the opportunity it offers for personal growth. Avoid denial of anger, depression, and anxiety in response to the caregiving burden, which heightens stress.
Seek social support.	Confide in family members and friends about the stress of caregiving, seeking their encouragement and help. So far as possible, avoid quitting work to care for an ill parent; doing so is associated with social isolation and loss of financial resources.
Make use of community resources.	Contact community organizations to seek information and assistance, in the form of caregiver support groups, in-home respite help, home-delivered meals, transportation, and adult day care.
Press for workplace and public policies that relieve the emotional and financial burdens of caring for an aging parent.	Encourage your employer to provide care benefits, such as flexible work hours and employment leave for caregiving. Communicate with lawmakers and other citizens about the need for improved health insurance plans that reduce the financial strain of caring for an aging parent on middle- and low-income families.

Siblings

A survey of a large sample of ethnically diverse Americans revealed that sibling contact and support decline from early to middle adulthood, rebounding only after age 70 for siblings living near each other (White, 2001). Decreased midlife contact is probably due to the demands of middle-aged adults' diverse roles. However, most adult siblings report getting together or talking on the phone at least monthly (Antonucci, Akiyama, & Merline, 2002).

Despite reduced contact, many siblings feel closer in midlife, often in response to major life events (Stewart et al., 2001).

© JEFF GREENBERG/THE IMAGE WORKS

These brothers, both in their fifties, express their mutual affection at a family reunion. Even when they have only limited contact, siblings often feel closer in midlife.

Launching and marriage of children seem to prompt siblings to think more about each other. When a parent becomes seriously ill, brothers and sisters who previously had little to do with one another may find themselves in touch about parental care. And when parents die, adult children realize they have become the oldest generation and must look to each other to sustain family ties.

Not all sibling bonds improve, of course. Recall Trisha's negative encounters with her sister, Dottie (see page 409 in Chapter 15). Dottie's difficult temperament had made her hard to get along with since childhood, and her temper flared when their father died and problems arose over family finances. Large inequities in division of labor in parental caregiving can also unleash intense sibling conflict (Silverstein & Giarrusso, 2010). As siblings grow older, good relationships often get better and poor relationships get worse.

In industrialized nations, sibling relationships are voluntary. In village societies, they are generally involuntary and basic to family functioning. For example, among Asian Pacific Islanders, family social life is organized around strong brother–sister attachments. A brother–sister pair is often treated as a unit in exchange marriages with another family. After marriage, brothers are expected to protect sisters, and sisters serve as spiritual mentors to brothers (Cicirelli, 1995). Cultural norms reduce sibling conflict, thereby ensuring family cooperation.

Friendships

As family responsibilities declined in middle age, Devin found he had more time to spend with friends. On Friday afternoons, he met several male friends at a coffee house, and they chatted for a couple of hours. But most of Devin's friendships were couple-based—relationships he shared with Trisha. Compared with Devin, Trisha more often got together with friends on her own.

Middle-aged friendships reflect the same trends discussed in Chapter 14. At all ages, men's friendships are less intimate than women's. Men tend to talk about sports, politics, and business, whereas women focus on feelings and life problems. Women report a greater number of close friends and say they both receive and provide their friends with more emotional support (Antonucci, Akiyama, & Takahashi, 2004).

Over the past decade, the average number of friendships rose among U.S. midlifers, perhaps because of ease of keeping in touch through social media (Wang & Wellman, 2010). Though falling short of young adults' use, connecting regularly with friends through Facebook or other social networking sites has risen rapidly among middle-aged adults (see Figure 16.3) (Brenner, 2013; Hampton et al., 2011). As in early adulthood, women are more active users. And users have more offline close relationships, sometimes using Facebook to revive "dormant" friendships.

Still, for both sexes, number of friends declines from middle to late adulthood, probably because people become less willing to invest in nonfamily ties unless they are very rewarding. As selectivity of friendship increases, older adults try harder to get along with friends (Antonucci & Akiyama, 1995). Having chosen a friend, middle-aged people attach great value to the relationship and take extra steps to protect it.

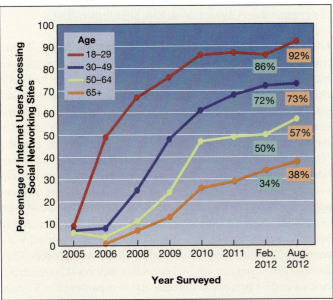

FIGURE 16.3 Gains in use of social networking sites by age group from 2005 to 2012. Repeated surveys of large representative samples of U.S. adults who use the Internet revealed that social networking site use increased substantially for all age groups. Though not as avid users as young adults, most middle-aged adults use social networking sites, primarily Facebook. (From J. Brenner, 2013, "Pew Internet: Social Networking." Pew Research Center's Internet & American Life Project, Washington, D.C. February 14, 2013, *www.pewinternet.org*. Adapted by permission.)

By midlife, family relationships and friendships support different aspects of psychological well-being. Family ties protect against serious threats and losses, offering security within a long-term timeframe. In contrast, friendships serve as current sources of pleasure and satisfaction (Levitt & Cici-Gokaltun, 2011). As middle-aged couples renew their sense of companionship, they may combine the best of family and friendship.

Vocational Life

Work continues to be a salient aspect of identity and self-esteem in middle adulthood. More so than in earlier or later years, people attempt to increase the personal meaning and self-direction of their vocational lives. The large tide of baby boomers currently moving through midlife and (as we will see in Chapter 18) the desire of most to work longer than the previous generation means that the number of older workers will rise dramatically over the next few decades (Leonesio et al., 2012). Yet a favorable transition from adult worker to older worker is hindered by negative stereotypes of aging—incorrect assumptions of limited learning capacity, slower decision making, and resistance to change and supervision (Posthuma & Campion, 2009). Furthermore, gender discrimination continues to restrict the career attainments of many women. Let's take a close look at middle-aged work life.

Job Satisfaction

Job satisfaction increases in midlife in diverse nations and at all occupational levels, from executives to hourly workers. The trend is weaker for women than for men, probably because women's reduced chances for advancement result in a sense of unfairness. It is also weaker for blue-collar than for white-collar workers, perhaps because blue-collar workers have less control over their own work schedules and activities (Avolio & Sosik, 1999). When different aspects of jobs are considered, intrinsic satisfaction—happiness with the work itself—shows a strong age-related gain. Extrinsic satisfaction—contentment with supervision, pay, and promotions—changes very little (Barnes-Farrell & Matthews, 2007).

What explains the rise in job satisfaction during middle adulthood? An improved capacity to cope effectively with difficult situations and a broader time perspective probably contribute. "When I first started teaching, I complained a lot," remarked Devin. "Now, I can tell a big problem from a trivial one." Moving out of unrewarding work roles, as Trisha did, can also boost morale. And older people tend to have greater access to key job characteristics that predict well-being—involvement in decision making, reasonable workloads, and good physical working conditions. Furthermore, having fewer alternative positions into which they can move, older workers generally reduce their career aspirations (Barnes-Farrell & Matthews, 2007). As the perceived gap between actual and possible achievements narrows, job involvement—importance of one's work to self-esteem—increases (Warr, 2001).

Although emotional engagement with work is usually psychologically healthy, it can also result in **burnout**—a condition in which long-term job stress leads to mental exhaustion, a sense of loss of personal control, and feelings of reduced accomplishment. Burnout occurs more often in the helping professions, including health care, human services, and teaching, which place high emotional demands on employees. And it is especially likely to occur in unsupportive work environments, where work assignments exceed time available to complete them and encouragement and feedback from supervisors are scarce (Schmidt, Neubach, & Heuer, 2007). Burnout tends to occur more often in the United States than in Western Europe, perhaps because of Americans' greater achievement orientation (Maslach, Schaufeli, & Leiter, 2001).

To prevent burnout, employers can make sure workloads are reasonable, provide opportunities for workers to take time out from stressful situations, limit hours of stressful work, and offer social support. Interventions that enlist employees' participation in designing higher-quality work environments show promise for increasing work engagement and effectiveness and reducing burnout (Leiter, Gascón, & Martínez-Jarreta, 2010). And provisions for working at home may respond to the needs of some people for a calmer, quieter work atmosphere.

Career Development

After several years as a parish nurse, Anya felt a need for additional training to do her job better. Trisha appreciated her firm's generous support of workshop and course attendance, which helped her keep abreast of new legal developments. As

these experiences reveal, career development is vital throughout work life.

Job Training. When Anya asked her supervisor, Roy, for time off to upgrade her skills, he replied, "You're in your fifties. What're you going to do with so much new information at this point in your life?" Roy's insensitive, narrow-minded response, though usually unspoken, is all too common among managers—even some who are older themselves! Training and on-the-job career counseling are less available to older workers. And when career development activities are offered, older employees may be less likely to volunteer for them (Barnes-Farrell & Matthews, 2007; Hedge, Borman, & Lammlein, 2006). What influences willingness to engage in job training and updating?

Personal characteristics are important: With age, growth needs give way somewhat to security needs. Perhaps for this reason, older employees depend more on co-worker and supervisor encouragement for vocational development. Yet as we have seen, they are less likely to have supportive supervisors. Furthermore, negative stereotypes of aging reduce older workers' self-efficacy, or confidence that they can get better at their jobs (Maurer, 2001; Maurer, Wrenn, & Weiss, 2003).

Workplace characteristics matter, too. An employee given work that requires new learning must pursue that learning to complete the assignment. Unfortunately, older workers sometimes receive more routine tasks than younger workers. In companies with a more favorable *age climate* (view of older workers), mature employees participate frequently in further education and report greater self-efficacy and commitment to the organization (Bowen, Noack, & Staudinger, 2011).

Gender and Ethnicity: The Glass Ceiling. In her thirties, Jewel became a company president by starting her own business. Having concluded that, as a woman, she had little chance of rising to a top executive position in a large corporation, she didn't even try. Although women and ethnic minorities have gradually gained in access to managerial careers, they remain a long distance from gender and ethnic equality (Huffman, 2012). From career entry on, inequalities in promotion between men and women and between whites and blacks become more pronounced over time—findings still evident after education, work skills, and work productivity have been controlled (Barreto, Ryan, & Schmitt, 2009; Maume, 2004). When the most prestigious high-level management jobs are considered, white men are overwhelmingly advantaged: They account for 70 percent of chief executive officers at large corporations and 93 percent at Fortune 500 companies (U.S. Census Bureau, 2013).

Women and ethnic minorities face a **glass ceiling,** or invisible barrier to advancement up the corporate ladder. Why is this so? Management is an art and skill that must be taught. Yet women and ethnic minorities have less access to mentors, role models, and informal networks that serve as training routes (Baumgartner & Schneider, 2010). And stereotyped doubts about women's career commitment and managerial ability

Facebook executive Sheryl Sandberg is among a handful of women who have attained top positions in major corporations. In her best-selling book, *Lean In*, she urges women to be more assertive in demonstrating qualities linked to leadership at work.

(especially women with children) also contribute, leading supervisors to underrate their competence and not to recommend them for formal management training programs (Hoobler, Lemmon, & Wayne, 2011).

Furthermore, women who demonstrate qualities linked to leadership and advancement—assertiveness, confidence, forcefulness, and ambition—encounter prejudice because they deviate from traditional gender roles, even though they more often combine these traits with a democratic, collaborative style of leading than do men (Cheung & Halpern, 2010; Eagly & Carli, 2007). To overcome this bias, women in line for top positions must demonstrate greater competence than their male counterparts. In an investigation of several hundred senior managers at a multinational financial services corporation, promoted female managers had earned higher performance ratings than promoted male managers (Lyness & Heilman, 2006). In contrast, no gender difference existed in performance of managers not selected for promotion.

Like Jewel, many women have dealt with the glass ceiling by going around it, leaving the corporate environment and going into business for themselves. Today, more than half of all startup businesses in the United States are owned and successfully operated by women (Ahuja, 2005; U.S. Census Bureau, 2013). But when women and ethnic minorities leave the corporate world, companies not only lose valuable talent but also fail to address the leadership needs of an increasingly diverse work force.

Planning for Retirement

One evening, Devin and Trisha met Anya and her husband, George, for dinner. Halfway through the meal, Devin inquired, "George, tell us what you and Anya are going to do

about retirement. Are you planning to work part-time or stop entirely? Do you think you'll stay here or move out of town?"

Three or four generations ago, the two couples would not have had this conversation. In 1900, about 70 percent of American men age 65 and over were in the labor force. By 1970, however, the figure had dropped to 27 percent, and in the early twenty-first century it declined to 16 percent (U.S. Census Bureau, 2013). Because of government-sponsored retirement benefits (begun in the United States in 1935), retirement is no longer a privilege reserved for the wealthy. The federal government pays Social Security to the majority of the aged, and others are covered by employer-based private pension plans.

As the trend just noted suggests, the average age of retirement has declined over the past several decades. Currently, it is age 63 in the United States and hovers between 60 and 63 in other Western nations (U.S. Census Bureau, 2013). The recent recession led to an increase in the number of Americans at risk for being unable to sustain their preretirement standard of living after leaving the workforce. Consequently, a survey of a large, nationally representative sample of baby boomers revealed that the majority expect to delay retirement (Jones, 2012). But current estimates indicate that most will need to work just a few extra years to be financially ready to retire (Munnell et al., 2012). For the healthy, active, long-lived baby-boom generation, up to one-fourth of their lives may lie ahead after they leave their jobs.

Retirement is a lengthy, complex process that begins as soon as the middle-aged person first thinks about it (Kim & Moen, 2002b). Planning is important because retirement leads to a loss of two important work-related rewards—income and status—and to a change in many other aspects of life. Yet nearly half of middle-aged people engage in no concrete retirement planning (Hershey et al., 2007).

Because income typically drops by 50 percent, more people engage in financial planning than in other forms of preparation. But even those who attend financial education programs often fail to look closely at their financial well-being and to make wise decisions (Keller & Lusardi, 2012). Many could benefit from an expert's financial analysis and counsel.

LOOK AND LISTEN

Contact the human resources division of a company or institution in your community, and inquire about the retirement planning services it offers. How comprehensive are those services, and what percentage of its recent retirees made use of them? ●

Retirement leads to ways of spending time that are largely guided by one's interests rather than one's obligations. Planning for an active life has an even greater impact on happiness after retirement than financial planning. Participation in activities promotes many factors essential for psychological well-being, including a structured time schedule, social contact, and self-esteem (Schlossberg, 2004). Carefully considering whether or not to relocate at retirement is related to an active life, since it affects access to health care, friends, family, recreation, entertainment, and part-time work.

Devin retired at age 62, George at age 66. Though several years younger, Trisha and Anya—like many married women—coordinated their retirements with those of their husbands. In contrast, Jewel—in good health but without an intimate partner to share her life—kept her consulting business going until age 75. Tim took early retirement and moved to be near Elena, where he devoted himself to public service—tutoring second graders in a public school and coaching after-school and weekend youth sports.

Unfortunately, less well-educated people with lower lifetime earnings are least likely to attend retirement preparation programs—yet they stand to benefit the most. And compared with men, women do less planning for retirement, instead relying on their husband's preparations. This gender gap seems to be narrowing, however, as women increasingly contribute to family income (Adams & Rau, 2011). Employers must take extra steps to encourage lower-paid workers and women to participate in planning activities. In addition, enhancing retirement adjustment among the economically disadvantaged depends on access to better vocational training, jobs, and health care at early ages. Clearly, a lifetime of opportunities and experiences affects the transition to retirement. In Chapter 18, we will consider the decision to retire and retirement adjustment in greater detail.

ASK YOURSELF

REVIEW What factors contribute to the rise in job satisfaction with age?

APPLY An executive wonders how his large corporation can foster advancement of women and ethnic minorities to upper management positions. What strategies would you recommend?

SUMMARY

Erikson's Theory: Generativity versus Stagnation (p. 423)

According to Erikson, how does personality change in middle age?

- Generativity expands as middle-aged adults face Erikson's psychological conflict of **generativity versus stagnation.** Personal desires and cultural demands jointly shape adults' generative activities.

JEAN-MARC GIBOUX/GETTY IMAGES

- Highly generative people, who contribute to society through parenthood, other family relationships, the workplace, and volunteer endeavors, appear especially well-adjusted. Stagnation occurs when people become self-centered and self-indulgent in midlife.

Other Theories of Psychosocial Development in Midlife (p. 425)

Describe Levinson's and Vaillant's views of psychosocial development in middle adulthood, and discuss similarities and differences between men and women.

- According to Levinson, middle-aged adults confront four developmental tasks, each requiring them to reconcile two opposing tendencies within the self: young–old, destruction–creation, masculinity–femininity, and engagement–separateness.

- Middle-aged men show greater acceptance of "feminine" traits of nurturance and caring, while women are more open to "masculine" characteristics of autonomy and assertiveness. Men and successful career-oriented women may reduce their concern with ambition and achievement. Women who have devoted themselves to child rearing or an unfulfilling job often seek rewarding work or community engagement.

- Vaillant found that adults in their late forties and fifties become guardians of their culture, seeking to "pass the torch" to later generations.

Does the term midlife crisis *reflect most people's experience of middle adulthood, and is middle adulthood accurately characterized as a stage?*

- Most people respond to midlife with changes that are better described as "turning points" than as a crisis. Only a minority experience a **midlife crisis** characterized by intense self-doubt and stress that lead to drastic life alterations.

Stability and Change in Self-Concept and Personality (p. 427)

Describe changes in self-concept, personality, and gender identity in middle adulthood.

- Middle-aged individuals maintain self-esteem and stay motivated by revising their **possible selves,** which become fewer in number as well as more modest and concrete.

- Midlife typically brings enhanced psychological well-being, through greater self-acceptance, autonomy, and environmental mastery. Factors contributing to well-being, however, vary widely among cohorts and cultures.

- Daily stressors plateau in early to mid-adulthood, and then decline as work and family responsibilities ease. Midlife gains in emotional stability and confidence in handling life's problems lead to increased effectiveness in coping with stressors.

- Both men and women become more androgynous in middle adulthood. Biological explanations, such as **parental imperative theory,** are controversial. A combination of social roles and life conditions is more likely responsible.

Discuss stability and change in the "big five" personality traits in adulthood.

- Among the **"big five" personality traits,** agreeableness and conscientiousness increase into middle age, while neuroticism declines, and extroversion and openness to experience do not change or decrease slightly. Individual differences are large and highly stable: Although adults change in overall organization and integration of personality, they do so on a foundation of basic, enduring dispositions.

Relationships at Midlife
(p. 431)

Describe the middle adulthood phase of the family life cycle.

- "Launching children and moving on" is the midlife phase of the family life cycle. Adults must adapt to many entries and exits of family members as their children launch–return–relaunch, marry, and produce grandchildren, and as their own parents age and die.

- When divorce occurs, middle-aged adults seem to adapt more easily than younger people. For women, midlife marital breakup often severely reduces standard of living, contributing to the **feminization of poverty.**

- Most middle-aged parents adjust well to launching adult children, especially if positive parent–child relationships are sustained, but adult children who are "off-time" in development can prompt parental strain. As children marry, middle-aged parents, especially mothers, often become **kinkeepers.**

- Grandparents' contact and closeness with grandchildren depend on proximity, number of grandchild sets, sex of grandparent and grandchild, and in-law relationships. In low-income families and in some ethnic groups, grandparents provide essential financial and child-care assistance. When serious family problems exist, grandparents may become primary caregivers in **skipped-generation families.**

- Middle-aged adults reassess their relationships with aging parents, often becoming more appreciative. Mother–daughter relationships tend to be closer than other parent–child ties. The more positive the history of the parent–child tie and the greater the need for assistance, the more help exchanged.

- Middle-aged adults, often caught between caring for aging parents, assisting young-adult children and grandchildren, and meeting work and community responsibilities, are called the **sandwich generation.** The burden of caring for ill or frail parents falls most heavily on adult daughters, though the sex difference declines in later middle age.

- Parental caregiving has emotional and health consequences, especially in cultures and subcultures where adult children feel a particularly strong obligation to provide care. Social support is highly effective in reducing caregiver stress.

Describe midlife sibling relationships and friendships.

- Sibling contact and support decline from early to middle adulthood, probably because of the demands of diverse roles. But many middle-aged siblings feel closer, often in response to major life events. Sister–sister ties are typically closest in industrialized nations. In nonindustrialized societies, strong brother–sister attachments may be basic to family functioning.

- In midlife, friendships become fewer, more selective, and more deeply valued. Men continue to be less expressive with their friends than women, who have more close friendships. Viewing a spouse as a best friend can contribute greatly to marital happiness.

Vocational Life (p. 439)

Discuss job satisfaction and career development in middle adulthood, with special attention to sex differences and experiences of ethnic minorities.

- Vocational readjustments are common as middle-aged people seek to increase the personal meaning and self-direction of their work lives. Job satisfaction increases, more so for men than for women. **Burnout** is a serious occupational hazard, especially for those in helping professions and in unsupportive work environments.

- Both personal and workplace characteristics influence the extent to which older workers engage in career development. In companies with a more favorable age climate, mature employees report greater self-efficacy and commitment to the organization.

- Women and ethnic minorities face a **glass ceiling** because of limited access to management training and prejudice against women who demonstrate strong leadership qualities. Many women further their careers by leaving the corporate world, often to start their own businesses.

Discuss the importance of planning for retirement.

- Retirement brings major life changes, including loss of income and status and increase in free time. Besides financial planning, planning for an active life is vital, with a strong impact on happiness after retirement. Low-paid workers and women need extra encouragement to participate in retirement planning.

Important Terms and Concepts

"big five" personality traits (p. 430)
burnout (p. 440)
feminization of poverty (p. 432)
generativity versus stagnation (p. 423)

glass ceiling (p. 440)
kinkeeper (p. 433)
midlife crisis (p. 426)
parental imperative theory (p. 430)

possible selves (p. 427)
sandwich generation (p. 436)
skipped-generation family (p. 435)

milestones

Development in Middle Adulthood

- General factual knowledge, knowledge related to one's occupation, and metacognitive knowledge remain unchanged or may increase. (416)

40–50 years

PHYSICAL

- Accommodative ability of the lens of the eye, ability to see in dim light, and color discrimination decline; sensitivity to glare increases. (402)
- Hearing loss at high frequencies occurs. (402)
- Hair grays and thins. (401)
- Lines on the face become more pronounced; skin loses elasticity and begins to sag. (402–403)
- Weight gain continues, accompanied by a rise in fatty deposits in the torso, while fat beneath the skin declines. (403)
- Loss of lean body mass (muscle and bone) occurs. (403)
- In women, production of estrogen drops, leading to shortening and irregularity of the menstrual cycle. (403)

- In men, quantity of semen and sperm declines. (406)
- Intensity of sexual response declines, but frequency of sexual activity drops only slightly. (407)
- Rates of cancer and cardiovascular disease increase. (407–408)

COGNITIVE

- Consciousness of aging increases. (401, 425)
- Crystallized intelligence increases; fluid intelligence declines. (413–414)
- Speed of processing declines, but adults can compensate through experience and practice. (415)

- Ability to attend selectively and to adapt attention—switching from one task to another—declines, but adults can compensate through experience and practice. (415–416)
- Amount of information retained in working memory declines, in part because of reduced use of memory strategies. (416)
- Retrieving information from long-term memory becomes more difficult. (416)

- Practical problem solving and expertise increase. (417–418)
- Creativity may become more deliberately thoughtful, emphasize integrating ideas, and shift from self-expression to more altruistic goals. (418)

Note: Numbers in parentheses indicate the page or pages on which each milestone is discussed.

EMOTIONAL/SOCIAL

- Generativity increases. (423–424)
- Focus shifts toward personally meaningful living. (425)

© JEFF GREENBERG/PHOTOEDIT

© JIM WEST/PHOTOEDIT

50–65 years

COGNITIVE

- Cognitive changes previously listed continue.

THINKSTOCK/GETTY IMAGES

- Possible selves become fewer in number and more modest and concrete. (427)
- Self-acceptance, autonomy, and environmental mastery increase. (428)
- Strategies for coping with stressors become more effective. (428)
- Gender identity becomes more androgynous; "masculine" traits increase in women, "feminine" traits in men. (425, 428, 430)
- Agreeableness and conscientiousness increase, while neuroticism declines. (430)
- May launch children. (432)
- May become a kinkeeper, especially if a mother. (433)
- May become a parent-in-law and a grandparent. (433)
- Becomes more appreciative of parents' strengths and generosity; quality of relationships with parents increase. (434–436)
- May care for a parent with a disability or chronic illness. (436–438)
- Siblings may feel closer. (438)

PHYSICAL

- Lens of the eye loses its capacity to adjust to objects at varying distances entirely. (402)
- Hearing loss gradually extends to all frequencies but remains greatest for high frequencies. (402)
- Skin continues to wrinkle and sag, "age spots" increase, and blood vessels in the skin become more visible. (402–403)
- In women, menopause occurs; as estrogen declines further, genitals are less easily stimulated, and the vagina lubricates more slowly during arousal. (403)
- In men, inability to attain an erection when desired becomes more common. (406)
- Loss of bone mass continues; rates of osteoporosis rise. (403, 408–409)
- Collapse of disks in the spinal column causes height to drop by as much as 1 inch. (403)
- Rates of cancer and cardiovascular disease continue to increase. (407–408)

EMOTIONAL/SOCIAL

- Emotional and social changes previously listed continue.

© JEFF GREENBERG/THE IMAGE WORKS

- Parent-to-child help-giving declines, and child-to-parent support and practical assistance increase. (435–437)

JUAN MONINO/GETTY IMAGES

- Number of friends generally declines. (439)
- Intrinsic job satisfaction—happiness with one's work—typically increases. (439–440)

KIDSTOCK/BLEND IMAGES/GETTY IMAGES

© LISA F. YOUNG/ALAMY

- May retire. (441–442)

chapter 17

Physical and Cognitive Development in Late Adulthood

AP IMAGES/KHIN MAUNG WIN

Cultures around the world connect age with wisdom. Older adults' life experience enhances their ability to solve human problems and fill leadership positions. These are endeavors of South African anti-apartheid activist Archbishop Desmond Tutu and Myanmar opposition leader Aung San Suu Kyi. Each is a Nobel Peace laureate.

chapter outline

At age 67, Walt gave up his photography business and looked forward to more spare time with 64-year-old Ruth, who retired from her position as a social worker at the same time. For Walt and Ruth, this culminating period of life was filled with volunteer work, golfing three times a week, and joint vacations with Walt's older brother Dick and his wife, Goldie. Walt also took up activities he had always loved but had little time to pursue—writing poems and short stories, attending theater performances, enrolling in a class on world politics, and cultivating a garden that became the envy of the neighborhood. Ruth read voraciously, served on the board of directors of an adoption agency, and had more time to visit her sister Ida in a nearby city.

Over the next 20 years, Walt and Ruth amazed nearly everyone who met them with their energy and vitality. Then, in their early eighties, the couple's lives changed profoundly. Walt had surgery to treat a cancerous prostate gland and within 3 months was hospitalized again after a heart attack. He lingered for 6 weeks and then died. Ruth's grieving was interrupted by the need to care for Ida. Alert and spry at age 78, Ida deteriorated mentally in her seventy-ninth year, despite otherwise excellent physical health. Meanwhile, Ruth's arthritis worsened, and her vision and hearing weakened.

As Ruth turned 85, certain activities had become difficult—but not impossible. "It just takes a little adjustment!" Ruth exclaimed in her usual upbeat manner. Reading was harder, so she downloaded audiobooks to her MP3 player. At dinner in a noisy restaurant with her daughter and family, Ruth felt overwhelmed and participated little in the fast-moving conversation. But in one-to-one interactions in a calm environment, she showed the same intelligence, wit, and astute insights that she had displayed all her life.

Late adulthood stretches from age 65 to the end of the lifespan. Unfortunately, popular images fail to capture the quality of these final decades. Instead, many myths prevail—that older people have entered a period of deterioration and dependency and that they are no longer able to learn. Young people who have little contact with older adults are often surprised that those like Walt and Ruth even exist—active and involved in the world around them.

© JEFF GREENBERG/ THE IMAGE WORKS

As we trace physical and cognitive development in late adulthood, we will see that the balance of gains and declines shifts as death approaches. But in industrialized nations, the typical 65-year-old can anticipate nearly two healthy, rewarding decades before this shift affects everyday life. And as Ruth illustrates, even after older adults become frail, many find ways to surmount physical and cognitive challenges.

Late adulthood is best viewed as an extension of earlier periods, not a break with them. As long as social and cultural contexts give older adults support, respect, and purpose in life, these years are a time of continued potential. ●

PHYSICAL DEVELOPMENT

TAKE A MOMENT... Do you know an older person who "seems young" or "seems old" for his or her age? In using these descriptors, we acknowledge that chronological age is an imperfect indicator of **functional age**, or actual competence and performance. Because people age biologically at different rates, some 80-year-olds appear younger than many 65-year-olds. Also, recall from Chapter 13 that within each person, change differs across parts of the body. For example, Ruth became infirm physically but remained active mentally, whereas Ida, though physically fit for her age, found it hard to engage in familiar tasks.

So much variation exists between and within individuals that researchers have not yet identified any single biological measure that predicts the overall rate at which a person will age. But we do have estimates of how much longer older adults can expect to live, and our knowledge of factors affecting longevity in late adulthood has increased rapidly.

Life Expectancy

"I wonder how many years I have left," Ruth asked herself each time a major life event, such as retirement or widowhood, occurred. Dramatic gains in **average life expectancy**—the number of years that an individual born in a particular year can expect to live, starting at any given age—provide powerful support for the multiplicity of factors considered in previous chapters that slow biological aging, including improved

© BORDERLANDS/ALAMY

Two friends enjoy a stroll in Tokyo, Japan. How old are they? How old do they look and feel? Because people age biologically at different rates, the woman on the right appears younger, though both are in their early eighties.

nutrition, medical treatment, sanitation, and safety. Recall from Chapter 1 that in 1900, life expectancy was just under 50 years; in the United States today, it is 78.5—nearly 76 for men and 81 for women. A major factor in this extraordinary gain is a steady decline in infant mortality (see Chapter 3), but death rates among adults have decreased as well, due mostly to advances in medical treatment (U.S. Department of Health and Human Services, 2011c).

Variations in Life Expectancy

Consistent group differences in life expectancy underscore the joint contributions of heredity and environment to biological aging. In almost all cultures, women can look forward to 2 to 7 more years of life than men—a life expectancy advantage that characterizes females of most species (Kirkwood, 2010). The protective value of the female's extra X chromosome (see Chapter 2) is believed to be responsible. Yet since the early 1970s, the gender gap in life expectancy has narrowed in industrialized nations (Leung, Zhang, & Zhang, 2004). Because men are at higher risk for disease and early death, they reap somewhat larger generational gains from positive lifestyle changes and new medical discoveries.

Life expectancy varies substantially with SES, ethnicity, and nationality. As education and income increase, so does length of life (Whitfield, Thorpe, & Szanton, 2011). In the United States, a white child born in 2010 is likely to live 3 to 6 years longer than an African-American child (U.S. Department of Health and Human Services, 2011c). Accounting for this difference are higher rates of infant mortality, unintentional injuries, life-threatening disease, stress, and violent death linked to low SES.

Length of life—and, even more important, *quality of life* in old age—can be predicted by a country's health care, housing, and social services, along with lifestyle factors. When researchers

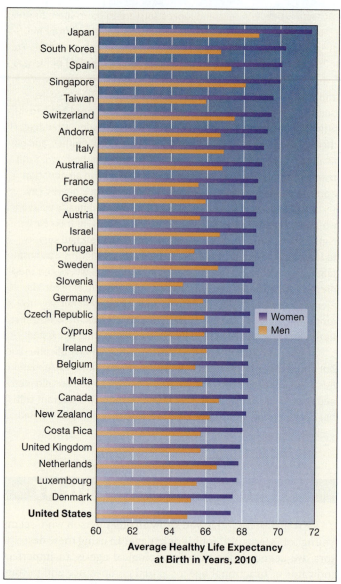

FIGURE 17.1 **Average healthy life expectancy at birth in 30 nations, ranked on basis of measures for women.** Japan ranks first, the United States a disappointing thirtieth. In each nation, women's healthy life expectancy is about 2 to 3 years longer than men's. (From Salomon et al., 2012.)

estimate **average healthy life expectancy**, the number of years a person born in a particular year can expect to live in full health, without disease or injury, Japan ranks first, with the United States below the overwhelming majority of industrialized nations (see Figure 17.1). Japan's leading status in this overall measure of population health has been attributed to its low rates of obesity and heart disease, linked to its low-fat diet, along with its favorable health-care policies.

In developing nations with widespread poverty, malnutrition, disease, and armed conflict, average life expectancy hovers around 55 years. And healthy life expectancy is reduced by 3 to 4 decades compared with the industrialized world—for example, for males, 69 years in Japan, 67 years in Sweden, 65 years in the United States, but only 48 in Afghanistan, 47 in

In a Japanese seaside city, a spry aging couple practice their local tradition of net fishing. Japan's low rates of obesity and heart disease and favorable health-care policies contribute to its worldwide leading status in healthy life expectancy.

Sierra Leone, and 28 in Haiti, where overall health recently declined because of the 2010 catastrophic earthquake (Salomon et al., 2012).

Life Expectancy in Late Adulthood

Although poverty-stricken groups lag behind the economically advantaged, the proportion of older adults has risen dramatically in the industrialized world. Because of aging baby boomers, older adults are projected to rise from 13 percent of the U.S. population today to nearly 20 percent by 2030. Among older Americans, the fastest-growing segment is the 85-and-older group, who currently make up nearly 3.5 percent of the U.S. population. By 2050, they are expected to swell to over three times their current number (U.S. Census Bureau, 2013).

Americans reaching age 65 in the early twenty-first century can look forward, on average, to 19 more years of life. Although women outnumber men by a greater margin as older adults advance in age, differences in average life expectancy between the sexes are declining. An American newborn girl can expect to live about 5 years longer than a newborn boy. At age 65, the difference narrows to just under 3 years; at age 85, to just over 1 year. Over age 100, the gender gap in life expectancy disappears (U.S. Census Bureau, 2013). Similarly, differences in rates of chronic illness and in life expectancy between higher-SES whites and low-SES ethnic minorities decline with age. Around age 87, a *life expectancy crossover* occurs—surviving members of low-SES ethnic minority groups live longer than members of the white majority (Herd, Robert, & House, 2011; Masters, 2012; Sautter et al., 2012). Researchers speculate that among males and members of low-SES groups, only the biologically sturdiest survive into very old age.

Throughout this book, we have seen that genetic and environmental factors jointly affect aging. With respect to heredity, identical twins typically die within 3 years of each other, whereas fraternal twins of the same sex differ by more than 6 years. Also, longevity runs in families. When both parents survive to age 70 or older, the chances that their children will live to 90 or 100 are double that of the general population (Cevenini et al., 2008; Hayflick, 1994; Mitchell et al., 2001). At the same time, evidence from twin studies suggests that once people pass 75 to 80 years, the contribution of heredity to length of life decreases in favor of environmental factors—a healthy diet; normal body weight; regular exercise; little or no tobacco, alcohol, and drug use; an optimistic outlook; low psychological stress; and social support (Yates et al., 2008; Zaretsky, 2003). As the Biology and Environment box on page 450 reveals, the study of centenarians—people who cross the 100-year mark—offers special insights into how biological, psychological, and social influences work together to promote a long, satisfying life.

Maximum Lifespan

Finally, perhaps you are wondering: For humans, what is the **maximum lifespan**, or species-specific biological limit to length of life (in years), corresponding to the age at which the oldest known individual died? As the Biology and Environment box indicates, the oldest verified age is 122 years.

Does this figure actually reflect the upper bound of human longevity, or can it be extended? At present, scientists disagree on the answer (Carnes, Olshansky, & Hayflick, 2013). But the controversy raises another issue: *Should* maximum lifespan be increased as far as possible? **TAKE A MOMENT...** How would you answer this question? Many people respond that the important goal is not just quantity of life, but quality—that is, doing everything possible to extend healthy life expectancy. Most experts agree that only after reducing the high rates of preventable illness and disability among low-SES individuals and wiping out age-related diseases should we invest in lengthening the maximum lifespan.

 ## Physical Changes

Physical declines become more apparent in late adulthood, as more organs and systems of the body are affected. The majority of people age 65 and older are capable of living active, independent lives, but with age, growing numbers need assistance. After age 75, about 9 percent of Americans have difficulty carrying out **activities of daily living (ADLs)**—basic self-care tasks required to live on one's own, such as bathing, dressing, getting in and out of bed or a chair, or eating. And about 17 percent cannot carry out **instrumental activities of daily living (IADLs)**—tasks necessary to conduct the business of daily life and also requiring some cognitive competence, such as telephoning, shopping, food preparation, housekeeping, and paying bills. The proportion of older adults with these limitations rises sharply with age (U.S. Department of Health and Human Services, 2011c). Nevertheless, most body structures can last into our eighties and beyond, if we take good care of them. For an overview of the physical changes we are about to discuss, return to Table 13.1 on page 347.

Nervous System

On a routine office visit, 80-year-old Ruth told her doctor, "I think I might be losing my mind. Yesterday, I forgot the name of the family who just moved in next door. And the day before, I had trouble finding the right words to explain to a delivery service how to get to my house."

"Ruth, everyone forgets those sorts of things from time to time," Dr. Wiley reassured her. "When we were young and had a memory lapse, we thought little about it. Now, when we do the same thing, we attribute it to having 'a senior moment,' and we worry."

Aging of the central nervous system affects a wide range of complex activities. Although brain weight declines throughout adulthood, brain-imaging research and after-death autopsies reveal that the loss becomes greater starting in the sixties and may amount to as much as 5 to 10 percent by age 80, due to withering of the myelin coating on neural fibers, loss of synaptic connections, death of neurons, and enlargement of ventricles

Biology and Environment

What Can We Learn About Aging from Centenarians?

Jeanne Louise Calment, listed in *Guinness World Records* as the longest-lived person whose age could be documented, was born in Arles, France, in 1875 and died there in 1997, 122 years later. Heredity undoubtedly contributed to her longevity: Her father lived to age 94, her mother to 86. As a young woman, she was healthy and energetic; she bicycled, swam, roller-skated, played tennis, and ran up the steps of the cathedral to attend daily Mass.

Jeanne's friends attributed her longevity to her easy-going disposition and resistance to stress. "If you can't do anything about it," she once said, "don't worry about it." Jeanne took up fencing at age 85 and rode a bicycle until age 100. Shortly thereafter, she moved into assisted living (see page 467), where she blossomed, becoming a celebrity because of both her age and her charming personality. Alert and quick-witted until her final year, she recommended laughter as the best recipe for long life.

The past 30 years have seen a 65 percent increase in centenarians in the industrialized world. Currently, American centenarians, though still rare (a fraction of one percent of the population), number about 53,000 (Meyer, 2012). Women centenarians outnumber men by five to one. About 60 to 70 percent have physical and mental impairments that interfere with independent functioning (Perls & Terry, 2003). The rest lead active, autonomous lives.

These robust centenarians are of special interest because they represent the ultimate potential of the human species. Results of several longitudinal studies reveal that they are diverse in years of education (none to postgraduate), economic well-being (very poor to very rich), and ethnicity. At the same time, their physical condition and life stories reveal common threads.

Health

Centenarians usually have grandparents, parents, and siblings who reached very old age, indicating a genetically based survival advantage (Coles, 2004; Perls et al., 2002). Some centenarians share with siblings a segment of identical DNA on the fourth chromosome, suggesting that a certain gene, or several genes, may increase the likelihood of exceptionally long life (Perls & Terry, 2003).

Most robust centenarians greatly delay or escape age-related chronic illnesses. Genetic testing reveals a low incidence of genes associated with immune-deficiency disorders, cancer, and Alzheimer's disease. Consistent with these findings, robust centenarians usually have efficiently functioning immune systems, and after-death examinations reveal few brain abnormalities (Silver & Perls, 2000). Others function effectively despite underlying chronic disease—typically atherosclerosis, other cardiovascular problems, and brain pathology (Berzlanovich et al., 2005).

As a group, robust centenarians are of average or slender build and practice moderation in eating. Many have most or all of their own teeth—another sign of unusual physical health. The large majority have never smoked, and most report lifelong physical activity extending past age 100 (Hagberg & Samuelson, 2008; Kropf & Pugh, 1995).

Personality

In personality, these very senior citizens appear highly optimistic (Jopp & Rott, 2006). In a study in which robust centenarians retook personality tests after 18 months, they reported more fatigue and depression, perhaps in response to increased frailty at the very end of their lives. But they also scored higher in toughmindedness, independence, emotional security, and openness to experience—traits that may be vital for surviving beyond 100 (Martin, Long, & Poon, 2002). An important contributor to their favorable mental health and longevity is social support, especially close family bonds and a long and happy marriage (Margrett et al., 2011; Velkoff, 2000). An unusually large percentage of centenarian men—about one-fourth—are still married.

Jeanne Louise Calment, shown here at age 121, took up fencing at age 85, rode a bicycle until age 100, and maintained a quick wit until her final year. The longest-lived person on record, she died at age 122.

Activities

Robust centenarians have a history of community involvement—working for personally rewarding just causes. Their past and current activities often include stimulating work, leisure pursuits, and learning, which may help sustain their good cognition and life satisfaction (Antonini et al., 2008). Writing letters, poems, plays, and memoirs; making speeches; teaching music lessons and Sunday school; nursing the sick; chopping wood; selling merchandise, bonds, and insurance; painting; practicing medicine; and preaching sermons are among robust centenarians' varied involvements.

In sum, robust centenarians illustrate typical development at its best. These independent, mentally alert, happy 100-year-olds reveal how a healthy lifestyle, personal resourcefulness, and close ties to family and community can build on biological strengths, thereby pushing the limits of an active, fulfilling life.

(spaces) within the brain (Rodrigue & Kennedy, 2011; Zelazo & Lee, 2010).

Neuron loss occurs throughout the cerebral cortex but at different rates among different regions. In longitudinal studies, the frontal lobes, especially the prefrontal cortex (responsible for inhibition, integration of information, strategic thinking, and other aspects of executive function), and the corpus callosum (which connects the two cortical hemispheres) tended to show the greatest shrinkage (Fabiani, 2012; Smith et al., 2007). The cerebellum (which controls balance and coordination and supports cognitive processes) also loses neurons—in all, about 25 percent. And EEG measures reveal gradual slowing and reduced intensity of brain waves—signs of diminished efficiency of the central nervous system (Kramer, Fabiani, & Colcombe, 2006).

But brain-imaging research reveals wide individual differences in the extent of these losses, which are moderately associated with cognitive functioning (Raz et al., 2010). And the brain can overcome some decline. In several studies, growth of neural fibers in the brains of older adults unaffected by illness took place at the same rate as in middle-aged people. Aging neurons established new synapses after other neurons had degenerated (Flood & Coleman, 1988). Furthermore, the aging cerebral cortex can, to a limited degree, generate new neurons (Gould, 2007; Snyder & Cameron, 2012). And fMRI evidence reveals that compared with younger adults, older people who do well on memory and other cognitive tasks show more widely distributed activity across areas of the cerebral cortex (Fabiani, 2012; Reuter-Lorenz & Cappell, 2008). This suggests that one way older adults compensate for neuron loss is to call on additional brain regions to support cognitive processing.

The autonomic nervous system, involved in many life-support functions, also performs less well, putting the older adults at risk during heat waves and cold spells. For example, Ruth's reduced tolerance for hot weather was due to decreased sweating. And her body found it harder to raise its core temperature during cold exposure. However, among physically fit older people who are free of disease, these declines are mild (Blatteis, 2012). The autonomic nervous system also releases higher levels of stress hormones into the bloodstream than it did earlier, perhaps to arouse body tissues that have become less responsive to these hormones over the years (Whitbourne, 2002). As we will see, this change may contribute to decreased immunity and to sleep problems.

Sensory Systems

Changes in sensory functioning become increasingly noticeable in late life. Older adults see and hear less well, and their taste, smell, and touch sensitivity may also decline. As Figure 17.2 shows, in late life, hearing impairments are more common than visual impairments. Extending trends in middle adulthood, more women than men report being visually impaired, more men than women hearing impaired.

Vision. In Chapter 15, we noted that structural changes in the eye make it harder to focus on nearby objects, see in dim light, and perceive color. In late adulthood, vision diminishes further. The cornea (clear covering of the eye) becomes more translucent and scatters light, which blurs images and increases sensitivity to glare. The lens continues to yellow, leading to further impairment in color discrimination. The number of individuals with **cataracts**—cloudy areas in the lens, resulting in foggy vision and (without surgery) eventual blindness—

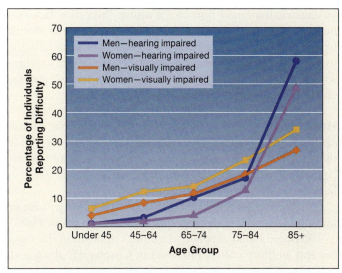

FIGURE 17.2 Rates of visual and hearing impairments among U.S. men and women by age. Among a large, nationally representative sample, those reporting that they had trouble seeing, even when wearing glasses or contact lenses, were judged visually impaired; those reporting "a lot of trouble" hearing were judged hearing impaired. Women report more visual impairments; men report more hearing impairments, a gap that widens considerably in late adulthood. In late life, hearing impairments become more common than visual impairments. (Adapted from U.S. Department of Health and Human Services, 2012d.)

increases tenfold from middle to late adulthood, affecting 25 percent of people in their seventies and 50 percent of those in their eighties (Owsley, 2011; U.S. Census Bureau, 2013). Besides biological aging, heredity, sun exposure, cigarette smoking, alcohol consumption, and certain diseases (such as hypertension and diabetes) increase the risk of cataracts (Sacca et al., 2009). Fortunately, removal of the lens and replacement with an artificial lens implant are highly successful in restoring vision.

Impaired eyesight in late adulthood largely results from a reduction in light reaching the retina and from cell loss in the retina and optic nerve (refer again to Chapter 15). Dark adaptation—moving from a brightly lit to a dim environment, such as a movie theater—becomes harder. A decline in binocular vision (the brain's ability to combine images received from both eyes) makes depth perception less reliable. And visual acuity (fineness of discrimination) worsens, dropping sharply after age 70 (Owsley, 2011).

When light-sensitive cells in the macula, or central region of the retina, break down, older adults may develop **macular degeneration**, in which central vision blurs and gradually is lost. Macular degeneration is the leading cause of blindness among older adults. About 10 percent of 65- to 74-year-olds, and 30 percent of 75- to 85-year-olds, have symptoms. If diagnosed early, macular degeneration can sometimes be treated with laser therapy. As with cataracts, heredity (including several identified genes) increases risk, especially when combined with cigarette smoking or obesity (Chu et al., 2008; Rhone & Basu, 2008; Wysong, Lee, & Sloan, 2009). Atherosclerosis also contributes by constricting blood flow to the retina. Protective factors—believed to exert their effects by shielding cells in the macula from free-radical damage—include regular, brisk physical activity and a diet rich in green, leafy vegetables, which are excellent sources of vitamins A, C, E, and carotenoids (yellow and red plant pigments) (Feret et al., 2007).

Hearing. "Mom, I'd like you to meet Joe's cousin Leona," said Ruth's daughter Sybil at a Thanksgiving gathering. But in the clamor of boisterous children, television sounds, and nearby conversations, 85-year-old Ruth didn't catch Leona's name or her relationship to Sybil's husband, Joe.

"Tell me your name again?" Ruth asked, adding, "Let's go into the other room, where it's quieter, so we can speak a bit."

Reduced blood supply and natural cell death in the inner ear and auditory cortex, discussed in Chapter 15, along with stiffening of membranes (such as the eardrum), cause hearing to decline in late adulthood. Decrements are greatest at high frequencies, although detection of soft sounds diminishes throughout the frequency range (see page 402). In addition, responsiveness to startling noises lessens, and discriminating complex tone patterns becomes harder (Hietanen et al., 2004; Kidd & Bao, 2012).

Although hearing loss has less impact on self-care than vision loss, it affects safety and enjoyment of life. In the din of city traffic, 80-year-old Ruth didn't always correctly interpret warnings, whether spoken ("Watch it, don't step out yet") or nonspoken (the beep of a horn). And when she turned up the radio or television volume, she sometimes missed the ring of the telephone or a knock at the door.

As hearing declines, older people report lower self-efficacy, more loneliness and depressive symptoms, and a smaller social network than their normally hearing peers (Kramer et al., 2002). Of all hearing difficulties, the age-related decline in speech perception has the greatest impact on life satisfaction. After age 70, ability to detect the content and emotionally expressive features of conversation declines, especially in noisy settings

(Gosselin & Gagne, 2011). Although Ruth used problem-centered coping to increase her chances of hearing conversation, she wasn't always successful. And sometimes people were inconsiderate. On a dinner outing, Joe raised his voice impatiently when Ruth asked him to repeat himself. At the family's Thanksgiving reunion, fewer relatives took time to talk with Ruth, and she felt pangs of loneliness.

Most older adults do not suffer from hearing loss great enough to disrupt their daily lives until after age 85. For those who do, compensating with a hearing aid and minimizing background noise are helpful. Furthermore, recall from Chapter 4 that beginning at birth, our perception is *intermodal*. By attending to facial expressions, gestures, and lip movements, older adults often use vision to help interpret the spoken word.

Taste and Smell. Walt's brother Dick was a heavy smoker. In his sixties, he poured salt and pepper over his food and asked for "extra hot" in Mexican and Indian restaurants.

Dick's reduced sensitivity to the four basic tastes—sweet, salty, sour, and bitter—is evident in many adults after age 60. Older adults also have greater difficulty recognizing familiar foods by taste alone (Fukunaga, Uematsu, & Sugimoto, 2005; Methven et al., 2012). But no change in the number or distribution of taste buds occurs late in life, so this drop in taste sensitivity may be due to factors other than aging. Cigarette smoking, dentures, medications, and environmental pollutants can affect taste perception (Drewnowski & Shultz, 2001). When taste is harder to detect, food is less enjoyable, increasing the likelihood of dietary deficiencies. Flavor additives can help make food more attractive.

Besides enhancing food enjoyment, smell has a self-protective function. An aging person who has difficulty detecting rancid food, gas fumes, or smoke may be in a life-threatening situation. A decrease in the number of smell receptors after age 60 contributes to declines in odor sensitivity (Seiberling & Conley, 2004). Researchers believe that odor perception not only wanes but becomes distorted, a change that may promote complaints that "food no longer smells and tastes right." But older adults experiencing greater difficulty with verbal recall, including retrieval of odor labels, have greater difficulty with odor recognition tasks (Larsson, Öberg, & Bäckman, 2005). So cognitive changes may make the decline in odor perception appear greater than it actually is.

Touch. Touch sensitivity is especially crucial for certain adults, such as the severely visually impaired reading Braille and people making fine judgments about texture—for example, in art and handicraft activities. In later life, capacity to discriminate detailed surface properties and identify unfamiliar objects by touch declines. Waning of touch perception on the hands, especially the fingertips—believed to be due to loss of touch receptors in certain regions of the skin and slowing of blood circulation to the extremities—contributes (Stevens & Cruz, 1996). In addition, decrements in fluid abilities, especially spatial orientation, are influential (see page 413 in Chapter 15)

This adult son's patient guidance helps his father feel included at a boisterous family reunion. Declines in hearing make it difficult for older adults to socialize in noisy settings.

© JEFF GREENBERG/THE IMAGE WORKS

(Kalisch et al., 2012). Fluid skills are strongly correlated with older adults' tactile performance.

Cardiovascular and Respiratory Systems

In late adulthood, signs of change in the cardiovascular and respiratory systems become more apparent. In their sixties, Ruth and Walt noticed that they felt more physically stressed after running to catch a bus or to cross a street before the light changed.

As the years pass, the heart muscle becomes more rigid, and some of its cells die while others enlarge, leading the walls of the left ventricle (the largest heart chamber, from which blood is pumped to the body) to thicken. In addition, artery walls stiffen and accumulate some plaque (cholesterol and fats) due to normal aging (much more in those with atherosclerosis). Finally, the heart muscle becomes less responsive to signals from pacemaker cells within the heart, which initiate each contraction (Larsen, 2009; Smith & Cotter, 2008). As a combined result of these changes, the heart pumps with less force, maximum heart rate decreases, and blood flow throughout the circulatory system slows. This means that sufficient oxygen may not be delivered to body tissues during high physical activity.

Changes in the respiratory system compound the effects of reduced oxygenation. Because lung tissue gradually loses its elasticity, vital capacity (amount of air that can be forced in and out of the lungs) is reduced by half between ages 25 and 80. As a result, the lungs fill and empty less efficiently, causing the blood to absorb less oxygen and give off less carbon dioxide. This explains why older people increase their breathing rate more and feel more out of breath while exercising—deficiencies that are more extreme in lifelong smokers and in people who have failed to reduce dietary fat or have had many years of exposure to environmental pollutants.

These mountain hikers need frequent rests to catch their breath and regain their energy. With aging of the cardiovascular and respiratory systems, sufficient oxygen may not be delivered to body tissues during physical exertion.

Immune System

As the immune system ages, T cells, which attack antigens (foreign substances) directly, become less effective (see Chapter 13, page 348). In addition, the immune system is more likely to malfunction by turning against normal body tissues in an **autoimmune response**. A less competent immune system can increase the risk of a variety of illnesses, including infectious diseases (such as the flu), cardiovascular disease, certain forms of cancer, and various autoimmune disorders, such as rheumatoid arthritis and diabetes (Larbi, Fülöp, & Pawelec, 2008).

Although older adults vary greatly in immunity, most experience some loss, ranging from partial to profound (Ponnappan & Ponnappan, 2011). The strength of the aging person's immune system seems to be a sign of overall physical vigor. Certain immune indicators, such as high T cell activity, predict better physical functioning and survival over the next two years in very old people (Moro-Garcia et al., 2012; Wikby et al., 1998). A healthy diet and exercise help protect the immune response in old age, whereas obesity aggravates the age-related decline.

Sleep

When Walt went to bed at night, he usually lay awake for a half-hour to an hour before falling asleep, remaining in a drowsy state longer than when he was younger. During the night, he spent less time in the deepest phase of NREM sleep (see Chapter 3, page 83) and awoke several times.

Older adults require about as much total sleep as younger adults: around 7 hours per night. Yet as people age, they have more difficulty falling asleep, staying asleep, and sleeping deeply. Insomnia affects nearly half of older adults at least a few nights per month. The timing of sleep tends to change as well, toward earlier bedtime and earlier morning wakening (Edwards et al., 2010). Changes in brain structures controlling sleep and higher levels of stress hormones in the bloodstream, which have an alerting effect on the central nervous system, are believed to be responsible. Insomnia in older adults is of special concern because it increases the risk of falls and cognitive impairments (Crowley, 2011). Those who are poor sleepers more often report slower reaction times and attention and memory difficulties.

Fortunately, there are ways to foster restful sleep, such as establishing a consistent bedtime and waking time, exercising regularly, and using the bedroom only for sleep (not for eating, reading, or watching TV) (McCurry et al., 2007). Older adults receive more prescription sedatives for sleep complaints than do people under age 60. Used briefly, these drugs can help relieve temporary insomnia. But long-term medication can make matters worse by inducing rebound insomnia after the drug is discontinued.

Physical Appearance and Mobility

In earlier chapters, we saw that changes leading to an aged appearance are under way as early as the twenties and thirties. Because these occur gradually, older adults may not notice that they look older until changes have become obvious.

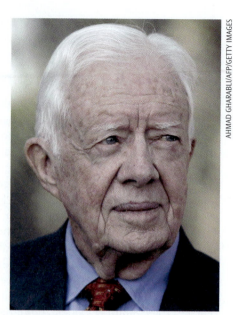

Aging brings changes in appearance, evident in these portraits of Jimmy Carter, former U.S. president, at ages 52, 63, and 88. The skin creases and sags, "age spots" increase, the nose and ears broaden, and hair on the head thins.

Creasing and sagging of the skin, described in Chapter 15, extends into old age. In addition, oil glands that lubricate the skin become less active, leading to dryness and roughness. "Age spots" increase; in some individuals, the arms, backs of the hands, and face may be dotted with these pigmented marks. Blood vessels can be seen beneath the more transparent skin, which has largely lost its layer of fatty support (Whitbourne, 2002).

The face is especially likely to show these effects because it is frequently exposed to the sun, which accelerates aging. Other factors that contribute to facial wrinkling and age spots include long-term alcohol use, cigarette smoking, and psychological stress. Additional facial changes occur: The nose and ears broaden as new cells are deposited on the outer layer of the skeleton. And especially in older adults with a history of poor dental care, teeth may be yellowed, cracked, and chipped, and gums may have receded. As hair follicles under the skin's surface die, hair on the head thins in both sexes, and the scalp may be visible (Whitbourne, 2002). In men with hereditary pattern baldness, follicles do not die but, instead, begin to produce fine, downy hair.

Body build changes as well. Height continues to decline, especially in women, as loss of bone mineral content leads to further collapse of the spinal column. Weight generally drops after age 60 because of additional loss of lean body mass (bone density and muscle), which is heavier than the fat deposits accumulating on the torso.

Several factors affect mobility. The first is muscle strength, which generally declines at a faster rate in late adulthood than in middle age (Reid & Fielding, 2012). Second, bone strength deteriorates because of reduced bone mass. Third, strength and flexibility of the joints and the ligaments and tendons (which connect muscle to bone) diminish. In her eighties, Ruth's reduced ability to support her body, flex her limbs, and rotate her hips made walking at a steady, moderate pace, climbing stairs, and rising from a chair difficult. A carefully planned exercise program can minimize declines in strength, joint flexibility, and range of movement.

Adapting to Physical Changes of Late Adulthood

Great diversity exists in older adults' adaptation to the physical changes of aging. People who are more anxious about growing older monitor their physical state more closely and are more concerned about their appearance (Montepare, 2006). Dick and Goldie took advantage of an enormous industry designed to stave off outward signs of old age, including cosmetics, wigs, and plastic surgery, plus various "anti-aging" dietary supplements, herbal products, and hormonal medications offered by "longevity" clinics—none with any demonstrated benefits and some of them harmful (Olshansky, Hayflick, & Perls, 2004). In contrast, Ruth and Walt were relatively unconcerned about their thinning white hair and wrinkled skin. Their identities were less bound up with their appearance than with their ability to remain active.

Most older people sustain a favorable *subjective age*—say they feel younger than they look and than they actually are (Kleinspehn-Ammerlahn, Kotter-Grühn, & Smith, 2008; Uotinen et al., 2006; Westerhof, 2008). In several investigations, 75-year-olds reported feeling about 15 years younger! A youthful self-evaluation is linked to satisfaction with growing older—better mental health and psychological well-being (Keyes & Westerhof, 2012).

The most obvious outward signs of aging—graying hair, facial wrinkles, and baldness—bear no relationship to sensory, cognitive, and motor functioning or to longevity (Schnohr et al., 1998). In contrast, neurological, sensory, cardiovascular, respiratory, immune-system, and skeletal and muscular health are strongly associated with cognitive performance and both quality and length of later life (Bergman, Blomberg, & Almkvist, 2007; Lin et al., 2011; Reyes-Ortiz et al., 2005; Schäfer, Huxhold, & Lindenberger, 2006). Furthermore, people can do more to prevent declines in the functioning of these internal body systems than they can do to prevent gray hair and baldness!

Effective Coping Strategies. Think back to our discussion of problem-centered and emotion-centered coping in Chapter 15. It applies here as well. As Walt and Ruth prevented and compensated for age-related changes through diet, exercise, environmental adjustments, and an active, stimulating lifestyle, they felt a sense of personal control over their fates. This prompted additional active coping and improved physical functioning. In contrast, older adults who consider age-related declines inevitable and uncontrollable tend to be passive when faced with them and to report more physical and psychological adjustment difficulties (Kempen et al., 2006; Lachman, Neupert, & Agrigoroaei, 2011).

When physical disabilities become severe, sense of control has diminishing returns, no longer having as much impact on health status. Older adults with substantial physical impairments cope more effectively when they acknowledge reduced control and accept the need for caregiver or equipment assistance (Clarke & Smith, 2011; Ross & Sastry, 1999). But doing so may be difficult for many older Americans, who—because of U.S. individualistic values—are accustomed to a "culture of personal control."

Assistive Technology. A rapidly expanding **assistive technology**, or array of devices that permit people with disabilities to improve their functioning, is available to help older people cope with physical declines. Computers are the great-

est source of these innovative products. People with sensory impairments can use special software to enlarge text or have it read aloud. Phones that can be dialed and answered by voice commands help those with difficulty pushing buttons or getting across a room to answer the phone. And for older people who take multiple medications, a tiny computer chip called a "smart cap" can be placed on medicine bottles. It beeps on a programmed schedule as a reminder to take the drug and tracks how many and at what time pills have been taken.

Architects have also designed homes that can adapt to changing physical needs—equipping them with movable walls that expand and contract, plumbing that enables a full bathroom to be added on the main floor, and "smart-home" technologies that promote safety and mobility, such as sensors in floors that activate room lights when an older person gets up at night and alarm systems that detect falls. Use of assistive devices slows physical declines and reduces the need for personal caregiving (Hoenig, Taylor, & Sloan, 2003; Wilson et al., 2009). Do older adults with disabilities regard some technologies as invasions of privacy? The overwhelming majority emphasize potential benefits—saying for example, "If this [monitoring system] would keep me independent longer, I wouldn't mind" (Melenhorst et al., 2004; Rogers & Fisk, 2005). As these findings indicate, sustaining an effective *person–environment fit,* or match between older people's current capabilities and the demands of their living environments, contributes to sense of competence and the quality life.

Yet U.S. government-sponsored health-care coverage is largely limited to essential medical equipment. Sweden's health-care system, in contrast, covers many assistive devices that promote function and safety, and its building code requires that new homes include a full bathroom on the main floor (Hooyman & Kiyak, 2011). In this way, Sweden strives to maximize person–environment fit for its older adults, helping them remain as independent as possible.

Overcoming Stereotypes of Aging. Negative stereotypes of late adulthood, which view older adults as weak, boring, and debilitated and "deterioration as inevitable," are widespread in Western nations (Staudinger & Bowen, 2010). Overcoming this pessimistic picture is vital for helping people adapt favorably to late-life physical changes.

Like gender stereotypes, aging stereotypes often operate automatically, without awareness; people "see" older adults in stereotypical ways, even when they appear otherwise (Kite et al., 2005). As seniors encounter these negative messages, they experience *stereotype threat,* which results in diminished performance on tasks related to the stereotype (see page 246 in Chapter 9). In several studies, researchers exposed older adults to words associated with either negative aging stereotypes ("decrepit," "confused") or positive aging stereotypes ("sage," "enlightened"). Those in negative-stereotype conditions displayed a more intense physiological response to stress, greater help-seeking and feelings of loneliness, and worse physical performance, recall memory, self-efficacy, and appraisals of their own health (Coudin & Alexopoulos, 2010; Hess & Hinson,

A physical therapist helps a stroke patient master use of a tool for reaching and gripping small objects. Assistive devices help older adults with disabilities maintain their independence.

WILL & DENI MCINTYRE/PHOTO RESEARCHERS/GETTY IMAGES

2006; Hess, Hinson, & Statham, 2004; Levy & Leifheit-Limson, 2009; Mazerolle et al., 2012).

Clearly, negative stereotypes have a stressful, disorganizing impact on older adults' functioning. Positive stereotypes, in contrast, reduce stress and foster physical and mental competence (Bolkan & Hooker, 2012). In a longitudinal investigation, people with positive self-perceptions of aging—who, for example, agreed with such statements as "As I get older, things are better than I thought they'd be"—lived, on average, 7½ years longer than those with negative self-perceptions. This survival advantage remained after gender, SES, loneliness, and physical health status were controlled (Levy et al., 2002). Adults with less education are especially susceptible to the detrimental effects of aging stereotypes, perhaps because they tend to accept those messages uncritically (Andreoletti & Lachman, 2004).

In cultures where older adults are treated with deference and respect, an aging appearance can be a source of pride. In one study, Chinese adults diverse in age were less likely than Canadian adults to stereotype older people, either positively or negatively (Ryan et al., 2004). In the native language of the Inuit people of Canada, the closest word to "elder" is *isumataq*, or "one who knows things"—a high status that begins when a couple becomes head of the extended family unit. When Inuit older adults were asked for their thoughts on aging well, they mentioned attitudes—a positive approach to life, interest in transmitting cultural knowledge to young people, and community involvement—nearly twice as often as physical health (Collings, 2001).

Despite inevitable declines, physical aging can be viewed with either optimism or pessimism. As Walt commented, "You can think of your glass as half full or half empty." Cultural valuing of older adults greatly increases the likelihood that they will adopt the "half full" alternative.

An Inuit senior of northern Canada teaches a young adult how to make sealskin kamiks, or boots. In Inuit culture, aging is associated with expert knowledge and high status. Hence, changes in physical appearance can be a source of pride.

ASK YOURSELF

REVIEW Cite examples of how older adults can compensate for age-related physical declines.

APPLY "The best way to adjust to this is to learn to like it," thought 65-year-old Herman, inspecting his thinning hair in the mirror. "I remember reading that bald older men are regarded as leaders." What type of coping is Herman using, and why is it effective?

REFLECT While watching TV during the coming week, keep a log of portrayals of older adults. How many images were positive? How many conveyed negative stereotypes of aging?

Health, Fitness, and Disability

At Walt and Ruth's fiftieth wedding anniversary, 77-year-old Walt thanked a roomful of well-wishers for joining in the celebration. Then, with emotion, he announced, "I'm so grateful Ruth and I are still healthy enough to give to our family, friends, and community."

As Walt's remarks affirm, health is central to psychological well-being in late life. When researchers ask older adults about possible selves (see Chapter 16, page 427), number of hoped-for physical selves declines with age and number of feared physical selves increases. Nevertheless, because older people compare themselves to same-age peers, the majority rate their health favorably (U.S. Department of Health and Human Services, 2011c). As for protecting their health, older adults' sense of self-efficacy is as high as that of young adults and higher than that of middle-aged people. Self-efficacy and optimism about one's health promote continued health-enhancing behaviors (Frazier, 2002; Morrison, 2008).

As mentioned earlier, SES and ethnic variations in health diminish in late adulthood. Nevertheless, SES continues to predict physical functioning (House, Lantz, & Herd, 2005; Yao & Robert, 2008). African-American and Hispanic older people (one-fifth of whom live in poverty) remain at greater risk for various health problems, including cardiovascular disease, diabetes, and certain cancers. Native-American older adults are even worse off. The majority are poor, and chronic health conditions—including diabetes, kidney disease, liver disease, tuberculosis, and hearing and vision impairments—are so widespread that in the United States, the federal government grants Native Americans special health benefits. These begin as early as age 45, reflecting a much harder and shorter lifespan.

Unfortunately, low-SES older adults are more likely than their higher-SES counterparts to delay seeking medical treatment (Lee, Hasnain-Wynia, & Lau, 2011). Part of the reason is cost: On average, U.S. Medicare beneficiaries devote an estimated one-tenth of their income to out-of-pocket health-care expenses—a proportion that escalates among those with the fewest resources (Johnson & Mommaerts, 2010). Furthermore, low-SES older people often do not comply with doctors' directions because they feel less in control of their health and less optimistic that treatment will work.

The sex differences noted in Chapter 15 extend into late adulthood: Men are more prone to fatal diseases, women to non-life-threatening disabling conditions. By very old age (80 to 85 and beyond), women are more impaired than men because only the sturdiest men have survived (Crimmins, Kim, & Solé-Auró, 2011; Morrison, 2008). In addition, with fewer physical limitations, older men are better able to remain independent and to engage in exercise, hobbies, and involvement in the social world, all of which promote better health.

Widespread health-related optimism among older people suggests that substantial inroads into preventing disability can be made even in the last few decades of life. Ideally, as life expectancy extends, we want the average period of diminished vigor before death—especially, the number of months or years of ill-health and suffering—to decrease. This public health goal is called the **compression of morbidity**. Several large-scale studies indicate that over the past several decades, compression of morbidity has occurred in industrialized nations (Fries, Bruce, & Chakravarty, 2011). Medical advances in treatment of disease and improved socioeconomic conditions are largely responsible.

In addition, the impact of good health habits on postponement of disability is large. In a longitudinal investigation, researchers followed university alumni from their late sixties over the next two decades. In those who were low risk (no risk factors of smoking, obesity, or lack of exercise), disability was delayed by nearly 5 years compared with those who were moderate risk (had one of these risk factors). Compared to high-risk participants (with two or three risk factors), postponement of disability in the low-risk group exceeded 8 years (Chakravarty et al., 2012). Those who were obese, sedentary, and addicted to tobacco surged to extremely high levels of disability in the two years before death. And although good health habits lengthened life by about 3½ years, their impact on functional ability was greater.

More comprehensive strategies are needed in the developing world, where 70 percent of older people will reside by 2025. In these nations, poverty is rampant, chronic diseases occur earlier, even routine health interventions are unavailable or too costly for all but a few, and most public health programs do not focus on late adulthood (Rinaldo & Ferraro, 2012). As a result, disability rates among older adults are especially high, and as yet, no progress has been made in compression of morbidity.

Nutrition and Exercise

The physical changes of late life lead to an increased need for certain nutrients—calcium and vitamin D to protect the bones; zinc and vitamins B$_6$, C, and E to protect the immune system;

and vitamins A, C, and E to prevent free radicals (see Chapter 13, page 344). Yet declines in physical activity, in the senses of taste and smell, and in ease of chewing (because of deteriorating teeth) can reduce the quantity and quality of food eaten. Furthermore, the aging digestive system has greater difficulty absorbing certain nutrients, such as protein, calcium, and vitamin D. And older adults who live alone may have problems shopping or cooking and may feel less like eating by themselves. Together, these physical and environmental conditions increase the risk of dietary deficiencies, which are common among U.S. older adults.

Except for calcium and vitamin D, a daily vitamin–mineral supplement is recommended only for older adults suffering from malnutrition. Vitamin–mineral supplements do not protect against cardiovascular disease or cancer (Neuhouser et al., 2009). Furthermore, supplemental nutrients and herbs identified as "cognitive enhancers"—including B and E vitamins, folic acid, and ginkgo biloba—do not improve cognitive functioning (Aisen et al., 2008; DeKosky et al., 2008). However, regularly eating fish high in polyunsaturated fatty acids (which promote vascular health) offers some protection against mental disabilities (Cannella, Savina, & Donini, 2009; Skully & Saleh, 2011).

In addition to a healthy diet, exercise continues to be a powerful health intervention. Sedentary healthy older adults up to age 80 who begin endurance training (walking, cycling, aerobic dance) show gains in vital capacity that compare favorably with those of much younger individuals. And weight-bearing

© BOB DAEMMRICH/PHOTOEDIT

This spectacularly fit participant in the Senior Olympics has likely been exercising for most of her life. But even exercise programs begun in late adulthood can promote muscle size and strength and preservation of brain structures and behavioral capacities.

exercise begun in late adulthood—even as late as age 90—promotes muscle size and strength (deJong & Franklin, 2004; Goldberg, Dengel, & Hagberg, 1996; Pyka et al., 1994). This translates into improved walking speed, balance, posture, and ability to carry out everyday activities.

Exercise also increases blood circulation to the brain, which helps preserve brain structures and behavioral capacities. Brain scans show that physically fit older people experience less tissue loss in the cerebral cortex (Erickson et al., 2010; Miller et al., 2012). And compared with physically inactive agemates, previously sedentary older adults who initiated a program of regular, moderate to vigorous exercise displayed increased activity in areas of the prefrontal cortex governing control of attention, as well as improved attention during mental testing, yielding better performance (Colcombe et al., 2004). They also showed gains in volume of the cerebral cortex—clear biological evidence for the role of physical activity in preserving central nervous system health (Colcombe et al., 2006).

Although good nutrition and physical activity are most beneficial when they are lifelong, it is never too late to change. Older people who come to value the intrinsic benefits of exercise—feeling stronger, healthier, and more energetic—are likely to engage in it. Yet about 65 percent of U.S. 65- to 74-year-olds and 75 percent of those over age 75 are not active enough (U.S. Department of Health and Human Services, 2011c).

Sexuality

When Walt turned 60, he asked his 90-year-old Uncle Louie at what age sexual desire and activity cease. Walt's question stemmed from a widely held myth that sex drive disappears in late adulthood. Louie corrected this impression. "My sexual interest has never gone away," he explained to Walt. "I can't do

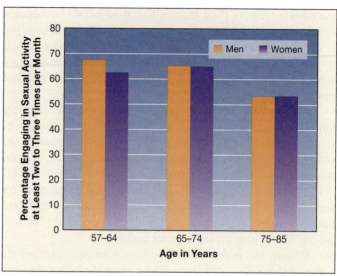

FIGURE 17.3 **Age-related changes in sexual activity among adults with an intimate partner.** In the National Social Life, Health, and Aging Project, which surveyed more than 3,000 U.S. 57- to 85-year-olds, most men and women with an intimate partner reported engaging in sexual activity (usually intercourse) at least two to three times per month. Sexual activity declined during late adulthood. Still, more than half of partnered 75- to 85-year-olds reported regular sexual activity. (Adapted from Waite et al., 2009.)

it as often, and it's a quieter experience than it was in my youth. But Rachella and I have led a happy intimate life, and it's still that way."

As in other cross-sectional studies, the National Social Life, Health, and Aging Project, which surveyed a large, nationally representative sample of U.S. 57- to 85-year-olds, reported a decline in frequency of sexual activity in late adulthood—especially among women, who are less likely than men to be in a marital or other intimate relationship. At the same time, the majority of respondents attributed at least some importance to sex, and those who had been sexually active in the previous year mostly rated sex as "very" or "extremely" important. Consistent with these attitudes, most healthy couples reported continued, regular sexual enjoyment. More than half of the oldest respondents with an intimate partner indicated that they engaged in some type of sexual activity (usually intercourse) at least two to three times per month (see Figure 17.3) (Waite et al., 2009). Note that these trends are probably influenced by cohort effects: A new generation of older adults, accustomed to viewing sexuality positively, will probably be more sexually active.

The same generalization we discussed for midlife applies to late life: Good sex in the past predicts good sex in the future. Furthermore, using intercourse as the only measure of sexual activity promotes a narrow view of pleasurable sex. Even at the most advanced ages, there is more to sexuality than the sex act itself—feeling sensual, enjoying close companionship, and being loved and wanted. Both older men and older women report that the male partner is usually the one who ceases to interact sexually (DeLamater, 2012; DeLamater & Moorman,

Most healthy older couples report continued, regular sexual enjoyment. In addition to intercourse, feeling sensual, enjoying close companionship, and being loved and wanted are all part of sexuality at the most advanced ages.

2007). In a culture that emphasizes an erection as necessary for being sexual, a man may withdraw from all erotic activity when he finds that erections are harder to achieve and more time must elapse between them.

Disabilities that disrupt blood flow to the penis—most often, disorders of the autonomic nervous system, cardiovascular disease, and diabetes—are largely responsible for dampening sexuality in older men. But as noted in Chapter 15, availability of drug treatments, such as Viagra, has increased men's willingness to discuss erectile dysfunction with their doctors. Cigarette smoking, excessive alcohol intake, and a variety of prescription medications also lead to diminished sexual performance (DeLamater, 2012; Huang et al., 2009). And because the sex ratio increasingly favors females, aging heterosexual women have fewer and fewer opportunities for sexual encounters.

Physical Disabilities

TAKE A MOMENT... Compare the death rates shown in Figure 17.4 with those in Figure 15.2 on page 407. You will see that illness and disability climb as the end of the lifespan approaches. Cardiovascular disease and cancer remain the leading causes of death, increasing dramatically from mid- to late life. As before, death rates from heart disease and cancer are higher for men than for women, although the sex difference declines with advancing age (U.S. Census Bureau, 2013).

Respiratory diseases, which rise sharply with age, are the third most common cause of death among the aged. Among such diseases is *emphysema,* caused by extreme loss of elasticity in lung tissue, with most cases resulting from long-term cigarette smoking. *Stroke* and *Alzheimer's disease* follow; both are

unique in being more prevalent among women, largely because women live longer. Stroke occurs when a blood clot blocks a blood vessel or a blood vessel hemorrhages in the brain, causing damage to brain tissue. It is a major cause of late-life disability and, after age 75, death. Alzheimer's disease, the leading cause of dementia, also rises sharply with age; we will consider it in-depth shortly.

Other diseases are less frequent killers, but they limit older adults' ability to live fully and independently. We have already noted the increase after age 65 in macular degeneration, which severely impairs vision and leads to blindness (see page 451). Osteoporosis, discussed in Chapter 15, continues to rise in late adulthood; recall that it affects the majority of men and women after age 70. Yet another bone disorder—*arthritis*—adds to the physical limitations of many older people. And *type 2 diabetes* and *unintentional injuries* also multiply in late adulthood. In the following sections, we take up these last three conditions.

Finally, an important point must be kept in mind as we discuss physical and mental disabilities of late adulthood: That these conditions are strongly *related to age* does not mean that they are *entirely caused by aging.* To clarify this distinction, experts distinguish between **primary aging** (another term for *biological aging*), or genetically influenced declines that affect all members of our species and take place even in the context of overall good health, and **secondary aging**, declines due to hereditary defects and negative environmental influences, such as poor diet, lack of exercise, disease, substance abuse, environmental pollution, and psychological stress.

Throughout this book, we have seen that it is difficult to distinguish primary from secondary aging. Undoubtedly you have, at one time or another, encountered a *frail older adult*—a person of extreme infirmity who displays wasted muscle mass and strength, weight loss, severe mobility problems, and perhaps cognitive impairment. **Frailty** involves weakened functioning of diverse organs and body systems, which profoundly interferes with everyday competence and leaves older people highly vulnerable in the face of infection, extremely hot or cold weather, or injury (Masoro, 2011; Walston et al., 2006). Although primary aging contributes to frailty, researchers agree that secondary aging plays a larger role, through genetic disorders, unhealthy lifestyle, and chronic disease (Bergman et al., 2007; Fried et al., 2009). The serious conditions we are about to discuss are major sources of frailty in late adulthood.

Arthritis. Beginning in her late fifties, Ruth felt a slight morning stiffness in her neck, back, hips, and knees. In her sixties, she developed bony lumps on the end joints of her fingers. As the years passed, she experienced periodic joint swelling and some loss of flexibility—changes that affected her ability to move quickly and easily.

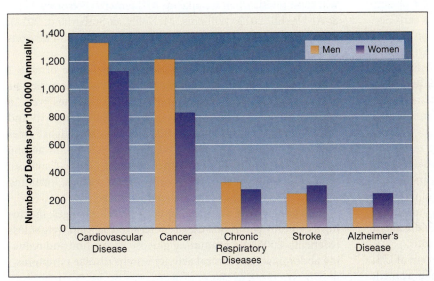

FIGURE 17.4 Leading causes of death among people age 65 and older in the United States. In late adulthood, heart disease is the leading cause of death, followed by cancer. Stroke (unique in being more prevalent among women), chronic respiratory diseases, pneumonia and flu, Alzheimer's disease, and unintentional injuries also claim the lives of many older adults. (Adapted from U.S. Census Bureau, 2013.)

This frail 80-year-old, working with a physical therapist, suffers from wasted muscle mass and strength, weight loss, and severe mobility problems. In addition to biological aging, secondary aging—through genetic disorders, unhealthy lifestyle, and chronic disease—plays a major role in his frailty.

Arthritis, a condition of inflamed, painful, stiff, and sometimes swollen joints and muscles, becomes more common in late adulthood. It occurs in several forms. Ruth has **osteoarthritis**, the most common type, which involves deteriorating cartilage on the ends of bones of frequently used joints. Otherwise known as "wear-and-tear arthritis" or "degenerative joint disease," it is one of the few age-related disabilities in which years of use make a difference. Although a genetic proneness exists, the disease usually does not appear until the forties or fifties. In frequently used joints, cartilage on the ends of the bones, which reduces friction during movement, gradually deteriorates. Or obesity places abnormal pressure on the joints and damages cartilage. Almost all older adults show some osteoarthritis on X-rays, although wide individual differences in severity exist (Zhang & Jordan, 2010). It is the most common cause of mobility problems and of surgical hip and knee replacements in older adults.

Unlike osteoarthritis, which is limited to certain joints, **rheumatoid arthritis** involves the whole body. An autoimmune response leads to inflammation of connective tissue, particularly the membranes that line the joints, resulting in overall stiffness, inflammation, and aching. Tissue in the cartilage tends to grow, damaging surrounding ligaments, muscles, and bones. The result is deformed joints and often serious loss of mobility. Sometimes other organs, such as the heart and lungs, are affected (Goronzy, Shao, & Weyand, 2010). Worldwide, about ½ to 1 percent of older adults have rheumatoid arthritis.

Overall, disability due to arthritis affects 45 percent of U.S. men over age 65 and rises modestly with age. Among women, the incidence is higher and increases sharply with age: About 50 percent of 65- to 84-year-olds and 70 percent of those over age 85 are affected (U.S. Census Bureau, 2013). Although rheumatoid arthritis can strike at any age, it rises after age 60. Twin studies support a strong hereditary contribution. Presence of certain genes heightens disease risk, possibly by triggering a late-life defect in the immune system (Turesson & Matteson, 2006). However, identical twins differ widely in disease severity, indicating that environment makes a difference. So far, cigarette smoking is the only confirmed lifestyle influence (Klareskog et al., 2006). Early treatment with powerful anti-inflammatory medications helps slow progression of rheumatoid arthritis.

Managing arthritis requires a balance of rest when the disease flares, pain relief, and physical activity. Regular aerobic exercise and strength training lessen pain and improve physical functioning (Semanik, Chang, & Dunlop, 2012). With proper analgesic medication, joint protection, lifestyle changes, and surgery to replace badly damaged hip or knee joints, many people with either form of the illness lead long, productive lives.

Diabetes. After a meal, the body breaks down the food, releasing glucose (the primary energy source for cell activity) into the bloodstream. Insulin, produced by the pancreas, keeps the blood concentration of glucose within set limits by stimulating muscle and fat cells to absorb it. When this balance system fails, either because not enough insulin is produced or because body cells become insensitive to it, *type 2 diabetes* (otherwise known as *diabetes mellitus*) results. Over time, abnormally high blood glucose damages the blood vessels, increasing the risk of heart attack, stroke, circulatory problems in the legs (which impair balance and gait), and injury to the eyes, kidneys, and nerves.

Excessive blood glucose also reduces blood flow to the hippocampus, a brain structure that plays an important role in memory (see page 169 in Chapter 7) (Wu et al., 2008). In several longitudinal studies, diabetes was associated with more rapid cognitive declines in older people and an elevated risk of dementia, especially Alzheimer's disease—an association we will soon revisit when we take up Alzheimer's (Petrofsky, Berk, & Al-Nakhli, 2012; Williams, McNeilly, & Sutherland, 2012). Impaired glucose tolerance accelerates degeneration of neurons and synapses.

From middle to late adulthood, the incidence of type 2 diabetes nearly doubles; it affects 20 percent of Americans age 65 and older (U.S. Census Bureau, 2013). Diabetes runs in families, suggesting that heredity is involved. But inactivity and abdominal fat deposits greatly increase the risk. Higher rates of type 2 diabetes—exceeding 30 percent—are found among African-American, Mexican-American, and Native-American seniors for both genetic and environmental reasons, including high-fat diets and obesity associated with poverty.

Treating type 2 diabetes requires lifestyle changes, including a carefully controlled diet, regular exercise, and weight loss (Meneilly, 2006). By promoting glucose absorption and reducing abdominal fat, physical activity lessens disease symptoms.

Unintentional Injuries. At age 65 and older, the death rate from unintentional injuries is at an all-time high—more than twice as great as in adolescence and early adulthood. Motor vehicle collisions and falls are largely responsible.

Visual processing difficulties, slowed reaction time, and declines in selective attention contribute to the high rates of traffic violations, accidents, and fatalities per mile driven among older people. Still, seniors usually try to drive as long as possible.

Motor Vehicle Accidents. Older adults have higher rates of traffic violations, accidents, and fatalities per mile driven than any other age group, with the exception of drivers under age 25 (U.S. Census Bureau, 2013). The high rate of injury persists, even though many older people, especially women, limit their driving after noticing that their ability to drive safely is slipping.

The greater older adults' visual processing difficulties, the higher their rate of moving violations and crashes (Friedman et al., 2013). Compared with young drivers, older people are less likely to drive quickly and recklessly but more likely to fail to heed signs, yield the right of way, and turn appropriately. They often try to compensate for their difficulties by being more cautious. Slowed reaction time, declines in capacity to attend selectively and engage in two activities at once, and resulting indecisiveness pose hazards, too (Makishita & Matsunaga, 2008). Seniors are at high risk for collisions at busy intersections and in other complex traffic situations.

Nevertheless, older people usually try to drive as long as possible. Giving up driving results in loss of freedom, control over one's life, and self-esteem. Specially trained driver rehabilitation consultants—affiliated with hospitals, drivers licensing agencies, or U.S. Area Agencies on Aging (see page 51 in Chapter 2)—can help assess older adults' capacity to continue driving, provide driver retraining, or counsel them to retire from driving and to arrange other transportation options.

Older adults also make up more than 30 percent of all U.S. pedestrian deaths (U.S. Census Bureau, 2013). Confusing intersections, especially signals that do not allow older people enough time to cross the street, are often involved.

Falls. One day, Ruth fell down the basement steps and lay there with a broken ankle until Walt arrived home an hour later. Ruth's tumble represents the leading type of accident in late life. About 30 percent of adults over age 65 and 50 percent over age 80 have experienced a fall within the last year. Declines in vision, hearing, mobility, muscle strength, and cognitive func-

tioning; depressed mood; use of medications that affect mental processing; and development of certain chronic illnesses (such as arthritis) increase the risk of falling (Rubenstein, Stevens, & Scott, 2008).

Because of weakened bones and difficulty breaking a fall, serious injury results about 10 percent of the time. Among the most common is hip fracture. It increases fifteenfold from age 65 to 85 and is associated with a 20 percent increase in mortality (Centers for Disease Control and Prevention, 2010). Of those who survive, half never regain the ability to walk without assistance.

Falling can also impair health indirectly, by promoting fear of falling. Almost half of older adults who have fallen admit that they purposefully avoid activities because they are afraid of falling again. In this way, a fall can limit mobility and social contact, undermining both physical and psychological well-being (Painter et al., 2012). Although an active lifestyle may expose older people to more situations that can cause a fall, the health benefits of activity far outweigh the risk of serious injury due to falling.

Mental Disabilities

Normal age-related cell death in the brain, described earlier, does not lead to loss of ability to engage in everyday activities. But when cell death and structural and chemical abnormalities are profound, serious deterioration of mental and motor functions occurs.

Dementia refers to a set of disorders occurring almost entirely in old age in which many aspects of thought and behavior are so impaired that everyday activities are disrupted. Dementia strikes 13 percent of adults over age 65. Approximately 2 to 3 percent of people age 65 to 69 are affected; the rate doubles every 5 to 6 years until it reaches about 22 percent among those age 85 to 89 and over half after age 90—trends that apply to the United States and other Western nations (Prince et al., 2013). Beyond age 80, a larger proportion of women than men have dementia, perhaps reflecting the biological sturdiness of the oldest men. Although dementia rates are similar across most ethnic groups, older African Americans have about twice the incidence, and Hispanics about one and one-half times the incidence, as whites (Alzheimer's Association, 2012b). Associated risk factors, not race, are responsible, as we will see shortly.

About a dozen types of dementia have been identified. Some are reversible with proper treatment, but most are irreversible and incurable. A few forms, such as Parkinson's disease,[1] involve deterioration in subcortical brain regions (primitive structures below the cortex) that often extends to the cerebral cortex and, in many instances, results in brain abnormalities resembling

---

[1]In Parkinson's disease, neurons in the part of the brain that controls muscle movements deteriorate. Symptoms include tremors, shuffling gait, loss of facial expression, rigidity of limbs, difficulty maintaining balance, and stooped posture.

Alzheimer's disease (Cai et al., 2012). But in the large majority of dementia cases, subcortical brain regions are intact, and progressive damage occurs only to the cerebral cortex. The two most common forms of *cortical dementia* are Alzheimer's disease and cerebrovascular dementia.

Alzheimer's Disease.

When Ruth took 79-year-old Ida to the ballet, an occasion the two sisters anticipated eagerly each year, she noticed a change in Ida's behavior. Ida, who had forgotten the engagement, reacted angrily when Ruth arrived unannounced at her door. Driving to the theater, which was in a familiar part of town, Ida got lost—all the while insisting that she knew the way perfectly. As the lights dimmed and the music began, Ida talked loudly and dug noisily in her purse.

"Shhhhhh," responded a dozen voices from surrounding seats.

"It's just the music!" Ida snapped at full volume. "You can talk all you want until the dancing starts." Ruth was astonished and embarrassed at the behavior of her once socially sensitive sister.

Six months later, Ida was diagnosed with **Alzheimer's disease,** the most common form of dementia, in which structural and chemical brain deterioration is associated with gradual loss of many aspects of thought and behavior. Alzheimer's accounts for 60 percent of all dementia cases and, at older ages, for an even higher percentage. Approximately 8 to 10 percent of people over age 65—about 5.2 million Americans—have the disorder. Of those over age 85, close to 45 percent are affected. In 2030, when all baby boomers will have reached late adulthood, the number of Americans with Alzheimer's is expected to rise to 7.7 million—an increase of more than 50 percent. About 5 to 15 percent of all deaths among older adults involve Alzheimer's, making it a significant cause of late-life mortality (Alzheimer's Association, 2012b).

Symptoms and Course of the Disease. The earliest symptoms are often severe memory problems—forgetting names, dates, appointments, familiar routes of travel, or the need to turn off the kitchen stove. At first, recent memory is most impaired, but as serious disorientation sets in, recall of distant events and such basic facts as time, date, and place evaporates. Faulty judgment puts the person in danger. For example, Ida insisted on driving after she was no longer competent to do so. Personality changes occur—loss of spontaneity and sparkle, anxiety in response to uncertainties created by mental problems, aggressive outbursts, reduced initiative, and social withdrawal. Depression often appears in the early phase of Alzheimer's and other forms of dementia and worsen (Serra et al., 2010; Yaari & Corey-Bloom, 2007).

As the disease progresses, skilled and purposeful movements disintegrate. When Ruth took Ida into her home, she had to help her dress, bathe, eat, brush her teeth, and (eventually) walk and use the bathroom. Ida's sleep was disrupted by delusions and imaginary fears. She often awoke in the night and banged on the wall, insisting that it was dinnertime, or cried out

that someone was choking her. Over time, Ida lost the ability to comprehend and produce speech. And when her brain ceased to process information, she could no longer recognize objects and familiar people. In the final months, Ida became increasingly vulnerable to infections, lapsed into a coma, and died.

The course of Alzheimer's varies greatly, from a year to as long as 20 years, with those diagnosed in their sixties and early seventies typically surviving longer than those diagnosed at later ages (Brodaty, Seeher, & Gibson, 2012; Rait et al., 2010). The average life expectancy for a 70-year-old man with the disease is about 4½ years, for a 70-year-old woman about 8 years.

Brain Deterioration. A diagnosis of Alzheimer's disease is made through exclusion, after ruling out other causes of dementia by a physical examination and psychological testing—an approach that is more than 90 percent accurate. To confirm Alzheimer's, doctors inspect the brain after death for a set of abnormalities that either cause or result from the disease (Hyman et al., 2012). In the overwhelming majority of cases brain-imaging techniques (MRI and PET), which yield three-dimensional pictures of brain volume and activity, can predict whether individuals will receive an after-death confirmation of Alzheimer's (Vitali et al., 2008). Two major structural changes in the cerebral cortex, especially in memory and reasoning areas, are associated with Alzheimer's. Inside neurons, **neurofibrillary tangles** appear—bundles of twisted threads that are the product of collapsed neural structures and that contain abnormal forms of a protein called *tau*. Outside neurons, **amyloid plaques,** dense deposits of a deteriorated protein called *amyloid,* surrounded by clumps of dead nerve and glial cells, develop. Although some neurofibrillary tangles and amyloid plaques are present in the brains of normal middle-aged and older people

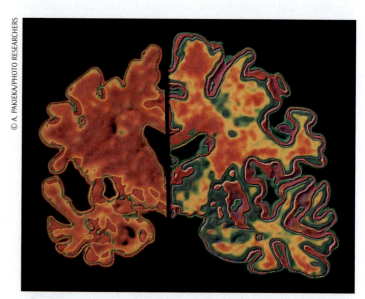

Computer images compare a brain scan of an Alzheimer's patient (left) with one of a healthy older adult (right). The Alzheimer's brain is shrunken, due to massive degeneration and death of neurons. Activity and blood flow (coded yellow and green in the right scan) are also greatly reduced in the Alzheimer's brain.

© A. PAKIEKA/PHOTO RESEARCHERS

and increase with age, they are far more abundant in Alzheimer's victims.

Recent findings indicate that a major culprit in the disease is abnormal breakdown of amyloid remaining *within* neurons and that plaques reflect the brain's effort to eject harmful amyloid from neurons (National Institute on Aging, 2012). In both Alzheimer's disease and Parkinson's disease, disruptions occur in a key neuronal process responsible for chopping up and disposing of abnormal proteins (Cai et al., 2012). These damaged proteins (including amyloid) build to toxic levels. Studies suggest that abnormal amyloid causes the generation of signals within neurons and their transfer across synapses to malfunction (Kopeikina et al., 2011; Palop et al., 2007). Eventually, damaged amyloid induces heightened, abnormal electrical activity throughout the brain.

Abnormal tau in neurofibrillary tangles adds to neuronal breakdown. Tangles disrupt the transport of nutrients and signals from the neuron to its connective fibers. Furthermore, abnormal tau triggers disintegration of nearby normal tau (de Calignon et al., 2012; Liu et al., 2012). Gradually, tau pathology moves across synapses, spreading from neuron to neuron and, over time, from one brain region to the next—thereby amplifying damage.

As synapses deteriorate, levels of neurotransmitters decline, neurons die in massive numbers, and brain volume shrinks. Destruction of neurons that release the neurotransmitter acetylcholine, involved in transporting messages between distant brain regions, further disrupts neuronal networks. A drop in serotonin, a neurotransmitter that regulates arousal and mood, may contribute to sleep disturbances, aggressive outbursts, and depression (Rothman & Mattson, 2012).

Risk Factors. Alzheimer's disease comes in two types: *familial,* which runs in families, and *sporadic,* which has no obvious family history. Familial Alzheimer's generally has an early onset—between ages 30 and 60—and progresses more rapidly than the later-appearing sporadic type, which typically appears after age 65. Researchers have identified genes on chromosomes 1, 14, and 21, involved in generation of harmful amyloid, that are related to familial Alzheimer's. In each case, the abnormal gene is dominant; if it is present in only one of the pair of genes inherited from parents, the person will develop early-onset Alzheimer's (Ertekin-Tanner, 2007; National Institute on Aging, 2012). Recall that chromosome 21 is involved in Down syndrome. Individuals with this chromosomal disorder who live past age 40 almost always have the brain abnormalities and symptoms of Alzheimer's.

Heredity plays a different role in sporadic Alzheimer's, through somatic mutation. About half of people with this form of the disease have an abnormal gene on chromosome 19, which results in excess levels of *ApoE4,* a blood protein that carries cholesterol throughout the body. Researchers believe that a high blood concentration of ApoE4 affects the expression of a gene involved in regulating insulin. Deficient insulin and resulting glucose buildup in the bloodstream (conditions that, when

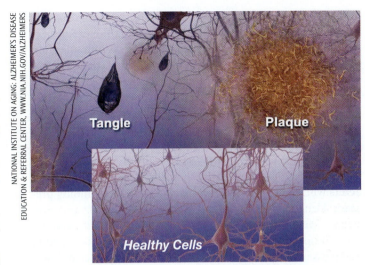

NATIONAL INSTITUTE ON AGING: ALZHEIMER'S DISEASE EDUCATION & REFERRAL CENTER, WWW.NIA.NIH.GOV/ALZHEIMERS

Tangle **Plaque**

Healthy Cells

An image of tissue in the Alzheimer's brain reveals amyloid plaques between neurons, and dead and dying neurons containing neurofibrillary tangles. Compare these cell changes with healthy brain cells.

extreme, lead to diabetes) are linked to brain damage, especially in areas regulating memory, and to high buildup of harmful amyloid in brain tissue (Liu et al., 2013; National Institute on Aging, 2012). In line with these findings, individuals with diabetes have a greatly increased risk of developing Alzheimer's.

At present, the abnormal ApoE4 gene is the most commonly known risk factor for sporadic Alzheimer's. Nevertheless, many sporadic Alzheimer's victims show no known genetic marker, and some individuals with the ApoE4 gene do not develop the disease. Evidence is increasing for the role of a variety of other factors, including excess dietary fat, physical inactivity, overweight and obesity, smoking, chronic psychological stress, cardiovascular disease, and stroke (Kivipelto et al., 2008; Pendlebury & Rothwell, 2009; Whitmer et al., 2008; Yaffe et al., 2011). Head injuries, possibly by accelerating deterioration of amyloid and tau, also increase Alzheimer's risk, especially among people with the ApoE4 gene (Jellinger, 2004). Individuals subjected to repeated instances, such as boxers, football players, and combat veterans, are especially likely to be affected.

The high incidence of Alzheimer's and other forms of dementia among African Americans illustrates the complexity of potential causes. Compared with African Americans, Yoruba village dwellers of Nigeria show a much lower Alzheimer's incidence and no association between the ApoE4 gene and the disease (Gureje et al., 2006). Some investigators speculate that intermarriage with Caucasians heightened genetic risk among African Americans and that environmental factors translated that risk into reality (Hendrie, 2001). Whereas the Yoruba of Nigeria eat a low-fat diet, the African-American diet is high in fat. Eating fatty foods may increase the chances that the ApoE4 gene will lead to Alzheimer's (Hall et al., 2006). The more fat consumed and the higher the blood level of "bad" cholesterol (low-density lipoproteins), the greater the incidence of Alzheimer's.

Protective Factors. Researchers are testing both drug and nondrug approaches to preventing or slowing the progress of Alzheimer's. Among promising drug therapies is immune globulin, a blood product delivered intravenously that contains naturally occurring antibodies against harmful amyloid (National Institute on Aging, 2012). Preliminary research suggests that it improves cognitive functioning and reduces amyloid buildup in the brain. Insulin therapy, delivered via a nasal spray to the brain, helps regulate neuronal use of glucose (Craft et al., 2012). New findings indicate that it has memory benefits and slows cognitive decline—at least in the short term—among older adults with mild cognitive impairment, which commonly precedes Alzheimer's.

A "Mediterranean diet" emphasizing fish, unsaturated fat (olive oil), and moderate consumption of red wine is linked to a 13 percent reduced incidence of Alzheimer's disease, to slower disease progression in diagnosed individuals, and also to a reduction in cerebrovascular dementia (which we will turn to next) (Scarmeas et al., 2007; Sofi et al., 2008). These foods contain fatty acids, antioxidants, and other substances that help promote the health of the cardiovascular and central nervous systems.

Education and an active lifestyle are beneficial as well. The rate of Alzheimer's is reduced by more than half in older adults with higher education, though this protective effect is not as great for those with the ApoE4 gene (Seeman et al., 2005; Stern, 2009). Some researchers speculate that the complex cognitive activities of better-educated people lead to more synaptic connections, which act as a *cognitive reserve,* giving the aging brain greater tolerance for injury before it crosses the threshold into mental disability. In support of this view, compared to their less educated counterparts, the highly educated display a faster rate of decline following an Alzheimer's diagnosis, suggesting that they show symptoms only after very advanced brain deterioration (Hall et al., 2007). Late-life engagement in cognitively stimulating social and leisure activities also reduces the risk of Alzheimer's and of dementia in general, perhaps by stimulating synaptic growth (Bennett et al., 2006; Hall et al., 2009).

Finally, persistence, intensity, and variety of physical activity are associated with decreased risk of Alzheimer's and cerebrovascular dementia (Ahlskog et al., 2011; Smith et al., 2013). Benefits are greatest for older people with the ApoE4 gene.

Helping Alzheimer's Victims and Their Caregivers. As Ida's Alzheimer's worsened, the doctor prescribed a mild sedative and an antidepressant to help control her behavior. Drugs that increase levels of the neurotransmitters acetylcholine and serotonin show promise in limiting challenging dementia symptoms—especially agitation and disruptiveness, which are particularly stressful for caregivers (National Institute on Aging, 2012).

But with no cure available, family interventions ensure the best adjustment possible for the Alzheimer's victim, spouse, and other relatives. Dementia caregivers devote substantially more time to caregiving and experience more stress than do people caring for older adults with physical disabilities (Alzheimer's

Association, 2012b). They need assistance and encouragement from extended-family members, friends, and community agencies. The Social Issues: Health box on the following page describes a variety of helpful interventions for family caregivers. In addition to these strategies, avoiding dramatic changes in living conditions, such as moving to a new location, rearranging furniture, or modifying daily routines, helps people with Alzheimer's disease feel as secure as possible in a cognitive world that is disintegrating.

LOOK AND LISTEN

Investigate formal respite services, providing temporary relief to caregivers of older adults with dementia, in your community. Visit a respite program, and talk to several family caregivers about its impact on the patient's and their own adjustment. ●

Cerebrovascular Dementia. In **cerebrovascular dementia,** a series of strokes leaves areas of dead brain cells, producing step-by-step degeneration of mental ability, with each step occurring abruptly after a stroke. Approximately 10 to 20 percent of all cases of dementia in Western nations are cerebrovascular, and about 10 percent are due to a combination of Alzheimer's and repeated strokes (Gorelick et al., 2011). Heredity indirectly affects cerebrovascular dementia, through high blood pressure, cardiovascular disease, and diabetes, each of which increases the risk of stroke. And environmental influences—including cigarette smoking, heavy alcohol use, high salt intake, very low dietary protein, obesity, inactivity, and psychological stress—also heighten stroke risk (Sahathevan, Brodtmann, & Donnan, 2011).

Because of their greater susceptibility to cardiovascular disease, more men than women have cerebrovascular dementia

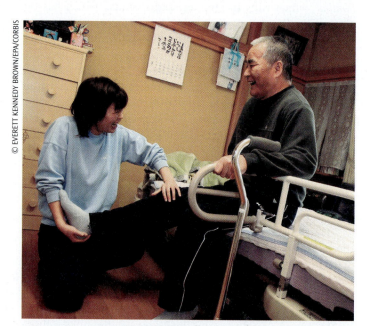

A stroke victim receives physical therapy at home in Japan. High intake of alcohol and salt, coupled with low intake of animal protein, increase the risk of stroke among the Japanese.

Social Issues: Health

Interventions for Caregivers of Older Adults with Dementia

Margaret, wife and caregiver of a 71-year-old Alzheimer's patient, sent a desperate plea to an advice columnist at her local newspaper: "My husband can't feed or bathe himself, or speak to anyone or ask for assistance. I must constantly anticipate his needs and try to meet them. Please help me. I'm at the end of my rope."

The effects of Alzheimer's disease are devastating not just to victims but also to family members who provide care with little or no outside assistance. Caregiving under these conditions has been called the "36-hour day." Although the majority of home caregivers are middle-aged, an estimated nearly 25 percent are older adults caring for a spouse or an aging parent. One-third are in poor health themselves, yet the number of hours dedicated to caregiving increases with caregiver age and is especially high among ethnic minority older adults, whose cultures emphasize care as a family obligation (Alzheimer's Association, 2012a).

Family members who exceed their caregiving capacities suffer greatly in physical and mental health (Sörensen & Pinquart, 2005). The close relationship between the caregiver and the suffering individual—involving shared memories, experiences, and emotions—seems to heighten these risks (Monin & Schulz, 2009).

Most communities offer interventions designed to support family caregivers, but they need to be expanded and made more cost-effective. Those that work best address multiple needs: knowledge, coping strategies, caregiving skills, and respite.

Knowledge

Virtually all interventions try to enhance knowledge about the disease, caregiving challenges, and available community assistance. Knowledge is usually delivered through classes, but websites with wide-ranging caregiver information and online message boards and chat rooms also exist. Gains in knowledge, however, must be combined with other approaches to improve caregivers' well-being.

Coping Strategies

Many interventions teach caregivers everyday problem-solving strategies for managing

the dependent person's behavior, along with techniques for dealing with their own negative thoughts and feelings, such as resentment about having to provide constant care. Modes of delivery include support groups, individual therapy, and "coping with frustration" classes. All yield improvements in caregivers' adjustment and in patients' disturbing behaviors, both immediately and in follow-ups more than a year later (Selwood et al., 2007). Individual approaches are most effective because assistance can be tailored to the specific situation.

Caregiving Skills

Caregivers benefit from lessons in how to communicate with older adults who can no longer express thoughts and emotions clearly and handle everyday tasks—for example, sustaining good eye contact to convey interest and caring; speaking slowly, with short, simple words; using gestures to reinforce meaning; waiting patiently for a response; refraining from interrupting, correcting, or criticizing; and introducing pleasant activities, such as music and slow-paced children's TV programs, that relieve agitation (Alzheimer's Association, 2012a). Interventions that teach communication skills through active practice reduce patients' troublesome behavior and, as a result, lessen caregivers' distress and boost their sense of self-efficacy (Done & Thomas, 2001; Irvine, Ary, & Bourgeois, 2003).

Respite

Caregivers usually say that *respite*—time away from providing care—is the assistance they most desire. But they may be reluctant to accept friends' and relatives' informal offers to help because of guilt, or to use formal services (such as adult day care or temporary placement in a care facility) because of cost or worries about the older adult's adjustment. Yet respite at least twice a week for several hours improves physical and mental health by enabling caregivers to maintain friendships, engage in enjoyable activities, and sustain a balanced life (Jeon, Brodaty, & Chesterson, 2005; Lund et al., 2010).

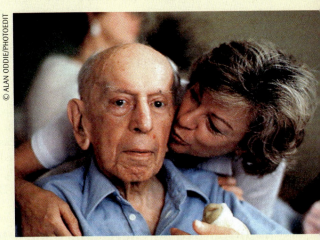

This daughter cares for her father, who has Alzheimer's disease. Although the task has compensating rewards, it is physically demanding and emotionally draining. A great need exists for interventions that support caregivers.

For respite time to be most effective, planning how best to use it is crucial. Caregivers who end up spending respite hours doing housework, shopping, or working usually remain dissatisfied (Lund et al., 2009). Those who engage in activities they had wanted and planned to do gain in psychological well-being.

Intervention Programs

Multifaceted intervention programs that are tailored to caregivers' individual needs make a substantial difference in caregivers' lives. The Resources for Enhancing Alzheimer's Caregiver Health (REACH) initiative was an evaluation of nine "active" intervention programs, each including some or all of the ingredients just described, versus five "passive" interventions providing only information and referral to community agencies. Among more than 1,200 participating caregivers, those receiving six months of active intervention declined more in self-reported burden. And one program providing family therapy in the home—through a telephone system facilitating frequent communication among therapist, caregiver, family members, and other support systems—substantially reduced caregiver depressive symptoms (Gitlin et al., 2003; Schultz et al., 2003). In an additional evaluation with more than 600 participants, REACH active intervention programs enhanced quality of life among caregivers of diverse ethnicities—African American, Caucasian, and Hispanic (Belle et al., 2006).

(Ruitenberg et al., 2001). The disease also varies among countries. For example, deaths due to stroke are high in Japan. Although a low-fat diet reduces Japanese adults' risk of cardiovascular disease, high intake of alcohol and salt and a diet very low in animal protein increase the risk of stroke. As Japanese consumption of alcohol and salt declined and intake of meat rose in recent decades, rates of cerebrovascular dementia and stroke-caused deaths improved (Jellinger, 2008; Sekita et al., 2010).

Although Japan presents a unique, contradictory picture (there, cardiovascular disease is low, and stroke is high), in most cases cerebrovascular dementia is caused by atherosclerosis. Prevention is the only effective way to stop the disease. The U.S. incidence of cerebrovascular dementia has dropped in the last two decades, largely as a result of the decline in heart disease and more effective stroke prevention methods (U.S. Department of Health and Human Services, 2011c).

Misdiagnosed and Reversible Dementia.

Careful diagnosis of dementia is crucial because other disorders can be mistaken for it. And some forms of dementia can be treated and a few reversed.

Depression is the disorder most often misdiagnosed as dementia. The depressed (but not demented) older adult is likely to exaggerate his or her mental difficulties, whereas the demented person minimizes them and is not fully aware of cognitive declines. About 1 to 2 percent of people over age 65 are severely depressed, and another 2 percent are moderately depressed—rates lower than those for young and middle-aged adults (Nordhus, 2008). As we will see in Chapter 18, however, depression rises with age. It is often related to physical illness and pain and can lead to cognitive deterioration. However, U.S. older adults often do not receive the mental health services they need—partly because Medicare offers reduced coverage for treating mental health problems and partly because doctors rarely refer seniors for mental health services (Robinson, 2010). These circumstances increase the chances that depression will deepen and be confused with dementia.

The older we get, the more likely we are to be taking drugs that may have side effects resembling dementia. For example, some medications for coughs, diarrhea, and nausea inhibit the neurotransmitter acetylcholine, leading to Alzheimer's-like symptoms. In addition, some diseases can cause temporary memory loss and mental symptoms (Fong, Tulevaev, & Inouye, 2009). Treatment of the underlying illness relieves the problem. Finally, environmental changes and social isolation can trigger mental declines (Hawton et al., 2011). When supportive ties are restored, cognitive functioning usually bounces back.

Health Care

Health-care professionals and lawmakers in industrialized nations worry about the economic consequences of rapid increase in the older population. Rising government-supported health-care costs and demand for certain health-care services, particularly long-term care, are of greatest concern.

Cost of Health Care for Older Adults.

Adults age 65 and older make up just 13 percent of the American population but account for over 40 percent of government health-care spending (U.S. Department of Health and Human Services, 2012d). According to current estimates, the cost of government-sponsored health insurance, or Medicare, for older people will nearly double by 2020 as more baby boomers enter late adulthood and average life expectancy extends further (Centers for Medicare and Medicaid Services, 2012).

Because Medicare funds only about half of older adults' medical needs, American seniors spend several times as much on health care as their counterparts do in other industrialized nations (OECD, 2012b). And Medicare provides far less support for long-term care than U.S. older people with severe disabilities need.

Long-Term Care.

When Ida moved into Ruth's home, Ruth promised never to place Ida in an institution. But as Ida's condition worsened and Ruth faced health problems of her own, she couldn't keep her word. Reluctantly, Ruth placed her in a nursing home.

Advancing age is strongly associated with use of long-term care services, especially nursing homes. Nearly half of U.S. nursing home residents are age 85 and older (Centers for Medicare and Medicaid Services, 2012). Among disorders of aging, dementia—especially Alzheimer's disease—most often leads to nursing home placement, followed by arthritis, hip fracture, and stroke (Agüero-Torres et al., 2001).

Overall, only 5 percent of Americans age 65 and older are institutionalized, about half the rate in other industrialized nations, such as the Netherlands and Sweden, which provide more generous public financing of institutional care (OECD, 2012b). Unless nursing home placement follows hospitalization for an acute illness, older adults must pay for it until their resources are exhausted. At that point, Medicaid (health insur-

In a nursing home in the Netherlands, a patient enjoys moving landscapes displayed on a screen in an area resembling a train compartment. Institutional care is more common in other industrialized nations than in the United States, where Medicare usually does not cover it.

© ROBIN VAN LONKHUIJSEN/REUTERS/CORBIS

A resident greets a server in the dining room of an assisted living facility. This homelike environment enhances older adults' autonomy, social life, community involvement, and life satisfaction.

ance for the poor) takes over. Consequently, the largest users of nursing homes in the United States are people with either very low or high incomes. Middle-income seniors and their families are more likely to try to protect their savings from being drained by high nursing home costs.

Nursing home use also varies across ethnic groups. For example, Caucasian Americans are nearly twice as likely as African Americans to be institutionalized. African-American older adults are more likely to have large, close-knit extended families with a strong sense of caregiving responsibility. Similarly, Asian, Hispanic, and Native-American seniors use nursing homes less often than Caucasian Americans (Andel, Hyer, & Slack, 2007; Yaffe et al., 2002). Overall, families provide at least 60 to 80 percent of all long-term care in Australia, Canada, New Zealand, the United States, and Western Europe.

To reduce institutionalized care of older adults and its associated high cost, experts advocate alternatives, such as publicly funded in-home help for family caregivers (see Chapter 16, page 437). Another option that has increased dramatically over the past two decades is **assisted living**—a homelike housing arrangement for seniors who require more care than can be provided at home but less than is usually provided in nursing homes. Assisted living is a cost-effective alternative to nursing homes that prevents unnecessary institutionalization (Stone & Reinhard, 2007). It also can enhance residents' autonomy, social life, community involvement, and life satisfaction—benefits that we will take up in Chapter 18.

In Denmark, the combination of a government-sponsored home-helper system and expansion of assisted-living housing resulted in a 30 percent reduction in the need for nursing home beds over a 15-year period. At the same time, the Danish government saved money: Public expenditures for long-term care declined by 8 percent (Hastrup, 2007; Stuart & Weinrich, 2001).

When nursing home placement is necessary, steps can be taken to improve its quality. For example, the Netherlands has established separate facilities designed to meet the differ-

ent needs of patients with mental and physical disabilities. Institutionalized individuals—like older people everywhere—desire a sense of personal control, gratifying social relationships, and meaningful and enjoyable daily activities (Alkema, Wilber, & Enguidanos, 2007). As Chapter 18 will reveal, designing nursing homes to meet these needs promotes both physical and psychological well-being.

ASK YOURSELF

REVIEW Cite evidence that both genetic and environmental factors contribute to Alzheimer's disease and cerebrovascular dementia.

APPLY Marissa complained to a counselor that at age 68, her husband, Wendell, no longer initiated sex or cuddled her. Why might Wendell have ceased to interact sexually? What interventions—both medical and educational—could be helpful to Marissa and Wendell?

REFLECT What care and living arrangements have been made for seniors needing assistance in your family? How did culture, personal values, financial means, health, and other factors influence those decisions?

COGNITIVE DEVELOPMENT

Ruth's complaints to her doctor about difficulties with memory and verbal expression reflect common concerns about cognitive functioning in late adulthood. Decline in speed of processing, under way throughout the adult years, is believed to affect many aspects of cognition in old age. In Chapter 15, we noted that reduced efficiency of thinking contributes to (but may not fully explain) decrements in certain basic aspects of executive function, including attention and memory. Declines in working-memory capacity, inhibition of irrelevant information, use of memory strategies, and retrieval from long-term memory continue in the final decades of life, affecting many aspects of cognitive aging.

TAKE A MOMENT... Return to Figure 15.3 on page 414, and note that the more a mental ability depends on fluid intelligence (biologically based information-processing skills), the earlier it starts to decline. In contrast, mental abilities that rely on crystallized intelligence (culturally based knowledge) are sustained longer. But maintenance of crystallized intelligence depends on continued opportunities to enhance cognitive skills. When these are available, crystallized abilities—vocabulary, general information, and expertise in specific endeavors—can offset losses in fluid intelligence.

Look again at Figure 15.3. In advanced old age, decrements in fluid intelligence limit what people can accomplish even with cultural supports, including a rich background of experience, knowledge of how to remember and solve problems, and a

Older adults can sustain high levels of functioning through selective optimization with compensation. This retired theater teacher has done so by creating a studio at home where he focuses on composing music.

stimulating daily life (Berg & Sternberg, 2003; Kaufman, 2001). Consequently, crystallized intelligence shows a modest decline.

Generally, loss outweighs improvement and maintenance as people approach the end of life, but plasticity is still possible: Some individuals display high maintenance and minimal loss at very old ages (Baltes & Smith, 2003; Schaie, 2011). Research reveals greater individual variation in cognitive functioning in late adulthood than at any other time of life (Hultsch, MacDonald, & Dixon, 2002; Riediger, Li, & Lindenberger, 2006). Besides fuller expression of genetic and lifestyle influences, increased freedom to pursue self-chosen courses of action—some that enhance and others that undermine cognitive skills—may be responsible.

How can older adults make the most of their cognitive resources? According to one view, those who sustain high levels of functioning engage in **selective optimization with compensation:** Narrowing their goals, they select personally valued activities to optimize (or maximize) returns from their diminishing energy. They also find new ways to *compensate* for losses (Baltes & Freund. 2003; Baltes, Lindenberger, & Staudinger, 2006). When 80-year-old concert pianist Arthur Rubinstein was asked how he managed to sustain such extraordinary piano playing at his advanced age, he described being *selective;* he played fewer pieces. This enabled him to *optimize* his energy; he could practice each piece more. Finally, he developed new, *compensatory* techniques for a decline in playing speed. For example, before a fast passage, he played extra slowly, so the fast section appeared to his audience to move more quickly.

In late adulthood, personal goals—while still including gains—increasingly focus on maintaining abilities and preventing losses (Ebner, Freund, & Baltes, 2006). As we review major changes in memory, language processing, and problem solving, we will consider ways that older adults optimize and compensate in the face of declines. We will also see that certain abilities that depend on extensive life experience, not processing efficiency, are sustained or increase in old age.

© JOURNAL-COURIER/STEVE WARMOWKSI/THE IMAGE WORKS

LOOK AND LISTEN

Interview an older adult about memory and other cognitive challenges, asking for examples. For each instance, invite the older person to describe his or her efforts to optimize cognitive resources and compensate for losses. ●

Memory

As older adults take in information more slowly, retain less in working memory, and find it harder to inhibit irrelevant information, apply strategies, and retrieve relevant knowledge from long-term memory, the chances of memory failure increase (Luo & Craik, 2008; Naveh-Benjamin, 2012; Verhaeghen, 2012). A reduced capacity to hold material in working memory while operating on it means that memory problems are especially evident on complex tasks.

Deliberate versus Automatic Memory

"Ruth, you know that movie we saw—the one with the little 5-year-old boy who did such a wonderful acting job. I'd like to suggest it to Dick and Goldie. But what was it called?" asked Walt.

"I can't think of it, Walt. We've seen a few movies lately. Which theater was it at? Who'd we go with? Tell me more about the little boy—maybe it'll come to me."

Although we all occasionally have memory failures like this, difficulties with diverse aspects of *episodic memory,* or recall of everyday experiences, rise substantially in old age. When Ruth and Walt watched the movie, their slower cognitive processing meant that they retained fewer details. And because their working memories could hold less at once, they attended poorly to *context*—where they saw the movie and who went with them (Wegesin et al., 2000; Zacks & Hasher, 2006). When we try to remember, context serves as an important retrieval cue.

These memory difficulties mean that older adults sometimes cannot distinguish an imagined event from one they actually experienced (Rybash & Hrubi-Bopp, 2000). They also find it harder to remember the source of information—which member of their bridge club made a certain statement, in what magazine they read about a particular news event, and to whom and on which occasion they previously told a certain joke or story (Simons et al., 2004). Temporal memory—recall of the order in which events occurred or how recently they happened—suffers as well (Dumas & Hartman, 2003; Hartman & Warren, 2005).

Older adults' limited working memories increase the likelihood of another type of episodic memory difficulty: They may, for example, travel from the den to the kitchen intending to get something but then not recall what they intended to get. When the context in which they formed the memory intention (the den) differs from the retrieval context (the kitchen), they often experience memory lapses (Verhaeghen, 2012). When they return to the first context (the den), it serves as a strong cue for their memory intention because that is where they first encoded it, and they say, "Oh, now I remember why I went to the kitchen!"

A few days later, when Ruth saw a TV ad for the movie whose title she had forgotten, she recognized its name immediately. Recognition—a fairly automatic type of memory that demands little mental effort—suffers less than recall in late adulthood because a multitude of environmental supports for remembering are present (Hoyer & Verhaeghen, 2006).

Consider another automatic form of memory: **implicit memory**, or memory without conscious awareness. In a typical implicit memory task, you would be shown a list of words and then asked to fill in a word fragment (such as *t– –k*). You would probably complete the sequence with a word you had just seen *(task)* rather than another word *(took* or *teak)*. Without trying to do so, you would engage in recall.

Age differences in implicit memory are much smaller than in explicit, or deliberate, memory. Memory that depends on familiarity rather than on conscious use of strategies is largely spared in old age (Fleischman et al., 2004; Hudson, 2008). This helps explain why recall of vocabulary and general information—which are mostly well-learned and highly familiar—decline far less, and do so at later ages, than recall of everyday experiences (Small et al., 2012). The episodic memory problems seniors report—for names of people, places where they put important objects, directions for getting from one place to another, and (as we will see) appointments and medication schedules—all place high demands on their more limited working memories.

Associative Memory

The memory deficits just described are part of a general, age-related decline in binding information into complex memories (Naveh-Benjamin, 2012). Researchers call this an **associative memory deficit**, or difficulty creating and retrieving links between pieces of information—for example, two items or an item and its context, such as Ruth's attempt to remember the name of the movie with the child actor or where she had seen the movie.

To find out whether older adults have greater difficulty with associative memory than younger adults, researchers showed them pairs of unrelated words or pictures of objects (such as *table–overcoat* or *sandwich–radio*) and asked that they study the pairs for an upcoming memory test. During the test, one group of participants was given a page of *single items,* some that had appeared in the study phase and some that had not, and asked to circle the ones they had studied. The other group was given a page of *item pairs,* some intact from the study phase *(table–overcoat)* and some that had been rearranged *(overcoat–radio),* and asked to circle pairs they had studied. Older adults did almost as well as younger adults on the single-item memory test. But they performed far worse on the item-pair test—findings that support an associative memory deficit (Naveh-Benjamin, 2000, 2012; Naveh-Benjamin et al., 2003). Older people have greater difficulty remembering widely varying associations, including face–name, face–face, word–voice, and person–action pairings.

Reducing task demands by providing older adults with helpful memory cues improves their associative memory (Naveh-Benjamin, 2012). For example, to associate names with faces, older people profit from mention of relevant facts about those individuals. And when older adults are directed to use the memory strategy of *elaboration* (relating word pairs by generating a sentence linking them) during both study and retrieval, the young–old difference in memory is greatly reduced (Naveh-Benjamin, Brav, & Levy, 2007). Clearly, associative deficits are greatly affected by lack of strategy use that helps bind information into integrated wholes.

Remote Memory

Although older people often say that their **remote memory**, or very long-term recall, is clearer than their memory for recent events, research does not support this conclusion. For example, to assess autobiographical memory, researchers typically give a series of words (such as *book, machine, sorry, surprised*) and ask adults to report a personal memory cued by each. Or they present participants with a time line on a piece of paper, representing birth to present age, and ask them to place important life events on the line and note the age at which each occurred. People between ages 50 and 90 recall both remote and recent events more frequently than intermediate events, with recent events mentioned most often in the word-cue studies (see Figure 17.5). Among remote events recalled using either word-cue or

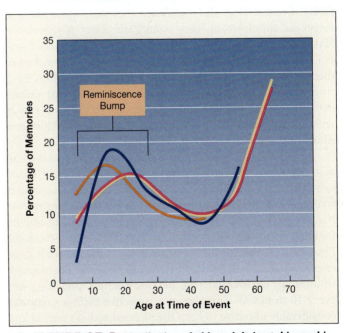

FIGURE 17.5 Distribution of older adults' autobiographical memories by reported age at time of the event. In the four studies of 50- to 90-year-olds represented here, later events were remembered better than early events. Among early events, most of those recalled occurred between ages 10 and 30. (From D. C. Rubin, T. A. Rahhal, & L. W. Poon, 1998, "Things Learned in Early Adulthood Are Remembered Best," *Memory and Cognition, 26,* p. 4. Copyright © 1998 by the Psychonomic Society, Inc. Adapted by permission of the Psychonomic Society.)

time-line procedures, most happened between ages 10 and 30—a period of heightened autobiographical memory called the **reminiscence bump** (Janssen, Rubin, & St. Jacques, 2011; Rubin, 2002; Schroots, van Dijkum, & Assink, 2004).

The reminiscence bump is evident in the autobiographical recall of older adults from diverse cultures—Bangladesh, China, Japan, Turkey, and the United States (Conway et al., 2005; Demiray, Gülgöz, & Bluck, 2009). Why do older adults recall youthful events? Adolescence and early adulthood are also times of identity development, when many personally significant experiences occur (Glück & Bluck, 2007). Furthermore, the reminiscence bump characterizes emotionally positive, but not negative, memories. Culturally shared, important life events—school proms, graduations, marriage, birth of children—are usually positive and cluster earlier in life (Dickson, Pillemer, & Bruehl, 2011).

Nevertheless, older people recall recent personal experiences more readily than remote ones, probably because of interference produced by years of additional experience (Verhaeghen, 2012). As we accumulate more memories, some inevitably resemble others. As a result, certain early memories become less clear than they once were.

Prospective Memory

So far, we have considered various aspects of *retrospective memory* (remembrance of things past). **Prospective memory** refers to remembering to engage in planned actions in the future. Because Walt and Ruth knew they were more likely to forget an appointment, they would ask about it repeatedly. "Sybil, what time is our dinner engagement?" Walt asked several times during the two days before the event. The amount of mental effort required determines whether older adults have trouble with prospective memory. Remembering the dinner date was challenging for Walt because he typically ate dinner with his daughter on Thursday evenings at 6 P.M., but this time, dinner was set for Tuesday at 7:15 P.M.

In the laboratory, older adults do better on *event-based* than on *time-based* prospective memory tasks. In an event-based task, an event (such as a certain word appearing on a computer screen) serves as a cue for remembering to do something (pressing a key) while the participant engages in an ongoing activity (reading paragraphs) (Kliegel, Jäger, & Phillips, 2008; McDaniel, Einstein, & Rendell, 2007). In time-based tasks, the adult must engage in an action after a certain time interval has elapsed, without any obvious external cue (for example, pressing a key every 10 minutes). Time-based prospective memory requires considerable initiative to keep the planned action in mind and monitor the passage of time while also performing an ongoing activity (Einstein, McDaniel, & Scullin, 2012). Consequently, declines in late adulthood are considerable.

But difficulties with prospective memory evident in the laboratory do not appear in real life, where adults are highly motivated to remember and good at setting up event-based reminders for themselves, such as a buzzer ringing in the kitchen or a note tacked up prominently (Henry et al., 2004). In

this way, seniors compensate for their reduced-capacity working memories and the challenge of dividing attention between what they are doing now and what they must do in the future.

Nevertheless, once a prospective memory task is finished, older adults find it harder than younger adults to deactivate, or inhibit, their intention to engage in the future action, especially when cues are still present after the task has been performed. Hence, they sometimes repeat the task again (Scullin et al., 2011). Whereas forgetting whether one has washed one's hair and doing so a second time is harmless, repeating a dose of medication can be dangerous. Older adults benefit from a system of reminders that regularly scheduled tasks have been completed, and they often arrange such systems themselves.

Language Processing

Language and memory skills are closely related. In language comprehension (understanding the meaning of spoken or written prose), we recollect what we have heard or read without conscious awareness. Like implicit memory, language comprehension changes little in late life, as long as conversational partners do not speak too quickly and older adults are given enough time to process written text accurately, enabling them to compensate for reduced working-memory capacity (Stine-Morrow & Miller, 2009). Older readers make a variety of adjustments to ensure comprehension, such as attending more closely to features of text prose, pausing more often to integrate infor-

In Alberta, Canada, a senior speaks out against environmental destruction caused by the oil industry. To compensate for language production problems, older adults speak more slowly and use simplified grammatical structures.

mation, and making good use of story organization to help them recall both main ideas and details. Those who have invested more time in reading and literacy activities over their lifetimes display faster and more accurate reading comprehension (Payne et al., 2012). They benefit from years of greater practice of this highly skilled activity.

Two aspects of language production show age-related losses. The first is retrieving words from long-term memory (Connor et al., 2004). When conversing with others, Ruth and Walt sometimes had trouble finding the right words to convey their thoughts—even well-known words they had used many times in the past. Consequently, their speech contained more pronouns and other unclear references than it did at younger ages. They also spoke more slowly and paused more often, partly because they needed time to search their memories for certain words (Burke & Shafto, 2004). And compared to younger people, they more often reported a *tip-of-the-tongue state*—certainty that they knew a word accompanied by an inability to produce it.

Second, planning what to say and how to say it is harder in late adulthood. As a result, Walt and Ruth displayed slightly more hesitations, false starts, word repetitions, and sentence fragments as they aged (Bortfeld et al., 2001). Their statements were also less grammatically complex and less well-organized than before (Kemper, 2012).

As with memory, older adults develop compensatory techniques for their language production problems. For example, they speak more slowly so they can devote more effort to retrieving words and organizing their thoughts. Sacrificing efficiency for greater clarity, they use more sentences, but shorter ones, to convey their message (Griffin & Spieler, 2006). As older people monitor their word-retrieval failures and try hard to overcome them, they show a greater frequency of tip-of-the-tongue states—but they resolve tip-of-the-tongues at a higher rate than do younger people (Schwartz & Frazier, 2005).

 ## Problem Solving

Problem solving is yet another cognitive skill that illustrates how aging brings not only deterioration but also adaptive changes. Problem solving in the laboratory declines in late adulthood (Finucane et al., 2005). Older adults' memory limitations make it hard to keep all relevant facts in mind when dealing with a complex hypothetical problem.

Yet the everyday problems seniors encounter differ from hypothetical problems devised by researchers—and also from the problems they experienced at earlier ages. After retirement, older adults do not have to deal with workplace problems. Their children are typically grown and living on their own, and their marriages have endured long enough to have fewer difficulties. With age, major concerns involve dealing with extended-family relationships (for example, expectations of adult children that they babysit grandchildren) and managing IADLs, such as preparing nutritious meals, handling finances, and attending to health concerns.

As long as they perceive problems as under their control and as important, older people are active and effective in solving problems of everyday life (Berg & Strough, 2011). Older adults generate a smaller number of strategies compared to young and middle-aged adults, but this may be due to their greater life experience (Strough et al., 2008). The health arena illustrates the adaptiveness of everyday problem solving in late adulthood. Older adults make faster decisions about whether they are ill, seek medical care sooner, and select treatments more quickly than young and middle-aged adults (Meyer, Russo, & Talbot, 1995). This swift response of older people is interesting in view of their slower cognitive processing. Research reveals that they have accumulated more health-related knowledge, which enables them to move ahead with greater certainty (Meyer, Talbot, & Ranalli, 2007). Acting decisively when faced with health risks is sensible in old age.

Finally, older adults report that they often consult others—generally spouses and adult children, but also friends, neighbors, and members of their religious congregation—for advice about everyday problems (Strough et al., 2003). And compared with younger married couples, older married couples more often collaborate in problem solving, and researchers judge their jointly generated strategies as highly effective—even on demanding tasks that require complex memory and reasoning (Meegan & Berg, 2002; Peter-Wight & Martin, 2011). In jointly solving problems, older people seem to compensate for moments of cognitive difficulty.

 ## Wisdom

A wealth of life experience underlies another capacity believed to reach its height in old age: **wisdom**. When researchers ask people to describe wisdom, most mention breadth and depth of practical knowledge, ability to reflect on and apply that knowledge in ways that make life more bearable and worthwhile; emotional maturity, including the ability to listen patiently and empathetically and give sound advice; and altruistic creativity that contributes to humanity and enriches others' lives. One group of researchers summed up the multiple cognitive and personality traits that make up wisdom as "expertise in the conduct and meaning of life" (Baltes & Smith, 2008; Baltes & Staudinger, 2000, p. 124; Staudinger, Dörner, & Mickler, 2005).

During her college years, Ruth and Walt's granddaughter Marci telephoned with a pressing personal dilemma. Ruth's advice reflected the features of wisdom just mentioned. After her boyfriend Ken moved to another city to attend medical school, Marci, unsure whether her love for Ken would endure, had begun dating another student. "I can't stand being pulled in two directions," she exclaimed. "I'm thinking of calling Ken and telling him about Steve. Do you think I should?"

"This is not a good time, Marci," Ruth advised. "You'll break Ken's heart before you've had a chance to size up your feelings for Steve. And you said Ken's taking some important exams in two weeks. If you tell him now and he's distraught, it could affect the rest of his life."

TONY KARUMBA/AFP/GETTY IMAGES

Renowned British primatologist Dr. Jane Goodall—speaking with admirers after a presentation at the National Museum in Nairobi, Kenya—exemplifies wisdom. At age 79, she continues to be a tireless leader in efforts to protect chimpanzees and their African habitats and to promote humane treatment of animals everywhere.

Wisdom—whether applied to personal problems or to community, national, and international concerns—requires the "pinnacle of insight into the human condition" (Baltes & Staudinger, 2000; Birren, 2009). Not surprisingly, cultures around the world assume that age and wisdom go together. In village and tribal societies, the most important social positions, such as chieftain and shaman (religious leader), are reserved for the old. Similarly, in industrialized nations, older adults are chief executive officers of large corporations, high-level religious leaders, members of legislatures, and supreme court justices. According to an evolutionary view, the genetic program of our species grants health, fitness, and strength to the young. Culture tames this youthful advantage in physical power with the insights of the old, ensuring balance and interdependence between generations (Csikszentmihalyi & Nakamura, 2005; Csikszentmihalyi & Rathunde, 1990).

In the most extensive research to date on development of wisdom, adults ranging in age from 20 to 89 responded to uncertain real-life situations—for example, what to consider and do if a good friend is about to commit suicide or if, after reflecting on your life, you discover that you have not achieved your goals (Staudinger, 2008; Staudinger, Dörner, & Mickler, 2005). Responses were rated for five ingredients of wisdom:

- Knowledge about fundamental concerns of life, including human nature, social relations, and emotions
- Effective strategies for applying that knowledge to making life decisions, handling conflict, and giving advice
- A view of people that considers the multiple demands of their life contexts
- A concern with ultimate human values, such as the common good, as well as respect for individual differences in values
- Awareness and management of the uncertainties of life—that many problems have no perfect solution

Results revealed that age is no guarantee of wisdom. A small number of adults of diverse ages ranked among the wise. But type of life experience made a difference. People in human-service careers who had extensive training and practice in grappling with human problems tended to attain high wisdom scores. Other high-scorers held leadership positions (Staudinger, Smith, & Baltes, 1992; Staudinger, 1996). And when age and relevant life experiences were considered together, more older than younger people scored in the top 20 percent.

In addition to age and life experience, having faced and overcome adversity appears to be an important contributor to late-life wisdom (Brugman, 2006; Linley, 2003). In an investigation of people who were young adults during the Great Depression of the 1930s, those who experienced economic hardship and surmounted it scored especially high in wisdom nearly 40 years later, as indicated by reflections on life events, insights into their own motives and behavior, and compassionate concern for the welfare of others (Ardelt, 1998).

Compared to their agemates, older adults with the cognitive, reflective, and emotional qualities that make up wisdom are better educated and physically healthier, forge more positive relations with others, and score higher on the personality dimension of openness to experience (Kramer, 2003). Wisdom also predicts sense of personal growth, generativity, favorable adjustment to aging, marital happiness, and life satisfaction (Ardelt, 2011; Le, 2011). Wise older people seem to flourish, even when faced with physical and cognitive challenges. This suggests that finding ways to promote wisdom would be a powerful means of both contributing to human welfare and fostering a gratifying old age.

Factors Related to Cognitive Maintenance and Change

Heritability research suggests a modest genetic contribution to individual differences in cognitive change in late adulthood (Deary et al., 2012). At the same time, a mentally active life is vital for preserving cognitive resources. Above-average education, frequent contact with family members and friends, stimulating leisure pursuits, community participation, and a flexible personality predict higher mental test scores and reduced cognitive decline into advanced old age (Bielak et al., 2012; Schaie, 2011). Today's seniors in industrialized nations are better educated than any previous generation. Since 1950, the rate of high school completion among U.S. adults age 65 and older has quadrupled, reaching 80 percent. Those with at least a bachelor's degree have increased sixfold, to 23 percent (U.S. Department of Health and Human Services, 2012d). As more baby boomers enter late adulthood, these trends are expected to continue, forecasting improved preservation of cognitive functions.

As noted earlier, health status powerfully predicts older adults' cognitive functioning. A wide variety of chronic conditions, including vision and hearing impairments, cardiovascular disease, diabetes, osteoporosis, and arthritis, are strongly associated with cognitive declines (Baltes, Lindenberger, & Staudinger, 2006). But we must be cautious in interpreting this link between physical and cognitive deterioration, which may be exaggerated by the fact that brighter adults are more likely to engage in health-protective behaviors.

Retirement also affects cognitive change, both positively and negatively. When people leave routine jobs for stimulating leisure activities, outcomes are favorable. In contrast, retiring from a highly complex job without developing challenging substitutes accelerates intellectual declines (Schaie, 1996). In fact, complex, challenging work has a strong, facilitating impact on intellectual functioning in late adulthood (Hertzog et al., 2009; Schooler, Mulatu, & Oates, 1999).

As seniors grow older, their cognitive scores show larger fluctuations from one occasion to the next. This rising instability of performance—especially in speed of response—accelerates in the seventies and is associated with cognitive declines, along with neurobiological signs of shrinkage in the prefrontal cortex and deficient brain functioning (Bielak et al., 2010; Lövdén et al., 2012; MacDonald, Li, & Bäckman, 2009). It seems to signal end-of-life brain degeneration.

Terminal decline refers to acceleration in deterioration of cognitive functioning prior to death. Some longitudinal studies indicate that it is limited to a few aspects of intelligence, others that it occurs generally, across many abilities. Findings also differ greatly in its estimated length—from 1 to 3 to as long as 14 years, with an average of 4 to 5 years (Lövdén et al., 2005; MacDonald, Hultsch, & Dixon, 2011; Rabbitt, Lunn, & Wong, 2008; Wilson et al., 2003). In one investigation, a sharp drop in life satisfaction predicted mortality. The downturn appeared, on average, four years in advance of death, was especially steep in people age 85 and older, and showed only a weak relationship to mental deterioration or chronic illnesses (Gerstorf et al., 2008).

Perhaps different kinds of terminal decline exist—one type arising from disease processes, another reflecting general biological breakdown due to normal aging. What we do know is that an extended falloff in cognitive performance or in emotional investment in life is a sign of loss of vitality and impending death.

 # Cognitive Interventions

For most of late adulthood, cognitive declines are gradual. Although aging of the brain contributes to them, recall from our earlier discussion that the brain can compensate by growing new neural fibers. Furthermore, some cognitive decrements may be due to disuse of particular skills rather than biological aging. If plasticity of development is possible, then interventions that train older people in cognitive strategies should at least partially reverse the age-related declines we have discussed.

Older adults' relatively well-preserved *metacognition* is a powerful asset in training efforts. Most, for example, are aware of memory declines and know they must take extra steps to ensure recall of important information (Castel, McGillivray, & Friedman, 2011). Their impressive metacognitive understanding is also evident in the wide-ranging techniques they devise to compensate for everyday cognitive challenges.

The Adult Development and Enrichment Project (ADEPT) is the most extensive cognitive intervention program conducted to date (Schaie, 2005). By using participants in the Seattle Longitudinal Study (see Chapter 15, page 414), researchers were able to do what no other investigation has done: assess the effects of cognitive training on long-term development.

Intervention began with adults over age 64, some of whom had maintained their scores on tests of two mental abilities (inductive reasoning and spatial orientation) over the previous 14 years and others who had shown declines. After just five one-hour training sessions in one of two types of mental test items, two-thirds of participants improved their performance on the trained skill. Gains for decliners were dramatic: Forty percent returned to the level at which they had been functioning 14 years earlier! A follow-up after 7 years revealed that although scores dropped somewhat, participants remained advantaged in their trained skill over agemates trained in the other ability. Finally, "booster" training at this time led to further gains, although these were smaller than the earlier gains.

In another large-scale intervention study called ACTIVE (Advanced Cognitive Training for Independent and Vital Elderly), more than 2,800 65- to 84-year-olds were randomly assigned to a 10-session training program focusing on one of three abilities—speed of processing, memory, or reasoning—or to a no-intervention control group. Again, trained older adults showed an immediate advantage in the trained skill over controls that was still evident—though smaller in magnitude—at one- and two-year follow-ups (Ball et al., 2002). Transfer to everyday functioning, unfortunately, was disappointing: For example, participants who improved on a laboratory processing-speed task were no faster at looking up numbers in a phone book. Nevertheless, five years after intervention, cognitive training was associated with reduced declines in general health and ability to perform IADLs—outcomes that were strongest for the speed-of-processing group (Wolinsky et al., 2006). The investigators speculated that speed-of-processing training induces a broad pattern of brain activation, affecting many regions.

Clearly, many cognitive skills can be enhanced in old age. A vital goal is to transfer intervention from the laboratory to the community, weaving it into the daily experiences of older people (Stine-Morrow & Basak, 2011).

 # Lifelong Learning

The competencies that older adults need to live in our complex, changing world are the same as those of younger people—communicating effectively through spoken and written systems; locating information, sorting through it, and selecting what is needed; using math strategies, such as estimation; planning and organizing activities, including making good use of time

Applying What We Know

Increasing the Effectiveness of Educational Experiences for Older Adults

Technique	Description
Provide a positive learning environment.	Many older adults have internalized negative stereotypes of their own abilities and come to the learning environment with low self-efficacy. A supportive group atmosphere helps convince older adults that they can learn.
Allow ample time to learn new information.	Rate of learning varies widely among older adults, and some master new material at a fairly slow rate. Presenting information over multiple sessions or allowing for self-paced instruction aids mastery.
Present information in a well-organized fashion.	Older adults do not organize information as effectively as younger adults. Material that is outlined, presented, and then summarized enhances memory and understanding. Digressions make a presentation harder to comprehend.
Relate information to older adults' experiences.	Relating new material to what older adults have already learned, by drawing on their extensive knowledge and experiences and giving many vivid examples, enhances recall.
Adapt the learning environment to fit changes in sensory systems.	Adequate lighting, availability of large-print reading materials, appropriate sound amplification, reduction in background noise, and clear, well-organized visual aids to supplement verbal teaching ease information processing.

and resources; mastering new technologies; and understanding past and current events and the relevance of each to their own lives. Seniors also need to develop new, problem-centered coping strategies—ways to sustain health and operate their households efficiently and safely—and updated vocational skills, for those who continue to work.

Participation of older adults in continuing education has increased substantially over the past few decades. In its most recently reported year, Road Scholar (formerly called Elderhostel) campus-based programs, and their recent exten-sion to travel experiences around the world, attracted nearly 100,000 American and Canadian older adults. Some programs make use of community resources through classes on local ecology or folk life. Others focus on innovative topics and experiences—writing one's own life story, discussing contemporary films with screenwriters, whitewater rafting, Chinese painting and calligraphy, or acquiring French language skills. Travel programs are enriched by in-depth lectures and expert-led field trips.

Similar educational programs have sprung up in the United States and elsewhere. The Bernard Osher Foundation collaborates with more than 120 U.S. universities to establish Osher Lifelong Learning Institutes on campuses. Each offers older adults a wide array of stimulating learning experiences, from auditing regular courses, to forming learning communities that address common interests, to helping to solve community problems.

LOOK AND LISTEN

Find out if your college or university hosts Road Scholar or Osher Foundation programs. Attend a session of an on-campus program. What did you observe about older adults' capacity for complex learning? ●

Participants in these programs tend to be active, well-educated, and financially well-off. Much less is available for older people with little education and limited income. Community senior centers with inexpensive offerings related to everyday living attract more low-SES people than programs such as Road Scholar. Regardless of course content and which seniors attend, using the techniques summarized in Applying What We Know above increases the effectiveness of educational experiences.

PHOTO BY CARL STUDNA/ROAD SCHOLAR

Active, adventurous seniors explore the sights, sounds, streets, and monuments of Dublin's authors, poets, and playwrights as part of a Road Scholar travel program to Ireland.

Older participants in continuing education report a rich array of benefits—understanding new ideas in many disciplines, learning new skills that enrich their lives, making new friends, and developing a broader perspective on the world (Preece & Findsen, 2007). Furthermore, seniors come to see themselves differently. Many abandon their own ingrained stereotypes of aging when they realize that adults in late life—including themselves—can still engage in complex learning.

Older adults' willingness to acquire new knowledge and skills is apparent in the recent, rapid rise in their use of online technology as they discover its many practical benefits, including assistance with shopping, banking, health-care management, and communication. Currently, just over half of adults age 65 and older access the Internet, with 86 percent using e-mail and 38 percent social networking sites such as Facebook (Brenner, 2013; Zickuhr & Madden, 2012). Still, older people have joined the computer and Internet community to a lesser extent than younger people (see page 439 in Chapter 16). But with patient training, support, and modified equipment and software to suit their physical and cognitive needs, older adults readily enter the online world, becoming devoted users.

The educational needs of seniors are likely to be given greater attention in coming decades, as their numbers grow and they assert their right to lifelong learning. Once this happens, false stereotypes—"the elderly are too old to learn" or "education is for the young"—are likely to weaken and, perhaps, disappear.

ASK YOURSELF

REVIEW Describe cognitive functions that are maintained or improve in late adulthood. What aspects of aging contribute to them?

APPLY Estelle complained that she had recently forgotten two of her regular biweekly hair appointments and sometimes had trouble finding the right words to convey her thoughts. What cognitive changes account for Estelle's difficulties? What can she do to compensate?

REFLECT Interview an older adult in your family, asking about ways the individual engages in selective optimization with compensation to make the most of declining cognitive resources. Describe several examples.

SUMMARY

PHYSICAL DEVELOPMENT

Life Expectancy (p. 447)

Distinguish between chronological age and functional age, and discuss changes in life expectancy over the past century.

- People age biologically at different rates, making chronological age an imperfect indicator of **functional age.** Dramatic twentieth-century gains in **average life expectancy** confirm that biological aging can be modified by environmental factors, including improved nutrition, medical treatment, sanitation, and safety.

- Length of life and, especially, **average healthy life expectancy** can be predicted by a country's health care, housing, and social services, along with lifestyle factors.

- With advancing age, the gender gap in average life expectancy declines, as do differences between higher-SES whites and low-SES ethnic minorities.

- Longevity runs in families, but environmental factors become increasingly important with age. Scientists disagree on whether **maximum lifespan** can be extended beyond 122 years— the oldest verified age.

Physical Changes (p. 449)

Describe physical declines of late adulthood, including changes in the nervous and sensory systems.

- With age, growing numbers of older adults experience physical declines, evident in difficulties carrying out **activities of daily living (ADLs),** or basic self-care tasks, and **instrumental activities of daily living (IADLs),** which are necessary to conduct the business of daily life.

- Neuron loss occurs throughout the cerebral cortex, with greater shrinkage in the frontal lobes and the corpus callosum. The cerebellum also loses neurons. The brain compensates by forming new synapses and, to some extent, generating new neurons. The autonomic nervous system functions less well in old age and releases more stress hormones.

- Older adults—more women than men—tend to suffer from impaired vision and may experience **cataracts** and **macular degeneration.** Hearing impairments are more common than visual impairments, especially in men, with decline in speech perception having the greatest impact on life satisfaction.

- Taste and odor sensitivity wane, making food less appealing. Touch sensitivity also deteriorates, particularly on the fingertips.

Describe cardiovascular, respiratory, and immune system changes and sleep difficulties in late adulthood.

- Reduced capacity of the cardiovascular and respiratory systems becomes more apparent in late adulthood, especially in lifelong smokers and in people who have not reduced dietary fat or who have had extensive exposure to environmental pollutants. Exercise can slow cardiovascular aging and facilitate respiratory functioning.

© JUICE IMAGES/ALAMY

- The immune system functions less effectively in late life, permitting diseases to progress and making **autoimmune responses** and stress-induced infection more likely.

- Older adults find it harder to fall asleep, stay asleep, and sleep deeply. Timing of sleep shifts toward earlier bedtime and morning wakening.

Describe changes in physical appearance and mobility in late adulthood, along with effective adaptations to these changes.

- Outward signs of aging—white hair, wrinkled and sagging skin, age spots, and decreased height and weight—become more noticeable. Mobility diminishes as muscle and bone strength and joint flexibility decline. Sense of personal control prompts active coping with physical changes and improved functioning.

- A rapidly expanding **assistive technology** helps older people cope with physical declines, sustaining an effective person–environment fit that enhances psychological well-being.

- Negative stereotypes of aging have a stressful, disorganizing impact on older adults' functioning, whereas positive stereotypes foster physical and mental competence.

JOHN EASTCOTT & YVA MOMATIUK/
NATIONAL GEOGRAPHIC/GETTY IMAGES

Health, Fitness, and Disability (p. 456)

Discuss health and fitness in late life, paying special attention to nutrition, exercise, and sexuality.

- Most older adults rate their health favorably and have a high sense of self-efficacy about protecting it. Low-SES ethnic minority older people remain at greater risk for certain health problems and are less likely to believe they can control their health.

- In late life, men continue to be more prone to fatal diseases and women to disabling conditions. In industrialized nations, **compression of morbidity** has occurred, largely as a result of medical advances and improved socioeconomic conditions; further gains will depend on reducing negative lifestyle factors. In the developing world, comprehensive strategies are needed.

- Risk of dietary deficiencies increases in late life, but except for calcium and vitamin D, a daily vitamin–mineral supplement is recommended only for those suffering from malnutrition. Exercise, even when begun in late adulthood, is a powerful health intervention.

- Though sexual activity declines, especially among women, most older couples report continued, regular sexual enjoyment.

Discuss physical disabilities common in late adulthood.

- Illness and disability increase toward the end of life. Cardiovascular disease and cancer are the leading causes of death, followed by respiratory diseases. **Primary aging** contributes to **frailty** in the elderly, but **secondary aging** (declines due to hereditary defects and negative environmental influences) plays a larger role.

- **Osteoarthritis** and **rheumatoid arthritis** are widespread among older adults, especially women. Type 2 diabetes also increases.

- The death rate from unintentional injuries reaches an all-time high from age 65 on, largely due to motor vehicle collisions and falls. Visual declines and slowed reaction time often contribute.

Discuss mental disabilities common in late adulthood.

- **Alzheimer's disease**, the most common form of **dementia**, often starts with severe memory problems. It brings personality changes, depression, disintegration of purposeful movements, loss of ability to comprehend and produce speech, and death. Underlying these changes are abundant **neurofibrillary tangles** and **amyloid plaques** and reduced neurotransmitter levels in the brain.

- Familial Alzheimer's, related to genes involved in generation of harmful amyloid, generally has an early onset and progresses rapidly. About half of sporadic Alzheimer's victims have an abnormal gene that results in insulin deficiency linked to brain damage.

- Diverse environmental factors, including a high-fat diet, physical inactivity, overweight and obesity, smoking, chronic psychological stress, cardiovascular disease, stroke, diabetes, and head injuries increase the risk of Alzheimer's. A "Mediterranean diet," education, and an active lifestyle are associated with lower incidence.

- Heredity contributes to **cerebrovascular dementia** indirectly, through high blood pressure, cardiovascular disease, and diabetes. Many environmental influences also heighten stroke risk.

- Treatable problems, such as depression, side effects of medication, and reactions to social isolation, can be mistaken for dementia.

Discuss health-care issues that affect senior citizens.

- Only a small percentage of U.S. seniors are institutionalized, about half the rate in other industrialized nations with more generous public financing of institutional care. Though ethnic differences exist, family members provide most long-term care in Western nations. Publicly funded in-home help and **assisted living** can reduce the high costs of institutional placement and increase older adults' life satisfaction.

COGNITIVE DEVELOPMENT

Describe overall changes in cognitive functioning in late adulthood.

- Individual differences in cognitive functioning are greater in late adulthood than at any other time of life. Older adults can make the most of their cognitive resources through **selective optimization with compensation**.

© JOURNAL-COURIER/
STEVE WARMOWSKI/THE IMAGE WORKS

Memory (p. 468)

How does memory change in late life?

- Memory failure is more likely in older adults, especially on tasks that are complex and require deliberate processing. Recall of context, source, and temporal order of episodic events declines. Automatic forms of memory, such as recognition and **implicit memory**, suffer less. In general, an **associative memory deficit**, or difficulty creating and retrieving links between pieces of information, characterizes older adults' memory deficits.

- Contrary to what older people often report, **remote memory** is not clearer than recent memory. Autobiographical memory is best for recent experiences, followed by personally meaningful events that occurred between ages 10 and 30, a period of heightened recall called the **reminiscence bump**. In the laboratory, older adults do better on event-based than on time-based **prospective memory** tasks. In everyday life, they compensate for declines in prospective memory by using external memory aids.

Language Processing (p. 470)

Describe changes in language processing in late adulthood.

- Language comprehension changes little in late life. Age-related losses occur in two aspects of language production: retrieving words from long-term memory and planning what to say and how to say it. Older people compensate by speaking more slowly, using shorter sentences, and communicating gist rather than details.

Problem Solving (p. 471)

How does problem solving change in late life?

- Hypothetical problem solving declines in late adulthood. In everyday problem solving, older adults are effective as long as they perceive problems as important and under their control. Older people make faster decisions about health than younger people and more often consult others about everyday problems.

Wisdom (p. 471)

What capacities make up wisdom, and how is it affected by age and life experience?

- **Wisdom** involves extensive practical knowledge, ability to reflect on and apply that knowledge in ways that make life more bearable and worthwhile, emotional maturity, and altruistic creativity. When age and life experience in grappling with human problems are combined, more older than younger people rank among the wise.

TONY KARUMBA/AFP/GETTY IMAGES

Factors Related to Cognitive Maintenance and Change (p. 472)

Cite factors related to cognitive maintenance and change in late adulthood.

- Mentally active people are likely to maintain their cognitive abilities into advanced old age. A wide array of chronic health conditions are associated with cognitive decline. Retirement can bring about either positive or negative changes. Stimulating leisure activities and complex, challenging work facilitate intellectual functioning.

- With age, older adults' cognitive scores become increasingly unstable. As death approaches, **terminal decline**—a marked acceleration in deterioration of cognitive functioning—often occurs.

Cognitive Interventions (p. 473)

Can cognitive interventions help older adults sustain their mental abilities?

- Large-scale interventions like ADEPT and ACTIVE demonstrate that training in cognitive skills can offer large benefits for older people who have experienced cognitive declines.

Lifelong Learning (p. 473)

Discuss types of continuing education and benefits of such programs in late life.

- Increasing numbers of older people continue their education through university courses, community offerings, and programs such as Road Scholar and Osher Lifelong Learning Institutes. Participants acquire new knowledge and skills, new friends, a broader perspective on the world, and an image of themselves as more competent.

Important Terms and Concepts

activities of daily living (ADLs) (p. 449)
Alzheimer's disease (p. 462)
amyloid plaques (p. 462)
assisted living (p. 467)
assistive technology (p. 455)
associative memory deficit (p. 469)
autoimmune response (p. 453)
average healthy life expectancy (p. 448)
average life expectancy (p. 447)
cataracts (p. 451)
cerebrovascular dementia (p. 464)

compression of morbidity (p. 457)
dementia (p. 461)
frailty (p. 459)
functional age (p. 447)
implicit memory (p. 469)
instrumental activities of daily living (IADLs)
   (p. 449)
macular degeneration (p. 451)
maximum lifespan (p. 449)
neurofibrillary tangles (p. 462)
osteoarthritis (p. 460)

primary aging (p. 459)
prospective memory (p. 470)
reminiscence bump (p. 470)
remote memory (p. 469)
rheumatoid arthritis (p. 460)
secondary aging (p. 459)
selective optimization with compensation
   (p. 468)
terminal decline (p. 473)
wisdom (p. 471)

Emotional and Social Development in Late Adulthood

© DESIGN PICS/CORBIS

As family responsibilities and vocational pressures lessen, friendships—like the relaxed companionship of these Guatemalan seniors—take on increasing importance. Having friends is an especially strong predictor of mental health in late adulthood.

chapter outline

With Ruth at his side, Walt spoke to the guests at their sixtieth-anniversary party. "Even when things were hard," he reflected, "the time of life I liked best always seemed to be the current one. When I was a kid, I adored playing baseball. In my twenties, I loved learning the photography business. And of course," Walt continued, glancing affectionately at Ruth, "our wedding was the most memorable day of all."

He went on: "And then Sybil was born. Looking back at my parents and grandparents and forward at Sybil, Marci, and Marci's son Jamel, I feel a sense of unity with past and future generations."

Walt and Ruth greeted old age with calm acceptance, grateful for the gift of long life and loved ones. Yet not all older adults find such peace of mind. Walt's brother Dick was contentious, complaining about petty issues and major disappointments alike: "Goldie, why'd you serve cheesecake? No one eats cheesecake on birthdays!" "Know why we've got financial worries? Uncle Louie wouldn't lend me the money to keep the bakery going, so I *had* to retire."

A mix of gains and losses characterizes these twilight years, extending the multidirectionality of development. On one hand,

old age is a time of pleasure and tranquility, when children are grown, life's work is nearly done, and responsibilities are lightened. On the other hand, it brings concerns about declining physical functions, unwelcome loneliness, and the growing specter of imminent death.

In this chapter, we consider how older adults reconcile these opposing forces. Although some are weary and discontented, most attach deeper significance to life and reap great benefits from family and friendship bonds, leisure activities, and community involvement. We will see how personal attributes and life history combine with home, neighborhood, community, and societal conditions to mold emotional and social development in late life. ●

Erikson's Theory: Ego Integrity versus Despair

The final psychological conflict of Erikson's (1950) theory, **ego integrity versus despair**, involves coming to terms with one's life. Adults who arrive at a sense of integrity feel whole, complete, and satisfied with their achievements. They have adapted to inevitable triumphs and disappointments and realize that the paths they followed, abandoned, and never selected were necessary for fashioning a meaningful life course.

The capacity to view one's life in the larger context of all humanity—as the chance combination of one person and one segment in history—contributes to the serenity and contentment that accompany integrity. "These last few decades have been the happiest," Walt murmured, clasping Ruth's hand—only weeks before the heart attack that would end his life. At peace with himself, his wife, and his children, Walt had accepted his life course as something that had to be the way it was. In a study that followed a sample of women diverse in SES throughout adulthood, midlife generativity predicted ego integrity in late adulthood. Ego integrity, in turn, was associated with more favorable psychological well-being—a more upbeat mood, greater self-acceptance, higher marital satisfaction, closer relationships with adult children, greater community involvement, and increased ease in accepting help from others when it is needed (James & Zarrett, 2007).

Scanning the newspaper, Walt pondered, "I keep reading these percentages: One out of five people will get heart disease, one out of three will get cancer. But the truth is, one out of one will die. We are all mortal and must accept this fate." The

year before, Walt had given his granddaughter, Marci, his collection of prized photos, which had absorbed him for over half a century. With the realization that the integrity of one's own life is part of an extended chain of human existence, Erikson

Erik Erikson and his wife Joan exemplified the ideal of Erikson's final stage. They aged gracefully, felt satisfied with their achievements, and were often seen together, contented and deeply in love.

suggested, death loses its sting. In support of this view, older adults who report having attained intrinsic (personally gratifying) life goals typically express acceptance of their own death (Van Hiel & Vansteenkiste, 2009). Those who emphasize attainment of extrinsic goals (such as money or prestige) more often fear life's end.

The negative outcome of this stage, despair, occurs when aging adults feel they have made many wrong decisions, yet time is too short to find an alternate route to integrity. Without another chance, the despairing person is overwhelmed with bitterness, defeat, and hopelessness. According to Erikson, these attitudes are often expressed as anger and contempt for others, which disguise contempt for oneself. Dick's argumentative, fault-finding behavior, tendency to blame others for his personal failures, and regretful view of his own life reflect this deep sense of despair.

Other Theories of Psychosocial Development in Late Adulthood

As with Erikson's stages of early and middle adulthood, other theorists have clarified and refined his vision of late adulthood, specifying the tasks and thought processes that contribute to a sense of ego integrity. All agree that optimal development involves greater integration and deepening of the personality.

Peck's Tasks of Ego Integrity and Joan Erikson's Gerotranscendence

According to Robert Peck (1968), attaining ego integrity involves three distinct tasks:

- *Ego differentiation:* For those who invested heavily in their careers, finding other ways to affirm self-worth—through family, friendship, and community life
- *Body transcendence:* Surmounting physical limitations by emphasizing the compensating rewards of cognitive, emotional, and social powers
- *Ego transcendence:* As contemporaries die, facing the reality of death constructively through efforts to make life more secure, meaningful, and gratifying for younger generations

In Peck's theory, ego integrity requires older adults to move beyond their life's work, their bodies, and their separate identities. Research suggests that as seniors grow older, both *body transcendence* (focusing on psychological strengths) and *ego transcendence* (orienting toward a larger, more distant future) increase. In a study of women, those in their eighties and nineties stated with greater certainty than those in their sixties that they "accept the changes brought about by aging," "have moved beyond fear of death," "have a clearer sense of the meaning of life," and "have found new, positive spiritual gifts to explore" (Brown & Lowis, 2003).

Erikson's widow Joan Erikson suggested that these attainments actually represent development beyond ego integrity (which requires satisfaction with one's past life) to an additional psychosocial stage that she calls gerotranscendence—a cosmic and transcendent perspective directed forward and outward, beyond the self. Drawing on her own experience of aging, her observations of her husband's final years, and the work of others on the positive potential of the years shortly before death, Joan Erikson speculated that success in attaining gerotranscendence is apparent in heightened inner calm and contentment and additional time spent in quiet reflection (Erikson, 1998; Tornstam, 2000, 2011).

Although interviews with people in their ninth and tenth decades reveal that many (but not all) experience this peaceful, contemplative state, more research is needed to confirm the existence of a distinct, transcendent late-life stage. Besides focusing more intently on life's meaning, many of the very old continue to report investments in the real world—visiting friends, keeping up with current events, striving to be a good neighbor, and engaging in leisure and volunteer pursuits.

Labouvie-Vief's Emotional Expertise

In Chapter 13, we discussed Gisella Labouvie-Vief's research on development of adults' reasoning about emotion (see page 359). Recall that cognitive-affective complexity (awareness and coordination of positive and negative feelings into an organized self-description) increases from adolescence through middle adulthood and then declines as basic information-processing skills diminish in late adulthood.

But older people display a compensating emotional strength: They gain in affect optimization, the ability to maximize positive emotion and dampen negative emotion (Labouvie-Vief, 2005; Labouvie-Vief et al., 2007; Labouvie-Vief, Grühn, & Studer, 2010). Compared with younger people, older adults selectively attend to and better recall emotionally positive over negative information, which contributes to their remarkable resilience (Mather & Carstensen, 2005). Despite physical declines, increased health problems, a restricted future, and death of loved ones, most older people sustain a sense of optimism, emotional stability, and good psychological well-being—an upbeat attitude linked to longer survival (Boyle et al., 2009; Carstensen et al., 2011). Furthermore, about 30 to 40 percent not only are high in affect optimization but also retain considerable capacity for cognitive-affective complexity—a combination related to especially effective emotional self-regulation.

Furthermore, many aging individuals describe their emotional reactions to personal experiences more vividly than younger people—evidence of being more in touch with their feelings. Older adults' emotional perceptiveness helps them separate interpretations from objective aspects of situations. Consequently, their coping strategies often include making sure they fully understand their own feelings before deciding on a

Despite serious medical problems, this aging adult asserts, "Being an invalid does not invalidate your life." Her adopted rescue dog gives her great pleasure. The ability to maximize positive emotion and dampen negative emotion contributes to older people's remarkable resilience.

course of action. And they readily use emotion-centered coping strategies (controlling distress internally) in negatively charged situations (Blanchard-Fields, 2007). In sum, a significant late-life psychosocial attainment is becoming expert at reflecting on one's own feelings and regulating negative affect.

Reminiscence

We often think of older adults as engaged in **reminiscence**—telling stories about people and events from their past and reporting associated thoughts and feelings. Indeed, the widespread image of a reminiscing older person ranks among negative stereotypes of aging. In this common view, older people live in the past to escape the realities of a shortened future. Yet research consistently reveals no age differences exist in total quantity of reminiscing! Rather, younger and older adults often use reminiscence for different purposes (Westerhof, Bohlmeijer, & Webster, 2010). And certain types of reminiscence are positive and adaptive.

In his comments on major events in his life at the beginning of this chapter, Walt was engaging in a special form of reminiscence called *life review*—calling up past experiences with the goal of achieving greater self-understanding. According to Robert Butler (1968), most older adults engage in life review as part of attaining ego integrity. Older adults who participate in counselor-led life review report increased self-esteem, greater sense of purpose in life, and reduced depression (O'Rourke, Cappeliez, & Claxton, 2011; Westerhof, Bohlmeijer, & Webster, 2010).

But many older people who are high in self-acceptance and life satisfaction spend little time evaluating their past (Wink,

2007; Wink & Schiff, 2002). Indeed, in several studies in which older people were asked what they considered to be the best time of life, 10 to 30 percent identified one of the decades of late adulthood. Early and middle adulthood received especially high marks, whereas childhood and adolescence ranked as less satisfying (Field, 1997; Mehlson, Platz, & Fromholt, 2003). These findings challenge the widespread belief that older adults inevitably focus on the past and wish to be young again. To the contrary, today's seniors in industrialized nations are largely present- and future-oriented: They seek avenues for personal growth and fulfillment (see the Cultural Influences box on page 482).

Clearly, life review is not essential for adapting well to late adulthood. Indeed, reminiscence that is *self-focused,* engaged in to reduce boredom and revive bitter events, is linked to adjustment problems. Compared with younger people, older adults less often engage in this ruminative form of reminiscence (Bohlmeijer et al., 2007; O'Rourke, Cappeliez, & Claxton, 2011). Rather, extroverted seniors favor *other-focused* reminiscence directed at social goals, such as solidifying family and friendship ties and reliving relationships with lost loved ones. And at times, older adults—especially those who score high in openness to experience—engage in *knowledge-based* reminiscence, drawing on their past for effective problem-solving strategies and for teaching younger people (Cappeliez, Rivard, & Guindon, 2007). These socially engaged, mentally stimulating forms of reminiscence help make life rich and rewarding.

For young and old alike, reminiscence often occurs during times of life transition. Older adults who have recently retired, been widowed, or moved to a new residence may turn temporarily to the past to sustain a sense of personal continuity (Cappeliez & Robitaille, 2010). During these times, reminiscing about positive memories probably helps them recapture a sense of meaning.

Stability and Change in Self-Concept and Personality

Longitudinal research reveals continuing stability of the "big five" personality traits from mid- to late life (see Chapter 16, page 431). Yet the ingredients of ego integrity—wholeness, contentment, and image of the self as part of a larger world order—are reflected in several significant late-life changes in both self-concept and personality.

Secure and Multifaceted Self-Concept

Older adults have accumulated a lifetime of self-knowledge, leading to more secure and complex conceptions of themselves than at earlier ages (Diehl et al., 2011; Labouvie-Vief & Diehl, 1999). Ruth, for example, knew with certainty that she was good at growing a flower garden, budgeting money, counseling

Cultural Influences

The New Old Age

For many, late adulthood is a time of personal enrichment. Since retiring from her university faculty position, 82-year-old Freda Briggs continues as an advocate for abused children while also embracing new adventures, such as parasailing.

After retiring, pediatrician Jack McConnell tried a relaxing lifestyle near a lake and golf course, but it worked poorly for the energetic 64-year-old. As his desire for a more fulfilling retirement grew, he noticed that outside his comfortable, gated neighborhood were many people serving community needs as gardeners, laborers, fast-food workers, and the like, yet who lived in or near poverty. The contrast galvanized Jack to found Volunteers in Medicine, a free clinic for working-poor adults and their families who lack health insurance (Croker, 2007). Five years later, at age 69, Jack was overseeing a highly cost-effective operation involving 200 retired doctors, nurses, and lay volunteers, who treat 6,000 patients a year.

Increasingly, older adults are using their freedom from work and parenting responsibilities to pursue personally enriching interests and goals. In doing so, they are giving back to their communities in significant ways and serving as role models for younger generations.

Added years of longevity and health plus financial stability have granted this active, opportunistic time of life to so many contemporary seniors that some experts believe a new phase of late adulthood has evolved called the **Third Age**—a term originating over a decade ago in France that spread through Western Europe and recently has stretched to North America. According to this view, the First Age is childhood, the Second Age is the adult period of earning a living and rearing children, and the Third Age—extending from ages 65 to 79, and sometimes longer—is a time of personal fulfillment (James & Wink, 2007). The Fourth Age brings physical decline and need for care.

The baby boomers—healthier and financially better off than any preceding aging generation—are approaching late life with the conviction that their old age will not begin until 80 (Gergen & Gergen, 2003). This self-perception has helped define the Third Age as a time of self-realization and high life satisfaction. As we will see later in this chapter, retirement is no longer a one-way, age-graded event. In one survey of 300 older Americans, very few self-identified as retired (Trafford, 2004). Instead, they were building hybrid lives—leaving career jobs to work at different jobs that utilized their skills and devoting themselves to community service (Moen & Altobelli, 2007).

Although policy makers often express concern about the huge, impending baby-boomer burden on Social Security and Medicare, this large pool of vigorous, publicly minded future seniors has the potential to make enormous economic and social contributions. Today's Third Agers donate billions to the global economy in volunteer work and continue to participate in the work force in large numbers.

But as midlife roles shrink and terminate, too few alternatives are available for the many aging adults eager to make a difference (Bass, 2011). Societies need to provide abundant volunteer, national service, and other public interest opportunities, thereby harnessing their rich elder resources to solve pressing problems. The U.S. Serve America Act, signed into law in 2009, offers expanded service incentives and options to American adults of all ages and, thus, is a major step in that direction.

---

others, giving dinner parties, and figuring out who could be trusted and who couldn't. Furthermore, when young and older adults were asked for several life-defining memories, 65- to 85-year-olds were more likely to mention events with a consistent theme—such as the importance of relationships or personal independence—and to explain how the events were interrelated (McLean, 2008). Their autobiographical selves emphasized coherence and consistency, despite physical, cognitive, and occupational changes.

Ruth's firm and multifaceted self-concept allowed for self-acceptance—a key feature of integrity. In a study of old (70 to 84 years) and very old (85 to 103 years) German seniors asked to respond to the question "Who am I?," participants mentioned more positive than negative self-evaluations. And positive, multifaceted self-definitions predicted psychological well-being (Freund & Smith, 1999).

As the future shortens, most older adults, into their eighties and nineties, continue to mention—and actively pursue—hoped-for selves in the areas of physical health, cognitive functioning, personal characteristics, relationships, social responsibility, and leisure (Frazier, 2002; Markus & Herzog, 1992). At the same time, possible selves reorganize well into old age. When the German 70- to 103-year-olds just mentioned were followed longitudinally for four years, the majority deleted some possible selves and replaced them with new ones (Smith & Freund, 2002). Older adults often characterize hoped-for selves in terms of "improving," "achieving," or "attaining," and those with hoped-for goals usually take concrete steps to attain them. Engaging in hope-related activities, in turn, is associated with gains in life satisfaction and with longer life (Hoppmann et al., 2007). Clearly, late adulthood is not a time of withdrawal from future planning!

Agreeableness, Acceptance of Change, and Openness to Experience

A flexible, optimistic approach to life, which fosters resilience in the face of adversity, is common in old age. Both open-ended interviews and personality tests reveal that older adults gain in *agreeableness*, becoming increasingly generous, acquiescent, and good-natured well into late life (Allemand, Zimprich, & Martin, 2008; Field & Millsap, 1991; Weiss et al., 2005). Agreeableness seems to characterize people who have come to terms with life despite its imperfections.

At the same time, older adults show modest age-related dips in *extroversion*, perhaps reflecting a narrowing of social contacts as people become more selective about relationships—a trend we will take up in a later section. Older people also tend to decline in *openness to experience*, likely due to their awareness of cognitive declines (Allemand, Zimprich, & Martin, 2008; Donnellan & Lucas, 2008). But engaging in cognitively challenging activities can promote openness to experience! In one study, 60- to 94-year-olds participated in a 16-week cognitive training program in reasoning, which included experience in solving challenging but enjoyable puzzles. During the program, the trained group showed steady gains in both reasoning and openness to experience not displayed by untrained controls. Sustained intellectual engagement seemed to induce seniors to view themselves as more open (Jackson et al., 2012). Openness, in turn, predicts pursuit of intellectual stimulation, thereby contributing to enhanced cognitive functioning.

Another late-life development is greater *acceptance of change* (Rossen, Knafl, & Flood, 2008). When asked about dissatisfactions in their lives, many seniors respond that they are not unhappy about anything! Acceptance of change is also evident in most older people' effective coping with the loss of loved ones, including death of a spouse, which they describe as the most stressful event they ever experienced (Lund, Caserta, & Dimond, 1993). The capacity to accept life's twists and turns, many of which are beyond one's control, is vital for adaptive functioning in late adulthood.

Most older adults are resilient, bouncing back in the face of adversity—especially if they did so earlier in their lives. And their heightened capacity for positive emotion contributes greatly to their resilience. Older adults' general cheerfulness strengthens their physiological resistance to stress, enabling them to conserve physical and mental resources needed for effective coping (Ong, Mroczek, & Riffin, 2011). The minority who are high in neuroticism—emotionally negative, short-

tempered, and dissatisfied—tend to cope poorly with stressful events, experience mounting negative affect, and are at risk for health problems and earlier death (Mroczek & Spiro, 2007; Mroczek, Spiro, & Turiano, 2009).

Spirituality and Religiosity

How do older adults manage to accept declines and losses yet still feel whole and complete and anticipate death with calm composure? One possibility, consistent with Peck's and Erikson's emphasis on a transcendent perspective among seniors, is the development of a more mature sense of spirituality. Spirituality is not the same as religion: An inspirational sense of life's meaning can be found in art, nature, and social relationships. But for many people, religion provides beliefs, symbols, and rituals that guide this quest for meaning.

Older adults attach great value to religious beliefs and behaviors. In recent national surveys, over 70 percent of Americans age 65 and older said that religion is very important in their lives—the highest of any age group (Gallup News Service, 2006, 2012). Although health and transportation difficulties reduce organized religious participation in advanced old age, U.S. seniors generally become more religious or spiritual as they age.

The late-life increase in religiosity, however, is modest, and it is far from universal. Longitudinal research reveals that the majority of people show stability in religiosity throughout adulthood (Ai, Wink, & Ardelt, 2010; Dillon & Wink, 2007). Furthermore, in a British investigation following adults for two decades, one-fourth of seniors said they had become less religious, with some citing disappointment at the support they had received from their religious institution during stressful times (such as bereavement) as the reason (Coleman, Ivani-Chalian, & Robinson, 2004). Despite these differences, spirituality and faith may advance to a higher level in late adulthood—away from prescribed beliefs toward a more reflective approach that emphasizes links to others and is at ease with mystery and uncertainty and that accepts one's own belief system as one of many possible worldviews (Fowler & Dell, 2006).

Involvement in both organized and informal religious activities is especially high among low-SES ethnic minority older people, including African-American, Hispanic, and Native-American groups. African-American seniors look to religion as a powerful resource for social support beyond the family and for the inner strength to withstand daily stresses and physical impairments (Armstrong & Crowther, 2002). Compared with their Caucasian agemates, more African-American older adults report collaborating with God to overcome life problems (Lee & Sharpe, 2007).

Throughout adulthood, women are more likely than men to say that religion is very important to them, to participate in religious activities, and to engage in a personal quest for connectedness with a higher power (Gallup News Service, 2012; Wink & Dillon, 2002). Women's higher rates of poverty, widowhood, and participation in caregiving expose them to higher levels of stress and anxiety. As with ethnic minorities, they turn to religion for social support and for a larger vision of community that places life's challenges in perspective.

Religious involvement is associated with diverse benefits, including better physical and psychological well-being, more time devoted to exercising and leisure activities, greater sense of closeness to family and friends, and greater generativity (care for others) (Boswell, Kahana, & Dilworth-Anderson, 2006; Gillum et al., 2008; Krause, 2012; Wink, 2006, 2007). In longitudinal research, both organized and informal religious participation predicted longer survival, after many factors known to affect mortality were controlled (Helm et al., 2000; Strawbridge et al., 2001).

Contextual Influences on Psychological Well-Being

Personal and situational factors often combine to affect psychological well-being. Identifying these contextual influences is vital for designing interventions that foster positive adjustment.

Control versus Dependency

As Ruth's eyesight, hearing, and mobility declined in her eighties, Sybil visited daily to help with self-care and household tasks. During the hours mother and daughter were together, Sybil interacted most often with Ruth when she asked for help with activities of daily living. When Ruth handled tasks on her own, Sybil usually withdrew.

Observations of people interacting with older adults in both private homes and institutions reveal two highly predictable, complementary behavior patterns. In the first, called the **dependency–support script,** dependent behaviors are attended to immediately. In the second, the **independence–ignore script,** independent behaviors are mostly ignored. Notice how these sequences reinforce dependent behavior at the expense of independent behavior, regardless of the older person's competencies (Baltes, 1995, 1996). Even a self-reliant individual like Ruth did not always resist Sybil's unnecessary help because it brought about social contact.

Among older people who experience no difficulty with daily activities, opportunities to interact with others are related to high satisfaction with everyday life. In contrast, among older adults who have trouble performing daily activities, social contact is linked to a less positive everyday existence (Lang & Baltes, 1997). This suggests that social interaction while assisting seniors with physical care, household chores, and errands is often not meaningful and rewarding but, rather, demeaning and unpleasant. Consider these typical reactions of care recipients to a spouse's help with daily activities: "felt indebted," "felt like a weak, incapable person" (Newsom, 1999).

Longitudinal research shows that negative reactions to caregiving can result in persisting depression (Newsom &

By letting her son help with grocery shopping, will this Mexican 80-year-old become too dependent? Not necessarily. When older adults assume personal control over areas of dependency, they can conserve their strength and invest it in highly valued activities.

Schulz, 1998). But whether assistance from others undermines well-being depends on many factors, including the quality of help, the caregiver–older adult relationship, and the social and cultural context in which helping occurs. In Western societies, which highly value independence, many older adults fear relinquishing control and becoming dependent on others (Curtiss, Hayslip, & Dolan, 2007; Frazier, 2002). As physical and cognitive limitations increase, granting older adults the freedom to choose those areas in which they desire help preserves their autonomy (Lachman, Neupert, & Agrigoroaei, 2011). Dependency can be adaptive if it permits older people to remain in control by choosing those areas in which they desire help. In this way, they can conserve their strength by investing it in self-chosen, highly valued activities, using a set of strategies considered in Chapter 17: *selective optimization with compensation.*

Assistance aimed at enabling older adults use their capacities fully in pursuit of their goals sustains an effective **person–environment fit**—a good match between their abilities and the demands of their living environments, which promotes adaptive behavior and psychological well-being. When people cannot maximize use of their capacities (have become excessively dependent), they react with boredom and passivity. When they encounter environmental demands that are too great (receive too little assistance), they experience overwhelming stress.

Physical Health

Physical declines and chronic disease can lead to a sense of loss of personal control—a powerful contributor to mental health problems. Physical illness resulting in disability is among the strongest risk factors for late-life depression (Morrison, 2008; Whitbourne & Meeks, 2011). Although fewer older than young and middle-aged adults are depressed (see Chapter 17), profound feelings of hopelessness rise with age as physical disability and consequent social isolation increase. But more than actual physical limitations, *perceived negative physical health* predicts depressive symptoms (Jang et al., 2007; Weinberger & Whitbourne, 2010). This helps explain the stronger physical impairment–depression relationship among higher-SES aging adults (Schieman & Plickert, 2007). Because of their lifetime of better physical health, they probably experience physical limitations as more unexpected and challenging.

Depression in old age is often lethal. People age 65 and older have the highest suicide rate of all age groups (see the Social Issues: Health box on page 486). What factors enable seniors like Ruth to surmount the physical impairment–depression relationship, remaining content? Personal characteristics discussed in this and earlier chapters—optimism, sense of self-efficacy, and effective coping—are vitally important (Morrison, 2008). But for frail aging adults to display these attributes, families and caregivers must avoid the dependency–support script and, instead, grant them autonomy.

Unfortunately, older adults generally do not get the mental health care they need—even in nursing homes, where depression and other mental health problems are widespread (Grabowski et al., 2010; Karel, Gatz, & Smyer, 2012). More than half of U.S. nursing home residents receive no regular mental health intervention.

Negative Life Changes

Ruth lost Walt to a heart attack, cared for her sister Ida as her Alzheimer's symptoms worsened, and faced health problems of her own—all within a span of a few years. Older adults are at risk for a variety of negative life changes—death of loved ones, illness and physical disabilities, declining income, and greater dependency. Negative life changes are difficult for everyone but may actually evoke less stress and depression in older than in younger adults (Charles, 2011). Many older people have learned to cope with hard times and to appraise negative changes as common and expected in late life.

Still, when negative changes pile up, they test the coping skills of older adults. In very old age, such changes are greater for women than for men. Women over age 75 are far less likely to be married, more often have lower incomes, and suffer from more illnesses—especially ones that restrict mobility. Furthermore, older women (as at younger ages) more often say that others depend on them for caregiving and emotional support. Thus, their social relations, even in very old age, are more often a source of stress (Antonucci, Ajrouch, & Birditt, 2008). And because of their own declining health, older women may not be able to meet others' needs for care—circumstances associated with chronic, high distress (Charles, 2010). Not surprisingly, women of advanced age tend to report lower psychological well-being than do men (Pinquart & Sörensen, 2001).

Social Support

In late adulthood, social support continues to reduce stress, thereby promoting physical health, psychological well-being, and longevity (Fry & Debats, 2006; Temkin-Greener et al., 2004). Usually, older adults receive informal assistance with tasks of daily living from family members—first from their spouse or, if none exists, from children and then from siblings.

Nevertheless, many older people place such high value on independence that they do not want extensive help from others close to them unless they can reciprocate. When assistance is excessive or cannot be returned, it often results in reduced self-efficacy and psychological stress (Liang, Krause, & Bennett, 2001; Warner et al., 2011). Perhaps for this reason, adult children express a deeper sense of obligation toward their aging parents than their parents expect from them. Formal support—a paid home helper or agency-provided services—as a complement to informal assistance not only helps relieve caregiving burden but also spares aging adults from feeling overly dependent in their close relationships.

Ethnic minority older adults are more willing to accept assistance when home helpers are connected to a familiar neighborhood organization, especially the church (Coke, 1992; Taylor, Lincoln, & Chatters, 2005). Support from religious congregants has psychological benefits for older people of all backgrounds, perhaps because recipients feel that it is motivated by genuine care and concern, not just obligation (Krause, 2001). Also, the warm atmosphere of religious organizations fosters a sense of social acceptance and belonging.

Overall, for social support to foster well-being, older adults must take personal control of it. As suggested earlier, this means consciously giving up primary control in some areas to remain in control of other, highly valued pursuits (Heckhausen, Wrosch, & Schultz, 2010). Help that is not wanted or needed or that exaggerates weaknesses results in poor person–environment fit, undermines mental health, and—if existing skills fall into disuse—accelerates physical disability. In contrast, help that increases autonomy—that frees up energy for endeavors that are personally satisfying and that lead to growth—enhances quality of life. These findings clarify why *perceived social support* (older adults' sense of being able to count on family or friends in times of need) is associated with a positive outlook in older adults with disabilities, whereas sheer *amount* of help family and friends provide has little impact (Uchino, 2009).

Finally, besides tangible assistance, older adults benefit from social support that offers affection, affirmation of their self-worth, and sense of belonging. As we will see in the next section, supportive social ties in old age have little to do with quantity of contact. Instead, high-quality relationships, involving expressions of kindness, encouragement, respect, and emotional closeness, have the greatest impact on mental health in late life.

Social Issues: Health

Elder Suicide

When 65-year-old Abe's wife died, he withdrew from life. Living far from his two daughters, he spent his nonworking days alone, watching television and reading mystery novels. As grandchildren were born, Abe visited his daughters' homes from time to time, carrying his despondent behavior with him.

After arthritis made walking difficult, Abe retired. With more empty days, his depression deepened. Gradually, he developed painful digestive difficulties, but he refused to see a doctor. "Don't need to," he said abruptly when one of his daughters begged him to get medical attention. Answering her invitation to a grandchild's tenth birthday party, Abe wrote, "Maybe—if I'm still around next month." Two weeks later, Abe died from an intestinal blockage. His body was found in the living room chair where he habitually spent his days. Although it may seem surprising, Abe's self-destructive acts are a form of suicide.

Factors Related to Elder Suicide

Recall from Chapter 12 that suicide increases over the lifespan. Although age differences in adulthood rates are shrinking, suicide continues to climb in late adulthood. Older adults are at increased risk in most countries throughout the world (World Health Organization, 2013b).

The higher suicide rate among males persists in late life. Five times as many U.S. aging men as women take their own lives. Suicide among white men age 70 and older rises steeply with age, whereas it actually declines after age 75 in women (U.S. Census Bureau, 2013). Compared with the white majority, most ethnic minority older adults have low suicide rates.

What explains these trends? Despite the lifelong pattern of higher rates of depression and more suicide attempts among females, older women's closer ties to family and friends, greater willingness to seek social support, and religiosity prevent many from taking their own lives. High levels of social support through extended families and church affiliations also may prevent suicide among ethnic minorities (Conwell, Van

Orden, & Caine, 2011). And within certain minority groups, such as Alaskan Natives, deep respect for older adults strengthens self-esteem and social integration (Kettl, 1998). This reduces elder suicide, making it nonexistent after age 80.

As in earlier years, the methods favored by older males (firearms, hanging) offer less chance of revival than those by older females (poisoning or drug overdose). Nevertheless, failed suicides are much rarer in old age than in adolescence (Conwell, Van Orden, & Caine, 2011). When seniors decide to die, they seem especially determined to succeed.

Underreporting of suicides probably occurs at all ages, but it is more common in old age. Medical examiners are less likely to pursue suicide as a cause of death when a person is old. And many older adults, like Abe, engage in indirect self-destructive acts rarely classified as suicide—refusing to eat or take prescribed medications. Among institutionalized seniors, these efforts to hasten death are widespread (Reiss & Tishler, 2008). Consequently, elder suicide is an even larger problem than official statistics indicate.

Two types of events prompt suicide in late life. Losses—retirement from a highly valued occupation, widowhood, or social isolation—place seniors who have difficulty coping with change at risk for persistent depression. Risks of another type arise when chronic and terminal illnesses severely reduce physical functioning or cause intense pain (Conwell et al., 2010). As comfort and quality of life diminish, feelings of hopelessness and helplessness deepen.

Prevention and Treatment

Warning signs of suicide in late adulthood, like those at earlier ages, include efforts to put personal affairs in order, statements about dying, despondency, and sleep and appetite changes. But family members, friends, and caregivers must also watch for indirect self-destructive acts that are unique to old age, such as refusing food or medical treatment. Too often, people in close touch with the elderly incorrectly assume that these symptoms are a "natural" consequence of aging.

Suicide reaches its highest rate among people age 75 and older. Warning signs include despondency, sleep and appetite changes, statements about dying, and efforts to put personal affairs in order.

When suicidal aging adults are depressed, the most effective treatment combines antidepressant medication with therapy, including help in coping with role transitions, such as retirement, widowhood, and dependency brought about by illness. Distorted ways of thinking ("I'm old—nothing can be done about my problems") must be countered and revised. Meeting with the family to find ways to reduce loneliness and desperation is also helpful.

Communities are beginning to recognize the importance of additional preventive steps, such as programs that help older adults cope with life transitions, telephone hot lines with trained volunteers who provide emotional support, and agencies that arrange for regular home visitors or "buddy system" phone calls (Lapierr et al., 2011). But so far, most of these efforts benefit women more than men because women are more likely to tell health professionals about high-risk symptoms and to use social resources.

Finally, elder suicide raises a controversial ethical issue: Do people with incurable illnesses have the right to take their own lives? We will take up this topic in Chapter 19.

ASK YOURSELF

REVIEW Many older people adapt effectively to negative life changes. List personal and situational factors that facilitate this generally positive outcome.

APPLY At age 85, Miriam took a long time to get dressed. Joan, her home helper, said, "From now on, don't get dressed until I get there. Then I can help, and it won't take so long." What impact is Joan's approach likely to have on Miriam's mental health? What alternative approach would you recommend?

REFLECT Among older people you know, do any fit the description of a Third Ager? Explain.

A Changing Social World

In late adulthood, extroverted individuals (like Walt and Ruth) continue to interact with a wider range of people than do introverts and people (like Dick) with poor social skills. Nevertheless, both cross-sectional and longitudinal research reveals that size of social networks and, therefore, amount of social interaction decline for virtually everyone (Antonucci, Akiyama, & Takahashi, 2004; Charles & Carstensen, 2009). This finding presents a curious paradox: If social interaction and social support are essential for mental health, how is it possible for older adults to interact less yet be generally satisfied with life and less depressed than younger adults?

Social Theories of Aging

Social theories of aging offer explanations for changes in aging adults' social activity. Two older perspectives—disengagement theory and activity theory—interpret declines in social interaction in opposite ways. More recent approaches—continuity theory and socioemotional selectivity theory—account for a wider range of findings.

Disengagement Theory.

According to **disengagement theory,** mutual withdrawal between older adults and society takes place in anticipation of death (Cumming & Henry, 1961). Older people decrease their activity levels and interact less frequently, becoming more preoccupied with their inner lives. At the same time, society frees the old from employment and family responsibilities. The result is viewed as beneficial for both sides. Aging adults are granted a life of tranquility. And once they disengage, their deaths are less disruptive to society.

Clearly, however, most aging adults don't disengage! As we saw in Chapter 17 when we discussed wisdom, older people in many cultures move into new positions of prestige and power because of their long life experience. Even after retirement, many adults sustain aspects of their work; others develop new,

rewarding roles in their communities. Disengagement, then, may represent not older peoples' personal preference but, rather, a failure of the social world to provide opportunities for engagement. Indeed, an obvious application of disengagement theory—encouraging older people to withdraw from vital roles—can have profound negative consequences for their sense of self-worth and, at a societal level, waste valuable social resources!

As we will see shortly, older adults' retreat from interaction is more complex than disengagement theory implies. Instead of disengaging from all social ties, they let go of unsatisfying contacts and maintain satisfying ones.

Activity Theory.

Attempting to overcome the flaws of disengagement theory, **activity theory** states that social barriers to engagement, not the desires of aging adults, cause declining rates of interaction. When older people lose certain roles (for example, through retirement or widowhood), they try to find others in an effort to stay about as active and busy as they were in middle age (Maddox, 1963). In this view, older adults' life satisfaction depends on conditions that permit them to remain engaged in roles and relationships.

Although people do seek alternative sources of meaning in response to social losses, activity theory fails to acknowledge any psychological change in old age. Many studies show that merely offering seniors opportunities for social contact does not lead to greater social activity. In nursing homes, for example, where social partners are abundant, social interaction is very low, even among the healthiest residents—a circumstance we will examine when we discuss housing arrangements for aging adults. Especially troubling for activity theory is the repeated finding that when health status is controlled, older people who have larger social networks and engage in more activities are not necessarily happier (Charles & Carstensen, 2009). Recall that quality, not quantity, of relationships predicts psychological well-being in old age.

Continuity Theory.

According to **continuity theory,** rather than maintaining a certain activity level, most aging adults strive to maintain a personal system—an identity and a set of personality dispositions, interests, roles, and skills—that promotes life satisfaction by ensuring consistency between their past and anticipated future. This striving for continuity does not mean that older people's lives are static. To the contrary, aging produces inevitable change, but most older adults try to minimize stress and disruptiveness by integrating those changes into a coherent, consistent life path. As much as possible, they choose to use familiar skills and engage in familiar activities with familiar people—preferences that provide a secure sense of routine and direction in life.

Research confirms a high degree of continuity in older adults' everyday pursuits and relationships. Even after a change (such as retirement), people usually make choices that extend the previous direction of their lives, engaging in new activities but often within familiar domains. For example, a retired manager of a children's bookstore collaborated with friends to build a children's library and donate it to an overseas orphanage. A musician who, because of arthritis, could no longer play the violin arranged regular get-togethers with musically inclined friends to listen to and talk about music. Robert Atchley (1989), originator of continuity theory, noted, "Everyday life for most older people is like long-running improvisational theater in which . . . changes are mostly in the form of new episodes [rather] than entirely new plays" (p. 185).

Aging adults' reliance on continuity has many benefits. Participating in familiar activities with familiar people provides repeated practice that helps preserve physical and cognitive functioning, fosters self-esteem and mastery, and affirms identity (Finchum & Weber, 2000; Vacha-Haase, Hill, & Bermingham, 2012). Investing in long-standing, close relationships provides comfort, pleasure, and a network of social support. Finally, striving for continuity is essential for attaining Erikson's sense of ego integrity, which depends on preserving a sense of personal history (Atchley, 1999).

Socioemotional Selectivity Theory.

A final perspective addresses how people's social networks sustain continuity while also narrowing as they age. According to **socioemotional selectivity theory**, social interaction extends lifelong selection processes. In middle adulthood, marital relationships deepen, siblings feel closer, and number of friendships declines. In old

These sisters—ages 93 and 89—greet each other with enthusiasm. The one on the right traveled from Poland to New York City for this reunion. To preserve emotional equilibrium and reduce stress, older adults increasingly emphasize familiar, emotionally rewarding relationships.

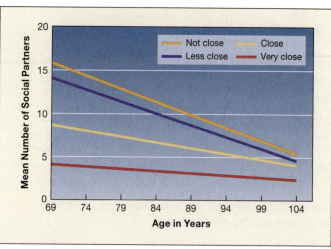

FIGURE 18.1 Age-related change in number of social partners varying in closeness. In interviews with over 500 older adults ranging in age from 69 to 104, the number of "not close" and "less close" partners fell off steeply with age, whereas the number of "close" and "very close" partners declined minimally. (From F. R. Lang, U. M. Staudinger, & L. L. Carstensen, 1998, "Perspectives on Socioemotional Selectivity in Late Life: How Personality and Social Context Do (and Do Not) Make a Difference," *Journal of Gerontology, 53B*, p. 24. Copyright © 1998 The Gerontological Society of America. Adapted by permission of Oxford University Press and F. R. Lang.)

age, contacts with family and long-term friends are sustained until the eighties, when they diminish gradually in favor of a few very close relationships. In contrast, as Figure 18.1 shows, contacts with acquaintances and willingness to form new social ties fall off steeply from middle through late adulthood (Carstensen, 2006; Carstensen, Fung, & Charles, 2003; Fung, Carstensen, & Lang, 2001).

What explains these changes? Socioemotional selectivity theory states that physical and psychological aspects of aging lead to changes in the functions of social interaction. ***TAKE A MOMENT...*** Consider the reasons you interact with members of your social network. At times, you approach them to get information. At other times, you seek affirmation of your worth as a person. You also choose social partners to regulate emotion, approaching those who evoke positive feelings and avoiding those who make you feel sad, angry, or uncomfortable. For older adults, who have gathered a lifetime of information, the information-gathering function becomes less significant. Also, they realize it is risky to approach people they do not know for self-affirmation: Negative stereotypes of aging increase the odds of receiving a condescending, hostile, or indifferent response.

Instead, as physical fragility makes it more important to avoid stress, older adults emphasize the emotion-regulating function of interaction. In one study, younger and older adults were asked to categorize their social partners. Younger people more often sorted them on the basis of information seeking and future contact, whereas older people emphasized anticipated feelings (Frederickson & Carstensen, 1990). They appeared highly motivated to approach pleasant relationships and avoid unpleasant ones. Interacting mostly with relatives and friends increases the chances that emotional equilibrium will be preserved. Within these close bonds, older adults actively apply their emotional expertise to promote harmony. They are less likely than younger people to respond to tensions with destructive tactics (yelling, arguing) and more likely to use constructive strategies, such as expressing affection or disengaging to calmly let the situation blow over (Birditt & Fingerman, 2005; Luong, Charles, & Fingerman, 2011). They also reinterpret conflict in less stressful ways—often by identifying something positive in the situation (Labouvie-Vief, 2003). Consequently, despite their smaller social networks, they are happier than younger people with their number of friends and report fewer problematic relationships (Blanchard-Fields & Coats, 2008; Fingerman & Birditt, 2003).

Research confirms that people's perception of time is strongly linked to their social goals. When remaining time is limited, adults *of all ages* shift from focusing on long-term goals to emphasizing emotionally fulfilling relationships in the here and now (Charles & Carstensen, 2010). Similarly, seniors—aware that time is "running out"—don't waste it on unlikely future payoffs but, instead, turn to close friends and family members. Furthermore, we generally take special steps to facilitate positive interaction with people dear to us whose time is limited—for example, treating older friends and relatives more kindly than younger ones, easily excusing or forgiving their social transgressions (Luong, Charles, & Fingerman, 2011). In this way, social partners contribute to older adults' gratifying relationship experiences. In sum, socioemotional selectivity theory views older adults' preference for high-quality, emotionally fulfilling relationships as resulting from changing life conditions.

Social Contexts of Aging: Communities, Neighborhoods, and Housing

The physical and social contexts in which aging adults live affect their social experiences and, consequently, their development and adjustment. Communities, neighborhoods, and housing arrangements vary in the extent to which they enable aging residents to satisfy their social needs.

Communities and Neighborhoods.
About half of U.S. ethnic minority older adults live in cities, compared with just one-third of Caucasians. The majority of seniors reside in suburbs, where they moved earlier in their lives and usually remain after retirement. Suburban older adults have higher incomes and report better health than their inner-city counterparts do. But inner-city older people are better off in terms of public transportation. As declines in physical functioning compromise out-of-home mobility, convenient bus, tram, and rail lines become increasingly important to life satisfaction and psychological well-being (Mollenkopf, Hieber, & Wahl, 2011;

Oswald et al., 2010). Furthermore, city-dwelling seniors fare better in terms of health, income, and proximity of social services and cultural activities than do the one-fifth of U.S. older people who live in small towns and rural areas (U.S. Department of Health and Human Services, 2012e). In addition, small-town and rural seniors are less likely to live near their children, who often leave these communities in early adulthood.

Yet small-town and rural aging adults compensate for distance from children and social services by establishing closer relationships with nearby extended family and by interacting more with neighbors and friends (Hooyman & Kiyak, 2011; Shaw, 2005). Smaller communities have features that foster gratifying relationships—stability of residents, shared values and lifestyles, willingness to exchange social support, and frequent social visits as country people "drop in" on one another. And many suburban and rural communities have responded to aging residents' needs by developing transportation programs (such as special buses and vans) to take them to health and social services, senior centers, and shopping centers.

Both urban and rural older adults report greater life satisfaction when many senior citizens reside in their neighborhood and are available as like-minded companions. Presence of family is less crucial when neighbors and nearby friends provide social support (Gabriel & Bowling, 2004). This does not mean that neighbors replace family relationships. But older adults are content as long as their children and other relatives who live far away arrange occasional visits (Hooyman & Kiyak, 2011).

Housing Arrangements.
Seniors' housing preferences reflect a strong desire for **aging in place**—remaining in a familiar setting where they have control over their everyday life. Overwhelmingly, older people in Western nations want to stay in the neighborhoods where they spent their adult lives; in fact, 90 percent remain in or near their old home. In the United States, fewer than 4 percent relocate to other communities (U.S.

Like many older adults, these dog lovers reap great satisfaction from residing in a neighborhood with like-minded senior residents. Presence of family is less crucial when neighbors and nearby friends provide social support.

Department of Health and Human Services, 2012e). These moves are usually motivated by a desire to live closer to children or, among the more economically advantaged and healthy, a desire for a more temperate climate and a place to pursue leisure interests.

Most aging adults' relocations occur within the same town or city and are prompted by declining health, widowhood, or disability (Sergeant, Ekerdt, & Chapin, 2008). As we look at housing arrangements for older adults, we will see that the more a setting deviates from home life, the harder it is for older people to adjust.

Ordinary Homes. For the majority of older adults, who are not physically impaired, staying in their own homes affords the greatest possible personal control. More seniors in Western countries live on their own today than ever before—a trend due to improved health and economic well-being (U.S. Department of Health and Human Services, 2012e). But when health and mobility problems appear, independent living poses risks to an effective person–environment fit. Most homes are not modified to suit the physical capacities of their aging residents. Living alone with a physical disability is linked to social isolation and loneliness (Adams, Sanders, & Auth, 2004).

When Ruth reached her mid-eighties, Sybil begged her to move into her home. Like many adult children of Southern, Central, and Eastern European descent (Greek, Italian, Polish, and others), Sybil felt an especially strong obligation to care for her frail mother. Older adults of these cultural backgrounds, as well as African Americans, Asians, Hispanics, and Native Americans, more often live in extended families (see page 434 in Chapter 16).

Yet increasing numbers of ethnic minority older adults want to live on their own. For example, two decades ago, most Asian-American older adults were living with their children, whereas today 65 percent live independently—a trend also evident in certain Asian nations, such as Japan (Federal Interagency Forum on Aging Related Statistics, 2012; Takagi, Silverstein, & Crimmins, 2007). With sufficient income to keep her home, Ruth refused to move in with Sybil. Continuity theory helps us understand why many older adults react this way, even after health problems accumulate. As the site of memorable life events, the home strengthens continuity with the past, sustaining a sense of identity in the face of physical declines and social losses. And it permits older adults to adapt to their surroundings in familiar, comfortable ways (Atchley, 1999). Older people also value their independence, privacy, and network of nearby friends and neighbors.

During the past half century, the number of unmarried, divorced, and widowed seniors living alone has risen dramatically. Approximately 30 percent of U.S. older adults live by themselves, a figure that rises to nearly 50 percent for those age 85 and older (U.S. Census Bureau, 2013). Over 40 percent of American seniors who live alone are poverty-stricken—rates many times greater than among older couples. More than 70 percent are widowed women. Because of lower earnings in

Residents of a retirement community join visiting Girl Scouts to bake dog treats for animal shelters. By sustaining an effective person–environment fit as capacities change, residential communities enable older adults to enjoy a more active lifestyle.

earlier years, some entered old age this way. Others became poor for the first time, often because they outlived a spouse who suffered a lengthy, costly illness. With age, their financial status worsens as their assets shrink and their own health-care costs rise (Biegel & Liebbrant, 2006; U.S. Census Bureau, 2013). Under these conditions, isolation, loneliness, and depression can pile up. Poverty among lone aging women is deeper in the United States than in other Western nations because of less generous government-sponsored income and health benefits.

Residential Communities. About 7 percent of U.S. adults age 65 and older live in residential communities, a proportion that rises with age as functional limitations increase. Among people age 85 and older, 22 percent live in these communities, which come in great variety (U.S. Department of Health and Human Services, 2012e). Housing developments for the aged, either single-dwelling or apartment complexes, differ from ordinary homes only in that they have been modified to suit older adults' capacities (featuring, for example, single-level living space and grab bars in bathrooms).

For older adults who need more help with everyday tasks, *assisted-living* arrangements are available (see Chapter 17, page 467). **Congregate housing**—an increasingly popular long-term care option—provides a variety of support services, including meals in a common dining room, along with watchful oversight of residents with physical and mental disabilities. **Life-care communities** offer a range of housing alternatives, from independent or congregate housing to full nursing home care. For a large initial payment and additional monthly fees, life care guarantees that seniors' changing needs will be met within the same facility as they age.

Dick and Goldie decided in their late sixties to move to nearby congregate housing. For Dick, the move was a positive turn of events that permitted him to set aside past failures and relate to peers on the basis of their current life together. Dick found gratifying leisure pursuits—leading an exercise class, organizing a charity drive with Goldie, and using his skills as a baker to make cakes for birthday and anniversary celebrations.

By sustaining an effective person–environment fit as older adults' capacities change, residential communities have positive effects on physical and mental health. A specially designed physical space and care on an as-needed basis help seniors overcome mobility limitations, enabling greater social participation and a more active lifestyle (Fonda, Clipp, & Maddox, 2002; Jenkins, Pienta, & Horgas, 2002). And in societies where old age leads to reduced status, age-segregated living can be gratifying, opening up useful roles and leadership opportunities. The more older adults perceive the environment as socially supportive, the more they collaborate with one another in coping with stressors of aging and in providing assistance to other residents (Lawrence & Schigelone, 2002).

Nevertheless, no U.S. federal regulations govern assisted-living facilities, which vary widely in quality. Low-income ethnic minority seniors are less likely to use assisted living, and, when they do, usually enter lower-quality settings—conditions associated with high stress (Ball et al., 2009). And in some states, assisted-living facilities are prohibited from providing any nursing care and monitoring, requiring seniors to leave when their health declines (Hernandez & Newcomer, 2007). Yet physical designs and support services that enable aging in place are vital for aging adults' well-being. These include homelike surroundings, division of large environments into smaller units to facilitate meaningful activities and social relationships, and the latest assistive technologies (Cutler, 2007; Oswald & Wahl, 2013).

Shared values and goals among residents with similar backgrounds also enhance life satisfaction. Older adults who feel socially integrated into the setting are more likely to consider it their home. But those who lack like-minded companions are at high risk for loneliness and depression (Adams, Sanders, & Auth, 2004; Cutchin, 2013).

LOOK AND LISTEN

Visit an assisted-living community, and explore its housing options, physical design, and social and leisure opportunities. How well does the living environment support aging in place and effective person–environment fit? ●

Nursing Homes. The 5 percent of Americans age 65 and older who live in nursing homes experience the most extreme restriction of autonomy and social integration. Although potential companions are abundant, interaction is low. To regulate emotion in social interaction (so important to aging adults), personal control over social experiences is vital. Yet nursing home residents have little opportunity to choose their social partners, and timing of contact is generally deter-

mined by staff. Social withdrawal is an adaptive response to these often overcrowded, hospital-like settings, which typically provide few ways for residents to use their competencies. Not surprisingly, nursing home residents with physical but not mental impairments are far more depressed, anxious, and lonely than their community-dwelling counterparts (Guildner et al., 2001).

Designing more homelike nursing homes could help increase residents' sense of security and control. U.S. nursing homes, usually operated for profit, are often packed with residents and institutional in their operation. In contrast, European facilities are liberally supported by public funds and resemble high-quality assisted living.

In a radically changed U.S. nursing home concept called THE GREEN HOUSE® model, a large, outdated nursing home in Mississippi was replaced by ten small houses, each with ten or fewer residents who live in private bedroom–bathroom suites surrounding a family-style communal space (Rabig et al., 2006). Besides providing personal care, a stable staff of nursing assistants fosters aging adults' control and independence. Residents determine their own daily schedules and are invited to join in both recreational and household activities. A professional support team—including licensed nurses, therapists, social workers, physicians, and pharmacists—visits regularly to serve residents' health needs.

In a comparison of Green House residents with traditional nursing home residents, Green House older adults reported

THE GREEN HOUSE® model blurs distinctions among nursing home, assisted living, and "independent" living. In this homelike setting, residents determine their own daily schedules and help with household tasks. Green House living environments now exist in more than 20 U.S. states.

substantially better quality of life, and they also showed less decline over time in ability to carry out activities of daily living (Kane et al., 2007). By making the home a central, organizing principle, the Green House approach includes all the aging-in-place and effective person–environment fit features that ensure late-life well-being.

ASK YOURSELF

REVIEW Cite features of neighborhoods and residential communities that enhance aging adults' life satisfaction.

APPLY Sam lives alone in the same home he has occupied for over 30 years. His adult children cannot understand why he won't move across town to a modern apartment. Using continuity theory, explain why Sam prefers to stay where he is.

REFLECT Imagine yourself as an aging resident in assisted living. List all the features you would want your living context to have, explaining how each helps ensure effective person–environment fit and favorable psychological well-being.

Relationships in Late Adulthood

The **social convoy** is an influential model of changes in our social networks as we move through life. *TAKE A MOMENT...* Picture yourself in the midst of a cluster of ships traveling together, granting one another safety and support. Ships in the inner circle represent people closest to you, such as a spouse, best friend, parent, or child. Those less close, but still important, travel on the outside. With age, ships exchange places in the convoy, and some drift off while others join the procession (Antonucci, Birditt, & Ajrouch, 2011; Antonucci, Birditt, & Akiyama, 2009). As long as the convoy continues to exist, you adapt positively.

In the following sections, we examine the ways older adults with diverse lifestyles sustain social networks of family members and friends. Although size of the convoy decreases as age-mates die, aging adults are rarely left without people in their inner circle who contribute to their well-being—a testament to their resilience in maintaining effective social networks (Fiori, Smith, & Antonucci, 2007). But for some, tragically, the social convoy breaks down. We will also explore the circumstances in which older people experience abuse and neglect at the hands of those close to them.

Marriage

Even with the high U.S. divorce rate, one in every four or five first marriages is expected to last at least 50 years. Walt's comment to Ruth that "the last few decades have been the happiest" characterizes the attitudes and behaviors of many aging couples

After retirement, couples have more time to devote to joint leisure activities, which contributes to the rise in marital satisfaction from middle to late adulthood.

who have spent their adult lives together. Marital satisfaction rises from middle to late adulthood, when it is at its peak (Ko et al., 2007). Several changes in life circumstance and couples' communication underlie this trend.

First, late-life marriages involve fewer stressful responsibilities that can negatively affect relationships, such as rearing children and balancing demands of career and family (Diamond, Fagundes, & Butterworth, 2010). Second, perceptions of fairness in the relationship increase as men participate more in household tasks after retirement (Kulik, 2001). Third, with extra time together, the majority of couples engage in more joint leisure activities, which—especially for women—enhances sense of marital closeness (Trudel et al., 2008).

Fourth, greater emotional understanding and emphasis on regulating emotion in relationships lead to more positive interactions between spouses. Compared to younger couples, aging couples rate their relationship as higher in quality, disagree less often, and resolve their differences in more constructive ways. Even in unhappy marriages, older adults are less likely to let their disagreements escalate into expressions of anger and resentment (Hatch & Bulcroft, 2004). As in other relationships, seniors protect themselves from stress by molding marital ties to make them as pleasant as possible.

Finally, compared to their single agemates, married seniors generally have larger social networks of both family members and friends, which provide for social engagement and support and are linked to higher psychological well-being (Birditt & Antonucci, 2007; Fiori, Smith, & Antonucci, 2007). When marital dissatisfaction exists, however, even having close, high-quality friendships cannot reduce its profoundly negative impact on adjustment. A poor marriage often takes a greater toll on women than on men (Birditt & Antonucci, 2007; Whisman et al., 2006). Recall from Chapter 14 that women more often try to work on a troubling relationship, yet in late life, expending energy in this way is especially taxing, both physically and mentally.

Gay and Lesbian Partnerships

Most older gays and lesbians in long-term partnerships report happy, highly fulfilling relationships, pointing to their partner as their most important source of social support. Compared with gay and lesbian seniors who live alone, couples rate their physical and mental health more favorably (Grossman, 2006).

A lifetime of effective coping with an oppressive social environment may have strengthened homosexuals' skill at dealing with late-life physical and social changes, thereby contributing to a satisfying partnership (Gabbay & Wahler, 2002). And changing social conditions, including the greater ease with which younger generations embrace their sexual minority identities and "come out," may have encouraged more older adults to do the same, with benefits for their well-being (Cohler & Hostetler, 2007). Also, greater gender-role flexibility enables gay and lesbian couples to adapt easily to sharing household tasks following retirement.

Nevertheless, because of continuing prejudice, aging gays and lesbians face unique challenges. Health-care systems are often unresponsive to their unique needs. And where gay and lesbian unions are not legally recognized (in most U.S. states), if one partner becomes frail or ill, the other may not be welcome in hospitals or nursing homes or be allowed to participate in health-care decisions—an issue we will return to in Chapter 19. These circumstances can make late-life declines and losses especially painful.

Divorce, Remarriage, and Cohabitation

When Walt's uncle Louie was 65, he divorced his wife Sandra after 32 years of marriage. Although she knew the marriage was far from perfect, Sandra had lived with Louie long enough that the divorce came as a shock. A year later, Louie married Rachella, a divorcée who shared his enthusiasm for sports and dance.

Couples who divorce in late adulthood constitute less than 5 percent of all U.S. divorces in any given year (Elliott & Simmons, 2011). But the divorce rate among people age 65 and older has increased over the past three decades as new generations of seniors—especially the baby boomers—have become accepting of marital breakup as a means of attaining self-fulfillment and as the divorce risk has risen for second and subsequent marriages.

Although one-fifth of older adults' dissolving marriages are of less than 10 years duration, about half are lengthy—30 years or more (Brown & Lin, 2012). Compared with younger adults, longtime married older people find it harder to separate their identity from that of their former spouse and, therefore, may experience a greater sense of personal failure. Relationships with family and friends shift at a time when close bonds are crucial for psychological well-being.

As in middle adulthood, aging women are more likely than men to initiate divorce. This is despite the fact that the financial consequences for women generally are severe—greater than for widowhood because many accumulated assets are lost in property settlements (McDonald & Robb, 2004; Wu & Schimmele, 2007). Still, older people of both genders seldom express regret over leaving an unhappy marriage (Bair, 2007). Usually, they experience a sense of relief.

Remarriage rates are low in late adulthood and decline with age, though remarriage is more likely after divorce than after widowhood. Aging baby boomers—accustomed to using the Internet for many purposes—are increasingly turning to contemporary ways of searching for new partners, including online dating services and personal ads, though they use dating sites far less often than younger people do. But older peoples' personal ads indicate that they are more selective with respect to the age, race, religion, and income of a potential dating partner (McIntosh et al., 2011). And as Figure 18.2 shows, they more often refer to their own health issues and loneliness and less often to romance, sex, desire for a soulmate, and adventure than middle-aged people do (Alterovitz & Mendelsohn, 2013). In their search for the right person, seniors seem to take a candid, no-nonsense approach!

Compared with younger people who remarry, seniors who do so enter more stable relationships, as their divorce rate is much lower. In Louie and Rachella's case, the second marriage lasted for 28 years! Perhaps late-life remarriages are more successful because they involve more maturity, patience, and a better balance of romantic with practical concerns. Remarried

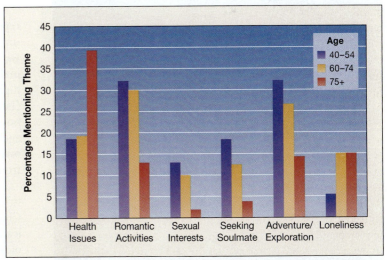

FIGURE 18.2 Themes in online personal ads of middle-aged and older adults seeking dating partners. An analysis of themes in 450 ads revealed that older adults more often mention health issues and loneliness, whereas middle-aged adults place greater emphasis on romance, sex, finding a soulmate, and adventure. Seniors appear to be practical and direct in their search for a partner. (From S. S. R. Alterovitz and G. A. Mendelsohn, 2013, "Relationship Goals of Middle-Aged, Young–Old, and Old–Old Internet Daters: An Analysis of Online Personal Ads." *Journal of Aging Studies, 27,* p. 163. Copyright © 2013, Elsevier. Reprinted by permission of Elsevier, Inc.)

older couples are generally very satisfied with their new relationships, although men tend to be more content than women (Clarke, 2005; Connidis, 2010). With fewer potential mates, perhaps women who remarry in late life settle for less desirable partners.

Rather than remarrying, seniors who enter a new relationship are increasingly choosing cohabitation. Like remarriage, cohabitation results in more stable relationships and higher relationship quality than it did at younger ages. And cohabiting seniors are as satisfied with their partnered lives as are their married counterparts (Brown & Kawamura, 2010). This suggests that cohabitation is distinctive in late adulthood, serving as a long-term alternative to marriage.

Widowhood

Walt died shortly after Ruth turned 80. Like over 70 percent of widowed seniors, Ruth described the loss of her spouse as the most stressful event of her life. As two researchers noted, being widowed means that the survivor has "lost the role and identity of being a spouse (being married and doing things as a couple), which is potentially one of the most pervasive, intense, intimate, and personal roles that they have ever had" (Lund & Caserta, 2004a, p. 29).

Widows make up about one-third of older adults in industrialized nations. Because women live longer than men and are less likely to remarry, more than 40 percent of U.S. women age 65 and older are widowed, compared with just 13 percent of men (U.S. Census Bureau, 2013). Ethnic minorities with

Because most men rely on their wives for social connectedness, they are less prepared than women to overcome the loneliness of widowhood. This widower, however, makes an effort to connect socially with neighbors by hosting a backyard barbecue.

high rates of poverty and chronic disease are more likely to be widowed.

The greatest problem for recently widowed older people is profound loneliness (Connidis, 2010). But adaptation varies widely, depending on age, social support, and personality. Aging adults have fewer lasting problems than younger individuals who are widowed, probably because death in later life is viewed as less unfair (Bennett & Soulsby, 2012). And most widowed seniors—especially those with outgoing personalities and high self-esteem—are resilient in the face of loneliness (Moore & Stratton, 2002; van Baarsen, 2002). To sustain continuity with their past, they try to preserve social relationships that were important before the spouse's death and report that relatives and friends respond in kind, contacting them at least as often as before (Utz et al., 2002). Also, the stronger aging adults' sense of self-efficacy in handling tasks of daily living, the more favorably they adjust (Fry, 2001).

Nevertheless, widowed individuals must reorganize their lives, reconstructing an identity that is separate from the deceased spouse. Overall, men show more physical and mental health problems and greater risk of mortality than women, for several reasons (Bennett, Smith, & Hughes, 2005; Shor et al., 2012). First, because most men relied on their wives for social connectedness, household tasks, promotion of healthy behaviors, and coping with stressors, they are less prepared than women for the challenges of widowhood. Second, because of gender-role expectations, men feel less free to express their emotions or to ask for help with meals, household tasks, and social relationships (Bennett, 2007; Lund & Caserta, 2004b). Finally, men tend to be less involved in religious activities—a vital source of social support and inner strength.

In two studies of older widowers, those in their seventies reported the most depression and showed the slowest rate of improvement over the following two years. The death of their wives occurred around the time they were adjusting to retirement, resulting in two major changes at once, with widowhood highly unexpected because most wives outlive their husbands (Lund & Caserta, 2001, 2004a). African-American widowers, however, show no elevated risk of mortality over their married agemates, and they report less depression than Caucasian widowers (Elwert & Christakis, 2006). Perhaps greater support from extended family and church is responsible.

Sex differences in the experience of widowhood contribute to men's higher remarriage rate. Women's kinkeeper role (see Chapter 16, page 433) and ability to form close friendships may lead them to feel less need to remarry. In addition, because many older women share the widowed state, they probably offer one another helpful advice and sympathy. In contrast, men often lack skills for maintaining family relationships, forming emotionally satisfying ties outside marriage, and handling the chores of their deceased wives.

Still, widowed seniors of both sexes who participated in several months of weekly classes providing information and support in acquiring daily living skills felt better prepared to

Applying What We Know

Fostering Adaptation to Widowhood in Late Adulthood

Suggestion	Description
Self	
Mastery of new skills of daily living	Especially for men, learning how to perform household tasks such as shopping and cooking, to sustain existing family and friendship ties, and to build new relationships is vital for positive adaptation.
Family and Friends	
Social support and interaction	Social support and interaction must extend beyond the grieving period to ongoing assistance and caring relationships. Family members and friends can help most by making support available while encouraging the widowed older adult to use effective coping strategies.
Community	
Senior centers	Senior centers offer communal meals and other social activities, enabling widowed and other older adults to connect with people in similar circumstances and to gain access to other community resources, such as listings of part-time employment and available housing.
Support groups	Support groups can be found in senior centers, religious institutions, and other agencies. Besides new relationships, they offer an accepting atmosphere for coming to terms with loss, effective role models, and assistance with developing skills for daily living.
Religious activities	Involvement in a church, synagogue, or mosque can help relieve the loneliness associated with loss of a spouse and offer social support, new relationships, and meaningful roles.
Volunteer activities	One of the best ways for widowed older adults to find meaningful roles is through volunteer activities. Some are sponsored by formal service organizations, such as the Red Cross or the Retired and Senior Volunteer Program. Other volunteer programs exist in hospitals, senior centers, schools, and charitable organizations.

manage the challenges of widowed life (Caserta, Lund, & Obray, 2004). Those who emerge from this traumatic event with a sense of purpose in life and with confidence in their ability to meet everyday challenges often experience stress-related personal growth (Caserta et al., 2009). Many report a newfound sense of inner strength, greater appreciation of close relationships, and reevaluation of life priorities. Applying What We Know above suggests a variety of ways to foster adaptation to widowhood in late adulthood.

Never-Married, Childless Older Adults

Shortly after Ruth and Walt's marriage in their twenties, Ruth's father died. Her sister Ida continued to live with and care for their mother, who was in ill health until she died 16 years later. When, at age 25, Ida received a marriage proposal, she responded, "I can't marry anybody while my mother is still living. I'm expected to look after her." Ida's decision was not unusual for a daughter of her day. She never married or had children.

About 5 percent of older Americans have remained unmarried and childless throughout their lives. Almost all are conscious of being different from the norm, but most have developed alternative meaningful relationships. Ida, for example, formed a strong bond with a neighbor's son. In his childhood, she provided emotional support and financial assistance, which

helped him overcome a stressful home life. He included Ida in family events and visited her regularly until she died. Other nonmarried seniors speak of the centrality of extended family and of younger people in their social networks—often nieces

SUSAN WATTS/NY DAILY NEWS VIA GETTY IMAGES

For this never-married older adult, a warm relationship with his great-nephew provides a sense of family connection and an opportunity to influence a member of a younger generation.

and nephews—and of influencing them in enduring ways (Wenger, 2009; Wenger & Burholdt, 2001). In addition, same-sex friendships are key in never-married older women's lives (McDill, Hall, & Turell, 2006). These tend to be unusually close and often involve joint travel, periods of coresidence, and associations with each other's extended families.

Never-married, childless men are more likely than women to feel lonely and depressed. And without pressure from a partner to maintain a healthy lifestyle, they engage in more unhealthy behaviors. Hence, their physical and mental health is poor compared with their married counterparts (Kendig et al., 2007). Never-married older women report a level of well-being equivalent to that of married older adults and greater than that of divorcées and recently widowed seniors. Only when they cannot maintain social contacts because of declining health do they report feeling lonely (Dykstra, 2009).

Because friendships are not the same as blood ties when it comes to caregiving, being unmarried and childless in very old age reduces the likelihood of informal personal care (Chang, Wilber, & Silverstein, 2010; Wenger, 2009). Still, most say that some informal support is available.

Siblings

Nearly 80 percent of Americans age 65 and older have at least one living sibling. Most live within 100 miles of each other, communicate regularly, and visit at least several times a year. Both men and women describe closer bonds with sisters than with brothers. Perhaps because of women's greater emotional expressiveness and nurturance, the closer the tie to a sister, the higher older people's psychological well-being (Van Volkom, 2006).

Aging siblings in industrialized nations are more likely to socialize than to provide one another with direct assistance because most turn first to their spouse and children. Nevertheless, siblings seem to be an important "insurance policy" in late adulthood. After age 70, aid from siblings living near one another rises (White, 2001). Widowed and never-married seniors have more contacts with siblings, perhaps because they have fewer competing family relationships, and they also are more likely to receive sibling support when their health declines (Connidis, 2010). For example, when Ida's Alzheimer's symptoms worsened, Ruth came to her aid. Although Ida had many friends, Ruth was her only living relative.

Friendships

As family responsibilities and vocational pressures lessen, friendships take on increasing importance. Having friends is an especially strong predictor of mental health among seniors (Rawlins, 2004). Older adults report more favorable experiences with friends than with family members, in part because of the pleasurable leisure activities shared with friends (Larson, Mannell, & Zuzanek, 1986). Unique qualities of friendship interaction—openness, spontaneity, mutual caring, and common interests—are also influential.

Functions of Late-Life Friendships. The diverse functions of friendship in late adulthood clarify its profound significance:

● *Intimacy and companionship.* As Ida and her best friend, Rosie, took walks, went shopping, or visited each other, they disclosed their deepest sources of happiness and worry. Mutual interests, feelings of belongingness, and opportunities to confide in each other sustain these bonds over time (Field, 1999).

● *A shield against negative judgments stemming from stereotypes of aging.* "Where's your cane, Rosie?" Ida asked when the two women were about to leave for a restaurant. "Come on, don't be self-conscious. When y'get one of those 'you're finished' looks from someone, just remember: In the Greek village where my mother grew up, there was no separation between generations, so the young ones got used to wrinkled skin and weak knees and recognized older women as the wise ones [Deveson, 1994]. Why, we were midwives, matchmakers, experts in herbal medicine; we knew about everything!"

● *A link to the larger community.* For seniors who cannot go out as often, interactions with friends can keep them abreast of events in the wider world. "Rosie," Ida reported, "did you know the Thompson girl was named high school valedictorian?" Friends can also open up new experiences, such as travel or participation in community activities.

● *Protection from the psychological consequences of loss.* Older people in declining health who remain in contact with friends through phone calls and visits show improved psychological well-being (Fiori, Smith, & Antonucci, 2007). Similarly, when close relatives die, friends offer compensating social supports.

On a village street in Cyprus, these older adults often meet to play backgammon. Even after physical mobility declines, many seniors find ways to sustain ties with friends, who offer companionship, links to the larger community, and social support.

Characteristics of Late-Life Friendships. Although older adults prefer familiar, established relationships over new ones, friendship formation continues throughout life. Ties to old and dear friends who live far away are maintained, with growing numbers of seniors staying in touch with the aid of e-mail and social networking sites, such as Facebook (see page 475 in Chapter 17). Nevertheless, with age, seniors report that the friends they interact with most often and feel closest to live in the same community. As in earlier years, older people tend to choose friends whose age, sex, ethnicity, and values resemble their own. Compared with younger people, fewer report other-sex friendships. But some have them—usually long-standing ones dating back several decades (Monsour, 2002). As agemates die, the very old report more intergenerational friends—both same- and other-sex (Johnson & Troll, 1994). In her eighties, Ruth spent time with Margaret, a 55-year-old widow she met while serving on the board of directors of an adoption agency. Two or three times a month, Margaret came to Ruth's home for tea and lively conversation.

Sex differences in friendship, discussed in previous chapters, extend into late adulthood. Women are more likely to have intimate friends; men depend on their wives and, to a lesser extent, their sisters for warm, open communication (Waite & Das, 2013). Also, older women have more secondary friends—people who are not intimates but with whom they spend time occasionally, such as a group that meets for lunch, bridge, or museum tours. Through these associates, older adults meet new people, remain socially involved, and gain in psychological well-being (Blieszner & Roberto, 2012).

Relationships with Adult Children

About 80 percent of older adults in Western nations are parents of living children, most of whom are middle-aged. In Chapter 16, we noted that exchanges of help vary with the closeness of the parent–child bond and the needs of the parent and adult child. Recall, also, that over time, parent-to-child help declines, whereas child-to-parent assistance increases. Older adults and their adult children are often in touch, even when they live far from each other. But as with other ties, quality rather than quantity of interaction affects older adults' life satisfaction. In diverse ethnic groups and cultures, warm bonds with adult children reduce the negative impact of physical impairments and other losses (such as death of a spouse) on psychological well-being (Ajrouch, 2007; Milkie, Bierman, & Schieman, 2008). Alternatively, conflict or unhappiness with adult children contributes to poor physical and mental health.

Although aging parents and adult children in Western nations provide each other with various forms of help, level of assistance is typically modest. Older adults in their sixties and seventies—especially those who own their own home and who are married or widowed as opposed to divorced—are more likely to be providers than recipients of help, suggesting SES variations in the balance of support (Grundy, 2005). This balance shifts as older adults age, but well into late adulthood, seniors in Western nations give more than they receive, especially in financial support but also in practical assistance—a circumstance that contradicts stereotypes of older adults as "burdens" on younger generations (HSBC & Oxford Institute of Ageing, 2007).

Interviews with parents age 75 and older in five Western nations revealed that in all countries, aid received from adult children most often took the form of emotional support. Fewer than one-third said their children assisted with household chores and errands. Aging parents who provided more help of various kinds than they received scored highest in life satisfaction, those receiving more help than they gave scored lowest, while those in a balanced exchange fell in between (Lowenstein, Katz, & Gur-Yaish, 2007). To avoid dependency, older people usually do not seek children's practical assistance in the absence of a pressing need, and they express annoyance when children are overprotective or help unnecessarily (Spitze & Gallant, 2004). Moderate support, with many opportunities to reciprocate, is beneficial, fostering self-esteem and sense of family connection.

As social networks shrink in size, relationships with adult children become more important sources of family involvement. People 85 years and older with children have substantially more contacts with relatives than do those without children (Hooyman & Kiyak, 2011). Why is this so? Consider Ruth, whose daughter Sybil linked her to grandchildren, great-grandchildren, and relatives by marriage. When childless adults reach their eighties, siblings, other same-age relatives, and close friends may have become frail or died and hence may no longer be available as companions.

Elder Maltreatment

Although the majority of older adults enjoy positive relationships with family members, friends, and professional caregivers, some suffer maltreatment at the hands of these individuals. Through recent media attention, elder maltreatment has become a serious public concern.

Reports from many industrialized nations reveal widely varying rates of maltreatment, from 3 to 28 percent in general population studies. Overall, 7 to 10 percent of U.S. older adults say they were targets during the past month, amounting to 3 to 4 million victims (Acierno et al., 2010). Elder maltreatment crosses ethnic lines, although it is lower in Asian, Hispanic, and Native-American groups with strong traditions of respect for and obligation to the aged and highly disapproving attitudes toward harming them (Sherman, Rosenblatt, & Antonucci, 2008). Yet all figures underestimate the actual incidence because most abusive acts take place in private, and victims are often unable or unwilling to complain.

Elder maltreatment usually takes the following forms:

- *Physical abuse.* Intentional infliction of pain, discomfort, or injury, through hitting, cutting, burning, physical force, restraint, sexual assault, and other acts

- *Physical neglect.* Intentional or unintentional failure to fulfill caregiving obligations, resulting in lack of food, medication, or health services or in the older person being left alone or isolated

- *Emotional abuse.* Verbal assaults (such as name calling), humiliation (being treated as a child), and intimidation (threats of isolation or placement in a nursing home)

- *Sexual abuse.* Unwanted sexual contact of any kind

- *Financial abuse.* Illegal or improper exploitation of the aging person's property or financial resources, through theft or use without consent

Financial abuse, emotional abuse, and neglect are the most frequently reported types. Often several forms occur in combination (Anetzberger, 2005; National Academies Committee on National Statistics, 2010). The perpetrator is usually a person the older adult trusts and depends on for care and assistance.

Most abusers are family members—spouses (usually men), followed by children of both sexes and then by other relatives. Some are friends, neighbors, and in-home caregivers (National Center on Elder Abuse, 2013). Abuse in nursing homes is a major concern: From 6 to 40 percent of caregivers admit to having committed at least one act in the previous year (Schiamberg et al., 2011).

Over the past several decades, another form of neglect—referred to in the media as "granny dumping"—has risen: abandonment of older adults with severe disabilities by family caregivers, usually at hospital emergency rooms (Fulmer, 2008). Overwhelmed, their caregivers seem to have concluded that they have no other option but to take this drastic step. (See page 437 in Chapter 16 and page 465 in Chapter 17 for related research.)

This older adult, who suffers from depression and physical disabilities, lives in a dilapidated rooming house. When conditions are ripe for elder maltreatment, those with severe impairments are least able to protect themselves.

© SIMON RAWLES/ALAMY

Risk Factors.
Characteristics of the victim, the abuser, their relationship, and its social context are related to the incidence and severity of elder maltreatment. The more of the following risk factors that are present, the greater the likelihood that abuse and neglect will occur.

Dependency of the Victim. When other conditions are ripe for maltreatment, older adults who are frail or severely disabled are at greater risk because they are least able to protect themselves (Reay & Browne, 2008; Selwood & Cooper, 2009). Those with physical or cognitive impairments may also have personality traits that make them vulnerable—a tendency to lash out when angry or frustrated, a passive or avoidant approach to handling problems, and a low sense of self-efficacy (Salari, 2011). The worse the caregiver–recipient relationship, the greater the risk of elder abuse of all kinds, particularly when that relationship has a long negative history.

Dependency of the Perpetrator. Many abusers are dependent, emotionally or financially, on their victims. Frequently the perpetrator–victim relationship is one of mutual dependency (Fryling, Summers, & Hoffman, 2006). The abuser needs the older person for money or housing, and the older person needs the abuser for assistance with everyday tasks or to relieve loneliness.

Psychological Disturbance and Stress of the Perpetrator. Abusers are more likely than other caregivers to have psychological problems and to be dependent on alcohol or other drugs (Nerenberg, 2010). Often they are socially isolated, have difficulties at work, or are unemployed. These factors increase the likelihood that they will lash out when caregiving is highly demanding or the behavior of an older adult with dementia is irritating or hard to manage.

History of Family Violence. Elder abuse is often part of a long history of family violence. Adults who were abused as children are at increased risk of harming older adults (Reay & Browne, 2008). In many instances, elder abuse is an extension of years of partner abuse (Walsh et al., 2007).

Institutional Conditions. Elder maltreatment is more likely to occur in nursing homes that are rundown and overcrowded and that have staff shortages, minimal staff supervision, high staff turnover, and few visitors (Schiamberg et al., 2011). Highly stressful work conditions combined with minimal oversight of caregiving quality set the stage for abuse and neglect.

Preventing Elder Maltreatment.
Preventing elder maltreatment by family members is especially challenging. Victims may fear retribution; wish to protect abusers who are spouses, sons, or daughters; or feel embarrassed that they cannot control the situation. And they may be intimidated into silence or not know where to turn for help (Summers & Hoffman, 2006). Once abuse is discovered, intervention involves immediate protection and provision of unmet needs for the older adult

and of mental health services and social support for the spouse or caregiver.

Prevention programs offer caregivers counseling, education, and respite services, such as adult day care and in-home help. Trained volunteer "buddies" who make visits to the home can combat social isolation of aging adults and assist them with problem solving to avoid further harm. Support groups help seniors identify abusive acts, practice appropriate responses, and form new relationships. And agencies that provide informal financial services to older people who are unable to manage on their own, such as writing and cashing checks and holding valuables in a safe, reduce financial abuse.

When elder abuse is extreme, legal action offers the best protection, yet many victims are reluctant to initiate court procedures or, because of mental impairments, cannot do so. In these instances, social service professionals must help caregivers rethink their role, even if it means that the aging person might be institutionalized. In nursing homes, improving staff selection, training, and working conditions can greatly reduce abuse and neglect.

LOOK AND LISTEN

Contact the your state's department of senior services. Find out about its policies and programs aimed at preventing elder abuse. ●

Combating elder maltreatment also requires efforts at the level of the larger society, including public education to encourage reporting of suspected cases and improved understanding of the needs of older people. As part of this effort, seniors benefit from information on where to go for help (National Center on Elder Abuse, 2013). Finally, countering negative stereotypes of aging reduces maltreatment because recognizing older adults' dignity, individuality, and autonomy is incompatible with acts of harm.

ASK YOURSELF

REVIEW Why is adjustment to late-life divorce usually more difficult for women and adjustment to widowhood more difficult for men?

APPLY At age 51, Mae lost her job, couldn't afford to pay rent, and moved in with her 78-year-old widowed mother, Beryl. Although Beryl welcomed Mae's companionship, Mae grew depressed, drank heavily, and stopped looking for work. When Beryl complained about Mae's behavior, Mae pushed and slapped her. Explain why this mother–daughter relationship led to elder abuse.

REFLECT Select one older member of your extended family whom you know well, and describe that person's social convoy, or cluster of close relationships providing safety and support. In what ways has the convoy changed over the past five to ten years?

Retirement

In Chapter 16, we noted that the period of retirement has lengthened because of increased life expectancy and a steady decline in average age of retirement—trends that have occurred in all Western industrialized nations. These changes have also led to a blurring of the distinction between work and retirement. Because mandatory retirement no longer exists for most workers in Western countries, older adults have more choices about when to retire and how they spend their time.

The late-2000s recession has had only a modest impact on raising the retirement age of the baby boomers (see page 441). Still, according to surveys of adults in many countries, the majority of baby boomers say they want to work longer, with one-third indicating that devoting some time to work is important for a happy retirement (HSBC & Oxford Institute of Ageing, 2007, 2011). Currently, nearly 40 percent of U.S. adults age 65 to 69, and nearly 20 percent of those in their seventies, are still working in some capacity.

As these figures suggest, the contemporary retirement process is highly variable: It may include a planning period, the decision itself, diverse acts of retiring, and continuous adjustment and readjustment of activities for the rest of the life course. The majority of U.S. older adults with career jobs retire gradually by cutting down their hours and responsibilities. Many take *bridge jobs* (new part-time jobs or full-time jobs of shorter duration) that serve as transitions between full-time career and retirement (Wang, 2011). Others leave their jobs but later return to paid work and even start new careers, desiring to introduce interest and challenge into their lives, to supplement limited financial resources, or both.

In the following sections, we examine factors that affect the decision to retire, happiness during the retirement years, and leisure and volunteer pursuits. We will see that the process of retirement and retired life reflect an increasingly diverse retired population.

The Decision to Retire

When Walt and Ruth retired, both had worked long enough to be eligible for comfortable income-replacement benefits—Walt's through the government-sponsored Social Security program, Ruth's through a private pension plan. In addition, they had planned for retirement (see Chapter 16, pages 441–442), with a projected date for leaving the work force. They wanted to retire early enough to pursue leisure activities while both were in good health. In contrast, Walt's brother Dick was forced to retire as the operating costs of his bakery rose while his clientele declined. He looked for temporary employment in sales while his wife, Goldie, kept her part-time job as a bookkeeper to help cover living expenses.

Affordability of retirement is usually the first consideration in the decision to retire. Yet despite economic concerns, many preretirees decide to let go of a steady work life in favor of alternative, personally meaningful work, leisure, or volunteer activities.

Retire

- Adequate retirement benefits
- Compelling leisure interests or family pursuits
- Low work commitment
- Declining health
- Spouse retiring
- Routine, boring job

A recent retiree enjoys an adult-education class in bookbinding.

Continue Working

- Limited or no retirement benefits
- Few leisure interests or family pursuits
- High work commitment
- Good health
- Spouse working
- Flexible job demands and work schedule
- Pleasant, stimulating work environment

This doctor, in her 60s, continues to enjoy her fulfilling career.

FIGURE 18.3 Personal and workplace factors that influence the decision to retire.

"I had been working since I was 10 years old," said one retired auto worker. "I wanted a rest." Exceptions to this favorable outlook are people like Dick—forced into retirement or earning very low wages—who often take bridge jobs reluctantly to make ends meet (Cahill, Giandrea, & Quinn, 2006).

Figure 18.3 summarizes personal and workplace factors in addition to income that influence the decision to retire. People in good health, for whom vocational life is central to self-esteem, and whose work environments are pleasant and interesting are likely to keep on working. For these reasons, individuals in high-earning professional occupations usually retire later than those in blue-collar or clerical positions. And when they do retire, they more often shift to stimulating bridge jobs, with some retiring and returning to the work force multiple times (Feldman & Beehr, 2011; Wang et al., 2009). Self-employed older adults also work longer, probably because they can flexibly adapt their working hours to changing needs (Feldman & Vogel, 2009). In contrast, people in declining health, who are engaged in routine, boring work, or who have pleasurable leisure or family pursuits often opt for retirement.

In most Western nations, generous social security benefits make retirement feasible for the economically disadvantaged and sustain the standard of living of most workers after they retire. The United States is an exception: Many U.S. retirees, especially those who held low-income jobs without benefits, experience falling living standards. Denmark, France, Germany, Finland, and Sweden have gradual retirement programs in which older employees reduce their work hours, receive a partial pension to make up income loss, and continue to accrue pension benefits. Besides strengthening financial security, this approach introduces a transitional phase that fosters retirement planning and well-being (Peiró, Tordera, & Potocnik, 2012). And some countries' retirement policies are sensitive to women's more interrupted work lives. In Canada, France, and Germany, for example, time devoted to child rearing is given some credit when figuring retirement benefits (Service Canada, 2009).

In sum, individual preferences shape retirement decisions. At the same time, older adults' opportunities and limitations greatly affect their choices.

Adjustment to Retirement

Because retirement involves giving up roles that are a vital part of identity and self-esteem, it is often assumed to be a stressful process that contributes to declines in physical and mental health. Consider Dick, who reacted to the closing of his bakery with anxiety and depression. But recall that Dick had a cranky, disagreeable personality. In this respect, his psychological well-being after retirement was similar to what it had been before!

We must be careful not to assume a cause-and-effect relationship each time retirement is paired with an unfavorable reaction. For example, a wealth of evidence confirms that physical health problems lead older adults to retire, rather than the reverse (Shultz & Wang, 2007). The widely held belief that retirement inevitably leads to adjustment problems is contradicted by countless research findings. Contemporary seniors view retirement as a time of opportunity and personal growth and describe themselves as active and socially involved—major determinants of retirement satisfaction (Kloep & Hendry, 2007; Wang & Shultz, 2010). Still, about 10 to 30 percent mention some adjustment difficulties.

Workplace factors—especially financial worries and having to give up one's job—predict stress following retirement. And older adults who find it hard to give up the predictable schedule and social contacts of the work setting experience discomfort with their less structured way of life. But a sense of personal control over life events, including deciding to retire for internally motivated reasons (to do other things), is strongly linked to retirement satisfaction (Kubicek et al., 2011; Quine et al., 2007). Well-educated people with complex jobs typically adjust favorably (Kim & Moen, 2002a). Perhaps the satisfactions derived from challenging, meaningful work readily transfer to nonwork pursuits.

As with other major life events, social support reduces stress associated with retirement. Although social-network size typically shrinks as relationships with co-workers decline, quality of relationships remains fairly stable. And many seniors add to their social networks through leisure and volunteer pursuits (Kloep & Hendry, 2007). In Dick's case, entering congregate housing eased a difficult postretirement period, leading to new friends and rewarding leisure activities, some of which he shared with Goldie.

Finally, earlier in this chapter we noted that marital happiness tends to rise after retirement. When a couple's relationship is positive, it can buffer the uncertainty of retirement (van Solinge & Henkens, 2008). And retirement can enhance marital satisfaction by granting husband and wife more time for companionship. Consequently, a good marriage not only promotes adjustment to retirement but also benefits from the greater freedom of the retirement years. In line with continuity theory, people try to sustain lifestyle patterns, self-esteem, and values following retirement (Atchley, 2003). In favorable economic and social contexts, they usually succeed.

Leisure and Volunteer Activities

After a "honeymoon period" of trying out new options, many discover that interests and skills do not develop suddenly. Instead, meaningful leisure and community service pursuits are usually formed earlier and sustained or expanded during retirement (HSBC & Oxford Institute of Ageing, 2007; Pinquart & Schindler, 2009). For example, Walt's fondness for writing, theater, and gardening dated back to his youth. And Ruth's strong focus on her social work career led her to become an avid community volunteer.

Time devoted to volunteering is higher in late adulthood than at any other time of life. As a Red Cross volunteer, this senior traveled to West, Texas, to provide services to those affected by the fertilizer plant explosion in April 2013.

Involvement in leisure activities and, especially, volunteer service is related to better physical and mental health and reduced mortality (Cutler, Hendricks, & O'Neill, 2011). But simply participating does not explain this relationship. Instead, older adults select these pursuits because they permit self-expression, new achievements, the rewards of helping others, or pleasurable social interaction. And those high in sense of self-efficacy are more engaged (Diehl & Berg, 2007). These factors account for gains in well-being.

Older people contribute enormously to society through volunteer work, a trend that is strengthening. About one-third of 60- and 70-year-olds in industrialized nations report volunteering. Of those who do, over half give 200 or more hours per year (HSBC & Oxford Institute of Ageing, 2007; Kloep & Hendry, 2007). Younger, better-educated, and financially secure seniors with social interests are more likely to volunteer, women more often than men. Although most extend an earlier pattern of civic engagement, nonvolunteers are especially receptive to volunteer activities in the first few years after retiring as they look for ways to compensate for work-role losses (Mutchler, Burr, & Caro, 2003). The retirement transition is a prime time to recruit seniors into these personally rewarding, socially useful pursuits.

LOOK AND LISTEN

Interview an older adult participating in a significant community service role about the personal meaning of the experience at this time of life. ●

In a survey of a large, nationally representative U.S. sample, time spent volunteering did not decline until the eighties (Hendricks & Cutler, 2004). Even then, it remained higher than at any other time of life! In accord with socioemotional selectivity theory, older adults eventually narrowed their volunteering to fewer roles, concentrating on one or two that meant the most to them (Windsor, Anstey, & Rodgers, 2008). They seemed to recognize that excessive volunteering reduces its emotional rewards and, thus, its benefits to life satisfaction.

Finally, older adults report greater awareness of and interest in public affairs and typically vote at a higher rate than any other age group. (The 2012 U.S. national election, in which 18- to 29-year-olds exceeded seniors in voter turnout, is an exception). After retiring, older people have more time to keep abreast of current events. Their political concerns are far broader than those that serve their own age group, and their voting behavior is not driven merely by self-interest (Campbell & Binstock, 2011). Rather, their political involvement may stem from a deep desire for a safer, more secure world for future generations.

 ## Optimal Aging

Walt, Ruth, Dick, Goldie, and Ida, and the research findings they illustrate, reveal great diversity in development during the final decades of life. Walt and Ruth fit contemporary experts' view of **optimal aging**, in which gains are maximized and losses minimized. Both were actively engaged with their families and communities, coped well with negative life changes, enjoyed a happy intimate partnership and other close relationships, and led daily lives filled with gratifying activities. Ida, too, experienced optimal aging until the onset of Alzheimer's symptoms overwhelmed her ability to manage life's challenges. As a single adult, she built a rich social network that sustained her into old age, despite the hardship of having spent many years caring for her ailing mother.

People age optimally when their growth, vitality, and striving limit and, at times, overcome physical, cognitive, and social declines. Researchers want to know more about factors that contribute to optimal aging so they can help more seniors experience it. Yet theorists disagree on the precise ingredients of a satisfying old age. Some focus on easily measurable outcomes, such as excellent cardiovascular functioning, absence of disability, superior cognitive performance, and creative achievements. But this view has been heavily criticized (Aldwin, Spiro, & Park, 2006). Not everyone can become an outstanding athlete, an innovative scientist, or a talented artist. And many older adults do not want to keep on accomplishing and producing—the main markers of success in Western nations.

Recent views of a contented, fulfilling late adulthood have turned away from specific achievements toward processes people use to reach personally valued goals (Freund & Baltes, 1998; Kahana et al., 2005; Lund, 1998). In research on three samples of adults followed over the lifespan, George Vaillant found that factors people could control to some degree (such as health habits, coping strategies, marital stability, and years of education) far outweighed uncontrollable factors (parental SES, family warmth in childhood, early physical health, and longevity of family members) in predicting a happy, active old age (Vaillant & Mukamal, 2001). Consider the following description of one participant, who in childhood had experienced low SES, parental discord, a depressed mother, and seven siblings crowded into a tenement apartment. Despite these early perils, he became happily married and, through the GI bill, earned an accounting degree. At 70, he was aging well:

> Anthony Pirelli may have been *ill* considering his heart attack and open-heart surgery, but he did not feel *sick*. He was physically active as ever, and he continued to play tennis. Asked what he missed about his work, he exulted, "I'm so busy doing other things that I don't have time to miss work. . . . Life is not boring for me." He did not smoke or abuse alcohol; he loved his wife; he used mature [coping strategies]; he obtained 14 years of education; he watched his waistline; and he exercised regularly. (Adapted from Vaillant, 2002, pp. 12, 305.)

Vaillant concluded, "The past often predicts but never determines our old age" (p. 12). Optimal aging is an expression of remarkable resilience during this final phase of the lifespan.

In this and the previous chapter, we have considered the many ways that older adults realize their goals. **TAKE A MOMENT...** Look back and review the most important ones:

- Optimism and sense of self-efficacy in improving health and physical functioning (page 456)

- Selective optimization with compensation to make the most of limited physical energies and cognitive resources (pages 468 and 484)
- Strengthening of self-concept, which promotes self-acceptance and pursuit of hoped-for possible selves (pages 481–482)
- Enhanced emotional understanding and emotional self-regulation, which support meaningful, rewarding social ties (page 480)
- Acceptance of change, which fosters life satisfaction (page 483)
- A mature sense of spirituality and faith, permitting anticipation of death with calmness and composure (pages 483–484)
- Personal control over domains of dependency and independence (pages 484–485)
- High-quality relationships, which offer social support and pleasurable companionships (pages 488–489)

Optimal aging is facilitated by societal contexts that promote effective person–environment fit, enabling seniors to manage life changes effectively. Older adults need well-funded social security plans, good health care, safe housing, and diverse social services. Yet because of inadequate funding and difficulties reaching rural communities, many older adults' needs remain unmet. Isolated aging adults with little education may not know how to gain access to available assistance. Furthermore, the U.S. Medicare system of sharing health-care costs with seniors strains the financial resources of many. And housing that adjusts to changes in older people's capacities, permitting them to age in place without disruptive and disorienting moves, is available only to the economically well-off.

Besides improving policies that meet older adults' basic needs, new future-oriented approaches must prepare for increased aging of the population. More emphasis on lifelong learning for workers of all ages would help people maintain and expand their skills as they grow older. Also, reforms that prepare for expected growth in the number of frail aging adults are vital, including affordable help for family caregivers, adapted housing, and sensitive nursing home care.

All these changes involve recognizing, supporting, and enhancing the contributions that seniors make to society. A nation that takes care of its aging maximizes the chances that each of us, when our time comes to be old, will age optimally.

ASK YOURSELF

REVIEW What psychological and workplace factors predict favorable adjustment to retirement?

APPLY Nate, happily married to Gladys, adjusted well to retirement, and his marriage became even happier. How can a good marriage ease the transition to retirement? How can retirement enhance marital satisfaction?

REFLECT Think of someone you know who is aging optimally. What personal qualities led you to select that person?

SUMMARY

Erikson's Theory: Ego Integrity versus Despair (p. 479)

According to Erikson, how does personality change in late adulthood?

- The final psychological conflict of Erikson's theory, **ego integrity versus despair,** involves coming to terms with one's life. Adults who arrive at a sense of integrity feel whole and satisfied with their achievements. Despair occurs when older people feel time is too short to find an alternate route to integrity.

Other Theories of Psychosocial Development in Late Adulthood (p. 480)

Describe Peck's, Joan Erikson's, and Labouvie-Vief's views of psychosocial development in late adulthood, and discuss reminiscence in older adults' lives.

- According to Robert Peck, attaining ego integrity involves three distinct tasks: ego differentiation, body transcendence, and ego transcendence.

- Joan Erikson believes these attainments represent an additional psychosocial stage, **gerotranscendence,** evident in inner calm and quiet reflection.

- Gisella Labouvie-Vief points out that older adults improve in **affect optimization,** the ability to maximize positive emotion and dampen negative emotion. This bias toward the emotionally positive contributes an upbeat attitude that is linked to longer survival.

- **Reminiscence** can be positive and adaptive for older people. But many well-adjusted older adults spend little time seeking greater self-understanding through life review. Rather, as the term **Third Age** conveys, they are largely present- and future-oriented, seeking opportunities for personal fulfillment.

Stability and Change in Self-Concept and Personality (p. 481)

Cite stable and changing aspects of self-concept and personality, and discuss spirituality and religiosity in late adulthood.

- The "big five" personality traits remain stable from mid- to late life. Older adults' accumulation of a lifetime of self-knowledge leads to more secure and complex self-concepts. Those who continue to actively pursue hoped-for possible selves gain in life satisfaction.

- In late adulthood, resilience is fostered by gains in agreeableness and acceptance of change. Engaging in cognitively challenging activities promotes openness to experience.

- While U.S. seniors generally become more religious or spiritual as they age, this increase is modest and not universal. For the majority of people, religiosity is stable throughout adulthood. Religious involvement is especially high among low-SES ethnic minority older people and women and is linked to better physical and psychological well-being and longer survival.

Contextual Influences on Psychological Well-Being (p. 484)

Discuss the influence of control versus dependency, physical health, negative life changes, and social support on older adults' psychological well-being.

- In patterns of behavior called the **dependency–support script** and the **independence–ignore script,** older adults' dependency behaviors are attended to immediately while their independent behaviors are ignored. Dependency can be adaptive if older adults remain in control by selecting areas in which they desire help while conserving their strength for highly valued activities. Assistance that enables older adults to pursue their goals sustains an effective **person–environment fit,** which fosters psychological well-being.

- Physical declines and chronic disease can lead to a loss of personal control and high risk for late-life depression. Older adults have the highest suicide rate of all age groups.

- Although aging adults are at risk for a variety of negative life changes, these events evoke less stress and depression in older than in younger people. But when negative changes pile up, they test older adults' coping resources.

- By easing stress, social support promotes physical health and psychological well-being. But assistance that is excessive or cannot be returned often results in reduced self-efficacy and psychological stress. Consequently, perceived social support, rather than sheer amount of help, is associated with a positive outlook.

A Changing Social World (p. 487)

Describe social theories of aging, including disengagement theory, activity theory, continuity theory, and socioemotional selectivity theory.

- **Disengagement theory** holds that mutual withdrawal between older adults and society occurs in anticipation of death. Most aging adults, however, do not disengage but let go of unsatisfying contacts and maintain satisfying ones.

- **Activity theory** states that social barriers to engagement, not the desires of older adults, cause declining rates of interaction. Yet opportunities for social contact do not guarantee greater social activity.

- **Continuity theory** proposes that most aging adults strive to maintain consistency between their past and anticipated future. By using familiar skills and engaging in familiar activities with familiar people, older people integrate late-life changes into a coherent, consistent life path.

- **Socioemotional selectivity theory** states that social networks become more selective with age. Older adults emphasize the emotion-regulating function of interaction, preferring high-quality, emotionally fulfilling relationships.

How do communities, neighborhoods, and housing arrangements affect older adults' social lives and adjustment?

- Suburban older adults have higher incomes and report better health than their inner-city counterparts, but the latter are better off in terms of public transportation. Small-town and rural aging adults, who are less likely to live near their children, compensate by interacting more with nearby relatives, neighbors, and friends. Living in neighborhoods with many like-minded seniors promotes life satisfaction.

- Most older people prefer **aging in place,** remaining in a familiar setting where they have control over everyday life. But for those with health and mobility problems, independent living poses risks, and many older adults who live alone are poverty-stricken.

- Residential communities for older adults who need help with everyday tasks include assisted-living arrangements such as **congregate housing** and **life-care communities,** which guarantee that residents' changing needs will be met as they age.

- The small number of U.S. older adults who live in nursing homes experience extreme restriction of autonomy. Typically, social interaction among residents is low. Homelike nursing homes that achieve an effective person–environment fit foster late-life well-being.

Relationships in Late Adulthood (p. 492)

Describe changes in social relationships in late adulthood, including marriage, gay and lesbian partnerships, divorce, remarriage, and widowhood, and discuss never-married, childless older adults.

- As we move through life, a **social convoy,** or cluster of family members and friends, provides safety and support. As ties are lost, aging adults seek ways to maintain gratifying relationships.

- Marital satisfaction peaks in late adulthood as stressful responsibilities decline and gains in perceptions of relationship fairness, joint leisure activities, and positive communication increase. Most gay and lesbian older adults also report happy, highly fulfilling relationships.

- Divorce in late life brings greater stress than for younger people. Although older adults' remarriage rates are low, those who do remarry enter into more stable relationships. Seniors are increasingly choosing cohabitation as a long-term alternative to marriage.

- Adaptation to widowhood varies widely. Older adults fare better than younger individuals, and women better than men. Efforts to maintain social ties, an outgoing personality, high self-esteem, and a sense of self-efficacy in handling tasks of daily living promote resilience.

- Most older adults who remain unmarried and childless throughout their lives develop alternative meaningful relationships. Never-married childless women are better-adjusted than men, but—despite smaller social networks—both find social support.

How do sibling relationships, friendships, and relationships with adult children change in late life?

- In late adulthood, most siblings live nearby, communicate regularly, and visit several times a year. Perhaps because of fewer competing family relationships, widowed and never-married older people have more contact with siblings.

- Friendships in late adulthood serve diverse functions: intimacy and companionship, a shield against negative judgments, a link to the larger community, and protection from the psychological consequences of loss. Women, more than men, tend to have both intimate friends and **secondary friends,** with whom they spend time occasionally.

- Older adults are often in touch with their adult children, who more often provide emotional support than direct assistance. Many opportunities for aging parents to reciprocate is beneficial to well-being. Aging parents typically provide more help than they receive, especially financial support and practical assistance.

Discuss elder maltreatment, including risk factors and strategies for prevention.

- Some older adults suffer maltreatment at the hands of family members, friends, or professional caregivers. Risk factors include a dependent perpetrator–victim relationship, perpetrator psychological disturbance and stress, a history of family violence, and inadequate institutional conditions.

- Elder-abuse prevention programs provide counseling, education, and respite services for caregivers. Trained volunteers and support groups can help older persons avoid future harm. Societal efforts that encourage reporting of suspected cases and increase understanding of older people's needs are also vital.

Retirement (p. 499)

Discuss the decision to retire, adjustment to retirement, and involvement in leisure and volunteer activities.

- The decision to retire depends on affordability, health status, nature of the work environment, and opportunities to pursue meaningful activities.

● Seniors who view retirement as a time of personal growth and who remain active and socially involved adapt especially well. Factors affecting adjustment include health status, satisfactions previously derived from work, a sense of personal control over life events (including the retirement decision), social support, and marital happiness.

● Meaningful leisure and volunteer pursuits are typically formed earlier and sustained or expanded during retirement. Involvement is related to better physical and mental health and to reduced mortality.

Optimal Aging (p. 501)

Discuss the meaning of optimal aging.

● Older adults who experience **optimal aging** have developed many ways to minimize losses and maximize gains. Societal contexts that permit older adults to manage life changes effectively foster optimal aging. These include well-funded social security plans, good health care, safe housing, diverse social services, and opportunities for lifelong learning.

Important Terms and Concepts

activity theory (p. 487)
affect optimization (p. 480)
aging in place (p. 489)
congregate housing (p. 490)
continuity theory (p. 487)
dependency–support script (p. 484)

disengagement theory (p. 487)
ego integrity versus despair (p. 479)
gerotranscendence (p. 480)
independence–ignore script (p. 484)
life-care communities (p. 490)
optimal aging (p. 501)

person–environment fit (p. 484)
reminiscence (p. 481)
secondary friends (p. 497)
social convoy (p. 492)
socioemotional selectivity theory (p. 488)
Third Age (p. 482)

milestones

Development in Late Adulthood

65–80 years

PHYSICAL

- Performance of autonomic nervous system declines, impairing tolerance for extremes of heat and cold. (451)
- Declines in vision continue, with increased sensitivity to glare and impaired color discrimination, dark adaptation, depth perception, and visual acuity. (451)
- Declines in hearing continue throughout the frequency range. (452)
- Sensitivity to taste and odor may decline. (452)
- Touch sensitivity declines on the hands, especially the fingertips. (452)
- Declines in cardiovascular and respiratory functioning lead to greater physical stress during exercise. (453)

- Aging of the immune system increases risk for a variety of illnesses, including infectious diseases, cardiovascular disease, certain forms of cancer, and several autoimmune disorders. (453)

- Timing of sleep shifts to earlier bedtime and earlier morning wakening; sleep difficulties increase. (453)
- Graying and thinning of the hair continue; the skin wrinkles and sags further and becomes more transparent as it loses its fatty layer of support; "age spots" increase. (454)
- Height and weight decline because of loss of lean body mass. (454)

- Continued loss of bone mass leads to rising rates of osteoporosis. (454, 460)
- Frequency of sexual activity and intensity of sexual response decline, although most healthy married couples report regular sexual enjoyment. (458–459)

COGNITIVE

- Processing speed continues to decline, but crystallized intelligence is largely sustained. (467)

- Ability to attend selectively and to adapt attention, switching from one task to another, continues to decline. (468)
- Amount of information that can be held in working memory, use of memory strategies, and retrieval from long-term memory diminish further; problems are greatest on tasks requiring deliberate processing and associative memory. (468–469)
- Modest forgetting of remote memories occurs. (469–470)
- Use of external aids for prospective memory increases. (470)
- Retrieving words from long-term memory and planning what to say and how to say it become more difficult. (471)

- More often represents to-be-communicated information in terms of gist rather than details. (471)
- Hypothetical problem solving declines, but everyday problem solving remains adaptive. (471)
- May hold an important position of leadership in society, such as chief executive officer, religious leader, or court justice. (472)
- May develop wisdom. (471–472)
- Can improve a wide range of cognitive skills through training. (473)

Note: Numbers in parentheses indicate the page or pages on which each milestone is discussed.

EMOTIONAL/SOCIAL

- Comes to terms with life, developing ego integrity. (479–480)
- Cognitive-affective complexity declines as basic information-processing skills diminish. (480)
- Affect optimization—the ability to maximize positive emotion and dampen negative emotion—increases. (480)
- May engage in reminiscence and life review, but continues to seek avenues for personal growth and fulfillment. (481)

AFP/GETTY IMAGES

- Self-concept strengthens, becoming more secure and complex. (481–482)
- Agreeableness and acceptance of change increase, while extroversion and openness to experience tend to decline modestly. (483)
- Spirituality and faith may advance to a higher level, away from prescribed beliefs toward a more reflective approach. (483–484)

- Size of social network and amount of social interaction decline. (487)
- Selection of social partners is based on anticipated feelings, including pursuit of pleasant relationships and avoidance of unpleasant ones. (488)
- Marital satisfaction increases, peaking in late adulthood. (492)
- May be widowed. (494)
- Visits and support from siblings living nearby may increase. (496)
- Friendships take on increasing importance. (496–497)

ALAN HICKS/STONE/GETTY IMAGES

- May retire. (499–500)
- Likely to increase involvement in leisure and volunteer activities (501)
- More likely to be knowledgeable about politics and to vote. (501)

80 years and older

PHYSICAL

- Physical changes previously listed continue.
- Mobility diminishes as muscle and bone strength and joint flexibility decline. (454)

© ROBERT W. GINN/PHOTOEDIT

COGNITIVE

- Cognitive changes previously listed continue.
- Fluid abilities decline further; crystallized abilities drop as well, though only modestly. (467)

© HERVÉ HUGHES/HEMIS/CORBIS

EMOTIONAL/SOCIAL

- Emotional and social changes previously listed continue.
- May develop gerotranscendence, a cosmic perspective directed beyond the self. (480)

© KEVIN RL HANSON/DK STOCK/CORBIS

- Relationships with adult children become more important. (497)
- Frequency and variety of leisure and volunteer activities decline slightly. (501)

chapter
19

Death, Dying, and Bereavement

Mourners on the island of Bali, Indonesia, perform a traditional Hindu ceremony marking the passage of the dead into the spirit realm. All cultures have rituals for celebrating the end of life and helping the bereaved cope with profound loss.

BRUNO MORANDI/ROBERT HARDING

chapter outline

How We Die

Physical Changes • Defining Death • Death with Dignity

Attitudes Toward Death

Thinking and Emotions of Dying People

Do Stages of Dying Exist? • Contextual Influences on Adaptations to Dying

A Place to Die

Home • Hospital • Nursing Home • The Hospice Approach

■ **BIOLOGY AND ENVIRONMENT** Music as Palliative Care for Dying Patients

The Right to Die

Passive Euthanasia • Voluntary Active Euthanasia • Assisted Suicide

Bereavement: Coping with the Death of a Loved One

Grief Process • Personal and Situational Variations • Bereavement Interventions

■ **CULTURAL INFLUENCES** Cultural Variations in Mourning Behavior

Death Education

As every life is unique, so each death is unique. The final forces of the human spirit separate themselves from the body in manifold ways.

My mother Sofie's death was the culmination of a five-year battle against cancer. In her last months, the disease invaded organs throughout her body, attacking the lungs in its final fury. She withered slowly, with the mixed blessing of time to prepare against certain knowledge that death was just around the corner. My father, Philip, lived another 18 years. At age 80, he was outwardly healthy, active, and about to depart on a long-awaited vacation when a heart attack snuffed out his life suddenly, without time for last words or death-bed reconciliations.

As I set to work on this chapter, my 65-year-old neighbor Nicholas gambled for a higher quality of life. To be eligible for a kidney transplant, he elected bypass surgery to strengthen his heart. Doctors warned that his body might not withstand the operation. But Nicholas knew that without taking a chance, he would live only a few years, in debilitated condition. Shortly after the surgery, infection set in, traveling throughout his system and so weakening him that only extreme measures—a respirator to sustain breathing and powerful drugs to elevate his fading blood pressure—could keep him alive.

"Come on, Dad, you can do it," encouraged Nicholas's daughter Sasha, standing by his bedside and stroking his hand. But Nicholas could not. After two months in intensive care, he experienced brain seizures and slipped into a coma. Three doctors met with his wife, Giselle, to tell her there was no hope. She asked them to disconnect the respirator, and within half an hour Nicholas drifted away.

Death is essential for the survival of our species. We die so that our own children and the children of others may live. As hard as it is to accept the reality that we too will die, our greatest solace lies in knowing that death is part of ongoing life.

In this chapter, we address the culmination of lifespan development. Over the past century, technology has provided so many means to keep death at bay that many people regard it as a forbidden topic. But pressing social and economic dilemmas that are an outgrowth of the dramatic

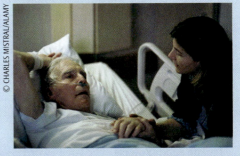

© CHARLES MISTRAL/ALAMY

increase in life expectancy are forcing us to attend to life's end—its quality, its timing, and ways to help people adjust to their own and others' final leave taking. The interdisciplinary field of **thanatology,** devoted to the study of death and dying, has expanded tremendously over the past 25 years.

Our discussion addresses the physical changes of dying; attitudes toward death, the thoughts and feelings of people as they stand face to face with death, where people die, hopelessly ill patients' right to die, and coping with the death of a loved one. The experiences of Sofie, Philip, Nicholas, their families, and others illustrate how each person's life history joins with social and cultural contexts to shape death and dying, lending great diversity to this universal experience. ●

How We Die

In industrialized countries, opportunities to witness the physical aspects of death are less available today than in previous generations. Most people in the developed world die in hospitals or nursing homes, where doctors and nurses, not loved ones, typically attend their last moments. Nevertheless, many want to know how we die, either to anticipate their own end or grasp what is happening to a dying loved one. As we look briefly at the physical dying, we must keep in mind that the dying person is more than a physical being requiring care of and attention to bodily functions. The dying are also mind and spirit—for whom the end of life is still life. They benefit profoundly in their last days and hours from social support responsive to their needs for emotional and spiritual closure.

Physical Changes

When asked how they would like to die, most people say they want "death with dignity"—either a quick, agony-free end during sleep or a clear-minded final few moments in which they can say farewell and review their lives. In reality, death is the culmination of a straightforward biological process. For about

20 percent of people, it is gentle—especially when narcotic drugs ease pain (Nuland, 1993). But most of the time it is not.

Of the one-quarter of deaths in industrialized nations that are sudden, 80 to 90 percent are due to heart attacks (American Heart Association, 2012; Winslow, Mehta, & Fuster, 2005). Though I longed for reassurance that my father's death had been painless, my wish was probably not fulfilled. Undoubtedly he felt the sharp, crushing sensation of a heart deprived of oxygen. As his heart twitched uncontrollably (called *fibrillation*) or stopped entirely, blood circulation slowed and ceased, and he was thrust into unconsciousness. A brain starved of oxygen for more than two to four minutes is irreversibly damaged. Other oxygen-deprived organs stop functioning as well.

Death is long and drawn out for three-fourths of people—many more than in times past, as a result of life-saving medical technology. Of those with heart disease, most have congestive heart failure, the cause of Nicholas's death (Gruenewald & White, 2006). His scarred heart could no longer contract with the force needed to deliver enough oxygen to his tissues. As it tried harder, its muscle weakened further. Without sufficient blood pressure, fluid backed up in Nicholas's lungs. This hampered his breathing and created ideal conditions for inhaled bacteria to multiply, enter the bloodstream, and run rampant in his system, leading many organs to fail.

Cancer also chooses diverse paths to inflict its damage. When it metastasizes, bits of tumor travel through the bloodstream and implant and grow in vital organs, disrupting their functioning. Medication made my mother's final days as comfortable as possible. But the preceding weeks involved physical suffering, including impaired breathing and digestion.

In the days or hours before death, activity declines; the person moves and communicates less and shows little interest in food, water, and surroundings. At the same time, body temperature, blood pressure, and circulation to the limbs fall, so the hands and feet feel cool and skin color changes to a duller, grayish hue (Hospice Foundation of America, 2005). When the transition from life to death is imminent, the person often moves through three phases:

1. The **agonal phase.** The Greek word *agon* means "struggle." Here agonal refers to gasps and muscle spasms during the first moments in which the regular heartbeat disintegrates (Manole & Hickey, 2006).
2. **Clinical death.** A short interval follows in which heartbeat, circulation, breathing, and brain functioning stop, but resuscitation is still possible.
3. **Mortality.** The individual passes into permanent death.

Defining Death

TAKE A MOMENT... Consider what we have said so far, and note the dilemma of identifying just when death occurs. Death is not an event that happens at a single point in time but, rather, a process in which organs stop functioning in a sequence that varies from person to person. Because the dividing line between life and death is fuzzy, societies need a definition of death to help doctors decide when life-saving measures should be terminated, to signal survivors that they must begin to grieve their loss and reorganize their lives, and to establish when donated organs can be removed.

A monk prays with mourners during a Shinto funeral in Japan. Shinto beliefs, emphasizing ancestor worship and time for the spirit to leave the corpse, may partly explain the Japanese discomfort with the brain death standard and organ donation.

Several decades ago, loss of heartbeat and respiration signified death. But these criteria are no longer adequate because resuscitation techniques frequently permit vital signs to be restored. Today, **brain death,** irreversible cessation of all activity in the brain and the brain stem (which controls reflexes), is used in most industrialized nations.

But not all countries accept this standard. In Japan, for example, doctors rely on traditional criteria—absence of heartbeat and respiration. This approach has hindered the development of a national organ transplant program because few organs can be salvaged from bodies without artificially maintaining vital signs. Buddhist, Confucian, and Shinto beliefs about death, which stress ancestor worship and time for the spirit to leave the corpse, may be partly responsible for the Japanese discomfort with brain death and organ donation. Today, Japanese law allows organ donation using the standard of brain death, even if the wishes of the deceased are not clear, as long as the family does not object (Ida, 2010). Otherwise, people are considered to be alive until the heart stops beating.

Often the brain death standard does not solve the problem of when to halt treatment. Consider Nicholas, who, though not brain dead, had entered a **persistent vegetative state,** in which the cerebral cortex no longer registered electrical activity but the brain stem remained active. Doctors were certain they could not restore consciousness or body movement. Because thousands of people in the United States and other nations are in a persistent vegetative state, with health-care costs totaling many millions of dollars annually, some experts believe that absence of activity in the cerebral cortex should be sufficient to declare a person dead. But others point to a few cases in which patients who had been vegetative for months regained cortical responsiveness and consciousness, though usually with very limited functioning (Laureys & Boly, 2007). In still other instances of illness, a fully conscious but suffering person refuses life-saving measures—an issue we will consider later when we take up the right to die.

Death with Dignity

We have seen that nature rarely delivers the idealized, easy end most people want, nor can medical science guarantee it. Therefore, the greatest dignity in death is in the integrity of the life that precedes it—an integrity we can foster by the way we communicate with and care for the dying person.

First, we can provide the majority of dying people, who succumb gradually, with the utmost in humane and compassionate care. This includes treating them through their physical and psychological distress. We can treat them with respect by taking interest in those aspects of their lives that they most value and by addressing their greatest concerns (Keegan & Drick, 2011).

Second, we can be candid about death's certainty. Unless people are aware that they are dying and understand (as far as possible) the likely circumstances of their death, they cannot plan for end-of-life care and decision making and share the

Dying patient Dick Warner's wife, Nancy, wears a nurse's hat she crafted from paper to symbolize her dual roles as medical and emotional caregiver. The evening of this photo, Nancy heard Dick's breaths shortening. She kissed him and whispered, "It's time to let go." Dick died as he wished, with his loving wife at his bedside.

sentiments that bring closure to relationships they hold most dear. Because Sofie knew how and when her death would probably take place, she chose a time when she and Philip could express what their lives had meant to each other. Among those precious bedside exchanges was Sofie's last wish that Philip remarry after her death so he would not live out his final years alone. Openness about impending death granted Sofie a final generative act, helped her let go of the person closest to her, and offered comfort as she faced death.

Finally, doctors and nurses can help dying people learn enough about their condition to make reasoned choices about whether to fight on or say no to further treatment. An understanding of how the normal body works simplifies comprehension of how disease affects it—education that can begin as early as the childhood years.

In sum, we can ensure the most dignified exit possible by offering the dying person care, affection, companionship, and esteem; the truth about diagnosis; and the maximum personal control over this final phase of life (American Hospice Foundation, 2013). These are essential ingredients of a "good death," and we will revisit them throughout this chapter.

Attitudes Toward Death

A century ago, when most deaths occurred at home, people of all ages, including children, helped with care of the dying family member and were present at the moment of death. They saw their loved one buried on family property or in the local cemetery, where the grave could be visited regularly. Because infant and childhood mortality rates were high, all people were likely to know someone their own age, or even younger, who had died. And it was common for children to experience the death of a parent.

Compared with earlier generations, today more young people reach adulthood without having experienced the death of someone they know well (Morgan, Laungani, & Palmer, 2009). When a death does occur, professionals in hospitals and funeral homes take care of most tasks that involve confronting it directly.

This distance from death undoubtedly contributes to a sense of uneasiness about it. Despite frequent images of death in television shows, movies, and news reports of accidents, murders, wars, and natural disasters, we live in a death-denying culture. Adults are often reluctant to talk about death. And substitute expressions, such as "passing away," "going out," or "departing," permit us to avoid acknowledging it candidly. Not surprisingly, **death anxiety**—fear and apprehension of death—is widespread.

Even people who clearly accept the reality of death may fear it. What predicts whether thoughts of our own demise trigger intense distress, relative calm, or something in between? To answer this question, researchers measure both general death anxiety and specific factors—fear of no longer existing, loss of control, a painful death, decay of the body, separation from loved ones, and the unknown (Neimeyer, 1994). Findings reveal large individual and cultural variations in aspects of death that arouse fear. For example, in a study of devout Islamic Saudi Arabians, certain factors that appear repeatedly in the responses of Westerners, such as fear of the body decaying and of the unknown, were entirely absent (Long, 1985).

Among Westerners, spirituality—a sense of life's meaning—seems to be more important than religious commitment in limiting death anxiety (Ardelt, 2003; Routledge & Juhl, 2010). People with a well-developed personal philosophy of death are also less fearful. And in two studies, Christian older adults whose religious beliefs and behavior were contradictory—who believed in a rewarding afterlife but rarely prayed or attended services, or who regularly prayed and attended services but doubted the existence of an afterlife—reported higher death anxiety (Wink, 2006; Wink & Scott, 2005). Together, these findings indicate that both firmness of beliefs and consistency between beliefs and practices, rather than religiousness itself, reduce fear of death. Death anxiety is especially low among adults with deep faith in some form of higher force or being—faith that may or may not be influenced by religion (Cicirelli, 2002; Neimeyer et al., 2011).

TAKE A MOMENT... From what you have learned about adult psychosocial development, how do you think death anxiety might change with age? If you predicted it would decline, reaching its lowest level in late adulthood, you are correct (see Figure 19.1 on page 512) (Russac et al., 2007; Tomer, Eliason, & Smith, 2000). This age-related drop has been found in many cultures and ethnic groups. Recall from Chapter 18 that older adults are especially effective at regulating negative emotion. As a result, most cope with anxieties, including fear of death, effectively. Furthermore, attainment of ego integrity reduces death anxiety. Older people have had more time to develop symbolic immortality—the belief that one will continue to live

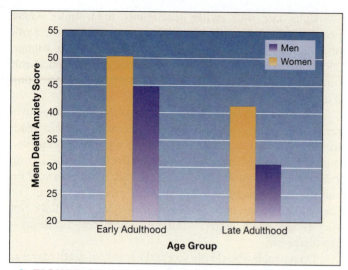

FIGURE 19.1 **Relationship of age and gender to death anxiety.** In this study comparing young and older adults, death anxiety declined with age. Women expressed greater fear of death than men. Many other studies show similar findings. (Adapted from Tomer, Eliason, & Smith, 2000.)

on through one's children or through one's work or personal influence (see Chapter 16, page 424).

As long as it is not overly intense, death anxiety can motivate people to live up to internalized cultural values—for example, to be kind to others and to work hard to reach one's goals. These efforts increase adults' sense of self-esteem, self-efficacy, and purpose in life—powerful antidotes against the terrifying thought that, in the overall scheme of things, they "are no more important or enduring than any individual potato, pineapple, or porcupine" (Fry, 2003; Pyszczynski et al., 2004,

Death anxiety declines in old age, and this 81-year-old from the Netherlands seems to have very little! She had this coffin made to serve as a bookshelf because, she said, "It's a waste to use a coffin just for burial." The pillow on the top will support her head after she dies.

p. 436). In a study of Israeli adults, symbolic immortality predicted reduced fear of death, especially among those with secure attachments (Florian & Mikulincer, 1998). Gratifying, close interpersonal ties seem to help people feel worthwhile and forge a sense of symbolic immortality. And people who view death as an opportunity to pass a legacy to future generations are less likely to fear it (Cicirelli, 2001; Mikulincer, Florian, & Hirschberger, 2003).

Regardless of age, in both Eastern and Western cultures, women appear more anxious about death than men do (refer again to Figure 19.1) (Madnawat & Kachhawa, 2007; Tomer, Eliason, & Smith, 2000). Women may be more likely to admit and men more likely to avoid troubled feelings about mortality—an explanation consistent with females' greater emotional expressiveness throughout the lifespan.

Experiencing some anxiety about death is normal and adaptive. But like other fears, very intense death anxiety can undermine effective adjustment. Although physical health in adulthood is not related to death anxiety, mental health clearly is. In cultures as different as China and the United States, people who are depressed or generally anxious are likely to have more severe death concerns (Neimeyer & Van Brunt, 1995; Wu, Tang, & Kwok, 2002). In contrast, people who are good at inhibition (keeping their minds from straying to irrelevant thoughts) and at emotional self-regulation report less death anxiety (Gailliot, Schmeichel, & Baumeister, 2006). They are better able to manage their concerns about death.

Death anxiety is largely limited to adolescence and adulthood. Children rarely display it unless they live in high-crime neighborhoods or war-torn areas where they are in constant danger (see the Cultural Influences box on the impact of ethnic and political violence on children on page 280 in Chapter 10). Terminally ill children are also at risk for high death anxiety. Compared with other same-age patients, children with cancer express more destructive thoughts and negative feelings about death (Malone, 1982). For those whose parents make the mistake of not telling them they are going to die, loneliness and death anxiety can be extreme (O'Halloran & Altmaier, 1996).

ASK YOURSELF

REVIEW Explain why death anxiety typically declines in late adulthood.

APPLY Considering factors that influence death anxiety, suggest several experiences that religious institutions or senior centers can offer that might reduce fear in highly death-anxious people.

REFLECT Ask members of earlier generations in your family about their childhood experiences with death. Compare these to your own experiences. What differences did you find, and how would you explain them?

Thinking and Emotions of Dying People

In the year before her death, Sofie did everything possible to surmount her illness. In between treatments to control the cancer, she tested her strength. She continued to teach high school, traveled to visit her children, cultivated a garden, and took weekend excursions with Philip. Hope pervaded Sofie's approach to her deadly condition, and she spoke often about the disease—so much so that her friends wondered how she could confront it so directly.

As Sofie deteriorated physically, she was frustrated, and at times angry and depressed, about her inability to keep on fighting. Once she asked when my husband and I, who were newly married, would have children. "If only I could live long enough to hold them in my arms!" she cried. In the last week, she appeared tired but free of struggle. Occasionally, she spoke of her love for us and commented on the beauty of the hills outside her window. But mostly, she looked and listened, rather than actively participating in conversation. One afternoon, she fell permanently unconscious.

Do Stages of Dying Exist?

As dying people move closer to death, are their reactions predictable? Do they go through a series of changes that are the same for everyone, or are their thoughts and feelings unique?

Kübler-Ross's Theory. Although her theory has been heavily criticized, Elisabeth Kübler-Ross (1969) is credited with awakening society's sensitivity to the psychological needs of dying patients. From interviews with over 200 terminally ill people, she devised a theory of five typical responses—initially proposed as stages—to the prospect of death and the ordeal of dying:

- *Denial.* On learning of the terminal illness, the person denies its seriousness. While the patient still feels reasonably well, denial is self-protective, allowing the individual to deal with the illness at his or her own pace. Kübler-Ross recommends that family members and health professionals not prolong denial by distorting the truth about the person's condition. In doing so, they prevent the dying person from adjusting to impending death and hinder necessary arrangements—for social support, for bringing closure to relationships, and for making decisions about medical interventions.

- *Anger.* Recognition that time is short promotes anger at having to die without having had a chance to do all one wants to do. Family members and health professionals may be targets of the patient's rage, resentment, and envy. Even so, they must tolerate rather than lash out at the patient's behavior, realizing that the underlying cause is the unfairness of death.

- *Bargaining.* Grasping the inevitability of death, the terminally ill person attempts to bargain for extra time—a deal he or she may try to strike with family members, friends, doctors, nurses, or God. The best response to these efforts to sustain hope is to listen sympathetically, as one doctor did to the pleas of a young AIDS-stricken father, whose wish was to live long enough to dance with his daughter—then 8 years old—at her wedding (Selwyn, 1996). Sometimes, bargains are altruistic acts. Tony, a 15-year-old leukemia patient, expressed to his mother:

  > I don't want to die yet. Gerry [youngest brother] is only 3 and not old enough to understand. If I could live just one more year, I could explain it to him myself and he will understand. Three is just too young. (Komp, 1996, pp. 69–70)

  Although many dying patients' bargains are unrealistic and impossible to fulfill, Tony lived for exactly one year—a gift to those who survived him.

- *Depression.* When denial, anger, and bargaining fail to postpone the illness, the person becomes depressed about the loss of his or her life. Unfortunately, many experiences associated with dying, including physical and mental deterioration, pain, lack of control, certain medications, and being hooked to machines, contribute to despondency. Compassionate medical and psychological treatment, aimed at clarifying and alleviating the patients concerns, can limit despair.

- *Acceptance.* Most people who reach acceptance, a state of peace and quiet about upcoming death, do so only in the last weeks or days. The weakened patient yields to death, disengaging from all but a few family members, friends, and caregivers. Some dying people, in an attempt to pull away from all they have loved, withdraw. "I'm getting my mental and emotional house in order," one patient explained (Samarel, 1995, p. 101).

Evaluation of Kübler-Ross's Theory. Kübler-Ross cautioned that her five stages should not be viewed as a fixed sequence and that not all people display each response. But her use of the term *stages* has made it easy for her theory to be interpreted simplistically, as the series of steps a "normal" dying person follows. Some health professionals, unaware of diversity in dying experiences, have insensitively tried to push patients through Kübler-Ross's sequence. And caregivers, through callousness or ignorance, can too easily dismiss a dying patient's legitimate complaints about treatment as "just what you would expect in Stage 2" (Corr & Corr, 2013; Kastenbaum, 2012).

Rather than stages, the five reactions Kübler-Ross observed are best viewed as coping strategies that anyone may call on in the face of threat. Furthermore, dying people react in many additional ways—for example, through efforts to conquer the disease, as Sofie displayed; through an overwhelming need to control what happens to their bodies during the dying process; through acts of generosity and caring, as seen in Tony's concern for his 3-year-old brother, Gerry; and through shifting their focus to living in a fulfilling way—"seizing the day" because so little time is left (Silverman, 2004; Wright, 2003).

As these examples suggest, the most serious drawback to Kübler-Ross's theory is that it looks at dying patients' thoughts and feelings outside the contexts that give them meaning. As we will see next, people's adaptations to impending death can be understood only in relation to the multidimensional influences that have contributed to their life course and that also shape this final phase.

Contextual Influences on Adaptations to Dying

From the moment of her diagnosis, Sofie spent little time in denial. Instead, she met the deadly disease head on, just as she had dealt with other challenges of life. Her impassioned plea to hold her grandchildren in her arms was less a bargain with fate than an expression of profound defeat that on the threshold of late adulthood, she would not live to enjoy its rewards. At the end, her quiet, withdrawn demeanor was probably resignation, not acceptance. All her life, she had been a person with a fighting spirit.

According to recent theorists, a single strategy, such as acceptance, is not best for every dying patient. Rather, an **appropriate death** is one that makes sense in terms of the individual's pattern of living and values and, at the same time, preserves or restores significant relationships and is as free of suffering as possible (Worden, 2000). When asked about a "good death," most patients mention the following goals:

- Maintaining a sense of identity, or inner continuity with one's past
- Clarifying the meaning of one's life and death

On September 18, 2007, Carnegie Mellon University computer science professor Randy Pausch, diagnosed with pancreatic cancer, gave his final lecture to a packed house. His message, which focused on achieving one's childhood dreams and enabling the dreams of others, can be viewed at *www.cmu.edu/homepage/multimedia/randy-pausch-lecture.shtml*. He died nine months later, at age 47, having approached his death in a way that suited his pattern of living and deepest values.

- Maintaining and enhancing relationships
- Achieving a sense of control over the time that remains
- Confronting and preparing for death (Goldsteen et al., 2006; Kleespies, 2004; Proulx & Jacelon, 2004)

Research reveals that biological, psychological, and social and cultural forces affect people's coping with dying and, therefore, the extent to which they attain these goals.

Nature of the Disease. The course of the illness and its symptoms affect the dying person's reactions. For example, the extended nature of Sofie's illness and her doctor's initial optimism about achieving a remission undoubtedly contributed to her attempts to try to conquer the disease. During the final month, when cancer had spread to Sofie's lungs and she could not catch her breath, she was agitated and fearful until oxygen and medication relieved her uncertainty about being able to breathe. In contrast, Nicholas's weakened heart and failing kidneys so depleted his strength that he responded only with passivity.

Because of the toll of the disease, about one-third of cancer patients experience severe depression—reactions distinct from the sadness, grief, and worry that typically accompany the dying process. Profound depression amplifies pain, impairs the immune response, interferes with the patient's capacity for pleasure, meaning, and connection, and is associated with poorer survival (Satin, Linden, & Phillips, 2009; Williams & Dale, 2006). It therefore requires immediate treatment. Among the most successful approaches are counselor-led life review (see page 481 in Chapter 18), medical control of pain, and advance care planning with the patient that ensures his or her end-of-life wishes are known and respected (Rosenstein, 2011).

Personality and Coping Style. Understanding the way individuals view stressful life events and have coped with them in the past helps us appreciate the way they manage the dying process. In a study in which terminally ill patients discussed their images of dying, responses varied greatly.

- Beth regarded *dying as imprisonment:* "I felt like the clock started ticking . . . like the future has suddenly been taken. . . . In a way, I feel like I'm already dead."
- To Faith, dying was *a mandate to live ever more fully:* "I have a saying: . . . 'You're not ready to live until you're ready to die.' . . . It never meant much to me until I . . . looked death in the eye, and now I'm living. . . . This life is a lot better than the one before."
- Dawn viewed dying as *part of life's journey:* "I learned all about my disease. . . . I would read, read, read. . . . I wanted to know as much as I can about it, and I don't think hiding . . . behind the door . . . could help me at all. And, I realized for the first time in my life—*really, really, really realized* that I could handle anything."

- Patty approached dying as *an experience to be transformed* so as to make it more bearable: "I am an avid, rabid fan of *Star Trek*, a trekkie like there never has been. . . . I watch it to the point that I've memorized it. . . . [In my mind, I play the various characters so] I'm not [always] thinking about cancer or dying. . . . I think that's how I get through it." (Wright, 2003, pp. 442–444, 447)

Each patient's view of dying helps explain her responses to worsening illness. Poorly adjusted individuals—those with conflict-ridden relationships and many disappointments in life—are usually more distressed (Kastenbaum, 2012).

Family Members' and Health Professionals' Behavior.
Earlier we noted that a candid approach, in which everyone close to and caring for the dying person acknowledges the terminal illness, is best. Yet this also introduces the burden of participating in the work of dying with the patient—bringing relationships to closure, reflecting on life, and dealing with fears and regrets.

People who find it hard to engage in these tasks may pretend that the disease is not as bad as it is. In patients inclined toward denial, a "game" can be set in motion in which participants are aware that the patient is dying but act as though it were not so. Though this game softens psychological pain for the moment, it makes dying much more difficult. Besides impeding communication, it frequently leads to futile medical interventions, in which the patient has little understanding of what is happening and is subjected to great physical and emotional suffering. One attending physician provided this account of a cancer patient's death:

> The problem was that she had a young husband and parents who were pretty much in complete denial. We were trying to be aggressive up to the end. To the point that we actually hung a new form of chemotherapy about four hours before she died, even though everybody knew except her immediate family that she was going to die within the next four to eight hours. (Jackson et al., 2005, p. 653)

When doctors do want to inform patients of their prognosis, they may encounter resistance, especially within certain ethnic groups. Withholding information is common in Southern and Eastern Europe, Central and South America, much of Asia, and the Middle East. Japanese terminally ill cancer patients are seldom told the truth about their condition, partly because dying disrupts important interdependent relationships (Yamamoto, 2004). Many Mexican Americans and Korean Americans believe that informing patients is wrong and will hasten death (Blackhall et al., 1995, 2001). In these instances, providing information is complex. When a family insists that a patient not be told, the doctor can first offer information to the patient and then, if the patient refuses, ask who should receive information and make health-care decisions (Zane & Yeh, 2002). The patient's preference can be honored and reassessed at regular intervals.

A doctor listens patiently to the concerns of a terminally ill 94-year-old. Through sensitive, open communication, health professionals help dying people prepare for death by bringing relationships to closure, reflecting on life, and dealing with fears and regrets.

Social support from family members also affects adaptation to dying. Dying patients who feel they have much unfinished business to attend to are more anxious about impending death. But family contact reduces their sense of urgency to prolong life (Mutran et al., 1997; Zimmerman, 2012). Perhaps it permits patients to work through at least some incomplete tasks.

Effective communication with the dying person is honest, fostering a trusting relationship, yet also oriented toward maintaining hope. Many dying patients move through a hope trajectory—at first, hope for a cure; later, hope for prolonging life; and finally, hope for a peaceful death with as few burdens as possible (Fanslow, 1981). Once patients near death stop expressing hope, those close to them must accept this. Family members who find letting go very difficult may benefit from expert guidance.

Spirituality, Religion, and Culture.
Earlier we noted that a sense of spirituality reduces fear of death. Research indicates that this is as true for the dying as for people in general. Terminally ill patients who score higher in spiritual well-being (belief in life's meaning) experience less end-of-life despair (desire for a hastened death and suicidal thoughts) (McClain, Rosenfeld, & Breitbard, 2003; McClain-Jacobson et al., 2004). Vastly different cultural beliefs, guided by religious ideas, also shape people's dying experiences:

- Buddhism, widely practiced in China, India, and Southeast Asia, fosters acceptance of death. By reading sutras (teachings of Buddha) to the dying person to calm the mind and emphasizing that dying leads to rebirth in a heaven of peace and relaxation, Buddhists believe that it is possible to reach Nirvana, a state beyond the world of suffering (Kubotera, 2004; Yeung, 1996).

- In many Native-American groups, death is met with stoic self-control, an approach taught at an early age through stories that emphasize a circular, rather than linear, relationship between life and death and the importance of making way for others (Cox, 2002).

- For African Americans, a dying loved one signals a crisis that unites family members in caregiving (Crawley et al., 2000; Jenkins et al., 2005). The terminally ill person remains an active and vital force within the family until he or she can no longer carry out this role—an attitude of respect that undoubtedly eases the dying process.

- Among the Maori of New Zealand, relatives and friends gather around the dying person to give spiritual strength and comfort. Older adults, clergy, and other experts in tribal customs conduct a *karakia* ceremony, in which they recite prayers asking for peace, mercy, and guidance from the creator. After the ceremony, the patient is encouraged to discuss important matters with those closest to her—giving away of personal belongings, directions for interment, and completion of other unfinished tasks (Ngata, 2004).

In sum, dying prompts a multitude of thoughts, emotions, and coping strategies. Which ones are emphasized depends on a wide array of contextual influences. A vital assumption of the lifespan perspective—that development is multidimensional and multidirectional—is just as relevant to this final phase as to each earlier period.

A Place to Die

Whereas in the past most deaths occurred at home, in the United States today about 40 percent take place in hospitals and another 20 percent in long-term care facilities, mostly nursing homes (Centers for Disease Control and Prevention, 2013). In the large, impersonal hospital environment, meeting the human needs of dying patients and their families is secondary, not because professionals lack concern, but because the work to be done focuses on saving lives. A dying patient represents a failure.

In the 1960s, a death awareness movement arose as a reaction to hospitals' death-avoiding practices—attachment of complicated machinery to patients with no chance of survival and avoidance of communication with dying patients. This movement soon led to medical care better suited to the needs of dying people and also to hospice programs, which have spread to many countries in the industrialized world. Let's visit each of these settings for dying.

Home

Had Sofie and Nicholas been asked where they wanted to die, undoubtedly each would have responded, "At home"—the preference of 80 to 90 percent of Americans (NHPCO, 2005; O'Connor, 2003). The reason is clear: The home offers an atmo-sphere of intimacy and loving care in which the terminally ill person is unlikely to feel abandoned.

However, only about one-fourth of Americans experience home death (Centers for Disease Control and Prevention, 2013). And it is important not to romanticize dying at home. Because of dramatic improvements in medicine, dying people tend to be sicker or much older than in the past. Consequently, their bodies may be extremely frail, making ordinary activities—eating, sleeping, taking a pill, toileting, and bathing—major ordeals for informal caregivers (Singer et al., 2005).

For many people, the chance to be with the dying person until the very end is a rewarding tradeoff for the high demands of caregiving. But to make dying at home feasible, adequate support for the caregiver is essential (Karlsson & Berggren, 2011; Newbury, 2011). A specially trained home health aide is usually necessary—a service (as we will see shortly) that hospice programs have made more accessible. Still, when family relationships are conflict-ridden, a dying patient introduces additional family strains and is subjected to increased distress, negating the benefits of home death. Furthermore, even with professional help, most homes are poorly equipped to handle the medical and comfort-care needs of the dying. Hospital-based equipment and technical support often must be transported to the home.

For all these reasons, older adults—although they view home as their ideal place to die—express concerns about quality of care, about burdening family and friends, and about the need for adult children to engage in unduly intimate caregiving tasks (Gott et al., 2004). And 10 months after a home death, family members continue to report more psychological stress than do family members whose loved one died elsewhere (Addington-Hall, 2000).

Hospital

Hospital dying takes many forms. Each is affected by the physical state of the dying person, the hospital unit in which it takes place, and the goal and quality of care.

Sudden deaths, due to injury or critical illness, typically occur in emergency rooms. Doctors and nurses must evaluate the problem and take action quickly. Little time is available for contact with family members. When staff break the news of death in a sympathetic manner and provide explanations, family members are grateful. Otherwise, feelings of anger, frustration, and confusion can add to their grief (Walsh & McGoldrick, 2004). Crisis intervention services are needed to help survivors cope with sudden death.

Nicholas died on an intensive care ward focused on preventing death in patients whose condition can worsen quickly. Privacy and communication with the family were secondary to monitoring his condition. To prevent disruption of nurses' activities, Giselle and Sasha could be at Nicholas's side only at scheduled times. Dying in intensive care—an experience unique to technologically sophisticated societies—is especially deper-

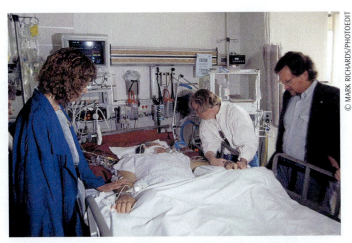

Dying in intensive care is a depersonalizing experience unique to technologically sophisticated societies. In such settings, medical responses supersede privacy and communication with patient and family.

sonalizing for patients like Nicholas, who linger between life and death while hooked to machines often for months.

Cancer patients, who account for most cases of prolonged dying, typically die in general or specialized cancer care hospital units. When hospitalized for a long time, they reach out for help with physical and emotional needs, too often with mixed success. In these settings, as in intensive care, a conflict of values is apparent (Costello, 2006). The tasks associated with dying must be performed efficiently so that all patients can be served and health professionals are not drained emotionally by repeated attachments and separations.

Although hospital comprehensive treatment programs aimed at easing physical, emotional, and spiritual suffering at the end of life have increased steadily over the past decade, one-third of hospitals still do not have them (Center to Advance Palliative Care, 2012). And because just 16 percent of U.S. and Canadian medical schools offer even a single pain-focused course (usually an elective), few doctors and nurses are specially trained in managing pain in chronically ill and dying people (Mezei & Murinson, 2011). At present, many people die in painful, frightening, and depersonalizing hospital conditions, without their wishes being met.

Nursing Home

Though deaths in U.S. nursing homes—mostly elderly patients—are common, care emphasizes rehabilitation rather than high-quality terminal care. The few studies that have addressed what it is like to die in nursing homes concur that many patients suffer from inattention to their emotional and spiritual needs and from high levels of untreated pain (Massachusetts Expert Panel on End of Life Care, 2010).

In one investigation, researchers conducted in-depth interviews with a nationally representative sample of nearly 600 family members whose loved one had spent at least 48 hours

of the final month of life in a nursing home. Respondents frequently mentioned unsatisfactory physical care of the dying patient, difficulty obtaining basic information from staff members on the patient's condition, staff members' lack of compassion and attentiveness to the patient's medical deterioration, and physicians who were "missing in action"—rarely seen in the nursing home (Shield et al., 2010; Wetle et al., 2005). Relatives often felt the need to advocate for their dying relative, though their efforts met with limited success—circumstances that greatly increased both patient and family distress.

The hospice approach—which we consider next—aims to reduce profound caregiving failures in hospitals and nursing homes. When combined with hospice, nursing home care of the dying improves greatly in pain management, emotional and spiritual support, and family satisfaction. But referrals of dying nursing home residents to hospice, though increasing, are often not made—or made too late to be useful (Zheng et al., 2012).

The Hospice Approach

In medieval times, a *hospice* was a place where travelers could find rest and shelter. In the nineteenth and twentieth centuries, the word referred to homes for dying patients. Today, **hospice** is not a place but a comprehensive program of support services for terminally ill people and their families. It aims to provide a caring community sensitive to the dying person's needs so patients and family members can prepare for death in ways that are satisfying to them. Quality of life is central to the hospice approach, which includes these main features:

- The patient and family as a unit of care
- Emphasis on meeting the patient's physical, emotional, social, and spiritual needs, including controlling pain, retaining dignity and self-worth, and feeling cared for and loved

A son and his dying mother share recollections as he shows her a photograph of her long-ago graduation. By creating opportunities for unpressured closeness and connection, hospice care enhances dying patients' quality of life rather than extending life.

Biology and Environment

Music as Palliative Care for Dying Patients

When Peter visits 82-year-old Stuart to play the harp, Stuart reports being transported to an idyllic place with water, children, and trees—far from the lung tumors that will soon take his life. "When Peter plays for me, . . . I am no longer frightened," Stuart says.

Peter is a specialist in *music thanatology,* an emerging specialty in music therapy that focuses on providing palliative care to the dying through music. He uses his harp, and sometimes his voice, to induce calm and give solace to the dying, their families, and their caregivers. Peter applies music systematically—matching it to each patient's breathing patterns and other responses, delivering different sounds to uplift or comfort, depending on his assessment of the patient's moment-by-moment needs.

Chaplains and counselors informally report that after music vigils, patients' conversations indicate that they more easily come to terms with their own death (Fyfe,

2006). And in a study of 65 dying patients in which pre- and post-intervention physiological measures were compared, music vigils averaging an hour in length resulted in decreased agitation and wakefulness and slower, deeper, less effortful breathing (Freeman et al., 2006). These physiological benefits extended to patients who, on the basis of their behavior, were clearly in pain.

Why is music effective in easing the distress of those who are dying? In patients close to death, hearing typically functions longer than other senses. Thus, responsiveness to music may persist until the individual's final moments. Besides reducing anxiety, music

LYNN JOHNSON. *A SONG FOR THE DYING.* 1994. LYNN JOHNSON COLLECTION. MAHN CENTER FOR ARCHIVES AND SPECIAL COLLECTIONS, OHIO UNIVERSITY LIBRARIES.

Music thanatology focuses on providing palliative care for the dying through music. This practitioner uses her harp, and sometimes her voice, to induce calm and provide solace.

can, in some instances, enhance the effects of medication administered to control pain (Starr, 1999). For these reasons, music vigils may be an especially effective end-of-life therapy.

- Care provided by an interdisciplinary team: a doctor, a nurse or home health aide, a chaplain, a counselor or social worker, and a trained volunteer

- The patient kept at home or in an inpatient setting with a homelike atmosphere where coordination of care is possible

- Focus on protecting the quality of remaining life with **palliative,** or **comfort, care** that relieves pain and other symptoms (nausea, breathing difficulties, insomnia, and depression) rather than prolonging life

- In addition to regularly scheduled home care visits, on-call services available 24 hours a day, 7 days a week

- Follow-up bereavement services offered to families in the year after a death

Hospice programs everywhere encompass a continuum of care, from home to inpatient options, including hospitals and nursing homes. Central to the hospice approach is that the dying person and his or her family be offered choices that guarantee an appropriate death. Some programs offer hospice day care, which enables caregivers to continue working or be relieved of

the stresses of long-term care (Kernohan et al., 2006). Contact with others facing terminal illness is a supportive byproduct of many hospice arrangements. And to find out about a comforting musical intervention for patients near death, consult the Biology and Environment box above.

LOOK AND LISTEN

Contact a nearby hospice program, and find out about the varied ways it delivers comprehensive services to meet the needs of dying patients and their families. ●

Currently, the United States has over 5,300 hospice programs serving approximately 1.6 million terminally ill patients annually (NHPCO, 2012). Because hospice care is a cost-effective alternative to expensive life-saving treatments, U.S. government health-care benefits (Medicare and Medicaid) cover it, as do most private insurance plans. In addition, community and foundation contributions allow many hospices to provide free services to uninsured patients who cannot pay (Hospice Foundation of America, 2013). Consequently hospice is affordable for most dying patients and their families. Hospices also serve dying children—a tragedy so devastating that social support and bereavement intervention are vital.

Besides reducing patient physical suffering, hospice contributes to improved family functioning. The majority of patients and families report high satisfaction with quality of care and pain management, enhanced sense of social support, and (in the case of home hospice) increased ability to sustain patient care at home (Candy et al., 2011). In one study, family members experiencing hospice scored higher than nonhospice family members in psychological well-being one to two years after their loved one's death (Ragow-O'Brien, Hayslip, & Guarnaccia, 2000).

As a long-range goal, hospice organizations are striving for broader acceptance of their patient- and family-centered approach. Culturally sensitive approaches are needed to reach more ethnic minority patients, who are far less likely than white patients to participate in hospice (NHPCO, 2012). In developing countries, where millions die of cancer and other devastating illnesses each year, community-based teams working under a nurse's supervision sometimes deliver palliative care. But they face many obstacles, including lack of funding, pain-relieving drugs, and professional and public education about hospice (Ddungu, 2011).

ASK YOURSELF

REVIEW Why is the stage notion an inaccurate account of dying patients' mental and emotional reactions?

APPLY When 5-year-old Timmy's kidney failure was diagnosed as terminal, his parents could not accept the tragic news. Their hospital visits became shorter, and they evaded his anxious questions. Eventually, Timmy blamed himself. He died with little physical pain, but alone, and his parents suffered prolonged guilt. How could hospice care have helped Timmy and his family?

REFLECT If you were terminally ill, where would you want to die? Explain.

The Right to Die

In 1990, 26-year-old Terri Schiavo's heart stopped briefly, temporarily cutting off oxygen to her brain. Terri lay in a persistent vegetative state. Her husband and guardian, Michael, claimed that she had earlier told him she would not want to be kept alive artificially, but Terri's parents disagreed. In 1998, the Florida Circuit Court granted Michael's petition to have Terri's feeding tube removed. In 2001, after her parents had exhausted their appeals, the tube was taken out. But on the basis of contradic-

tory medical testimony, Terri's parents convinced a circuit court judge to order the feeding tube reinserted, and the legal wrangling continued. In 2002, Michael won a second judgment to remove the tube.

By that time, publicity over the case and its central question—who should make end-of-life decisions when the patient's wishes are unclear—had made Terri a political issue. In 2003, the Florida legislature passed a law allowing the governor to stay the circuit court's order to keep Terri alive, but on appeal, the law was declared unconstitutional. In 2005, the U.S. Congress entered the fray, passing a bill that transferred Terri's fate to the U.S. District Court. When the judge refused to intervene, the feeding tube was removed for a third time. In 2005—15 years after losing consciousness—Terri Schiavo died. The autopsy confirmed the original persistent vegetative state diagnosis: Her brain was half normal size.

The Schiavo case—and others like it—have brought right-to-die issues to the forefront of public attention. Today, all U.S. states have laws that honor patients' wishes concerning withdrawal of treatment in cases of terminal illness and, sometimes, in cases of a persistent vegetative state. But no uniform right-to-die policy exists, and heated controversy persists over how to handle the diverse circumstances in which patients and family members make requests.

Euthanasia is the practice of ending the life of a person suffering from an incurable condition. Its various forms are summarized in Table 19.1. As we will see, public acceptance of euthanasia is high, except when it involves ending the life of an anguished, terminally ill patient without his or her expressed permission.

TABLE 19.1 Forms of Euthanasia

FORM	DESCRIPTION
Passive euthanasia	At the patient's request, the doctor withholds or withdraws treatment, thereby permitting the patient to die naturally. For example, the doctor does not perform surgery or administer medication that could prolong life, or the doctor turns off the respirator of a patient who cannot breathe independently.
Voluntary active euthanasia	The doctor ends a suffering patient's life at the patient's request. For example, the doctor administers a lethal dose of drugs.
Assisted suicide	The doctor helps a suffering patient take his or her own life. For example, the doctor enables the patient to swallow or inject a lethal dose of drugs.
Involuntary active euthanasia	The doctor ends a suffering patient's life without the patient's permission. For example, without obtaining the patient's consent, the doctor administers a lethal dose of drugs.

Passive Euthanasia

In **passive euthanasia**, life-sustaining treatment is withheld or withdrawn, permitting a patient to die naturally. **TAKE A MOMENT...** Do you think Terri Schiavo should have been allowed to die sooner? Was it right for Nicholas's doctors to turn off his respirator at Giselle's request? When an Alzheimer's victim has lost all awareness and bodily functions, should life support be withheld?

In recent polls, more 70 percent of U.S. adults and 95 percent of physicians supported the right of patients or family members to end treatment when there is no hope of recovery (Curlin et al., 2008; Pew Research Center, 2006). In 1986, the American Medical Association endorsed withdrawing all forms of treatment from the terminally ill when death is imminent and from those in a permanent vegetative state. Consequently, passive euthanasia is widely practiced as part of ordinary medical procedure, in which doctors exercise professional judgment.

Still, a minority of citizens oppose passive euthanasia. Religious denomination has surprisingly little effect on people's opinions. For example, most Catholics hold favorable views, despite slow official church acceptance because of fears that passive euthanasia might be a first step toward government-approved mercy killing. However, ethnicity makes a difference: Nearly twice as many African Americans as Caucasian Americans desire all medical means possible, regardless of the patient's condition, and African Americans more often receive life-sustaining intervention, such as feeding tubes (Haley, 2013; Johnson et al., 2008). Their reluctance to forgo treatment reflects strong cultural and religious beliefs in overcoming adversity and in the power of God to promote healing (Johnson, Elbert-Avila, & Tulsky, 2005).

Because of controversial court cases like Terri Schiavo's, some doctors and health-care institutions are unwilling to end treatment without legal protection. In the absence of national consensus on passive euthanasia, people can best ensure that their wishes will be followed by preparing an **advance medical directive**—a written statement of desired medical treatment should they become incurably ill. U.S. states recognize two types of advance directives: a *living will* and a *durable power of attorney for health care* (U.S. Living Will Registry, 2005). Sometimes these are combined into one document.

In a **living will,** people specify the treatments they do or do not want in case of a terminal illness, coma, or other near-death situation. For example, a person might state that without reasonable expectation of recovery, he or she should not be kept alive through medical intervention of any kind. In addition, a living will sometimes specifies that pain-relieving medication be given, even though it might shorten life. In Sofie's case, her doctor administered a powerful narcotic to relieve labored breathing and quiet her fear of suffocation. The narcotic suppressed respiration, causing death to occur hours or days earlier than if the medication had not been prescribed, but without distress. Such palliative care is accepted as appropriate and ethical medical practice.

This couple discusses a durable power of attorney with a hospital chaplain. This advance directive authorizes a trusted spokesperson to make health-care decisions and helps ensure that one's desires will be granted.

Although living wills help ensure personal control, they do not guarantee it. Recognition of living wills is usually limited to patients who are terminally ill or are otherwise expected to die shortly. Only a few U.S. states cover people in a persistent vegetative state or aging adults who linger with many chronic problems, including Alzheimer's disease, because these conditions are not classified as terminal. Even when terminally ill patients have living wills, doctors sometimes do not follow them for a variety of reasons (van Asselt, 2006). These include fear of lawsuits, their own moral beliefs, failure to inquire about patients' directives, and inaccessibility of those directives—for example, located in the family safe or family members unaware of them.

Because living wills cannot anticipate all future medical conditions and can easily be ignored, a second form of advance directive has become common. The **durable power of attorney for health care** authorizes appointment of another person (usually, though not always, a family member) to make health-care decisions on one's behalf. It is more flexible than the living will because it permits a trusted spokesperson to confer with the doctor as medical circumstances arise. Because authority to speak for the patient is not limited to terminal illnesses, more latitude exists for dealing with unexpected situations. And in gay and lesbian and other close relationships not sanctioned by law, the durable power of attorney can ensure the partner's role in decision making and in advocating for the patient's health-care needs.

Whether or not a person supports passive euthanasia, it is important to have a living will, durable power of attorney, or both, because most deaths occur in hospitals or nursing homes. Yet only about 30 percent of Americans have executed such documents, perhaps because of widespread uneasiness about bringing up the topic of death, especially with relatives (Harris Interactive, 2011; Pew Research Center, 2006). The percentage with advance directives does increase with age; almost two-thirds of adults over age 65 have them. To encourage people to make decisions about potential treatment while they are able, U.S. federal law now requires that all medical facilities receiving federal funds provide information at admission about state laws and institutional policies on patients' rights and advance directives.

As happened with Terri Schiavo, health-care professionals—unclear about a patient's intent and fearing liability—will probably decide to continue treatment regardless of cost and a person's prior oral statements. Perhaps for this reason, some U.S. states permit appointment of a health-care proxy, or substitute decision maker, if a patient failed to provide an advance medical directive while competent. Proxies are an important means of covering children and adolescents, who cannot legally execute advance medical directives.

Voluntary Active Euthanasia

In recent years, the right-to-die debate has shifted from withdrawal of treatment for the hopelessly ill to more active alternatives. In **voluntary active euthanasia,** doctors or others act directly, at a patient's request, to end suffering before a natural end to life. The practice, a form of mercy killing, is a criminal offense in most countries, including almost all U.S. states. But support for voluntary active euthanasia has grown. As Figure 19.2 shows, about 70 to 90 percent of people in Western nations approve of it (World Federation of Right to Die Societies, 2006). When doctors engage in voluntary active euthanasia, judges are

usually lenient, granting suspended sentences or probation—a trend reflecting rising public interest in self-determination in death as in life.

Nevertheless, attempts to legalize voluntary active euthanasia have prompted heated controversy. Supporters believe it represents the most compassionate option for terminally ill people in severe pain. Opponents stress the moral difference between "letting die" and "killing" and point out that at times, even very sick patients recover. They also argue that involving doctors in taking the lives of suffering patients may impair people's trust in health professionals. Finally, a fear exists that legalizing this practice—even when strictly monitored to make sure it does not arise out of depression, loneliness, coercion, or a desire to diminish the burden of illness on others—could lead to a broadening of euthanasia. Initially limited to the terminally ill, it might be applied involuntarily to the frail, demented, or disabled—outcomes that most people find unacceptable and immoral. These concerns are warranted, as events in the Netherlands—where voluntary active euthanasia has been practiced for several decades and became legal in 2002—make clear. Dutch doctors are allowed to engage in it under the following conditions: when physical or mental suffering is severe, with no prospect of relief; when no doubt exists about the patient's desire to die; when the patient's decision is voluntary, well-informed, and stable over time; when all other options for care have been exhausted or refused; and when another doctor has been consulted. But despite these safeguards, some doctors admit to having actively caused a death when a patient did not ask for it (Rurup et al., 2005; von Tol, Rietjens, & van der Heide, 2010). They defend their actions by referring to the impossibility of treating pain, a low quality of life, or drawn-out dying in a patient near death. A small minority say they granted the euthanasia requests of physically healthy patients—usually older people who felt "weary of life."

Nevertheless, terminally ill individuals in severe pain continue to plead for legalization of voluntary active euthanasia. Probably all would agree that when doctors feel compelled to relieve suffering and honor self-determination by assisting a patient in dying, they should be subject to the most stringent monitoring possible.

Assisted Suicide

After checking Diane's blood count, Dr. Timothy Quill gently broke the news: leukemia. If she were to have any hope of survival, a strenuous course of treatment with only a 25 percent success rate would have to begin immediately. Convinced that she would suffer unspeakably from side effects and lack of control over her body, Diane chose not to undergo chemotherapy and a bone marrow transplant.

Dr. Quill made sure that Diane understood her options. As he adjusted to her decision, Diane raised another issue: She calmly insisted that when the time came, she desired to take her own life in the least painful way possible—a choice she had discussed with her husband and son, who respected it. Realizing that Diane could get the most out of the time she had left only

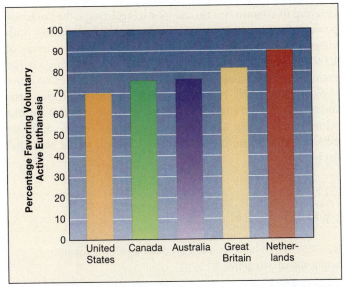

FIGURE 19.2 Public opinion favoring voluntary active euthanasia in five nations. A struggle exists between public opinion, which has increasingly favored voluntary active euthanasia over the past 30 years, and legal statutes, which prohibit it. The majority of people in Western nations believe that a hopelessly ill, suffering patient who asks for a lethal injection should be granted that request. Public support for voluntary active euthanasia is highest in the Netherlands—the only nation in the world where the practice is legal under certain conditions. (From Harris Interactive, 2011; Pew Research Center, 2006.)

In a prestigious medical journal, Dr. Timothy Quill explained how and why he aided a terminally ill patient in taking her own life. Doctor-assisted suicide is legal in the states of Oregon, Washington, Montana, and Vermont and in several Western European countries.

if her fears of prolonged pain were allayed, Dr. Quill granted her request for sleeping pills, making sure she knew the amounts needed for both sleep and suicide.

Diane's next few months were busy and fulfilling. Her son took leave from college to be with her, and her husband worked at home as much as possible. Gradually, bone pain, fatigue, and fever set in. Saying goodbye to her family and friends, Diane asked to be alone for an hour, took a lethal dose of medication, and died at home (Quill, 1991).

Assisting a suicide is illegal in Canada and in most, but not all, U.S. states. In Western Europe, doctor-assisted suicide is legal in Belgium, the Netherlands, Luxembourg, and Switzerland and is tacitly accepted in many other countries. In the United States, Oregon's 1997 Death with Dignity Act explicitly allows physicians to prescribe drugs so terminally ill patients can end their lives. To get a prescription, patients must have two doctors agree that they have less than six months to live and must request the drugs at least twice, with an interval of at least 15 days. In January 2006, the U.S. Supreme Court rejected a challenge to the Oregon law, but the Court has also upheld the right of other states to ban assisted suicide. In 2008, the state of Washington passed legislation—similar to Oregon's—permitting assisted suicide. In 2013, the Montana and Vermont legislatures also legalized the practice.

Nearly 60 percent of Americans approve of assisted suicide for terminally ill patients in great pain (Harris Interactive, 2011). In a review of studies carried out in the United States, Canada, and Western Europe, level of support among terminally ill patients was about the same as for the general public, with about one-third of patients saying they would consider it for themselves in particular circumstances (Hendry et al., 2012). In Oregon, assisted suicide accounts for only one-fifth of 1 percent of deaths (Oregon Public Health Division, 2013). But thousands of Oregonians say they find comfort in knowing the option is available (Hedberg et al., 2009).

Public interest in assisted suicide was sparked in the 1990s by Dr. Jack Kevorkian, a vigorous proponent of euthanasia who devised "suicide machines" that permitted more than 100 terminally ill patients, after brief counseling, to self-administer lethal drugs and carbon monoxide. Less publicity surrounded Dr. Quill's decision to assist Diane—a patient he knew well after serving for years as her personal doctor. After he told her story in a prestigious medical journal, reactions were mixed, as they are toward assisted suicide in general. Some view doctors who help suffering people who want to die as compassionate and respectful of patients' personal choices. Others oppose assisted suicide on religious and moral grounds or believe that the role of doctors should be limited to saving, not taking, lives.

Like euthanasia, assisted suicide poses grave dilemmas. Juries have seldom returned guilty verdicts in cases involving doctor-assisted suicide. Yet in April 1999, Kevorkian—after giving a terminally ill man a lethal injection, videotaping the death, and permitting the event to be broadcast on the CBS television program *60 Minutes*—was convicted of second-degree murder and served 8 years of a 10- to 25-year sentence. The murder indictment prevented Kevorkian from introducing evidence indicating that the man wanted to kill himself—evidence that would have been permissible had the charge been assisted suicide or voluntary active euthanasia.

Public opinion consistently favors voluntary active euthanasia over assisted suicide. Yet in assisted suicide, the final act is solely the patient's, reducing the possibility of coercion. For this reason, some experts believe that legalizing assisted suicide is preferable to legalizing voluntary active euthanasia. However, in an atmosphere of high family caregiving burdens and intense pressure to contain health-care costs, legalizing either practice poses risks. The American Medical Association opposes both voluntary active euthanasia and assisted suicide. In a survey of 1,140 U.S. doctors, only 18 percent objected to sedating a dying patient to unconsciousness if pain can be controlled in no other way, whereas nearly 70 percent opposed assisted suicide—attitudes resembling those of physicians in other Western nations (Curlin et al., 2008; Seale, 2009). Helping incurable, suffering patients who yearn for death poses profound moral and legal problems.

ASK YOURSELF

REVIEW What benefits and risks does legalizing voluntary active euthanasia pose?

APPLY Ramón is certain that, if he ever became terminally ill, he would want doctors to halt life-saving treatment. To best ensure that his wish will be granted, what should Ramón do?

REFLECT Do you approve of passive euthanasia, voluntary active euthanasia, or assisted suicide? If you were terminally ill, would you consider any of these practices? Explain.

Bereavement: Coping with the Death of a Loved One

Loss is an inevitable part of existence throughout the lifespan. Even when change is for the better, we must let go of some aspects of experience so we can embrace others. In this way, our development prepares us for profound loss.

Bereavement is the experience of losing a loved one by death. The root of this word means "to be robbed," suggesting unjust and injurious theft of something valuable. Consistent with this image, we respond to loss with **grief**—intense physical and psychological distress. When we say someone is grief-stricken, we imply that his or her total way of being is affected.

Because grief can be overwhelming, cultures have devised ways of helping their members move beyond it to deal with the life changes demanded by death of a loved one. **Mourning** is the culturally specified expression of the bereaved person's thoughts and feelings. Customs—such as gathering with family and friends, dressing in black, attending the funeral, and observing a prescribed mourning period with special rituals—vary greatly among societies and ethnic groups. But all have in common the goal of helping people work through their grief and learn to live in a world that does not include the deceased.

Clearly, grief and mourning are closely linked—in everyday language, we often use the two words interchangeably. Let's look closely at how people respond to the death of a loved one.

Grief Process

Theorists formerly believed that bereaved individuals—both children and adults—moved through three phases of grieving, each characterized by a different set of responses (Bowlby, 1980; Rando, 1995). In reality, however, people vary greatly in behavior and timing and often move back and forth between these reactions. A more accurate account compares grief to a roller-coaster ride, with many ups and downs and, over time, gradual resolution (Lund, 1996). Rather than phases, the grieving process can be conceived as a set of *tasks*—actions the person must take to recover and return to a fulfilling life: (1) to accept the reality of the loss; (2) to work through the pain of grief; (3) to adjust to a world without the loved one; and (4) to develop an inner bond with the deceased and move on with life (Worden, 2009). According to this view, people can take active steps to overcome grief—a powerful remedy for the overwhelming feelings of vulnerability that the bereaved often experience.

Avoidance. On hearing the news, the survivor experiences shock followed by disbelief, which may last from hours to weeks. A numbed feeling serves as "emotional anesthesia" while the person begins the first task of grieving: becoming painfully aware of the loss.

Confrontation. As the mourner confronts the reality of the death, grief is most intense. The person often experiences a cascade of emotional reactions, including anxiety, sadness, protest, anger, helplessness, frustration, abandonment, and yearning for the loved one. Common responses include obsessively reviewing the circumstances of death, asking how it might have been prevented, and searching for meaning in it (Neimeyer, 2001). In addition, the grief-stricken person may be absent-minded, unable to concentrate, and preoccupied with thoughts of the deceased, and may experience loss of sleep and appetite. Self-destructive behaviors, such as taking drugs or driving too fast, may occur. Most of these responses are symptoms of depression—an invariable component of grieving.

Although confrontation is difficult, it enables the mourner to grapple with the second task: working through the pain of grief. Each surge of anguish brings the mourner closer to acceptance that the loved one is gone. As a result, the mourner makes progress on the third task: adjusting to a world in which the deceased is missing.

Restoration. Bereaved individuals must also deal with stressors that are secondary outcomes of the death—overcoming loneliness by reaching out to others; mastering skills (such as finances or cooking) that the deceased had performed; reorganizing daily life without the loved one; and revising one's identity from "spouse" to "widow" or from "parent" to "parent of a deceased child."

According to a recent perspective, called the **dual-process model of coping with loss**, effective coping requires people to oscillate between dealing with the emotional consequences of loss and attending to life changes, which—when handled successfully—have restorative, or healing, effects (Hansson & Stroebe, 2007; Stroebe & Schut, 1999, 2010). Much research indicates that confronting grief without relief has severe negative consequences for physical and mental health (Corr & Corr, 2007). Consistent with the dual-process model, in a study that assessed widowed older adults at 6, 18, and 48 months after the death of their spouses, both loss-oriented and restoration-oriented activities occurred throughout bereavement. As predicted, restoration-oriented activities—such as visiting friends, attending religious services, and volunteering—reduced the stress of grieving (Richardson, 2007). Using the dual-process approach, one 14-session intervention for older adults grieving the loss of a spouse addresses both emotional and life-change issues, alternating between them (Lund et al., 2004, 2010).

As grief subsides, emotional energies increasingly shift toward the fourth task—forging a symbolic bond with the deceased and moving on with life by meeting everyday responsibilities, investing in new activities and goals, strengthening old ties, and building new relationships. On certain days, such as family celebrations or the anniversary of death, grief reactions may resurface and require attention, but they do not interfere with a healthy, positive approach to life.

In fact, throughout the grieving process, individuals report experiencing positive as well as negative emotions, with expressions of happiness and humor aiding in coping with grief (Ong, Bergeman, & Bisconti, 2004). In an investigation of several hundred people age 50 and older whose spouse or partner had died within the previous six months, 90 percent agreed that "feeling happy" and "having humor" in daily life are important, and more than 75 percent said they had experienced humor, laughter, or happiness during the past week. The greater participants' valuing and experience of positive emotion, the better their bereavement adjustment, as indicated by reduced levels of grief and depression (Lund et al., 2008–2009). Expressions of happiness can be viewed as a restoration-oriented activity, offering distraction from grieving and strengthening bonds with others.

How long does grieving last? There is no single answer. Sometimes confrontation continues for a few months, at other times for several years. An occasional upsurge of grief may persist for a lifetime and is a common response to losing a much-loved spouse, partner, child, or friend.

Personal and Situational Variations

Like dying, grieving is affected by many factors, including personality, coping style, and religious and cultural background. Sex differences are also evident. Compared with women, men typically express distress and depression less directly and seek social support less readily—factors that may contribute to the much higher mortality rate among bereaved men than women (Doka & Martin, 2010; Lund & Caserta, 2004b; McGoldrick, 2004).

Furthermore, the quality of the mourner's relationship with the deceased is important. An end to a loving, fulfilling bond leads to more anguished grieving, but it is less likely to leave a long-term residue of anger, guilt, and regret than the dissolution of a conflict-ridden, ambivalent tie (Abakoumkin, Stroebe, & Stroebe, 2010; Mikulincer & Shaver, 2008). And end-of-life care makes a difference: Widowed older adults whose spouses experienced a painful death reported more anxiety, intrusive thoughts, and yearning for the loved one six months later (Carr, 2003).

Circumstances surrounding the death—whether it is sudden and unanticipated or follows a prolonged illness—also shape mourners' responses. The nature of the lost relationship and the timing of the death within the life course make a difference as well.

Sudden, Unanticipated Deaths versus Prolonged, Expected Deaths.
In instances of sudden, unexpected deaths—usually the result of murder, suicide, war, accident, or natural disaster—avoidance may be especially pronounced and confrontation highly traumatic because shock and disbelief are extreme. In contrast, during prolonged dying, the bereaved person has had time to engage in **anticipatory grieving—** acknowledging that the loss is inevitable and preparing emotionally for it. Survivors may feel less overwhelmed immediately following the death (Johansson & Grimby, 2013). But they may

display more persistent anxiety due to long-term stressors, such as highly demanding caregiving and having watched a loved one suffer from a debilitating illness (Carr et al., 2001).

Adjusting to a sudden death is easier when the survivor understands the reasons for it. This barrier to confronting loss is tragically apparent in cases of sudden infant death syndrome (SIDS), in which doctors cannot tell parents exactly why their apparently healthy baby died (see Chapter 3, page 84). That death seems "senseless" also complicates grieving after suicides, terrorist attacks, school and drive-by shootings, and natural disasters. In Western societies, people tend to believe that momentous events should be comprehensible and non-random (Lukas & Seiden, 2007). A death that is sudden and unexpected can threaten basic assumptions about a just, benevolent, and controllable world.

Suicide, particularly that of a young person, is especially hard to bear. Compared with survivors of other sudden deaths, people grieving a suicidal loss are more likely to conclude that they contributed to or could have prevented it—self-blame that can trigger profound guilt and shame. These reactions are likely to be especially intense and persisting when a mourner's culture or religion condemns suicide as immoral (Dunne & Dunne-Maxim, 2004). Typically, recovery from grief after a suicide is prolonged.

Parents Grieving the Loss of a Child.
The death of a child, whether unexpected or foreseen, is the most difficult loss an adult can face (Dent & Stewart, 2004). Children are extensions of parents' feelings about themselves—the focus of hopes and dreams, including parents' sense of immortality. Also, because children depend on, admire, and appreciate their parents in a deeply gratifying way, they are an unmatched source

A father weeps while holding the body of his son, killed during the Syrian armed conflict in 2012. The death of a child, whether unexpected or foreseen, is the most difficult loss an adult can face.

of love. Finally, the death of a child is unnatural: Children are not supposed to die before their parents. Parents who have lost a child often report considerable distress many years later, along with frequent thoughts of the deceased.

If parents can reestablish a sense of life's meaning through valuing the lost child's impact on their lives and investing in other children and activities, then the result can be firmer family commitments and personal growth. The process, which often takes years, is associated with improved physical and mental health and gains in marital satisfaction (Murphy, 2008; Price et al., 2011). Five years after her son's death, one parent reflected on her progress:

> I was afraid to let go [of my pain, which was] a way of loving him. . . . Finally I had to admit that his life meant more than pain, it also meant joy and happiness and fun—and living. . . . When we release pain we make room for happiness in our lives. My memories of S. became lighter and more spontaneous. Instead of hurtful, my memories brought comfort, even a chuckle. . . . realized S. was still teaching me things. (Klass, 2004, p. 87)

Children and Adolescents Grieving the Loss of a Parent or Sibling.

The loss of an attachment figure has long-term consequences for children. When a parent dies, children's basic sense of security and being cared for is threatened. And the death of a sibling not only deprives children of a close emotional tie but also informs them, often for the first time, of their own vulnerability.

Children grieving a family loss describe frequent crying, trouble concentrating in school, sleep difficulties, headaches, and other physical symptoms several months to years after a death. And clinical studies reveal that persistent depression, anxiety, angry outbursts, social withdrawal, loneliness, and worries about dying themselves are common (Luecken, 2008; Marshall & Davies, 2011). At the same time, many children say they have actively maintained mental contact with their dead parent or sibling, dreaming about and speaking to them frequently (Silverman & Nickman, 1996). These images, reported by bereaved adults as well, seem to facilitate coping with loss.

Cognitive development contributes to the ability to grieve. Children with an immature understanding of death may believe the dead parent left voluntarily, perhaps in anger, and that the other parent may also disappear. For these reasons, young children need careful, repeated explanations assuring them that the parent did not want to die and was not angry at them (Christ, Siegel, & Christ, 2002). Keeping the truth from children isolates them and often leads to profound regrets. One 8-year-old who learned only a half-hour in advance that his sick brother was dying reflected, "If only I'd known, I could have said goodbye."

Regardless of children's level of understanding, honesty, affection, and reassurance help them tolerate painful feelings of loss. Grief-stricken school-age children are usually more willing than adolescents to confide in parents. To appear normal, teenagers tend to keep their grieving from both adults and peers. Consequently, they are more likely than children to

become depressed or to escape from grief through acting-out behavior (Granot, 2005). Overall, effective parenting—warmth combined with rational discipline—fosters adaptive coping and positive long-term adjustment in both children and adolescents (Luecken, 2008).

Adults Grieving the Loss of an Intimate Partner.

Recall from Chapter 18 that after the death of a spouse, adaptation to widowhood varies greatly, with age, social support, and personality making a difference. After a period of intense grieving, most widowed older adults in Western nations fare well, while younger individuals display more negative outcomes (see page 494 to review). Older widows and widowers have many more contemporaries in similar circumstances. And most have already attained important life goals or adjusted to the fact that some goals will not be attained.

In contrast, loss of a spouse or partner in early or middle adulthood is a nonnormative event that profoundly disrupts life plans. Interviews with a large, U.S. nationally representative sample of adults who had been widowed from less than 1 to 64 years previously (typically in middle adulthood) revealed that thoughts about and conversations with the lost spouse occurred often in the first few years, then declined gradually (Carnelley et al., 2006). But they did not reach their lowest level for several decades, when the typical respondent still thought about the deceased partner once every week or two and conversed with him or her about once a month.

In addition to dealing with feelings of loss, young and middle-aged widows and widowers often must assume a greater role in comforting others, especially children. They also face the stresses of single parenthood and rapid shrinking of the social network established during their life as a couple. The death of an intimate partner in a gay or lesbian relationship presents unique challenges. When relatives limit or bar the partner from participating in funeral services, the survivor experiences *disenfranchised grief*—a sense of loss without the opportunity to mourn publicly and benefit from others' support—which can profoundly disrupt the grieving process (Doka, 2008). Fortunately, gay and lesbian communities provide helpful alternative support in the form of memorial services and other rituals.

Bereavement Overload.

When a person experiences several deaths at once or in close succession, bereavement overload can occur. Multiple losses deplete the coping resources of even well-adjusted people, leaving them emotionally overwhelmed and unable to resolve their grief (Lattanzi-Licht & Doka, 2003).

Because old age often brings the death of spouse, siblings, and friends in close succession, aging adults are at risk for bereavement overload (Kastenbaum, 2008). But recall from Chapter 18 that compared with young people, older adults are often better equipped to handle these losses.

Public tragedies—terrorist attacks, natural disasters, random murders in schools, or widely publicized kidnappings—can

Applying **What We Know**

Suggestions for Resolving Grief After a Loved One Dies

Suggestion	Description
Give yourself permission to feel the loss.	Permit yourself to confront all thoughts and emotions associated with the death. Make a conscious decision to overcome your grief, recognizing that this will take time.
Accept social support.	In the early part of grieving, let others reach out to you by making meals, running errands, and keeping you company. Be assertive; ask for what you need so people who would like to help will know what to do.
Be realistic about the course of grieving.	Expect to have some negative and intense reactions, such as feeling anguished, sad, and angry, that last from weeks to months and may occasionally resurface years after the death. There is no one way to grieve, so find the best way for you.
Remember the deceased.	Review your relationship to and experiences with the deceased, permitting yourself to see that you can no longer be with him or her as before. Form a new bond based on memories, keeping it alive through photographs, commemorative donations, prayers, and other symbols and actions.
When ready, invest in new activities and relationships, and master new tasks of daily living.	Identify which roles you must give up and which ones you must assume as a consequence of the death, and take deliberate steps to modify daily life accordingly. Set small goals at first, such as a night at the movies, a dinner date with a friend, a cooking or household repair class, or a week's vacation.

spark bereavement overload (Rynearson & Salloum, 2011). Many survivors who lost loved ones, co-workers, or friends in the September 11, 2001, terrorist attacks (including an estimated 3,000 children who lost a parent) experienced repeated images of horror and destruction, which impeded coming to terms with loss. The greater the bereaved individual's exposure to the catastrophic death scene, the more severe these reactions.

Funerals and other bereavement rituals, illustrated in the Cultural Influences box on the following page, assist mourners of all ages in resolving grief with the help of family and friends.

Villagers in Sichuan Province, China, grieve for relatives who died in a massive earthquake in 2013 that left nearly 200 dead. Public tragedies can spark bereavement overload, leaving mourners at risk for prolonged, overwhelming grief.

Bereaved individuals who remain preoccupied with loss and who have difficulty resuming interest in everyday activities benefit from special interventions designed to help them adjust.

Bereavement Interventions

Sympathy and understanding are sufficient to enable most people to undertake the tasks necessary to recover from grief (see Applying What We Know above). Yet effective support is often difficult to provide, and relatives and friends can benefit from training in how to respond. Sometimes they give advice aimed at hastening recovery or ask questions aimed at managing their own anxiety ("Were you expecting him to die?" Was she in a lot of pain?")—approaches that most bereaved people dislike (Kastenbaum, 2012). Listening patiently and assuring the bereaved of "being there" for them—"I'm here if you need to talk," "Let me know what I can do"—are among the best ways to help.

Bereavement interventions typically encourage people to draw on their existing social network, while providing additional social support through group or individual counseling. Controversy exists over whether grief counseling benefits most bereaved people, or whether it helps only those experiencing profound difficulties (CFAH, 2003; Jordan & Neimeyer, 2003). One analysis of research expressed optimism about broadly favorable effects (Larson & Hoyt, 2007). Furthermore, evidence is mounting that bereaved adults who struggle with and surmount challenges and losses often experience stress-related personal growth, including greater awareness of their own strengths, enhanced appreciation of close relationships, and new spiritual insights (Calhoun et al., 2010).

Cultural Influences

Cultural Variations in Mourning Behavior

The ceremonies that commemorated Sofie's and Nicholas's deaths—the first Jewish, the second Quaker—were strikingly different. Yet they served common goals: announcing that a death had occurred, ensuring social support, commemorating the deceased, and conveying a philosophy of life after death.

At the funeral home, Sofie's body was washed and shrouded, a Jewish ritual signifying return to a state of purity. Then it was placed in a plain wooden (not metal) coffin, so as not to impede the natural process of decomposition. To underscore the finality of death, Jewish tradition does not permit viewing of the body; it remains in a closed coffin. Traditionally, the coffin is not left alone until burial; in honor of the deceased, the community maintains a day-and-night vigil.

To return the body quickly to the life-giving earth from which it sprang, Sofie's funeral was scheduled as soon as relatives could gather—just three days after death. Sofie's husband and children symbolized their anguish by cutting a black ribbon and pinning it to their clothing. The rabbi recited psalms of comfort, followed by a eulogy. The service continued at the graveside. Once the coffin had been lowered into the ground, relatives and friends took turns shoveling earth onto it, each participating in the irrevocable act of burial. The service concluded with the *Kaddish* prayer, which affirms life while accepting death.

At home, the family lit a memorial candle, which burned throughout *shiva*, the seven-day mourning period. A meal of consolation prepared by others followed, creating a warm feeling of community. Jewish custom prescribes that after 30 days, life should gradually return to normal. When a parent dies, the mourning period is extended to 12 months.

In the Quaker tradition of simplicity, Nicholas was cremated promptly. During the next week, relatives and close friends gathered with Giselle and Sasha at their home. Together, they planned a memorial service to celebrate Nicholas's life.

When people arrived on the appointed day, a clerk of the Friends (Quaker) Meeting welcomed them and explained to newcomers the Quaker custom of worshipping silently, with those who feel moved to speak rising at any time to share thoughts and feelings. Many mourners offered personal statements about Nicholas or read poems and selections from Scripture. After concluding comments from Giselle and Sasha, everyone joined hands to close the service. A reception for the family followed.

Variations in mourning behavior are vast, both within and across societies. At African-American funerals, for example, grief is expressed freely: Eulogies and music are usually designed to trigger release of deep emotion (McGoldrick et al., 2004). In contrast, the Balinese of Indonesia believe they must remain calm in the face of death so that the gods can hear their prayers. While acknowledging their underlying grief, Balinese mourners work hard to maintain their composure (Rosenblatt, 2008).

In recent years, a new ritual has arisen: "virtual cemeteries" on the Internet, which allow postings whenever bereaved individuals feel ready to convey their thoughts and feelings, creation of tributes at little or no cost, and continuous, easy access to the memorial. Most creators of Web tributes choose to tell personal stories, highlighting a laugh, a favorite joke, or a touching moment. Some survivors use Web memorials to grieve openly, others to converse with the lost loved one. Cemetery guestbooks offer a place for visitors to connect with other mourners. Web cemeteries also provide a means for people excluded from traditional death rituals to engage in public mourning (Roberts, 2006; Stroebe, van der Houwen, & Schut, 2008). The following "gravesite" message captures the unique qualities of this highly flexible medium for mourning:

I wish I could maintain contact with you, to keep alive the vivid memories of your impact on my life. . . . Because I cannot visit your grave today, I use this means to tell you how much you are loved.

Mourners light candles at a memorial service for six Sikhs who died in a shooting rampage in Wisconsin in 2012. Sikh funeral customs include singing hymns, saying prayers, and offering remembrances of the deceased, followed by cremation and scattering of the ashes.

Support groups that bring together mourners who have experienced the same type of loss seem highly effective in promoting recovery. In a program for recently widowed older adults based on the dual-process model of coping with loss, a participant expressed the many lasting benefits:

We shared our anger at being left behind, . . . our fright of that aloneness. We shared our favorite pictures, so each of us could know the others' families and the fun we used to have. We shared our feelings of guilt if we had fun . . . and found out that it was okay to keep on living! . . . We cheered when one of us accomplished a new task. We also tried to lend a helping hand and heart when we would have one of our bad days! . . . This group will always be there for me and I will always be there for them. I love you all! (Lund, 2005)

Follow-up research suggests that group sessions are best suited for fostering loss-oriented coping (confronting and resolving grief), whereas an individually tailored approach works best for restoration-oriented coping (reorganizing daily life) (Lund et al., 2010). Bereaved adults differ widely in the new roles, relationships, and life skills they need most, and in the formats and schedules best suited to acquiring them.

LOOK AND LISTEN

Arrange to sit in on a bereavement support group session sponsored by a local hospice program or hospital, noting both emotional and daily living challenges expressed by group members. Ask participants to explain how the group has helped them. ●

Interventions for children and adolescents following violent deaths must protect them from unnecessary reexposure and assist parents and teachers with their own distress so they can effectively offer comfort (Dowd, 2013). In the aftermath of horrific tragedies—such as the December 14, 2012, mass shooting at Sandy Hook Elementary School in Newtown, Connecticut, or the April 15, 2013, Boston Marathon bombings—nurturing and caring relationships with adults are the most powerful way to help children recover from trauma.

A sudden, violent, and unexplainable death; the loss of a child; a death that the mourner feels he or she could have prevented; or an ambivalent or dependent relationship with the deceased makes it harder for bereaved people to overcome their loss. In these instances, grief therapy, or individual counseling with a specially trained professional, can be helpful. Assisting bereaved adults in finding some value in the grieving experience—for example, gaining insight into the meaning of relationships, discovering their own capacity to cope with adversity, or crystallizing a sense of purpose in their lives—is particularly effective (Neimeyer et al., 2010).

Nevertheless, most bereaved individuals do not participate in bereavement interventions. In several studies, only 30 to 50 percent of family caregivers of dying patients made use of bereavement services—such as phone support, support groups, and referrals for counseling—even though these were readily available through hospice, hospitals, or other community organizations (Bergman, Haley, & Small, 2010, 2011; Cherlin et al., 2007). Many who refused bereavement services were severely distressed yet did not realize that intervention could be helpful.

Death Education

Preparatory steps can help people of all ages cope with death more effectively. The death awareness movement that sparked increased sensitivity to the needs of dying patients has also led to the rise of college and university courses in death, dying, and bereavement. Instruction has been integrated into the training of doctors, nurses, psychologists, and social workers, although most professional offerings are limited to only a few lectures (Wass, 2004). Death education is also found in adult education programs in many communities and even in a few elementary and secondary schools.

Death education at all levels has the following goals:

- Increasing students' understanding of the physical and psychological changes that accompany dying
- Helping students learn how to cope with the death of a loved one
- Preparing students to be informed consumers of medical and funeral services
- Promoting understanding of social and ethical issues involving death

Educational format varies widely. Although using a lecture approach focused on conveying information leads to gains in knowledge, it often leaves students more uncomfortable about death than when they entered. In contrast, experiential programs that help people confront their own mortality—through discussions with the terminally ill, visits to mortuaries and cemeteries, and personal awareness exercises—are less likely to heighten death anxiety and may sometimes reduce it (Hurtig & Stewin, 2006; Maglio & Robinson, 1994).

Whether acquired in the classroom or in our daily lives, our thoughts and feelings about death are forged through interactions with others. Dying people have at times confided in those close to them that awareness of the limits of their lifespan permitted them to focus on what is truly important in their lives. As one terminally ill patient summed up, "[It's] kind of like life, just speeded up"—an accelerated process in which, over a period of weeks to months, one grapples with issues that normally would have taken years or decades to resolve (Selwyn, 1996, p. 36). Applying this lesson to ourselves, we learn that by being in touch with death and dying, we can live ever more fully.

ASK YOURSELF

REVIEW What circumstances are likely to induce bereavement overload? Cite examples.

APPLY List features of self-help groups likely to contribute to their effectiveness in helping people cope with loss.

REFLECT Visit a Web cemetery, such as Virtual Memorials (*virtualmemorials.com*). Select examples of Web tributes, guest book entries, and testimonials that illustrate the unique ways in which virtual cemeteries help people cope with death.

SUMMARY

How We Die (p. 509)

Describe the physical changes of dying, along with their implications for defining death and the meaning of death with dignity.

- Death is long and drawn-out for three-fourths of people, many more than in times past, as a result of life-saving medical technology. Of those who die suddenly, 80 to 90 percent are victims of heart attacks.

- In general, dying takes place in three phases: the **agonal phase,** in which regular heartbeat disintegrates; **clinical death,** a short interval in which resuscitation is still possible; and **mortality,** or permanent death.

- In most industrialized nations, **brain death** is accepted as the definition of death. But for incurable patients who remain in a **persistent vegetative state,** the brain death standard does not solve the problem of when to halt treatment.

- We can best ensure death with dignity by supporting dying patients through their physical and psychological distress, being candid about death's certainty, and helping them learn enough about their condition to make reasoned choices about treatment.

Attitudes Toward Death (p. 511)

Discuss factors that influence attitudes toward death, including death anxiety.

- Compared with earlier generations, more young people reach adulthood having had little contact with death, contributing to a sense of unease about it.

- Wide individual and cultural variations exist in **death anxiety.** People with a sense of spirituality or a well-developed personal philosophy of death are less fearful, as are those with deep faith in a higher force or being. Older adults' greater ability to regulate negative emotion and their sense of symbolic immortality reduce death anxiety. Women exhibit more death anxiety than men.

Thinking and Emotions of Dying People (p. 513)

Describe and evaluate Kübler-Ross's theory, citing factors that influence dying patients' responses.

- Elisabeth Kübler-Ross proposed that dying people typically express five responses, initially proposed as stages: denial, anger, bargaining, depression, and acceptance. These reactions do not occur in fixed sequence, and dying people often display other coping strategies.

- An **appropriate death** is one that makes sense in terms of the individual's pattern of living and values, preserves or restores significant relationships, and is as free of suffering as possible. The extent to which people attain these goals depends on many contextual variables—nature of the disease, personality and coping style, family members' and health professionals' behavior, and spirituality, religion, and cultural background.

A Place to Die (p. 516)

Evaluate the extent to which homes, hospitals, nursing homes, and the hospice approach meet the needs of dying people and their families.

- Although most people say they want to die at home, only about one-fourth of Americans do. Even with professional help and hospital-supplied equipment, caring for a dying patient is highly demanding.

- Sudden deaths typically occur in hospital emergency rooms, where sympathetic explanations from staff can reduce family members' anger, frustration, and confusion. Intensive care is especially depersonalizing for patients, lingering between life and death while hooked to machines. Many U.S. hospitals still lack comprehensive treatment programs aimed at easing end-of-life suffering.

- Though deaths in U.S. nursing homes are common, high-quality terminal care is lacking. Too many patients die in pain without having their needs met.

- The **hospice** approach is a comprehensive program of support services designed to meet the dying person's physical, emotional, social, and spiritual needs by providing **palliative,** or **comfort, care,** rather than prolonging life. Hospice care also contributes to improved family functioning and better psychological well-being among family survivors.

The Right to Die (p. 519)

Discuss controversies surrounding euthanasia and assisted suicide.

- **Euthanasia**—ending the life of a person suffering from an incurable condition—takes various forms.

- **Passive euthanasia,** withholding or withdrawing life-sustaining treatment from a hopelessly ill patient, is widely accepted and practiced. People can best ensure that their wishes will be followed by preparing an **advance medical directive. A living will** contains instructions for treatment, whereas the **durable power of attorney for health care** names another person to make health care decisions on one's behalf.

- Public support for **voluntary active euthanasia,** in which doctors or others act directly, at a patient's request, to end suffering before a natural end to life, is high. Nevertheless, the practice remains a criminal offense in most countries and has sparked heated controversy.

- Less public support exists for assisted suicide. But because the final act is solely the patient's, some experts believe that legalizing assisted suicide is preferable to legalizing voluntary active euthanasia.

Bereavement: Coping with the Death of a Loved One
(p. 523)

Describe the phases of grieving, factors that underlie individual variations, and bereavement interventions.

- **Bereavement** refers to the experience of losing a loved one by death, **grief** to the intense physical and psychological distress that accompanies loss. **Mourning** is the culturally prescribed expression of the bereaved person's thoughts and feelings.

- Although theorists previously believed that grieving occurred in orderly phases—avoidance, confrontation, and finally restoration—a more accurate image is a roller-coaster ride, with the mourner engaging in a set of tasks to overcome grief. According to the **dual-process model of coping with loss,** effective coping involves oscillating between dealing with the emotional consequences of loss and attending to life changes, which can have restorative effects. Bereaved individuals who experience positive as well as negative emotions cope more effectively.

- Like dying, grieving is affected by many personal and situational factors. Bereaved men express grief less directly than bereaved women. After a sudden, unanticipated death, avoidance may be especially pronounced and confrontation highly traumatic. In contrast, a prolonged, expected death grants the bereaved person time to engage in **anticipatory grieving.**

AP IMAGES/MANU BRABO

- When a parent loses a child or a child loses a parent or sibling, grieving is generally intense and prolonged. Because early loss of a life partner is a nonnormative event with a major impact on life plans, younger widowed individuals usually fare less well than widowed older people. Disenfranchised grief can profoundly disrupt the process of grieving.

- People who experience several deaths at once or in close succession may suffer from bereavement overload.

- Sympathy and understanding are sufficient for most people to recover from grief. Support groups are highly effective in aiding recovery, whereas individually tailored approaches help mourners reorganize their daily lives. Interventions for children and adolescents following violent deaths must protect them from unnecessary reexposure and assist parents and teachers in offering comfort.

Death Education (p. 528)

Explain how death education can help people cope with death more effectively.

- Today, instruction in death, dying, and bereavement is integrated into training programs for doctors, nurses, psychologists, and social workers. It is also found in adult education programs and in a few elementary and secondary schools. Courses with an experiential component may reduce death anxiety.

Important Terms and Concepts

advance medical directive (p. 520)
agonal phase (p. 510)
anticipatory grieving (p. 524)
appropriate death (p. 514)
bereavement (p. 523)
brain death (p. 510)
clinical death (p. 510)

death anxiety (p. 511)
dual-process model of coping with loss (p. 523)
durable power of attorney for health care (p. 520)
euthanasia (p. 519)
grief (p. 523)
hospice (p. 517)
living will (p. 520)

mortality (p. 510)
mourning (p. 523)
palliative, or comfort, care (p. 518)
passive euthanasia (p. 520)
persistent vegetative state (p. 510)
thanatology (p. 509)
voluntary active euthanasia (p. 521)

Glossary

A

academic programs Preschool and kindergarten programs in which teachers structure children's learning, teaching academic skills through formal lessons that often involve repetition and drill. Distinguished from *child-centered programs*. (p. 190)

accommodation In Piaget's theory, that part of adaptation in which new schemes are created and old ones adjusted to produce a better fit with the environment. Distinguished from *assimilation*. (p. 119)

acculturative stress Psychological distress resulting from conflict between an individual's minority culture and the host culture. (p. 322)

activities of daily living (ADLs) Basic self-care tasks required to live on one's own, such as bathing, dressing, getting in and out of bed or a chair, and eating. (p. 449)

activity theory A social theory of aging that states that declining rates of interaction in late adulthood reflect social barriers to engagement, not the desires of aging adults. Older people try to preserve life satisfaction by finding roles that allow them to remain about as active and busy as they were in middle age. Distinguished from *disengagement theory, continuity theory,* and *socioemotional selectivity theory*. (p. 487)

adaptation In Piaget's theory, the process of building schemes through direct interaction with the environment. Consists of two complementary activities: *assimilation* and *accommodation*. (p. 118)

adolescence The transition between childhood and adulthood that begins with puberty. It involves accepting one's full-grown body, acquiring adult ways of thinking, attaining greater independence from one's family, developing more mature ways of relating to peers of both sexes, and beginning to construct an identity. (p. 287)

advance medical directive A written statement of desired medical treatment should a person become incurably ill. (p. 520)

affect optimization The ability to maximize positive emotion and dampen negative emotion. An emotional strength of late adulthood. (p. 480)

age-graded influences Influences on lifespan development that are strongly related to age and therefore fairly predictable in when they occur and how long they last. (p. 7)

age of viability The age at which the fetus can first survive if born early. Occurs sometime between 22 and 26 weeks. (p. 65)

aging in place In late adulthood, remaining in a familiar setting where one has control over one's everyday life. (p. 489)

agonal phase The phase of dying in which gasps and muscle spasms occur during the first moments in which the regular heart beat disintegrates. Distinguished from *clinical death* and *mortality*. (p. 510)

alcohol-related neurodevelopmental disorder (ARND) The least severe form of fetal alcohol spectrum disorder, involving brain injury but with typical physical growth and absence of facial abnormalities. Distinguished from *fetal alcohol syndrome (FAS)* and *partial fetal alcohol syndrome (p-FAS)*. (p. 69)

allele Each of two or more forms of a gene located at the same place on corresponding pairs of chromosomes. (p. 38)

Alzheimer's disease The most common form of dementia, in which structural and chemical brain deterioration is associated with gradual loss of many aspects of thought and behavior, including memory, skilled and purposeful movements, and comprehension and production of speech. (p. 462)

amnion The inner membrane that that encloses the prenatal organism in amniotic fluid, which helps keep temperature constant and provides a cushion against jolts caused by the mother's movements. (p. 63)

amyloid plaques A structural change in the cerebral cortex associated with Alzheimer's disease, in which dense deposits of a deteriorated protein called *amyloid* develop, surrounded by clumps of dead nerve and glial cells. (p. 462)

androgyny The gender identity held by individuals who score high on both traditionally masculine and traditionally feminine personality characteristics. (p. 215)

anorexia nervosa An eating disorder in which young people, mainly females, starve themselves because of a compulsive fear of getting fat and an extremely distorted body image. (p. 296)

anoxia Inadequate oxygen supply. (p. 77)

anticipatory grieving Before a prolonged, expected death, acknowledging the inevitability of the loss and preparing emotionally for it. (p. 524)

Apgar Scale A rating system used to assess a newborn baby's physical condition immediately after birth on the basis of five characteristics: heart rate, respiratory effort, reflex irritability, muscle tone, and color. (p. 76)

appropriate death A death that makes sense in terms of the individual's pattern of living and values, preserves or restores significant relationships, and is as free of suffering as possible. (p. 514)

assimilation In Piaget's theory, that part of adaptation in which the external world is interpreted in terms of current schemes. Distinguished from *accommodation*. (p. 118)

assisted living A homelike housing arrangement for older adults who require more care than can be provided at home but less than is usually provided in nursing homes. (p. 467)

assistive technology An array of devices that permits people with disabilities, including older adults, to improve their functioning. (p. 455)

associative memory deficit Age-related difficulty creating and retrieving links between pieces of information—for example, two items or an item and its context. (p. 469)

associative play A form of social interaction in which children engage in separate activities but interact by exchanging toys and commenting on one another's behavior. Distinguished from *nonsocial activity, parallel play,* and *cooperative play*. (p. 204)

attachment The strong affectionate tie that humans have with special people in their lives, which leads them to feel pleasure when interacting with those people and to be comforted by their nearness in times of stress. (p. 152)

Attachment Q-Sort A method for assessing the quality of attachment in children between 1 and 4 years of age through home observations of a variety of attachment-related behaviors. (p. 154)

attention-deficit hyperactivity disorder (ADHD) A childhood disorder involving inattention, impulsivity, and excessive motor activity, resulting in academic and social problems. (p. 239)

authoritarian child-rearing style A child-rearing style that is low in acceptance and involvement, high in coercive control, and low in autonomy granting. Distinguished from *authoritative, permissive,* and *uninvolved child-rearing styles*. (p. 218)

authoritative child-rearing style A child-rearing style that is high in acceptance and involvement, emphasizes adaptive control techniques, and includes gradual, appropriate autonomy granting. Distinguished from *authoritarian, permissive,* and *uninvolved child-rearing styles*. (p. 217)

autobiographical memory Long-lasting recollections of personally meaningful one-time events from both the recent and the distant past. (p. 129)

autoimmune response A malfunction of the immune system in which it turns against normal body tissues. (p. 453)

automatic processes Cognitive activities that are so well-learned that they require no space in working memory and, therefore, permit an individual to focus on other information while performing them. (p. 126)

autonomy At adolescence, a sense of oneself as a separate, self-governing individual. Involves relying more on oneself and less on parents for support and guidance and engaging in careful, well-reasoned decision making. (p. 329)

autonomy versus shame and doubt In Erikson's theory, the psychological conflict of toddlerhood, which is resolved favorably when parents provide young children with suitable guidance and reasonable choices. (p. 143)

autosomes The 22 matching chromosome pairs in each human cell. (p. 37)

average healthy life expectancy The number of years that an individual born in a particular year can expect to live in full health, without disease or injury. Distinguished from *maximum lifespan* and *average life expectancy*. (p. 448)

average life expectancy The number of years that an individual born in a particular year can expect to live, starting at any given age. Distinguished from *maximum lifespan* and *average healthy life expectancy*. (p. 447)

avoidant attachment The attachment pattern characterizing infants who seem unresponsive to the parent when she is present, are usually not distressed by parental separation, react to the stranger in much the same way as to the parent, and avoid or are slow to greet the parent when she returns. Distinguished from *secure, resistant,* and *disorganized/disoriented attachment.* (p. 154)

B

babbling Repetition of consonant–vowel combinations in long strings, beginning around 6 months of age. (p. 137)

basal metabolic rate (BMR) The amount of energy the body uses at complete rest. (p. 350)

basic emotions Emotions such as happiness, interest, surprise, fear, anger, sadness, and disgust that are universal in humans and other primates and have a long evolutionary history of promoting survival. (p. 144)

basic trust versus mistrust In Erikson's theory, the psychological conflict of infancy, which is resolved positively when the balance of care is sympathetic and loving. (p. 143)

behavioral genetics A field devoted to uncovering the contributions of nature and nurture to the diversity of human traits and abilities. (p. 53)

behaviorism An approach that regards directly observable events—stimuli and responses—as the appropriate focus of study and views the development of behavior as taking place through classical and operant conditioning. (p. 13)

behavior modification Procedures that combine conditioning and modeling to eliminate undesirable behaviors and increase desirable responses. (p. 14)

bereavement The experience of losing a loved one by death. (p. 523)

bicultural identity The identity constructed by individuals who explore and adopt values from both their family's subculture and the dominant culture. (p. 322)

"big five" personality traits Five basic factors into which hundreds of personality traits have been organized: neuroticism, extroversion, openness to experience, agreeableness, and conscientiousness. (p. 430)

biological aging, or senescence Genetically influenced, age-related declines in the functioning of organs and systems that are universal in all members of our species. Sometimes called *primary aging.* (p. 343)

blended, or reconstituted, family A family structure resulting from remarriage or cohabitation that includes parent, child, and steprelatives. (p. 276)

body image Conception of and attitude toward one's physical appearance. (p. 294)

brain death Irreversible cessation of all activity in the brain and the brain stem. The definition of death accepted in most industrialized nations. (p. 510)

brain plasticity The capacity of various parts of the cerebral cortex to take over functions of damaged regions. Declines as hemispheres of the cerebral cortex lateralize. (p. 96)

breech position A position of the baby in the uterus that would cause the buttocks or feet to be delivered first. (p. 77)

bulimia nervosa An eating disorder in which individuals, mainly females, engage in strict dieting and excessive exercise accompanied by binge eating, often followed by deliberate vomiting and purging with laxatives. (p. 296)

burnout A condition in which long-term job stress leads to mental exhaustion, a sense of loss of personal control, and feelings of reduced accomplishment. (p. 440)

C

cardinality The mathematical principle specifying that the last number in a counting sequence indicates the quantity of items in the set. (p. 189)

carrier A heterozygous individual who can pass a recessive trait to his or her offspring. (p. 38)

cataracts Cloudy areas in the lens of the eye that increase from middle to old age, resulting in foggy vision and (without surgery) eventual blindness. (p. 451)

categorical self Classification of the self according to prominent ways in which people differ, such as age, sex, physical characteristics, and goodness and badness. Develops between 18 and 30 months. (p. 160)

central executive In information processing, the conscious, reflective part of our mental system that directs the flow of information, coordinating incoming information with information already in the system and selecting, applying, and monitoring strategies that facilitate memory storage, comprehension, reasoning, and problem solving. (p. 126)

centration In Piaget's theory, the tendency of preoperational children to focus on one aspect of a situation while neglecting other important features. (p. 178)

cephalocaudal trend An organized pattern of physical growth that proceeds from the upper to the lower part of the body ("head to tail"). Distinguished from *proximodistal trend.* (p. 93)

cerebellum A structure at the rear and base of the brain that aids in balance and control of body movements. (p. 169)

cerebral cortex The largest, most complex structure of the human brain, containing the greatest number of neurons and synapses and accounting for the highly developed intelligence of the human species. (p. 95)

cerebrovascular dementia A form of dementia that develops when a series of strokes leaves areas of dead brain cells, producing step-by-step degeneration of mental ability, with each step occurring abruptly after a stroke. (p. 464)

cesarean delivery A surgical delivery in which the doctor makes an incision in the mother's abdomen and lifts the baby out of the uterus. (p. 78)

child-centered programs Preschool and kindergarten programs in which teachers provide a variety of activities from which children select, and much learning takes place through play. Distinguished from *academic programs.* (p. 190)

child-rearing styles Combinations of parenting behaviors that occur over a wide range of situations, creating an enduring child-rearing climate. (p. 217)

chorion The outer membrane that forms a protective covering around the prenatal organism. It sends out tiny hairlike villi, from which the placenta begins to develop. (p. 63)

chromosomes Rodlike structures in the cell nucleus that store and transmit genetic information. (p. 36)

chronosystem In ecological systems theory, temporal changes in environments, either externally imposed or arising from within the person, that produce new conditions affecting development. Distinguished from *microsystem, mesosystem, exosystem,* and *macrosystem.* (p. 20)

circular reaction In Piaget's theory, a means of building schemes in which infants try to repeat a chance event caused by their own motor activity. (p. 119)

classical conditioning A form of learning that involves associating a neutral stimulus with a stimulus that leads to a reflexive response. Once the nervous system makes the connection between the two stimuli, the neutral stimulus alone produces the behavior. (p. 103)

climacteric The midlife transition in which fertility declines, bringing an end to reproductive capacity in women and diminished fertility in men. (p. 403)

clinical death The phase of dying in which heartbeat, circulation, breathing, and brain functioning stop, but resuscitation is still possible. Distinguished from *agonal phase* and *mortality.* (p. 510)

clinical interview An interview method in which the researcher uses a flexible, conversational style to probe for the participant's point of view. Distinguished from *structured interview.* (p. 24)

clinical, or case study, method A research method in which the aim is to obtain as complete a picture as possible of one individual's psychological functioning by bringing together interview data, observations, and sometimes test scores. (p. 24)

clique A group of about five to seven members who are good friends and, therefore, usually resemble one another in family background, attitudes, and values. (p. 332)

cognitive-affective complexity A form of thinking that increases from adolescence through middle adulthood, involving awareness of conflicting positive and negative feelings and coordination of them into a complex, organized structure that recognizes the uniqueness of individual experiences. (p. 359)

cognitive-developmental theory An approach introduced by Piaget that views children as actively constructing knowledge as they manipulate and explore their world and that regards cognitive development as taking place in stages. (p. 15)

cognitive maps Mental representations of familiar large-scale spaces, such as neighborhood or school. (p. 235)

cognitive self-regulation The process of continuously monitoring progress toward a goal, checking outcomes, and redirecting unsuccessful efforts. (p. 240)

cohabitation The lifestyle of unmarried couples who have a sexually intimate relationship and who share a residence. (p. 389)

cohort effects The effects of cultural–historical change on the accuracy of longitudinal and cross-sectional research findings. Results based on one cohort—individuals developing in the same time period, who are influenced by particular historical and cultural conditions—may not apply to other cohorts. (p. 29)

collectivist societies Societies in which people define themselves as part of a group and stress group goals over individual goals. Distinguished from *individualistic societies*. (p. 50)

commitment within relativistic thinking In Perry's theory, the mature individual's formulation of a perspective that synthesizes contradictions between opposing views, rather than choosing between them. (p. 358)

companionate love Love based on warm, trusting affection and caregiving. Distinguished from *passionate love*. (p. 377)

compliance Voluntary obedience to requests and commands. (p. 161)

compression of morbidity The public health goal of reducing the average period of diminished vigor before death as life expectancy extends. Medical advances, improved socioeconomic conditions, and good health habits all promote this goal. (p. 457)

concrete operational stage Piaget's third stage of cognitive development, extending from about 7 to 11 years of age, during which thought becomes logical, flexible, and organized in its application to concrete information, but the capacity for abstract thinking is not yet present. (p. 234)

conditioned response (CR) In classical conditioning, a new response produced by a conditioned stimulus (CS) that is similar to the unconditioned, or reflexive, response (UCR). (p. 103)

conditioned stimulus (CS) In classical conditioning, a neutral stimulus that, through pairing with an unconditioned stimulus (UCS), leads to a new, conditioned response. (CR). (p. 103)

congregate housing Housing for older adults that provides a variety of support services, including meals in a common dining room, along with watchful oversight of residents with physical and mental disabilities. (p. 490)

conservation The understanding that certain physical characteristics of objects remain the same, even when their outward appearance changes. (p. 178)

constructivist classroom A classroom grounded in Piaget's view of children as active agents who construct their own knowledge. Features include richly equipped learning centers, small groups and individuals solving self-chosen problems, a teacher who guides and supports in response to children's needs, and evaluation based on individual students' progress in relation to their own prior development. Distinguished from *traditional* and *social-constructivist classrooms*. (p. 250)

contexts Unique combinations of personal and environmental circumstances that can result in different paths of development. (p. 4)

continuity theory A social theory of aging that states that most aging adults, in their choice of everyday activities and social relationships, strive to maintain a personal system—an identity and a set of personality dispositions, interests, roles, and skills—that promotes life satisfaction by ensuring consistency between their past and anticipated future. Distinguished from *disengagement theory, activity theory,* and *socioemotional selectivity theory.* (p. 487)

continuous development The view that development is a process of gradually augmenting the same types of skills that were there to begin with. Distinguished from *discontinuous development.* (p. 4)

controversial children Children who receive many votes, both positive and negative, on self-report measures of peer acceptance, indicating that they are both liked and disliked. Distinguished from *popular, neglected,* and *rejected children.* (p. 269)

conventional level Kohlberg's second level of moral development, in which moral understanding is based on conforming to social rules to ensure positive human relationships and maintain societal order. (p. 324)

convergent thinking The type of cognition emphasized on intelligence tests, which involves arriving at a single correct answer to a problem. Distinguished from *divergent thinking.* (p. 254)

cooing Pleasant vowel-like noises made by infants beginning around 2 months of age. (p. 137)

cooperative learning Collaboration on a task by a small group of classmates who work toward common goals by resolving differences of opinion, sharing responsibilities, and providing one another with sufficient explanation to correct misunderstandings. (p. 251)

cooperative play A form of social interaction in which children orient toward a common goal, such as acting out a make-believe theme. Distinguished from *nonsocial activity, parallel play,* and *associative play.* (p. 204)

coparenting Parents' mutual support of each other's parenting behaviors. (p. 46)

coregulation A form of supervision in which parents exercise general oversight while letting children take charge of moment-by-moment decision making. (p. 273)

core knowledge perspective A perspective that states that infants are born with a set of innate knowledge systems, or core domains of thought, each of which permits a ready grasp of new, related information and therefore supports early, rapid development of certain aspects of cognition. (p. 125)

corpus callosum The large bundle of fibers connecting the two hemispheres of the cerebral cortex. (p. 170)

correlational design A research design in which the investigator gathers information on individuals without altering their experiences and then examines relationships between participants' characteristics and their behavior or development. Does not permit inferences about cause and effect. (p. 25)

correlation coefficient A number, ranging from +1.00 to –1.00, that describes the strength and direction of the relationship between two variables. (p. 27)

creativity The ability to produce work that is original yet appropriate—something others have not thought of that is useful in some way. (p. 254)

cross-linkage theory of aging A theory of biological aging asserting that the formation of bonds, or links, between normally separate protein fibers causes the body's connective tissue to become less elastic over time, leading to many negative physical outcomes. (p. 345)

cross-sectional design A research design in which groups of participants of different ages are studied at the same point in time. Distinguished from *longitudinal design.* (p. 29)

crowd A large, loosely organized social group consisting of several cliques with similar values. Membership is based on reputation and stereotype. (p. 332)

crystallized intelligence Intellectual skills that depend on accumulated knowledge and experience, good judgment, and mastery of social conventions—abilities acquired because they are valued by the individual's culture. Distinguished from *fluid intelligence.* (p. 413)

D

death anxiety Fear and apprehension of death. (p. 511)

deferred imitation The ability to remember and copy the behavior of models who are not present. (p. 121)

delay of gratification The ability to wait for an appropriate time and place to engage in a tempting act. (p. 161)

dementia A set of disorders occurring almost entirely in old age in which many aspects of thought and behavior are so impaired that everyday activities are disrupted. (p. 461)

deoxyribonucleic acid (DNA) Long, double-stranded molecules that make up chromosomes. (p. 36)

dependency–support script A typical pattern of interaction in which caregivers attend to older adults' dependent behaviors immediately, thereby reinforcing those behaviors. Distinguished from *independence-ignore script*. (p. 484)

dependent variable The variable the researcher expects to be influenced by the independent variable in an experiment. Distinguished from *independent variable*. (p. 27)

developmental cognitive neuroscience An area of investigation that brings together researchers from psychology, biology, neuroscience, and medicine to study the relationship between changes in the brain and the developing person's cognitive processing and behavior patterns. (p. 17)

developmentally appropriate practice A set of standards devised by the U.S. National Association for the Education of Young Children, specifying program characteristics that meet the developmental and individual needs of young children of varying ages, based on current research and consensus among experts. (p. 135)

developmental science An interdisciplinary field devoted to understanding constancy and change throughout the lifespan. (p. 3)

differentiation theory The view that perceptual development involves the detection of increasingly fine-grained, invariant features in the environment. (p. 114)

difficult child A child whose temperament is characterized by irregular daily routines, slow acceptance of new experiences, and a tendency to react negatively and intensely. Distinguished from *easy child* and *slow-to-warm-up child*. (p. 148)

discontinuous development The view that development is a process in which new ways of understanding and responding to the world emerge at specific times. Distinguished from *continuous development*. (p. 4)

disengagement theory A social theory of aging that states that declines in social interaction in late adulthood are due to mutual withdrawal between older adults and society in anticipation of death. Distinguished from *activity theory, continuity theory,* and *socioemotional selectivity theory*. (p. 487)

disorganized/disoriented attachment The attachment pattern reflecting the greatest insecurity, characterizing infants who show confused, contradictory responses when reunited with the parent after a separation. Distinguished from *secure, avoidant,* and *resistant attachment*. (p. 154)

displaced reference The realization that words can be used to cue mental images of things that are not physically present. (p. 123)

divergent thinking The type of thinking associated with creativity, which involves generating multiple and unusual possibilities when faced with a task or problem. Distinguished from *convergent thinking*. (p. 254)

dominant cerebral hemisphere The hemisphere of the cerebral cortex responsible for skilled motor action and other important abilities. In right-handed individuals, the left hemisphere is dominant; in left-handed individuals, motor and language skills are often shared between the hemispheres. (p. 169)

dominant–recessive inheritance A pattern of inheritance in which, under heterozygous conditions, the influence of only one allele is apparent. (p. 38)

dualistic thinking In Perry's theory, the cognitive approach typical of younger college students, who divide information, values, and authority into right and wrong, good and bad, we and they. Distinguished from *relativistic thinking*. (p. 358)

dual-process model of coping with loss A perspective that assumes that people cope most effectively with loss when they oscillate between dealing with the emotional consequences of loss and attending to life changes, which—when handled successfully—have restorative, or healing, effects. (p. 523)

dual representation The ability to view a symbolic object as both an object in its own right and a symbol. (p. 177)

durable power of attorney for health care A written statement authorizing appointment of another person (usually, though not always, a family member) to make health care decisions on one's behalf. (p. 520)

dynamic assessment An approach to testing consistent with Vygotsky's zone of proximal development, in which purposeful teaching is introduced into the testing situation to find out what the child can attain with social support. (p. 247)

dynamic systems theory of motor development A theory that views new motor skills as reorganizations of previously mastered skills, which lead to more effective ways of exploring and controlling the environment. Each new skill is a joint product of central nervous system development, the body's movement capacities, the child's goals, and environmental supports for the skill. (p. 107)

E

easy child A child whose temperament is characterized by quick establishment of regular routines in infancy, general cheerfulness, and easy adaptation to new experiences. Distinguished from *difficult child* and *slow-to-warm-up child*. (p. 148)

ecological systems theory Bronfenbrenner's approach, which views the person as developing within a complex system of relationships affected by multiple levels of the surrounding environment, from immediate settings of family and school to broad cultural values and programs. (p. 19)

educational self-fulfilling prophecies Teachers' positive or negative views of individual children, who tend to adopt and start to live up to those views. (p. 252)

effortful control The self-regulatory dimension of temperament, involving the capacity to voluntarily suppress a dominant response in order to plan and execute a more adaptive response. (p. 149)

egalitarian marriage A form of marriage in which partners relate as equals, sharing power and authority. Both try to balance the time and energy they devote to their occupations, their children, and their relationship. Distinguished from *traditional marriage*. (p. 382)

egocentrism Failure to distinguish others' symbolic viewpoints from one's own. (p. 177)

ego integrity versus despair In Erikson's theory, the psychological conflict of late adulthood, which is resolved positively when older adults come to terms with their lives and feel whole, complete, and satisfied with their achievements, recognizing that the paths they followed, abandoned, or never selected were necessary for fashioning a meaningful life course. (p. 479)

elaboration A memory strategy that involves creating a relationship, or shared meaning, between two or more pieces of information that do not belong to the same category in order to improve recall. (p. 238)

embryo The prenatal organism from 2 to 8 weeks after conception—the period when the groundwork for all body structures and internal organs is laid down. (p. 63)

emergent literacy Children's active efforts to construct literacy knowledge through informal experiences. (p. 187)

emerging adulthood A new transitional period of development, extending from the late teens to the mid- to late twenties, during which young people have left adolescence but have not yet assumed adult responsibilities. Rather, they continue to explore alternatives in education, work, personal beliefs and values, and love. (p. 369)

emotional self-regulation Strategies for adjusting our emotional state to a comfortable level of intensity so we can accomplish our goals. (p. 147)

emotion-centered coping A strategy for managing emotion that is internal, private, and aimed at controlling distress when little can be done to change an outcome. Distinguished from *problem-centered coping*. (p. 265)

empathy The ability to understand another's emotional state and to *feel with* that person, or respond emotionally in a similar way. (p. 160)

epigenesis Development resulting from ongoing, bidirectional exchanges between heredity and all levels of the environment. (p. 56)

episodic memory Memory for everyday experiences. (p. 185)

epistemic cognition Reflections on how one arrived at facts, beliefs, and ideas. (p. 358)

ethnic identity A sense of ethnic group membership and attitudes and feelings associated with that membership, as an enduring aspect of the self. (p. 322)

ethnography A method in which the researcher attempts to understand a culture or a distinct social group through participant observation—

living with its members and taking field notes for an extended time. (p. 25)

ethological theory of attachment Bowlby's theory, the most widely accepted view of attachment, which regards the infant's emotional tie to the caregiver as an evolved response that promotes survival. (p. 153)

ethology An approach concerned with the adaptive, or survival, value of behavior and its evolutionary history. (p. 17)

euthanasia The practice of ending the life of a person suffering from an incurable condition. (p. 519)

evolutionary developmental psychology An area of research that seeks to understand the adaptive value of specieswide cognitive, emotional, and social competencies as those competencies change with age. (p. 18)

executive function In information processing, the diverse cognitive operations and strategies that enable us to achieve our goals in cognitively challenging situations. Includes controlling attention, suppressing impulses, coordinating information in working memory, and flexibly directing and monitoring thought and behavior. (p. 127)

exosystem In ecological systems theory, social settings that do not contain the developing person but nevertheless affect experiences in immediate settings. Distinguished from *microsystem, mesosystem, macrosystem,* and *chronosystem.* (p. 20)

expansions Adult responses that elaborate on children's speech, increasing its complexity. (p. 196)

experience-dependent brain growth Growth and refinement of established brain structures as a result of specific learning experiences that vary widely across individuals and cultures. Distinguished from *experience-expectant brain growth.* (p. 98)

experience-expectant brain growth The young brain's rapidly developing organization, which depends on ordinary experiences—opportunities to explore the environment, interact with people, and hear language and other sounds. Distinguished from *experience-dependent brain growth.* (p. 98)

experimental design A research design in which the investigator randomly assigns participants to two or more treatment conditions and studies the effect that manipulating an independent variable has on a dependent variable. Permits inferences about cause and effect. (p. 27)

expertise Acquisition of extensive knowledge in a field or endeavor. (p. 360)

extended-family household A household in which three or more generations live together. (p. 50)

F

family life cycle A series of phases characterizing the development of most families around the world. In early adulthood, people typically live on their own, marry, and bear and rear children. In middle age, parenting responsibilities diminish. Late adulthood brings retirement, growing old, and (more often for women) death of one's spouse. (p. 381)

fantasy period Period of vocational development in which children gain insight into career options by fantasizing about them. Distinguished from *tentative period* and *realistic period.* (p. 362)

fast-mapping Children's ability to connect new words with their underlying concepts after only a brief encounter. (p. 193)

feminization of poverty A trend in which women who support themselves or their families have become the majority of the adult population living in poverty, regardless of age and ethnic group. (p. 432)

fetal alcohol spectrum disorder (FASD) A range of physical, mental, and behavioral outcomes caused by prenatal alcohol exposure, including *fetal alcohol syndrome (FAS), partial fetal alcohol syndrome (p-FAS),* and *alcohol-related neurodevelopmental disorder (ARND).* (p. 68)

fetal alcohol syndrome (FAS) The most severe form of fetal alcohol spectrum disorder, distinguished by slow physical growth, facial abnormalities, and brain injury. Usually affects children whose mothers drank heavily throughout pregnancy. Distinguished from *partial fetal alcohol syndrome (p-FAS)* and *alcohol-related neurodevelopmental disorder (ARND).* (p. 69)

fetal monitors Electronic instruments that track the baby's heart rate during labor. (p. 78)

fetus The prenatal organism from the ninth week to the end of pregnancy—the period during which body structures are completed and dramatic growth in size occurs. (p. 64)

fluid intelligence Intellectual skills that largely depend on basic information-processing skills—ability to detect relationships among visual stimuli, speed of analyzing information, and capacity of working memory. Influenced less by culture than by conditions in the brain and by learning unique to the individual. Distinguished from *crystallized intelligence.* (p. 413)

formal operational stage Piaget's highest stage, beginning around 11 years of age, in which adolescents develop the capacity for abstract, systematic, scientific thinking. (p. 304)

frailty Weakened functioning of diverse organs and body systems, which profoundly interferes with everyday competence and leaves older adults highly vulnerable in the face of infection, extremely hot or cold weather, or injury. (p. 459)

fraternal, or dizygotic, twins Twins resulting from the release and fertilization of two ova. They are genetically no more alike than ordinary siblings. Distinguished from *identical,* or *monozygotic, twins.* (p. 37)

free radicals Naturally occurring, highly reactive chemicals that form in the presence of oxygen and destroy nearby cellular material, including DNA, proteins, and fats essential for cell functioning. Believed to be involved in many disorders of aging. (p. 344)

functional age Actual competence and performance of an older adult, as distinguished from chronological age. (p. 447)

G

gametes Sex cells, or sperm and ova, which contain half as many chromosomes as regular body cells. (p. 37)

gender constancy A full understanding of the biologically based permanence of one's gender, including the realization that sex remains the same even if clothing, hairstyle, and play activities change. (p. 215)

gender identity An image of oneself as relatively masculine or feminine in characteristics. (p. 215)

gender intensification Increased gender stereotyping of attitudes and behavior and movement toward a more traditional gender identity, typical of early adolescence. (p. 328)

gender schema theory An information-processing approach to gender typing that explains how environmental pressures and children's cognitions work together to shape gender-role development. (p. 216)

gender typing Any association of objects, roles, or traits with one sex or the other in ways that conform to cultural stereotypes. (p. 213)

gene A segment of a DNA molecule that contains instructions for production of various proteins that contribute to growth and functioning of the body. (p. 36)

gene–environment correlation The idea that heredity influences the environments to which individuals are exposed. (p. 55)

gene–environment interaction The view that people have unique, genetically influenced reactions to particular experiences and qualities of the environment. (p. 54)

generativity versus stagnation In Erikson's theory, the psychological conflict of midlife, which is resolved positively if the adult can integrate personal goals with the welfare of the larger social world. The resulting strength is the capacity to give to and guide the next generation. (p. 423)

genetic counseling A communication process designed to help couples assess their chances of giving birth to a baby with a hereditary disorder and choose the best course of action in view of risks and family goals. (p. 42)

genomic imprinting A pattern of inheritance in which alleles are imprinted, or chemically marked, in such a way that one pair member is activated, regardless of its makeup. (p. 40)

genotype An individual's genetic makeup. Distinguished from *phenotype.* (p. 36)

gerotranscendence According to Joan Erikson, a psychosocial stage characterizing the very old and representing development beyond ego integrity. Involves a cosmic, transcendent perspective directed forward and outward, beyond the self. Apparent in heightened inner calm and contentment and in additional time spent in quiet reflection. (p. 480)

gifted Displaying exceptional intellectual strengths, such as high IQ, high potential for creativity, and specialized talent. (p. 254)

glass ceiling Invisible barrier to advancement up the corporate ladder, faced by women and ethnic minorities. (p. 440)

glaucoma A disease in which poor fluid drainage leads to a buildup of pressure within the eye, damaging the optic nerve. A leading cause of blindness among older adults. (p. 402)

glial cells Cells that are responsible for myelination of neural fibers, improving the efficiency of message transfer. (p. 94)

goodness-of-fit model A model that describes how favorable adjustment depends on an effective match, or good fit, between a child's temperament and the child-rearing environment. (p. 151)

grief Intense physical and psychological distress following the death of a loved one. (p. 523)

growth hormone (GH) A pituitary hormone that affects the development of all body tissues except the central nervous system and the genitals. (p. 170)

growth spurt Rapid gain in height and weight that is the first outward sign of puberty. (p. 288)

guided participation Shared endeavors between more expert and less expert participants, without specifying the precise features of communication in order to allow for variations across situations and cultures. A broader concept than *scaffolding*. (p. 183)

H

habituation A gradual reduction in the strength of a response due to repetitive stimulation. (p. 104)

hardiness A set of three personal qualities—control, commitment, and challenge—that, together, help people cope adaptively with stress brought on by inevitable life changes. (p. 411)

heritability estimate A statistic that measures the extent to which individual differences in complex traits, such as intelligence or personality, in a specific population are due to genetic factors. (p. 53)

heterozygous Having two different alleles at the same place on a pair of chromosomes. Distinguished from *homozygous*. (p. 38)

hierarchical classification The organization of objects into classes and subclasses on the basis of similarities and differences. (p. 178)

hippocampus An inner-brain structure that plays a vital role in memory and in images of space that help us find our way. (p. 169)

history-graded influences Influences on lifespan development that are unique to a particular historical era and explain why people born around the same time (called a *cohort*) tend to be alike in ways that set them apart from people born at other times. (p. 9)

Home Observation for Measurement of the Environment (HOME) A checklist for gathering information about the quality of children's home lives through observation and parental interview. (p. 133)

homozygous Having two identical alleles at the same place on a pair of chromosomes. Distinguished from *heterozygous*. (p. 38)

hormone therapy Low daily doses of estrogen, either alone or in combination with progesterone, aimed at reducing the physical discomforts of menopause. (p. 405)

hospice A comprehensive program of support services for terminally ill people and their families, which regards the patient and family as a unit of care and emphasizes meeting the patient's physical, emotional, social, and spiritual needs while also providing follow-up bereavement services to the family. (p. 517)

hypothetico-deductive reasoning A formal operational problem-solving strategy in which adolescents begin with a *hypothesis*, or prediction, about variables that might affect an outcome. From the hypothesis, they *deduce* logical, testable inferences. Then they systematically isolate and combine variables to see which of those inferences are confirmed in the real world. (p. 304)

I

identical, or monozygotic, twins Twins that result when a zygote, during early cell duplication, separates into two clusters of cells with the same genetic makeup, which develop into two individuals. Distinguished from *fraternal, or dizygotic, twins*. (p. 38)

identity A well-organized conception of the self, consisting of values, beliefs, and goals, to which the individual is solidly committed. (p. 318)

identity achievement The identity status of individuals who, after a period of exploration, have committed themselves to a clearly formulated set of self-chosen values and goals. Distinguished from *identity moratorium, identity foreclosure,* and *identity diffusion*. (p. 319)

identity diffusion The identity status of individuals who do not engage in exploration and are not committed to values and goals. Distinguished from *identity achievement, identity moratorium,* and *identity foreclosure*. (p. 319)

identity foreclosure The identity status of individuals who do not engage in exploration but, instead, are committed to ready-made values and goals chosen for them by authority figures. Distinguished from *identity achievement, identity moratorium,* and *identity diffusion*. (p. 319)

identity moratorium The identity status of individuals who are exploring but not yet committed to self-chosen values and goals. Distinguished from *identity achievement, identity foreclosure,* and *identity diffusion*. (p. 319)

identity versus role confusion In Erikson's theory, the psychological conflict of adolescence, which is resolved positively when adolescents achieve an identity through a process of exploration and inner soul-searching. (p. 318)

imaginary audience Adolescents' belief that they are the focus of everyone else's attention and concern. (p. 308)

imitation Learning by copying the behavior of another person. Also known as *modeling* or *observational learning*. (p. 104)

implantation Attachment of the blastocyst to the uterine lining, which occurs 7 to 9 days after fertilization. (p. 63)

implicit memory Memory without conscious awareness. (p. 469)

inclusive classrooms Classrooms in which students with learning difficulties learn alongside typical students in a regular educational setting for all or part of the school day—a practice designed to prepare them for participation in society and to combat prejudices against individuals with disabilities. (p. 252)

incomplete dominance A pattern of inheritance in which both alleles are expressed in the phenotype, resulting in a combined trait, or one that is intermediate between the two. (p. 39)

independence–ignore script A typical pattern of interaction in which older adults' independent behaviors are mostly ignored and, as a result, occur less often. Distinguished from *dependency–support script*. (p. 484)

independent variable In an experiment, the variable the investigator expects to cause changes in another variable and that the researcher manipulates by randomly assigning participants to treatment conditions. Distinguished from *dependent variable*. (p. 27)

individualistic societies Societies in which people think of themselves as separate entities and are largely concerned with their own personal needs. Distinguished from *collectivist societies*. (p. 50)

induction A type of discipline in which an adult helps the child notice feelings by pointing out the effects of the child's misbehavior on others. (p. 207)

industry versus inferiority In Erikson's theory, the psychological conflict of middle childhood, which is resolved positively when experiences lead children to develop a sense of competence at useful skills and tasks. (p. 260)

infant-directed speech (IDS) A form of communication used by adults to speak to infants and toddlers, consisting of short sentences with high-pitched, exaggerated expression, clear pronunciation, distinct pauses between speech segments, and repetition of new words in a variety of contexts. (p. 139)

infantile amnesia The inability of most older children and adults to retrieve events that happened before age 3. (p. 129)

infant mortality The number of deaths in the first year of life per 1,000 live births. (p. 81)

information-loss view A view that attributes age-related slowing of cognitive processing to greater loss of information as it moves through the system. As a result, the whole system must slow down to inspect and interpret the information. Distinguished from *neural network view*. (p. 415)

information processing A perspective that views the human mind as a symbol-manipulating system through which information flows and that regards cognitive development as a continuous process. (p. 16)

inhibited, or shy, child A child whose temperament is such that he or she reacts negatively to and withdraws from novel stimuli. Distinguished from *uninhibited, or sociable, child.* (p. 149)

initiative versus guilt In Erikson's theory, the psychological conflict of early childhood, which is resolved positively through play experiences that foster a healthy sense of initiative and through development of a superego, or conscience, that is not overly strict and guilt-ridden. (p. 200)

instrumental activities of daily living (IADLs) Tasks necessary to conduct the business of daily life and also requiring some cognitive competence, such as telephoning, shopping, food preparation, housekeeping, and paying bills. (p. 449)

intelligence quotient (IQ) A score that permits an individual's performance on an intelligence test to be compared to the performances of other individuals of the same age. (p. 132)

intentional, or goal-directed, behavior A sequence of actions in which schemes are deliberately coordinated to solve a problem. (p. 120)

intermodal perception The process of making sense of simultaneous input from more than one modality, or sensory system, perceiving them as an integrated whole. (p. 113)

internal working model A set of expectations about the availability of attachment figures and the likelihood that they will provide support in times of stress. It becomes a vital part of personality, serving as a guide for all future close relationships. (p. 153)

intimacy versus isolation In Erikson's theory, the psychological conflict of early adulthood, reflected in the young person's thoughts and feelings about making a permanent commitment to an intimate partner. (p. 374)

irreversibility The inability to mentally go through a series of steps in a problem and then reverse direction, returning to the starting point. Distinguished from *reversibility.* (p. 178)

J

joint attention A state in which the child attends to the same object or event as the caregiver, who often labels it. Supports language development. (p. 137)

K

kinkeeper Role assumed by members of the middle generation, especially mothers, who take responsibility for gathering the family for celebrations and making sure everyone stays in touch. (p. 433)

kinship studies Studies that compare the characteristics of family members to determine the importance of heredity in complex human characteristics. (p. 53)

kwashiorkor A disease caused by an unbalanced diet very low in protein that usually appears after weaning, between 1 and 3 years of age. Symptoms include an enlarged belly, swollen feet, hair loss, skin rash, and irritable, listless behavior. (p. 102)

L

language acquisition device (LAD) In Chomsky's theory, an innate system containing a universal grammar, or set of rules common to all languages, that enables children, no matter which language they hear, to understand and speak in a rule-oriented fashion as soon as they pick up enough words. (p. 136)

lanugo White, downy hair that covers the entire body of the fetus, helping the vernix stick to the skin. (p. 64)

lateralization Specialization of functions in the two hemispheres of the cerebral cortex. (p. 96)

learned helplessness Attribution of success to external factors, such as luck, and failure to low ability, which is fixed and cannot be improved through effort. Distinguished from *mastery-oriented attributions.* (p. 263)

learning disabilities Great difficulty with one or more aspects of learning, usually reading, resulting in achievement considerably behind what would be expected on the basis of a child's IQ. (p. 253)

life-care communities Housing for older adults that offers a range of alternatives, from independent or congregate housing to full nursing home care, guaranteeing that residents' changing needs will be met within the same facility as they age. (p. 490)

lifespan perspective A dynamic systems approach to development that assumes development is lifelong, multidimensional and multidirectional, highly plastic, and affected by multiple interacting forces. (p. 5)

living will A written statement specifying the treatments a person does or does not want in case of a terminal illness, coma, or other near-death situation. (p. 520)

longitudinal design A research design in which participants are studied repeatedly, and changes are noted as they get older. Distinguished from *cross-sectional design.* (p. 28)

long-term memory In information processing, the largest storage area in memory, containing our permanent knowledge base. (p. 126)

M

macrosystem In ecological systems theory, cultural values, laws, customs, and resources that influence experiences and interactions at inner levels of the environment. Distinguished from *microsystem, mesosystem, exosystem,* and *chronosystem.* (p. 20)

macular degeneration Blurring and eventual loss of central vision due to a breakdown of light-sensitive cells in the macula, or central region of the retina. (p. 451)

make-believe play A type of play in which children act out everyday and imaginary activities. (p. 121)

marasmus A wasted condition of the body caused by a diet low in all essential nutrients, which usually appears in the first year of life. (p. 101)

mastery-oriented attributions Attributions that credit success to ability, which can be improved through effort, and failure to insufficient effort. Distinguished from *learned helplessness.* (p. 263)

matters of personal choice Concerns that do not involve rights or others' welfare and, therefore, are up to the individual, such as choice of friends, hairstyle, and leisure activities. Distinguished from *moral imperatives* and *social conventions.* (p. 210)

maximum lifespan The species-specific biological limit to length of life (in years), corresponding to the age at which the oldest known individual died. Distinguished from *average life expectancy* and *average healthy life expectancy.* (p. 449)

meiosis The process of cell division through which gametes are formed and in which the number of chromosomes in each cell is halved. (p. 37)

memory strategies Deliberate mental activities that improve the likelihood of remembering. (p. 185)

menarche First menstruation. (p. 290)

menopause The end of menstruation and, therefore, of a woman's reproductive capacity. (p. 403)

mental representation An internal depiction of information that the mind can manipulate, including images and concepts. (p. 120)

mesosystem In ecological systems theory, connections between a person's microsystems, or immediate settings. Distinguished from *microsystem, exosystem, macrosystem,* and *chronosystem.* (p. 20)

metacognition Thinking about thought; a theory of mind, or coherent set of ideas about mental activities. (p. 186)

microsystem In ecological systems theory, the innermost level of the environment, consisting of activities and interaction patterns in the person's immediate surroundings. Distinguished from *mesosystem, exosystem, macrosystem,* and *chronosystem.* (p. 20)

midlife crisis Self-doubt and stress that prompt major restructuring of the personality during the transition to middle adulthood. Characterizes the experience of only a minority of adults. (p. 426)

mirror neurons Specialized cells in motor areas of the cerebral cortex in primates that underlie the ability to imitate by firing identically when a primate hears or sees an action and when it carries out the action on its own. (p. 105)

mitosis The process of cell duplication, in which each new cell receives an exact copy of the original chromosomes. (p. 37)

moral identity The degree to which morality is central to an individual's self-concept. (p. 327)

moral imperatives Rules and expectations that protect people's rights and welfare. Distinguished from *social conventions* and *matters of personal choice.* (p. 210)

mortality The phase of dying in which the individual passes into permanent death. Distinguished from *agonal phase* and *clinical death.* (p. 510)

mourning The culturally specified expression of the bereaved person's thoughts and feelings through funerals and other rituals. (p. 523)

mutation A sudden but permanent change in a segment of DNA. (p. 40)

myelination The coating of neural fibers with an insulating fatty sheath, called *myelin,* that improves the efficiency of message transfer. (p. 94)

N

naturalistic observation A research method in which the researcher goes into the field, or natural environment, and records the behavior of interest. Distinguished from *structured observation.* (p. 22)

natural, or **prepared, childbirth** A group of techniques designed to reduce pain and medical intervention and to make childbirth as rewarding an experience as possible. (p. 77)

nature–nurture controversy Disagreement among theorists about whether genetic or environmental factors are more important influences on development. (p. 5)

neglected children Children who are seldom mentioned, either positively or negatively, on self-report measures of peer acceptance. Distinguished from *popular, rejected,* and *controversial children.* (p. 269)

neural network view A view that attributes age-related slowing of cognitive processing to breaks in neural networks as neurons die. The brain adapts by forming bypasses—new synaptic connections that go around the breaks but are less efficient. Distinguished from *information-loss view.* (p. 415)

neural tube During the period of the embryo, the primitive spinal cord that develops from the ectoderm, the top of which swells to form the brain. (p. 63)

neurofibrillary tangles A structural change in the cerebral cortex associated with Alzheimer's disease, in which bundles of twisted threads appear that are the product of collapsed neural structures. (p. 462)

neurons Nerve cells that store and transmit information. (p. 93)

neurotransmitters Chemicals released by neurons that cross the synapse to send messages to other neurons. (p. 94)

niche-picking A type of gene–environment correlation in which individuals actively choose environments that complement their heredity. (p. 55)

nonnormative influences Influences on lifespan development that are irregular, in that they happen to just one or a few individuals and do not follow a predictable timetable. (p. 9)

non-rapid-eye-movement (NREM) sleep A "regular" sleep state during which the body is almost motionless and heart rate, breathing, and brain-wave activity are slow and even. Distinguished from *rapid-eye-movement (REM) sleep.* (p. 83)

nonsocial activity Unoccupied, onlooker behavior and solitary play. Distinguished from *parallel, associative,* and *cooperative play.* (p. 203)

normal distribution The bell-shaped distribution that results when individual differences are measured in large samples. Most scores cluster around the mean, or average, with progressively fewer falling toward the extremes. (p. 132)

normative approach An approach in which measures of behavior are taken on large numbers of individuals, and age-related averages are computed to represent typical development. (p. 11)

O

obesity A greater-than-20-percent increase over healthy body weight, based on body mass index, a ratio of weight to height associated with body fat. (p. 228)

object permanence The understanding that objects continue to exist when out of sight. (p. 120)

operant conditioning A form of learning in which a spontaneous behavior is followed by a stimulus that changes the probability that the behavior will occur again. (p. 104)

optimal aging Aging in which gains are maximized and losses minimized. (p. 501)

ordinality The mathematical principle specifying order relationships (more than and less than) between quantities. (p. 189)

organization In Piaget's theory, the internal rearrangement and linking together of schemes to create a strongly interconnected cognitive system. In information processing, a memory strategy that involves grouping related items together to improve recall. (p. 119, p. 238)

osteoarthritis A form of arthritis that involves deteriorating cartilage on the ends of bones of frequently used joints, which leads to swelling, stiffness, and loss of flexibility. Also known as "wear-and-tear" arthritis or "degenerative joint disease." Distinguished from *rheumatoid arthritis.* (p. 460)

osteoporosis Severe age-related bone loss, which greatly magnifies the risk of bone fractures. (p. 408)

overextension An early vocabulary error in which young children apply a word too broadly, to a wider collection of objects and events than is appropriate. Distinguished from *underextension.* (p. 138)

overregularization Overextension of regular grammatical rules to words that are exceptions. (p. 195)

P

palliative, or **comfort, care** Care for terminally ill, suffering patients that relieves pain and other symptoms (such as nausea, breathing difficulties, insomnia, and depression), with the goal of protecting the patient's quality of remaining life rather than prolonging life. (p. 518)

parallel play A form of limited social participation in which a child plays near other children with similar materials but does not try to influence their behavior. Distinguished from *nonsocial, associative,* and *cooperative play.* (p. 204)

parental imperative theory A theory that claims that identification with traditional gender roles is maintained during the active parenting years to help ensure the survival of children but that after children reach adulthood, parents are free to express the "other-gender" side of their personalities. (p. 430)

partial fetal alcohol syndrome (p-FAS) A form of fetal alcohol spectrum disorder characterized by facial abnormalities and brain injury, but less severe than fetal alcohol syndrome. Usually affects children whose mothers drank alcohol in smaller quantities during pregnancy. Distinguished from *fetal alcohol syndrome (FAS)* and *alcohol-related neurodevelopmental disorder (ARND).* (p. 69)

passionate love Love based on intense sexual attraction. Distinguished from *companionate love.* (p. 377)

passive euthanasia The practice of withholding or withdrawing life-sustaining treatment, permitting a patient to die naturally. Distinguished from *voluntary active euthanasia.* (p. 520)

peer acceptance Likability, or the extent to which a child is viewed by a group of agemates as a worthy social partner. (p. 269)

peer group A collective of peers who generate unique values and standards for behavior and a social structure of leaders and followers. (p. 267)

peer victimization A destructive form of peer interaction in which certain children become frequent targets of verbal and physical attacks or other forms of abuse. (p. 270)

perceptual narrowing effect Perceptual sensitivity that becomes increasingly attuned with age to information most often encountered. (p. 110)

permissive child-rearing style A child-rearing style that is warm and accepting but uninvolved, low in control (either overindulgent or inattentive), and lenient rather than appropriate in autonomy granting. Distinguished from *authoritative, authoritarian,* and *uninvolved child-rearing styles.* (p. 218)

persistent vegetative state A state in which the cerebral cortex no longer registers electrical activity but the brain stem remains active. The person is unconscious and displays no voluntary movements. (p. 510)

personal fable Adolescents' inflated opinion of their own importance—a feeling that they are special and unique. (p. 308)

person–environment fit A good match between older adults' abilities and the demands of their living environments. Promotes adaptive behavior and psychological well-being. (p. 484)

phenotype An individual's directly observable physical and behavioral characteristics, which are determined by both genetic and environmental factors. Distinguished from *genotype*. (p. 36)

phobia An intense, unmanageable fear that leads to persistent avoidance of the feared situation. (p. 279)

phonics approach An approach to beginning reading instruction that emphasizes coaching children on phonics—the basic rules for translating written symbols into sounds—before exposing them to complex reading material. Distinguished from the *whole-language approach*. (p. 241)

phonological awareness The ability to reflect on and manipulate the sound structure of spoken language, as indicated by sensitivity to changes in sounds within words, to rhyming, and to incorrect pronunciation. A strong predictor of emergent literacy knowledge. (p. 188)

physical aggression A form of aggression that harms others through physical injury to themselves or their property. Distinguished from *verbal aggression* and *relational aggression*. (p. 211)

pituitary gland A gland located at the base of the brain that releases hormones that induce physical growth. (p. 170)

placenta The organ that permits exchange of nutrients and waste products between the bloodstreams of the mother and the embryo, while also preventing the mother's and embryo's blood from mixing directly. (p. 63)

plasticity Openness of development to change in response to influential experiences. (p. 5)

polygenic inheritance A pattern of inheritance in which many genes influence a characteristic. (p. 40)

popular-antisocial children A subgroup of popular children who are admired for their socially adept yet belligerent behavior. Includes "tough" boys who are athletically skilled, aggressive, and poor students, as well as relationally aggressive boys and girls. Distinguished from *popular-prosocial children*. (p. 269)

popular children Children who receive many positive votes on self-report measures of peer acceptance, indicating they are well-liked. Distinguished from *rejected, controversial,* and *neglected children*. (p. 269)

popular-prosocial children A subgroup of popular children who combine academic and social competence. Distinguished from *popular-antisocial children*. (p. 269)

possible selves Future-oriented representations of what one hopes to become and what one is afraid of becoming. The temporal dimension of self-concept. (p. 427)

postconventional level Kohlberg's highest level of moral development, in which individuals define morality in terms of abstract principles and values that apply to all situations and societies. (p. 324)

postformal thought Cognitive development beyond Piaget's formal operational stage. (p. 358)

practical problem solving Problem solving that requires people to size up real-world situations and analyze how best to achieve goals that have a high degree of uncertainty. (p. 418)

pragmatics The practical, social side of language, concerned with how to engage in effective and appropriate communication. (p. 195)

pragmatic thought In Labouvie-Vief 's theory, a structural advance in thinking in adulthood, in which logic becomes a tool for solving real-world problems and contradictions are accepted as part of existence. (p. 359)

preconventional level Kohlberg's first level of moral development, in which children accept the rules of authority figures and judge actions by their consequences, viewing behaviors that result in punishment as bad and those that lead to rewards as good. (p. 323)

prefrontal cortex The region of the cerebral cortex, lying in front of areas controlling body movement, that is responsible for thought—in particular, for consciousness, inhibition of impulses, integration of information, and use of memory, reasoning, planning, and problem-solving strategies. (p. 96)

prenatal diagnostic methods Medical procedures that permit detection of developmental problems before birth. (p. 43)

preoperational stage Piaget's second stage of cognitive development, extending from about 2 to 7 years of age, in which children undergo an extraordinary increase in representational, or symbolic, activity, although thought is not yet logical. (p. 175)

presbycusis Age-related hearing impairment, beginning around age 50 with a noticeable decline in sensitivity to high-frequency sounds, which gradually extends to all frequencies. (p. 402)

presbyopia A condition of aging in which, around age 60, the lens of the eye loses its capacity to adjust to objects at varying distances. (p. 402)

preterm infants Infants born several weeks or more before their due date. (p. 79)

primary aging Genetically influenced age-related declines in the functioning of organs and systems that affect all members of our species and occur even in the context of overall good health. Also called *biological aging*. Distinguished from *secondary aging*. (p. 459)

primary sexual characteristics Physical features that involve the reproductive organs (ovaries, uterus, and vagina in females; penis, scrotum, and testes in males). Distinguished from *secondary sexual characteristics*. (p. 290)

private speech Self-directed speech that children use to plan and guide their own behavior. (p. 182)

proactive aggression A type of aggression in which children act to fulfill a need or desire—obtain an object, privilege, space, or social reward, such as adult or peer attention—and unemotionally attack a person to achieve their goal. Also called *instrumental aggression*. Distinguished from *reactive aggression*. (p. 211)

problem-centered coping A strategy for managing emotion that involves appraising the situation as changeable, identifying the difficulty, and deciding what to do about it. Distinguished from *emotion-centered coping*. (p. 265)

programmed cell death An aspect of brain growth whereby, as synapses form, many surrounding neurons die, making space for these connective structures. (p. 94)

Project Head Start A U.S. federal early intervention program that provides children from low-income families with a year or two of preschool, along with nutritional and health services, and that encourages parent involvement in children's learning and development. (p. 191)

propositional thought A type of formal operational reasoning involving the ability to evaluate the logic of propositions, or verbal statements, without referring to real-world circumstances. (p. 305)

prosocial, or altruistic, behavior Actions that benefit another person without any expected reward for the self. (p. 203)

prospective memory Recall that involves remembering to engage in planned actions in the future. (p. 470)

proximodistal trend An organized pattern of physical growth that proceeds from the center of the body outward. Distinguished from *cephalocaudal trend*. (p. 93)

psychoanalytic perspective An approach to personality development introduced by Freud that assumes people move through a series of stages in which they confront conflicts between biological drives and social expectations. How these conflicts are resolved determines the person's ability to learn, to get along with others, and to cope with anxiety. (p. 12)

psychological control Parental behaviors that intrude on and manipulate children's verbal expressions, individuality, and attachments to parents. (p. 218)

psychosexual theory Freud's theory, which emphasizes that how parents manage children's sexual and aggressive drives in the first few years is crucial for healthy personality development. (p. 12)

psychosocial theory Erikson's theory, which emphasizes that in each Freudian stage, individuals not only develop a unique personality but also acquire attitudes and skills that make them active, contributing members of their society. Recognizes the lifespan nature of development and the impact of culture. (p. 12)

puberty Biological changes at adolescence that lead to an adult-sized body and sexual maturity. (p. 287)

public policies Laws and government programs designed to improve current conditions. (p. 50)

punishment In operant conditioning, removal of a desirable stimulus or presentation of an unpleasant one to decrease the occurrence of a response. (p. 104)

R

random assignment An unbiased procedure for assigning participants to treatment conditions in an experiment, such as drawing numbers out of a hat or flipping a coin. Increases the chances that participants' characteristics will be equally distributed across treatment groups. (p. 27)

rapid-eye-movement (REM) sleep An "irregular" sleep state in which brain-wave activity is similar to that of the waking state. Distinguished from *non-rapid-eye-movement (NREM) sleep.* (p. 83)

reactive aggression An angry, defensive response to provocation or a blocked goal that is meant to hurt another person. Also called *hostile aggression.* Distinguished from *proactive aggression.* (p. 211)

realistic period Period of vocational development in which older adolescents and young adults narrow their vocational options, engaging in further exploration before focusing on a general vocational category and, slightly later, settling on a single occupation. Distinguished from *fantasy period* and *tentative period.* (p. 362)

recall A type of memory that involves remembering something that is not present. Distinguished from *recognition.* (p. 128)

recasts Adult responses that restructure children's grammatically inaccurate speech into correct form. (p. 196)

recognition A type of memory that involves noticing whether a stimulus is identical or similar to one previously experienced. Distinguished from *recall.* (p. 128)

recovery Following habituation, an increase in responsiveness to a new stimulus. (p. 104)

reflex An inborn, automatic response to a particular form of stimulation. (p. 82)

rehearsal A memory strategy that involves repeating information to oneself to improve recall. (p. 238)

reinforcer In operant conditioning, a stimulus that increases the occurrence of a response. (p. 104)

rejected-aggressive children A subgroup of rejected children who show high rates of conflict, physical and relational aggression, and hyperactive, inattentive, and impulsive behavior. Distinguished from *rejected-withdrawn children.* (p. 269)

rejected children Children who receive many negative votes on self-report measures of peer acceptance, indicating they are actively disliked. Distinguished from *popular, controversial,* and *neglected children.* (p. 269)

rejected-withdrawn children A subgroup of rejected children who are passive and socially awkward. Distinguished from *rejected-aggressive children.* (p. 269)

relational aggression A form of aggression that damages another's peer relationships through social exclusion, malicious gossip, or friendship manipulation. Distinguished from *physical aggression* and *verbal aggression.* (p. 211)

relativistic thinking In Perry's theory, the cognitive approach typical of older college students, who view all knowledge as embedded in a framework of thought and, therefore, give up the possibility of absolute truth in favor of multiple truths, each relative to its context. Distinguished from *dualistic thinking.* (p. 358)

reminiscence The process of telling stories about people and events from the past and reporting associated thoughts and feelings. (p. 481)

reminiscence bump Older adults' heightened autobiographical memory for events that occurred between ages 10 and 30. (p. 470)

remote memory Very long-term recall. (p. 469)

resilience The ability to adapt effectively in the face of threats to development. (p. 8)

resistant attachment The attachment pattern characterizing infants who remain close to the parent and fail to explore before separation, are usually distressed when the parent leaves, and combine clinginess with angry, resistive behavior when the parent returns. Distinguished from *secure, avoidant,* and *disorganized/disoriented attachment.* (p. 154)

reticular formation A structure in the brain stem that maintains alertness and consciousness. (p. 169)

reversibility The ability to think through a series of steps in a problem and then mentally reverse direction, returning to the starting point. Distinguished from *irreversibility.* (p. 234)

rheumatoid arthritis A form of arthritis in which an autoimmune response leads to inflammation of connective tissue, particularly the membranes that line the joints, resulting in overall stiffness, inflammation, and aching. Leads to deformed joints and often serious loss of mobility. Distinguished from *osteoarthritis.* (p. 460)

Rh factor incompatibility A condition that arises when the Rh protein is present in the fetus's blood but not in the mother's, causing the mother to build up antibodies. If these enter the fetus's system, they destroy red blood cells, reducing the oxygen supply to organs and tissues. Mental retardation, miscarriage, heart damage, and infant death can occur. (p. 72)

rough-and-tumble play A form of peer interaction involving friendly chasing and play-fighting that emerges in the preschool years and peaks in middle childhood. In our evolutionary past, it may have been important for developing fighting skill. (p. 232)

S

sandwich generation A term used to describe middle-aged adults who must care for multiple generations above and below them at the same time. (p. 436)

scaffolding Adjusting the support offered during a teaching session to fit the learner's current level of performance. Direct instruction is offered when a task is new; less help is provided as competence increases, thereby keeping the task within the zone of proximal development. (p. 182)

scale errors Toddlers' attempts to do things that their body size makes impossible, possibly indicating lack of an accurate understanding of their own body dimensions. (p. 160)

scheme In Piaget's theory, a specific psychological structure, or organized way of making sense of experience, that changes with age. (p. 118)

scripts General descriptions of what occurs and when it occurs in a particular situation, used to organize and interpret everyday experiences. (p. 185)

secondary aging Age-related declines due to hereditary defects and environmental influences, such as poor diet, lack of exercise, disease, substance abuse, environmental pollution, and psychological stress. Distinguished from *primary aging.* (p. 459)

secondary friends People who are not intimates but with whom an individual spends time occasionally, such as a group that meets for lunch, bridge, or museum tours. (p. 497)

secondary sexual characteristics Physical features visible on the outside of the body that serve as signs of sexual maturity but do not involve the reproductive organs (for example, breast development in females, appearance of underarm and pubic hair in both sexes). Distinguished from *primary sexual characteristics.* (p. 290)

secular trend A change from one generation to the next in an aspect of development, such as body size or pubertal timing. (p. 291)

secure attachment The attachment pattern characterizing infants who use the parent as a secure base from which to explore, may be distressed by parental separation, but actively seek contact and are easily comforted by the parent when she returns. Distinguished from *avoidant, resistant,* and *disorganized/disoriented attachment.* (p. 154)

secure base The familiar caregiver as a point from which the baby explores, venturing into the environment and then returning for emotional support. (p. 146)

selective optimization with compensation A set of strategies used by older adults who sustain high levels of functioning. Narrowing their goals, they *select* personally valued activities to *optimize* returns from their diminishing energy and also find new ways to *compensate* for losses. (p. 468)

self-care children Children who are without adult supervision for some period of time after school. (p. 278)

self-concept The set of attributes, abilities, attitudes, and values that an individual believes defines who he or she is. (p. 201)

self-conscious emotions Emotions involving injury to or enhancement of the sense of self, including guilt, shame, embarrassment, envy, and pride. (p. 147)

self-esteem An aspect of self-concept that involves judgments about one's own worth and the feelings associated with those judgments. (p. 201)

self-recognition Identification of the self as a physically unique being. (p. 160)

sensitive caregiving Caregiving that involves responding promptly, consistently, and appropriately to infants and holding them tenderly and carefully. (p. 156)

sensitive period A time that is optimal for certain capacities to emerge and in which the individual is especially responsive to environmental influences. (p. 18)

sensorimotor stage Piaget's first stage, spanning the first two years of life, during which infants and toddlers "think" with their eyes, ears, hands, and other sensorimotor equipment. (p. 118)

sensory register The part of the information-processing system in which sights and sounds are represented directly and stored briefly. (p. 126)

separation anxiety An infant's distressed reaction to the departure of the familiar caregiver. (p. 153)

seriation The ability to order items along a quantitative dimension, such as length or weight. (p. 234)

sequential designs Developmental designs in which investigators conduct several similar cross-sectional or longitudinal studies (called *sequences*) at varying times, sometimes combining longitudinal and cross-sectional strategies. (p. 30)

sex chromosomes The twenty-third pair of chromosomes, which determines the sex of the individual. In females, it is called *XX*; in males, *XY*. (p. 37)

short-term memory store The part of the mind in which attended-to-information is retained briefly so that we can actively "work" on it to achieve our goals. (p. 126)

skipped-generation family A family structure in which children live with grandparents but apart from parents. (p. 435)

slow-to-warm-up child A child whose temperament is characterized by inactivity; mild, low-key reactions to environmental stimuli; negative mood; and slow adjustment to new experiences. Distinguished from *easy child* and *difficult child*. (p. 148)

small-for-date infants Infants whose birth weight is below their expected weight considering length of the pregnancy. Some are full-term; others are preterm infants who are especially underweight. (p. 79)

social clock Age-graded expectations for major life events, such as beginning a first job, getting married, birth of the first child, buying a home, and retiring. (p. 376)

social comparisons Judgments of one's own appearance, abilities, and behavior in relation to those of others. (p. 260)

social-constructivist classroom A classroom grounded in Vygotsky's sociocultural theory, in which children participate in a wide range of challenging activities with teachers and peers, with whom they jointly construct understandings. Distinguished from *traditional* and *constructivist classrooms*. (p. 251)

social conventions Customs determined solely by consensus within a society, such as table manners and politeness rituals. Distinguished from *moral imperatives* and *matters of personal choice*. (p. 210)

social convoy A model of age-related changes in social networks, which views the individual as moving through life within a cluster of relationships, with close ties in the inner circle and less close ties on the outside. With age, people change places in the convoy, new ties are added, and some are lost entirely. (p. 492)

social learning theory An approach that emphasizes the role of modeling, otherwise known as imitation or observational learning, in the development of behavior. (p. 14)

social referencing Actively seeking emotional information from a trusted person in an uncertain situation. (p. 146)

social smile The infant's broad grin, evoked by the parent's communication, that first appears between 6 and 10 weeks of age. (p. 144)

sociocultural theory Vygotsky's theory, in which children acquire the ways of thinking and behaving that make up their community's culture through social interaction—in particular, cooperative dialogues with more knowledgeable members of society. (p. 18)

sociodramatic play The make-believe with others that is under way by the end of the second year and increases rapidly in complexity during early childhood. (p. 176)

socioeconomic status (SES) A measure of an individual's or a family's social position and economic well-being that combines three related, but not completely overlapping, variables: years of education, the prestige of one's job and the skill it requires, and income. (p. 47)

socioemotional selectivity theory A social theory of aging that states that social interaction in late adulthood extends lifelong selection processes. Physical and psychological aspects of aging lead to an increased emphasis on the emotion-regulating function of social interaction, leading older adults to prefer familiar social partners with whom they have developed pleasurable relationships. Distinguished from *disengagement theory*, *activity theory*, and *continuity theory*. (p. 488)

spermarche First ejaculation of seminal fluid. (p. 290)

stage A qualitative change in thinking, feeling, and behaving that characterizes a specific period of development. (p. 4)

standardization The practice of giving a newly constructed test to a large, representative sample and using the results as the standard for interpreting individual scores. (p. 132)

states of arousal Different degrees of sleep and wakefulness. (p. 83)

statistical learning capacity The capacity to analyze the speech stream for regularly occurring sound sequences, through which infants acquire a stock of speech structures for which they will later learn meanings. (p. 109)

stereotype threat The fear of being judged on the basis of a negative stereotype, which can trigger anxiety that interferes with performance. (p. 246)

stranger anxiety The infant's expression of fear in response to unfamiliar adults, which appears in many babies in the second half of the first year. (p. 146)

Strange Situation A laboratory procedure used to assess the quality of attachment between 1 and 2 years of age by observing the baby's response to eight short episodes involving brief separations from and reunions with the caregiver in an unfamiliar playroom. (p. 154)

structured interview An interview method in which each participant is asked the same questions in the same way. Distinguished from *clinical interview*. (p. 24)

structured observation A research method in which the investigator sets up a laboratory situation that evokes the behavior of interest so that every participant has an equal opportunity to display the response. Distinguished from *naturalistic observation*. (p. 23)

subculture A group of people with beliefs and customs that differ from those of the larger culture. (p. 50)

sudden infant death syndrome (SIDS) The unexpected death, usually during the night, of an infant under 1 year of age that remains unexplained after thorough investigation. (p. 84)

sympathy Feelings of concern or sorrow for another's plight. (p. 203)

synapses The gaps between neurons, across which chemical messages are sent. (p. 94)

synaptic pruning Loss of synapses by seldom-stimulated neurons, a process that returns them to an uncommitted state so they can support future development. (p. 94)

T

talent Outstanding performance in a specific field. (p. 254)

telegraphic speech Toddlers' two-word utterances that, like a telegram, focus on high-content words while omitting smaller, less important words. (p. 138)

telomeres A special type of DNA located at the ends of chromosomes—serving as a "cap" to protect the ends from destruction—that shortens with each cell duplication. Eventually, so little remains that the cells no longer duplicate at all. (p. 344)

temperament Early-appearing, stable individual differences in reactivity (quickness and intensity of emotional arousal, attention, and motor activity) and self-regulation (strategies that modify that reactivity). (p. 148)

tentative period Period of vocational development in which adolescents begin to evaluate vocational options in terms of their interests, abilities, and values. Distinguished from *fantasy period* and *realistic period*. (p. 362)

teratogen Any environmental agent that causes damage during the prenatal period. (p. 66)

terminal decline Acceleration in deterioration of cognitive functioning prior to death. (p. 473)

thanatology An interdisciplinary field devoted to the study of death and dying. (p. 509)

theory An orderly, integrated set of statements that describes, explains, and predicts behavior. (p. 3)

theory of multiple intelligences Gardner's theory, which identifies eight independent intelligences, defined in terms of distinct sets of processing operations that permit individuals to engage in a wide range of culturally valued activities: linguistic, logico-mathematical, musical, spatial, bodily-kinesthetic, naturalist, interpersonal, and intrapersonal. (p. 244)

Third Age A new phase of late adulthood extending from ages 65 to 79 or longer, resulting from added years of longevity plus good health and financial stability, in which older adults pursue personally enriching interests and goals. (p. 482)

thyroid-stimulating hormone (TSH) A pituitary hormone that stimulates the thyroid gland to release thyroxine, which is necessary for brain development and for growth hormone to have its full impact on body size. (p. 170)

time out A form of mild punishment that involves removing children from the immediate setting until they are ready to act appropriately. (p. 208)

traditional classroom A classroom in which the teacher is the sole authority for knowledge, rules, and decision making and students are relatively passive learners whose progress is evaluated in relation to how well they keep pace with a uniform set of standards for their grade. Distinguished from *constructivist* and *social-constructivist classrooms*. (p. 250)

traditional marriage A form of marriage involving clear division of husband's and wife's roles, in which the man is the head of household and economic provider, and the woman devotes herself to caring for her husband and children and creating a nurturant, comfortable home. Distinguished from *egalitarian marriage*. (p. 382)

transitive inference The ability to seriate, or order items along a quantitative dimension, mentally. (p. 234)

triarchic theory of successful intelligence Sternberg's theory, in which intelligent behavior involves balancing three broad, interacting intelligences—analytical intelligence, creative intelligence, and practical intelligence—to achieve success in life according to one's personal goals and the requirements of one's cultural community. (p. 243)

triangular theory of love Sternberg's view of love as including three components—intimacy, passion, and commitment—that shift in emphasis as romantic relationships develop. (p. 377)

trimesters Three equal time periods, each lasting three months, into which prenatal development is sometimes divided. (p. 64)

Type A behavior pattern A behavior pattern characterized by extreme competitiveness, ambition, impatience, hostility, angry outbursts, and a sense of time pressure. (p. 409)

U

umbilical cord The long cord connecting the prenatal organism to the placenta that delivers nutrients and removes waste products. (p. 63)

unconditioned response (UCR) In classical conditioning, a reflexive response that is produced by an unconditioned stimulus (UCS). Distinguished from *conditioned response*. (p. 103)

unconditioned stimulus (UCS) In classical conditioning, a stimulus that leads to a reflexive response. Distinguished from *conditioned stimulus*. (p. 103)

underextension An early vocabulary error in which young children apply a word too narrowly, to a smaller number of objects and events than is appropriate. Distinguished from *overextension*. (p. 138)

uninhibited, or sociable, child A child whose temperament is such that he or she displays positive emotion to and approaches novel stimuli. Distinguished from *inhibited, or shy, child*. (p. 149)

uninvolved child-rearing style A child-rearing style that combines low acceptance and involvement with little control and general indifference to issues of autonomy. Distinguished from *authoritative, authoritarian,* and *permissive child-rearing styles*. (p. 219)

V

verbal aggression A type of aggression that harms others through threats of physical aggression, name-calling, or hostile teasing. Distinguished from *physical aggression* and *relational aggression*. (p. 211)

vernix A white, cheeselike substance that covers the fetus, preventing the skin from chapping due to constant exposure to amniotic fluid. (p. 64)

video deficit effect In toddlers, poorer performance on tasks after watching a video than after seeing a live demonstration. (p. 124)

violation-of-expectation method A method in which researchers show babies an expected event (one that follows physical laws) and an unexpected event (a variation of the first event that violates physical laws). Heightened attention to the unexpected event suggests that the infant is "surprised" by a deviation from physical reality and, therefore, is aware of that aspect of the physical world. (p. 121)

visual acuity Fineness of visual discrimination. (p. 87)

voluntary active euthanasia The practice of acting directly, at a patient's request, to end suffering before a natural end to life. Distinguished from *passive euthanasia*. (p. 521)

W

whole-language approach An approach to beginning reading instruction that exposes children to text in its complete form, using reading materials that are whole and meaningful, to promote appreciation of the communicative function of written language. Distinguished from *phonics approach*. (p. 241)

wisdom A capacity made up of multiple cognitive and personality traits, combining breadth and depth of practical knowledge; ability to reflect on and apply that knowledge in ways that make life more bearable and worthwhile; emotional maturity, including the ability to listen, evaluate, and give advice; and altruistic creativity, which involves contributing to humanity and enriching others' lives. (p. 471)

working memory The number of items that can be briefly held in mind while also engaging in some effort to monitor or manipulate those items—a "mental workspace" that we use to accomplish many activities in daily life. A contemporary view of the short-term memory store. (p. 126)

X

X-linked inheritance A pattern of inheritance in which a recessive gene is carried on the X chromosome, so that males are more likely than females to be affected. (p. 39)

Z

zone of proximal development In Vygotsky's theory, a range of tasks too difficult for a child to do alone but possible with the help of more-skilled partners. (p. 130)

zygote The newly fertilized cell formed by the union of sperm and ovum at conception. (p. 37)

References

A

Aalsma, M., Lapsley, D. K., & Flannery, D. J. (2006). Personal fables, narcissism, and adolescent adjustment. *Psychology in the Schools, 43*, 481–491.

Aarnoudse-Moens, C. S., Weisglas-Kuperus, N., & van Goudoever, J. B. (2009). Meta-analysis of neurobehavioral outcomes in very preterm and/or very low birth weight children. *Pediatrics, 124*, 717–728.

AARP. (2002). *The Grandparent Study 2002 report.* Washington, DC: Author.

Abakoumkin, G., Stroebe, W., & Stroebe, M. (2010). Does relationship quality moderate the impact of marital bereavement on depressive symptoms? *Journal of Social and Clinical Psychology, 29*, 510–526.

Abbey, A., & Jacques-Tiura, A. J. (2011). Sexual assault perpetrators' tactics: Associations with their personal characteristics and aspects of the incident. *Journal of Interpersonal Violence, 26*, 2866–2889.

Abbey, A., & McAuslan, P. (2004). A longitudinal examination of male college students' perpetration of sexual assault. *Journal of Consulting and Clinical Psychology, 72*, 747–756.

Abela, J. R. Z., Hankin, B. L., Haigh, E. A. P., Adams, P., Vinokuroff, T., & Trayhern, L. (2005). Interpersonal vulnerability to depression in high-risk children: The role of insecure attachment and reassurance seeking. *Journal of Clinical Child and Adolescent Psychology, 34*, 182–192.

Abele, A. E., & Spurk, D. (2011). The dual impact of gender and the influence of timing of parenthood on men's and women's career development: Longitudinal findings. *International Journal of Behavioral Development, 35*, 225–232.

Abelson, H., Ledeen, K., & Lewis, H. (2008). *Blown to bits: Your life, liberty and happiness after the digital explosion.* New York: Addison-Wesley.

Aber, J. L., Jones, S. M., & Raver, C. C. (2007). Poverty and child development: New perspectives on a defining issue. In J. L. Aber, S. J. Bishop-Josef, S. M. Jones, K. T. McLearn, & D. Phillips (Eds.), *Child development and social policy: Knowledge for action* (pp. 149–166). Washington, DC: American Psychological Association.

Aboud, F. E. (2008). A social-cognitive developmental theory of prejudice. In S. M. Quintana & C. McKown (Eds.), *Handbook of race, racism, and the developing child* (pp. 55–71). Hoboken, NJ: Wiley.

Aboud, F. E., & Doyle, A. (1996). Parental and peer influences on children's racial attitudes. *International Journal of Intercultural Relations, 20*, 371–383.

Abrams, K. Y., Rifkin, A., & Hesse, E. (2006). Examining the role of parental frightened/frightening subtypes in predicting disorganized attachment within a brief observational procedure. *Development and Psychopathology, 18*, 345–361.

Achenbach, T. M., Phares, V., Howell, C. T., Rauh, V. A., & Nurcombe, B. (1990). Seven-year outcome of the Vermont program for low-birthweight infants. *Child Development, 61*, 1672–1681.

Acierno R., Hernandez, M. A., Amstadter, A. B., Resnick, H. S., Steve, K., Muzzy, W., et al. (2010). Prevalence and correlates of emotional, physical, sexual, and financial abuse and potential neglect in the United States: The national elder mistreatment study. *American Journal of Public Health, 100*, 292–297.

Acker, M. M., & Davis, M. H. (1992). Intimacy, passion, and commitment in adult romantic relationships: A test of the triangular love theory. *Journal of Social and Personal Relationships, 9*, 21–50.

Acker, M. M., & O'Leary, S. G. (1996). Inconsistency of mothers' feedback and toddlers' misbehavior and negative affect. *Journal of Abnormal Child Psychology, 24*, 703–714.

Ackerman, S., Zuroff, D. C., & Moskowitz, D. S. (2000). Generativity in midlife and young adults: Links to agency, communion, and subjective wellbeing. *International Journal of Aging and Human Development, 50*, 17–41.

ACT. (2010). *2010 retention/completion summary tables.* Retrieved from www.act.org/research/policymakers/pdf/10retain_trends.pdf

Adachi-Mejia, A. M., Longacre, M. R., Gibson, J. J., Beach, M. L., Titus-Ernstoff, L. T., & Dalton, M. A. (2007). Children with a TV in their bedroom at higher risk for being overweight. *International Journal of Obesity, 31*, 644–651.

Adams, G. A., Rau, B. L. (2011). Putting off tomorrow to do what you want today: Planning for retirement. *American Psychologist, 66*, 180–192.

Adams, K. B., Sanders, S., & Auth, E. A. (2004). Loneliness and depression in independent living retirement communities: Risk and resilience factors. *Aging and Mental Health, 8*, 475–485.

Adams, R. G., & Laursen, B. (2001). The organization and dynamics of adolescent conflict with parents and friends. *Journal of Marriage and the Family, 63*, 97–110.

Adamson, D. (2005). Regulation of assisted reproductive technologies in the United States. *Family Law Quarterly, 39*, 727–744.

Addington-Hall, J. (2000). Do home deaths increase distress in bereavement? *Palliative Medicine, 14*, 161–162.

Adhikari, B., Kahende, J., Malarcher, A., Pechacek, T., & Tong, V. (2009). Smoking-attributable mortality, years of potential life lost, and productivity losses. *Oncology Times, 31*, 40–43.

Adolph, K. E. (2008). Learning to move. *Current Directions in Psychological Science, 17*, 213–218.

Adolph, K. E., & Berger, S. E. (2006). Motor development. In D. Kuhn & R. Siegler (Eds.), *Handbook of child psychology: Vol. 2. Cognition, perception, and language* (6th ed., pp. 161–213). Hoboken, NJ: Wiley.

Adolph, K. E., & Eppler, M. A. (1998). Development of visually guided locomotion. *Ecological Psychology, 10*, 303–321.

Adolph, K. E., & Eppler, M. A. (1999). Obstacles to understanding: An ecological approach to infant problem solving. In E. Winograd, R. Fivush, & W. Hirst (Eds.), *Ecological approaches to cognition* (pp. 31–58). Mahwah, NJ: Erlbaum.

Adolph, K. E., Karasik, L. B., & Tamis-LeMonda, C. S. (2010). Motor skill. In M. H. Bornstein (Ed.), *Handbook of cultural developmental science* (pp. 61–88). New York: Psychology Press.

Adolph, K. E., Tamis-LeMonda, C. S., Ishak, S., Karasik, L. B., & Lobo, S. A. (2008). Locomotor experience and use of social information are posture specific. *Developmental Psychology, 44*, 1705–1714.

Adolph, K. E. A., Vereijken, B., & Shrout, P. E. (2003). What changes in infant walking and why. *Child Development, 74*, 475–497.

Afifi, T. O., Brownridge, D. A., Cox, B. J., & Sareen J. (2006). Physical punishment, childhood abuse and psychiatric disorders. *Child Abuse and Neglect, 30*, 1093–1103.

Afterschool Alliance. (2009). *America after 3 PM.* Retrieved from www.kidsdeservebetter.org/AA3PM.cfm

Aggarwal, R., Sentz, J., & Miller, M. A. (2007). Role of zinc administration in prevention of childhood diarrhea and respiratory illnesses: A meta-analysis. *Pediatrics, 119*, 1120–1130.

Agronick, G., Stueve, A., Vargo, S., & O'Donnell, L. (2007). New York City young adults' psychological reactions to 9/11: Findings from the Reach for Health longitudinal study. *American Journal of Community Psychology, 39*, 79–90.

Agüero-Torres, H., von Strauss, E., Viitanen, M., Winblad, B., & Fratiglioni, L. (2001). Institutionalization in the elderly: The role of chronic diseases and dementia. Cross-sectional and longitudinal data from a population-based study. *Journal of Clinical Epidemiology, 54*, 795–801.

Aguiar, A., & Baillargeon, R. (2002). Developments in young infants' reasoning about occluded objects. *Cognitive Psychology, 45*, 267–336.

Ahlskog, J. E., Geda, Y. E., Graff-Radford, N. R., & Petersen, R. C. (2011). Physical exercise as a preventive or disease-modifying treatment of dementia and brain aging. *Mayo Clinics Proceedings, 86*, 876–884.

Ahrens, C. J. C., & Ryff, C. D. (2006). Multiple roles and well-being: Sociodemographic and psychological moderators. *Sex Roles, 55*, 801–815.

Ahuja, J. (2005). *Women's entrepreneurship in the United States.* Kansas City, MO: Kauffman Center for Entrepreneurial Leadership, Clearinghouse on Entrepreneurship Education. Retrieved from www.celcee.edu

Ai, A. L., Wink, P., & Ardelt, M. (2010). Spirituality and aging: A journey for meaning through deep interconnection in humanity. In J. C. Cavanaugh & C. K. Cavanaugh (Eds.), *Aging in America: Vol. 3. Societal issues* (pp. 222–246). Santa Barbara, CA: Praeger.

Aikens, J. W., Bierman, K. L., & Parker, J. G. (2005). Navigating the transition to junior high school: The influence of pre-transition friendship and self-system characteristics. *Social Development, 14*, 42–60.

Aikens, J. W., Howes, C., & Hamilton, C. (2009). Attachment stability and the emergence of unresolved representations in adolescence. *Attachment & Human Development, 11*, 491–512.

Ainsworth, M. D. S., Blehar, M. C., Waters, E., & Wall, S. (1978). *Patterns of attachment.* Hillsdale, NJ: Erlbaum.

Aisen, P. S., Schneider, L. S., Sano, M., Diaz-Arrastia, R., van Dyck, C. H., & Weiner, M. F. (2008). High-dose B vitamin supplementation and cognitive decline in Alzheimer disease: A randomized controlled trial. *Journal of the American Medical Association, 15*, 1774–1783.

Ajrouch, K. (2007). Health disparities and Arab-American elders: Does intergenerational support buffer the inequality–health link? *Journal of Social Issues, 63*, 745–758.

Akimoto, S. A., & Sanbonmatsu, D. M. (1999). Differences in self-effacing behavior between European and Japanese Americans: Effect on competence evaluations. *Journal of Cross-Cultural Psychology, 30*, 159–177.

Akinbami, L. J., Moorman, J. E., Garbe, P. L., & Sondik, E. J. (2009). Status of childhood asthma in the United States, 1980–2007. *Pediatrics, 123*, S123–S145.

Aksan, N., & Kochanska, G. (2004). Heterogeneity of joy in infancy. *Infancy, 6*, 79–94.

Akshoomoff, N. A., Feroleto, C. C., Doyle, R. E., & Stiles, J. (2002). The impact of early unilateral brain injury on perceptual organization and visual memory. *Neuropsychologia, 40*, 539–561.

Albers, C. A., & Grieve, A. J. (2007). Test review: Bayley, N. (2006). Bayley Scales of Infant and Toddler Development–Third Edition. San Antonio, TX: Harcourt Assessment. *Journal of Psychoeducational Assessment, 25*, 180–190.

Aldwin, C. M., Spiro, A., III, & Park, C. L. (2006). Health, behavior, and optimal aging: A life span developmental perspective. In J. E. Birren & K. W. Schaie (Eds.), *Handbook of the psychology of aging* (6th ed., pp. 85–104). Burlington, MA: Elsevier Academic Press.

Aldwin, C. M., & Yancura, L. (2011). Stress, coping, and adult development. In R. J. Contrada & A. Baum (Eds.), *Handbook of stress science: Biology, psychology, and health* (pp. 263–274). New York: Springer.

Aldwin, C. M., Yancura, L. A., & Boeninger, D. K. (2010). Coping across the life span. In M. E. Lamb, A. M. Freund, & R. M. Lerner (Eds.), *Handbook of life-span development. Vol. 2: Social and emotional development* (pp. 298–340). Hoboken, NJ: Wiley.

Alessandri, S. M., Sullivan, M. W., & Lewis, M. (1990). Violation of expectancy and frustration in early infancy. *Developmental Psychology, 26*, 738–744.

Alexander, J. M., Fabricius, W. V., Fleming, V. M., Zwahr, M., & Brown, S. A. (2003). The development of metacognitive causal explanations. *Learning and Individual Differences, 13*, 227–238.

Alink, L. R. A., Mesman, J., van Zeijl, J., Stolk, M. N., Juffer, F., & Koot, H. M. (2006). The early childhood aggression curve: Development of physical aggression in 10- to 50-month-old children. *Child Development, 77*, 954–966.

Alkema, G. E., Wilber, K. H., & Enguidanos, S. M. (2007). Community- and facility-based care. In J. A. Blackburn & C. N. Dulmus (Eds.), *Handbook of gerontology: Evidence-based approaches to theory, practice, and policy* (pp. 455–497). Hoboken, NJ: Wiley.

Allemand, M., Zimprich, D., & Martin, M. (2008). Long-term correlated change in personality traits in old age. *Psychology and Aging, 23*, 545–557.

Allen, J. P., Philliber, S., Herrling, S., & Kuperminc, G. P. (1997). Preventing teen pregnancy and academic failure: Experimental evaluation of a developmentally based approach. *Child Development, 64*, 729–742.

Allen, J. P., Seitz, V., & Apfel, N. H. (2007). The sexually mature teen as a whole person. In J. L. Aber, S. J. Bishop-Josef, S. M. Jones, K. T. McLearn, & D. A. Phillips (Eds.), *New directions in prevention and intervention for teen pregnancy and parenthood* (pp. 185–199). Washington, DC: American Psychological Association.

Allen, M., & Burrell, N. (1996). Comparing the impact of homosexual and heterosexual parents on children: Meta-analysis of existing research. *Journal of Homosexuality, 32*, 19–35.

Allen, P. A., Ruthruff, E., & Lien, M.-C. (2007). Attention. In J. E. Birren (Ed.), *Encyclopedia of gerontology* (2nd ed., pp. 120–129). San Diego: Academic Press.

Allen, S. E. M., & Crago, M. B. (1996). Early passive acquisition in Inuktitut. *Journal of Child Language, 23*, 129–156.

Allen, T. D., & Finkelstein, L. M. (2003). Beyond mentoring: Alternative sources and functions of developmental support. *Career Development Quarterly, 51*, 346–355.

Allison, B. N., & Schultz, J. B. (2004). Parent–adolescent conflict in early adolescence. *Adolescence, 39*, 101–119.

Alloway, T. P. (2009). Working memory, but not IQ, predicts subsequent learning in children with learning difficulties. *European Journal of Psychological Assessment, 25*, 92–98.

Almeida, D. M., & Horn, M. C. (2004). Is daily life more stressful during middle adulthood? In O. G. Brim, C. D. Ryff, & R. C. Kessler (Eds.), *How healthy are we? A national study of well-being at midlife* (pp. 425–451). Chicago: University of Chicago Press.

Almeida, D. M., Neupert, S. D., Banks, S. R., & Serido, J. (2005). Do daily stress processes account for socioeconomic health disparities? *Journal of Gerontology, 60B*, 34–39.

Almeida, J., Johnson, R. M., Corliss, H. L., Molnar, B. E., & Azrael, D. (2009). Emotional distress among LGBT youth: The influence of perceived discrimination based on sexual orientation. *Journal of Youth and Adolescence, 38*, 1001–1014.

Al-Namlah, A. S., Fernyhough, C., & Meins, E. (2006). Sociocultural influences on the development of verbal mediation: Private speech and phonological recoding in Saudi Arabian and British samples. *Developmental Psychology, 42*, 117–131.

Alonso-Fernández, P., & De la Fuente, M. (2011). Role of the immune system in aging and longevity. *Current Aging Science, 4*, 78–100.

Alsaker, F. D. (1995). Timing of puberty and reactions to pubertal changes. In M. Rutter (Ed.), *Psychosocial disturbances in young people* (pp. 37–82). New York: Cambridge University Press.

Alterovitz, S. S. R., & Mendelsohn, G. A. (2013). Relationship goals of middle-aged, young-old, and old-old Internet daters: An analysis of online personal ads. *Journal of Aging Studies, 27*, 159–165.

Althaus, J., & Wax, J. (2005). Analgesia and anesthesia in labor. *Obstetrics and Gynecology Clinics of North America, 32*, 231–244.

Alzheimer's Association. (2012a). *Communication: Best ways to interact with a person with dementia.* Chicago: Author.

Alzheimer's Association. (2012b). 2012 Alzheimer's disease facts and figures. *Alzeimer's and Dementia, 8* (Issue 2).

Amato, P. R. (2000). The consequences of divorce for adults and children. *Journal of Marriage and Family, 62*, 1269–1287.

Amato, P. R. (2001). Children of divorce in the 1990s: An update of the Amato and Keith (1991) meta-analysis. *Journal of Family Psychology, 15*, 355–370.

Amato, P. R. (2006). Marital discord, divorce, and children's well-being: Results from a 20-year longitudinal study of two generations. In A. Clarke-Stewart & J. Dunn (Eds.), *Families count: Effects on child and adolescent development* (pp. 179–202). New York: Cambridge University Press.

Amato, P. R. (2010). Research on divorce: Continuing trends and new developments. *Journal of Marriage and Family, 72*, 650–666.

Amato, P. R., & Booth, A. (1995). Change in gender role attitudes and perceived marital quality. *American Sociological Review, 60*, 58–66.

Amato, P. R., & Cheadle, J. (2005). The long reach of divorce: Divorce and child well-being across three generations. *Journal of Marriage and Family, 67*, 191–206.

Amato, P. R., & Dorius, C. (2010). Father, children, and divorce. In M. E. Lamb (Ed.), *The role of the father in child development* (5th ed., pp. 177–200). Hoboken, NJ: Wiley.

Amato, P. R., & Fowler, F. (2002). Parenting practices, child adjustment, and family diversity. *Journal of Marriage and the Family, 64*, 703–716.

Amato, P. R., & Rogers, S. J. (1997). A longitudinal study of marital problems and subsequent divorce. *Journal of Marriage and the Family, 59*, 612–624.

Amato, P. R., & Sobolewski, J. M. (2004). The effects of divorce on fathers and children: Nonresidential fathers and stepfathers. In M. E. Lamb (Ed.), *The role of the father in child development* (4th ed., pp. 341–367). Hoboken, NJ: Wiley.

Amba, J. C., & Martinez, G. M. (2006). Childlessness among older women in the United States: Trends and profiles. *Journal of Marriage and Family, 68*, 1045–1056.

American Academy of Orthopaedic Surgeons. (2009). *Position statement: Osteoporosis/bone health in adults as a national health priority.* Retrieved from www.aaos.org/about/papers/position/1113.asp

American Academy of Pediatrics. (2001). Committee on Public Education: Children, adolescents, and television. *Pediatrics, 104*, 341–343.

American Academy of Pediatrics. (2005). Breastfeeding and the use of human milk. *Pediatrics, 115*, 496–506.

American Academy of Pediatrics. (2006). Folic acid for the prevention of neural tube defects. *Pediatrics, 104*, 325–327.

American Academy of Pediatrics. (2012). SIDS and other sleep-related infant deaths: Expansion of recommendations for a safe sleep environment. *Pediatrics, 128*, e1341.

American Cancer Society. (2012). *Stay healthy.* Retrieved from www.cancer.org/healthy/index

American College of Sports Medicine. (2011). Quantity and quality of exercise for developing and maintaining cardiorespiratory, musculoskeletal, and neuromotor fitness in apparently healthy adults: Guidance for prescribing exercise. *Medicine and Science in Sports and Exercise, 43*, 1334–1359.

American Heart Association. (2012). Heart disease and stroke statistics—2012 update. *Circulation, 125*, e2–e220.

American Hospice Foundation. (2013). *Talking about hospice: Tips for physicians.* Washington, DC: Author.

American Psychiatric Association. (2013). Diagnostic and statistical manual of mental disorders (5th ed.). Washington, DC: Author.

American Psychological Association. (2002). Ethical principles of psychologists and code of conduct. *American Psychologist, 57*, 1060–1073.

Amsel, E., & Brock, S. (1996). The development of evidence evaluation skills. *Cognitive Development, 11*, 523–550.

Amsterlaw, J., & Wellman, H. M. (2006). Theories of mind in transition: A micro-genetic study of the development of false belief understanding. *Journal of Cognition and Development, 7*, 139–172.

An, J. S., & Cooney, T. M. (2006). Psychological well-being in mid to late life: The role of generativity development and parent–child relationships across the lifespan. *International Journal of Behavioral Development, 30*, 410–421.

Anand, S. S., Yusuf, S., Jacobs, R., Davis, A. D., Yi, Q., & Gerstein, H. (2001). Risk factors, atherosclerosis, and cardiovascular disease among Aboriginal people in Canada: The study of health assessment and risk evaluation in Aboriginal peoples (SHARE-AP). *Lancet, 358*, 1147–1153.

Andel, R., Hyer, K., & Slack, A. (2007). Risk factors for nursing home placement in older adults with and without dementia. *Journal of Aging and Health, 19*, 213–228.

Anderson, C. A., Sakamoto, A., Gentile, D. A., Ihori, N., Shibuya, A., Yukawa, S., et al. (2008). Longitudinal effects of violent video games on aggression in Japan and the United States. *Pediatrics, 122*, e1067–e1072.

Anderson, D. M., Huston, A. C., Schmitt, K. L., Linebarger, D. L., & Wright, J. C. (2001). Early childhood television viewing and adolescent behavior. *Monographs of the Society for Research in Child Development, 66*(1, Serial No. 264).

Anderson, E. (2000). Exploring register knowledge: The value of "controlled improvisation." In L. Menn & N. B. Ratner (Eds.), *Methods for studying language production* (pp. 225–248). Mahwah, NJ: Erlbaum.

Anderson, J. L., Morgan, J. L., & White, K. S. (2003). A statistical basis for speech sound discrimination. *Language and Speech, 46*, 155–182.

Anderson, P. B., & Savage, J. S. (2005). Social, legal, and institutional context of heterosexual aggression by college women. *Trauma, Violence, and Abuse, 6*, 130–140.

Andreoletti, C., & Lachman, M. E. (2004). Susceptibility and resilience to memory aging stereotypes: Education matters more than age. *Experimental Aging Research, 30*, 129–148.

Andrews, G., & Halford, G. S. (1998). Children's ability to make transitive inferences: The importance of premise integration and structural complexity. *Cognitive Development, 13,* 479–513.

Andrews, G., & Halford, G. S. (2002). A cognitive complexity metric applied to cognitive development. *Cognitive Psychology, 45,* 475–506.

Aneshensel, C. S., Wight, R. G., Miller-Martinez, D., Botticello, A. L., Karlamangla, A. S., & Seeman, T. E. (2007). Urban neighborhoods and depressive symptoms among older adults. *Journal of Gerontology, 62B,* S52–S59.

Anetzberger, G. J. (2005). The reality of elder abuse. *Clinical Gerontologist, 28,* 2–25.

Anisfeld, M., Turkewitz, G., Rose, S. A., Rosenberg, F. R., Shelber, F. J., Couturier-Fagan, D. A., Ger, J. S., & Sommer, I. (2001). No compelling evidence that newborns imitate oral gestures. *Infancy, 2,* 111–122.

Annett, M. (2002). *Handedness and brain asymmetry: The right shift theory.* Hove, UK: Psychology Press.

Antonini, F. M., Magnolfi, S. U., Petruzzi, E., Pinzani, P., Malentacchi, F., Petruzzi, I., & Masotti, G. (2008). Physical performance and creative activities of centenarians. *Archives of Gerontology and Geriatrics, 46,* 253–261.

Antonucci, T. C., Ajrouch, K. J., & Birditt, K. (2008). Social relations in the Third Age: Assessing strengths and challenges using the convoy model. In J. B. James & P. Wink (Eds.), *Annual review of gerontology and geriatrics* (Vol. 26, pp. 193–209). New York: Springer.

Antonucci, T. C., & Akiyama, H. (1995). Convoys of social relations: Family and friendships within a life span context. In R. Blieszner & V. H. Bedford (Eds.), *Handbook of aging and the family* (pp. 355–371). Westport, CT: Greenwood Press.

Antonucci, T. C., Akiyama, H., & Merline, A. (2002). Dynamics of social relationships in midlife. In M. E. Lachman (Ed.), *Handbook of midlife development* (pp. 571–598). New York: Wiley.

Antonucci, T. C., Akiyama, H., & Takahashi, K. (2004). Attachment and close relationships across the lifespan. *Attachment and Human Development, 6,* 353–370.

Antonucci, T. C., Birditt, K. S., & Ajrouch, K. (2011). Convoys of social relations: Past, present, and future. In K. L. Fingerman, C. A. Berg, J. Smith, & T. C. Antonucci (Eds.), *Handbook of life-span development* (pp. 161–182). New York: Springer.

Antonucci, T. C., Birditt, K. S., & Akiyama, H. (2009). Convoys of social relations: An interdisciplinary approach. In V. Bengston, M. Silverstein, N. Putney, & D. Gans (Eds.), *Handbook of theories of aging* (pp. 247–260). New York: Springer.

Antonucci, T. C., Blieszner, R., & Denmark, F. L. (2010). Psychological perspectives on older women. In H. Landrine & N. F. Russo (Eds.), *Handbook of diversity in feminist psychology* (pp. 233–257). New York: Springer.

Anzuini, F., Battistella, A., & Izzotti, A. (2011). Physical activity and cancer prevention: A review of current evidence and biological mechanisms. *Journal of Preventive Medicine and Hygiene, 52,* 174–180.

Apgar, V. (1953). A proposal for a new method of evaluation in the newborn infant. *Current Research in Anesthesia and Analgesia, 32,* 260–267.

Aquilino, W. S. (2006). Family relationships and support systems in emerging adulthood. In J. J. Arnett & J. L. Tanner (Eds.), *Emerging adults in America: Coming of age in the 21st century* (pp. 193–218). Washington, DC: American Psychological Association.

Archer, J. (2002). Sex differences in aggression between heterosexual partners: A meta-analytic review. *Psychological Bulletin, 126,* 651–681.

Archibald, A. B., Graber, J. A., & Brooks-Gunn, J. (2006). Pubertal processes and physiological growth in adolescence. In G. R. Adams & M. D. Berzonsky (Eds.), *Blackwell handbook of adolescence* (pp. 24–48). Malden, MA: Blackwell.

Arcus, D., & Chambers, P. (2008). Childhood risks associated with adoption. In T. P. Gullotta & G. M Blau (Eds.), *Family influences on childhood behavior and development* (pp. 117–142). New York: Routledge.

Ardelt, M. (1998). Social crisis and individual growth: The long-term effects of the Great Depression. *Journal of Aging Studies, 12,* 291–314.

Ardelt, M. (2003). Effects of religion and purpose in life on elders' subjective well-being and attitudes toward death. *Journal of Religious Gerontology, 14,* 55–77.

Ardelt, M. (2011). Wisdom, age, and well-being. In K. W. Schaie & S. L. Willis (Eds.), *Handbook of the psychology of aging* (7th ed., pp. 279–291). San Diego, CA: Academic Press.

Arking, R. (2006). *Biology of aging: Observations and principles* (3rd ed.). New York: Oxford University Press.

Armstrong, T. D., & Crowther, M. R. (2002). Spirituality among older African Americans. *Journal of Adult Development, 9,* 3–12.

Arnett, J. J. (2000). Emerging adulthood: A theory of development from the late teens through the twenties. *American Psychologist, 55,* 469–480.

Arnett, J. J. (2001). Conceptions of the transition to adulthood: Perspectives from adolescence to midlife. *Journal of Adult Development, 8,* 133–143.

Arnett, J. J. (2003). Conceptions of the transition to adulthood among emerging adults in American ethnic groups. In J. J. Arnett & N. L. Galambos (Eds.), *New directions for child and adolescent development* (No. 100, pp. 63–75). San Francisco: Jossey-Bass.

Arnett, J. J. (2006). Emerging adulthood: Understanding the new way of coming of age. In J. J. Arnett & J. L. Tanner (Eds.), *Emerging adults in America: Coming of age in the 21st century* (pp. 3–19). Washington, DC: American Psychological Association.

Arnett, J. J. (2007a). Emerging adulthood, a 21st century theory: A rejoinder to Hendry and Kloep. *Child Development Perspectives, 1,* 80–82.

Arnett, J. J. (2007b). Emerging adulthood: What is it and what is it good for? *Child Development Perspectives, 1,* 68–73.

Arnett, J. J. (2010). Oh, grow up! Generational grumbling and the new life stage of emerging adulthood—commentary on Trzesniewski & Donnellan (2010). *Perspectives on Psychological Science, 5,* 89–92.

Arnett, J. J. (2011). Emerging adulthood(s): The cultural psychology of a new life stage. In L. A. Jensen (Ed.), *Bridging cultural and developmental psychology: New syntheses in theory, research, and policy* (pp. 255–275). New York: Oxford University Press.

Arnett, J. J. (2012). *New Clark Poll: 18- to 29-year-olds are traditional about roles in sex, marriage and raising children.* Retrieved from http://news.clarku.edu/news/2012/08/07/new-clark-poll-18-to-29-year-olds-are-traditional-about-roles-in-sex-marriage-and-raising-children

Arnon, S., Shapsa, A., Forman, L., Regev, R., Bauer, S., & Litmanovitz, I. (2006). Live music is beneficial to preterm infants in the neonatal intensive care unit. *Birth, 33,* 131–136.

Artman, L., & Cahan, S. (1993). Schooling and the development of transitive inference. *Developmental Psychology, 29,* 753–759.

Artman, L., Cahan, S., & Avni-Babad, D. (2006). Age, schooling, and conditional reasoning. *Cognitive Development, 21,* 131–145.

Asher, S. R., & Rose, A. J. (1997). Promoting children's social-emotional adjustment with peers. In P. Salovey & D. J. Sluyter (Eds.), *Emotional development and emotional intelligence* (pp. 193–195). New York: Basic Books.

Aslin, R. N., Jusczyk, P. W., & Pisoni, D. B. (1998). Speech and auditory processing during infancy: Constraints on and precursors to language. In D. Kuhn & R. S. Siegler (Eds.), *Handbook of child psychology: Vol. 2. Cognition, perception, and language* (5th ed., pp. 147–198). New York: Wiley.

Aslin, R. N., & Newport, E. L. (2009). What statistical learning can and can't tell us about language acquisition. In J. Colombo, P. McCardle, & L. Freund (Eds.), *Infant pathways to language: Methods, models, and research directions* (pp. 15–29). New York: Psychology Press.

Astington, J. W., Pelletier, J., & Homer, B. (2002). Theory of mind and epistemological development: The relation between children's second-order false belief understanding and their ability to reason about evidence. *New Ideas in Psychology, 20,* 131–144.

Atchley, R. C. (1989). A continuity theory of normal aging. *Gerontologist, 29,* 183–190.

Atchley, R. C. (1999). *Continuity and adaptation in aging: Creating positive experiences.* Baltimore, MD: Johns Hopkins University Press.

Atchley, R. C. (2003). Why people cope well with retirement. In J. L. Ronch & J. A. Goldfield (Eds.), *Mental wellness in aging: Strengths-based approaches* (pp. 123–138). Baltimore, MD: Health Professions Press.

Atkins, R., Hart, D., & Donnelly, T. M. (2004). Moral identity development and school attachment. In D. Lapsley & D. Narvaez (Eds.), *Moral development, self, and identity* (pp. 65–82). Mahwah, NJ: Erlbaum.

Au, T. K., Sidle, A. L., & Rollins, K. B. (1993). Developing an intuitive understanding of conservation and contamination: Invisible particles as a plausible mechanism. *Developmental Psychology, 29,* 286–299.

Aunola, K., Stattin, H., & Nurmi, J.-E. (2000). Parenting styles and adolescents' achievement strategies. *Journal of Adolescence, 23,* 205–222.

Averhart, C. J., & Bigler, R. S. (1997). Shades of meaning: Skin tone, racial attitudes, and constructive memory in African-American children. *Journal of Experimental Child Psychology, 67,* 368–388.

Aveyard, P., & Raw, M. (2012). Improving smoking cessation approaches at the individual level. *Tobacco Control, 21,* 252–257.

Avis, N. E., Crawford, S., & Johannes, C. B. (2002). Menopause. In G. M. Wingood & R. J. DeClemente (Eds.), *Handbook of women's sexual and reproductive health* (pp. 367–391). New York: Kluwer.

Avolio, B. J., & Sosik, J. J. (1999). A lifespan framework for assessing the impact of work on white-collar workers. In S. L. Willis & J. D. Reid (Eds.), *Life in the middle* (pp. 249–274). San Diego, CA: Academic Press.

Axelin, A., Salanterä, S., & Lehtonen, L. (2006). 'Facilitated tucking by parents' in pain management of preterm infants—a randomized crossover trial. *Early Human Development, 82,* 241–247.

Axia, G., & Baroni, R. (1985). Linguistic politeness at different age levels. *Child Development, 56,* 918–927.

Ayala, G. X., Rogers, M., Arredondo, E. M., Campbell, N. R., Baquero, B., Duerksen, S. C., & Elder, J. P. (2008). Away-from-home food intake and risk for obesity: Examining the influence of context. *Obesity, 16,* 1002–1008.

B

Bacallao, M. L., & Smokowski, P. R. (2007). The costs of getting ahead: Mexican family system changes after immigration. *Family Relations, 56,* 52–66.

Bagwell, C. L., & Coie, J. D. (2004). The best friendships of aggressive boys: Relationship quality, conflict management, and rule-breaking behavior. *Journal of Experimental Child Psychology, 88,* 5–24.

Bahrick, L. E. (2010). Intermodal perception and selective attention to intersensory redundancy: Implications for typical social development and autism. In G. Bremner & T. D. Wachs (Eds.), *Wiley-Blackwell handbook of infant development: Vol. 1. Basic research* (2nd ed., pp. 120–166). Malden, MA: Blackwell.

Bahrick, L. E., Gogate, L. J., & Ruiz, I. (2002). Attention and memory for faces and actions in infancy: The salience of actions over faces in dynamic events. *Child Development, 73,* 1629–1643.

Bahrick, L. E., Hernandez-Reif, M., & Flom, R. (2005). The development of infant learning about specific face–voice relations. *Developmental Psychology, 41,* 541–552.

Bahrick, L. E., Hernandez-Reif, M., & Pickens, J. N. (1997). The effect of retrieval cues on visual preferences and memory in infancy: Evidence for a four-phase attention function. *Journal of Experimental Child Psychology, 67,* 1–20.

Bahrick, L. E., Lickliter, R., & Flom, R. (2004). Intersensory redundancy guides the development of selective attention, perception, and cognition in infancy. *Current Directions in Psychological Science, 13,* 99–102.

Bahrick, L. E., Netto, D., & Hernandez-Reif, M. (1998). Intermodal perception of adult and child faces and voices by infants. *Child Development, 69,* 1263–1275.

Bailey, J. M., Bobrow, D., Wolfe, M., & Mikach, S. (1995). Sexual orientation of adult sons of gay fathers. *Developmental Psychology, 31,* 124–129.

Baillargeon, R. (2004). Infants' reasoning about hidden objects: Evidence for event-general and event-specific expectations. *Developmental Science, 7,* 391–424.

Baillargeon, R., & DeVos, J. (1991). Object permanence in young infants: Further evidence. *Child Development, 62,* 1227–1246.

Baillargeon, R., Scott, R. M., & He, Z. (2010). False-belief understanding in infants. *Trends in Cognitive Sciences, 14,* 110–118.

Baillargeon, R. H., Zoccolillo, M., Keenan, K., Côté, S., Pérusse, D., Wu, H.-X., & Boivin, M. (2007). Gender differences in physical aggression: A prospective population-based survey of children before and after 2 years of age. *Developmental Psychology, 43,* 13–26.

Bair, D. (2007). *Calling it quits: Late-life divorce and starting over.* New York: Random House.

Baird, B. M., & Bergeman, C. S. (2011). Life-span developmental behavior genetics. In K. L. Fingerman, C. A. Berg, J. Smith, & T. C. Antonucci (Eds.), *Handbook of life-span development* (pp. 701–744). New York: Springer.

Balasch, J. (2010). Ageing and infertility: An overview. *Gynecological Endocrinology, 26,* 855–860.

Bale, J. F. (2009). Fetal infections and brain development. *Clinical Perinatology, 36,* 639–653.

Balis, T., & Postolache, T. T. (2008). Ethnic differences in adolescent suicide in the United States. *International Journal of Child Health and Human Development, 1,* 282–296.

Ball, K., Berch, D. B., Helmers, K. F., Jobe, J. B., Leveck, M. D., & Marsiske, M. (2002). Effects of cognitive training interventions with older adults: A randomized controlled trial. *Journal of the American Medical Association, 288,* 2271–2281.

Ball, M. M., Perkins, M. M., Hollingsworth, C., Whittington, F. J., & King, S. V. (2009). Pathways to assisted living: The influence of race and class. *Journal of Applied Gerontology, 28,* 81–108.

Balsam, K. F., Beauchaine, T. P., Rothblum, E. D., & Solomon, S. E. (2008). Three-year follow-up of same-sex couples who had civil unions in Vermont, same-sex couples not in civil unions, and heterosexual married couples. *Developmental Psychology, 44,* 102–116.

Baltes, M. M. (1995, February). Dependency in old age: Gains and losses. *Psychological Science, 4*(1), 14–19.

Baltes, M. M. (1996). *The many faces of dependency in old age.* New York: Cambridge University Press.

Baltes, P. B., & Freund, A. M. (2003). Human strengths as the orchestration of wisdom and selective optimization with compensation (SOC). In L. G. Aspinwall & U. M. Staudinger (Eds.), *A psychology of human strengths: Fundamental questions and future directions for a positive psychology* (pp. 23–25). Washington, DC: American Psychological Association.

Baltes, P. B., Lindenberger, U., & Staudinger, U. M. (2006). Life span theory in developmental psychology. In R. M. Lerner (Ed.), *Handbook of child psychology: Vol. 1. Theoretical models of human development* (6th ed., pp. 569–664). Hoboken, NJ: Wiley.

Baltes, P. B., & Smith, J. (2003). New frontiers in the future of aging: From successful aging of the young old to the dilemmas of the fourth age. *Gerontology, 49,* 123–135.

Baltes, P. B., & Smith, J. (2008). The fascination of wisdom. *Perspectives on Psychological Science, 3,* 56–64.

Baltes, P. B., & Staudinger, U. M. (2000). Wisdom: A metaheuristic (pragmatic) to orchestrate mind and virtue toward excellence. *American Psychologist, 55,* 122–136.

Bancroft, J. (2002). The medicalization of female sexual dysfunction: The need for caution. *Archives of Sexual Behavior, 31,* 451–455.

Bandstra, E. S., Morrow, C. E., Accornero, V. H., Mansoor, E., Xue, L., & Anthony, J. C. (2011). Estimated effects of in utero cocaine exposure on language development through early adolescence. *Neurotoxicology and Teratology, 33,* 25–35.

Bandstra, E. S., Morrow, C. E., Mansoor, E., & Accornero, V. H. (2010). Prenatal drug exposure: Infant and toddler outcomes. *Journal of Addictive Diseases, 29,* 245–258.

Bandura, A. (1977). *Social learning theory.* Englewood Cliffs, NJ: Prentice-Hall.

Bandura, A. (1992). Perceived self-efficacy in cognitive development and functioning. *Educational Psychologist, 28,* 117–148.

Bandura, A. (1999). Social cognitive theory of personality. In L. A. Pervin (Ed.), *Handbook of personality: Theory and research* (2nd ed., pp. 154–196). New York: Guilford.

Bandura, A. (2001). Social cognitive theory: An agentic perspective. *Annual Review of Psychology, 52,* 1–26.

Banish, M. T., & Heller, W. (1998). Evolving perspectives on lateralization of function. *Current Directions in Psychological Science, 7,* 1–2.

Banks, M. S. (1980). The development of visual accommodation during early infancy. *Child Development, 51,* 646–666.

Banse, R., Gawronski, B., Rebetez, C., Gutt, H., & Morton, J. B. (2010). The development of spontaneous gender stereotyping in childhood: Relations to stereotype knowledge and stereotype flexibility. *Developmental Science, 13,* 298–306.

Barber, B. K., & Olsen, J. A. (1997). Socialization in context: Connection, regulation, and autonomy in the family, school, and neighborhood, and with peers. *Journal of Adolescent Research, 12,* 287–315.

Barber, B. K., & Olsen, J. A. (2004). Assessing the transitions to middle and high school. *Journal of Adolescent Research, 19,* 3–30.

Barber, B. K., Stolz, H. E., & Olsen, J. A. (2005). Parental support, psychological control, and behavioral control: Assessing relevance across time, culture, and method. *Monographs of the Society for Research in Child Development, 70*(4, Serial No. 282).

Barber, B. L., Stone, M. R., Hunt, J. E., & Eccles, J. S. (2005). Benefits of activity participation: The roles of identity affirmation and peer group norm sharing. In J. L. Mahoney, R. W. Larson, & J. S. Eccles (Eds.), *Organized activities as contexts of development: Extracurricular activities, after-school and community programs* (pp. 185–210). Mahwah, NJ: Erlbaum.

Bard, K. A., Todd, B. K., Bernier, C., Love, J., & Leavens, D. A. (2006). Self-awareness in human and chimpanzee infants: What is measured and what is meant by the mark and mirror test? *Infancy, 9,* 191–219.

Barelds, D. P. H., & Dijkstra, P. (2011). Positive illusions about a partner's personality and relationship quality. *Journal of Research in Personality, 45,* 37–43.

Barenbaum, J., Ruchkin, V., & Schwab-Stone, M. (2004). The psychosocial aspects of children exposed to war: Practice and policy initiatives. *Journal of Child Psychology and Psychiatry, 45,* 41–62.

Bar-Haim, Y., Ziv, T., Lamy, D., & Hodes, R. M. (2006). Nature and nurture in own-race face processing. *Psychological Science, 17,* 159–163.

Barker, D. J. (2008). Human growth and cardiovascular disease. *Nestlé Nutrition Workshop Series, 61,* 21–38.

Barkley, R. A. (2002). Psychosocial treatments of attention-deficit/hyperactivity disorder in children. *Journal of Clinical Psychology, 63*(Suppl. 12), 36–43.

Barkley, R. A. (2003a). Attention-deficit/hyperactivity disorder. In E. J. Mash & R. A. Barkley (Eds.), *Child psychopathology* (2nd ed., pp. 75–143). New York: Guilford Press.

Barkley, R. A. (2003b). Issues in the diagnosis of attention-deficit hyperactivity disorder in children. *Brain and Development, 25,* 77–83.

Barkley, R. A. (2008). Attention-deficit/hyperactivity disorder. In R. A. Barkley, D. A. Wolfe, & E. J. Mash (Eds.), *Behavioral and emotional disorders in adolescents: Nature, assessment, and treatment* (pp. 91–152). New York: Guilford.

Barnes, G. M., Hoffman, J. H., Welte, J. W., Farrell, M. P., & Dintcheff, B. A. (2006). Effects of parental monitoring and peer deviance on substance use and delinquency. *Journal of Marriage and Family, 68,* 1084–1104.

Barnes, J., Katz, I., Korbin, J. E., & O'Brien, M. (2007). *Children and families in communities: Theory, research, policy and practice.* Hoboken, NJ: Wiley.

Barnes-Farrell, J., & Matthews, R. A. (2007). Age and work attitudes. In K. S. Shultz & G. A. Adams (Eds.), *Aging and work in the 21st century* (pp. 139–162). Mahwah, NJ: Erlbaum.

Barnett, D., & Vondra, J. I. (1999). Atypical patterns of early attachment: Theory, research, and current directions. In J. I Vondra & D. Barnett (Eds.), *Atypical attachment in infancy and early childhood among children at developmental risk. Monographs of the Society for Research in Child Development, 64*(3, Serial No. 258), 1–24.

Barnett, W. S. (2011). Effectiveness of early educational intervention. *Science, 333,* 975–978.

Baron, I. S., & Rey-Casserly, C. (2010). Extremely preterm birth outcome: A review of four decades of cognitive research. *Neuropsychology Review, 20,* 430–452.

Baron-Cohen, S., & Belmonte, M. K. (2005). Autism: A window onto the development of the social and the analytic brain. *Annual Review of Neuroscience, 28,* 109–126.

Barr, H. M., Bookstein, F. L., O'Malley, K. D., Connor, P. D., Huggins, J. E., & Streissguth, A. P. (2006). Binge drinking during pregnancy as a predictor of psychiatric disorders on the structured clinical interview for DSM-IV in young adult offspring. *American Journal of Psychiatry, 163,* 1061–1065.

Barr, H. M., Streissguth, A. P., Darby, B. L., & Sampson, P. D. (1990). Prenatal exposure to alcohol, caffeine, tobacco, and aspirin: Effects on fine and gross motor performance in 4-year-old children. *Developmental Psychology, 26,* 339–348.

Barr, R., Marrott, H., & Rovee-Collier, C. (2003). The role of sensory preconditioning in memory retrieval by preverbal infants. *Learning and Behavior, 31,* 111–123.

Barr, R., Muentener, P., & Garcia, A. (2007). Age-related changes in deferred imitation from television by 6- to 18-month-olds. *Developmental Science, 10,* 910–921.

Barr, R. G. (2001). "Colic" is something infants do, rather than a condition they "have": A developmental approach to crying phenomena patterns, pacification and (patho)genesis. In R. G. Barr, I. St. James-Roberts, & M. R. Keefe (Eds.), *New evidence on unexplained infant crying* (pp. 87–104). St. Louis: Johnson & Johnson Pediatric Institute.

Barr, R. G., Paterson, J. A., MacMartin, L. M., & Lehtonen, L. (2005). Prolonged and unsoothable crying bouts in infants with and without colic. *Journal of Developmental and Behavioral Pediatrics, 26*, 14–23.

Barreto, M., Ryan, M. K., & Schmitt, M. T. (2009). *The glass ceiling in the 21st century: Understanding barriers to gender equality.* Washington, DC: American Psychological Association.

Barrett, K. C. (2005). The origins of social emotions and self-regulation in toddlerhood: New evidence. *Cognition and Emotion, 19*, 953–979.

Barrett, T. M., Traupman, E., & Needham, E. (2008). Infants' visual anticipation in grasp planning. *Infant Behavior and Development, 31*, 1–9.

Barros, R. M., Silver, E. J., & Stein, R. E. K. (2009). School recess and group classroom behavior. *Pediatrics, 123*, 431–436.

Barry, C. M., & Madsen, S. D. (2010). Friends and friendships in emerging adulthood. In T. Clydesdale (Ed.), *Who are emerging adults?* Washington, DC: Changing Spirituality of Emerging Adults Project. Retrieved from changingsea.org/barry.htm

Barry, C. M., & Nelson, L. J. (2008). The role of religious beliefs and practices in emerging adults' perceived competencies, perceived importance ratings, and global self-worth. *International Journal of Behavioral Development, 32*, 509–521.

Barry, C. M., Nelson, L., Davarya, S., & Urry, S. (2010). Religiosity and spirituality during the transition to adulthood. *International Journal of Behavioral Development, 34*, 311–324.

Bartlik, B., & Goldstein, M. Z. (2001). Men's sexual health after midlife. *Practical Geriatrics, 52*, 291–306.

Bartocci, M., Berggvist, L. L., Lagercrantz, H., & Anand, K. J. (2006). Pain activates cortical areas in the preterm newborn brain. *Pain, 122*, 109–117.

Bartrip, J., Morton, J., & de Schonen, S. (2001). Responses to mother's face in 3-week- to 5-month-old infants. *British Journal of Developmental Psychology, 19*, 219–232.

Bartsch, K., & Wellman, H. (1995). *Children talk about the mind.* New York: Oxford University Press.

Basak, C., & Verhaeghen, P. (2011). Aging and switching the focus of attention in working memory: Age differences in item availability but not in item accessibility. *Journal of Gerontology, 66B*, 519–526.

Basow, S. A., & Rubin, L. R. (1999). Gender influences on adolescent development. In N. G. Johnson & M. C. Roberts (Eds.), *Beyond appearance: A new look at adolescent girls* (pp. 25–52). Washington, DC: American Psychological Association.

Bass, S. (2011). From retirement to "productive aging" and back to work again. In D. C. Carr & K. Komp (Eds.), *Gerontology in the era of the Third Age: Implications and next steps* (pp. 169–188). New York: Springer.

Bassuk, S. S., & Manson, J. E. (2005). Epidemiological evidence for the role of physical activity in reducing risk of type 2 diabetes and cardiovascular disease. *Journal of Applied Physiology, 99*, 1193–1204.

Bates, E. (2004). Explaining and interpreting deficits in language development across clinical groups: Where do we go from here? *Brain and Language, 88*, 248–253.

Bates, J. E., Wachs, T. D., & Emde, R. N. (1994). Toward practical uses for biological concepts. In J. E. Bates & T. D. Wachs (Eds.), *Temperament: Individual differences at the interface of biology and behavior*

(pp. 275–306). Washington, DC: American Psychological Association.

Bauer, C. R., Langer, J. C., Shakaran, S., Bada, H. S., & Lester, B. (2005). Acute neonatal effects of cocaine exposure during pregnancy. *Archives of Pediatrics and Adolescent Medicine, 159*, 824–834.

Bauer, P. J. (2002). Early memory development. In U. Goswami (Ed.), *Blackwell handbook of child cognitive development* (pp. 127–150). Malden, MA: Blackwell.

Bauer, P. J. (2006). Event memory. In D. Kuhn & R. Siegler (Eds.), *Handbook of child psychology: Vol. 2. Cognition, perception, and language* (6th ed., pp. 373–425). Hoboken, NJ: Wiley.

Bauer, P. J. (2007). Recall in infancy: A neuro-developmental account. *Current Directions in Psychological Science, 16*, 142–146.

Baum, N., Rahav, G., & Sharon, D. (2005). Changes in the self-concepts of divorced women. *Journal of Divorce and Remarriage, 43*, 47–67.

Baumeister, R. F. (1998). Inducing guilt. In J. Bybee (Ed.), *Guilt and children* (pp. 185–213). San Diego: Academic Press.

Baumeister, R. F., Campbell, J. D., Krueger, J. I., & Vohs, K. D. (2003). Does high self-esteem cause better performance, interpersonal success, happiness, or healthier lifestyles? *Psychological Science in the Public Interest, 4*(1), 1–44.

Baumgartner, M. S., & Schneider, D. E. (2010). Perceptions of women in management: A thematic analysis of razing the glass ceiling. *Journal of Career Development, 37*, 559–576.

Baumrind, D. (1971). Current patterns of parental authority. *Developmental Psychology Monograph, 4*(No. 1, Pt. 2).

Baumrind, D., Lazelere, R. E., & Owens, E. B. (2010). Effects of preschool parents' power assertive patterns and practices on adolescent development. *Parenting, 10*, 157–201.

Bauserman, R. (2002). Child adjustment in joint-custody versus sole-custody arrangements: A meta-analytic review. *Journal of Family Psychology, 16*, 91–102.

Baydar, N., Greek, A., & Brooks-Gunn, J. (1997). A longitudinal study of the effects of the birth of a sibling during the first 6 years of life. *Journal of Marriage and the Family, 59*, 939–956.

Bayer, A., & Tadd, W. (2000). Unjustified exclusion of elderly people from studies submitted to research ethics committee for approval: Descriptive study. *British Medical Journal, 321*, 992–993.

Bayley, N. (1969). *Bayley Scales of Infant Development.* New York: Psychological Corporation.

Bayley, N. (1993). *Bayley Scales of Infant Development* (2nd ed.). San Antonio, TX: Psychological Corporation.

Bayley, N. (2005). *Bayley Scales of Infant and Toddler Development, Third Edition* (Bayley-III). San Antonio, TX: Harcourt Assessment.

Bean, R. A., Barber, B. K., & Crane, D. R. (2007). Parental support, behavioral control, and psychological control among African American youth: The relationships to academic grades, delinquency, and depression. *Journal of Family Issues, 27*, 1335–1355.

Bearman, P. S., & Moody, J. (2004). Suicide and friendships among American adolescents. *American Journal of Public Health, 94*, 89–95.

Beautrais, A. L. (2003). Life course factors associated with suicidal behaviors in young people. *American Behavioral Scientist, 46*, 1137–1156.

Becker, G., Beyene, Y., Newsome, E., & Mayen, N. (2003). Creating continuity through mutual assistance: Intergenerational reciprocity in four ethnic groups. *Journal of Gerontology, 38B*, S151–S159.

Becker, K., El-Faddagh, M., Schmidt, M. H., Esser, G., & Laucht, M. (2008). Interaction of dopamine transporter genotype with prenatal smoke exposure

on ADHD symptoms. *Journal of Pediatrics, 152*, 263–269.

Beckerman, M. B. (1990). Leos Janáček and "the late style" in music. *Gerontologist, 30*, 632–635.

Beckett, C., Maughan, B., Rutter, M., Castle, J., Colvert, E., & Groothues, C. (2006). Do the effects of early severe deprivation on cognition persist into early adolescence? Findings from the English and Romanian adoptees study. *Child Development, 77*, 696–711.

Bedford, O. A. (2004). The individual experience of guilt and shame in Chinese culture. *Culture and Psychology, 10*, 29–52.

Behnke, M., Smith, V., C., Committee on Substance Abuse, and Committee on Fetus and Newborn. (2013). Prenatal substance abuse: Short-and long-term effects on the exposed fetus. *American Academy of Pediatrics, 131*, e1009–e1024.

Behrens, K. Y., Hesse, E., & Main, M. (2007). Mothers' attachment status as determined by the Adult Attachment Interview predicts their 6-year-olds' reunion responses: A study conducted in Japan. *Developmental Psychology, 43*(6), 1553–1567.

Beier, M. E., & Ackerman, P. L. (2005). Age, ability, and the role of prior knowledge on the acquisition of new domain knowledge: Promising results in a real-world learning environment. *Psychology and Aging, 20*, 341–355.

Bekkouche, N. S., Holmes, S., Whittaker, K. S., & Krantz, D. S. (2011). Stress and the heart: Psychosocial stress and coronary heart disease. In R. J. Contrada & A. Baum (Eds.), *Handbook of stress science: Biology, psychology, and health* (pp. 385–398). New York: Springer.

Belcher, D., Lee, A., Solmon, M., & Harrison, L. (2003). The influence of gender-related beliefs and conceptions of ability on women learning the hockey wrist shot. *Research Quarterly for Exercise and Sport, 74*, 183–192.

Bell, J. H., & Bromnick, R. D. (2003). The social reality of the imaginary audience: A grounded theory approach. *Adolescence, 38*, 205–219.

Bell, M. L. (1995). Attitudes toward menopause among Mexican American women. *Health Care for Women International, 16*, 425–435.

Belle, S. H., Burgio, L., Burns, R., Coon, D., Czaja, S. J., Gallagher-Thompson, D., & Gitlin, L. N. (2006). Enhancing quality of life of dementia caregivers from different ethnic or racial groups: A randomized, controlled trial. *Annals of Internal Medicine, 145*, 727–738.

Bell-Scriber, M. J. (2008). Warming the nursing education climate for traditional-age nurses who are male. *Nursing Education Perspectives, 29*, 143–150.

Belsky, J. (2006). Early child care and early child development: Major findings of the NICHD Study of Early Child Care. *European Journal of Developmental Psychology, 3*, 95–110.

Belsky, J., & Fearon, R. M. P. (2002a). Early attachment security, subsequent maternal sensitivity, and later child development: Does continuity in development depend on caregiving? *Attachment and Human Development, 4*, 361–387.

Belsky, J., & Fearon, R. M. P. (2008). Precursors of attachment security. In J. Cassidy & P. R. Shaver (Eds.), *Handbook of attachment: Theory, research, and clinical applications* (2nd ed., pp. 295–316). New York: Guilford.

Belsky, J., Steinberg, L. D., Houts, R. M., Friedman, S. L., DeHart, G., Cauffman, E., Roisman, G. I., & Halpern-Felsher, B. (2007a). Family rearing antecedents of pubertal timing. *Child Development, 78*, 1302–1321.

Belsky, J., Steinberg, L., Houts, R. M., & Halpern-Felsher, B. L. (2010). The development of reproductive strategy in females: Early maternal harshness → earlier menarche → increased sexual risk taking. *Developmental Psychology, 46*, 120–128.

Belsky, J., Vandell, D. L., Burchinal, M., Clarke-Stewart, K. A., McCartney, K., & Owen, M. T. (2007b). Are there long-term effects of early child care? *Child Development, 78,* 681–701.

Bender, H. L., Allen, J. P., McElhaney, K. B., Antonishak, J., Moore, C. M., Kelly, H. L., & Davis, S. M. (2007). Use of harsh physical discipline and developmental outcomes in adolescence. *Development and Psychopathology, 19,* 227–242.

Benenson, J. F., & Christakos, A. (2003). The greater fragility of females' versus males' closest same-sex friendships. *Child Development, 74,* 1123–1129.

Bengtsson, H. (2005). Children's cognitive appraisal of others' distressful and positive experiences. *International Journal of Behavioral Development, 29,* 457–466.

Benner, A. D., & Graham, S. (2009). The transition to high school as a developmental process among multiethnic urban youth. *Child Development, 80,* 356–376.

Bennett, D. A., Schneider, J. A., Tang, Y., Arnold, S. E., & Wilson, R. S. (2006). The effect of social networks on the relation between Alzheimer's disease pathology and level of cognitive function in old people: A longitudinal cohort study. *Lancet Neurology, 5,* 406–412.

Bennett, K. M. (2007). "No sissy stuff": Toward a theory of masculinity and emotional expression in older widowed men. *Journal of Aging Studies, 21,* 347–356.

Bennett, K. M., Smith, P. T., & Hughes, G. M. (2005). Coping, depressive feelings and gender differences in late life widowhood. *Aging and Mental Health, 9,* 348–353.

Bennett, K. M., & Soulsby, L. K. (2012). Well-being in bereavement and widowhood. *Illness, Crisis & Loss, 20,* 321–337.

Bennett, M., Barrett, M., Karakozov, R., Kipiani, G., Lyons, E., Pavlenko, V., & Riazanova, T. (2004). Young children's evaluations of the ingroup and outgroup: A multi-national study. *Social Development, 13,* 124–141.

Benson, P. L., Scales, P. C., Hamilton, S. F., & Sesma, A., Jr. (2006). Positive youth development: Theory, research, and applications. In R. M. Lerner (Ed.), *Handbook of child psychology: Vol. 1. Theoretical models of human development* (6th ed., pp. 894–941). Hoboken, NJ: Wiley.

Berg, C. A., & Sternberg, R. J. (2003). Multiple perspectives on the development of adult intelligence. In J. Demick & C. Andreoletti (Eds.), *Handbook of adult development* (pp. 103–119). New York: Springer.

Berg, C. A., & Strough, J. (2011). Problem solving across the life span. In K. L. Fingerman, C. A. Berg, J. Smith, & T. C. Antonucci (Eds.), *Handbook of life-span development* (pp. 239–267). New York: Springer.

Berger, L. M., Paxson, C., & Waldfogel, J. (2009). Income and child development. *Children and Youth Services Review, 31,* 978–989.

Berger, S. E., Theuring, C., & Adolph, K. E. (2007). How and when infants learn to climb stairs. *Infant Behavior and Development, 30,* 36–49.

Bergman, E. J., Haley, W. E., & Small, B. J. (2010). The role of grief, anxiety, and depressive symptoms in the utilization of bereavement services. *Death Studies, 34,* 441–458.

Bergman, E. J., Haley, W. E., & Small, B. J. (2011). Who uses bereavement services? An examination of service use by bereaved dementia caregivers. *Aging and Mental Health, 15,* 531–540.

Bergman, H., Ferrucci, L., Guralnik, J., Hogan, D. B., Hummel, S., Karunananthan, S., & Wolfson. C. (2007). Frailty: An emerging research and clinical paradigm—issues and controversies. *Journal of Gerontology, 62A,* 731–737.

Bergman, I., Blomberg, M., & Almkvist, O. (2007). The importance of impaired physical health and age in normal cognitive aging. *Scandinavian Journal of Psychology, 48,* 115–125.

Berk, L. E. (2001). *Awakening children's minds: How parents and teachers can make a difference.* New York: Oxford University Press.

Berk, L. E. (2006). Looking at kindergarten children. In D. Gullo (Ed.), *K today: Teaching and learning in the kindergarten year* (pp. 11–25). Washington, DC: National Association for the Education of Young Children.

Berk, L. E., & Harris, S. (2003). Vygotsky, Lev. In L. Nadel (Ed.), *Encyclopedia of cognitive science.* London: Macmillan.

Berk, L. E., Mann, T., & Ogan, A. (2006). Make-believe play: Wellspring for development of self-regulation. In D. Singer, K. Hirsh-Pasek, & R. Golinkoff (Eds.), *Play = learning.* New York: Oxford University Press.

Berk, L. E., & Spuhl, S. (1995). Maternal interaction, private speech, and task performance in preschool children. *Early Childhood Research Quarterly, 10,* 145–169.

Berkowitz, M. W., & Gibbs, J. C. (1983). Measuring the developmental features of moral discussion. *Merrill-Palmer Quarterly, 29,* 399–410.

Berlin, L. J., Ipsa, J. M., Fine, M. A., Malone, P. S., Brooks-Gunn, J., Brady-Smith, C., et al. (2009). Correlates and consequences of spanking and verbal punishment for low-income white, African-American, and Mexican-American toddlers. *Child Development, 80,* 1403–1420.

Berman, R. A. (2007). Developing linguistic knowledge and language use across adolescence. In K. Hirsh-Pasek & R. M. Golinkoff (Eds.), *Action meets word: How children learn verbs* (pp. 347–367). New York: Oxford University Press.

Berndt, T. J., & Murphy, L. M. (2002). Influences of friends and friendships: Myths, truths, and research recommendations. In R. V. Kail (Ed.), *Advances in child development and behavior* (Vol. 30, pp. 275–310). San Diego, CA: Academic Press.

Berner, M. M., Leiber, C., Kriston, L., Stodden, V., & Gunzler, C. (2008). Effects of written information material on help-seeking behavior in patients with erectile dysfunction: A longitudinal study. *Journal of Sexual Behavior, 5,* 436–447.

Bernier, J. C., & Siegel, D. H. (1994). Attention-deficit hyperactivity disorder: A family ecological systems perspective. *Families in Society, 75,* 142–150.

Bert, S. C., Farris, J. R., & Borkowski, J. G. (2008). Parent training: Implementation strategies for adventures in parenting. *Journal of Primary Prevention, 29,* 243–261.

Bertenthal, B. I. (1993). Infants' perception of biomechanical motions: Instrinsic image and knowledge-based constraints. In C. Granrud (Ed.), *Visual perception and cognition in infancy* (pp. 175–214). Hillsdale, NJ: Erlbaum.

Bertenthal, B. I., & Longo, M. R. (2007). Is there evidence of a mirror neuron system from birth? *Developmental Science, 10,* 513–523.

Bertenthal, B. I., Longo, M. R., & Kenny, S. (2007). Phenomenal permanence and the development of predictive tracking in infancy. *Child Development, 78,* 350–363.

Berzin, S. C., & De Marco, A. C. (2010). Understanding the impact of poverty on critical events in emerging adulthood. *Youth and Society, 42,* 278–300.

Berzlanovich, A. M., Keil, W. W., Sim, T., Fasching, P., & Fazeny-Dorner, B. (2005). Do centenarians die healthy? An autopsy study. *Journal of Gerontology, 60A,* 862–865.

Berzonsky, M. D. (2003). Identity style and well-being: Does commitment matter? *Identity: An International Journal of Theory and Research, 3,* 131–142.

Berzonsky, M. D. (2004). Identity style, parental authority, and identity commitment. *Journal of Youth and Adolescence, 33,* 213–220.

Berzonsky, M. D. (2011). A social-cognitive perspective on identity construction. In S. J. Schwartz, K. Luyckx, & V. L. Vignoles (Eds.), *Handbook of identity theory and research* (pp. 55–76). New York: Springer.

Berzonsky, M. D., Cieciuch, J., Duriez, B., & Soenens, B. (2011). The how and what of identity formation: Associations between identity styles and value orientations. *Personality and Individual Differences, 50,* 295–299.

Berzonsky, M. D., & Kuk, L. S. (2000). Identity status, identity processing style, and the transition to university. *Journal of Adolescent Research, 15,* 81–98.

Best, D. (2009). From the American Academy of Pediatrics: Technical report—Secondhand and prenatal tobacco smoke exposure. *Pediatrics, 124,* e1017–e1044.

Best, D. L. (2001). Gender concepts: Convergence in cross-cultural research and methodologies. *Cross-cultural Research: The Journal of Comparative Social Science, 35,* 23–43.

Beyers, J. M., Bates, J. E., Pettit, G. S., & Dodge, K. A. (2003). Neighborhood structure, parenting processes, and the development of youths' externalizing behaviors: A multilevel analysis. *American Journal of Community Psychology, 31,* 35–53.

Beyers, W., & Seiffge-Krenke, I. (2010). Does identity precede intimacy? Testing Erikson's theory of romantic development in emerging adults of the 21st century. *Journal of Adolescent Research, 25,* 387–415.

Bhanot, R., & Jovanovic, J. (2005). Parents' academic gender stereotypes influence whether they intrude on their children's work. *Sex Roles, 52,* 597–607.

Bhat, A., Heathcock, J., & Galloway, J. C. (2005). Toy-oriented changes in hand and joint kinematics during the emergence of purposeful reaching. *Infant Behavior and Development, 28,* 445–465.

Bhatt, R. S., Rovee-Collier, C., & Weiner, S. (1994). Developmental changes in the interface between perception and memory retrieval. *Developmental Psychology, 30,* 151–162.

Bhatt, R. S., Wilk, A., Hill, D., & Rovee-Collier, C. (2004). Correlated attributes and categorization in the first half-year of life. *Developmental Psychobiology, 44,* 103–115.

Bherer, L. (2012). Physical activity and exercise in older adults. In E. O. Acevedo (Ed.), *Oxford handbook of exercise psychology* (pp. 359–384). New York: Oxford University Press.

Bherer, L., Kramer, A. F., Peterson, M. S., Colcombe, S., Erickson, K., & Becic, E. (2006). Training effects on dual-task performance: Are there age-related differences in plasticity of attentional control? *Psychology and Aging, 20,* 695–709.

Bhopal, K. (2011). "Education makes you have more say in the way your life goes": Indian women and arranged marriages in the United Kingdom. *British Journal of Sociology of Education, 32,* 431–447.

Bialystok, E., Craik, F. I. M., Green, D. W., & Gollan, T. H. (2009). Bilingual minds. *Psychological Science in the Public Interest, 3,* 89–129.

Bialystok, E., & Martin, M. M. (2003). Notation to symbol: Development in children's understanding of print. *Journal of Experimental Child Psychology, 86,* 223–243.

Bianco, A., Stone, J., Lynch, L., Lapinski, R., Berkowitz, G., & Berkowitz, R. L. (1996). Pregnancy outcome at age 40 and older. *Obstetrics and Gynecology, 87,* 917–922.

Biederman, J., Kwon, A., Aleardi, M., Chouinard, V. A., Marino, T., & Cole, H. (2005). Absence of gender effects on attention-deficit hyperactivity disorder: Findings in nonreferred subjects. *American Journal of Psychiatry, 162,* 1083–1089.

Biegel, D., & Liebbrant, S. (2006). Elders living in poverty. In B. Berkman & S. D'Ambruoso (Eds.),

Handbook of social work in health and aging (pp. 161–180). New York: Oxford University Press.

Bielak, A. A. M., Anstey, K. J., Christensen, H., & Windsor, T. D. (2012). Activity engagement is related to level, but not change, in cognitive ability across adulthood. *Psychology and Aging, 27,* 219–228.

Bielak, A. A. M., Hultsch, D. F., Strauss, E., MacDonald, S. W. S., & Hunter, M. A. (2010). Intraindividual variability in reaction time predicts cognitive outcomes 5 years later. *Neuropsychology, 24,* 731–741.

Bielawska-Batorowicz, E., & Kossakowska-Petrycka, K. (2006). Depressive mood in men after the birth of their offspring in relation to a partner's depression, social support, fathers' personality and prenatal expectations. *Journal of Reproductive and Infant Psychology, 24,* 21–29.

Bierman, K. L., & Powers, L. M. (2009). Social skills training to improve peer relations. In K. H. Rubin, W. M. Bukowski, & B. Laursen (Eds.), *Handbook of peer interactions, relationships, and groups* (pp. 603–621). New York: Guilford Press.

Bifulco, R., Cobb, C. D., & Bell, C. (2009). Can interdistrict choice boost student achievement? The case of Connecticut's interdistrict magnet school program. *Educational Evaluation and Policy Analysis, 31,* 323–345.

Bigler, R. S. (2007, June). Personal communication.

Bigler, R. S., Brown, C. S., & Markell, M. (2001). When groups are not created equal: Effects of group status on the formation of intergroup attitudes in children. *Child Development, 72,* 1151–1162.

Bimmel, N., Juffer, F., van IJzendoorn, M. H., & Bakermans-Kranenburg, M. J. (2003). Problem behavior of internationally adopted adolescents: A review and meta-analysis. *Harvard Review of Psychiatry, 11,* 64–77.

Birch, L. L., & Fisher, J. A. (1995). Appetite and eating behavior in children. *Pediatric Clinics of North America, 42,* 931–953.

Birch, L. L., Fisher, J. O., & Davison, K. K. (2003). Learning to overeat: Maternal use of restrictive feeding practices promotes girls' eating in the absence of hunger. *American Journal of Clinical Nutrition, 78,* 215–220.

Bird, A., & Reese, E. (2006). Emotional reminiscing and the development of an autobiographical self. *Developmental Psychology, 42,* 613–626.

Birditt, K. S., & Antonucci, T. C. (2007). Relationship quality profiles and well-being among married adults. *Journal of Family Psychology, 21,* 595–604.

Birditt, K. S., Brown, E., Orbuch, T. L., & McIlvane, J. M. (2010). Marital conflict behaviors and implications for divorce over 16 years. *Journal of Marriage and Family, 72,* 1188–1204.

Birditt, K. S., & Fingerman, K. L. (2005). Do we get better at picking our battles? Age group differences in descriptions of behavioral reactions to interpersonal tensions. *Journal of Gerontology, 60B,* P121–P128.

Biringen, Z., Emde, R. N., Campos, J. J., & Appelbaum, M. I. (1995). Affective reorganization in the infant, the mother, and the dyad: The role of upright locomotion and its timing. *Child Development, 66,* 499–514.

Birkett, M., Espelage, D. L., & Koenig, B. (2009). LGB and questioning students in schools: The moderating effects of homophobic bullying and school climate on negative outcomes. *Journal of Youth and Adolescence, 38,* 989–1000.

Birney, D. P., & Sternberg, R. J. (2006). Intelligence and cognitive abilities as competencies in development. In E. Bialystok & F. I. M. Craik (Eds.), *Lifespan cognition: Mechanisms of change* (pp. 315–330). New York: Oxford University Press.

Birney, D. P., & Sternberg, R. J. (2011). The development of cognitive abilities. In M. H. Bornstein & M. E.

Lamb (Eds.), *Developmental science: An advanced textbook* (6th ed., pp. 353–388). New York: Psychology Press.

Birren, J. E. (2009). Gifts and talents of elderly people: The persimmon's promise. In F. D. Horowitz, R. F. Subotnik, & D. J. Matthews (Eds.), *The development of giftedness and talent across the life span* (pp. 171–185). Washington, DC: American Psychological Association.

Bjorklund, D. F. (2012). *Children's thinking* (5th ed.). Belmont, CA: Wadsworth Cengage Learning.

Bjorklund, D. F., Causey, K., & Periss, V. (2009). The evolution and development of human social cognition. In P. Kappeler & J. Silk (Eds.), *Mind the gap: Racing the origins of human universals* (pp. 351–371). Berlin: Springer Verlag.

Bjorklund, D. F., Schneider, W., Cassel, W. S., & Ashley, E. (1994). Training and extension of a memory strategy: Evidence for utilization deficiencies in high- and low-IQ children. *Child Development, 65,* 951–965.

Black, M. C., Basile, K. C., Breiding, M. J., Smith, S. G., Walters, M. L., et al. (2011). *National intimate partner and sexual violence survey: 2010 summary report.* Atlanta, GA: Centers for Disease Control and Prevention.

Black, R. E., Williams, S. M., Jones, I. E., & Goulding, A. (2002). Children who avoid drinking cow milk have low dietary calcium intakes and poor bone health. *American Journal of Clinical Nutrition, 76,* 675–680.

Blackhall, L. J., Frank, G., Murphy, S., & Michel, V. (2001). Bioethics in a different tongue: The case of truth-telling. *Journal of Urban Health, 78,* 59–71.

Blackhall, L. J., Murphy, S. T., Frank, G., Michel, V., & Azen, S. (1995). Ethnicity and attitudes toward patient autonomy. *Journal of the American Medical Association, 274,* 820–825.

Blackwell, L. S., Trzesniewski, K. H., & Dweck, C. S. (2007). Implicit theories of intelligence predict achievement across an adolescent transition: A longitudinal study and an intervention. *Child Development, 78,* 246–263.

Blair, C., & Raver, C. C. (2012). Child development in the context of adversity: Experiential canalization of brain and behavior. *American Psychologist, 67,* 309–318.

Blair, C., & Razza, R. P. (2007). Relating effortful control, executive function, and false belief understanding to emerging math and literacy ability in kindergarten. *Developmental Psychology, 78,* 647–663.

Blair-Loy, M., & DeHart, G. (2003). Family and career trajectories among African-American female attorneys. *Journal of Family Issues, 24,* 908–933.

Blakemore, J. E. O. (2003). Children's beliefs about violating gender norms: Boys shouldn't look like girls, and girls shouldn't act like boys. *Sex Roles, 48,* 411–419.

Blakemore, S.-J., & Choudhury, S. (2006). Development of the adolescent brain: Implications for executive function and social cognition. *Journal of Child Psychology and Psychiatry, 47,* 296–312.

Blanchard, R., & Bogaert, A. F. (2004). Proportion of homosexual men who owe their sexual orientation to fraternal birth order: An estimate based on two national probability samples. *American Journal of Human Biology, 16,* 151–157.

Blanchard-Fields, F. (2007). Everyday problem solving and emotion: An adult developmental perspective. *Current Directions in Psychological Science, 16,* 26–31.

Blanchard-Fields, F., & Coats, A. H. (2008). The experience of anger and sadness in everyday problems impacts age differences in emotion regulation. *Developmental Psychology, 44,* 1547–1556.

Blanchard-Fields, F., Mienaltowski, A., & Baldi, R. (2007). Age differences in everyday problem-solving effectiveness: Older adults select more

effective strategies for interpersonal problems. *Journal of Gerontology, 62B,* P61–P64.

Blandon, A. Y., & Volling, B. L. (2008). Parental gentle guidance and children's compliance within the family: A replication study. *Journal of Family Psychology, 22,* 355–366.

Blass, E. M., Ganchrow, J. R., & Steiner, J. E. (1984). Classical conditioning in newborn humans 2–48 hours of age. *Infant Behavior and Development, 7,* 223–235.

Blatteis, C. M. (2012). Age-dependent changes in temperature regulation—a mini review. *Gerontology, 58,* 289–295.

Bleeker, M. M., & Jacobs, J. E. (2004). Achievement in math and science: Do mothers' beliefs matter 12 years later? *Journal of Educational Psychology, 96,* 97–109.

Bleses, D., Vach, W., Slott, M., Wehberg, S., Thomsen, P., Madsen, T., et al. (2008). Early vocabulary development in Danish and other languages: A CDI-based comparison. *Journal of Child Language, 35,* 619–650.

Bleske, A. L., & Buss, D. M. (2000). Can men and women be just friends? *Personal Relationships, 7,* 131–151.

Blieszner, R., & Roberto, K. A. (2012). Partners and friends in adulthood. In S. K. Whitbourne & M. J. Sliwinski (Eds.), The Wiley-Blackwell handbook of adulthood and aging (pp. 381–398). Malden, MA: Wiley-Blackwell.

Block, J. (2011). The five-factor framing of personality and beyond: Some ruminations. *Psychological Inquiry, 21,* 2–25.

Blood-Siegfried, J. (2009). The role of infection and inflammation in sudden infant death syndrome. *Immunopharmacology and Immunotoxicology, 31,* 516–523.

Bloom, L. (1998). Language acquisition in its developmental context. In D. Kuhn & R. S. Siegler (Eds.), *Handbook of child psychology: Vol. 2. Cognition, perception, and language* (5th ed., pp. 309–370). New York: Wiley.

Blumenfeld, P. C., Marx, R. W., & Harris, C. J. (2006). Learning environments. In K. A. Renninger & I. E. Sigel (Eds.), *Handbook of child psychology: Vol. 4. Child psychology in practice* (6th ed., pp. 297–342). Hoboken, NJ: Wiley.

Blumenthal, H., Leen-Feldner, E. W., Babson, K. A., Gahr, J. L., Trainor, C. D., & Frala, J. L. (2011). Elevated social anxiety among early maturing girls. *Developmental Psychology, 47,* 1133–1140.

Boardman, J. D. (2004). Stress and physical health: The role of neighborhoods as mediating and moderating mechanisms. *Social Science and Medicine, 58,* 2473–2483.

Bobb, A. J., Castellanos, F. X., Addington, A. M., & Rapoport, J. L. (2006). Molecular genetic studies of ADHD: 1991 to 2004. *American Journal of Medical Genetics Part B (Neuropsychiatric Genetics), 141B,* 551–565.

Bodrova, E., & Leong, D. J. (2007). *Tools of the mind: The Vygotskian approach to early childhood education* (2nd ed.). Upper Saddle River, NJ: Merrill/Prentice Hall.

Body, J. J., Bergmann, P., Boonen, S., Boutsen, Y., Bruyere, O., Devogelaer, J. P., et al. (2011). Non-pharmacological management of osteoporosis: A consensus of the Belgian Bone Club. *Osteoporosis International, 22,* 2769–2788.

Bogaert, A. F. (2005). Age at puberty and father absence in a national probability sample. *Journal of Adolescence, 28,* 541–546.

Bogin, B. (2001). *The growth of humanity.* New York: Wiley-Liss.

Bohannon, J. N., & Bonvillian, J. D. (2009). Theoretical approaches to language acquisition. In J. B. Gleason & B. Ratner (Ed.), *The development of language* (7th ed., pp. 227–284). Boston: Allyn and Bacon.

Bohannon, J. N., III, & Stanowicz, L. (1988). The issue of negative evidence: Adult responses to children's language errors. *Developmental Psychology, 24,* 684–689.

Bohlmeijer, E. T., Roemer, M., Cuijpers, P., & Smit, F. (2007). The effects of life-review on psychological well-being in older adults: A meta-analysis. *Aging and Mental Health, 11,* 291–300.

Boldizar, J. P. (1991). Assessing sex typing and androgyny in children: The children's sex role inventory. *Developmental Psychology, 27,* 505–515.

Bolen, R. M. (2001). *Child sexual abuse.* New York: Kluwer Academic.

Bolkan, C., & Hooker, K. (2012). Self-regulation and social cognition in adulthood: The gyroscope of personality. In S. K. Whitbourne & M. J. Sliwinski (Eds.), *Wiley-Blackwell handbook of adulthood and aging* (pp. 357–380). Malden, MA: Wiley-Blackwell.

Bonilla, S., Kehl, S., Kwong, K. Y., Morphew, T., Kachru, R., & Jones, C. A. (2005). School absenteeism in children with asthma in a Los Angeles inner-city school. *Journal of Pediatrics, 147,* 802–806.

Bonnick, S. L. (2008). Osteoporosis in men and women. *Management of Osteoporosis, 8,* 28–36.

Bono, M. A., & Stifter, C. A. (2003). Maternal attention-directing strategies and infant focused attention during problem solving. *Infancy, 4,* 235–250.

Bookman, A., & Kimbrel, D. (2011). Families and elder care in the twenty-first century. *Future of Children, 21,* 117–140.

Boom, J., Wouters, H., & Keller, M. (2007). A cross-cultural validation of stage development: A Rasch re-analysis of longitudinal socio-moral reasoning data. *Cognitive Development, 22,* 213–229.

Booth, A., Scott, M. E., & King, V. (2010). Father residence and adolescent problem behavior: Are youth always better off in two-parent families? *Journal of Family Issues, 31,* 585–605.

Borduin, C. M. (2007). Multisystemic treatment of violent youth and their families. In T. A. Cavell & K. T. Malcolm (Eds.), *Anger, aggression and interventions for interpersonal violence* (pp. 239–265). Mahwah, NJ: Erlbaum.

Bornstein, M. H. (1989). Sensitive periods in development: Structural characteristics and causal interpretations. *Psychological Bulletin, 105,* 179–197.

Bornstein, M. H., & Arterberry, M. E. (1999). Perceptual development. In M. H. Bornstein & M. E. Lamb (Eds.), *Developmental psychology: An advanced textbook* (pp. 231–274). Mahwah, NJ: Erlbaum.

Bornstein, M. H., & Arterberry, M. E. (2003). Recognition, discrimination, and categorization of smiling by 5-month-old infants. *Developmental Science, 6,* 585–599.

Bornstein, M. H., Arterberry, M. E., & Mash, C. (2010). Infant object categorization transcends object–context relations. *Infant Behavior and Development, 33,* 7–15.

Bornstein, M. H., & Sawyer, J. (2006). Family systems. In K. McCartney & D. Phillips (Eds.), *Blackwell handbook of early childhood development* (pp. 381–398). Malden, MA: Blackwell.

Bornstein, M. H., Vibbert, M., Tal, J., & O'Donnell, K. (1992). Toddler language and play in the second year: Stability, covariation, and influences of parenting. *First Language, 12,* 323–338.

Boroughs, D. S. (2004). Female sexual abusers of children. *Children and Youth Services Review, 26,* 481–487.

Borst, C. G. (1995). *Catching babies: The professionalization of childbirth, 1870–1920.* Cambridge, MA: Harvard University Press.

Bortfeld, H., Leon, S., Bloom, J., Schober, M., & Brennan, S. (2001). Disfluency rates in conversation: Effects of age, relationship, topic, role, and gender. *Language and Speech, 44,* 123–147.

Bos, H. M. W., & Sandfort, T. G. M. (2010). Children's gender identity in lesbian and heterosexual two-parent families. *Sex Roles, 62,* 114–126.

Bos, H. M. W., van Balen, F., & van den Boom, D. C. (2007). Child adjustment and parenting in planned lesbian-parent families. *American Journal of Orthopsychiatry, 77,* 38–48.

Bosacki, S. L., & Moore, C. (2004). Preschoolers' understanding of simple and complex emotions: Links with gender and language. *Sex Roles, 50,* 659–675.

Bost, K. K., Shin, N., McBride, B. A., Brown, G. L., Vaughn, B. E., & Coppola, G. (2006). Maternal secure base scripts, children's attachment security, and mother–child narrative styles. *Attachment and Human Development, 8,* 241–260.

Boswell, G. H., Kahana, E., & Dilworth-Anderson, P. (2006). Spirituality and healthy lifestyle behaviors: Stress counter-balancing effects on the well-being of older adults. *Journal of Religion and Health, 45,* 587–602.

Botton, J., Heude, B., Maccario, J., Ducimetiére, P., & Charles, M. A. (2008). Postnatal weight and height growth velocities at different ages between birth and 5y and body composition in adolescent boys and girls. *American Journal of Clinical Nutrition, 87,* 1760–1768.

Bouchard, T. J. (2004). Genetic influence on human psychological traits: A survey. *Current Directions in Psychological Science, 13,* 148–151.

Bouchard, T. J., & Loehlin, J. C. (2001). Genes, evolution, and personality. *Behavior Genetics, 31,* 243–274.

Boucher, O., Bastien, C. H., Saint-Amour, D., Dewailly, E., Ayotte, P., Jacobson, J. L., Jacobson, et al. (2010). Prenatal exposure to methylmercury and PCBs affects distinct stages of information processing: An event-related potential study with Inuit children. *Neurotoxicology, 31,* 373–384.

Boucher, O., Muckle, G., & Bastien, C. H. (2009). Prenatal exposure to polychlorinated biphenyls: A neuropsychologic analysis. *Environmental Health Perspectives, 117,* 7–16.

Boukydis, C. F. Z., & Lester, B. M. (1998). Infant crying, risk status and social support in families of preterm and term infants. *Early Development and Parenting, 7,* 31–39.

Boulton, M. J. (1999). Concurrent and longitudinal relations between children's playground behavior and social preference, victimization, and bullying. *Child Development, 70,* 944–954.

Bowen, C. E., Noack, M. G., & Staudinger, U. M. (2011). Aging in the work context. In K. W. Schaie & S. L. Willis (Eds.), *Handbook of the psychology of aging* (7th ed., pp. 263–277). San Diego, CA: Academic Press.

Bowen, N. K., Bowen, G. L., & Ware, W. B. (2002). Neighborhood social disorganization, families, and the educational behavior of adolescents. *Journal of Adolescent Research, 17,* 468–490.

Bowlby, J. (1969). *Attachment and loss: Vol. 1. Attachment.* New York: Basic Books.

Bowlby, J. (1980). *Attachment and loss: Vol. 3. Loss: Sadness and depression.* New York: Basic Books.

Bowman, N. A. (2011a). College diversity experiences and cognitive development: A meta-analysis. *Review of Educational Research, 80,* 4–33.

Bowman, N. A. (2011b). Promoting participation in a diverse democracy: A meta-analysis of college diversity experiences and civic engagement. *Review of Educational Research, 81,* 29–68.

Bowman, S. A., Gortmaker, S. L., Ebbeling, C. B., Pereira, M. A., & Ludwig, D. S. (2004). Effects of fast-food consumption on energy intake and diet quality among children in a national household survey. *Pediatrics, 113,* 112–113.

Boyce, W., Doherty-Poirier, M., MacKinnon, D., Fortin, C., Saab, H., King, M., & Gallupe, O. (2006). Sexual health of Canadian youth: Findings from the Canadian Youth, Sexual Health and HIV/AIDS Study. *Canadian Journal of Human Sexuality, 15,* 59–68.

Boyle, P. A., Barnes, L. L., Buchman, A. S., & Bennett, D. A. (2009). Purpose in life is associated with mortality among community-dwelling older persons. *Psychosomatic Medicine, 71,* 574–579.

Boysson-Bardies, B. de, & Vihman, M. M. (1991). Adaptation to language: Evidence from babbling and first words in four languages. *Language, 67,* 297–319.

Bozionelos, N., Bozionelos, G., Kostopoulos, K., & Polychroniou, P. (2011). How providing mentoring relates to career success and organizational commitment: A study in the general managerial population. *Career Development International, 16,* 446–468.

Bracci, R., Perrone, S., & Buonocore, G. (2006). The timing of neonatal brain damage. *Biology of the Neonate, 90,* 145–155.

Bradbury, J. C. (2009). Peak athletic performance and ageing: Evidence from baseball. *Journal of Sports Sciences, 27,* 599–610.

Bradford, K., Barber, B. K., Olsen, J. A., Maughan, S. L., Erickson, L. D., Ward, D., & Stolz, H. E. (2003). A multi-national study of interparental conflict, parenting, and adolescent functioning: South Africa, Bangladesh, China, India, Bosnia, Germany, Palestine, Colombia, and the United States. *Marriage and Family Review, 35,* 107–137.

Bradley, R. H., & Caldwell, B. M. (1982). The consistency of the home environment and its relation to child development. *International Journal of Behavioral Development, 5,* 445–465.

Bradley, R. H., Whiteside, L., Mundfrom, D. J., Casey, P. H., Kelleher, K. J., & Pope, S. K. (1994). Early indications of resilience and their relation to experiences in the home environments of low birthweight, premature children living in poverty. *Child Development, 65,* 346–360.

Braine, L. G., Schauble, L., Kugelmass, S., & Winter, A. (1993). Representation of depth by children: Spatial strategies and lateral biases. *Developmental Psychology, 29,* 466–479.

Brame, B., Nagin, D. S., & Tremblay, R. E. (2001). Developmental trajectories of physical aggression from school entry to late adolescence. *Journal of Child Psychology and Psychiatry, 42,* 503–512.

Brand, S., Gerber, M., Beck, J., Hatzinger, M., Puhse, U., & Holsboer-Trachsler, E. (2010). High exercise levels are related to favorable sleep and psychological functioning in adolescence: A comparison of athletes and controls. *Journal of Adolescent Health, 46,* 133–141.

Braswell, G. S., & Callanan, M. A. (2003). Learning to draw recognizable graphic representations during mother–child interactions. *Merrill-Palmer Quarterly, 49,* 471–494.

Braungart-Rieker, J. M., Hill-Soderlund, A. L., & Karrass, J. (2010). Fear and anger reactivity trajectories from 4 to 16 months: The roles of temperament, regulation, and maternal sensitivity. *Developmental Psychology, 46,* 791–804.

Braveman, P., Cubbin, C., Egerter, S., Williams, D. R., & Pamuk, E. (2010). Socioeconomic disparities in health in the United States: What the patterns tell us. *American Journal of Public Health, 100,* S186–S196.

Bray, J. H. (1999). From marriage to remarriage and beyond: Findings from the Developmental Issues in Stepfamilies Research Project. In E. M. Hetherington (Ed.), *Coping with divorce, single parenting, and remarriage: A risk and resiliency perspective* (pp. 295–319). Mahwah, NJ: Erlbaum.

Bremner, J. G. (2010). Cognitive development: Knowledge of the physical world. In J. G. Bremner & T. D. Wachs (Eds.), *Wiley-Blackwell handbook of infant development: Vol. 1. Basic research* (2nd ed., pp. 204–242). Oxford, UK: Wiley.

Brendgen, M., Markiewicz, D., Doyle, A. B., & Bukowski, W. M. (2001). The relations between friendship quality, ranked-friendship preference, and adolescents' behavior with their friends. *Merrill-Palmer Quarterly, 47,* 395–415.

Brenner, E., & Salovey, P. (1997). Emotional regulation during childhood: Developmental, interpersonal, and individual considerations. In P. Salovey & D. Sluyter (Eds.), *Emotional literacy and emotional development* (pp. 168–192). New York: Basic Books.

Brenner, J. (2013). *Pew Internet: Social Networking.* Washington, DC: Pew Research Center.

Brent, R. L., Christian, M. S., & Diener, R. M. (2011). Evaluation of the reproductive and developmental risks of caffeine. *Developmental and Reproductive Toxicology, 92,* 152–187.

Bretherton, I., & Munholland, K. A. (2008). Internal working models in attachment relationships. In J. Cassidy & P. R. Shaver (Eds.), *Handbook of attachment: Theory, research, and clinical applications* (2nd ed., pp. 102–127). New York: Guilford.

Brewaeys, A., Ponjaert, I., Van Hall, E. V., & Golombok, S. (1997). Donor insemination: Child development and family functioning in lesbian mother families. *Human Reproduction, 12,* 1349–1359.

Bridge, J. A., Goldstein, T. R., & Brent, D. A. (2006). Adolescent suicide and suicidal behavior. *Journal of Child Psychology and Psychiatry, 47,* 372–394.

Bridgett, D. J., Gartstein, M. A., Putnam, S. P., McKay, T., Iddins, R., Robertson, C., et al. (2009). Maternal and contextual influences and the effect of temperament development during infancy on parenting in toddlerhood. *Infant Behavior and Development, 32,* 103–116.

Bright, G. M., Mendoza, J. R., & Rosenfeld, R. G. (2009). Recombinant human insulin-like growth factor-1 treatment: Ready for primetime. *Endocrinology and Metabolism Clinics of North America, 38,* 625–638.

Bright, J. E. H., Pryor, R. G. L., Wilkenfeld, S., & Earl, J. (2005). The role of social context and serendipitous events in career decision making. *International Journal for Educational and Vocational Guidance, 5,* 19–36.

Brim, O. G., Ryff, C. D., & Kessler, R. C. (2005). The MIDUS National Survey: An overview. In O. G. Brim, C. D. Ryff, & R. C. Kessler (Eds.), *How healthy are we? A national study of well-being at midlife* (pp. 1–34). Chicago: University of Chicago Press.

Brodaty, H., Seeher, K., & Gibson, L. (2012). Dementia time to death: A systematic literature review on survival time and years of life lost in people with dementia. *International Psychogeriatrics, 24,* 1034–1045.

Brody, G. H., & Flor, D. L. (1998). Maternal resources, parenting practices, and child competence in rural, single-parent African American families. *Child Development, 69,* 803–816.

Brody, G. H., & Murry, V. M. (2001). Sibling socialization of competence in rural, single-parent African American families. *Journal of Marriage and Family, 63,* 996–1008.

Brody, G. H., Stoneman, Z., & McCoy, J. K. (1994). Forecasting sibling relationships in early adolescence from child temperaments and family processes in middle childhood. *Child Development, 65,* 771–784.

Brody, L. (1999). *Gender, emotion, and the family.* Cambridge, MA: Harvard University Press.

Brody, L. R. (1997). Gender and emotion: Beyond stereotypes. *Journal of Social Issues, 53,* 369–393.

Brodzinsky, D. M. (2011). Children's understanding of adoption: Developmental and clinical implications. *Professional Psychology: Research and Practice, 42,* 200–207.

Broidy, L. M., Nagin, D. S., Tremblay, R. E., Bates, J. E., Brame, B., Dodge, K. A., et al. (2003). Developmental trajectories of childhood disruptive behaviors and adolescent delinquency: A six-site, cross-national study. *Developmental Psychology, 39,* 222–245.

Bronfenbrenner, U., & Morris, P. A. (2006). The bioecological model of human development. In R. M. Lerner (Ed.), *Handbook of child psychology: Vol. 1. Theoretical models of human development* (6th ed., pp. 297–342). Hoboken, NJ: Wiley.

Bronson, G. W. (1994). Infants' transitions toward adult-like scanning. *Child Development, 65,* 1243–1261.

Bronstein, P. (2006). The family environment: Where gender role socialization begins. In J. Worell & C. D. Goodheart (Eds.), *Handbook of girls' and women's psychological health: Gender and well-being across the lifespan* (pp. 262–271). New York: Oxford University Press.

Bronte-Tinkew, J., Moore, K. A., & Carrano, J. (2006). The father–child relationship, parenting styles, and adolescent risk behaviors in intact families. *Journal of Family Issues, 27,* 850–881.

Brooks, L., McCabe, P., & Schneiderman, N. (2011). Stress and cardiometabolic syndrome. In R. J. Contrada & A. Baum (Eds.), *Handbook of stress science: Biology, psychology, and health* (pp. 399–410). New York: Springer.

Brooks, P. J., Hanauere, J. B., Padowska, B., & Rosman, H. (2003). The role of selective attention in preschoolers' rule use in a novel dimensional card sort. *Cognitive Development, 18,* 195–215.

Brooks, R., & Meltzoff, A. N. (2008). Infant gaze following and pointing predict accelerated vocabulary growth through two years of age: A longitudinal, growth curve modeling study. *Journal of Child Language, 35,* 207–220.

Brooks-Gunn, J. (1988). Antecedents and consequences of variations in girls' maturational timing. *Journal of Adolescent Health Care, 9,* 365–373.

Brooks-Gunn, J. (2003). Do you believe in magic? What we can expect from early childhood intervention programs. *Social Policy Report of the Society for Research in Child Development, 17,* 3–14.

Brooks-Gunn, J. (2004). Intervention and policy as change agents for young children. In P. L. Chase-Lansdale, K. Kiernan, & R. J. Friedman (Eds.), *Human development across lives and generations: The potential for change* (pp. 293–340). New York: Cambridge University Press.

Brooks-Gunn, J., Han, W.-J., & Waldfogel, J. (2002). Maternal employment and child cognitive outcomes in the first three years of life: The NICHD study of early child care. *Child Development, 73,* 1052–1072.

Brooks-Gunn, J., Han, W.-J., & Waldfogel, J. (2010). First-year maternal employment and child development in the first 7 years. *Monographs of the Society for research in Child Development, 75*(No. 2, Serial No. 296), 59–69.

Brooks-Gunn, J., Klebanov, P. K., Smith, J., Duncan, G. J., & Lee, K. (2003). The black–white test score gap in young children. Contributions of test and family characteristics. *Applied Developmental Science, 7,* 239–252.

Brown, A. M., & Miracle, J. A. (2003). Early binocular vision in human infants: Limitations on the generality of the Superposition Hypothesis. *Vision Research, 43,* 1563–1574.

Brown, A. S. (2006). Prenatal infection as a risk factor for schizophrenia. *Schizophrenia Bulletin, 32,* 200–202.

Brown, B. B., & Dietz, E. L. (2009). Informal peer groups in middle childhood and adolescence. In K. H. Rubin, W. M. Bukowski, & B. Laursen (Eds.), *Handbook of peer interactions, relationships, and groups* (pp. 361–376). New York: Guilford Press.

Brown, B. B., Herman, M., Hamm, J. V., & Heck, D. (2008). Ethnicity and image: Correlates of minority adolescents' affiliation with individual-based versus ethnically defined peer crowds. *Child Development, 79,* 529–546.

Brown, C., & Lowis, M. J. (2003). Psychosocial development in the elderly: An investigation into Erikson's ninth stage. *Journal of Aging Studies, 17,* 415–426.

Brown, C. S., & Bigler, R. S. (2004). Children's perceptions of gender discrimination. *Developmental Psychology, 40,* 714–726.

Brown, G. L., Schoppe-Sullivan, S. J., Mangelsdorf, S. C., & Neff, C. (2010). Observed and reported supportive coparenting as predictors of infant–mother and infant–father attachment security. *Early Child Development and Care, 180,* 121–137.

Brown, J. D., & L'Engle, K. L. (2009). X-rated: Attitudes and behaviors associated with U.S. early adolescents' exposure to sexually explicit media. *Communication Research, 36,* 129–151.

Brown, L. H., & Rodin, P. A. (2004). Grandparent–grandchild relationships and the life course perspective. In J. Demick & C. Andreoletti (Eds.), *Handbook of adult development* (pp. 459–474). New York: Springer.

Brown, R. W. (1973). *A first language: The early stages.* Cambridge, MA: Harvard University Press.

Brown, S. A., & Ramo, D. E. (2005). Clinical course of youth following treatment for alcohol and drug problems. In H. A. Liddle & C. L. Rowe (Eds.), *Adolescent substance abuse: Research and clinical advances* (pp. 79–103). Cambridge, UK: Cambridge University Press.

Brown, S. L., & Kawamura, S. (2010). Relationships quality among cohabitors and marrieds in older adulthood. *Social Science Research, 39,* 777–786.

Brown, S. L., & Lin, I.-F. (2012). *Divorce in middle and later life: New estimates from the 2009 American Community Survey.* Bowling Green, OH: Center for Family and Demographic Research, Bowling Green University.

Brown, T. M., & Rodriguez, L. F. (2009). School and the co-construction of dropout. *International Journal of Qualitative Studies in Education, 22,* 221–242.

Browne, C. A., & Woolley, J. D. (2004). Preschoolers' magical explanations for violations of physical, social, and mental laws. *Journal of Cognition and Development, 5,* 239–260.

Brownell, C. A., Zerwas, S., & Ramani, G. B. (2007). "So big": The development of body self-awareness in toddlers. *Child Development, 78,* 1426–1440.

Brugman, G. M. (2006). Wisdom and aging. In J. E. Birren & K. W. Schaie (Eds.), *Handbook of the psychology of aging* (6th ed., pp. 445–476). Burlington, MA: Elsevier Academic Press.

Brussoni, M. J., and Boon, S. D. (1998). Grandparental impact in young adults' relationships with their closest grandparents: The role of relationship strength and emotional closeness. *International Journal of Aging and Human Development, 45,* 267–286.

Bruzzese, J.-M., & Fisher, C. B. (2003). Assessing and enhancing the research consent capacity of children and youth. *Applied Developmental Science, 7,* 13–26.

Bryan, A. E., & Dix, T. (2009). Mothers' emotions and behavioral support during interactions with toddlers: The role of child temperament. *Social Development, 18,* 647–670.

Bryant, B. K., Zvonkovic, A. M., & Reynolds, P. (2006). Parenting in relation to child and adolescent vocational development. *Journal of Vocational Behavior, 69,* 149–175.

Bryant, P., & Nunes, T. (2002). Children's understanding of mathematics. In U. Goswami (Ed.), *Blackwell handbook of childhood cognitive development* (pp. 412–439). Malden, MA: Blackwell.

Buchanan, C. M., Eccles, J. S., & Becker, J. B. (1992). Are adolescents the victims of raging hormones? Evidence for activational effects of hormones on moods and behavior at adolescence. *Psychological Bulletin, 111,* 62–107.

Buchanan, C. M., Maccoby, E. E., & Dornbusch, S. M. (1996). *Adolescents after divorce.* Cambridge, MA: Harvard University Press.

Buchanan-Barrow, E., & Barrett, M. (1998). Children's rule discrimination within the context of the school. *British Journal of Developmental Psychology, 16,* 539–551.

Buehler, C., & O'Brien, M. (2011). Mothers' part-time employment: Associations with mother and family well-being. *Journal of Family Psychology, 25,* 895–906.

Bugental, D. B., Ellerson, P. C., Lin, E. K., Rainey, B., & Kokotovic, A. (2002). A cognitive approach to child abuse prevention. *Journal of Family Psychology, 16,* 243–258.

Bugental, D. B., & Happaney, K. (2004). Predicting infant maltreatment in low-income families: The interactive effects of maternal attributions and child status at birth. *Developmental Psychology, 40,* 234–243.

Buhl, H. M., & Lanz, M. (2007). Emerging adulthood in Europe: Common traits and variability across five European countries. *Journal of Adolescent Research, 22,* 439–443.

Buhrmester, D. (1996). Need fulfillment, interpersonal competence, and the developmental contexts of early adolescent friendship. In W. M. Bukowski, A. F. Newcomb, & W. W. Hartup (Eds.), *The company they keep: Friendship during childhood and adolescence* (pp. 158–185). New York: Cambridge University Press.

Buhrmester, D., & Furman, W. (1990). Perceptions of sibling relationships during middle childhood and adolescence. *Child Development, 61,* 1387–1398.

Buhs, E. S., Ladd, G. W., & Herald-Brown, S. L. (2010). Victimization and exclusion: Links to peer rejection, classroom engagement, and achievement. In S. R. Jimerson, S. M. Swearer, & D. L. Espelage (Eds.), *Handbook of bullying in schools: An international perspective* (pp. 163–172). New York: Routledge.

Bukowski, W. M. (2001). Friendship and the worlds of childhood. In D. W. Nangle & C. A. Erdley (Eds.), *The role of friendship in psychological adjustment* (pp. 93–105). San Francisco: Jossey-Bass.

Bullo, M., Lamuela-Raventos, R., & Salas-Salvadó, J. (2011). Mediterranean diet and oxidation: Nuts and olive oil as important sources of fat and antioxidants. *Current Topics in Medicinal Chemistry, 11,* 1797–1810.

Bumpus, M. F., Crouter, A. C., & McHale, S. M. (2006). Linkages between negative work-to-family spillover and mothers' and fathers' knowledge of their young adolescents' daily lives. *Journal of Early Adolescence, 26,* 36–59.

Bunge, S. A., & Wright, S. B. (2007). Neurodevelopmental changes in working memory and cognitive control. *Current Opinion in Neurobiology, 17,* 243–250.

Bunting, L., & McAuley, C. (2004). Teenage pregnancy and parenthood: The role of fathers. *Child and Family Social Work, 9,* 295–303.

Burchinal, M., Vandergrift, N., & Pianta, R. (2010). Threshold analysis of association between child care quality and child outcomes for low-income children in prekindergarten programs. *Early Childhood Research Quarterly, 25,* 166–176.

Burden, M. J., Jacobson, S. W., & Jacobson, J. L. (2005). Relation of prenatal alcohol exposure to cognitive processing speed and efficiency in childhood. *Alcoholism: Clinical and Experimental Research, 29,* 1473–1483.

Burgess-Champoux, T. L., Larson, N., Neumark-Sztainer, D., Hannan, P. J., & Story, M. (2009). Are family meal patterns associated with overall diet quality during the transition from early to middle adolescence? *Journal of Nutrition Education and Behavior, 41,* 79–86.

Burke, D. M., & Shafto, M. A. (2004). Aging and language production. *Current Directions in Psychological Science, 13,* 21–24.

Burleson, B. R., & Kunkel, A. W. (2006). Revisiting the different cultures thesis: An assessment of sex differences and similarities in communication. In K. Dindia & D. J. Canary (Eds.), *Sex differences and similarities in communication* (2nd ed., pp. 137–159). Mahwah, NJ: Erlbaum.

Burts, D.C., Hart, C. H., Charlesworth, R., Fleege, P. O., Mosely, J., & Thomasson, R. H. (1992). Observed activities and stress behaviors of children in developmentally appropriate and inappropriate kindergarten classrooms. *Early Childhood Research Quarterly, 7,* 297–318.

Buscemi, L., & Turchi, C. (2011). An overview of the genetic susceptibility to alcoholism. *Medicine, Science, and the Law, 51,* S2–S6.

Bush, K. R., & Peterson, G. W. (2008). Family influences on child development. In T. P. Gullotta & G. M. Blau (Eds.), *Handbook of child behavioral issues: Evidence-based approaches to prevention and treatment* (pp. 43–67). New York: Routledge.

Bushman, B. J., & Huesmann, L. R. (2001). Effects of televised violence on aggression. In D. G. Singer & J. L. Singer (Eds.), *Handbook of children and the media* (pp. 223–254). Thousand Oaks, CA: Sage.

Bushnell, E. W., & Boudreau, J. P. (1993). Motor development and the mind: The potential role of motor abilities as a determinant of aspects of perceptual development. *Child Development, 64,* 1005–1021.

Buss, D. (2012). *Evolutionary psychology: The new science of the mind* (4th ed.). Upper Saddle River, NJ: Pearson.

Buss, D. M., Shackelford, T. K., Kirkpatrick, L. A., & Larsen, R. J. (2001). A half century of mate preferences: The cultural evolution of values. *Journal of Marriage and Family, 63,* 491–503.

Bussey, K. (1992). Lying and truthfulness: Children's definitions, standards, and evaluative reactions. *Child Development, 63,* 129–137.

Bussey, K. (1999). Children's categorization and evaluation of different types of lies and truths. *Child Development, 70,* 1338–1347.

Buswell, S. D., & Spatz, D. L. (2007). Parent–infant co-sleeping and its relationship to breastfeeding. *Journal of Pediatric Health Care, 21,* 22–28.

Butler, M., & Meaney, J. (Eds.). (2005). *Genetics of developmental disabilities.* Boca Raton, FL: Taylor & Francis.

Butler, R. N. (1968). The life review: An interpretation of reminiscence in the aged. In B. Neugarten (Ed.), *Middle age and aging* (pp. 486–496). Chicago: University of Chicago Press.

Buttelmann, D., Carpenter, M., & Tomasello, M. (2009). Eighteen-month-old infants show false belief understanding in an active helping paradigm. *Cognition, 112,* 337–342.

Buunk, B. P. (2002). Age and gender differences in mate selection criteria for various involvement levels. *Personal Relationships, 9,* 271–278.

Bybee, J. A., & Wells, Y. V. (2003). The development of possible selves during adulthood. In J. Demick & C. Andreoletti (Eds.), *Handbook of adult development* (pp. 257–270). New York: Springer.

Byrnes, J. P. (2003). Cognitive development during adolescence. In G. R. Adams & M. D. Berzonsky (Eds.), *Blackwell handbook of adolescence* (pp. 227–246). Malden, MA: Blackwell.

C

Cabrera, N. J., & Bradley, R. H. (2012). Latino fathers and their children. *Child Development Perspectives, 6,* 232–238.

Cabrera, N. J., & García-Coll, C. (2004). Latino fathers: Uncharted territory in need of much exploration. In M. E. Lamb (Ed.), *The role of the father in child development* (4th ed., pp. 98–120). Hoboken, NJ: Wiley.

Cahill, K. E., Giandrea, M. D., & Quinn, J. F. (2006). Retirement patterns from career employment. *Gerontologist, 46,* 514–523.

Cai, H., Cong, W., Ji, S., Rathman, S., Maudsley, S., & Martin, B. (2012). Metabolic dysfunction in Alzheimer's disease and related neurodegenerative disorders. *Current Alzheimer Research, 9,* 5–17.

Cain, K. M., & Dweck, C. S. (1995). The relation between motivational patterns and achievement cognitions through the elementary school years. *Merrill-Palmer Quarterly, 41,* 25–52.

Cairns, R. B., & Cairns, B. D. (2006). The making of developmental psychology. In R. M. Lerner (Ed.), *Handbook of child psychology: Vol. 1. Theoretical models of human development* (6th ed., pp. 89–165). Hoboken, NJ: Wiley.

Caldera, Y. M., & Lindsey, E. W. (2006). Coparenting, mother–infant interaction, and infant–parent attachment relationships in two-parent families. *Journal of Family Psychology, 20,* 275–283.

Caldwell, B. M., & Bradley, R. H. (1994). Environmental issues in developmental follow-up research. In S. L. Friedman & H. C. Haywood (Eds.), *Developmental follow-up* (pp. 235–256). San Diego: Academic Press.

Calhoun, L. G., Tedeschi, R. G., Cann, A., & Hanks, E. A. (2010). Positive outcomes following bereavement: Paths to posttraumatic growth. *Psychologica Belgica, 50,* 125–143.

Callanan, M. A., & Oakes, L. M. (1992). Preschoolers' questions and parents' explanations: Causal thinking in everyday activity. *Cognitive Development, 7,* 213–233.

Calvert, S. L., Rideout, V. J., Woolard, J. L., Barr, R. F., & Strouse, G. A. (2005). Age, ethnicity, and socioeconomic patterns in early computer use: A national survey. *American Behavioral Scientist, 48,* 590–607.

Cameron, C. A., & Lee, K. (1997). The development of children's telephone communication. *Journal of Applied Developmental Psychology, 18,* 55–70.

Cameron-Faulkner, T., Lieven, E., & Tomasello, M. (2003). A construction based analysis of child-directed speech. *Cognitive Science, 27,* 843–873.

Campbell, A., Shirley, L., & Candy, J. (2004). A longitudinal study of gender-related cognition and behaviour. *Developmental Science, 7,* 1–9.

Campbell, A. L., & Binstock, R. H. (2011). Politics and aging in the United States. In R. H. Binstock & L. K. George (Eds.), *Handbook of aging and the social sciences* (pp. 265–280). San Diego, CA: Academic Press.

Campbell, D. A., Lake, M. F., Falk, M., & Backstrand, J. R. (2006). A randomized control trial of continuous support in labor by a lay doula. *Journal of Obstetrics and Gynecology and Neonatal Nursing, 35,* 456–464.

Campbell, D. A., Scott, K. D., Klaus, M. H., & Falk, M. (2007). Female relatives or friends trained as labor doulas: Outcomes at 6 to 8 weeks postpartum. *Birth, 34,* 220–227.

Campbell, F. A., Pungello, E. P., Miller-Johnson, S., Burchinal, M., & Ramey, C. T. (2001). The development of cognitive and academic abilities: Growth curves from an early childhood educational experiment. *Developmental Psychology, 37,* 231–242.

Campbell, F. A., & Ramey, C. T. (2010). Carolina Abecedarian Project. In A. Reynolds, A. J. Rolick, M. M. Englund, & J. A. Temple (Eds.), *Childhood* programs and practices in the first decade of life: A human capital integration (pp. 76–98). New York: Cambridge University Press.

Campbell, F. A., Ramey, C. T., Pungello, E. P., Sparling, J., & Miller-Johnson, S. (2002). Early childhood education: Young adult outcomes from the Abecedarian Project. *Applied Developmental Science, 6*, 42–57.

Campbell, J., & Glass, N. (2009). Safety planning, danger, and lethality assessment. In C. Mitchell & D. Anglin (Eds.), *Intimate partner violence: A healthbased perspective* (pp. 319–334). New York: Oxford University Press.

Campbell, S. B., Brownell, C. A., Hungerford, A., Spieker, S. J., Mohan, R., & Blessing, J. S. (2004). The course of maternal depressive symptoms and maternal sensitivity as predictors of attachment security at 36 months. *Development and Psychopathology, 16*, 231–252.

Campos, J. J., Anderson, D. I., Barbu-Roth, M. A., Hubbard, E. M., Hertenstein, J. J., & Witherington, D. (2000). Travel broadens the mind. *Infancy, 1*, 149–219.

Campos, J. J., Witherington, D., Anderson, D. I., Frankel, C. I., Uchiyama, I., & Barbu-Roth, M. (2008). Rediscovering development in infancy. *Child Development, 79*, 1625–1632.

Camras, L. A., Oster, H., Campos, J. J., & Bakeman, R. (2003). Emotional facial expressions in European-American, Japanese, and Chinese infants. *Annals of the New York Academy of Sciences, 1000*, 1–17.

Camras, L. A., Oster, H., Campos, J. J., Campos, R., Ujie, T., Miyake, K., Wang, L., & Meng, Z. (1998). Production of emotional and facial expressions in European American, Japanese, and Chinese infants. *Developmental Psychology, 34*, 616–628.

Camras, L. A., Oster, H., Campos, J. J., Miyake, K., & Bradshaw, D. (1992). Japanese and American infants' responses to arm restraint. *Developmental Psychology, 28*, 578–583.

Canada Campaign 2000. (2009). *2009 Report Card on Child and Family Poverty in Canada: 1989–2009.* Retrieved from www.campaign2000.ca/reportcards .html

Candy, B., Holman, A., Leurent, S., & Jones, D. L. (2011). Hospice care delivered at home, in nursing homes and in dedicated hospice facilities: A systematic review of quantitative and qualitative evidence. *International Journal of Nursing Studies, 48*, 121–133.

Cannella, C., Savina, C., & Donini, L. M. (2009). Nutrition, longevity and behavior. *Archives of Gerontology and Geriatrics, 49*(Suppl. 1), 19–27.

Canobi, K. H. (2004). Individual differences in children's addition and subtraction knowledge. *Cognitive Development, 19*, 81–93.

Canobi, K. H., Reeve, R. A., & Pattison, P. E. (2003). The role of conceptual understanding in children's addition problem solving. *Developmental Psychology, 39*, 521–534.

Capaldi, D., DeGarmo, D., Patterson, G. R., & Forgatch, M. (2002). Contextual risk across the early life span and association with antisocial behavior. In J. B. Reid, G. R. Patterson, & J. Snyder (Eds.), *Antisocial behavior in children and adolescents* (pp. 123–145). Washington, DC: American Psychological Association.

Cappeliez, P., Rivard, V., & Guindon, S. (2007). Functions of reminiscence in later life: Proposition of a model and applications. European *Review of Applied Psychology, 57*, 151–156.

Cappeliez, P., & Robitaille, A. (2010). Coping mediates the relationships between reminiscence and psychological well-being among older adults. *Aging and Mental Health, 14*, 807–818.

Card, N. A., Stucky, B. D., Sawalani, G. M., & Little, T. D. (2008). Direct and indirect aggression during childhood and adolescence: A meta-analytic review of gender differences, intercorrelations, and relations to maladjustment. *Child Development, 79*, 1185–1229.

Carek, P. J., Laibstain, S. E., & Carek, S. M. (2011). Exercise for the treatment of depression and anxiety. *International Journal of Psychiatry in Medicine, 41*, 15–28.

Carey, S., & Markman, E. M. (1999). Cognitive development. In B. M. Bly & D. E. Rumelhart (Eds.), *Cognitive science* (pp. 201–254). San Diego: Academic Press.

Carlo, G., Koller, S. H., Eisenberg, N., Da Silva, M., & Frohlich, C. (1996). A cross-national study on the relations among prosocial moral reasoning, gender role orientations, and prosocial behaviors. *Developmental Psychology, 32*, 231–240.

Carlo, G., Mestre, M. V., Samper, P., Tur, A., & Armenta, B. E. (2011). The longitudinal relations among dimensions of parenting styles, sympathy, prosocial moral reasoning, and prosocial behaviors. *International Journal of Behavioral Development, 35*, 116–124.

Carlson, S. M., & Meltzoff, A. N. (2008). Bilingual experience and executive functioning in young children. *Developmental Science, 11*, 282–298.

Carlson, V. J., & Harwood, R. L. (2003). Attachment, culture, and the caregiving system: The cultural patterning of everyday experiences among Anglo and Puerto Rican mother–infant pairs. *Infant Mental Health Journal, 24*, 53–73.

Carnelley, K. B., Wortman, C. B., Bolger, N., & Burke, C. T. (2006). The time course of grief reactions to spousal loss: Evidence from a national probability sample. *Journal of Personality and Social Psychology, 91*, 476–492.

Carnes, B. A., Olshansky, S. J., & Hayflick, L. (2013). Can human biology allow most of us to become centenarians? *Journal of Gerontology, 68A*, 136–142.

Carpenter, M., Akhtar, N., & Tomasello, M. (1998). Fourteen- through eighteen-month-old infants differentially imitate intentional and accidental actions. *Infant Behavior and Development, 21*, 315–330.

Carr, D. (2003). A "good death" for whom? Quality of spouse's death and psychological distress among older widowed persons. *Journal of Health and Social Behavior, 44*, 215–232.

Carr, D. (2004). Psychological well-being across three cohorts: A response to shifting work–family opportunities and expectations? In O. G. Brim, C. D. Ryff & R. C. Kessler (Eds.), *How healthy are we? A national study of well-being at midlife* (pp. 452–484). Chicago: University of Chicago Press.

Carr, D., House, J. S., Wortman, C., Nesse, R., & Kessler, R. C. (2001). Psychological adjustment to sudden and anticipated spousal loss among older widowed persons. *Journal of Gerontology, 56B*, S237–S248.

Carroll, D., Phillips, A. C., Hunt, K., & Der, G. (2007). Symptoms of depression and cardiovascular reactions to acute psychological stress: Evidence from a population study. *Biological Psychology, 75*, 68–74.

Carroll, J. B. (2005). The three-stratum theory of cognitive abilities. In D. P. Flanagan & P. L. Harrison (Eds.), *Contemporary intellectual assessment: Theories, tests, and issues* (2nd ed., pp. 69–76). New York: Guilford.

Carroll, J. S., Badger S., Willoughby, B. J., Nelson, L. J., Madsen, S. D., & Barry, C. M. (2009). Ready or not?: Criteria for marriage readiness among emerging adults. *Journal of Adolescent Research, 24*, 349–375.

Carstensen, L. L. (2006). The influence of sense of time on human development. *Science, 312*, 1913–1915.

Carstensen, L. L., Fung, H. H., & Charles, S. T. (2003). Socioemotional selectivity theory and the regulation of emotion in the second half of life. *Motivation and Emotion, 27*, 103–123.

Carstensen, L. L., Turan, B., Scheibe, S., Ram, N., Ersner-Hershfield, H., Samanez-Larkin, G. R., et al.

(2011). Emotional experience improves with age: Evidence based on over 10 years of experience sampling. *Psychology and Aging, 26*, 21–33.

Carter, C. S., Hofer, T., Seo, A. Y., & Leeuwenburgh, C. (2007). Molecular mechanisms of life- and health-span extension: Role of calorie restriction and exercise intervention. *Applied Physiology, Nutrition, and Metabolism, 32*, 954–966.

Carver, C. S. (2011). Coping. In R. J. Contrada & A. Baum (Eds.), *Handbook of stress science: Biology, psychology, and health* (pp. 221–245). New York: Springer.

Carver, K., Joyner, K., & Udry, J. R. (2003). National estimates of adolescent romantic relationships. In P. Florsheim (Ed.), *Adolescent romantic relations and sexual behavior: Theory, research, and practical implications* (pp. 23–56). Mahwah, NJ: Erlbaum.

Carver, P. R., Egan, S. K., & Perry, D. G. (2004). Children who question their heterosexuality. *Developmental Psychology, 40*, 43–53.

Casalis, S., & Cole, P. (2009). On the relationship between morphological and phonological awareness: Effects of training in kindergarten and in first-grade reading. *First Language, 29*, 113–142.

Casas, J. F., Weigel, S. M., Crick, N. R., Ostrov, J. M., Woods, K. E., Yeh, E. A. J., & Huddleston-Casas, C. A. (2006). Early parenting and children's relational and physical aggression in the preschool and home contexts. *Applied Developmental Psychology, 27*, 209–227.

Casasola, M., Cohen, L. B., & Chiarello, E. (2003). Six-month-old infants' categorization of containment spatial relations. *Child Development, 74*, 679–693.

Casavant, M. J., Blake, K., Griffith, J., Yates, A., & Copley, L. M. (2007). Consequences of use of anabolic androgenic steroids. *Pediatric Clinics of North America, 54*, 677–690.

Case, R. (1996). Introduction: Reconceptualizing the nature of children's conceptual structures and their development in middle childhood. In R. Case & Y. Okamoto (Eds.), The role of central conceptual structures in the development of children's thought. *Monographs of the Society for Research in Child Development, 246*(61, Serial No. 246), pp. 1–26.

Case, R. (1998). The development of central conceptual structures. In D. Kuhn & R. Siegler (Eds.), *Handbook of child psychology: Vol. 2. Cognition, perception, and language* (5th ed., pp. 745–800). New York: Wiley.

Case, R., & Okamoto, Y. (Eds.). (1996). The role of central conceptual structures in the development of children's thought. *Monographs of the Society for Research in Child Development, 61*(1–2, Serial No. 246).

Caserta, M., Lund, D., Utz, R., & de Vries, B. (2009). Stress-related growth among the recently bereaved. *Aging and Mental Health, 13*, 463–476.

Caserta, M. S., Lund, D. A., & Obray, S. J. (2004). Promoting self-care and daily living skills among older widows and widowers: Evidence from the Pathfinders Demonstration Project. *Omega, 49*, 217–236.

Casper, L. M., & Smith, K. E. (2002). Dispelling the myths: Self-care, class, and race. *Journal of Family Issues, 23*, 716–727.

Caspi, A., Elder, G. H., Jr., & Bem, D. J. (1987). Moving against the world: Life-course patterns of explosive children. *Developmental Psychology, 23*, 308–313.

Caspi, A., Elder, G. H., Jr., & Bem, D. J. (1988). Moving away from the world: Life-course patterns of shy children. *Developmental Psychology, 24*, 824–831.

Caspi, A., Harrington, H., Milne, B., Amell, J. W., Theodore, R. F., & Moffitt, T. E. (2003). Children's behavioral styles at age 3 are linked to their adult personality traits at age 26. *Journal of Personality, 71*, 495–513.

Caspi, A., Lynam, D., Moffitt, T. E., & Silva, P. A. (1993). Unraveling girls' delinquency: Biological, dispositional, and contextual contributions to adolescent misbehavior. *Developmental Psychology, 29,* 19–30.

Caspi, A., McClay, J., Moffitt, T. E., Mill, J., Martin, J., & Craig, I. W. (2002). Role of genotype in the cycle of violence in maltreated children. *Science, 297,* 851–854.

Caspi, A., Moffitt, T. E., Morgan, J., Rutter, M., Taylor, A., Kim-Cohen, J., & Polo-Tomas, M. (2004). Maternal expressed emotion predicts children's antisocial behavior problems: Using monozygotic-twin differences to identify environmental effects on behavioral development. *Developmental Psychology, 40,* 149–161.

Caspi, A., & Roberts, B. W. (2001). Personality development across the life course: The argument for change and continuity. *Psychological Inquiry, 12,* 49–66.

Caspi, A., & Shiner, R. L. (2006). Personality development. In N. Eisenberg (Ed.), *Handbook of child psychology: Vol. 3. Social, emotional, and personality development* (6th ed., pp. 300–365). Hoboken, NJ: Wiley.

Cassia, V. M., Turati, C., & Simion, F. (2004). Can a nonspecific bias toward top-heavy patterns explain newborns' face preference? *Psychological Science, 15,* 379–383.

Cassidy, J. (2001). Adult romantic attachments: A developmental perspective on individual differences. *Review of General Psychology, 4,* 111–131.

Cassidy, J., & Berlin, L. J. (1994). The insecure/ambivalent pattern of attachment: Theory and research. *Child Development, 65,* 971–991.

Castel, A. D., McGillivray, S., & Friedman, M. C. (2011). Metamemory and memory efficiency in older adults: Learning about the benefits of priority processing and value-directed remembering. In M. Naveh-Benjamin & N. Ohta (Eds.), *Memory and aging: Current issues and future directions* (pp. 245–270). New York: Psychology Press.

Castillo, E. M., & Comstock, R. D. (2007). Prevalence of use of performance-enhancing substances among United States adolescents. *Pediatric Clinics of North America, 54,* 663–675.

Caton, D., Corry, M. P., Frigoletto, F. D., Hokins, D. P., Liberman, E., & Mayberry, L. (2002). The nature and management of labor pain: Executive summary. *American Journal of Obstetrics and Gynecology, 186,* S1–S15.

Cauley, J. A. (2011). Defining ethnic and racial differences in osteoporosis and fragility fractures. *Clinical Orthopedics and Related Research, 469,* 1891–1899.

Ceci, S. J. (1991). How much does schooling influence general intelligence and its cognitive components? A reassessment of the evidence. *Developmental Psychology, 27,* 703–722.

Ceci, S. J. (1999). Schooling and intelligence. In S. J. Ceci & W. M. Williams (Eds.), *The nature–nurture debate: The essential readings* (pp. 168–175). Oxford, UK: Blackwell.

Ceci, S. J., Rosenblum, T. B., & Kumpf, M. (1998). The shrinking gap between high- and low-scoring groups: Current trends and possible causes. In U. Neisser (Ed.), *The rising curve* (pp. 287–302). Washington, DC: American Psychological Association.

Ceci, S. J., & Williams, W. M. (1997). Schooling, intelligence, and income. *American Psychologist, 52,* 1051–1058.

Ceci, S. J., & Williams, W. M. (2010). *The mathematics of sex: How biology and society conspire to limit talented women and girls.* New York: Oxford University Press.

Cecil, J. E., Watt, P., Murrie, I. S. L., Wrieden, W., Wallis, D. J., Hetherington, M. M., Bolton-Smith, C., & Palmer, C. N. A. (2005). Childhood obesity and socioeconomic status: A novel role for height

growth limitation. *International Journal of Obesity, 29,* 1199–1203.

Center for Communication and Social Policy. (Ed.). (1998). *National Television Violence Study* (Vol. 2). Newbury Park, CA: Sage.

Center for Hearing and Communication. (2012). *Facts about hearing loss.* Retrieved from www.chchearing.org/about-hearing-loss/facts-about-hearing-loss

Center to Advance Palliative Care. (2012). *Growth of palliative care in U.S. hospitals: 2012 snapshot.* Retrieved from www.capc.org/capc-growthanalysis-snapshot-2011.pdf

Centers for Disease Control and Prevention. (2007). *School Health Policies and Programs Study.* Atlanta, GA: Author.

Centers for Disease Control and Prevention. (2010). *Hip fractures in older adults.* Retrieved from www.cdc.gov/homeandrecreationalsafety/falls/adulthipfx.html

Centers for Disease Control and Prevention. (2011a). *Breastfeeding report card—United States 2011.* Retrieved from www.cdc.gov/breastfeeding/pdf/2011BreastfeedingReportCard.pdf

Centers for Disease Control and Prevention. (2011b). *HIV Surveillance Report: Diagnoses of HIV infection and AIDS in the United States and dependent areas, 2009.* Atlanta, GA: U.S. Department of Health and Human Services.

Centers for Disease Control and Prevention. (2011c). *Sexually transmitted disease surveillance 2010.* Atlanta, GA: U.S. Department of Health and Human Services.

Centers for Disease Control and Prevention. (2011d). *2009 assisted reproductive technology success rates: National summary and fertility clinic reports.* Atlanta, GA: Author.

Centers for Disease Control and Prevention. (2012a). *CDC vital signs: Child injury.* Retrieved from www.cdc.gov/vitalsigns/ChildInjury

Centers for Disease Control and Prevention. (2012b). Vital signs: Current cigarette smoking among adults aged ≥18 years—United States, 2005–2010. *Morbidity and Mortality Weekly Report, 60,* 1207–1212.

Centers for Disease Control and Prevention. (2013). *Multiple cause of death, 1999–2010.* Retrieved from wonder.cdc.gov/wonder/help/mcd.html

Centers for Medicare and Medicaid Services. (2012a). *National health expenditure projections.* Retrieved from www.cms.gov/Research-Statistics-Data-and-Systems/Statistics-Trends-and-Reports/NationalHealthExpendData/NationalHealthAccountsProjected.html

Centers for Medicare and Medicaid Services. (2012b). *Nursing home data compendium: 2012 edition.* Retrieved from www.cms.gov/Medicare/Provider-Enrollment-and-Certification/CertificationandComplianc/downloads/nursinghomedatacompendium_508.pdf

Cerella, J. (1990). Aging and information processing rate. In J. E. Birren & K. W. Schaie (Eds.), *Handbook of the psychology of aging* (3rd ed.), (pp. 201–221). San Diego: Academic Press.

Cernoch, J. M., & Porter, R. H. (1985). Recognition of maternal axillary odors by infants. *Child Development 56,* 1593–1598.

Cevenini, E., Invidia, L., Lescai, F., Salvioli, S., Tieri, P., Castellani, G., & Franceschi, G. (2008). Human models of aging and longevity. *Expert Opinion on Biological Therapy, 8,* 1393–1405.

CFAH (Center for Advancement of Health). (2003). *Report on Phase 1 of the Grief Research Gaps, Needs and Actions Project.* Washington, DC: Author.

Chakravarty, E. F., Hubert, H. B., Krishnan, E., Bruce, B. B., Lingala, V. B., & Fries, J. F. (2012). Lifestyle risk factors predict disability and death in healthy aging adults. *American Journal of Medicine, 125,* 190–197.

Chalabaev, A., Sarrazin, P., & Fontayne, P. (2009). Stereotype endorsement and perceived ability as mediators of the girls' gender orientation–soccer performance relationship. *Psychology of Sport and Exercise, 10,* 297–299.

Chamberlain, P. (2003). Antisocial behavior and delinquency in girls. In P. Chamberlain (Ed.), *Treating chronic juvenile offenders* (pp. 109–127). Washington, DC: American Psychological Association.

Champion, T. B. (2003a). "A matter of vocabulary": Performances of low-income African-American Head Start children on the Peabody Picture Vocabulary Test. *Communication Disorders Quarterly, 24,* 121–127.

Champion, T. B. (2003b). *Understanding storytelling among African-American children: A journey from Africa to America.* Mahwah, NJ: Erlbaum.

Chan, A., Meints, K., Lieven, E., & Tomasello, M. (2010). Young children's comprehension of English SVO word order revisited: Testing the same children in act-out and intermodal preferential looking tasks. *Cognitive Development, 25,* 30–45.

Chan, L. K. S., & Moore, P. J. (2006). Development of attributional beliefs and strategic knowledge in years 5–9: A longitudinal analysis. *Educational Psychology, 26,* 161–185.

Chan, R. W., Raboy, B., & Patterson, C. J. (1998). Psychosocial adjustment among children conceived via donor insemination by lesbian and heterosexual mothers. *Child Development, 69,* 443–457.

Chan, S. M. (2010). Aggressive behaviour in early elementary school children: Relations to authoritarian parenting, children's negative emotionality and coping strategies. *Early Child Development and Care, 180,* 1253–1269.

Chandola, T., & Marmot, M. G. (2011). Socioeconomic status and stress. In R. J. Contrada & A. Baum (Eds.), *Handbook of stress science: Biology, psychology, and health* (pp. 185–193). New York: Springer.

Chandra, A., Martino, S. C., Collins, R. L., Elliott, M. N., Berry, S. H., Kanouse, D. E., & Miu, A. (2008). Does watching sex on television predict teen pregnancy? Findings from a national longitudinal survey of youth. *Pediatrics, 122,* 1047–1054.

Chang, E., Wilber, K. H., & Silverstein, M. (2010). The effects of childlessness on the care and psychological well-being of older adults with disabilities. *Aging and Mental Health, 14,* 712–719.

Chang, L., Schwartz, D., Dodge, D. A., & McBride-Chang, C. (2003). Harsh parenting in relation to child emotion regulation and aggression. *Journal of Family Psychology, 17,* 598–606.

Chao, R. K. (1994). Beyond parental control and authoritarian parenting style: Understanding Chinese parenting through the cultural notion of training. *Child Development, 65,* 1111–1119.

Chao, R. K., & Good, G. E. (2004). Nontraditional students' perspectives on college education: A qualitative study. *Journal of College Counseling, 7,* 5–12.

Chao, R. K., & Tseng, V. (2002). Parenting of Asians. In M. H. Bornstein (Ed.), *Handbook of parenting: Vol. 4* (2nd ed., pp. 59–94). Mahwah, NJ: Erlbaum.

Charles, S. T. (2010). Strength and vulnerability integration: A model of emotional well-being across adulthood. *Psychological Bulletin, 136,* 1068–1091.

Charles, S. T. (2011). Emotional experience and regulation in later life. In K. W. Schaie & S. L. Willis (Eds.), *Handbook of the psychology of aging* (7th ed., pp. 295–310). San Diego, CA: Academic Press.

Charles, S. T., & Carstensen, L. L. (2009). Socio-emotional selectivity theory. In H. Reis & S. Sprecher (Eds.), *Encyclopedia of human relationships* (pp. 1578–1581). Thousand Oaks, CA: Sage.

Charles, S. T., & Carstensen, L. L. (2010). Social and emotional aging. *Annual Review of Psychology, 61,* 383–409.

Charman, T., Baron-Cohen, S., Swettenham, J., Baird, G., Cox, A., & Drew, A. (2001). Testing joint attention, imitation, and play as infancy precursors to language and theory of mind. *Cognitive Development, 15,* 481–49.

Charman, W. N. (2008). The eye in focus: Accommodation and presbyopia. *Optometry, 91,* 207–225.

Charpak, N., Ruiz-Peláez, J. G., & Figueroa, Z. (2005). Influence of feeding patterns and other factors on early somatic growth of healthy, preterm infants in home-based kangaroo mother care: A cohort study. *Journal of Pediatric Gastroenterology and Nutrition, 41,* 430–437.

Chase-Lansdale, P. L., Gordon, R., Brooks-Gunn, J., & Klebanov, P. K. (1997). Neighborhood and family influences on the intellectual and behavioral competence of preschool and early school-age children. In J. Brooks-Gunn, G. Duncan, & J. L. Aber (Eds.), *Neighborhood poverty: Context and consequences for development* (pp. 79–118). New York: Russell Sage Foundation.

Chauhan, G. S., Shastri, J., & Mohite, P. (2005). Development of gender constancy in preschoolers. *Psychological Studies, 50,* 62–71.

Chavajay, P., & Rogoff, B. (1999). Cultural variation in management of attention by children and their caregivers. *Developmental Psychology, 35,* 1079–1090.

Chavajay, P., & Rogoff, B. (2002). Schooling and traditional collaborative social organization of problem solving by Mayan mothers and children. *Developmental Psychology, 38,* 55–66.

Chawarska, K., & Shic, F. (2009). Looking but not seeing: Atypical visual scanning and recognition of faces in 2- and 4-year-old children with autism spectrum disorder. *Journal of Autism and Developmental Disorders, 39,* 1663–1672.

Cheadle, J. E., & Amato, P. R. (2011). A quantitative assessment of Lareau's qualitative conclusions about class, race, and parenting. *Journal of Family Issues, 32,* 679–706.

Cheah, C. S. L., Leung, C. Y. Y., Tahseen, M., & Schultz, D. (2009). Authoritative parenting among immigrant Chinese mothers of preschoolers. *Journal of Family Psychology, 23,* 311–320.

Checkley, W., Epstein, L. D., Gilman, R. H., Cabrera, L., & Black, R. E. (2003). Effects of acute diarrhea on linear growth in Peruvian children. *American Journal of Epidemiology, 157,* 166–175.

Chen, E. S. L., & Rao, N. (2011). Gender socialization in Chinese kindergartens: Teachers' contributions. *Sex Roles, 64,* 103–116.

Chen, J. J. (2005). Relation of academic support from parents, teachers, and peers to Hong Kong adolescents' academic achievement: The mediating role of academic engagement. *Genetic, Social, and General Psychology Monographs, 131,* 77–127.

Chen, J. J., Howard, K. S., & Brooks-Gunn, J. (2011). How do neighborhoods matter across the life span? In K. L. Fingerman, C. A. Berg, J. Smith, & T. C. Antonucci (Eds.), *Handbook of life-span development* (pp. 805–836). New York: Springer.

Chen, R. (2012). Institutional characteristics and college student dropout risks: A multilevel event history analysis. *Research in Higher Education, 53,* 487–505.

Chen, X., & French, D. C. (2008). Children's social competence in cultural context. *Annual Review of Psychology, 59,* 591–616.

Chen, X., Wang, L., & DeSouza, A. (2006). Temperament, socioemotional functioning, and peer relationships in Chinese and North American children. In X. Chen, D. C. French, & B. H. Schneider (Eds.), *Peer relationships in cultural context* (pp. 123–147). New York: Cambridge University Press.

Chen, X., Wu, H., Chen, H., Wang, L., & Cen, G. (2001). Parenting practices and aggressive behavior in Chinese children. *Parenting: Science and Practice, 1,* 159–184.

Chen, Y.-C., Yu, M.-L., Rogan, W., Gladen, B., & Hsu, C.-C. (1994). A 6-year follow-up of behavior and activity disorders in the Taiwan Yu-cheng children. *American Journal of Public Health, 84,* 415–421.

Chen, Y.-J., & Hsu, C.-C. (1994). Effects of prenatal exposure to PCBs on the neurological function of children: A neuropsychological and neurophysiological study. *Developmental Medicine and Child Neurology, 36,* 312–320.

Cherlin, A. J. (2009). *The marriage-go-round.* New York: Knopf.

Cherlin, E. J., Barry, C. L., Prigerson, H. G., Schulman-Green, D., Johnson-Hurzeler, R., Kasl, S. V., & Bradley, E. H. (2007). Bereavement services for family caregivers: How often used, why, and why not. *Journal of Palliative Medicine, 10,* 148–158.

Chess, S., & Thomas, A. (1984). *Origins and evolution of behavior disorders.* New York: Brunner/Mazel.

Cheung, F. M., & Halpern, D. F. (2010). Women at the top: Powerful leaders define success as work + family in a culture of gender. *American Psychologist, 65,* 182–193.

Chhin, C. S., Bleeker, M. M., & Jacobs, J. E. (2008). Gender-typed occupational choices: The long-term impact of parents' beliefs and expectations. In H. M. G. Watt & J. S. Eccles (Eds.), *Gender and occupational outcomes: Longitudinal assessments of individual, social, and cultural influences* (pp. 215–234). Washington, DC: American Psychological Association.

Chi, M. T. H. (2006). Laboratory methods for assessing experts' and novices' knowledge. In K. A. Ericsson, N. Charness, P. J. Feltovich, & R. R. Hoffman (Eds.), *The Cambridge handbook of expertise and expert performance* (pp. 167–184). New York: Cambridge University Press.

Chi, M. T. H., Glaser, R., & Farr, M. J. (Eds.). (1988). *The nature of expertise.* Hillsdale, NJ: Erlbaum.

Child Trends. (2007). *Late or no prenatal care.* Retrieved from www.childtrendsdatabank.org/indicators/25PrenatalCare.cfm

Child Trends. (2011). *Teen births.* Retrieved from www.childtrendsdatabank.org/?q=node/52

Child Trends. (2012). *Late or no prenatal care.* Retrieved from www.childtrendsdatabank.org/sites/default/files/25_Prenatal_Care.pdf

Chin, T., & Phillips, M. (2004). Social reproduction and child-rearing practices: Social class, children's agency, and the summer activity gap. *Sociology of Education, 77*(3), 185–210.

Chinn, C. A., & Malhotra, B. A. (2002). Children's responses to anomalous scientific data: How is conceptual change impeded? *Journal of Educational Psychology, 94,* 327–343.

Choi, J., Fauce, S. R., & Effros, R. B. (2008). Reduced telomerase activity in human T lymphocytes exposed to cortisol. *Brain, Behavior, and Immunity, 22,* 600–605.

Choi, N., & Kim, J. (2011). The effect of time volunteering and charitable donations in later life on psychological well-being. *Ageing and Society, 31,* 590–611.

Chomsky, C. (1969). *The acquisition of syntax in children from five to ten.* Cambridge, MA: MIT Press.

Chomsky, N. (1957). *Syntactic structures.* The Hague: Mouton.

Chomtho, S., Wells, J. C., Williams, J. E., Davies, P. S., Lucas, A., & Fewtrell, M. S. (2008). Infant growth and later body composition: Evidence from the 4-component model. *American Journal of Clinical Nutrition, 87,* 1776–1784.

Chouinard, M. M. (2007). Children's questions: A mechanism for cognitive development. *Monographs of the Society for Research in Child Development, 72*(1, Serial No. 286).

Chouinard, M. M., & Clark, E. V. (2003). Adult reformulations of child errors as negative evidence. *Journal of Child Language, 30,* 637–669.

Christ, G. H., Siegel, K., & Christ, A. E. (2002). "It never really hit me . . . until it actually happened." *Journal of the American Medical Association, 288,* 1269–1278.

Christakis, D. A., Zimmerman, F. J., DiGiuseppe, D. L., & McCarty, C. A. (2004). Early television exposure and subsequent attentional problems in children. *Pediatrics, 113,* 708–713.

Christensen, A.-D., & Larsen, J. E. (2008). Gender, class, and family: Men and gender equality in a Danish context. *Social Politics: International Studies in Gender, State and Society, 15,* 53–78.

Christenson, S. L., & Thurlow, M. L. (2004). School dropouts: Prevention considerations, interventions, and challenges. *Current Directions in Psychological Science, 13,* 36–39.

Christiansen, M. H., & Chater, N. (2008). Language as shaped by the brain. *Behavioral and Brain Sciences, 31,* 489–558.

Chu, J., Zhou, C. C., Lu, N., Zhang, X., & Dong, F. T. (2008). Genetic variants in three genes and smoking show strong associations with susceptibility to exudative age-related macular degeneration in a Chinese population. *Chinese Medical Journal, 121,* 2525–2533.

Chudley, A. E., Conry, J., Cook, J. L., Loock, C., Rosales, T., & LeBlanc, N. (2005). Fetal alcohol spectrum disorder: Canadian guidelines for diagnosis. *Canadian Medical Association Journal, 172,* S1–S21.

Chumlea, W. C., Schubert, C. M., Roche, A. F., Kulin, H. E., Lee, P. A., Himes, J. H., & Sun, S. S. (2003). Age at menarche and racial comparisons in U.S. girls. *Pediatrics, 111,* 110–113.

Chung, H. L., Mulvey, E. P., & Steinberg, L. (2011). Understanding the school outcomes of juvenile offenders: An exploration of neighborhood influences and motivational resources. *Journal of Youth and Adolescence, 40,* 1025–1038.

Church, E. (2004). *Understanding stepmothers: Women share their struggles, successes, and insights.* Toronto: HarperCollins.

CIA (Central Intelligence Agency). (2012). *World fact book.* Retrieved from www.cia.gov/library/publications/download/download-2012/index.html

Cicchetti, D. (2007). Intervention and policy implications of research on neurobiological functioning in maltreated children. In J. L. Aber, S. J. Bishop-Josef, S. M. Jones, K. T. McLearn, & D. A. Phillips (Eds.), *Child development and social policy* (pp. 167–184). Washington, DC: American Psychological Association.

Cicirelli, V. G. (1995). *Sibling relationships across the life span.* New York: Plenum.

Cicirelli, V. G. (2001). Personal meanings of death in older adults and young adults in relation to their fears of death. *Death Studies, 25,* 663–683.

Cicirelli, V. G. (2002). *Older adults' views on death.* New York: Springer.

Cillessen, A. H. N., & Bellmore, A. D. (2004). Social skills and interpersonal perception in early and middle childhood. In P. K. Smith & C. H. Hart (Eds.), *Blackwell handbook of childhood social development* (pp. 355–374). Malden, MA: Blackwell.

Cipriano, E. A., & Stifter, C. A. (2010). Predicting preschool effortful control from toddler temperament and parenting behavior. *Journal of Applied Developmental Psychology, 31,* 221–230.

Clark, C. A., Woodward, L. J., Horwood, L. J., & Moor, S. (2008). Development of emotional and behavioral regulation in children born extremely preterm and very preterm: Biological and social influences. *Child Development, 79,* 1444–1462.

Clark, K. E., & Ladd, G. W. (2000). Connectedness and autonomy support in parent–child relationships: Links to children's socio-emotional orientation and peer relationships. *Developmental Psychology, 36,* 485–498.

Clarke, B. L., & Khosla, S. (2010). Physiology of bone loss. *Radiologic Clinics of North America, 48,* 483–495.

Clarke, L. H. (2005). Remarriage in later life: Older women's negotiations of power, resources and domestic labor. *Journal of Women and Aging, 17,* 21–41.

Clarke, P., & Smith, J. (2011). Aging in a cultural context: Cross-national differences in disability and the moderating role of personal control among older adults in the United States and England. *Journal of Gerontology, 66B,* 457–467.

Clarkson, T. W., Magos, L., & Myers, G. J. (2003). The toxicology of mercury—current exposures and clinical manifestations. *New England Journal of Medicine, 349,* 1731–1737.

Clarke-Stewart, K. A., & Brentano, C. (2006). *Divorce: Causes and consequences.* New Haven: Yale University Press.

Clarke-Stewart, K. A., & Hayward, C. (1996). Advantages of father custody and contact for the psychological well-being of school-age children. *Journal of Applied Developmental Psychology, 17,* 239–270.

Claxton, A., O'Rourke, N., Smith, J. Z., & DeLongis, A. (2011). Personality traits and marital satisfaction within enduring relationships: An intra-couple discrepancy approach. *Journal of Social and Personal Relationships, 29,* 375–396.

Clay, R. A. (2009). Mini-multitaskers. *Monitor on Psychology, 40*(2), 38–40.

Clearfield, M. W., & Nelson, N. M. (2006). Sex differences in mothers' speech and play behavior with 6-, 9-, and 14-month-old infants. *Sex Roles, 54,* 127–137.

Clearfield, M. W., Obsborn, C. N., & Mullen, M. (2008). Learning by looking: Infants' social looking behavior across the transition from crawling to walking. *Journal of Experimental Child Psychology, 100,* 297–307.

Clegg, L. X., Reichman, M. E., Miller, B. A., Hankey, B. F., Singh, G. K., Lin, Y. D., et al. (2009). Impact of socioeconomic status on cancer incidence and stage at diagnosis: Selected findings from the surveillance, epidemiology, and end results: National Longitudinal Mortality Study. *Cancer Causes and Control, 20,* 417–435.

Clements, D. H., & Sarama, J. (2003). Young children and technology: What does the research say? *Young Children, 58*(6), 34–40.

Cleveland, E. S., & Reese, E. (2005). Maternal structure and autonomy support in conversations about the past: Contributions to children's autobiographical memory. *Developmental Psychology, 41,* 376–388.

Clinchy, B. M. (2002). Revisiting women's ways of knowing. In B. K. Hofer & P. R. Pintrich (Eds.), *Personal epistemology: The psychological beliefs about knowledge and knowing* (pp. 63–87). Mahwah, NJ: Erlbaum.

Clingempeel, W. G., & Henggeler, S. W. (2003). Aggressive juvenile offenders transitioning into emerging adulthood: Factors discriminating persistors and desistors. *American Journal of Orthopsychiatry, 73,* 310–323.

Coatsworth, J. D., Sharp, E. H., Palen, L., Darling, N., Cumsille, P., & Marta, M. (2005). Exploring adolescent self-defining leisure activities and identity experiences across three countries. *International Journal of Behavioral Development, 29,* 361–370.

Cohen, L. B. (2003). Commentary on Part I: Unresolved issues in infant categorization. In D. H. Rakison & L. M. Oakes (Eds.), *Early category and concept development: Making sense of the blooming, buzzing confusion* (pp. 193–209). New York: Oxford University Press.

Cohen, L. B. (2010). A bottom-up approach to infant perception and cognition: A summary of evidence and discussion of issues. In S. P. Johnson (Ed.), *Neoconstructivism: The new science of cognitive development* (pp. 335–346). New York: Oxford University Press.

Cohen, L. B., & Brunt, J. (2009). Early word learning and categorization: Methodological issues and recent empirical evidence. In J. Colombo, P. McCardle, & L. Freund (Eds.), *Infant pathways to language: Methods, models, and research disorders* (pp. 245–266). New York: Psychology Press.

Cohen, L. B., & Cashon, C. H. (2006). Infant cognition. In D. Kuhn & R. Siegler (Eds.), *Handbook of child psychology: Vol. 2. Cognition, perception, and language* (6th ed., pp. 214–251). Hoboken, NJ: Wiley.

Cohen-Bendahan, C. C. C., van de Beek, C., & Berenbaum, S. A. (2005). Prenatal sex hormones effects on child and adult sex-typed behavior: Methods and findings. *Neuroscience and Biobehavioral Reviews, 29,* 353–384.

Cohen-Shalev, A. (1986). Artistic creativity across the adult life span: An alternative approach. *Interchange, 17*(4), 1–16.

Cohler, B. J., & Hostetler, A. J. (2007). Gay lives in the Third Age: Possibilities and paradoxes. In J. B. James & P. Wink (Eds.), *Annual review of gerontology and geriatrics* (Vol. 26, pp. 193–209). New York: Springer.

Coie, J. D., Dodge, K. A., & Coppotelli, H. (1982). Dimensions and types of social status: A cross-age perspective. *Developmental Psychology, 18,* 557–570.

Coke, M. M. (1992). Correlates of life satisfaction among elderly African Americans. *Journal of Gerontology, 47,* P316–P320.

Coker, A. D. (2003). African American female adult learners: Motivations, challenges, and coping strategies. *Journal of Black Studies, 33,* 654–674.

Colby, A., Kohlberg, L., Gibbs, J., & Lieberman, M. (1983). A longitudinal study of moral judgment. *Monographs of the Society for Research in Child Development, 48*(1–2, Serial No. 200).

Colcombe, S. J., Erickson, K. I., Scalf, P. E., Kim, J. S., Prakash, R., & McAuley, E. (2006). Aerobic exercise training increases brain volume in aging humans. *Journal of Gerontology, 61A,* 1166–1170.

Colcombe, S. J., Kramer, A. F., Erickson, K. I., Scalf, P., McAuley, E., & Cohen, N. J. (2004). Cardiovascular fitness, cortical plasticity, and aging. *Proceedings of the National Academy of Sciences, 101,* 3316–3321.

Cole, D. A., Martin, J. M., Peeke, L. A., Seroczynski, A. D., & Fier, J. (1999). Children's over- and underestimation of academic competence: A longitudinal study of gender differences, depression, and anxiety. *Child Development, 70,* 459–473.

Cole, E. R., & Stewart, A. J. (1996). Meanings of political participation among black and white women: Political identity and social responsibility. *Journal of Personality and Social Psychology, 71,* 130–140.

Cole, M. (1990). Cognitive development and formal schooling: The evidence from cross-cultural research. In L. C. Moll (Ed.), *Vygotsky and education* (pp. 89–110). New York: Cambridge University Press.

Cole, P. M., Armstrong, L. M., & Pemberton, C. K. (2010). The role of language in the development of emotion regulation. In S. D. Calkins & M. A. Bell (Eds.), *Child development at the intersection of emotion and cognition* (pp. 59–77). Washington, DC: American Psychological Association.

Coleman, M., Ganong, L., & Leon, K. (2006). Divorce and postdivorce relationships. In A. L. Vangelisti & D. Perlman (Eds.), *The Cambridge handbook of personal relationships* (pp. 157–173). New York: Cambridge University Press.

Coleman, P. G., Ivani-Chalian, C., & Robinson, M. (2004). Religious attitudes among British older people: Stability and change in a 20-year longitudinal study. *Ageing and Society, 24,* 167–188.

Coles, C. D., Goldstein, F. C., Lynch, M. E., Chen, X., Kable, J. A., Johnson, K. C., et al. (2011). Memory and brain volume in adults prenatally exposed to alcohol. *Brain and Cognition, 75,* 67–77.

Coles, L. (2004). Demography of human super-centenarians. *Journal of Gerontology, 59A,* 579–586.

Coley, R. L., Morris, J. E., & Hernandez, D. (2004). Out-of-school care and problem behavior trajectories among low-income adolescents: Individual, family, and neighborhood characteristics as added risks. *Child Development, 75,* 948–965.

Coley, R. L., Votruba-Drzal, E., & Schindler, H. S. (2009). Fathers' and mothers' parenting predicting and responding to adolescent sexual risk behaviors. *Child Development, 80,* 808–827.

Collings, P. (2001). "If you got everything, it's good enough": Perspectives on successful aging in a Canadian Inuit community. *Journal of Cross-Cultural Gerontology, 16,* 127–155.

Collins, N. L., Guichard, A. C., Ford, M. B., & Feeney, B. C. (2006). Responding to need in intimate relationships: Normative processes and individual differences. In M. Mikulincer & G. S. Goodman (Eds.), *Dynamics of romantic love* (pp. 149–189). New York: Guilford.

Collins, W. A., & Laursen, B. (2004). Parent–adolescent relationships and influences. In R. M. Lerner & L. Steinberg (Eds.), *Handbook of adolescent psychology* (2nd ed., pp. 331–361). New York: Wiley.

Collins, W. A., & Madsen, S. D. (2006). Personal relationships in adolescence and early adulthood. In A. L. Vangelisti & D. Perlman (Eds.), *The Cambridge handbook of personal relationships* (pp. 191–209). New York: Cambridge University Press.

Collins, W. A., Madsen, S. D., & Susman-Stillman, A. (2002). Parenting during middle childhood. In M. H. Bornstein (Ed.), *Handbook of parenting: Vol. 1* (2nd ed., pp. 73–101). Mahwah, NJ: Erlbaum.

Collins, W. A., & van Dulmen, M. (2006a). "The course of true love(s) . . .": Origins and pathways in the development of romantic relationships. In A. Booth & A. Crouter (Eds.), *Romance and sex in adolescence and emerging adulthood: Risks and opportunities* (pp. 63–86). Mahwah, NJ: Erlbaum.

Collins, W. A., & van Dulmen, M. (2006b). Friendships and romantic relationships in emerging adulthood: Continuities and discontinuities. In J. J. Arnett & J. Tanner (Eds.), *Emerging adults in America: Coming of age in the 21st century* (pp. 219–234). Washington, DC: American Psychological Association.

Collins, W. A., Welsh, D. P., & Furman, W. (2009). Adolescent romantic relationships. *Annual Review of Psychology, 60,* 631–652.

Collins, W. K., & Steinberg, L. (2006). Adolescent development in interpersonal context. In N. Eisenberg (Ed.), *Handbook of child psychology: Vol. 3. Social, emotional, and personality development* (6th ed., pp. 1003–1067). Hoboken, NJ: Wiley.

Colman, R. A., Hardy, S. A., Albert, M., Raffaelli, M., & Crockett, L. (2006). Early predictors of self-regulation in middle childhood. *Infant and Child Development, 15,* 421–437.

Colom, R., Escorial, S., Shih, P. C., & Privado, J. (2007). Fluid intelligence, memory span, and temperament difficulties predict academic performance of young adolescents. *Personality and Individual Differences, 42,* 1503–1514.

Colombo, J. (2002). Infant attention grows up: The emergence of a developmental cognitive neuroscience perspective. *Current Directions in Psychological Science, 11,* 196–199.

Colombo, J., Shaddy, D. J., Richman, W. A., Maikranz, J. M., & Blaga, O. M. (2004). The developmental course of habituation in infancy and preschool outcome. *Infancy, 5,* 1–38.

Commission on Adolescent Suicide Prevention. (2005). Targeted youth suicide prevention programs. In D. L. Evans, E. B. Foa, R. E. Gur, H. Hending, & C. P. O'Brien (Eds.), *Treating and preventing adolescent mental health disorders: What we know and what we don't know* (pp. 463–469). New York: Oxford University Press.

Commission on Children at Risk. (2008). Hardwired to connect: The new scientific case for authoritative communities. In K. K. Kline (Ed.), *Authoritative communities: The scientific case for nurturing the whole child* (pp. 3–68). New York: Springer.

Compton, J. I., Cox, E., & Laanan, F. S. (2006). Adult learners in transition. In F. S. Lanaan (Eds.), *New directions for student services* (Vol. 114, pp. 73–800). San Francisco: Jossey-Bass.

Comunian, A. L., & Gielen, U. P. (2000). Sociomoral reflection and prosocial and antisocial behavior: Two Italian studies. *Psychological Reports, 87,* 161–175.

Comunian, A. L., & Gielen, U. P. (2006). Promotion of moral judgment maturity through stimulation of social role-taking and social reflection: An Italian intervention study. *Journal of Moral Education, 35,* 51–69.

Conboy, B. T., & Thal, D. J. (2006). Ties between the lexicon and grammar: Cross-sectional and longitudinal studies of bilingual toddlers. *Child Development, 77,* 712–735.

Conchas, G. Q. (2006). *The color of success: Race and high-achieving urban youth.* New York: Teachers College Press.

Conde-Agudelo, A., Belizan, J. M., and Diaz-Rossello, J. (2011). Kangaroo mother care to reduce morbidity and mortality in low birthweight infants. *Cochrane Database of Systematic Reviews, 3,* CD002771.

Conger, K. J., Stocker, C., & McGuire, S. (2009). Sibling socialization: The effects of stressful life events and experiences. In L. Kramer & K. J. Conger (Eds.), *Siblings as agents of socialization: New directions for child and adolescent development* (No. 126, pp. 44–60). San Francisco: Jossey-Bass.

Conger, R. D., & Donnellan, M. B. (2007). An interactionist perspective on the socioeconomic context of human development. *Annual Review of Psychology, 58,* 175–199.

Connell, M. W., Sheridan, K., & Gardner, H. (2003). On abilities and domains. In R. J. Sternberg & E. Grigorenko (Eds.), *Perspectives on the psychology of abilities, competencies, and expertise* (pp. 126–155). New York: Cambridge University Press.

Conner, D. B., & Cross, D. R. (2003). Longitudinal analysis of the presence, efficacy, and stability of maternal scaffolding during informal problem-solving interactions. *British Journal of Developmental Psychology, 21,* 315–334.

Connidis, I. A. (2010). *Family ties and aging* (2nd ed.). Thousand Oaks, CA: Pine Forge Press.

Connolly, J., Craig, W., Goldberg, A., & Pepler, D. (2004). Mixed-gender groups, dating, and romantic relationships in early adolescence. *Journal of Research on Adolescence, 14,* 185–207.

Connolly, J., & Goldberg, A. (1999). Romantic relationships in adolescence: The role of friends and peers in their emergence and development. In W. Furman, B. B. Brown, & C. Feiring (Eds.), *The development of romantic relationships in adolescence* (pp. 266–290). New York: Cambridge University Press.

Connolly, J. A., & Doyle, A. B. (1984). Relations of social fantasy play to social competence in preschoolers. *Developmental Psychology, 20,* 797–806.

Connor, L. T., Spiro, A., Obler, L. K., & Albert, M. L. (2004). Change in object naming ability during adulthood. *Journal of Gerontology, 59B,* P203–P209.

Conway, C. C., Rancourt, D., Adelman, C. B., Burk, W. J., & Prinstein, M. J. (2011). Depression socialization within friendship groups at the transition to adolescence: The roles of gender and group centrality as moderators of peer influence. *Journal of Abnormal Psychology, 120,* 857–867.

Conway, L. (2007, April 5). Drop the Barbie: Ken Zucker's reparatist treatment of gender-variant children. *Trans News Updates.* Retrieved from ai.eecs.umich.edu/people/conway/TS/News/Drop%20the%20Barbie.htm

Conway, M. A., Wang, Q., Hanyu, K., & Haque, S. (2005). A cross-cultural investigation of autobiographical memory. On the universality and cultural variation of the reminiscence bump. *Journal of Cross-Cultural Psychology, 36,* 739–749.

Conwell, Y., Duberstein, P. R., Hirsch, J., & Conner, K. R. (2010). Health status and suicide in the second half of life. *Geriatric Psychiatry, 25,* 371–379.

Conwell, Y., Van Orden, K., & Caine, E. D. (2011). Suicide in older adults. *Psychiatric Clinics of North America, 34,* 451–468.

Cook, C. R., Williams, K. R., Guerra, N. G., & Kim, T. E. (2010). Variability in the prevalence of bullying and victimization: A cross-national and methodological analysis. In S. R. Jimerson, S. M. Swearer, & D. L. Espelage (Eds.), *Handbook of bullying in schools: An international perspective* (pp. 347–362). New York: Routledge.

Cooke, L. P. (2010). The politics of housework. In J. Treas & S. Drobnic (Eds.), *Dividing the Domestic: Men, women, and household work in cross-national perspective* (pp. 59–78). Stanford, CA: Stanford University Press.

Cooney, T. M., & Mortimer, J. T. (1999). Family structure differences in the timing of leaving home: Exploring mediating factors. *Journal of Research on Adolescence, 9,* 367–393.

Cooper, C., Harvey, N., Cole, Z., Hanson, M., & Dennison, E. (2009). Developmental origins of osteoporosis: The role of maternal nutrition. In B. Koletzko, T. Decsi, D. Molnár, & A. de la Hunty (Eds.), *Early nutrition programming and health outcomes in later life: Obesity and beyond* (pp. 31–39). New York: Springer Science + Business Media.

Cooper, C., Sayer, A. A., & Dennison, E. M. (2006). The developmental environment: Clinical perspectives on effects on the musculoskeletal system. In P. Gluckman & M. Hanson (Eds.), *Developmental origins of health and disease* (pp. 392–405). Cambridge, UK: Cambridge University Press.

Cooper, R., & Huh, C. R. (2008). Improving academic possibilities of students of color during the middle school to high school transition: Conceptual and strategic considerations in a U.S. context. In J. K. Asamen, M. L. Ellis, & G. L. Berry (Eds.), *Sage handbook of child development, multiculturalism, and media* (pp. 143–162). Thousand Oaks, CA: Sage.

Copen, C. E., Chandra A., & Martinez G. (2012). *Prevalence and timing of oral sex with opposite-sex partners among females and males aged 15–24 years: United States, 2007–2010.* National Health Statistics Reports, No. 56. Hyattsville, MD: U.S. Department of Health and Human Services.

Coplan, R. J., & Arbeau, K. A. (2008). The stresses of a "brave new world": Shyness and school adjustment in kindergarten. *Journal of Research in Childhood Education, 22,* 377–389.

Coplan, R. J., Arbeau, K. A., & Armer, M. (2008). "Don't fret, be supportive!" Maternal characteristics linking child shyness to psychosocial and school adjustment in kindergarten. *Journal of Abnormal Child Psychology, 36,* 359–371.

Coplan, R. J., & Armer, M. (2007). A "multitude" of solitude: A closer look at social withdrawal and nonsocial play in early childhood. *Child Development Perspectives, 1,* 26–32.

Coplan, R. J., Gavinsky-Molina, M. H., Lagace-Seguin, D., & Wichmann, C. (2001). When girls versus boys play alone: Gender differences in the associates of nonsocial play in kindergarten. *Developmental Psychology, 37,* 464–474.

Coplan, R. J., Prakash, K., O'Neil, K., & Armer, M. (2004). Do you "want" to play? Distinguishing between conflicted shyness and social disinterest in early childhood. *Developmental Psychology, 40,* 244–258.

Copple, C., & Bredekamp, S. (2009). *Developmentally appropriate practice in early childhood programs* (3rd ed.). Washington, DC: National Association for the Education of Young Children.

Corenblum, B. (2003). What children remember about ingroup and outgroup peers: Effects of stereotypes on children's processing of information about group members. *Journal of Experimental Child Psychology, 86,* 32–66.

Cornish, A. M., McMahon, C. A., Ungerer, J. A., Barnett, B., Kowalenko, N., & Tennant, C. (2005). Postnatal depression and infant cognitive and motor development in the second postnatal year: The impact of depression chronicity and infant gender. *Infant Behavior and Development, 28,* 407–417.

Cornwell, A. C., & Feigenbaum, P. (2006). Sleep biological rhythms in normal infants and those at high risk for SIDS. *Chronobiology International, 23,* 935–961.

Corr, C. A., & Corr, D. M. (2007). Historical and contemporary perspectives on loss, grief, and mourning. In C. A. Corr & D. M. Corr (Eds.), *Handbook of thanatology* (pp. 131–142). New York: Routledge.

Corr, C. A., & Corr, D. M. (2013). *Death and dying, life and living* (2nd ed.). Belmont, CA: Cengage.

Correa-Chávez, M., Rogoff, B., & Mejía-Arauz, R. (2005). Cultural patterns in attending to two events at once. *Child Development, 76,* 664–678.

Costello, J. (2006). Dying well: Nurses' experiences of "good and bad" deaths in hospital. *Journal of Advanced Nursing, 54,* 594–601.

Côté, J. E. (2006). Emerging adulthood as an institutionalized moratorium: Risks and benefits to identity formation. In J. J. Arnett (Ed.), *Emerging adults in America: Coming of age in the 21st century* (pp. 85–116). Washington, DC: American Psychological Association.

Côté, J. E. (2009). Identity formation and self-development in adolescence. In R. M. Lerner & L. Steinberg (Eds.), *Handbook of adolescent psychology: Vol. 1. Individual bases of adolescent development* (3rd ed., pp. 266–304). Hoboken, NJ: Wiley.

Côté, J. E., & Bynner, J. M. (2008). Changes in the transition to adulthood in the UK and Canada: The role of structure and agency in emerging adulthood. *Journal of Youth Studies, 11,* 251–268.

Côté, S. M., Vaillancourt, T., Barker, E. D., Nagin, D., & Tremblay, R. E. (2007). The joint development of physical and indirect aggression: Predictors of continuity and change during childhood. *Development and Psychopathology, 19,* 37–55.

Coudin, G., & Alexopoulos, T. (2010). "Help me! I'm old": How negative aging stereotypes create dependency among older adults. *Aging and Mental Health, 14,* 516–523.

Coulton, C. J., Crampton, D. S., Irwin, M., Spilsbury, J. C., & Korbin, J. E. (2007). How neighborhoods influence child maltreatment: A review of the literature and alternative pathways. *Child Abuse and Neglect, 31,* 1117–1142.

Courage, M. L., & Howe, M. L. (1998). The ebb and flow of infant attentional preferences: Evidence for longterm recognition memory in 3-month-olds. *Journal of Experimental Child Psychology, 18,* 98–106.

Courage, M. L., & Howe, M. L. (2002). From infant to child: The dynamics of cognitive change in the second year of life. *Psychological Bulletin, 128,* 250–277.

Courchesne, E., Carper, R., & Akshoomoff, N. (2003). Evidence of brain overgrowth in the first year of life in autism. *Journal of the American Medical Association, 290,* 337–344.

Couturier, J. L., & Lock, J. (2006). Denial and minimization in adolescents with anorexia nervosa. *International Journal of Eating Disorders, 39,* 212–216.

Cowan, C. P., & Cowan, P. A. (2000). *When partners become parents: The big life change for couples.* Mahwah, NJ: Erlbaum.

Cowan, N., & Alloway, T. (2009). Development of working memory in childhood. In M. L. Courage & N. Cowan (Eds.), *Development of memory in infancy and childhood* (pp. 303–342). Hove, UK: Psychology Press.

Cowan, P. A., & Cowan, C. P. (2002). Interventions as tests of family systems theories: Marital and family relationships in children's development and psychopathology. *Development and Psychopathology, 14,* 731–759.

Cowan, P. A., & Cowan, C. P. (2004). From family relationships to peer rejection to antisocial behavior in middle childhood. In J. B. Kupersmidt & K. A. Dodge (Eds.), *Children's peer relations: From development to intervention* (pp. 159–177). Washington, DC: American Psychological Association.

Cox, G. (2002). The Native American patient. In R. B. Gilbert (Ed.), *Health care and spirituality: Listening, assessing, caring* (pp. 107–127). Amityville, NY: Baywood.

Coyl, D. D., Newland, L. A., & Freeman, H. (2010). Predicting preschoolers' attachment security from parenting behaviours, parents' attachment relationships and their use of social support. *Early Child Development and Care, 180,* 499–512.

Coyne, S. M., Robinson, S. L., & Nelson, D. A. (2010). Does reality backbite? Verbal and relational aggression in reality television programs. *Journal of Broadcasting and Electronic Media, 54,* 282–298.

Craft, S., Baker, L. D., Montine, T. J., Minoshima, S., Watson, G. S., Arbuckle, M., et al. (2012). Intranasal insulin therapy for Alzheimer disease and amnestic mild cognitive impairment: A pilot clinical trial. *Archives of Neurology, 69,* 29–38.

Crago, M. B., Annahatak, B., & Ningiuruvik, L. (1993). Changing patterns of language socialization in Inuit homes. *Anthropology and Education Quarterly, 24,* 205–223.

Craig, C. M., & Lee, D. N. (1999). Neonatal control of sucking pressure: Evidence for an intrinsic tau guide. *Experimental Brain Research, 124,* 371–382.

Crain, W. (2005). *Theories of development* (5th ed.). Upper Saddle River, NJ: Prentice-Hall.

Crair, M. C., Gillespie, D. C., & Stryker, M. P. (1998). The role of visual experience in the development of columns in cat visual cortex. *Science, 279,* 566–570.

Cramer, R. E., Schaefer, J. T., & Reid, S. (2003). Identifying the ideal mate: More evidence for male-female convergence. In N. J. Pallone (Ed.), *Love, romance, sexual interaction: Research perspectives from current psychology* (pp. 61–73). New Brunswick, NJ: Transaction Publishers.

Cratty, B. J. (1986). *Perceptual and motor development in infants and children* (3rd ed.), Englewood Cliffs, NJ: Prentice-Hall.

Crawford, N. (2003, September). Understanding children's atypical gender behavior. *APA Monitor,* p. 40.

Crawley, L., Payne, R., Bolden, J., Payne, T., Washington, P., & Williams, S. (2000). Palliative and end-of-life care in the African American community. *Journal of the American Medical Association, 284,* 2518–2521.

Creasey, G., & Jarvis, P. (2009). Attachment and marriage. In M. C. Smith & N. DeFrates-Densch

(Eds.), *Handbook of research on adult learning and development* (pp. 269–304). New York: Routledge/ Taylor & Francis Group.

Creasey, G. L., Jarvis, P. A., & Berk, L. E. (1998). Play and social competence. In O. N. Saracho & B. Spodek (Eds.), *Multiple perspectives on play in early childhood education* (pp. 116–143). Albany: State University of New York Press.

Crick, N. R., & Nelson, D. A. (2002). Relational and physical victimization within friendships: Nobody told me there'd be friends like these. *Journal of Abnormal Child Psychology, 30,* 599–607.

Crick, N. R., Ostrov, J. M., Appleyard, K., Jansen, E., & Casas, J. F. (2004). Relational aggression in early childhood: You can't come to my birthday party unless. . . . In M. Putallaz & K. Bierman (Eds.), *Aggression, antisocial behavior, and violence among girls: A developmental perspective* (pp. 71–89). New York: Guilford.

Crick, N. R., Ostrov, J. M., Burr, J. E., Cullerton-Sen, C., Jansen-Yeh, E., & Ralston, P. (2006). A longitudinal study of relational and physical aggression in preschool. *Journal of Applied Developmental Psychology, 27,* 254–268.

Crick, N. R., Ostrov, J. M., & Werner, N. E. (2006). A longitudinal study of relational aggression, physical aggression, and social-psychological adjustment. *Journal of Abnormal Child Psychology, 34,* 131–142.

Crimmins, E. M., Kim, J. K., & Solé-Auró, A. (2011). Gender differences in health: Results from SHARE, ELSA and HRS. *European Journal of Public Health, 21,* 81–91.

Criss, M. M., & Shaw, D. S. (2005). Sibling relationships as contexts for delinquency training in low income families. *Journal of Family Psychology, 19,* 592–600.

Crockenberg, S., & Leerkes, E. (2003). Infant negative emotionality, caregiving, and family relationships. In A. C. Crouter & A. Booth (Eds.), *Children's influence on family dynamics* (pp. 57–78). Mahwah, NJ: Erlbaum.

Crockenberg, S., & Leerkes, E. (2004). Infant and maternal behaviors regulate infant reactivity to novelty at 6 months. *Developmental Psychology, 40,* 1123–1132.

Crockett, L. J., Raffaelli, M., & Shen, Y.-L. (2006). Linking self-regulation and risk proneness to risky sexual behavior: Pathways through peer pressure and early substance use. *Journal of Research on Adolescence, 16,* 503–525.

Croker, R. (2007). *The boomer century: 1946–2046: How America's most influential generation changed everything.* New York: Springboard Press.

Cross, S., & Markus, H. (1991). Possible selves across the life span. *Human Development, 34,* 230–255.

Crouch, J. L., Skowronski, J. J., Milner, J. S., & Harris, B. (2008). Parental responses to infant crying: The influence of child physical abuse risk and hostile priming. *Child Abuse and Neglect, 32,* 702–710.

Crouter, A. C., & Bumpus, M. F. (2001). Linking parents' work stress to children's and adolescents' psychological adjustment. *Current Directions in Psychological Science, 10,* 156–159.

Crouter, A. C., & Head, M. R. (2002). Parental monitoring and knowledge of children. In M. H. Bornstein (Ed.), *Handbook of parenting: Vol. 3. Being and becoming a parent* (2nd ed., pp. 461–483). Mahwah, NJ: Erlbaum.

Crouter, A. C., Whiteman, S. D., McHale, S. M., & Osgood, D. W. (2007). Development of gender attitude traditionality across middle childhood and adolescence. *Child Development, 78,* 911–926.

Crowley, K. (2011). Sleep and sleep disorders in older adults. *Neuropsychological Review, 21,* 41–53.

Crystal, D. S., Killen, M., & Ruck, M. D. (2008). It is who you know that counts: Intergroup contact and judgments about race-based exclusion. *British Journal of Developmental Psychology, 26,* 51–70.

Crystal, D. S., Killen, M., & Ruck, M. D. (2010). Fair treatment by authorities is related to children's and adolescents' evaluations of interracial exclusion. *Applied Developmental Science, 14,* 125–136.

Csikszentmihalyi, M., & Nakamura, J. (2005). The role of emotions in the development of wisdom. In R. J. Sternberg & J. Jordan (Eds.), *A handbook of wisdom: Psychological perspectives* (pp. 220–242). New York: Cambridge University Press.

Csikszentmihalyi, M., & Rathunde, K. (1990). The psychology of wisdom: An evolutionary interpretation. In R. J. Sternberg (Ed.), *Wisdom: Its nature, origins, and development* (pp. 25–51). New York: Cambridge University Press.

Culbertson, F. M. (1997). Depression and gender: An international review. *American Psychologist, 52,* 25–51.

Cumming, E., & Henry, W. E. (1961). *Growing old: The process of disengagement.* New York: Basic Books.

Cummings, E. M., Goeke-Morey, M. C., & Papp, L. M. (2004). Everyday marital conflict and child aggression. *Journal of Abnormal Child Psychology, 32,* 91–202.

Cummings, E. M., & Merrilees, C. E. (2010). Identifying the dynamic processes underlying links between marital conflict and child adjustment. In M. S. Schulz, M. K. Pruett, P. K. Kerig, & R. D. Parke (Eds.), *Strengthening couple relationships for optimal child development* (pp. 27–40). Washington, DC: American Psychological Association.

Curby, T. W., LoCasale-Crouch, J., Konold, T. R., Pianta, R. C., Howes, C., Burchinal, M., et al. (2009). The relations of observed pre-K classroom quality profiles to children's achievement and social competence. *Early Education and Development, 20,* 346–372.

Curlin, F. A., Nwodim, C., Vance, J. L., Chin, M. H., & Lantos, J. D. (2008). To die, to sleep: U.S. physicians' religious and other objections to physician-assisted suicide, terminal sedation, and withdrawal of life support. *American Journal of Hospice and Palliative Medicine, 25,* 112–120.

Curtiss, K., Hayslip, B., Jr., & Dolan, D. C. (2007). Motivational style, length of residence, voluntariness, and gender as influences on adjustment to long term care: A pilot study. *Journal of Human Behavior in the Social Environment, 15,* 13–34.

Cutchin, M. P. (2013). The complex process of becoming at-home in assisted living. In G. D. Rowles & M. Bernard (Eds.), *Environmental gerontology: Making meaningful places in old age* (pp. 105–124). New York: Springer.

Cutler, L. J. (2007). Physical environments of assisted living: Research needs and challenges. *Gerontologist, 47*(Special Issue III), 68–82.

Cutler, R. G., & Mattson, M. P. (2006). Introduction: The adversities of aging. *Ageing Research Reviews, 5,* 221–238.

Cutler, S. J., Hendricks, J., & O'Neill, G. (2011). Civic engagement and aging. In R. H. Binstock & L. K. George (Eds.), *Handbook of aging and the social sciences* (7th ed., pp. 221–233). San Diego, CA: Academic Press.

Cutrona, C. E., Hessling, R. M., Bacon, P. L., & Russell, D. W. (1998). Predictors and correlates of continuing involvement with the baby's father among adolescent mothers. *Journal of Family Psychology, 12,* 369–387.

Cutter, W. J., Daly, E. M., Robertson, D. M. W., Chitnis, X. A., van Amelsvoort, T. A. M. J., & Simmons, A. (2006). Influence of X chromosome and hormones on human brain development: A magnetic resonance imaging and proton magnetic resonance spectroscopy study of Turner syndrome. *Biological Psychiatry, 59,* 273–283.

Cvencek, D., Meltzoff, A. N., & Greenwald, A. G. (2011). Math–gender stereotypes in elementary school children. *Child Development, 82,* 766–779.

Cyr, M., McDuff, P., & Wright, J. (2006). Prevalence and predictors of dating violence among adolescent female victims of child sexual abuse. *Journal of Interpersonal Violence, 21,* 1000–1017.

D

Dabrowska, E. (2000). From formula to schema: The acquisition of English questions. *Cognitive Linguistics, 11,* 1–20.

Daher, M. (2012). Cultural beliefs and values in cancer patients. *Annals of Oncology, 23*(Suppl. 3), 66–69.

Dahl, R. E., & Lewin, D. S. (2002). Pathways to adolescent healthy sleep regulation and behavior. *Journal of Adolescent Health, 31,* 175–184.

Dahlberg, L. L., & Simon, T. R. (2006). Predicting and preventing youth violence: Developmental pathways and risk. In L. L. Dahlberg & T. R. Simon (Eds.), *Preventing violence: Research and evidence-based intervention strategies* (pp. 97–124). Washington, DC: American Psychological Association.

Dal Santo, J. A., Goodman, R. M., Glik, D., & Jackson, K. (2004). Childhood unintentional injuries: Factors predicting injury risk among preschoolers. *Journal of Pediatric Psychology, 29,* 273–283.

Damjanovic, A. M., Yang, Y., Glaser, R., Kiecolt-Glaser, J. K., & Nguyen, H. (2007). Accelerated telomere erosion is associated with a declining immune function of caregivers of Alzheimer's disease patients. *Journal of Immunology, 179,* 4249–4254.

Damon, W. (1988a). *The moral child.* New York: Free Press.

Damon, W. (1988b). *Self-understanding in childhood and adolescence.* New York: Cambridge University Press.

Damon, W. (1990). Self-concept, adolescent. In R. M. Lerner, A. C. Petersen, & J. Brooks-Gunn (Eds.), *The encyclopedia of adolescence* (Vol. 2, pp. 87–91). New York: Garland.

Damon, W. (2004). *The moral advantage: How to succeed in business by doing the right thing.* San Francisco: Berrett-Koehler.

Damon, W., & Hart, D. (1988). *Self-understanding in childhood and adolescence.* New York: Cambridge University Press.

Dane, E., Baer, M., Pratt, M. G., & Oldham, G. R. (2011). Rational versus intuitive problem solving: How thinking "off the beaten path" can stimulate creativity. *Psychology of Aesthetics, Creativity, and the Arts, 5,* 3–12.

Daniels, E., & Leaper, C. (2006). A longitudinal investigation of sport participation, peer acceptance, and self-esteem among adolescent girls and boys. *Sex Roles, 55,* 875–880.

Daniels, P., Noe, G. F., & Mayberry, R. (2006). Barriers to prenatal care among black women of low socioeconomic status. *American Journal of Health Behavior, 30,* 188–198.

Dannemiller, J. L., & Stephens, B. R. (1988). A critical test of infant pattern preference models. *Child Development, 59,* 210–216.

Darling-Hammond, L. (2010). *The flat world and education: How America's commitment to equity will determine our future.* New York: Teachers College Press.

Darroch, J. E., Frost, J. J., & Singh, S. (2001). *Teenage sexual and reproductive behavior in developed countries: Can more progress be made?* New York: Alan Guttmacher Institute.

Darwin, C. (1936). *On the origin of species by means of natural selection.* New York: Modern Library. (Original work published 1859)

Daubenmier, J., Lin, J., Blackburn, E., Hecht, F. M., Kristeller, J., Maninger, N., et al. (2012). Changes in stress, eating, and metabolic factors are related to changes in telomerase activity in a randomized mindfulness intervention pilot study. *Psychoneuroendocrinology, 37,* 917–928.

D'Augelli, A. R. (2002). Mental health problems among lesbian, gay, and bisexual youths ages 14 to 21. *Clinical Child Psychology and Psychiatry, 7,* 433–456.

D'Augelli, A. R. (2006). Developmental and contextual factors and mental health among lesbian, gay, and bisexual youths. In A. M. Omoto & H. S. Howard (Eds.), *Sexual orientation and mental health: Examining identity and development in lesbian, gay, and bisexual people* (pp. 37–53). Washington, DC: American Psychological Association.

D'Augelli, A. R., Grossman, A. H., Salter, N. P., Vasey, J. J., Starks, M. T., & Sinclair, K. O. (2005). Predicting the suicide attempts of lesbian, gay, and bisexual youth. *Suicide and Life-Threatening Behavior, 35,* 646–660.

D'Augelli, A. R., Grossman, A. H., & Starks, M. T. (2008). Families of gay, lesbian, and bisexual youth: What do parents and siblings know and how do they react? *Journal of GBLT Family Studies, 4,* 95–115.

Davey, A., & Takagi, E. (2013). Adulthood and aging in families. In G. W. Peterson & K. R. Bush (Eds.), *Handbook of marriage and family* (pp. 377–399). New York: Springer.

Davidov, M., & Grusec, J. E. (2006). Untangling the links of parental responsiveness to distress and warmth to child outcomes. *Child Development, 77,* 44–58.

Davies, J. (2008). Differential teacher positive and negative interactions with male and female pupils in the primary school setting. *Educational and Child Psychology, 25,* 17–26.

Davis, K. F., Parker, K. P., & Montgomery, G. L. (2004). Sleep in infants and young children. Part 1: Normal sleep. *Journal of Pediatric Health Care, 18,* 65–71.

Dawley, K., Loch, J., & Bindrich, I. (2007). The Nurse-Family Partnership. *American Journal of Nursing, 107,* 60–67.

Dawson, G., Ashman, S. B., Panagiotides, H., Hessl, D., Self, J., Yamada, E., & Embry, L. (2003). Preschool outcomes of children of depressed mothers: Role of maternal behavior, contextual risk, and children's brain activity. *Child Development, 74,* 1158–1175.

Dawson, T. L. (2002). New tools, new insights: Kohlberg's moral judgment stages revisited. *International Journal of Behavioral Development, 26,* 154–166.

Ddungu, H. (2011). Palliative care: What approaches are suitable in developing countries? *British Journal of Haematology, 154,* 728–735.

Deák, G. O., Ray, S. D., & Brenneman, K. (2003). Children's perseverative appearance–reality errors are related to emerging language skills. *Child Development, 74,* 944–964.

DeAngelo, L., Hurtado, S., & Pryor, J. H. (2010). *Your first college year: National norms for the 2008 YFCY survey.* Los Angeles: Higher Education Research Institute, UCLA.

Dearing, E., Wimer, C., Simpkins, S. D., Lund, T., Bouffard, S. M., Caronongan, P., & Kreider, H. (2009). Do neighborhood and home contexts help explain why low-income children miss opportunities to participate in activities outside of school? *Developmental Psychology, 45,* 1545–1562.

Deary, I. J. (2001). *g* and cognitive elements of information progressing: An agnostic view. In R. J. Sternberg & E. L. Grigorenko (Eds.), *The general factor of intelligence: How general is it?* (pp. 447–479). Mahwah, NJ: Erlbaum.

Deary, I. J., Strand, S., Smith, P., & Fernandes, C. (2007). Intelligence and educational achievement. *Intelligence, 35,* 13–21.

Deary, I. J., Yang, J., Davies, G., Harris, S. E., Tenesa, A., Liewald, D., et al. (2012). Genetic contributions to stability and change in intelligence from childhood to old age. *Nature, 481,* 212–215.

Deater-Deckard, K., Lansford, J. E., Dodge, K. A., Pettit, G. S., & Bates, J. E. (2003). The development of attitudes about physical punishment: An 8-year longitudinal study. *Journal of Family Psychology, 17,* 351–360.

Deater-Deckard, K., Pike, A., Petrill, S. A., Cutting, A. L., Hughes, C., & O'Connor, T. G. (2001). Nonshared environmental processes in socialemotional development: An observational study of identical twin differences in the preschool period. *Developmental Science, 4,* F1–F6.

Debes, F., Budtz-Jorgensen, E., Weihe, P., White, R. F., & Grandjean, P. (2006). Impact of prenatal methylmercury exposure on neurobehavioral function at age 4 years. *Neurotoxicology and Teratology, 28,* 536–547.

DeBoer, T., Scott, L. S., & Nelson, C. A. (2007). Methods for acquiring and analyzing infant eventrelated potentials. In M. de Haan (Ed.), *Infant EEG and event-related potentials* (pp. 5–37). New York: Psychology Press.

de Bruyn, E. H. (2005). Role strain, engagement and academic achievement in early adolescence. *Educational Studies, 31,* 15–27.

de Bruyn, E. H., & Cillessen, A. H. N. (2006). Popularity in early adolescence: Prosocial and antisocial subtypes. *Journal of Adolescent Research, 21,* 607–627.

de Calignon, A., Polydoro, M., Suárez-Calvet, M., William, C., Adamowicz, D. H., Kopeikina, K. J., et al. (2012). Propagation of tau pathology in a model of early Alzheimer's disease. *Neuron, 73,* 685–697.

Dechanet, C., Anahory, T., Mathieu, T., Mathieu, D. J. C., Quantin, X., Ryftmann, L., et al. (2011). Effects of cigarette smoking on reproduction. *Human Reproduction Update, 17,* 76–95.

Deci, E. L., La Guardia, J. G., Moller, A. C., Scheiner, M. J., & Ryan, R. M. (2006). On the benefits of giving as well as receiving autonomy support: Mutuality in close friendships. *Personality and Social Psychology Bulletin, 32,* 313–327.

Degner, J., & Wentura, D. (2010). Automatic prejudice in childhood and early adolescence. *Journal of Personality and Social Psychology, 98,* 356–374.

De Goede, I. H. A., Branje, S. J. T., & Meeus, W. H. J. (2009). Developmental changes and gender differences in adolescents' perceptions of friendships. *Journal of Adolescence, 32,* 1105–1123.

de Haan, M., & Johnson, M. H. (2003). Mechanisms and theories of brain development. In M. de Haan & M. H. Johnson (Eds.), *The cognitive neuroscience of development* (pp. 1–18). Hove, UK: Psychology Press.

Deissinger, T. (2007). "Making schools practical": Practice firms and their function in the full-time vocational school system in Germany. *Education + Training, 49,* 364–378.

deJong, A., & Franklin, B. A. (2004). Prescribing exercise for the elderly: Current research and recommendations. *Current Sports Medicine Reports, 3,* 337–343.

Dekker, M. C., Ferdinand, R. F., van Lang, D. J., Bongers, I. L., van der Ende, J., & Verhulst, F. C. (2007). Developmental trajectories of depressive symptoms from early childhood to late adolescence: Gender differences and adult outcome. *Journal of Child Psychology and Psychiatry, 48,* 657–666.

DeKosky, S. T., Williamson, J. D., Fitzpatrick, A. L., Kronmal, R. A., Ives, D. G., & Saxton, J. A. (2008). Ginkgo biloba for prevention of dementia: A randomized controlled trial. *Journal of the American Medical Association, 300,* 2253–2262.

Dekovi?, M., & Buist, K. L. (2005). Multiple perspectives within the family: Family relationship patterns. *Journal of Family Issues, 26,* 467–490.

DeLamater, J. (2012). Sexual expression in later life: A review and synthesis. *Journal of Sex Research, 49,* 125–141.

DeLamater, J., & Moorman, S. M. (2007). Sexual behavior in later life. *Journal of Aging and Health, 19,* 921–945.

DeLoache, J. S. (1987). Rapid change in symbolic functioning of very young children. *Science, 238,* 1556–1557.

DeLoache, J. S. (2002). The symbol-mindedness of young children. In W. Hartup & R. A. Weinberg (Eds.), *Minnesota Symposia on Child Psychology* (Vol. 32, pp. 73–101). Mahwah, NJ: Erlbaum.

DeLoache, J. S., Uttal, D. H., & Rosengren, K. S. (2004). Scale errors offer evidence for a perception–action dissociation early in life. *Science, 304,* 1027–1029.

Delobel-Ayoub, M., Arnaud, C., White-Koning, M., Casper, C., Pierrat, V., Garel, M., et al. (2009). Behavioral problems and cognitive performance at 5 years of age after very preterm birth: The EPIPAGE Study. *Pediatrics, 123,* 485–1492.

De Marco, A. C., & Berzin, S. C. (2008). The influence of family economic status on home-leaving patterns during emerging adulthood. *Families in Society, 89,* 208–218.

DeMarie, D., Miller, P. H., Ferron, J., & Cunningham, W. R. (2004). Path analysis tests of theoretical models of children's memory performance. *Journal of Cognition and Development, 5,* 461–492.

Demetriou, A., Christou, C., Spanoudis, G., & Platsidou, M. (2002). The development of mental processing: Efficiency, working memory, and thinking. *Monographs of the Society for Research in Child Development, 67*(1, Serial No. 268).

Demiray, B., Gülgöz, S., & Bluck, S. (2009). Examining the life story account of the reminiscence bump: Why we remember more from young adulthood. *Memory, 17,* 708–723.

DeNavas-Walt, C., Proctor, B. D., & Smith, J. C. (2011). Income, poverty, and health insurance coverage in the United States: 2010. *U.S. Census Bureau, Current Population Reports,* P60–P239. Washington, DC: U.S. Government Printing Office.

Denissen, J. J. A., Zarrett, N. R., & Eccles, J. S. (2007). I like to do it, I'm able, and I know I am: Longitudinal couplings between domain-specific achievement, self-concept, and interest. *Child Development, 78,* 430–447.

Denmark, F. L., & Klara, M. D. (2007). Empowerment: A prime time for women over 50. In V. Mulhbauer & J. C. Chrisler (Eds.), *Women over 50* (pp. 182–203). New York: Springer.

Dennerstein, L., & Lehert, P. (2004). Modeling midaged women's sexual functioning: A prospective, population-based study. *Journal of Sex and Marriage Therapy, 30,* 173–183.

Denney, N. W. (1990). Adult age differences in traditional and practical problem solving. *Advances in Psychology, 72,* 329–349.

Denney, N. W., & Pearce, K A. (1989). A developmental study of practical problem solving in adults. *Psychology and Aging, 4,* 438–442.

Dennis, T., Bendersky, M., Ramsay, D., & Lewis, M. (2006). Reactivity and regulation in children prenatally exposed to cocaine. *Developmental Psychology, 42,* 688–697.

Dent, A., & Stewart, A. (2004). *Sudden death in childhood: Support for the bereaved family.* London: Butterworth-Heinemann.

Deocampo, J. A. (2003, April). *Tools on TV: A new paradigm for testing dual representational understanding.* Poster presented at the biennial meeting of the Society for Research in Child Development, Tampa, FL.

DePaulo, B. M., & Morris, W. L. (2005). Singles in society and in science. *Psychological Inquiry, 16,* 142–149.

Deprest, J. A., Devlieger, R., Srisupundit, K., Beck, V., Sandaite, I., Rusconi, S., et al. (2010). Fetal surgery is a clinical reality. *Seminars in Fetal and Neonatal Medicine, 15,* 58–67.

Der, G., Batty, G. D., & Deary, I. J. (2006). Effect of breastfeeding on intelligence in children: Prospective study, sibling pairs analysis, and meta-analysis. *British Medical Journal, 333,* 945.

Der, G., & Deary, I. J. (2006). Age and sex differences in reaction time in adulthood: Results from the United Kingdom Health and Lifestyle Survey. *Psychology and Aging, 21,* 62–73.

deRegnier, R.-A. (2005). Neurophysiologic evaluation of early cognitive development in high-risk infants and toddlers. *Mental Retardation and Developmental Disabilities, 11,* 317–324.

deRegnier, R.-A., Long, J. D., Geogieff, M. K., & Nelson, C. A. (2007). Using event-related potentials and brain development in infants of diabetic mothers. *Developmental Neuropsychology, 31,* 379–396.

DeRoche, K., & Welsh, M. (2008). Twenty-five years of research on neurocognitive outcomes in early-treated phenylketonuria: Intelligence and executive function. *Developmental Neuropsychology, 33,* 474–504.

DeRose, L. M., & Brooks-Gunn, J. (2006). Transition into adolescence: The role of pubertal processes. In L. Balter & C. S. Tamis-LeMonda (Eds.), *Child psychology: A handbook of contemporary issues* (2nd ed., pp. 385–414). New York: Psychology Press.

DeRosier, M. E. (2007). Peer-rejected and bullied children: A safe schools initiative for elementary school students. In J. E. Zins, M. J. Elias, & C. A. Maher (Eds.), *Bullying, victimization, and peer harassment* (pp. 257–276). New York: Haworth.

DeRosier, M. E., & Thomas, J. M. (2003). Strengthening sociometric prediction: Scientific advances in the assessment of children's peer relations. *Child Development, 75,* 1379–1392.

de Rosnay, M., Copper, P. J., Tsigaras, N., & Murray, L. (2006). Transmission of social anxiety from mother to infant: An experimental study using a social referencing paradigm. *Behavior Research and Therapy, 44,* 1165–1175.

de Rosnay, M., & Hughes, C. (2006). Conversation and theory of mind: Do children talk their way to socio-cognitive understanding? *British Journal of Developmental Psychology, 24,* 7–37.

Derwinger, A., Neely, A. S., & Bäckman, L. (2005). Design your own memory strategies! Self-generated strategy training versus mnemonic training in old age: An 8-month follow-up. *Neuropsychological Rehabilitation, 15,* 37–54.

De Souza, E., Alberman, E., & Morris, J. K. (2009). Down syndrome and paternal age, a new analysis of case-control data collected in the 1960s. *American Journal of Medical Genetics, 149A,* 1205–1208.

Dessel, A. (2010). Prejudice in schools: Promotion of an inclusive culture and climate. *Education and Urban Society, 42,* 407–429.

Deutsch, N. L., & Schmertz, B. (2011). Starting from Ground Zero: Constraints and experiences of adult women returning to college. *Review of Higher Education, 34,* 477–504.

Deveson, A. (1994). *Coming of age: Twenty-one interviews about growing older.* Newham, Australia: Scribe.

Devi, N. P. G., Shenbagvalli, R., Ramesh, K., & Rathinam, S. N. (2009). Rapid progression of HIV infection in infancy. *Indian Pediatrics, 46,* 53–56.

de Villiers, J. G., & de Villiers, P. A. (1973). A cross-sectional study of the acquisition of grammatical morphemes in child speech. *Journal of Psycholinguistic Research, 2,* 267–278.

DeVries, R. (2001). Constructivist education in preschool and elementary school: The sociomoral atmosphere as the first educational goal. In S. L. Golbeck (Ed.), *Psychological perspectives on early childhood education* (pp. 153–180). Mahwah, NJ: Erlbaum.

De Weerd, A. W., & van den Bossche, A. S. (2003). The development of sleep during the first months of life. *Sleep Medicine Reviews, 7,* 179–191.

de Weerth, C., & Buitelaar, J. K. (2005). Physiological stress reactivity in human pregnancy—a review. *Neuroscience and Biobehavioral Reviews, 29,* 295–312.

De Wolff, M. S., & van IJzendoorn, M. H. (1997). Sensitivity and attachment: A meta-analysis on parental antecedents of infant attachment. *Child Development, 68,* 571–591.

Dey, J. G., & Hill, C. A. (2007). *Behind the pay gap.* Washington, DC: American Association of University Women.

Diamond, A. (2009). The interplay of biology and the environment broadly defined. *Developmental Psychology, 45,* 1–8.

Diamond, L. M. (1998). Development of sexual orientation among adolescent and young adult women. *Developmental Psychology, 34,* 1085–1095.

Diamond, L. M. (2003). Love matters: Romantic relationships among sexual-minority adolescents. In P. Florsheim (Ed.), *Adolescent romantic relations and sexual behavior* (pp. 85–108). Mahwah, NJ: Erlbaum.

Diamond, L. M. (2006). The intimate same-sex relationships of sexual minorities. In A. L. Vangelisti & D. Perlman (Eds.), *The Cambridge handbook of personal relationships* (pp. 293–312). New York: Cambridge University Press.

Diamond, L. M. (2008). Female bisexuality from adolescence to adulthood: Results from a 10-year longitudinal study. *Developmental Psychology, 44,* 5–14.

Diamond, L. M., Fagundes, C. P., & Butterworth, M. R. (2010). Intimate relationships across the lifespan. In M. E. Lamb, A. M. Freund, & R. M. Lerner, (Eds.), *The handbook of life-span development, Vol. 2: Social and emotional development* (pp. 379–433). Hoboken, NJ: Wiley.

Diamond, L. M., & Lucas, S. (2004). Sexual-minority and heterosexual youths' peer relationships: Experiences, expectations, and implications for well-being. *Journal of Research on Adolescence, 14,* 313–340.

Dias, M. G., & Harris, P. L. (1988). The effect of makebelieve play on deductive reasoning. *British Journal of Developmental Psychology, 6,* 207–221.

Dias, M. G., & Harris, P. L. (1990). The influence of the imagination on reasoning by young children. *British Journal of Developmental Psychology, 8,* 305–318.

Dick, D. M., Prescott, C., & McGue, M. (2008). The genetics of substance use and substance use disorders. In Y.-K. Kim (Ed.), *Handbook of behavior genetics* (pp. 433–453). New York: Springer.

Dick, D. M., Rose, R. J., Viken, R. J., & Kaprio, J. (2000). Pubertal timing and substance use: Associations between and within families across late adolescence. *Developmental Psychology, 36,* 180–189.

Dickinson, D. K., Golinkoff, R. M., & Hirsh-Pasek, K. (2010). Speaking out for language: Why language is central to reading development. *Educational Researcher, 39,* 305–310.

Dickinson, D. K., & McCabe, A. (2001). Bringing it all together: The multiple origins, skills, and environmental supports of early literacy. *Learning Disabilities Research and Practice, 16,* 186–202.

Dick-Read, G. (1959). *Childbirth without fear.* New York: Harper & Row.

Dickson, R. A., Pillemer, D. B., & Bruehl, E. C. (2011). The reminiscence bump for salient personal memories: Is a cultural life script required? *Memory and Cognition, 39,* 977–991.

Dickstein, M. (1992). After utopia: The 1960s today. In B. L. Tischler (Ed.), *Sights on the sixties* (pp. 13–24). New Brunswick, NJ: Rutgers University Press.

DiDonato, M. D., & Berenbaum, S. A. (2011). The benefits and drawbacks of gender typing: How different dimensions are related to psychological adjustment. *Archives of Sexual Behavior, 40,* 457–463.

Diehl, M., & Berg, K. M. (2007). Personality and involvement in leisure activities during the Third Age: Findings from the Ohio Longitudinal Study. In J. B. James & P. Wink (Eds.), *Annual review of gerontology and geriatrics* (Vol. 26, pp. 211–226). New York: Springer.

Diehl, M., Coyle, N., & Labouvie-Vief, G. (1996). Age and sex differences in strategies of coping and defense across the life span. *Psychology and Aging, 11,* 127–139.

Diehl, M., Youngblade, L. M., Hay, E. L., & Chui, H. (2011). The development of self-representations across the life span. In K. L. Fingergman, C. A. Berg, J. Smith, & H. Chui (Eds.), *Handbook of lifespan development* (pp. 611–646). New York: Springer.

Diener, E., Gohm, C. L., Suh, E., & Oishi, S. (2000). Similarity of the relations between marital status and subjective well-being across cultures. *Journal of Cross-Cultural Psychology, 31,* 419–436.

Dildy, G. A., Jackson, G. M., Fowers, G. K., Oshiro, B. T., Varner, M. W., & Clark, S. L. (1996). Very advanced maternal age. Pregnancy after age 45. *American Journal of Obstetrics and Gynecology, 175,* 668–674.

Dillon, M., & Wink, P. (2004). American religion, generativity, and the therapeutic culture. In E. de St. Aubin & D. P. McAdams (Eds.), *The generative society: Caring for future generations* (pp. 15–31). Washington, DC: American Psychological Association.

Dillon, M., & Wink, P. (2007). *In the course of a lifetime: Tracing religious belief, practice, and change.* Berkeley: University of California Press.

Dilworth-Anderson, P., Goodwin, P. Y., & Williams, S. W. (2004). Can culture help explain the physical health effects of caregiving over time among African American caregivers? *Journal of Gerontology, 59B,* S138–S145.

DiPietro, J. A., Bornstein, M. H., Costigan, K. A., Pressman, E. K., Hahn, C.-S., & Painter, K. (2002). What does fetal movement predict about behavior during the first two years of life? *Developmental Psychobiology, 40,* 358–371.

DiPietro, J. A., Hodgson, D. M., Costigan, K. A., & Hilton, S. C. (1996). Fetal neurobehavioral development. *Child Development, 67,* 2553–2567.

Dirix, C. E. H., Nijhuis, J. G., Jongsma, H. W., & Hornstra, G. (2009). Aspects of fetal learning and memory. *Child Development, 80,* 1251–1258.

Dirks, J. (1982). The effect of a commercial game on children's Block Design scores on the WISC-R test. *Intelligence, 6,* 109–123.

Dishion, T. J., Shaw, D., Connell, A., Gardner, F., Weaver, C., & Wilson, M. (2008). The Family Check-Up with high-risk indigent families: Preventing problem behavior by increasing parents' positive behavior support in early childhood. *Child Development, 79,* 1395–1414.

Dix, T., Stewart, A. D., Gershoff, E. T., & Day, W. H. (2007). Autonomy and children's reactions to being controlled: Evidence that both compliance and defiance may be positive markers in early development. *Child Development, 78,* 1204–1221.

Djahanbakhch, O., Ezzati, M., & Zosmer, A. (2007). Reproductive ageing in women. *Journal of Pathology, 211,* 219–231.

Dodd, V. L. (2005). Implications of kangaroo care for growth and development in preterm infants. *JOGNN, 34,* 218–232.

Dodge, K. A., Coie, J. D., & Lynam, D. (2006). Aggression and antisocial behavior in youth. In N. Eisenberg (Ed.), *Handbook of child psychology: Vol. 3. Social, emotional, and personality development* (6th ed., pp. 719–788). New York: Wiley.

Dodge, K. A., McLoyd, V. C., & Lansford, J. E. (2006). The cultural context of physically disciplining children. In V. C. McLoyd, N. E. Hill, & K. A.

Dodge (Eds.), *African-American family life: Ecological and cultural diversity* (pp. 245–263). New York: Guilford.

Dodson, T. A., & Borders, L. D. (2006). Men in traditional and nontraditional careers: Gender role attitudes, gender role conflict, and job satisfaction. *Career Development Quarterly, 54,* 283–296.

Dohnt, H., & Tiggemann, M. (2006). The contribution of peer and media influences to the development of body satisfaction and self-esteem in young girls: A prospective study. *Developmental Psychology, 42,* 929–936.

Doka, K. J. (2008). Disenfranchised grief in historical and cultural perspective. In M. S. Stroebe, R. O. Hansson, H. Schut, & W. Stroebe (Eds.), *Handbook of bereavement research and practice* (pp. 223–240). Washington, DC: American Psychological Association.

Doka, K. J., & Martin, T. L. (2010). *Grieving beyond gender: Understanding the ways men and women mourn* (rev. ed.). New York: Routledge.

Dolbin-MacNab, M. L. (2006). Just like raising your own? Grandmothers' perceptions of parenting a second time around. *Family Relations, 55,* 564–575.

Dombrowski, S. C., Noonan, K., & Martin, R. P. (2007). Low birth weight and cognitive outcomes: Evidence for a gradient relationship in an urban, poor, African American birth cohort. *School Psychology Quarterly, 22,* 26–43.

Donatelle, R. J. (2012). *Health: The basics* (10th ed.). San Francisco: Benjamin Cummings.

Dondi, M., Simion, F., & Caltran, G. (1999). Can newborns discriminate between their own cry and the cry of another newborn infant? *Developmental Psychology, 35,* 418–426.

Done, D. J., & Thomas, J. A. (2001). Training in communication skills for informal carers of people suffering from dementia: A cluster randomized clinic trial comparing a therapist led workshop and booklet. *International Journal of Geriatric Psychiatry, 16,* 816–821.

Donnellan, M. B., Larsen-Rife, D., & Conger, R. D. (2005). Personality, family history, and competence in early adult romantic relationships. *Journal of Personality and Social Psychology, 88,* 562–576.

Donnellan, M. B., & Lucas, R. E. (2008). Age differences in the big five across the life span: Evidence from two national samples. *Psychology and Aging, 23,* 558–566.

D'Onofrio, B. M., Turkheimer, E., Emery, R. E., Slutske, W. S., Heath, A. C., Madden, P. A., & Martin, N. G. (2006). A genetically informed study of the processes underlying the association between parental marital instability and offspring adjustment. *Developmental Psychology, 42,* 486–499.

Dorris, M. (1989). *The broken cord.* New York: Harper & Row.

Doss, B. D., Rhoades, G. K., Stanley, S. M., & Markman, H. J. (2009). The effect of the transition to parenthood on relationship quality: An 8-year prospective study. *Journal of Personality and Social Psychology, 96,* 601–619.

Double, E. B., Mabuchi, K., Cullings, H. M., Preston, D. L., Kodama, K., Shimizu, Y., et al. (2011). Long-term radiation-related health effects in a unique human population: Lessons learned from the atomic bomb survivors of Hiroshima and Nagasaki. *Disaster Medicine and Public Health Preparedness, 5*(Suppl. 1), S122–S133.

Dowd, M. D. (2013). Prevention and treatment of traumatic stress in children: Few answers, many questions. *Pediatrics, 31,* 591–592.

Dowling, E. M., Gestsdottir, S., Anderson, P. M., von Eye, A., Almerigi, J., & Lerner, R. M. (2004). Structural relations among spirituality, religiosity, and thriving in adolescence. *Applied Developmental Psychology, 8,* 7–16.

Downing, J. E. (2010). *Academic instruction for students with moderate and severe intellectual disabilities.* Thousand Oaks, CA: Corwin.

Drayton, S., Turley-Ames, K. J., & Guajardo, N. R. (2011). Counterfactual thinking and false belief: The role of executive function. *Journal of Experimental Child Psychology, 108,* 532–548.

Drewnowski, A., & Shultz, J. M. (2001). Impact of aging on eating behaviors, food choices, nutrition, and health status. *Journal of Nutrition, Health, and Aging, 5,* 75–79.

Driscoll, M. C. (2007). Sickle cell disease. *Pediatrics in Review, 28,* 259–268.

Driver, J., Tabares, A., Shapiro, A. F., & Gottman, J. M. (2012). Couple interaction in happy and unhappy marriages: Gottman Laboratory studies. In F. Walsh (Ed.), *Normal family processes: Growing diversity and complexity* (pp. 57–77). New York: Guilford.

Drotar, D., Witherspoon, D. O., Zebracki, K., & Peterson, C. C. (2006). *Psychological interventions in childhood chronic illness.* Washington, DC: American Psychological Association.

Dubé, E. M., Savin-Williams, R. C., & Diamond, L. M. (2001). Intimacy development, gender, and ethnicity among sexual-minority youths. In A. R. D'Augelli & C. J. Patterson (Eds.), *Lesbian, gay, and bisexual identities and youth* (pp. 129–152). New York: Oxford University Press.

DuBois, D. L., Burk-Braxton, C., Swenson, L. P., Tevendale, H. D., Lockerd, E. M., & Moran, B. L. (2002). Getting by with a little help from self and others: Self-esteem and social support as resources during early adolescence. *Developmental Psychology, 38,* 822–939.

DuBois, D. L., Felner, R. D., Brand, S., & George, G. R. (1999). Profiles of self-esteem in early adolescence: Identification and investigation of adaptive correlates. *American Journal of Community Psychology, 27,* 899–932.

Dubois, M-F., Bravo, C., Graham, J., Wildeman, S., Cohen, C., Painter, K., et al. (2011). Comfort with proxy consent to research involving decisionally impaired older adults: Do type of proxy and risk–benefit profile matter? *International Psychogeriatrics, 23,* 1479–1488.

Duckworth, A. L., & Seligman, M. E. P. (2005). Self-discipline outdoes IQ in predicting academic performance of adolescents. *Psychological Science, 12,* 939–944.

Dudani, A., Macpherson, A., & Tamim, H. (2010). Childhood behavior problems and unintentional injury: A longitudinal, population-based study. *Journal of Developmental and Behavioral Pediatrics, 31,* 276–285.

Duggan, A., McFarlane, E., Fuddy, L., Burrell, L., Higman, S. M., Windham, A., & Sia, C. (2004). Randomized trial of a statewide home visiting program: Impact in preventing child abuse and neglect. *Child Abuse and Neglect, 28,* 597–622.

Dumas, J. A., & Hartman, M. (2003). Age differences in temporal and item memory. *Psychology and Aging, 18,* 573–586.

Duncan, G. J., Dowsett, C. J., Claessens, A., Magnuson, K., Huston, A. C., Klebanov, P., et al. (2007). School readiness and later achievement. *Developmental Psychology, 43,* 1428–1446.

Duncan, G. J., & Magnuson, K. A. (2003). Off with Hollingshead: Socioeconomic resources, parenting, and child development. In M. H. Bornstein & R. H. Bradley (Eds.), *Socioeconomic status, parenting, and child development* (pp. 83–106). Mahwah, NJ: Erlbaum.

Duncan, S. R., Paterson, D. S., Hoffman, J. M., Mokler, D. J., Borenstein, M. S., Belliveau, R. A., et al. (2010). Brainstem serotonergic deficiency in sudden infant death syndrome. *Journal of the American Medical Association, 303,* 430–437.

Dunham, Y., Baron, A. S., & Banaji, M. R. (2006). From American city to Japanese village: A cross-cultural investigation of implicit race attitudes. *Child Development, 77,* 1129–1520.

Dunham, Y., Baron, A. S., & Carey, S. (2011). Consequences of "minimal" group affiliations in children. *Child Development, 82,* 793–811.

Dunlosky, J., & Hertzog, C. (2001). Measuring strategy production during associative learning: The relative utility of concurrent versus retrospective reports. *Memory and Cognition, 29,* 247–253.

Dunn, J. (1989). Siblings and the development of social understanding in early childhood. In P. G. Zukow (Ed.), *Sibling interaction across cultures* (pp. 106–116). New York: Springer-Verlag.

Dunn, J. (1994). Temperament, siblings, and the development of relationships. In W. B. Carey & S. C. McDevitt (Eds.), *Prevention and early intervention* (pp. 50–58). New York: Brunner/Mazel.

Dunn, J. (2002). The adjustment of children in stepfamilies: Lessons from community studies. *Child and Adolescent Mental Health, 7,* 154–161.

Dunn, J. (2004). Sibling relationships. In P. K. Smith & C. H. Hart (Eds.), *Handbook of childhood social development* (pp. 223–237). Malden, MA: Blackwell.

Dunn, J. (2005). Moral development in early childhood and social interaction in the family. In M. Killen & J. G. Smetana (Eds.), *Handbook of moral development* (pp. 331–350). Mahwah, NJ: Erlbaum.

Dunn, J., Brown, J. R., & Maguire, M. (1995). The development of children's moral sensibility: Individual differences and emotion understanding. *Developmental Psychology, 31,* 649–659.

Dunn, J., Cheng, H., O'Connor, T. G., & Bridges, L. (2004). Children's perspectives on their relationships with their nonresident fathers: Influences, outcomes and implications. *Journal of Child Psychology and Psychiatry, 45,* 553–566.

Dunn, J. R., Schaefer-McDaniel, N. J., & Ramsay, J. T. (2010). Neighborhood chaos and children's development: Questions and contradictions. In G. W. Evans & T. D. Wachs (Eds.), *Chaos and its influence on children's development: An ecological perspective* (pp. 173–189). Washington, DC: American Psychological Association.

Dunne, E. J., & Dunne-Maxim, K. (2004). Working with families in the aftermath of suicide. In F. Walsh & M. McGoldrick (Eds.), *Living beyond loss: Death in the family* (2nd ed., pp. 272–284). New York: Norton.

Durbin, D. L., Darling, N., Steinberg, L., & Brown, B. B. (1993). Parenting style and peer group membership among European-American adolescents. *Journal of Research on Adolescence, 3,* 87–100.

Durlak, J. A., & Weissberg, R. P. (2007). *The impact of after-school programs that promote personal and social skills.* Chicago: Collaborative for Academic, Social, and Emotional Learning.

Durston, S., & Casey, B. J. (2006). What have we learned about cognitive development from neuroimaging? *Neuropsychologia, 44,* 2149–2157.

Durston, S., & Conrad, K. (2007). Integrating genetic, psychopharmacological and neuroimaging studies: A converging methods approach to understanding the neurobiology of ADHD. *Developmental Review, 27,* 374–395.

Dusek, J. B. (1987). Sex roles and adjustment. In D. B. Carter (Ed.), *Current conceptions of sex roles and sex typing* (pp. 211–222). New York: Praeger.

Duszak, R. S. (2009). Congenital rubella syndrome—major review. *Optometry, 80,* 36–43.

Dutta, A., Henley, W., Lang, I., Llewellyn, D., Guralnik, J., Wallace, R. B., et al. (2011). Predictors of extraordinary survival in the Iowa Established Populations for Epidemiological Study of the Elderly: Cohort follow-up to "extinction." *Journal of the American Geriatrics Society, 59,* 963–971.

Dutton, D. G. (2007). *The abusive personality: Violence and control in intimate relationships* (2nd ed.). New York: Guilford.

Dutton, D. G. (2012). The case against the role of gender in intimate partner violence. *Aggression and Violent Behavior, 17,* 99–104.

Dutton, D. G., Nicholls, T. L., & Spidel, A. (2005). Female perpetrators of intimate abuse. In F. P. Buttell & M. M. Carney (Eds.), *Women who perpetrate relationship violence: Moving beyond political correctness* (pp. 1–31). New York: Haworth Press.

Dweck, C. S. (2002). Messages that motivate: How praise molds students' beliefs, motivation, and performance (in surprising ways). In J. Aronson (Ed.), *Improving academic achievement: Impact of psychological factors on education* (pp. 37–60). San Diego, CA: Academic Press.

Dweck, C. S. (2009). Prejudice: How it develops and how it can be undone. *Human Development, 52,* 371–376.

Dykiert, D., Der, G., Starr, J. M., & Deary, I. J. (2012). Sex differences in reaction time mean and intraindividual variability across the life span. *Developmental Psychology, 48,* 1262–1276.

Dykstra, P. A. (2009). Older adult loneliness: Myths and realities. *European Journal of Ageing, 6,* 91–100.

E

Eagly, A. H., & Carli, L. L. (2007). *Through the labyrinth: The truth about how women become leaders.* Boston, MA: Harvard Business School Press.

Eagly, A. H., & Wood, W. (2012). Social role theory. In P. A. M. Van Lange, A. W. Kruglanski, & E. T. Higgins (Eds.), *Handbook of theories of social psychology* (Vol. 2, pp. 458–476). Thousand Oaks, CA: Sage.

Eaker, E. D., Sullivan. L. M., Kelly-Hayes, M., D'Agostino, R. B., & Benjamin, E. J. (2004). Anger and hostility predict the development of atrial fibrillation in men in the Framingham Offspring Study. *Circulation, 109,* 1267–1271.

Eaker, E. D., Sullivan, L. M., Kelly-Hayes, M., D'Agostino, R. B., & Benjamin, E. J. (2007). Marital status, marital strain, and risk of coronary heart disease or total mortality: The Framingham Offspring Study. *Psychosomatic Medicine, 69,* 509–513.

Early Head Start National Resource Center. (2013). *Early Head Start program facts for Fiscal Year 2012.* Retrieved from eclkc.ohs.acf.hhs.gov/hslc/tta-system/ehsnrc/Early Head Start/about.html

Eaton, D. K., Davis, K. S., Barrios, L., Brener, N. D., & Noonan, R. K. (2007). Associations of dating violence victimization with lifetime participation, cooccurrence, and early initiation of risk behaviors among U.S. high school students. *Journal of Interpersonal Violence, 22,* 585–602.

Eaves, L., Silberg, J., Foley, D., Bulik, C., Maes, H., & Erkanli, A. (2004). Genetic and environmental influences on the relative timing of pubertal change. *Twin Research, 7,* 471–481.

Ebner, N. C., Freund, A. M., & Baltes, P. B. (2006). Developmental changes in personal goal orientation from young to late adulthood: From striving for gains to maintenance and prevention of losses. *Psychology and Aging, 21,* 664–678.

Eccles, J. S. (2004). Schools, academic motivation, and stage–environment fit. In R. M. Lerner & L. Steinberg (Eds.), *Handbook of Adolescent Psychology* (2nd ed., pp. 125–154). Hoboken, N. J.: Wiley.

Eccles, J. S., & Gootman, J. (Eds.). (2002). *Community programs to promote youth development.* Washington, DC: National Academy Press.

Eccles, J. S., Jacobs, J. E., & Harold, R. D. (1990). Gender-role stereotypes, expectancy effects, and parents' role in the socialization of gender differences in self-perceptions and skill acquisition. *Journal of Social Issues, 46,* 183–201.

Eccles, J. S., & Roeser, R. W. (2009). Schools, academic motivation, and stage–environment fit. In R. M. Lerner & L. Steinberg (Eds.), *Handbook of adolescent psychology* (Vol. 1, pp. 404–434). Hoboken, NJ: Wiley.

Eccles, J. S., Templeton, J., Barber, B., & Stone, M. (2003). Adolescence and emerging adulthood: The critical passageways to adulthood. In M. H. Bornstein, L. Davidson, C. L. M., Keyes, K. A. Moore, & the Center for Child Well-Being (Eds.), *Well-being: Positive development across the life course* (pp. 383–406). Mahwah, NJ: Erlbaum.

Eder, R. A., & Mangelsdorf, S. C. (1997). The emotional basis of early personality development: Implications for the emergent self-concept. In R. Hogan, J. Johnson, & S. Briggs (Eds.), *Handbook of personality psychology* (pp. 209–240). San Diego, CA: Academic Press.

Edwards, B. A., O'Driscoll, D. M., Ali A., Jordan, A. S., Trinder, J., & Malhotra, A. (2010). Aging and sleep: Physiology and pathophysiology. *Seminars in Respiratory Critical Care Medicine, 31,* 618–633.

Edwards, O. W., & Oakland, T. D. (2006). Factorial invariance of Woodcock-Johnson III scores for African Americans and Caucasian Americans. *Journal of Psychoeducational Assessment, 24,* 358–366.

Egan, S. K., & Perry, D. G. (2001). Gender identity: A multidimensional analysis with implications for psychosocial adjustment. *Developmental Psychology, 37,* 451–463.

Eggebeen, D. J., Dew, J., & Knoester, C. (2010). Fatherhood and men's lives at middle age. *Journal of Family Issues, 31,* 113–130.

Eggebeen, D. J., & Sturgeon, S. (2006). Demography of the baby boomers. In S. K. Whitbourne & S. L. Willis (Eds.), *The baby boomers grow up: Contemporary perspectives on midlife* (pp. 3–21). Mahwah, NJ: Erlbaum.

Ehrensaft, M. K. (2009). Family and relationship predictors of psychological and physical aggression. In D. K. O'Leary & E. M. Woodin (Eds.), *Psychological and physical aggression in couples: Causes and interventions* (pp. 99–118). Washington, DC: American Psychological Association.

Ehrensaft, M. K., Moffitt, T. E., & Caspi, A. (2004). Clinically abusive relationships in an unselected birth cohort: Men's and women's participation and developmental antecedents. *Journal of Abnormal Psychology, 113,* 258–270.

Ehri, L. C., & Roberts, T. (2006). The roots of learning to read and write: Acquisition of letters and phonemic awareness. In D. K. Dikinson & S. B. Neuman (Eds.), *Handbook of early literacy research* (Vol. 2, pp. 113–131). New York: Guildford.

Einstein, G. O., McDaniel, M. A., & Scullin, M. K. (2012). Prospective memory and aging: Understanding the variability. In M. Naveh-Benjamin & N. Ohta (Eds.), *Memory and aging: Current issues and future directions* (pp. 153–179). New York: Psychology Press.

Eisenberg, N. (2003). Prosocial behavior, empathy, and sympathy. In M. H. Bornstein & L. Davidson (Eds.), *Well-being: Positive development across the life course* (pp. 253–265). Mahwah, NJ: Erlbaum.

Eisenberg, N. (2010). Empathy-related responding: Links with self-regulation, moral judgment, and moral behavior. In M. Mikulincer & P. R. Shaver (Eds.), *Prosocial motives, emotions, and behavior: The better angels of our nature* (pp. 129–148). Washington, DC: American Psychological Association.

Eisenberg, N., Eggum, N. D., & Edwards, A. (2010). Empathy-related responding and moral development. In W. F. Arsenio & E. A. Lemerise (Eds.), *Emotions, aggression, and morality in children* (pp. 115–135). Washington, DC: American Psychological Association.

Eisenberg, N., Fabes, R. A., Shepard, S. A., Murphy, B. C., Jones, S., & Guthrie, I. K. (1998). Contemporaneous and longitudinal prediction of children's sympathy from dispositional regulation and emotionality. *Developmental Psychology, 34,* 910–924.

Eisenberg, N., Sadovsky, A., Spinrad, T. L., Fabes, R. A., Losoya, S., & Valiente, C. (2005a). The relations of problem behavior status to children's negative emotionality, effortful control, and impulsivity: Concurrent relations and prediction of change. *Developmental Psychology, 41,* 193–211.

Eisenberg, N., & Silver, R. C. (2011). Growing up in the shadow of terrorism. *American Psychologist, 66,* 468–481.

Eisenberg, N., Smith, C. L., Sadovsky, A., & Spinrad, T. L. (2004). Effortful control: Relations with emotion regulation, adjustment, and socialization in childhood. In R. Baumeister & K. D. Vohs (Eds.), *Handbook of self-regulation: Research, theory, and applications* (pp. 259–282). New York: Guilford.

Eisenberg, N., Zhou, Q., Spinrad, T. L., Valiente, C., Fabes, R. A., & Liew, J. (2005b). Relations among positive parenting, children's effortful control, and externalizing problems: A three-wave longitudinal study. *Child Development, 76,* 1055–1071.

Elavsky, S., & McAuley, E. (2007). Physical activity and mental health outcomes during menopause: A randomized controlled trial. *Annals of Behavioral Medicine, 33,* 132–142.

Elder, G. H., Jr., & Conger, R. (2000). *Children of the land: Adversity and success in rural America.* Chicago: University of Chicago Press.

Elder, G. H., Jr., Nguyen, T. V., & Caspi, A. (1985). Linking family hardship to children's lives. *Child Development, 56,* 361–375.

Elfenbein, D. S., & Felice, M. E. (2003). Adolescent pregnancy. *Pediatric Clinics of North America, 50,* 781–800.

Elias, C. L., & Berk, L. E. (2002). Self-regulation in young children: Is there a role for sociodramatic play? *Early Childhood Research Quarterly, 17,* 1–17.

Elkind, D. (1994). *A sympathetic understanding of the child: Birth to sixteen* (3rd ed.). Boston: Allyn and Bacon.

Elkind, D., & Bowen, R. (1979). Imaginary audience behavior in children and adolescents. *Developmental Psychology, 15,* 33–44.

Elliott, D. B., & Simmons, T. (2011, August). *Marital events of Americans: 2009. American Community Survey Reports, ACS-13.* Washington, DC: U.S. Census Bureau. Retrieved from www.census.gov/prod/2011pubs/acs-13.pdf

Elliott, J. G. (1999). School refusal: Issues of conceptualization, assessment, and treatment. *Journal of Child Psychology and Psychiatry and Allied Disciplines, 40,* 1001–1012.

Ellis, A. E., & Oakes, L. M. (2006). Infants flexibly use different dimensions to categorize objects. *Developmental Psychology, 42,* 1000–1011.

Ellis, B. J. (2004). Timing of pubertal maturation in girls: An integrated life history approach. *Psychological Bulletin, 130,* 920–958.

Ellis, B. J., & Essex, M. J. (2007). Family environments, adrenarche, and sexual maturation: A longitudinal test of a life history model. *Child Development, 78,* 1799–1817.

Ellis, L., & Bonin, S. L. (2003). Genetics and occupation-related preferences: Evidence from adoptive and non-adoptive families. *Personality and Individual Differences, 35,* 929–937.

Ellis, W. E., & Zarbatany, L. (2007). Explaining friendship formation and friendship stability: The role of children's and friends' aggression and victimization. *Merrill-Palmer Quarterly, 53,* 79–104.

Else-Quest, N. M., Hyde, J. S., Goldsmith, H. H., & Van Hulle, C. A. (2006). Gender differences in temperament: A meta-analysis. *Psychological Bulletin, 132,* 33–72.

El-Sheikh, M., Cummings, E. M., & Reiter, S. (1996). Preschoolers' responses to ongoing interadult conflict: The role of prior exposure to resolved versus unresolved arguments. *Journal of Abnormal Child Psychology, 24,* 665–679.

Eltzschig, H. K., Lieberman, E. S., & Camann, W. R. (2003). Regional anesthesia and analgesia for labor and delivery. *New England Journal of Medicine, 384,* 319–332.

Eluvathingal, T. J., Chugani, H. T., Behen, M. E., Juhasz, C., Muzik, O., Maqbook, M., et al. (2006). Abnormal brain connectivity in children after early severe socioemotional deprivation: A diffusion tensor imaging study. *Pediatrics, 117,* 2093–2100.

Elwert, F., & Christakis, N. A. (2006). Widowhood and race. *American Sociological Review, 71,* 16–41.

Emery, R. E., Sbarra, D., & Grover, T. (2005). Divorce mediation: Research and reflections. *Family Court Review, 43,* 22–37.

Englund, M. E., Egeland, B., & Collins, W. A. (2008). Exceptions to high school dropout predictions in a low-income sample: Do adults make a difference? *Journal of Social Issues, 64,* 77–93.

Ennemoser, M., & Schneider, W. (2007). Relations of television viewing and reading: Findings from a 4-year longitudinal study. *Journal of Educational Psychology, 99,* 349–368.

Entringer, S., Kumsta, R., Hellhammer, D. H., Wadhwa, P. D., & Wüst, S. (2009). Prenatal exposure to maternal psychosocial stress and HPA axis regulation in young adults. *Hormones and Behavior, 55,* 292–298.

Entwisle, D. R., Alexander, K. L., & Olson, L. S. (2005). First grade and educational attainment by age 22: A new story. *American Journal of Sociology, 110,* 1458–1502.

Epel, E. S., Linn, J., Wilhelm, F., Mendes, W., Adler, N., & Dolbier, C. (2006). Cell aging in relation to stress arousal and cardiovascular disease risk factors. *Psychoneuroendocrinology, 31,* 277–287.

Epel, E. S., Merkin, S. S., Cawthon, R., Blackburn, E. H., Adler, N. E., Pletcher, M. J., & Seeman, T. S. (2009). The rate of leukocyte telomere shortening predicts mortality from cardiovascular disease in elderly men: A novel demonstration. *Aging, 1,* 81–88.

Epstein, L. H., Roemmich, J. N., & Raynor, H. A. (2001). Behavioral therapy in the treatment of pediatric obesity. *Pediatric Clinics of North America, 48,* 981–983.

Erath, S. A., Bierman, K. L., & the Conduct Problems Prevention Research Group. (2006). Aggressive marital conflict, maternal harsh punishment, and child aggressive-disruptive behavior: Evidence for direct and mediate relations. *Journal of Family Psychology, 20,* 217–226.

Erickson, K. I., Colcombe, S. J., Wadhwa, R., Bherer, L., Peterson, M. S., & Scalf, P. E. (2007). Training-induced plasticity in older adults: Effects of training on hemispheric asymmetry. *Neurobiology of Aging, 28,* 272–283.

Erickson, K. I., Raji, C. A., Lopez, O. L., Becker, J. T., Rosano, C., Newman, A. B., et al. (2010). Physical activity predicts gray matter volume in late adulthood: The Cardiovascular Health Study. *Neurology, 75,* 1415–1422.

Erikson, E. H. (1950). *Childhood and society.* New York: Norton.

Erikson, E. H. (1968). *Identity, youth, and crisis.* New York: Norton.

Erikson, E. H. (1998). *The life cycle completed. Extended version with new chapters on the ninth stage by Joan M. Erikson.* New York: Norton.

Ernst, M., Moolchan, E. T., & Robinson, M. L. (2001). Behavioral and neural consequences of prenatal exposure to nicotine. *Journal of the American Academy of Child and Adolescent Psychiatry, 40,* 630–641.

Ernst, M., & Spear, L. (2009). Reward systems. In M. de Haan & M. Gunnar (Eds.), *Handbook of developmental social neuroscience* (pp. 324–341). New York: Guilford.

Erol, R. Y., & Orth, U. (2011). Self-esteem development from age 14 to 30 years: A longitudinal study. *Journal of Personality and Social Psychology, 101,* 607–619.

Ertekin-Tanner, N. (2007). Genetics of Alzheimer's disease: A centennial review. *Neurologic Clinics, 25,* 611–667.

Espy, K. A., Fang, H., Johnson, C., Stopp, C., & Wiebe, S. A. (2011). Prenatal tobacco exposure: Developmental outcomes in the neonatal period. *Developmental Psychology, 47,* 153–156.

Espy, K. A., Molfese, V. J., & DiLalla, L. F. (2001). Effects of environmental measures on intelligence in young children: Growth curve modeling of longitudinal data. *Merrill-Palmer Quarterly, 47,* 42–73.

Estourgie-van Burk, G. F., Bartels, M., van Beijsterveldt, T. C., Delemarre-van de Waal, H. A., & Boomsma, D. I. (2006). Body size in five-year-old twins: Heritability and comparison to singleton standards. *Twin Research and Human Genetics, 9,* 646–655.

Ethier, K. A., Kershaw, T., Niccolai, L., Lewis, J. B., & Ickovics, J. R. (2003). Adolescent women underestimate their susceptibility to sexually transmitted infections. *Sexually Transmitted Infections, 79,* 408–411.

Etnier, J. L., & Labban, J. D. (2012). Physical activity and cognitive function: Theoretical bases, mechanisms, and moderators. In E. O. Acebedo (Ed.), *Oxford Handbook of exercise psychology* (pp. 76–96). New York: Oxford University Press.

Evans, A. M. (2008). Growing pains: Contemporary knowledge and recommended practice. *Journal of Foot and Ankle Research, 1,* 4.

Evans, E., Hawton, K., & Rodham, K. (2004). Factors associated with suicidal phenomena in adolescents: A systematic review of population-based studies. *Clinical Psychology Review, 24,* 957–979.

Evans, G. W., & Schamberg, M A. (2009). Childhood poverty, chronic stress, and adult working memory. *Proceedings of the National Academy of Sciences, 106,* 6545–6549.

Evans, N., & Levinson, S. C. (2009). The myth of language universals: Language diversity and its importance for cognitive science. *Behavioral and Brain Sciences, 32,* 429–492.

F

Fabes, R. A., Eisenberg, N., Hanish, L. D., & Spinrad, T. L. (2001). Preschoolers' spontaneous emotion vocabulary: Relations to likeability. *Early Education and Development, 12,* 11–27.

Fabes, R. A., Eisenberg, N., McCormick, S. E., & Wilson, M. S. (1988). Preschoolers' attributions of the situational determinants of others' naturally occurring emotions. *Developmental Psychology, 24,* 376–385.

Fabes, R. A., Martin, C. L., & Hanish, L. D. (2003). Young children's play qualities in same-, other-, and mixed-sex peer groups. *Child Development, 74,* 921–932.

Fabiani, M. (2012). It was the best of times, it was the worst of times: A psychophysiologist's view of cognitive aging. *Psychophysiology, 49,* 283–304.

Fagan, J. F., Holland, C. R., & Wheeler, K. (2007). The prediction, from infancy, of adult IQ and achievement. *Intelligence, 35,* 225–231.

Fagard, J., Spelke, E., & von Hofsten, C. (2009). Reaching and grasping a moving object in 6-, 8-, and 10-month-old infants: Laterality and performance. *Infant Behavior and Development, 32,* 137–146.

Fagot, B. I. (1985). Changes in thinking about early sex role development. *Developmental Review, 5,* 83–98.

Fagot, B. I., & Hagan, R. I. (1991). Observations of parent reactions to sex-stereotyped behaviors: Age and sex effects. *Child Development, 62,* 617–628.

Fagot, B. I., & Leinbach, M. D. (1989). The young child's gender schema: Environmental input, internal organization. *Child Development, 60,* 663–672.

Fagundes, C. P., Bennett, J. M., Derry, H. M., & Kiecolt-Glaser, J. K. (2011). Relationships and inflammation across the lifespan: Social developmental pathways to disease. *Social and Personality Psychology Compass, 5,* 891–903.

Fahrmeier, E. D. (1978). The development of concrete operations among the Hausa. *Journal of Cross-Cultural Psychology, 9,* 23–44.

Fairburn, C. G., & Harrison, P. J. (2003). Eating disorders. *Lancet, 361,* 407–416.

Faircloth, B. S., & Hamm, J. V. (2005). Sense of belonging among high school students representing four ethnic groups. *Journal of Youth and Adolescence, 34,* 293–309.

Falagas, M. E., & Zarkadoulia, E. (2008). Factors associated with suboptimal compliance to vaccinations in children in developed countries: A systematic review. *Current Medical Research and Opinion, 24,* 1719–1741.

Falbo, T. (1992). Social norms and the one-child family: Clinical and policy implications. In F. Boer & J. Dunn (Eds.), *Children's sibling relationships* (pp. 71–82). Hillsdale, NJ: Erlbaum.

Falbo, T., & Poston, D. L., Jr. (1993). The academic, personality, and physical outcomes of only children in China. *Child Development, 64,* 18–35.

Falbo, T., Poston, D. L., Jr., Triscari, R. S., & Zhang, X. (1997). Self-enhancing illusions among Chinese schoolchildren. *Journal of Cross-Cultural Psychology, 28,* 172–191.

Falk, D. (2005). Brain lateralization in primates and its evolution in hominids. *American Journal of Physical Anthropology, 30,* 107–125.

Family Caregiver Alliance. (2009). *Fact sheet: Selected caregiver statistics.* Retrieved from www.caregiver.org/caregiver/jsp/content_node.jsp?nodeid=439

Fanslow, C. A. (1981). Death: A natural facet of the life continuum. In D. Krieger (Ed.), *Foundations for holistic health nursing practices: The renaissance nurse* (pp. 249–272). Philadelphia: Lippincott.

Fantz, R. L. (1961, May). The origin of form perception. *Scientific American, 204*(5), 66–72.

Farah, M. J., Shera, D. M., Savage, J. H., Betancourt, L., Giannetta, J. M., Brodsky, N. L., et al. (2006). Childhood poverty: Specific associations with neurocognitive development. *Brain Research, 110,* 166–174.

Faraone, S. V., & Mick, E. (2010). Molecular genetics of attention deficit hyperactivity disorder. *Psychiatric Clinics of North America, 33,* 159–180.

Farmer, T. W., Irvin, M. J., Leung, M.-C., Hall, C. M., Hutchins, B. C., & McDonough, E. (2010). Social preference, social prominence, and group membership in late elementary school: Homophilic concentration and peer affiliation configurations. *Social Psychology of Education, 13,* 271–293.

Farr, R. J., Forssell, S. L., & Patterson, C. J. (2010). Parenting and child development in adoptive families: Does parental sexual orientation matter? *Applied Developmental Science, 14,* 164–178.

Farrant, K., & Reese, E. (2000). Maternal style and children's participation in reminiscing: Stepping stones in children's autobiological memory development. *Journal of Cognition and Development, 1,* 193–225.

Farrington, D. P. (2009). Conduct disorder, aggression and delinquency. In R. M. Lerner & L. Steinberg (Eds.), *Handbook of adolescent psychology: Vol. 1. Individual bases of adolescent development* (3rd ed., pp. 683–722). Hoboken, NJ: Wiley.

Farroni, T., Massaccesi, S., Menon, E., & Johnson, M. H. (2007). Direct gaze modulates face recognition in young infants. *Cognition, 102,* 396–404.

Farver, J. M., & Branstetter, W. H. (1994). Preschoolers' prosocial responses to their peers' distress. *Developmental Psychology, 30,* 334–341.

Farver, J. M., Kim, Y. K., & Lee, Y. (1995). Cultural differences in Korean- and Anglo-American preschoolers' social interaction and play behaviors. *Child Development, 66,* 1088–1099.

Fattibene, P., Mazzei, F., Nuccetelli, C., & Risica, S. (1999). Prenatal exposure to ionizing radiation: Sources, effects, and regulatory aspects. *Acta Paediatrica, 88,* 693–702.

Fearon, R. P., Bakermans-Kranenburg, M. J., Lapsley, A., & Roisman, G. I. (2010). The significance of insecure attachment and disorganization in the development of children's externalizing behavior: A meta-analytic study. *Child Development, 81,* 435–456.

Federal Interagency Forum on Aging Related Statistics. (2012). *Older Americans: Key indicators of well-being.* Washington, DC: U.S. Government Printing Office.

Federal Interagency Forum on Child and Family Statistics. (2011). *America's children: Key national indicators of well-being, 2011.* Retrieved from www.childstats.gov

Federico, M. J., & Liu, A. H. (2003). Overcoming childhood asthma disparities of the inner-city poor. *Pediatric Clinics of North America, 50,* 655–675.

Feeney, J. A. (1999). Adult romantic attachment and couple relationships. In J. Cassidy & P. R. Shaver (Eds.), *Handbook of attachment* (pp. 355–377). New York: Guilford.

Feeney, J. A., Hohaus, L., Noller, P., & Alexander, R. P. (2001). *Becoming parents: Exploring the bonds between mothers, fathers, and their infants.* New York: Cambridge University Press.

Fehr, B. (1994). Prototype based assessment of laypeoples' views of love. *Personal Relationships, 1,* 309–331.

Feigelman, W., & Gorman, B. S. (2008). Assessing the effects of peer suicide on youth suicide. *Suicide and Life-Threatening Behavior, 38,* 181–194.

Feinberg, M. E., McHale, S. M., Crouter, A. C., & Cumsille, P. (2003). Sibling differentiation: Sibling and parent relationship trajectories in adolescence. *Child Development, 74,* 1261–1274.

Feldman, A. F., & Matjasko, J. L. (2007). Profiles and portfolios of adolescent school-based extracurricular activity participation. *Journal of Adolescence, 30,* 313–332.

Feldman, D. C., & Beehr, T. A. (2011). A three-phase model of retirement decision making. *American Psychologist, 66,* 193–203.

Feldman, D. C., & Vogel, R. M. (2009). The aging process and person–environment fit. In S. G. Baugh & S. E. Sullivan (Eds.), *Research in careers* (pp. 1–25). Charlotte, NC: Information Age Press.

Feldman, P. J., & Steptoe, A. (2004). How neighborhoods and physical functioning are related: The roles of neighborhood socioeconomic status, perceived neighborhood strain, and individual health risk factors. *Annals of Behavioral Medicine, 27,* 91–99.

Feldman, R. (2003). Infant–mother and infant–father synchrony: The coregulation of positive arousal. *Infant Mental Health Journal, 24,* 1–23.

Feldman, R. (2006). From biological rhythms to social rhythms: Physiological precursors of mother–infant synchrony. *Developmental Psychology, 42,* 175–188.

Feldman, R. (2007). Maternal versus child risk and the development of parent–child and family relationships in five high-risk populations. *Development and Psychopathology, 19,* 293–312.

Feldman, R., Eidelman, A. I., & Rotenberg, N. (2004). Parenting stress, infant emotion regulation, maternal sensitivity, and the cognitive development of triplets: A model for parent and child influences in a unique ecology. *Child Development, 75,* 1774–1791.

Feldman, R., Gordon, I., Schneiderman, I., Weisman, O., & Zagoory-Sharon, O. (2010). Natural variations in maternal and paternal care are associated with systematic changes in oxytocin following parent–infant contact. *Psychoneuroendocrinology, 35,* 1133–1141.

Feldman, R., Granat, A., Pariente, C., Kanety, H., Kuint, J., & Gilboa-Schechtman, E. (2009). Maternal depression and anxiety across the postpartum year and infant social engagement, fear regulation, and stress reactivity. *Journal of the American Academy of Child and Adolescent Psychiatry, 48,* 919–927.

Feldman, R., Greenbaum, C. W., & Yirmiya, N. (1999). Mother–infant affect synchrony as an antecedent of the emergence of self-control. *Developmental Psychology, 35,* 223–231.

Feldman, R., & Klein, P. S. (2003). Toddlers' self-regulated compliance to mothers, caregivers, and fathers: Implications for theories of socialization. *Developmental Psychology, 39,* 680–692.

Feldman, R., Sussman, A. L., & Zigler, E. (2004). Parental leave and work adaptation at the transition to parenthood: Individual, marital, and social correlates. *Applied Developmental Psychology, 25,* 459–479.

Felner, R. D., Favazza, A., Shim, M., Brand, S., Gu, K., & Noonan, N. (2002). Whole school improvement and restructuring as prevention and promotion: Lessons from STEP and the Project on High Performance Learning Communities. *Journal of School Psychology, 39,* 177–202.

Felsman, D. E., & Blustein, D. L. (1999). The role of peer relatedness in late adolescent career development. *Journal of Vocational Behavior, 54,* 279–295.

Feret, A., Steinweg, S., Griffin, H. C., & Glover, S. (2007). Macular degeneration: Types, causes, and possible interventions. *Geriatric Nursing, 28,* 387–392.

Ferguson, L. R. (2010). Meat and cancer. *Meat Science, 84,* 308–313.

Fergusson, D. M., & Woodward, L. J. (1999). Breastfeeding and later psychosocial adjustment. *Paediatric and Perinatal Epidemiology, 13,* 144–157.

Fernald, A., Perfors, A., & Marchman, V. A. (2006). Picking up speed in understanding: Speech processing efficiency and vocabulary growth across the 2nd year. *Developmental Psychology, 42,* 98–116.

Fernald, A., Taeschner, T., Dunn, J., Papousek, M., Boysson-Bardies, B., & Fukui, I. (1989). A cross-language study of prosodic modifications in mothers' and fathers' speech to preverbal infants. *Journal of Child Language, 16,* 477–502.

Fernald, L. C., & Grantham-McGregor, S. M. (1998). Stress response in school-age children who have been growth-retarded since early childhood. *American Journal of Clinical Nutrition, 68,* 691–698.

Ferrari, P. F., & Coudé, G. (2011). Mirror neurons and imitation from a developmental and evolutionary perspective. In A. Vilain, C. Abry, J.-L. Schwartz, & J. Vauclair (Eds.), *Primate communication and human language* (pp. 121–138). Amsterdam, Netherlands: John Benjamins.

Ferrari, P. F., Visalberghi E., Paukner A., Fogassi L., Ruggiero A., Suomi, S. (2006). Neonatal imitation in rhesus macaques. *PLoS Biology, 4,* e302.

Ferry, A. L., Hespos, S. J., & Waxman, S. R. (2010). Categorization in 3- and 4-month-old infants: An advantage of words over tones. *Child Development, 81,* 472–479.

Ficca, G., Fagioli, I., Giganti, F., & Salzarulo, P. (1999). Spontaneous awakenings from sleep in the first year of life. *Early Human Development, 55,* 219–228.

Field, D. (1997). "Looking back, what period of your life brought you the most satisfaction?" *International Journal of Aging and Human Development, 45,* 169–194.

Field, D. (1999). Stability of older women's friendships: A commentary on Roberto. *International Journal of Aging and Human Development, 48,* 81–83.

Field, D., & Millsap, R. E. (1991). Personality in advanced old age: Continuity or change? *Journal of Gerontology, 46,* 299–308.

Field, T. (2001). Massage therapy facilitates weight gain in preterm infants. *Current Directions in Psychological Science, 10,* 51–54.

Field, T. (2011). Prenatal depression effects on early development: A review. *Infant Behavior and Development, 34,* 1–14.

Field, T., Hernandez-Reif, M., Feijo, L., & Freedman, J. (2006). Prenatal, perinatal and neonatal stimulation: A survey of neonatal nurseries. *Infant Behavior and Development, 29,* 24–31.

Field, T., Hernandez-Reif, M., & Freedman, J. (2004). Stimulation programs for preterm infants. *Social Policy Report of the Society for Research in Child Development, 18*(1).

Fiese, B. H., & Schwartz, M. (2008). Reclaiming the family table: Mealtimes and child health and well-being. *Social Policy Report of the Society for Research in Child Development, 22*(4), 3–18.

Fifer, W. P., Byrd, D. L., Kaku, M., Eigsti, I. M., Isler, J. R., Grose-Fifer, J., et al. (2010). Newborn infants learn during sleep. *Proceedings of the National Academy of Sciences, 107,* 10320–10323.

Figner, B., Mackinlay, R. J., Wilkening, F., & Weber, E. U. (2009). Affective and deliberative processes in risky choice: Age differences in risk taking in the Columbia Card Task. *Journal of Experimental Psychology: Learning, Memory, and Cognition, 35,* 709–770.

Fincham, F. D., & Bradbury, T. N. (2004). Marital satisfaction, depression, and attributions: A longitudinal analysis. In R. M. Kowalski & M. R. Leary (Eds.), *The interface of social and clinical psychology: Key readings* (pp. 129–146). New York: Psychology Press.

Finchum, T., & Weber, J. A. (2000). Applying continuity theory to elder adult friendships. *Journal of Aging and Identity, 5,* 159–168.

Findlay, L. C., & Coplan, R. J. (2008). Come out and play: Shyness in childhood and the benefits of organized sports participation. *Canadian Journal of Behavioural Science, 40,* 153–161.

Fine, M. A., Ganong, L. H., & Demo, D. H. (2010). Divorce: A risk and resilience perspective. In S. J. Price, C. A. Price, & P. C. McKenry (Eds.), *Families and change: Coping with stressful events and transitions* (pp. 211–234). Thousand Oaks, CA: Sage.

Fingerman, K. L. (2004). The role of offspring and in-laws in grandparents' ties to their grandchildren. *Journal of Family Issues, 25,* 1026–1049.

Fingerman, K. L., & Birditt, K. S. (2003). Do we get better at picking our battles? Age group differences in descriptions of behavioral reactions to interpersonal tensions. *Journal of Gerontology, 60B,* P121–P128.

Fingerman, K. L., & Birditt, K. S. (2011). Relationships between adults and their aging parents. In K. W. Schaie & S. L. Willis (Eds.), *Handbook of the psychology of aging* (pp. 219–232). San Diego, CA: Academic Press.

Fingerman, K. L., Cheng, Y.-P., Birditt, K., & Zarit, S. (2012a). Only as happy as the least happy child: Multiple grown children's problems and successes and middle-aged parents' well-being. *Journal of Gerontology, 67B,* 184–193.

Fingerman, K. L., Cheng, Y-P., Tighe, L., Birditt, K. S., & Zarit, S. (2012b). Relationships between young adults and their parents. In A. Booth, S. L. Brown, N. S. Landale, W. D. Manning, & S. M. McHale (Eds.), *Early adulthood in a family context* (pp. 59–85). New York: Springer.

Fingerman, K. L., Cheng, Y-P., Wesselmann, D., Zarit, S., Furstenberg, F., & Birditt, K. S. (2012c).

Helicopter parents and landing pad kids: Intense parental support of grown children. *Journal of Marriage and Family, 74,* 880–896.

Fingerman, K. L., Hay, E. L., Dush, C. M. K., Cichy, K. E., & Hosterman, S. J. (2007). Parents' and offspring's perceptions of change and continuity when parents experience the transition to old age. *Advances in Life Course Research, 12,* 275–305.

Fingerman, K. L., Pitzer, L. M., Chan, W., Birditt, K., Franks, M. M., & Zarit, S. (2011a). Who gets what and why? Help middle-aged adults provide to parents and grown children. *Journal of Gerontology, 66B,* 87–98.

Fingerman, K. L., Pitzer, L., Lefkowitz, E. S., Birditt, K. S., & Mroczek, D. (2008). Ambivalent relationship qualities between adults and their parents: Implications for both parties' well-being. *Journal of Gerontology, 63B,* P362–P371.

Fingerman, K. L., VanderDrift, L. E., Dotterer, A. M., Birditt, K. S., & Zarit, S. H. (2011b). Support to aging parents and grown children in black and white families. *Gerontologist, 51,* 441–452.

Finkel, D., Reynolds, C. A., McArdle, J. J., & Pedersen, N. L. (2007). Age changes in processing speed as a leading indicator of cognitive aging. *Psychology and Aging, 22,* 558–568.

Finkel, E. J., Eastwick, P. W., Karney, B. R., Reis, H. T., & Sprecher, S. (2012). Online dating: A critical analysis from the perspective of psychological science. *Psychological Science in the Public Interest, 13,* 3–66.

Finkelhor, D. (2009). The prevention of childhood sexual abuse. *Future of Children, 19,* 169–194.

Finucane, M. L., Mertz, C. K., Slovic, P., & Schmidt, E. S. (2005). Task complexity and older adults' decision-making competence. *Psychology and Aging, 20,* 71–84.

Fiori, K. L., Antonucci, T., & Cortina, K. S. (2006). Social network typologies and mental health among older adults. *Journal of Gerontology, 61B,* 25–32.

Fiori, K. L., Smith, J., & Antonucci, T. C. (2007). Social network types among older adults: A multidimensional approach. *Journal of Gerontology, 62B,* P322–P330.

Fischer, K. W., & Bidell, T. R. (2006). Dynamic development of action and thought. In R. M. Lerner (Ed.), *Handbook of child psychology: Vol. 1. Theoretical models of human development* (6th ed., pp. 313–399). Hoboken, NJ: Wiley.

Fischman, M. G., Moore, J. B., & Steele, K. H. (1992). Children's one-hand catching as a function of age, gender, and ball location. *Research Quarterly for Exercise and Sport, 63,* 349–355.

Fish, M. (2004). Attachment in infancy and preschool in low socioeconomic status rural Appalachian children: Stability and change and relations to preschool and kindergarten competence. *Development and Psychopathology, 16,* 293–312.

Fisher, C. B. (1993, Winter). Integrating science and ethics in research with high-risk children and youth. *Social Policy Report of the Society for Research in Child Development, 7*(4), 1–27.

Fisher, S. E., Francks, C., McCracken, J. T., McGough, J. J., Marlow, A. J., & MacPhie, I. L. (2002). A genomewide scan for loci involved in attention-deficit/hyperactivity disorder. *American Journal of Human Genetics, 70,* 1183–1196.

Fisher, S. K., Easterly, S., & Lazear, K. J. (2008). Lesbian, gay, bisexual and transgender families and their children. In T. P. Gullotta & G. M. Blau (Eds.), *Family influences on child behavior and development: Evidence-based prevention and treatment approaches* (pp. 187–208). New York: Routledge.

Fitzpatrick, J., & Sollie, D. L. (1999). Influence of individual and interpersonal factors on satisfaction and stability in romantic relationships. *Personal Relationships, 6,* 337–350.

Fivush, R., & Haden, C. A. (2005). Parent–child reminiscing and the construction of a subjective self. In B. D. Homer & C. S. Tamis-LeMonda (Eds.), *The development of social cognition and communication* (pp. 315–336). Mahwah, NJ: Erlbaum.

Flanagan, C. A., Stout, M., & Gallay, L. S. (2008). It's my body and none of your business: Developmental changes in adolescents' perceptions of rights concerning health. *Journal of Social Issues, 64,* 815–834.

Flannery, D. J., Hussey, D. L., Biebelhausen, L., & Wester, K. L. (2003). Crime, delinquency, and youth gangs. In G. R. Adams & M. D. Berzonsky (Eds.), *Blackwell handbook of adolescence* (pp. 502–522). Malden, MA: Blackwell.

Flannery, K. A., & Liederman, J. (1995). Is there really a syndrome involving the co-occurrence of neurodevelopmental disorder, talent, non–right handedness and immune disorder among children? *Cortex, 31,* 503–515.

Flavell, J. H., Flavell, E. R., & Green, F. L. (2001). Development of children's understanding of connections between thinking and feeling. *Psychological Science, 12,* 430–432.

Flavell, J. H., Green, F. L., & Flavell, E. R. (1987). Development of knowledge about the appearance-reality distinction. *Monographs of the Society for Research in Child Development, 51*(1, Serial No. 212).

Flavell, J. H., Green, F. L., & Flavell, E. R. (1995). Young children's knowledge about thinking. *Monographs of the Society for Research in Child Development, 60*(1, Serial No. 243).

Flegal, K. M., Carroll, M. D., Kit, B. K., & Ogden, C. L. (2012). Prevalence of obesity and trends in the distribution of body mass index among U.S. adults, 1999–2010. *Journal of the American Medical Association, 307,* 491–497.

Fleischman, D. A., Wilson, R. S., Gabrieli, J. D. E., Bienias, J. L., & Bennett, D. A. (2004). A longitudinal study of implicit and explicit memory in old persons. *Psychology and Aging, 19,* 617–625.

Fletcher, A. C., Nickerson, P., & Wright, K. L. (2003). Structured leisure activities in middle childhood: Links to well-being. *Journal of Community Psychology, 31,* 641–659.

Flom, R., & Bahrick, L. E. (2010). The effects of intersensory redundancy on attention and memory: Infants' long-term memory for orientation in audiovisual events. *Developmental Psychology, 46,* 428–436.

Flom, R., & Pick, A. D. (2003). Verbal encouragement and joint attention in 18-month-old infants. *Infant Behavior and Development, 26,* 121–134.

Flood, D. G., & Coleman, P. D. (1988). Cell type heterogeneity of changes in dendritic extent in the hippocampal region of the human brain in normal aging and in Alzheimer's disease. In T. L. Petit & G. O. Ivy (Ed.), *Neural plasticity: A lifespan approach* (pp. 265–281). New York: Alan R. Liss.

Florian, V., & Mikulincer, M. (1998). Symbolic immortality and the management of the terror of death: The moderating role of attachment style. *Journal of Personality and Social Psychology, 74,* 725–734.

Florsheim, P., & Smith, A. (2005). Expectant adolescent couples' relations and subsequent parenting behavior. *Infant Mental Health Journal, 26,* 533–548.

Flynn, E. (2006). A microgenetic investigation of stability and continuity in theory of mind development. *British Journal of Developmental Psychology, 24,* 631–654.

Flynn, J. R. (2007). *What is intelligence? Beyond the Flynn effect.* New York: Cambridge University Press.

Flynn, J. R. (2011). Secular changes in intelligence. In R. J. Sternberg & S. B. Kaufman (Eds.), *Cambridge handbook of intelligence* (pp. 647–665). New York: Cambridge University Press.

Foehr, U. G. (2006). *Media multitasking among American youth: Prevalence, predictors, and pairings.* Menlo Park. CA: Kaiser Family Foundation.

Foerde, K., Knowlton, B. J., & Poldrack, R. A. (2006). Modulation of competing memory systems by distraction. *Proceedings of the National Academy of Sciences, 103,* 11778–11783.

Fogel, A. (1993). *Developing through relationships: Origins of communication, self and culture.* New York: Harvester Wheatsheaf.

Fomon, S. J., & Nelson, S. E. (2002). Body composition of the male and female reference infants. *Annual Review of Nutrition, 22,* 1–17.

Fonda, S. J., Clipp, E. C., & Maddox, G. L. (2002). Patterns in functioning among residents of an affordable assisted living housing facility. *Gerontologist, 42,* 178–187.

Fong, T. G., Tulebaev, S. R., & Inouye, S. K. (2009). Delirium in elderly adults: Diagnosis, prevention and treatment. *Nature Reviews Neurology, 5,* 210–220.

Fontana, L. (2008). Calorie restriction and cardiometabolic health. *European Journal of Cardiovascular Prevention and Rehabilitation, 15,* 3–9.

Fontana, L. (2009). The scientific basis of caloric restriction leading to longer life. *Current Opinion in Gastroenterology, 25,* 144–150.

Fontana, L., Klein, S., & Holloszy, J. O. (2010). Effects of long-term calorie restriction and endurance exercise on glucose tolerance, insulin action, and adipokine production. *Age, 32,* 97–108.

Fontana, L., Meyer, T. E., Klein, S., & Holloszy, J. O. (2004). Long-term calorie restriction is highly effective in reducing the risk for atherosclerosis in humans. *Proceedings of the National Academy of Sciences, 101,* 6659–6663.

Forman, D. R., Aksan, N., & Kochanska, G. (2004). Toddlers' responsive imitation predicts preschoolage conscience. *Psychological Science, 15,* 699–704.

Forman, D. R., O'Hara, M. W., Stuart, S., Gorman, L. L., Larsen, K. E., & Coy, K. C. (2007). Effective treatment for postpartum depression is not sufficient to improve the developing mother–child relationship. *Development and Psychopathology, 19,* 585–602.

Forry, N. D., Leslie, L. A., & Letiecq, B. L. (2007). Marital quality in interracial relationships: The role of sex role ideology and perceived fairness. *Journal of Family Issues, 28,* 1538–1552.

Forste, R., & Heaton, T. B. (2004). The divorce generation: Well-being, family attitudes, and socioeconomic consequences of marital disruption. *Journal of Divorce and Remarriage, 42,* 95–114.

Fortenberry, J. D. (2010). Fate, desire, and the centrality of the relationship to adolescent condom use. *Journal of Adolescent Health, 47,* 219–220.

Foster, M. A., Lambert, R., Abbott-Shim, M., McCarty, F., & Franze, S. (2005). A model of home learning environment and social risk factors in relation to children's emergent literacy and social outcomes. *Early Childhood Research Quarterly, 20,* 13–36.

Fowler, J. W., & Dell, M. L. (2006). Stages of faith from infancy through adolescence: Reflections on three decades of faith development theory. In E. C. Roehlkepartain, P. E. King, L. Wagener, & P. L. Benson (Eds.), *Handbook of spiritual development in childhood and adolescence* (pp. 34–45). Thousand Oaks, CA: Sage.

Fox, C. L., & Boulton, M. J. (2006). Friendship as a moderator of the relationship between social skills problems and peer victimization. *Aggressive Behavior, 32,* 110–121.

Fox, N. A. (1991). If it's not left, it's right: Electroencephalograph asymmetry and the development of emotion. *American Psychologist, 46,* 863–872.

Fox, N. A., & Calkins, S. D. (2003). The development of self-control of emotion: Intrinsic and extrinsic influences. *Motivation and Emotion, 27,* 7–26.

Fox, N. A., & Davidson, R. J. (1986). Taste-elicited changes in facial signs of emotion and the asymmetry of brain electrical activity in newborn infants. *Neuropsychologia, 24,* 417–422.

Fox, N. A., Henderson, H. A., Pérez-Edgar, K., & White, L. K. (2008). The biology of temperament: An integrative approach. In C. A. Nelson & M. Luciana (Eds.), *Handbook of developmental cognitive neuroscience* (2nd ed., pp. 839–853). Cambridge, MA: MIT Press.

Franchak, J. M., & Adolph, K. E. (2012). What infants know and what they do: Perceiving possibilities for walking through openings. *Developmental Psychology, 48,* 1254–1261.

Frankenburg, E., & Orfield, G. (2007). *Lessons in integration: Realizing the promise of racial diversity in American schools.* Charlottesville: University of Virginia Press.

Franklin, V. P. (2012). "The teachers' unions strike back?" No need to wait for "Superman": Magnet schools have brought success to urban public school students for over 30 years. In D. T. Slaughter-Defoe, H. C. Stevenson, E. G. Arrington, & D. J. Johnson (Eds.), *Black educational choice: Assessing the private and public alternatives to traditional K–12 public schools* (pp. 217–220). Santa Barbara, CA: Praeger.

Frazier, L., Barreto, M., & Newman, F. (2012). Self-regulation and eudaimonic well-being across adulthood. *Experimental Aging Research, 38,* 394–410.

Frazier, L. D. (2002). Perceptions of control over health: Implications for sense of self in healthy and ill older adults. In S. P. Shohov (Ed.), *Advances in psychology research* (Vol. 10, pp. 145–163). Huntington, NY: Nova Science Publishers.

Frazier, L. D., & Hooker, K. (2006). Possible selves in adult development: Linking theory and research. In C. Dunkel & J. Kerpelman (Eds.), *Possible selves: Theory, research and applications* (pp. 41–59). Hauppauge, NY: Nova Science.

Frederickson, B. L., & Carstensen, L. L. (1990). Relationship classification using grade of membership analysis: A typology of sibling relationships in later life. *Journal of Gerontology, 45,* S43–S51.

Fredricks, J. A. (2012). Extracurricular participation and academic outcomes: Testing the overscheduling hypothesis. *Journal of Youth and Adolescence, 41,* 295–306.

Fredricks, J. A., & Eccles, J. S. (2002). Children's competence and value beliefs from childhood through adolescence: Growth trajectories in two male-sex-typed domains. *Developmental Psychology, 38,* 519–533.

Fredricks, J. A., & Eccles, J. S. (2006). Is extracurricular participation associated with beneficial outcomes? Concurrent and longitudinal relations. *Developmental Psychology, 42,* 698–713.

Freedman, M. (1999). *Prime time: How baby boomers will revolutionize retirement and transform America.* New York: Public Affairs.

Freeman, D. (1983). *Margaret Mead and Samoa: The making and unmaking of an anthropological myth.* Cambridge, MA: Harvard University Press.

Freeman, H., & Newland, L. A. (2010). New directions in father attachment. *Early Child Development and Care, 180,* 1–8.

Freeman, L., Caserta, M., Lund, D., Rossa, S., Dowdy, A., & Partenheimer, A. (2006). Music thanatology: Prescriptive harp music as palliative care for the dying patient. *American Journal of Hospice and Palliative Care, 23,* 100–104.

Freitag, C. M., Rohde, L. A., Lempp, T., & Romanos, M. (2010). Phenotypic and measurement influences on heritability estimates in childhood ADHD.

European Child and Adolescent Psychiatry, 19, 311–323.

Freud, A. (1969). Adolescence as a developmental disturbance. In G. Caplan & S. Lebovici (Eds.), *Adolescence* (pp. 5–10). New York: Basic Books.

Freud, S. (1973). *An outline of psychoanalysis.* London: Hogarth. (Original work published 1938)

Freud, S. (1974). *The ego and the id.* London: Hogarth. (Original work published 1923)

Freund, A. M., & Baltes, P. B. (1998). Selection, optimization, and compensation as strategies of life management: Correlations with subjective indicators of successful aging. *Psychology and Aging, 13,* 531–543.

Freund, A. M., & Smith, J. (1999). Content and function of the self-definition in old and very old age. *Journal of Gerontology, 54B,* P55–P67.

Frey, A., Ruchkin, V., Martin, A., & Schwab-Stone, M. (2009). Adolescents in transition: School and family characteristics in the development of violent behaviors entering high school. *Child Psychiatry and Human Development, 40,* 1–13.

Fried, L. P., Xue, Q.-L., Cappola, A. R., Ferrucci, L., Chaves, P., Varadhan, R., et al. (2009). Nonlinear multisystem physiological dysregulation associated with frailty in older women: Implications for etiology and treatment. *Journal of Gerontology, 64A,* 1049–1052.

Friedman, C., McGwin, G., Jr., Ball, K. K., & Owsley, C. (2013). Association between higher-order visual processing abilities and a history of motor vehicle collision involvement by drivers age 70 and over. *Investigative Ophthalmology and Visual Science, 54,* 778–782.

Friedman, E. M., & Lawrence, D. A. (2002). Environmental stress mediates changes in neuroimmunological interactions. *Toxicological Sciences, 67,* 4–10.

Fries, J. F., Bruce, B., & Chakravarty, E. (2011). Compression of morbidity 1980–2011: A focused review of paradigms and progress. *Journal of Aging Research,* Article ID 261702. Retrieved from www.hindawi.com/journals/jar/2011/261702

Frith, U. (2003). *Autism: Explaining the enigma* (2nd ed.). Malden, MA: Blackwell.

Fry, C. L. (1985). Culture, behavior, and aging in the comparative perspective. In J. E. Birren & K. W. Schaie (Eds.), *Handbook of the psychology of aging* (2nd ed., pp. 216–244). New York: Van Nostrand Reinhold.

Fry, P. S. (2001). Predictors of health-related quality of life perspectives, self-esteem, and life satisfactions of older adults following spousal loss: An 18-month follow-up study of widows and widowers. *Gerontologist, 41,* 787–798.

Fry, P. S. (2003). Perceived self-efficacy domains as predictors of fear of the unknown and fear of dying among older adults. *Psychology and Aging, 18,* 474–486.

Fry, P. S., & Debats, D. L. (2006). Sources of life strengths as predictors of late-life mortality and survivorship. *International Journal of Aging and Human Development, 62,* 303–334.

Fryer, S. L., Crocker, N. A., & Mattson, S. N. (2008). Exposure to teratogenic agents as a risk factor for psychopathology. In T. P. Beauchaine & S. P. Hinshaw (Eds.), *Child and adolescent psychopathology* (pp. 180–207). Hoboken, NJ: Wiley.

Fryling, T., Summers, R., & Hoffman, A. (2006). Elder abuse: Definition and scope of the problem. In R. W. Summers & A. M. Hoffman (Eds.), *Elder abuse: A public health perspective* (pp. 5–18). Washington, DC: American Public Health Association.

Fuchs, D., Fuchs, L. S., Mathes, P. G., & Martinez, E. A. (2002a). Preliminary evidence on the standing of students with learning disabilities in PALS and no-PALS classrooms. *Learning Disabilities Research and Practice, 17,* 205–215.

Fuchs, L. S., Fuchs, D., Yazkian, L., & Powell, S. R. (2002b). Enhancing first-grade children's mathematical development with peer-assisted learning strategies. *School Psychology Review, 31,* 569–583.

Fukunaga, A., Uematsu, H., & Sugimoto, K. (2005). Influences of aging on taste perception and oral somatic sensation. *Journal of Gerontology, 60A,* 109–113.

Fuligni, A. J. (1998). The adjustment of children from immigrant families. *Current Directions in Psychological Science, 7,* 99–103.

Fuligni, A. J. (2004). The adaptation and acculturation of children from immigrant families. In U. P. Gielen & J. Roopnarine (Eds.), *Childhood and adolescence: Cross-cultural perspectives* (pp. 297–318). Westport, CT: Praeger.

Fuligni, A. J., Yip. T., & Tseng, V. (2002). The impact of family obligation on the daily activities and psychological well-being of Chinese-American adolescents. *Child Development, 73,* 302–314.

Fuller, C., Keller, L., Olson, J., Plymale, A., & Gottesman, M. (2005). Helping preschoolers become healthy eaters. *Journal of Pediatric Health Care, 19,* 178–182.

Fuller-Iglesias, H. (2010, November). Coping across borders: Transnational families in Mexico. In M. Mulso, *Families Coping across Borders*. Paper symposium presented at the National Council on Family Relations Annual Conference, Minneapolis, MN.

Fuller-Thomson, E., & Minkler, M. (2000). The mental and physical health of grandmothers who are raising their grandchildren. *Journal of Mental Health and Aging, 6,* 311–323.

Fuller-Thomson, E., & Minkler, M. (2005). Native American grandparents raising grandchildren: Findings from the Census 2000 Supplementary Survey and implications for social work practice. *Social Work, 50,* 131–139.

Fuller-Thomson, E., & Minkler, M. (2007). Mexican American grandparents raising grandchildren: Findings from the Census 2000 American Community Survey. *Families in Society, 88,* 567–574.

Fullerton, J. T., Navarro, A. M., & Young, S. H. (2007). Outcomes of planned home birth: An integrative review. *Journal of Midwifery and Women's Health, 52,* 323–333.

Fulmer, T. (2008). Screening for mistreatment of older adults. *American Journal of Nursing, 108,* 52–56.

Fülöp, T., Larbi, A., Kotb, R., de Angelis, F., & Pawelec, G. (2011). Aging, immunity, and cancer. *Discovery Medicine, 11,* 537–550.

Fung, H. H., Carstensen, L. L., & Lang, F. R. (2001). Age-related patterns in social networks among European Americans and African Americans: Implications for socioemotional selectivity across the life span. *International Journal of Aging and Human Development, 52,* 185–206.

Furchtgott-Roth, D. (2009). *Testimony on the gender pay gap* (testimony before the Joint Economic Committee, U.S. House of Representatives). Washington, DC: Hudson Institute.

Furnham, A. (2009). Sex differences in mate selection preferences. *Personality and Individual Differences, 47,* 262–267.

Furstenberg, F. F. (2010). On a new schedule: Transitions to adulthood and family change. *Future of Children, 20,* 67–87.

Furstenberg, F. F., Jr., & Harris, K. M. (1993). When and why fathers matter: Impact of father involvement on children of adolescent mothers. In R. I. Lerman & T. J. Ooms (Eds.), *Young unwed fathers* (pp. 117–138). Philadelphia: Temple University Press.

Fuson, K. C. (2009). Avoiding misinterpretations of Piaget and Vygotsky: Mathematical teaching without learning, learning without teaching, or

helpful learning-path teaching? *Cognitive Development, 24,* 343–361.

Fuson, K. C., & Burghard, B. H. (2003). Multidigit addition and subtraction methods invented in small groups and teacher support of problem solving and reflection. In J. J. Baroody & A. Dowker (Eds.), *The development of arithmetic concepts and skills* (pp. 267–304). Mahwah, NJ: Erlbaum.

Fussell, E., & Furstenberg, F. F., Jr. (2005). The transition to adulthood during the twentieth century. In R. A. Settersten, Jr., F. F. Furstenberg, Jr., & R. G. Rumbaut (Eds.), *On the frontier of adulthood* (pp. 29–75). Chicago: University of Chicago Press.

Fussell, E., & Gauthier, A. H. (2005). American women's transition to adulthood in comparative perspective. In R. A. Settersten, Jr., F. F. Furstenberg, Jr., & R. G. Rumbaut (Eds.), *On the frontier of adulthood: Theory, research, and public policy* (pp. 76–109). Chicago: University of Chicago Press.

Fuster, J. J., & Andres, V. (2006). Telomere biology and cardiovascular disease. *Circulation Research, 99,* 1167–1180.

Fyfe, M. (2006, April). Music and love help defy the doctors. Retrieved from www.theage.com.au/news/national/music-and-love-help-dying-defythedoctors/2006/03/31/1143441339517.html

G

Gabbay, S. G., & Wahler, J. J. (2002). Lesbian aging: Review of a growing literature. *Journal of Gay and Lesbian Social Services, 14,* 1–21.

Gabriel, Z., & Bowling, A. (2004). Quality of life from the perspectives of older people. *Ageing and Society, 24,* 675–691.

Gailliot, M. T., Schmeichel, B. J., & Baumeister, R. F. (2006). Self-regulatory processes defend against the threat of death: Effects of self-control depletion and trait self-control on thoughts and fears of dying. *Journal of Personality and Social Psychology, 91,* 49–62.

Galambos, N. L., Almeida, D. M., & Petersen, A. C. (1990). Masculinity, femininity, and sex role attitudes in early adolescence: Exploring gender intensification. *Child Development, 61,* 1905–1914.

Galambos, N. L., & Maggs, J. L. (1991). Children in self-care: Figures, facts, and fiction. In J. V. Lerner & N. L. Galambos (Eds.), *Employed mothers and their children* (pp. 131–157). New York: Garland.

Galambos, N. L., & Martinez, M. L. (2007). Poised for emerging adulthood in Latin America: A pleasure for the privileged. *Child Development Perspectives, 1,* 109–114.

Galinsky, E., Aumann, K., & Bond, J. T. (2009). *Times are changing: Gender and generation at work and at home.* New York: Families and Work Institute.

Galler, J. R., Ramsey, C. F., Morley, D. S., Archer, E., & Salt, P. (1990). The long-term effects of early kwashiorkor compared with marasmus. IV. Performance on the National High School Entrance Examination. *Pediatric Research, 28,* 235–239.

Galloway, J., & Thelen, E. (2004). Feet first: Object exploration in young infants. *Infant Behavior and Development, 27,* 107–112.

Gallup News Service. (2006). *Religion most important to blacks, women, and older Americans.* Retrieved from www.gallup.com/poll/25585/Religion-Most-Important-Blacks-Women-Older-Americans.aspx?version=print

Gallup News Service. (2012). *Seven in 10 Americans are very or moderately religious.* Retrieved from www.gallup.com/poll/159050/sevenamericansmoderatelyreligious.aspx

Ganea, P. A., Allen, M. L., Butler, L., Carey, S., & DeLoache, J. S. (2009). Toddlers' referential understanding of pictures. *Journal of Experimental Child Psychology, 104,* 283–295.

Ganea, P. A., Pickard, M. B., & DeLoache, J. S. (2008). Transfer between picture books and the real world

by very young children. *Journal of Cognition and Development, 9,* 46-66.

Ganea, P. A., Shutts, K., Spelke, E., & DeLoache, J. S. (2007). Thinking of things unseen: Infants' use of language to update object representations. *Psychological Science, 8,* 734–739.

Ganger, J., & Brent, M. R. (2004). Reexamining the vocabulary spurt. *Developmental Psychology, 40,* 621–632.

Ganong, L., Coleman, M., Fine, M., & Martin, P. (1999). Step-parents' affinity-seeking and affinity-maintaining strategies with stepchildren. *Journal of Family Issues, 20,* 299–327.

Ganong, L. H., & Coleman, M. (1994). *Remarried family relationships.* Thousand Oaks, CA: Sage.

Ganong, L. H., & Coleman, M. (2004). *Stepfamily relationships: Development, dynamics, and interventions.* New York: Kluwer/Plenum.

Ganong, L. H., Coleman, M., & Jamison, Y. (2011). Patterns of stepchild–stepparent relationship development. *Journal of Marriage and Family, 73,* 396–413.

Gans, D., & Silverstein, M. (2006). Norms of filial responsibility for aging parents across time and generations. *Journal of Marriage and Family, 68,* 961–976.

Garces, E., Thomas, D., & Currie, J. (2002). Longer-term effects of Head Start. *American Economic Review, 92,* 999–1012.

Garcia, M. M., Shaw, D. S., Winslow, E. B., & Yaggi, K. E. (2000). Destructive sibling conflict and the development of conduct problems in young boys. *Developmental Psychology, 36,* 44–53.

Garcia-Bournissen, F., Tsur, L., Goldstein, L. H., Staroselsky, A., Avner, M., & Asrar, F. (2008). Fetal exposure to isotretinoin—an international problem. *Reproductive Toxicology, 25,* 124–128.

García Coll, C., & Magnuson, K. (1997). The psychological experience of immigration: A developmental perspective. In A. Booth, A. C. Crouter, & N. Landale (Eds.), *Immigration and the family* (pp. 91–131). Mahwah, NJ: Erlbaum.

Gardner, H. (1982). *Artful Scribbles.* New York: Basic Books.

Gardner, H. (1983). *Frames of mind: The theory of multiple intelligences.* New York: Basic Books.

Gardner, H. (1993). *Multiple intelligences: The theory in practice.* New York: Basic Books.

Gardner, H. E. (1998). Are there additional intelligences? The case of the naturalist, spiritual, and existential intelligences. In J. Kane (Ed.), *Educational information and transformation.* Upper Saddle River, NJ: Prentice-Hall.

Gardner, H. E. (2000). *Intelligence reframed: Multiple intelligences for the twenty-first century.* New York: Basic Books.

Gardner, J. P., Li, S., Srinivasan, S. R., Chen, W., Kimura, M., & Lu, X. (2005). Rise in insulin resistance is associated with escalated telomere attrition. *Circulation, 111,* 2171–2177.

Garner, P. W. (2003). Child and family correlates of toddlers' emotional and behavioral responses to a mishap. *Infant Mental Health Journal, 24,* 580–596.

Garner, P. W., & Estep, K. (2001). Emotional competence, emotion socialization, and young children's peer-related social competence. *Early Education and Development, 12,* 29–48.

Gartstein, M. A., & Rothbart, M. K. (2003). Studying infant temperament via the revised infant behavior questionnaire. *Infant Behavior and Development, 26,* 64–86.

Gartstein, M. A., Slobodskaya, H. R., Zylicz, P. O., Gosztyla, D., & Nakagawa, A. (2010). A crosscultural evaluation of temperament: Japan, USA, Poland and Russia. *International Journal of Psychology and Psychological Therapy, 10,* 55–75.

Gasden, V. (1999). Black families in intergenerational and cultural perspective. In M. E. Lamb (Ed.),

Parenting and child development in "nontraditional" families (pp. 221–246). Mahwah, NJ: Erlbaum.

Gaskill, R. L., & Perry, B. D. (2012). Child sexual abuse, traumatic experiences, and their impact on the developing brain. In P. Goodyear-Brown (Ed.), *Handbook of child sexual abuse: Identification, assessment, and treatment* (pp. 29–47). Hoboken, NJ: Wiley.

Gaskins, S. (1999). Children's daily lives in a Mayan village: A case study of culturally constructed roles and activities. In R. Göncü (Ed.), *Children's engagement in the world: Sociocultural perspectives* (pp. 25–61). Cambridge, UK: Cambridge University Press.

Gaskins, S. (2000). Children's daily activities in a Mayan village: A culturally grounded description. *Cross-Cultural Research, 34,* 375–389.

Gaskins, S., Haight, W., & Lancy, D. F. (2007). The cultural construction of play. In A. Göncü & S. Gaskins (Eds.), *Play and development: Evolutionary, sociocultural, and functional perspectives* (pp. 179–202). Mahwah, NJ: Erlbaum.

Gates, G. J. (2011). *How many people are lesbian, gay, bisexual, and transgender?* Berkeley: The Williams Institute, University of California School of Law.

Gates, G. J., Badgett, M. V. L., Macomber, J. E., & Chambers, K. (2007). *Adoption and foster care by gay and lesbian parents in the United States.* Los Angeles, CA: Williams Institute of the UCLA School of Law.

Gathercole, S. E., Adams, A.-M., & Hitch, G. (1994). Do young children rehearse? An individual-differences analysis. *Memory and Cognition, 22,* 201–207.

Gathercole, S. E., & Alloway, T. P. (2008). Working memory and classroom learning. In S. K. Thurman & C. A. Fiorello (Eds.), *Applied cognitive research in K-3 classrooms* (pp. 17–40). New York: Routledge/Taylor & Francis Group.

Gathercole, S. E., Lamont, E., & Alloway, T. P. (2006). Working memory in the classroom. In S. Pickering (Ed.), *Working memory and education* (pp. 219–240). San Diego: Elsevier.

Gathercole, S. E., Tiffany, C., Briscoe, J., Thorn, A., & ALSPAC Team. (2005). Developmental consequences of poor phonological short-term memory function in childhood: A longitudinal study. *Journal of Child Psychology and Psychiatry, 46,* 598–611.

Gathercole, V., Sebastián, E., & Soto, P. (1999). The early acquisition of Spanish verb morphology: Across-the-board or piecemeal knowledge? *International Journal of Bilingualism, 3,* 133–182.

Gauvain, M. (2004). Bringing culture into relief: Cultural contributions to the development of children's planning skills. In R. V. Kail (Ed.), *Advances in child development and behavior* (pp. 39–71). San Diego, CA: Elsevier.

Gauvain, M., de la Ossa, J. L., & Hurtado-Ortiz, M. T. (2001). Parental guidance as children learn to use cultural tools: The case of pictorial plans. *Cognitive Development, 16,* 551–575.

Gavrilova, N. S., & Gavrilov, L. A. (2012). Comments on dietary restriction, Okinawa diet and longevity. *Gerontology, 58,* 221–223.

Gazzaley, A., Cooney, J. W., Rissman, J., & D'Esposito, M. (2005). Top-down suppression deficit underlies working memory impairment in normal aging. *Nature Neuroscience, 8,* 1298–1300.

Ge, X., Brody, G. H., Conger, R. D., Simons, R. L., & Murry, V. (2002). Contextual amplification of the effects of pubertal transition on African American children's deviant peer affiliation and externalized behavioral problems. *Developmental Psychology, 38,* 42–54.

Ge, X., Conger, R. D., & Elder, G. H., Jr. (1996). Coming of age too early: Pubertal influences on girls' vulnerability to psychological distress. *Child Development, 67,* 3386–3400.

Ge, X., Conger, R. D., & Elder, G. H., Jr. (2001). The relation between puberty and psychological distress in adolescent boys. *Journal of Research on Adolescence, 11,* 49–70.

Ge, X., Jin, R., Natsuaki, M. N., Frederick, X., Brody, G. H., Cutrona, C. E., & Simons, R. L. (2006). Pubertal maturation and early substance use risks among African American children. *Psychology of Addictive Behaviors, 20,* 404–414.

Ge, X., Natsuaki, M. N., Jin, R., & Biehl, M. C. (2011). A contextual amplification hypothesis: Pubertal timing and girls' emotional and behavior problems. In M. Kerr, H. Stattin, R. C. M. E. Engels, G. Overbeek, & A.-K. Andershed (Eds.), *Understanding girls' problem behavior* (pp. 11–28). Chichester, UK: Wiley-Blackwell.

Geangu, E., Benga, O., Stahl, D., & Striano, T. (2010). Contagious crying beyond the first days of life. *Infant Behavior and Development, 33,* 279–288.

Geary, D. C. (2006a). Development of mathematical understanding. In D. Kuhn & R. Siegler (Eds.), *Handbook of child psychology: Vol. 2. Cognition, perception, and language* (pp. 777–810). Hoboken, NJ: Wiley.

Geary, D. C. (2006b). Evolutionary developmental psychology: Current status and future directions. *Developmental Review, 26,* 113–119.

Gee, C. B., & Rhodes, J. E. (2003). Adolescent mothers' relationship with their children's biological fathers: Social support, social strain, and relationship continuity. *Journal of Family Psychology, 17,* 370–383.

Geerts, C. C., Bots, M. L., van der Ent, C. K., Grobbee, D. E., & Uiterwaal, C. S. (2012). Parental smoking and vascular damage in their 5-year-old children. *Pediatrics, 129,* 45–54.

Geist, C. (2010). Men's and women's reports about housework. In J. Treas & S. Drobnic (Eds.), *Dividing the Domestic: Men, women, and household work in cross-national perspective* (pp. 217–240). Stanford, CA: Stanford University Press.

Gelman, R. (1972). Logical capacity of very young children: Number invariance rules. *Child Development, 43,* 75–90.

Gelman, S. A. (2003). *The essential child.* New York: Oxford University Press.

Gelman, S. A., & Kalish, C. W. (2006). Conceptual development. In D. Kuhn & R. Siegler (Eds.), *Handbook of child psychology: Vol. 2. Cognition, perception, and language* (6th ed., pp. 687–733). Hoboken, NJ: Wiley.

Gelman, S. A., Taylor, M. G., & Nguyen, S. P. (2004). Mother–child conversations about gender. *Monographs of the Society for Research in Child Development, 69*(1, Serial No. 275), pp. 1–127.

Genesee, F., & Nicoladis, E. (2007). Bilingual first language acquisition. In E. Hoff & M. Shatz (Eds.), *Blackwell handbook of language development* (pp. 324–342). Malden, MA: Blackwell.

Gentile, B., Twenge, J. M., & Campbell, W. K. (2010). Birth cohort differences in self-esteem, 1988–2008: A cross-temporal meta-analysis. *Review of General Psychology, 14,* 261–268.

George, S. A. (2002). The menopause experience: A woman's perspective. *Journal of Obstetric, Gynecologic, and Neonatal Nursing, 31,* 71–85.

Gere, J., Schimmack, U., Pinkus, R. T., & Lockwood, P. (2011). The effects of romantic partners' goal congruence on affective well-being. *Journal of Research in Personality, 45,* 549–559.

Gergely, G., & Watson, J. (1999). Early socioemotional development: Contingency perception and the social-biofeedback model. In P. Rochat (Ed.), *Early social cognition: Understanding others in the first months of life* (pp. 101–136). Mahwah, NJ: Erlbaum.

Gergen, M., & Gergen, K. J. (2003). Positive aging. In J. F. Gubrim & J. A. Holstein (Eds.), *Ways of aging* (pp. 203–224). Malden: Blackwell Publishers Ltd.

Gershoff, E. T. (2002a). Corporal punishment by parents and associated child behaviors and experiences: A meta-analytic and theoretical review. *Psychological Bulletin, 128,* 539–579.

Gershoff, E. T., Grogan-Kaylor, A., Lansford, J. E., Chang, L., Zelli, A., Deater-Deckard, K., et al. (2010). Parent discipline practices in an international sample: Associations with child behaviors and moderation by perceived normativeness. *Child Development, 81,* 487–502.

Gershoff, E. T., Lansford, J. E., Sexton, H. R., Davis-Kean, P., & Sameroff, A. J. (2012). Longitudinal links between spanking and children's externalizing behaviors in a national sample of white, black, Hispanic, and Asian American families. *Child Development, 83,* 838–843.

Gerstorf, D., Ram, N., Estabrook, R., Schupp, J., Wagner, G. G., & Lindenberger, U. (2008). Life satisfaction shows terminal decline in old age: Longitudinal evidence from the German socioeconomic panel study. *Developmental Psychology, 44,* 1148–1159.

Gervai, J. (2009). Environmental and genetic influences on early attachment. *Child and Adolescent Psychiatry and Mental Health, 3,* 25. Retrieved from www.capmh.com/content/3/1/25

Gesell, A. (1933). Maturation and patterning of behavior. In C. Murchison (Ed.), *A handbook of child psychology.* Worcester, MA: Clark University Press.

Gest, S. D., Domitrovich, C. E., & Welsh, J. A. (2005). Peer academic reputation in elementary school: Associations with changes in self-concept and academic skills. *Journal of Educational Psychology, 97,* 337–346.

Geuze, R. H., Schaafsma, S. M., Lust, J. M., Bouma, A., Schiefenhovel, W., Groothuis, T. G. G., et al. (2012). Plasticity of lateralization: Schooling predicts hand preference but not hand skill asymmetry in a nonindustrial society. *Neuropsychologia, 50,* 612–620.

Gewirtz, A., Forgatch, M. S., & Wieling, E. (2008). Parenting practices as potential mechanisms for child adjustment following mass trauma. *Journal of Marital and Family Therapy, 34,* 177–192.

Ghavami, N., Fingerhut, A., Peplau, L. A., Grant, S. K., & Wittig, M. A. (2011). Testing a model of minority identity achievement, identity affirmation, and psychological well-being among ethnic minority and sexual minority individuals. *Cultural Diversity and Ethnic Minority Psychology, 17,* 79–88.

Gibbs, J. C. (2006). Should Kohlberg's cognitive developmental approach to morality be replaced with a more pragmatic approach? Comment on Krebs and Denton (2005). *Psychological Review, 113,* 666–671.

Gibbs, J. C. (2013). *Moral development & reality: Beyond the theories of Kohlberg, Hoffman, and Haidt* (3rd ed.) New York: Oxford University Press.

Gibbs, J. C., Basinger, K. S., Grime, R. L., & Snarey, J. R. (2007). Moral judgment development across cultures: Revisiting Kohlberg's universality claims. *Developmental Review, 24,* 443–500.

Gibbs, J. C., Moshman, D., Berkowitz, M. W., Basinger, K. S., & Grime, R. L. (2009). Taking development seriously: Critique of the 2008 *JME* special issue on moral functioning. *Journal of Moral Education, 38,* 271–282.

Gibson, E. J. (1970). The development of perception as an adaptive process. *American Scientist, 58,* 98–107.

Gibson, E. J. (2000). Perceptual learning in development: Some basic concepts. *Ecological Psychology, 12,* 295–302.

Gibson, E. J. (2003). The world is so full of a number of things: On specification and perceptual learning. *Ecological Psychology, 15,* 283–287.

Gibson, E. J., & Walk, R. D. (1960). The "visual cliff." *Scientific American, 202,* 64–71.

Gibson, J. J. (1979). *The ecological approach to visual perception.* Boston: Houghton Mifflin.

Gibson, P. A. (2005). Intergenerational parenting from the perspective of American grandmothers. *Family Relations, 54,* 280–297.

Giles, J. W., & Heyman, G. D. (2005). Young children's beliefs about the relationship between gender and aggressive behavior. *Child Development, 76,* 107–121.

Gill, M., Daly, G., Heron, S., Hawi, Z., & Fitzgerald, M. (1997). Confirmation of association between attention deficit hyperactivity disorder and a dopamine transporter polymorphism. *Molecular Psychiatry, 2,* 311–313.

Gillet, J.-P., Macadangdang, B., Rathke, R. L., Gottesman, M. M., & Kimchi-Sarfaty, C. (2009). The development of gene therapy: From monogenic recessive disorders to complex diseases such as cancer. *Methods in Molecular Biology, 542,* 5–54.

Gillies, R. M. (2000). The maintenance of cooperative and helping behaviours in cooperative groups. *British Journal of Educational Psychology, 70,* 97–111.

Gillies, R. M. (2003). The behaviors, interactions, and perceptions of junior high school students during small-group learning. *Journal of Educational Psychology, 95,* 137–147.

Gilligan, C. F. (1982). *In a different voice.* Cambridge, MA: Harvard University Press.

Gilliom, M., Shaw, D. S., Beck, J. E., Schonberg, M. A., & Lukon, J. L. (2002). Anger regulation in disadvantaged preschool boys: Strategies, antecedents, and the development of self-control. *Developmental Psychology, 38,* 222–235.

Gillum, R. F., Dana, E. K., Thomas, O. O., & Harold, G. K. (2008). Frequency of attendance at religious services and mortality in a U.S. national cohort. *Annals of Epidemiology, 18,* 124–129.

Ginsburg, H. P., Lee, J. S., & Boyd, J. S. (2008). Mathematics education for young children: What it is and how to promote it. *Social Policy Report of the Society for Research in Child Development, 12*(1).

Ginsburg, K. R. (2007). The importance of play in promoting healthy child development and maintaining strong parent–child bonds. *Pediatrics, 119,* 182–191.

Ginsburg-Block, M. D., Rohrbeck, C. A., & Fantuzzo, J. W. (2006). A meta-analytic review of social, self-concept, and behavioral outcomes of peer-assisted learning. *Journal of Educational Psychology, 98,* 732–749.

Gitlin, L. N., Belle, S. H., Burgio, L. D., Szaja, S. J., Mahoney, D., & Gallagher-Thompson, D. (2003). Effect of multicomponent interventions on caregiver burden and depression: The REACH multisite initiative at 6-month follow-up. *Psychology and Aging, 18,* 361–374.

Gladstone, I. M., & Katz, V. L. (2004). The morbidity of the 34- to 35-week gestation: Should we reexamine the paradigm? *American Journal of Perinatology, 21,* 9–13.

Glasgow, K. L., Dornbusch, S. M., Troyer, L., Steinberg, L., & Ritter, P. L. (1997). Parenting styles, adolescents' attributions, and educational outcomes in nine heterogeneous high schools. *Child Development, 68,* 507–523.

Gleitman, L. R., Cassidy, K., Nappa, R., Papfragou, A., & Trueswell, J. C. (2005). Hard words. *Language Learning and Development, 1,* 23–64.

Glover, V., Bergman, K., & O'Connor, T. G. (2008). The effects of maternal stress, anxiety, and depression during pregnancy on the neurodevelopment of the child. In S. D. Stone & A. E. Menken (Eds.), *Perinatal and postpartum mood disorders: Perspectives and treatment guide for the health care practitioner* (pp. 3–5). New York: Springer.

Glowinski, A. L., Madden, P. A. F., Bucholz, K. K., Lynskey, M. T., & Heath, A. C. (2003). Genetic epidemiology of self-reported lifetime DSM-IV major depressive disorder in a population-based twin sample of female adolescents. *Journal of Child Psychology and Psychiatry and Allied Disciplines, 44,* 988–996.

Glück, J., & Bluck, S. (2007). Looking back across the lifespan: A life story account of the reminiscence bump. *Memory and Cognition, 35,* 1928–1939.

Gluckman, P. D., Sizonenko, S. V., & Bassett, N. S. (1999). The transition from fetus to neonate—an endocrine perspective. *Acta Paediatrica Supplement, 88*(428), 7–11.

Go, A. S., Mozaffarian, V. L., Roger, E. J., Benjmin, J. D., Berry, J. D., Borden, W. B, et al. (2013). Heart disease and stroke statistics—2013 update. A report from the American Heart Association. *Circulation, 127,* e1–e241.

Goering, J. (Ed.). (2003). *Choosing a better life? How public housing tenants selected a HUD experiment to improve their lives and those of their children: The Moving to Opportunity Demonstration Program.* Washington, DC: Urban Institute Press.

Gögele, M., Pattaro, C., Fuchsberger, C., Minelli, C., Pramstaller, P. P., & Wjst, M. (2011). Heritability analysis of life span in a semi-isolated population followed across four centuries reveals the presence of pleiotropy between life span and reproduction. *Journal of Gerontology, 66A,* 26–37.

Goldberg, A. E. (2010). *Lesbian and gay parents and their children: Research on the family life cycle.* Washington, DC: American Psychological Association.

Goldberg, A. P., Dengel, D. R., & Hagberg, J. M. (1996). Exercise physiology and aging. In E. L. Schneider & J. W. Rowe (Eds.), *Handbook of the biology of aging* (pp. 331–354). San Diego: Academic Press.

Goldenberg, C., Gallimore, R., Reese, L., & Garnier, H. (2001). Cause or effect? Immigrant Latino parents' aspirations and expectations, and their children's school performance. *American Educational Research Journal, 38,* 547–582.

Goldschmidt, L., Richardson, G. A., Cornelius, M. D., & Day, N. L. (2004). Prenatal marijuana and alcohol exposure and academic achievement at age 10. *Neurotoxicology and Teratology, 26,* 521–532.

Goldsmith, H. H., Pollak, S. D., & Davidson, R. J. (2008). Developmental neuroscience perspectives on emotion regulation. *Child Development Perspectives, 2,* 132–140.

Goldsmith, L. T. (2000). Tracking trajectories of talent: Child prodigies growing up. In R. C. Friedman & B. M. Shore (Eds.), *Talents unfolding: Cognition and development* (pp. 89–122). Washington, DC: American Psychological Association.

Goldsteen, M., Houtepen, R., Proot, I. M., Abu-Saad, H. H., Spreeuwenberg, C., & Widdershoven, G. (2006). What is a good death? Terminally ill patients dealing with normative expectations around death and dying. *Patient Education and Counseling, 64,* 378–386.

Goldstein, M. H., & Schwade, J. A. (2008). Social feedback to infants' babbling facilitates rapid phonological learning. *Psychological Science, 19,* 515–523.

Goldstein, S. (2011). Attention-deficit/hyperactivity disorder. In S. Goldstein & C. R. Reynolds (Eds.), *Handbook of neurodevelopmental and genetic disorders in children* (2nd ed., pp. 131–150). New York: Guilford.

Goldston, D. B., Molock, S. D., Whitbeck, L. B., Murakami, J. L., Zayas, L. H., & Hall, G. C. N. (2008). Cultural considerations in adolescent suicide prevention and psychosocial treatment. *American Psychologist, 63,* 14–31.

Golinkoff, R. M., & Hirsh-Pasek, K. (2008). How toddlers begin to learn verbs. *Trends in Cognitive Sciences, 12,* 397–403.

Golomb, C. (2004). *The child's creation of a pictorial world* (2nd ed.). Mahwah, NJ: Erlbaum.

Golombok, S., Lycett, E., MacCallum, F., Jadva, V., Murray, C., Rust, J., Abdalla, H., Jenkins, J., & Margar, R. (2004). Parenting of infants conceived by gamete donation. *Journal of Family Psychology, 18,* 443–452.

Golombok, S., Perry, B., Burston, A., Murray, C., Mooney-Somers, J., Stevens, M., & Golding, J. (2003). Children with lesbian parents: A community study. *Developmental Psychology, 39,* 20–33.

Göncü, A., Patt, M. B., & Kouba E. (2004). Understanding young children's pretend play in context. In P. K. Smith & C. H. Hart (Eds.), *Blackwell handbook of childhood social development* (pp. 418–437). Malden, MA: Blackwell.

Gonzalez, A.-L., & Wolters, C. A. (2006). The relation between perceived parenting practices and achievement motivation in mathematics. *Journal of Research in Childhood Education, 21,* 203–217.

Good, T. L., & Brophy, J. (2003). *Looking in classrooms* (9th ed.). Boston: Allyn and Bacon.

Goode, V., & Goode, J. D. (2007). De facto zero tolerance: An exploratory study of race and safe school violations. In J. L. Kincheloe & K. Hayes (Eds.), *Teaching city kids: Understanding and appreciating them* (pp. 85–96). New York: Peter Lang.

Goodman, A. Schorge, J., & Greene, M. F. (2011). The long-term effects of in utero exposures—the DES story. *New England Journal of Medicine, 364,* 2083–2084.

Goodman, C. C. (2012). Caregiving grandmothers and their grandchildren: Well-being nine years later. *Children and Youth Services Review, 34,* 648–654.

Goodman, J., Dale, P., & Li, P. (2008). Does frequency count? Parental input and the acquisition of vocabulary. *Journal of Child Language, 35,* 515–531.

Goodnow, J. J. (2010). Culture. In M. H. Bornstein (Ed.), *Handbook of cultural developmental science* (pp. 3–20). New York: Psychology Press.

Goodvin, R., Meyer, S., Thompson, R. A., & Hayes, R. (2008). Self-understanding in early childhood: Associations with child attachment security and maternal negative affect. *Attachment and Human Development, 10,* 433–450.

Goodwin, R., & Pillay, U. (2006). Relationships, culture, and social change. In A. L. Vangelisti & D. Perlman (Eds.), *The Cambridge handbook of personal relationships* (pp. 760–779). New York: Cambridge University Press.

Goodyear-Brown, P., Fath, A., & Myers, L. (2012). Child sexual abuse: The scope of the problem. In P. Goodyear-Brown (Ed.), *Handbook of child sexual abuse: Identification, assessment, and treatment* (pp. 3–28). Hoboken, NJ: Wiley.

Gooren, E. M. J. C., Pol, A. C., Stegge, H., Terwogt, M. M., & Koot, H. M. (2011). The development of conduct problems and depressive symptoms in early elementary school children: The role of peer rejection. *Journal of Clinical Child and Adolescent Psychology, 40,* 245–253.

Gopnik, A., & Nazzi, T. (2003). Words, kinds, and causal powers: A theory theory perspective on early naming and categorization. In D. H. Rakison & L. M. Oakes (Eds.), *Early category and concept development* (p. 303–329). New York: Oxford University Press.

Gopnik, A., & Tenenbaum, J. B. (2007). Bayesian networks, Bayesian learning and cognitive development. *Developmental Science, 10,* 281–287.

Gorelick, P. B., Scuteri A., Black S. E., DeCarli, C., Greenberg, S. M., Costantino, I., et al. (2011). Vascular contributions to cognitive impairment and dementia: A statement for healthcare professionals from the American Heart Association/American Stroke Association. *Stroke, 42,* 2672–2713.

Gormally, S., Barr, R. G., Wertheim, L., Alkawaf, R., Calinoiu, N., & Young, S. N. (2001). Contact and nutrient caregiving effects on newborn infant pain responses. *Developmental Medicine and Child Neurology, 43,* 28–38.

Goronzy, J. J., Shao, L., & Weyand, C. M. (2010). Immune aging and rheumatoid arthritis. *Rheumatoid Disease Clinics of North America, 36,* 297–310.

Gosselin, P. A., & Gagne, J.-P. (2011). Older adults expend more listening effort than young adults recognizing audiovisual speech in noise. *International Journal of Audiology, 50,* 786–792.

Goswami, U. (1996). Analogical reasoning and cognitive development. In H. Reese (Ed.), *Advances in child development and behavior* (Vol. 26, pp. 91–138). New York: Academic Press.

Gothe, N., Mullen, S. P., Wójcicki, T. R., Mailey, E. L., White, S. M., Olson, E. A. (2011). Trajectories of change in self-esteem in older adults: Exercise intervention effects. *Journal of Behavioral Medicine, 34,* 298–306.

Gott, M., & Hinchliff, S. (2003). How important is sex in later life? The views of older people. *Social Science and Medicine, 56,* 1617–1628.

Gott, M., Seymour, J., Bellamy, G., Clark, D., & Ahmedzai, S. (2004). Older people's views about home as a place of care at the end of life. *Palliative Medicine, 18,* 460–467.

Gottfredson, G. D., & Duffy, R. D. (2008). Using a theory of vocational personalities and work environments to explore subjective well-being. *Journal of Career Assessment, 16,* 44–59.

Gottfredson, L. S. (2005). Applying Gottfredson's theory of circumscription and compromise in career guidance and counseling. In S. D. Brown & R. W. Lent (Eds.), *Career development and counseling* (pp. 71–100). Hoboken, NJ: Wiley.

Gottfried, A. E., Gottfried, A. W., & Bathurst, K. (2002). Maternal and dual-earner employment status and parenting. In M. H. Bornstein (Ed.), *Handbook of parenting. Vol. 2: Biology and ecology of parenting* (2nd ed., pp. 207–229). Mahwah, NJ: Erlbaum.

Gottlieb, G. (2007). Probabilistic epigenesis. *Developmental Science, 10,* 1–11.

Gottlieb, G., Wahlsten, D., & Lickliter, R. (2006). The significance of biology for human development: A developmental psychobiological systems view. In R. M. Lerner (Ed.), *Handbook of child psychology: Vol. 1. Theoretical models of human development* (6th ed., pp. 210–257). Hoboken, NJ: Wiley.

Gottman, J. M. (2011). *The science of trust: Emotional attunement for couples.* New York: Norton.

Gottman, J. M., & Levenson, R. W. (2000). The timing of divorce: Predicting when a couple will divorce over a 14-year period. *Journal of Marriage and Family, 62,* 737–745.

Gould, E. (2007). How widespread is adult neurogenesis in mammals? *Nature Reviews: Neuroscience, 8,* 481–488.

Gould, F., Clarke, J., Heim, C., Harvey, P. D., Majer, M., & Nemeroff, C. B. (2010). The effects of child abuse and neglect on cognitive functioning in adulthood. *Journal of Psychiatric Research, 46,* 500–506.

Gould, J. L., & Keeton, W. T. (1996). *Biological science* (6th ed.). New York: Norton.

Graber, J. A. (2003). Puberty in context. In C. Hayward (Ed.), *Gender differences at puberty* (pp. 307–325). New York: Cambridge University Press.

Graber, J. A. (2004). Internalizing problems during adolescence. In R. M. Lerner & L. Steinberg (Eds.), *Handbook of adolescent psychology* (2nd ed., pp. 587–626). Hoboken, NJ: Wiley.

Graber, J. A., Brooks-Gunn, J., & Warren, M. P. (2006). Pubertal effects on adjustment in girls: Moving from demonstrating effects to identifying pathways. *Journal of Youth and Adolescence, 35,* 413–423.

Graber, J. A., Nichols, T., Lynne, S. D., Brooks-Gunn, J., & Botwin, G. J. (2006). A longitudinal examination of family, friend, and media influences on competent

versus problem behaviors among urban minority youth. *Applied Developmental Science, 10,* 75–85.

Graber, J. A., Seeley, J. R., Brooks-Gunn, J., & Lewinsohn, P. M. (2004). Is pubertal timing associated with psychopathology in young adulthood? *Journal of the American Academy of Child and Adolescent Psychiatry, 43,* 718–726.

Graber, J. A., & Sontag, L. M. (2009). Internalizing problems during adolescence. In R. M. Lerner & L. Steinberg (Eds.), *Handbook of adolescent psychology: Vol. 1. Individual bases of adolescent development* (3rd ed., pp. 642–682). Hoboken, NJ: Wiley.

Grabowski, D. C., Aschbrenner, K. A., Rome, V. F., & Bartels, S. J. (2010). Quality of mental health care for nursing home residents: A literature review. *Medical Care Research and Review, 67,* 627–656.

Graham-Bermann, S. A., & Howell, K. H. (2011). Child maltreatment in the context of intimate partner violence. In J. E. B. Myers (Ed.), *Child maltreatment* (3rd ed., pp. 167–180). Thousand Oaks, CA: Sage.

Gralinski, J. H., & Kopp, C. B. (1993). Everyday rules for behavior: Mothers' requests to young children. *Developmental Psychology, 29,* 573–584.

Grall, T. S. (2011, December). *Custodial mothers and fathers and their child support: 2007. Current Population Reports,* P60–240. Washington, DC: U.S. Department of Commerce.

Granger, R. C. (2008). After-school programs and academics: Implications for policy, practice, and research. *Social Policy Report of the Society for Research in Child Development, 22*(2), 3–11.

Granier-Deferre, C., Bassereau, S., Ribeiro, A., Jacquet, A.-Y., & Lecanuet, J.-P. (2003). Cardiac "orienting" response in fetuses and babies following in utero melody-learning. Paper presented at the 11th European Conference on Developmental Psychology, Milan, Italy.

Granillo, T., Jones-Rodriguez, G., & Carvajal, S. C. (2005). Prevalence of eating disorders in Latina adolescents: Associations with substance use and other correlates. *Journal of Adolescent Health, 36,* 214–220.

Granot, T. (2005). *Without you: Children and young people growing up with loss and its effects.* London: Jessica Kingsley.

Grantham-McGregor, S., Powell, C., Walker, S., Chang, S., & Fletcher, P. (1994). The long-term follow-up of severely malnourished children who participated in an intervention program. *Child Development, 65,* 428–439.

Grantham-McGregor, S., Schofield, W., & Powell, C. (1987). Development of severely malnourished children who received psychosocial stimulation: Six-year follow-up. *Pediatrics, 79,* 247–254.

Grantham-McGregor, S., Walker, S. P., & Chang, S. (2000). Nutritional deficiencies and later behavioral development. *Proceedings of the Nutrition Society, 59,* 47–54.

Graves, L. M., Ohlott, P. J., & Ruderman, M. N. (2007). Commitment to family roles: Effects on managers' attitudes and performance. *Journal of Applied Psychology, 92,* 44–56.

Gray, K. A., Day, N. L., Leech, S., & Richardson, G. A. (2005). Prenatal marijuana exposure: Effect on child depression symptoms at ten years of age. *Neurotoxicology and Teratology, 27,* 439–448.

Gray, M. R., & Steinberg, L. (1999). Unpacking authoritative parenting: Reassessing a multidimensional construct. *Journal of Marriage and the Family, 61,* 574–587.

Gray-Little, B., & Carels, R. (1997). The effects of racial and socioeconomic consonance on self-esteem and achievement in elementary, junior high, and high school students. *Journal of Research on Adolescence, 7,* 109–131.

Gray-Little, B., & Hafdahl, A. R. (2000). Factors influencing racial comparisons of self-esteem:

A quantitative review. *Psychological Bulletin, 126,* 26–54.

Green, G. E., Irwin, J. R., & Gustafson, G. E. (2000). Acoustic cry analysis, neonatal status and longterm developmental outcomes. In R. G. Barr, B. Hopkins, & J. A. Green (Eds.), *Crying as a sign, a symptom, and a signal* (pp. 137–156). Cambridge, UK: Cambridge University Press.

Greenberger, E., O'Neil, R., & Nagel, S. K. (1994). Linking workplace and homeplace: Relations between the nature of adults' work and their parenting behavior. *Developmental Psychology, 30,* 990–1002.

Greendorfer, S. L., Lewko, J. H., & Rosengren, K. S. (1996). Family and gender-based socialization of children and adolescents. In F. L. Smoll & R. E. Smith (Eds.), *Children and youth in sport: A biopsychological perspective* (pp. 89–111). Dubuque, IA: Brown & Benchmark.

Greene, M. L., Way, N., & Pahl, K. (2006). Trajectories of perceived adult and peer discrimination among black, Latino, and Asian American adolescents: Patterns and psychological correlates. *Developmental Psychology, 42,* 218–238.

Greene, S. M., Anderson, E., Hetherington, E. M., Forgath, M. S., & DeGarmo, D. S. (2003). Risk and resilience after divorce. In R. Walsh (Ed.), *Normal family processes* (pp. 96–120). New York: Guilford.

Greenfield, P. (1992, June). *Notes and references for developmental psychology.* Conference on Making Basic Texts in Psychology More Culture-Inclusive and Culture-Sensitive, Western Washington University, Bellingham, WA.

Greenfield, P. M. (2004). *Weaving generations together: Evolving creativity in the Maya of Chiapas.* Santa Fe, NM: School of American Research.

Greenfield, P. M., Suzuki, L. K., & Rothstein-Fish, C. (2006). Cultural pathways through human development. In K. A. Renninger & I. E. Sigel (Eds.), *Handbook of child psychology: Vol. 4. Child psychology in practice* (6th ed., pp. 655–699). Hoboken, NJ: Wiley.

Greenhill, L. L., Halperin, J. M., & Abikoff, H. (1999). Stimulant medications. *Journal of the American Academy of Child and Adolescent Psychiatry, 38,* 503–512.

Greenough, W. T., & Black, J. E. (1992). Induction of brain structure by experience: Substrates for cognitive development. In M. R. Gunnar & C. A. Nelson (Eds.), *Minnesota Symposia on Child Psychology* (pp. 155–200). Hillsdale, NJ: Erlbaum.

Gregg, V., Gibbs, J. C., & Fuller, D. (1994). Patterns of developmental delay in moral judgment by male and female delinquents. *Merrill-Palmer Quarterly, 40,* 538–553.

Gregory, A., & Weinstein, R. S. (2004). Connection and regulation at home and in school: Predicting growth in achievement for adolescents. *Journal of Adolescent Research, 19,* 405–427.

Greve, W., & Bjorklund, D. F. (2009). The Nestor effect: Extending evolutionary developmental psychology to a lifespan perspective. *Developmental Review, 29,* 163–179.

Griffin, Z. M., & Spieler, D. H. (2006). Observing the what and when of language production for different age groups by monitoring speakers' eye movements. *Brain and Language, 99,* 272–288.

Grob, A., Krings, F., & Bangerter, A. (2001). Life markers in biographical narratives of people from three cohorts: A life span perspective in its historical context. *Human Development, 44,* 171–190.

Grolnick, W. S., Kurowski, C. O., Dunlap, K. G., & Hevey, C. (2000). Parental resources and the transition to junior high. *Journal of Research on Adolescence, 10,* 466–488.

Grossbaum, M. F., & Bates, G. W. (2002). Correlates of psychological well-being at midlife: The role of generativity, agency and communion, and narrative themes. *International Journal of Behavioral Development, 26,* 120–127.

Grossman, A. H. (2006). Physical and mental health of older lesbian, gay, and bisexual adults. In D. Kimmel, T. Rose, & S. David (Eds.), *Lesbian, gay, bisexual, and transgender aging* (pp. 53–69). New York: Columbia University Press.

Grossmann, K., Grossmann, K. E., Spangler, G., Suess, G., & Unzner, L. (1985). Maternal sensitivity and newborns' orientation responses as related to quality of attachment in Northern Germany. In I. Bretherton & E. Waters (Eds.), Growing points of attachment theory and research. *Monographs of the Society for Research in Child Development, 50*(1–2, Serial No. 209).

Gruendel J., & Aber, J. L. (2007). Bridging the gap between research and child policy change: The role of strategic communications in policy advocacy. In J. L. Aber, S. J. Bishop-Josef, S. M. Jones, K. T. McLearn, & D. Phillips (Eds.), *Child development and social policy: Knowledge for action* (pp. 43–58). Washington, DC: American Psychological Association.

Gruenewald, D. A., & White, E. J. (2006). The illness experience of older adults near the end of life: A systematic review. *Anesthesiology Clinics of North America, 24,* 163–180.

Grundy, E. (2005). Reciprocity in relationships: Socio-economic and health influences on intergenerational exchanges between Third Age parents and their adult children in Great Britain. *British Journal of Sociology, 56,* 233–255.

Grundy, E., & Henretta, J. C. (2006). Between elderly parents and adult children: A new look at the "sandwich generation." *Aging and Society, 26,* 707–722.

Grusec, J. E. (1988). *Social development: History, theory, and research.* New York: Springer.

Grusec, J. E. (2006). The development of moral behavior and conscience from a socialization perspective. In M. Killen & J. Smetana (Eds.), *Handbook of moral development* (pp. 243–265). Philadelphia: Erlbaum.

Guedes, G., Tsai, J. C., & Loewen, N. A. (2011). Glaucoma and aging. *Current Aging Science, 4,* 110–117.

Guerra, N. G., Graham, S., & Tolan, P. H. (2011). Raising healthy children: Translating child development research into practice. *Child Development, 82,* 7–16.

Guglielmi, R. S. (2008). Native language proficiency, English literacy, academic achievement, and occupational attainment in limited-English-proficient students: A latent growth modeling perspective. *Journal of Educational Psychology, 100,* 322–342.

Guignard, J.-H., & Lubart, T. I. (2007). A comparative study of convergent and divergent thinking in intellectually gifted children. *Gifted and Talented International, 22*(1), 9–15.

Guildner, S. H., Loeb, S., Morris, D., Penrod, J., Bramlett, M., Johnston, L., & Schlotzhauer, P. (2001). A comparison of life satisfaction and mood in nursing home residents and community-dwelling elders. *Archives of Psychiatric Nursing, 15,* 232–240.

Guilford, J. P. (1985). The structure-of-intellect model. In B. B. Wolman (Ed.), *Handbook of intelligence* (pp. 225–266). New York: Wiley.

Gullone, E. (2000). The development of normal fear: A century of research. *Clinical Psychology Review, 20,* 429–451.

Gulotta, T. P. (2008). How theory influences treatment and prevention practice within the family. In T. P. Gulotta (Ed.), *Family influences on child behavior and development: Evidence-based prevention and treatment approaches* (pp. 1–20). New York: Routledge.

Gunnar, M. R., & Cheatham, C. L. (2003). Brain and behavior interfaces: Stress and the developing brain. *Infant Mental Health Journal, 24,* 195–211.

Gunnar, M. R., Morison, S. J., Chisholm, K., & Schuder, M. (2001). Salivary cortisol levels in children adopted from Romanian orphanages. *Development and Psychopathology, 13,* 611–628.

Gunnarsdottir, I., Schack-Nielsen, L., Michaelson, K. F., Sørensen, T. I., & Thorsdottir, I. (2010). Infant weight gain, duration of exclusive breast-feeding, and childhood BMI—two similar follow-up cohorts. *Public Health Nutrition, 13,* 201–207.

Gunnoe, M. L., & Mariner, C. L. (1997). Toward a developmental-contextual model of the effects of parental spanking on children's aggression. *Archives of Pediatrics and Adolescent Medicine, 151,* 768–775.

Gunstad, J., Spitznagel, M. B., Luyster, F., Cohen, R. A., & Paul, R. H. (2007). Handedness and cognition across the healthy lifespan. *International Journal of Neuroscience, 117,* 477–485.

Gure, A., Ucanok, Z., & Sayil, M. (2006). The associations among perceived pubertal timing, parental relations and self-perception in Turkish adolescents. *Journal of Youth and Adolescence, 35,* 541–550.

Gureje, O., Ogunniyi, A., Baiyewu, O., Price, B., Unverzagt, F. W., & Evans, R. M. (2006). APOE epsilon-4 is not associated with Alzheimer's disease in elderly Nigerians. *Annals of Neurology, 59,* 182–185.

Gustafson, G. E., Wood, R. M., & Green, J. A. (2000). Can we hear the causes of infants' crying? In R. G. Barr & B. Hopkins (Eds.), *Crying as a sign, a symptom, and a signal: Clinical, emotional, and developmental aspects of infant and toddler crying* (pp. 8–22). New York: Cambridge University Press.

Guterman, N. B., Lee, S. J., Taylor, C. A., & Rathouz, P. J. (2009). Parental perceptions of neighborhood processes, stress, personal control, and risk for physical child abuse and neglect. *Child Abuse and Neglect, 33,* 897–906.

Gutman, L. M. (2006). How student and parent goal orientations and classroom goal structures influence the math achievement of African Americans during the high school transition. *Contemporary Educational Psychology, 31,* 44–63.

Gutman, L. M., & Midgley, C. (2000). The role of protective factors in supporting the academic achievement of poor African-American students during the middle school transition. *Journal of Youth and Adolescence, 29,* 223–248.

Gutmann, D. (1977). The cross-cultural perspective: Notes toward a comparative psychology of aging. In J. E. Birren & K. W. Schaie (Eds.), *Handbook of the psychology of aging* (pp. 302–326). New York: Van Nostrand Reinhold.

Gutmann, D. L., & Huyck, M. H. (1994). Development and pathology in post-parental men: A community study. In E. Thompson, Jr. (Ed.), *Older men's lives* (pp. 65–84). Thousand Oaks, CA: Sage.

Gutteling, B. M., de Weerth, C., Zandbelt, N., Mulder, E. J. H., Visser, G. H. A., & Buitelaar, J. K. (2006). Does maternal prenatal stress adversely affect the child's learning and memory at age six? *Journal of Abnormal Child Psychology, 34,* 789–798.

Guttuso, T., Jr. (2012). Effective and clinically meaningful non-hormonal hot flash therapies. *Maturitas, 72,* 6–12.

Gwiazda, J., & Birch, E. E. (2001). Perceptual development: Vision. In E. B. Goldstein (Ed.), *Blackwell handbook of perception* (pp. 636–668). Oxford, UK: Blackwell.

H

Haentjens, P., Magaziner, J., Colón-Emeric, C. S., Vanderschueren, D., Milisen, K., Velkeniers, B., et al. (2010). Meta-analysis: Excess mortality after hip fracture among older women and men. *Annals of Internal Medicine, 16,* 380–390.

Hagberg, B., & Samuelsson, G. (2008). Survival after 100 years of age: A multivariate model of exceptional survival in Swedish centenarians. *Journal of Gerontology, 63A,* 1219–1226.

Hagerman, R. J., Berry-Kravis, E., Kaufmann, W. E., Ono, M. Y., Tartaglia, N., & Lachiewicz, A. (2009). Advances in the treatment of fragile X syndrome. *Pediatrics, 123,* 378–390.

Hahn, S., & Chitty, L. S. (2008). Noninvasive prenatal diagnosis: Current practice and future perspectives. *Current Opinion in Obstetrics and Gynecology, 20,* 146–151.

Haidt, J. (2001). The emotional dog and its rational tail: A social intuitionist approach to moral judgment. *Psychological Review, 108,* 814–834.

Haidt, J., & Kesebir, S. (2010). Morality. In S. T. Fiske & D. Gilbert (Eds.), *Handbook of social psychology* (5th ed., pp. 797–832). Hoboken, NJ: Wiley.

Haight, W. L., & Miller, P. J. (1993). *Pretending at home: Early development in a sociocultural context.* Albany: State University of New York Press.

Hainline, L. (1998). The development of basic visual abilities. In A. Slater (Ed.), *Perceptual development: Visual, auditory, and speech perception in infancy* (pp. 37–44). Hove, UK: Psychology Press.

Hakman, M., & Sullivan, M. (2009). The effect of task and maternal verbosity on compliance in toddlers. *Infant and Child Development, 18,* 195–205.

Hakuta, K., Bialystok, E., & Wiley, E. (2003). Critical evidence: A test of the critical-period hypothesis for second-language acquisitions. *Psychological Science, 14,* 31–38.

Hale, C. M., & Tager-Flusberg, H. (2003). The influence of language on theory of mind: A training study. *Developmental Science, 6,* 346–359.

Hale, S., Rose, N. S., Myerson, J., Strube, M. J., Sommers, M., Tye-Murray, N., et al. (2011). The structure of working memory abilities across the adult life span. *Psychology and Aging, 26,* 92–110.

Hales, C. N., & Ozanne, S. E. (2003). The dangerous road of catch-up growth. *Journal of Physiology, 547,* 5–10.

Haley, W. E. (2013). Family caregiving at end-of-life: Current status and future directions. In R. C. Talley & R. J. V. Montgomery (Eds.), *Caregiving across the lifespan: Research, practice, and policy* (pp. 157–175). New York: Springer.

Halfon, N., & McLearn, K. T. (2002). Families with children under 3: What we know and implications for results and policy. In N. Halfon & K. T. McLearn (Eds.), *Child rearing in America: Challenges facing parents with young children* (pp. 367–412). New York: Cambridge University Press.

Halford, G. S., & Andrews, G. (2006). Reasoning and problem solving. In D. Kuhn & R. Siegler (Eds.), *Handbook of child psychology: Vol. 2. Cognition, perception, and language* (6th ed., pp. 557–608). Hoboken, NJ: Wiley.

Halgunseth, L. C., Ispa, J. M., & Rudy, D. (2006). Parental control in Latino families: An integrated review of the literature. *Child Development, 77,* 1282–1297.

Hall, C. B., Derby, C., LeValley, A., Katz, M. J., Verghese, J., & Lipton, R. B. (2007). Education delays accelerated decline on a memory test in persons who develop dementia. *Neurology, 69,* 1657–1664.

Hall, C. B., Lipton, R. B., Sliwinski, M., Katz, M. J., Derby, C. A., & Verghese, J. (2009). Cognitive activities delay onset of memory decline in persons who develop dementia. *Neurology, 73,* 356–361.

Hall, G. S. (1904). *Adolescence.* New York: Appleton.

Hall, J. G. (2003). Twinning. *Lancet, 362,* 735–743.

Hall, K., Murrell, J., Ogunniyi, A., Deeg, M., Baiyewu, O., & Gao, S. (2006). Cholesterol, APOE genotype, and Alzheimer disease: An epidemiologic study of Nigerian Yoruba. *Neurology, 66,* 223–227.

Halle, T. G. (2003). Emotional development and wellbeing. In M. H. Bornstein, L. Davidson,

C. L. M. Keyes, K. A. Moore, & the Center for Child Well-Being (Eds.), *Well-being: Positive development across the life course* (pp. 125–138). Mahwah, NJ: Erlbaum.

Haller, J. (2005). Vitamins and brain function. In H. R. Lieberman, R. B. Kanarek, & C. Prasad (2005). *Nutritional neuroscience* (pp. 207–233). Philadelphia: Taylor & Francis.

Hallinan, M. T., & Kubitschek, W. N. (1999). Curriculum differentiation and high school achievement. *Social Psychology of Education, 3,* 41–62.

Halpern, C. T., Udry, J. R., & Suchindran, C. (1997). Testosterone predicts initiation of coitus in adolescent females. *Psychosomatic Medicine, 59,* 161–171.

Halpern, D. F. (2004). A cognitive-process taxonomy for sex differences in cognitive abilities. *Current Directions in Psychological Science, 13,* 135–139.

Halpern, D. F. (2005a). How time-flexible work policies can reduce stress, improve health, and save money. *Stress and Health, 21,* 157–168.

Halpern, D. F. (2005b). Psychology at the intersection of work and family: Recommendations for employers, working families, and policymakers. *American Psychologist, 60,* 397–409.

Halpern, D. F., Wai, J., & Saw, A. (2005). A psychobiological model: Why females are sometimes greater than and sometimes less than males in math achievement. In D. F. Halpern, J. Wai, & A. Saw (Eds.), *Gender differences in mathematics: An integrative psychological approach* (pp. 48–72). New York: Cambridge University Press.

Halpern-Felsher, B. L., Biehl, M., Kropp, R. Y., & Rubinstein, M. L. (2004). Perceived risks and benefits of smoking: Differences among adolescents with different smoking experiences and intentions. *Preventive Medicine, 39,* 559–567.

Haltzman, S., Holstein, N., & Moss, S. B. (2007). Men, marriage, and divorce. In J. E. Grant & M. N. Potenza (Eds.), *Textbook of men's mental health* (pp. 283–305). Washington, DC: American Psychiatric Publishing.

Hamberger, L. K., Lohr, J. M., Parker, L. M., & Witte, T. (2009). Treatment approaches for men who batter their partners. In C. Mitchell & D. Anglin (Eds.), *Intimate partner violence: A health-based perspective* (pp. 459–471). New York: Oxford University Press.

Hamer, D. H., Hu, S., Magnuson, V. L., Hu, N., & Pattatucci, A. M. L. (1993). A linkage between DNA markers on the X chromosome and male sexual orientation. *Science, 261,* 321–327.

Hammes, B., & Laitman, C. J. (2003). Diethylstilbestrol (DES) update: Recommendations for the identification and management of DES-exposed individuals. *Journal of Midwifery and Women's Health, 48,* 19–29.

Hampton, K. N., Goulet, L. S., Rainie, L., & Purcell, K. (2011). *Social networking sites and our lives.* Washington, DC: Pew Research Center Internet & American Life Project. Retrieved from www.pewinternet.org/Reports/2011/Technology-and-social-networks.aspx

Hane, A. A., Cheah, C., Rubin, K. H., & Fox, N. A. (2008). The role of maternal behavior in the relation between shyness and social reticence in early childhood and social withdrawal in middle childhood. *Social Development, 17,* 795–811.

Hanioka, T., Ojima, M., Tanaka, K., & Yamamoto, M. (2011). Does secondhand smoke affect the development of dental caries in children? A systematic review. *International Journal of Environmental Research and Public Health, 8,* 1503–1509.

Hankin, B. L., & Abela, J. R. Z. (2005). Depression from childhood through adolescence and adulthood: A developmental vulnerability and stress perspective. In B. L. Hankin & J. R. Z. Abela (Eds.), *Development of psychopathology: A vulnerability-stress perspective* (pp. 245–288). Thousand Oaks, CA: Sage.

Hankin, B. L., Stone, L., & Wright, P. A. (2010). Corumination, interpersonal stress generation, and internalizing symptoms: Accumulating effects and transactional influences in a multiwave study of adolescents. *Development and Psychopathology, 22,* 217–235.

Hannon, E. E., & Johnson, S. P. (2004). Infants use meter to categorize rhythms and melodies: Implications for musical structure learning. *Cognitive Psychology, 50,* 354–377.

Hannon, E. E., & Trehub, S. E. (2005a). Metrical categories in infancy and adulthood. *Psychological Science, 16,* 48–55.

Hannon, E. E., & Trehub, S. E. (2005b). Tuning in to musical rhythms: Infants learn more readily than adults. *Proceedings of the National Academy of Sciences, 102,* 12639–12643.

Hannon, T. S., Rao, G., & Arslanian, S. A. (2005). Childhood obesity and type 2 diabetes mellitus. *Pediatrics, 116,* 473–480.

Hansell, N. K., Wright, M. J., Geffen, G. M., Geffen, L. B., Smith, G. A., & Martin, N. G. (2001). Genetic influence on ERP slow wave measures of working memory. *Behavioral Genetics, 31,* 603–614.

Hansen, M., Janssen, I., Schiff, A., Zee, P. C., & Dubocovich, M. L. (2005). The impact of school daily schedule on adolescent sleep. *Pediatrics, 115,* 1555–1561.

Hansen, M. B., & Markman, E. M. (2009). Children's use of mutual exclusivity to learn labels for parts of objects. *Developmental Psychology, 45,* 592–596.

Hansson, R. O., & Stroebe, M. S. (2007). The dual process model of coping with bereavement and development of an integrative risk factor framework. In R. O. Hansson & M. S. Stroebe (Eds.), *Bereavement in late life: Coping, adaptation, and developmental influences* (pp. 41–60). Washington, DC: American Psychological Association.

Hao, L., & Woo, H. S. (2012). Distinct trajectories in the transition to adulthood: Are children of immigrants advantaged? *Child Development, 83,* 1623–1639.

Harachi, T. W., Fleming, C. B., White, H. R., Ensminger, M. E., Abbott, R. D., Catalano, R. F., & Haggerty, K. P. (2006). Aggressive behavior among girls and boys during middle childhood: Predictors and sequelae of trajectory group membership. *Aggressive Behavior, 32,* 279–293.

Harden, K. Paige, & Tucker-Drob, E. M. (2011). Individual differences in the development of sensation seeking and impulsivity during adolescence: Further evidence for a dual systems model. *Developmental Psychology, 47,* 739–746.

Hardy, S. A., & Carlo, G. (2005). Religiosity and prosocial behaviours in adolescence: The mediating role of prosocial values. *Journal of Moral Education, 34,* 231–249.

Hardy, S. A., & Carlo, G. (2011). Moral identity: What is it, how does it develop, and is it linked to moral action? *Child Development Perspectives, 5,* 212–218.

Hardy, S. A., Pratt, M. W., Pancer, S. M., Olsen, J. A., & Lawford, H. L. (2011). Community and religious involvement as contexts of identity change across late adolescence and emerging adulthood. *International Journal of Behavioral Development, 35,* 125–135.

Harley, B., & Jean, G. (1999). Vocabulary skills of French immersion students in their second language. *Zeitschrift für Interkulturellen Fremdsprachenunterricht, 4*(2). Retrieved from www.ualberta.ca

Harley, K., & Reese, E. (1999). Origins of autobiographical memory. *Developmental Psychology, 35,* 1338–1348.

Harlow, H. F., & Zimmerman, R. (1959). Affectional responses in the infant monkey. *Science, 130,* 421–432.

Harris, R. C., Robinson, J. B., Chang, F., & Burns, B. M. (2007). Characterizing preschool children's attention regulation in parent–child interactions: The roles of effortful control and motivation. *Journal of Applied Developmental Psychology, 28,* 25–39.

Harris, Y. R., & Graham, J. A. (2007). *The African American child: Development and challenges.* New York: Springer.

Harris Interactive. (2011). *Large majorities support doctor-assisted suicide for terminally ill patients in great pain.* Retrieved from www.harrisinteractive.com/NewsRoom/HarrisPolls/tabid/447/mid/1508/articleId/677/ctl/ReadCustom%20Default/Default.aspx

Hart, B., & Risley, T. R. (1995). *Meaningful differences in the everyday experience of young American children.* Baltimore: Paul H. Brookes.

Hart, C. H., Burts, D. C., Durland, M. A., Charlesworth, R., DeWolf, M., & Fleege, P. O. (1998). Stress behaviors and activity type participation of preschoolers in more and less developmentally appropriate classrooms: SES and sex differences. *Journal of Research in Childhood Education, 13,* 176–196.

Hart, C. H., Newell, L. D., & Olsen, S. F. (2003). Parenting skills and social–communicative competence in childhood. In J. O. Greene & B. R. Burleson (Eds.), *Handbook of communication and social interaction skills* (pp. 753–797). Mahwah, NJ: Erlbaum.

Hart, C. H., Yang, C., Nelson, L. J., Robinson, C. C., Olsen, J. A., Nelson, D. A., Porter, C. L., Jin, S., Olsen, S. F., & Wu, P. (2000). Peer acceptance in early childhood and subtypes of socially withdrawn behavior in China, Russia, and the United States. *International Journal of Behavioral Development, 24,* 73–81.

Hart, D., & Fegley, S. (1995). Prosocial behavior and caring in adolescence: Relations to self-understanding and social judgment. *Child Development, 66,* 1346–1359.

Hart, H., & Rubia, K. (2012). Neuroimaging of child abuse: A review. *Frontiers in Human Neuroscience, 6,* 52.

Hart, H. M., McAdams, D. P., Hirsch, B. J., & Bauer, J. J. (2001). Generativity and social involvement among African Americans and white adults. *Journal of Research in Personality, 35,* 208–230.

Harter, S. (1999). *The construction of self: A developmental perspective.* New York: Guilford.

Harter, S. (2003). The development of self-representations during childhood and adolescence. In M. R. Leary & J. P. Tangney (Eds.), *Handbook of self and identity* (pp. 610–642). New York: Guilford.

Harter, S. (2006). The self. In N. Eisenberg (Ed.), *Handbook of child psychology: Vol. 3. Social, emotional, and personality development* (6th ed., pp. 505–570). Hoboken, NJ: Wiley.

Harter, S., & Whitesell, N. (1989). Developmental changes in children's understanding of simple, multiple, and blended emotion concepts. In C. Saarni & P. Harris (Eds.), *Children's understanding of emotion* (pp. 81–116). Cambridge, UK: Cambridge University Press.

Hartley, A. (2006). Changing role of the speed of processing construct. In J. E. Birren & K. W. Schaie (Eds.), *Handbook of the psychology of aging* (6th ed., pp. 183–207). Burlington, MA: Academic Press.

Hartman, J., & Warren, L. H. (2005). Explaining age differences in temporal working memory. *Psychology and Aging, 20,* 645–656.

Hartshorn, K., Rovee-Collier, C., Gerhardstein, P., Bhatt, R. S., Wondoloski, T. L., Klein, P., Gilch, J., Wurtzel, N., & Campos-de-Carvalho, M. (1998). The ontogeny of long-term memory over the first year-and-a-half of life. *Developmental Psychobiology, 32,* 69–89.

Hartup, W. W. (2006). Relationships in early and middle childhood. In A. L. Vangelisti & D. Perlman (Eds.), *Cambridge handbook of personal relationships* (pp. 177–190). New York: Cambridge University Press.

Hartup, W. W., & Abecassis, M. (2004). Friends and enemies. In P. K. Smith & C. H. Hart (Eds.), *Blackwell handbook of childhood social development* (pp. 285–306). Malden, MA: Blackwell.

Hartup, W. W., & Stevens, N. (1999). Friendships and adaptation across the life span. *Current Directions in Psychological Science, 8,* 76–79.

Harvey, M. W. (2001). Vocational-technical education: A logical approach to dropout prevention for secondary special education. *Preventing School Failure, 45,* 108–113.

Harwood, M. D., & Farrar, M. J. (2006). Conflicting emotions: The connection between affective perspective taking and theory of mind. *British Journal of Developmental Psychology, 24,* 401–418.

Harwood, R., Leyendecker, B., Carlson, V., Asencio, M., & Miller, A. (2002). Parenting among Latino families in the U.S. In M. H. Bornstein (Ed.), *Handbook of parenting: Vol. 4. Social conditions and applied parenting* (4th ed., pp. 21–46). Mahwah, NJ: Erlbaum.

Hasebe, Y., Nucci, L., & Nucci, M. S. (2004). Parental control of the personal domain and adolescent symptoms of psychopathology: A cross-national study in the United States and Japan. *Child Development, 75,* 815–828.

Hasher, L., Lustig, C., & Zacks, R. T. (2007). Inhibitory mechanisms and the control of attention. In A. R. A. Conway, C. Jarrold, M. Kane, A. Miyake, & J. N. Towse (Eds.), *Variation in working memory* (pp. 227–249). New York: Oxford University Press.

Hastrup, B. (2007). Healthy aging in Denmark? In M. Robinson, W. Novelli, C. Pearson, & L. Norris (Eds.), *Global health and global aging* (pp. 71–84). San Francisco: Jossey-Bass.

Hatch, L. R., & Bulcroft, K. (2004). Does long-term marriage bring less frequent disagreements? *Journal of Family Issues, 25,* 465–495.

Hatfield, E., Rapson, R. L, & Martel, L. D. (2007). Passionate love and sexual desire. In S. Kitayama & D. Cohen (Eds.), *Handbook of cultural psychology* (pp. 760–779). New York: Guilford.

Hatfield, E., & Sprecher, S. (1995). Men's and women's mate preferences in the United States, Russia, and Japan. *Journal of Cross-Cultural Psychology, 26,* 728–750.

Hau, K.-T., & Ho, I. T. (2010). Chinese students' motivation and achievement. In M. H. Bond (Ed.), *Oxford handbook of Chinese psychology* (pp. 187–204). New York: Oxford University Press.

Hauf, P., Aschersleben, G., & Prinz, W. (2007). Baby do-baby see! How action production influences action perception in infants. *Cognitive Development, 22,* 16–32.

Haukkala, A., Konttinen, H., Laatikainen, T., Kawachi, I., & Uutela, A. (2010). Hostility, anger control, and anger expression as predictors of cardiovascular disease. *Psychosomatic Medicine, 72,* 556–562.

Hausfather, A., Toharia, A., LaRoche, C., & Engelsmann, F. (1997). Effects of age of entry, day-care quality, and family characteristics on preschool behavior. *Journal of Child Psychology and Psychiatry, 38,* 441–448.

Hawkins, J. N. (1994). Issues of motivation in Asian education. In H. F. O'Neil, Jr., & M. Drillings (Eds.), *Motivation: Theory and research* (pp. 101–115). Hillsdale, NJ: Erlbaum.

Hawkley, L. C., & Cacioppo, J. T. (2004). Stress and the aging immune system. *Brain, Behavior and Immunity, 18,* 114–119.

Haworth, C. M. A., Wright, M. J., Luciano, M., Martin, N. G., de Geus, E. J. C., van Beijsterveldt, C. E. M., et al. (2010). The heritability of general cognitive ability increases linearly from childhood to young adulthood. *Molecular Psychiatry, 15,* 1112–1120.

Haws, R. A., Yakoob, M. Y., Soomro, T., Menezes, E. V., Darmstadt, G. L., & Bhutta, Z. A. (2009). Reducing stillbirths: Screening and monitoring during pregnancy and labour. *BMC Pregnancy and Childbirth, 9*(Suppl. S1).

Hawton, A., Green, C., Dickens, A. P., Richards, S. H., Taylor, R. S., & Edwards, R. (2011). The impact of social isolation on the health status and healthrelated quality of life of older people. *Quality of Life Research, 20,* 57–67.

Hay, D. F., Pawlby, S., Waters, C. S., Perra, O., & Sharp, D. (2010). Mothers' antenatal depression and their children's antisocial outcomes. *Child Development, 81,* 149–165.

Hay, E. L., & Diehl, M. (2010). Reactivity to daily stressors in adulthood: The importance of stressor type in characterizing risk factors. *Psychology and Aging, 25,* 118–131.

Hay, P., & Bacaltchuk, J. (2004). Bulimia nervosa. *Clinical Evidence, 12,* 1326–1347.

Haycock, P. C. (2009). Fetal alcohol spectrum disorders: The epigenetic perspective. *Biology of Reproduction, 81,* 607–617.

Hayflick, L. (1994). *How and why we age.* New York: Ballantine.

Hayflick, L. (1998). How and why we age. *Experimental Gerontology, 33,* 639–653.

Hayne, H., Herbert, J., & Simcock, G. (2003). Imitation from television by 24- and 30-month-olds. *Developmental Science, 6,* 254–261.

Hayne, H., Rovee-Collier, C., & Perris, E. E. (1987). Categorization and memory retrieval by three-month-olds. *Child Development, 58,* 750–767.

Hayslip, B., Jr., & Kaminski, P. L. (2005). Grandparents raising their grandchildren. *Marriage and Family Review, 37,* 147–169.

Haywood, H. C., & Lidz, C. S. (2007). *Dynamic assessment in practice.* New York: Cambridge University Press.

Haywood, K. M., & Getchell, N. (2005). *Life span motor development* (4th ed.). Champaign, IL: Human Kinetics.

Haywood, K. M., & Getchell, N. (2009). *Life span motor development* (5th ed.). Champaign, IL: Human Kinetics.

Hazen, N. L., McFarland, L., Jacobvitz, D., & Boyd-Soisson, E. (2010). Fathers' frightening behaviours and sensitivity with infants: Relations with fathers' attachment representations, father–infant attachment, and children's later outcomes. *Early Child Development and Care, 180,* 51–69.

Head Start Bureau. (2010). *Head Start Program fact sheet.* Retrieved from eclkc.ohs.acf.hhs.gov/hslc/mr/factsheets/fHeadStartProgr.htm

Healthy Families America. (2011). *Healthy Families America FAQ.* Retrieved from www.healthyfamiliesamerica.org/about_us/faq.shtml

Heath, S. B. (1990). The children of Trackton's children: Spoken and written in social change. In J. Stigler, G. Herdt, & R. A. Shweder (Eds.), *Cultural psychology: Essays on comparative human development* (pp. 496–519). New York: Cambridge University Press.

Hebblethwaite, S., & Norris, J. (2011). Expressions of generativity through family leisure: Experiences of grandparents and adult grandchildren. *Family Relations, 60,* 121–133.

Heckhausen, J., Wrosch, C., & Schultz, R. (2010). A motivational theory of life-span development. *Psychological Review, 117,* 32–60.

Heckman, J. J., Seong, H. M., Pinto, R., Savelyev, P., & Yavitz, A. (2010). A new cost–benefit and rate of return for the Perry Preschool Program: A summary. In A. J. Reynolds, A. J. Rolnick, M. M. Englund, & J. Temple (Eds.), *Childhood programs and practices in the first decade of life: A human capital integration* (pp. 199–213). New York: Cambridge University Press.

Hedberg, K., Hopkins, D., Leman, R., & Kohn, M. (2009). The 10-year experience of Oregon's Death with Dignity Act: 1998–2007. *Journal of Clinical Ethics, 20,* 124–132.

Hedge, J. W., Borman, W. C., & Lammlein, S. E. (2006). *The aging workforce: Realities, myths, and implications for organizations.* Washington, DC: American Psychological Association.

Hediger, M. L., Overpeck, M. D., Ruan, W. J., & Troendle, J. F. (2002). Birthweight and gestational age effects on motor and social development. *Paediatric and Perinatal Epidemiology, 16,* 33–46.

Heino, R., Ellison, N., & Gibbs, J. (2010). Relationshopping: Investigating the market metaphor in online dating. *Journal of Social and Personal Relationships, 27,* 427–447.

Hellemans, K. G., Sliwowska, J. H., Verma, P., & Weinberg, J. (2010). Prenatal alcohol exposure: Fetal programming and later life vulnerability to stress, expression and anxiety disorders. *Neuroscience and Biobehavioral Reviews, 34,* 791–807.

Helm, H. M., Hays, J. C., Flint, E. P., Koenig, H. G., & Blazer, D. G. (2000). Does private religious activity prolong survival? A six-year follow-up study of 3,851 older adults. *Journal of Gerontology, 55A,* M400–M405.

Helson, R. (1992). Women's difficult times and the rewriting of the life story. *Psychology of Women Quarterly, 16,* 331–347.

Helson, R., Jones, C. J., & Kwan, V. S. Y. (2002). Personality change over 40 years of adulthood: Hierarchical linear modeling analyses of two longitudinal samples. *Journal of Personality and Social Psychology, 83,* 752–766.

Helson, R., & Picano, J. (1990). Is the traditional role bad for women? *Journal of Personality and Social Psychology, 59,* 311–320.

Helson, R., Soto, C. J., & Cate, R. A. (2006). From young adulthood through the middle ages. In D. K. Mroczek & T. D. Little (Eds.), *Handbook of personality development* (pp. 337–352). Mahwah, NJ: Erlbaum.

Heltzner, E. P., Cauley, J. A., Pratt, S. R., Wisniewski, S. R., Zmuda, J. M., & Talbott, E. O. (2005). Race and sex differences in age-related hearing loss: The health, aging and body composition study. *Journal of the American Geriatrics Society, 53,* 2119–2127.

Helwig, C. C. (2006). Rights, civil liberties, and democracy across cultures. In M. Killen & J. G. Smetana (Eds.), *Handbook of moral development* (pp. 185–210). Philadelphia: Erlbaum.

Helwig, C. C., & Jasiobedzka, U. (2001). The relation between law and morality: Children's reasoning about socially beneficial and unjust laws. *Child Development, 72,* 1382–1393.

Helwig, C. C., & Prencipe, A. (1999). Children's judgments of flags and flag-burning. *Child Development, 70,* 132–143.

Helwig, C. C., Zelazo, P. D., & Wilson, M. (2001). Children's judgments of psychological harm in normal and canonical situations. *Child Development, 72,* 66–81.

Henggeler, S. W., Schoenwald, S. K., Bourduin, C. M., Rowland, M. D., & Cunningham, P. B. (2009). *Multisystemic therapy for antisocial behavior in children and adolescents* (2nd ed.). New York: Guilford.

Hendrick, S. S., & Hendrick, C. (2002). Love. In C. R. Snyder & S. J. Lopez (Eds.), *Handbook of positive psychology* (pp. 472–484). New York: Oxford University Press.

Hendricks, J., & Cutler, S. J. (2004). Volunteerism and socioemotional selectivity in later life. *Journal of Gerontology, 59B,* S251–S257.

Hendrie, H. H. (2001). Exploration of environmental and genetic risk factors for Alzheimer's disease: The value of cross-cultural studies. *Current Directions in Psychological Science, 10,* 98–101.

Hendry, L. B., & Kloep, M. (2007). Conceptualizing emerging adulthood: Inspecting the emperor's new clothes? *Child Development Perspectives, 1,* 74–79.

Hendry, L. B., & Kloep, M. (2010). How universal is emerging adulthood? An empirical example. *Journal of Youth Studies, 13,* 169–179.

Hendry, M., Paserfield, D., Lewis, R., Carter, B., Hodgson, D., & Wilinson, C. (2012). Why do we want the right to die? A systematic review of the international literature on the views of patients, carers and the public on assisted dying. *Palliative Medicine, 27,* 13–26.

Henig, R. M., & Henig, S. (2012). *Twenty something: Why do young adults seem stuck?* New York: Hudson Street Press.

Henning, K., Jones, A. R., & Holdford, R. (2005). Attributions of blame among male and female domestic violence offenders. *Journal of Family Violence, 20,* 131–139.

Henrich, C. C., Brookmeyer, K. A., Shrier, L. A., & Shahar, G. (2006). Supportive relationships and sexual risk behavior in adolescence: An ecological–transactional approach. *Journal of Pediatric Psychology, 31,* 286–297.

Henrich, C. C., Kuperminc, G. P., Sack, A., Blatt, S. J., & Leadbeater, B. J. (2000). Characteristics and homogeneity of early adolescent friendship groups: A comparison of male and female clique and nonclique members. *Applied Developmental Science, 4,* 15–26.

Henricsson, L., & Rydell, A.-M. (2004). Elementary school children with behavior problems: Teacher–child relations and self-perception. A prospective study. *Merrill-Palmer Quarterly, 50,* 111–138.

Henry, J. D., MacLeod, M. S., Phillips, L. H., & Crawford, J. R. (2004). A meta-analytic review of prospective memory and aging. *Psychology and Aging, 19,* 27–39.

Herbenick, D., Reece, M., Schick, V., Sanders, S. A., Dodge, B., & Fortenberry, J. D. (2010). Sexual behavior in the United States: Results from a national probability sample of men and women ages 14–94. *Journal of Sexual Medicine, 7*(Suppl. 5), 255–265.

Herbst, J. H., McCrae, R. R., Costa, P. T., Jr., Feaganes, J. R., & Siegler, I. C. (2000). Self-perceptions of stability and change in personality at midlife: The UNC Alumni Heart Study. *Assessment, 7,* 379–388.

Herd, P., Robert, S. A., & House, J. S. (2011). Health disparities among older adults: Life course influences and policy solutions. *Handbook of aging and the social sciences* (7th ed., pp. 121–134). San Diego: Academic Press.

Herman, M. (2004). Forced to choose: Some determinants of racial identification in multiracial adolescents. *Child Development, 75,* 730–748.

Herman-Giddens, M. E. (2006). Recent data on pubertal milestones in United States children: The secular trend toward earlier development. *International Journal of Andrology, 29,* 241–246.

Herman-Giddens, M. E., Steffes, J., Harris, D., Slora, E., Hussey, M., Dowshen, S. A., et al. (2012). Secondary sexual characteristics in boys: Data from the Pediatric Research in Office Settings Network. *Pediatrics, 130,* e1058–e1068.

Hernandez, D. J., Denton, N. A., & Macartney, S. E. (2008). Children in immigrant families: Looking to America's future. *Social Policy Report of the Society for Research in Child Development, 12*(11).

Hernandez, M., & Newcomer, R. (2007). Assisted living and special populations: What do we know about differences in use and potential access barriers? *Gerontologist, 47*(Special Issue III), 110–117.

Herrnstein, R. J., & Murray, C. (1994). *The bell curve.* New York: Free Press.

Hershey, D. A., Jacobs-Lawson, J. M., McArdle, J. J., & Hamagami, F. (2007). Psychological foundations of financial planning for retirement. *Journal of Adult Development, 14,* 26–36.

Hertzog, C., & Dunlosky, J. (2011). Metacognition in later adulthood: Spared monitoring can benefit older adults' self-regulation. *Current Directions in Psychological Science, 20,* 167–173.

Hertzog, C., Kramer, A. F., Wilson, R. S., & Lindenberger, U. (2009). Enrichment effects on adult cognitive development. *Psychological Science in the Public Interest, 9*(1), 1–65.

Herzog, D. B., Eddy, K. T., & Beresin, E. V. (2006). Anorexia and bulimia nervosa. In M. K. Dulcan & J. M. Wiener (Eds.), *Essentials of child and adolescent psychiatry* (pp. 527–560). Washington, DC: American Psychiatric Publishing.

Hespos, S. J., & Baillargeon, R. (2008). Young infants' actions reveal their developing knowledge of support variables: Converging evidence for violation-ofexpectation findings. *Cognition, 107,* 304–316.

Hespos, S. J., Ferry, A. L., Cannistraci, C. J., Gore, J., & Park, S. (2010). Using optical imaging to investigate functional cortical activity in human infants. In A. W. Roe (Ed.), *Imaging the brain with optical methods* (pp. 159–176). New York: Springer Science + Business Media.

Hess, T. M., & Hinson, J. T. (2006). Age-related variation in the influences of aging stereotypes on memory in adulthood. *Psychology and Aging, 21,* 621–625.

Hess, T. M., Hinson, J. T., & Statham, J. A. (2004). Explicit and implicit stereotype activation effects on memory: Do age and awareness moderate the impact of priming? *Psychology and Aging, 19,* 495–505.

Hetherington, E. M. (1999). Should we stay together for the sake of the children? In E. M. Hetherington (Ed.), *Coping with divorce, single-parenting, and remarriage: A risk and resiliency perspective* (pp. 93–116). Hillsdale, NJ: Erlbaum.

Hetherington, E. M., Henderson, S. H., & Reiss, D. (1999). Adolescent siblings in stepfamilies: Family functioning and adolescent adjustment. *Monographs of the Society for Research in Child Development, 64*(4, Serial No. 259).

Hetherington, E. M., & Kelly, J. (2002). *For better or for worse: Divorce reconsidered.* New York: Norton.

Hetherington, E. M., & Stanley-Hagan, M. (2000). Diversity among stepfamilies. In D. H. Demo, K. R. Allen, & M. A. Fine (Eds.), *Handbook of family diversity* (pp. 173–196). New York: Oxford University Press.

Hewlett, B. S. (2004). Fathers in forager, farmer, and pastoral cultures. In M. E. Lamb (Ed.), *The role of the father in child development* (4th ed., pp. 182–195). Hoboken, NJ: Wiley.

Hewlett, S. (2003). *Creating a life.* New York: Miramax.

Heyman, G. D., & Dweck, C. S. (1998). Children's thinking about traits: Implications for judgments of the self and others. *Child Development, 69,* 391–403.

Heyman, G. D., & Legare, C. H. (2004). Children's beliefs about gender differences in the academic and social domains. *Sex Roles, 50,* 227–239.

Hickling, A. K., & Wellman, H. M. (2001). The emergence of children's causal explanations and theories: Evidence from everyday conversation. *Developmental Psychology, 37,* 668–683.

Hietanen, A., Era, P., Sorri, M., & Heikkinen, E. (2004). Changes in hearing in 80-year-old people: A 10-year follow-up study. *International Journal of Audiology, 43,* 126–135.

Higginbottom, G. M. A. (2006). "Pressure of life": Ethnicity as a mediating factor in mid-life and older peoples' experience of high blood pressure. *Sociology of Health and Illness, 28,* 583–610.

Higgins, C. A., Duxbury, L. E., & Lyons, S. T. (2010). Coping with overload and stress: Men and women in dual-earner families. *Journal of Marriage and Family 72,* 847–859.

High, P. C., LaGasse, L., Becker, S., Ahlgren, I., & Gardner, A. (2000). Literacy promotion in primary care pediatrics: Can we make a difference? *Pediatrics, 105,* 927–934.

Hildreth, K., & Rovee-Collier, C. (2002). Forgetting functions of reactivated memories over the first year of life. *Developmental Psychobiology, 41,* 277–288.

Hildreth, K., Sweeney, B., & Rovee-Collier, C. (2003). Differential memory-preserving effects of reminders at 6 months. *Journal of Experimental Child Psychology, 84,* 41–62.

Hilgers, K. K., Akridge, M., Scheetz, J. P., & Kinance, D. E. (2006). Childhood obesity and dental development. *Pediatric Dentistry, 28,* 18–22.

Hill, J. L., Brooks-Gunn, J., & Waldfogel, J. (2003). Sustained effects of high participation in an early intervention for low-birth-weight premature infants. *Developmental Psychology, 39,* 730–744.

Hill, N. E., & Taylor, L. C. (2004). Parental school involvement and children's academic achievement: Pragmatics and issues. *Current Directions in Psychological Science, 13,* 161–164.

Hill, N. M., & Schneider, W. (2006). Brain changes in the development of expertise: Neuroanatomical and neurophysiological evidence about skill-based adaptations. In K. A. Ericsson, N. Charness, P. J. Feltovich, & R. R. Hoffman (Eds.), *The Cambridge handbook of expertise and expert performance* (pp. 653–682). New York: Cambridge University Press.

Hillis, S. D., Anda, R. F., Dube, S. R., Felitti, V. J., Marchbanks, P. A., & Marks, J. S. (2004). The association between adverse childhood experiences and adolescent pregnancy, long-term psychosocial consequences, and fetal death. *Pediatrics, 113,* 320–327.

Hilt, L. M. (2004). Attribution retaining for therapeutic change: Theory, practice, and future directions. *Imagination, Cognition, and Personality, 23,* 289–307.

Hinojosa, T., Sheu, C.-F., & Michael, G. F. (2003). Infant hand-use preference for grasping objects contributes to the development of a hand-use preference for manipulating objects. *Developmental Psychobiology, 43,* 328–334.

Hirasawa, R., & Feil, R. (2010). Genomic imprinting and human disease. *Essays in Biochemistry, 48,* 187–200.

Hirsch, C. (1996). Understanding the influence of gender role identity on the assumption of family caregiving roles by men. *International Journal of Aging and Human Development, 42,* 103–121.

Hirsh-Pasek, K., & Golinkoff, R. M. (2003). *Einstein never used flash cards.* New York: Rodale.

Hirsh-Pasek, K., Golinkoff, R. M., Berk, L. E., & Singer, D. G. (2009). *A mandate for playful learning in preschool: Presenting the evidence.* New York: Oxford University Press.

Hoch-Espada, A., Ryan, E., & Deblinger, E. (2006). Child sexual abuse. In J. E. Fisher & W. T. O'Donohue (Eds.), *Practitioner's guide to evidence-based psychotherapy* (pp. 177–188). New York: Springer.

Hodges, R. M., & French, L. A. (1988). The effect of class and collection labels on cardinality, class inclusion, and number conservation tasks. *Child Development, 59,* 1387–1396.

Hodnett, E. D., Gates, S., Hofmeyr, G. J., & Sakala, C. (2003). Continuous support for women during childbirth. *Cochrane Database of Systematic Reviews, 3,* CD003766.

Hoenig, H., Taylor, D. H., Jr., & Sloan, F. A. (2003). Does assistive technology substitute for personal assistance among the disabled elderly? *American Journal of Public Health, 93,* 330–337.

Hoerr, T. (2004). How MI informs teaching at New City School. *Teachers College Record, 106,* 40–48.

Hoff, B. (2001). *Full report of the prevalence, incidence, and consequences of violence against women.* Washington, DC: U.S. Department of Justice.

Hoff, E. (2003). The specificity of environmental influence: Socioeconomic status affects early vocabulary development via maternal speech. *Child Development, 74,* 1368–1378.

Hoff, E. (2006). How social contexts support and shape language development. *Developmental Review, 26,* 55–88.

Hoff, E. (2013). Interpreting the early language trajectories of children from low-SES and language minority homes: Implications for closing achievement gaps. *Developmental Psychology, 49,* 4–14.

Hoff, E., Laursen, B., & Tardif, T. (2002). Socioeconomic status and parenting. In M. H. Bornstein (Ed.), *Handbook of parenting* (pp. 231–252). Mahwah, NJ: Erlbaum.

Hofferth, S. L. (2010). Home media and children's achievement and behavior. *Child Development, 81,* 1598–1619.

Hoffman, L. W. (2000). Maternal employment: Effects of social context. In R. D. Taylor & M. C. Wang (Eds.), *Resilience across contexts: Family, work, culture, and community* (pp. 147–176). Mahwah, NJ: Erlbaum.

Hoffman, M. L. (2000). *Empathy and moral development.* New York: Cambridge University Press.

Hogan, B. E., & Linden, W. (2004). Anger response styles and blood pressure: At least don't ruminate about it! *Annals of Behavioral Medicine, 27,* 38–49.

Hogan, M. J., & Strasburger, V. C. (2008). Body image, eating disorders, and the media. *Adolescent Medicine, 19,* 521–546.

Holditch-Davis, D., Belyea, M., & Edwards, L. J. (2005). Prediction of 3-year developmental outcomes from sleep development over the preterm period. *Infant Behavior and Development, 79,* 49–58.

Holdren, J. P., & Lander, E. (2012). *Engage to excel: Producing one million additional college graduates with degrees in science, technology, engineering, and mathematics.* Washington, DC: President's Council of Advisors on Science and Technology.

Holland, J. L. (1985). *Making vocational choices: A theory of vocational personalities and work environments.* Englewood Cliffs, NJ: Prentice-Hall.

Holland, J. L. (1997). *Making vocational choices: A theory of vocational personalities and work environments* (3rd ed.). Odessa, FL: Psychological Assessment Resources.

Hollich, G. J., Hirsh-Pasek, K., & Golinkoff, R. M. (2000). Breaking the language barrier: An emergentist coalition model for the origins of word learning. *Monographs of the Society for Research in Child Development, 65*(3, Serial No. 262).

Holobow, N., Genesee, F., & Lambert, W. (1991). The effectiveness of a foreign language immersion program for children from different ethnic and social class backgrounds: Report 2. *Applied Psycholinguistics, 12,* 179–198.

Honein, M. A., Paulozzi, L. J., & Erickson, J. D. (2001). Continued occurrence of Accutane exposed pregnancies. *Teratology, 64,* 142–147.

Hong, Z.-R., Veach, P. M., & Lawrenz, F. (2003). An investigation of the gender stereotyped thinking of Taiwanese secondary school boys and girls. *Sex Roles, 48,* 495–504.

Hoobler, J. M., Lemmon, G., & Wayne, S. J. (2011). Women's underrepresentation in upper management: New insights on a persistent problem. *Organizational Dynamics, 40,* 151–156.

Hooper, L., Summerbell, C. D., Thompson, R., Sills, F., Roberts, F. G., Moore, H. J., et al. (2012). Reduced

or modified dietary fat for preventing cardiovascular disease. *Cochrane Database of Systematic Reviews* [Online], 5: CD002137.

Hooyman, N. R., & Kiyak, H. A. (2011). *Social gerontology: A multidisciplinary perspective* (9th ed.). Boston, MA: Pearson.

Hopkins, B., & Westra, T. (1988). Maternal handling and motor development: An intracultural study. *Genetic, Social and General Psychology Monographs, 14,* 377–420.

Hoppmann, C. A., Gerstorf, D., Smith, J., & Klumb, P. L. (2007). Linking possible selves and behavior: Do domain-specific hopes and fears translate into daily activities in very old age? *Journal of Gerontology, 62B,* P104–P111.

Horn, J. L., Donaldson, G., & Engstrom, R. (1981). Apprehension, memory, and fluid intelligence decline through the "vital years" of adulthood. *Research on Aging, 3,* 33–84.

Horn, J. L., & Noll, J. (1997). Human cognitive capabilities: Gf-Gc theory. In D. P. Flanagan, J. L. Genshaft, & P. L. Harrison (Eds.), *Beyond traditional intellectual assessment* (pp. 53–91). New York: Guilford.

Horner, T. M. (1980). Two methods of studying stranger reactivity in infants: A review. *Journal of Child Psychology and Psychiatry, 21,* 203–219.

Hornor, G. (2010). Child sexual abuse: Consequences and implications. *Journal of Pediatric Health Care, 24,* 358–364.

Hospice Foundation of America. (2005). *The dying process: A guide for caregivers.* Washington, DC: Author.

Hospice Foundation of America. (2013). *Hospice services and expenses.* Retrieved from www .hospicefoundation.org/servicesandexpenses

Hostetler, A. J., & Sweet, S., & Moen, P. (2007). Gendered career paths: A life course perspective on returning to school. *Sex Roles, 56,* 85–103.

Houlihan, J., Kropp. T., Wiles, R., Gray, S., & Campbell, C. (2005). *Body burden: The pollution in newborns.* Washington, DC: Environmental Working Group.

House, J. S., Lantz, P. M., & Herd, P. (2005). Continuity and change in the social stratification of aging and health over the life course: Evidence from a nationally representative longitudinal study from 1986 to 2001/2002 (Americans' Changing Lives Study). *Journal of Gerontology, 60B*(Special Issue II), 15–26.

Houts, R. M., Barnett-Walker, K. C., Paley, B., & Cox, M. J. (2008). Patterns of couple interaction during the transition to parenthood. *Personal Relationships, 15,* 103–122.

Howard, A. L., Galambos, N. L., & Krahn, H. J. (2010). Paths to success in young adulthood from mental health and life transitions in emerging adulthood. *International Journal of Behavioral Development, 34,* 538–546.

Howard, B. V., Manson, J. E., Stefanick, M. L., Beresford, S. A., Frank, G., & Jones, B. (2006). Low-fat dietary pattern and weight change over 7 years: The Women's Health Initiative Dietary Modification Trial. *Journal of the American Medical Association, 295,* 39–49.

Howard, K., & Walsh, M. E. (2010). Conceptions of career choice and attainment: Developmental levels in how children think about careers. *Journal of Vocational Behavior, 76,* 143–152.

Howe, M. L., Courage, M. L., & Rooksby, M. (2009). The genesis and development of autobiographical memory. In M. L. Courage & N. Cowan (Eds.), *The development of memory in infancy and childhood* (pp. 177–196). Hove, UK: Psychology Press.

Howe, N., Aquan-Assee, J., & Bukowski, W. M. (2001). Predicting sibling relations over time: Synchrony between maternal management styles and sibling relationship quality. *Merrill-Palmer Quarterly, 47,* 121–141.

Howell, K. K., Coles, C. D., & Kable, J. A. (2008). The medical and developmental consequences of prenatal drug exposure. In J. Brick (Ed.), *Handbook of the medical consequences of alcohol and drug abuse* (2nd ed., pp. 219–249). New York: Haworth Press.

Howell, K. K., Lynch, M. E., Platzman, K. A., Smith, G. H., & Coles, C. D. (2006). Prenatal alcohol exposure and ability, academic achievement, and school functioning in adolescence: A longitudinal follow-up. *Journal of Pediatric Psychology, 31,* 116–126.

Howell, L. C., & Beth, A. (2002). Midlife myths and realities: Women reflect on their experiences. *Journal of Women and Aging, 14,* 189–204.

Hoyer, W. J., & Verhaeghen, P. (2006). Memory aging. In J. E. Birren & K. W. Schaie (Eds.), *Handbook of the psychology of aging* (6th ed., pp. 209–232). Burlington, MA: Elsevier Academic Press.

Hoza, B., Gerdes, A. C., Hinshaw, S. P., Bukowski, W. M., Gold, J. A., Kraemer, H. C., Pelham, W. E., Jr., Wigal, T., & Arnold, L. E. (2005). What aspects of peer relationships are impaired in children with attention-deficit/hyperactivity disorder? *Journal of Consulting and Clinical Psychology, 73,* 411–423.

HSBC & Oxford Institute of Ageing. (2007). *The future of retirement.* London: HSBC Insurance.

HSBC & Oxford Institute of Ageing. (2011). *The future of retirement: The power of planning.* London: HSBC Insurance.

Huang, A. Subak, L., Thom, D., Van Den Eeden, S., Ragins, A., Kuppermann, M., et al. (2009). Sexual function and aging in racially and ethnically diverse women. *Journal of the American Geriatrics Society, 57,* 1362–1368.

Huang, C. Y., & Stormshak, E. A. (2011). A longitudinal examination of early adolescence ethnic identity trajectories. *Cultural Diversity and Ethnic Minority Psychology, 17,* 261–270.

Huang, Q., & Sverke, M. (2007). Women's occupational career patterns over 27 years: Relations to family of origin, life careers, and wellness. *Journal of Vocational Behavior, 70,* 369–397.

Hubbs-Tait, L., Nation, J. R., Krebs, N. F., & Bellinger, D. C. (2005). Neurotoxicants, micronurtrients, and social environments: Individual and combined effects on children's development. *Psychological Science in the Public Interest, 6,* 57–121.

Huddleston, J., & Ge, X. (2003). Boys at puberty: Psychosocial implications. In C. Hayward (Ed.), *Gender differences at puberty* (pp. 113–134). New York: Cambridge University Press.

Hudson, J. A., Fivush, R., & Kuebli, J. (1992). Scripts and episodes: The development of event memory. *Applied Cognitive Psychology, 6,* 483–505.

Hudson, J. A., & Mayhew, E. M. Y. (2009). The development of memory for recurring events. In M. L. Courage & N. Cowan (Eds.), *The development of memory in infancy and childhood* (pp. 69–91). Hove, UK: Psychology Press.

Hudson, J. M. (2008). Automatic memory processes in normal ageing and Alzheimer's disease. *Cortex, 44,* 345–349.

Hudziak, J. J., & Rettew, D. C. (2009). Genetics of ADHD. In T. E. Brown (Ed.), *ADHD comorbidties: Handbook for ADHD complications in children and adults* (pp. 23–36). Arlington, VA: American Psychiatric Publishing.

Huebner, C. E., & Payne, K. (2010). Home support for emergent literacy: Follow-up of a community-based implementation of dialogic reading. *Journal of Applied Developmental Psychology, 31,* 195–201.

Huesmann, L. R. (1986). Psychological processes promoting the relation between exposure to media violence and aggressive behavior by the viewer. *Journal of Social Issues, 42,* 125–139.

Huesmann, L. R., Moise-Titus, J., Podolski, C. & Eron, L. D. (2003). Longitudinal relations between children's exposure to TV violence and their aggressive and violent behavior in young adulthood: 1977–1992. *Developmental Psychology, 39,* 201–221.

Huffman, M. L. (2012). Introduction: Gender, race, and management. *Annals of the American Academy of Political and Social Science, 639,* 6–12.

Hughes, C. (2010). Conduct disorder and antisocial behavior in the under-5s. In C. L. Cooper, J. Field, U. Goswami, R. Jenkins, & B. J. Sahakian (Eds.), *Mental capital and well-being* (pp. 821–827). Malden, MA: Wiley-Blackwell.

Hughes, C., & Dunn, J. (1998). Understanding mind and emotion: Longitudinal associations with mental-state talk between young friends. *Developmental Psychology, 34,* 1026–1037.

Hughes, C., & Ensor, R. (2007). Executive function and theory of mind: Predictive relations from ages 2 to 4. *Developmental Psychology, 43,* 1447–1459.

Hughes, C., & Ensor, R. (2010). Do early social cognition and executive function predict individual differences in preschoolers' prosocial and antisocial behavior? In B. W. Sokol, U. Müller, J. I. M. Carpendale, A. R. Young, & G. Iarocci (Eds.), *Social interaction and the development of social understanding and executive functions* (pp. 418–441). New York: Oxford University Press.

Hughes, C., Ensor, R., & Marks, A. (2010). Individual differences in false belief understanding are stable from 3 to 6 years of age and predict children's mental state talk with school friends. *Journal of Experimental Child Psychology, 108,* 96–112.

Hughes, D., Rodriguez, J., Smith, E. P., Johnson, D. J., Stevenson, H. C., & Spicer, P. (2006). Parents' ethnic-racial socialization practices: A review of research and directions for future study. *Developmental Psychology, 42,* 747–770.

Hughes, J. N., Cavell, T. A., & Grossman, P. B. (1997). A positive view of self: Risk or protection for aggressive children? *Development and Psychopathology, 9,* 75–94.

Hughes, J. N., & Kwok, O. (2006). Classroom engagement mediates the effect of teacher–student support on elementary students' peer acceptance. *Journal of School Psychology, 43,* 465–480.

Hughes, J. N., & Kwok, O. (2007). Influence of student–teacher and parent–teacher relationships on lower achieving readers' engagement and achievement in the primary grades. *Journal of Educational Psychology, 99,* 39–51.

Huizenga, H., Crone, E. A., & Jansen, B. (2007). Decision making in healthy children, adolescents and adults explained by the use of increasingly complex proportional reasoning rules. *Developmental Science, 10,* 814–825.

Huizink, A. C., Bartels, M., Rose, R. J., Pulkkinen, L., Eriksson, C. J., & Kaprio, J. (2008). Chernobyl exposure as a stressor during pregnancy and hormone levels in adolescent offspring. *Journal of Epidemiology and Community Health, 62,* e5.

Huizink, A. C., & Mulder, E. J. (2006). Maternal smoking, drinking or cannabis use during pregnancy and neurobehavioral and cognitive functioning in human offspring. *Neuroscience and Biobehavioral Reviews, 30,* 24–41.

Hultsch, D. F., Hertzog, C., Dixon, R. A., & Small, B. J. (1998). *Memory change in the aged.* New York: Cambridge University Press.

Hultsch, D. F., MacDonald, S. W. S., & Dixon, R. A. (2002). Variability in reaction time performance of younger and older adults. *Journal of Gerontology, 57B,* P101–P115.

Human Genome Project. (2008). *How many genes are in the human genome?* Retrieved from www.ornl .gov/sci/techresources/Human_Genome/faq/ genenumber.shtml

Human Rights Campaign. (2008). *Surrogacy laws: State by state.* Retrieved from http://66.151.111.225/ issues/parenting/surrogacy/surrogacy_laws.asp

Humes, L. E., Dubno, J. R., Gordon-Salant, S., Lister, J. J., Cacace, A. T., Cruickshanks, K. J., et al. (2012). Central presbycusis: A review and evaluation of the evidence. *Journal of the American Academy of Audiology, 23,* 635–666.

Humphrey, T. (1978). Function of the nervous system during prenatal life. In U. Stave (Ed.), *Perinatal physiology* (pp. 651–683). New York: Plenum.

Hunnius, S., & Geuze, R. H. (2004a). Developmental changes in visual scanning of dynamic faces and abstract stimuli in infants: A longitudinal study. *Infancy, 6,* 231–255.

Hunnius, S., & Geuze, R. H. (2004b). Gaze shifting in infancy: A longitudinal study using dynamic faces and abstract stimuli. *Infant Behavior and Development, 27,* 397–416.

Hunt, C. E., & Hauck, F. R. (2006). Sudden infant death syndrome. *Canadian Medical Association Journal, 174,* 1861–1869.

Huotilainen, M., Kujala, A., Hotakainen, M., Parkkonen, L., Taulu, S., & Simola, J. (2005). Short-term memory functions of the human fetus recorded with magneto-encephalography. *NeuroReport, 16,* 81–84.

Hursti, U. K. (1999). Factors influencing children's food choice. *Annals of Medicine, 31,* 26–32.

Hurt, H., Betancourt, L. M., Malmud, E. K., Shera, D. M., Giannetta, J. M., Brodsky, N. L., et al. (2009). Children with and without gestational cocaine exposure: A neurocognitive systems analysis. *Neurotoxicology and Teratology, 31,* 334–341.

Hurtig, W. A., & Stewin, L. (2006). The effect of death education and experience on nursing students' attitude toward death. *Journal of Advanced Nursing, 15,* 29–34.

Huston, A. C., & Alvarez, M. M. (1990). The socialization context of gender role development in early adolescence. In R. Montemayor, G. R. Adams, & T. P. Gullotta (Eds.), *From childhood to adolescence: A transitional period?* (pp. 156–179). Newbury Park, CA: Sage.

Huttenlocher, P. R. (2002). *Neural plasticity: The effects of environment on the development of the cerebral cortex.* Cambridge, MA: Harvard University Press.

Huyck, M. H. (1990). Gender differences in aging. In J. E. Birren & K. W. Schaie (Eds.), *Handbook of the psychology of aging* (3rd ed., pp. 124–134). New York: Academic Press.

Huyck, M. H. (1996). Continuities and discontinuities in gender identity in midlife. In V. L. Bengtson (Ed.), *Adulthood and aging* (pp. 98–121). New York: Springer-Verlag.

Huyck, M. H. (1998). Gender roles and gender identity in midlife. In S. L. Willis & J. D. Reid (Eds.), *Life in the middle* (pp. 209–232). San Diego: Academic Press.

Hyde, J. S., Essex, M. J., Clark, R., & Klein, M. H. (2001). Maternity leave, women's employment, and marital incompatibility. *Journal of Family Psychology, 15,* 476–491.

Hyde, J. S., Mezulis, A. H., & Abramson, L. Y. (2008). The ABCs of depression: Integrating affective, biological, and cognitive models to explain the emergence of the gender difference in depression. *Psychological Review, 115,* 291–313.

Hyman, B. T., Phelps, C. H., Beach, T. G., Bigio, E. H., Cairns, N. J., Carrillo, M. C., et al. (2012). National Institute on Aging–Alzheimer's Association guidelines for the neuropathologic assessment of Alzheimer's disease. *Alzheimer's and Dementia, 8,* 1–13.

Hymel, S., Vaillancourt, T., McDougall, P., & Renshaw, P. D. (2004). Peer acceptance and rejection in childhood. In P. K. Smith & C. H. Hart (Eds.), *Blackwell handbook of childhood social development* (pp. 265–284). Malden, MA: Blackwell.

I

Iacoboni, M. (2009). Imitation, empathy, and mirror neurons. *Annual Review of Psychology, 60,* 653–670.

Ickes, M. J. (2011). Stigmatization of overweight and obese individuals: Implications for mental health promotion. *International Journal of Mental Health Promotion, 13,* 37–45.

Ida, M. (2010). [The concept of death in the revised Organ Transplant Law in Japan.] *Nihon Rinsho [Japanese Journal of Clinical Medicine], 68,* 2223–2228.

Iglowstein, I., Jenni, O. G., Molinari, L., & Largo, R. H. (2003). Sleep duration from infancy to adolescence: Reference values and generational trends. *Pediatrics, 111,* 302–307.

Imai, M., & Haryu, E. (2004). The nature of wordlearning biases and their roles for lexical development: From a cross-linguistic perspective. In D. G. Hall & S. R. Waxman (Eds.), *Weaving a lexicon* (pp. 411–444). Cambridge, MA: MIT Press.

Impett, E. A., Sorsoli, L., Schooler, D., Henson, J. M., & Tolman, D. L. (2008). Girls' relationship authenticity and self-esteem across adolescence. *Developmental Psychology, 44,* 722–733.

Inhelder, B., & Piaget, J. (1958). *The growth of logical thinking from childhood to adolescence: An essay on the construction of formal operational structures.* New York: Basic Books. (Original work published 1955)

Irvine, A. B., Ary, D. V., & Bourgeois, M. S. (2003). An interactive multimedia program to train professional caregivers. *Journal of Applied Gerontology, 22,* 269–288.

Isabella, R. (1993). Origins of attachment: Maternal interactive behavior across the first year. *Child Development, 64,* 605–621.

Isabella, R., & Belsky, J. (1991). Interactional synchrony and the origins of infant–mother attachment: A replication study. *Child Development, 62,* 373–384.

Ishihara, K., Warita, K., Tanida, T., Sugawara, T., Kitagawa, H., & Hoshi, N. (2007). Does paternal exposure to 2, 3, 7, 8-tetrachlorodibenzo-p-dioxin (TCDD) affect the sex ratio of offspring? *Journal of Veterinary Medical Science, 69,* 347–352.

Israel, M., Johnson, C., & Brooks, P. J. (2000). From states to events: The acquisition of English passive participles. *Cognitive Linguistics, 11,* 103–129.

Itti, E., Gaw, G. I. T., Pawlikowska-Haddal, A., Boone, K. B., Mlikotic, A., & Itti, L. (2006). The structural brain correlates of cognitive deficits in adults with Klinefelter's syndrome. *Journal of Clinical Endocrinology and Metabolism, 91,* 1423–1427.

Ivorra, J. L., Sanjuan, J., Jover, M., Carot, J. M., de Frutos, R., & Molto, M. D. (2010). Gene–environment interaction of child temperament. *Journal of Developmental and Behavioral Pediatrics, 31,* 545–554.

Izard, C. E., & Ackerman, B. P. (2000). Motivational, organizational, and regulatory functions of discrete emotions. In M. Lewis & J. M. Haviland-Jones (Eds.), *Handbook of emotions* (2nd ed., pp. 253–264). New York: Guilford.

J

Jaccard, J., Dodge, T., & Dittus, P. (2002). Parent-adolescent communication about sex and birth control: A conceptual framework. In S. S. Feldman & D. A. Rosenthal (Eds.), *Talking sexuality: Parent-adolescent communication* (pp. 9–41). San Francisco: Jossey-Bass.

Jaccard, J., Dodge, T., & Dittus, P. (2003). Maternal discussions about pregnancy and adolescents' attitudes toward pregnancy. *Journal of Adolescent Health, 33,* 84–87.

Jackson, G. R., & Owsley, C. (2000). Scotopic sensitivity during adulthood. *Vision Research, 40,* 2467–2473.

Jackson, J. J., Hill, P. L., Payne, B. R., Roberts, B. W., & Steine-Morrow, E. A. L. (2012). Can an old dog learn (and want to experience) new tricks? Cognitive training increases openness to experience in older adults. *Psychology and Aging, 27,* 286–292.

Jackson, V. A., Sullivan, A. M., Gadmer, N. M., Seltzer, D., Mitchell, A. M., & Lakoma, M. D. (2005). "It was haunting . . .": Physicians' descriptions of emotionally powerful patient deaths. *Academic Medicine, 80,* 648–656.

Jacobs, J. A., & King, R. B. (2002). Age and college completion: A life-history analysis of women aged 15–44. *Sociology of Education, 75,* 211–230.

Jacobs, J. E., & Klaczynski, P. A. (2002). The development of judgment and decision making during childhood and adolescence. *Current Directions in Psychological Science, 11,* 145–149.

Jacobs, J. E., Lanza, S., Osgood, D. W., Eccles, J. S., & Wigfield, A. (2002). Changes in children's self-competence and values: Gender and domain differences across grades one through twelve. *Child Development, 73,* 509–527.

Jacobs, J. N., & Kelley, M. L. (2006). Predictors of paternal involvement in childcare in dual-earner families with young children. *Fathering, 4,* 23–47.

Jacobson, J. L., & Jacobson, S. W. (2003). Prenatal exposure to polychlorinated biphenyls and attention at school age. *Journal of Pediatrics, 143,* 780–788.

Jacobson, K. C., & Crockett, L. J. (2000). Parental monitoring and adolescent adjustment: An ecological perspective. *Journal of Research on Adolescence, 10,* 65–97.

Jacobson, S. W., Jacobson, J. L., Sokol, R. J., Chiodo, L. M., & Corobana, R. (2004). Maternal age, alcohol abuse history, and quality of parenting as moderators of the effects of prenatal alcohol exposure on 7.5-year intellectual function. *Alcoholism: Clinical and Experimental Research, 28,* 1732–1745.

Jadack, R. A., Hyde, J. S., Moore, C. F., & Keller, M. L. (1995). Moral reasoning about sexually transmitted diseases. *Child Development, 66,* 167–177.

Jaffee, S. R., & Hyde, J. S. (2000). Gender differences in moral orientation: A meta-analysis. *Psychological Bulletin, 126,* 703–706.

James, J., Ellis, B. J., Schlomer, G. L., & Garber, J. (2012). Sex-specific pathways to early puberty, sexual debut, and sexual risk taking: Tests of an integrated evolutionary–developmental model. *Developmental Psychology, 48,* 687–702.

James, J. B., Lewkowicz, C., Libhaber, J., & Lachman, M. (1995). Rethinking the gender identity crossover hypothesis: A test of a new model. *Sex Roles, 32,* 185–207.

James, J. B., & Wink, P. (2007). The Third Age: A rationale for research. In J. B. James & P. Wink (Eds.), *Annual review of gerontology and geriatrics* (Vol. 26, pp. xix–xxxii). New York: Springer.

James, J. B., & Zarrett, N. (2007). Ego integrity in the lives of older women. *Journal of Adult Development, 13,* 61–75.

Jang, Y., Bergman, E., Schonfeld, L., & Molinari, V. (2007). The mediating role of health perceptions in the relation between physical and mental health: A study of older residents in assisted living facilities. *Journal of Aging and Health, 19,* 439–452.

Janosz, M., Le Blanc, M., Boulerice, B., & Tremblay, R. E. (2000). Predicting different types of school dropouts: A typological approach with two longitudinal samples. *Journal of Educational Psychology, 92,* 171–190.

Jansen, A., Theunissen, N., Slechten, K., Nederkoorn, C., Boon, B., Mulkens, S., & Roefs, A. (2003). Overweight children overeat after exposure to food cues. *Eating Behaviors, 4,* 197–209.

Jansen, J., de Weerth, C., & Riksen-Walraven, J. M. (2008). Breastfeeding and the mother–infant relationship. *Developmental Review, 28,* 503–521.

Janssen, S. M., Rubin, D. C., & St. Jacques, P. L. (2011). The temporal distribution of autobiographical memory: Changes in reliving and vividness over the life span do not explain the reminiscence bump. *Memory and Cognition, 39,* 1–11.

Janssens, J. M. A. M., & Dekovi?, M. (1997). Child rearing, prosocial moral reasoning, and prosocial behaviour. *International Journal of Behavioral Development, 20,* 509–527.

Jarvis, J. F., & van Heerden, H. G. (1967). The acuity of hearing in the Kalahari Bushman: A pilot study. *Journal of Laryngology and Otology, 81,* 63–68.

Jaudes, P. K., & Mackey-Bilaver, L. (2008). Do chronic conditions increase young children's risk of being maltreated? *Child Abuse and Neglect, 32,* 671–681.

Jayakody, R., & Kalil, A. (2002). Social fathering in low-income, African-American families with preschool children. *Journal of Marriage and Family, 64,* 504–516.

Jedrychowski, W., Perera, F. P., Jankowski, J., Mrozek-Budzyn, D., Mroz, E., Flak, E., et al. (2009). Very low prenatal exposure to lead and mental development of children in infancy and early childhood. *Neuroepidemiology, 32,* 270–278.

Jellinger, K. A. (2004). Head injury and dementia. *Current Opinion in Neurology, 17,* 719–723.

Jellinger, K. A. (2008). Morphologic diagnosis of "vascular dementia"—a critical update. *Journal of the Neurological Sciences, 270,* 1–12.

Jenkins, C., Lapelle, N., Zapka, J. G., & Kurent, J. E. (2005). End-of-life care and African Americans: Voices from the community. *Journal of Palliative Medicine, 8,* 585–592.

Jenkins, J. M., Rasbash, J., & O'Connor, T. G. (2003). The role of the shared family context in differential parenting. *Developmental Psychology, 39,* 99–113.

Jenkins, K. R., Pienta, A. M., & Horgas, A. L. (2002). Activity and health-related quality of life in continuing care retirement communities. *Research on Aging, 24,* 124–149.

Jenni, O. G., Achermann, P., & Carskadon, M. A. (2005). Homeostatic sleep regulation in adolescents. *Sleep, 28,* 1446–1454.

Jennings, B. J., Ozanne, S. E., Dorling, M. W., & Hales, C. N. (1999). Early growth determines longevity in male rats and may be related to telomere shortening in the kidney. *FEBS Letters, 448,* 4–8.

Jensen, A. R. (1969). How much can we boost IQ and scholastic achievement? *Harvard Educational Review, 39,* 1–123.

Jensen, A. R. (1998). *The g factor: The science of mental ability.* New York: Praeger.

Jensen, A. R. (2001). Spearman's hypothesis. In J. M. Collis & S. Messick (Eds.), *Intelligence and personality: Bridging the gap in theory and measurement* (pp. 3–24). Mahwah, NJ: Erlbaum.

Jeon, Y.-H., Brodaty, H., & Chesterson, J. (2005). Respite care for caregivers and people with severe mental illness: Literature review. *Journal of Advanced Nursing, 49,* 297–306.

Jeong, S.-H., & Fishbein, M. (2007). Predictors of multitasking with media: Media factors and audience factors. *Media Psychology, 10,* 364–384.

Jerome, E. M., Hamre, B. K., & Pianta, R. C. (2009). Teacher–child relationships from kindergarten to sixth grade: Early childhood predictors of teacher-perceived conflict and closeness. *Social Development, 18,* 915–945.

Jeynes, W. (2012). A meta-analysis of the efficacy of different types of parental involvement programs for urban students. *Urban Education, 47,* 706–742.

Jeynes, W. H. (2007). The impact of parental remarriage on children: A meta-analysis. *Marriage and Family Review, 40,* 75–102.

Jiao, S., Ji, G., & Jing, Q. (1996). Cognitive development of Chinese urban only children and children with siblings. *Child Development, 67,* 387–395.

Jipson, J. L., & Gelman, S. A. (2007). Robots and rodents: Children's inferences about living and nonliving kinds. *Child Development, 78,* 1675–1688.

Joh, A. S., & Adolph, K. E. (2006). Learning from falling. *Child Development, 77,* 89–102.

Johansson, A. K., & Grimby, A. (2013). Anticipatory grief among close relatives of patients in hospice and palliative wards. *American Journal of Hospice and Palliative Medicine, 29,* 134–138.

Johnson, C. L., & Troll, L. E. (1994). Constraints and facilitators to friendships in late life. *Gerontologist, 34,* 79–87.

Johnson, E. K., & Seidl, A. (2008). Clause segmentation by 6-month-old infants: A crosslinguistic perspective. *Infancy, 13,* 440–455.

Johnson, J. G., Cohen, P., Smailes, E. M., Kasen, S., & Brook, J. S. (2002). Television viewing and aggressive behavior during adolescence and adulthood. *Science, 295,* 2468–2471.

Johnson, K. S., Elbert-Avila, K. I., & Tulsky, J. A. (2005). The influence of spiritual beliefs and practices on the treatment preferences of African Americans: A review of the literature. *Journal of the American Geriatrics Society, 53,* 711–719.

Johnson, K. S., Juchibhatla, M., Tanis, D., & Tulsky, J. A. (2008). Racial differences in hospice revocation to pursue aggressive care. *Archives of Internal Medicine, 168,* 218–224.

Johnson, M. D., Cohan, C. L., Davila, J., Lawrence, E., Rogge, R. D., Karney, B. R., Sullivan, K. T., & Bradbury, T. N. (2005). Problem-solving skills and affective expressions as predictors of change in marital satisfaction. *Journal of Consulting and Clinical Psychology, 73,* 15–27.

Johnson, M. H. (1999). Ontogenetic constraints on neural and behavioral plasticity: Evidence from imprinting and face processing. *Canadian Journal of Experimental Psychology, 55,* 77–90.

Johnson, M. H. (2011). Developmental neuroscience, psychophysiology, and genetics. In M H. Bornstein & M. E. Lamb (Eds.), *Developmental science: An advanced textbook* (6th ed., pp. 187–222). Mahwah, NJ: Erlbaum.

Johnson, M. H., & Mareschal, D. (2001). Cognitive and perceptual development during infancy. *Current Opinion in Neurobiology, 11,* 213–218.

Johnson, R. W., & Mommaerts, C. (2010). *Will health care costs bankrupt aging boomers?* Washington, DC: Urban Institute.

Johnson, S. P., Slemmer, J. A., & Amso, D. (2004). Where infants look determines how they see: Eye movements and object perception performance in 3-month-olds. *Infancy, 6,* 185–201.

Johnston, L. D., O'Malley, P. M., Bachman, J. G., & Schulenberg, J. E. (2011). *Monitoring the future: National results on adolescent drug use. Overview of key findings, 2010.* Bethesda, MD: National Institute on Drug Abuse.

Johnston, L. D., O'Malley, P. M., Bachman, J. G., & Schulenberg, J. E. (2012). *Monitoring the Future: National results on adolescent drug use: Overview of key findings, 2011.* Ann Arbor: Institute for Social Research, University of Michigan.

Jokhi, R. P., & Whitby, E. H. (2011). Magnetic resonance imaging of the fetus. *Developmental Medicine and Child Neurology, 53,* 18–28.

Jome, L. M., Surething, N. A., & Taylor, K. K. (2005). Relationally oriented masculinity, gender nontraditional interests, and occupational traditionality of employed men. *Journal of Career Development, 32,* 183–197.

Jones, F. (2003). *Religious commitment in Canada, 1997 and 2000. Religious Commitment Monograph No. 3.* Ottawa: Christian Commitment Research Institute.

Jones, J., Lopez, A., & Wilson, M. (2003). Congenital toxoplasmosis. *American Family Physician, 67,* 2131–2137.

Jones, J. M. (2012). *Expected retirement age in U.S.: Up to 67.* Princeton, NJ: Gallup. Retrieved from www.gallup.com/poll/154178/expected-retirement-age.aspx

Jones, K. M., Whitbourne, S. K., & Skultety, K. M. (2006). Identity processes and the transition to midlife among the baby boomers. In S. K. Whitbourne & S. L. Willis (Eds.), *The baby boomers grow up: Contemporary perspectives on midlife* (pp. 149–164). Mahwah, NJ: Erlbaum.

Jones, M. C., & Mussen, P. H. (1958). Self-conceptions, motivations, and interpersonal attitudes of early- and late-maturing girls. *Child Development, 29,* 491–501.

Jones, S. (2009). The development of imitation in infancy. *Philosophical Transactions of the Royal Society B, 364,* 2325–2335.

Jopp, D., & Rott, C. (2006). Adaptation in very old age: Exploring the role of resources, beliefs, and attitudes for centenarians' happiness. *Psychology and Aging, 21,* 266–280.

Jordan, B. (1993). *Birth in four cultures.* Prospect Heights, IL: Waveland.

Jordon, J., & Neimeyer, R. (2003). Does grief counseling work? *Death Studies, 27,* 765–786.

Jose, A., O'Leary, D., & Moyer, A. (2010). Does premarital cohabitation predict subsequent marital stability and martial quality? A meta-analysis. *Journal of Marriage and Family, 72,* 105–116.

Joseph, R. M., & Tager-Flusberg, H. (2004). The relationship of theory of mind and executive functions to symptom type and severity in children with autism. *Development and Psychopathology, 16,* 137–155.

Juby, H., Billette, J.-M., Laplante, B., & Le Bourdais, C. (2007). Nonresident fathers and children: Parents' new unions and frequency of contact. *Journal of Family Issues, 28,* 1220–1245.

Julkunen, J., & Ahlström, R. (2006). Hostility, anger, and sense of coherence as predictors of health-related quality of life. Results of an ASCOT substudy. *Journal of Psychosomatic Research, 61,* 33–39.

Jürgensen, M., Hiort, O., Holterhus, P.-M., & Thyen, U. (2007). Gender role behavior in children with XY karyotype and disorders of sex development. *Hormones and Behavior, 51,* 443–453.

Jusczyk, P. W. (2002). Some critical developments in acquiring native language sound organization. *Annals of Otology, Rhinology and Laryngology, 189,* 11–15.

Jusczyk, P. W., & Hohne, E. A. (1997). Infants' memory for spoken words. *Science, 277,* 1984–1986.

Jutras-Aswad, D., DiNieri, J. A., Harkany, T., & Hurd, Y. L. (2009). Neurobiological consequences of maternal cannabis on human fetal development and its neuropsychiatric outcome. *European Archives of Psychiatry and Clinical Neuroscience, 259,* 395–412.

K

Kaczmarczyk, M. M., Miller, M. J., & Freund, G. G. (2012). The health benefits of dietary fiber: Beyond the usual suspects of type 2 diabetes mellitus, cardiovascular disease and colon cancer. *Metabolism: Clinical and Experimental, 61,* 1058–1066.

Kagan, J. (2003). Behavioral inhibition as a temperamental category. In R. J. Davidson, K. R. Scherer, & H. H. Goldsmith (Eds.), *Handbook of affective science* (pp. 320–331). New York: Oxford University Press.

Kagan, J. (2008a). Behavioral inhibition as a risk factor for psychopathology. In T. P. Beauchaine & S. P. Hinshaw (Eds.), *Child and adolescent psychopathology* (pp. 157–179). Hoboken, NJ: Wiley.

Kagan, J. (2008b). In defense of qualitative changes in development. *Child Development, 79,* 1606–1624.

Kagan, J. (2010). Emotions and temperament. In M. H. Bornstein (Ed.), *Handbook of cultural developmental science* (pp. 175–194). New York: Psychology Press.

Kagan, J., Arcus, D., Snidman, N., Feng, W. Y. Hendler, J., & Greene, S. (1994). Reactivity in infants: A cross-national comparison. *Developmental Psychology, 30,* 342–345.

Kagan, J., & Fox, N. A. (2006). Biology, culture, and temperamental biases. In N. Eisenberg (Ed.), *Handbook of child psychology: Vol. 3. Social, emotional, and personality development* (6th ed., pp. 167–225). Hoboken, NJ: Wiley.

Kagan, J., & Saudino, K. J. (2001). Behavioral inhibition and related temperaments. In R. N. Emde & J. K. Hewitt (Eds.), *Infancy to early childhood: Genetic and environmental influences on developmental change* (pp. 111–119). New York: Oxford University Press.

Kagan, J., Snidman, N., Kahn, V., & Towsley, S. (2007). The preservation of two infant temperaments into adolescence. *Monographs of the Society for Research in Child Development, 72*(2, Serial No. 287).

Kagan, J., Snidman, N., Zentner, M., & Peterson, E. (1999). Infant temperament and anxious symptoms in school-age children. *Development and Psychopathology, 11,* 209–224.

Kahana, E., King, C., Kahana, B., Menne, H., Webster, N. J., & Dan, A. (2005). Successful aging in the face of chronic disease. In M. L. Wykle, P. J. Whitehouse, & D. L. Morris (Eds.), *Successful aging through the life span* (pp. 101–126). New York: Springer.

Kahn, R. S., Khoury, J., Nichols, W. C., & Lanphear, B. M. (2003). Role of dopamine transporter genotype and maternal prenatal smoking in childhood hyperactive–impulsive, inattentive, and oppositional behaviors. *Journal of Pediatrics, 143,* 104–110.

Kail, R. (1993). The role of a global mechanism in developmental change in speed of processing. In M. L. Howe & R. Pasnak (Eds.), *Emerging themes in cognitive development: Vol. 1. Foundations.* New York: Springer-Verlag.

Kail, R. (1997). Processing time, imagery, and spatial memory. *Journal of Experimental Child Psychology, 64,* 67–78.

Kail, R. V. (2003). Information processing and memory. In M. H. Bornstein, L. Davidson, C. L. M. Keyes, K. A. Moore, and the Center for Child Well-Being (Eds.), *Well-being: Positive development across the life course* (pp. 269–280). Mahwah, NJ: Erlbaum.

Kaisa, A., Stattin, H., & Nurmi, J. (2000). Parenting styles and adolescents' achievement strategies. *Journal of Adolescence, 23,* 205–222.

Kakihara, F., Tilton-Weaver, L., Kerr, M., & Stattin, H. (2010). The relationship of parental control to youth adjustment: Do youths' feelings about their parents play a role? *Journal of Youth and Adolescence, 39,* 1442–1456.

Kalil, A., Levine, J. A., & Ziol-Guest, K. M. (2005). Following in their parents' footsteps: How characteristics of parental work predict adolescents' interest in parents' working jobs. In B. Schneider & L. J. Waite (Eds.), *Being together, working apart: Dual-career families and the work–life balance* (pp. 422–442). New York: Cambridge University Press.

Kalisch, T., Kattenstroth, J.-C., Kowalewski, R., Tegenthoff, M., & Dinse, H. R. (2012). *PLoS ONE, 7*(1), e30420.

Kalpouzos, G., & Nyberg, L. (2012). *Multimodal neuroimaging in normal aging: Structure–function interactions* (pp. 273–304). New York: Psychology Press.

Kaminski, J. W., Puddy, R. W., Hall, D. M., Cashman, S. Y., Crosby, A. E., & Ortega, L. G. (2010). The relative influence of different domains of social connectedness on self-directed violence in adolescence. *Journal of Youth and Adolescence, 39,* 460–473.

Kamo, Y. (1998). Asian grandparents. In M. E. Szinovacz (Ed.), *Handbook on grandparenthood* (pp. 97–112). Westport, CT: Greenwood Press.

Kane, P., & Garber, J. (2004). The relations among depression in fathers, children's psychopathology, and father–child conflict: A meta-analysis. *Clinical Psychology Review, 24,* 339–360.

Kane, R. A., Lum, T. Y., Cutler, L. J., Degenholtz, H. B., & Yu, T.-C. (2007). Resident outcomes in small-house nursing homes: A longitudinal evaluation of the initial Green House program. *Journal of the American Geriatrics Society, 55,* 836–839.

Kang, N. H., & Hong, M. (2008). Achieving excellence in teacher workforce and equity in learning opportunities in South Korea. *Educational Researcher, 37,* 200–207.

Kaplow, J. B., & Widom, C. S. (2007). Age of onset of child maltreatment predicts long-term mental health outcomes. *Journal of Abnormal Psychology, 116,* 176–187.

Kaplowitz, P. (2006). Pubertal development in girls: Secular trends. *Current Opinion in Obstetrics and Gynecology, 18,* 487–491.

Kaplowitz, P. B. (2007). Link between body fat and the timing of puberty. *Pediatrics, 121,* S208–S217.

Karafantis, D. M., & Levy, S. R. (2004). The role of children's lay theories about the malleability of human attributes in beliefs about and volunteering for disadvantaged groups. *Child Development, 75,* 236–250.

Karasawa, M., Curhan, K. B., Markus, H. R., Kitayama, S. S., Love, G. D., Radler, B. T., et al. (2011). Cultural perspectives on aging and well-being: A comparison of Japan and the U.S. *International Journal of Aging and Human Development, 73,* 73–98.

Karasik, L. B., Tamis-LeMonda, C. S., & Adolph, K. E. (2011). Transition from crawling to walking affects infants' social actions with objects. *Child Development, 82,* 1199–1209.

Karasik, L. B., Tamis-LeMonda, C. S., Adolph, K. E., & Dimitroupoulou, K. A. (2008). How mothers encourage and discourage infants' motor actions. *Infancy, 13,* 366–392.

Karel, M. J., Gatz, M., & Smyer, M. A. (2012). Aging and mental health in the decade ahead: What psychologists need to know. *American Psychologist, 67,* 184–198.

Karevold, E., Ystrom, E., Coplan, R. J., Sanson, A. V., & Mathiesen, K. S. (2012). A prospective longitudinal study of shyness from infancy to adolescence: Stability, age-related changes, and prediction of socio-emotional functioning. *Journal of Abnormal Child Psychology, 40,* 1167–1177.

Karger, H. J., & Stoesz, D. (2010). *American social welfare policy* (6th ed.). Upper Saddle River, NJ: Pearson Education.

Karlsson, C., & Berggren, I. (2011). Dignified end-of-life care in the patients' own homes. *Nursing Ethics, 18,* 374–385.

Kassel, J. D., Weinstein, S., Skitch, S. A., Veilleux, J., & Mermelstein, R. (2005). The development of substance abuse in adolescence: Correlates, causes, and consequences. In J. D. Kassel, S. Weinstein, S. A. Skitch, J. Veilleux, & R. Mermelstein (Eds.), *Development of psychopathology: A vulnerability-stress perspective* (pp. 355–384). Thousand Oaks, CA: Sage.

Kastenbaum, R. (2008). Grieving in contemporary society. In M. S. Stroebe, R. O. Hansson, H. Schut, & W. Stroebe (Eds.), *Handbook of bereavement research and practice* (pp. 67–85). Washington, DC: American Psychological Association.

Kastenbaum, R. J. (2012). *Death, society, and human experience* (11th ed.). Upper Saddle River, NJ: Pearson.

Kato, I., Franco, P., Groswasser, J., Scaillet, S., Kelmanson, I., Togari, H., & Kahn, A. (2003). Incomplete arousal processes in infants who were victims of sudden death. *American Journal of Respiratory and Critical Care, 168,* 1298–1303.

Katzman, D. K. (2005). Medical complications in adolescents with anorexia nervosa: A review of the literature. *International Journal of Eating Disorders, 37,* S52–S59.

Katz-Wise, S. L., Priess, H. A., & Hyde, J. S. (2010). Gender-role attitudes and behavior across the transition to parenthood. *Developmental Psychology, 46,* 18–28.

Kaufman, A. S. (2001). WAIS-III IQs, Horn's theory, and generational changes from young adulthood to old age. *Intelligence, 29,* 131–167.

Kaufman, A. S., & Horn, J. L. (1996). Age changes on tests of fluid and crystallized intelligence for females and males on the Kaufman Adolescent and Adult Intelligence Test (KAIT) at ages 17 to 94 years. *Archives of Clinical Neuropsychology, 11,* 97–121.

Kaufman, J. C., & Sternberg, R. J. (2007, July/August). Resource review: Creativity. *Change, 39,* 55–58.

Kavanaugh, R. D. (2006). Pretend play. In B. Spodek & O. N. Saracho (Eds.), *Handbook of research on the education of young children* (2nd ed., pp. 269–278). Mahwah, NJ: Erlbaum.

Kavšek, M. (2004). Predicting later IQ from infant visual habituation and dishabituation: A metaanalysis. *Journal of Applied Developmental Psychology, 25,* 369–393.

Kavšek, M., Yonas, A., & Granrud, C. E. (2012). Infants' sensitivity to pictorial depth cues: A review and meta-analysis. *Infant Behavior and Development, 35,* 109–128.

Kaya, Y., & Cook, K. J. (2010). A cross-national analysis of physical intimate partner violence against women. *International Journal of Comparative Sociology, 51,* 423–444.

Kaye, W. (2008). Neurobiology of anorexia and bulimia nervosa. *Physiology and Behavior, 94,* 121–135.

Keegan, L., & Drick, C. A. (2011). *End of life: Nursing solutions for death with dignity.* New York: Springer.

Keil, F. C. (1986). Conceptual domains and the acquisition of metaphor. *Cognitive Development, 1,* 73–96.

Keil, F. C., & Lockhart, K. L. (1999). Explanatory understanding in conceptual development. In E. K. Scholnick, K. Nelson, S. A. Gelman, & P. H. Miller (Eds.), *Conceptual development: Piaget's legacy* (pp. 103–130). Mahwah, NJ: Erlbaum.

Keith, P. M., & Schafer, R. B. (1991). *Relationships and well-being over the life stages.* New York: Praeger.

Keith, T. Z., Keith, P. B., Quirk, K. J., Sperduto, J., Santillo, S., & Killings, S. (1998). Longitudinal effects of parent involvement on high school grades: Similarities and differences across gender and ethnic groups. *Journal of School Psychology, 36,* 335–363.

Keller, H., Borke, Y. J., Kärtner, J., Jensen, H., & Papaligoura, Z. (2004). Developmental consequences of early parenting experiences: Self-recognition and self-regulation in three cultural communities. *Child Development, 75,* 1745–1760.

Keller, H., Kärtner, J., Borke, J., Yovsi, R., & Kleis, A. (2005). Parenting styles and the development of the categorical self: A longitudinal study on mirror self-recognition in Cameroonian Nso and German families. *International Journal of Behavioral Development, 29,* 496–504.

Keller, P. A., & Lusardi, A. (2012). Employee retirement savings: What we know and are discovering for helping people prepare for life after work. In G. D. Mick, S. Pettigrew, C. Pechmann, & J. L. Ozanne (Eds.), *Transformative consumer research for personal and collective well-being* (pp. 445–464). New York: Routledge.

Kelley, S. A., Brownell, C. A., & Campbell, S. B. (2000). Mastery motivation and self-evaluative affect in toddlers: Longitudinal relations with maternal behavior. *Child Development, 71,* 1061–1071.

Kellman, P. J., & Arterberry, M. E. (2006). Infant visual perception. In D. Kuhn & R. Siegler (Eds.), *Handbook of child psychology: Vol. 2. Cognition, perception, and language* (6th ed., pp. 109–160). Hoboken, NJ: Wiley.

Kelly, D. J., Liu, S., Ge, L., Quinn, P. C., Slater, A. M., Lee, K., Liu, Q., & Pascalis, O. (2007). Cross-race preferences for same-race faces extend beyond the African versus Caucasian contrast in 3-month-old infants. *Infancy, 11,* 87–95.

Kelly, D. J., Quinn, P. C., Slater, A. M., Lee, K., Ge, L., & Pascalis, O. (2009). Development of the other-race effect during infancy: Evidence toward universality? *Journal of Experimental Child Psychology, 104,* 105–114.

Kelly, N., & Norwich, B. (2004). Pupils' perceptions of self and of labels: Moderate learning difficulties in mainstream and special schools. *British Journal of Educational Psychology, 74,* 411–435.

Kemkes-Grottenthaler, A. (2003). Postponing or rejecting parenthood? Results of a survey among female academic professionals. *Journal of Biosocial Science, 35,* 213–226.

Kempen, G., Ranchor, A. V., van Sonderen, E., van Jaarsveld, C. H. M., & Sanderman, R. (2006). Risk and protective factors of different functional trajectories in older persons: Are these the same? *Journal of Gerontology, 61B,* P95–P101.

Kemper, S. (2012). The interaction of linguistic constraints, working memory, and aging on language production and comprehension. In M. Naveh-Benjamin & N. Ohta (Eds.), *Memory and aging: Current issues and future directions* (pp. 31–47). New York: Psychology Press.

Kendig, H., Dykstra, P. A., van Gaalen, R. I., & Melkas, T. (2007). Health of aging parents and childless individuals. *Journal of Family Issues, 28,* 1457–1486.

Kendler, K. S., Thornton, L. M., Gilman, S. E., & Kessler, R. C. (2000). Sexual orientation in a U.S. national sample of twin and non-twin sibling pairs. *American Journal of Psychiatry, 157,* 1843–1846.

Kendrick, D., Barlow, J., Hampshire, A., Stewart-Brown, S., & Polnay, L. (2008). Parenting interventions and the prevention of unintentional injuries in childhood: Systematic review and meta-analysis. *Child: Care, Health and Development, 34,* 682–695.

Kennedy, G. E., & Kennedy, C. E. (1993). Grandparents: A special resource for children in stepfamilies. *Journal of Divorce and Remarriage, 19,* 45–68.

Kenney, G. M., Lynch, V., Cook, A., & Phong, S. (2010). Who and where are the children yet to enroll in Medicaid and the Children's Health Insurance Program? *Health Affairs, 29,* 1920–1929.

Kerckhoff, A. C. (2002). The transition from school to work. In J. T. Mortimer & R. Larson (Eds.), *The changing adolescent experience* (pp. 52–87). New York: Cambridge University Press.

Keren, M., Feldman, R., Namdari-Weinbaum, I., Spitzer, S., & Tyano, S. (2005). Relations between parents' interactive style in dyadic and triadic play and toddlers' symbolic capacity. *American Journal of Orthopsychiatry, 75,* 599–607.

Kerestes, M., & Youniss, J. E. (2003). Rediscovering the importance of religion in adolescent development. In R. M. Lerner, F. Jacobs, & D. Wertlieb (Eds.), *Handbook of applied developmental science* (Vol. 1, pp. 165–184). Thousand Oaks, CA: Sage.

Kerestes, M., Youniss, J., & Metz, E. (2004). Longitudinal patterns of religious perspective and civic integration. *Applied Developmental Science, 8,* 39–46.

Kernis, M. H. (2002). Self-esteem as a multifaceted construct. In T. M. Brinthaupt & R. P. Lipka (Eds.), *Understanding early adolescent self and identity* (pp. 57–88). Albany: State University of New York Press.

Kernohan, W. G., Hasson, F., Hutchison, P., & Cochrane, B. (2006). Patient satisfaction with hospice day care. *Supportive Care in Cancer, 14,* 462–468.

Kerr, D. C. R., Lopez, N. L., Olson, S. L., & Sameroff, A. J. (2004). Parental discipline and externalizing behavior problems in early childhood: The roles of moral regulation and child gender. *Journal of Abnormal Child Psychology, 32,* 369–383.

Kesler, S. R. (2007). Turner syndrome. *Child and Adolescent Psychiatric Clinics of North America, 16,* 709–722.

Kettl, P. (1998). Alaska Native suicide: Lessons for elder suicide. *International Psychogeriatrics, 10,* 205–211.

Key, J. D., Gebregziabher, M. G., Marsh, L. D., & O'Rourke, K. M. (2008). Effectiveness of an intensive, school-based intervention for teen mothers. *Journal of Adolescent Health, 42,* 394–400.

Keyes, C. L. M., Shmotkin, D., & Ryff, C. D. (2002). Optimizing well-being: The empirical encounter of two traditions. *Journal of Personality and Social Psychology, 82,* 1007–1022.

Keyes, C. L. M., & Westerhof, G. J. (2012). Chronological and subjective age differences in flourishing mental health and major depressive episode. *Aging and Mental Health, 16,* 67–74.

Khashan, A. S., Baker, P. N., & Kenny, L. C. (2010). Preterm birth and reduced birthweight in first and second teenage pregnancies: A register-based cohort study. *BMC Pregnancy and Childbirth, 10,* 36.

Khavkin, J., & Ellis, D. A. (2011). Aging skin: Histology, physiology, and pathology. *Facial Plastic Surgery Clinics of North America, 19,* 229–234.

Kidd, A. R., III, & Bao, J. (2012). Recent advances in the study of age-related hearing loss: A mini-review. *Gerontology, 58,* 490–496.

Kieffer, M. J. (2008). Catching up or falling behind? Initial English proficiency, concentrated poverty and the reading growth of language minority learners in the United States. *Journal of Educational Psychology, 100,* 851–868.

Killen, M., Crystal, D., & Watanabe, H. (2002). The individual and the group: Japanese and American children's evaluations of peer exclusion, tolerance of difference, and prescriptions for conformity. *Child Development, 73,* 1788–1802.

Killen, M., Henning, A., Kelly, M. C., Crystal, D., & Ruck, M. (2007). Evaluations of interracial peer encounters by majority and minority U.S. children and adolescents. *International Journal of Behavioral Development, 31,* 491–500.

Killen, M., Kelly, M. C., Richardson, C., Crystal, D., & Ruck, M. (2010). European American children's and adolescents' evaluations of interracial exclusion. *Group Processes and Intergroup Relations, 13,* 283–300.

Killen, M., Lee-Kim, J., McGlothlin, H., & Stangor, C. (2002). How children and adolescents evaluate gender and racial exclusion. *Monographs of the Society for Research in Child Development, 67*(4, Serial No. 271).

Killen, M., Margie, N. G., & Sinno, S. (2006). Morality in the context of intergroup relationships. In M. Killen & J. G. Smetana (Eds.), *Handbook of moral development* (pp. 155–183). Mahwah, NJ: Erlbaum.

Killen, M., & Nucci, L. P. (1995). Morality, autonomy, and social conflict. In M. Killen & D. Hart (Eds.), *Morality in everyday life: Developmental perspectives* (pp. 52–86). Cambridge, UK: Cambridge University Press.

Killoren, S. E., Thayer, S. M., & Updegraff, K. A. (2008). Conflict resolution between Mexican origin adolescent siblings. *Journal of Marriage and Family, 70,* 1200–1212.

Kilpatrick, S. W., & Sanders, D. M. (1978). Body image stereotypes: A developmental comparison. *Journal of Genetic Psychology, 132,* 87–95.

Kim, J. E., & Moen, P. (2002a). Is retirement good or bad for subjective well-being? *Current Directions in Psychological Science, 10,* 83–86.

Kim, J. E., & Moen, P. (2002b). Moving into retirement: Preparation and transitions in late midlife. In M. E. Lachman (Ed.), *Handbook of midlife development* (pp. 487–527). New York: Wiley.

Kim, J. M. (1998). Korean children's concepts of adult and peer authority and moral reasoning. *Developmental Psychology, 34,* 947–955.

Kim, J. M., & Turiel, E. (1996). Korean children's concepts of adult and peer authority. *Social Development, 5,* 310–329.

Kim, J.-Y., McHale, S. M., Crouter, A. C., & Osgood, D. W. (2007). Longitudinal linkages between sibling relationships and adjustment from middle childhood through adolescence. *Developmental Psychology, 43,* 960–973.

Kim, J.-Y., McHale, S. M., Osgood, D. W., & Crouter, A. C. (2006). Longitudinal course and family correlates of sibling relationships from childhood through adolescence. *Child Development, 77,* 1746–1761.

Kim, M., McGregor, K. K., & Thompson, C. K. (2000). Early lexical development in English- and Korean-speaking children: Language-general and language-specific patterns. *Journal of Child Language, 27,* 225–254.

Kim, S., & Hasher, L. (2005). The attraction effect in decision making: Superior performance by older adults. *Quarterly Journal of Experimental Psychology, 58A,* 120–133.

Kimbro, R. T. (2006). On-the-job moms: Work and breastfeeding initiation and duration for a sample of low-income women. *Maternal and Child Health Journal, 10,* 19–26.

King, A. C. (2001). Interventions to promote physical activity by older adults. *Journal of Gerontology, 56A,* 36A–46A.

King, A. C., & Bjorklund, D. F. (2010). Evolutionary developmental psychology. *Psicothema, 22,* 22–27.

King, A. C., Kiernan, M., Oman, R. F., Kraemer, H., Hull, M., & Ahn, D. (1997). Can we identify who will adhere to long-term physical activity? Signal detection methodology as a potential aid to clinical decision making. *Health Psychology, 16,* 380–389.

King, L. A., & Hicks, J. A. (2007). Whatever happened to "What might have been"? *American Psychologist, 62,* 625–636.

King, P. E., & Furrow, J. L. (2004). Religion as a resource for positive youth development: Religion, social capital, and moral outcomes. *Developmental Psychology, 40,* 703–713.

King, P. M., & Kitchener, K. S. (1994). *Developing reflective judgment: Understanding and promoting intellectual growth and critical thinking in adolescents and adults.* San Francisco: Jossey-Bass.

King, P. M., & Kitchener, K. S. (2002). The reflective judgment model: Twenty years of research on epistemic cognition. In B. K. Hofer & P. R. Pintrich (Eds.), *Personal epistemology: The psychological beliefs about knowledge and knowing* (pp. 37–61). Mahwah, NJ: Erlbaum.

King, V. (2007). When children have two mothers: Relationships with nonresident mothers, stepmothers, and fathers. *Journal of Marriage and Family, 69,* 1178–1193.

King, V. (2009). Stepfamily formation: Implications for adolescent ties to mothers, nonresident fathers, and stepfathers. *Journal of Marriage and Family, 71,* 954–968.

Kingsbery, S. A. (2002). The impact of aging on sexual function in women and their partners. *Archives of Sexual Behavior, 31,* 431–437.

Kinney, D. (1999). From "headbangers" to "hippies": Delineating adolescents' active attempts to form an alternative peer culture. In J. A. McLellan & M. J. V. Pugh (Eds.), *The role of peer groups in adolescent social identity: Exploring the importance of stability and change* (pp. 21–35). San Francisco: Jossey-Bass.

Kinney, H. C. (2009). Brainstem mechanisms underlying the sudden infant death syndrome: Evidence from human pathologic studies. *Developmental Psychobiology, 51,* 223–233.

Kinnunen, M.-L., Pietilainen, K., & Rissanen, A. (2006). Body size and overweight from birth to adulthood. In L. Pulkkinen & J. Kaprio (Eds.), *Socioemotional development and health from adolescence to adulthood* (pp. 95–107). New York: Cambridge University Press.

Kinsella, M. T., & Monk, C. (2009). Impact of maternal stress, depression and anxiety on fetal neurobehavioral development. *Clinical Obstetrics and Gynecology, 52,* 425–440.

Kinser, K., & Deitchman, J. (2007). Tenacious persisters: Returning adult students in higher education. *Journal of College Student Retention, 9,* 75–94.

Kirby, D. (2002a). Antecedents of adolescent initiation of sex, contraceptive use, and pregnancy. *American Journal of Health Behavior, 26,* 473–485.

Kirby, D. (2002b). Effective approaches to reducing adolescent unprotected sex, pregnancy, and childbearing. *Journal of Sex Research, 39,* 51–57.

Kirby, D., & Laris, B. A. (2009). Effective curriculumbased sex and STD/HIV education programs for adolescents. *Child Development Perspectives, 3,* 21–29.

Kirchner, G. (2000). *Children's games from around the world.* Boston: Allyn and Bacon.

Kiriakidis, S. P., & Kavoura, A. (2010). Cyberbullying: A review of the literature on harassment through the Internet and other electronic means. *Family and Community Health, 33,* 82–93.

Kirk, K. M., Bailey, J. M., Dunne, M. P., & Martin, N. G. (2000). Measurement models for sexual orientation in a community twin sample. *Behavior Genetics, 30,* 345–356.

Kirkham, N. Z., Cruess, L., & Diamond, A. (2003). Helping children apply their knowledge to their behavior on a dimension-switching task. *Developmental Science, 6,* 449–476.

Kirkham, N. Z., Slemmer, J. A., & Johnson, S. P. (2002). Visual statistical learning in infancy: Evidence for a domain general learning mechanism. *Cognition, 83,* B35–B42.

Kirkwood, T. (2010, November). Why women live longer. *Scientific American, 303,* 34–35.

Kirshenbaum, A. P., Olsen, D. M., & Bickel, W. K. (2009). A quantitative review of the ubiquitous relapse curve. *Journal of Substance Abuse Treatment, 36,* 8–17.

Kisilevsky, B. S., Hains, S. M. J., Brown, C. A., Lee, C. T., Cowperthwaite, B., & Stutzman, S. S. (2009). Fetal sensitivity to properties of maternal speech and language. *Infant Behavior and Development, 32,* 59–71.

Kisilevsky, B. S., Hains, S. M. J., Lee, K., Xie, X., Huang, H., Ye, H. H., Zhang, K., & Wang, Z. (2003). Effects of experience on fetal voice recognition. *Psychological Science, 14,* 220–224.

Kisilevsky, B. S., & Low, J. A. (1998). Human fetal behvior: 100 years of study. *Developmental Review, 18,* 1–29.

Kite, M. E., Stockdale, G. D., Whitley, B. E., Jr., & Johnson, B. T. (2005). Attitudes toward younger and older adults: An updated meta-analytic review. *Journal of Social Issues, 61,* 241–266.

Kito, M. (2005). Self-disclosure in romantic relationships and friendships among American and Japanese college students. *Journal of Social Psychology, 145,* 127–145.

Kitzman, H. J., Olds, D. L., Cole, R. E., Hanks, C. A., Anson, E. A., Arcoleo, K. J., et al. (2010). Enduring effects of prenatal and infancy home visiting by nurses on children: Follow-up of a randomized trial among children at age 12 years. *Archives of Pediatric and Adolescent Medicine, 164,* 412–418.

Kitzmann, K. M., Cohen, R., & Lockwood, R. L. (2002). Are only children missing out? Comparison of the peer-related social competence of only children and siblings. *Journal of Social and Personal Relationships, 19,* 299–316.

Kiuru, N., Aunola, K., Vuori, J., & Nurmi, J.-E. (2009). The role of peer groups in adolescents' educational expectation and adjustment. *Journal of Youth and Adolescence, 36,* 995–1009.

Kivipelto, M., Rovio, S., Ngandu, T., Karenhold, I., Eskelinen, M., & Winblad, B. (2008). Apolipoprotein E epsilon4 magnifies lifestyle risks for dementia: A population-based study. *Journal of Cellular and Molecular Medicine, 12,* 2762–2771.

Kjønniksen, L., Anderssen, N., & Wold, B. (2009). Organized youth sport as a predictor of physical activity in adulthood. *Scandinavian Journal of Medicine and Science in Sports, 19,* 646–654.

Kjønniksen, L., Torsheim, T., & Wold, B. (2008). Tracking of leisure-time physical activity during adolescence and young adulthood: A 10-year longitudinal study. *International Journal of Behavioral Nutrition and Physical Activity, 5,* 69.

Klaczynski, P. A. (2001). Framing effects on adolescent task representations, analytic and heuristic processing, and decision making: Implications for the normative/descriptive gap. *Applied Developmental Psychology, 22,* 289–309.

Klaczynski, P. A., & Narasimham, G. (1998). Development of scientific reasoning biases: Cognitive versus ego-protective explanations. *Developmental Psychology, 34,* 175–187.

Klaczynski, P. A., Schuneman, M. J., & Daniel, D. B. (2004). Theories of conditional reasoning: A developmental examination of competing hypotheses. *Developmental Psychology, 40,* 559–571.

Klareskog, L., Padyukov, L., Rönnelid, J., & Alfredsson, L. (2006). Genes, environment and immunity in the development of rheumatoid arthritis. *Current Opinion in Immunology, 18,* 650–655.

Klass, D. (2004). The inner representation of the dead child in the psychic and social narratives of bereaved parents. In R. A. Neimeyer (Ed.), *Meaning reconstruction and the experience of loss* (pp. 77–94). Washington, DC: American Psychological Association.

Klaw, E. L., Rhodes, J. E., & Fitzgerald, L. F. (2003). Natural mentors in the lives of African-American adolescent mothers: Tracking relationships over time. *Journal of Youth and Adolescence, 32,* 223–232.

Klebanov, P. K., Brooks-Gunn, J., McCarton, C., & McCormick, M. C. (1998). The contribution of neighborhood and family income to developmental test scores over the first three years of life. *Child Development, 69,* 1420–1436.

Kleespies, P. M. (2004). Concluding thoughts on suffering, dying and choice. In P. M. Kleespies (Ed.), *Life and death decisions: Psychological and ethical considerations in end-of-life care* (pp. 163–167). Washington, DC: American Psychological Association.

Klein, P. J., & Meltzoff, A. N. (1999). Long-term memory, forgetting, and deferred imitation in 12-month-old infants. *Developmental Science, 2,* 102–113.

Kleinspehn-Ammerlahn, A., Kotter-Grühn, D., & Smith, J. (2008). Self-perceptions of aging: Do subjective age and satisfaction with aging change during old age? *The Journals of Gerontology Series B: Psychological Sciences and Social Sciences, 63,* 377–385.

Klesges, L. M., Johnson, K. C., Ward, K. D., & Barnard, M. (2001). Smoking cessation in pregnant women. *Obstetrics and Gynecology Clinics of North America, 28,* 269–282.

Kliegel, M., Jäger, T., & Phillips, L. H. (2008). Adult age differences in event-based prospective memory: A meta-analysis on the role of focal versus nonfocal cues. *Psychology and Aging, 23,* 203–208.

Kliewer, W., Fearnow, M. D., & Miller, P. A. (1996). Coping socialization in middle childhood: Tests of maternal and paternal influences. *Child Development, 67,* 2339–2357.

Klimstra, T. A., Hale, W. W., III, Raaijmakers, Q. A. W., Branje, S. J. T., & Meeus, W. H. J. (2010). Identity formation in adolescence: Change or stability? *Journal of Youth and Adolescence, 39,* 150–162.

Kline, G. H., Stanley, S. M., Markman, H. J., Olmos-Gallo, P. A., St. Peters, M., Whitton, S. W., & Prado, L. M. (2004). Timing is everything: Preengagement cohabitation and increased risk for poor marital outcomes. *Journal of Family Psychology, 18,* 311–318.

Klingman, A. (2006). Children and war trauma. In K. A. Renninger & I. E. Sigel (Eds.), *Handbook of child psychology: Vol. 4. Child psychology in practice* (6th ed., pp. 619–652). Hoboken, NJ: Wiley.

Kloep, M., & Hendry, L. B. (2007). Retirement: A new beginning? *The Psychologist, 20,* 742–745.

Klomsten, A. T., Skaalvik, E. M., & Espnes, G. A. (2004). Physical self-concept and sports: Do gender differences exist? *Sex Roles, 50,* 119–127.

Klump, K. L., Kaye, W. H., & Strober, M. (2001). The evolving foundations of eating disorders. *Psychiatric Clinics of North America, 24,* 215–225.

Kluwer, E. S., & Johnson, M. D. (2007). Conflict frequency and relationship quality across the transition to parenthood. *Journal of Marriage and Family, 69,* 1089–1106.

Knafo, A., Zahn-Waxler, C., Davidov, M., Hulle, C. V., Robinson, J. L., & Rhee, S. H. (2009). Empathy in early childhood: Genetic, environmental, and affective contributions. In O. Vilarroya, S. Altran, A. Navarro, K. Ochsner, & A. Tobena (Eds.), *Values, empathy, and fairness across social barriers* (pp. 103–114). New York: New York Academy of Sciences.

Knickmeyer, R. C., Gouttard, S., Kang, C., Evans, D., Wilber, K., Smith, J. K., et al. (2008). A structural MRI study of human brain development from birth to 2 years. *Journal of Neuroscience, 28,* 12176–12182.

Knight, B. J., & Sayegh, P. (2010). Cultural values and caregiving: The updated sociocultural stress and coping model. *Journal of Gerontology, 65B,* 5–13.

Knopf, M., Kraus, U., & Kressley-Mba, R. A. (2006). Relational information processing of novel unrelated actions by infants. *Infant Behavior and Development, 29,* 44–53.

Knox, D., Langehaugh, S. O., & Walters, C. (1998). Religiosity and spirituality among college students. *College Student Journal, 32,* 430–432.

Ko, K. J., Berg, C. A., Butner, J., Uchino, B. N., & Smith, T. W. (2007). Profiles of successful aging in middle-age and older adult married couples. *Psychology and Aging, 22,* 705–718.

Kobayashi, T., Hiraki, K., & Hasegawa, T. (2005). Auditory-visual intermodal matching of small numerosities in 6-month-old infants. *Developmental Science, 8,* 409–419.

Kobayashi, T., Kazuo, H., Ryoko, M., & Hasegawa, T. (2004). Baby arithmetic: One object plus one tone. *Cognition, 91,* B23–B34.

Kobayashi, Y. (1994). Conceptual acquisition and change through social interaction. *Human Development, 37,* 233–241.

Kochanska, G. (1991). Socialization and temperament in the development of guilt and conscience. *Child Development, 62,* 1379–1392.

Kochanska, G., & Aksan, N. (2006). Children's conscience and self-regulation. *Journal of Personality, 74,* 1587–1617.

Kochanska, G., Aksan, N., & Joy, M. E. (2007). Children's fearfulness as a moderator of parenting in early socialization: Two longitudinal studies. *Developmental Psychology, 43,* 222–237.

Kochanska, G., Aksan, N., & Nichols, K. E. (2003). Maternal power assertion in discipline and moral discourse contexts: Commonalities, differences, and implications for children's moral conduct and cognition. *Developmental Psychology, 39,* 949–963.

Kochanska, G., Aksan, N., Prisco, T. R., & Adams, E. E. (2008). Mother–child and father–child mutually

responsive orientation in the first 2 years and children's outcomes at preschool age: Mechanisms of influence. *Child Development, 79,* 30–44.

Kochanska, G., Casey, R. J., & Fukumoto, A. (1995). Toddlers' sensitivity to standard violations. *Child Development, 66,* 643–656.

Kochanska, G., Forman, D. R., Aksan, N., & Dunbar, S. B. (2005). Pathways to conscience: Early mother–child mutually responsive orientation and children's moral emotion, conduct, and cognition. *Journal of Child Psychology and Psychiatry, 46,* 19–34.

Kochanska, G., Gross, J. N., Lin, M.-H., & Nichols, K. E. (2002). Guilt in young children: Development, determinants, and relations with broader system standards. *Child Development, 73,* 461–482.

Kochanska, G., & Knaack, A. (2003). Effortful control as a personality characteristic of young children: Antecedents, correlates, and consequences. *Journal of Personality, 71,* 1087–1112.

Kochanska, G., Murray, K. T., & Harlan, E. T. (2000). Effortful control in early childhood: Continuity and change, antecedents, and implications for social development. *Developmental Psychology, 36,* 220–232.

Kochanska, G., Philibert, R. A., & Barry, R. A. (2009). Interplay of genes and early other–child relationship in the development of self-regulation from toddler to preschool age. *Journal of Child Psychology and Psychiatry, 50,* 1331–1338.

Koestner, R., Franz, C., & Weinberger, J. (1990). The family origins of empathic concern: A 26-year longitudinal study. *Journal of Personality and Social Psychology, 58,* 709–717.

Kohen, D. E., Leventhal, T., Dahinten, V. S., & McIntosh, C. N. (2008). Neighborhood disadvantage: Pathways of effects for young children. *Child Development, 79,* 156–169.

Kohlberg, L. (1969). Stage and sequence: The cognitivedevelopmental approach to socialization. In D. A. Goslin (Ed.), *Handbook of socialization theory and research* (pp. 347–480). Chicago: Rand McNally.

Kohlberg, L., Levine, C., & Hewer, A. (1983). *Moral stages: A current formulation and a response to critics.* Basel, Switzerland: Karger. Kohn, M. L. (2006). *Change and stability: A cross-national analysis of social structure and personality.* Greenbrae, CA: Paradigm Press.

Komp, D. M. (1996). The changing face of death in children. In H. M. Spiro, M. G. M. Curnen, & L. P. Wandel (Eds.), *Facing death: Where culture, religion, and medicine meet* (pp. 66–76). New Haven: Yale University Press.

Konner, M. (2010). *The evolution of childhood: Relationships, emotion, mind.* Cambridge, MA: Harvard University Press.

Konold, T. R., & Pianta, R. C. (2005). Empirically derived, person-oriented patterns of school readiness in typically developing children: Description and prediction to first-grade achievement. *Applied Developmental Science, 9,* 174–187.

Kopp, C. B., & Neufeld, S. J. (2003). Emotional development during infancy. In R. Davidson, K. R. Scherer, & H. H. Goldsmith (Eds.), *Handbook of affective sciences* (pp. 347–374). Oxford, UK: Oxford University Press.

Kooijman, V., Hagoort, P., & Cutler, A. (2009). Prosodic structure in early word segmentation: ERP evidence from Dutch ten-month-olds. *Infancy, 14,* 591–612.

Kopeikina, K. J., Carlson, G. A., Pitstick, R., Ludvigson, A. E., Peters, A., et al. (2011). Tau accumulation causes mitochondrial distribution deficits in neurons in a mouse model of tauopathy and in human Alzheimer's disease brain. *American Journal of Pathology 179,* 2071–2082.

Kornhaber, M. L. (2004). Using multiple intelligences to overcome cultural barriers to identification for gifted education. In D. Boothe & J. C. Stanley

(Eds.), *In the eyes of the beholder: Critical issues for diversity in gifted education* (pp. 215–225). Waco, TX: Prufrock Press.

Kotkin, J. (2012, July 16). Are Millennials the screwed generation? *Newsweek.* Retrieved from www.thedailybeast.com/newsweek/2012/07/15/aremillennials-the-screwed-generation.html

Kotre, J. (1999). *Make it count: How to generate a legacy that gives meaning to your life.* New York: Free Press.

Kozer, E., Costei, A. M., Boskovic, R., Nulman, I., Nikfar, S., & Koren, G. (2003). Effects of aspirin consumption during pregnancy on pregnancy outcomes: Meta-analysis. *Birth Defects Research, Part B, Developmental and Reproductive Toxicology, 68,* 70–84.

Kozol, J. (2005). *The shame of the nation: The restoration of apartheid schooling in America.* New York: Three Rivers Press.

Kragstrup, T. W., Kjaer, M., & Mackey, A. L. (2011). Structural, biochemical, cellular, and functional changes in skeletal muscle extracellular matrix with aging. *Scandinavian Journal of Medicine and Science in Sports, 21,* 749–757.

Kral, T. V. E., & Faith, M. S. (2009). Influences on child eating and weight development from a behavioral genetics perspective. *Journal of Pediatric Psychology, 34,* 596–605.

Kramer, A. F., Fabiani, M., & Colcombe, S. J. (2006). Contributions of cognitive neuroscience to the understanding of behavior and aging. In J. E. Birren & K. W. Schaie (Eds.), *Handbook of the psychology of aging* (6th ed., pp. 57–83). Burlington, MA: Elsevier Academic Press.

Kramer, A. F., Hahn, S., & Gopher, D. (1998). Task coordination and aging: Explorations of executive control processes in the task switching paradigm. *Acta Psychologica, 101,* 339–378.

Kramer, A. F., & Kray, J. (2006). Aging and attention. In E. Bialystok & F. I. M. Fergus (Eds.), *Lifespan cognition: Mechanisms of change* (pp. 57–69). New York: Oxford University Press.

Kramer, A. F., & Madden, D. J. (2008). Attention. In F. I. M. Craik & T. A. Salthouse (Eds.), *Handbook of aging and cognition* (pp. 189–249). New York: Psychology Press.

Kramer, D. A. (2003). The ontogeny of wisdom in its variations. In J. Demick & C. Andreoletti (Eds.), *Handbook of adult development* (pp. 131–151). New York: Springer.

Kramer, S. E., Kapteyn, T. S., Kuik, D. J., & Deeg, D. J. (2002). The association of hearing impairment and chronic diseases with psychosocial health status in older age. *Journal of Aging and Health, 14,* 122–137.

Krampe, R. T., & Charness, N. (2007). Aging and expertise. In K. A. Ericsson, N. Charness, P. J. Feltovich, & R. R. Hoffman (Eds.), *Cambridge handbook of expertise and expert performance* (pp. 723–742). New York: Cambridge University Press.

Krause, N. (2001). Social support. In R. H. Binstock & L. K. George (Eds.), *Handbook of aging and the social sciences* (5th ed., pp. 272–294). San Diego, CA: Academic Press.

Krause, N. (2012). Religious involvement, humility, and change in self-rated health over time. *Journal of Psychology and Theology, 40,* 199–210.

Krcmar, M., Grela, B., & Linn, K. (2007). Can toddlers learn vocabulary from television? An experimental approach. *Media Psychology, 10,* 41–63.

Krebs, D., & Denton, K. (2005). Toward a more pragmatic approach to morality: A critical evaluation of Kohlberg's model. *Psychological Review, 112,* 629–649.

Kreppner, J. M., Kumsta, R., Rutter, M., Beckett, C., Castle, J., Stevens, S., et al. (2010). Developmental course of deprivation specific psychological patterns: Early manifestations, persistence to age 15, and clinical features. *Monographs of the Society for Research in Child Development, 75*(1, Serial No. 295), 79–101.

Kreppner, J. M., Rutter, M., Beckett, C., Castle, J., Colvert, E., Groothues, C., Hawkins, A., & O'Connor, T. G. (2007). Normality and impairment following profound early institutional deprivation: A longitudinal follow-up into early adolescence. *Developmental Psychology, 43,* 931–946.

Krettenauer, T. (2005). The role of epistemic cognition in adolescent identity formation: Further evidence. *Journal of Youth and Adolescence, 34,* 185–198.

Krevans, J., & Gibbs, J. C. (1996). Parents' use of inductive discipline: Relations to children's empathy and prosocial behavior. *Child Development, 67,* 3263–3277.

Krishnamoorthy, J. S., Hart, C., & Jelalian, E. (2006). The epidemic of childhood obesity: Review of research and implications for public policy. *Social Policy Report of the Society for Research in Child Development, 9*(2).

Kroger, J. (2007). *Identity development: Adolescence through adulthood* (2nd ed.). Thousand Oaks, CA: Sage.

Kroger, J., Martinussen, M., & Marcia, J. E. (2010). Identity status change during adolescence and young adulthood: A meta-analysis. *Journal of Adolescence, 33,* 683–698.

Kropf, N. P., & Pugh, K. L. (1995). Beyond life expectancy: Social work with centenarians. *Journal of Gerontological Social Work, 23,* 121–137.

Krumhansl, C. L., & Jusczyk, P. W. (1990). Infants' perception of phrase structure in music. *Psychological Science, 1,* 70–73.

Kubicek, B., Korunka, C., Raymo, J. M., & Hoonakker, P. (2011). Psychological well-being in retirement: The effects of personal and gendered contextual resources. *Journal of Occupational Health Psychology, 16,* 230–246.

Kubik, M. Y., Lytle, L. A., Hannan, P. J., Perry, C. L., & Story, M. (2003). The association of the school food environment with dietary behaviors of young adolescents. *American Journal of Public Health, 93,* 1168–1173.

Kübler-Ross, E. (1969). *On death and dying.* New York: Macmillan.

Kubotera, T. (2004). Japanese religion in changing society: The spirits of the dead. In J. D. Morgan & P. Laungani (Eds.), *Death and bereavement around the world: Vol. 4. Asia, Australia, and New Zealand* (pp. 95–99). Amityville, NY: Baywood Publishing Company.

Kuchner, J. (1989, April). *Chinese-American and European-American mothers and infants: Cultural influences in the first three months of life.* Paper presented at the biennial meeting of the Society for Research in Child Development, Kansas City, MO.

Kuczynski, L. (1984). Socialization goals and mother–child interaction: Strategies for long-term and short-term compliance. *Developmental Psychology, 20,* 1061–1073.

Kuczynski, L., & Lollis, S. (2002). Four foundations for a dynamic model of parenting. In J. R. M. Gerris (Ed.), *Dynamics of parenting.* Hillsdale, NJ: Erlbaum.

Kudo, N., Nonaka, Y., Noriko, M., Katsumi, M., & Okanoya, K. (2011). On-line statistical segmentation of a non-speech auditory stream in neonates as demonstrated by event-related brain potentials. *Developmental Science, 14,* 1100–1106.

Kuebli, J., Butler, S., & Fivush, R. (1995). Mother–child talk about past emotions: Relations of maternal language and child gender over time. *Cognition and Emotion, 9,* 265–283.

Kugelmass, J., & Ainscow, M. (2004). Leadership for inclusion: A comparison of international practices. *Journal of Research in Special Educational Needs, 4,* 133–141.

Kuhl, P. K., Tsao, F.-M., & Liu, H.-M. (2003). Foreign language experience in infancy: Effects of short-term exposure and social interaction on phonetic learning. *Proceedings of the National Academy of Sciences, 100,* 9096–9101.

Kuhn, D. (2000). Theory of mind, metacognition, and reasoning: A life-span perspective. In P. Mitchell & K. J. Riggs (Eds.), *Children's reasoning and the mind* (pp. 301–326). Hove, UK: Psychology Press.

Kuhn, D. (2002). What is scientific thinking, and how does it develop? In U. Goswami (Ed.), *Blackwell handbook of childhood cognitive development* (pp. 371–393). Malden, MA: Blackwell.

Kuhn, D. (2009). Adolescent thinking. In R. M. Lerner & L. Steinberg (Eds.), *Handbook of adolescent psychology, Vol. 1: Individual bases of adolescent development* (3rd ed., pp. 152–186). Hoboken, NJ: Wiley.

Kuhn, D., Amsel, E., & O'Loughlin, M. (1988). *The development of scientific thinking skills.* Orlando, FL: Academic Press.

Kuhn, D., & Dean, D. (2004). Connecting scientific reasoning and causal inference. *Journal of Cognition and Development, 5,* 261–288.

Kuhn, D., & Franklin, S. (2006). The second decade: What develops (and how)? In D. Kuhn & R. S. Siegler (Eds.), *Handbook of child psychology: Vol. 2. Cognition, perception, and language* (6th ed.). Hoboken, NJ: Wiley.

Kuhn, D., Iordanou, K., Pease, M., & Wirkala, C. (2008). Beyond control of variables: What needs to develop to achieve skilled scientific thinking? *Cognitive Development, 23,* 435–451.

Kuhn, D., & Pease, M. (2006). Do children and adults learn differently? *Journal of Cognition and Development, 7,* 279–293.

Kuklinski, M. R., & Weinstein, R. S. (2001). Classroom and developmental differences in a path model of teacher expectancy effects. *Child Development, 72,* 1554–1578.

Kulik, K. (2001). Marital relationships in late adulthood: Synchronous versus asynchronous couples. *International Journal of Aging and Human Development, 52,* 323–339.

Kumar, S., & O'Brien, A. (2004). Recent developments in fetal medicine. *British Medical Journal, 328,* 1002–1006.

Kunemund, H., Motel-Klingebiel, A., & Kohli, M. (2005). Do intergenerational transfers from elderly parents increase social inequality among their middle-aged children? Evidence from the German Aging Survey. *Journal of Gerontology, 60B,* S30-S36.

Kunnen, E. S., & Bosma, H. A. (2003). Fischer's skill theory applied to identity development: A response to Kroger. *Identity, 3,* 247–270.

Kunnen, E. S., Sappa, V., van Gert, P. L. C., & Bonica, L. (2008). The shapes of commitment development in emerging adulthood. *Journal of Adult Development, 15,* 113–131.

Kuppens, S., Grietens, H., Onghena, P., & Michiels, D. (2009). Associations between parental control and children's overt and relational aggression. *British Journal of Developmental Psychology, 27,* 607–623.

Kurdek, L. A. (2005). Gender and marital satisfaction early in marriage: A growth curve approach. *Journal of Marriage and Family, 67,* 68–84.

Kurdek, L. A. (2006). Differences between partners from heterosexual, gay, and lesbian cohabiting couples. *Journal of Marriage and Family, 68,* 509–528.

Kurdek, L. A., & Fine, M. A. (1994). Family acceptance and family control as predictors of adjustment in young adolescents: Linear, curvilinear, or interactive effects? *Child Development, 65,* 1137–1146.

Kurtz-Costes, B., Rowley, S. J., Harris-Britt, A., & Woods, T. A. (2008). Gender stereotypes about mathematics and science and self-perceptions of ability in late childhood and early adolescence. *Merrill-Palmer Quarterly, 54,* 386–409.

Kwon, Y. H., Fingert, J. H., Kuehn, M. H., & Alward, W. L. (2009). Primary open-angle glaucoma. *New England Journal of Medicine, 360,* 1113–1124.

L

Labouvie-Vief, G. (1980). Beyond formal operations: Uses and limits of pure logic in life-span development. *Human Development, 23,* 141–160.

Labouvie-Vief, G. (1985). Logic and self-regulation from youth to maturity: A model. In M. Commons, F. Richards, & C. Armon (Eds.), *Beyond formal operations: Late adolescent and adult cognitive development* (pp. 158–180). New York: Praeger.

Labouvie-Vief, G. (2003). Dynamic integration: Affect, cognition, and the self in adulthood. *Current Directions in Psychological Science, 12,* 201–206.

Labouvie-Vief, G. (2005). Self-with-other representations and the organization of the self. *Journal of Research in Personality, 39,* 185–205.

Labouvie-Vief, G. (2006). Emerging structures of adult thought. In J. J. Arnett & J. L. Tanner (Eds.), *Emerging adults in America: Coming of age in the 21st century* (pp. 59–84). Washington, DC: American Psychological Association.

Labouvie-Vief, G. (2008). When differentiation and negative affect lead to integration and growth. *American Psychologist, 63,* 564–565.

Labouvie-Vief, G., Chiodo, L. M., Goguen, L. A., Diehl, M., & Orwoll, L. (1995). Representations of self across the life span. *Psychology and Aging, 10,* 404–415.

Labouvie-Vief, G., & Diehl, M. (1999). Self and personality development. In J. C. Kavanaugh & S. K. Whitbourne (Eds.), *Gerontology: An interdisciplinary perspective* (pp. 238–268). New York: Oxford University Press.

Labouvie-Vief, G., & Diehl, M. (2000). Cognitive complexity and cognitive-affective integration: Related or separate domains of adult development? *Psychology and Aging, 15,* 490–504.

Labouvie-Vief, G., Diehl, M., Jain, E., & Zhang, F. (2007). Six-year change in affect optimization and affect complexity across the adult life span: A further examination. *Psychology and Aging, 22,* 738–751.

Labouvie-Vief, G., Grühn, S., & Studer, J. (2010). Dynamic integration of emotion and cognition: Equilibrium regulation in development and aging. In W. Overton & R. M. Lerner (Eds.), *Handbook of life-span development: Vol. 2. Social and emotional development* (pp. 79–115). Hoboken, NJ: Wiley.

Lachance-Grzela, M., & Bouchard, G. (2010). Why do women do the lion's share of housework? A decade of research. *Sex Roles, 63,* 767–780.

Lachman, M. E. (2004). Development in midlife. *Annual Review of Psychology, 55,* 305–331.

Lachman, M. E., Neupert, S. D., & Agrigoroaei, S. (2011). The relevance of control beliefs for health and aging. In K. W. Schaie & S. L. Willis (Eds.), *Handbook of the psychology of aging* (7th ed., pp. 175–190). San Diego, CA: Elsevier.

Lacourse, E., Nagin, D., Tremblay, R. E., Vitaro, F., & Claes, M. (2003). Developmental trajectories of boys' delinquent group membership and facilitation of violent behaviors during adolescence. *Development and Psychopathology, 15,* 183–197.

Ladd, G. W. (2005). *Children's peer relationships and social competence: A century of progress.* New Haven, CT: Yale University Press.

Ladd, G. W., Birch, S. H., & Buhs, E. S. (1999). Children's social and scholastic lives in kindergarten: Related spheres of influence? *Child Development, 70,* 1373–1400.

Ladd, G. W., Buhs, E. S., & Seid, M. (2000). Children's initial sentiments about kindergarten: Is school liking an antecedent of early classroom participation and achievement? *Merrill-Palmer Quarterly, 46,* 255–279.

Ladd, G. W., & Burgess, K. B. (1999). Charting the relationship trajectories of aggressive, withdrawn, and aggressive/withdrawn children during early grade school. *Child Development, 70,* 910–929.

Ladd, G. W., Herald, S. L., & Kochel, K. P. (2006). School readiness: Are there social prerequisites? *Early Education and Development, 17,* 115–150.

Ladd, G. W., Kochenderfer-Ladd, B., Eggum, N. D., Kochel, K. P., & McConnell, E. M. (2011). Characterizing and comparing the friendships of anxious-solitary and unsociable preadolescents. *Child Development, 82,* 1434–1453.

Ladd, G. W., LeSieur, K., & Profilet, S. M. (1993). Direct parental influences on young children's peer relations. In S. Duck (Ed.), *Learning about relationships* (Vol. 2, pp. 152–183). London: Sage.

Ladd, G. W., & Pettit, G. S. (2002). Parenting and the development of children's peer relationships. In M. Bornstein (Ed.), *Handbook of parenting* (2nd ed.). Mahwah, NJ: Erlbaum.

Ladd, G. W., & Price, J. M. (1987). Predicting children's social and school adjustment following the transition from preschool to kindergarten. *Child Development, 58,* 1168–1189.

LaFraniere, S. (2011, April 6). As China ages, birthrate policy may prove difficult to reverse. *New York Times.* Retrieved from www.nytimes.com/2011/04/07/world/asia/07population.html?pagewanted=all

Lagattuta, K. H., Wellman, H. M., & Flavell, J. H. (1997). Preschoolers' understanding of the link between thinking and feeling: Cognitive cuing and emotional change. *Child Development, 68,* 1081–1104.

Lagnado, L. (2001, November 2). Kids confront Trade Center trauma. *Wall Street Journal,* pp. B1, B6.

Laible, D. (2004). Mother–child discourse in two contexts: Links with child temperament, attachment security, and socioemotional competence. *Developmental Psychology, 40,* 979–992.

Laible, D. (2007). Attachment with parents and peers in late adolescence: Links with emotional competence and social behavior. *Personality and Individual Differences, 43,* 1185–1197.

Laible, D., & Song, J. (2006). Constructing emotional and relational understanding: The role of affect and mother–child discourse. *Merrill-Palmer Quarterly, 52,* 44–69.

Laird, R. D., Jordan, K. Y., Dodge, K. A., Pettit, G. S., & Bates, J. E. (2001). Peer rejection in childhood, involvement with antisocial peers in early adolescence, and the development of externalizing behavior problems. *Development and Psychopathology, 13,* 337–354.

Laird, R. D., Pettit, G. S., Dodge, K. A., & Bates, J. E. (2005). Peer relationship antecedents of delinquent behavior in late adolescence: Is there evidence of demographic group differences in developmental processes? *Development and Psychopathology, 17,* 127–144.

Lamarche, V., Brendgen, M., Boivin, M., Vitaro, F., Perusse, D., & Dionne, G. (2006). Do friendships and sibling relationships provide protection against peer victimization in a similar way? *Social Development, 15,* 373–393.

Lamaze, F. (1958). *Painless childbirth.* London: Burke.

Lamb, M. E., & Ahnert, L. (2006). Nonparental child care: Context, concepts, correlates, and consequences. In K. A. Renninger & I. E. Sigel (Eds.), *Handbook of child psychology: Vol. 4. Child psychology in practice* (6th ed., pp. 700–778). Hoboken, NJ: Wiley.

Lamb, M. E., & Lewis, C. (2004). The development and significance of father–child relationships in twoparent families. In M. E. Lamb (Ed.), *The role of the father in child development* (4th ed., pp. 272–306). Hoboken, NJ: Wiley.

Lamb, M. E., Thompson, R. A., Gardner, W., Charnov, E. L., & Connell, J. P. (1985). Infant–mother attachment: The origins and developmental

significance of individual differences in the Strange Situation: Its study and biological interpretation. *Behavioral and Brain Sciences, 7,* 127–147.

Lamberg, L. (2007). Menopause not always to blame for sleep problems in midlife women. *Journal of the American Medical Association, 297,* 1865–1866.

Lambert, S. M., Masson, P., & Fisch, H. (2006). The male biological clock. *World Journal of Urology, 24,* 611–617.

Lang, F. R., & Baltes, M. M. (1997). Being with people and being alone in later life: Costs and benefits for everyday functioning. *International Journal of Behavioral Development, 21,* 729–749.

Lang, F. R., Rohr, M. K., & Williger, B. (2010). Modeling success in life-span psychology: The principles of selection, optimization, and compensation. In L. Fingerman, C. A. Berg, J. Smith, & T. C. Antonucci (Eds.), *Handbook of life-span development* (pp. 57–85). New York: Springer.

Lang, F. R., Staudinger, U. M., & Carstensen, L. L. (1998). Perspectives on socioemotional selectivity in late life: How personality and social context do (and do not) make a difference. *Journal of Gerontology, 53B,* P21–P30.

Lang, I. A., Llewellyn, D. J., Langa, K. M., Wallace, R. B., Huppert, F. A., & Melzer, D. (2008). Neighborhood deprivation, individual socioeconomic status, and cognitive function in older people: Analyses from the English Longitudinal Study of Ageing. *Journal of the American Geriatric Society, 56,* 191–198.

Lang, M. (2010). Can mentoring assist in the school-to-work transition? *Education + Training, 52,* 359–367.

Langer, G. (2004). *ABC New Prime Time Live Poll: The American Sex Survey.* Retrieved from abcnews.go.com/Primetime/News/story?id=174461&page=1

Langer, J., Gillette, P., & Arriaga, R. I. (2003). Toddlers' cognition of adding and subtracting objects in action and in perception. *Cognitive Development, 18,* 233–246.

Langhinrichsen-Rohling, J., Friend, J., & Powell, A. (2009). Adolescent suicide, gender, and culture: A rate and risk factor analysis. *Aggression and Violent Behavior, 14,* 402–414.

Langosch, D. (2012). Grandparents parenting again: Challenges, strengths, and implications for practice. *Psychoanalytic Inquiry, 32,* 163–170.

Langsetmo, L., Hitchcock, C. L., Kingwell, E. J., Davison, K. S., Berger, C., Forsmo, S., et al. (2012). Physical activity, body mass index and bone mineral density-associations in a prospective population-based cohort of women and men: The Canadian Multicentre Osteoporosis Study. *Bone, 50,* 401–408.

Lansford, J. E. (2009). Parental divorce and children's adjustment. *Perspectives on Psychological Science, 4,* 140–152.

Lansford, J. E., Antonucci, T. C., Akiyama, H., & Takahashi, K. (2005). A quantitative and qualitative approach to social relationships and well-being in the United States and Japan. *Journal of Comparative Family Studies, 36,* 1–22.

Lansford, J. E., Criss, M. M., Dodge, K. A., Shaw, D. S., Pettit, G. S., & Bates, J. E. (2009). Trajectories of physical discipline: Early childhood antecedents and developmental outcomes. *Child Development, 80,* 1385–1402.

Lansford, J. E., Criss, M. M., Laird, R. D., Shaw, D. S., Pettit, G. S., Bates, J. E., et al. (2011). Reciprocal relations between parents' physical discipline and children's externalizing behavior during middle childhood and adolescence. *Development and Psychopathology, 23,* 225–238.

Lansford, J. E., Criss, M. M., Pettit, G. S., Dodge, K. A., & Bates, J. E. (2003). Friendship quality, peer group affiliation, and peer antisocial behavior as moderators of the link between negative parenting and adolescent externalizing behavior. *Journal of Research on Adolescence, 13,* 161–184.

Lansford, J. E., Deater-Deckard, K., Dodge, K. A., Bates, J. E., & Pettit, G. S. (2004). Ethnic differences in the link between physical discipline and later adolescent externalizing behaviors. *Journal of Child Psychology and Psychiatry, 45,* 801–812.

Lansford, J. E., Malone, P. S., Castellino, D. R., Dodge, K. A., Pettit, G., & Bates, J. E. (2006). Trajectories of internalizing, externalizing, and grades for children who have and have not experienced their parents' divorce or separation. *Journal of Family Psychology, 20,* 292–301.

Lapierr, S., Erlangsen, A., Waern, M., De Leo, D., Oyama, H., Scocco, P., et al. (2011). A systematic review of elderly suicide prevention programs. *Crisis, 32,* 88–98.

Larbi, A., Fülöp, T., & Pawelec, G. (2008). Immune receptor signaling, aging and autoimmunity. In A. B. Sigalov (Ed.), *Multichain immune recognition receptor signaling: From spatiotemporal organization to human disease* (pp. 312–324). New York: Springer.

Largo, R. H., Caflisch, J. A., Hug, F., Muggli, K., Molnar, A. A., & Molinari, L. (2001). Neuromotor development from 5 to 18 years. Part 1: Timed performance. *Developmental Medicine and Child Neurology, 43,* 436–443.

Larsen, J. A., & Nippold, M. A. (2007). Morphological analysis in school-age children: Dynamic assessment of a word learning strategy. *Language, Speech, and Hearing Services in Schools, 38,* 201–212.

Larsen, J. T., To, Y. M., & Fireman, G. (2007). Children's understanding and experience of mixed emotions. *Psychological Science, 18,* 186–191.

Larsen, P. (2009, January). A review of cardiovascular changes in the older adult. *Gerontology Update, December 2008/January 2009, 3,* 9.

Larson, D. G., & Hoyt, W. T. (2007). What has become of grief counseling? An evaluation of the empirical foundations of the new pessimism. *Professional Psychology: Research and Practice, 38,* 347–355.

Larson, R. W. (2001). How U.S. children and adolescents spend time: What it does (and doesn't) tell us about their development. *Current Directions in Psychological Science, 10,* 160–164.

Larson, R. W., & Lampman-Petraitis, C. (1989). Daily emotional states as reported by children and adolescents. *Child Development, 60,* 1250–1260.

Larson, R. W., Mannell, R., & Zuzanek, J. (1986). Daily well-being of older adults with friends and family. *Psychology and Aging, 1,* 117–126.

Larson, R. W., Moneta, G., Richards, M. H., & Wilson, S. (2002). Continuity, stability, and change in daily emotional experience across adolescence. *Child Development, 73,* 1151–1165.

Larson, R. W., & Richards, M. (1998). Waiting for the weekend: Friday and Saturday night as the emotional climax of the week. In A. C. Crouter & R. Larson (Eds.), *Temporal rhythms in adolescence: Clocks, calendars, and the coordination of daily life* (pp. 37–51). San Francisco: Jossey-Bass.

Larsson, M., Öberg, C., & Bäckman, L. (2005). Odor identification in old age: Demographic, sensory and cognitive correlates. *Aging, Neuropsychology, and Cognition, 12,* 231–244.

Larzelere, R. E., Schneider, W. N., Larson, D. B., & Pike, P. L. (1996). The effects of discipline responses in delaying toddler misbehavior recurrences. *Child and Family Behavior Therapy, 18,* 35–57.

Lashley, F. R. (2007). Essentials of clinical genetics in nursing practice. New York: Springer.

Lattanzi-Licht, M., & Doka, K. J. (Eds.). (2003). *Living with grief: Coping with public tragedy.* New York: Brunner-Routledge.

Latz, S., Wolf, A. W., & Lozoff, B. (1999). Sleep practices and problems in young children in Japan and the United States. *Archives of Pediatric and Adolescent Medicine, 153,* 339–346.

Lau, C. Q. (2012). The stability of same-sex cohabitation, different-sex cohabitation, and marriage. *Journal of Marriage and Family, 74*, 973–988.

Lauer, P. A., Akiba, M., Wilkerson, S. B., Apthorp, H. S., Snow, D., & Martin-Glenn, M. (2006). Out-of-school time programs: A meta-analysis of effects for at-risk students. *Review of Educational Research, 76*, 275–313.

Laumann, E. O., Gagnon, J. H., Michael, R. T., & Michaels, S. (1994). *The social organization of sexuality*. Chicago: University of Chicago Press.

Laumann, E. O., Paik, A., & Rosen, R. C. (1999). Sexual dysfunction in the United States: Prevalence and predictors. *Journal of the American Medical Association, 281*, 537–544.

Laureys, S., & Boly, M. (2007). What is it like to be vegetative or minimally conscious? *Current Opinion in Neurology, 20*, 609–613.

Laursen, B., & Collins, W. A. (2009). Parent–child relationships during adolescence. In R. M. Lerner (Ed.), *Handbook of adolescent psychology: Vol. 2. Contextual influences on adolescent development* (3rd ed., pp. 3–42). Hoboken, NJ: Wiley.

Lavelli, M., & Fogel, A. (2005). Developmental changes in the relationship between the infant's attention and emotion during early face-to-face communication: The 2-month transition. *Developmental Psychology, 41*, 265–280.

Lavner, J. A., & Bradbury, T. N. (2012). Why do even satisfied newlyweds eventually go on to divorce? *Journal of Family Psychology, 26*, 1–10.

Law, K. L., Stroud, L. R., Niaura, R., LaGasse, L. L., Giu, J., & Lester, B. M. (2003). Smoking during pregnancy and newborn neurobehavior. *Pediatrics, 111*, 1318–1323.

Lawn, J. E., Mwansa-Kambafwile J., Horta, B. L., Barros, F. C., & Cousens, S. (2010). Kangaroo mother care to prevent neonatal deaths due to preterm birth complications. *International Journal of Epidemiology, 39*(Supplement 1), i144–i154.

Lawrence, A. R., & Schigelone, A. R. S. (2002). Reciprocity beyond dyadic relationships: Aging-related communal coping. *Research on Aging, 24*, 684–704.

Lawrence, E., Rothman, A., Cobb, R. J., & Bradbury, T. N. (2010). Marital satisfaction across the transition to parenthood. In M. S. Schulz, M. K. Pruett, P. K. Kerig, & R. D. Parke (Eds.), *Strengthening couple relationships for optimal child development* (pp. 97–114). Washington, DC: American Psychological Association.

Lawson, K. R., & Ruff, H. A. (2004). Early attention and negative emotionality predict later cognitive and behavioral function. *International Journal of Behavioral Development, 28*, 157–165.

Lawton, J. S. (2011). Sex and gender differences in coronary artery disease. *Seminars in Thoracic Surgery, 23*, 126–130.

Lazar, I., & Darlington, R. (1982). Lasting effects of early education: A report from the Consortium for Longitudinal Studies. *Monographs of the Society for Research in Child Development, 47*(2–3, Serial No. 195).

Lazarus, R. S., & Lazarus, B. N. (1994). *Passion and reason*. New York: Oxford University Press.

Lazinski, M. J., Shea, A. K., & Steiner, M. (2008). Effects of maternal prenatal stress on offspring development: A commentary. *Archives of Women's Mental Health, 11*, 363–375.

Le, T. N. (2011). Life satisfaction, openness value, selftranscendence, and wisdom. *Journal of Happiness Studies, 12*, 171–182.

Leaper, C. (1994). Exploring the correlates and consequences of gender segregation: Social relationships in childhood, adolescence, and adulthood. In C. Leaper (Ed.), *New directions for child development* (No. 65, pp. 67–86). San Francisco: Jossey-Bass.

Leaper, C., Anderson, K. J., & Sanders, P. (1998). Moderators of gender effects on parents' talk to their children: A meta-analysis. *Developmental Psychology, 34*, 3–27.

Leaper, C., & Friedman, C. K. (2007). The socialization of gender. In J. E. Grusec & P. D. Hastings (Eds.), *Handbook of socialization: Theory and research* (pp. 561–587). New York: Guilford.

Leaper, C., Tenenbaum, H. R., & Shaffer, T. G. (1999). Communication patterns of African-American girls and boys from low-income, urban backgrounds. *Child Development, 70*, 1489–1503.

LeBlanc, L. A., Goldsmith, T., & Patel, D. R. (2003). Behavioral aspects of chronic illness in children and adolescents. *Pediatric Clinics of North America, 50*, 859–878.

Lecanuet, J.-P., Granier-Deferre, C., Jacquet, A.-Y., Capponi, I., & Ledru, L. (1993). Prenatal discrimination of a male and female voice uttering the same sentence. *Early Development and Parenting, 2*, 217–228.

Lecuyer, E., & Houck, G. M. (2006). Maternal limitsetting in toddlerhood: Socialization strategies for the development of self-regulation. *Infant Mental Health Journal, 27*, 344–370.

Lee, C.-Y. S., & Doherty, W. J. (2007). Marital satisfaction and father involvement during the transition to parenthood. *Fathering, 5*, 75–96.

Lee, E. E., & Farran, C. J. (2004). Depression among Korean, Korean American, and Caucasian American family caregivers. *Journal of Transcultural Nursing, 15*, 18–25.

Lee, E. O., & Sharpe, T. (2007). Understanding religious/spiritual coping and support resources among African American older adults: A mixed method approach. *Journal of Religion, Spirituality and Aging, 19*, 55–75.

Lee, J. C., Hasnain-Wynia, R., & Lau, D. T. (2011). Delay in seeing a doctor due to cost: Disparity between older adults with and without disabilities in the United States. *Health Services Research, 47*, 698–720.

Lee, J. M., Appulgiese, D., Kaciroti, N., Corwyn, R. F., Bradley, R. H., & Lumeng, J. C. (2007). Weight status in young girls and the onset of puberty. *Pediatrics, 119*, e624–e630.

Lee, S. J., Ralston, H. J., Partridge, J. C., & Rosen, M. A. (2005). Fetal pain: A systematic multidisciplinary review of the evidence. *Journal of the American Medical Association, 294*, 947–954.

Lee, V. E., & Burkam, D. T. (2002). *Inequality at the starting gate*. Washington, DC: Economic Policy Institute.

Leerkes, E. M. (2010). Predictors of maternal sensitivity to infant distress. *Parenting: Science and Practice, 10*, 219–239.

Legacy Project. (2012). *Fast facts on grandparenting and intergenerational mentoring*. Retrieved from www .legacyproject.org/specialreports/fastfacts.html

Lehman, D. R., & Nisbett, R. E. (1990). A longitudinal study of the effects of undergraduate training on reasoning. *Developmental Psychology, 26*, 952–960.

Lehman, M., & Hasselhorn, M. (2007). Variable memory strategy use in children's adaptive intratask learning behavior: Developmental changes and working memory influences in free recall. *Child Development, 78*, 1068–1082.

Lehman, M., & Hasselhorn, M. (2010). The dynamics of free recall and their relation to rehearsal between 8 and 10 years of age. *Child Development, 81*, 1006–1020.

Lehr, V. T., Zeskind, P. S., Ofenstein, J. P., Cepeda, E., Warrier, I., & Aranda, J. V. (2007). Neonatal facial coding system scores and spectral characteristics of infant crying during newborn circumcision. *Clinical Journal of Pain, 23*, 417–424.

Lehrer, E. L., & Chen, Y. (2011). *Women's age at first marriage and marital instability: Evidence from the 2006–2008 National Survey of Family Growth*.

Discussion Paper No. 5954. Chicago: University of Illinois at Chicago.

Lehrer, J. A., Pantell, R., Tebb, K., & Shafer, M. A. (2007). Forgone health care among U.S. adolescents: Associations between risk characteristics and confidentiality. *Journal of Adolescent Health, 40*, 218–226.

Leiter, M. P., Gascón, S., & Martínez-Jarreta, B. (2010). Making sense of work life: A structural model of burnout. *Journal of Applied Social Psychology, 40*, 57–75.

Lemaitre, H., Goldman, A. L., Sambataro, F., Verchinski, B. A., Meyer-Lindenberg, A., & Mattay, V. S. (2012). Normal age-related brain morphometric changes: Nonuniformity across cortical thickness, surface area and gray matter volume? *Neurobiology of Aging, 33*, 617.

Leman, P. J. (2005). Authority and moral reasons: Parenting style and children's perceptions of adult rule justifications. *International Journal of Behavioral Development, 29*, 265–270.

Lempert, H. (1990). Acquisition of passives: The role of patient animacy, salience, and lexical accessibility. *Journal of Child Language, 17*, 677–696.

Lengua, L. J., Wolchik, S., Sandler, I. N., & West, S. G. (2000). The additive and interactive effects of parenting and temperament in predicting problems of children of divorce. *Journal of Clinical Psychology, 29*, 232–244.

Lenhart, A., Ling, R., Campbell, S., & Purcell, K. (2010). *Teens and mobile phones*. Washington, DC: Pew Internet & American Life Project.

Lenroot, R. K., & Giedd, J. N. (2006). Brain development in children and adolescents: Insights from anatomical magnetic resonance imaging. *Neuroscience and Biobehavioral Reviews, 30*, 718–729.

Leon, K. (2003). Risk and protective factors in young children's adjustment to parental divorce: A review of the research. *Family Relations, 52*, 258–270.

Leonesio, M. V., Bridges, B., Gesumaria, R., & Del Bene, L. (2012). The increasing labor force participation of older workers and its effect on the income of the aged. *Social Security Bulletin, 72*(1). Retrieved from www.ssa.gov/policy/docs/ssb/v72n1/v72n1p59.html

Lepage, J.-F., & Théoret, H. (2007). The mirror neuron system: Grasping others' actions from birth? *Developmental Science, 10*, 513–523.

Lerman, R. I. (2010). Capabilities and contributions of unwed fathers. *Future of Children, 20*, 63–85.

Lerner, R. M. (2006). Developmental science, developmental systems, and contemporary theories of human development. In R. M. Lerner (Ed.), *Handbook of child psychology: Vol. 1. Theoretical models of human development* (6th ed., pp. 1–17). Hoboken, NJ: Wiley.

Lerner, R. M., Leonard, K., Fay, K., & Issac, S. S. (2011). Continuity and discontinuity in development across the life span: A developmental systems perspective. In K. L. Fingerman, C. A. Berg, J. Smith, & T. C. Antonucci (Eds.), *Handbook of life-span development* (pp. 141–160). New York: Springer.

Lerner, R. M., & Overton, W. F. (2008). Exemplifying the integrations of the relational developmental system. *Journal of Adolescent Research, 23*, 245–255.

Leslie, A. M. (2004). Who's for learning? *Developmental Science, 7*, 417–419.

Lester, B. M., & Lagasse, L. L. (2010). Children of addicted women. *Journal of Addictive Diseases, 29*, 259–276.

Letherby, G. (2002). Childless and bereft? Stereotypes and realities in relation to "voluntary" and "involuntary" childlessness and womanhood. *Sociological Inquiry, 72*, 7–20.

Leuner, B., Glasper, E. R., & Gould, E. (2010). Parenting and plasticity. *Trends in Neurosciencess, 33*, 465–473.

Leung, M. C. M., Zhang, J., & Zhang, J. (2004). An economic analysis of life expectancy by gender with application to the United States. *Journal of Health Economics, 23*, 737–759.

LeVay, S. (1993). *The sexual brain.* Cambridge, MA: MIT Press.

Levendosky, A. A., Bogat, G. A., Huth-Bocks, A. C., Rosenblum, K., & von Eye, A. (2011). The effects of domestic violence on the stability of attachment from infancy to preschool. *Journal of Clinical Child and Adolescent Psychology, 40*, 398–410.

Leventhal, T., & Brooks-Gunn, J. (2003). Children and youth in neighborhood contexts. *Current Directions in Psychological Science, 12*, 27–31.

Leventhal, T., Dupere, V., & Brooks-Gunn, J. (2009). Neighborhood influences on adolescent development. In R. M. Lerner & L. Steinberg (Eds.), *Handbook of adolescent psychology: Vol. 2* (3rd ed., pp. 411–443). Hoboken, NJ: Wiley.

Levi, J., Vinter, S., Richardson, L., St. Laurent, R., & Segal, L. M. (2009). *F as in fat: How obesity policies are failing in America.* Washington, DC: Trust for America's Health.

Levine, L. J. (1995). Young children's understanding of the causes of anger and sadness. *Child Development, 66*, 697–709.

LeVine, R. A., Dixon, S., LeVine, S., Richman, A., Leiderman, P. H., Keefer, C. H., & Brazelton, T. B. (1994). *Child care and culture: Lessons from Africa.* New York: Cambridge University Press.

Levinson, D. J. (1978). *The seasons of a man's life.* New York: Knopf.

Levinson, D. J. (1996). *The seasons of a woman's life.* New York: Knopf.

Levitt, M. J., & Cici-Gokaltun, A. (2011). Close relationships across the lifespan. In K. Fingerman, C. A. Berg, J. Smith, & T. C. Antonucci (Eds.), *Handbook of life-span development* (pp. 457–486). New York: Springer.

Levy, B. R., & Leifheit-Limson, E. (2009). The stereotype-matching effect: Greater influence on functioning when age stereotypes correspond to outcomes. *Psychology and Aging, 24*, 230–233.

Levy, B. R., Slade, M. D., Kunkel, S. R., & Kasl, S. V. (2002). Longevity increased by positive self-perceptions of aging. *Journal of Personality and Social Psychology, 83*, 261–270.

Levy, S. R., & Dweck, C. S. (1999). The impact of children's static vs. dynamic conceptions of people on stereotype formation. *Child Development, 70*, 1163–1180.

Lewis, M. (1992). *Shame: The exposed self.* New York: Free Press.

Lewis, M. (1995). Embarrassment: The emotion of self-exposure and evaluation. In J. P. Tangney & K. W. Fischer (Eds.), *Self-conscious emotions* (pp. 198–218). New York: Guilford.

Lewis, M. (1998). Emotional competence and development. In D. Pushkar, W. M. Bukowski, A. E. Schwartzman, E. M. Stack, & D. R. White (Eds.), *Improving competence across the lifespan* (pp. 27–36). New York: Plenum.

Lewis, M., & Brooks-Gunn, J. (1979). *Social cognition and the acquisition of self.* New York: Plenum.

Lewis, M., Ramsay, D. S., & Kawakami, K. (1993). Differences between Japanese infants and Caucasian American infants in behavioral and cortisol response to inoculation. *Child Development, 64*, 1722–1731.

Lewis, M., Sullivan, M. W., Stanger, C., & Weiss, M. (1989). Self development and self-conscious emotions. *Child Development, 60*, 146–156.

Leyk, D., Rüther, T., Wunderlich, M., Sievert, A., Ebfeld, D., Witzki, A., et al. (2010). Physical performance in middle age and old age. *Deutsches Ärzteblatt International, 107*, 809–816.

Li, D.-K., Willinger, M., Petitti, D. B., Odouli, R., Liu, L., & Hoffman, H. J. (2006). Use of a dummy (pacifier) during sleep and risk of sudden infant death syndrome (SIDS): Population based casecontrol study. *British Medical Journal, 332*, 18–21.

Li, S.-C., Lindenberger, U., Hommel, B., Aschersleben, G., Prinz, W., & Baltes, P. B. (2004). Transformation in the couplings among intellectual abilities and constituent cognitive processes across the life span. *Psychological Science, 15*, 155–163.

Liang, J., Krause, N. M., & Bennett, J. M. (2001). Social exchange and well-being: Is giving better than receiving? *Psychology and Aging, 16*, 511–523.

Liben, L. S. (2006). Education for spatial thinking. In K. A. Renninger & I. E. Sigel (Eds.), *Handbook of child psychology: Vol. 4. Child psychology in practice* (6th ed., pp. 197–247). Hoboken, NJ: Wiley.

Liben, L. S. (2009). The road to understanding maps. *Current Directions in Psychological Science, 18*, 310–315.

Liben, L. S., & Bigler, R. S. (2002). The developmental course of gender differentiation: Conceptualizing, measuring, and evaluating constructs and pathways. *Monographs of the Society for Research in Child Development, 6*(4, Serial No. 271).

Liben, L. S., Bigler, R. S., & Krogh, H. R. (2001). Pink and blue collar jobs: Children's judgments of job status and job aspirations in relation to sex of worker. *Journal of Experimental Child Psychology, 79*, 346–363.

Liben, L. S., & Downs, R. M. (1993). Understanding person–space–map relations: Cartographic and developmental perspectives. *Developmental Psychology, 29*, 739–752.

Lidstone, J. S. M., Meins, E., & Fernyhough, C. (2010). The roles of private speech and inner speech in planning during middle childhood: Evidence from a dual task paradigm. *Journal of Experimental Child Psychology, 107*, 438–451.

Lidz, J. (2007). The abstract nature of syntactic representations. In E. Hoff & M. Shatz (Eds.), *Blackwell handbook of language development* (pp. 277–303). Malden, MA: Blackwell.

Lieven, E., Pine, J., & Baldwin, G. (1997). Lexically based learning and early grammatical development. *Journal of Child Language, 24*, 187–220.

Li-Grining, C. P. (2007). Effortful control among low-income preschoolers in three cities: Stability, change, and individual differences. *Developmental Psychology, 43*, 208–221.

Lillard, A. (2003). Pretend play and cognitive development. In U. Goswami (Ed.), *Blackwell handbook of childhood cognitive development* (pp. 189–205). Malden, MA: Blackwell.

Lillard, A. (2007). *Montessori: The science behind the genius.* New York: Oxford University Press.

Lillard, A., & Else-Quest, N. (2006). Evaluating Montessori education. *Science, 313*, 1893–1894.

Lin, F. R., Ferrucci, L., Metter, E. J., An, Y., Zonderman, A. B., & Resnick, S. M. (2011). Hearing loss and cognition in the Baltimore Longitudinal Study of Aging. *Neuropsychology, 25*, 763–770.

Linares, T. J., Singer, L. T., Kirchner, H., Lester, H., Short, E. J., & Min, M. O. (2006). Mental health outcomes of cocaine-exposed children at 6 years of age. *Journal of Pediatric Psychology, 31*, 85–97.

Lindblad, F., & Hjern, A. (2010). ADHD after fetal exposure to maternal smoking. *Nicotine and Tobacco Research, 12*, 408–415.

Lindau, S. T., Schumm, L. P., Laumann, E. O., Levinson, W., O'Muircheartaigh, C. A., & Waite, L. J. (2007). A study of sexuality and health among older adults in the United States. *New England Journal of Medicine, 357*, 762–774.

Lindauer, M. S., Orwoll, L., & Kelley, M. C. (1997). Aging artists on the creativity of their old age. *Creativity Research Journal, 10*, 133–152.

Lindsay-Hartz, J., de Rivera, J., & Mascolo, M. F. (1995). Differentiating guilt and shame and their effects on motivation. In J. P. Tangney & K. W. Fischer (Eds.), *Self-conscious emotions* (pp. 274–300). New York: Guilford.

Lindsey, E. W., Colwell, M. J., Frabutt, J. M., Chambers, J. C., & MacKinnon-Lewis, C. (2008). Mother–child dyadic synchrony in European-American families during early adolescence: Relations with self-esteem and prosocial behavior. *Merrill-Palmer Quarterly, 54*, 289–315.

Lindsey, E. W., & Mize, J. (2000). Parent–child physical and pretense play: Links to children's social competence. *Merrill-Palmer Quarterly, 46*, 565–591.

Linebarger, D. L., Kosanic, A. Z., Greenwood, C. R., & Doku, N. S. (2004). Effects of viewing the television program *Between the Lions* on the emergent literacy skills of young children. *Journal of Educational Psychology, 96*, 297–308.

Linebarger, D. L., & Piotrowski, J. T. (2010). Structure and strategies in children's educational television: The roles of program type and learning strategies in children's learning. *Child Development, 81*, 1582–1597.

Linley, P. A. (2003). Positive adaptation to trauma: Wisdom as both process and outcome. *Journal of Traumatic Stress, 16*, 601–610.

Linn, R. L., & Welner, K. G. (2007). *Race-conscious policies for assigning students to schools: Social science research and the Supreme Court cases.* Washington, DC: National Academy Press.

Linver, M. R., Martin, A., & Brooks-Gunn, J. (2004). Measuring infants' home environment: The ITHOME for infants between birth and 12 months in four national data sets. *Parenting: Science and Practice, 4*, 115–137.

Lippe, T. van der (2010). Women's employment and housework. In J. Treas & S. Drobnic (Eds.), *Dividing the Domestic: Men, women, and household work in cross-national perspective* (pp. 41–58). Stanford, CA: Stanford University Press.

Lips, H. M. (2013). The gender pay gap: Challenging the rationalizations. Perceived equity, discrimination, and the limits of human capital models. *Sex Roles, 68*, 169–185.

Lipsitt, L. P. (2003). Crib death: A biobehavioral phenomenon? *Psychological Science, 12*, 164–170.

Lipton, J., & Spelke, E. (2004). Discrimination of large and small numerosities by human infants. *Infancy, 5*, 271–290.

Liu, C-C., Kanekiyo, T., Xu, H., & Bu, G. (2013). Apolipoprotein E and Alzheimer disease: Risk, mechanisms and therapy. *Nature Reviews Neurology, 9*, 106–118.

Liu, J., Raine, A., Venables, P. H., Dalais, C., & Mednick, S. A. (2003). Malnutrition at age 3 years and lower cognitive ability at age 11 years. *Archives of Paediatric and Adolescent Medicine, 157*, 593–600.

Liu, K., Daviglus, M. L., Loria, C. M., Colangelo, L. A., Spring, B., Moller, A. C., et al. (2012). Healthy lifestyle through young adulthood and the presence of low cardiovascular disease risk profile in middle age: The Coronary Artery Risk Development in (Young) Adults (CARDIA) study. *Circulation, 125*, 996–1004.

Liu, L., Drouet, V., Wu, J. W., Witter, M. P., Small, S. A., Clelland C., et al. (2012). Trans-synaptic spread of tau pathology in vivo. *PLoS One, 7*, e31302.

Livingston, G., & Cohn, D. (2010). *Childlessness up among all women; down among women with advanced degrees.* Washington, DC: Pew Research Center. Retrieved from pewresearch.org/pubs/1642/more-women-without-children

Lloyd, M. E., Doydum, A. O., & Newcombe, N. S. (2009). Memory binding in early childhood: Evidence for a retrieval deficit. *Child Development, 80*, 1321–1328.

Lochman, J. E., & Dodge, K. A. (1998). Distorted perceptions in dyadic interactions of aggressive and nonaggressive boys: Effects of prior expectations, context, and boys' age. *Development and Psychopathology, 10*, 495–512.

Lock, J., & Kirz, N. (2008). Eating disorders: Anorexia nervosa. In W. E. Graighead, D. J. Miklowitz, & L. W. Craighead (Eds.), *Psychopathology: History, diagnosis, and empirical foundations* (pp. 467–494). Hoboken, NJ: Wiley.

Loehlin, J. C., Horn, J. M., & Willerman, L. (1997). Heredity, environment, and IQ in the Texas Adoption Project. In R. J. Sternberg & E. L. Grigorenko (Eds.), *Intelligence, heredity, and environment* (pp. 105–125). New York: Cambridge University Press.

Loehlin, J. C., Jonsson, E. G., Gustavsson, J. P., Stallings, M. C., Gillespie, N. A., Wright, M. J., & Martin, N. G. (2005). Psychological masculinity–femininity via the gender diagnosticity approach: Heritability and consistency across ages and populations. *Journal of Personality, 73*, 1295–1319.

Loehlin, J. C., & Martin, N. G. (2001). Age changes in personality traits and their heritabilities during the adult years: Evidence from Australian twin registry samples. *Personality and Individual Differences, 30*, 1147–1160.

Loganovskaja, T. K., & Loganovsky, K. N. (1999). EEG, cognitive and psychopathological abnormalities in children irradiated in utero. *International Journal of Psychophysiology, 34*, 211–224.

Loganovsky, K. N., Loganovskaja, T. K., Nechayev, S. Y., Antipchuk, Y. Y., & Bomko, M. A. (2008). Disrupted devlopment of the dominant hemisphere following prenatal irradiation. *Journal of Neuropsychiatry and Clinical Neurosciences, 20*, 274–291.

Lohman, D. F. (2000). Measures of intelligence: Cognitive theories. In A. E. Kazdin (Ed.), *Encyclopedia of psychology: Vol. 5* (pp. 147–150). Washington, DC: American Psychological Association.

Lohrmann, S., & Bambara, L. M. (2006). Elementary education teachers' beliefs about essential supports needed to successfully include students with developmental disabilities who engage in challenging behaviors. *Research and Practice for Persons with Severe Disabilities, 31*, 157–173.

Loman, M. M., & Gunnar, M. R. (2010). Early experience and the development of stress reactivity and regulation in children. *Neuroscience and Biobehavioral Reviews, 34*, 867–876.

Long, D. D. (1985). A cross-cultural examination of fears of death among Saudi Arabians. *Omega, 16*, 43–50.

Loock, C., Conry, J., Cook, J. L., Chudley, A. E., & Rosales, T. (2005). Identifying fetal alcohol spectrum disorder in primary care. *Canadian Medical Association Journal, 172*, 628–630.

Loomans, E. M. Van der Stelt, O., van Eijsden, M., Gemke, R. J., Vrijkotte, T., & den Bergh, B. R. (2011). Antenatal maternal anxiety is associated with problem behaviour at age five. *Early Human Development, 87*, 565–570.

Lopez, C. M., Driscoll, K. A., & Kistner, J. A. (2009). Sex differences and response styles: Subtypes of rumination and associations with depressive symptoms. *Journal of Clinical Child and Adolescent Psychology, 38*, 27–35.

Lorenz, K. (1952). *King Solomon's ring*. New York: Crowell.

Lou, E., Lalonde, R. N., & Giguère, B. (2012). Making the decision to move out: Bicultural young adults and the negotiation of cultural demands and family relationships. *Journal of Cross-Cultural Psychology, 43*, 663–670.

Louie, V. (2001). Parents' aspirations and investment: The role of social class in the educational experiences of 1.5- and second-generation Chinese Americans. *Harvard Educational Review, 71*, 438–474.

Louis, J., Cannard, C., Bastuji, H., & Challemel, M. J. (1997). Sleep ontogenesis revisited: A longitudinal 24-hour home polygraphic study on 15 normal infants during the first two years of life. *Sleep, 20*, 323–333.

Lourenco, O. (2003). Making sense of Turiel's dispute with Kohlberg: The case of the child's moral competence. *New Ideas in Psychology, 21*, 43–68.

Lövdén, M., Bergman, L., Adolfsson, R., Lindenberger, U., & Nilsson, L.-G. (2005). Studying individual aging in an interindividual context: Typical paths of age-related, dementia-related, and mortality-related cognitive development in old age. *Psychology and Aging, 20*, 303–316.

Lövdén, M., Schmiedek, F., Kennedy, K. M., Rodrigue, K. M., Lindenberger, U., & Raz, N. (2012). Does variability in cognitive performance correlated with frontal brain volume? *NeuroImage, 64*, 209–215.

Love, J. M., Chazan-Cohen, R., & Raikes, H. (2007). Forty years of research knowledge and use: From Head Start to Early Head Start and beyond. In J. L. Aber, S. J. Bishop-Josef, S. M. Jones, K. T. McLearn, & D. Phillips (Eds.), *Child development and social policy: Knowledge for action* (pp. 79–95). Washington, DC: American Psychological Association.

Love, J. M., Harrison, L., Sagi-Schwartz, A., van IJzendoorn, M. H., Ross, C., & Ungerer, J. A. (2003). Child care quality matters: How conclusions may vary with context. *Child Development, 74*, 1021–1033.

Love, J. M., Kisker, E. E., Ross, C., Raikes, H., Constantine, J., Boller, K., & Brooks-Gunn, J. (2005). The effectiveness of Early Head Start for 3-year-old children and their parents: Lessons for policy and programs. *Developmental Psychology, 41*, 885–901.

Love, J. M., Tarullo, L. B., Raikes, H., & Chazan-Cohen, R. (2006). Head Start: What do we know about its effectiveness? What do we need to know? In K. McCartney & D. Phillips (Eds.), *Blackwell handbook of early childhood development* (pp. 550–575). Malden, MA: Blackwell.

Low, S. M., & Stocker, C. (2012). Family functioning and children's adjustment: Associations among parents' depressed mood, marital hostility, parent–child hostility, and children's adjustment. *Journal of Family Psychology, 19*, 394–403.

Lowenstein, A., Katz, R., & Gur-Yaish, N. (2007). Reciprocity in parent–child exchange and life satisfaction among the elderly: A cross-national perspective. *Journal of Social Issues, 63*, 865–883.

Lown, A. E., Nayak, M. B., Korcha, R. A., & Greenfield, T. K. (2011). Child physical and sexual abuse: A comprehensive look at alcohol consumption patterns, consequences, and dependence from the National Alcohol Survey. *Alcoholism: Clinical and Experimental Research, 35*, 317–325.

Lubart, T. I. (2003). In search of creative intelligence. In R. J. Sternberg, J. Lautrey, & T. I. Lubart (Eds.), *Models of intelligence: International perspectives* (pp. 279–292). Washington, DC: American Psychological Association.

Lubart, T. I., Georgsdottir, A., & Besançon, M. (2009). The nature of creative giftedness and talent. In T. Balchin, B. Hymer, & D. J. Matthews (Eds.), *The Routledge international companion to gifted education* (pp. 42–49). New York: Routledge.

Lubart, T. I., & Sternberg, R. J. (1998). Life span creativity: An investment theory approach. In C. E. Adams-Price (Ed.), *Creativity and successful aging*. New York: Springer.

Luby, J., Belden, A., Sullivan, J., Hayen, R., McCadney, A., & Spitznagel, E. (2009). Shame and guilt in preschool depression: Evidence for elevations in self-conscious emotions in depression as early as age 3. *Journal of Child Psychology and Psychiatry, 50*, 1156–1166.

Lucas, R. E., Clark, A. E., Georgellis, Y., & Diener, E. (2003). Reexamining adaptation and the set point model of happiness: Reactions to changes in marital status. *Journal of Personality and Social Psychology, 84*, 803–805.

Lucas, S. R., & Behrends, M. (2002). Sociodemographic diversity, correlated achievement, and de facto tracking. *Sociology of Education, 75*, 328–348.

Lucas-Thompson, R., & Clarke-Stewart, K. A. (2007). Forecasting friendship: How marital quality, maternal mood, and attachment security are linked to children's peer relationships. *Journal of Applied Developmental Psychology, 28*, 499–514.

Luciana, M. (2003). The neural and functional development of the human prefrontal cortex. In M. de Haan & M. H. Johnson (Eds.), *The cognitive neuroscience of development* (pp. 157–180). New York: Psychology Press.

Luciana, M. (2007). Special issue: Developmental cognitive neuroscience. *Developmental Review, 27*, 277–282.

Ludemann, P. M. (1991). Generalized discrimination of positive facial expressions by seven-and ten-month-old infants. *Child Development, 62*, 55–67.

Luecken, L. J. (2008). Long-term consequences of parental death in childhood: Psychological and physiological manifestations. In M. S. Stroebe, R. O. Hansson, H. Schut, & W. Stroebe (Eds.), *Handbook of bereavement research and practice* (pp. 397–416). Washington, DC: American Psychological Association.

Lukas, C., & Seiden, H. M. (2007). *Silent grief: Living in the wake of suicide* (rev. ed.). London, U.K.: Jessica Kingsley.

Luke, A., Cooper, R. S., Prewitt, T. E., Adeyemo, A. A., & Forrester, T. E. (2001). Nutritional consequences of the African diaspora. *Annual Review of Nutrition, 21*, 47–71.

Lukowski, A. F., Koss, M., Burden, M. J., Jonides, J., Nelson, C. A., Kaciroti, N., et al. (2010). Iron deficiency in infancy and neurocognitive functioning at 19 years: Evidence of long-term deficits in executive function and recognition memory. *Nutritional Neuroscience, 13*, 54–70.

Luna, B., Garver, K. E., Urban, T. A., Lazar, N. A., & Sweeney, J. A. (2004). Maturation of cognitive processes from late childhood to adulthood. *Child Development, 75*, 1357–1372.

Luna, B., Thulborn, K. R., Monoz, D. P., Merriam, E. P., Garver, K. E., Minshew, N. J., Keshavan, M. S., Genovese, C. R., Eddy, W. F., & Sweeney, J. A. (2001). Maturation of widely distributed brain function subserves cognitive development. *Neuroimage, 13*, 786–793.

Lund, D., Caserta, M., Utz, R., & de Vries, B. (2010). Experiences and early coping of bereaved spouses/partners in an intervention based on the dual process model (DPM). *Omega, 61*, 291–313.

Lund, D. A. (1996). Bereavement and loss. In J. E. Birren (Ed.), *Encyclopedia of gerontology* (pp. 173–183). San Diego: Academic Press.

Lund, D. A. (1998). Statements and perspectives from leaders in the field of aging in Utah. In *Utah sourcebook on aging*. Salt Lake City: Empire Publishing.

Lund, D. A. (2005). *My journey* [Sue's letter]. Unpublished document. Salt Lake City, UT: University of Utah.

Lund, D. A., & Caserta, M. S. (2001). When the unexpected happens: Husbands coping with the deaths of their wives. In D. Lund (Ed.), *Men coping with grief* (pp. 147–166). Amityville, NY: Baywood.

Lund, D. A., & Caserta, M. S. (2004a). Facing life alone: Loss of a significant other in later life. In D. Doda (Ed), *Living with grief: Loss in later life* (pp. 207–223). Washington, DC: Hospice Foundation of America.

Lund, D. A., & Caserta, M. S. (2004b). Older men coping with widowhood. *Geriatrics and Aging, 7*(6), 29–33.

Lund, D. A., Caserta, M. S., de Vries, B., & Wright, S. (2004). Restoration after bereavement. *Generations Review, 14*, 9–15.

Lund, D. A., Caserta, M. S., & Dimond, M. F. (1993). The course of spousal bereavement in later life. In M. S. Stroebe, W. Stroebe, & R. O. Hansson (Eds.), *Handbook of bereavement* (pp. 240–245). New York: Cambridge University Press.

Lund, D. A., Utz, R., Caserta, M., & de Vries, B. (2008–2009). Humor, laughter, and happiness in the daily lives of recently bereaved spouses. *Omega, 58,* 87–105.

Lund, D. A., Utz, R., Caserta, M. S., & Wright, S. D. (2009). Examining what caregivers do during respite time to make respite more effective. *Journal of Applied Gerontology, 28,* 109–131.

Lund, D. A., Wright, S. D., Caserta, M. S., Utz, R. L., Lindfelt, C., Bright, O., et al. (2010). *Respite services: Enhancing the quality of daily life for caregivers and care receivers.* San Bernardino, CA: California State University at San Bernardino.

Lund, N., Pedersen, L. H., & Henriksen, T. B. (2009). Selective serotonin reuptake inhibitor exposure in utero and pregnancy outcomes. *Archives of Pediatrics and Adolescent Medicine, 163,* 949–954.

Lundy, B. L. (2003). Father– and mother–infant face-to-face interactions: Differences in mind-related comments and infant attachment? *Infant Behavior and Development, 26,* 200–212.

Luo, L., & Craik, F. I. M. (2008). Aging and memory: A cognitive approach. *Canadian Journal of Psychiatry, 53,* 346–353.

Luo, Y., & Baillargeon, R. (2005). When the ordinary seems unexpected: Evidence for incremental physical knowledge in young infants. *Cognition, 95,* 297–328.

Luong, G., Charles, S. T., & Fingerman, K. L. (2011). Better with age: Social relationships across adulthood. *Journal of Social and Personal Relationships, 28,* 9–23.

Luster, T., & Haddow, J. L. (2005). Adolescent mothers and their children: An ecological perspective. In T. Luster & J. L. Haddow (Eds.), *Parenting: An ecological perspective* (2nd ed., pp. 73–101). Mahwah, NJ: Erlbaum.

Luthar, S. S., & Becker, B. E. (2002). Privileged but pressured: A study of affluent youth. *Child Development, 73,* 1593–1610.

Luthar, S. S., & Goldstein, A. S. (2008). Substance use and related behaviors among suburban late adolescents: The importance of perceived parent containment. *Development and Psychopathology, 20,* 591–614.

Luthar, S. S., & Latendresse, S. J. (2005). Children of the affluent: Challenges to well-being. *Current Directions in Psychological Science, 14,* 49–53.

Luxembourg Income Study. (2011). *LIS key figures.* Retrieved from www.lisdatacenter.org/data-access/key-figures/download-key-figures

Luyckx, K., Goossens, L., & Soenens, B. (2006). A developmental contextual perspective on identity construction in emerging adulthood: Change dynamics in commitment formation and commitment evaluation. *Developmental Psychology, 42,* 366–380.

Luyckx, K., Goossens, L., Soenens, B., & Beyers, W. (2006). Unpacking commitment and exploration: Preliminary validation of an integrative model of late adolescent identity formation. *Journal of Adolescence, 29,* 361–378.

Luyckx, K., Soenens, B., Vansteenkiste, M., Goossens, L., & Berzonsky, M. D. (2007). Parental psychological control and dimensions of identity formation in emerging adulthood. *Journal of Family Psychology, 21,* 546–550.

Lynch, S. K., Turkheimer, E., D'Onofrio, B. M., Mendle, J., Emery, R. E., Slutske, W. S., & Martin, N. G. (2006). A genetically informed study of the association between harsh punishment and offspring behavioral problems. *Journal of Family Psychology, 20,* 190–198.

Lyness, K. S., & Heilman, M. E. (2006). When fit is fundamental: Performance evaluations and promotions of upper-level female and male managers. *Journal of Applied Psychology, 90,* 777–785.

Lyon, T. D., & Flavell, J. H. (1994). Young children's understanding of "remember" and "forget." *Child Development, 65,* 1357–1371.

Lytton, H., & Gallagher, L. (2002). Parenting twins and the genetics of parenting. In M. H. Bornstein (Ed.), *Handbook of parenting* (Vol. 1, pp. 227–253). Mahwah, NJ: Erlbaum.

M

Ma, F., Xu, F., Heyman, G. D., & Lee, K. (2011). Chinese children's evaluations of white lies: Weighing the consequences for recipients. *Journal of Experimental Child Psychology, 108,* 308–321.

Maas, F. K. (2008). Children's understanding of promising, lying, and false belief. *Journal of General Psychology, 13,* 301–321.

Maas, F. K., & Abbeduto, L. J. (2001). Children's judgments about intentionally and unintentionally broken promises. *Journal of Child Language, 28,* 517–529.

Macaluso, A., & De Vito, G. (2004). Muscle strength, power and adaptations to resistance training in older people. *European Journal of Applied Physiology, 91,* 450–472.

Maccoby, E. E. (1984). Socialization and developmental change. *Child Development, 55,* 317–328.

Maccoby, E. E. (1998). *The two sexes: Growing up apart, coming together.* Cambridge, MA: Belknap.

Maccoby, E. E. (2002). Gender and group process: A developmental perspective. *Current Directions in Psychological Science, 11,* 54–58.

MacDonald, S. W. S., Hultsch, D. F., & Dixon, R. A. (2011). Aging and the shape of cognitive change before death: Terminal decline or terminal drop? *Journal of Gerontology, 66,* 292–301.

MacDonald, S. W. S., Li, S-C., & Bäckman, L. (2009). Neural underpinnings of within-person variability in cognitive functioning. *Psychology and Aging, 24,* 792–808.

MacDonald, W. L., & DeMaris, A. (1996). The effects of stepparent's gender and new biological children. *Journal of Family Issues, 17,* 5–25.

Macek, P., Bejček, J., & Vaníčková, J. (2007). Contemporary Czech emerging adults: Generation growing up in the period of social changes. *Journal of Adolescent Research, 22,* 444–475.

Machin, G. A. (2005). Multiple birth. In H. W. Taeusch, R. A. Ballard, & C. A. Gleason (Eds.), *Avery's diseases of the newborn* (8th ed., pp. 57–62). Philadelphia: Saunders.

Mackey, K., Arnold, M. L., & Pratt, M. W. (2001). Adolescents' stories of decision making in more and less authoritative families: Representing the voices of parents in narrative. *Journal of Adolescent Research, 16,* 243–268.

Mackie, S., Show, P., Lenroot, R., Pierson, R., Greenstein, D. K., & Nugent, T. F., III. (2007). Cerebellar development and clinical outcome in attention deficit hyperactivity disorder. *American Journal of Psychiatry, 164,* 647–655.

Mackinnon, S. P., Nosko, A., Pratt, M. W., & Norris, J. E. (2011). Intimacy in young adults' narratives of romance and friendship predicts Eriksonian generativity: A mixed mother analysis. *Journal of Personality, 79,* 587–617.

MacLean, P. S., Bergouignan, A., Cornier, M-A., & Jackman, M. R. (2011). Biology's response to dieting: The impetus for weight gain. *American Journal of Physiology—Regular, Integrated, and Comparative Physiology, 301,* R581–R600.

MacWhinney, B. (2005). Language development. In M. H. Bornstein & M. E. Lamb (Eds.), *Developmental science: An advanced textbook* (5th ed., pp. 359–387). Mahwah, NJ: Erlbaum.

Maddi, S. R. (2005). On hardiness and other pathways to resilience. *American Psychologist, 60,* 261–262.

Maddi, S. R. (2006). Hardiness: The courage to be resilient. In J. C. Thomas, D. L. Segal, & M. Hersen (Eds.), *Comprehensive handbook of personality and psychopathology: Vol. 1. Personality and everyday functioning* (pp. 306–321). Hoboken, NJ: Wiley.

Maddi, S. R. (2007). The story of hardiness: Twenty years of theorizing, research, and practice. In A. Monat, R. S. Lazarus, & G. Reevy (Eds.), *Praeger handbook on stress and coping* (Vol. 2, pp. 327–340). Wastport, CT: Praeger.

Maddi, S. R. (2011). Personality hardiness as a pathway to resilience under educational stresses. In G. M. Reevy & E. Frydenberg (Eds.), *Personality, stress, and coping: Implications for education* (pp. 293–313). Charlotte, NC: Information Age Publishing.

Maddox, G. L. (1963). Activity and morale: A longitudinal study of selected elderly subjects. *Social Forces, 42,* 195–204.

Madey, S. F., & Rodgers, L. (2009). The effect of attachment and Sternberg's triangular theory of love on relationship satisfaction. *Individual Differences Research, 7,* 76–84.

Madigan, S., Bakermans-Kranenburg, M. J., van IJzendoorn, M. H., Moran, G., Pederson, D. R., & Benoit, D. (2006). Unresolved states of mind, anomalous parental behavior, and disorganized attachment: A review and meta-analysis of a transmission gap. *Attachment and Human Development, 8,* 89–111.

Madnawat, A. V. S., & Kachhawa, P. S. (2007). Age, gender, and living circumstances: Discriminating older adults on death anxiety. *Death Studies, 31,* 763–769.

Madon, S., Jussim, L., & Eccles, J. (1997). In search of the powerful self-fulfilling prophecy. *Journal of Personality and Social Psychology, 72,* 791–809.

Madsen, S. A., & Juhl, T. (2007). Paternal depression in the postnatal period assessed with traditional and male depression scales. *Journal of Men's Health and Gender, 4,* 26–31.

Maglio, C. J., & Robinson, S. E. (1994). The effects of death education on death anxiety: A meta-analysis. *Omega, 29,* 319–335.

Magnuson, K., & Shager H. (2010). Early education: Progress and promise for children from low-income families. *Children and Youth Services Review, 32,* 1186–1198.

Magolda, M. B., Abes, E., & Torres, V. (2009). Epistemological, intrapersonal, and interpersonal development in the college years and young adulthood. In M. C. Smith & N. DeFrates-Densch (Eds.), *Handbook of research on adult learning and development* (pp. 183–219). New York: Routledge.

Mahanran, L. G., Bauman, P. A., Kalman, D., Skolnik, H., & Pele, S. M. (1999). Master athletes: Factors affecting performance. *Sports Medicine, 28,* 273–285.

Main, M., & Goldwyn, R. (1998). *Adult attachment classification system.* London: University College.

Main, M., & Solomon, J. (1990). Procedures for identifying infants as disorganized/disoriented during the Ainsworth Strange Situation. In M. Greenberg, D. Cicchetti, & M. Cummings (Eds.), *Attachment in the preschool years: Theory, research, and intervention* (pp. 121–160). Chicago: University of Chicago Press.

Majdandžić, M., & van den Boom, D. C. (2007). Multimethod longitudinal assessment of temperament in early childhood. *Journal of Personality, 75,* 12.

Makishita, H., & Matsunaga, K. (2008). Differences of drivers' reaction times according to age and mental workload. *Accident Analysis Prevention, 40,* 567–575.

Makrantonaki, E., & Xouboulis, C. C. (2007). Molecular mechanisms of skin aging: State of the art. *Annals of the New York Academy of Sciences, 1119,* 40–50.

Malatesta, C. Z., Grigoryev, P., Lamb, C., Albin, M., & Culver, C. (1986). Emotion socialization and expressive development in preterm and full-term infants. *Child Development, 57,* 316–330.

Malina, R. M., & Bouchard, C. (1991). *Growth, maturation, and physical activity.* Champaign, IL: Human Kinetics.

Malone, M. M. (1982). Consciousness of dying and projective fantasy of young children with malignant disease. *Developmental and Behavioral Pediatrics, 3,* 55–60.

Mandara, J., Varner, F., Greene, N., & Richman, S. (2009). Intergenerational family predictors of the black–white achievement gap. *Journal of Educational Psychology, 101,* 867–878.

Mandler, J. M. (2004). Thought before language. *Trends in Cognitive Sciences, 8,* 508–513.

Mandler, J. M., & McDonough, L. (1998). On developing a knowledge base in infancy. *Developmental Psychology, 34,* 1274–1288.

Mangelsdorf, S. C., Schoppe, S. J., & Buur, H. (2000). The meaning of parental reports: A contextual approach to the study of temperament and behavior problems. In V. J. Molfese & D. L. Molfese (Eds.), *Temperament and personality across the life span* (pp. 121–140). Mahwah, NJ: Erlbaum.

Mani, T. M., Bedwell, J. S., & Miller, L. S. (2005). Age-related decrements in performance on a brief continuous performance task. *Archives of Clinical Neuropsychology, 20,* 575–586.

Manole, M. D., & Hickey, R. W. (2006). Preterminal gasping and effects on the cardiac function. *Critical Care Medicine, 34*(Suppl.), S438–S441.

Maquestiaux, F., Lagué-Beauvais, M., Ruthruff, E., Hartley, A., & Bherer, L. (2010). Learning to bypass the central bottleneck: Declining automaticity with advancing age. *Psychology and Aging, 25,* 177–192.

Maratsos, M. (2000). More overregularizations after all: New data and discussion on Marcus, Pinker, Ullman, Hollander, Rosen, & Xu. *Journal of Child Language, 27,* 183–212.

Marcon, R. A. (1999a). Differential impact of preschool models on development and early learning of inner-city children: A three-cohort study. *Developmental Psychology, 35,* 358–375.

Marcon, R. A. (1999b). Positive relationships between parent–school involvement and public school inner-city preschoolers' development and academic performance. *School Psychology Review, 28,* 395–412.

Marcus, G. F. (1995). Children's overregularization of English plurals: A quantitative analysis. *Journal of Child Language, 22,* 447–459.

Marcus-Newhall, A., Thompson, S., & Thomas, C. (2001). Examining a gender stereotype: Menopausal women. *Journal of Applied Social Psychology, 31,* 698–719.

Margrett, J. A., Daugherty, K., Martin, P., MacDonald, M., Davey, A., Woodard, J. L., et al. (2011). Affect and loneliness among centenarians and the oldest old: The role of individual and social resources. *Aging and Mental Health, 15,* 385–396.

Marian, V., Neisser, U., & Rochat, P. (1996). *Can 2-month-old infants distinguish live from videotaped interactions with their mothers?* (Emory Cognition Project, Report #33). Atlanta, GA: Emory University.

Mariano, K. A., & Harton, H. C. (2005). Similarities in aggression, inattention/hyperactivity, depression, and anxiety in middle childhood friendships. *Journal of Social and Clinical Psychology, 24,* 471–496.

Marjoribanks, J., Farquhar, C., Roberts, H., & Lethaby, A. (2012). Long term hormone therapy for perimenopausal and postmenopausal women. *Cochrane Database of Systematic Reviews, Issue 7,* Art. No.: CD004143.

Markey, P. M., & Markey, C. N. (2007). Romantic ideas, romantic obtainment, and relationship experiences: The complementarity of interpersonal traits among romantic partners. *Journal of Social and Personal Relationships, 24,* 517–533.

Markman, E. M. (1992). Constraints on word learning: Speculations about their nature, origins, and domain specificity. In M. R. Gunnar & M. P.

Markova, G., & Legerstee, M. (2006). Contingency, imitation, and affect sharing: Foundations of infants' social awareness. *Developmental Psychology, 42,* 132–141.

Markovits, H., Benenson, J., & Dolensky, E. (2001). Evidence that children and adolescents have internal models of peer interactions that are gender differentiated. *Child Development, 72,* 879–886.

Markovits, H., & Vachon, R. (1990). Conditional reasoning, representation, and level of abstraction. *Developmental Psychology, 26,* 942–951.

Marks, G. N., Cresswell, J., & Ainley, J. (2006). Explaining socioeconomic inequalities in student achievement: The role of home and school factors. *Educational Research and Evaluation, 12,* 105–128.

Marks, N. F. (1996). Caregiving across the lifespan: National prevalence and predictors. *Family Relations, 45,* 27–36.

Marks, N. F., Bumpass, L. L., & Jun, H. (2004). Family roles and well-being during the middle life course. In O. G. Brim, C. D. Ryff, & R.C. Kessler (Eds.), *How healthy are we? A national study of well-being at midlife* (pp. 514–549). Chicago: University of Chicago Press.

Marks, N. F., & Greenfield, E. A. (2009). The influence of family relationships on adult psychological well-being and generativity. In M. C. Smith & N. DeFrates-Densch (Eds.), *Handbook of research on adult learning and development* (pp. 306–349). New York: Routledge.

Marks, N. F., & Lambert, J. D. (1998). Marital status continuity and change among young and midlife adults. *Journal of Family Issues, 19,* 652–686.

Marks, R. (2010). Hip fracture epidemiological trends, outcomes, and risk factors, 1970–2009. *International Journal of General Medicine, 3,* 1–17.

Markstrom, C. A., & Kalmanir, H. M. (2001). Linkages between the psychosocial stages of identity and intimacy and the ego strengths of fidelity and love. *Identity, 1,* 179–196.

Markstrom, C. A., Sabino, V., Turner, B., & Berman, R. (1997). The Psychosocial Inventory of Ego Strengths: Development and validation of a new Eriksonian measure. *Journal of Youth and Adolescence, 26,* 705–732.

Markus, H. R., & Herzog, A. R. (1992). The role of self-concept in aging. In K. W. Schaie & M. P. Lawton (Eds.), *Annual review of gerontology and geriatrics* (pp. 110–143). New York: Springer.

Marlier, L., & Schaal, B. (2005). Human newborns prefer human milk: Conspecific milk odor is attractive without postnatal exposure. *Child Development, 76,* 155–168.

Marra, R., & Palmer, B. (2004). Encouraging intellectual growth: Senior college student profiles. *Journal of Adult Development, 11,* 111–122.

Marsee, M. A., & Frick, P. J. (2010). Callous-unemotional traits and aggression in youth. In W. F. Arsenio & E. A. Lemerise (Eds.), *Emotions, aggression, and morality in children: Bridging development and psychopathology* (pp. 137–156). Washington, DC: American Psychological Association.

Marsh, H. W. (1990). The structure of academic self-concept: The Marsh/Shavelson model. *Journal of Educational Psychology, 82,* 623–636.

Marsh, H. W., & Ayotte, V. (2003). Do multiple dimensions of self-concept become more differentiated with age? The differential distinctiveness hypothesis. *Journal of Educational Psychology, 95,* 687–706.

Marsh, H. W., Craven, R., & Debus, R. (1998). Structure, stability, and development of young children's self-concepts: A multicohort–multioccasion study. *Child Development, 69,* 1030–1053.

Marsh, H. W., Ellis, L. A., & Craven, R. G. (2002). How do preschool children feel about themselves? Unraveling measurement and multidimensional self-concept structure. *Developmental Psychology, 38,* 376–393.

Marsh, H. W., Gerlach, E., Trautwein, U., Lüdtke, O., & Brettschneider, W.-D. (2007). Longitudinal study of predadolescent sport self-concept and performance: Reciprocal effects and causal ordering. *Child Development, 78,* 1640–1656.

Marsh, H. W., Trautwein, U., Lüdtke, O., Koller, O., & Baumert, J. (2005). Academic self-concept, interest, grades, and standardized test scores: Reciprocal effects models of causal ordering. *Child Development, 76,* 397–416.

Marshall, B. J., & Davies, B. (2011). Bereavement in children and adults following the death of a sibling. In R. Neimeyer, D. Harris, H. Winokuer, G. Thornton (Eds.), *Grief and bereavement in contemporary society: Bridging research and practice* (pp. 107–116). New York: Routledge.

Marshall-Baker, A., Lickliter, R. & Cooper, R. P. (1998). Prolonged exposure to a visual pattern may promote behavioral organization in preterm infants. *Journal of Perinatal and Neonatal Nursing, 12,* 50–62.

Martin, C. L., & Fabes, R. A. (2001). The stability and consequences of young children's same-sex peer interactions. *Developmental Psychology, 37,* 431–446.

Martin, C. L., & Halverson, C. F. (1987). The role of cognition in sex role acquisition. In D. B. Carter (Ed.), *Current conceptions of sex roles and sex typing: Theory and research* (pp. 123–137). New York: Praeger.

Martin, C. L., & Ruble, D. (2004). Children's search for gender cues: Cognitive perspectives on gender development. *Current Directions in Psychological Science, 13,* 67–70.

Martin, C. L., Ruble, D. N., & Szkrybalo, J. (2002). Cognitive theories of early gender development. *Psychological Bulletin, 128,* 903–933.

Martin, G. L., & Pear, J. (2011). *Behavior modification: What it is and how to do it* (9th ed.). Upper Saddle River, NJ: Pearson.

Martin, K. A. (1996). *Puberty, sexuality and the self: Girls and boys at adolescence.* New York: Routledge.

Martin, P., Long, M. V., & Poon, L. W. (2002). Age changes and differences in personality traits and states of the old and very old. *Journal of Gerontology, 57B,* P144–P152.

Martin, R. (2008). Meiotic errors in human oogenesis and spermatogenesis. *Reproductive Biomedicine Online, 16,* 523–531.

Martinez-Frias, M. L., Bermejo, E., Rodríguez-Pinilla, E., & Frías, J. L. (2004). Risk for congenital anomalies associated with different sporadic and daily doses of alcohol consumption during pregnancy: A case-control study. *Birth Defects Research, Part A, Clinical and Molecular Teratology, 70,* 194–200.

Martinot, D., & Désert, M. (2007). Awareness of a gender stereotype, personal beliefs, and self-perceptions regarding math ability: When boys do not surpass girls. *Social Psychology of Education, 10,* 455–471.

Maruta, T., Colligan, R. C., Malinchoc, M., & Offord, K. P. (2002). Optimism–pessimism assessed in the 1960s and self-reported health status 30 years later. *Mayo Clinic Proceedings, 77,* 748–753.

Marzolf, D. P., & DeLoache, J. S. (1994). Transfer in young children's understanding of spatial representations. *Child Development, 65,* 1–15.

Masataka, N. (1996). Perception of motherese in a signed language by 6-month-old deaf infants. *Developmental Psychology, 32,* 874–879.

Mascolo, M. F., & Fischer, K. W. (2007). The codevelopment of self and sociomoral emotions during the toddler years. In C. A. Brownell & C. B. Kopp (Eds.), *Socioemotional development in the toddler years: Transitions and transformations* (pp. 66–99). New York: Guilford.

Mashburn, A. J. (2008). Quality of social and physical environments in preschools and children's development of academic, language, and literacy skills. *Applied Developmental Science, 12,* 113–127.

Mashburn, A. J., Pianta, R. C., Mamre, B. K., Downer, J. T., Barbarin, O. A., Bryant, D., et al. (2008). Measures of classroom quality in prekindergarten and children's development of academic, language, and social skills. *Child Development, 79,* 732–749.

Maslach, C., Schaufeli, W. B., & Leiter, M. P. (2001). Job burnout. *Annual Review of Psychology, 52,* 397–422.

Mason, M. G., & Gibbs, J. C. (1993a). Role-taking opportunities and the transition to advanced moral judgment. *Moral Education Forum, 18,* 1–12.

Mason, M. G., & Gibbs, J. C. (1993b). Social perspective taking and moral judgment among college students. *Journal of Adolescent Research, 8,* 109–123.

Masoro, E. J. (2011). Terminal weight loss, frailty, and mortality. In E. J. Masoro & S. N. Austad (Eds.), *Handbook of the biology of aging* (7th ed., pp. 321–331). San Diego, CA: Academic Press.

Massachusetts Expert Panel on End-of-Life Care. (2010, October). *Patient-centered care and human mortality: The urgency of health system reforms to ensure respect for patients' wishes and accountability for excellence in care.* Retrieved from www.mass .gov/hqcc/docs/expert-panel/final-expert-panel-report.pdf

Masten, A. S. (2001). Ordinary magic: Resilience processes in development. *American Psychologist, 56,* 227–238.

Masten, A. S., Burt, K. B., Roisman, G. I., Obradovic, J., Long, J. D., & Tellegen, A. (2004). Resources and resilience in the transition to adulthood: Continuity and change. *Development and Psychopathology, 16,* 1071–1094.

Masten, A. S., & Gewirtz, A. H. (2006). Vulnerability and resilience in early child development. In K. McCartney & D. Phillips (Eds.), *Blackwell handbook of early childhood development* (pp. 22–43). Malden, MA: Blackwell.

Masten, A. S., & Powell, J. L. (2003). A resilience framework for research, policy, and practice. In S. S. Luthar (Ed.), *Resilience and vulnerability* (pp. 1–25). New York: Cambridge University Press.

Masten, A. S., & Reed, M. J. (2002). Resilience in development. In C. R. Snyder & S. J. Lopez (Eds.), *Handbook of positive psychology* (pp. 74–88). New York: Oxford University Press.

Masten, A. S., & Shaffer, A. (2006). How families matter in child development: Reflections from research on risk and resilience. In A. S. Masten & A. Shaffer (Eds.), *Families count: Effects on child and adolescent development* (pp. 5–25). New York: Cambridge University Press.

Masters, R. K. (2012). Uncrossing the U.S. black–white mortality crossover: The role of cohort forces in life course mortality risk. *Demography, 49,* 773–796.

Mastropieri, D., & Turkewitz, G. (1999). Prenatal experience and neonatal responsiveness to vocal expression of emotion. *Developmental Psychobiology, 35,* 204–214.

Mather, M. (2010, May). *U.S. children in single-mother families* (PRB Data Brief). Washington, DC: Population Reference Bureau.

Mather, M., & Carstensen, L. L. (2005). Aging and motivated cognition: The positivity effect in attention and memory. *Trends in Cognitive Sciences, 9,* 496–502.

Mathews, T. J., & MacDorman, M. F. (2008). Infant mortality statistics from the 2005 period linked birth/infant death data set. *National Vital Statistics Reports, 57*(2), 1–32.

Matthews, K. A., Gump, B. B., Harris, K. F., Haney, T. L., & Barefoot, J. C. (2004). Hostile behaviors predict cardiovascular mortality among men enrolled in the Multiple Risk Factor Intervention Trial. *Circulation, 109,* 66–70.

Mattison, J. A., Roth, G. S., Beasley, T. M., Tilmont, E. M., Handy, A. M., Herbert, R. L., et al. (2012). Impact of caloric restriction on health and survival in rhesus monkeys from the NIA study. *Nature, 489,* 318–321.

Mattson, S. N., Calarco, K. E., & Lang, A. R. (2006). Focused and shifting attention in children with heavy prenatal alcohol exposure. *Neuropsychology, 20,* 361–369.

Maume, D. J., Jr. (2004). Is the glass ceiling a unique form of inequality? *Work and Occupations, 31,* 250–274.

Maurer, T. J. (2001). Career-relevant learning and development, worker age, and beliefs about self-efficacy for development. *Journal of Management, 27,* 123–140.

Maurer, T. J., Wrenn, K. A., & Weiss, E. M. (2003). Toward understanding and managing stereotypical beliefs about older workers' ability and desire for learning and development. In J. J. Martocchio & G. R. Ferris (Eds.), *Research in personnel and human resources management* (Vol. 22, pp. 253–285). Stamford, CT: JAI Press.

Mayberry, R. I. (2010). Early language acquisition and adult language ability: What sign language reveals about the critical period for language. In M. Marshark & P. E. Spencer (Eds.), *Oxford handbook of deaf studies, language, and education* (Vol. 2, pp. 281–291). New York: Oxford University Press.

Mayeux, L., & Cillessen, A. H. N. (2003). Development of social problem solving in early childhood: Stability, change, and associations with social competence. *Journal of Genetic Psychology, 164,* 153–173.

Maynard, A. E. (2002). Cultural teaching: The development of teaching skills in Maya sibling interactions. *Child Development, 73,* 969–982.

Maynard, A. E., & Greenfield, P. M. (2003). Implicit cognitive development in cultural tools and children: Lessons from Maya Mexico. *Cognitive Development, 18,* 489–510.

Maynard, A. E., Subrahmanyam, K., & Greenfield, P. M. (2005). Technology and the development of intelligence: From the loom to the computer. In R. J. Sternberg & D. D. Preiss (Eds.), *Intelligence and technology: The impact of tools in the nature and development of human abilities* (pp. 29–53). Mahwah, NJ: Erlbaum.

Mazerolle, M., Régner, I., Morisset, P., Rigalleau, F., & Huguet, P. (2012). Stereotype threat strengthens automatic recall and undermines controlled processes in older adults. *Psychological Science, 23,* 723–727.

McAdams, D. P., & Cox, K. S. (2010). Self and identity across the life span. In M. Lamb & A. Freund (Eds.), *Handbook of life-span development: Vol. 2. Social and emotional development* (pp. 158–207). Hoboken, NJ: Wiley.

McAdams, D. P., & de St. Aubin, E. (1992). A theory of generativity and its assessment through self-report, behavioral acts, and narrative themes in autobiography. *Journal of Personality and Social Psychology, 62,* 1003–1015.

McAdams, D. P., Hart, H. M., & Maruna, S. (1998). The anatomy of generativity. In D. P. McAdams & E. de St. Aubin (Eds.), *Generativity and adult development* (pp. 7–43). Washington, DC: American Psychological Association.

McAdams, D. P., & Logan, R. L. (2004). What is generativity? In E. de St. Aubin & D. P. McAdams (Eds.), *The generative society: Caring for future generations* (pp. 15–31). Washington, DC: American Psychological Association.

McAlister, A., & Peterson, C. C. (2006). Mental playmates: Siblings, executive functioning and theory of mind. *British Journal of Developmental Psychology, 24,* 733–751.

McAlister, A., & Peterson, C. C. (2007). A longitudinal study of child siblings and theory of mind development. *Cognitive Development, 22,* 258–270.

McAuley, E., & Elavsky, S. (2008). Self-efficacy, physical activity, and cognitive function. In W. W. Spirduso, L. W. Poon, & W. Chodzko-Zajko (Eds.), *Exercise and its mediating effects on cognition* (pp. 69–84). Champaign, IL: Human Kinetics.

McBee, M. T. (2006). A descriptive analysis of referral sources for gifted identification screening by race and socioeconomic status. *Journal of Secondary Gifted Education, 17,* 103–111.

McBride-Chang, C., & Kail, R. V. (2002). Cross-cultural similarities in the predictors of reading acquisition. *Child Development, 73,* 1392–1407.

McCabe, A. (1997). Developmental and cross-cultural aspects of children's narration. In M. Bamberg (Ed.), *Narrative development: Six approaches* (pp. 137–174). Mahwah, NJ: Erlbaum.

McCall, R. B., & Carriger, M. S. (1993). A meta-analysis of infant habituation and recognition memory performance as predictors of later IQ. *Child Development, 64,* 57–79.

McCartney, K., Dearing, E., Taylor, B., & Bub, K. (2007). Quality child care supports the achievement of low-income children: Direct and indirect pathways through caregiving and the home environment. *Journal of Applied Developmental Psychology, 28,* 411–426.

McCartney, K., Harris, M. J., & Bernieri, F. (1990). Growing up and growing apart: A developmental meta-analysis of twin studies. *Psychological Bulletin, 107,* 226–237.

McCartney, K., Owen, M., Booth, C., Clarke-Stewart, A., & Vandell, D. (2004). Testing a maternal attachment model of behavior problems in early childhood. *Journal of Child Psychology and Psychiatry, 45,* 765–778.

McCarton, C. (1998). Behavioral outcomes in low birth weight infants. *Pediatrics, 102,* 1293–1297.

McCarty, M. E., & Ashmead, D. H. (1999). Visual control of reaching and grasping in infants. *Developmental Psychology, 35,* 620–631.

McCarty, M. E., & Keen, R. (2005). Facilitating problem-solving performance among 9- and 12-month-old infants. *Journal of Cognition and Development, 6,* 209–228.

McClain, C. S., Rosenfeld, B., & Breitbart, W. (2003). Effect of spiritual well-being on end-of-life despair in terminally ill cancer patients. *Lancet, 361,* 1603–1607.

McClain-Jacobson, C., Rosenfeld, B., Kosinski, A., Pessin, H., Cimino, J. E., & Breitbart, W. (2004). Belief in an afterlife, spiritual well-being and end-of-life despair in patients with advanced cancer. *General Hospital Psychiatry, 26,* 484–486.

McClure, S., Laibson, D., Loewenstein, G., & Cohen, J. (2004). Separate neural systems value immediate and delayed monetary rewards. *Science, 306,* 503–507.

McColgan, K. L., & McCormack, T. (2008). Searching and planning: Young children's reasoning about past and future event sequences. *Child Development, 79,* 1477–1479.

McCrae, R., & Costa, P. T., Jr. (2006). Cross-cultural perspectives on adult personality trait development. In D. K. Mroczek & T. D. Little (Eds.), *Handbook of personality development* (pp. 129–146). Mahwah, NJ: Erlbaum.

McCrae, R. R. (2011). Personality theories for the 21st century. *Teaching of Psychology, 38,* 209–214.

McCune, L. (1993). The development of play as the development of consciousness. In M. H. Bornstein & A. O'Reilly (Eds.), *New directions for child development* (No. 59, pp. 67–79). San Francisco: Jossey-Bass.

McCurry, S. M., Logsdon, R. G., Teri, L., & Vitello, M. V. (2007). Evidence-based psychological treatments for insomnia in older adults. *Psychology and Aging, 22,* 18–27.

McDaniel, M. A., Einstein, G. O., & Rendell, P. G. (2007). The puzzle of inconsistent age-related declines in prospective memory: A multiprocess explanation. In M. Kliegel, M. A. McDaniel, & G. O. Einstein (Eds.), *Prospective memory: Cognitive, neuroscience, developmental, and applied perspectives* (pp. 141–160). Mahwah, NJ: Erlbaum.

McDill, T., Hall, S. K., & Turell, S. C. (2006). Aging and creating families: Never-married heterosexual women over forty. *Journal of Women and Aging, 18,* 37–50.

McDonagh, M. S., Osterweil, P., & Guise, J. M. (2005). The benefits and risks of inducing labour in patients with prior cesarean delivery: A systematic review. *BJOG, 112,* 1007–1015.

McDonald, L., & Robb, A. L. (2004). The economic legacy of divorce and separation for women in old age. *Canadian Journal on Aging, 23*(Suppl. 1), S83–S97.

McDonough, L. (1999). Early declarative memory for location. *British Journal of Developmental Psychology, 17,* 381–402.

McElhaney, K. B., Allen, J. P., Stephenson, J. C., & Hare, A. L. (2009). Attachment and autonomy during adolescence. In R. M. Lerner & L. Steinberg (Eds.), *Handbook of adolescent psychology: Vol. 1. Individual bases of adolescent development* (3rd ed., pp. 358–403). Hoboken, NJ: Wiley.

McElwain, N. L., & Booth-LaForce, C. (2006). Maternal sensitivity to infant distress and nondistress as predictors of infant–mother attachment security. *Journal of Family Psychology, 20,* 247–255.

McEwen, B. S. (2007). Physiology and neurobiology of stress an adaptation: Central role of the brain. *Physiological Reviews, 87,* 873–904.

McFarlane, J., Malecha, A., Watson, K., Gist, J., Batten, E., Hall, I., & Smith, S. (2005). Intimate partner assault against women: Frequency, health consequences, and treatment outcomes. *Obstetrics and Gynecology, 105,* 99–108.

McGee, L. M., & Richgels, D. J. (2012). *Literacy's beginnings: Supporting young readers and writers* (6th ed.). Boston: Allyn and Bacon.

McGoldrick, M. (2004). Echoes from the past: Helping families deal with their ghosts. In F. Walsh & M. McGoldrick (Eds.), *Living beyond loss* (pp. 99–118). New York: Norton.

McGoldrick, M., Schlesinger, J. M., Lee, E., Hines, P. M., Chan, J., & Almeida, R. (2004). Mourning in different cultures. In F. Walsh & M. McGoldrick (Eds.), *Living beyond loss* (pp. 1119–160). New York: Norton.

McGoldrick, M., & Shibusawa, T. (2012). The family life cycle. In F. Walsh (Ed.), *Normal family processes: Growing diversity and complexity* (pp. 375–398). New York: Guilford.

McGrath, S. K., & Kennell, J. H. (2008). A randomized controlled trial of continuous labor support for middle-class couples: Effect on cesarean delivery rates. *Birth: Issues in Perinatal Care, 35,* 9–97.

McGue, M., Elkins, I., Walden, B., & Iacono, W. G. (2005). Perceptions of the parent–adolescent relationship: A longitudinal investigation. *Developmental Psychology, 41,* 971–984.

McHale, J. P., Khazan, I., Erera, P., Rotman, T., DeCourcey, W., & McConnell, M. (2002a). Coparenting in diverse family systems. In M. H. Bornstein (Ed.), *Handbook of parenting: Vol. 3* (2nd ed., pp. 75–107). Mahwah, NJ: Erlbaum.

McHale, J. P., Kuersten-Hogan, R., & Rao, N. (2004). Growing points for coparenting theory and research. *Journal of Adult Development, 11,* 221–234.

McHale, J. P., Lauretti, A., Talbot, J., & Pouquette, C. (2002b). Retrospect and prospect in the psychological study of coparenting and family group process. In J. P. McHale & W. S. Grolnick (Eds.), *Retrospect and prospect in the psychological study of families* (pp. 127–165). Mahwah, NJ: Erlbaum.

McHale, J. P., & Rotman, T. (2007). Is seeing believing? Expectant parents' outlooks on coparenting and later coparenting solidarity. *Infant Behavior and Development, 30,* 63–81.

McHale, S. M., Crouter, A. C., Kim, J.-Y., Burton, L. M., Davis, K. D., Dotterer, A. M., & Swanson, D. P. (2006). Mothers' and fathers' racial socialization in African-American families: Implications for youth. *Child Development, 77,* 1387–1402.

McIntosh, H., Metz, E., & Youniss, J. (2005). Community service and identity formation in adolescents. In J. S. Mahoney, R. W. Larson, & J. S. Eccles (Eds.), *Organized activities as contexts of development: Extracurricular activities, after-school and community programs* (pp. 331–351). Mahwah, NJ: Erlbaum.

McIntosh, W. D., Locker, L., Briley, K., Ryan, R., & Scott, A. J. (2011). What do older adults seek in their potential romantic partners? Evidence from online personal ads. *International Journal of Aging and Human Development, 72,* 67–82.

McKenna, J. J. (2001). Why we never ask "Is it safe for infants to sleep alone?" *Academy of Breast Feeding Medicine News and Views, 7*(4), 32, 38.

McKenna, J. J. (2002, September/October). Breastfeeding and bedsharing still useful (and important) after all these years. *Mothering, 114.* Retrieved from www.mothering.com/articles/new_baby/sleep/mckenna.html

McKenna, J. J., & McDade, T. (2005). Why babies should never sleep alone: A review of the co-sleeping controversy in relation to SIDS, bedsharing, and breastfeeding. *Paediatric Respiratory Reviews, 6,* 134–152.

McKenna, J. J., & Volpe, L. E. (2007). Sleeping with baby: An Internet-based sampling of parental experiences, choices, perceptions, and interpretations in a Western industrialized context. *Infant and Child Development, 16,* 359–385.

McKeown, M. G., & Beck, I. L. (2009). The role of metacognition in understanding and supporting reading comprehension. In D. J. Hacker, J. Dunlosky, & A. C. Graesser (Eds.), *Handbook of metacognition in education* (pp. 7–25). New York: Routledge.

McKim, W. A., & Hancock, S. (2013). *Drugs and behavior* (7th ed.). Upper Saddle River, NJ: Pearson.

McKinney, C., Donnelly, R., & Renk, K. (2008). Perceived parenting, positive and negative perceptions of parents, and late adolescent emotional adjustment. *Child and Adolescent Mental health, 13,* 66–73.

McKown, C., & Strambler, M. J. (2009). Developmental antecedents and social and academic consequences of stereotype-consciousness in middle childhood. *Child Development, 80,* 1643–1659.

McKown, C., & Weinstein, R. S. (2003). The development and consequences of stereotype consciousness in middle childhood. *Child Development, 74,* 498–515.

McKown, C., & Weinstein, R. S. (2008). Teacher expectations, classroom context, and the achievement gap. *Journal of School Psychology, 46,* 235–261.

McKusick, V. A. (2011). *Online Mendelian inheritance in man.* Retrieved from www.nslij-genetics.org/search_omim.html

McLanahan, S. (1999). Father absence and the welfare of children. In E. M. Hetherington (Ed.), *Coping with divorce, single parenting, and remarriage: A risk and resiliency perspective* (pp. 117–145). Mahwah, NJ: Erlbaum.

McLaughlin, K. A., Fox, N. A., Zeanah, C. H., & Nelson, C. A. (2011). Adverse rearing environments and neural development in children: The development of frontal electroencephalogram asymmetry. *Biological Psychiatry, 70,* 1008–1015.

McLean, K. C. (2008). Stories of the young and the old: Personal continuity and narrative identity. *Developmental Psychology, 44,* 254–264.

McLoyd, V. C., Aikens, N. L., & Burton, L. M. (2006). Child poverty, policy, and practice. In K. A. Renninger & I. E. Sigel (Eds.), *Handbook of child psychology: Vol. 4. Child psychology in practice* (6th ed., pp. 700–778). Hoboken, NJ: Wiley.

McLoyd, V. C., Kaplan, R., Hardaway, C. R., & Wood, D. (2007). Does endorsement of physical discipline matter? Assessing moderating influences on the maternal and child psychological correlates of physical discipline in African-American families. *Journal of Family Psychology, 21,* 165–175.

McLoyd, V. C., & Smith, J. (2002). Physical discipline and behavior problems in African-American, European-American, and Hispanic children: Emotional support as a moderator. *Journal of Marriage and Family, 64,* 40–53.

McMahon, C. A., Barnett, B., Kowalenko, N. M., & Tennant, C. C. (2006). Maternal attachment state of mind moderates the impact of postnatal depression on infant attachment. *Journal of Child Psychology and Psychiatry, 47,* 660–669.

Mead, M. (1928). *Coming of age in Samoa.* Ann Arbor, MI: Morrow.

Meade, C. S., Kershaw, T. S., & Ickovics, J. R. (2008). The intergenerational cycle of teenage motherhood: An ecological approach. *Health Psychology, 27,* 419–429.

Meadus, R. J., & Twomey, J. C. (2011). Men student nurses: The nursing education experience. *Nursing Forum, 46,* 269–279.

Meegan, S. P., & Berg, C. A. (2002). Contexts, functions, forms, and processes of collaborative everyday problem solving in older adulthood. *International Journal of Behavioral Development, 26,* 6–15.

Meeus, W., Oosterwegel, A., & Vollebergh, W. (2002). Parental and peer attachment and identity development in adolescence. *Journal of Adolescence, 25,* 93–106.

Meeus, W., van de Schoot, R., Keijsers, L., & Branje, S. (2012). Identity statuses as developmental trajectories: A five-wave longitudinal study in early-to-middle and middle-to-late adolescents. *Journal of Youth and Adolescence, 41,* 1008–1021.

Meeus, W. H. J., Branje, S. J. T., van der Valk, I., & de Wied, M. (2007). Relationships with intimate partner, best friend, and parents in adolescence and early adulthood: A study of the saliency of the intimate partnership. *International Journal of Behavioral Development, 31,* 569–580.

Mehlmadrona, L., & Madrona, M. M. (1997). Physician- and midwife-attended home births—effects of breech, twin, and post-dates outcome data on mortality rates. *Journal of Nurse-Midwifery, 42,* 91–98.

Mehlson, M., Platz, M., & Fromholt, P. (2003). Life satisfaction across the life course: Evaluations of the most and least satisfying decades of life. *International Journal of Aging and Human Development, 57,* 217–236.

Meier, A., & Allen, G. (2009). Romantic relationships from adolescence to young adulthood: Evidence from the National Longitudinal Study of Adolescent Health. *Sociological Quarterly, 50,* 308–335.

Meins, E., Fernyhough, C., Russell, J., & Clark-Carter, D. (1998). Security of attachment as a predictor of symbolic and mentalizing abilities: A longitudinal study. *Social Development, 7,* 1–24.

Meins, E., Fernyhough, C., Wainwright, R., Clark-Carter, D., Gupta, M. D., Fradley, E., & Tucker, M. (2003). Pathways to understanding mind: Construct validity and predictive validity of maternal mind-mindedness. *Child Development, 74,* 1194–1211.

Melby, M. K., Lock, M., & Kaufert, P. (2005). Culture and symptom reporting at menopause. *Human Reproduction Update, 11,* 495–512.

Melby-Lervag, M., & Hulme, C. (2010). Serial and free recall in children can be improved by training: Evidence for the importance of phonological and semantic representations in immediate memory tasks. *Psychological Science, 21,* 1694–1700.

Melenhorst, A. S., Fisk, A. D., Mynatt, E. D., & Rogers, W. A. (2004). Potential intrusiveness of aware home technology: Perceptions of older adults. In *Proceedings of the Human Factors and Ergonomics Society 48th annual meeting* (pp. 266–270). Santa Monica, CA: Human Factors and Ergonomics Society.

Meltzoff, A. N. (2007). "Like me": A foundation for social cognition. *Developmental Science, 10,* 126–134.

Meltzoff, A. N., & Kuhl, P. K. (1994). Faces and speech: Intermodal processing of biologically relevant signals in infants and adults. In D. J. Lewkowicz & R. Lickliter (Eds.), *The development of intersensory perception* (pp. 335–369). Hillsdale, NJ: Erlbaum.

Meltzoff, A. N., & Moore, M. K. (1977). Imitation of facial and manual gestures by human neonates. *Science, 198,* 75–78.

Meltzoff, A. N., & Moore, M. K. (1994). Imitation, memory, and the representation of persons. *Infant Behavior and Development, 17,* 83–99.

Meltzoff, A. N., & Moore, M. K. (1999). Persons and representations: Why infant imitation is important for theories of human development. In J. Nadel & G. Butterworth (Eds.), *Imitation in infancy* (pp. 9–35). Cambridge, UK: Cambridge University Press.

Meltzoff, A. N., & Williamson, R. A. (2010). The importance of imitation for theories of social-cognitive development. In J. G. Bremner & T. D. Wachs (Eds.), *Wiley-Blackwell handbook of infant development* (2nd ed., pp. 345–364). Oxford, UK: Wiley.

Melzi, G., & Ely, R. (2009). Language development in the school years. In J. B. Gleason & N. B. Ratner (Eds.), *The development of language* (7th ed., pp. 391–435). Boston: Allyn and Bacon.

Mendle, J., Turkheimer, E., & Emery, R. E. (2007). Detrimental psychological outcomes associated with early pubertal timing in adolescent girls. *Developmental Review, 27,* 151–171.

Meneilly, G. S. (2006). Diabetes in the elderly. *Medical Clinics of North America, 90,* 909–923.

Mennella, J. A., & Beauchamp, G. K. (1998). Early flavor experiences: Research update. *Nutrition Reviews, 56,* 205–211.

Menon, U. (2001). Middle adulthood in cultural perspective: The imagined and the experienced in three cultures. In M. E. Lachman (Ed.), *Handbook of midlife development* (pp. 40–74). New York: Wiley.

Ment, L. R., Vohr, B., Allan, W., Katz, K. H., Schneider, K. C., Westerveld, M., Cuncan, C. C., & Makuch, R. W. (2003). Change in cognitive function over time in very low-birth-weight infants. *Journal of the American Medical Association, 289,* 705–711.

Merikangas, K. R., He, J-P. Burstein, M., Swanson, S. A. Avenevoli, S., Cui, L., Benjet, C., et al. (2010). Lifetime prevalence of mental disorders in U.S. adolescents: Results from the National Comorbidity Survey Replication—Adolescent Supplement (NCS-A). *Journal of the American Academy of Child and Adolescent Psychiatry, 49,* 980–989.

Messman, S. J., Canary, D. J., & Hause, K. S. (2000). Motives to remain platonic, equity, and the use of maintenance strategies in opposite-sex friendships. *Journal of Social and Personal Relationships, 17,* 67–94.

Methven, L., Allen, V. J., Withers, C. A., & Gosney, M. A. (2012). Aging and taste. *Proceedings of the Nutrition Society, 71,* 556–565.

MetLife. (2011). *MetLife study of caregiving costs to working caregivers: Double jeopardy for baby boomers caring for their parents.* Westport, CT: National Alliance for Caregiving and MetLife Mature Market Institute.

Meyer, B. J. F., Russo, C., & Talbot, A. (1995). Discourse comprehension and problem solving: Decisions about the treatment of breast cancer by women across the lifespan. *Psychology and Aging, 10,* 84–103.

Meyer, B. J. F., Talbot, A. P., & Ranalli, C. (2007). Why older adults make more immediate treatment decisions about cancer than younger adults. *Psychology and Aging, 22,* 505–524.

Meyer, I. H. (2003). Prejudice, social stress, and mental health in lesbian, gay, and bisexual populations: Conceptual issues and research evidence. *Psychological Bulletin, 129,* 674–697.

Meyer, J. (2012). *Centenarians: 2010.* Washington, DC: U.S. Government Printing Office.

Meyer, R. (2009). Infant feeding in the first year. 1: Feeding practices in the first six months of life. *Journal of Family Health Care, 19,* 13–16.

Meyer-Bahlburg, H. F. L., Ehrhardt, A. A., Rosen, L. R., Gruen, R. S., Veridiano, N. P., Vann, F. H., & Neuwalder, H. F. (1995). Prenatal estrogens and the development of homosexual orientation. *Developmental Psychology, 31,* 12–21.

Meyers, A. B., & Berk, L. E. (2014). In L. Brooker, S. Edwards, & M. Blaise (Eds.), *Sage Handbook of play and learning in early childhood.* London: Sage.

Mezei, L., & Murinson, B. B. (2011). Pain education in North American medical schools. *Journal of Pain, 12,* 1199–1208.

Mezulis, A. H., Hyde, J. S., & Clark, R. (2004). Father involvement moderates the effect of maternal depression during a child's infancy on child behavior problems in kindergarten. *Journal of Family Psychology, 18,* 575–588.

Michael, R. T., Gagnon, J. H., Laumann, E. O., & Kolata, G. (1994). *Sex in America.* Boston: Little, Brown.

Michalik, N. M., Eisenberg, N., Spinrad, T. L., Ladd, B., Thompson, M., & Valiente, C. (2007). Longitudinal relations among parental emotional expressivity and sympathy and prosocial behavior in adolescence. *Social Development, 16,* 286–309.

Michels, K. B., Willett, W. C., Graubard, B. I., Vaidya, R. L., Cantwell, M. M., Sansbury, L. B., & Forman, M. R. (2007). A longitudinal study of infant feeding and obesity throughout the life course. *International Journal of Obesity, 31,* 1078–1085.

Mienaltowski, A. (2011). Everyday problem solving across the adult life span. *Annals of the New York Academy of Sciences, 1235,* 75–85.

Mikami, A. Y., Lerner, M. D., & Lun, J. (2010). Social context influences on children's rejection by their peers. *Child Development Perspectives, 4,* 123–130.

Mikulincer, M., Florian, V., & Hirschberger, G. (2003). The existential function of close relationships: Introducing death into the science of love. *Personality and Social Psychology Review, 7,* 20–40.

Mikulincer, M., & Shaver, P. R. (2008). An attachment perspective on bereavement. In M. S. Stroebe, R. O. Hansson, H. Schut, & W. Stroebe (Eds.), *Handbook of bereavement research and practice* (pp. 87–112). Washington, DC: American Psychological Association.

Milevsky, A., Schlechter, M., Netter, S., & Keehn, D. (2007). Maternal and paternal parenting styles in adolescents: Associations with self-esteem, depression, and life satisfaction. *Journal of Child and Family Studies, 16,* 39–47.

Milkie, M. A., Bierman, A., & Schieman, S. (2008). How adult children influence older parents' mental health: Integrating stress-process and life-course perspectives. *Social Psychology Quarterly, 71,* 86–105.

Miller, D. I., Taler, V., Davidson, P. S. R., & Messier, C. (2012). Measuring the impact of exercise on

cognitive aging: Methodological issues. *Neurobiology of Aging, 33,* 622.e29–622.e43.

Miller, D. N. (2011). *Child and adolescent suicidal behavior: School-based prevention, assessment, and intervention.* New York: Guilford.

Miller, J. G. (2006). Insights into moral development from cultural psychology. In M. Killen & J. Smetana (Eds.), *Handbook of moral development* (pp. 375–398). Philadelphia: Erlbaum.

Miller, J. G., & Bersoff, D. M. (1995). Development in the context of everyday family relationships: Culture, interpersonal morality, and adaptation. In M. Killen & D. Hart (Eds.), *Morality in everyday life: Developmental perspectives* (pp. 259–282). Cambridge, UK: Cambridge University Press.

Miller, L. T., & Vernon, P. A. (1992). The general factor in short-term memory, intelligence, and reaction time. *Intelligence, 16,* 5–29.

Miller, P. H. (2009). *Theories of developmental psychology* (5th ed.). New York: Worth.

Miller, P. J., Fung, H., Lin, S., Chen, E. C., & Boldt, B. R. (2012). How socialization happens on the ground: Narrative practices as alternate socializing pathways in Taiwanese and European-American families. *Monographs of the Society for Research in Child Development, 77*(1, Serial No. 302).

Miller, P. J., Hengst, J. A., & Wang, S. (2003). Ethnographic methods: Applications from developmental cultural psychology. In P. M. Carnic & J. E. Rhodes (Eds.), *Qualitative research in psychology* (pp. 219–242). Washington, DC: American Psychological Association.

Miller, P. J., Wang, S., Sandel, T., & Cho, G. E. (2002). Self-esteem as folk theory: A comparison of European American and Taiwanese mothers' beliefs. *Parenting: Science and Practice, 2,* 209–239.

Miller, P. J., Wiley, A. R., Fung, H., & Liang, C. H. (1997). Personal storytelling as a medium of socialization in Chinese and American families. *Child Development, 68,* 557–568.

Miller, S., Lansford, J. E., Costanzo, P., Malone, P. S., Golonka, M., & Killeya-Jones, L. A. (2009). Early adolescent romantic partner status, peer standing, and problem behaviors. *Journal of Early Adolescence, 29,* 839–861.

Miller, S. A., Hardin, C. A., & Montgomery, D. E. (2003). Young children's understanding of the conditions for knowledge acquisition. *Journal of Cognition and Development, 4,* 325–356.

Milligan, K., Astington, J. W., & Dack, L. A. (2007). Language and theory of mind: Meta-analysis of the relation between language ability and false-belief understanding. *Child Development, 78,* 622–646.

Mills, D., Plunkett, K., Prat, C., & Schafer, G. (2005). Watching the infant brain learn words: Effects of language and experience. *Cognitive Development, 20,* 19–31.

Mills, R., & Grusec, J. (1989). Cognitive, affective, and behavioral consequences of praising altruism. *Merrill-Palmer Quarterly, 35,* 299–326.

Mills, R. S. L. (2005). Taking stock of the developmental literature on shame. *Developmental Review, 25,* 26–63.

Mills, T. L., Gomez-Smith, Z., & De Leon, J. M. (2005). Skipped generation families: Sources of psychological distress among grandmothers of grandchildren who live in homes where neither parent is present. *Marriage and Family Review, 37,* 191–212.

Miner-Rubino, K., Winter, D. G., & Stewart, A. J. (2004). Gender, social class, and the subjective experience of aging: Self-perceived personality change from early adulthood to late midlife. *Personality and Social Psychology Bulletin, 30,* 1599–1610.

Minkler, M., & Fuller-Thomson, E. (2005). African American grandparents raising grandchildren: A national study using the Census 2000 American Community Survey. *Journal of Gerontology, 60B,* S82–S92.

Misailidi, P. (2006). Young children's display rule knowledge: Understanding the distinction between apparent and real emotions and the motives underlying the use of display rules. *Social Behavior and Personality, 34,* 1285–1296.

Mishra, G., & Kuh, D. (2006). Perceived change in quality of life during the menopause. *Social Science and Medicine, 62,* 93–102.

Mistry, R. S., Biesanz, J. C., Chien, N., Howes, C., & Benner, A. D. (2008). Socioeconomic status, parental investments, and the cognitive and behavioral outcomes of low-income children from immigrant and native households. *Early Childhood Research Quarterly, 23,* 193–212.

Mitchell, A., & Boss, B. J. (2002). Adverse effects of pain on the nervous systems of newborns and young children: A review of the literature. *Journal of Neuroscience Nursing, 34,* 228–235.

Mitchell, B. A., & Lovegreen, L. D. (2009). The empty nest syndrome in midlife families: A multimethod exploration of parental gender differences and cultural dynamics. *Journal of Family Issues, 30,* 1651–1670.

Mitchell, B. D., Hsueh, W. C., King, T. M., Pollin, T. I., Sorkin, J., Agarwala, R., Schäffer, A. A., & Shuldiner, A. R. (2001). Heritability of life span in the Old Order Amish. *American Journal of Medical Genetics, 102,* 346–352.

Mitchell, P., Teucher, U., Kikuno, H., & Bennett, M. (2010). Cultural variations in developing a sense of knowing your own mind: A comparison between British and Japanese children. *International Journal of Behavioral Development, 34,* 248–258.

Miura, I. T., & Okamoto, Y. (2003). Language supports for mathematics understanding and performance. In A. J. Baroody & A. Dowker (Eds.), *The development of arithmetic concepts and skills* (pp. 229–242). Mahwah, NJ: Erlbaum.

Mize, J., & Pettit, G. S. (2010). The mother–child playgroup as socialisation context: A short-term longitudinal study of mother–child–peer relationship dynamics. *Early Child Development and Care, 180,* 1271–1284.

Moen, P., & Altobelli, J. (2007). Strategic selection as a retirement project: Will Americans develop hybrid arrangements? In J. B. James & P. Wink (Eds.), *Annual review of gerontology and geriatrics* (Vol. 26, pp. 61–82). New York: Springer.

Moen, P., & Roehling, P. V. (2005). *The career mystique.* Boulder, CO: Rowman & Littlefield.

Moens, E., Braet, C., & Soetens, B. (2007). Observation of family functioning at mealtime: A comparison between families of children with and without overweight. *Journal of Pediatric Psychology, 32,* 52–63.

Moffitt, T. E. (2007). Life-course-persistent vs. adolescence-limited antisocial behavior. In D. Cicchetti & D. J. Cohen (Eds.), *Developmental psychopathology* (2nd ed., pp. 570–598). Hoboken, NJ: Wiley.

Mohr, J. J., & Daly, C. A. (2008). Sexual minority stress and changes in relationship quality in same-sex couples. *Journal of Social and Personal Relationships, 25,* 989–1007.

Mohr, J. J., & Fassinger, R. E. (2006). Sexual orientation identity and romantic relationship quality in same-sex couples. *Personality and Social Psychology Bulletin, 32,* 1085–1099.

Mok, M. M. C., Kennedy, K. J., & Moore, P. J. (2011). Academic attribution of secondary students: Gender, year level and achievement level. *Educational Psychology, 31,* 87–104.

Moll, H., & Meltzoff, A. N. (2011). How does it look? Level 2 perspective-taking at 36 months of age. *Child Development, 82,* 661–673.

Moll, H., & Tomasello, M. (2006). Level I perspective-taking at 24 months of age. *British Journal of Developmental Psychology, 24,* 603–613.

Mollenkopf, H., Hieber, A., & Wahl, H.-W. (2011). Continuity and change in older adults' perceptions of out-of-home mobility over ten years: A qualitative–quantitative approach. *Ageing and Society, 31,* 782–802.

Moller, K., Hwang, C. P., & Wickberg, B. (2008). Couple relationship and transition to parenthood: Does workload at home matter? *Journal of Reproductive and Infant Psychology, 26,* 57–68.

Mondloch, C. J., Lewis, T., Budreau, D. R., Maurer, D., Dannemiller, J. L., Stephens, B. R., & Kleiner-Gathercoal, K. A. (1999). Face perception during early infancy. *Psychological Science, 10,* 419–422.

Monin, J. K., & Schulz, R. (2009). Interpersonal effects of suffering in older adult caregiving relationships. *Psychology and Aging, 24,* 681–695.

Monk, C., Sloan, R., Myers, M. M., Ellman, L., Werner, E., Jeon, J., et al. (2010). Neural circuitry of emotional face processing in autism spectrum disorders. *Journal of Psychiatry and Neuroscience, 35,* 105–114.

Monsour, M. (2002). *Women and men as friends.* Mahwah, NJ: Erlbaum.

Montemayor, R., & Eisen, M. (1977). The development of self-conceptions from childhood to adolescence. *Developmental Psychology, 37,* 826–838.

Montepare, J. M. (2006). Body consciousness across the adult years: Variations with actual and subjective age. *Journal of Adult Development, 13,* 102–107.

Montgomery, M. J. (2005). Psychosocial intimacy and identity: From early adolescence to emerging adulthood. *Journal of Adolescent Research, 20,* 346–374.

Montgomery, M. J., & Côté, J. E. (2003). College as a transition to adulthood. In G. R. Adams & M. D. Berzonsky (Eds.), *Blackwell handbook of adolescence* (pp. 149–172). Malden, MA: Blackwell.

Montgomery-Goodnough, A., & Gallagher, S. J. (2007). Review of research on spiritual and religious formation in higher education. In S. M. Nielsen & M. S. Plakhotnik (Eds.), *Proceedings of the sixth annual College of Education Research Conference: Urban and international education section* (pp. 60–65). Miami, FL: International University.

Montorsi, F. (2005). Assessment, diagnosis, and investigation of erectile dysfunction. *Clinical Cornerstone, 7,* 29–35.

Montoya, A. G., Sorrentino, R., Lukas, S. E., & Price, B. H. (2002). Long-term neuropsychiatric consequences of "ecstasy" (MDMA): A review. *Harvard Review of Psychiatry, 10,* 212–220.

Moon, C., Cooper, R. P., & Fifer, W. P. (1993). Two-day-old infants prefer their native language. *Infant Behavior and Development, 16,* 495–500.

Moon, R. Y., Horne, R. S. C., & Hauck, F. R. (2007). Sudden infant death syndrome. *Lancet, 370,* 1578–1587.

Moore, A., & Stratton, D. C. (2002). *Resilient widowers.* New York: Springer.

Moore, D. R., & Florsheim, P. (2001). Interpersonal processes and psychopathology among expectant and nonexpectant adolescent couples. *Journal of Consulting and Clinical Psychology, 69,* 101–113.

Moore, E. G. J. (1986). Family socialization and the IQ test performance of traditionally and transracially adopted black children. *Developmental Psychology, 22,* 317–326.

Moore, K. L., & Persaud, T. V. N. (2008). *Before we are born* (7th ed.). Philadelphia: Saunders.

Moore, K. L., Persaud, T. V. N., & Torchia, M. G. (2013). *Before we are born: Essentials of embryology and birth defects* (8th ed.). Philadelphia, PA: Saunders.

Moore, M. K., & Meltzoff, A. N. (2004). Object permanence after a 24-hr delay and leaving the locale of disappearance: The role of memory, space, and identity. *Developmental Psychology, 40,* 606–620.

Moore, M. K., & Meltzoff, A. N. (2008). Factors affecting infants' manual search for occluded objects and the genesis of object permanence. *Infant Behavior and Development, 31,* 168–180.

Moore, M. R., & Brooks-Gunn, J. (2002). Adolescent parenthood. In M. H. Bornstein (Ed.), *Handbook of parenting: Vol. 3* (2nd ed., pp. 173–214). Mahwah, NJ: Erlbaum.

Moore, W. S. (2002). Understanding learning in a postmodern world: Reconsidering the Perry scheme of ethical and intellectual development. In B. K. Hofer & P. R. Pintrich (Eds.), *Personal epistemology* (pp. 17–36). Mahwah, NJ: Erlbaum.

Moran, G., Forbes, L., Evans, E., Tarabulsy, G. M., & Madigan, S. (2008). Both maternal sensitivity and atypical maternal behavior independently predict attachment security and disorganization in adolescent mother–infant relationships. *Infant Behavior and Development, 31,* 321–325.

Moran, S., & Gardner, H. (2006). Extraordinary achievements: A developmental and systems analysis. In D. Kuhn & R. Siegler (Eds.), *Handbook of child psychology: Vol. 2. Cognition, perception, and language* (6th ed., pp. 905–949). Hoboken, NJ: Wiley.

Morawska, A., & Sanders, M. (2011). Parental use of time out revisited: A useful or harmful parenting strategy? *Journal of Child and Family Studies, 20,* 1–8.

Morelli, G., Rogoff, B., Oppenheim, D., & Goldsmith, D. (1992). Cultural variation in infants' sleeping arrangements: Questions of independence. *Developmental Psychology, 28,* 604–613.

Morelli, G. A., Rogoff, B., & Angelillo, C. (2003). Cultural variation in young children's access to work or involvement in specialized child-focused activities. *International Journal of Behavioral Development, 27,* 264–274.

Moreno, A. J., Klute, M. M., & Robinson, J. L. (2008). Relational and individual resources as predictors of empathy in early childhood. *Social Development, 17,* 613–637.

Morgan, J. D., Laungani, P., & Palmer, S. (2009). General introduction to series. In J. D. Morgan, P. Laungani, & S. Palmer (Eds.), *Death and bereavement around the world: Vol. 5. Reflective essays* (pp. 1–4). Amityville, NY: Baywood.

Morgan, P. L., Farkas, G., Hillemeier, M. M., & Maczuga, S. (2009). Risk factors for learning-related behavior problems at 24 months of age: Population-based estimates. *Journal of Abnormal Child Psychology, 37,* 401–413.

Moro-García, M. A., Alonso-Arias, R., López-Vázquez, A., Suárez-García, F. M., Solano-Jaurrieta, J. J., Baltar, J., et al. (2012). Relationship between functional ability in older people, immune system status, and intensity of response to CMV. *Age, 34,* 479–495.

Morrill, M. I., Hines, D. A., Mahmood, S., & Córdova, J. V. (2010). Pathways between marriage and parenting for wives and husbands: The role of coparenting. *Family Process, 49,* 59–73.

Morris, A. S., Silk, J. S., Morris, M. D. S., & Steinberg, L. (2011). The influence of mother–child emotion regulation strategies on children's expression of anger and sadness. *Developmental Psychology, 47,* 213–225.

Morris, W. L., DePaulo, B. M., Hertel, J., & Taylor, L. C. (2008). Singlism—another problem that has no name: Prejudice, stereotypes and discrimination against singles. In M. A. Morrison & T. G. Morrison (Eds.), *The psychology of modern prejudice* (pp. 165–194). Hauppauge, NY: Nova Science Publishers.

Morrison, V. (2008). Ageing and physical health. In B. Woods & L. Clare (Eds.), *Handbook of the clinical psychology of ageing* (2nd ed., pp. 57–74). Chichester, UK: Wiley.

Morrongiello, B. A., Fenwick, K. D., & Chance, G. (1998). Crossmodal learning in newborn infants:

Inferences about properties of auditory-visual events. *Infant Behavior and Development, 21,* 543–554.

Morrongiello, B. A., Midgett, C., & Shields, R. (2001). Don't run with scissors: Young children's knowledge of home safety rules. *Journal of Pediatric Psychology, 26,* 105–115.

Morrongiello, B. A., Ondejko, L., & Littlejohn, A. (2004). Understanding toddlers' in-home injuries: I. Context, correlates, and determinants. *Journal of Pediatric Psychology, 29,* 415–431.

Morrow, D. F. (2006). Gay, lesbian, and transgender adolescents. In D. F. Morrow & L. Messinger (Eds.), *Sexual orientation and gender expression in social work practice* (pp. 177–195). New York: Columbia University Press.

Morse, S. B., Zheng, H., Tang, Y., & Roth, J. (2009). Early school-age outcomes of late preterm infants. *Pediatrics, 123,* e622–e629.

Mosby, L., Rawls, A. W., Meehan, A. J., Mays, E., & Pettinari, C. J. (1999). Troubles in interracial talk about discipline: An examination of African American child rearing narratives. *Journal of Comparative Family Studies, 30,* 489–521.

Mosca, L., Barrett-Connor, E., & Wenger, N. K. (2012). Sex/gender differences in cardiovascular disease prevention: What a difference a decade makes. *Circulation, 124,* 2145–2154.

Moses, L. J., Baldwin, D. A., Rosicky, J. G., & Tidball, G. (2001). Evidence for referential understanding in the emotions domain at twelve and eighteen months. *Child Development, 72,* 718–735.

Mosher, W. D., Chandra, A., & Jones, J. (2005). *Sexual behavior and selected health measures: Men and women 15–44 years of age, United States 2002,* Vol. 362. Atlanta: Centers for Disease Control and Prevention.

Moshman, D. (1998). Identity as a theory of oneself. *Genetic Epistemologist, 26*(3), 1–9.

Moshman, D. (2003). Developmental change in adulthood. In J. Demick & C. Andreoletti (Eds.), *Handbook of adult development* (pp. 43–61). New York: Plenum.

Moshman, D. (2005). *Adolescent psychological development: Rationality, morality, and identity* (2nd ed.). Mahwah, NJ: Erlbaum.

Moshman, D. (2011). *Adolescent rationality and development: Cognition, morality, and identity* (3rd ed.). New York: Psychology Press.

Moshman, D., & Franks, B. A. (1986). Development of the concept of inferential validity. *Child Development, 57,* 153–165.

Moshman, D., & Geil, M. (1998). Collaborative reasoning: Evidence for collective rationality. *Thinking and Reasoning, 4,* 231–248.

Moss, E., Cyr, C., Bureau, J.-F., Tarabulsy, G. M., & Dubois-Comtois, K. (2005). Stability of attachment during the preschool period. *Developmental Psychology, 41,* 773–783.

Mossey, P. A., Little, J., Munger, R. G., Dixon, M. J., & Shaw, W. C. (2009). Cleft lip and palate. *Lancet, 374,* 1773–1785.

Moss-Racusin, C. A., Dovidio, J. F., Brescoll, V. L., Graham, M. J., & Handelsman, J. (2012). Science faculty's subtle gender biases favor male students. *Proceedings of the National Academy of Sciences, 109,* 16474–16479.

Mottus, R., Indus, K., & Allik, J. (2008). Accuracy of only children stereotype. *Journal of Research in Personality, 42,* 1047–1052.

Mounts, N. S., Valentiner, D. P., Anderson, K. L., & Boswell, M. K. (2006). Shyness, sociability, and parental support for the college transition: Relation to adolescents' adjustment. *Journal of Youth and Adolescence, 35,* 71–80.

Moxley, D. P., Najor-Durack, A., & Dumbrigue, C. (2001). *Keeping students in higher education.* London: Kogan Page.

Mroczek, D. K., & Spiro, A., III. (2007). Personality change influences mortality in older men. *Psychological Science, 18,* 371–376.

Mroczek, D. K., Spiro, A., & Turiano, N. A. (2009). Do health behaviors explain the effect of neuroticism on mortality? *Journal of Research in Personality, 43,* 653–659.

Mrug, S., Hoza, B., & Gerdes, A. C. (2001). Children with attention-deficit/hyperactivity disorder: Peer relationships and peer-oriented interventions. In D. W. Nangle & C. A. Erdley (Eds.), *The role of friendship in psychological adjustment* (pp. 51–77). San Francisco: Jossey-Bass.

Mueller, C. M., & Dweck, C. S. (1998). Intelligence praise can undermine motivation and performance. *Journal of Personality and Social Psychology, 75,* 33–52.

Muenchow, S., & Marsland, K. W. (2007). Beyond baby steps: Promoting the growth and development of U.S. child-care policy. In J. L. Aber, S. J. Bishop-Josef, S. M. Jones, K. T. McLearn, & D. Phillips (Eds.), *Child development and social policy: Knowledge for action* (pp. 97–112). Washington, DC: American Psychological Association.

Müller, O., & Krawinkel, M. (2005). Malnutrition and health in developing countries. *Canadian Medical Association Journal, 173,* 279–286.

Müller, U., Liebermann-Finestone, D. P., Carpendale, J. I. M., Hammond, S. I., & Bibok, M. B. (2012). Knowing minds, controlling actions: The developmental relations between theory of mind and executive function from 2 to 4 years of age. *Journal of Experimental Child Psychology, 111,* 331–348.

Müller, U., Overton, W. F., & Reese, K. (2001). Development of conditional reasoning: A longitudinal study. *Journal of Cognition and Development, 2,* 27–49.

Mulvaney, M. K., McCartney, K., Bub, K. L., & Marshall, N. L. (2006). Determinants of dyadic scaffolding and cognitive outcomes in first graders. *Parenting: Science and Practice, 6,* 297–310.

Mumme, D. L., Bushnell, E. W., DiCorcia, J. A., & Lariviere, L. A. (2007). Infants' use of gaze cues to interpret others' actions and emotional reactions. In R. Flom, K. Lee, & D. Muir (Eds.), *Gaze-following: Its development and significance* (pp. 143–170). Mahwah, NJ: Erlbaum.

Munakata, Y. (2001). Task-dependency in infant behavior: Toward an understanding of the processes underlying cognitive development. In F. Lacerda, C. von Hofsten, & M. Heimann (Eds.), *Emerging cognitive abilities in early infancy* (pp. 29–52). Mahwah, NJ: Erlbaum.

Munakata, Y. (2006). Information processing approaches to development. In D. Kuhn & R. S. Siegler (Eds.), *Handbook of child psychology: Vol. 3. Cognition, perception, and language* (6th ed., pp. 426–463). Hoboken, NJ: Wiley.

Mundy, P., & Stella, J. (2000). Joint attention, social orienting, and nonverbal communication in autism. In A. M. Wetherby & B. M. Prizant (Eds.), *Autism spectrum disorders* (Vol. 9, pp. 55–77). Baltimore, MD: Paul H. Brookes.

Munnell, A. H., Webb, A., Delorme, L., & Golub-Sass, F. (2012). *National retirement risk index: How much longer do we need to work?* Chestnut Hill, MA: Center for Retirement Research at Boston College. Retrieved from crr.bc.edu/briefs/national-retirement-risk-index-how-much-longer-do-we-need-to-work

Munroe, R. L., & Romney, A. K. (2006). Gender and age differences in same-sex aggregation and social behavior. *Journal of Cross-Cultural Psychology, 37,* 3–19.

Muris, P., Merckelbach, H., Ollendick, T. H., King, N. J., & Bogie, N. (2001). Children's nighttime fears: Parent–child ratings of frequency, content, origins,

coping behaviors, and severity. *Behaviour Research and Therapy, 39,* 13–28.

Murphy, S. A. (2008). The loss of a child: Sudden death and extended illness perspectives. In M. S. Stroebe, R. O. Hansson, H. Schut, & W. Stroebe (Eds.), *Handbook of bereavement research and practice* (pp. 375–396). Washington, DC: American Psychological Association.

Murray, S. L. (2008). Risk regulation in relationships: Self-esteem and the if–then contingencies of interdependent life. In J. V. Wood, A. Tesser, & J. G. Holmes (Eds.), *The self and social relationships* (pp. 3–25). New York: Psychology Press.

Mussen, P., & Eisenberg-Berg, N. (1977). *Roots of caring, sharing, and helping.* San Francisco: Freeman.

Mustanski, B. S., Viken, R. J., Kaprio, J., Pulkkinen, L., & Rose, R. J. (2004). Genetic and environmental influences on pubertal development: Longitudinal data from Finnish twins at ages 11 and 14. *Developmental Psychology, 40,* 1188–1198.

Mutchler, J. E., Burr, J. A., & Caro, F. G. (2003). From paid worker to volunteer: Leaving the paid workforce and volunteering in later life. *Social Forces, 81,* 1267–1293.

Mutran, E. J., Danis, M., Bratton, K. A., Sudha, S., & Hanson, L. (1997). Attitudes of the critically ill toward prolonging life: The role of social support. *Gerontologist, 37,* 192–199.

Myers, D. G. (2000). The funds, friends, and faith of happy people. *American Psychologist, 55,* 56–67.

Myers, M. G., Brown, S. A., Tate, S., Abrantes, A., & Tomlinson, K. (2001). *Adolescents, alcohol, and substance abuse* (pp. 275–296). New York: Guilford.

Myerson, J., Hale, S., Wagstaff, D., Poon, L. W., & Smith, G. A. (1990). The information-loss model: A mathematical theory of age-related cognitive slowing. *Psychological Review, 97,* 475–487.

Myowa-Yamakoshi, M., Tomonaga, M., Tanaka, M., & Matsuzawa, T. (2004). Imitation in neonatal chimpanzees *(Pan troglodytes). Developmental Science, 7,* 437–442.

N

Nadel, J., Prepin, K., & Okanda, M. (2005). Experiencing contingency and agency: First step toward self-understanding in making a mind? *Interaction Studies, 6,* 447–462.

Nader, P. R., Bradley, R. H., Houts, R. M., McRitchie, S. L., & O'Brien, M. (2008). Moderate-to-vigorous physical activity from ages 9 to 15 years. *Journal of the American Medical Association, 16,* 295–305.

Nagy, E., Compagne, H., Orvos, H., Pal, A., Molnar, P., & Janszky, I. (2005). Index finger movement imitation by human neonates: Motivation, learning, and left-hand preference. *Pediatric Research, 58,* 749–753.

Nagy, W. E., & Scott, J. A. (2000). Vocabulary processes. In M. L. Kamil & P. B. Mosenthal (Eds.), *Handbook of reading research* (Vol. 3, pp. 269–284). Mahwah, NJ: Erlbaum.

Naigles, L. R., & Swenson, L. D. (2007). Syntactic supports for word learning. In E. Hoff & M. Shatz (Eds.), *Blackwell handbook of language development* (pp. 212–231). Malden, MA: Blackwell.

Naito, M., & Seki, Y. (2009). The relationship between second-order false belief and display rules reasoning: Integration of cognitive and affective social understanding. *Developmental Science, 12,* 150–164.

Nakamura, J., & Csikszentmihalyi, M. (2009). Flow theory and research. In C. R. Snyder & S. J. Lopez (Eds.), *Oxford handbook of positive psychology* (2nd ed., pp. 195–206). New York: Oxford University Press.

Nánez, J., Sr., & Yonas, A. (1994). Effects of luminance and texture motion on infant defensive reactions to optical collision. *Infant Behavior and Development, 17,* 165–174.

Narayan, C. (2008). Is there a double standard of aging? Older men and women and ageism. *Educational Gerontology, 34,* 782–787.

Narr, K. L., Woods, R. P., Lin J., Kim, J., Phillips, O. R., Del'Homme, M., et al. (2009). Widespread cortical thinning is a robust anatomical marker for attention-deficit/hyperactivity disorder. *Journal of the American Academy of Child and Adolescent Psychiatry, 48,* 1014–1022.

Nastasi, B. K., & Clements, D. H. (1994). Effectance motivation, perceived scholastic competence, and higher-order thinking in two cooperative computer environments. *Journal of Educational Computing Research, 10,* 249–275.

Natale, R., & Dodman, N. (2003). Birth can be a hazardous journey: Electronic fetal monitoring does not help. *JOGC, 25,* 1007–1009.

National Academies Committee on National Statistics. (2010, January). *Meeting on research issues in elder mistreatment and abuse and financial fraud: Meeting report.* Washington, DC: National Institute on Aging.

National Association for Sport and Physical Education. (2010). *2010 Shape of the nation report: Status of physical education in the USA.* Reston, VA: Author.

National Center on Elder Abuse, U.S. Administration on Aging. (2013). *Frequently asked questions.* Retrieved from www.ncea.aoa.gov/faq/index.aspx

National Council of Youth Sports. (2008). *Report on trends and participation in organized youth sports.* Stuart, FL: Author.

National Institute on Aging. (2012). *2011–2012 Alzheimer's disease progress report: Intensifying the research effort.* Retrieved from www.nia.nih.gov/alzheimers/publication/2011-2012-alzheimers-disease-progress-report

National Institute on Drug Abuse. (2012). *Drug facts: MDMA (Ecstasy).* Retrieved from www.drugabuse.gov/publications/drugfacts/mdma-ecstasy

National Institutes of Health. (2011). *Dental caries (tooth decay) in children (age 2 to 11).* Retrieved from www.nidcr.nih.gov/DataStatistics/FindDataByTopic/DentalCaries/DentalCariesChildren2to11

National Institutes of Health. (2012). *Genes and disease.* Retrieved from www.ncbi.nlm.nih.gov/books/NBK22183

National Research Council. (2007). *Race conscious policies for assigning students to schools: Social science research and the Supreme Court cases.* Washington, DC: National Academy Press.

National Women's Law Center. (2007). *When girls don't graduate we all fail.* Washington, DC: Author.

Natsuaki, M. N., Biehl, M. C., & Ge, X. (2009). Trajectories of depressed mood from early adolescence to young adulthood: The effects of pubertal timing and adolescent dating. *Journal of Research on Adolescence, 19,* 47–74.

Naveh-Benjamin, M. (2000). Adult age differences in memory performance: Tests of an associative deficit hypothesis. *Journal of Experimental Psychology: Learning, Memory, and Cognition, 26,* 1170–1187.

Naveh-Benjamin, M. (2012). Age-related differences in explicit associative memory: Contributions of effortful-strategic and automatic processes. In M. Naveh-Benjamin & N. Ohta (Eds.), *Memory and aging: Current issues and future directions* (pp. 71–95). New York: Psychology Press.

Naveh-Benjamin, M., Brav, T. K., & Levy, D. (2007). The associative memory deficit of older adults: The role of strategy utilization. *Psychology and Aging, 22,* 202–208.

Naveh-Benjamin, M., Hussain, Z., Guez, J., & Bar-On, M. (2003). Adult age differences in episodic memory: Further support for an associative-deficit hypothesis. *Journal of Experimental Psychology: Learning, Memory, and Cognition, 29,* 826–837.

Neal, M. B., & Hammer, L. B. (2007). *Working couples caring for children and aging parents.* Mahwah, NJ: Erlbaum.

Needham, B. L., & Austin, E. L. (2010). Sexual orientation, parental support, and health during the transition to young adulthood. *Journal of Youth and Adolescence, 39,* 1189–1198.

Neff, K. D., & Helwig, C. C. (2002). A constructivist approach to understanding the development of reasoning about rights and authority within cultural contexts. *Cognitive Development, 17,* 1429–1450.

Neff, L. A., & Karney, B. R. (2008). Compassionate love in early marriage. In B. Fehr, S. Sprecher, & L. G. Underwood, (Eds.), *The science of compassionate love: Theory, research, and applications* (pp. 201–221). Malden, MA: Wiley-Blackwell.

Neimeyer, R., Currier, J. M., Coleman, R., Tomer, A., & Samuel, E. (2011). Confronting suffering and death at the end of life: The impact of religiosity, psychosocial factors, and life regret among hospice patients. *Death Studies, 35,* 777–800.

Neimeyer, R. A. (Ed.). (1994). *Death anxiety handbook.* Washington, DC: Taylor & Francis.

Neimeyer, R. A., Burke, L. A., Mackay, M. M., & Stringer, J G. van D. (2010). Grief therapy and the reconstruction of meaning: From principles to practice. *Journal of Contemporary Psychotherapy, 40,* 73–83.

Neimeyer, R. A., & Van Brunt, D. (1995). Death anxiety. In H. Waas & R. A. Neimeyer (Eds.), *Dying: Facing the facts* (3rd ed., pp. 49–88). Washington, DC: Taylor & Francis.

Neitzel, C., & Stright, A. D. (2003). Mothers' scaffolding of children's problem solving: Establishing a foundation of academic self-regulatory competence. *Journal of Family Psychology, 17,* 147–159.

Nelson, C. A. (1995). The ontogeny of human memory: A cognitive neuroscience perspective. *Developmental Psychology, 31,* 723–738.

Nelson, C. A. (2001). The development and neural bases of face recognition. *Infant and Child Development, 10,* 3–18.

Nelson, C. A. (2002). Neural development and lifelong plasticity. In R. M. Lerner, F. Jacobs, & D. Wertlieb (Eds.), *Handbook of applied developmental science* (Vol. 1, pp. 31–60). Thousand Oaks, CA: Sage.

Nelson, C. A. (2007b). A neurobiological perspective on early human deprivation. *Child Development Perspectives, 1,* 13–18.

Nelson, C. A. (2011). Neural development and lifelong plasticity. In D. P. Keating (Ed.), *Nature and nurture in early child development* (pp. 45–69). New York: Cambridge University Press.

Nelson, C. A., & Bosquet, M. (2000). Neurobiology of fetal and infant development: Implications for infant mental health. In C. H. Zeanah, Jr. (Ed.), *Handbook of infant mental health* (2nd ed., pp. 37–59). New York: Guilford.

Nelson, C. A., Thomas, K. M., & de Haan, M. (2006). Neural bases of cognitive development. In D. Kuhn & R. Siegler (Eds.), *Handbook of child psychology: Vol. 2. Cognition, perception, and language* (6th ed., pp. 3–57). Hoboken, NJ: Wiley.

Nelson, C. A., Zeanah, C. H., Fox, N. A., Marshall, P. J., Smyke, A. T., & Guthrie, D. (2007). Cognitive recovery in socially deprived young children: The Bucharest Early Intervention Project. *Science, 318,* 1937–1940.

Nelson, D. A., Hart, C. H., Yang, C., Olsen, J. A., & Jin, S. (2006a). Aversive parenting in China: Associations with child physical and relational aggression. *Child Development, 77,* 554–572.

Nelson, D. A., Nelson, L. J., Hart, C. H., Yang, C., & Jin, S. (2006b). Parenting and peer-group behavior in cultural context. In X. Chen, D. French, & B. Schneider (Eds.), *Peer relations in cultural context* (pp. 213–246). New York: Cambridge University Press.

Nelson, D. A., Robinson, C. C., & Hart, C. H. (2005). Relational and physical aggression of preschool-age children: Peer status linkages across informants. *Early Education and Development, 16,* 115–139.

Nelson, H. D. (2008). Menopause. *Lancet, 371,* 760–770.

Nelson, K. (2003). Narrative and the emergence of a consciousness of self. In G. D. Fireman & T. E. McVay, Jr. (Eds.). *Narrative and consciousness: Literature, psychology, and the brain* (pp. 17–36). London: Oxford University Press.

Nelson, L. J. (2009). An examination of emerging adulthood in Romanian college students. *International Journal of Behavioral Development, 33,* 402–411.

Nelson, L. J., & Chen, X. (2007). Emerging adulthood in China: The role of social and cultural factors. *Child Development Perspectives, 1,* 86–91.

Nelson, L. J., Padilla-Walker, L. M., Carroll, J. S., Madsen, S. D., Barry, C. M., & Badger, S. (2007). "If you want me to treat you like an adult, start acting like one!" Comparing the criteria that emerging adults and their parents have for adulthood. *Journal of Family Psychology, 21,* 665–674.

Nelson, L. J., Padilla-Walker, L. M., Christensen, K. J., Evans, C. A., & Carroll, J. S. (2011). Parenting in emerging adulthood: An examination of parenting clusters and correlates. *Journal of Youth and Adolescence, 40,* 730–743.

Nemet, D., Barkan, S., Epstein, Y., Friedland, O., Kowen, G., & Eliakim, A. (2005). Short- and long-term beneficial effects of a combined dietary–behavioral–physical activity intervention for the treatment of childhood obesity. *Pediatrics, 115,* e443–e449.

Nepomnyaschy, L., & Waldfogel, J. (2007). Paternity leave and fathers' involvement with their young children. *Community, Work and Family, 10,* 427–453.

Nerenberg, L. (2010). Elder abuse prevention: A review of the field. In J. C. Cavanaugh & C. K. Cavanaugh (Eds.), *Aging in America. Vol. 3: Societal issues* (pp. 53–80). Santa Barbara, CA: Praeger.

Neri, Q., Takeuchi, T., & Palermo, G. D. (2008). An update of assisted reproductive technologies in the United States. *Annals of the New York Academy of Sciences, 1127,* 41–48.

Nesdale, D., Durkin, K., Maas, A., & Griffiths, J. (2004). Group status, outgroup ethnicity, and children's ethnic attitudes. *Applied Developmental Psychology, 25,* 237–251.

Nesdale, D., Durkin, K., Maas, A., & Griffiths, J. (2005). Threat, group identification, and children's ethnic prejudice. *Social Development, 14,* 189–205.

Nettelbeck, T., & Burns, N. R. (2010). Processing speed, working memory and reasoning ability from childhood to old age. *Personality and Individual Differences, 48,* 379–384.

Netz, Y., Wu, M.-J., Becker, B. J., & Tenenbaum, G. (2005). Physical activity and psychological well-being in advanced age: A meta-analysis of intervention studies. *Psychology and Aging, 20,* 272–284.

Neugarten, B. L. (1968a). Adult personality: Toward a psychology of the life cycle. In B. Neugarten (Ed.), *Middle age and aging* (pp. 137–147). Chicago: University of Chicago Press.

Neugarten, B. L. (1968b). The awareness of middle aging. In B. L. Neugarten (Ed.), *Middle age and aging* (pp. 93–98). Chicago: University of Chicago Press.

Neugarten, B. L. (1979). Time, age, and the life cycle. *American Journal of Psychiatry, 136,* 887–894.

Neuhouser, M. L., Wasserthel-Smoller, S., Thomson, C., Aragaki, A., Anderson, G. L., & Manson, J. E. (2009). Multivitamin use and risk of cancer and cardiovascular disease in the Women's Health Initiative cohorts. *Archives of Internal Medicine, 169,* 294–304.

Neuman, S. B. (2003). From rhetoric to reality: The case for high-quality compensatory prekindergarten programs. *Phi Delta Kappan, 85*(4), pp. 286–291.

Neville, H. J., & Bavelier, D. (2002). Human brain plasticity: Evidence from sensory deprivation and altered language experience. In M. A. Hofman, G. J. Boer, A. J. G. D. Holtmaat, E. J. W. van Someren, J. Berhaagen, & D. F. Swaab (Eds.), *Plasticity in the adult brain: From genes to neurotherapy* (pp. 177–188). Amsterdam: Elsevier Science.

Newbury, J. (2011). The drama of end of life care at home. *Nursing Times, 107*(11), 20–23.

Newcomb, A. F., Bukowski, W. M., & Pattee, L. (1993). Children's peer relations: A meta-analytic review of popular, rejected, neglected, controversial, and average sociometric status. *Psychological Bulletin, 113,* 99–128.

Newcomb, M. D., Abbott, R. D., Catalano, R. F., Hawkins, J. D., Battin-Pearson, S., & Hill, K. (2002). Mediational and deviance theories of late high school failure: Process roles of structural strains, academic competence, and general versus specific problem behavior. *Journal of Counseling Psychology, 49,* 172–186.

Newland, L. A., Coyl, D. D., & Freeman, H. (2008). Predicting preschoolers' attachment security from fathers' involvement, internal working models, and use of social support. *Early Child Development and Care, 178,* 785–801.

Newnham, C. A., Milgrom, J., & Skouteris, H. (2009). Effectiveness of a modified mother–infant transaction program on outcomes for preterm infants from 3 to 24 months of age. *Infant Behavior and Development, 32,* 17–26.

Newport, E. L. (1991). Contrasting conceptions of the critical period for language. In S. Cary & R. Gelman (Eds.), *The epigenesis of mind: Essays on biology and cognition* (pp. 111–130). Hillsdale, NJ: Erlbaum.

Newsom, J. T. (1999). Another side to caregiving: Negative reactions to being helped. *Current Directions in Psychological Science, 8,* 183–187.

Newsom, J. T., & Schulz, R. (1998). Caregiving from the recipient's perspective: Negative reactions to being helped. *Health Psychology, 17,* 172–181.

Newton, N. J., & Stewart, A. J. (2010). The middle ages: Change in women's personalities and social roles. *Psychology of Women Quarterly, 34,* 75–84.

Ng, F. F., Pomerantz, E. M., & Lam, S. (2007). European American and Chinese parents' responses to children's success and failure: Implications for children's responses. *Developmental Psychology, 43,* 1239–1255.

Ngata, P. (2004). Death, dying, and grief: A Maori perspective. In J. D. Morgan & P. Laungani (Eds.), *Death and bereavement around the world: Vol. 4. Asia, Australia, and New Zealand* (pp. 95–99). Amityville, NY: Baywood.

Nguyen, U.-S. D. T., Rothman, K. J., Demissie, S., Jackson, D. J., Lang, J. M., & Ecker, J. L. (2010). Epidural analgesia and risks of cesarean and operative vaginal deliveries in nulliparous and multiparous women. *Maternal and Child Health Journal, 14,* 705–712.

NHPCO (National Hospice and Palliative Care Organization). (2005). 83% of *Americans want to die at home.* Retrieved from www.nhpco.org/templates/1/homepage.cfm

NHPCO (National Hospice and Palliative Care Organization). (2012). *Hospice care in America.* Retrieved from www.nhpco.org/sites/default/files/public/Statistics_Research/2012_Facts_Figures.pdf

Ni, Y. (1998). Cognitive structure, content knowledge, and classificatory reasoning. *Journal of Genetic Psychology, 159,* 280–296.

NICHD (National Institute of Child Health and Human Development) Early Child Care Research Network. (1997). The effects of infant child care on infant–mother attachment security: Results of the NICHD Study of Early Child Care. *Child Development, 68,* 860–879.

NICHD (National Institute of Child Health and Human Development) Early Child Care Research Network. (1998). Relations between family predictors and child outcomes: Are they weaker for children in child care? *Developmental Psychology, 34,* 1119–1128.

NICHD (National Institute of Child Health and Human Development) Early Child Care Research Network. (1999). Child care and mother–child interaction in the first 3 years of life. *Developmental Psychology, 35,* 1399–1413.

NICHD (National Institute of Child Health and Human Development) Early Child Care Research Network. (2000a). Characteristics and quality of child care for toddlers and preschoolers. *Applied Developmental Science, 4,* 116–135.

NICHD (National Institute of Child Health and Human Development) Early Child Care Research Network. (2000b). The relation of child care to cognitive and language development. *Child Development, 71,* 960–980.

NICHD (National Institute of Child Health and Human Development) Early Child Care Research Network. (2001). Before Head Start: Income and ethnicity, family characteristics, child care experiences, and child development. *Early Education and Development, 12,* 545–575.

NICHD (National Institute of Child Health and Human Development) Early Child Care Research Network. (2003a). Does amount of time spent in child care predict socioemotional adjustment during the transition to kindergarten? *Child Development, 74,* 976–1005.

NICHD (National Institute of Child Health and Human Development) Early Child Care Research Network. (2003b). Does quality of child care affect child outcomes at age 4½? *Developmental Psychology, 39,* 451–469.

NICHD (National Institute of Child Health and Human Development) Early Child Care Research Network. (2004). Trajectories of physical aggression from toddlerhood to middle childhood. *Monographs of the Society for Research in Child Development, 69*(4, Serial No. 278).

NICHD (National Institute of Child Health and Human Development) Early Child Care Research Network. (2006). Child-care effect sizes for the NICHD Study of Early Child Care and Youth Development. *American Psychologist, 61,* 99–116.

Nichols, W. C., & Pace-Nichols, M. A. (2000). Childless married couples. In W. C. Nichols, M. A. Pace-Nichols, D. S. Becvar, & A. Y. Napier (Eds.), *Handbook of family development and intervention* (pp. 171–188). New York: Wiley.

Nicholson, J. M., Sanders, M. R., Halford, W. K., Phillips, M., & Whitton, S. W. (2008). The prevention and treatment of children's adjustment problems in stepfamilies. In J. Pryor (Ed.), *International handbook of stepfamilies: Policy and practice in legal, research, and clinical environments* (pp. 485–521). Hoboken, NJ: Wiley.

Nickman, S. L., Rosenfeld, A. A., Fine, P., MacIntyre, J. C., Pilowsky, D. J., & Howe, R. A. (2005). Children in adoptive families: Overview and update. *Journal of the American Academy of Child and Adolescent Psychiatry, 44,* 987–995.

Niehaus, M. D., Moore, S. R., Patrick, P. D., Derr, L. L., Lorntz, B., Lima, A. A., & Gurerrant, R. L. (2002). Early childhood diarrhea is associated with diminished cognitive function 4 to 7 years later in children in a northeast Brazilian shanty-town. *American Journal of Tropical Medicine and Hygiene, 66,* 590–593.

Nielsen, L. S., Danielsen, K. V., & Sørensen, T. I. (2011). Short sleep duration as a possible cause of obesity: Critical analysis of the epidemiological evidence. *Obesity Reviews, 12,* 78–92.

Nielsen, N. M., Hansen, A. V., Simonsen, J., & Hviid, A. (2011). Prenatal stress and risk of infectious diseases in offspring. *American Journal of Epidemiology, 173,* 990–997.

Nippold, M. A., Taylor, C. L., & Baker, J. M. (1996). Idiom understanding in Australian youth: A cross-cultural comparison. *Journal of Speech and Hearing Research, 39,* 442–447.

Nisbett, R. E. (2009). *Intelligence and how to get it.* New York: Norton.

Nishitani, S., Miyamura, T., Tagawa, M., Sumi, M., Takase, R., Doi, H., et al. (2009). The calming effect of a maternal breast milk odor on the human newborn infant. *Neuroscience Research, 63,* 66–71.

Noble, K. G., Fifer, W. P., Rauh, V. A., Nomura, Y., & Andrews, H. F. (2012). Academic achievement varies with gestational age among children born at term. *Pediatrics, 130,* e257–e264.

Noble, K. G., McCandliss, B. D., & Farah, M. J. (2007). Socioeconomic gradients predict individual differences in neurocognitive abilities. *Developmental Science, 10,* 464–480.

Noice, H., & Noice, T. (2006). What studies of actors and acting can tell us about memory and cognitive functioning. *Current Directions in Psychological Science, 15,* 14–18.

Noice, H., Noice, T., & Staines, G. (2004). A short-term intervention to enhance cognitive and affective functioning in older adults. *Journal of Aging and Health, 16,* 562–585.

Nolen-Hoeksema, S. (2006). The etiology of gender differences in depression. In C. M. Mazure & G. Puryear (Eds.), *Understanding depression in women: Applying empirical research to practice and policy* (pp. 9–43). Washington, DC: American Psychological Association.

Nolen-Hoeksema, S., & Aldao, A. (2011). Gender and age differences in emotion regulation and their relationship to depressive symptoms. *Personality and Individual Differences, 51,* 704–708.

Noller, P., Feeney, J. A., Sheehan, G., Darlington, Y., & Rogers, C. (2008). Conflict in divorcing and continuously married families: A study of marital, parent–child and sibling relationships. *Journal of Divorce and Remarriage, 49,* 1–24.

Nomaguchi, K. M., & Brown, S. L. (2011). Parental strains and rewards among mothers: The role of education. *Journal of Marriage and Family, 73,* 621–636.

Nomaguchi, K. M., & Milkie, M. A. (2003). Costs and rewards of children: The effects of becoming a parent on adults' lives. *Journal of Marriage and Family, 65,* 356–374.

Nordhus, I. H. (2008). Manifestations of depression and anxiety in older adults. In B. Woods & L. Clare (Eds.), *Handbook of the clinical psychology of ageing* (pp. 97–110). Hoboken, NJ: Wiley-Interscience.

Nosarti, C., Walshe, M., Rushe, T. M., Rifkin, L., Wyatt, J., Murray, R. M., et al. (2011). Neonatal ultrasound results following very preterm birth predict adolescent behavioral and cognitive outcome. *Developmental Neuropsychology, 36,* 118–135.

Noterdaeme, M., Mildenberger, K., Minow, F., & Amorosa, H. (2002). Evaluation of neuromotor deficits in children with autism and children with a specific speech and language disorder. *European Child and Adolescent Psychiatry, 11,* 219–225.

Nucci, L. (2008). *Nice is not enough: Facilitating moral development.* Upper Saddle River, NJ: Prentice Hall.

Nucci, L. P. (1996). Morality and the personal sphere of action. In E. Reed, E. Turiel, & T. Brown (Eds.), *Values and knowledge* (pp. 41–60). Hillsdale, NJ: Erlbaum.

Nucci, L. P. (2001). *Education in the moral domain.* New York: Cambridge University Press.

Nucci, L. P. (2002). The development of moral reasoning. In U. Goswami (Ed.), *Blackwell handbook of childhood cognitive development* (pp. 303–325). Malden, MA: Blackwell.

Nucci, L. P. (2005). Culture, context, and the psychological sources of human rights concepts. In W. Edelstein & G. Nunner-Winkler (Eds.), *Morality in context* (pp. 365–394). Amsterdam, Netherlands: Elsevier.

Nuland, S. B. (1993). *How we die.* New York: Random House.

Numan, M., & Insel, T. (2003). *Neurobiology of parental behavior.* New York: Springer-Verlag.

Nunez-Smith, M., Wolf, E., Huang, H. M., Chen, P. G., Lee, L., Emanuel, E. J., et al. (2008). *The impact of media on child and adolescent health.* Retrieved from www.commonsensemedia.org/sites/default/files/media_child_health_exec_summary_0.pdf

O

Oakes, L. M., Coppage, D. J., & Dingel, A. (1997). By land or by sea: The role of perceptual similarity in infants' categorization of animals. *Developmental Psychology, 33,* 396–407.

Oakes, L. M., Horst, J. S., Kovack-Lesh, K. A., & Perone, S. (2009). How infants learn categories. In A. Woodward & A. Needham (Eds.), *Learning and the infant mind* (pp. 144–171). New York: Oxford University Press.

Oberecker, R., & Friederici, A. D. (2006). Syntactic event-related potential components in 24-month-olds' sentence comprehension. *NeuroReport, 17,* 1017–1021.

Oberecker, R., Friedrich, M., & Friederici, A. D. (2005). Neural correlates of syntactic processing in two-year-olds. *Journal of Cognitive Neuroscience, 17,* 1667–1678.

Obermeyer, C. M. (2000). Menopause across cultures: A review of the evidence. *Menopause, 7,* 184–192.

Obradović, J., Long, J. D., Cutuli, J. J., Chan, C. K., Hinz, E., Heistad, D., & Masten, A. S. (2009). Academic achievement of homeless and highly mobile children in an urban school district: Longitudinal evidence on risk, growth, and resilience. *Development and Psychopathology, 21,* 493–518.

O'Brien, M. A., Hsing, C., & Konrath, S. (2010, May). *Empathy is declining in American college students.* Poster presented at the annual meeting of the Association for Psychological Science, Boston.

O'Connor, E., & McCartney, K. (2007). Examining teacher–child relationships and achievement as part of an ecological model of development. *American Educational Research Journal, 44,* 340–369.

O'Connor, P. (2003). Dying in the hospital. In I. Corless, B. B. Germino, & M. A. Pitman (Eds.), *Dying, death, and bereavement: A challenge for the living* (2nd ed., pp. 87–103). New York: Springer.

O'Connor, P. G. (2012). Alcohol abuse and dependence. In L. Goldman & D. A. Ausiello (Eds.), *Cecil Medicine* (23rd ed.), Philadelphia, PA: Elsevier.

O'Connor, T. G., Rutter, M., Beckett, C., Keaveney, L., Dreppner, J. M., & the English and Romanian Adoptees Study Team. (2000). The effects of global severe privation on cognitive competence: Extension and longitudinal follow-up. *Child Development, 71,* 376–390.

OECD (Organisation for Economic Cooperation and Development). (2006). *Starting strong II: Early childhood education and care.* Paris: OECD Publishing. Retrieved from www.sourceoecd.org/education/9264035451

OECD (Organisation for Economic Cooperation and Development). (2010a). *Education at a glance 2010: OECD indicators.* Paris: Author. Retrieved from www.oecd.org/document/52/0,3746,en_2649_39263238_45897844_1_1_1_1,00.html

OECD (Organisation for Economic Cooperation and Development). (2010b). *OECD Health data: 2010.* Retrieved from www.oecd.org/document/44/0,3746,en_2649_37407_2085228_1_1_1_37407,00.html

OECD (Organisation for Economic Cooperation and Development). (2011). *OECD health data 2011.* Retrieved from stats.oecd.org/index.aspx?DataSetCode=HEALTH_STAT

OECD (Organisation for Economic Cooperation and Development). (2012a). *Education at a glance 2012: OECD indicators.* Paris: Author.

OECD (Organisation for Economic Cooperation and Development). (2012b). *Health data: 2012.* Retrieved from www.oecd.org/health/healthpoliciesanddata/oecdhealthdata2012.htm

Ogan, A., & Berk, L. E. (2009, April). *Effects of two approaches to make-believe play training on self-regulation in Head Start children.* Paper presented at the biennial meeting of the Society for Research in Child Development, Denver, CO.

Ogawa, J. R., Sroufe, L. A., Weinfield, N. S., Carlson, E. A., & Egeland, B. (1997). Development and the fragmented self: Longitudinal study of dissociative symptomatology in a nonclinical sample. *Development and Psychopathology, 9,* 855–879.

Ogden, C. L., Carroll, M. D., Curtin, L. R., Lamb, M. M., & Flegal, K. M. (2010). Prevalence of high body mass index in U.S. children and adolescents, 2007–2008. *Journal of the American Medical Association, 303,* 242–249.

O'Halloran, C. M., & Altmaier, E. M. (1996). Awareness of death among children: Does a life-threatening illness alter the process of discovery? *Journal of Counseling and Development, 74,* 259–262.

Ohannessian, C. M., & Hesselbrock, V. M. (2008). Paternal alcoholism and youth substance abuse: The indirect effects of negative affect, conduct problems, and risk taking. *Journal of Adolescent Health, 42,* 198–200.

Okagaki, L., & Sternberg, R. J. (1993). Parental beliefs and children's school performance. *Child Development, 64,* 36–56.

Okami, P., Weisner, T., & Olmstead, R. (2002). Outcome correlates of parent–child bedsharing: An eighteen-year longitudinal study. *Developmental and Behavioral Pediatrics, 23,* 244–253.

O'Keefe, M. J., O'Callaghan, M., Williams, G. M., Najman, J. M., & Bor, W. (2003). Learning, cognitive, and attentional problems in adolescents born small for gestational age. *Pediatrics, 112,* 301–307.

O'Laughlin, E. M., & Anderson, V. N. (2001). Perceptions of parenthood among young adults: Implications for career and family planning. *American Journal of Family Therapy, 29,* 95–108.

Old, S. R., & Naveh-Benjamin, M. (2008). Age-related changes in memory: Experimental approaches. In S. M. Hofer & D. F. Alwin (Eds.), *Handbook of cognitive aging: Interdisciplinary perspectives* (pp. 151–167). Thousand Oaks, CA: Sage.

Olds, D. L., Kitzman, H., Cole, R., Robinson, J., Sidora, K., Luckey, D. W., et al. (2004). Effects of nurse home-visiting on maternal life course and child development: Age 6 follow-up results of a randomized trial. *Pediatrics, 114,* 1550–1559.

Olds, D. L., Kitzman, H., Hanks, C., Cole, R., Anson, E., Sidora-Arcoleo, K., et al. (2007). Effects of nurse home visiting on maternal and child functioning: Age-9 follow-up of a randomized trial. *Pediatrics, 120,* e832–e845.

Olfman, S., & Robbins, B. D. (Eds.). (2012). *Drugging our children.* New York: Praeger.

Olineck, K. M., & Poulin-Dubois, D. (2007). Imitation of intentional actions and internal state language in infancy predict preschool theory of mind skills. *European Journal of Developmental Psychology, 4,* 14–30.

Olineck, K. M., & Poulin-Dubois, D. (2009). Infants' understanding of intention from 10 to 14 months: Interrelations among violation of expectancy and imitation tasks. *Infant Behavior and Development, 32,* 404–415.

Oliveira, F. L., Patin, R. V., & Escrivao, M. A. (2010). Atherosclerosis prevention and treatment in children and adolescents. *Expert Review of Cardiovascular Therapy, 8,* 513–528.

Ollendick, T. H., King, N. J., & Muris, P. (2002). Fears and phobias in children: Phenomenology, epidemiology, and aetiology. *Child and Adolescent Mental Health, 7,* 98–106.

Olshansky, S. J., Hayflick, L., & Perls, T. T. (2004). Antiaging medicine: The hype and the reality—Part II. *Journal of Gerontology, 59A,* 649–651.

Omar, H., McElderry, D., & Zakharia, R. (2003). Educating adolescents about puberty: What are we missing? *International Journal of Adolescent Medicine and Health, 15,* 79–83.

Ondrusek, N., Abramovitch, R., Pencharz, P., & Koren, G. (1998). Empirical examination of the ability of children to consent to clinical research. *Journal of Medical Ethics, 24,* 158–165.

O'Neill, M., Bard, K. A., Kinnell, M., & Fluck, M. (2005). Maternal gestures with 20-month-old infants in two contexts. *Developmental Science, 8,* 352–359.

Ong, A. D., Bergeman, C. S., & Bisconti, T. L. (2004). The role of daily positive emotions during conjugal bereavement. *Journal of Gerontology, 59B,* 168–176.

Ong, A. D., Mroczek, D. K., & Riffin, C. (2011). The health significance of positive emotions in adulthood and later life. *Social and Personality Psychology Compass, 5/8,* 538–551.

Ontai, L. L., & Thompson, R. A. (2008). Attachment, parent–child discourse and theory-of-mind development. *Social Development, 17,* 47–60.

Ophir, E., Nass, C., & Wagner, A. D. (2009). Cognitive control in media multitaskers. *Proceedings of the National Academy of Sciences, 106,* 15583–15587.

Oosterwegel, A., & Oppenheimer, L. (1993). *The self-system: Developmental changes between and within self-concepts.* Hillsdale, NJ: Erlbaum.

Orbio de Castro, B., Veerman, J. W., Koops, W., Bosch, J. D., & Monshouwer, H. J. (2002). Hostile attribution of intent and aggressive behavior: A meta-analysis. *Child Development, 73,* 916–934.

Oregon Public Health Division. (2013). *Oregon's Death with Dignity Act—2012.* Retrieved from public.health.oregon.gov/ProviderPartnerResources/EvaluationResearch/DeathwithDignityAct/Documents/year15.pdf

O'Rourke, N., Cappeliez, P., & Claxton, A. (2011). Functions of reminiscence and the psychological well-being of young-old and older adults over time. *Aging and Mental Health, 15,* 272–281.

Orth, U., Robins, R. W., & Widaman, K. F. (2012). Lifespan development of self-esteem and its effects on important life outcomes. *Personality Processes and Individual Differences, 102,* 1271–1288.

Orth, U., Trzesniewski, K. H., & Robins, R. W. (2010). Self-esteem development from young adulthood to old age: A cohort-sequential longitudinal study. *Journal of Personality and Social Psychology, 98,* 645–658.

Osherson, D. N., & Markman, E. M. (1975). Language and the ability to evaluate contradictions and tautologies. *Cognition, 2,* 213–226.

Ostrov, J. M., Crick, N. R., & Stauffacher, K. (2006). Relational aggression in sibling and peer relationships during early childhood. *Applied Developmental Psychology, 27,* 241–253.

Ostrov, J. M., Gentile, D. A., & Crick, N. R. (2006). Media exposure, aggression, and prosocial behavior during early childhood: A longitudinal study. *Social Development, 15,* 612–627.

Oswald, F., Jopp, D., Rott, C., & Wahl, H.-W. (2010). Is aging in place a resource for or risk to life satisfaction? *Gerontologist, 51*, 238–250.

Oswald, F., & Wahl, H.-W. (2013). Creating and sustaining homelike places in residential living. In G. D. Rowles & M. Bernard (Eds.), *Environmental gerontology: Making meaningful places in old age* (pp. 53–78). New York: Springer.

Otis, N., Grouzet, F. M. E., & Pelletier, L. G. (2005). Latent motivational change in an academic setting: A three-year longitudinal study. *Journal of Educational Psychology, 97*, 170–183.

Otto, M. W., Henin, A., Hirshfeld-Becker, D. R., Pollack, M. H., Biederman, J., & Rosenbaum, J. (2007). Posttraumatic stress disorder symptoms following media exposure to tragic events: Impact of 9/11 on children at risk for anxiety disorders. *Journal of Anxiety Disorders, 21*, 888–902.

Oude, L. H., Baur, L., Jansen, H., Shrewsbury, V. A., O'Malley, C., Stolk, R. P., & Summerbell, C. D. (2009). Interventions for treating obesity in children. *Cochrane Database of Systematic Reviews, Issue 4*. Chichester, UK: Wiley.

Ouko, L. A., Shantikumar, K., Knezovich, J., Haycock, P., Schnugh, D. J., & Ramsay, M. (2009). Effect of alcohol consumption on CpG methylation in the differentially methylated regions of H19 and IGDMR in male gametes: Implications for fetal alcohol spectrum disorders. *Alcoholism, Clinical and Experimental Research, 33*, 1615–1627.

Ovando, C. J., & Collier, V. P. (1998). *Bilingual and ESL classrooms: Teaching in multicultural contexts*. Boston: McGraw-Hill.

Overton, W. F. (2010). Life-span development: Concepts and issues. In W. F. Overton (Ed.), *Handbook of lifespan development: Cognition, biology, and methods* (pp. 1–29). Hoboken, NJ: Wiley.

Owen, C. G., Whincup, P. H., Kaye, S. J., Martin, R. M., Smith, G. D., Cook, D. G., et al. (2008). Does initial breastfeeding lead to lower blood cholesterol in adult life? A quantitative review of the evidence. *American Journal of Clinical Nutrition, 88*, 305–314.

Owsley, C. (2011). Aging and vision. *Vision Research, 51*, 1610–1622.

Oyserman, D., Bybee, D., Mowbray, C., & Hart-Johnson, T. (2005). When mothers have serious mental health problems: Parenting as a proximal mediator. *Journal of Adolescence, 28*, 443–463.

Özçaliskan, S. (2005). On learning to draw the distinction between physical and metaphorical motion: Is metaphor an early emerging cognitive and linguistic capacity? *Journal of Child Language, 32*, 291–318.

Özçaliskan, S., & Goldin-Meadow, S. (2005). Gesture is at the cutting edge of early language development. *Cognition, 96*, B101–B113.

Ozer, E. M., & Irwin, C. E., Jr. (2009). Adolescent and young adult health: From basic health status to clinical interventions. In R. M. Lerner & L. Steinberg (Eds.), *Handbook of adolescent psychology: Vol. 1. Individual bases of adolescent development* (pp. 618–641). Hoboken, NJ: Wiley.

P

Padilla-Walker, L. M., & Nelson, L. J. (2012). Black Hawk down?: Establishing helicopter parenting as a distinct construct from other forms of parental control during emerging adulthood. *Journal of Adolescence, 35*, 1177–1190.

Pagani, L. S., Japel, C., Vitaro, F., Tremblay, R. E., Larose, S., & McDuff, P. (2008). When predictions fail: The case of unexpected pathways toward high school dropout. *Journal of Social Issues, 64*, 175–193.

Pager, D., & Shepherd, H. (2008). The sociology of discrimination: Racial discrimination in employment, housing, credit, and consumer markets. *Annual Review of Sociology, 34*, 181–209.

Pager, D., Western, B., & Bonkowski, B. (2009). Discrimination in a low-wage labor market: A field experiment, *American Sociological Review, 74*, 777–799.

Paik, A. (2010). "Hookups," dating, and relationship quality: Does the type of sexual involvement matter? *Social Science Research, 39*, 739–753.

Painter, J. A., Allison, L., Dhingra, P., Daughtery, J., Cogdill, K., & Trujillo, L. G. (2012). Fear of falling and its relationship with anxiety, depression, and activity engagement among community-dwelling older adults. *American Journal of Occupational Therapy, 66*, 169–176.

Palincsar, A. S. (2003). Advancing a theoretical model of learning and instruction. In B. J. Zimmerman (Ed.), *Educational psychology: A century of contributions* (pp. 459–475). Mahwah, NJ: Erlbaum.

Palop, J. J., Chin, J., Roberson, E. D., Wang, J., Thwin, M. T., & Bien-Ly, N. (2007). Aberrant excitatory neuronal activity and compensatory remodeling of inhibitory hippocampal circuits in mouse models of Alzheimer's disease. *Neuron, 55*, 697–711.

Pan, B. A., & Snow, C. E. (1999). The development of conversation and discourse skills. In M. Barrett (Ed.), *The development of language* (pp. 229–249). Hove, UK: Psychology Press.

Pan, H. W. (1994). Children's play in Taiwan. In J. L. Roopnarine, J. E. Johnson, & F. H. Hooper (Eds.), *Children's play in diverse cultures* (pp. 31–50). Albany, NY: SUNY Press.

Panish, J. B., & Stricker, G. (2002). Perceptions of childhood and adult sibling relationships. *NYS Psychologist, 14*, 33–36.

Papadakis, A. A., Prince, R. P., Jones, N. P., & Strauman, T. J. (2006). Self-regulation, rumination, and vulnerability to depression in adolescent girls. *Development and Psychopathology, 18*, 815–829.

Paquette, D. (2004). Theorizing the father–child relationship: Mechanisms and developmental outcomes. *Human Development, 47*, 193–219.

Paradis, J. (2007). Second language acquisition in childhood. In E. Hoff & M. Shatz (Eds.), *Blackwell handbook of language development* (pp. 387–405). Malden, MA: Blackwell.

Paradise, R., & Rogoff, B. (2009). Side by side: Learning by observing and pitching in. *Ethos, 27*, 102–138.

Paramei, G. V. (2012). Color discrimination across four life decades assessed by the Cambridge Color Test. *Journal of the Optical Society of America, 29*, A290–A297.

Pardini, D. A., Fite, P. J., & Burke, J. D. (2008). Bidirectional associations between parenting practices and conduct problems in boys from childhood to adolescence: The moderating effect of age and African-American ethnicity. *Journal of Abnormal Child Psychology, 36*, 647–662.

Parent, A., Teilmann, G., Juul, A., Skakkebaek, N. E., Toppari, J., & Bourguignon, J. (2003). The timing of normal puberty and the age limits of sexual precocity: Variations around the world, secular trends, and changes after migration. *Endocrine Reviews, 24*, 668–693.

Paris, S. G., & Paris, A. H. (2006). Assessments of early reading. In K. A. Renninger & I. E. Sigel (Eds.), *Handbook of child psychology: Vol. 4. Child psychology in practice* (6th ed., pp. 48–74). Hoboken, NJ: Wiley.

Park, D. C. (2002). Judging meaning improves function in the aging brain. *Trends in Cognitive Sciences, 6*, 227–229.

Park, D. C., Lautenschlager, G., Hedden, T., Davidson, N. S., Smith, A. D., & Smith, P. K. (2002). Models of visuospatial and verbal memory across the adult life span. *Psychology and Aging, 17*, 299–320.

Park, W. (2009). Acculturative stress and mental health among Korean adolescents in the United States. *Journal of Human Behavior in the Social Environment, 19*, 626–634.

Parke, R. D., & Buriel, R. (2006). Socialization in the family: Ethnic and ecological perspectives. In N. Eisenberg (Ed.), *Handbook of child psychology: Vol. 3. Social, emotional, and personality development* (6th ed., pp. 429–504). Hoboken, NJ: Wiley.

Parke, R. D., Simpkins, S. D., McDowell, D. J., Kim, M., Killian, C., Dennis, J., Flyr, M. L., Wild, M., & Rah, Y. (2004). Relative contributions of families and peers to children's social development. In P. K. Smith & C. H. Hart (Eds.), *Blackwell handbook of childhood social development* (pp. 156–177). Malden, MA: Blackwell.

Parker, F. L., Boak, A. Y., Griffin, K. W., Ripple, C., & Peay, L. (1999). Parent–child relationship, home learning environment, and school readiness. *School Psychology Review, 28*, 413–425.

Parker, J. G., Low, C. M., Walker, A. R., & Gamm, B. K. (2005). Friendship jealousy in young adolescents: Individual differences and links to sex, self-esteem, aggression, and social adjustment. *Developmental Psychology, 41*, 235–250.

Parker, P. D., Schoon, I., Tsai, Y-M., Nagy, G., Trautwein, U., & Eccles, J. (2012). Achievement, agency, gender, and socioeconomic background as predictors of postschool choices: A multicontext study. *Developmental Psychology, 48*, 1629–1642.

Parten, M. (1932). Social participation among preschool children. *Journal of Abnormal and Social Psychology, 27*, 243–269.

Pascalis, O., de Haan, M., & Nelson, C. A. (2002). Is face processing species-specific during the first year of life? *Science, 296*, 1321–1323.

Pascarella, E. T., & Terenzini, P. T. (1991). *How college affects students*. San Francisco: Jossey-Bass.

Pascarella, E. T., & Terenzini, P. T. (2005). *How college affects students: Vol. 2. A third decade of research*. San Francisco: Jossey-Bass.

Pasterski, V. L., Geffner, M. E., Brain, C., Hindmarsh, P., & Brook, C. (2005). Prenatal hormones and postnatal socialization by parents as determinants of male-typical toy play in girls with congenital adrenal hyperplasia. *Child Development, 76*, 264–278.

Patock-Peckam, J. A., & Morgan-Lopez, A. A. (2009). Mediational links among parenting styles, perceptions of parental confidence, self-esteem, and depression on alcohol-related problems in emerging adulthood. *Journal of Studies on Alcohol and Drugs, 70*, 215–226.

Patrick, R. B., & Gibbs, J. C. (2011). Inductive discipline, parental expression of disappointed expectations, and moral identity in adolescence. *Journal of Youth and Adolescence, 41*, 973–983.

Pattenden, S., Antova, T., Neuberger, M., Nikiforov, B., De Sario, M., Grize, L., & Heinrich, J. (2006). Parental smoking and children's respiratory health: Independent effects of prenatal and postnatal exposure. *Tobacco Control, 15*, 294–301.

Patterson, C. J., & Riskind, R. G. (2010). To be a parent: Issues in family formation among gay and lesbian adults. *Journal of GLBT Family Studies, 6*, 326–340.

Patterson, G. R., & Fisher, P. A. (2002). Recent developments in our understanding of parenting: Bidirectional effects, causal models, and the search for parsimony. In M. H. Bornstein (Ed.), *Handbook of parenting* (Vol. 5, pp. 59–88). Mahwah, NJ: Erlbaum.

Patterson, G. R., & Yoerger, K. (2002). A developmental model for early- and late-onset delinquency. In J. B. Reid & G. R. Patterson (Eds.), *Antisocial behavior in children and adolescents* (pp. 147–172). Washington, DC: American Psychological Association.

Paukner, A., Ferrari, P. F., & Suomi, S. J. (2011). Delayed imitation of lipsmacking gestures by infant rhesus macaques (*Macaca mulatta*). *PLoS ONE 6(12)*, e28848.

Paul, J. J., & Cillessen, A. H. N. (2003). Dynamics of peer victimization in early adolescence: Results from a four-year longitudinal study. *Journal of Applied School Psychology, 19,* 25–43.

Pauli, S. A., Berga, S. L., Shang, W., & Session, D. R. (2009). Current status of the approach to assisted reproduction. *Pediatric Clinics of North America, 56,* 467–488.

Paulussen-Hoogeboom, M. C., Stams, G. J. J. M., Hermanns, J. M. A., & Peetsma, T. T. D. (2007). Child negative emotionality and parenting from infancy to preschool: A meta-analytic review. *Developmental Psychology, 43,* 438–453.

Payne, B. R., Gao, X., Noh, S. R., Anderson, C. J., & Stine-Morrow, E. A. L. (2012). The effects of print exposure on sentence processing and memory in older adults: Evidence for efficiency and reserve. *Aging, Neuropsychology, and Cognition, 19,* 122–149.

Pea, R., Nass, C., Meheula, L., Rance, M., Kumar, A., Bamford, H., et al. (2012). Media use, face-to-face communication, media multitasking, and social well-being among 8- to 12-year-old girls. *Developmental Psychology, 48,* 327–336.

Peake, A., & Harris, K. L. (2002). Young adults' attitudes toward multiple role planning: The influence of gender, career traditionality, and marriage plans. *Journal of Vocational Behavior, 60,* 405–421.

Pearlman, D. N., Zierler, S., Meersman, S., Kim, H. K., Viner-Brown, S. I., & Caron, C. (2006). Race disparities in childhood asthma: Does where you live matter? *Journal of the National Medical Association, 98,* 239–247.

Peck, R. C. (1968). Psychological developments in the second half of life. In B. L. Neugarten (Ed.), *Middle age and aging* (pp. 88–92). Chicago: University of Chicago Press.

Pederson, D. R., & Moran, G. (1996). Expressions of the attachment relationship outside of the Strange Situation. *Child Development, 67,* 915–927.

Peets, K., Hodges, E. V. E., Kikas, E., & Salmivalli, C. (2007). Hostile attributions and behavioral strategies in children: Does relationship type matter? *Developmental Psychology, 43,* 889–900.

Peirano, P., Algarin, C., & Uauy, R. (2003). Sleep–wake states and their regulatory mechanisms throughout early human development. *Journal of Pediatrics, 43,* S70–S79.

Peiró, J., Tordera, N., & Potocnik, K. (2012). Retirement practices in different countries. In M. Wang (Ed.), *Oxford handbook of retirement* (pp. 509–540). New York: Oxford University Press.

Pellegrini, A. D. (1992). Kindergarten children's social cognitive status as a predictor of first grade success. *Early Childhood Research Quarterly, 7,* 565–577.

Pellegrini, A. D. (2003). Perceptions and functions of play and real fighting in early adolescence. *Child Development, 74,* 1522–1533.

Pellegrini, A. D. (2004). Rough-and-tumble play from childhood through adolescence: Development and possible functions. In P. K. Smith & C. H. Hart (Eds.), *Blackwell handbook of childhood social development* (pp. 438–453). Malden, MA: Blackwell.

Pellegrini, A. D., & Holmes, R. M. (2006). The role of recess in primary school. In D. G. Singer, R. M. Golinkoff, & K. Hirsh-Pasek (Eds.), *Play = learning* (pp. 36–53). New York: Oxford University Press.

Pellegrini, A. D., Huberty, P. D., & Jones, I. (1995). The effects of recess timing on children's playground and classroom behaviors. *American Educational Research Journal, 32,* 845–864.

Pellegrini, A. D., Kato, K., Blatchford, P., & Baines, E. (2002). A short-term longitudinal study of children's playground games across the first year of school: Implications for social competence and adjustment to school. *American Educational Research Journal, 39,* 991–1015.

Pellegrini, A. D., & Smith, P. K. (1998). Physical activity play: The nature and function of a neglected aspect of play. *Child Development, 69,* 577–598.

Pendlebury, S. T., Rothwell, P. M. (2009). Prevalence, incidence, and factors associated with pre-stroke and post-stroke dementia: A systematic review and meta-analysis. *Lancet Neurology, 8,* 1006–1018.

Pennington, B. F., Snyder, K. A., & Roberts, R. J., Jr. (2007). Developmental cognitive neuroscience: Origins, issues, and prospects. *Developmental Review, 27,* 428–441.

Penny, H., & Haddock, G. (2007). Anti-fat prejudice among children: The "mere proximity" effect in 5–10 year olds. *Journal of Experimental Social Psychology, 43,* 678–683.

Pepler, D. J., Craig, W. M., Connolly, J. A., Yuile, A., McMaster, L., & Jiang, D. (2006). A developmental perspective on bullying. *Aggressive Behavior, 32,* 376–384.

Peralta de Mendoza, O. A., & Salsa, A. M. (2003). Instruction in early comprehension and use of a symbol–referent relation. *Cognitive Development, 18,* 269–284.

Perelli-Harris, B., & Gassen, N. S. (2012). How similar are cohabitation and marriage? Legal approaches to cohabitation across Western Europe. *Population and Development Review, 38,* 435–467.

Perkins, H. W. (1991). Religious commitment, yuppie values, and well-being in post-collegiate life. *Review of Religious Research, 32,* 244–251.

Perlmutter, M. (1984). Continuities and discontinuities in early human memory: Paradigms, processes, and performances. In R. V. Kail, Jr., & N. R. Spear (Eds.), *Comparative perspectives on the development of memory* (pp. 253–287). Hillsdale, NJ: Erlbaum.

Perlmutter, M., Kaplan, M., & Nyquist, L. (1990). Development of adaptive competence in adulthood. *Human Development, 33,* 185–197.

Perls, T., Levenson, R., Regan, M., & Puca, A. (2002). What does it take to live to 100? *Mechanisms of Ageing and Development, 123,* 231–242.

Perls, T., & Terry, D. (2003). Understanding the determinants of exceptional longevity. *Annals of Internal Medicine, 139,* 445–449.

Perone, S., Madole, K. L., Ross-Sheehy, S., Carey, M., & Oakes, L. M. (2008). The relation between infants' activity with objects and attention to object appearance. *Developmental Psychology, 44,* 1242–1248.

Perry, W. G., Jr. (1981). Cognitive and ethical growth. In A. Chickering (Ed.), *The modern American college* (pp. 76–116). San Francisco: Jossey-Bass.

Perry, W. G., Jr. (1998). *Forms of intellectual and ethical development in the college years: A scheme.* San Francisco: Jossey-Bass. (Originally published 1970)

Perry-Jenkins, M., Repetti, R. L., & Crouter, A. C. (2000). Work and family in the 1990s. *Journal of Marriage and the Family, 62,* 981–998.

Peshkin, A. (1997). *Places of memory: Whiteman's schools and Native American communities.* Mahwah, NJ: Erlbaum.

Pesonen, A.-K., Räikkönen, K., Heinonen, K., & Komsi, N. (2008). A transactional model of temperamental development: Evidence of a relationship between child temperament and maternal stress over five years. *Social Development, 17,* 326–340.

Peters, R. D. (2005). A community-based approach to promoting resilience in young children, their families, and their neighborhoods. In R. D. Peters, B. Leadbeater, & R. J. McMahon (Eds.), *Resilience in children, families, and communities: Linking context to practice and policy* (pp. 157–176). New York: Kluwer Academic.

Peters, R. D., Petrunka, K., & Arnold, R. (2003). The Better Beginnings, Better Futures Project: A universal, comprehensive, community-based prevention approach for primary school children and their families. *Journal of Clinical Child and Adolescent Psychology, 32,* 215–227.

Peterson, B. E. (2002). Longitudinal analysis of midlife generativity, intergenerational roles, and caregiving. *Psychology and Aging, 17,* 161–168.

Peterson, B. E. (2006). Generativity and successful parenting: An analysis of young adult outcomes. *Journal of Personality, 74,* 847–869.

Peterson, B. E., & Duncan, L. E. (2007). Midlife women's generativity and authoritarianism: Marriage, motherhood, and 10 years of aging. *Psychology and Aging, 22,* 411–419.

Peterson, B. E., Smirles, K. A., & Wentworth, P. A. (1997). Generativity and authoritarianism: Implications for personality, political involvement, and parenting. *Journal of Personality and Social Psychology, 72,* 1202–1216.

Peterson, C., Warren, K. L., & Short, M. M. (2011). Infantile amnesia across the years: A 2-year follow-up of children's earliest memories. *Child Development, 82,* 1092–1105.

Peter-Wight, M., & Martin, M. (2011). Older spouses' individual and dyadic problem solving. *European Psychologist, 16,* 288–294.

Petitto, L. A., Holowka, S., Sergio, L. E., Levy, B., & Ostry, D. J. (2004). Baby hands that move to the rhythm of language: Hearing babies acquiring sign languages babble silently on the hands. *Cognition, 93,* 43–73.

Petitto, L. A., Holowka, S., Sergio, L. E., & Ostry, D. (2001, September 6). Language rhythms in babies' hand movements. *Nature, 413,* 35–36.

Petitto, L. A., & Marentette, P. F. (1991). Babbling in the manual mode: Evidence for the ontogeny of language. *Science, 251,* 1493–1496.

Petrofsky, J., Berk, L., & Al-Nakhli, H. (2012). The influence of autonomic dysfunction associated with aging and type 2 diabetes on daily life activities. *Experimental Diabetes Research,* Article ID 657103.

Pettigrew, T. F., & Tropp, L. R. (2006). A meta-analytic test of intergroup contact theory. *Journal of Personality and Social Psychology, 90,* 751–783.

Pettit, G. S., Keiley, M. K., Laird, R. D., Bates, J. E., & Dodge, K. A. (2007). Predicting the developmental course of mother-reported monitoring across childhood and adolescence from early proactive parenting, child temperament, and parents' worries. *Journal of Family Psychology, 21,* 206–217.

Pew Forum on Religion and Public Life. (2010). *Religion among the Millennials.* Washington, DC: Pew Research Center.

Pew Research Center. (2006). *Strong public support for right to die.* Retrieved from www.people-press.org/2006/01/05/strong-public-support-for-right-to-die

Pew Research Center. (2010a). *The decline of marriage and rise of new families.* Washington, DC: Author.

Pew Research Center. (2010b). *Religion among the millennials.* Washington, DC: Pew Form on Religion and Public Life.

Pew Research Center. (2013). *Growing support for gay marriage: Changed minds and changing demographics.* Washington, DC: Author. Retrieved from www.people-press.org/files/legacy-pdf/3-20-13%20Gay%20Marriage%20Release%20UPDATE.pdf

Pharo, H., Sim, C., Graham, M., Gross, J., & Hayne, H. (2011). Risky business: Executive function, personality, and reckless behavior during adolescence and emerging adulthood. *Behavioral Neuroscience, 125,* 970–978.

Phinney, J. S. (2007). Ethnic identity exploration in emerging adulthood. In J. J. Arnett & J. L. Tanner (Eds.), *Emerging adults in America: Coming of age in the 21st century* (pp. 117–134). Washington, DC: American Psychological Association.

Phinney, J. S., & Chavira, V. (1995). Parental ethnic socialization and adolescent outcomes in ethnic minority families. *Journal of Research on Adolescence, 5,* 31–53.

Phinney, J. S., Horenczyk, G., Liebkind, K., & Vedder, P. (2001). Ethnic identity, immigration, and well-being: An interactional perspective. *Journal of Social Issues, 57*, 493–510.

Phinney, J. S., Ong, A., & Madden, T. (2000). Cultural values and intergenerational value discrepancies in immigrant and non-immigrant families. *Child Development, 71*, 528–539.

Phuong, D. D., Frank, R., & Finch, B. R. (2012). Does SES explain more of the black/white health gap than we thought? Revisiting our approach toward understanding racial disparities in health. *Social Science and Medicine, 74*, 1385–1393.

Piaget, J. (1926). *The language and thought of the child*. New York: Harcourt, Brace & World. (Original work published 1923)

Piaget, J. (1930). *The child's conception of the world*. New York: Harcourt, Brace, & World. (Original work published 1926)

Piaget, J. (1951). *Play, dreams, and imitation in childhood*. New York: Norton. (Original work published 1945)

Piaget, J. (1952). *The origins of intelligence in children*. New York: International Universities Press. (Original work published 1936)

Piaget, J. (1967). *Six psychological studies*. New York: Vintage.

Piaget, J. (1971). *Biology and knowledge*. Chicago: University of Chicago Press.

Pianta, R., Egeland, B., & Erickson, M. F. (1989). The antecedents of maltreatment: Results of the Mother–Child Interaction Research Project. In D. Cicchetti & V. Carlson (Eds.), *Child maltreatment* (pp. 203–253). New York: Cambridge University Press.

Pierroutsakos, S. L., & Troseth, G. L. (2003). Video verité: Infants' manual investigation of objects on video. *Infant Behavior and Development, 26*, 183–199.

Pietz, J., Peter, J., Graf, R., Rauterberg, R. I., Rupp, A., & Sontheimer, D. (2004). Physical growth and neurodevelopmental outcome of nonhandicapped low-risk children born preterm. *Early Human Development, 79*, 131–143.

Piirto, J. (2007). *Talented children and adults* (3rd ed.). Waco, TX: Prufrock Press.

Pillow, B. (2002). Children's and adults' evaluation of the certainty of deductive inferences, inductive inferences, and guesses. *Child Development, 73*, 779–792.

Pinquart, M. (2003). Loneliness in married, widowed, divorced, and never-married older adults. *Journal of Social and Personal Relationships, 20*, 31–53.

Pinquart, M., & Schindler, I. (2009). Change of leisure satisfaction in the transition to retirement: A latent-class analysis. *Leisure Sciences, 31*, 311–329.

Pinquart, M., & Sörensen, S. (2001). Gender differences in self-concept and psychological well-being in old age: A meta-analysis. *Journal of Gerontology, 56B*, P195–P213.

Pinquart, M., & Sörensen, S. (2006). Gender differences in caregiver stressor, social resources, and health: An updated meta-analysis. *Journal of Gerontology, 61B*, P33–P45.

Pirie, K., Peto, R., Reeves, G. K., Green, J., Beral, V., & the Million Women Study Collaborators. (2012). The 21st century hazards of smoking and benefits of stopping: A prospective study of one million women in the UK. *Lancet, 308*, 133–141.

Pitkin, J. (2010). Cultural issues and the menopause. *Menopause International, 16*, 156–161.

Pizarro, D. A., & Bloom, P. (2003). The intelligence of the moral intuitions: Comment on Haidt (2001). *Psychological Review, 110*, 193–196.

Plante, I., Théoret, M., & Favreau, O. E. (2009). Student gender stereotypes: Contrasting the perceived maleness and femaleness of mathematics and language. *Educational Psychology, 29*, 385–405.

Pleck, J. H., & Masciadrelli, B. P. (2004). Paternal involvement by U.S. residential fathers: Levels, sources, and consequences. In M. E. Lamb (Ed.), *The role of the father in child development* (4th ed., pp. 222–271). Hoboken, NJ: Wiley.

Plomin, R. (1994). *Genetics and experience: The interplay between nature and nurture*. Thousand Oaks, CA: Sage.

Plomin, R. (2009). The nature of nurture. In K. McCartney & R. A. Weinberg (Eds.), *Experience and development: A festschrift in honor of Sandra Wood Scarr* (pp. 61–80). New York: Psychology Press.

Plomin, R., & Davis, O. S. P. (2009). The future of genetics in psychology and psychiatry: Microarrays, genome-wide association, and non-coding RNA. *Journal of Child Psychology and Psychiatry, 50*, 63–71.

Plomin, R., & Spinath, F. M. (2004). Intelligence: Genetics, genes, and genomics. *Journal of Personality and Social Psychology, 86*, 112–129.

Plucker, J. A., & Makel, M. C. (2010). Assessment of creativity. In J. C. Kaufman & R. J. Sternberg (Eds.), *Cambridge handbook of creativity* (pp. 48–73). New York: Cambridge University Press.

Pluess, M., & Belsky, J. (2011). Prenatal programming of postnatal plasticity? *Development and Psychopathology, 23*, 29–38.

Poehlmann, J., Schwichtenberg, A. J. M., Shlafer, R. J., Hahn, E., Bianchi, J.-P., & Warner, R. (2011). Emerging self-regulation in toddlers born preterm or low birth weight: Differential susceptibility to parenting. *Developmental and Psychopathology, 23*, 177–193.

Pogarsky, G., Thornberry, T. P., & Lizotte, A. J. (2006). Developmental outcomes for children of young mothers. *Journal of Marriage and Family, 68*, 332–344.

Polderman, T. J. C., de Geus, J. C., Hoekstra, R. A., Bartels, M., van Leeuwen, M., Verhulst, F. C., et al. (2009). Attention problems, inhibitory control, and intelligence index overlapping genetic factors: A study in 9-, 12-, and 18-year-old twins. *Neuropsychology, 23*, 381–391.

Polka, L., & Werker, J. F. (1994). Developmental changes in perception of non-native vowel contrasts. *Journal of Experimental Psychology: Human Perception and Performance, 20*, 421–435.

Pomerantz, E. M., & Dong, W. (2006). Effects of mothers' perceptions of children's competence: The moderating role of mothers' theories of competence. *Developmental Psychology, 42*, 950–961.

Pomerantz, E. M., & Eaton, M. M. (2000). Developmental differences in children's conceptions of parental control: "They love me, but they make me feel incompetent." *Merrill-Palmer Quarterly, 46*, 140–167.

Pomerantz, E. M., Ng, F. F., & Wang, Q. (2008). Culture, parenting, and motivation: The case of East Asia and the United States. In M. L. Maehr, S. A., Karabenick, & T. C. Urdan (Eds.), *Advances in motivation and achievement: Social psychological perspectives* (Vol. 15, pp. 209–240). Bingley, UK: Emerald Group.

Pomerantz, E. M., & Ruble, D. N. (1998). The multidimensional nature of control: Implications for the development of sex differences in self-evaluation. In J. Heckhausen & C. S. Dweck (Eds.), *Motivation and self-regulation across the lifespan* (pp. 159–184). New York: Cambridge University Press.

Pomerantz, E. M., & Saxon, J. L. (2001). Conceptions of ability as stable and self-evaluative processes: A longitudinal examination. *Child Development, 72*, 152–173.

Pomerleau, A., Scuccimarri, C., & Malcuit, G. (2003). Mother–infant behavioral interactions in teenage and adult mothers during the first six months

postpartum: Relations with infant development. *Infant Mental Health Journal, 24*, 495–509.

Pong, S., Johnston, J., & Chen, V. (2010). Authoritarian parenting and Asian adolescent school performance. *International Journal of Behavioral Development, 34*, 62–72.

Pong, S., & Landale, N. S. (2012). Academic achievement of legal immigrants' children: The roles of parents' pre- and postmigration characteristics in origin-group differences. *Child Development, 83*, 1543–1559.

Ponnappan, S., & Ponnappan, U. (2011). Aging and immune function: Molecular mechanisms to interventions. *Antioxidants & Redox Signaling, 14*, 1551–1585.

Pons, F., Lawson, J., Harris, P. L., & de Rosnay, M. (2003). Individual differences in children's emotion understanding: Effects of age and language. *Scandinavian Journal of Psychology, 44*, 347–353.

Poobalan, A. S., Aucott, L. S., Precious, E., Crombie, I. K., & Smith, W. C. S. (2010). Weight loss interventions in young people (18 to 25 year olds): A systematic review. *Obesity Reviews, 11*, 580–592.

Poon, S., Goodman, S. G., Bugiardini, R., Bierman, A. S., Eagle, K. A., Johnston, N., et al. (2012). Bridging the gender gap: Insights from a contemporary analysis of sex-related differences in the treatment and outcomes of patients with acute coronary syndromes. *American Heart Journal, 163*, 66–73.

Portes, A., & Rumbaut, R. G. (2005). Introduction: The second generation and the Children of Immigrants Longitudinal Study. *Ethnic and Racial Studies, 28*, 983–999.

Posner, M. I., & Rothbart, M. K. (2007). Temperament and learning. In M. I. Posner & M. K. Rothbart (Eds.), *Educating the human brain* (pp. 121–146). Washington, DC: American Psychological Association.

Posthuma, R. A., & Campion, M. A. (2009). Age stereotypes in the workplace: Common stereotypes, moderators, and future research directions. *Journal of Management, 35*, 158–188.

Poti, J. M., & Popkin, B. M. (2011). Trends in energy intake among U.S. children by eating location and food source, 1977–2006. *Journal of the American Dietetic Association, 111*, 1156–1164.

Poulin-Dubois, D., Serbin, L. A., Eichstedt, J. A., Sen, M. G., & Beissel, C. F. (2002). Men don't put on make-up: Toddlers' knowledge of the gender stereotyping of household activities. *Social Development, 11*, 166–181.

Powdthavee, N. (2008). Putting a price tag on friends, relatives, and neighbors: Using surveys of life satisfaction to value social relationships. *Journal of Socio-economics, 37*, 1459–1480.

Powlishta, K. K., Serbin, L. A., & Moller, L. C. (1993). The stability of individual differences in gender typing: Implications for understanding gender segregation. *Sex Roles, 29*, 723–737.

Prager, K. J., & Bailey, J. M. (1985). Androgyny, ego development, and psychological crisis resolution. *Sex Roles, 13*, 525–535.

Pratt, M. W., Norris, J. E., Hebblethwaite, S., & Arnold, M. L. (2008). Intergenerational transmission of values: Family generativity and adolescents' narratives of parent and grandparent value teaching. *Journal of Personality, 76*, 171–198.

Pratt, M. W., Skoe, E. E., & Arnold, M. L. (2004). Care reasoning development and family socialization patterns in later adolescence: A longitudinal analysis. *International Journal of Behavioral Development, 28*, 139–147.

Preece, J., & Findsen, B. (2007). Keeping people active: Continuing education programs that work. In M. Robinson, W. Novelli, C. Pearson, & L. Norris (Eds.), *Global health and global aging* (pp. 313–322). San Francisco: Jossey-Bass.

Pressley, M., & Hilden, D. (2006). Cognitive strategies. In D. Kuhn & R. Siegler (Eds.), *Handbook of child psychology: Vol. 2. Cognition, perception, and language* (6th ed., pp. 511–556). Hoboken, NJ: Wiley.

Pressley, M., Wharton-McDonald, R., Raphael, L. M., Bogner, K., & Roehrig, A. (2002). Exemplary first-grade teaching. In B. M. Taylor & P. D. Pearson (Eds.), *Teaching reading: Effective schools, accomplished teachers* (pp. 73–88). Mahwah, NJ: Erlbaum.

Prevatt, F. (2003). Dropping out of school: A review of intervention programs. *Journal of School Psychology, 41,* 377–399.

Previc, F. H. (1991). A general theory concerning the prenatal origins of cerebral lateralization. *Psychological Review, 98,* 299–334.

Price, J., Jordan, J., Prior, L., & Parkes, J. (2011). Living through the death of a child: A qualitative study of bereaved parents' experiences. *International Journal of Nursing Studies, 48,* 1384–1392.

Priess, H. A., Lindberg, S. M., & Hyde, J. S. (2009). Adolescent gender-role identity and mental health: Gender intensification revisited. *Child Development, 80,* 1531–1544.

Prince, M., Bryce, R., Albanese, E., Wimo, A., Ribeiro, W., & Ferri, C. P. (2013). The global prevalence of dementia: A systematic review and meta-analysis. *Alzheimer's and Dementia, 9,* 63–75.

Prinstein, M. J., Boergers, J., & Vernberg, E. M. (2001). Overt and relational aggression in adolescents: Social–psychological adjustment of aggressors and victims. *Journal of Clinical Child Psychology, 30,* 479–491.

Prinstein, M. J., & Cillessen, A. H. N. (2003). Forms and functions of adolescent peer aggression associated with high levels of peer status. *Merrill-Palmer Quarterly, 49,* 310–342.

Prinstein, M. J., & La Greca, A. M. (2002). Peer crowd affiliation and internalizing distress in childhood and adolescence: A longitudinal follow-back study. *Journal of Research on Adolescence, 12,* 325–351.

Proctor, M. H., Moore, L. L., Gao, D., Cupples, L. A., Bradlee, M. L., Hood, M. Y., & Ellison, R. C. (2003). Television viewing and change in body fat from preschool to early adolescence: The Framingham Children's Study. *International Journal of Obesity, 27,* 827–833.

Programme for International Student Assessment. (2009). *PISA profiles by country/economy.* Retrieved from stats.oecd.org/PISA2009Profiles

Proulx, K., & Jacelon, C. (2004). Dying with dignity: The good patient versus the good death. *American Journal of Hospice and Palliative Care, 21,* 116–120.

Pruden, S. M., Hirsh-Pasek, K., Golinkoff, R. M., & Hennon, E. A. (2006). The birth of words: Ten-month-olds learn words through perceptual salience. *Child Development, 77,* 266–280.

Pryor, J. H., Hurtado, S., DeAngelo, L., Blake, L. P., & Tran, S. (2009). *The American freshman: National norms for fall 2009.* Los Angeles: Higher Education Research Institute, UCLA.

Prysak, M., Lorenz, R. P., & Kisly, A. (1995). Pregnancy outcome in nulliparous women 35 years and older. *Obstetrics and Gynecology, 85,* 65–70.

Puhl, R. M., & Heuer, C. A. (2010). Obesity stigma: Important considerations for public health. *American Journal of Public Health, 100,* 1019–1028.

Puhl, R. M., Heuer, C. A., & Brownell, D. K. (2010). Stigma and social consequences of obesity. In P. G. Kopelman, I. D. Caterson, & W. H. Dietz (Eds.), *Clinical obesity in adults and children* (3rd ed., pp. 25–40). Hoboken, NJ: Wiley.

Puhl, R. M., & Latner, J. D. (2007). Stigma, obesity, and the health of the nation's children. *Psychological Bulletin, 133,* 557–580.

Pujol, J., Soriano-Mas, C., Ortiz, H., Sebastián-Gallés, N., Losilla, J. M., & Deus, J. (2006). Myelination of language-related areas in the developing brain. *Neurology, 66,* 339–343.

Punamaki, R. L. (2006). Ante- and perinatal factors and child characteristics predicting parenting experience among formerly infertile couples during the child's first year: A controlled study. *Journal of Family Psychology, 20,* 670–679.

Putallaz, M., Grimes, C. L., Foster, K. J., Kupersmidt, J. B., Coie, J. D., & Dearing, K. (2007). Overt and relational aggression and victimization: Multiple perspectives within the school setting. *Journal of School Psychology, 45,* 523–547.

Putnam, S. P., Samson, A. V., & Rothbart, M. K. (2000). Child temperament and parenting. In V. J. Molfese & D. L. Molfese (Eds.), *Temperament and personality across the life span* (pp. 255–277). Mahwah, NJ: Erlbaum.

Pyka, G., Lindenberger, E., Charette, S., & Marcus, R. (1994). Muscle strength and fiber adaptations to a year-long resistance training program in elderly men and women. *Journal of Gerontology, 49,* M22–27.

Pyszczynski, T., Greenberg, J., Solomon, S., Arndt, J., & Schimel, J. (2004). Why do people need self-esteem? A theoretical and empirical view. *Psychological Bulletin, 130,* 435–468.

Q

Qian, Z., & Lichter, D. T. (2011). Changing patterns of interracial marriage in a multiracial society. *Journal of Marriage and Family, 73,* 1065–1084.

Quill, T. E. (1991). Death and dignity: A case of individualized decision making. *New England Journal of Medicine, 324,* 691–694.

Quine, S., Wells, Y., de Vaus, D., & Kendig, H. (2007). When choice in retirement decisions is missing: Qualitative and quantitative findings of impact on well-being. *Australasian Journal on Ageing, 26,* 173–179.

Quinn, P. C. (2008). In defense of core competencies, quantitative change, and continuity. *Child Development, 79,* 1633–1638.

Quinn, P. C., Kelly, D. J., Lee, K., Pascalis, O., & Slater, A. (2008). Preference for attractive faces extends beyond conspecifics. *Developmental Science, 11,* 76–83.

Quinn, P. C., Yahr, J., Kuhn, A., Slater, A. M., & Pascalis, O. (2002). Representation of the gender of human faces by infants: A preference for female. *Perception, 31,* 1109–1121.

R

Raaijmakers, Q. A. W., Engels, R. C. M. E., & van Hoof, A. (2005). Delinquency and moral reasoning in adolescence and young adulthood. *International Journal of Behavioral Development, 29,* 247–258.

Rabbitt, P., Lunn, M., & Wong, D. (2008). Death, dropout, and longitudinal measurements of cognitive change in old age. *Journal of Gerontology, 63B,* P271–P278.

Rabig, J., Thomas, W., Kane, R., Cutler, L. J., & McAlilly, S. (2006). Radical redesign of nursing homes: Applying the Green House concept in Tupelo, Mississippi. *Gerontologist, 46,* 533–539.

Radler, B. T., & Ryff, C. D. (2010). Who participates? Accounting for longitudinal retention in the MIDUS national study of health and well-being. *Journal of Aging and Health, 22,* 307–331.

Ragow-O'Brien, D., Hayslip, B., Jr., & Guarnaccia, C. A. (2000). The impact of hospice on attitudes toward funerals and subsequent bereavement adjustment. *Omega, 41,* 291–305.

Rahman, Q., & Wilson, G. D. (2003). Born gay? The psychobiology of human sexual orientation. *Personality and Individual Differences, 34,* 1337–1382.

Raikes, H. A., Robinson, J. L., Bradley, R. H., Raikes, H. H., & Ayoub, C. C. (2007). Developmental trends in self-regulation among low-income toddlers. *Social Development, 16,* 128–149.

Raikes, H. A., & Thompson, R. A. (2006). Family emotional climate, attachment security, and young children's emotion knowledge in a high-risk sample. *British Journal of Developmental Psychology, 24,* 89–104.

Raikes, H. H., Chazan-Cohen, R., Love, J. M., & Brooks-Gunn, J. (2010). Early Head Start impacts at age 3 and a description of the age 5 follow-up study. In A. J. Reynolds, A. J. Rolnick, M. M. Englund, & J. Temple (Eds.), *Childhood programs and practices in the first decade of life: A human capital integration* (pp. 99–118). New York: Cambridge University Press.

Räikkönen, K., Matthews, K. A., Flory, J. D., Owens, J. F., & Gump, B. B. (1999). Effects of optimism, pessimism, and trait anxiety on ambulatory blood pressure and mood during everyday life. *Journal of Personality and Social Psychology, 76,* 104–113.

Rait, G., Walters, K., Bottomley, C., Petersen, I., Iliffe, S., & Nazareth, I. (2010). Survival of people with clinical diagnosis of dementia in primary care: Cohort study. *British Medical Journal, 341,* c3584.

Rakison, D. H. (2005). Developing knowledge of objects' motion properties in infancy. *Cognition, 96,* 183–214.

Rakison, D. H. (2006). Make the first move: How infants learn about self-propelled objects. *Developmental Psychology, 42,* 900–912.

Rakison, D. H. (2010). Perceptual categorization and concepts in infancy. In J. G. Bremner & T. D. Wachs (Eds.), *Wiley-Blackwell handbook of infant development* (2nd ed., pp. 243–270). Oxford, UK: Wiley.

Rakison, D. H., & Lupyan, G. (2008). Developing object concepts in infancy: An associative learning perspective. *Monographs of the Society for Research in Child Development, 73*(1, Serial No. 289).

Rakoczy, H., Tomasello, M., & Striano, T. (2004). Young children know that trying is not pretending: A test of the "behaving-as-if" construal of children's early concept of pretense. *Developmental Psychology, 40,* 388–399.

Rakoczy, H., Tomasello, M., & Striano, T. (2005). How children turn objects into symbols: A cultural learning account. In L. Namy (Ed.), *Symbol use and symbol representation* (pp. 67–97). New York: Erlbaum.

Ralston, S. H., & Uitterlinden, A. G. (2010). Genetics of osteoporosis. *Endocrine Reviews, 31,* 629–662.

Ramaswami, A., & Dreher, G. F. (2007). The benefits associated with workplace mentoring relationships. In T. D. Allen & L. T. Eby (Eds.), *Blackwell handbook of mentoring: A multiple perspectives approach* (pp. 211–231). Malden, MA: Blackwell.

Ramaswami, A., Dreher, G. F., Bretz, R., & Wiethoff, C. (2010). Gender, mentoring, and career success: The importance of organizational context. *Personnel Psychology, 63,* 385–405.

Ramchandani, P. G., Stein, A., O'Connor, T. G., Heron, J., Murray, L., & Evans, J. (2008). Depression in men in the postnatal period and later child psychopathology: A population cohort study. *Journal of the American Academy of Child and Adolescent Psychiatry, 47,* 390–398.

Ramey, C. T., Ramey, S. L., & Lanzi, R. G. (2006). Children's health and education. In K. A. Renninger & I. E. Sigel (Eds.), *Handbook of child psychology: Vol. 4. Child psychology in practice* (6th ed., pp. 864–892). Hoboken, NJ: Wiley.

Ramirez, A., & Zhang, S. (2007). When online meets offline: The effect of modality switching on relational communication. *Communication Monographs, 74,* 287–310.

Ramos, E., Frontera, W. R., Llorpart, A., & Feliciano, D. (1998). Muscle strength and hormonal levels in adolescents: Gender related differences. *International Journal of Sports Medicine, 19,* 526–531.

Ramos, M. C., Guerin, D. W., Gottfried, A. W., Bathurst, K., & Oliver, P. H. (2005). Family conflict and children's behavior problems: The moderating role of child temperament. *Structural Equation Modeling, 12,* 278–298.

Rampell, C. (2010, March 9). The gender wage gap, around the world. *New York Times online.* Retrieved from economix.blogs.nytimes.com/2010/03/09/the-gender-wage-gap-around-the-world

Ramsey-Rennels, J. L., & Langlois, J. H. (2006). Differential processing of female and male faces. *Current Directions in Psychological Science, 15,* 59–62.

Ramus, F. (2002). Language discrimination by newborns: Teasing apart phonotactic, rhythmic, and intonational cues. *Annual Review of Language Acquisition, 2,* 85–115.

Rando, T. A. (1995). Grief and mourning: Accommodating to loss. In H. Wass & R. A. Neimeyer (Eds.), *Dying: Facing the facts* (3rd ed., pp. 211–241). Washington, DC: Taylor & Francis.

Raqib, R., Alam, D. S., Sarker, P., Ahmad, S. M., Ara, G., & Yunus, M. (2007). Low birth weight is associated with altered immune function in rural Bangladeshi children: A birth cohort study. *American Journal of Clinical Nutrition, 85,* 845–852.

Rasmussen, C., Ho, E., & Bisanz, J. (2003). Use of the mathematical principle of inversion in young children. *Journal of Experimental Child Psychology, 85,* 89–102.

Rasmussen, E. R., Neuman, R. J., Heath, A. C., Levy, F., Hay, D. A., & Todd, R. D. (2004). Familial clustering of latent class and DSM-IV defined attention-deficit hyperactivity disorder (ADHD) subtypes. *Journal of Child Psychology and Psychiatry, 45,* 589–598.

Rathunde, K., & Csikszentmihalyi, M. (2005). The social context of middle school: Teachers, friends, and activities in Montessori and traditional school environments. *Elementary School Journal, 106,* 59–79.

Rauber, M. (2006, May 18). Parents aren't sitting still as recess disappears. *Parents in Action.* Retrieved from http://healthyschoolscampaign.org/news/media/food/2006-05_recess_disappears.php

Ravid, D., & Tolchinsky, L. (2002). Developing linguistic literacy: A comprehensive model. *Journal of Child Language, 29,* 417–447.

Ravitch, D. (2010). *The death and life of the great American school system: How testing and choice are undermining education.* New York: Basic Books.

Rawlins, W. K. (2004). Friendships in later life. In J. F. Nussbaum & J. Coupland (Eds.), *Handbook of communication and aging research* (2nd ed., pp. 273–299). Mahwah, NJ: Erlbaum.

Rayner, K., Pollatsek, A., & Starr, M. S. (2003). Reading. In A. F. Healy & R. W. Proctor (Eds.), *Handbook of psychology: Experimental psychology* (Vol. 4, pp. 549–574). New York: Wiley.

Raz, N., Ghisletta, P., Rodrigue, K. M., Kennedy, K. M., & Lindenberger, U. (2010). Trajectories of brain aging in middle-aged and older adults: Regional and individual differences. *NeuroImage, 51,* 501–511.

Reay, A. C., & Browne, K. D. (2008). Elder abuse and neglect. In B. Woods & L. Clare (Eds.), *Handbook of the clinical psychology of ageing* (pp. 311–322). Chichester, UK: Wiley.

Reddin, J. (1997). High-achieving women: Career development patterns. In H. S. Farmer (Ed.), *Diversity and women's career development* (pp. 95–126). Thousand Oaks, CA: Sage.

Redman, L. M., Martin, C. K., Williamson, D. A., & Ravussin, E. (2008). Effect of caloric restriction in non-obese humans on physiological, psychological and behavioral outcomes. *Physiology and Behavior, 94,* 643–648.

Redman, L. M., & Ravussin, E. (2011). Caloric restriction in humans: Impact on physiological, psychological, and behavioral outcomes. *Antioxidants & Redox Signaling, 14,* 275–287.

Reich, S. M., Subrahmanyam, K., & Espinoza, G. (2012). Friending, IMing, and hanging out face-to-face: Overlap in adolescents' online and offline social networks. *Developmental Psychology, 48,* 356–368.

Reid, H. M., & Fine, A. (1992). Self-disclosure in men's friendships: Variations associated with intimate relations. In P. M. Nardi (Ed.), *Men's friendships* (pp. 153–171). Newbury Park, CA: Sage.

Reid, K. F., & Fielding, R. A. (2012). Skeletal muscle power: A critical determinant of physical functioning in older adults. *Exercise and Sports Sciences Reviews, 40,* 4–12.

Reis, O., & Youniss, J. (2004). Patterns in identity change and development in relationships with mothers and friends. *Journal of Adolescent Research, 19,* 31–44.

Reis, S. M. (2004). We can't change what we don't recognize: Understanding the special needs of gifted females. In S. Baum (Ed.), *Twice-exceptional and special populations of gifted students* (pp. 67–80). Thousand Oaks, CA: Corwin Press.

Reiss, D. (2003). Child effects on family systems: Behavioral genetic strategies. In A. C. Crouter & A. Booth (Eds.), *Children's influence on family dynamics: The neglected side of family relationships* (pp. 3–36). Mahwah, NJ: Erlbaum.

Reiss, N. S., & Tishler, C. L. (2008). Suicidality in nursing home residents: Part II. Prevalence, risk factors, methods, assessment, and management. *Professional Psychology: Research and Practice, 39,* 271–275.

Reitzes, D. C., & Mutran, E. J. (2002). Self-concept as the organization of roles: Importance, centrality, and balance. *Sociological Quarterly, 43,* 647–667.

Reitzes, D. C., & Mutran, E. J. (2004). Grandparenthood: Factors influencing frequency of grandparent–grandchildren contact and grandparent role satisfaction. *Journal of Gerontology, 59,* S9–S16.

Repacholi, B. M., & Gopnik, A. (1997). Early reasoning about desires: Evidence from 14- and 18-month-olds. *Developmental Psychology, 33,* 12–21.

Reppucci, N. D., Meyer, J. R., & Kostelnik, J. O. (2011). Tales of terror from juvenile justice and education. In M. S. Aber, K. I. Maton, & E. Seidman (Eds.), *Empowering settings and voices for social change* (pp. 155–172). New York: Oxford University Press.

Resnick, M., & Silverman, B. (2005). *Some reflections on designing construction kits for kids.* Proceedings of the Conference on Interaction Design and Children, Boulder, CO.

Rest, J. R. (1979). *Development in judging moral issues.* Minneapolis: University of Minnesota Press.

Reuter-Lorenz, P. A., & Cappell, K. A. (2008). Neurocognitive aging and the compensation hypothesis. *Current Directions in Psychological Science, 17,* 177–182.

Reyes-Ortiz, C. A., Kuo, Y.-F., DiNuzzo, A. R., Ray, L. A., Raji, M. A., & Markides, K. S. (2005). Near vision impairment predicts cognitive decline: Data from the Hispanic established populations for epidemiologic studies of the elderly. *Journal of the American Geriatric Society, 53,* 681–686.

Reyna, V. F., & Farley, F. (2006). Risk and rationality in adolescent decision making: Implications for theory, practice, and public policy. *Psychological Science in the Public Interest, 7,* 1–44.

Rhoades, B. L., Greenberg, M. T., & Domitrovich, C. E. (2009). The contribution of inhibitory control to preschoolers' social-emotional competence. *Journal of Applied Developmental Psychology, 30,* 310–320.

Rhoades, G. K., Stanley, S. M., & Markman, H. J. (2006). Pre-engagement cohabitation and gender asymmetry in marital commitment. *Journal of Family Psychology, 20,* 553–560.

Rhone, M., & Basu, A. (2008). Phytochemicals and age-related eye diseases. *Nutrition Reviews, 66,* 465–472.

Richardson, H. L., Walker, A. M., & Horne, R. S. C. (2008). Sleep position alters arousal processes maximally at the high-risk age for sudden infant death syndrome. *Journal of Sleep Research, 17,* 450–457.

Richardson, H. L., Walker, A. M., & Horne, R. S. C. (2009). Maternal smoking impairs arousal patterns in sleeping infants. *Pediatric Sleep, 32,* 515–521.

Richardson, V. E. (2007). A dual process model of grief counseling: Findings from the changing lives of older couples (CLOC) study. *Journal of Gerontological Social Work, 48,* 311–329.

Richie, B. S., Fassinger, R. E., Linn, S. G., Johnson, J., Prosser, J., & Robinson, S. (1997). Persistence, connection, and passion: A qualitative study of the career development of highly achieving African American–black and white women. *Journal of Counseling Psychology, 44,* 133–148.

Richler, J., Luyster, R., Risi, S., Hsu, W.-L., Dawson, G., & Bernier, R. (2006). Is there a "regressive phenotype" of autism spectrum disorder associated with the measles-mumps-rubella vaccine? A CPEA study. *Journal of Autism and Developmental Disorders, 36,* 299–316.

Richmond, J., Colombo, M., & Hayne, H. (2007). Interpreting visual preferences in the visual paired-comparison task. *Journal of Experimental Psychology: Learning, Memory, and Cognition, 33,* 823–831.

Rideout, V., & Hamel, E. (2006). *The media family: Electronic media in the lives of infants, toddlers, preschoolers and their parents.* Menlo Park, CA: Henry J. Kaiser Family Foundation.

Rideout, V. J., Foehr, U. G., & Roberts, D. F. (2010). *Generation M2: Media in the lives of 8- to 18-year-olds.* Menlo Park. CA: Henry J. Kaiser Family Foundation.

Riediger, M., Li, S.-C., & Lindenberger, U. (2006). Selection, optimization, and compensation as developmental mechanisms of adaptive resource allocation: Review and preview. In J. E. Birren & K. W., Schaire (Eds.), *Handbook of the psychology of aging* (6th ed.) (pp. 289–313). Burlington, MA: Academic Press.

Riley, J. R., & Masten, A. S. (2004). Resilience in context. In R. D. Peters, B. Leadbeater, & R. McMahon (Eds.), *Resilience in children, families, and communities: Linking context to practice and policy* (pp. 13–25). New York: Kluwer Academic.

Riley, L. D., & Bowen, C. P. (2005). The sandwich generation: Challenges and coping strategies of multigenerational families. *Counseling and Therapy for Couples and Families, 13,* 52–58.

Rinaldo, L. A., & Ferraro, K. F. (2012). Inequality, health. In G. Ritzer (Ed.), *Wiley-Blackwell encyclopedia of globalization.* Hoboken, NJ: Wiley-Blackwell.

Ripple, C. H., & Zigler, E. (2003). Research, policy, and the federal role in prevention initiatives for children. *American Psychologist, 58,* 482–490.

Ritchie, L. D., Spector, P., Stevens, M. J., Schmidt, M. M., Schreiber, G. B., Striegel-Moore, R. H., et al. (2007). Dietary patterns in adolescence are related to adiposity in young adulthood in black and white females. *Journal of Nutrition, 137,* 399–406.

Riva, D., & Giorgi, C. (2000). The cerebellum contributes to higher functions during development: Evidence from a series of children surgically treated for posterior fossa tumours. *Brain, 123,* 1051–1061.

Rivlin, R. S. (2007). Keeping the young–elderly healthy: Is it too late to improve our health through nutrition? *American Journal of Clinical Nutrition, 86*(Suppl.), 1572S–1576S.

Rizvi, S. I., & Jha, R. (2011). Strategies for the discovery of anti-aging compounds. *Expert Opinion on Drug Discovery, 6,* 89–102.

Rizzolatti, G., & Craighero, L. (2004). The mirror-neuron system. *Annual Review of Neuroscience, 27,* 169–192.

Roberts, B. W., & DelVecchio, W. E. (2000). The rank-order consistency of personality traits from childhood to old age: A quantitative review of longitudinal studies. *Psychological Bulletin, 126,* 3–25.

Roberts, B. W., Kuncel, N., Shiner, R., Caspi, A., & Goldberg, L. R. (2007). The power of personality: A comparative analysis of the predictive validity of personality traits, SES, and IQ. *Perspectives on Psychological Science, 2,* 313–345.

Roberts, B. W., & Mroczek, D. (2008). Personality and trait change in adulthood. *Current Directions in Psychological Science, 17,* 31–35.

Roberts, B. W., Walton, K. E., & Viechtbauer, W. (2006). Patterns of mean-level change in personality traits across the life course: A meta-analysis of longitudinal studies. *Psychological Bulletin, 132,* 3–25.

Roberts, D. F., Henriksen, L., & Foehr, U. G. (2004). Adolescents and media. In R. M. Lerner & L. Steinberg (Eds.), *Handbook of adolescent psychology* (2nd ed., pp. 627–664). Hoboken, NJ: Wiley.

Roberts, D. F., Henriksen, L., & Foehr, U. G. (2009). Adolescence, adolescents, and media. In R. M. Lerner & L. Steinberg (Eds.), *Handbook of adolescent psychology: Vol. 2. Contextual influences on adolescent development* (3rd ed., pp. 314–344). Hoboken, NJ: Wiley.

Roberts, J. E., Burchinal, M. R., & Durham, M. (1999). Parents' report of vocabulary and grammatical development of American preschoolers: Child and environment associations. *Child Development, 70,* 92–106.

Roberts, P. (2006). From my space to our space: The functions of Web memorials in bereavement. *The Forum, 32,* 1–4.

Robertson, J. (2008). Stepfathers in families. In J. Pryor (Ed.), *International handbook of stepfamilies: Policy and practice in legal, research, and clinical environments* (pp. 125–150). Hoboken, NJ: Wiley.

Robertson, K. F., Smeets, S., Lubinski, D., & Benbow, C. P. (2010). Beyond the threshold hypothesis: Even among the gifted and top math/science graduate students, cognitive abilities, vocational interests, and lifestyle preferences matter for career choice, performance, and persistence. *Current Directions in Psychological Science, 19,* 346–351.

Robin, A. L., & Le Grange, D. (2010). Family therapy for adolescents with anorexia nervosa. In J. R. Weisz & A. E. Kazdin (Eds.), *Evidence-based psychotherapies for children and adolescents* (2nd ed., pp. 359–374). New York: Guilford.

Robinson, C. C., Anderson, G. T., Porter, C. L., Hart, C. H., & Wouden-Miller, M. (2003). Sequential transition patterns of preschoolers' social interactions during child-initiated play: Is parallel-aware play a bi-directional bridge to other play states? *Early Childhood Research Quarterly, 18,* 3–21.

Robinson, K. M. (2010). Policy issues in mental health among the elderly. *Nursing Clinics of North America, 45,* 627–634.

Robinson, S., Goddard, L., Dritschel, B., Wisley, M., & Howlin, P. (2009). Executive functions in children with autism spectrum disorders. *Brain and Cognition, 71,* 362–368.

Robles, T. F., & Carroll, J. E. (2011). Restorative biological processes and health. *Social and Personality Psychology Compass, 5,* 518–537.

Roca, A. Carcia-Esteve, L., Imaz, M. L., Torres, A., Hernández, S., & Botet, F. (2011). Obstetrical and neonatal outcomes after prenatal exposure to selective serotonin reuptake inhibitors: The relevance of dose. *Journal of Affective Disorders, 135,* 208–215.

Rochat, P. (1989). Object manipulation and exploration in 2- to 5-month-old infants. *Developmental Psychology, 25,* 871–884.

Rochat, P. (2003). Five levels of self-awareness as they unfold early in life. *Consciousness and Cognition, 12,* 717–731.

Rochat, P., & Goubet, N. (1995). Development of sitting and reaching in 5- to 6-month-old infants. *Infant Behavior and Development, 18,* 53–68.

Rochat, P., & Hespos, S. J. (1997). Differential rooting responses by neonates: Evidence for an early sense of self. *Early Development and Parenting, 6,* 105–112.

Rochat, P., & Striano, T. (2002). Who's in the mirror? Self–other discrimination in specular images by four- and nine-month-old infants. *Infant and Child Development, 11,* 289–303.

Rochat, P., Striano, T., & Blatt, L. (2002). Differential effects of happy, neutral, and sad still-faces on 2-, 4-, and 6-month-old infants. *Infant and Child Development, 11,* 289–303.

Rodkin, P. C., Farmer, T. W., Pearl, R., & Van Acker, R. (2000). Heterogeneity of popular boys: Antisocial and prosocial configurations. *Developmental Psychology, 36,* 14–24.

Rodrigue, K. M., & Kennedy, K. M. (2011). The cognitive consequences of structural changes to the aging brain. In K. W. Schaie & S. L. Willis (Eds.), *Handbook of the psychology of aging* (7th ed., pp. 73–91). San Diego, CA: Academic Press.

Rodríguez, B., & López, M. J. R. (2011). El "nido repleto": La resolución de conflictos familiares cuando los hijos mayores se quedan en el hogar. [The "full nest": The resolution of family conflicts when older children remain in the home.] *Cultura y Educación, 23,* 89–104.

Roelfsema, N. M., Hop, W. C., Boito, S. M., & Wladimiroff, J. W. (2004). Three-dimensional sonographic measurement of normal fetal brain volume during the second half of pregnancy. *American Journal of Obstetrics and Gynecology, 190,* 275–280.

Roeser, R. W., Eccles, J. S., & Freedman-Doan, C. (1999). Academic functioning and mental health in adolescence: Patterns, progressions, and routes from childhood. *Journal of Adolescent Research, 14,* 135–174.

Rogers, W. A., & Fisk, A. D. (2005). Aware home technology: Potential benefits for older adults. *Public Policy and Aging Report, 15*(4), 28–30.

Rogoff, B. (1998). Cognition as a collaborative process. In D. Kuhn & R. S. Siegler (Eds.), *Handbook of child psychology: Vol. 2. Cognition, perception, and language* (5th ed., pp. 679–744). New York: Wiley.

Rogoff, B. (2003). *The cultural nature of human development.* New York: Oxford University Press.

Rogoff, B., & Chavajay, P. (1995). What's become of research on the cultural basis of cognitive development? *American Psychologist, 50,* 859–877.

Rogoff, B., Malkin, C., & Gibride, K. (1984). Interaction with babies as guidance in development. In B. Rogoff & J. V. Wertsch (Eds.), *Children's learning in the "zone of proximal development" (New directions for child development,* No. 23, pp. 31–44). San Francisco: Jossey-Bass.

Rogoff, B., Paradise, R., Arauz, R. M., Correa-Chávez, M., & Angelillo, C. (2003). Firsthand learning through intent participation. *Annual Review of Psychology, 54,* 175–203.

Rogoff, B., & Waddell, K. J. (1982). Memory for information organized in a scene by children from two cultures. *Child Development, 53,* 1224–1228.

Rogol, A. D., Roemmich, J. N., & Clark, P. A. (2002). Growth at puberty. *Journal of Adolescent Health, 31,* 192–200.

Rohner, R. P., & Veneziano, R. A. (2001). The importance of father love: History and contemporary evidence. *Review of General Psychology, 5,* 382–405.

Roid, G. (2003). *The Stanford-Binet Intelligence Scales, Fifth Edition, interpretive manual.* Itasca, IL: Riverside Publishing.

Roisman, G. I., Madsen, S. D., Hennighausen, K. H., Sroufe, L. A., & Collins, W. A. (2001). The coherence of dyadic behavior across parent–child and romantic relationships as mediated by the internalized representation of experience. *Attachment and Human Development, 3,* 156–172.

Roisman, G. I., Padron, E., Sroufe, L. A., & Egeland, B. (2002). Earned-secure attachment status in retrospect and prospect. *Child Development, 73,* 1204–1219.

Rokach, A. (2001). Perceived causes of loneliness in adulthood. *Journal of Social Behavior and Personality, 15,* 67–84.

Rokach, A. (2003). Strategies of coping with loneliness throughout the lifespan. In N. J. Pallone (Ed.), *Love, romance, sexual interaction: Research perspectives from current psychology* (pp. 225–344). New Brunswick, NJ: Transaction.

Rokach, R., Cohen, O., & Dreman, S. (2004). Who pulls the trigger? Who initiates divorce among over 45-year-olds. *Journal of Divorce and Remarriage, 42,* 61–83.

Romano, E., Babchishin, L., Pagani, L. S., & Kohen, D. (2010). School readiness and later achievement: Replication and exgtension using a nationwide Canadian survey. *Developmental Psychology, 46,* 995–1007.

Rome-Flanders, T., & Cronk, C. (1995). A longitudinal study of infant vocalizations during mother–infant games. *Journal of Child Language, 22,* 259–274.

Romero, A. J., & Roberts, R. E. (2003). The impact of multiple dimensions of ethnic identity on discrimination and adolescents' self-esteem. *Journal of Applied Social Psychology, 33,* 2288–2305.

Rönnqvist, L., & Domellöf, E. (2006). Quantitative assessment of right and left reaching movements in infants: A longitudinal study from 6 to 36 months. *Developmental Psychobiology, 48,* 444–459.

Roopnarine, J. L., & Evans, M. E. (2007). Family structural organization, mother–child and father–child relationships and psychological outcomes in English-speaking African Caribbean and Indo Caribbean families. In M. Sutherland (Ed.), *Psychological of development in the Caribbean.* Kingston, Jamaica: Ian Randle.

Roopnarine, J. L., Hossain, Z., Gill, P., & Brophy, H. (1994). Play in the East Indian context. In J. L. Roopnarine, J. E. Johnson, & F. H. Hooper (Eds.), *Children's play in diverse cultures* (pp. 9–30). Albany: State University of New York Press.

Roopnarine, J. L., Krishnakumar, A., Metindogan, A., & Evans, M. (2006). Links between parenting styles, parent–child academic interaction, parent–school interaction, and early academic skills and social behaviors in young children of English-speaking Caribbean immigrants. *Early Childhood Research Quarterly, 21,* 238–252.

Roopnarine, J. L., Talukder, E., Jain, D., Joshi, P., & Srivastav, P. (1990). Characteristics of holding, patterns of play, and social behaviors between parents and infants in New Delhi, India. *Developmental Psychology, 26,* 667–673.

Rosander, K., & von Hofsten, C. (2004). Infants' emerging ability to represent occluded object motion. *Cognition, 91,* 1–22.

Rose, A. J., Carlson, W., & Waller, E. M. (2007). Prospective associations of co-rumination with friendship and emotional adjustment: Considering the socioemotional trade-offs of corumination. *Developmental Psychology, 43,* 1019–1031.

Rose, A. J., Swenson, L. P., & Waller, E. M. (2004). Overt and relational aggression and perceived popularity:

Developmental differences in concurrent and prospective relations. *Developmental Psychology, 40,* 378–387.

Rose, S. A., Feldman, J. F., & Jankowski, J. J. (2001). Attention and recognition memory in the 1st year of life: A longitudinal study of preterm and full-term infants. *Developmental Psychology, 37,* 135–151.

Rose, S. A., Jankowski, J. J., & Senior, G. J. (1997). Infants' recognition of contour-deleted figures. *Journal of Experimental Psychology: Human Perception and Performance, 23,* 1206–1216.

Rosen, A. B., & Rozin, P. (1993). Now you see it, now you don't: The preschool child's conception of invisible particles in the context of dissolving. *Developmental Psychology, 29,* 300–311.

Rosen, C. S., & Cohen, M. (2010). Subgroups of New York City children at high risk of PTSD after the September 11 attacks: A signal detection analysis. *Psychiatric Services, 61,* 64–69.

Rosen, D. (2003). Eating disorders in children and young adolescents: Etiology, classification, clinical features, and treatment. *Adolescent Medicine: State of the Art Reviews, 14,* 49–59.

Rosen, S., Bergman, M., & Plester, D. (1962). Presbycusis study of a relatively noise-free population in the Sudan. *Transactions of the American Otological Society, 50,* 135–152.

Rosenbaum, J. E. (2009). Patient teenagers? A comparison of the sexual behavior of virginity pledgers and matched nonpledgers. *Pediatrics, 123,* e110–e120.

Rosenblatt, P. C. (2008). Grief across cultures: A review and research agenda. In M. S. Stroebe, R. O. Hansson, H. Schut, & W. Stroebe (Eds.), *Handbook of bereavement research and practice* (pp. 207–222). Washington, DC: American Psychological Association.

Rosenman, R. H., Brand, R. J., Jenkins, C. D., Friedman, M., Strauss, R., & Wurm, M. (1975). Coronary heart disease in the Western Collaborative Group Study: Final follow-up experience of 8½ years. *Journal of the American Medical Association, 223,* 872–877.

Rosenstein, D. L. (2011). Depression and end-of-life care for patients with cancer. *Dialogues in Clinical Neuroscience, 13,* 101–108.

Roseth, C. J., Pellegrini, A. D., Bohn, C. M., van Ryzin, M., & Vance, N. (2007). Preschoolers' aggression, affiliation, and social dominance relationships: An observational, longitudinal study. *Journal of School Psychology, 45,* 479–497.

Rosetta, L., & Baldi, A. (2008). On the role of breastfeeding in health promotion and the prevention of allergic diseases. *Advances in Experimental Medicine and Biology, 606,* 467–483.

Ross, C. E., & Sastry, J. (1999). The sense of personal control: Social-structural causes and emotional consequences. In C. S. Aneshensel & J. C. Phelan (Eds.), *Handbook of the sociology of mental health* (pp. 369–394). New York: Springer.

Rossen, E. K., Knafl, K. A., & Flood, M. (2008). Older women's perceptions of successful aging. *Activities, Adaptation and Aging, 32,* 73–88.

Rossi, A. S. (2005). The menopausal transition and aging processes. In O. G. Brim, C. D. Ryff, & R. C. Kessler (Eds.), *How healthy are we? A national study of well-being at midlife* (pp. 153–201). Chicago: University of Chicago Press.

Rothbart, M. K. (2003). Temperament and the pursuit of an integrated developmental psychology. *Merrill-Palmer Quarterly, 50,* 492–505.

Rothbart, M. K., Ahadi, S. A., & Evans, D. E. (2000). Temperament and personality: Origins and outcome. *Journal of Personality and Social Psychology, 78,* 122–135.

Rothbart, M. K., & Bates, J. E. (2006). Temperament. In N. Eisenberg (Ed.), *Handbook of child psychology: Vol. 3. Social, emotional, and personality development* (6th ed., pp. 99–166). Hoboken, NJ: Wiley.

Rothbart, M. K., Posner, M. I., & Kieras, J. (2006). Temperament, attention, and the development of self-regulation. In K. McCartney & D. Phillips (Eds.), *Blackwell handbook of early childhood development* (pp. 338–357). Malden, MA: Blackwell.

Rothbaum, F., Kakinuma, M., Nagaoka, R., & Azuma, H. (2007). Attachment and amae: Parent–child closeness in the United States and Japan. *Journal of Cross-Cultural Psychology, 38,* 465–486.

Rothbaum, F., Pott, M., Azuma, H., Miyake, K., & Weisz, J. (2000a). The development of close relationships in Japan and the United States: Paths of symbiotic harmony and generative tension. *Child Development, 71,* 1121–1142.

Rothblum, E. D., Balsam, K. F., & Solomon, S. E. (2011). The longest "legal" U.S. same-sex couples reflect on their relationships. *Journal of Social Issues, 67,* 302–315.

Rothman, S. M., & Mattson, M. P. (2012). Sleep disturbances in Alzheimer's and Parkinson's diseases. *Neuromolecular Medicine, 14,* 194–204.

Routledge, C., & Juhl, J. (2010). When death thoughts lead to death fears: Mortality salience increases death anxiety for individuals who lack meaning in life. *Cognition and Emotion, 24,* 848–854.

Rovee-Collier, C. K. (1999). The development of infant memory. *Current Directions in Psychological Science, 8,* 80–85.

Rovee-Collier, C. K., & Bhatt, R. S. (1993). Evidence of long-term memory in infancy. *Annals of Child Development, 9,* 1–45.

Rovee-Collier, C. K., & Cuevas, K. (2009). Multiple memory systems are unnecessary to account for infant memory development: An ecological model. *Developmental Psychology, 45,* 160–174.

Rowe, M. L. (2008). Child-directed speech: Relation to socioeconomic status, knowledge of child development and child vocabulary skill. *Journal of Child Language, 35,* 185–205.

Rowe, M. L., & Goldin-Meadow, S. (2009). Early gesture selectively predicts later language learning. *Developmental Science, 12,* 182–187.

Rowland, C. F. (2007). Explaining errors in children's questions. *Cognition, 104,* 106–134.

Rowland, C. F., & Pine, J. M. (2000). Subject-auxiliary inversion errors and wh-question acquisition: "What children do know?" *Journal of Child Language, 27,* 157–181.

Rowley, S. J., Kurtz-Costes, B., Mistry, R., & Feagans, L. (2007). Social status as a predictor of race and gender stereotypes in late childhood and early adolescence. *Social Development, 16,* 150–168.

Roy, K. M., & Lucas, K. (2006). Generativity as second chance: Low-income fathers and transformation of the difficult past. *Research in Human Development, 3,* 139–159.

Rubenstein, L. Z., Stevens, J. A., & Scott, V. (2008). Interventions to prevent falls among older adults. In L. S. Doll, S. E. Bonzo, D. A. Sleet, J. A. Mercy, & E. N. Haas (Eds.), *Handbook of injury and violence prevention* (pp. 37–53). New York: Springer.

Rubin, C., Maisonet, M., Kieszak, S., Monteilh, C., Holmes A., Flanders, D., et al. (2009). Timing of maturation and predictors of menarche in girls enrolled in a contemporary British cohort. *Paediatric and Perinatal Epidemiology, 23,* 492–504.

Rubin, D., Downes, K., O'Reilly, A., Mekonnen, R., Luan, X., & Localio, R. (2008). Impact of kinship care on behavioral well-being for children in out of home care. *Archives of Pediatrics and Adolescent Medicine, 162,* 550–556.

Rubin, D. C. (2002). Autobiographical memory across the lifespan. In P. Graf & N. Ohta (Eds.), *Lifespan development of human memory* (pp. 159–184). Cambridge, MA: MIT Press.

Rubin, D. C., Rahhal, T. A., & Poon, L. W. (1998). Things learned in early adulthood are remembered best. *Memory and Cognition, 26,* 3–19.

Rubin, D. M., O'Reilly, A. L., Luan, X., Dai, D., Localio, A. R., et al. (2011). Variation in pregnancy outcomes following statewide implementation of a prenatal home visitation program. *Archives of Pediatrics and Adolescent Medicine, 165,* 198–204.

Rubin, K. H., Bowker, J., & Gazelle, H. (2010). Social withdrawal in childhood and adolescence: Peer relationships and social competence. In K. H. Rubin & R. J. Coplan (Eds.), *The development of shyness and social withdrawal* (pp. 131–156). New York: Guilford.

Rubin, K. H., Bukowski, W. M., & Parker, J. G. (2006). Peer interactions, relationships, and groups. In N. Eisenberg (Ed.), *Handbook of child psychology: Vol. 3. Social, emotional, and personality development* (6th ed., pp. 571–645). Hoboken, NJ: Wiley.

Rubin, K. H., & Burgess, K. B. (2002). Parents of aggressive and withdrawn children. In M. Bornstein (Ed.), *Handbook of parenting* (2nd ed., pp. 383–418). Hillsdale, NJ: Erlbaum.

Rubin, K. H., Coplan, J., Chen, X., Buskirk, A. A., & Wojslawowicz, J. C. (2005). Peer relationships in childhood. In M. H. Bornstein & M. E. Lamb (Eds.), *Developmental science: An advanced textbook* (pp. 469–512). Mahwah, NJ: Erlbaum.

Rubin, K. H., Fein, G. G., & Vandenberg, B. (1983). Play. In E. M. Hetherington (Ed.), *Handbook of child psychology: Vol. 4. Socialization, personality, and social development* (4th ed., pp. 693–744). New York: Wiley.

Rubin, K. H., Watson, K. S., & Jambor, T. W. (1978). Free-play behaviors in preschool and kindergarten children. *Child Development, 49,* 539–536.

Ruble, D. N., Alvarez, J., Bachman, M., Cameron, J., Fuligni, A., García Coll, C., & Rhee, E. (2004). The development of a sense of "we": The emergence and implications of children's collective identity. In M. Bennett & F. Sani (Eds.), *The development of the social self* (pp. 29–76). Hove, UK: Psychology Press.

Ruble, D. N., Martin, C. L., & Berenbaum, S. A. (2006). Gender development. In N. Eisenberg (Ed.), *Handbook of child psychology: Vol. 3. Social, emotional, and personality development* (6th ed., pp. 226–299). Hoboken, NJ: Wiley.

Ruble, D. N., Taylor, L. J., Cyphers, L., Greulich, F. K., Lurye, L. E., & Shrout, P. E. (2007). The role of gender constancy in early gender development. *Child Development, 78,* 1121–1136.

Rudolph, K. D., Lambert, S. F., Clark, A. G., & Kurlakowsky, K. D. (2001). Negotiating the transition to middle school: The role of self-regulatory processes. *Child Development, 72,* 929–946.

Ruff, H. A., & Capozzoli, M. C. (2003). Development of attention and distractibility in the first 4 years of life. *Developmental Psychology, 39,* 877–890.

Ruffman, T., & Langman, L. (2002). Infants' reaching in a multi-well A not B task. *Infant Behavior and Development, 25,* 237–246.

Ruffman, T., Perner, J., Olson, D. R., & Doherty, M. (1993). Reflecting on scientific thinking: Children's understanding of the hypothesis–evidence relation. *Child Development, 64,* 1617–1636.

Ruffman, T., Slade, L., Devitt, K., & Crowe, E. (2006). What mothers say and what they do: The relation between parenting, theory of mind, language, and conflict/cooperation. *British Journal of Developmental Psychology, 24,* 105–124.

Ruitenberg, A., Ott, A., van Swieten, J. C., Hofman, A., & Breteler, M. M. B. (2001). Incidence of dementia: Does gender make a difference? *Neurobiology of Aging, 22,* 575–580.

Runco, M. A. (1992). Children's divergent thinking and creative ideation. *Developmental Review, 12,* 233–264.

Runco, M. A., Cramond, B., & Pagnani, A. R. (2010). Gender and creativity. In J. C. Chrisler & D. R. McCreary (Eds.), *Handbook of gender research in psychology* (Vol. 1, pp. 343–357). New York: Springer.

Rurup, M. L., Muller, M. T., Onwuteaka-Philipsen, B. D., van der Heide, A., van der Wal, G., & van der Maas, P. J. (2005). Requests for euthanasia or physician-assisted suicide from older persons who do not have a severe disease: An interview study. *Psychological Medicine, 35,* 665–671.

Rusconi, A. (2004). Different pathways out of the parental home: A comparison of West Germany and Italy. *Journal of Comparative Family Studies, 35,* 627–649.

Rushton, J. L., Forcier, M., & Schectman, R. M. (2002). Epidemiology of depressive symptoms in the National Longitudinal Study of Adolescent Health. *Journal of the American Academy of Child and Adolescent Psychiatry, 41,* 199–205.

Rushton, J. P., & Bons, T. A. (2005). Mate choice and friendship in twins. *Psychological Science, 16,* 555–559.

Rushton, J. P., & Jensen, A. R. (2005). Thirty years of research on race differences in cognitive ability. *Psychology, Public Policy, and Law, 11,* 235–294.

Rushton, J. P., & Jensen, A. R. (2006). The totality of available evidence shows the race IQ gap still remains. *Psychological Science, 17,* 921–924.

Rushton, J. P., & Jensen, A. R. (2010). The rise and fall of the Flynn effect as a reason to expect a narrowing of the black–white IQ gap. *Intelligence, 38,* 213–219.

Russac, R. J., Gatliff, C., Reece, M., & Spottswood, D. (2007). Death anxiety across the adult years: An examination of age and gender effects. *Death Studies, 31,* 549–561.

Russell, A., Mize, J., & Bissaker, K. (2004). Parent–child relationships. In P. K. Smith & C. H. Hart (Eds.), *Blackwell handbook of childhood social development* (pp. 204–222). Malden, MA: Blackwell.

Russell, J. A. (1990). The preschooler's understanding of the causes and consequences of emotion. *Child Development, 61,* 1872–1881.

Russell, J. A., Douglas, A. J., & Ingram, C. D. (2001). Brain preparations for maternity—adaptive changes in behavioral and neuroendocrine systems during pregnancy and lactation. *Progress in Brain Research, 133,* 1–38.

Russell, R. B., Petrini, J. R., Damus, K., Mattison, D. R., & Schwarz, R. H. (2003). The changing epidemiology of multiple births in the United States. *Obstetrics and Gynecology, 101,* 129–135.

Rutland, A., Killen, M., & Abrams, D. (2010). A new social-cognitive developmental perspective on prejudice: The interplay between morality and group identity. *Perspectives on Psychological Science, 5,* 279–291.

Rutter, M. (2007). Gene–environment interdependence. *Developmental Science, 10,* 12–18.

Rutter, M. (2011). Biological and experiential influences on psychological development. In D. P. Keating (Ed.), *Nature and nurture in early child development* (pp. 7–44). New York: Cambridge University Press.

Rutter, M., Colvert, E., Kreppner, J., Beckett, C., Castle, J., & Groothues, C. (2007). Early adolescent outcomes for institutionally deprived and nondeprived adoptees. I: Disinhibited attachment. *Journal of Child Psychology and Psychiatry, 48,* 17–30.

Rutter, M., & the English and Romanian Adoptees Study Team. (1998). Developmental catch-up, and deficit, following adoption after severe global early privation. *Journal of Child Psychology and Psychiatry, 39,* 465–476.

Rutter, M., O'Connor, T. G., & English and Romanian Adoptees (ERA) Study Team. (2004). Are there biological programming effects for psychological development? Findings from a study of Romanian adoptees. *Developmental Psychology, 40,* 81–94.

Rutter, M., Pickles, A., Murray, R., & Eaves, L. (2001). Testing hypotheses on specific environmental causal effects on behavior. *Psychological Bulletin, 127,* 291–324.

Rutter, M., Sonuga-Barke, E. J, Beckett, C., Castle, J., Kreppner, J., Kumsta, R., et al. (2010). Deprivation-specific psychological patterns: Effects of institutional deprivation. *Monographs of the Society for Research in Child Development, 75*(1, Serial No. 295), 48–78.

Ryan, E. B., Jin, Y., Anas, A. P., & Luh, J. J. (2004). Communication beliefs about youth and old age in Asia and Canada. *Journal of Cross-Cultural Gerontology, 19,* 343–360.

Rybash, J. M., & Hrubi-Bopp, K. L. (2000). Isolating the neural mechanisms of age-related changes in human working memory. *Nature Neuroscience, 3,* 509–515.

Ryff, C. D. (1991). Possible selves in adulthood and old age: A tale of shifting horizons. *Psychology and Aging, 6,* 286–295.

Ryff, C. D., Friedman, E., Fuller-Rowell, T., Love, G., Miyamoto, Y., Morozink, J., et al. (2012). Varieties of resilience in MIDUS. *Social and Personality Psychology Compass, 6,* 792–806.

Ryff, C. D., & Keyes, C. L. M. (1995). The structure of psychological well-being revisited. *Journal of Personality and Social Psychology, 69,* 719–727.

Ryff, C. D., Singer, B. H., & Seltzer, M. M. (2002). Pathways through challenge: Implications for well-being and health. In L. Pulkkinen & A. Caspi (Eds.), *Paths to successful development* (pp. 302–328). Cambridge, UK: Cambridge University Press.

Rynearson, E. K., & Salloum, A. (2011). Restorative retelling: Revising the narrative of violent death. In R. A. Neimeyer, D. L. Harris, H. R. Winokuer, & G. F. Thornton (Eds.), *Grief and bereavement in contemporary society: Bridging research and practice* (pp. 177–188). New York: Routledge.

S

Saarni, C. (2000). Emotional competence: A developmental perspective. In R. Bar-On & J. D. A. Parker (Eds.), *Handbook of emotional intelligence* (pp. 68–91). San Francisco: Jossey-Bass.

Saarni, C., Campos, J. J., Camras, L. A., & Witherington, D. (2006). Emotional development: Action, communication, and understanding. In N. Eisenberg (Ed.), *Handbook of child psychology: Vol. 3. Social, emotional, and personality development* (6th ed., pp. 226–299). Hoboken, NJ: Wiley.

Sabo, D. and Veliz, P. (2011). *Progress without equity: The provision of high school athletic opportunity in the United States, by gender 1993–94 through 2005–06.* East Meadow, NY: Women's Sports Foundation.

Sacca, S. C., Bolognesi, C., Battistella, A., Bagnis, A., & Izzotti, A. (2009). Gene–environment interactions in ocular diseases. *Mutation Research, 667,* 98–117.

Sacks, P. (2005). "No child left": What are schools for in a democratic society? In S. Olfman (Ed.), *Childhood lost: How American culture is failing our kids* (pp. 185–202). Westport, CT: Praeger.

Sadeh, A. (1997). Sleep and melatonin in infants: A preliminary study. *Sleep, 20,* 185–191.

Sadeh, A., Flint-Ofir, E., Tirosh, T., & Tikotzky, L. (2007). Infant sleep and parental sleep-related cognitions. *Journal of Family Psychology, 21,* 74–87.

Sadler, P., Ethier, N., & Woody, E. (2011). Interpersonal complementarity. In L. M. Horowitz & S. Strack (Eds.), *Handbook of interpersonal psychology* (pp. 123–156). Hoboken, NJ: Wiley.

Sadler, T. W. (2010). *Langman's medical embryology* (11th ed.). Baltimore, MD: Lippincott Williams & Wilkins.

Safe Kids USA. (2008). *Report to the nation: Trends in unintentional childhood injury mortality and parental views on child safety.* Retrieved from www.safekids.org/assets/docs/ourwork/research/research-report-safe-kids-week-2008.pdf

Safe Kids USA. (2011a). *A look inside American family vehicles: National study of 79,000 car seats, 2009–2010.* Retrieved from www.safekids.org/assets/docs/safety-basics/safety-tips-by-risk-area/sk-car-seat-report-2011.pdf

Safe Kids USA. (2011b). *Injury trends fact sheet.* Retrieved from www.safekids.org/our-work/research/fact-sheets/injury-trends-fact-sheet.html

Saffran, J. R. (2009). Acquiring grammatical patterns: Constraints on learning. In J. Colombo, P. McCardle, & L. Freund (Eds.), *Infant pathways to language: Methods, models, and research disorders* (pp. 31–47). New York: Psychology Press.

Saffran, J. R., Aslin, R. N., & Newport, E. L. (1996). Statistical learning by 8-month-old infants. *Science, 27,* 1926–1928.

Saffran, J. R., & Thiessen, E. D. (2003). Pattern induction by infant language learners. *Developmental Psychology, 39,* 484–494.

Saffran, J. R., Werker, J. F., & Werner, L. A. (2006). The infant's auditory world: Hearing, speech, and the beginnings of language. In D. Kuhn & R. Siegler (Eds.), *Handbook of child psychology: Vol. 2. Cognition, perception, and language* (6th ed., pp. 58–108). Hoboken, NJ: Wiley.

Safren, S. A., & Pantalone, D. W. (2006). Social anxiety and barriers to resilience among lesbian, gay, and bisexual adolescents. In A. M. Omoto & H. S. Kurtzman (Eds.), *Sexual orientation and mental health: Examining identity and development in lesbian, gay, and bisexual young people* (pp. 55–71). Washington, DC: American Psychological Association.

Saginak, K. A., & Saginak, M. A. (2005). Balancing work and family: Equity, gender, and marital satisfaction. *Counseling and Therapy for Couples and Families, 13,* 162–166.

Sahathevan, R., Brodtmann, A., & Donnan, G. (2011). Dementia, stroke, and vascular risk factors: A review. *International Journal of Stroke, 7,* 61–73.

Sahlberg, P. (2010). Educational change in Finland. In A. Hargreaves, M. Fullan, A. Lieberman, & D. Hopkins (Eds.), *Second international handbook of educational change.* New York: Springer.

Saito, Y., Auestad, R. A., & Waerness, K. (2010). *Meeting the challenges of elder care: Japan and Norway.* Kyoto, Japan: Kyoto University Press.

Salari, S. (2011). Elder mistreatment. In R. A. Settersten, Jr., & J. L. Angel (Eds.), *Handbook of sociology of aging* (pp. 415–430). New York: Springer.

Sale, A., Berardi, N., & Maffei, L. (2009). Enrich the environment to empower the brain. *Trends in Neurosciences, 32,* 233–239.

Salerno, M., Micillo, M., Di Maio, S., Capalbo, D., Ferri, P., & Lettiero, T. (2001). Longitudinal growth, sexual maturation and final height in patients with congenital hypothyroidism detected by neonatal screening. *European Journal of Endocrinology, 145,* 377–383.

Salihu, H. M., Shumpert, M. N., Slay, M., Kirby, R. S., & Alexander, G. R. (2003). Childbearing beyond maternal age 50 and fetal outcomes in the United States. *Obstetrics and Gynecology, 102,* 1006–1014.

Salley, B. J., & Dixon, W. E., Jr. (2007). Temperamental and joint attentional predictors of language development. *Merrill-Palmer Quarterly, 53,* 131–154.

Salmivalli, C., & Voeten, M. (2004). Connections between attitudes, group norms, and behaviour in bullying situations. *International Journal of Behavioral Development, 28,* 246–258.

Salomon, J. A., Wang, H., Freeman, M. K., Vos, T., Flaxman, A. D., Lopez, A. D., et al. (2012). Healthy life expectancy for 187 countries, 1990–2010: A systematic analysis for the Global Burden Disease Study 2010. *Lancet, 380,* 2144–2162.

Salter, D., McMillan, D., Richards, M., Talbot, T., Hodges, J., Bentovim, A., & Hastings, R. (2003). Development of sexually abusive behavior in sexually victimized males: A longitudinal study. *Lancet, 361,* 471–476.

Salthouse, T. A. (1996). Constraints on theories of cognitive aging. *Psychonomic Bulletin and Review, 3,* 287–299.

Salthouse, T. A. (2006). Aging of thought. In E. Bialystok & F. I. M. Craik (Eds.), *Lifespan cognition: Mechanisms of change* (pp. 274–284). New York: Oxford University Press.

Salthouse, T. A. (2011). Neuroanatomical substrates of age-related cognitive decline. *Psychological Bulletin, 137,* 753–784.

Salthouse, T. A., & Caja, S. J. (2000). Structural constraints on process explanations in cognitive aging. *Psychology and Aging, 15,* 44–55.

Salvioli, S., Capri, M., Santoro, A., Raule, N., Sevini, F., & Lukas, S. (2008). The impact ofd mitochondrial DNA on human lifespan: A view from studies on centenarians. *Biotechnology Journal, 3,* 740–749.

Samarel, N. (1995). The dying process. In H. Wass & R. A. Neimeyer (Eds.), *Dying: Facing the facts* (3rd ed., pp. 89–116). Washington, DC: Taylor & Francis.

Samek, D. R., & Rueter, M. A. (2011). Considerations of elder sibling closeness in predicting younger sibling substance use: Social learning versus social bonding explanations. *Journal of Family Psychology, 25,* 931–941.

Sameroff, A. (2006). Identifying risk and protective factors for healthy child development. In A. Clarke-Stewart & J. Dunn (Eds.), *Families count: Effects on child and adolescent development* (pp. 53–76). New York: Cambridge University Press.

Sampselle, C. M., Harris, V., Harlow, S. D., & Sowers, M. (2002). Midlife development and menopause in African-American and Caucasian women. *Health Care for Women International, 23,* 351–363.

Sanchez, M. M., & Pollak, S. D. (2009). Socioemotional development following early abuse and neglect: Challenges and insight from translational research. In M. de Haan & M. R. Gunnar (Eds.), *Handbook of developmental social neuroscience* (pp. 497–520). New York: Guilford.

Sanders, O. (2006). *Evaluating the Keeping Ourselves Safe Programme.* Wellington, NZ: Youth Education Service, New Zealand Police. Retrieved from www.nzfvc.org.nz/accan/papers-presentations /abstract11v.shtml

Sanderson, J. A., & Siegal, M. (1988). Conceptions of moral and social rules in rejected and nonrejected preschoolers. *Journal of Clinical Child Psychology, 17,* 66–72.

Sangrigoli, S., Pallier, C., Argenti, A. M., Ventureyra, V. A. G., & de Schonen, S. (2005). Reversibility of the other-race effect in face recognition during childhood. *Psychological Science, 16,* 440–444.

San Juan, V., & Astington, J. W. (2012). Bridging the gap between implicit and explicit understanding: How language development promotes the processing and representation of false belief. *British Journal of Developmental Psychology, 30,* 105–122.

Sann, C., & Streri, A. (2007). Perception of object shape and texture in human newborns: Evidence from cross-modal transfer tasks. *Developmental Science, 10,* 399–410.

Sann, C., & Streri, A. (2008). The limits of newborn's grasping to detect texture in a cross-modal transfer task. *Infant Behavior and Development, 31,* 523–531.

Sansavini, A., Bertoncini, J., & Giovanelli, G. (1997). Newborns discriminate the rhythm of multisyllabic stressed words. *Developmental Psychology, 33,* 3–11.

Santtila, P., Wager, I., Witting, K., Harlaar, N., Jern, P., Johansson, A., Varjonen, M., & Sandnabba, K. (2008). Discrepancies between sexual desire and sexual activity: Gender differences and associations with relationship satisfaction. *Journal of Sex and Marital Therapy, 34,* 31–44.

Sanz, A., Pamplona, R., & Barja, G. (2006). Is the mitochondrial free radical theory of aging intact? *Antioxidants and Redox Signaling, 8,* 582–599.

Sarnecka, B. W., & Gelman, S. A. (2004). Six does not just mean a lot: Preschoolers see number words as specific. *Cognition, 92,* 329–352.

Satin, J. R., Linden, W., Phillips, M. J. (2009). Depression as a predictor of disease progression and mortality in cancer patients. *Cancer, 115,* 5349–5361.

Sato, T., Matsumoto, T., Kawano, H., Watanabe, T., Uematsu, Y., & Semine, K. (2004). Brain masculinization requires androgen receptor function. *Proceedings of the National Academy of Sciences, 101,* 1673–1678.

Saucier, J. F., Sylvestre, R., Doucet, H., Lambert, J., Frappier, J. Y., Charbonneau, L., & Malus, M. (2002). Cultural identity and adaptation to adolescence in Montreal. In F. J. C. Azima & N. Grizenko (Eds.), *Immigrant and refugee children and their families: Clinical, research, and training issues* (pp. 133–154). Madison, WI: International Universities Press.

Saudino, K. J. (2003). Parent ratings of infant temperament: Lessons from twin studies. *Infant Behavior and Development, 26,* 100–107.

Saunders, B. E. (2012). Determining best practice for treating sexually victimized children. In P. Goodyear-Brown (Ed.), *Handbook of child sexual abuse: Identification, assessment, and treatment* (pp. 173–198). Hoboken, NJ: Wiley.

Sautter, J. M., Thomas, P. A., Dupre, M., & George, L. K. (2012). Socioeconomic status and the black–white mortality crossover. *American Journal of Public Health, 102,* 1566–1571.

Savin-Williams, R. C. (2001). A critique of research on sexual minority youths. *Journal of Adolescence, 24,* 5–13.

Savin-Williams, R. C., & Diamond, L. M. (2004). Sex. In R. M. Lerner & L. Steinberg (Eds.), *Handbook of adolescent development* (2nd ed., pp. 189–231). Hoboken, NJ: Wiley.

Savin-Williams, R. C., & Ream, G. L. (2003). Sex variations in the disclosure to parents of same-sex attractions. *Journal of Family Psychology, 17,* 429–438.

Sawyer, A. M., & Borduin, C. M. (2011). Effects of multisystemic therapy through midlife: A 21.9-year follow-up to a randomized clinical trial with serious and violent juvenile offenders. *Journal of Consulting and Clinical Psychology, 79,* 643–652.

Sayer, L. C. (2010). Trends in housework. In J. Treas & S. Drobnic (Eds.), *Dividing the domestic: Men, women, and household work in cross-national perspective* (pp. 19–38). Stanford, CA: Stanford University Press.

Saygin, A. P., Leech, R., & Dick, F. (2010). Nonverbal auditory agnosia with lesion to Wernicke's area. *Neuropsychologia, 48,* 107–113.

Saylor, M. M. (2004). Twelve- and 16-month-old infants recognize properties of mentioned absent things. *Developmental Science, 7,* 599–611.

Saylor, M. M., Baldwin, D. A., & Sabbagh, M. A. (2005). Word learning: A complex product. In G. Hall & S. Waxman (Eds.), *Weaving a lexicon.* Cambridge, MA: MIT Press.

Saylor, M. M., & Troseth, G. L. (2006). Preschoolers use information about speakers' desires to learn new words. *Cognitive Development, 21,* 214–231.

Scarlett, W. G., & Warren, A. E. A. (2010). Religious and spiritual development across the life span: A behavioral and social science perspective. In M. Lamb & A. Freund (Eds.), *Handbook of lifespan development: Vol. 2. Social and emotional development* (pp. 631–682). Hoboken, NJ: Wiley.

Scarmeas, N., Luchsinger, J. A., Mayeux, R., & Stern, Y. (2007). Mediterranean diet and Alzheimer disease mortality. *Neurology, 69,* 1084–1093.

Scarr, S., & McCartney, K. (1983). How people make their own environments: A theory of genotype environment effects. *Child Development, 54,* 424–435.

Scarr, S., & Weinberg, R. A. (1983). The Minnesota Adoption Studies: Genetic differences and malleability. *Child Development, 54,* 260–267.

Schaal, B., Marlier, L., & Soussignan, R. (2000). Human fetuses learn odours from their pregnant mother's diet. *Chemical Senses, 25,* 729–737.

Schacht, P. M., Cummings, E. M., & Davies, P. T. (2009). Fathering in family context and child adjustment: A longitudinal analysis. *Journal of Family Psychology, 23,* 790–797.

Schäfer, S., Huxhold, O., & Lindenberger, U. (2006). Healthy mind in healthy body? A review of sensorimotor–cognitive interdependencies in old age. *European Review of Aging and Physical Activity, 3,* 45–54.

Schaie, K. W. (1994). The course of adult intellectual development. *American Psychologist, 49,* 304–313.

Schaie, K. W. (1996). *Intellectual development in adulthood: The Seattle Longitudinal Study.* New York: Cambridge University Press.

Schaie, K. W. (1998). The Seattle Longitudinal Studies of Adult Intelligence. In M. P. Lawton & T. A. Salthouse (Eds.), *Essential papers on the psychology of aging* (pp. 263–271). New York: New York University Press.

Schaie, K. W. (2005). *Developmental influences on adult intelligence: The Seattle Longitudinal Study.* New York: Oxford University Press.

Schaie, K. W. (2011). Historical influences on aging and behavior. In K. W. Schaie & S. L. Willis (Eds.), *Handbook of the psychology of aging* (7th ed., pp. 41–55). San Diego, CA: Academic Press.

Schalet, A. (2007). Adolescent sexuality viewed through two different cultural lenses. In M. S. Tepper & A. F. Owens (Eds.), *Sexual health: Vol. 3. Moral and cultural foundations* (pp. 365–387). Westport, CT: Praeger.

Scheibe, S., Freund, A. M., & Baltes, P. B. (2007). Toward a developmental psychology of Sehnsucht (life longings): The optimal (utopian) life. *Developmental Psychology, 43,* 778–795.

Schewe, P. A. (2007). Interventions to prevent sexual violence. In L. S. Doll, S. E. Bonzo, D. A. Sleet, & J. A. Mercy (Eds.), *Handbook of injury and violence prevention* (pp. 223–240). New York: Springer Science + Business Media.

Schiamberg, L. B., Barboza, G. G., Oehmke, J., Zhang, Z., Griffore, R. J., Weatherhill, R. P., et al. (2011). Elder abuse in nursing homes: An ecological perspective. *Journal of Elder Abuse and Neglect, 23,* 190–211.

Schieman, S., & Plickert, G. (2007). Functional limitations and changes in levels of depression among older adults: A multiple-hierarchy stratification perspective. *Journal of Gerontology, 62B,* S36–S42.

Schindler, H. S. (2010). The importance of parenting and financial contributions in promoting fathers' psychological health. *Journal of Marriage and Family, 72,* 318–332.

Schlaggar, B. L., & McCandliss, B. D. (2007). Development of neural systems for reading. *Annual Review of Neuroscience, 30,* 475–503.

Schlegel, A., & Barry, H., III. (1991). *Adolescence: An anthropological inquiry.* New York: Free Press.

Schlossberg, N. (2004). *Retire smart, retire happy: Finding your true path in life.* Washington, DC: American Psychological Association.

Schmidt, K.-H., Neubach, B., & Heuer, H. (2007). Self-control demands, cognitive control deficits, and burnout. *Work and Stress, 21,* 142–154.

Schmidt, L. A., Fox, N. A., Rubin, K. H., Sternberg, E. M., Gold, P. W., & Smith, C. C. (1997). Behavioral and neuroendocrine responses in shy children. *Developmental Psychobiology, 35,* 119–135.

Schmidt, L. A., Fox, N. A., Schulkin, J., & Gold, P. W. (1999). Behavioral and psychophysiological correlates of self-presentation in temperamentally shy children. *Developmental Psychobiology, 30,* 127–140.

Schmidt, L. A., Santesso, D. L., Schulkin, J., & Segalowitz, S. J. (2007). Shyness is a necessary but not sufficient condition for high salivary cortisol in typically developing 10-year-old children. *Personality and Individual Differences, 43,* 1541–1551.

Schmitt, D. P., Allik, J., McCrae, R. R., & Benet-Martínez, V. (2007). The geographic distribution of the Big Five personality traits: Patterns and profiles of human self-description across 56 countries. *Journal of Cross-Cultural Psychology, 38,* 173–212.

Schmitz, S., Fulker, D. W., Plomin, R., Zahn-Waxler, C., Emde, R. N., & DeFries, J. C. (1999). Temperament and problem behaviour during early childhood. *International Journal of Behavioural Development, 23,* 333–355.

Schneewind, K. A., & Gerhard, A. (2002). Relationship personality, conflict resolution, and marital satisfaction in the first 5 years of marriage. *Family Relations, 51,* 63–71.

Schneider, B. H., Atkinson, L., & Tardif, C. (2001). Child–parent attachment and children's peer relations: A quantitative review. *Developmental Psychology, 37,* 87–100.

Schneider, W. (2002). Memory development in childhood. In U. Goswami (Ed.), *Blackwell handbook of childhood cognitive development* (pp. 236–256). Malden, MA: Blackwell.

Schneider, W., & Bjorklund, D. F. (1992). Expertise, aptitude, and strategic remembering. *Child Development, 63,* 461–473.

Schneider, W., & Bjorklund, D. F. (1998). Memory. In D. Kuhn & R. S. Siegler (Eds.), *Handbook of child psychology: Vol. 2. Cognition, perception, and language* (5th ed., pp. 467–521). New York: Wiley.

Schneider, W., & Pressley, M. (1997). *Memory development between two and twenty* (2nd ed.). Mahwah, NJ: Erlbaum.

Schneiders, J., Nicolson, N. A., Berkhof, J., Feron, F. J., van Os, J., & deVries, M. W. (2006). Mood reactivity to daily negative events in early adolescence: Relationship to risk for psychopathology. *Developmental Psychology, 42,* 543–554.

Schneller, D. P., & Arditti, J.A. (2004). After the breakup: Interpreting divorce and rethinking intimacy. *Journal of Divorce and Remarriage, 42,* 1–37.

Schnohr, P., Nyboe, J., Lange, P., & Jensen, G. (1998). Longevity and gray hair, baldness, facial wrinkles, and arcus senilis in 13,000 men and women: The Copenhagen City Heart Study. *Journal of Gerontology, 53,* M347–350.

Scholl, B. J., & Leslie, A. M. (2000). Minds, modules, and meta-analysis. *Child Development, 72,* 696–701.

Scholnick, E. K. (1995, Fall). Knowing and constructing plans. *SRCD Newsletter,* pp. 1–2, 17.

Schonberg, R. L., & Tifft, C. J. (2007). Birth defects and prenatal diagnosis. In M. L. Batshaw, L. Pellegrino, & N. J. Roizen (Eds.), *Children with disabilities* (6th ed., pp. 83–96). Baltimore: Paul H. Brookes.

Schooler, C., Mulatu, M. S., & Oates, G. (1999). The continuing effects of substantively complex work on the intellectual functioning of older workers. *Psychology and Aging, 14,* 483–506.

Schoon, L., & Parsons, S. (2002). Teenage aspirations for future careers and occupational outcomes. *Journal of Vocational Behavior, 60,* 262–288.

Schoppe-Sullivan, S. J., Brown, G. L., Cannon, E. A., Mangelsdorf, S. C., & Sokolowski, M. S. (2008). Maternal gatekeeping, coparenting quality, and fathering behavior in families with infants. *Journal of Family Psychology, 22,* 389–398.

Schoppe-Sullivan, S. J., Mangelsdorf, S. C., Frosch, C. A., & McHale, J. (2004). Associations between coparenting and marital behavior from infancy to the preschool years. *Journal of Family Psychology, 18,* 194–207.

Schott, J. M., & Rossor, M. N. (2003). The grasp and other primitive reflexes. *Journal of Neurological and Neurosurgical Psychiatry, 74,* 558–560.

Schroeder, R. D., Bulanda, R. E., Giordano, P. C., & Cernkovich, S. A. (2010). Parenting and adult criminality: An examination of direct and indirect effects by race. *Journal of Adolescent Research, 25,* 64–98.

Schroots, J. J. F., van Dijkum, C., & Assink, M. H. J. (2004). Autobiographical memory from a life span perspective. *International Journal of Aging and Human Development, 58,* 69–85.

Schuckit, M. A. (2009). Alcohol-use disorders. *Lancet, 373,* 492–501.

Schuetze, P., & Eiden, R. D. (2006). The association between maternal cocaine use during pregnancy and physiological regulation in 4- to 8-week-old infants: An examination of possible mediators and moderators. *Journal of Pediatric Psychology, 31,* 15–26.

Schull, W. J. (2003). The children of atomic bomb survivors: A synopsis. *Journal of Radiological Protection, 23,* 369–394.

Schulte-Ruther, M., Markowitsch, H. J., Fink, G. R., & Piefke, M. (2007). Mirror neuron and theory of mind mechanisms involved in face-to-face interactions: A functional magnetic resonance imaging approach to empathy. *Journal of Cognitive Neuroscience, 19,* 1354–1372.

Schultz, R., Burgio, L., Burns, R., Eisdorfer, C., Gallagher-Thompson, D., Gitlin, L. N., & Mahoney, D. F. (2003). Resources for enhancing Alzheimer's caregiver health (REACH): Overview, site-specific outcomes, and future directions. *Gerontologist, 43,* 514–520.

Schulz, R., & Curnow, C. (1988). Peak performance and age among superathletes: Track and field, swimming, baseball, tennis, and golf. *Journal of Gerontology, 43,* P113–P120.

Schumann, C. M., & Amaral, D. G. (2010). The human amygdala in autism. In P. J. Whalen & E. A. Phelps (Eds.), *The human amygdala* (pp. 362–381). New York: Guilford.

Schumann, C. M., Barnes, C. C., Lord, C., & Courchesne, E. (2009). Amygdala enlargement in toddlers and autism related to severity of social and communication impairments. *Biological Psychiatry, 66,* 942–949.

Schwanenflugel, P. J., Henderson, R. L., & Fabricius, W. V. (1998). Developing organization of mental verbs and theory of mind in middle childhood: Evidence from extensions. *Developmental Psychology, 34,* 512–524.

Schwartz, B. L., & Frazier, L. D. (2005). Tip-of-the-tongue states and aging: Contrasting psycholinguistic and metacognitive perspectives. *Journal of General Psychology, 132,* 377–391.

Schwartz, J. P., & Waldo, M. (2004). Group work with men who have committed partner abuse. In J. L. DeLucia-Waack, D. A. Gerrity, C. R. Kalodner, & M. T. Riva (Eds.), *Handbook of group counseling and psychotherapy* (pp. 576–592). Thousand Oaks, CA: Sage.

Schwartz, S. J., Beyers, W., Luyckz, K., Soenens, B. Zamboanga, B. L., Forthun, L. F., et al. (2011). Examining the light and dark sides of emerging adults' identity: A study of identity status differences in positive and negative psychosocial functioning. *Journal of Youth and Adolescence, 40,* 839–859.

Schwartz, S. J., Côté, J. E., & Arnett, J. J. (2005). Identity and agency in emerging adulthood: Two developmental routes in the individualization process. *Youth and Society, 37,* 201–229.

Schwartz, S. J., Pantin, H., Prado, G., Sullivan, S., & Szapocznik, J. (2005). Family functioning, identity, and problem behavior: Immigrant early adolescents. *Journal of Early Adolescence, 25,* 392–420.

Schwebel, D. C., & Brezausek, C. M. (2007). Father transitions in the household and young children's injury risk. *Psychology of Men and Masculinity, 8,* 173–184.

Schweiger, W. K., & O'Brien, M. (2005). Special needs adoption: An ecological systems approach. *Family Relations, 54,* 512–522.

Schweinhart, L. J. (2010). The challenge of the High/Scope Perry Preschool study. In A. J. Reynolds, A. J. Rolnick, M. M. Englund, & J. Temple (Eds.), *Childhood programs and practices in the first decade of life: A human capital integration* (pp. 199–213). New York: Cambridge University Press.

Schweinhart, L. J., Montie, J., Xiang, Z., Barnett, W. S., Belfield, C. R., & Nores, M. (2005). *Lifetime effects: The High/Scope Perry Preschool Study through age 40.* Ypsilanti, MI: High/Scope Press.

Schweizer, K., Moosbrugger, H., & Goldhammer, F. (2006). The structure of the relationship between attention and intelligence. *Intelligence, 33,* 589–611.

Schwenck, C., Bjorklund, D. F., & Schneider, W. (2007). Factors influencing the incidence of utilization deficiencies and other patterns of recall/strategy-use relations in a strategic memory task. *Child Development, 22,* 197–212.

Schwier, C., van Maanen, C., Carpenter, M., & Tomasello, M. (2006). Rational imitation in 12-month-old infants. *Infancy, 10,* 303–311.

Scott, L. D. (2003). The relation of racial identity and racial socialization to coping with discrimination among African Americans. *Journal of Black Studies, 20,* 520–538.

Scott, L. S., & Monesson, A. (2009). The origin of biases in face perception. *Psychological Science, 20,* 676–680.

Scullin, M. K., Bugg, J. M., McDaniel, M. A., & Einstein, G. O. (2011). Prospective memory and aging: Preserved spontaneous retrieval, but impaired deactivation, in older adults. *Memory and Cognition, 39,* 1232–1240.

Seale, C. (2009). Legalisation of euthanasia or physician-assisted suicide: Survey of doctors' attitudes. *Palliative Medicine, 23,* 205–212.

Seaton, E. K., Scottham, K. M., & Sellers, R. M. (2006). The status model of racial identity development in African American adolescents: Evidence of structure, trajectories, and well-being. *Child Development, 77,* 1416–1426.

Seeman, E. (2008). Structural basis of growth-related gain and age-related loss of bone strength. *Rheumatology, 47,* iv2–iv8.

Seeman, T. E., Huang, M.-H., Bretsky, P., Crimmins, E., Launer, L., & Guralnik, J. M. (2005). Education and APOE-e4 in longitudinal cognitive decline: MacArthur Studies of Successful Aging. *Journal of Gerontology, 60B,* P74–P83.

Seiberling, K. A., & Conley, D. B. (2004). Aging and olfactory and taste function. *Otolaryngologic Clinics of North America, 37,* 1209–1228.

Seibert, A. C., & Kerns, K. A. (2009). Attachment figures in middle childhood. *International Journal of Behavioral Development, 33,* 347–355.

Seidman, E., Aber, J. L., & French, S. E. (2004). Assessing the transitions to middle and high school. *Journal of Adolescent Research, 19,* 3–30.

Seidman, E., Lambert, L. E., Allen, L., & Aber, J. L. (2003). Urban adolescents' transition to junior high school and protective family transactions. *Journal of Early Adolescence, 23,* 166–193.

Seitz, V., & Apfel, N. H. (2005). Creating effective school-based interventions for pregnant teenagers. In R. DeV. Peters, B. Leadbeater, & R. J. McMahon

(Eds.), *Resilience in children, families, and communities: Linking context to practice and policy* (pp. 65–82). New York: Kluwer Academic.

Sekita, A., Ninomiya, T., Tanizaki, Y., Doi, Y., Hata, J., Yonemoto, K., et al. (2010). Trends in prevalence of Alzheimer's disease and vascular dementia in a Japanese community: The Hisayama Study. *Acta Psychiatrica Scandivavica, 122,* 319–325.

Selfhout, M. H. W., Branje, S. J. T., & Meeus, W. H. J. (2008). The development of delinquency and perceived friendship quality in adolescent best friendship dyads. *Journal of Abnormal Child Psychology, 36,* 471–485.

Selwood, A., & Cooper, C. (2009). Abuse of people with dementia. *Reviews in Clinical Gerontology, 19,* 35–43.

Selwood, A., Johnston, K., Katona, C., Lyketsos, C., & Livingston, G. (2007). Systematic review of the effect of psychological interventions on family caregivers of people with dementia. *Journal of Affective Disorders, 101,* 75–89.

Selwyn, P. A. (1996). Before their time: A clinician's reflections on death and AIDS. In H. M. Spiro, M. G. M. Curnen, & L. P. Wandel (Eds.), *Facing death: Where culture, religion, and medicine meet* (pp. 33–37). New Haven, CT: Yale University Press.

Semanik, P. A., Chang, R. W., & Dunlop, D. D. (2012). Aerobic activity in prevention and symptom control of osteoarthritis. *PM&R, 4,* S37–S44.

Senju, A., Csibra, G., & Johnson, M. H. (2008). Understanding the referential nature of looking: Infants' preference for object-directed gaze. *Cognition, 108,* 303–319.

Senju, A., Southgate, V., Snape, C., Leonard, M., & Csibra, G. (2011). Do 18-month-olds really attribute mental states to others? A critical test. *Psychological Science, 22,* 878–880.

Serafini, T. E., & Adams, G. R. (2002). Functions of identity: Scale construction and validation. *Identity: An International Journal of Theory and Research, 2,* 361–389.

Serbin, L. A., Powlishta, K. K., & Gulko, J. (1993). The development of sex typing in middle childhood. *Monographs of the Society for Research in Child Development, 58*(2, Serial No. 232).

Sergeant, J. F., Ekerdt, D. J., & Chapin, R. (2008). Measurement of late-life residential relocation: Why are rates for such a manifest event so varied? *Journal of Gerontology, 63B,* S92–S98.

Serra, L., Perri, R., Cercignani, M., Spano, B., Fadda, L., Marra, C. et al. (2010). Are behavioral symptoms of Alzheimer's disease directly associated with neurodegeneration? *Journal of Alzheimer's Disease, 21,* 627–639.

Service Canada. (2009). *Guide to Canada Pension Plan disability benefits.* Retrieved from www.servicecanada.gc.ca/eng/isp/pub/cpp/disability/guide/sectionb.shtml

Sesame Workshop. (2009). *Sesame Workshop Annual Report 2009.* Retrieved from www.sesameworkshop.org/assets/290/src/Annual%20Report%202009.pdf

Settersten, R. A. (2003). Age structuring and the rhythm of the life course. In J. T. Mortimer & M. J. Shanahan (Eds.), *Handbook of the life course* (pp. 81–98). New York: Kluwer Academic.

Settersten, R. A. (2007). The new landscape of adult life: Road maps, signposts, and speed lines. *Research in Human Development, 4,* 239–252.

Settles, I. H., Cortina, L. M., Malley, J., & Stewart, A. J. (2006). The climate for women in academic science: The good, the bad, and the changeable. *Psychology of Women Quarterly, 30,* 47–58.

Sevigny, P. R., & Loutzenhiser, L. (2010). Predictors of parenting self-efficacy in mothers and fathers of toddlers. Child Care, *Health and Development, 36,* 179–189.

Seymour, S. C. (1999). *Women, family, and child care in India.* Cambridge, UK: Cambridge University Press.

Shaeer, O., & Shaeer, K. (2012). The Global Online Sexual Survey (GOSS): The United States of America in 2011. Chapter I: Erectile dysfunction among English-speakers. *Journal of Sexual Medicine, 9,* 3018–3027.

Shah, T., Sullivan, K., & Carter, J. (2006). Sudden infant death syndrome and reported maternal smoking during pregnancy. *American Journal of Public Health, 96,* 1757–1759.

Shalev, I. (2012). Early life stress and telomere length: Investigating the connection and possible mechanisms. *BioEssays, 34,* 943–952.

Shanahan, L., McHale, S. M., Crouter, A. C., & Osgood, D. W. (2007). Warmth with mothers and fathers from middle childhood to late adolescence: Within- and between-families comparisions. *Developmental Psychology, 43,* 551–563.

Shapka, J. D., & Keating, D. P. (2005). Structure and change in self-concept during adolescence. *Canadian Journal of Behavioural Science, 37,* 83–96.

Sharp, E. A., & Ganong, L. (2011). "I'm a loser, I'm not married, let's just all look at me": Ever-single women's perceptions of their social environment. *Journal of Family Issues, 32,* 956–980.

Shatz, M. (2007). On the development of the field. In E. Hoff & M. Shatz (Eds.), *Blackwell handbook of language development* (pp. 1–20). Malden, MA: Blackwell.

Shaver, P., Furman, W., & Buhrmester, D. (1985). Transition to college: Network changes, social skills, and loneliness. In S. Duck & D. Perlman (Eds.), *Understanding personal relationships: An interdisciplinary approach* (pp. 193–219). London: Sage.

Shaw, B. A. (2005). Anticipated support from neighbors and physical functioning during later life. *Research on Aging, 27,* 503–525.

Shaw, D. S., Gilliom, M., Ingoldsby, E. M., & Nagin, D. S. (2003). Trajectories leading to school-age conduct problems. *Developmental Psychology, 39,* 189–200.

Shaw, P., Eckstrand, K., Sharp, W., Blumenthal, J., Lerch, J. P., & Greenstein, D. (2007, November 16). Attention-deficit/hyperactivity disorder is characterized by a delay in cortical maturation. *Proceedings of the National Academy of Sciences Online.* Retrieved from www.pnas.org/cgi/content/abstract/0707741104v1

Shay, J. W., & Wright, W. E. (2011). Role of telomeres and telomerase in cancer. *Seminars in Cancer Biology, 21,* 349–353.

Shea, J. L. (2006). Cross-cultural comparison of women's midlife symptom-reporting: A China study. *Culture, Medicine, and Psychiatry, 30,* 331–362.

Shedler, J., & Block, J. (1990). Adolescent drug use and psychological health: A longitudinal inquiry. *American Psychologist, 45,* 612–630.

Sherman, A. M., de Vries, B., & Lansford, J. E. (2000). Friendship in childhood and adulthood: Lessons across the life span. *International Journal of Aging and Human Development, 51,* 31–51.

Sherman, A. M., Lansford, J. E., & Volling, B. L. (2006). Sibling relationships and best friendships in young adulthood: Warmth, conflict, and well-being. *Personal Relationships, 13,* 151–165.

Sherman, C. W., Rosenblatt, D. E., & Antonucci, T. C. (2008). Elder abuse and mistreatment: A life span and cultural context. *Indian Journal of Gerontology, 22.*

Sherman, S. L., Freeman, S. B., Allen, E. G., & Lamb, N. E. (2005). Risk factors for nondisjunction of trisomy 21. *Cytogenetic Genome Research, 111,* 273–280.

Sherrod, L. R., & Spiewak, G. S. (2008). Possible interrelationships between civic engagement, positive youth development, and spirituality/religiosity. In R. M. Lerner, R. W. Roeser, & E. Phelps

(Eds.), *Positive youth development and spirituality: From theory to research* (pp. 322–338). West Conshohocken, PA: Templeton Foundation Press.

Sherry, B., McDivitt, J., Brich, L. L., Cook, F. H., Sanders, S., Prish, J. L., et al. (2004). Attitudes, practices, and concerns about child feeding and child weight status among socioeconomically diverse white, Hispanic, and African-American mothers. *Journal of the American Dietetic Association, 104,* 215–221.

Shield, R. R., Wetle, T., Teno, J., Miller, S. C., & Welch, L. C. (2010). Vigilant at the end of life: Family advocacy in the nursing home. *Journal of Palliative Medicine, 13,* 573–579.

Shields, G., King, W., Fulks, S., & Fallon, L. F. (2002). Determinants of perceived safety among the elderly: An exploratory study. *Journal of Gerontological Social Work, 38,* 73–83.

Shierholz, H., Sabadish, N., & Wething, H. (2012, May 3). *The class of 2012: Labor market for young graduates remains grim.* EPI Briefing Paper #340. Washington, DC: Economic Policy Institute.

Shifren, J. L., Monz, B. U., Russo, P. A., Segreti, A., & Johannes, C. B. (2008). Sexual problems and distress in United States women. *Obstetrics and Gynecology, 112,* 970–978.

Shimizu, H. (2001). Japanese adolescent boys' senses of empathy (omoiyari) and Carol Gilligan's perspectives on the morality of care: A phenomenological approach. *Culture and Psychology, 7,* 453–475.

Shin, J. S., Hong, A., Solomon, M. J., & Lee, C. S. (2006). The role of telomeres and telomerase in the pathology of human cancer and aging. *Pathology, 38,* 103–113.

Shonkoff, J. P., & Bales, S. N. (2011). Science does not speak for itself: Translating child development research for the public and its policymakers. *Child Development, 82,* 17–32.

Shonkoff, J. P., & Phillips, D. (Eds.). (2001). *Neurons to neighborhoods: The science of early childhood development.* Washington, DC: National Academy Press.

Shor, E., Roelfs, D. J., Curreli, M., Clemow, L., Burg, M. M., & Schwartz, J. E. (2012). Widowhood and mortality: A meta-analysis and meta-regression. *Demography, 49,* 575–606.

Shuey, K., & Hardy, M. A. (2003). Assistance to aging parents and parents-in-law: Does lineage affect family allocation decisions? *Journal of Marriage and Family, 65,* 418–431.

Shultz, K. S., & Wang, M. (2007). The influence of specific physical health conditions on retirement decisions. *International Journal of Aging and Human Development, 65,* 149–161.

Shure, M. B., & Aberson, B. (2005). Enhancing the process of resilience through effective thinking. In S. Goldstein & R. B. Brooks (Eds.), *Handbook of resilience in children* (pp. 373–394). New York: Kluwer Academic.

Shuwairi, S. M., Albert, M. K., & Johnson, S. P. (2007). Discrimination of possible and impossible objects in infancy. *Psychological Science, 18,* 303–307.

Shwalb, D. W., Nakawaza, J., Yamamoto, T., & Hyun, J.-H. (2004). Fathering in Japanese, Chinese, and Korean cultures: A review of the research literature. In M. E. Lamb (Ed.), *The role of the father in child development* (4th ed., pp. 146–181). Hoboken, NJ: Wiley.

Shweder, R. A., Goodnow, J. J., Hatano, G., LeVine, R. A., Markus, H. R., & Miller, P. J. (2006). The cultural psychology of development: One mind, many mentalities. In R. M. Lerner (Ed.), *Handbook of child psychology: Vol. 1. Theoretical models of human development* (6th ed., pp. 716–792). Hoboken, NJ: Wiley.

Sibley, C. G., & Overall, N. C. (2010). Modeling the hierarchical structure of personality–attachment associations: Domain diffusion versus domain differentiation. *Journal of Social and Personal Relationships, 27,* 47–70.

Sidebotham, P., Heron, J., & the ALSPAC Study Team. (2003). Child maltreatment in the "children of the nineties": The role of the child. *Child Abuse and Neglect, 27,* 337–352.

Siebenbruner, J., Zimmer-Gembeck, M. J., & Egeland, B. (2007). Sexual partners and contraceptive use: A 16-year prospective study predicting abstinence and risk behavior. *Journal of Research on Adolescence, 17,* 179–206.

Siegal, M., Iozzi, L., & Surian, L. (2009). Bilingualism and conversational understanding in young children. *Cognition, 110,* 115–122.

Siega-Riz, A. M., Deming, D. M., Reidy, K. C., Fox, M. K., Condon, E., & Briefel, R. R. (2010). Food consumption patterns of infants and toddlers: Where are we now? *Journal of the American Dietetic Association, 110,* S38–S51.

Siegel, R., Naishadham, D., & Jemal, A. (2012). Cancer statistics, 2012. *CA: A Cancer Journal for Clinicians, 62,* 10–29.

Sieger, K., & Renk, K. (2007). Pregnant and parenting adolescents: A study of ethnic identity, emotional and behavioral functioning, child characteristics, and social support. *Journal of Youth and Adolescence, 36,* 567–581.

Siegler, R. S. (1996). *Emerging minds: The process of change in children's thinking.* New York: Oxford University Press.

Siegler, R. S. (2007). Cognitive variability. *Developmental Science, 10,* 104–109.

Siegler, R. S. (2009). Improving preschoolers' number sense using information-processing theory. In O. A. Barbarin & B. H. Wasik (Eds.), *Handbook of child development and early education* (pp. 429–454). New York: Guilford.

Siegler, R. S., & Mu, Y. (2008). Chinese children excel on novel mathematics problems even before elementary school. *Psychological Science, 19,* 759–763.

Siegler, R. S., & Svetina, M. (2006). What leads children to adopt new strategies? A microgenetic/cross-sectional study of class inclusion. *Child Development, 77,* 997–1015.

Siervogel, R. M., Maynard, L. M., Wisemandle, W. A., Roche, A. F., Guo, S. S., Chumlea, W. C., & Towne, B. (2000). Annual changes in total body fat and fat-free mass in children from 8 to 18 years in relation to changes in body mass index: The Fels Longitudinal Study. *Annals of the New York Academy of Sciences, 904,* 420–423.

Silk, J. S., Morris, A. S., Kanaya, T., & Steinberg, L. (2003). Psychological control and autonomy granting: Opposite ends of a continuum or distinct constructs? *Journal of Research on Adolescence, 13,* 113–128.

Silvén, M. (2001). Attention in very young infants predicts learning of first words. *Infant Behavior and Development, 24,* 229–237.

Silver, M. H., & Perls, T. T. (2000). Is dementia the price of a long life? An optimistic report from centenarians. *Journal of Geriatric Psychiatry, 33,* 71–79.

Silverman, P. R. (2004). Dying and bereavement in historical perspective. In J. Berzoff & P. R. Silverman (Eds.), *Living with dying: A handbook for end-of-life healthcare practitioners* (pp. 128–149). New York: Columbia University Press.

Silverman, P. R., & Nickman, S. L. (1996). Children's construction of their dead parents. In D. Klass, P. R. Silverman, & S. L. Nickman (Eds.), *Continuing bonds: New understandings of grief* (pp. 73–86). Washington, DC: Taylor & Francis.

Silverman, W. K., & Pina, A. A. (2008). Psychosocial treatments for phobic and anxiety disorders in youth. In R. G. Steele, T. D. Elkin, & M. Roberts (Eds.), *Handbook of evidence-based therapies for*

children and adolescents: Bridging science and practice* (pp. 65–82). New York: Springer.

Silverstein, M., Conroy, S., Wang, H., Giarrusso, R., & Bengtson, V. L. (2002). Reciprocity in parent–child relations over the adult life course. *Journal of Gerontology, 57B,* S3–S13.

Silverstein, M., & Giarrusso, R. (2010). Aging and family life: A decade review. *Journal of Marriage and Family, 72,* 1039–1058.

Silverstein, M., & Marenco, A. (2001). How Americans enact the grandparent role across the family life course. *Journal of Family Issues, 22,* 493–522.

Simcock, G., & DeLoache, J. (2006). Get the picture? The effects of iconicity on toddlers' reenactment from picture books. *Developmental Psychology, 42,* 1352–1357.

Simcock, G., & Hayne, H. (2002). Breaking the barrier? Children fail to translate their preverbal memories into language. *Psychological Science, 13,* 225–231.

Simcock, G., & Hayne, H. (2003). Age-related changes in verbal and nonverbal memory during early childhood. *Developmental Psychology, 39,* 805–814.

Simon, N. M., Smoller, J. W., McNamara, K. L., Maser, R. S., Zlata, A. K., & Pollack, M. H. (2006). Telomere shortening and mood disorders: Preliminary support for a chronic stress model of accelerated aging. *Biological Psychiatry, 60,* 432–435.

Simoneau, M., & Markovits, H. (2003). Reasoning with premises that are not empirically true: Evidence for the role of inhibition and retrieval. *Developmental Psychology, 39,* 964–975.

Simons, J. S., Dodson, C. S., Bell, D., & Schachter, D. L. (2004). Specific-and partial-source memory: Effects of aging. *Psychology and Aging, 19,* 689–694.

Simonton, D. K. (2000). Creativity: Cognitive, personal, developmental, and social aspects. *American Psychologist, 55,* 151–158.

Simonton, D. K. (2006). Historiometric methods. In K. A. Ericsson, N. Charness, P. J. Feltovich, & R. R. Hoffman (Eds.), *The Cambridge handbook of expertise and expert performance* (pp. 319–335). New York: Cambridge University Press.

Simonton, D. K. (2012). Creative productivity and aging. In S. K. Whitbourne & M. J. Sliwinski (Eds.), *Wiley-Blackwell handbook of adulthood and aging* (pp. 477–496). Malden, MA: Blackwell Publishing.

Simpson, E. A., Varga, K., Frick, J. E., & Fragaszy, D. (2011). Infants experience perceptual narrowing for nonprimate faces. *Infancy, 16,* 318–328.

Simpson, J. A., & Harris, B. A. (1994). Interpersonal attraction. In A. L. Weber & J. H. Harvey (Eds.), *Perspectives on close relationships* (pp. 45–66). Boston: Allyn and Bacon.

Simpson, J. A., Rholes, W. S., Campbell, L., Tran, S., & Wilson, C. L. (2003). Adult attachment, the transition to parenthood, and depressive symptoms. *Journal of Personality and Social Psychology, 84,* 1172–1187.

Simpson, R. (2004). Masculinity at work: The experiences of men in female dominated occupations. *Work, Employment and Society, 18,* 349–368.

Simpson, R. (2005). Men in non-traditional occupations: Career entry, career orientation and experience of role strain. *Gender, Work and Organization, 12,* 363–380.

Singer, D. G., & Singer, J. L. (2005). *Imagination and play in the electronic age.* Cambridge, MA: Harvard University Press.

Singer, Y., Bachner, Y. G., Shvartzman, P., & Carmel, S. (2005). Home death—the caregivers' experiences. *Journal of Pain and Symptom Management, 30,* 70–74.

Singleton, J. L., & Newport, E. L. (2004). When learners surpass their models: The acquisition of American Sign Language from inconsistent input. *Cognitive Psychology, 49,* 370–407.

Sinkkonen, J., Anttila, R., & Siimes, M. A. (1998). Pubertal maturation and changes in self-image in early adolescent Finnish boys. *Journal of Youth and Adolescence, 27,* 209–218.

Sirsch, U., Erher, E., Mayr, E., & Willinger, U. (2009). What does it take to be an adult in Austria? *Journal of Adolescent Research, 24,* 275–292.

Skully, R., & Saleh, A. S. (2011). Aging and the effects of vitamins and supplements. *Clinical Geriatric Medicine, 27,* 591–607.

Slack, K. S., & Yoo, J. (2005). Food hardship and child behavior problems among low-income children. *Social Service Review, 79,* 511–536.

Slater, A., Brown, E., Mattock, A., & Bornstein, M. H. (1996). Continuity and change in habituation in the first 4 months from birth. *Journal of Reproductive and Infant Psychology, 14,* 187–194.

Slater, A., Quinn, P. C., Kelly, D. J., Lee, K., Longmore, C. A., McDonald, P. R., & Pascalis, O. (2011). The shaping of the face space in early infancy: Becoming a native face processor. *Child Development Perspectives, 4,* 205–211.

Slater, A., Riddell, P., Quinn, P. C., Pascalis, O., Lee, K., & Kelly, D. J. (2010). Visual perception. In J. G. Bremner & T. D. Wachs (Eds.), *Wiley-Blackwell handbook of infant development: Vol. 1. Basic research* (2nd ed., pp. 40–80). Chichester, UK: Wiley-Blackwell.

Sloter, E., Schmid, T. E., Marchetti, F., Eskenazi, B., & Nath, J. (2006). Quantitative effects of male age on sperm motion. *Human Reproduction, 21,* 2868–2875.

Slutske, W. S., Hunt-Carter, E. E., Nabors-Oberg, R. E., Sher, K. J., Bucholz, K. K., & Madden, P. A. F. (2004). Do college students drink more than their non-college-attending peers? Evidence from a population-based longitudinal female twin study. *Journal of Abnormal Psychology, 113,* 530–540.

Smahel, D., Brown, B. B., & Blinka, L. (2012). Associations between online friendship and Internet addiction among adolescents and emerging adults. *Developmental Psychology, 48,* 381–388.

Small, B. J., Rawson, K. S., Eisel, S., & McEvoy, C. L. (2012). Memory and aging. In S. K. Whitbourne & M. J. Sliwinski (Eds.), *Wiley-Blackwell handbook of adulthood and aging* (pp. 174–189). Malden, MA: Wiley-Blackwell.

Smart, J., & Hiscock, H. (2007). Early infant crying and sleeping problems: A pilot study of impact on parental well-being and parent-endorsed strategies for management. *Journal of Paediatrics and Child Health, 43,* 284–290.

Smetana, J. G. (2002). Culture, autonomy, and personal jurisdiction in adolescent–parent relationships. In R. V. Kail & H. W. Reese (Eds.), *Advances in child development and behavior* (Vol. 29, pp. 51–87). San Diego, CA: Academic Press.

Smetana, J. G. (2006). Social-cognitive domain theory: Consistencies and variations in children's moral and social judgments. In M. Killen & J. G. Smetana (Eds.), *Handbook of moral development* (pp. 119–154). Mahwah, NJ: Erlbaum.

Smetana, J. G., Metzger, A., & Campione-Barr, N. (2004). African-American late adolescents' relationships with parents: Developmental transitions and longitudinal patterns. *Child Development, 75,* 932–947.

Smith, A. N., Brief, A. P., & Colella, A. (2010). Bias in organizations. In J. F. Dovidio, M. Hewstone, P. Glick, & V. M. Esses (Eds.), *Treatment of childhood disorders* (3rd ed., pp. 65–136). New York: Guilford.

Smith, B. H., Barkley, R. A., & Shapiro, C. J. (2006). Attention-deficit/hyperactivity disorder. In E. J. Mash & R. A. Barkley (Eds.), *Treatment of childhood disorders* (3rd ed., pp. 65–136). New York: Guilford.

Smith, C., Perou, R., & Lesesne, C. (2002). Parent education. M. H. Bornstein (Ed.), *Handbook of* parenting (Vol. 4, pp. 389–410). Mahwah, NJ: Erlbaum.

Smith, C., & Snell, P. (2009). *Souls in transition: The religious & spiritual lives of emerging adults*. New York: Oxford University Press.

Smith, C. D., Chebrolu, H., Wekstein, D. R., Schmitt, F. A., & Markesbery, W. R. (2007). Age and gender effects on human brain anatomy: A voxel-based morphometric study in healthy elderly. *Neurobiology of Aging, 28*, 1075–1087.

Smith, C. L., Calkins, S. D., Keane, S. P., Anastopoulos, A. D., & Shelton, T. L. (2004). Predicting stability and change in toddler behavior problems: Contributions of maternal behavior and child gender. *Developmental Psychology, 40*, 29–42.

Smith, C. M., & Cotter, V. T. (2008). Age-related changes in health. In E. Capezuti, D. Zwicker, M. Mezey, T. T. Fulmer, & D. Gray-Miceli (Eds.), *Evidence-based geriatric nursing protocols for best practice* (3rd ed., pp. 431–458). New York: Springer.

Smith, D. G., Xiao, L., & Bechara, A. (2012). Decision making in children and adolescents: Impaired Iowa gambling task performance in early adolescence. *Developmental Psychology, 48*, 1180–1187.

Smith, G. C., Rodriguez, J. M., & Palmieri, P. A. (2010). Patterns and predictors of support group use by custodial grandmothers and grandchildren. *Families in Society, 91*, 385–393.

Smith, J., & Freund, A. M. (2002). The dynamics of possible selves in old age. *Journal of Gerontology, 57B*, P492–P500.

Smith, J., & Infurna, F. J. (2011). Early precursors of later health. In K. L. Fingerman, C. A. Berg, J. Smith, & T. C. Antonucci (Eds.), *Handbook of life-span development* (pp. 213–238). New York: Springer.

Smith, J. C., Nielson, K. A., Woodard, J. L., Seidenberg, M., & Rao, S. M. (2013). Physical activity and brain function in older adults at increased risk for Alzheimer's disease. *Brain Science, 3*, 54–83.

Smith, L. B., Jones, S. S., Gershkoff-Stowe, L., & Samuelson, L. (2002). Object name learning provides on-the-job training for attention. *Psychological Science, 13*, 13–19.

Smith, N., Young, A., & Lee, C. (2004). Optimism, health-related hardiness and well-being among older Australian women. *Journal of Health Psychology, 9*, 741–752.

Smith, T. W. (2011a). *Cross-national differences in attitudes toward homosexuality*. Chicago: National Opinion Research Center/University of Chicago.

Smith, T. W. (2011b). *Public attitudes toward homosexuality*. Chicago: National Opinion Research Center/University of Chicago.

Smith, T. W., & Cundiff, J. M. (2011). An interpersonal perspective on risk for coronary heart disease. In L. Horowitz & S. Strack (Eds.), *Handbook of interpersonal psychology: Theory, research, assessment, and therapeutic interventions* (pp. 471–489). Hoboken, NJ: Wiley.

Smith, T. W., Glazer, K., Ruiz, J. M., & Gallo, L. C. (2004). Hostility, anger, aggressiveness, and coronary heart disease: An interpersonal perspective on personality, emotion, and health. *Journal of Personality, 72*, 1217–1270.

Smith, T. W., Uchino, B. N., Berg, C. A., & Florsheim, P. (2012). Marital discord and coronary artery disease: A comparison of behaviorally defined discrete groups. *Journal of Consulting and Clinical Psychology, 80*, 87–92.

Smyke, A. T., Zeanah, C. H., Fox, N. A., & Nelson, C. A. (2009). A new model of foster care for young children: The Bucharest Early Intervention Project. *Child and Adolescent Psychiatric Clinics of North America, 18*, 721–734.

Smyke, A. T., Zeanah, C. H., Fox, N. A., Nelson, C. A., & Guthrie, D. (2010). Placement in foster care enhances quality of attachment among young institutionalized children. *Child Development, 81*, 212–223.

Snarey, J., Son, L., Kuehne, V. S., Hauser, S., & Vaillant, G. (1987). The role of parenting in men's psychosocial development: A longitudinal study of early adulthood infertility and midlife generativity. *Developmental Psychology, 23*, 593–603.

Sneed, J. R., Whitbourne, S. K., & Culang, M. E. (2006). Trust, identity, and ego integrity: Modeling Erikson's core stages over 34 years. *Journal of Adult Development, 13*, 148–157.

Sneed, J. R., Whitbourne, S. K., Schwartz, S. J., & Huang, S. (2012). The relationship between identity, intimacy, and midlife well-being: Findings from the Rochester Adult Longitudinal Study. *Psychology and Aging, 27*, 318–323.

Snidman, N., Kagan, J., Riordan, L., & Shannon, D. C. (1995). Cardiac function and behavioral reactivity. *Psychophysiology, 32*, 199–207.

Snow, C. E., & Beals, D. E. (2006). Mealtime talk that supports literacy development. In R. W. Larson, A. R. Wiley, & K. R. Branscomb (Eds.), *Family mealtime as a context of development and socialization* (pp. 51–66). San Francisco: Jossey-Bass.

Snow, C. E., & Kang, J. Y. (2006). Becoming bilingual, biliterate, and bicultural. In K. A. Renninger & I. E. Sigel (Eds.), *Handbook of child psychology: Vol. 4. Child psychology in practice* (6th ed., pp. 75–102). Hoboken, NJ: Wiley.

Snyder, J., Brooker, M., Patrick, M. R., Snyder, A., Schrepferman, L., & Stoolmiller, M. (2003). Observed peer victimization during early elementary school: Continuity, growth, and relation to risk for child antisocial and depressive behavior. *Child Development, 74*, 1881–1898.

Snyder, J. S., & Cameron, H. A. (2012). Could adult hippocampal neurogenesis be relevant for human behavior? *Behavioural Brain Research, 227*, 384–390.

Soares, C. N. (2007). Menopausal transition and depression: Who is at risk and how to treat it? *Expert Review of Neurotherapeutics, 7*, 1285–1293.

Sobel, D. M. (2006). How fantasy benefits young children's understanding of pretense. *Developmental Science, 9*, 63–75.

Society for Research in Child Development. (2007). *SRCD ethical standards for research with children*. Retrieved from www.srcd.org/about-us/ethical-standards-research

Soderstrom, M., Dolbier, C., Leiferman, J., & Steinhardt, M. (2000). The relationship of hardiness, coping strategies, and perceived stress to symptoms of illness. *Journal of Behavioral Medicine, 23*, 311–328.

Soderstrom, M., Seidl, A., Nelson, D. G. K., & Jusczyk, P. W. (2003). The prosodic bootstrapping of phrases: Evidence from prelinguistic infants. *Journal of Memory and Language, 49*, 249–267.

Sofi, F., Cesari, F., Abbate, R., Gensini, G. F., & Casini, A. (2008). Adherence to Mediterranean diet and health status: Meta-analysis. *British Medical Journal, 337*, a1344.

Soli, A. R., McHale, S. M., & Feinberg, M. E. (2009). Risk and protective effects of sibling relationships among African American adolescents. *Family Relations, 58*, 578–592.

Solomon, J. C., & Marx, J. (1995). "To grandmother's house we go": Health and school adjustment of children raised solely by grandparents. *Gerontologist, 35*, 386–394.

Son, J., & Wilson, J. (2011). Generativity and volunteering. *Sociological Forum, 26*, 644–667.

Sondergaard, C., Henriksen, T. B., Obel, C., & Wisborg, K. (2002). Smoking during pregnancy and infantile colic. *Journal of the American Academy of Child and Adolescent Psychiatry, 41*, 147.

Sörensen, S., & Pinquart, M. (2005). Racial and ethnic differences in the relationship of caregiving stressors, resources, and sociodemographic variables to caregiver depression and perceived physical health. *Aging and Mental Health, 9*, 482–495.

Soska, K. C., Adolph, K. E., & Johnson, S. P. (2010). Systems in development: Motor skill acquisition facilitates three-dimensional object completion. *Developmental Psychology, 46*, 129–138.

Soto, C. J., John, O. P., Gosling, S. D., & Potter, J. (2011). Age differences in personality traits from 10 to 65: Big five domains and facets in a large cross-sectional sample. *Journal of Personality and Social Psychology, 100*, 330–348.

South African Department of Health. (2009). *2008 National Antenatal Sentinel HIV and Syphilis Prevalence Survey*. Retrieved from www.info.gov.za/view/DownloadFileAction?id=109007

Sowell, E. R., Thompson, P. M., Welcome, S. E., Henkenius, A. L., Toga, A. W., & Peterson, B. S. (2003). Cortical abnormalities in children and adolescents with attention-deficit hyperactivity disorder. *Lancet, 362*, 1699–1707.

Sowell, E. R., Trauner, D. A., Gamst, A., & Jernigan, T. (2002). Development of cortical and subcortical brain structures in childhood and adolescence: A structural MRI study. *Developmental Medicine and Child Neurology, 44*, 4–16.

Sowers, M. F., Zheng, H., Tomey, K., Karvonen-Gutierrez, M. J., Li, X., Matheos, Y., & Symons, J. (2007). Changes in body composition in women over six years at midlife: Ovarian and chronological aging. *Journal of Clinical Endocrinology and Metabolism, 92*, 895–901.

Speakman, J. R., & Selman, C. (2011). The free-radical damage theory: Accumulating evidence against a simple link of oxidative stress to ageing and lifespan. *Bioessays, 33*, 255–259.

Speece, D. L., Ritchey, K. D., Cooper, D. H., Roth, F. P., & Schatschneider, C. (2004). Growth in early reading skills from kindergarten to third grade. *Contemporary Educational Psychology, 29*, 312–332.

Spelke, E. S. (2000). Core knowledge. *American Psychologist, 55*, 1233–1242.

Spelke, E. S. (2004). Core knowledge. In N. Kanwisher & J. Duncan (Eds.), *Attention and performance* (Vol. 20, pp. 29–56). Oxford, UK: Oxford University Press.

Spelke, E. S., & Kinzler, K. D. (2007). Core knowledge. *Developmental Science, 10*, 89–96.

Spence, M. J., & DeCasper, A. J. (1987). Prenatal experience with low-frequency maternal voice sounds influences neonatal perception of maternal voice samples. *Infant Behavior and Development, 10*, 133–142.

Spencer, J. P., & Perone, S. (2008). Defending qualitative change: The view from dynamical systems theory. *Child Development, 79*, 1639–1647.

Spencer, J. P., Verejiken, B., Diedrich, F. J., & Thelen, E. (2000). Posture and the emergence of manual skills. *Developmental Science, 3*, 216–233.

Spera, C. (2005). A review of the relationship among parenting practices, parenting styles, and adolescent school achievement. *Educational Psychology Review, 17*, 125–146.

Spere, K. A., Schmidt, L. A., Theall-Honey, L. A., & Martin-Chang, S. (2004). Expressive and receptive language skills of temperamentally shy preschoolers. *Infant and Child Development, 13*, 123–133.

Spielmann, G., McFarlin, B. K., O'Connor, D. P., Smith, P. J., Pircher, H., & Simpson, R. J. (2011). Aerobic fitness is associated with lower proportions of senescent blood T-cells in man. *Brain, Behavior, and Immunity, 25*, 1521–1529.

Spinrad, T. L., & Eisenberg, N. (2009). Empathy, prosocial behavior, and positive development in schools. In R. Gilman, E. S. Huebner, & M. J. Furlong (Eds.), *Handbook of positive psychology in schools* (pp. 119–129). New York: Routledge

Spitze, G., & Gallant, M. P. (2004). "The bitter with the sweet": Older adults' strategies for handling ambivalence in relations with their adult children. *Research on Aging, 26*, 387–412.

Spock, B., & Needlman, R. (2012). *Dr. Spock's baby and child care* (9th ed.). New York: Gallery Books.

Spokane, A. R., & Cruza-Guet, M. C. (2005). Holland's theory of vocational personalities in work environments. In S. D. Brown & R. W. Lent (Eds.), *Career development and counseling* (pp. 24–41). Hoboken, NJ: Wiley.

Sprecher, S. (1999). "I love you more today than yesterday": Romantic partners' perceptions of changes in love and related affect over time. *Journal of Personality and Social Psychology, 76,* 46–53.

Sprecher, S., & Fehr, B. (2011). Dispositional attachment and relationship-specific attachment as predictors of compassionate love for partner. *Journal of Social and Personal Relationships, 28,* 558–574.

Srivastava, S., John, O. P., Gosling, S. D., & Potter, J. (2003). Development of personality in early and middle adulthood: Set like plaster or persistent change? *Journal of Personality and Social Psychology, 84,* 1041–1053.

Sroufe, L. A., Coffino, B., & Carlson, E. A. (2010). Conceptualizing the role of early experience: Lessons from the Minnesota Longitudinal Study. *Developmental Review, 30,* 36–51.

Sroufe, L. A., Egeland, B., Carlson, E., & Collins, W. (2005). *Minnesota Study of Risk and Adaptation from birth to maturity: The development of the person.* New York: Guilford.

Sroufe, L. A., & Waters, E. (1976). The ontogenesis of smiling and laughter: A perspective on the organization of development in infancy. *Psychological Review, 83,* 173–189.

Sroufe, L. A., & Wunsch, J. P. (1972). The development of laughter in the first year of life. *Child Development, 43,* 1324–1344.

Stackert, R. A., & Bursik, K. (2003). Why am I unsatisfied? Adult attachment style, gendered irrational relationship beliefs, and young adult romantic relationship satisfaction. *Personality and Individual Differences, 34,* 1419–1429.

Stahl, S. A., & Miller, P. D. (2006). Whole language and language experience approaches for beginning reading: A quantitative research synthesis. In K. A. Dougherty Stahl & M. C. McKenna (Eds.), *Reading research at work: Foundations of effective practice* (pp. 9–35). New York: Guilford.

Stams, G. J. M., Brugman, D., Deković, M., van Rosmalen, L., van der Laan, P., & Gibbs, J. C. (2006). The moral judgment of juvenile delinquents: A meta-analysis. *Journal of Abnormal Child Psychology, 34,* 697–713.

Stams, G. J. M., Juffer, F., & van IJzendoorn, M. H. (2002). Maternal sensitivity, infant attachment, and temperament in early childhood predict adjustment in middle childhood: The case of adopted children and their biologically unrelated parents. *Developmental Psychology, 38,* 806–821.

Stanovich, K. E. (2013). *How to think straight about psychology* (10th ed.). Upper Saddle River, NJ: Pearson.

Starr, R. J. (1999). Music therapy in hospice care. *American Journal of Hospice and Palliative Care, 16,* 739–742.

Stattin, H., & Magnusson, D. (1990). *Pubertal maturation in female development.* Hillsdale, NJ: Erlbaum.

Staudinger, U. M. (1996). Wisdom and the social-interactive foundation of the mind. In P. B. Baltes & U. M. Staudinger (Eds.), *Interactive minds: Life-span perspectives on the social foundation of cognition* (pp. 276–315). New York: Cambridge University Press.

Staudinger, U. M. (2008). A psychology of wisdom: History and recent developments. *Research in Human Development, 5,* 107–120.

Staudinger, U. M., & Bowen, C. E. (2010). Life-span perspectives on positive personality development in adulthood and old age. In M. E. Lamb, A. M. Freund, & R. M. Lerner (Eds.), *Handbook of lifespan*

development: Vol. 2. Social and emotional development* (pp. 254–297). Hoboken, NJ: Wiley.

Staudinger, U. M., Dörner, J., & Mickler, C. (2005). Wisdom and personality. In R. J. Sternberg & J. Jordan (Eds.), *A handbook of wisdom: Psychological perspectives* (pp 191–219). New York: Cambridge University Press.

Staudinger, U. M., & Lindenberger, U. (2003). Understanding human development takes a metatheory and multiple disciplines. In U. M. Staudinger & U. Lindenberger (Eds.), *Understanding human development: Dialogues with life span psychology* (pp. 1–13). Norwell, MA: Kluwer.

Staudinger, U. M., Smith, J., & Baltes, P. B. (1992). Wisdom-related knowledge in a life-review task: Age differences and the role of professional specialization. *Psychology and Aging, 7,* 271–281.

Steele, C. M. (1997). A threat in the air: How stereotypes shape intellectual identity and performance. *American Psychologist, 52,* 613–629.

Steele, H., Steele, M., & Fonagy, P. (1996). Associations among attachment classifications of mothers, fathers, and their infants. *Child Development, 67,* 541–555.

Steele, S., Joseph, R. M., & Tager-Flusberg, H. (2003). Developmental change in theory of mind abilities in children with autism. *Journal of Autism and Developmental Disorders, 33,* 461–467.

Stein, C. H. (2009). "I owe it to them": Understanding felt obligation toward parents in adulthood. In K. Shifren (Ed.), *How caregiving affects development* (pp. 119–145). Washington, DC: American Psychological Association.

Stein, J. H., & Reiser, L. W. (1994). A study of white middle-class adolescent boys' responses to "semenarche" (the first ejaculation). *Journal of Youth and Adolescence, 23,* 373–384.

Stein, N., & Levine, L. J. (1999). The early emergence of emotional understanding and appraisal: Implications for theories of development. In T. Dalgleish & M. J. Power (Eds.), *Handbook of cognition and emotion* (pp. 383–408). Chichester, UK: Wiley.

Steinberg, L. (2008). A social neuroscience perspective on adolescent risk-taking. *Developmental Review, 28,* 78–106.

Steinberg, L., Albert, D., Cauffman, E., Banich, M., & Graham, S. (2008). Age differences in sensation seeking and impulsivity as indexed by behavior and self-report: Evidence for a dual systems model. *Developmental Psychology, 44,* 1764–1778.

Steinberg, L., Blatt-Eisengart, I., & Cauffman, E. (2006). Patterns of competence and adjustment among adolescents from authoritative, authoritarian, indulgent, and neglectful homes: A replication in a sample of serious juvenile offenders. *Journal of Research on Adolescence, 16,* 47–58.

Steinberg, L., Graham, S., O'Brien, L., Woolard, J., Cauffman, E., & Banich, M. (2009). Age differences in future orientation and delay discounting. *Child Development, 80,* 28–44.

Steinberg, L., & Monahan, K. C. (2011). Adolescents' exposure to sexy media does not hasten the initiation of sexual intercourse. *Developmental Psychology, 47,* 562–576.

Steinberg, L. D., Darling, N. E., & Fletcher, A. C. (1995). Authoritative parenting and adolescent development: An ecological journey. In P. Moen, G. H. Elder, Jr., & K. Luscher (Eds.), *Examining lives in context* (pp. 423–466). Washington, DC: American Psychological Association.

Steinberg, L. D., & Silk, J. S. (2002). Parenting adolescents. In M. H. Bornstein (Ed.), *Handbook of parenting* (Vol. 1, pp. 103–134). Mahwah, NJ: Erlbaum.

Steiner, J. E. (1979). Human facial expression in response to taste and smell stimulation. In H. W. Reese & L. P. Lipsitt (Eds.), *Advances in child development and behavior* (Vol. 13, pp. 257–295). New York: Academic Press.

Steiner, J. E., Glaser, D., Hawilo, M. E., & Berridge, D. C. (2001). Comparative expression of hedonic impact: Affective reactions to taste by human infants and other primates. *Neuroscience and Biobehavioral Review, 25,* 53–74.

Steinhausen, C. (2006). Eating disorders: Anorexia nervosa and bulimia nervosa. In C. Gillberg, R. Harrington, & H. Steinhausen (Eds.), *A clinician's handbook of child and adolescent psychiatry* (pp. 272–303). New York: Cambridge University Press.

Stenberg, C. (2003). Effects of maternal inattentiveness on infant social referencing. *Infant and Child Development, 12,* 399–419.

Stenberg, C., & Campos, J. J. (1990). The development of anger expressions in infancy. In N. Stein, B. Leventhal, & T. Trabasso (Eds.), *Psychological and biological approaches to emotion* (pp. 247–282). Hillsdale, NJ: Erlbaum.

Stephens, B. E., & Vohr, B. R. (2009). Neurodevelopmental outcome of the premature infant. *Pediatric Clinics of North America, 56,* 631–646.

Stephens, M. A. P., Franks, M. M., Martire, L. M., Norton, T. R., & Atienza, A. A. (2009). Women at midlife: Stress and rewards of balancing parent care with employment and family roles. In K. Shifren (Ed.), *How caregiving affects development* (pp. 147–167). Washington, DC: American Psychological Association.

Stephens, P. C., Sloboda, Z., Stephens, R. C., Teasdale, B., Grey, S. F., Hawthorne, R. D., & Williams, J. (2009). Universal school-based substance abuse prevention programs: Modeling targeted mediators and outcomes for adolescent cigarette, alcohol, and marijuana use. *Drug and Alcohol Dependence, 102,* 19–29.

Stern, D. (1985). *The interpersonal world of the infant.* New York: Basic Books.

Stern, Y. (2009). Cognitive reserve. *Neuropsychologia, 47,* 2015–2028.

Sternberg, R. J. (1988). Triangulating love. In R. J. Sternberg & M. L. Barnes (Eds.), *The psychology of love* (pp. 119–138). New Haven, CT: Yale University Press.

Sternberg, R. J. (2000). *Cupid's arrow: The course of love through time.* Cambridge, UK: Cambridge University Press.

Sternberg, R. J. (2001). Why schools should teach for wisdom: The balance theory of wisdom in educational settings. *Educational Psychologist, 36,* 227–245.

Sternberg, R. J. (2003). The development of creativity as a decision-making process. In R. K. Sawyer, V. John-Steiner, S. Moran, R. J. Sternberg, D. H. Feldman, J. Nakamura, & M. Csikszentmihalyi (Eds.), *Creativity and development* (pp. 91–138). New York: Oxford University Press.

Sternberg, R. J. (2005). The triarchic theory of successful intelligence. In D. P. Flanagan & P. L. Harrison (Eds.), *Contemporary intellectual assessment: Theories, tests, and issues* (pp. 103–119). New York: Guilford.

Sternberg, R. J. (2006). A duplex theory of love. In R. J. Sternberg & K. Weis (Eds.), *The new psychology of love* (pp. 184–199). New Haven, CT: Yale University Press.

Sternberg, R. J. (2008). The triarchic theory of successful intelligence. In N. Salkind (Ed.), *Encyclopedia of educational psychology* (Vol. 2, pp. 988–994). Thousand Oaks, CA: Sage.

Sternberg, R. J., Forsythe, G. B., Hedlund, J., Horvath, J. A., Wagner, R. K., Williams, W. M., Snook, S. A., & Grigorenko, E. L. (2000). *Practical intelligence in everyday life.* Cambridge, UK: Cambridge University Press.

Sternberg, R. J., & Grigorenko, E. L. (2002). *Dynamic testing.* New York: Cambridge University Press.

Sternberg, R. J., & Lubart, T. I. (2001). Wisdom and creativity. In J. E. Birren & K. W. Schaie (Eds.),

Handbook of the psychology of aging (pp. 500–522). San Diego: Academic Press.

Stevens, J., Katz, E. G., & Huxley, R. R. (2010). Associations between gender, age and waist circumference. *European Journal of Clinical Nutrition, 64*, 6–15.

Stevens, J. C., & Cruz, L. A. (1996). Spatial acuity of touch: Ubiquitous decline with aging revealed by repeated threshold testing. *Somatosensory and Motor Research, 13*, 1–10.

Stevenson, H. W., Lee, S., & Mu, X. (2000). Successful achievement in mathematics: China and the United States. In C. F. M. van Lieshout & P. G. Heymans (Eds.), *Developing talent across the life span* (pp. 167–183). Philadelphia: Psychology Press.

Stewart, A. J., & Malley, J. E. (2004). Women of the greatest generation. In C. Daiute & C. Lightfoot (Eds.), *Narrative analysis: Studying the development of individuals in society* (pp. 223–244). Thousand Oaks, CA: Sage.

Stewart, A. J., Ostrove, J. M., & Helson, R. (2001). Middle aging in women: Patterns of personality change from the 30s to the 50s. *Journal of Adult Development, 8*, 23–37.

Stewart, A. J., & Vandewater, E. A. (1999). "If I had to do over again . . .": Midlife review, midcourse corrections, and women's well-being in midlife. *Journal of Personality and Social Psychology, 76*, 270–283.

Stewart, A. L., Verboncoeur, C. J., McLellan, B. Y., Gillis, D. E., Rush, S., & Mills, K. M. (2001). Physical activity outcomes of CHAMPS II: A physical activity promotion program for older adults. *Journal of Gerontology, 56A*, M465–M470.

Stewart, P. W., Lonky, E., Reihman, J., Pagano, J., Gump, B. B., & Darvill, T. (2008). The relationship between prenatal PCB exposure and intelligence (IQ). *Environmental Health Perspectives, 116*, 1416–1422.

Stewart, R. B., Jr. (1990). *The second child: Family transition and adjustment.* Newbury Park, CA: Sage.

Stewart, S., Stinnett, H., & Rosenfeld, L. B. (2000). Sex differences in desired characteristics of short-term and long-term relationship partners. *Journal of Social and Personal Relationships, 17*, 843–853.

Stice, E. (2003). Puberty and body image. In C. Hayward (Ed.), *Gender differences at puberty* (pp. 61–76). New York: Cambridge University Press.

Stice, E., Presnell, K., & Bearman, S. K. (2001). Relation of early menarche to depression, eating disorders, substance abuse, and comorbid psychopathology among adolescent girls. *Developmental Psychology, 37*, 608–619.

Stiles, J. (2008). *Fundamentals of brain development.* Cambridge, MA: Harvard University Press.

Stiles, J. (2012). The effects of injury to dynamic neural networks in the mature and developing brain. *Developmental Psychobiology, 54*, 343–349.

Stiles, J., Reilly, J., Paul, B., & Moses, P. (2005). Cognitive development following early brain injury: Evidence for neural adaptation. *Trends in Cognitive Sciences, 9*, 136–143.

Stiles, J., Stern, C., Appelbaum, M., & Nass, R. (2008). Effects of early focal brain injury on memory for visuospatial patterns: Selective deficits of global–local processing. *Neuropsychology, 22*, 61–73.

Stilson, S. R., & Harding, C. G. (1997). Early social context as it relates to symbolic play: A longitudinal investigation. *Merrill-Palmer Quarterly, 43*, 682–693.

Stinchcomb, J. B., Bazemore, G., & Riestenberg, N. (2006). Beyond zero tolerance: Restoring justice in secondary schools. *Youth Violence and Juvenile Justice, 4*, 123–147.

Stine-Morrow, E. A. L., & Basak, C. (2011). Cognitive interventions. In K. W. Schaie & S. L. Willis (Eds.), *Handbook of the psychology of aging* (7th ed.,pp. 153–171). New York: Elsevier.

Stine-Morrow, E. A. L., & Miller, L. M. S. (2009). Aging, self-regulation, and learning from text. *Psychology of Learning and Motivation, 51*, 255–285.

Stipek, D. J., Feiler, R., Daniels, D., & Milburn, S. (1995). Effects of different instructional approaches on young children's achievement and motivation. *Child Development, 66*, 209–223.

Stipek, D. J., Gralinski, J. H., & Kopp, C. B. (1990). Self-concept development in the toddler years. *Developmental Psychology, 26*, 972–977.

St James-Roberts, I. (2007). Helping parents to manage infant crying and sleeping: A review of the evidence and its implications for services. *Child Abuse Review, 16*, 47–69.

St James-Roberts, I., Alvarez, M., Csipke, E., Abramsky, T., Goodwin, J., & Sorgenfrei, E. (2006). Infant crying and sleeping in London, Copenhagen and when parents adopt a "proximal" form of care. *Pediatrics, 117*, e1146–e1155.

St James-Roberts, I., Goodwin, J., Peter, B., Adams, D., & Hunt, S. (2003). Individual differences in responsivity to a neurobehavioural examination predict crying patterns of 1-week-old infants at home. *Developmental Medicine and Child Neurology, 45*, 400–407.

St. Louis, G. R., & Liem, J. H. (2005). Ego identity, ethnic identity, and the psychosocial well-being of ethnic minority and majority college students. *Identity, 5*, 227–246.

Stoch, M. B., Smythe, P. M., Moodie, A. D., & Bradshaw, D. (1982). Psychosocial outcome and CT findings after growth undernourishment during infancy: A 20-year developmental study. *Developmental Medicine and Child Neurology, 24*, 419–436.

Stocker, C. M., Burwell, R. A., & Briggs, M. L. (2002). Sibling conflict in middle childhood predicts children's adjustment in early adolescence. *Journal of Family Psychology, 16*, 50–57.

Stohs, S. J. (2011). The role of free radicals in toxicity and disease. *Journal of Basic and Clinical Physiology and Pharmacology, 6*, 205–228.

Stone, A. A., Schwartz, J. E., Broderick, J. E., & Deaton, A. (2010). A snapshot of the age distribution of psychological well-being in the United States. *Proceedings of the National Academy of Sciences, 107*, 9985–9990.

Stone, M. R., & Brown, B. B. (1999). Identity claims and projections: Descriptions of self and crowds in secondary school. In J. A. McLellan & M. J. V. Pugh (Eds.), *The role of peer groups in adolescent social identity: Exploring the importance of stability and change* (pp. 7–20). San Francisco: Jossey-Bass.

Stone, R. I., & Reinhard, S. C. (2007). The place of assisted living in long-term care and related service systems. *Gerontologist, 47*, 23–32.

Stoppa, T. M., & Lefkowitz, E. S. (2010). Longitudinal changes in religiosity among emerging adult college students. *Journal of Research on Adolescence, 20*, 23–38.

Stormshak, E. A., Bierman, K. L., McMahon, R. J., Lengua, L. J., & the Conduct Problems Prevention Research Group. (2000). Parenting practices and child disruptive behavior problems in early elementary school. *Journal of Clinical Child Psychology, 29*, 17–29.

Story, R. (2007). Asthma and obesity in children. *Current Opinion in Pediatrics, 19*, 680–684.

Stouthamer-Loeber, M., Wei, E., Loeber, R., & Masten, A. S. (2004). Desistance from persistent serious delinquency in the transition to adulthood. *Development and Psychopathology, 16*, 897–918.

Strapp, C. M., & Federico, A. (2000). Imitations and repetitions: What do children say following recasts? *First Language, 20*, 273–290.

Straus, M. A., & Stewart, J. H. (1999). Corporal punishment by American parents: National data on prevalence, chronicity, severity, and duration, in relation to child and family characteristics. *Clinical Child and Family Psychology Review, 2*, 55–70.

Strawbridge, W. J., Shema, S. J., Cohen, R. D., & Kaplan, G. A. (2001). Religious attendance increases survival by improving and maintaining good health behaviors. *Annals of Behavioral Medicine, 23*, 68–74.

Strazdins, L., Clements, M. S., Korda, R. J., Broom, D. H., & D'Souza, R. M. (2006). Unsociable work? Nonstandard work schedules, family relationships, and children's well-being. *Journal of Marriage and the Family, 68*, 394–410.

Street, A. E., Bell, M., & Ready, C. B. (2011). Sexual assault. In D. Benedek & G. Wynn (Eds.), *Clinical manual for the management of PTSD* (pp. 325–348). Arlington, VA: American Psychiatric Press.

Streissguth, A. P., Bookstein, F. L., Barr, H. M., Sampson, P. D., O'Malley, K., & Young, J. K. (2004). Risk factors for adverse life outcomes in fetal alcohol syndrome and fetal alcohol effects. *Journal of Developmental and Behavioral Pediatrics, 25*, 228–238.

Streissguth, A. P., Treder, R., Barr, H. M., Shepard, T., Bleyer, W. A., Sampson, P. D., & Martin, D. (1987). Aspirin and acetaminophen use by pregnant women and subsequent child IQ and attention decrements. *Teratology, 35*, 211–219.

Striano, T., & Rochat, P. (2000). Emergence of selective social referencing in infancy. *Infancy, 1*, 253–264.

Striegel-Moore, R. H., & Franko, D. L. (2006). Adolescent eating disorders. In R. H. Striegel-Moore & D. L. Franko (Eds.), *Child and adolescent psychopathology: Theoretical and clinical implications* (pp. 160–183). New York: Routledge.

Stright, A. D., Herr, M. Y., & Neitzel, C. (2009). Maternal scaffolding of children's problem solving and children's adjustment in kindergarten: Hmong families in the United States. *Journal of Educational Psychology, 101*, 207–218.

Stright, A. D., Neitzel, C., Sears, K. G., & Hoke-Sinex, L. (2002). Instruction begins in the home: Relations between parental instruction and children's self-regulation in the classroom. *Journal of Educational Psychology, 93*, 456–466.

Stringer, K., Kerpelman, J., & Skorikov, V. (2011). Career preparation: A longitudinal, process-oriented examination. *Journal of Vocational Behavior, 79*, 158–169.

Stringer, K. J., & Kerpelman, J. L. (2010). Career identity development in college students: Decision making, parental support, and work experience. *Identity, 10*, 181–200.

Stroebe, M., & Schut, H. (2010). The dual process model of coping with bereavement: A decade on. *Omega, 61*, 273–289.

Stroebe, M. S., & Schut, H. (1999). The dual process model of coping with bereavement: Rationale and description. *Death Studies, 23*, 197–224.

Stroebe, M. S., van der Houwen, K., & Schut, H. (2008). Bereavement support, intervention, and research on the Internet: A critical review. In M. S. Stroebe, R. O. Hansson, H. Schut, & W. Stroebe (Eds.), *Handbook of bereavement research and practice* (pp. 551–574). Washington, DC: American Psychological Association.

Strohschein, L. (2005). Parental divorce and child mental health trajectories. *Journal of Marriage and Family, 67*, 1286–1300.

Strough, J., Hicks, P. J., Swenson, L. M., Cheng, S., & Barnes, K. A. (2003). Collaborative everyday problem solving: Interpersonal relationships and problem dimensions. *International Journal of Aging and Human Development, 56*, 43–66.

Strough, J., Leszczynski, J. P., Neely, T. L., Flinn, J. A., & Margrett, J. (2007). From adolescence to later adulthood: Femininity, masculinity, and androgyny in six age groups. *Sex Roles, 57*, 385–396.

Strough, J., McFall, J. P., Flinn, J. A., & Schuller, K. L. (2008). Collaborative everyday problem solving among same-gender friends in early and later adulthood. *Psychology and Aging, 23,* 517–530.

Strouse, D. L. (1999). Adolescent crowd orientations: A social and temporal analysis. In J. A. McLellan & M. J. V. Pugh (Eds.), *The role of peer groups in adolescent social identity: Exploring the importance of stability and change* (pp. 37–54). San Francisco: Jossey-Bass.

Stuart, M., & Weinrich, M. (2001). Home- and community-based long-term care: Lessons from Denmark. *Gerontologist, 41,* 474–480.

Sturaro, C., van Lier, P. A. C., Cuijpers, P., & Koot, H. M. (2011). The role of peer relationships in the development of early school-age externalizing problems. *Child Development, 82,* 758–765.

Sturge-Apple, M. L., Davies, P. T., Winter, M. A., Cummings, E. M., & Schermerhorn, A. (2008). Interparental conflict and children's school adjustment: The explanatory role of children's internal representations of interparental and parent–child relationships. *Developmental Psychology, 44,* 1678–1690.

Styne, D. M. (2003). The regulation of pubertal growth. *Hormone Research, 60*(Suppl. 1), 22–26.

Su, T. F., & Costigan, C. L. (2008). The development of children's ethnic identity in immigrant Chinese families in Canada: The role of parenting practices and children's perceptions of parental family obligation expectations. *Journal of Early Adolescence, 29,* 638–663.

Suarez-Morales, L., & Lopez, B. (2009). The impact of acculturative stress and daily hassles on preadolescent psychological adjustment: Examining anxiety symptoms. *Journal of Primary Prevention, 30,* 335–349.

Suárez-Orozco, C., Todorova, I., & Qin, D. B. (2006). The well-being of immigrant adolescents: A longitudinal perspective on risk and protective factors. In F. A. Villarruel & T. Luster (Eds.), *The crisis in youth mental health: Critical issues and effective programs: Vol. 2. Disorders in adolescence* (pp. 53–83). Westport, CT: Praeger.

Subbotsky, E. (2004). Magical thinking in judgments of causation: Can anomalous phenomena affect ontological causal beliefs in children and adults? *British Journal of Developmental Psychology, 22,* 123–152.

Subrahmanyam, K., Gelman, R., & Lafosse, A. (2002). Animate and other separably moveable things. In G. Humphreys (Ed.), *Category-specificity in brain and mind* (pp. 341–371). London: Psychology Press.

Subrahmanyam, K., & Greenfield, P. M. (2008). Online communication and adolescent relationships. *Future of Children, 18,* 119–146.

Subrahmanyam, K., Smahel, D., & Greenfield, P. (2006). Connecting developmental constructions to the Internet: Identity presentation and sexual exploration in online teen chat rooms. *Developmental Psychology, 42,* 395–406.

Substance Abuse and Mental Health Services Administration. (2011). *Results from the 2010 National Survey on Drug Use and Health: Vol. 1. Summary of national findings.* Rockville, MD: Author.

Sullivan, M. C., McGrath, M. M. Hawes, K., & Lester, B. M. (2008). Growth trajectories of preterm infants: Birth to 12 years. *Journal of Pediatric Health Care, 22,* 83–93.

Sullivan, M. W., & Lewis, M. (2003). Contextual determinants of anger and other negative expressions in young infants. *Developmental Psychology, 39,* 693–705.

Summers, R. W., & Hoffman, A. M. (Eds.). (2006). *Elder abuse: A public health perspective.* Washington, DC: American Public Health Association.

Super, C. M. (1981). Behavioral development in infancy. In R. H. Monroe, R. L. Monroe, & B. B. Whiting (Eds.), *Handbook of cross-cultural human development* (pp. 181–270). New York: Garland.

Super, C. M., & Harkness, S. (2002). Culture structures the environment for development. *Human Development 45,* 270–274.

Super, C. M., & Harkness, S. (2010). Culture and infancy. In J. G. Bremner & T. D. Wachs (Eds.), *Wiley-Blackwell handbook of infant development: Vol. 1. Basic research* (2nd ed., pp. 623–649). Chichester, UK: Wiley-Blackwell.

Super, D. E. (1990). A life span, life space approach to career development. In D. Brown & L. Brooks (Eds.), *Career choice and development* (2nd ed., pp. 197–261). San Francisco: Jossey-Bass.

Super, D. E. (1994). A life span, life space perspective on convergence. In M. L. Savikas & R. W. Lent (Eds.), *Convergence in career development theories* (pp. 62–71). Palo Alto, CA: Consulting Psychologists Press.

Supple, A. J., Ghazarian, S. R., Peterson, G. W., & Bush, K. R. (2009). Assessing the cross-cultural validity of a parental autonomy granting measure: Comparing adolescents in the United States, China, Mexico, and India. *Journal of Cross-Cultural Psychology, 40,* 816–833.

Supple, A. J., & Small, S. A. (2006). The influence of parental support, knowledge, and authoritative parenting on Hmong and European American adolescent development. *Journal of Family Issues, 27,* 1214–1232.

Susman, E. J., & Dorn, L. D. (2009). Puberty: Its role in development. In R. M. Lerner & L. Steinberg (Eds.), *Handbook of adolescent psychology: Vol. 1. Individual bases of adolescent development* (3rd ed., pp. 116–151). Hoboken, NJ: Wiley.

Sussman, S., Skara, S., & Ames, S. L. (2008). Substance abuse among adolescents. *Substance Use and Misuse, 43,* 1802–1828.

Sutton, M. J., Brown, J. D., Wilson, K. M., & Klein, J. D. (2002). Shaking the tree of forbidden fruit: Where adolescents learn about sexuality and contraception. In J. D. Brown, J. R. Steele, & K. Walsh-Childers (Eds.), *Sexual teens, sexual media* (pp. 25–55). Mahwah, NJ: Erlbaum.

Swartz, T. T. (2009). Intergenerational family relations in adulthood: Patterns, variations, and implictions in the contemporary United States. *Annual Review of Sociology, 25,* 191–212.

Sweet, S., & Moen, P. (2007). Integrating educational careers in work and family. *Community, Work and Family, 10,* 231–250.

Swinson, J., & Harrop, A. (2009). Teacher talk directed to boys and girls and its relationship to their behaviour. *Educational Studies, 35,* 515–524.

Symons, D. K. (2001). A dyad-oriented approach to distress and mother–child relationship outcomes in the first 24 months. *Parenting: Science and Practice, 1,* 101–122.

Szaflarski, J. P., Rajogopal, A., Altaye, M., Byars, A. W., Jacola, L., Schmithorst, V. J., et al. (2012). Lefthandedness and language lateralization in children. *Brain Research, 1433,* 85–97.

Szlemko, W. J., Wood, J. W., & Thurman, P. J. (2006). Native Americans and alcohol: Past, present, and future. *Journal of General Psychology, 133,* 435–451.

T

Tabibi, Z., & Pfeffer, K. (2007). Finding a safe place to cross the road: The effect of distractors and the role of attention in children's identification of safe and dangerous road-crossing sites. *Infant and Child Development, 16,* 193–206.

Taga, G., Asakawa, K., Maki, A., Konishi, Y., & Koizumi, H. (2003). Brain imaging in awake infants by near-infrared optical topography. *Proceedings of the National Academy of Sciences, 100,* 10722–10727.

Tager-Flusberg, H., & Zukowski, A. (2009). Putting words together: Morphology and syntax in the preschool years. In J. B. Gleason & B. Ratner (Ed.), *The development of language* (7th ed., pp. 139–191). Boston: Allyn and Bacon.

Tahir, L., & Gruber, H. E. (2003). Developmental trajectories and creative work in late life. In J. Demick & C. Andreoletti (Eds.), *Handbook of adult development* (pp. 239–255). New York: Springer.

Takagi, E., Silverstein, M., & Crimmins, E. (2007). Intergenerational coresidence of older adults in Japan: Conditions for cultural plasticity. *Journal of Gerontology, 62B,* S330–S339.

Takahashi, K. (1990). Are the key assumptions of the "Strange Situation" procedure universal? A view from Japanese research. *Human Development, 33,* 23–30.

Takamura, J., & Williams, B. (2002). *Informal caregiving: Compassion in action.* Arlington, TX: Arc of the United States.

Talbot, L. S., McGlinchey, E. L., Kaplan, K. A., & Dahl, R. E. (2010). Sleep deprivation in adolescents and adults: Changes in affect. *Emotion, 10,* 831–841.

Tamis-LeMonda, C. S., & Bornstein, M. H. (1989). Habituation and maternal encouragement of attention in infancy as predictors of toddler language, play, and representational competence. *Child Development, 60,* 738–751.

Tamis-LeMonda, C. S., Shannon, J. D., Cabrera, N. J., & Lamb, M. E. (2004). Fathers and mothers at play with their 2- and 3-year-olds: Contributions to language and cognitive development. *Child Development, 75,* 1806–1820.

Tamis-LeMonda, C. S., Way, N., Hughes, D., Yoshikawa, H., Kalman, R. K., & Niwa, E. Y. (2008). Parents' goals for children: The dynamic coexistence of individualism and collectivism in cultures and individuals. *Social Development, 17,* 183–209.

Tammelin, T., Näyhä, S., Hills, A. P., & Järvelin, M. (2003). Adolescent participation in sports and adult physical activity. *American Journal of Preventive Medicine, 24,* 22–28.

Tamrouti-Makkink, I. D., Dubas, J. S., Gerris, J. R. M., & van Aken, A. G. (2004). The relation between the absolute level of parenting and differential parental treatment with adolescent siblings' adjustment. *Journal of Child Psychology and Psychiatry, 45,* 1397–1406.

Tanaka, H., & Seals, D. R. (2003). Dynamic exercise performance in master athletes: Insight into the effects of primary human aging on physiological functional capacity. *Journal of Applied Physiology, 95,* 2152–2162.

Tangney, J. P., Stuewig, J., & Mashek, D. J. (2007). Moral emotions and moral behavior. *Annual Review of Psychology, 58,* 345–372.

Tanimura, M., Takahashi, K., Kataoka, N., Tomita, K., Tanabe, I., Yasuda, M., et al. (2004). Proposal: Heavy television and video viewing poses a risk for infants and young children. *Nippon Shonika Gakkai Zasshi, 108,* 709–712 (in Japanese).

Tanner, J. M., Healy, M., & Cameron, N. (2001). *Assessment of skeletal maturity and prediction of adult height (TW3 method)* (3rd ed.). Philadelphia: Saunders.

Tanner, J. L., & Arnett, J. J. (2011). Presenting "emerging adulthood": What makes it developmentally distinctive? In J. J. Arnett, M. Kloep, L. B. Hendry, & J. L. Tanner (Eds.), *Debating emerging adulthood: Stage or process?* (pp. 13–30). New York: Oxford University Press.

Tanner, J. L., Arnett, J. J., & Leis, J. A. (2009). Emerging adulthood: Learning and development during the first stage of adulthood. In M. C. Smith & N. DeFrates-Densch (Eds.), *Handbook of research on adult learning and development* (pp. 34–67). New York: Routledge.

Tardif, T. (2006). But are they really verbs? Chinese words for action. In K. Hirsh-Pasek & R. M. Golinkoff (Eds.), *Action meets word: How children learn verbs* (pp. 477–498). New York: Oxford University Press.

Tardif, T., Fletcher, P., Liang, W., & Kaciroti, N. (2009). Early vocabulary development in Mandarin (Putonghua) and Cantonese. *Journal of Child Language, 36,* 1115–1144.

Tardif, T., Fletcher, P., Liang, W., Zhang, Z., Kaciroti, N., & Marchman, V. A. (2008). Baby's first 10 words. *Developmental Psychology, 44,* 929–938.

Tardif, T., Wellman, H. M., & Cheung, K. M. (2004). False belief understanding in Cantonese-speaking children. *Journal of Child Language, 31,* 779–800.

Tarry-Adkins, J. L., Martin-Gronert, M. S., Chen, J. H., Cripps, R. L., & Ozanne, S. E. (2008). Maternal diet influences DNA damage, aortic telomere length, oxidative stress, and antioxidant defense capacity in rats. *FASEB Journal, 22,* 2037–2044.

Tarter, R. E., Vanyukov, M., & Kirisci, L. (2008). Etiology of substance use disorder: Developmental perspective. In Y. Kaminer & O. G. Bukstein (Eds.), *Adolescent substance abuse: Psychiatric comorbidity and high-risk behaviors* (pp. 5–27). New York: Routledge.

Tasker, F. (2005). Lesbian mothers, gay fathers, and their children: A review. *Developmental and Behavioral Pediatrics, 26,* 224–240.

Taylor, C. A., Manganello, J. A., Lee, S. J., & Rice, J. C. (2010). Mother's spanking of 3-year-old children and subsequent risk of children's aggressive behavior. *Pediatrics, 125,* e1057–e1065.

Taylor, J. L. (2009). Midlife impacts of adolescent parenthood. *Journal of Family Issues, 30,* 484–510.

Taylor, M. C., & Hall, J. A. (1982). Psychological androgyny: Theories, methods, and conclusions. *Psychological Bulletin, 92,* 347–366.

Taylor, M. G., Rhodes, M., & Gelman, S. A. (2009). Boys will be boys; cows will be cows: Children's essentialist reasoning about gender categories and animal species. *Child Development, 80,* 461–481.

Taylor, P., Wang, W., Parker, K., Passel, J. S., Patten, E., & Motel, S. (2012). *The rise of intermarriage.* Washington, DC: Pew Research Center.

Taylor, R. D. (2010). Risk and resilience in low-income African American families: Moderating effects of kinship social support. *Cultural Diversity and Ethnic Minority Psychology, 16,* 344–351.

Taylor, R. J., Lincoln, K. D., & Chatters, L. M. (2005). Supportive relationships with church members among African Americans. *Family Relations, 54,* 501–511.

Taylor, W. C., Sallis, J. F., Lees, E., Hepworth, J. T., Feliz, K., Volding, D. C., Cassels, A., & Tobin, J. N. (2007). Changing social and built environments to promote physical activity: Recommendations from low-income, urban women. *Journal of Physical Activity and Health, 4,* 54–65.

Teasdale, B., & Bradley-Engen, M. S. (2010). Adolescent same-sex attraction and mental health: The role of stress and support. *Journal of Homosexuality, 57,* 287–309.

Teinonen, T., Fellman, V., Näätänen, R., Alku, P., & Huotilainen, M. (2009). Statistical language learning in neonates revealed by event-related brain potentials. *BMC Neuroscience, 10,* 21.

Temkin-Greener, H., Bajorska, A., Peterson, D. R., Kunitz, S. J., Gross, D., & Williams, T. F. (2004). Social support and risk-adjusted mortality in a frail older population. *Medical Care, 42,* 779–788.

Temple, J. L., Giacomelli, A. M., Roemmich, J. N., & Epstein, L. H. (2007). Overweight children habituate slower than nonoverweight children to food. *Physiology and Behavior, 9,* 250–254.

ten Brummelhuis, L. L., ter Hoeven, C. L., De Jong, M. D. T., & Peper, B. (2012). Exploring the linkage between the home domain and absence from work: Health, motivation, or both? *Journal of Organizational Behavior, 33.* Accessed online at http://onlinelibrary.wiley.com/doi/10.1002/job.1789/abstract

Tenenbaum, H. R., Hill, D., Joseph, N., & Roche, E. (2010). "It's a boy because he's painting a picture": Age differences in children's conventional and unconventional gender schemas. *British Journal of Psychology, 101,* 137–154.

Tenenbaum, H. R., & Leaper, C. (2002). Are parents' gender schemas related to their children's gender-related cognitions? A meta-analysis. *Developmental Psychology, 38,* 615–630.

Tenenbaum, H. R., & Leaper, C. (2003). Parent–child conversations about science: The socialization of gender inequities? *Developmental Psychology, 39,* 34–47.

Tenenbaum, H. R., Snow, C. E., Roach, K. A., & Kurland, B. (2005). Talking and reading science: Longitudinal data on sex differences in mother–child conversations in low-income families. *Journal of Applied Developmental Psychology, 26,* 1–19.

ten Tusscher, G. W., & Koppe, J. G. (2004). Perinatal dioxin exposure and later effects—a review. *Chemosphere, 54,* 1329–1336.

Terwel, J., Gillies, R. M., van den Eeden, P., & Hoek, D. (2001). Cooperative learning processes of students: A longitudinal multilevel perspective. *British Journal of Educational Psychology, 71,* 619–645.

Teti, D. M., Saken, J. W., Kucera, E., & Corns, K. M. (1996). And baby makes four: Predictors of attachment security among preschool-age firstborns during the transition to siblinghood. *Child Development, 67,* 579–596.

Teyber, E. (2001). *Helping children cope with divorce* (rev. ed.). San Francisco: Jossey-Bass.

Thacker, H. L. (2011). Assessing risks and benefits of nonhormonal treatments for vasomotor symptoms in perimenopausal and postmenopausal women. *Journal of Women's Health, 20,* 1007–1016.

Thacker, S. B., & Stroup, D. F. (2003). Revisiting the use of the electronic fetal monitor. *Lancet, 361,* 445–446.

Thatcher, R. W., Walker, R. A., & Giudice, S. (1987). Human cerebral hemispheres develop at different rates and ages. *Science, 236,* 1110–1113.

Thelen, E., Schöner, G., Scheier, C., & Smith, L. B. (2001). The dynamics of embodiment: A field theory of infant perseverative reaching. *Behavioral and Brain Sciences, 24,* 1–34.

Thelen, E., & Smith, L. B. (1998). Dynamic systems theories. In R. M. Lerner (Ed.), *Handbook of child psychology: Vol. 1. Theoretical models of human development* (5th ed., pp. 563–634). New York: Wiley.

Thelen, E., & Smith, L. B. (2006). Dynamic systems theories. In R. M. Lerner (Ed.), *Handbook of child psychology: Vol. 1. Theoretical models of human development* (6th ed., pp. 258–312). Hoboken, NJ: Wiley.

Thiessen, E. D., & Saffran, J. R. (2007). Learning to learn: Infants' acquisition of stress-based strategies for work segmentation. *Language Learning and Development, 3,* 73–100.

Thoermer, C., Sodian, B., Vuori, M., Perst, H., & Kristen, S. (2012). Continuity from an implicit to an explicit understanding of false belief from infancy to preschool age. *British Journal of Developmental Psychology, 30,* 172–187.

Thomaes, S., Stegge, H., Bushman, B. J., & Olthof, T. (2008). Trumping shame by blasts of noise: Narcissism, self-esteem, shame, and aggression in young adolescents. *Child Development, 79,* 1792–1801.

Thomas, A., & Chess, S. (1977). *Temperament and development.* New York: Brunner/Mazel.

Thomas, A., Chess, S., & Birch, H. G. (1968). *Temperament and behavior disorders in children.* New York: New York University Press.

Thomas, C. L., & Dimitrov, D. M. (2007). Effects of a teen pregnancy prevention program on teens' attitudes toward sexuality: A latent trait modeling approach. *Developmental Psychology, 43,* 173–185.

Thomas, K. A., & Tessler, R. C. (2007). Bicultural socialization among adoptive families: Where there is a will, there is a way. *Journal of Family Issues, 28,* 1189–1219.

Thomas, R. M. (2005). *Comparing theories of child development* (6th ed.). Belmont, CA: Wadsworth.

Thombs, B. D., Roseman, M., & Arthurs, E. (2010). Prenatal and postpartum depression in fathers and mothers. *Journal of the American Medical Association, 304,* 961.

Thompson, A., Hollis, C., & Richards, D. (2003). Authoritarian parenting attitudes as a risk for conduct problems: Results of a British national cohort study. *European Child and Adolescent Psychiatry, 12,* 84–91.

Thompson, P. M., Giedd, J. N., Woods, R. P., MacDonald, D., Evans, A. C., & Toga, A. W. (2000). Growth patterns in the developing brain detected by using continuum mechanical tensor maps. *Nature, 404,* 190–192.

Thompson, R. A. (2000). The legacy of early attachments. *Child Development, 71,* 145–152.

Thompson, R. A. (2006). The development of the person: Social understanding, relationships, conscience, self. In N. Eisenberg (Ed.), *Handbook of child psychology: Vol. 3. Social, emotional, and personality development* (6th ed., pp. 24–98). Hoboken, NJ: Wiley.

Thompson, R. A. (2008). Early attachment and later development. In J. Cassidy & P. R. Shaver (Eds.), *Handbook of attachment: Theory, research, and clinical applications* (2nd ed., pp. 348–365). New York: Guilford.

Thompson, R. A., & Goodman, M. (2010). Development of emotion regulation: More than meets the eye. In A. M. Kring & D. M. Sloan (Eds.), *Emotion regulation and psychopathology: A transdiagnostic approach to etiology and treatment* (pp. 38–58). New York: Guilford.

Thompson, R. A., & Goodvin, R. (2007). Taming the tempest in the teapot. In C. A. Brownell & C. B. Kopp (Eds.), *Socioemotional development in the toddler years: Transitions and transformations* (pp. 320–341). New York: Guilford.

Thompson, R. A., & Meyer, S. (2007). Socialization of emotion regulation in the family. In J. J. Gross (Ed.), *Handbook of emotion regulation* (pp. 249–268). New York: Guilford.

Thompson, R. A., Meyer, S., & McGinley, M. (2006). Understanding values in relationships: The development of conscience. In M. Killen & J. G. Smetana (Eds.), *Handbook of moral development* (pp. 267–298). Mahwah, NJ: Erlbaum.

Thompson, R. A., & Raikes, H. A. (2007). The social and emotional foundations of school readiness. In D. F. Perry, R. K. Kaufmann, & J. Knitzer (Eds.), *Social and emotional health in early childhood: Building bridges between services and systems* (pp. 13–35). Baltimore, MD: Paul H. Brookes.

Thompson, W. W., Price, C., Goodson, B., Shay, D. K., Benson, P., Hinrichsen, V. L., et al. (2007). Early thimerosal exposure and neuropsychological outcomes at 7 to 10 years. *New England Journal of Medicine, 357,* 1281–1292.

Thorne, B. (1993). *Gender play: Girls and boys in school.* New Brunswick, NJ: Rutgers University Press.

Thornton, J., Edwards, R., Mitchell, P., Harrison, R. A., Buchan, I., & Kelly, S. P. (2005). Smoking and age-related macular degeneration: A review of association. *Eye, 19,* 935–944.

Thornton, S. (1999). Creating conditions for cognitive change: The interaction between task structures and specific strategies. *Child Development, 70,* 588–603.

Tienari, P., Wahlberg, K. E., & Wynne, L. C. (2006). Finnish adoption study of schizophrenia: Implications for family interventions. *Families, Systems, and Health, 24,* 442–451.

Tiet, Q. Q., Huizinga, D., & Byrnes, H. F. (2010). Predictors of resilience among inner city youths. *Journal of Child and Family Studies, 19,* 360–378.

Tiggemann, M., & Anesbury, T. (2000). Negative stereotyping of obesity in children: The role of controllability beliefs. *Journal of Applied Social Psychology, 30,* 1977–1993.

Tofler, I. R., Knapp, P. K., & Drell, M. J. (1998). The achievement by proxy spectrum in youth sports: Historical perspective and clinical approach to pressured and high-achieving children and adolescents. *Child and Adolescent Psychiatric Clinics of North America, 7,* 803–820.

Tokunaga, R. S. (2010). Following you home from school: A critical review and synthesis of research on cyberbullying victimization. *Computers in Human behavior, 26,* 277–287.

Tomasello, M. (1999). Having intentions, understanding intentions, and understanding communicative intentions. In P. D. Zelazo, J. W. Astington, & J. Wilde (Eds.), *Developing theories of intention: Social understanding and self-control* (pp. 63–75). Mahwah, NJ: Erlbaum.

Tomasello, M. (2003). *Constructing a language: A usage-based theory of language acquisition.* Cambridge, MA: Harvard University Press.

Tomasello, M. (2006). Acquiring linguistic constructions. In D. Kuhn & R. Siegler (Eds.), *Handbook of child psychology: Vol. 2: Cognition, perception, and language* (6th ed., pp. 255–298). Hoboken, NJ: Wiley.

Tomasello, M. (2011). Language development. In U. Goswami (Ed.), *Wiley-Blackwell handbook of childhood cognitive development* (2nd ed., pp. 239–257). Malden, MA: Wiley-Blackwell.

Tomasello, M., & Akhtar, N. (1995). Two-year-olds use pragmatic cues to differentiate reference to objects and actions. *Cognitive Development, 10,* 201–224.

Tomasello, M., & Brandt, S. (2009). Flexibility in the semantics and syntax of children's early verb use. *Monographs of the Society for Research in Child Development, 72*(2, Serial No. 293), 113–126.

Tomasello, M., Carpenter, M., & Liszkowski, U. (2007). A new look at infant pointing. *Child Development, 78,* 705–722.

Tomer, A., Eliason, G., & Smith, J. (2000). Beliefs about the self, life, and death: Testing aspects of a comprehensive model of death anxiety and death attitudes. *Death attitudes and the older adult: Theories, concepts, and applications* (pp. 109–122). Philadelphia: Taylor & Francis.

Tong, V. T., Jones, J. R., Dietz, P. M., D'Angelo, D., & Bombard, J. M. (2009, May 29). Trends in smoking before, during, and after pregnancy—Pregnancy Risk Assessment Monitoring System (PRAMS), United States, 31 Sites, 2000–2005. *Morbidity and Mortality Weekly Report, 58* (No. SS-4).

Torges, C. M., Stewart, A. J., & Miner-Rubino, K. (2005). Personality after the prime of life: Men and women coming to terms with regrets. *Journal of Research in Personality, 39,* 148–165.

Tornstam, L. (2000). Transcendence in later life. *Generations, 23*(10), 10–14.

Tornstam, L. (2011). Maturing into gerotranscendence. *Journal of TransPersonal Psychology, 43,* 166–180.

Toro-Morn, M., & Sprecher, S. (2003). A cross-cultural comparison of mate preferences among university students: The United States vs. the People's Republic of China (PRC). *Journal of Comparative Family Studies, 34,* 151–170.

Torrance, E. P. (1988). The nature of creativity as manifest in its testing. In R. J. Sternberg (Ed.), *The nature of creativity: Contemporary psychological perspectives* (pp. 43–75). New York: Cambridge University Press.

Tottenham, N., Hare, T. A., Millner, A., Gilhooly, T., Zevin, J. D., & Casey, B. J. (2011). Elevated amygdala response to faces following early deprivation. *Developmental Science, 14,* 190–204.

Touwslager, R. N., Gielen, M., Derom, C., Mulder, A. L., Gerver, W. J., Zimmermann, L. J., et al. (2011). Determinants of infant growth in four age windows: A twin study. *Journal of Pediatrics, 158,* 566–572.

Tracy, J. L., Robins, R. W., & Lagattuta, K. H. (2005). Can children recognize pride? *Emotion, 5,* 251–257.

Trafford, A. (2004). *My time: Making the most of the rest of your life.* New York: Basic Books.

Trappe, S. (2007). Marathon runners: How do they age? *Sports Medicine, 37,* 302–305.

Trautner, H. M., Gervai, J., & Nemeth, R. (2003). Appearance–reality distinction and development of gender constancy understanding in children. *International Journal of Behavioral Development, 27,* 275–283.

Trautner, H. M., Ruble, D. N., Cyphers, L., Kirsten, B., Behrendt, R., & Hartmann, P. (2005). Rigidity and flexibility of gender stereotypes in childhood: Developmental or differential? *Infant and Child Development, 14,* 365–381.

Treasure, J., & Schmidt, U. (2005). Anorexia nervosa. *Clinical Evidence, 13,* 1148–1157.

Trehub, S. E. (2001). Musical predispositions in infancy. *Annals of the New York Academy of Sciences, 930,* 1–16.

Tremblay, L., & Frigon, J.-Y. (2005). Precocious puberty in adolescent girls: A biomarker of later psychosocial adjustment problems. *Child Psychiatry and Human Development, 36,* 73–94.

Tremblay, R. E. (2000). The development of aggressive behaviour during childhood: What have we learned in the past century? *International Journal of Behavioral Development, 24,* 129–141.

Tremblay, R. E., Japel, C., Perusse, D., Voivin, M., Zoccolillo, M., Montplaisir, J., & McDuff, P. (1999). The search for the age of "onset" of physical aggression: Rousseau and Bandura revisited. *Criminal Behavior and Mental Health, 9,* 8–23.

Trentacosta, C. J., & Shaw, D. S. (2009). Emotional self-regulation, peer rejection, and antisocial behavior: Developmental associations from early childhood to early adolescence. *Journal of Applied Developmental Psychology, 30,* 356–365.

Triandis, H. C. (1995). *Individualism and collectivism.* Boulder, CO: Westview Press.

Triandis, H. C. (2005). Issues in individualism and collectivism research. In R. M. Sorrentino, D. Cohen, J. M. Olson, & M. P. Zanna (Eds.), *Culture and social behavior: The Ontario Symposium* (Vol. 10, pp. 207–225). Mahwah, NJ: Erlbaum.

Triandis, H. C. (2007). Culture and psychology: A history of the study of their relationship. In S. Kitayama & D. Cohen (Eds.), *Handbook of cultural psychology* (pp. 59–76). New York: Guilford.

Trocmé, N., & Wolfe, D. (2002). *Child maltreatment in Canada: The Canadian Incidence Study of Reported Child Abuse and Neglect.* Retrieved from www.hc-sc .gc.ca/pphb-dgspsp/cm-vee

Tronick, E., Morelli, G., & Ivey, P. (1992). The Efe forager infant and toddler's pattern of social relationships: Multiple and simultaneous. *Developmental Psychology, 28,* 568–577.

Tronick, E. Z., Thomas, R. B., & Daltabuit, M. (1994). The Quechua manta pouch: A caretaking practice for buffering the Peruvian infant against the multiple stressors of high altitude. *Child Development, 65,* 1005–1013.

Troop-Gordon, W., & Asher, S. R. (2005). Modifications in children's goals when encountering obstacles to conflict resolution. *Child Development, 76,* 568–582.

Troseth, G. L., Saylor, M. M., & Archer, A. H. (2006). Young children's use of video as a source of socially relevant information. *Child Development, 77,* 786–799.

Troyer, A. K., Häfliger, A., Cadieux, M. J., & Craik, F. I. M. (2006). Name and face learning in older adults: Effects of level of processing, self-generation, and intention to learn. *Journal of Gerontology, 61B,* P67–P74.

Trudel, G., Villeneuve, V., Anderson, A., & Pilon, G. (2008). Sexual and marital aspects of old age: An update. *Sexual and Relationship Therapy, 23,* 161–169.

True, M. M., Pisani, L., & Oumar, F. (2001). Infant–mother attachment among the Dogon of Mali. *Child Development, 72,* 1451–1466.

Trusty, J. (1999). Effects of eighth-grade parental involvement on late adolescents' educational expectations. *Journal of Research and Development in Education, 32,* 224–233.

Trzesniewski, K. H., & Donnellan, M. B. (2009). Reevaluating the evidence for increasingly positive self-views among high school students: More evidence for consistency across generations. *Psychological Science, 20,* 920–922.

Trzesniewski, K. H., & Donnellan, M. B. (2010). Rethinking "generation me": A study of cohort effects from 1976–2006. *Perspectives on Psychological Science, 5,* 58–75.

Trzesniewski, K. H., Donnellan, M. B., & Robins, R. W. (2003). Stability of self-esteem across the life span. *Journal of Personality and Social Psychology, 84,* 205–220.

Tsang, P. S., & Shaner, T. L. (1998). Age, attention, expertise, and time-sharing performance. *Psychology and Aging, 13,* 323–347.

Tsujimoto, S. (2008). The prefrontal cortex: Functional neural development during early childhood. *Neuroscientist, 14,* 345–358.

Tucker, C. J., McHale, S. M., & Crouter, A. C. (2001). Conditions of sibling support in adolescence. *Journal of Family Psychology, 15,* 254–271.

Tucker, C. J., McHale, S. M., & Crouter, A. C. (2003). Dimensions of mothers' and fathers' differential treatment of siblings: Links with adolescents' sex-typed personal qualities. *Family Relations, 52,* 82–89.

Turati, C. (2004). Why faces are not special to newborns: An account of the face preference. *Current Directions in Psychological Science, 13,* 5–8.

Turesson, C., & Matteson, E. L. (2006). Genetics of rheumatoid arthritis. *Mayo Clinic Proceedings, 81,* 94–101.

Turiel, E. (2006). The development of morality. In N. Eisenberg (Ed.), *Handbook of child psychology: Vol. 3. Social, emotional, and personality development* (6th ed., pp. 789–857). Hoboken, NJ: Wiley.

Turiel, E., & Killen, M. (2010). Taking emotions seriously: The role of emotions in moral development. In W. F. Arsenio & E. A. Lemerise (Eds.), *Emotions, aggression, and morality in children: Bridging development and psychopathology* (pp. 33–52). Washington, DC: American Psychological Association.

Turnbull, K. P., Anthony, A. B., Justice, L., & Bowles, R. (2009). Preschoolers' exposure to language stimulation in classrooms serving at-risk children: The contribution of group size and activity context. *Early Education and Development, 20,* 53–79.

Turnbull, M., Hart, D., & Lapkin, S. (2003). Grade 6 French immersion students' performance on large-scale reading, writing, and mathematics tests: Building explanations. *Alberta Journal of Educational Research, 49,* 6–23.

Turner, B. F. (1982). Sex-related differences in aging. In B. B. Wolman (Ed.), *Handbook of developmental psychology* (pp. 912–936). Englewood Cliffs, NJ: Prentice-Hall.

Turner, L. B. (2011). A meta-analysis of fat intake, reproduction, and breast cancer risk: An evolutionary perspective. *American Journal of Human Biology, 23,* 601–608.

Turner, P. J., & Gervai, J. (1995). A multidimensional study of gender typing in preschool children and their parents: Personality, attitudes, preferences, behavior, and cultural differences. *British Journal of Developmental Psychology, 11,* 323–342.

Turner, R. N., Hewstone, M., & Voci, A. (2007). Reducing explicit and implicit outgroup prejudice via direct and extended contact: The mediating role of self-disclosure and intergroup anxiety. *Journal of Personality and Social Psychology, 93,* 369–388.

Tuyen, J. M., & Bisgard, K. (2003). *Community setting: Pertussis outbreak.* Atlanta, GA: Centers for Disease Control and Prevention. Retrieved from www.cdc.gov/pertussis/outbreaks/guide/downloads/chapter-10.pdf

Twenge, J. M. (1997). Changes in masculine and feminine traits over time: A meta-analysis. *Sex Roles, 36,* 305–325.

Twenge, J. M. (2001). Changes in women's assertiveness in response to status and roles: A cross-temporal meta-analysis, 1931–1993. *Journal of Personality and Social Psychology, 81,* 133–145.

Twenge, J. M., & Campbell, W. K. (2001). Age and birth cohort differences in self-esteem: A crosstemporal meta-analysis. *Personality and Social Psychology Review, 5,* 321–344.

Twenge, J. M., Campbell, W. K., & Freeman, E. C. (2012). Generational differences in young adults' life goals, concern for others, and civic orientation, 1966–2009. *Journal of Personality and Social Psychology, 102,* 1045–1062.

Twenge, J. M., & Crocker, J. (2002). Race and self-esteem: Meta-analyses comparing whites, blacks, Hispanics, Asians, and America Indians and comment on Gray-Little and Hafdahl (2000). *Psychological Bulletin, 128,* 371–408.

Tzuriel, D., & Kaufman, R. (1999). Mediated learning and cognitive modifiability: Dynamic assessment of young Ethiopian immigrant children to Israel. *Journal of Cross-Cultural Psychology, 30,* 359–380.

U

Uauy, R., Kain, J., Mericq, V., Rojas, J., & Corválan, C. (2008). Nutrition, child growth, and chronic disease prevention. *Annals of Medicine, 40,* 11–20.

Uchino, B. N. (2009). Understanding the links between social support and physical health. *Perspectives on Psychological Science, 4,* 236–255.

Udechuku, A., Nguyen, T., Hill, R., & Szego, K. (2010). Antidepressants in pregnancy: A systematic review. *Australian and New Zealand Journal of Psychiatry, 44,* 978–996.

Uhlenberg, P., & Hammill, B. G. (1998). Frequency of grandparent contact with grandchild sets: Six factors that make a difference. *Gerontologist, 38,* 276–285.

Ukrainetz, T. A., Justice, L. M., Kaderavek, J. N., Eisenberg, S. L., Gillam, R., & Harm, H. M. (2005). The development of expressive elaboration in fictional narratives. *Journal of Speech, Language, and Hearing Research, 48,* 1363–1377.

Umana-Taylor, A. J., & Alfaro, E. C. (2006). Ethnic identity among U.S. Latino adolescents: Measurement and implications for well-being. In F. A. Villarruel & T. Luster (Eds.), *The crisis in youth mental health: Critical issues and effective programs: Vol. 2. Disorders in adolescence* (pp. 195–211). Westport, CT: Praeger.

Umana-Taylor, A. J., & Updegraff, K. A. (2007). Latino adolescents' mental health: Exploring the interrelations among discrimination, ethnic identity, cultural orientation, self-esteem, and depressive symptoms. *Journal of Adolescence, 30,* 549–567.

Underhill, K., Montgomery, P., & Operario, D. (2007). Sexual abstinence only programmes to prevent HIV infection in high-income countries: Systematic review. *British Medical Journal, 335,* 248.

Underwood, M. K. (2003). *Social aggression among girls.* New York: Guilford.

UNICEF (United Nations Children's Fund). (2007). *An overview of child well-being in rich countries,* Innocenti Report Card 7. Florence, Italy: UNICEF Innocenti Research Centre.

UNICEF (United Nations Children's Fund). (2009). *Infant and young child feeding 2000–2007.* Retrieved from www.childinfo.org/breastfeeding_countrydata.php

UNICEF (United Nations Children's Fund). (2010a). *Children and AIDS: Fifth stocktaking report.* New York: United Nations.

UNICEF (United Nations Children's Fund). (2010b). *Young champions for education: A progress review.* Retrieved from www.ungei.org/resources/files/Young_Champions_Evaluation_7_Jan.pdf

UNICEF (United Nations Children's Fund). (2011). *Children in conflict and emergencies.* Retrieved from www.unicef.org/protection/armedconflict.html

United Nations. (2011). *World population prospects: The 2011 revision. Population database.* Retrieved from esa.un.org/wpp/unpp/panel_population.htm

Uotinen, V., Rantanen, T., Suutama, T., & Ruoppila, I. (2006). Change in subjective age among older people over an eight-year follow-up: "Getting older and feeling younger"? *Experimental Aging Research, 32,* 381–393.

U.S. Census Bureau. (2012a). International database. Retrieved from sasweb.ssd.census.gov/idb/ranks.html

U.S. Census Bureau. (2012b). *Statistical abstract of the United States* (131st ed.). Washington, DC: U.S. Government Printing Office.

U.S. Census Bureau. (2013). *Statistical abstract of the United States* (132nd ed.). Washington, DC: U.S. Government Printing Office.

U.S. Department of Agriculture. (2011a). *Food security in the United States: Key statistics and graphics.* Retrieved from www.ers.usda.gov/Briefing/FoodSecurity/stats_graphs.htm

U.S. Department of Agriculture. (2011b). *WIC: The Special Supplemental Nutrition Program for Women, Infants, and Children.* Nutrition Program Facts. Retrieved from www.fns.usda.gov/wic/wic-fact-sheet.pdf

U.S. Department of Agriculture. (2012). *Expenditures on children by families, 2011.* Retrieved from www.cnpp.usda.gov/Publications/CRC/crc2011.pdf

U.S. Department of Education. (2007). *The Nation's Report Card: Mathematics 2007.* Retrieved from nces.ed.gov/pubsearch/pubsinfo.asp?pubid=2007494

U.S. Department of Education. (2009). *The Nation's Report Card: Mathematics 2009.* Retrieved from nces.ed.gov/nationsreportcard/pdf/main2009/2010451.pdf

U.S. Department of Education. (2010). *The nation's report card: Reading 2009.* Retrieved from nces.ed.gov/pubsearch/pubsinfo.asp?pubid=2010458

U.S. Department of Education. (2012a). *The condition of education 2012.* Retrieved from nces.ed.gov/pubsearch/pubsinfo.asp?pubid=2012045

U.S. Department of Education. (2012b). *Digest of education statistics: 2011.* Washington, DC: U.S. Government Printing Office.

U.S. Department of Health and Human Services. (2010a). Births: Final data for 2008. *National Vital Statistics Reports, 59*(1).

U.S. Department of Health and Human Services. (2010b). *Breastfeeding.* Retrieved from www.womenshealth.gov/breastfeeding/index.cfm

U.S. Department of Health and Human Services. (2010c). *Drugs, brains, and behavior: The science of addiction.* Bethesda, MD: National Institute of Drug Abuse.

U.S. Department of Health and Human Services. (2010d). *Head Start Impact Study: Final report.* Washington, DC: U.S. Government Printing Office.

U.S. Department of Health and Human Services. (2010e). National, state, and local vaccination coverage among children aged 19–35 months—United States, 2009. *Morbidity and Mortality Weekly Report, 59,* 1171–1177.

U.S. Department of Health and Human Services. (2011a). *Births: Preliminary data for 2010.* Retrieved from www.cdc.gov/nchs/data/nvsr/nvsr60/nvsr60_02.pdf

U.S. Department of Health and Human Services. (2011b). *Child maltreatment 2010.* Retrieved from www.acf.hhs.gov/programs/cb/resource/child-maltreatment-2010

U.S. Department of Health and Human Services. (2011c). *Health, United States 2010: With special feature on death and dying.* Washington, DC: U.S. Government Printing Office.

U.S. Department of Health and Human Services. (2011d). *Results from the 2010 National Survey on Drug Use and Health: Summary of national findings.* Rockville, MD: Substance Abuse and Mental Health Services Administration.

U.S. Department of Health and Human Services. (2011e). *The Surgeon General's call to action to prevent and decrease overweight and obesity: Overweight children and adolescents.* Retrieved from www.surgeongeneral.gov/library/calls/obesity/fact_adolescents.html

U.S. Department of Health and Human Services. (2012a). *Facts about Down syndrome.* Retrieved from www.education.com/reference/article/Ref_Facts_About_Down

U.S. Department of Health and Human Services. (2012b). *Key statistics from the National Survey of Family Growth: Impaired fecundity.* Retrieved from www.cdc.gov/nchs/nsfg/abc_list_i.htm#impaired

U.S. Department of Health and Human Services. (2012c). *Morbidity and mortality: 2012 chart book on cardiovascular, lung and blood diseases.* Bethesda, MD: Author.

U.S. Department of Health and Human Services. (2012d). *Older persons' health: Health care utilization.* Retrieved from www.cdc.gov/nchs/fastats/older_americans.htm

U.S. Department of Health and Human Services. (2012e). *A profile of older Americans 2012: Key indicators of well-being.* Washington, DC: U.S. Government Printing Office.

U.S. Department of Health and Human Services. (2012f). Youth Risk Behavior Surveillance—United States, 2011. *Morbidity and Mortality Weekly Report, 61*(No. 4). Retrieved from www.cdc.gov/mmwr/pdf/ss/ss6104.pdf

U.S. Department of Justice. (2010). *Crime in the United States, 2009.* Retrieved from www2.fbi.gov/ucr/cius2009

U.S. Department of Transportation. (2012). *Traffic safety facts: Research note. 2011 motor vehicle crashes: Overview.* Retrieved from www-nrd.nhtsa.dot.gov/Pubs/811701.pdf

U.S. Living Will Registry. (2005). *Advance directive forms.* Retrieved from uslwr.com/formslist.shtm

Usher-Seriki, K. K., Bynum, M. S., & Callands, T. A. (2008). Mother–daughter communication about sex and sexual intercourse among middle- to upper-class African American girls. *Journal of Family Issues, 29,* 901–917.

Usta, I. M., & Nassar, A. H. (2008). Advanced maternal age. Part I: Obstetric complications. *American Journal of Perinatology, 25,* 521–534.

Utz, R. L., Carr, D., Nesse, R., & Wortman, C. B. (2002). The effect of widowhood on older adults' social participation: An evaluation of activity, disengagement, and continuity theories. *Gerontologist, 42,* 522–533.

V

Vacha-Haase, T., Hill, R. D., & Bermingham, D. W. (2012). Aging theory and research. In N. A. Fouad, J. A. Carter, & L. M. Subich (Eds.), *APA handbook of counseling psychology: Vol. 1. Theories, research, and methods* (pp. 491–505). Washington, DC: American Psychological Association.

Vaillancourt, T., Brittain, H., Bennett, L., Arnocky, S., McDougall, P., Hymel, S., et al. (2010a). Places to avoid: Population-based study of student reports of unsafe and high bullying areas at school. *Canadian Journal of School Psychology, 25,* 40–54.

Vaillancourt, T., Clinton, J., McDougall, P., Schmidt, L. A., & Hymel, S. (2010b). The neurobiology of peer victimization and rejection. In S. Jimerson, S. M. Swearer, & D. L. Espelage (Eds.), *Handbook of bullying in schools: An international perspective* (pp. 293–304). New York: Routledge.

Vaillancourt, T., & Hymel, S. (2006). Aggression and social status: The moderating roles of sex and peer-valued characteristics. *Aggressive Behavior, 32,* 396–408.

Vaillancourt, T., McDougall, P., Hymel, S., & Sunderani, S. (2010c). Respect or fear? The relationship between power and bullying behavior. In S. R. Jimerson, S. M. Swearer, & D. L. Espelage (Eds.), *Handbook of bullying in schools: An international perspective* (pp. 211–222). New York: Routledge.

Vaillant, G. E. (1977). *Adaptation to life.* Boston: Little, Brown.

Vaillant, G. E. (2002). *Aging well.* Boston: Little, Brown.

Vaillant, G. E., & Koury, S. H. (1994). Late midlife development. In G. H. Pollock & S. I. Greenspan (Eds.), *The course of life* (pp. 1–22). Madison, CT: International Universities Press.

Vaillant, G. E., & Mukamal, K. (2001). Successful aging. *American Journal of Psychiatry, 158,* 839–847.

Vaillant, G. E., & Vaillant, C. O. (1990). Determinants and consequences of creativity in a cohort of gifted women. *Psychology of Women Quarterly, 14,* 607–616.

Vakil, E., Blachstein, H., Sheinman, M., & Greenstein, Y. (2009). Developmental changes in attention tests norms: Implications for the structure of attention. *Child Neuropsychology, 15,* 21–39.

Valdés, G. (1998). The world outside and inside schools: Language and immigrant children. *Educational Researcher, 27*(6), 4–18.

Valentine, J. C., DuBois, D. L., & Cooper, H. (2004). The relation between self-beliefs and academic achievement: A meta-analytic review. *Educational Psychologist, 39,* 111–133.

Valian, V. (1999). Input and language acquisition. In W. C. Ritchie & T. K. Bhatia (Eds.), *Handbook of child language acquisition* (pp. 497–530). San Diego: Academic Press.

Valiente, C., Eisenberg, N., Fabes, R. A., Shepard, S. A., Cumberland, A., & Losoya, S. H. (2004). Prediction of children's empathy-related responding from their effortful control and parents' expressivity. *Developmental Psychology, 40,* 911–926.

Valiente, C., Lemery-Chalfant, K., Swanson, J., & Reiser, M. (2008). Prediction of children's academic competence from their effortful control, relationships, and classroom participation. *Journal of Educational Psychology, 100,* 67–77.

Valkenburg, P. M., & Peter, J. (2007a). Internet communication and its relation to well-being: Identifying some underlying mechanisms. *Media Psychology, 9,* 43–58.

Valkenburg, P. M., & Peter, J. (2007b). Preadolescents' and adolescents' online communication and their closeness to friends. *Developmental Psychology, 43,* 267–277.

Valkenburg, P. M., & Peter, J. (2009). Social consequences of the Internet for adolescents: A decade of research. *Current Directions in Psychological Science, 18,* 1–5.

Valkenburg, P. M., & Peter, J. (2011). Online communication among adolescents: An integrated model of its attraction, opportunities, and risks. *Journal of Adolescent Health, 48,* 121–127.

van Aken, C., Junger, M., Verhoeven, M., van Aken, M. A. G., & Dekovi?, M. (2007). The interactive effects of temperament and maternal parenting on toddlers' externalizing behaviours. *Infant and Child Development, 16,* 553–572.

van Asselt, D. (2006). Advance directives: Prerequisites and usefulness. *Zeitschrift für Gerontologie und Geriatrie, 39,* 371–375.

van Baarsen, B. (2002). Theories on coping with loss: The impact of social support and self-esteem on adjustment to emotional and social loneliness following a partner's death in later life. *Journal of Gerontology, 57B,* S33–S42.

Van Cleave, J., Gortmaker, S. L., & Perrin, J. M. (2010). Dynamics of obesity and chronic health conditions among children and youth. *Journal of the American Medical Association, 303,* 623–630.

Vandell, D. L., Belsky, J., Burchinal, M., Steinberg, L., Vandergrift, N., & NICHD Early Child Care Research Network. (2010). Do effects of early child care extend to age 15 years? Results from the NICHD Study of Early Child Care and Youth Development. *Child Development, 81,* 737–756.

Vandell, D. L., & Posner, J. K. (1999). Conceptualization and measurement of children's after-school environments. In S. L. Friedman & T. D. Wachs (Eds.), *Measuring environment across the life span* (pp. 167–196). Washington, DC: American Psychological Association.

Vandell, D. L., Reisner, E. R., & Pierce, K. M. (2007). *Outcomes linked to high-quality after-school programs: Longitudinal findings from the Study of Promising After-School Programs.* Retrieved from www.gse.uci .edu/childcare/pdf/afterschool/PP%20Longitudinal %20Findings%20Final%20Report.pdf

Vandell, D. L., Reisner, E. R., Pierce, K. M., Brown, B. B., Lee, D., Bolt, D., & Pechman, E. M. (2006). *The study of promising after-school programs: Examination of longer term outcomes after two years of program experiences.* Madison, WI: University of Wisconsin. Retrieved from www.wcer.wisc.edu/ childcare/statements.html

van den Akker, A. L. Deković, M., Prinzie, P., & Asscher, J. J. (2010). Toddlers' temperament profiles: Stability and relations to negative and positive parenting. *Journal of Abnormal Child Psychology, 38,* 485–495.

Van den Bergh, B. R. H., & De Rycke, L. (2003). Measuring the multidimensional self-concept and global self-worth of 6- to 8-year-olds. *Journal of Genetic Psychology, 164,* 201–225.

Van den Bergh, B. R. H., Van Calster, B., Smits, T., Van Huffel, S., & Lagae, L. (2008). Antenatal maternal anxiety is related to HPA-axis dysregulation and self-reported depressive symptoms in adolescence: A prospective study on the fetal origins of depressed mood. *Neuropsychopharmacology, 33,* 536–545.

van den Dries, L., Juffer, F., van IJzendoorn, M. H., & Bakermans-Kranenburg, M. J. (2009). Fostering security? A meta-analysis of attachment in adopted children. *Children and Youth Services Review, 31,* 410–421.

Vanderbilt-Adriance, E., & Shaw, D. S. (2008). Protective factors and the development of resilience in the context of neighborhood disadvantage. *Journal of Abnormal Child Psychology, 36,* 887–901.

van der Wal, M. F., van Eijsden, M., & Bonsel, G. J. (2007). Stress and emotional problems during pregnancy and excessive infant crying. *Developmental and Behavioral Pediatrics, 28,* 431–437.

Van de Vijver, P. J. R., Hofer, J., & Chasiotis, A. (2010). Methodology. In M. H. Bornstein (Ed.), *Handbook of cultural developmental science* (pp. 21–37). New York: Psychology Press.

Vandewater, E. A., & Stewart, A. J. (1997). Women's career commitment patterns and personality development. In M. E. Lachman & J. B. James (Eds.), *Multiple paths of midlife development* (pp. 375–410). Chicago: University of Chicago Press.

Van Eyk, J., & Dunn, M. J. (Eds.). (2008). *Clinical proteomics.* Weinheim, Germany: Wiley-VCH.

Van Eyken, E., Van Camp, G., & Van Laer, L. (2007). The complexity of age-related hearing impairment: Contributing environmental and genetic factors. *Audiology and Neurotology, 12,* 345–358.

Van Hiel, A., & Vansteenkiste, M. (2009). Ambitions fulfilled? The effects of intrinsic and extrinsic goal attainment on older adults' ego integrity and death attitudes. *International Journal of Aging and Human Development, 68,* 27–51.

Van Hulle, C. A., Goldsmith, H. H., & Lemery, K. S. (2004). Genetic, environmental, and gender effects on individual differences in toddler expressive language. *Journal of Speech, Language, and Hearing Research, 47,* 904–912.

van IJzendoorn, M. H. (1995). Adult attachment representations, parental responsiveness, and infant attachment: A meta-analysis on the predictive validity of the Adult Attachment Interview. *Psychological Bulletin, 117,* 387–403.

van IJzendoorn, M. H., & Bakermans-Kranenburg, M. J. (2006). DRD4 7-repeat polymorphism moderates the association between maternal unresolved loss or trauma and infant disorganization. *Attachment and Human Development, 8,* 291–307.

van IJzendoorn, M. H., Juffer, F., & Poelhuis, C. W. K. (2005). Adoption and cognitive development: A meta-analytic comparison of adopted and nonadopted children's IQ and school performance. *Psychological Bulletin, 131,* 301–316.

van IJzendoorn, M. H., & Kroonenberg, P. M. (1988). Cross-cultural patterns of attachment: A meta-analysis of the Strange Situation. *Child Development, 59,* 147–156.

van IJzendoorn, M. H., & Sagi-Schwartz, A. (2008). Cross-cultural patterns of attachment: Universal and contextual dimensions. In J. Cassidy & P. R. Shaver (Eds.), *Handbook of attachment* (2nd ed., pp. 880–905). New York: Guilford.

van IJzendoorn, M. H., Schuengel, C., & Bakermans-Kranenburg, M. J. (1999). Disorganized attachment in early childhood: Meta-analysis of precursors, concomitants, and sequelae. *Development and Psychopathology, 11,* 225–249.

van IJzendoorn, M. H., Vereijken, C. M. J. L., Bakermans-Kranenburg, M. J., & Riksen-Walraven, J. M. (2004). Assessing attachment security with the Attachment Q Sort: Meta-analytic evidence for the validity of the Observer AQS. *Child Development, 75,* 1188–1213.

van Solinge, H., & Henkens, K. (2008). Adjustment to and satisfaction with retirement: Two of a kind? *Psychology and Aging, 23,* 422–434.

van Tol, D., Rietjens, J., & van der Heide, A. (2010). Judgment of unbearable suffering and willingness to grant a euthanasia request by Dutch general practitioners. *Health Policy, 97,* 166–172.

Van Volkom, M. (2006). Sibling relationships in middle and older adulthood: A review of the literature. *Marriage and Family Review, 40,* 151–170.

Varendi, H., & Porter, R. H. (2001). Breast odour as the only maternal stimulus elicits crawling toward the odour source. *Acta Paediatrica, 90,* 372–375.

Varnhagen, C. (2007). Children and the Web. In J. Gackenbach (Ed.), *Psychology and the Internet* (2nd ed., pp, 37–54). Amsterdam: Elsevier.

Vartanian, L. R., & Powlishta, K. K. (1996). A longitudinal examination of the social-cognitive foundations of adolescent egocentrism. *Journal of Early Adolescence, 16,* 157–178.

Vaughn, B. E., Bost, K. K., & van IJzendoorn, M. H. (2008). Attachment and temperament. In J. Cassidy & P. R. Shaver (Eds.), *Handbook of attachment: Theory, research, and clinical applications* (2nd ed., pp. 192–216). New York: Guilford.

Vaughn, B. E., Kopp, C. B., & Krakow, J. B. (1984). The emergence and consolidation of self-control from eighteen to thirty months of age: Normative trends and individual differences. *Child Development, 55,* 990–1004.

Vazsonyi, A. T., Hibbert, J. R., & Snider, J. B. (2003). Exotic enterprise no more? Adolescent reports of family and parenting processes from youth in four countries. *Journal of Research on Adolescence, 13,* 129–160.

Veenstra, R., Lindenberg, S., Munniksma, A., & Dijkstra, J. K. (2010). The complex relation between bullying, victimization, acceptance, and rejection: Giving special attention to status, affection, and sex differences. *Child Development, 81,* 480–486.

Velderman, M. K., Bakermans-Kranenburg, M. J., Juffer, F., & van IJzendoorn, M. H. (2006). Effects of attachment-based interventions on maternal sensitivity and infant attachment: Differential susceptibility of highly reactive infants. *Journal of Family Psychology, 20,* 266–274.

Velleman, R. D. B., Templeton, L. J., & Copello, A. G. (2005). The role of the family in preventing and intervening with substance use and misuse: A comprehensive review of family interventions, with a focus on young people. *Drug and Alcohol Review, 24,* 93–109.

Venet, M., & Markovits, H. (2001). Understanding uncertainty with abstract conditional premises. *Merrill-Palmer Quarterly, 47,* 74–99.

Venezia, M., Messinger, D. S., Thorp, D., & Mundy, P. (2004). The development of anticipatory smiling. *Infancy, 6,* 397–406.

Veneziano, R. A. (2003). The importance of paternal warmth. *Cross-Cultural Research, 37,* 265–281.

Ventura, S. J., Curtin, S. C., & Abma, J. C. (2012). Estimated pregnancy rates and rates of pregnancy outcomes for the United States, 1990–2008. *National Vital Statistics Reports, 60*(7). Retrieved from www.cdc.gov/nchs/data/nvsr/nvsr60/nvsr60_07.pdf

Verhaeghen, P. (2012). Age-related differences in working-memory functioning and cognitive control. In M. Naveh-Benjamin & N. Ohta (Eds.), *Memory and aging: Current issues and future directions* (pp. 3–30). New York: Psychology Press.

Verhaeghen, P., & Cerella, J. (2008). Everything we know about aging and response times: A meta-analytic integration. In S. M. Hofer & D. F. Alwin (Eds.), *Handbook of cognitive aging: Interdisciplinary perspectives* (pp. 134–150). Thousand Oaks, CA: Sage.

Verhulst, F. C. (2008). International adoption and mental health: Long-term behavioral outcome. In M. E. Garralda & J.-P. Raynaud (Eds.), *Culture and conflict and adolescent mental health* (pp. 83–105). Lanham, MD: Jason Aronson.

Veríssimo, M., & Salvaterra, F. (2006). Maternal secure-base scripts and children's attachment security in an adopted sample. *Attachment and Human Development, 8,* 261–273.

Vernon-Feagans, L., Pancsofar, N., Willoughby, M., Odom, E., Quade, A., & Cox, M. (2008). Predictors of maternal language to infants during a picture book task in the home: Family SES, child characteristics and the parenting environment. *Journal of Applied Developmental Psychology, 29,* 213–226.

Vesco, K. K., Haney, E. M., Humphrey, L., Fu, R., & Nelson, H. D. (2007). Influence of menopause on mood: A systematic review of cohort studies. *Climacteric, 10,* 448–465.

Vidaeff, A. C., Carroll, M. A., & Ramin, S. M. (2005). Acute hypertensive emergencies in pregnancy. *Critical Care Medicine, 33,* S307–S312.

Vinden, P. G. (1996). Junín Quechua children's understanding of mind. *Child Development, 67,* 1707–1716.

Vinden, P. G. (2002). Understanding minds and evidence for belief: A study of Mofu children in Cameroon.

International Journal of Behavioral Development, 26, 445–452.

Visher, E. B., Visher, J. S., & Pasley, K. (2003). Remarriage, families and stepparenting. In F. Walsh (Ed.), *Normal family processes* (pp. 153–175). New York: Guilford.

Vitali, P., Migliaccio, R., Agosta, F., Rosen, H. J., & Geschwind, M. D. (2008). Neuroimaging in dementia. *Seminars in Neurology, 28,* 467–483.

Vitrup, B., & Holden, G. W. (2010). Children's assessments of corporal punishment and other disciplinary practices: The role of age, race, SES, and exposure to spanking. *Journal of Applied Developmental Psychology, 31,* 211–220.

Vivanti, G., Nadig, A., Ozonoff, S., & Rogers, S. J. (2008). What do children with autism attend to during imitation tasks? *Journal of Experimental Psychology, 101,* 186–205.

Vogels, N., Diepvens, K., & Westerterp-Plantenga, M. S. (2005). Predictors of long-term weight maintenance. *Obesity Research, 13,* 2162–2168.

Volling, B. L. (2001). Early attachment relationships as predictors of preschool children's emotion regulation with a distressed sibling. *Early Education and Development, 12,* 185–207.

Volling, B. L., & Belsky, J. (1992). Contribution of mother–child and father–child relationships to the quality of sibling interaction: A longitudinal study. *Child Development, 63,* 1209–1222.

Volling, B. L., McElwain, N. L., & Miller, A. L. (2002). Emotion regulation in context: The jealousy complex between young siblings and its relations with child and family characteristics. *Child Development, 73,* 581–600.

Volling, B. L., McElwain, N. L., Notaro, P. C., & Herrera, C. (2002). Parents' emotional availability and infant emotional competence: Predictors of parent–infant attachment and emerging self-regulation. *Journal of Family Psychology, 16,* 447–465.

Vondra, J. I., Shaw, D. S., Searingen, L., Cohen, M., & Owens, E. B. (2001). Attachment stability and emotional and behavioral regulation from infancy to preschool age. *Development and Psychopathology, 13,* 13–33.

von Hofsten, C. (2004). An action perspective on motor development. *Trends in Cognitive Sciences, 8,* 266–272.

Vouloumanos, A., & Werker, J. F. (2004). Tuned to the signal: The privileged status of speech for young infants. *Developmental Science, 7,* 270–276.

Vuoksimaa, E., Koskenvuo, M., Rose, R. J., & Kaprio, J. (2009). Origins of handedness: A nationwide study of 30,1671 adults. *Neuropsychologia, 47,* 1294–301.

Vygotsky, L. S. (1978). *Mind in society: The development of higher mental processes.* Cambridge, MA: Harvard University Press. (Original works published 1930, 1933, and 1935)

Vygotsky, L. S. (1987). Thinking and speech. In R. W. Rieber, & A. S. Carton (Eds.), & N. Minick (Trans.), *The collected works of L. S. Vygotsky: Vol. 1. Problems of general psychology* (pp. 37–285). New York: Plenum. (Original work published 1934)

W

Waber, D. P. (2010). *Rethinking learning disabilities.* New York: Guilford.

Wachs, T. D., & Bates, J. E. (2001). Temperament. In G. Bremner & A. Fogel (Eds.), *Blackwell handbook of infant development* (pp. 465–501). Oxford, UK: Blackwell.

Wadsworth, M. E., & Santiago, C. D. (2008). Risk and resiliency processes in ethnically diverse families in poverty. *Journal of Family Psychology, 22,* 399–410.

Wagenaar, K., van Wessenbruch, M. M., van Leeuwen, F. E., Cohen-Kettenis, P. T., Delemarre-van de Waal, H. A., Schats, R., et al. (2011). Self-reported behavioral and socioemotional functioning of

11- to 18-year-old adolescents conceived by in vitro fertilization. *Fertility and Sterility, 95,* 611–616.

Wainryb, C. (1997). The mismeasure of diversity: Reflections on the study of cross-cultural differences. In H. D. Saltzstein (Ed.), *New directions for child development* (No. 76, pp. 51–65). San Francisco: Jossey-Bass.

Waite, L., & Das, A. (2013). Families, social life, and well-being at older ages. *Demography, 47,* S87–S109.

Waite, L. J., Laumann, E. O., Das, A., & Schumm, L. P. (2009). Sexuality: Measures of partnerships, practices, attitudes, and problems in the National Social Life, Health, and Aging Study. *Journal of Gerontology, 64B,* i56–i66.

Wakeley, A., Rivera, S., & Langer, J. (2000). Can young infants add and subtract? *Child Development, 71,* 1477–1720.

Walberg, H. J. (1986). Synthesis of research on teaching. In M. C. Wittrock (Ed.), *Handbook of research on teaching* (3rd ed., pp. 214–229). New York: Macmillan.

Waldfogel, J. (2001). International policies toward parental leave and child care. *Future of Children 11,* 52–61.

Waldfogel, J., Craigie, T. A., & Brooks-Gunn, J. (2010). Fragile families and child well-being. *Future of Children, 20,* 87–112.

Waldman, I. D., Rowe, D. C., Abramowitz, A., Kozel, S. T., Mohr, J. H., & Sherman, S. L. (1998). Association and linkage of the dopamine transporter gene and attention-deficit hyperactivity disorder in children: Heterogeneity owing to diagnostic subtype and severity. *American Journal of Human Genetics, 63,* 1767–1776.

Waldrip, A. M. (2008). With a little help from your friends: The importance of high-quality friendships on early adolescent adjustment. *Social Development, 17,* 832–852.

Walenski, M., Tager-Flusberg, H., & Ullman, M. T. (2006). Language in autism. In S. O. Moldin & J. L. R. Rubenstein (Eds.), *Understanding autism: From basic neuroscience to treatment* (pp. 175–203). Boca Raton, FL: CRC Press.

Walker, L. J. (1995). Sexism in Kohlberg's moral psychology? In W. M. Kurtines & J. L. Gewirtz (Eds.), *Moral development: An introduction* (pp. 83–107). Boston: Allyn and Bacon.

Walker, L. J. (2004). Progress and prospects in the psychology of moral development. *Merrill-Palmer Quarterly, 50,* 546–557.

Walker, L. J. (2006). Gender and morality. In M. Killen & J. G. Smetana (Eds.), *Handbook of moral development* (pp. 93–118). Philadelphia: Erlbaum.

Walker, L. J., & Taylor, J. H. (1991a). Family interactions and the development of moral reasoning. *Child Development, 62,* 264–283.

Walker, L. J., & Taylor, J. H. (1991b). Stage transitions in moral reasoning: A longitudinal study of developmental processes. *Developmental Psychology, 27,* 330–337.

Wall, M., & Côté, J. (2007). Developmental activities that lead to dropout and investment in sport. *Physical Education and Sport Pedagogy, 12,* 77–87.

Walsh, C. A., Ploeg, J., Lohfeld, L., Horne, J., MacMillan, H., & Lai, D. (2007). Violence across the lifespan: Interconnections among forms of abuse as described by marginalized Canadian elders and their caregivers. *British Journal of Social Work, 37,* 491–514.

Walsh, F., & McGoldrick, M. (2004). Loss and the family: A systemic perspective. In F. Walsh & M. McGoldrick (Eds.), *Living beyond loss: Death in the family* (2nd ed., pp. 3–26). New York: Norton.

Walsh, K. E., & Berman, J. R. (2004). Sexual dysfunction in the older woman: An overview of the current understanding and management. *Therapy in Practice, 21,* 655–675.

Walston, J., Hadley, E. C., Ferrucci, L., Guralnik, J. M., Newman, A. B., Studenski, S. A., et al. (2006). Research agenda for frailty in older adults: Toward a better understanding of physiology and etiology: Summary from the American Geriatrics Society/National Institute on Aging Research Conference on Frailty in Older Adults. *Journal of the American Geriatrics Society, 54,* 991–1001.

Wang, H., & Amato, P. R. (2000). Predictors of divorce adjustment: Stressors, resources, and definitions. *Journal of Marriage and Family, 62,* 655–668.

Wang, H., & Wellman, B. (2010). Social connectivity in America: Changes in adult friendship network size from 2002 to 2007. *American Behavioral Scientist, 53,* 1148–1169.

Wang, M. (2011). Retirement: An adult development perspective. In S. K. Whitbourne & M. J. Sliwinski (Eds.), *Wiley-Blackwell handbook of adulthood and aging* (pp. 416–429). Malden, MA: Wiley-Blackwell.

Wang, M., Adams, G. A., Beehr, T. A., & Shultz, K. S. (2009). Career issues at the end of one's career: Bridge employment and retirement. In S. G. Baugh & S. E. Sullivan (Eds.), *Maintaining focus, energy, and options over the life span* (pp. 135–162). Charlotte, NC: Information Age Publishing.

Wang, M., & Shultz, K. (2010). Employee retirement: A review and recommendations for future investigation. *Journal of Management, 36,* 172–206.

Wang, Q. (2006). Relations of maternal style and child self-concept to autobiographical memories in Chinese, Chinese immigrant, and European American 3-year-olds. *Child Development, 77,* 1794–1809.

Wang, Q., Pomerantz, E. M., & Chen, H. (2007). The role of parents' control in early adolescents' psychological functioning: A longitudinal investigation in the United States and China. *Child Development, 78,* 1592–1610.

Wang, Q., Shao, Y., & Li, Y. J. (2010). "My way or mom's way?" The bilingual and bicultural self in Hong Kong Chinese children and adolescents. *Child Development, 81,* 555–567.

Wang, S., Baillargeon, R., & Paterson, S. (2005). Detecting continuity violations in infancy: A new account and new evidence from covering and tube events. *Cognition, 95,* 129–173.

Wang, Z., & Deater-Deckard, K. (2013). Resilience in gene–environment transactions. In S. Goldstein & R. Brooks (Eds.), *Handbook of resilience in children* (2nd ed., pp. 57–72). New York: Springer Science + Business Media.

Wark, G. R., & Krebs, D. L. (1996). Gender and dilemma differences in real-life moral judgment. *Developmental Psychology, 32,* 220–230.

Warner, L. A., Valdez, A., Vega, W. A., de la Rosa, M., Turner, R. J., & Canino, G. (2006). Hispanic drug abuse in an evolving cultural context: An agenda for research. *Drug and Alcohol Dependence, 84*(Suppl. 1), S8–S16.

Warner, L. M., Ziegelmann, J. P., Schüz, B., Wurm, S., Tesch-Römer, C., & Schwarzer, R. (2011). Maintaining autonomy despite multimorbidity: Self-efficacy and the two faces of social support. *European Journal of Ageing, 8,* 3–12.

Warnock, F., & Sandrin, D. (2004). Comprehensive description of newborn distress behavior in response to acute pain (newborn male circumcision). *Pain, 107,* 242–255.

Warr, P. (2001). Age and work behavior: Physical attributes, cognitive abilities, knowledge, personality traits, and motives. *International Review of Industrial and Organizational Psychology, 16,* 1–36.

Warren, A. R., & Tate, C. S. (1992). Egocentrism in children's telephone conversations. In R. M. Diaz & L. E. Berk (Eds.), *Private speech: From social interaction to self-regulation* (pp. 245–264). Hillsdale, NJ: Erlbaum.

Warshaw, C., Brashler, P., & Gil, J. (2009). Mental health consequences of intimate partner violence. In C. Mitchell & D. Anglin (Eds.), *Intimate partner violence: A health-based perspective* (pp. 147–171). New York: Oxford University Press.

Wass, H. (2004). A perspective on the current state of death education. *Death Studies, 28,* 289–308.

Wasserman, E. A., & Rovee-Collier, C. (2001). Pick the flowers and mind your As and 2s! Categorization by pigeons and infants. In M. E. Carroll & J. B. Overmier (Eds.), *Animal research and human health: Advancing human welfare through behavioral science* (pp. 263–279). Washington, DC: American Psychological Association.

Watamura, S. E., Phillips, D., Morrissey, T. W., McCartney, K., & Bub, K. (2011). Double jeopardy: Poorer social-emotional outcomes for children in the NICHD SECCYD experiencing home and childcare environments that confer risk. *Child Development, 82,* 48–65.

Waterman, A. S., & Whitbourne, S. K. (1982). Androgyny and psychosocial development among college students and adults. *Journal of Personality, 50,* 121–133.

Waters, E., & Cummings, E. M. (2000). A secure base from which to explore close relationships. *Child Development, 71,* 164–172.

Waters, E., Merrick, S., Treboux, D., Crowell, J., & Albersheim, L. (2000). Attachment security in infancy and early adulthood: A twenty-year longitudinal study. *Child Development, 71,* 684–689.

Waters, E., Vaughn, B. E., Posada, G., & Kondo-Ikemura, K. (Eds.). (1995). Caregiving, cultural, and cognitive perspectives on secure-base behavior and working models: New growing points of attachment theory and research. *Monographs of the Society for Research in Child Development, 60*(2–3, Serial No. 244).

Watson, J. B., & Raynor, R. (1920). Conditioned emotional reactions. *Journal of Experimental Psychology, 3,* 1–14.

Watson, M. (1990). Aspects of self-development as reflected in children's role playing. In D. Cicchetti & M. Beeghly (Eds.), *The self in transition: Infancy to childhood* (pp. 281–307). Chicago: University of Chicago Press.

Wax, J. R., Pinette, M. G., & Cartin, A. (2010). Home versus hospital birth—process and outcome. *Obstetric and Gynecological Survey, 65,* 132–140.

Waxman, S. R., & Senghas, A. (1992). Relations among word meanings in early lexical development. *Developmental Psychology, 28,* 862–873.

Webb, N. M., Franke, M. L., Ing, M., Chan, A., De, T., Freund, D., & Battey, D. (2008). The role of teacher instructional practices in student collaboration. *Contemporary Educational Psychology, 35,* 360–381.

Weber, C., Hahne, A., Friedrich, M., & Friederici, A. (2004). Discrimination of word stress in early infant perception: Electrophysiological evidence. *Cognitive Brain Research, 18,* 149–161.

Webster-Stratton, C., & Reid, M. J. (2010a). The Incredible Years Parents, Teachers, and Children Training Series: A multifaceted treatment approach for young children with conduct disorders. In J. R. Weisz & A. E. Kazdin (Eds.), *Evidence-based psychotherapies for children and adolescents* (2nd ed., pp. 194–210). New York: Guilford.

Webster-Stratton, C., & Reid, M. J. (2010b). The Incredible Years program for children from infancy to pre-adolescence: Prevention and treatment of behavior problems. In R. C. Murrihy, A. D. Kidman, & T. H. Ollendick (Eds.), *Clinical handbook of assessing and treating conduct problems in youth* (pp. 117–138). New York: Springer Science + Business Media.

Webster-Stratton, C., Rinaldi, J., & Reid, J. M. (2011). Long-term outcomes of Incredible Years parenting program: Predictors of adolescent adjustment. *Child and Adolescent Mental Health, 16,* 38–46.

Wechsler, D. (2002). *WPPSI-III: Wechsler Preschool and Primary Scale of Intelligence* (3rd ed.). San Antonio, TX: Psychological Corporation.

Wechsler, D. (2003). *WISC-IV: Wechsler Intelligence Scale for Children* (4th ed.). San Antonio, TX: Psychological Corporation.

Weems, C. F., & Costa, N. M. (2005). Developmental differences in the expression of childhood anxiety symptoms and fears. *Journal of the American Academy of Child and Adolescent Psychiatry, 44,* 656–663.

Wegesin, D. J., Jacobs, D. M., Zubin, N. R., & Ventura, P. R. (2000). Source memory and encoding strategy in normal aging. *Journal of Clinical and Experimental Neuropsychology, 22,* 455–464.

Wehren, A., De Lisi, R., & Arnold, M. (1981). The development of noun definition. *Journal of Child Language, 8,* 165–175.

Weikum, W. M., Vouloumanos, A., Navarra, J., Soto-Faraco, S., Sebastián-Gallés, N., & Werker, J. F. (2007). Visual language discrimination in infancy. *Science, 316,* 1159.

Weinberg, M. K., & Tronick, E. Z. (1994). Beyond the face: An empirical study of infant affective configurations of facial, vocal, gestural, and regulatory behaviors. *Child Development, 65,* 1503–1515.

Weinberger, M. I., & Whitbourne, S. K. (2010). Depressive symptoms, self-reported physical functioning, and identity in community-dwelling older adults. *Aging International, 35,* 276–285.

Weindruch, R., Keenan, K. P., Carney, J. M., Fernandes, G., Feuers, R. J., & Floyd, R. A. (2001). Caloric restriction mimetics: Metabolic interventions. *Journal of Gerontology, 56A,* 20–33.

Weiner, J., & Tardif, C. (2004). Social and emotional functioning of children with learning disabilities: Does special education placement make a difference? *Learning Disabilities Research and Practice, 19,* 20–32.

Weinfield, N. S., Sroufe, L. A., & Egeland, B. (2000). Attachment from infancy to early adulthood in a high-risk sample: Continuity, discontinuity, and their correlates. *Child Development, 71,* 695–702.

Weinfield, N. S., Whaley, G. J. L., & Egeland, B. (2004). Continuity, discontinuity, and coherence in attachment from infancy to late adolescence: Sequelae of organization and disorganization. *Attachment and Human Development, 6,* 73–97.

Weinstein, R. S. (2002). *Reaching higher: The power of expectations in schooling.* Cambridge, MA: Harvard University Press.

Weinstein, S. M., Mermelstein, R. J., Hedeker, D., Hankin, B. L., & Flay, B. R. (2006). The time-varying influences of peer and family support on adolescent daily positive and negative affect. *Journal of Clinical Child and Adolescent Psychology, 35,* 420–430.

Weinstock, M. (2008). The long-term behavioural consequences of prenatal stress. *Neuroscience and Biobehavioral Reviews, 32,* 1073–1086.

Weisfield, G. E. (1997). Puberty rites as clues to the nature of human adolescence. *Cross-Cultural Research, 31,* 27–54.

Weisgram, E. S., Bigler, R. S., & Liben, L. S. (2010). Gender, values, and occupational interests among children, adolescents, and adults. *Child Development, 81,* 778–796.

Weissberg, R. W. (2006). Modes of expertise in creative thinking: Evidence from case studies. In K. A. Ericsson, N. Charness, P. J. Feltovich, & R. R. Hoffman (Eds.), *The Cambridge handbook of expertise and expert performance* (pp. 761–787). New York: Cambridge University Press.

Weisz, A. N., & Black, B. M. (2002). Gender and moral reasoning: African American youths respond to dating dilemmas. *Journal of Human Behavior in the Social Environment, 6,* 17–34.

Weizman, Z. O., & Snow, C. E. (2001). Lexical output as related to children's vocabulary acquisition: Effects of sophisticated exposure and support for meaning. *Developmental Psychology, 37,* 265–279.

Wekerle, C., & Avgoustis, E. (2003). Child maltreatment, adolescent dating, and adolescent dating violence. In P. Florsheim (Ed.), *Adolescent romantic relations and sexual behavior: Theory, research, and practical implications* (pp. 213–242). Mahwah, NJ: Erlbaum.

Wekerle, C., Wall, A.-M., Leung, E., & Trocmé, N. (2007). Cumulative stress and substantiated maltreatment: The importance of caregiver vulnerability and adult partner violence. *Child Abuse and Neglect, 31,* 427–443.

Wellman, H. M. (2002). Understanding the psychological world: Developing a theory of mind. In U. Goswami (Ed.), *Blackwell handbook of child cognitive development* (pp. 167–187). Malden, MA: Blackwell.

Wellman, H. M. (2011). Developing a theory of mind. In U. Goswami (Ed.), *Wiley-Blackwell handbook of childhood cognitive development* (2nd ed., pp. 258–284). Malden, MA: Wiley-Blackwell.

Wellman, H. M., & Hickling, A. K. (1994). The mind's "I": Children's conception of the mind as an active agent. *Child Development, 65,* 1564–1580.

Welsh, M. C. (2002). Developmental and clinical variations in executive functions. In U. Kirk & D. Molfese (Eds.), *Developmental variations in language and learning* (pp. 139–185). Mahwah, NJ: Erlbaum.

Welsh, M. C., Friedman, S. L., & Spieker, S. J. (2008). Executive functions in developing children: Current conceptualizations and questions for the future. In K. McCartney & D. Phillips (Eds.), *Blackwell handbook of early childhood development* (pp. 167–187). Malden, MA: Blackwell Publishing.

Wenger, G. C. (2009). Childlessness at the end of life: Evidence from rural Wales. *Ageing and Society, 29,* 1243–1259.

Wenger, G. C., & Burholdt, V. (2001). Differences over time in older people's relationships with children, grandchildren, nieces and nephews in rural North Wales. *Ageing and Society, 21,* 567–590.

Wentworth, N., Benson, J. B., & Haith, M. M. (2000). The development of infants' reaches for stationary and moving targets. *Child Development, 71,* 576–601.

Wentzel, K. R., Barry, C. M., & Caldwell, K. A. (2004). Friendships in middle school: Influences on motivation and school adjustment. *Journal of Educational Psychology, 96,* 195–203.

Werner, E. E. (1991). Grandparent–grandchild relationships amongst U.S. ethnic groups. In P. K. Smith (Ed.), *The psychology of grandparenthood: An international perspective* (pp. 68–82). London: Routledge.

Werner, E. E. (2013). What can we learn about resilience from large-scale longitudinal studies? In S. Goldstein & R. Brooks (Eds.), *Handbook of resilience in children* (2nd ed., pp. 87–102). New York: Springer Science + Business Media.

Werner, N. E., & Crick, N. R. (2004). Maladaptive peer relationships and the development of relational and physical aggression during middle childhood. *Social Development, 13,* 495–514.

Westerhof, G. J. (2008). Age identity. In D. Carr (Ed.), *Encyclopedia of the life course and human development* (pp. 10–14). Farmington Hills, MI: Macmillan.

Westerhof, G. J., & Barrett, A. E. (2005). Age identity and subjective well-being: A comparison of the United States and Germany. *Journal of Gerontology, 60S,* 129–136.

Westerhof, G. J., Bohlmeijer, E., & Webster, J. D. (2010). Reminiscence and mental health: A review of recent progress in theory, research and interventions. *Ageing and Society, 30,* 697–721.

Westerhof, G. J., Whitbourne, S. K., & Freeman, G. P. (2012). The aging self in a cultural context: The relation of conceptions of aging to identity processes and self-esteem in the United States and the Netherlands. *Journal of Gerontology, 67B,* 52–60.

Westermann, G., Mareschal, D., Johnson, M. H., Sirois, S., Spratling, M. W., & Thomas, M. S. C. (2007). Neuroconstructivism. *Developmental Science, 10,* 75–83.

Westermann, G., Sirois, S., Shultz, T. R., & Mareschal, D. (2006). Modeling developmental cognitive neuroscience. *Trends in Cognitive Sciences, 10,* 227–232.

Westermeyer, J. F. (2004). Predictors and characteristics of Erikson's life cycle model among men: A 32-year longitudinal study. *International Journal of Aging and Human Development, 58,* 29–48.

Wethington, E. (2000). Expecting stress: Americans and the "midlife crisis." *Motivation and Emotion, 24,* 85–103.

Wethington, E., Kessler, R. C., & Pixley, J. E. (2004). Turning points in adulthood. In O. G. Brim, C. D. Ryff, & R. C. Kessler (Eds.), *How healthy are we? A national study of well-being at midlife* (pp. 586–613). Chicago: University of Chicago Press.

Wetle, T., Shield, R., Teno, J., Miller, S. C., & Welch, L. (2005). Family perspectives on end-of-life care experiences in nursing homes. *Gerontologist, 45,* 642–650.

Wetmore, C. M., & Mokdad, A. H. (2012). In denial: Misperceptions of weight change among adults in the United States. *Preventive Medicine, 55,* 93–100.

Whincup, P. H., Kaye, S. G., Owen, C. G., Huxley, R., Cook, D. G., Anazawa, S., et al. (2008). Birth weight and risk of type 2 diabetes: A systematic review. *Journal of the American Medical Association, 24,* 2886–2897.

Whipple, E. E. (2006). Child abuse and neglect: Consequences of physical, sexual, and emotional abuse of children. In H. E. Fitzgerald, B. M. Lester, & B. Zuckerman (Eds.), *The crisis in youth mental health: Critical issues and effective programs: Vol. 1. Childhood disorders* (pp. 205–229). Westport, CT: Praeger.

Whipple, N., Bernier, A., & Mageau, G. A. (2011). Broadening the study of infant security of attachment: Maternal autonomy-support in the context of infant exploration. *Social Development, 20,* 17–32.

Whisman, M. A., Uebelacker, L. A., Tolejko, N., Chatav, Y., & McKelvie, M. (2006). Marital discord and well-being in older adults: Is the association confounded by personality? *Psychology and Aging, 21,* 626–631.

Whitaker, D. J., Baker, C. K., & Arias, I. (2007). Interventions to prevent intimate partner violence. In L. S. Doll, S. E., Bonzo, D. A. Sleet, & J. A. Mercy (Eds.), *Handbook of injury and violence prevention* (pp. 203–221). New York: Springer Science + Business Media.

Whitbourne, S. K. (1996). *The aging individual: Physical and psychological perspectives.* New York: Springer.

Whitbourne, S. K. (2002). *The aging individual: Physical and psychological perspectives.* New York: Springer.

Whitbourne, S. K., & Meeks, S. (2011). Psychopathology, bereavement, and aging. In K. W. Schaie & S. L. Willis (Eds.), *Handbook of the psychology of aging* (7th ed., pp. 311–323). San Diego, CA: Elsevier.

Whitbourne, S. K., & Willis, S. L. (2006). Preface. In S. K. Whitbourne & S. L. Willis (Eds.), *The baby boomers grow up* (pp. vii–ix). Mahwah, NJ: Erlbaum.

Whitbourne, S. K., Zuschlag, M. K., Elliot, L. B., & Waterman, A. S. (1992). Psychosocial development in adulthood: A 22-year sequential study. *Journal of Personality and Social Psychology, 63,* 260–271.

White, H. R., McMorris, B. J., Catalano, R. F., Fleming, C. B., Haggerty, K. P., & Abbott, R. D. (2006). Increases in alcohol and marijuana use during the transition out of high school into emerging adulthood: The effects of leaving home, going to college, and high school protective factors. *Journal of Studies on Alcohol, 67,* 810–822.

White, L. (2001). Sibling relationships over the life course: A panel analysis. *Journal of Marriage and Family, 63,* 555–568.

White, Y. A., Woods, D. C., Takai, Y., Ishihara, O., Seki, H., & Tilly, J. L. (2012). Oocyte formation by mitotically active germ cells purified from ovaries of reproductive-age women. *Nature Medicine, 18,* 413–421.

Whiteman, S. D., & Loken, E. (2006). Comparing analytic techniques to classify dyadic relationships: An example using siblings. *Journal of Marriage and Family, 68,* 1370–1382.

Whiteman, S. D., McHale, S. M., & Crouter, A. C. (2010). Family relationships from adolescence to early adulthood: Changes in the family system following firstborns' leaving home. *Journal of Research on Adolescence, 21,* 461–474.

Whitesell, N. R., Mitchell, C. M., Spicer, P., and the Voices of Indian Teens Project Team. (2009). A longitudinal study of self-esteem, cultural identity, and academic success among American Indian adolescents. *Cultural Diversity and Ethnic Minority Psychology, 15,* 38–50.

Whiteside-Mansell, L., Bradley, R. H., Owen, M. T., Randolph, S. M., & Cauce, A. M. (2003). Parenting and children's behavior at 36 months: Equivalence between African-American and European-American mother–child dyads. *Parenting: Science and Practice, 3,* 197–234.

Whitfield, K. E., Thorpe, R., & Szanton, S. (2011). Health disparities, social class, and aging. In K. Warner Schaie & S. L. Willis (Eds.), *Handbook of the psychology of aging* (7th ed., pp. 207–218). San Diego, CA: Academic Press.

Whitlock, J. L., Powers, J. L., & Eckenrode, J. (2006). The virtual cutting edge: The Internet and adolescent self-injury. *Developmental Psychology, 42,* 407–417.

Whitmer, R. A., Gustafson, D. R., Barrett-Connor, E., Haan, M. N., Gunderson, E. P., & Yaffe, K. (2008). Central obesity and increased risk of dementia more than three decades later. *Neurology, 71,* 1057–1064.

Wichmann, C., Coplan, R. J., & Daniels, T. (2004). The social cognitions of socially withdrawn children. *Social Development, 13,* 377–392.

Wichstrøm, L. (2006). Sexual orientation as a risk factor for bulimic symptoms. *International Journal of Eating Disorders, 39,* 448–453.

Wickens, A. P. (2001). Aging and the free radical theory. *Respiration Physiology, 128,* 379–391.

Wigfield, A., Battle, A., Keller, L. B., & Eccles, J. S. (2002). Sex differences in motivation, self-concept, career aspiration, and career choice: Implications for cognitive development. In A. McGillicudy-De Lisi & R. De Lisi (Eds.), *Biology, society, and behavior: The development of sex differences in cognition* (pp. 93–124). Westport, CT: Ablex.

Wigfield, A., & Eccles, J. S. (1994). Children's competence beliefs, achievement values, and general self-esteem change across elementary and middle school. *Journal of Early Adolescence, 14,* 107–138.

Wigfield, A., Eccles, J. S., Schiefele, U., Roeser, R. W., & Davis-Kean, P. (2006). Development of achievement motivation. In N. Eisenberg (Ed.), *Handbook of child psychology: Vol. 3. Social, emotional, and personality development* (6th ed., pp. 933–1002). Hoboken, NJ: Wiley.

Wigfield, A., Eccles, J. S., Yoon, K. S., Harold, R. D., Arbreton, A. J., Freedman-Doan, C., & Blumenfeld, P. C. (1997). Changes in children's competence beliefs and subjective task values across the elementary school years: A three-year study. *Journal of Educational Psychology, 89,* 451–469.

Wikby, A., Maxson, P., Olsson, J., Johansson, B., & Ferguson, F. G. (1998). Changes in CD8 and CD4 lymphocyte subsets, T cell proliferation responses and non-survival in the very old: The Swedish longitudinal OCTO-immune study. *Mechanisms of Ageing and Development, 102,* 187–198.

Wilbur, J., Chandler, P. J., Dancy, B., & Lee, H. (2003). Correlates of physical activity in urban Midwestern African-American women. *American Journal of Preventive Medicine, 25,* 45–52.

Wilbur, J., Vassalo, A., Chandler, P., McDevitt, J., & Miller, A. M. (2005). Midlife women's adherence to home-based walking during maintenance. *Nursing Research, 54,* 33–40.

Wilcox, A. J., Weinberg, C. R., & Baird, D. D. (1995). Timing of sexual intercourse in relation to ovulation: Effects on the probability of conception, survival of the pregnancy, and sex of the baby. *New England Journal of Medicine, 333,* 1517–1519.

Wilkie, S. S., Guenette, J. A., Dominelli, P. B., & Sheel, A. W. (2012). Effects of an aging pulmonary system on expiratory flow limitation and dyspnoea during exercise in healthy women. *European Journal of Applied Physiology, 112,* 2195–2204.

Wilkinson, R. B. (2004). The role of parental and peer attachment in the psychological health and self-esteem of adolescents. *Journal of Youth and Adolescence, 33,* 479–493.

Wilkinson, R. G., & Pickett, K. E. (2006). Income inequality and population health: A review and explanation of the evidence. *Social Science and Medicine, 62,* 1768–1784.

Willatts, P. (1999). Development of means–end behavior in young infants: Pulling a support to retrieve a distant object. *Developmental Psychology, 35,* 651–667.

Williams, J. M., & Currie, C. (2000). Self-esteem and physical development in early adolescence: Pubertal timing and body image. *Journal of Early Adolescence, 20,* 129–149.

Williams, K., & Dunne-Bryant, A. (2006). Divorce and adult psychological well-being: Clarifying the role of gender and age. *Journal of Marriage and Family, 68,* 1178–1196.

Williams, N., & Torrez, D. J. (1998). Grandparenthood among Hispanics. In M. E. Szinovacz (Ed.), *Handbook on grandparenthood* (pp. 87–96). Westport, CT: Greenwood Press.

Williams, P. E., Weis, L. G., & Rolfhus, E. (2003). *WISC-IV: Theoretical model and test blueprint.* San Antonio, TX: Psychological Corporation.

Williams, R., McNeilly, A., & Sutherland, C. (2012). Insulin resistance in the brain: An old-age or new-age problem? *Biochemical Pharmacology, 84,* 737–745.

Williams, S., & Dale, J. (2006). The effectiveness of treatment for depression/depressive symptoms in adults with cancer: A systematic review. *British Journal of Cancer, 94,* 372–390.

Williams, T. S., Connolly, J., Pepler, D., Craig, W., & Loporte, L. (2008). Risk models of dating aggression across different adolescent relationships: A developmental psychopathology approach. *Journal of Consulting and Clinical Psychology, 76,* 622–632.

Williamson, J., Softas-Nall, B., & Miller, J. (2003). Grandmothers raising grandchildren: An exploration of their experiences and emotions. *Counseling and Therapy for Couples with Families, 11,* 23–32.

Willinger, M., Ko, C.-W., Hoffman, H. J., Kessler, R. C., & Corwin, M. J. (2003). Trends in infant bed sharing in the United States. *Archives of Pediatrics and Adolescent Medicine, 157,* 43–49.

Willis, S. L., & Schaie, K. W. (1999). Intellectual functioning in midlife. In S. L. Willis & J. D. Reid (Eds.), *Life in the middle* (pp. 105–146). San Diego: Academic Press.

Wilson, D. J., Mitchell, J. M., Kemp, B. J., Adkins, R. H., & Mann, W. (2009). Effects of assistive technology on functional decline in people aging with a disability. *Assistive Technology, 21,* 208–217.

Wilson, E. K., Dalberth, B. T., Koo, H. P., & Gard, J. C. (2010). Parents' perspectives on talking to preteenage children about sex. *Perspectives on Sexual and Reproductive Health, 42,* 56–63.

Wilson, R. S., Beckett, L. A., Evans, D. A., & Bennett, D. A. (2003). Terminal decline in cognitive function. *Neurology, 60,* 1782–1787.

Windsor, T. D., Anstey, K. J., & Rodgers, B. (2008). Volunteering and psychological well-being among young–old adults: How much is too much? *Gerontologist, 48,* 59–70.

Wink, P. (2006). Who is afraid of death? Religiousness, spirituality, and death anxiety in late adulthood. *Journal of Religion, Spirituality and Aging, 18,* 93–110.

Wink, P. (2007). Everyday life in the Third Age. In J. B. James & P. Wink (Eds.), *Annual review of gerontology and geriatrics* (Vol. 26, pp. 243–261). New York: Springer.

Wink, P., & Dillon, M. (2002). Spiritual development across the adult life course: Findings from a longitudinal study. *Journal of Adult Development, 9,* 79–94.

Wink, P., & Dillon, M. (2008). Religiousness, spirituality, and psychosocial functioning in late adulthood: Findings from a longitudinal study. *Psychology of Religion and Spirituality 5,* 102–115.

Wink, P., & Helson, R. (1993). Personality change in women and their partners. *Journal of Personality and Social Psychology, 65,* 597–605.

Wink, P., & Schiff, B. (2002). To review or not to review? The role of personality and life events in life review and adaptation to older age. In J. D. Webster & B. K. Haight (Eds.), *Critical advances in reminiscence work* (pp. 44–75). New York: Springer.

Wink, P., & Scott, J. (2005). Does religiousness buffer against the fear of death and dying in late adulthood? Findings from a longitudinal study. *Journal of Gerontology, 60B,* P207–P214.

Winkler, I., Háden, G. P., Ladinig, O., Sziller, I., & Honing, H. (2009). Newborn infants detect the beat in music. *Proceedings of the National Academy of Sciences, 106,* 2468–2471.

Winner, E. (1986, August). Where pelicans kiss seals. *Psychology Today, 20*(8), 25–35.

Winner, E. (1988). *The point of words: Children's understanding of metaphor and irony.* Cambridge, MA: Harvard University Press.

Winner, E. (2000). The origins and ends of giftedness. *American Psychologist, 55,* 159–169.

Winner, E. (2003). Creativity and talent. In M. H. Bornstein, L. Davidson, C. L. M. Keyes, K. A. Moore, & the Center for Child Well-Being (Eds.), *Well-being: Positive development across the life course* (pp. 371–380). Mahwah, NJ: Erlbaum.

Winsler, A. (2009). Still talking to ourselves after all these years: A review of current research on private speech. In A. Winsler, C. Fernyhough, & I. Montero (Eds.), *Private speech executive functioning, and the development of self-regulation.* New York: Cambridge University Press.

Winsler, A., Fernyhough, C., & Montero, I. (Eds.). (2009). *Private speech, executive functioning, and the development of verbal self-regulation.* New York: Cambridge University Press.

Winsler, A., Naglieri, J., & Manfra, L. (2006). Children's search strategies and accompanying verbal and motor strategic behavior: Developmental trends and relations with task performance among children age 5 to 17. *Cognitive Development, 21,* 232–248.

Winslow, R. D., Mehta, D., & Fuster, V. (2005). Sudden cardiac death: Mechanisms, therapies and challenges. *Cardiovascular Medicine, 2,* 352–360.

Wiseman, F. K., Alford, K. A., Tybulewicz, V. L. J., & Fisher, E. M. C. (2009). Down syndrome—recent progress and future prospects. *Human Molecular Genetics, 8,* R75–R83.

Wissink, I. B., Deković, M., & Meijer, A. M. (2006). Parenting behavior, quality of the parent–adolescent relationship, and adolescent functioning in four ethnic groups. *Journal of Early Adolescence, 26,* 133–159.

Witherington, D. C. (2005). The development of prospective grasping control between 5 and 7 months: A longitudinal study. *Infancy, 7,* 143–161.

Wolak, J., Finkelhor, D., Mitchell, K. J., & Ybarra, M. L. (2008). Online "predators" and their victims: Myths, realities, and implications for prevention and treatment. *American Psychologist, 63,* 111–128.

Wolak, J., Mitchell, K. J., & Finkelhor, D. (2003). Escaping or connecting? Characteristics of youth who form close online relationships. *Journal of Adolescence, 26,* 105–119.

Wolak, J., Mitchell, K., & Finkelhor, D. (2007). Unwanted and wanted exposure to online pornography in a national sample of youth Internet users. *Pediatrics, 119,* 247–257.

Wolchik, S. A., Wilcox, K. L., Tein, J.-Y. & Sandler, I. N. (2000). Maternal acceptance and consistency of discipline as buffers of divorce stressors on children's psychological adjustment problems. *Journal of Abnormal Child Psychology, 28,* 87–102.

Wolfe, V. V. (2006). Child sexual abuse. In E. J. Mash & R. A. Barkley (Eds.), *Treatment of childhood disorders* (3rd ed., pp. 647–727). New York: Guilford.

Wolff, P. H. (1966). The causes, controls and organization of behavior in the neonate. *Psychological Issues, 5*(1, Serial No. 17).

Wolff, P. H., & Fesseha, G. (1999). The orphans of Eritrea: A five-year follow-up study. *Journal of Child Psychology and Psychiatry and Allied Disciplines, 40,* 1231–1237.

Wolfinger, N. H. (2005). *Understanding the divorce cycle.* New York: Cambridge University Press.

Wolinsky, F. D., Unverzagt, F. W., Smith, D. M., Jones, R., Stoddard, A., & Tennstedt, S. L. (2006). The ACTIVE cognitive training trail and health-related quality of life: Protection that lasts for 5 years. *Journal of Gerontology, 61A,* 1324–1329.

Wong, C. A., Eccles, J. S., & Sameroff, A. (2003). The influence of ethnic discrimination and ethnic identification on African American adolescents' school and socioemotional adjustment. *Journal of Personality, 71,* 1197–1232.

Wood, E., Desmarais, S., & Gugula, S. (2002). The impact of parenting experience on gender stereotyped toy play of children. *Sex Roles, 47,* 39–49.

Wood, J. J., Emmerson, N. A., & Cowan, P. A. (2004). Is early attachment security carried forward into relationships with preschool peers? *British Journal of Developmental Psychology, 22,* 245–253.

Wood, J. T. (2009). Communication, gender differences in. In H. T. Reis & S. K. Sprecher (Eds.), *Encyclopedia of human relationships* (Vol. 1, pp. 252–256). Thousand Oaks, CA: Sage.

Wood, R. M. (2009). Changes in cry acoustics and distress ratings while the infant is crying. *Infant and Child Development, 18,* 163–177.

Woods, N. F., Smith-DiJulio, K., Percival, D. B., Tao, E. Y., Mariella, A., & Mitchell, E. S. (2008). Depressed mood during the menopausal transition and early postmenopause: Observations from the Seattle Midlife Women's Health Study. *Menopause, 15,* 223–232.

Woolley, J. D., & Cox, V. (2007). Development of beliefs about storybook reality. *Developmental Science, 10,* 681–693.

Woolley, M. E., Kol, K. L., & Bowen, G. L. (2009). The social context of school success for Latino middle school students: Direct and indirect influences of teachers, family, and friends. *Journal of Early Adolescence 29*, 43–70.

Worden, J. W. (2000). Toward an appropriate death. In T. A. Rando (Ed.), *Clinical dimensions of anticipatory mourning* (pp. 267–277). Champaign, IL: Research Press.

Worden, J. W. (2009). *Grief counseling and grief therapy* (4th ed.). New York: Springer.

World Cancer Research Fund/American Institute for Cancer Research. (2007). *Food, nutrition, physical activity, and the prevention of cancer: A global perspective.* Washington, DC: American Institute for Cancer Research.

World Federation of Right to Die Societies. (2006). *Public opinion.* Retrieved from www.worldrtd.net

World Health Organization. (2008). *World report on child injury prevention.* Geneva, Switzerland: Author.

World Health Organization. (2010). *World health statistics 2010.* Geneva, Switzerland: Author.

World Health Organization. (2011). *The world's women 2010: Trends and statistics.* Retrieved from unstats.un.org/unsd/demographic/products/ Worldswomen/Executive%20summary.htm

World Health Organization. (2012a). *Countdown to 2015: Building a future for women and children.* Geneva, Switzerland: Author.

World Health Organization. (2012b). *The World Health Organization's infant feeding recommendation.* Retrieved from www.who.int/nutrition/topics/ infantfeeding_recommendation/en/index.html

World Health Organization. (2012c). *World health statistics 2012.* Geneva: Author.

World Health Organization. (2013a). *Obesity and overweight.* Retrieved from www.who.int/ mediacentre/factsheets/fs311/en

World Health Organization. (2013b). *Suicide prevention (SUPRE).* Retrieved from www.who.int/mental_ health/prevention/suicide/suicideprevent/en

Worrell, F. C., & Gardner-Kitt, D. L. (2006). The relationship between racial and ethnic identity in black adolescents: The cross-racial identity scale and the multigroup ethnic identity measure. *Identity, 6*, 293–315.

Worthy, J., Hungerford-Kresser, H., & Hampton, A. (2009). Tracking and ability grouping. In L. Christenbury, R. Bomer, & P. Smargorinsky (Eds.), *Handbook of adolescent literacy research* (pp. 220–235). New York: Guilford.

Wright, B. C. (2006). On the emergence of the discriminative mode for transitive inference. *European Journal of Cognitive Psychology, 18*, 776–800.

Wright, J. C., Huston, A. C., Murphy, K. C., St. Peters, M., Pinon, M., Scantlin, R., & Kotler, J. (2001). The relations of early television viewing to school readiness and vocabulary of children from low-income families: The Early Window Project. *Child Development, 72*, 1347–1366.

Wright, K. (2003). Relationships with death: The terminally ill talk about dying. *Journal of Marital and Family Therapy, 29*, 439–454.

Wright, M. J., Gillespie, N. A., Luciano, M., Zhu, G., & Martin, N. G. (2008). Genetics of personality and cognition in adolescents. In J. J. Hudziak (Ed.), *Developmental psychology and wellness: Genetic and environmental influences* (pp. 85–107). Washington, DC: American Psychiatric Publishing.

Wright, M. O., & Masten, A. S. (2005). Resilience processes in development. In S. Goldstein & R. B. Brooks (Eds.), *Handbook of resilience in children* (pp. 17–37). New York: Springer.

Wrotniak, B. H., Epstein, L. H., Raluch, R. A., & Roemmich, J. N. (2004). Parent weight change as a predictor of child weight change in family-based behavioral obesity treatment. *Archives of Pediatric and Adolescent Medicine, 158*, 342–347.

Wu, A. M. S., Tang, C. S. K., & Kwok, T. C. Y. (2002). Death anxiety among Chinese elderly people in Hong Kong. *Journal of Aging and Health, 14*, 42–56.

Wu, L. L., Bumpass, L. L., & Musick, K. (2001). Historical and life course trajectories of nonmarital childbearing. In L. L. Wu & B. Wolfe (Eds.), *Out of wedlock: Causes and consequences of nonmarital fertility* (pp. 3–48). New York: Russell Sage Foundation.

Wu, P., Robinson, C. C., Yang, C., Hart, C. H., Olsen, S. F., Porter, C. L., Jin, S., Wo, J., & Wu, X. (2002). Similarities and differences in mothers' parenting of preschoolers in China and the United States. *International Journal of Behavioral Development, 26*, 481–491.

Wu, T., Mendola, P., & Buck, G. M. (2002). Ethnic differences in the presence of secondary sex characteristics and menarche among U.S. girls: The Third National Health and Nutrition Examination Survey, 1988–1994. *Pediatrics, 110*, 752–757.

Wu, W., Brickman, A. M., Luchsinger, J., Ferrazzano, P., Pichiule, P., Yoshita, M., & Brown, T. (2008). The brain in the age of old: The hippocampal formation is targeted differentially by diseases of late life. *Annals of Neurology, 64*, 698–706.

Wu, Z., & Schimmele, C. M. (2007). Uncoupling in late life. *Generations, 31*, 41–46.

Wulczyn, F. (2009). Epidemiological perspectives on maltreatment prevention. *Future of Children, 19*, 39–66.

Wyatt, J. M., & Carlo, G. (2002). What will my parents think? Relations among adolescents' expected parental reactions, prosocial moral reasoning, and prosocial and antisocial behaviors. *Journal of Adolescent Research, 16*, 646–666.

Wyman, E., Rakoczy, H., & Tomasello, M. (2009). Normativity and context in young children's pretend play. *Cognitive Development, 24*, 146–155.

Wynn, K., Bloom, P., & Chiang, W.-C. (2002). Enumeration of collective entities by 5-month-old infants. *Cognition, 83*, B55–B62.

Wynne-Edwards, K. E. (2001). Hormonal changes in mammalian fathers. *Hormones and Behavior, 40*, 139–145.

Wysong, A., Lee, P. P., & Sloan, F. A. (2009). Longitudinal incidence of adverse outcomes of age-related macular degeneration. *Archives of Ophthalmology, 127*, 320–327.

X

Xu, F., Spelke, E. S., & Goddard, S. (2005). Number sense in human infants. *Developmental Science, 8*, 88–101.

Xu, X., & Lai, S.-C. (2004). Gender ideologies, marital roles, and marital quality in Taiwan. *Journal of Family Issues, 25*, 318–355.

Xue, Y., & Meisels, S. J. (2004). Early literacy instruction and learning in kindergarten: Evidence from the early childhood longitudinal study—kindergarten classes of 1998–1999. *American Educational Research Journal, 41*, 191–229.

Y

Yaari, R., & Corey-Bloom, J. (2007). Alzheimer's disease. *Seminars in Neurology, 27*, 32–41.

Yaffe, K., Fox, P., Newcomer, R., Sands, L., Lindquist, K., Dane, K., & Covinsky, K. E. (2002). Patient and caregiver characteristics and nursing home placement in patients with dementia. *Journal of the American Medical Association, 287*, 2090–2097.

Yaffe, K., Lindquist K., Schwartz, A. V., Vitartas C., Vittinghoff, E., Satterfield, S., et al. (2011). Advanced glycation end product level, diabetes, and accelerated cognitive aging. *Neurology, 77*, 1351–1356.

Yale, M. E., Messinger, D. S., Cobo-Lewis, A. B., Oller, D. K., & Eilers, R. E. (1999). An event-based analysis of the coordination of early infant vocalizations and facial actions. *Developmental Psychology, 35*, 505–513.

Yamamoto, K. (2004). The care of the dying and the grieving in Japan. In J. D. Morgan & P. Laungani (Eds.), *Death and bereavement around the world: Vol. 4. Death and bereavement in Asia, Australia, and New Zealand* (pp. 101–107). Amityville, NY: Baywood Publishing Company.

Yang, B., Ollendick, T. H., Dong, Q., Xia, Y., & Lin, L. (1995). Only children and children with siblings in the People's Republic of China: Levels of fear, anxiety, and depression. *Child Development, 66*, 1301–1311.

Yang, C. (2008, April). *The influence of one-child policy on child rearing, family, and society in post-Mao China.* Invited address, Illinois State University.

Yang, C.-K., & Hahn, H.-M. (2002). Cosleeping in young Korean children. *Developmental and Behavioral Pediatrics, 23*, 151–157.

Yang, F.-Y., & Tsai, C.-C. (2010). Reasoning about science-related uncertain issues and epistemological perspectives among children. *Instructional Science, 38*, 325–354.

Yao, L., & Robert, S. A. (2008). The contributions of race, individual socioeconomic status, and neighborhood socioeconomic context to the self-rated health trajectories and mortality of older adults. *Research on Aging, 30*, 251–273.

Yap, M. B. H., Allen, N. B., & Ladouceur, C. D. (2008). Maternal socialization of positive affect: The impact of invalidation on adolescent emotion regulation and depressive symptomatology. *Child Development, 79*, 1415–1431.

Yates, L. B., Djouseé, L., Kurth, T., Buring, J. E., & Gaziano, J. M. (2008). Exceptional longevity in men: Modifiable factors associated with survival and function to age 90 years. *Archives of Internal Medicine, 168*, 284–290.

Yau, J. P., Tasopoulos-Chan, M., & Smetana, J. G. (2009). Disclosure to parents about everyday activities among American adolescents from Mexican, Chinese, and European backgrounds. *Child Development, 80*, 1481–1498.

Yeh, C. J., Kim, A. B., Pituc, S. T., & Atkins, M. (2008). Poverty, loss, and resilience: The story of Chinese immigrant youth. *Journal of Counseling Psychology, 55*, 34–48.

Yeh, S. S. (2010). Understanding and addressing the achievement gap through individualized instruction and formative assessment. *Assessment in Education: Principles, Policy and Practice, 17*, 169–182.

Yeung, W. (1996). Buddhism, death, and dying. In J. K. Parry & A. S. Ryan (Eds.), *A cross-cultural look at death, dying, and religion* (pp. 74–83). Chicago: Nelson-Hall.

Yirmiya, N., Erel, O., Shaked, M., & Solomonica-Levi, D. (1998). Meta-analyses comparing theory of mind abilities of individuals with autism, individuals with mental retardation, and normally developing individuals. *Psychological Bulletin, 124*, 283–307.

Yoshida, H., & Smith, L. B. (2003). Known and novel noun extensions: Attention at two levels of abstraction. *Child Development, 74*, 564–577.

Yoshikawa, H., Weisner, T. S., Kalil, A., & Way, N. (2008). Mixing qualitative and quantitative research in developmental science: Uses and methodological choices. *Developmental Psychology, 44*, 344–354.

Youn, G., Knight, B. G., Jeon, H., & Benton, D. (1999). Differences in familism values and caregiving outcomes among Korean, Korean American, and White American dementia caregivers. *Psychology and Aging, 14*, 355–364.

Young, J. F., & Mroczek, D. K. (2003). Predicting intraindividual self-concept trajectories during adolescence. *Journal of Adolescence, 26*, 589–603.

Young, S. E., Friedman, N. P., Miyake, A., Willcutt, E. G., Corley, R. P., Haberstick, B. C., et al. (2009). Behavioral disinhibition: Liability for externalizing spectrum disorders and its genetic and environmental relation to response inhibition across adolescence. *Journal of Abnormal Psychology, 118,* 117–130.

Young, T., Rabago, D., Zgierska, A., Austin, D., & Finn, L. (2002). Objective and subjective sleep quality in premenopausal, perimenoapusal, and postmenopausal women in the Wisconsin Sleep Cohort Study. *Epidemiology, 26,* 667–672.

Youngblade, L. M., & Dunn, J. (1995). Individual differences in young children's pretend play with mother and sibling: Links to relationships and understanding of other people's feelings and beliefs. *Child Development, 66,* 1472–1492.

Young-Hyman, D., Tanofsky-Kraff, M., Yanovski, S. Z., Keil, M., Cohen, M. L., & Peyrot, M. (2006). Psychological status and weight-related distress in overweight or at-risk-for-overweight children. *Obesity, 14,* 2249–2258.

Yu, B. P. (2006). Why calorie restriction would work for human longevity. *Biogerontology, 7,* 179–182.

Yuan, A. S. V., & Hamilton, H. A. (2006). Stepfather involvement and adolescent well-being: Do mothers and nonresidential fathers matter? *Journal of Family Issues, 27,* 1191–1213.

Yunger, J. L., Carver, P. R., & Perry, D. G. (2004). Does gender identity influence children's psychological well-being? *Developmental Psychology, 40,* 572–582.

Z

Zacks, R. T., & Hasher, L. (2006). Aging and long-term memory: Deficits are not inevitable. In E. Bialystok & F. I. M. Craik (Eds.), *Lifespan cognition: Mechanisms of change* (pp. 162–177). New York: Oxford University Press.

Zahn-Waxler, C., Radke-Yarrow, M., & King, R. M. (1979). Child-rearing and children's prosocial initiations toward victims of distress. *Child Development, 50,* 319–330.

Zakowski, S. G., Hall, M. H., Klein, L. C., & Baum, A. (2001). Appraised control, coping, and stress in a community sample: A test of the goodness-of-fit hypothesis. *Annals of Behavioral Medicine, 23,* 158–165.

Zane, N., & Yeh, M. (2002). The use of culturally based variables in assessment: Studies on loss of face. In K. Kurasaki, S. Okazaki, & S. Sue (Eds.), *Asian American mental health: Assessment theories and methods* (pp. 123–138). Dordrecht, Netherlands: Kluwer Academic.

Zaretsky, M. D. (2003). Communication between identical twins: Health behavior and social factors are associated with longevity that is greater among identical than fraternal U.S. World War II veteran twins. *Journal of Gerontology, 58,* 566–572.

Zaslow, M. J., Weinfield, N. S., Gallagher, M., Hair, E. C., Ogawa, J. R., Egeland, B., Tabors, P. O., & De Temple, J. M. (2006). Longitudinal prediction of child outcomes from differing measures of parenting in a low-income sample. *Developmental Psychology, 42,* 27–37.

Zeanah, C. H. (2000). Disturbances of attachment in young children adopted from institutions. *Journal of Developmental and Behavioral Pediatrics, 21,* 230–236.

Zeifman, D. M. (2003). Predicting adult responses to infant distress: Adult characteristics associated with perceptions, emotional reactions, and timing of intervention. *Infant Mental Health Journal, 24,* 597–612.

Zelazo, N. A., Zelazo, P. R., Cohen, K. M., & Zelazo, P. D. (1993). Specificity of practice effects on elementary neuromotor patterns. *Developmental Psychology, 29,* 686–691.

Zelazo, P. D., Carlson, S. M., & Kesek, A. (2008). The development of executive function in childhood. In C. A. Nelson & M. Luciana (Eds.), *Handbook of cognitive developmental neuroscience* (2nd ed., pp. 553–574). Cambridge, MA: MIT Press.

Zelazo, P. D., & Lee, W. S. C. (2010). Brain development: An overview. In W. Overton & R. M. Lerner (Eds.), *Handbook of life-span development: Vol. 1. Cognition biology, and methods* (pp. 89–114). Hoboken, NJ: Wiley.

Zelinski, E., & Kennison, R. F. (2007). Not your parents' test scores: Cohort reduces psychometric aging effects. *Psychology and Aging, 22,* 546–557.

Zeman, J., Shipman, K., & Suveg, C. (2002). Anger and sadness regulation: Predictions to internalizing and externalizing symptoms in children. *Journal of Clinical Child and Adolescent Psychology, 31,* 393–398.

Zeskind, P. S., & Barr, R. G. (1997). Acoustic characteristics of naturally occurring cries of infants with "colic." *Child Development, 68,* 394–403.

Zhan, H. J., & Montgomery, R. J. V. (2003). Gender and elder care in China: The influence of filial piety and structural constraints. *Gender and Society, 17,* 209–229.

Zhang, J., & Sternberg, R. J. (2011). Revisiting the investment theory of creativity. *Creativity Research Journal, 23,* 229–238.

Zhang, Q. F. (2004). Economic transition and new patterns of parent–adult child coresidence in urban China. *Journal of Marriage and Family, 66,* 1231–1245.

Zhang, T.-Y., & Meaney, M. J. (2010). Epigenetics and the environmental regulation of the genome and its function. *Annual Review of Psychology, 61,* 439–466.

Zhang, Y., & Jordan, J. M. (2010). Epidemiology of osteoarthritis. *Clinics of Geriatric Medicine, 26,* 355–369.

Zhao, J., Settles, B. H., & Sheng, X. (2011). Family-to-work conflict: Gender, equity and workplace policies. *Journal of Comparative Family Studies, 42,* 723–738.

Zheng, N. T., Mukamel, D. B., Caprio, T. V., & Temkin-Greener, H. (2012). Hospice utilization in nursing homes: Association with facility end-of-life care practices. *Gerontologist, 52.* Retrieved from gerontologist.oxfordjournals.org.libproxy.lib.ilstu .edu/search?fulltext=Zheng&submit=yes&x=13&y=9

Zhou, M., & Bankston, C. L. (1998). *Growing up American: How Vietnamese children adapt to life in the United States.* New York: Russell Sage Foundation.

Zhou, Q., Lengua, L. J., & Wang, Y. (2009). The relations of temperament reactivity and effortful control to children's adjustment problems in China and the United States. *Developmental Psychology, 45,* 724–739.

Zhou, X., Huang, J., Wang, Z., Wang, B., Zhao, Z., Yang, L., & Zheng-zheng, Y. (2006). Parent–child interaction and children's number learning. *Early Child Development and Care, 176,* 763–775.

Zhu, W. X., & Hesketh, T. (2009). China's excess males, sex selective abortion, and one child policy: Analysis of data from 2005 national intercensus survey. *British Medical Journal, 338,* b1211.

Zickuhr, K., & Madden, M. (2012). *Pew Internet: Older adults and Internet use.* Washington, DC: Pew Research Center.

Zimmer-Gembeck, M., & Helfand, M. J. (2008). Ten years of longitudinal research on U.S. adolescent sexual behavior: Developmental correlates of sexual intercourse, and the importance of age, gender and ethnic background. *Developmental Review, 28,* 153–224.

Zimmerman, B. J., & Cleary, T. J. (2009). Motives to self-regulate learning: A social cognitive account. In K. R. Wenzel & A. Wigfield (Eds.), *Handbook of motivation at school* (pp. 247–264). New York: Routledge.

Zimmerman, B. J., & Moylan, A. R. (2009). Self-regulation: Where metacognition and motivation intersect. In D. J. Hacker, J. Dunlosky, & A. C. Graesser (Eds.), *Handbook of metacognition in education* (pp. 299–315). New York: Routledge.

Zimmerman, C. (2007). The development of scientific thinking skills in elementary and middle school. *Developmental Review, 27,* 172–223.

Zimmerman, C. (2012). Acceptance of dying: A discourse analysis of palliative care literature. *Social Science and Medicine, 78,* 217–224.

Zimmerman, F. J., & Christakis, D. A. (2005). Children's television viewing and cognitive outcomes. *Archives of Pediatrics and Adolescent Medicine, 159,* 619–625.

Zimmerman, F. J., Christakis, D. A., & Meltzoff, A. N. (2007). Television and DVD/video viewing in children younger than 2 years. *Archives of Pediatrics and Adolescent Medicine, 161,* 473–479.

Zimmerman, F. J., Gilkerson, J., Richards, J. A., Christakis, D. A., Xu, D., Gray, S., & Yapanel, U. (2009). Teaching by listening: The importance of adult–child conversations to language development. *Pediatrics, 124,* 342–348.

Zimmerman, L. K., & Stansbury, K. (2004). The influence of emotion regulation, level of shyness, and habituation on the neuroendocrine response of three-year-old children. *Psychoneuroendocrinology, 29,* 973–982.

Zimmerman, P., & Becker-Stoll, F. (2002). Stability of attachment representations during adolescence: The influence of ego-identity status. *Journal of Adolescence, 25,* 107–124.

Zolotor, A. J., & Puzia, M. E. (2010). Bans against corporal punishment: A systematic review of the laws, changes in attitudes and behaviours. *Child Abuse Review, 19,* 229–247.

Zosuls, K. M., Ruble, D. N., Bornstein, M. H., & Greulich, F. K. (2009). The acquisition of gender labels in infancy: Implications for gender-typed play. *Developmental Psychology, 45,* 688–701.

Zucker, A. N., Ostrove, J. M., & Stewart, A. J. (2002). College-educated women's personality development in adulthood: Perceptions and age differences. *Psychology and Aging, 17,* 236–244.

Zukow-Golding, P. (2002). Sibling caregiving. In M. H. Bornstein (Ed.), *Handbook of parenting: Vol. 3* (2nd ed., pp. 253–286). Hillsdale, NJ: Erlbaum.

Name Index

Italic n *following page number indicates page with an illustration or table.*

Subject Index

Figures and tables are indicated by f and t following page numbers.